THE ENCYCLOPEDIA OF
THE VIETNAM WAR

Second Edition

THE ENCYCLOPEDIA OF
THE VIETNAM WAR

A Political, Social, and Military History,
Second Edition

VOLUME IV: DOCUMENTS

Dr. Spencer C. Tucker

Editor

Dr. Paul G. Pierpaoli Jr.

Associate Editor

Merle L. Pribbenow II

Dr. James H. Willbanks, Lieutenant Colonel, U.S. Army (retired)

Dr. David T. Zabecki, Major General, Army of the United States (retired)

Assistant Editors

A B C ⬥ C L I O

Santa Barbara, California Denver, Colorado Oxford, England

Library of Congress Cataloging-in-Publication Data

The encyclopedia of the Vietnam War : a political, social, and military history / Spencer C. Tucker, editor. — 2nd ed.
    p.   cm.
  Includes bibliographical references and index.
  ISBN 978-1-85109-960-3 (hard back : alk. paper) — ISBN 978-1-85109-961-0 (e-book)
 1. Vietnam War, 1961-1975—Encyclopedias.   I. Tucker, Spencer, 1937–
  DS557.7.E53   2011
  959.704'3—dc22

                                 2011007604

ISBN: 978-1-85109-960-3
EISBN: 978-1-85109-961-0

14 13 12 11 10 1 2 3 4 5

This book is also available on the World Wide Web as an eBook.
Visit www.abc-clio.com for details.

ABC-CLIO, LLC
130 Cremona Drive, P.O. Box 1911
Santa Barbara, California 93116–1911

This book is printed on acid-free paper ∞
Manufactured in the United States of America

To all those who fought in the Indochina and Vietnam Wars

About the Editor

Spencer C. Tucker, PhD, graduated from the Virginia Military Institute and was a Fulbright scholar in France. He was a U.S. Army captain and an intelligence analyst in the Pentagon during the Vietnam War and then taught for 30 years at Texas Christian University before returning to his alma mater for 6 years as the holder of the John Biggs Chair of Military History. He retired from teaching in 2003. He is now Senior Fellow of Military History at ABC-CLIO. Dr. Tucker has written or edited 38 books, including ABC-CLIO's award-winning *The Encyclopedia of the Cold War* and *The Encyclopedia of the Arab-Israeli Conflict* as well as the comprehensive *A Global Chronology of Conflict.*

Contents

List of Documents

Introduction

The documents in this volume cover a 75-year span, from 1920 through 1995. The introductions seek to place the individual documents in time and place. The documents include the views of national leaders in Vietnam, in France, and in the United States and trace the evolution of their national policies before and after the Indochina War and the Vietnam War. Certain documents discuss military tactics, while others detail the provisions of specific agreements.

I am especially pleased to have the assistance of Merle Pribbenow in the documents section. He is a former Central Intelligence Agency (CIA) Vietnamese specialist who served in Saigon during 1970–1975. Since his retirement from the CIA, Mr. Pribbenow has worked as an independent researcher and author specializing in the Vietnam War and as a translator of Vietnamese-language source materials. His translation of the official Vietnamese history of the war was published in 2002 under the title *Victory in Vietnam: The Official History of the People's Army of Vietnam, 1954–1975*. Mr. Pribbenow has provided translations of 13 Vietnamese docu-ments and the introductions for them. These fill gaps in policies of the Democratic Republic of Vietnam (DRV, North Vietnam) toward the war. These documents are nos. 109, 110, 111, 151, 161, 164, 171, 185, 195, 203, 219, 220, and 222.

Some of the documents in this volume are excerpted rather than reprinted in their entirety. A number of documents have punctuation problems and/or spelling errors or appear frag-mented; this is especially true with cables to and from Saigon. A number of the documents treating U.S. policy were made available in the publication of the so-called Pentagon Papers, which traced U.S. involvement in Indochina, and were released under the Free-dom of Information Act.

These documents provide insight on how government policies evolve. Studying them is a useful exercise in reminding us how our leaders can on occasion totally misread the intentions, determina-tion, and capabilities of another nation.

SPENCER C. TUCKER

Documents

---

1. Ho Chi Minh: Speech at the Tours Congress, December 1920

Introduction

Vietnamese nationalist Ho Chi Minh was in Paris during World War I and was active there in the Vietnamese community in France, which grew dramatically during the war. In 1919 Ho appealed without success to the leaders of the Great Powers at the Paris Peace Conference for the extension of self-determination to the peoples of Indochina. A member of the French Socialist Party, Ho was one of its prominent spokespersons on colonial affairs. In these remarks at the December 1920 French Socialist Party conference at Tours, he stresses the high costs of French rule for the people of Indochina and appeals to the delegates to oppose continued French rule there. Ho was among the majority of delegates at this conference who voted to break off from the Socialists and establish the French Communist Party.

Primary Source

Chairman: Comrade Indochinese Delegate, you have the floor.

Indochinese Delegate [Nguyen Ai Quoc]: Today, instead of contributing, together with you, to world revolution as I should wish, I come here with deep sadness and profound grief, as a Socialist, to protest against the abhorrent crimes committed my native land.

You all have known that French capitalism entered Indochina half a century ago. It conquered our country at bayonet point and in the nature of capitalism. Since then we have not only been oppressed and exploited shamelessly, but also tortured and poisoned pitilessly. (I would stress this fact that we have been poisoned with opium, alcohol, etc.) I cannot, in but a few minutes, reveal all the atrocities perpetrated by the predatory capitalists in Indochina. Prisons outnumber schools and are always overcrowded with detainees. Any native suspected of having socialist ideas is arrested and sometimes put to death without trial. So goes justice in Indochina for in there is one law for the Annamese [Vietnamese] and another for the Europeans or those holding European citizenship. The former do not enjoy the same safeguards as the latter. We have neither freedom of press, freedom of speech, freedom of assembly, nor freedom of association. We have no right to emigrate or travel abroad as tourists. We live in utter ignorance because we have no right to study. In Indochina the colonialists do all they can to poison us with opium and besot us with alcohol. Thousands of Vietnamese have been led to a slow death and thousands of others massacred to protect interests that are not theirs.

Comrades, such is the treatment inflicted upon more than 20 million Vietnamese, that is more than half the population of France. And yet they are said to be under French protection! The Socialist Party must act effectively in favour of the oppressed natives.

Jean Longuet: I have spoken in favor of the natives.

Indochinese Delegate: Right from the beginning of my speech I have imposed the dictatorship of silence. [*laughter*] The Party must make propaganda for socialism in all colonial countries. We shall see in the Socialist Party's joining the Third International the promise that from now on it will attach to the colonial questions the importance they deserve. We are very glad to learn that a Standing Delegation has been appointed for North Africa and we should be very happy if in the near future the Party sends one of its members to Indochina to study on-the-spot the relevant questions and what should be done about them.

A delegate: With Comrade Enver Pasha?

Indochinese Delegate: Silence, the Parliamentarians!

Chairman: Now all delegates must keep silence, including the non-Parliamentarians!

Indochinese Delegate: In the name of the whole of mankind, in the name of all Socialists, both those of the left and those of the right, we say to you: Comrades, save us!

Chairman: Through the applause which greeted him, the Indochinese Delegate can realize that the entire Socialist Party sides with him to oppose the crimes of the bourgeois.

Source: Ho Chi Minh, *Selected Writings: 1920–1969* (Hanoi: Foreign Languages Publishing House, 1977), 15–17.

2. Ho Chi Minh: Open Letter to Léon Archimbaud, January 15, 1923

Introduction

As a leading spokesperson on colonial affairs for the new French Communist Party, Vietnamese nationalist Ho Chi Minh, who was still residing in France, wrote to National Assembly deputy Léon Archimbaud. In the letter Ho blasts the Radical Party member for a speech in the Chamber of Deputies in which Archimbaud had glossed over the plight of hundreds of thousands of Vietnamese and other colonial peoples who had come to France during World War I to work as laborers. Ho also sharply criticizes Archimbaud for his claims that France had carried out a "generous" policy toward the peoples of its colonial empire.

Primary Source

Sir,

In your speech to the Chamber of Deputies you said that if you had wished to do so, you could have denounced colonial scandals, but you prefer to pass over in silence the crimes and offenses committed by your civilizers in the colonies. This is your right and it concerns only you, your conscience, and your electors. As for us who have suffered and will continue to suffer every day from these "blessings" of colonialism, we do not need you to tell us about them.

But when, writing in Le Rappel, you say that the facts pointed out by citizen Boumetont are false or exaggerated, you yourself "exaggerate"! First, the Minister of Colonies himself was obliged to recognize that a "contemptuous state of mind toward native life" exists. And that he "denied no act of brutality" denounced by Deputy Boisneuf. And then can you deny, M. Archimbaud, that during the last few years, that is to say, following the war for "the rule of law" for which 800,000 natives came to work "voluntarily" or to be killed in France, that your civilizers—with impunity—have robbed, swindled, murdered, or burnt alive Annamese, Tunisians, and Senegalese?

You write next that acts of injustice are more numerous in France than in the colonies. Then allow me to tell you, M. Archimbaud, that one should not pretend to give lessons in equality or justice to others when one is unable to apply them at home. This is the most elementary logic, isn't it?

According to you, the doings of your colonial administrators are known, commented upon, and controlled by the Governments General and the Ministry of Colonies. Hence it must be one of two things. Either you are harebrained and have forgotten the Baudoins, the Darles, the Lucases, and so many others making up the galaxy which is the honor and pride of your Colonial Administration, and who, after having committed heinous crimes, receive as punishment only promotions and decorations. Or else you are treating your readers as complete fools.

You state that if France has sinned in colonial matters it is rather from an excess of generous sentiment than anything else. Will you tell us, M. Archimbaud, whether it is out of these generous sentiments that the natives are deprived of all rights to write, speak, and travel, etc? Is it out of these same sentiments that the ignoble condition of "native" is imposed on them, that they are robbed of their land only to see it given to the conquerors, and forced thereafter to work as slaves? You yourselves have said that the Tahitian race has been decimated by alcoholism and is disappearing. Is it also from an excess of generosity that you are doing all you can to intoxicate the Annamese with your alcohol and stupefy them with your opium?

You speak finally of "duty," "humanity," and "civilization"! What is this duty? You showed what it is throughout your speech. It is markets, competition, interests, privileges. Trade and finance are things which express your "humanity." Taxes, forced labor, excessive exploitation, that is the summing up of your civilization!

While you are waiting to receive "one of the finest claims to glory that can be dreamt of," allow me to tell you, M. Archimbaud, that if Victor Hugo had known that you would write such stuff today in his newspaper, he would never have founded it.

Source: Ho Chi Minh, *On Revolution: Selected Writings, 1920–66,* edited by Bernard B. Fall (New York: Praeger, 1967), 18–19.

3. Ho Chi Minh: Appeal Made on the Occasion of the Founding of the Communist Party, February 18, 1930

Introduction

Vietnamese nationalist leader Ho Chi Minh traveled widely in the 1920s. In 1930 he was in the British colony of Hong Kong, where he was a key figure in merging the three Communist parties of Indochina into one organization. By the beginning of World War II, Ho's Communist Party of Indochina was the most prominent nationalist organization in Vietnam.

Primary Source

Workers, peasants, soldiers, youth, and school students! Oppressed and exploited fellow-countrymen!

Sisters and brothers! Comrades!

Imperialist contradictions were the cause of the 1914–18 World War. After this horrible slaughter, the world was divided into two camps: one is the revolutionary camp which includes the oppressed colonial peoples and the exploited working class throughout the world. Its vanguard is the Soviet Union. The other is the counterrevolutionary camp of international capitalism and imperialism, whose general staff is the League of Nations.

That war resulted in untold loss of life and property for the peoples. The French imperialists were the hardest hit. Therefore, in order to restore the capitalist forces in France, the French imperialists have resorted to every perfidious scheme to intensify capitalist exploitation in Indochina. They have built new factories to exploit the workers by paying them starvation wages. They plundered the peasants' land to establish plantations and drive them to destitution. They have levied new heavy taxes. They have forced our people to buy government bonds. In short, they have driven our people to utter misery. They increased their military forces, firstly to strangle the Vietnamese revolution, secondly to prepare for a new imperialist war in the Pacific aimed at conquering new colonies, thirdly to suppress the Chinese revolution, fourthly to attack the Soviet Union because she helps the oppressed nations and the exploited working class to wage revolution. World War II will break out. When it does, the French imperialists will certainly drive our people to an even more horrible slaughter. If we let them prepare for this war, oppose the Chinese revolution, and attack the Soviet Union, if we allow them to stifle the Vietnamese revolution, it is tantamount to giving them a free hand to wipe our race off the earth and drown our nation in the Pacific.

However, the French imperialists' barbarous oppression and ruthless exploitation have awakened our compatriots, who have all realized that revolution is the only road to survival and that without it they will die a slow death. This is why the Vietnamese revolutionary movement has grown even stronger with each passing day. The workers refuse to work, the peasants demand land, the students go on strike, the traders stop doing business. Everywhere the masses have risen to oppose the French imperialists.

The Vietnamese revolution has made the French imperialists tremble with fear. On the one hand, they use the feudalists and comprador bourgeois to oppress and exploit our people. On the other, they terrorize, arrest, jail, deport, and kill a great number of Vietnamese revolutionaries. If the French imperialists think that they can suppress the Vietnamese revolution by means of terror, they are grossly mistaken. For one thing the Vietnamese revolution is not isolated but enjoys the assistance of the world proletariat in general and that of the French working class in particular. Secondly, it is precisely at the very time when the French imperialists are frenziedly carrying out terrorist acts that the Vietnamese Communists, formerly working separately, have united into a single party, the Indochinese Communist Party, to lead the revolutionary struggle of our entire people.

Workers, peasants, soldiers, youth, school students!

Oppressed and exploited fellow-countrymen!

The Indochinese Communist Party has been founded. It is the party of the working class. It will help the proletariat lead the revolution waged for the sake of all oppressed and exploited people. From now on we must join the Party, help it and follow it in order to implement the following slogans:

1. To overthrow French imperialism and Vietnamese feudalism, and reactionary bourgeoisie.
2. To make Indochina completely independent.
3. To establish a worker-peasant-soldier government.
4. To confiscate the banks and other enterprises belonging to the imperialists and put them under the control of the worker-peasant-soldier government.
5. To confiscate the whole of the plantations and property belonging to the imperialists and the Vietnamese reactionary bourgeoisie and distribute them to the poor peasants.
6. To implement the eight-hour working day.
7. To abolish the forced buying of government bonds, the poll-tax and all unjust taxes hitting the poor.
8. To bring democratic freedoms to the masses.
9. To dispense education to all the people.
10. To realize equality between man and woman.

Source: Ho Chi Minh, *Selected Writings: 1920–1969* (Hanoi: Foreign Languages Publishing House, 1977), 39–41.

4. Ho Chi Minh: Letter from Abroad, June 6, 1941

Introduction

In the summer of 1940, German forces invaded and defeated France. The Japanese then took advantage of France's weakness to secure military bases in Indochina. This action, which brought Japanese bombers within range of the Philippines, caused the United States to tighten the economic screws on Japan, which in turn led to the preemptive Japanese strike at Pearl Harbor. In this letter to the Vietnamese people, Vietnamese nationalist leader Ho Chi Minh, then in China, notes the present military weakness of France and the occupation of Indochina by the Japanese. With the Japanese bogged down in China, Ho believes that it is the ideal time for Vietnamese to unite, rise up, and defeat both the French and Japanese and to reestablish their independence. Such calls for action were premature, for the Japanese retained a firm grip on Indochina.

Primary Source

Venerable elders!

Patriotic personalities!

Intellectuals, peasants, workers, traders and soldiers!

Dear fellow-countrymen!

Since France was defeated by Germany, its power has completely collapsed. Nevertheless, with regard to our people, the French rulers have become even more ruthless in carrying out their policy of exploitation, repression and massacre. They bleed us white and carry out a barbarous policy of all-out terrorism and massacre. In the foreign field, bowing their heads and bending their knees, they resign themselves to ceding part of our land to Siam and shamelessly surrendering our country to Japan. As a result our people are writhing under a double yoke of oppression. They serve not only as beasts of burden to the French bandits but also as slaves to the Japanese robbers. Alas! What sin have our people committed to be doomed to such a wretched fate? Plunged into such tragic suffering, are we to await death with folded arms?

No! Certainly not! The twenty-odd million descendants of the Lac and the Hong are resolved not to let themselves be kept in servitude. For nearly eighty years under the French pirates' iron heels we have unceasingly and selflessly struggled for national independence and freedom. The heroism of our predecessors, such as Phan Dinh Phung, Hoang Hoa Tham and Luong Ngoc Quyen and the glorious feats of the insurgents of Thai Nguyen, Yen Bai, Nghe An and Ha Tinh provinces will live forever in our memory. The recent uprisings in the South and at Do Luong and Bac Son testify to the determination of our compatriots to follow the glorious example of their ancestors and to annihilate the enemy. If we were not successful, it was not because the French bandits were strong, but only because the situation was not yet ripe and our people throughout the country were not yet of one mind.

Now, the opportunity has come for our liberation. France itself is unable to help the French colonialists rule over our country. As for the Japanese, on the one hand, bogged down in China, on the other, hampered by the British and American forces, they certainly cannot use all their strength against us. If our entire people are solidly united we can certainly get the better of the best-trained armies of the French and the Japanese.

Fellow-countrymen! Rise up! Let us emulate the dauntless spirit of the Chinese people! Rise up without delay! Let us organize the Association for National Salvation to fight the French and the Japanese!

Dear fellow-countrymen! A few hundred years ago, in the reign of Tran, when our country faced the great danger of invasion by Yuan armies the elders ardently called on their sons and daughters throughout the country to stand up as one man to kill the enemy. Finally they saved their people and their glorious memory will live forever. Let our elders and patriotic personalities follow the illustrious example set by our forefathers.

Notables, soldiers, workers, peasants, traders, civil servants, youth and women who warmly love your country! At present national liberation stands above everything. Let us unite and overthrow the Japanese, the French and their lackeys in order to save our people from their present dire straits.

Dear fellow-countrymen!

National salvation is the common cause of our entire people. Every Vietnamese must take part in it. He who has money will contribute his money, he who has strength will contribute his strength, he who has talent will contribute his talent. For my part I pledge to follow in your steps and devote all my modest abilities to the service of the country and am ready for the supreme sacrifice.

Revolutionary fighters!

The hour has struck! Raise aloft the banner of insurrection and lead the people throughout the country to overthrow the Japanese and the French! The sacred call of the Fatherland is resounding in our ears; the ardent blood of our heroic predecessors is seething in our hearts! The fighting spirit of the people is mounting before our eyes! Let us unite and unify our action to overthrow the Japanese and the French.

The Vietnamese revolution will certainly triumph! The world revolution will certainly triumph!

Source: Ho Chi Minh, *Selected Writings: 1920–1969* (Hanoi: Foreign Languages Publishing House, 1977), 44–46.

5. President Franklin D. Roosevelt: Memorandum to Secretary of State Cordell Hull, January 24, 1944 [Excerpts]

Introduction

U.S. president Franklin Roosevelt was sharply critical of French imperial rule, not only in North Africa but also in Southeast Asia. No friend of Free French leader General Charles de Gaulle and his pretension that France was still a Great Power, Roosevelt makes clear in this memorandum to Secretary of State Cordell Hull his firm belief that Indochina should become independent at the end of World War II. Roosevelt notes that the leaders of both the Soviet Union and Nationalist China supported this point of view. This should hardly have come as a surprise to the president, however: Chinese leaders hoped to dominate the region, and the Soviet Union wanted to weaken French power. Roosevelt also notes that the British opposed granting independence to the states of Indochina over concern for the effect that this might have on their own Southeast Asian possessions as well as those of the Dutch.

Primary Source

I saw Halifax [Lord Halifax, the British ambassador to the United States] last week and told him quite frankly that it was perfectly true that I had, for over a year, expressed the opinion that Indo-China should not go back to France, but that it should be administered by an international trusteeship. . . .

As a matter of interest, I am wholeheartedly supported in this view by Generalissimo Chiang Kai-Shek and by Marshall Stalin. . . . The only reason they [the British] seem to oppose it is that they fear the effect it would have on their possessions and those of the Dutch. They have never liked the idea of trusteeship because it is, in some instances, aimed at future independence. This is true in the case of Indo-China.

Each case must, of course, stand on its own feet, but the case of Indo-China is perfectly clear. France has milked it for one hundred years. The people of Indo-China are entitled to something better than that.

Source: *United States–Vietnam Relations, 1945–1967*, Book 7 (Washington, DC: U.S. Government Printing Office, 1971), 30.

6. Charles Taussig: Memorandum of Conversation with President Franklin D. Roosevelt by the Adviser on Caribbean Affairs, March 15, 1945 [Excerpt]

Introduction

Anticolonialism was a major tenant of U.S. president Franklin Roosevelt's foreign policy. In this memorandum, Charles Taussig, Roosevelt's adviser on Caribbean Affairs, reports on a meeting with the president in which Roosevelt directed that U.S. policy be aimed at helping the "brown people in the East" achieve independence from European colonial rule. Roosevelt also expressed his belief that self-government under France was an unacceptable solution and that Indochina should be entirely removed from its rule and placed under the trusteeship of a postwar international organization (the United Nations [UN]).

Primary Source

The Peoples of East Asia

The President said he was concerned about the brown people in the East. He said that there are 1,100,000,000 brown people. In many Eastern countries, they are ruled by a handful of whites and they resent it. Our goal must be to help them achieve independence—1,100,000,000 potential enemies are dangerous. He said he included the 450,000,000 Chinese in that. He then added, Churchill doesn't understand this.

Indo-China and New Caledonia

The President said he thought we might have some difficulties with France in the matter of colonies. I said that I thought that was quite probable and it was also probable the British would use France as a "stalking horse".

I asked the President if he had changed his ideas on French Indo-China as he had expressed them to us at the luncheon with Stanley. He said no he had not changed his ideas; that French Indo-China and New Caledonia should be taken from France and put under a trusteeship. The President hesitated a moment and then said—well if we can get the proper pledge from France to assume for herself the obligations of a trustee, then I would agree to France retaining these colonies with the proviso that independence was the ultimate goal. I asked the President if he would settle for self-government. He said no. I asked him if he would settle for dominion status. He said no—it must be independence. He said that is to be the policy and you can quote me in the State Department.

Source: *Foreign Relations of the United States: Diplomatic Papers, 1945*, Vol. 1 (Washington, DC: U.S. Government Printing Office, 1967), 124.

7. State Department Division of European Affairs: Draft Memorandum for President Harry S. Truman, April 20, 1945

Introduction

With the end of World War II in Europe only weeks away and with planning going forward in the Pacific theater for an expected bloody invasion of the Japanese home islands, the European Division of the State Department urged a reexamination of U.S. Indochina policy by new U.S. president Harry S. Truman. The European Division recommended a decided movement away from the policy of Truman's predecessor, President Franklin D. Roosevelt. Anxious about U.S. policy toward Indochina, the interim French government headed by Charles de Gaulle had been pressing Washington regarding the dispatch of French troops to the region. Officials in the European Division believed that circumstances had rendered moot the plan to put off the disposition of Indochina to "postwar determination." In this memorandum the division points out that the de Gaulle government has committed itself to the creation of an Indochinese federation within the new French Union. The authors therefore argue against the policy of the Roosevelt administration that Indochina be granted independence under a trusteeship and instead propose a neutral stance on the issue of the region's future. The United States should press France to liberalize its governance of Indochina, but at the same time U.S. military aid to the French in Indochina should be limited only to operations aimed at defeating Japan. As it worked out, with the Cold War Washington came to see the Soviet Union as the principal threat and France as the only major continental military power capable of maintaining the peace in Europe. Independence for Indochina thus lost out to a Europe-first strategy.

Primary Source

Subject: Suggested Reexamination of American Policy with Respect to Indo-China

General Observations

1. The Japanese aggression against the French in Indo-China last month has brought about a marked increase in the number of proposals advanced by the French for the use of French forces and resources in the Pacific.

2. The consequences of these military developments make it clear that our last policy, which held that the disposition of Indo-China was a matter for postwar determination and that the United States should not become involved in military effort for its liberation, is in urgent need for reexamination and clarification. This is particularly so in order that American military and naval authorities may have guidance to enable them to take appropriate action with respect to the French proposals referred to above.

3. The United States Government has publicly taken the position that it recognizes the sovereign jurisdiction of France over French possessions overseas when those possessions are resisting the enemy and had expressed the hope that it will see the reestablishment of the integrity of French territory. In spite of this general assurance, the negative policy so far pursued by this Government with respect to Indo-China has aroused French suspicions concerning our intentions with respect to the future of that territory. This has had and continues to have a harmful effect on American relations with the French Government and people.

4. On April 3, 1945, the Secretary of State with the approval of the President issued a statement of which the following excerpt is pertinent to the present problem:

"As to territorial trusteeship, it appeared desirable that the Governments represented at Yalta, in consultation with the Chinese Government and the French Provisional Government, should endeavor to formulate proposals for submission to the San Francisco Conference for a trusteeship structure as a part of the general organization. This trusteeship structure, it was felt, should be defined to permit the placing under it of the territories taken from the enemy in this war, as might be agreed upon at a later date, and also such other territories as might voluntarily be placed under trusteeship."

5. General de Gaulle and his Government have made it abundantly clear that they expect a proposed Indo-Chinese federation to function within the framework of the "French Union." There is consequently not the slightest possibility at the present time or in the foreseeable future that France will volunteer to place Indo-China under an international trusteeship, or will consent to any program of international accountability which is not applied to the colonial possessions of other powers. If an effort were made to exert pressure on the French Government, such action would have to be taken by the United States alone for France could rely upon the support of other colonial powers, notably, Great Britain and the Netherlands. Such action would likewise run counter to the established American policy of aiding France to regain her strength in order that she may be better fitted to share responsibility in maintaining the peace of Europe and the world.

Recommendations

In the light of the above considerations, the following recommendations, which have been communicated to the War and Navy Departments, are submitted for your approval.

1. The Government of the United States should neither oppose the restoration of Indo-China to France, with or without a program of international accountability, nor take any action toward French overseas possessions which it is not prepared to take or suggest with regard to the colonial possessions of our other Allies.

2. The Government of the United States should continue to exert its influence with the French in the direction of having them effect a liberalization of their past policy of limited opportunities for native participation in government and administration, as well as a liberalization of restrictive French economic policies formerly pursued in Indo-China.

3. The French Provisional Government should be informed confidentially that, owing to the need of concentrating all our resources in the Pacific on operations already planned, large-scale military operations aimed directly at the liberation of Indo-China cannot be contemplated at this time.

4. French offers of military and naval assistance in the Pacific should be considered on their merits as bearing upon the objective of defeating Japan, as in the case of British and Dutch proposals. The fact that acceptance of a specific proposal might serve to strengthen French claims for the restoration of Indo-China to France should not be regarded as grounds for rejection. On the contrary, acceptance of French proposals for military assistance in the defeat of Japan should be regarded as desirable in principle, subject always to military requirements in the theater of operations.

5. While avoiding specific commitments with regard to the amount or character of any assistance which the United States may give to the French resistance forces in Indo-China, this Government should continue to afford all possible assistance provided it does not interfere with the requirements of other planned operations.

6. In addition to the aid which we are able to bring from the China theater of operations to the French forces resisting the Japanese in Indo-China, the United States should oppose no obstacle to the implementation of proposals looking toward the despatch of assistance to those forces from the southeast Asia theater of operations, provided such assistance does not constitute a diversion of resources which the Combined Chiefs of Staff consider are needed elsewhere.

Source: *United States–Vietnam Relations, 1945–1967*, Book 8 (Washington, DC: U.S. Government Printing Office, 1971), 6–8.

8. State Department Division of Far East Affairs: Draft Memorandum for President Harry S. Truman, April 21, 1945

Introduction

In this memorandum, officials in the State Department Division of Far East Affairs move sharply away from former president Franklin D. Roosevelt's plan to grant Indochina immediate independence under a trusteeship (the United Nations [UN]) and move close to the views of the State Department's European Division. The memorandum notes the increasing number of proposals advanced by the interim French government to assist in the defeat of Japanese forces in the Pacific theater and reiterates the belief held by the European Division of the State Department that French cooperation will be essential in maintaining peace in Europe. The memorandum opposes placing restrictions on the restoration of French power in Indochina and urges dropping the insistence on a trusteeship there. Instead, U.S. policy should be directed at ensuring peace and stability in the region. The memorandum, however, calls for specific guarantees from France that it would permit the establishment of a government run by the Indochinese themselves. Prophetically, the memorandum warns that if France fails to adopt policies that have the real interests of the indigenous peoples of the region in mind, the result would be "substantial bloodshed and unrest for many years."

Primary Source

Subject: American Policy with Respect to Indochina General Observations

1. The Japanese aggression against the French in Indochina last month has brought about a marked increase in the number of proposals advanced by the French for the use of French forces and resources in the Pacific.

2. These proposals and recent military developments make it essential that the United States reach a definitive determination regarding its policy towards Indochina rather than, as heretofore considered, the disposition of Indochina a matter of postwar determination.

3. The joint State-War-Navy authorities have reached the decision that all American military efforts must be directed entirely to the major issue of defeating Japan in its homeland and that, for

military reasons, American troops should not be used or equipment needed in American operations be utilized for the liberation of Indochina.

4. It is established American policy to aid France to regain her strength in order that she may be better fitted to share responsibility in maintaining the peace of Europe—where her chief interests lie—and of the world. However, in pursuing this policy, the United States must not jeopardize its own increasingly important interests in Southeast Asia.

5. The United States Government has publicly taken the position that it recognizes the sovereign jurisdiction of France over French possessions overseas when those possessions are resisting the enemy, and has expressed the hope that it will see the reestablishment of the integrity of French territory.

6. Until the last few weeks the French administration of Indochina has collaborated with the Japanese in marked distinction to the administrations of colonial areas belonging to our other Allies.

7. President Roosevelt recognized the future increasing importance to the United States of Southeast Asia. He saw the necessity of aiding the 150,000,000 people there to achieve improved social, economic and political standards.

He realized that dynamic forces leading toward self-government are growing in Asia; that the United States—as a great democracy—cannot and must not try to retard this development but rather act in harmony with it; and that social, economic or political instability in the area may threaten the peace and stability of the Far East and indeed the world.

8. As his solution of this problem, as it relates to Indochina, President Roosevelt long favored placing Indochina under a trusteeship. However, on April 3 1945, the Secretary of State with the approval of the President issued a statement relative to the plans approved at Yalta which would indicate that Indochina could come under the trusteeship structure only by voluntary action of the French. It is abundantly clear that there is no possibility at the present time or in the foreseeable future that France will volunteer to place Indochina under trusteeship, or consent to any program of international accountability which is not applied to the colonial possessions of other powers. If an effort were made to exert pressure on the French Government, such action would have to be taken by the United States alone for France could rely upon the support of other colonial powers, notably Great Britain and the Netherlands.

9. The prewar French administration in Indochina was the least satisfactory colonial administration in Asia, both as regards the development and interests of the native peoples and as regards economic relations with other countries. Among the Annamites there is increasing opposition to French rule. The Chinese are giving active support to the independence movement. France will probably encounter serious difficulty in reimposing French control in Indochina.

10. If really liberal policies towards Indochina are not adopted by the French—policies which recognize the paramount interest of the native peoples and guarantee within the foreseeable future a genuine opportunity for true, autonomous self-government—there will be substantial bloodshed and unrest for many years, threatening the economic and social progress and the peace and stability of Southeast Asia.

11. On several occasions in the past few years, French authorities have issued policy statements on the future of Indochina. These show a growing trend toward greater autonomy for the French administration of Indochina, but even the recent statement of March 24 is vague and, when examined with care, indicates little intention of permitting genuine self-rule for the Indochinese. The change in French attitude towards Indochina is believed to have been occasioned by clearer realization of the anti-French sentiment among the Annamites and a belief that American approval of French restoration can be won only by a liberalization of its policies towards Indochina.

12. China is exercised at the economic stranglehold which France formerly exercised through control of the Yunan Railroad and the port of Haiphong, and is particularly perturbed at the danger to its southwest flank first made visible by the surrender of Indochina to the Japanese.

13. It is stated American policy that the cession of territory by Indochina to Thailand in 1941 is not recognized and that this territory must be returned to Indochina. This territory, however, had in earlier years been wrested by the French from Thailand and its inhabitants are culturally akin to the Thai. Similarly, parts of Laos are Thai in character. Whatever the legalistic background may be, the entire border region between Indochina and Thailand will be a source of potential conflict unless a fair and appropriate frontier is determined by an impartial international commission. The Thai Government will accept any frontier so determined.

14. It will be an American victory over Japan which will make possible the liberation of Indochina. We are fighting to assure peace and stability in the Far East, and will, in fact, bear the major responsibility for its maintenance after the war. Encouragement of and assistance to the peoples of Southeast Asia in developing autonomous, democratic self-rule in close, willing association with major Western powers would not only be in harmony with

political trends in that area, but would appear to be the one practical solution which will assure peace and stability in the Far East. If this policy is not followed, the millions who live in that area may well embrace ideologies contrary to our own—or ultimately develop a pan-Asiatic movement against the Western world. It is not unreasonable, therefore, for the United States to insist that the French give adequate assurances as to the implementing of policies in Indochina which we consider essential to assure peace and stability in the Far East.

In the light of the above considerations, the following recommendations, which have been communicated to the War and Navy Departments for their comment, are submitted for your approval:

1. The Government of the United States should not seek a trusteeship, international or French, over Indochina, unless it seeks similar trusteeship by the British and Dutch over Burma and the Netherlands Indies, nor should the United States seek international accountability which is not sought for the adjacent colonial areas. It should not oppose restoration of Indochina to France, provided the French give adequate assurances that they will meet the following conditions:

   a. Development of a democratic national or federal government to be run for and increasingly by the Indochinese themselves with no special privileges for French or other persons who are not inhabitants and citizens of Indochina so that within the forseeable future Indochina may be fully self-governing and autonomous, except in matters of imperial concern in which Indochina should be a partner in the French Union.
   b. Maintenance of a policy of non-discriminatory treatment and of complete economic and commercial equality.
   c. Establishment of Haiphong as a free port with tax-free transit facilities between Haiphong and China.
   d. Acceptance of a frontier between Indochina and Thailand, to be determined by an impartial international commission.
   e. Acceptance of such international security arrangements, including American or international bases, as may be determined to be necessary for international security, including protection of China's southwestern flank.

2. For the present, the policy of the United States with respect to the postwar status of Indochina should not be communicated to the Provincial French Government.

3. The French Provisional Government should be informed, confidentially, that owing to the need of concentrating all our resources in the Pacific on operations already planned, American military operations aimed directly at the liberation of Indochina cannot be contemplated until after the defeat of Japan, nor will it be possible to make any commitments for the furnishing of military equipment or supplies to resistance groups in Indochina or to French military forces in the Asiatic theatres of war.

4. French officers of military and naval assistance in the Pacific should be accepted or rejected by the military authorities solely on their military merits as bearing upon the defeat of Japan, as in the case of British and Dutch proposals.

Source: *United States–Vietnam Relations, 1945–1967*, Book 8 (Washington, DC: U.S. Government Printing Office, 1971), 13–17.

9. Joseph Grew, Acting Secretary of State: Telegram to Ambassador Jefferson Caffery in France, May 9, 1945

Introduction

In this telegram, U.S. acting secretary of state Joseph Grew discusses a meeting of the United Nations (UN) Conference on International Organization at San Francisco involving Secretary of State James Byrnes, French foreign minister Georges Bidault, and French ambassador to the United States Henri Bonnet. Byrnes informs Bidault and Bonnet that the United States will not insist on a trusteeship for Indochina, thus definitively reversing the stance taken by former president Franklin D. Roosevelt.

Primary Source

[Dated May 8, sent on May 9]

The subject of Indo-China came up in a recent conversation I had with Bidault and Bonnet. The latter remarked that although the French Government interprets Mr. Welles' statement of 1942 concerning the restoration of French sovereignty over the French Empire as including Indo-China, the press continues to imply that a special status will be reserved for this colonial area. It was made quite clear to Bidault that the record is entirely innocent of any official statement of this government questioning, even by implication, French sovereignty over Indo-China. Certain elements of American public opinion, however, condemned French governmental policies and practices in Indo-China. Bidault seemed relieved and has no doubt cabled Paris that he received renewed assurances of our recognition of French sovereignty over that area.

Source: *Foreign Relations of the United States: Diplomatic Papers, 1945*, Vol. 6 (Washington, DC: U.S. Government Printing Office, 1969), 307.

10. Joseph Grew, Acting Secretary of State: Telegram to Ambassador Patrick J. Hurley in Chungking, China, June 7, 1945 [Excerpt]

Introduction

Providing guidance to U.S. ambassador to China Patrick J. Hurley regarding U.S. policy toward Indochina, acting secretary of state Joseph Grew informs Hurley, who is in Chungking [Chongqing], that the United States will not seek a trusteeship over Indochina unless this has the support of the French government. At the same time, however, Grew states that the United States will insist that France create "increasing measures of self-government" for Indochina.

Primary Source

The President thanks you for your considered telegram in regard to the problems presented by the reestablishment of French control in Indochina and the British desire to reoccupy Hongkong and fully appreciates the difficulties in which you and General Wedemeyer may be placed on account of the lack of specific directives in respect to both of these problems which have been under careful study both here and in connection with the discussions at San Francisco.

I have also received your message No. 1548 of June 6 and regret that there has been delay in replying to your earlier one owing to the study which has been required of these matters in connection with present developments at the Conference. The President has asked me to say that there has been no basic change in the policy in respect to these two questions and that the present position is as follows:

The President assumes that you are familiar with the statement made by the Secretary of State on April 3, 1945 with the approval of President Roosevelt in which Mr. Stettinius declared that as a result of the Yalta discussions the "trusteeship structure, it was felt, should be defined to permit the placing under it of such of the territories taken from the enemy in this war, as might be agreed upon at a later date, and also such other territories as might voluntarily be placed under trusteeship". The position thus publicly announced has been confirmed by the conversations which are now taking place in San Francisco in regard to trusteeships. Throughout these discussions the American delegation has insisted upon the necessity of providing for a progressive measure of self-government for all dependent peoples looking toward their eventual independence or incorporation in some form of federation, according to circumstances and the ability of the peoples to assume these responsibilities. Such decisions would preclude the establishment of a trusteeship in Indochina except with the consent of the French Government. The latter seems unlikely. Nevertheless it is the President's intention at some appropriate time to ask that the French Government give some positive indication of its intentions in regard to the establishment of civil liberties and increasing measures of self-government in Indochina before formulating further declarations of policy in this respect. . . .

Source: *United States–Vietnam Relations, 1945–1967*, Book 8 (Washington, DC: U.S. Government Printing Office, 1971), 30–31.

11. U.S. State Department: Paper on U.S. Postwar Policy toward Asia and the Pacific, June 22, 1945 [Excerpts]

Introduction

Responding to a request from Secretary of War Henry L. Stimson for a position paper on U.S. policy toward Indochina, the U.S. State Department seeks to balance the need to preserve close ties with France in order to secure that government's postwar cooperation to preserve the peace in Europe with the oft-stated U.S. position that France must grant greater self-government to the peoples of Indochina. This position paper recognizes the likelihood of a violent struggle for independence against the French by Vietnamese nationalists led by Ho Chi Minh but notes that the United States had already recognized French sovereignty over Indochina.

Primary Source

An Estimate of Conditions in Asia and the Pacific at the Close of the War in the Far East and the Objectives and Policies of the United States

I. Introduction

[. . .]

Aside from the traditional American belief in the right of all peoples to independence, the largest possible measure of political freedom for the countries of Asia consistent with their ability to assume the responsibility thereof is probably necessary in order to achieve the chief objective of the United States in the Far East and the Pacific: continuing peace and security.

Another condition on which peace and security depend is cooperation among the peace-minded states of the world. One of the foremost policies of the United States is to maintain the unity of purpose and action of all the United Nations, especially of the leading powers. Two of these leading powers are Great Britain and France, each of which has dependencies in the Far East in which there is an insistent demand for a greater measure of self-government than the parent states have yet been willing to grant.

A problem for the United States is to harmonize, so far as possible, its policies in regard to the two objectives: increased political freedom for the Far East and the maintenance of the unity of the leading United Nations in meeting this problem. The United States Government may properly continue to state the political principle which it has frequently announced, that dependent peoples should be given the opportunity, if necessary after an adequate period of preparation, to achieve an increased measure of self-government, but it should avoid any course of action which would seriously impair the unity of the major United Nations.

The United States, also, may utilize either the force of its example or its influence or both. Its treatment of the Philippines has earned a rich reward for this country in the attitude and conduct of both the Filipinos and the nationals of other Far Eastern states. The American Government influenced the British Government to take parallel action with it in the renunciation of extraterritoriality and other exceptional rights in China.

The solution which would best harmonize these two policies of the United States would be a Far East progressively developing into a group of self-governing states—independent or with Dominion status—which would cooperate with each other and with the Western powers on a basis of mutual self-respect and friendship. The interests of the United States and of its European Allies require that the Far East be removed as a source of colonial rivalry and conflict, not only between the Great Powers, but between the Great Powers and the peoples of Asia.

[...]

V. French Indochina

A. Estimate of Conditions at the End of the War

1. Political

At the end of the war, political conditions in Indochina, and especially in the north, will probably be particularly unstable. The Indochinese independence groups, which may have been working against the Japanese, will quite possibly oppose the restoration of French control. Independence sentiment in the area is believed to be increasingly strong. The Indochinese Independence League, representing some ten different native political groups, is thought to carry substantial influence with between one-quarter and one-half million persons. The serious 1930 insurrection, in which over 100,000 peasants actively participated, and similar insurrections which took place in the fall of 1940 indicate that the supporters of independence are neither apathetic nor supine and are willing to

fight. It is believed that the French will encounter serious difficulty in overcoming this opposition and in reestablishing French control. What effect the Japanese declarations of independence for Annam, Cambodia, and Luang Prabang will have in the period immediately following the war cannot be estimated at this time, but clearly these declarations will make the French problem more difficult.

The French government recognizes that it will have very serious difficulties in reestablishing and maintaining its control in Indochina, and its several statements regarding the future of that country show an increasing trend toward autonomy for the French administration. Even the latest statement, however, shows little intention to give the Indochinese self-government. An increased measure of self-government would seem essential if the Indochinese are to be reconciled to continued French control.

2. Economic

Economically, Indochina has so far suffered least of all the countries involved in the war in the Far East. Bombing and fighting before the close of the war will probably, however, have resulted in the destruction of some of its railway system, key bridges, harbor installations, and the more important industrial and power plants. This will probably intensify already existing food shortages in the north and lack of consumer goods throughout the area.

Pre-war French policies involved economic exploitation of the colony for France. Indochina had to buy dear in the high, protected market of France and sell cheap in the unprotected markets of other nations. The French realize that this economic policy, which was very detrimental to Indochina, must be changed. They have pledged tariff autonomy and equality of tariff rates for other countries. There is no indication, however, that the French intend to pursue an open-door economic policy.

B. International Relations

French policy toward Indochina will be dominated by the desire to reestablish control in order to reassert her prestige in the world as a great power. This purpose will be augmented by the potent influence of the Banque de l'Indochine and other economic interests. Many French appear to recognize that it may be necessary for them to make further concessions to Indochinese self-government and autonomy primarily to assure native support but also to avoid unfriendly United States opinion. Chief French reliance, however, will continue to be placed upon the United Kingdom, which is almost as anxious as the French to see that no pre-war colonial power suffers diminution of power or prestige. Friction between France and China over Indochina will probably continue. The Chinese government, at least tacitly, is supporting the Independence League and is thought by the French, despite the Generalissimo's disclaimer of territorial ambitions, to desire to dominate, if not annex, northern Indochina. French economic policies interfered with all nations trading with China through its access to the sea at Haiphong. China particularly will look for a complete reversal of French policy in this respect.

The Thai consider the territory acquired from Indochina in 1941 as theirs by legal and historic right, but they have indicated they will accept any border determined by an Anglo-American commission. The French consider the territory theirs and there will doubtless be border conflict unless a fair settlement is reached which eliminates causes for serious discontent.

C. United States Policy

The United States recognizes French sovereignty over Indochina. It is, however, the general policy of the United States to favor a policy which would allow colonial peoples an opportunity to prepare themselves for increased participation in their own government with eventual self-government as the goal.

Source: *Foreign Relations of the United States: Diplomatic Papers, 1945*, Vol. 6 (Washington, DC: U.S. Government Printing Office, 1969), 557–558, 567–568.

1. At the Potsdam Conference the Prime Minister of Great Britain and I, in consultation with the Combined Chiefs of Staff, have had under consideration future military operations in South-East Asia.

2. On the advice of the Combined Chiefs of Staff we have reached the conclusion that for operational purposes it is desirable to include that portion of French Indo-China lying south of 160 north latitude in the Southeast Asia Command. This arrangement would leave in the China Theater that part of Indo-China which covers the flank of projected Chinese operations in China and would at the same time enable Admiral Mountbatten to develop operations in the southern half of Indo-China.

3. I greatly hope that the above conclusions will recommend themselves to Your Excellency and that, for the purpose of facilitating operations against the common enemy, Your Excellency will feel able to concur in the proposed arrangements.

4. I understand that the Prime Minister of Great Britain is addressing a communication to Your Excellency in a similar sense.

Source: *Foreign Relations of the United States: Diplomatic Papers; The Conference of Berlin (The Potsdam Conference), 1945*, Vol. 2 (Washington, DC: U.S. Government Printing Office, 1960), 1321.

12. President Harry S. Truman: Telegram to Generalissimo Jiang Jieshi, Transmitted via Ambassador to China Patrick J. Hurley, August 1, 1945

Introduction

At the end of World War II there were perhaps 70,000 Japanese troops in Indochina. During July 16–August 2, 1945, in Potsdam, Germany, the leaders of the Big Three Allied powers held their last summit conference of World War II. There British prime minister Clement Atlee and U.S. president Harry S. Truman agreed to establish a line at the 16th Parallel north latitude for the purposes of the surrender of Japanese forces in Indochina. In March 1945 the Japanese, aware of French plans for a coup d'état to restore their authority, had arrested all French administrators and French Army forces they could find and put them in prison camps. A Japanese surrender would thus create a political vacuum in Vietnam. According to the Potsdam Agreement on Indochina, Chinese forces were to occupy territory north of the 16th Parallel, while British imperial forces would take the Japanese surrender south of it. This decision had profound implications for the course of events in Vietnam.

Primary Source

Please deliver the following message from me to Generalissimo Chiang Kai-shek [Jiang Jieshi].

13. Abdication of Emperor Bao Dai of Annam, August 1945

Introduction

The last of the Nguyen dynasty emperors, Bao Dai (1913–1997) was educated in France and crowned emperor in 1926, although the French did not allow him to return to Vietnam until 1932. Initially enthusiastic about his role and attempting to introduce reforms, Bao Dai soon discovered that he was hamstrung by the French authorities and had little power. Disillusioned, he gave himself over to the pursuit of pleasure. Bao Dai cooperated with the Japanese during their occupation in World War II and in March 1945, at their behest, declared independence. Although he tried to govern, the Viet Minh seized power in northern Vietnam. Recognizing the inevitable, Bao Dai abdicated on August 25, becoming First Citizen Vinh Thuy. Elected to the new Viet Minh legislature, he soon became disillusioned with Communist control and departed his homeland for self-imposed exile in France.

Primary Source

The happiness of the people of Vietnam!

The Independence of Vietnam!

To achieve these ends, we have declared ourself ready for any sacrifice and we desire that our sacrifice be useful to the people.

Considering that the unity of all our compatriots is at this time our country's need, we recalled to our people on August 22: "In this decisive hour of our national history, union means life and division means death."

In view of the powerful democratic spirit growing in the north of our kingdom, we feared that conflict between north and south could be inevitable if we were to wait for a National Congress to decide for us, and we know that this conflict, if it occurred, would plunge our people into suffering and would play the game of the invaders.

We cannot but have a certain feeling of melancholy upon thinking of our glorious ancestors who fought without respite for 400 years to aggrandise our country from Thuan- hoa to Ha-tien.

Despite this, and strong in our convictions, we have decided to abdicate and we transfer power to the democratic Republican Government.

Upon leaving our throne, we have only three wishes to express:

1. We request that the new Government take care of the dynastic temples and royal tombs.
2. We request the new Government to deal fraternally with all the parties and groups which have fought for the independence of our country even though they have not closely followed the popular movement; to do this in order to give them the opportunity to participate in the reconstruction of the country, and to demonstrate that the new regime is built upon the absolute union of the entire population.
3. We invite all parties and groups, all classes of society, as well as the royal family, to solidarize in unreserved support of the democratic Government with a view to consolidating the national independence.

As for us, during twenty years' reign, we have known much bitterness. Henceforth, we shall be happy to be a free citizen in an independent country. We shall allow no one to abuse our name or the name of the royal family in order to sow dissent among our compatriots.

Long live the independence of Vietnam!

Long live our Democratic Republic!

Source: Harold R. Isaacs, ed., *New Cycle in Asia* (New York: Macmillan, 1947), 161–162.

14. Vietnamese Declaration of Independence, September 2, 1945

Introduction

In March 1945 the Japanese arrested French officials and the vast bulk of the French military throughout Indochina. Thus, on August 14 when Japan surrendered unconditionally to the Allies, there was a vacuum in Vietnam into which Nationalist leader Ho Chi Minh and his Viet Minh Nationalist/Communist organization now moved. On August 16 in Hanoi, Ho declared himself president of the provisional government of a "free Vietnam," and three days later the Viet Minh seized power in Hanoi. Emperor Bao Dai abdicated on August 25, and on September 2 in Hanoi Ho publicly announced the formation of a "Provisional Government of the Democratic Republic of Vietnam" with its capital at Hanoi. Then, in a clear bid to widen his base at home and win Western support abroad, on November 11 Ho dissolved the Indochinese Communist Party (ICP).

Primary Source

"All men are created equal. They are endowed by their Creator with certain inalienable rights; among these are Life, Liberty, and the pursuit of Happiness."

This immortal statement was made in the Declaration of Independence of the United States of America in 1776. In a broader sense, this means: All the peoples on the earth are equal from birth, all the peoples have a right to live, to be happy and free.

The Declaration of the French Revolution made in 1791 on the Rights of Man and the Citizen also states: "All men are born free and with equal rights, and must always remain free and have equal rights."

Those are undeniable truths.

Nevertheless, for more than eighty years, the French imperialists, abusing the standard of Liberty, Equality, and Fraternity, have violated our Fatherland and oppressed our fellow-citizens. They have acted contrary to the ideals of humanity and justice.

In the field of politics, they have deprived our people of every democratic liberty.

They have enforced inhuman laws; they have set up three distinct political regimes in the North, the Center and the South of Vietnam in order to wreck our national unity and prevent our people from being united.

They have built more prisons than schools. They have mercilessly slain our patriots, they have drowned our uprisings in rivers of blood.

They have fettered public opinion, they have practiced obscurantism against our people.

To weaken our race they have forced us to use opium and alcohol.

In the field of economics, they have fleeced us to the backbone, impoverished our people, and devastated our land.

They have robbed us of our rice fields, our mines, our forests, and our raw materials. They have monopolized the issuing of banknotes and the export trade.

They have invented numerous unjustifiable taxes and reduced our people, especially our peasantry, to a state of extreme poverty.

They have hampered the prospering of our national bourgeoisie; they have mercilessly exploited our workers.

In the autumn of 1940, when the Japanese Fascists violated Indochina's territory to establish new bases in their fight against the Allies, the French imperialists went down on their bended knees and handed over our country to them.

Thus, from that date, our people were subjected to the double yoke of the French and the Japanese. Their sufferings and miseries increased. The result was that from the end of last year to the beginning of this year, from Quang Tri Province to the North of Vietnam, more than two million of our fellow-citizens died from starvation. On March 9, the French troops were disarmed by the Japanese. The French colonialists either fled or surrendered showing that not only were they incapable of "protecting" us, but that, in the span of five years, they had twice sold our country to the Japanese.

On several occasions before March 9, the Viet Minh League urged the French to ally themselves with it against the Japanese. Instead of agreeing to this proposal, the French colonialists so intensified their terrorist activities against the Viet Minh members that before fleeing they massacred a great number of our political prisoners detained at Yen Bay and Cao Bang.

Notwithstanding all this, our fellow citizens have always manifested toward the French a tolerant and humane attitude. Even after the Japanese Putsch of March, 1945, the Viet Minh League helped many Frenchmen to cross the frontier, rescued some of them from Japanese jails, and protected French lives and property.

From the autumn of 1940, our country had in fact ceased to be a French colony and had become a Japanese possession.

After the Japanese had surrendered to the Allies, our whole people rose to regain our national sovereignty and to found the Democratic Republic of Viet-Nam.

The truth is that we have wrested our independence from the Japanese and not from the French.

The French have fled, the Japanese have capitulated, Emperor Bao Dai has abdicated. Our people have broken the chains which for nearly a century have fettered them and have independence for the Fatherland. Our people at the same time have overthrown the monarchic regime that has reigned supreme for dozens of centuries. In its place has been established the present Democratic Republic.

For these reasons, we, members of the Provisional Government, representing the whole Vietnamese people, declare that from now on we break off all relations of a colonial character with France; we repeal all the international obligation that France has so far subscribed to on behalf of Viet-Nam, and we abolish all the special rights the French have unlawfully acquired in our Fatherland.

The whole Vietnamese people, animated by a common purpose, are determined to fight to the bitter end against any attempt by the French colonialists to reconquer their country.

We are convinced that the Allied nations, which at Teheran and San Francisco have acknowledged the principles of self-determination and equality of nations, will not refuse to acknowledge the independence of Viet-Nam.

A people who have courageously opposed French domination for more than eighty years, a people who have fought side by side with the Allies against the fascists during these last years, such a people must be free and independent.

For these reasons, we, members of the Provisional Government of the Democratic Republic of Viet-Nam, solemnly declare to the world that Viet-Nam has the right to be a free and independent country—and in fact it is so already. The entire Vietnamese people are determined to mobilize all their physical and mental strength, to sacrifice their lives and property in order to safeguard their independence and liberty.

Source: Ho Chi Minh, *Selected Works*, Vol. 3 (Hanoi: Foreign Languages Publishing House, 1960–62), 17–21.

15. Dean Acheson, Acting Secretary of State: Telegram to Charge Walter Robertson in China, October 5, 1945

Introduction

With the end of World War II, the U.S. government found itself caught between a rock and a hard place regarding the unfolding situation in Indochina. In this first official statement of policy by the Harry S. Truman administration after Ho Chi Minh's declaration of the independence of the Democratic Republic of Vietnam (DRV, North Vietnam), Acting Secretary of State Dean Acheson in October 1945 restates the U.S. position of the previous August that the United States does not dispute French sovereignty over Vietnam but will not assist France's reestablishment militarily. He also states that the American position will be conditioned by whether the Vietnamese support French sovereignty.

Primary Source

US has no thought of opposing the reestablishment of French control in Indochina and no official statement by US Govt has questioned even by implication French sovereignty over Indochina. However, it is not the policy of this Govt to assist the French to reestablish their control over Indochina by force and the willingness of the US to see French control reestablished assumes that French claim to have the support of the population of Indochina is borne out by future events.

> **Source:** *United States–Vietnam Relations, 1945–1967,* Book 8 (Washington, DC: U.S. Government Printing Office, 1971), 49.

16. Ho Chi Minh: Letter to President Harry S. Truman, October 17, 1945

Introduction

New president of the Democratic Republic of Vietnam (DRV, North Vietnam) Ho Chi Minh found himself in a difficult position. The North Vietnamese government desperately needed both diplomatic support and capital. With the Soviet Union in no position to provide financial assistance, Ho turned to the United States. Using legalistic arguments, he presented the case to U.S. president Harry S. Truman that North Vietnam rather than France should be represented on the United Nations (UN) Advisory Commission for the Far East. In a clear bid to win Western support as well as to increase his base of support at home, on November 11, 1945, Ho dissolved the Indochinese Communist Party (ICP). How sincere Ho, the veteran Communist, was about this has been a matter of considerable debate. Regardless, he never received an answer to his letter of October 17 and subsequent appeals to Truman and other U.S. officials for a meeting with the American president.

Primary Source

Establishment of Advisory Commission for the Far East is heartily welcomed by Vietnamese people in principle. Taking into consideration primo the strategical and economical importance of Vietnam secundo the earnest desire which Vietnam deeply feels and has unanimously manifested to cooperate with the other democracies in the establishment and consolidation of world peace and

prosperity we wish to call the attention of the Allied nations on the following points:

First   absence of Vietnam and presence of France in the Advisory Commission leads to the conclusion that France is to represent the Vietnamese people at the Commission. Such representation is groundless either de jure or defacto. De jure no alliance exists any more between France and Vietnam: Baodai abolished treaties of 1884 and 1863 comma, Baodai voluntarily abdicated to hand over government to Democratic Republican Government, Provisional Government rectorated [sic] abolishment of treaties of 1884 and 1863. De facto since March ninth France having handed over governing rule to Japan has broken all administrative links with Vietnam, since August 18, 1945, Provisional Government has been a de facto independent government in every respect, recent incidents in Saigon instigated by the French roused unanimous disapproval leading to fight for independence.

Second   France is not entitled because she had ignominiously sold Indo China to Japan and betrayed the Allies.

Third   Vietnam is qualified by Atlantic Charter and subsequent peace agreement and by her goodwill and her unflinching stand for democracy to be represented at the Advisory Commission. We are convinced that Vietnam at Commission will be able to bring effective contribution to solution of pending problems in Far East whereas her absence would bring forth unstability [sic] and temporary character to solutions otherwise reached. Therefore we express earnest request to take part in Advisory Commission for Far East. We should be very grateful to your excellency and Premier Attlee Premier Stalin Generalissimo Tchang Kai Shek for the conveyance of our desiderata to the United Nations.

> **Source:** *United States–Vietnam Relations, 1945–1967,* Book 1 (Washington, DC: U.S. Government Printing Office, 1971), C73–C74.

17. Ho Chi Minh: Letter to Secretary of State James F. Byrnes, October 22, 1945 [Excerpts]

Introduction

Acting in accordance with the agreement reached at the Potsdam Conference regarding the surrender of Japanese forces in Indochina, the British dispatched to Vietnam south of the 16th Parallel some 5,000 troops of the 20th Indian Division. At the same time, the nationalist Viet Minh hoped to add southern Vietnam to the northern part of the country, now controlled by the Democratic Republic of Vietnam (DRV, North Vietnam). On August 29, 1945, the Viet Minh leader in the south, Tran Van Giau, led an insurrection against French rule in which atrocities were committed against French nationals, including the murders of women and children. On his own initiative, Major General Douglas Gracey, the commander of the 20th Division who detested the Viet Minh, rearmed French soldiers who had been imprisoned by the Japanese. French, British, and Japanese troops then crushed Viet Minh resistance in Saigon. In this letter to U.S. secretary of state James F. Byrnes, North Vietnamese president Ho Chi Minh calls for immediate United Nations (UN) intervention to halt the violence in southern Vietnam, which he claims has reached the "critical stage," and makes the case for a united, independent Vietnam.

Primary Source

Excellency: The situation in South Vietnam has reached its critical stage, and calls for immediate interference on the part of the United Nations. I wish by the present letter to bring your excellency some more light on the case of Vietnam which has come for the last three weeks into the international limelight. . . .

After 80 years of French oppression and unsuccessful though obstinate Vietnamese resistance, we at last saw France defeated in Europe, then her betrayal of the Allies successively on behalf of Germany and of Japan. Though the odds were at that time against the Allies, the Vietnamese, leaving aside all differences in political opinion, united in the Vietminh League and started on a ruthless fight against the Japanese. Meanwhile, the Atlantic Charter was concluded, defining the war aims of the Allies and laying the foundation of peace-work. The noble principles of international justice and equality of status laid down in that charter strongly appealed to the Vietnamese and contributed in making of the Vietminh resistance in the war zone a nation-wide anti-Japanese movement which found a powerful echo in the democratic aspirations of the people. The Atlantic Charter was looked upon as the foundation of future Vietnam. A nation-building program was drafted which was later found in keeping with San Francisco Charter and which has been fully carried out these last years: continuous fight against the Japanese bringing about the recovery of national independence on August 19th, voluntary abdication of Ex-Emperor Baodai, establishment of the Democratic Republic of Vietnam, assistance given to the Allied Nations in the disarmament of the Japanese, appointment of a provisional Government whose mission was to carry out the Atlantic and San Francisco Charters and have them carried out by other nations.

As a matter of fact, the carrying out of the Atlantic and San Francisco Charters implies the eradication of imperialism and all forms of colonial oppression. This was unfortunately contrary to the interests of some Frenchmen, and France, to whom the colonists have long concealed the truth on Indochina, instead of entering into peaceable negotiations, resorted to an aggressive invasion, with all the means at the command of a modern nation. Moreover, having persuaded the British that the Vietnamese are wishing for

a return of the French rule, they obtained, first from the British command in Southeast Asia, then from London, a tacit recognition of their sovereignty and administrative responsibility as far as South Vietnam is concerned. The British gave to understand that they had agreed to this on the ground that the reestablishment of French administration and, consequently, of Franco-Vietnamese collaboration would help them to speed up the demobilization and the disarmament of the Japanese. But subsequent events will prove the fallacy of the argument. The whole Vietnamese nation rose up as one man against French aggression. The first hours of September 23rd soon developed into real and organized warfare in which losses are heavy on both sides. The bringing in of French important reinforcements on board of the most powerful of their remaining warships will extend the war zone further. As murderous fighting is still going on in Indonesia, and as savage acts on the part of Frenchmen are reported every day, we may expect the flaring up of a general conflagration in the Far-East.

As it is, the situation in South Vietnam calls for immediate interference. The establishment of the Consultative Commission for the Far-East has been enthusiastically welcomed here as the first effective step toward an equitable settlement of the pending problems. The people of Vietnam . . . only asks for full independence and for the respect of truth and justice. . . .

Source: *United States–Vietnam Relations, 1945–1967*, Book 1 (Washington, DC: U.S. Government Printing Office, 1971), C80–C81.

18. Ho Chi Minh: Speech on the Resistance War in Southern Vietnam, November 1945

Introduction

Acting in accordance with the agreement reached at the earlier Potsdam Conference, the Guomindang (GMD, Nationalist) government of China dispatched 150,000–200,000 men into Vietnam to take the surrender of Japanese troops north of the 16th Parallel. The Chinese proceeded to bleed the region of much of its resources, but the new government of the Democratic Republic of Vietnam (DRV, North Vietnam) was able to buy off the Chinese, specifically General Lu Han and his staff, and in the process secured some weapons. At the same time, the North Vietnamese leaders gave full support to the Viet Minh effort in southern Vietnam to bring it into the fold. Fighting occurred in many places in southern Vietnam between the Viet Minh on the one hand and British, French, and even Japanese troops on the other. In this November 1945 speech, North Vietnamese president Ho Chi Minh seeks to rally all Vietnamese behind the southern resistance movement.

Primary Source

Compatriots!

During the Second World War, the French colonialists twice sold out our country to the Japanese. Thus they betrayed the Allied nations, and helped the Japanese to cause the latter many losses.

Meanwhile they also betrayed our people, exposing us to the destruction of bombs and bullets. In this way, the French colonialists withdrew of their own accord from the Allied ranks and tore up the treaties they had earlier compelled us to sign.

Notwithstanding the French colonialists' treachery, our people as a whole are determined to side with the Allies and oppose the invaders. When the Japanese surrendered, our entire people single-mindedly changed our country into a Democratic Republic and elected a provisional Government which is to prepare for a national congress and draw up our draft Constitution.

Not only is our act in line with the Atlantic and San Francisco Charters, etc. solemnly proclaimed by the Allies, but it entirely conforms with the glorious principles upheld by the French people, viz. Freedom, Equality and Fraternity.

It is thus clear that in the past the colonialists betrayed the Allies and our country, and surrendered to the Japanese. At present, in the shadow of the British and Indian troops, and behind the Japanese soldiers, they are attacking the South of our country.

They have sabotaged the peace that China, the United States, Britain and Russia won at the cost of scores of millions of lives. They have run counter to the promises concerning democracy and liberty that the Allied powers have proclaimed. They have of their own accord sabotaged their fathers' principles of liberty and equality. In consequence, it is for a just cause, for justice of the world, and for Viet Nam's land and people that our compatriots throughout the country have risen to struggle, and are firmly determined to maintain their independence. We do not hate the French people and France. We are energetically fighting slavery, and the ruthless policy of the French colonialists. We are not invading another's country. We only safeguard our own against the French invaders. Hence we are not alone. The countries which love peace and democracy, and the weaker nations all over the world, all sympathize with us. With the unity of the whole people within the country, and having many sympathizers abroad, we are sure of victory.

The French colonialists have behaved lawlessly in the South for almost one and a half months. Our southern compatriots have sacrificed their lives in a most valiant struggle. Public opinion in the great countries: China, the United States, Russia and Britain, has supported our just cause.

Compatriots throughout the country! Those in the South will do their utmost to resist the enemy. Those in the Centre and the North will endeavour to help their southern compatriots, and be on the alert.

The French colonialists should know that the Vietnamese people do not want bloodshed, that they love peace. But we are determined to sacrifice even millions of combatants, and fight a long-term war of resistance in order to safeguard Viet Nam's independence and free her children from slavery. We are sure that our war of resistance will be victorious!

Let the whole country be determined in the war of resistance!

Long live independent Viet Nam!

Source: Ho Chi Minh, *Selected Works*, Vol. 3 (Hanoi: Foreign Languages Publishing House, 1960–62), 48–49.

19. Ho Chi Minh: Declaration of the Policy of the Provisional Coalition Government, January 1, 1946

Introduction

Still in the hopes of securing recognition and aid from the United States, the new government of the Democratic Republic of Vietnam (DRV, North Vietnam) remained a coalition in name but was in fact controlled by the Communists. Here North Vietnamese president Ho Chi Minh stresses the coalition nature of the government and enumerates domestic and foreign policy goals. These include friendly relations with all countries (he especially singles out China) and opposition only to those French who seek to reestablish colonial control. Ho pledges to protect the lives and property of those who do not threaten Vietnamese independence.

Primary Source

With a view to winning complete independence and bringing about a close cooperation between the various political parties to further strengthen the Government, it is now named the Provisional Coalition Government. At this moment, if the parties unite together, the Government can overcome difficulties. All the Vietnamese people want the Provisional Government to hold office until the election of the National Assembly, which will change it into a definite Government. Meanwhile, the Provisional Coalition Government will discuss the following practical questions:

HOME POLICY

Political objectives: to carry out satisfactorily the general elections throughout the country; to unify the various administrative organs according to democratic principles.

Economic objectives: to endeavor to develop agriculture; to encourage cultivation and stock-breeding in order to check famine.

Military objectives: to unify the various armed forces under the command of the Government. Parties are not allowed to have armies of their own.

Cultural objectives: to give aid to various cultural organs. In short, in home policy, the Government must exert itself politically to unify the country, and intensify production in order to cope with famine and foreign invasion.

FOREIGN POLICY

Objectives: to induce other countries to recognize Viet-Nam's independence; to have friendly relations with foreign residents of Viet-Nam, particularly the Chinese. With regard to the Frenchmen, we only fight the colonialists. As for those who do not seek to prejudice our independence, we will protect their lives and property.

Such is the policy of the Provisional Coalition Government of the Democratic Republic of Viet-Nam. I hope that the entire people will support it to enable the Government to succeed.

Long live independent Viet-Nam!

> **Source:** Ho Chi Minh, *On Revolution: Selected Writings, 1920–66,* edited by Bernard B. Fall (New York: Praeger, 1967), 160–161.

20. Preliminary Franco–Viet Minh Convention, March 6, 1946 [Excerpts]

Introduction

On February 28, 1946, the governments of France and Guomindang (GMD, Nationalist) China reached agreement whereby the Chinese would withdraw from Vietnam north of the 16th Parallel in return for yielding certain concessions in China. The Chinese departed in March 1946, and with U.S. and Soviet support for the government of the Democratic Republic of Vietnam (DRV, North Vietnam) not forthcoming, President Ho Chi Minh had no alternative but to deal with France, which was now steadily augmenting its troop strength in Indochina. The result was the agreement of March 6, 1946, between Ho and French diplomatic representative Jean Sainteny. In it, France recognizes North Vietnam as a "free state" with its own institutions and as "part of the Indo-Chinese Federation of the French Union." In a key provision, France also agrees to the holding of a referendum in southern Vietnam to see if it wanted to join the North Vietnamese government in a unified state, although no date for the vote is specified. In a supplemental

agreement, France is allowed to introduce 15,000 French and 10,000 Vietnamese troops under unified French command ostensibly to protect French lives and property. The French government promises to withdraw 3,000 of them each year, with all to be gone by the end of 1951 with the possible exception of those guarding bases. France also agrees to train and equip units of the new Vietnamese Army. Had the Ho-Sainteny Agreement been allowed to stand, the Indochina War and the Vietnam War would not have occurred.

Primary Source

1. The French Government recognizes the Vietnamese Republic as a Free State having its own Government, its own Parliament, its own Army, and its own Finances, forming part of the Indochinese Federation and of the French Union. . . .

2. The Vietnamese Government declares itself ready to welcome amicably the French Army when, conforming to international agreements, it relieves the Chinese Troops. . . .

3. The stipulations formulated above will immediately enter into force. Immediately after the exchange of signatures, each of the High Contracting Parties will take all measures necessary to stop hostilities in the field, to maintain the troops in their respective positions, and to create the favorable atmosphere necessary to the immediate opening of friendly and sincere negotiations. These negotiations will deal particularly with:

   a. diplomatic relations of Viet-nam with Foreign States
   b. the future law of Indochina
   c. French interests, economic and cultural in Viet-nam

Hanoi, Saigon or Paris may be chosen as the seat of the conference.

Signed: Sainteny

Signed: Ho-chi Minh and Vu Hong Khanh

> **Source:** *The Pentagon Papers: The Defense Department History of United States Decisionmaking on Vietnam,* Vol. 1. Senator Gravel edition (Boston: Beacon, 1971), 18–19.

21. James F. Byrnes, Secretary of State: Note to French Ambassador Henri Bonnet, April 12, 1946

Introduction

In this note from U.S. secretary of state James Byrnes to French ambassador Henri Bonnet, Byrnes removes the caveat by Acting Secretary of State Dean Acheson in October 1945 that the U.S.

position regarding the restoration of French sovereignty in Indo-china would depend on whether the indigenous population supported it. The note also ignores the Ho-Sainteny Agreement of the previous month in which France agreed to recognize Vietnam as a "free state."

Primary Source

The Secretary of State presents his compliments to His Excellency the French Ambassador and has the honor to refer to the Ambassador's note no. 167 of March 7, 1946, enclosing a copy of the Franco-Chinese Agreement with regard to the relief of Chinese forces in northern Indo-China by French forces and requesting the approval of the Combined Chiefs of Staff thereto.

The Secretary of State is pleased to inform the Ambassador that the Combined Chiefs of Staff have no objection to the relief of Chinese troops in northern French Indo-China by French forces, since they consider that such arrangements are a matter for determination by the Governments of France and China.

Since the Franco-Chinese agreement completes the reversion of all Indo-China to French control, the Combined Chiefs of Staff consider that the French military commander in Indo-China should act as a medium for the French Government for coordination with the Supreme Commander for the Allied Powers on matters relating to the repatriation of Japanese from Indo-China, and that the Chinese Supreme Commander and Admiral Mountbatten should be relieved of their duties and responsibilities for disarmament and evacuation of Japanese in Indo-China.

Current repatriation schedules envisage the completion of the evacuation of the Japanese from northern Indo-China by April 15. The Combined Chiefs of Staff consider that it is most desirable to have the French commander in Indo-China conform to present schedules.

Accordingly, Admiral Mountbatten has been directed to make the necessary arrangements with the French military commander in Indo-China regarding the transfer of his share of the abovementioned responsibility at the earliest possible date.

The Supreme Commander for the Allied Powers and the appropriate Chinese authorities have been informed of the Combined Chiefs of Staff action on this matter.

It is understood that a memorandum has been addressed directly to the French Military Attaché to the United States informing him of the above and requesting that appropriate instructions be issued to the French military commander in Indo-China.

Source: *United States–Vietnam Relations, 1945–1967*, Book 8 (Washington, DC: U.S. Government Printing Office, 1971), 64–65.

22. Ho Chi Minh: Letter to Compatriots in Nam Bo, May 31, 1946

Introduction

Under terms of the Ho-Sainteny Agreement, French troops returned to Democratic Republic of Vietnam (DRV, North Vietnam). North Vietnamese president Ho Chi Minh now led a Vietnamese delegation to France to negotiate implementation of the agreement. Before departing, he addressed a letter to those living in southern Vietnam. In it he pledges to secure the unity of Vietnam and urges them to be generous to those who might oppose unification with North Vietnam. Nothing was accomplished at the Fontainebleau Conference, however, and on June 1 just after Ho's departure for France, on his own initiative French high commissioner in Indochina Admiral Georges Thierry d'Argenlieu torpedoed Sainteny's work by proclaiming in Saigon the establishment of the "Republic of Cochinchina." With an "independent" Republic of Cochin China there would be no need of a plebiscite in southern Vietnam.

Primary Source

Dear fellow-countrymen in Nam Bo,

The news of my going to France with a delegation for official negotiation has caused concern to our people, especially in Nam Bo. What does the future hold for Nam Bo?

Please, don't worry. I pledge my word that Ho Chi Minh will never sell his country.

You in Nam Bo have been fighting self-sacrificingly for many months now to safeguard the territorial integrity of Viet Nam; for this, our entire people are grateful to you.

You in Nam Bo are citizens of Viet Nam. Rivers may dry up, mountains may erode; but this truth can never change.

I advise you to unite closely and broadly. The five fingers are of unequal length but they are united in the hand.

The millions of our fellow-countrymen are not all alike; but they are descended from the same ancestors. We must therefore be generous and broadminded and admit the fact that the offspring of the Lac and the Hong are all more or less patriotic. With regard to those who have gone astray, we must use friendly persuasion. Only in this way can we achieve unity, and broad unity will bring us a bright future.

Through this short message written before my departure, I wish to convey my cordial greetings to all of you, dear fellow-countrymen in Nam Bo.

Source: Ho Chi Minh, *Selected Writings: 1920–1969* (Hanoi: Foreign Languages Publishing House, 1977), 66–67.

23. Ho Chi Minh: Reply at Luncheon Given by French Premier Georges Bidault, July 2, 1946

Introduction

In June 1946 Ho Chi Minh, president of the Democratic Republic of Vietnam (DRV, North Vietnam), led a delegation to France to discuss implementation of the March 6 Ho-Sainteny Agreement. The French government having fallen, it was weeks before this Fontainebleau Conference could commence, so Ho traveled in France. In these remarks in an official French government luncheon in his honor, he invokes French history, including the ideals enshrined by the French Revolution of 1789, and expresses hopes for a fruitful partnership between the North Vietnamese government and France within the framework of the French Union.

Primary Source

The reception given me by the French people and Government has moved me to my innermost heart. Please convey to the French Government and people the sincere thanks of the Vietnamese people for the sympathy and friendliness the French people and Government have expressed to me. Before officially greeting the French Government, I had the opportunity to visit the Basque provinces, a very beautiful region of France. The contact with the Basques taught me many lessons. While maintaining their peculiarities, dialect, and customs, the Basque people continue to be French citizens. Though France has many provinces which differ from each other, it remains unified and indivisible. In the future, the French Union will astonish the world with its solidarity and unity. The French Union that we will establish on a democratic basis can be set up only under a good omen. It is here in Paris, a heroic and generous city which proclaimed the principles of liberty, equality, and fraternity, a city which has the tradition to champion the equality of other peoples, it is in this very city that I solemnly declare that Viet-Nam will join this humanitarian organization.

Paris is the city which discovered the eternal ideals for the 1789 Revolution; it has remained loyal to its ideals in the bloodshed between the democratic and fascist blocs.

Paris has made no small contribution to the concord of Viet-Nam and France within the French Union including free and equal nations which cherish the same democratic ideals and are all for freedom. It is here in Paris that Viet-Nam will step forward to the path of independence. I am convinced that it will not be long before independent Viet-Nam plays its worthy role in the Pacific. No doubt many difficulties are awaiting the Fontainebleau Conference which has the responsibility to lay down the foundation for the relations between new France and new Viet-Nam. But sincerity and mutual confidence will level all obstacles. Have we not done away with aggressive imperialism and narrow chauvinism which

are no longer fit for the present world? We are all stimulated by the same spirit. The Confucian philosophy and the Western philosophy alike uphold an ethic principle which is "Do as you would be done by." I believe that in those conditions, the forthcoming conference will achieve satisfactory results.

Mr. Prime Minister, I believe that the sincere and friendly cooperation between our two countries will be a great example for the world to realize that with mutual confidence, free and equal nations can always solve the most difficult problems. Ladies and gentlemen, I beg to propose a toast in honor of the Prime Minister and members of the French Government.

Source: Ho Chi Minh, *On Revolution: Selected Writings, 1920–66*, edited by Bernard B. Fall (New York: Praeger, 1967), 166–167.

24. Abbot L. Moffat, Chief of the Division of Southeast Asian Affairs: Memorandum to John Carter Vincent, Director of the Office of Far Eastern Affairs, August 9, 1946

Introduction

In this memorandum, chief of the Division of Southeast Asian Affairs Abbot L. Moffat discusses recent developments in French policy toward Indochina, specifically suspension of the Fontainebleau Conference in France and the French government's torpedoing of the Ho-Sainteny Agreement of March 1946 to include the establishment of a "Republic of Cochinchina" and the convening of a conference at Dalat on August 1 with representatives of the kingdoms of Laos and Cambodia, the Republic of Cochin China, and minorities within southern Vietnam. He also notes fighting between "Annamese" and French forces.

Primary Source

Recent developments indicate that the French are moving to regain a large measure of their control of Indochina in violation of the spirit of the, March 6 convention. The evidence, as set forth below, suggests that the French are attempting to gain their objective by manoeuvres designed to confine and weaken Viet Nam. In. the event that Viet Nam decides to resist these encroachments, which is by no means unlikely, widespread hostilities may result.

The chief opposition to the reestablishment of French rule in Indochina has all along come from the Annamese, who inhabit the three east coastal provinces of Tonkin, Annam, and Cochinchina, which once comprised the Kingdom of Annam. The populations of the other two countries of Indochina—Cambodia and Laos—are not in a high state of political development or in any condition seriously to resist French control. A modus vivendi between the French and the Annamese was achieved in the preliminary convention of March 6, 1946, by which the Annamese "Republic of Viet Nam" was recognized as a free state within the Indochinese Federation and the Viet Nam Government declared its readiness to receive the French Army.

The convention left for future settlement two crucial problems: the status of Viet Nam in its external relations, and the geographical extent of Viet Nam. On the former point, the provisional agreement stated that "each contracting party will take all necessary measures to create the favorable atmosphere necessary for an immediate opening of amicable and free negotiations. These negotiations will bear particularly upon diplomatic relations between the Viet Nam and foreign states, the future status of Indochina, French economic and cultural interests in Viet Nam." On the latter point the agreement stated that "with respect to the bringing together of the three (provinces), the French Government pledges itself to ratify the decisions taken by the populations consulted by referendum." The crux of the present situation lies in the apparent intention of the French to settle both matters to their own advantage and without reference to Viet Nam.

The hostility of the Annamese toward the French began to mount to its present intensity when the French on June 1 announced the inauguration of the Provisional Government of the Republic of Cochinchina. Annamese leaders had long emphasized their view that the inclusion of Cochinchina in Viet Nam was a matter of life and death to their country. Cochinchina, it may be mentioned, contains the important mercantile cities of Saigon and Cholon, includes the mouths of the Mekong, and is the richest province in Indochina.

Called the Southern Province by the Viet Namese, it is racially indistinct from Tonkin and Annam. Statements by the French that the referendum in Cochinchina (as pledged in the March 6 convention) would still be held failed to reassure Viet Nam leaders, who pointed out that such a referendum could not possibly be fair owing to the suppression by the French of pro–Viet Nam political parties and of all anti-French opinion. SEA's information tends to substantiate this point of view.

Tension between the French and the Amnamese reached its present pitch when the French on August 1 convened a conference at Dalat (in southern Annam) to which the Royal Governments of Cambodia and Laos, the Government of the autonomous Republic of Cochinchina, and the native peoples of southern Annam and high plateau of Indochina (but not Viet Nam, recognized by the French as part of the Indochina Federation and French Union) to send delegates to "study the framework of the French Union". Subsequently published agenda of the conference indicated that the

salient aspects of the Indochina Federation would also be deliberated. As an immediate result of this conference, the Viet Nam delegation which had been discussing the future relation between France and Viet Nam with the representatives of the French at Fountainebleau since July 6 announced that they were suspending negotiations until the French should have cleared up the "equivocal" situation which had been created. The head of the Viet Nam delegation, who had opened the conference with a violent blast against French policies, charged that the French were now trying to engineer their own statute for the Indochinese Federation and their own settlement of the status of Cochinchina and other areas claimed by Viet Nam.

The view of Consul Saigon is not very different. He gave as his opinion that a front against Viet Nam was in the making, that the states participating in the Dalat Conference were at least tacitly recognized as free states by the French, and that France and these free states are now determining the status of the Indochinese federation without reference to Viet Nam. In his view it indicated double-dealing on the part of the French, and he reported that the French Commissioner for Cochinchina had forced the issue by threatening to resign unless his policy is carried out. Nothing has been said at the conference about a referendum. Finally, Consul Saigon added that he had learned that representatives of the southern regions of the Province of Annam (which has always been claimed by Viet Nam) will petition for inclusion of their territories in Cochinchina. In view of the completeness of the agenda of the Dalat Conference, which covers the essential framework of the Indochinese federation, and in view of the deliberate exclusion of Viet Nam from the conference, the conclusion is inescapable that the French are endeavoring to whittle down Viet Nam and to settle the future form of organization of Indochina with those who may be expected to be amenable to French influence.

Annamese reaction to French moves has been sharp, and following the suspension of the Fontainebleau negotiations, there were pro-Viet Nam manifestations in Saigon. The ambush of a French supply column near Hanoi by Annamese soldiers, during which the French suffered 52 casualties (one of the worst of many incidents during the past several months), may have been related to the opening of the Dalat Conference.

While it is to be doubted that the French will allow the Fontainebleau Conference to break down completely, Embassy Paris quotes Baudet as having stated that French officials are in no hurry to speed up negotiations until the pacification of Indochina, and particularly of Cochinchina, has been completed. In this connection Consul Saigon reports that more troops are arriving in Indochina and that the French military position has grown much stronger. Meanwhile, the Saigon press has been carrying vitriolic attacks against Viet Nam. Since this press is completely controlled by the French, there would appear to be no official objection to this line.

In his latest report, Consul Hanoi states that there now exists an imminent danger of an open break between the French and Viet Nam. He adds that a rupture of relations would probably be followed by a period of anarchy and that, although the French could quickly overrun the country, they could not—as they themselves admit—pacify it except through a long and bitter military operation.

In conclusion, it is SEA's view that the Annamese are faced with the choice of a costly submission to the French or of open resistance, and that the French may be preparing to resort to force in order to secure their position throughout Indochina. It may not be advisable for this Government to take official notice of this situation during the Peace Conference, but the Department should be prepared, SEA believes, to express to the French, in view of our interest in peace and orderly development of dependent peoples, our hope that they will abide by the spirit of the March 6 convention.

Source: *Foreign Relations of the United States, 1946,* Vol. 8 (Washington, DC: U.S. Government Printing Office, 1971), 52–54.

25. Franco-Vietnamese Modus Vivendi, September 14, 1946

Introduction

This innocuous document was the result of the Fontainebleau Conference between the Vietnamese delegation headed by President Ho Chi Minh of the Democratic Republic of Vietnam (DRV, North Vietnam) and the French government. While the modus vivendi makes reference to the Ho-Sainteny Agreement of the previous March, pledges both sides to implement a policy of "concord and conciliation," and sets out a number of key principles to be followed, in reality nothing was accomplished at the Fontainebleau Conference. The draft accord reinforced France's economic rights in North Vietnam without solving the problem of the French creation of the independent state of Cochin China, in clear violation of the Ho-Sainteny Agreement.

Primary Source

The Government of the French Republic and the Government of the Democratic Republic of Viet Nam have firmly decided to pursue, in a spirit of reciprocal confidence, the policy of concord and collaboration established by the Preliminary Convention of March 6 and outlined during the course of Franco-Viet Nam conferences at Dalat and Fontainebleau. Convinced that this policy alone represents the permanent interests of the two countries and the democratic traditions which they claim as theirs, the two Governments, while referring to the Convention of March 6 which continues in force, consider that the time has come to register new progress in the development of relations between France and Viet Nam, while

awaiting the time when circumstances will permit the conclusion of a complete and definitive agreement. In a spirit of friendship and mutual understanding, the Government of the French Republic and the Government of the Democratic Republic of Viet Nam have signed a Modus Vivendi providing, within the framework of the limited agreements, provisional solutions of the main issues of immediate interest which arise between France and Viet Nam. So far as the referendum provided for in the Convention of March 6 is concerned, the two Governments reserve the right to fix later its date and form. They are convinced that all the measures contained in the Modus Vivendi will contribute to the establishment, in the near future, of an atmosphere of calm and confidence which will permit the carrying on of definite negotiations in the near future. They believe, therefore, that it is possible to anticipate for the resumption in January 1947 of the work which has just taken place at the Franco-Vietnamese conference in Fontainebleau.

Franco-Vietnamese Modus Vivendi

Article 1—Viet Nam nationals in France and French nationals in Viet Nam shall enjoy the same freedom of establishment as nationals, as well as freedom of speech, freedom to teach, to trade and to circulate in general all the democratic freedoms.

Article 2—French property and concerns in Viet Nam shall not be subject to a stricter regime than the one reserved for Vietnamese property and concerns, particularly with respect to taxation and labor legislation. This equality of status shall be granted reciprocally to the property and enterprises of Viet Nam nationals in the territories of the French Union. The status of the French property and concerns in Viet Nam may not be changed except by common agreement between the French Republic and the Republic of Viet Nam. All French property requisitioned by the Government of Viet Nam or of which persons or enterprises have been deprived by the Viet Nam authorities shall be returned to their owners and parties entitled thereto. A mixed commission shall be appointed to fix procedure for such restitution.

Article 3—For the purpose of the resumption of the cultural relations which Viet Nam and France are equally desirous of developing, French educational institutions representing different categories shall be able to function freely in Viet Nam and they shall apply official French programs. The institutions in question shall receive, by special agreement, the buildings necessary for their functioning. They shall be open to Vietnamese students. Scientific research, the establishing and functioning of scientific institutions shall be unhindered for French nationals throughout Viet Nam territory. Viet Nam nationals shall enjoy the same privilege in France. The Pasteur Institute shall be secured in its rights and property. A mixed commission shall regulate the conditions under which the "Ecole Francaise d'Extrême Orient" (Far Eastern French School) shall resume its activity.

Article 4—The Government of the Republic of Viet Nam shall call, first on French nationals, whenever it needs advisers, technicians or experts. The priority granted to French nationals shall cease to be in effect only in cases where it is impossible for France to furnish the required personnel.

Article 5—As soon as the present problem of monetary standardization is settled, one and the same currency shall have circulation in the territories under the authority of the Government of the Democratic Republic of Viet Nam and in the other territories of Indochina. The said currency shall be the Indochinese piaster.

Article 6—Viet Nam shall form a Customs Union with the other members of the Federation. Therefore, there shall be no customs barrier within the country and the same tariffs shall be applied everywhere for entry into and departure from Indochinese territory. A coordinating customs and foreign trade committee which, moreover, may be the same as the one dealing with currency and exchange shall study the necessary means of application and prepare the organization of the Indochinese customs service.

Article 7—A mixed communications coordinating committee shall study the measures which will re-establish and improve communications between Viet Nam and the other countries of the Indochinese Federation and the French Union: land, sea and air transport, postal, telephone, telegraph and radio communications.

Article 8—Until such time as the French Government and the Government of the Democratic Republic of Viet Nam conclude a definitive agreement regulating the question of the diplomatic relations of Viet Nam with foreign countries, a mixed Franco–Viet Nam Commission shall determine the arrangements to be made to ensure the consular representation of Viet Nam in neighboring countries and its relations with foreign consuls.

Article 9—Desirous of ensuring as soon as possible, in Cochinchina and in Southern Annam, the restoration of public order as indispensable to the free development of democratic liberties as it is to the resumption of commercial transactions and aware of the fortunate effect that the cessation on the part of both of all acts of hostility or violence will have, the French Government and the Government of the Democratic Republic of Viet Nam have decided on the following measures:

(a) Acts of hostility and violence on the part of both shall cease.
(b) Agreements of the French and Viet Nam General Staff shall arrange the conditions of application and supervision of measures decided in common.
(c) It is specified that prisoners detained at the present time for political reasons shall be released with the exception of those prosecuted for crimes and offenses against the common law. The same shall apply for prisoners captured

in the course of operations. Viet Nam guarantees that no prosecution shall be initiated and no act of violence tolerated against any person by reason of his attachment or loyalty to France; reciprocally, the French Government guarantees that no prosecution shall be initiated and no act of violence tolerated toward any person because of his attachment to Viet Nam.
(d) The enjoyment of the democratic freedoms defined in Article I shall be reciprocally guaranteed.
(e) Unfriendly propaganda on both sides shall be terminated.
(f) A person of note designated by the Government of the Democratic Republic of Viet Nam and approved by the French Government shall be accredited to the High Commissioner to establish the cooperation indispensable for the carrying out of the present agreements.

Article 10—The Government of the French Republic and the Government of the Democratic Republic of Viet Nam agree to seek in common the conclusion of special agreements concerning all questions requiring them in order to strengthen friendly relations and prepare the way for a general, definitive treaty. Negotiations shall be resumed again for that purpose as soon as possible and in January 1947 at the latest.

Article 11—All the provisions of the present Modus Vivendi drawn up in duplicate, shall enter into force on October 30, 1946.

Source: Gareth Porter, ed., *Vietnam: A History in Documents* (New York: New American Library, 1981), 48–50.

26. Ho Chi Minh: Proclamation to the People upon His Return from France after Negotiations, October 23, 1946

Introduction

Fighting was already occurring in Vietnam between French troops and Vietnamese when Ho Chi Minh, president of the Democratic Republic of Vietnam (DRV, North Vietnam), returned from France and the fruitless Fontainebleau Conference with French government officials. On his return Ho issued this statement to the people of Vietnam, urging them to eschew violence and to exhibit correct behavior toward the French. Ho stresses that the Vietnamese must attempt to achieve their political aims in a democratic manner.

Primary Source

Compatriots throughout the country,

I left for France over four months ago. Today I am back home. I am very happy to see the Fatherland and you again. I have the following statements to make:

On my way to France, during my stay in France, and on my way back from France, the French Government, to show its desire to cooperate with Viet-Nam, received me ceremoniously. Out of sincere friendship for our people, the French people received me fraternally. On your behalf, I have the honor to thank the French Government and people.

In my absence, thanks to the clearsighted leadership of Acting President Huynh, the care and help of the Assembly, the efforts of the Government, and the unity and common effort of the people, many difficult questions were settled and much progress made in constructive work.

I thank the Government, the National Assembly, and all our compatriots.

I think constantly of our compatriots living abroad who have made many sacrifices in the struggle and are always faithful to their Fatherland, notwithstanding the hardships they have endured.

Thanks to the understanding of French personalities in the North and Center of Viet-Nam, most of the difficulties arising between the Vietnamese and the Frenchmen have lately been settled.

I hope that from now on cooperation between the two peoples will be closer.

My thoughts are also with the Chinese and other foreign residents who all bear in mind the sentence, "Brother countries, like passengers on the same boat, must help each other."

At various places, when I met friends of Chinese and Indian nationalities, we were very happy to see each other and to show our friendliness. Now, coming back to Viet-Nam, I witness the same sight.

Answering the kind invitation of the French Government, I went to France with the purpose of solving the question of Viet-Nam's independence and the unification of the North, Center, and South. Due to the present situation in France, these two questions have not yet been settled. We have to wait. But I dare to vouch that sooner or later Viet-Nam is sure to be independent, and its three parts, the North, the Center, and the South, will be unified.

What did the Delegation and I do during the months we spent in France?

We took Viet-Nam's flag to France. The French Government and people and foreign residents there looked on our flag with respect.

We drew greater attention from the French Government and people and made them understand the question of Viet-Nam better than before. We also drew the attention of the world and made it understand the question of Viet-Nam better than before.

We caused a great many Frenchmen to become friends of the Vietnamese people and approve of Viet-Nam's independence and sincere Vietnamese-French cooperation on an equal footing.

We further heightened the position of the Vietnamese youth, women's, and workers' organizations because respective international organizations have recognized our organizations as members.

The Vietnamese-French Conference has not ended yet. It will resume next May, but the September 14 modus vivendi has, firstly, permitted the Vietnamese and French to carry out their business easily, and secondly, it has paved the way for the next Conference to be conducted in a friendly manner.

What have we to do from now until January?

1. The Government and people must be singleminded in their efforts at organization and must work for a closer unity, economic development, national reconstruction, and realization of a new mode of life in all aspects. Men or women, old or young, intellectuals or peasants, producers or traders, everyone must endeavor to work. We must show to the French Government and people and to the world at large that the Vietnamese people are already in possession of all the required conditions to be independent and free, and that the recognition of our freedom and independence is a necessity.

2. The French in France are very friendly toward us. So the Vietnamese in Viet-Nam should also be friendly toward the French people.

Toward the French Army we must be correct.

Toward the French residents, we must be moderate.

Toward the Frenchmen who sincerely want to cooperate with us, we will sincerely cooperate, and that is advantageous to both parties.

All this is to show to the world that we are a civilized people, to get a greater number of Frenchmen to support us, and to further strengthen their support so that the provokers who intend to divide us may find themselves with no pretext, and our unity and independence will soon succeed.

3. Compatriots in the South and the southern part of Central Viet-Nam! The North, Center, and South are part and parcel of Viet-Nam. We have the same ancestors, we are of the same family, we are all brothers and sisters. Our country has three parts, which

are the North, the Center, and the South. They are just like three brothers in the same family. They are just like three regions of France: Normandy, Provence, and Beauce.

No one can divide the children of the same family. No one can divide France. Likewise, no one can divide Viet-Nam.

During the past year, in waging the Resistance War, our compatriots have seen their property destroyed, have sacrificed their lives, or were imprisoned and exiled. But their patriotism remains unshakable. This iron will will never be forgotten by the entire people, the Fatherland, and the Government.

I respectfully bow to the memory of the martyrs, and sympathize with the compatriots who are suffering and making sacrifices.

So long as the Fatherland is not yet unified and our compatriots are still suffering, I can neither eat with an appetite, nor sleep in peace. I solemnly promise you that with your determination and that of the entire people, our beloved South will surely come back into the bosom of our Fatherland.

The French Government has acknowledged the holding of a referendum by our southern compatriots to decide on the fate of the South. In the September 14 modus vivendi, the French Government agreed to implement the main points concerning the South as follows:

1. Political prisoners and those arrested for taking part in the resistance are to be released.
2. Our southern compatriots are to have freedom of organization, of meeting, of the press, of movement, etc.
3. Both parties are to stop fighting.

The French Government will undoubtedly respect its signature and implement the above clauses.

Now, what must our southern compatriots have to do?

1. The Vietnamese army, like the French army, must simultaneously stop fighting.
2. Our compatriots must carry out political actions in a democratic way.
3. Close unity must be realized with no discrimination as to political parties, social classes, and creeds. Unity means strength. Division means weakness.
4. Acts of reprisal are forbidden. Toward those who went astray, our compatriots must display a generous policy. We must let them hear the voice of reason. Everybody loves his country. It is only for petty interests that they forget the great cause. If we use the right words, they will certainly listen to us. Violent actions are absolutely forbidden. This is what you have to do at present to create

a peaceful atmosphere, paving the way democratically to reach the unification of our Viet-Nam.

Source: Ho Chi Minh, *On Revolution: Selected Writings, 1920–66,* edited by Bernard B. Fall (New York: Praeger, 1967), 168–171.

27. General Jean-Étienne Valluy: Telegram to Colonel Pierre-Louis Debès, November 22, 1946

Introduction

On November 22 fighting broke out between French forces and Vietnamese in the northern port of Haiphong after a French Navy patrol vessel seized a Chinese junk attempting to smuggle contraband. Although the fighting ended that afternoon, French high commissioner for Indochina Admiral Georges Thierry d'Argenlieu, then in Paris reporting to the French government, sought to use the clash to teach the Vietnamese a lesson. Premier Georges Bidault approved such a step, although in so doing he probably did not realize the likelihood of immediate action.

Primary Source

It appears clear that we are up against premeditated aggressions carefully staged by the Vietnamese regular army, which no longer seems to obey its government's orders. Under these circumstances, your commendable attempts at conciliation and division of quarters, as well as the inquiry that I asked you to make are out of season. The moment has come to give a severe lesson to those who have treacherously attacked you. Use all the means at your disposal to make yourself complete master of Haiphong and so bring the Vietnamese army around to a better understanding of the situations.

Source: Ellen J. Hammer, *The Struggle for Indochina, 1940–1955* (Stanford, CA: Stanford University Press, 1955), 183.

28. Colonel Pierre-Louis Debès, French Commander at Haiphong: Ultimatum to Haiphong Administrative Committee, November 22, 1946

Introduction

Having secured the approval of French premier Georges Bidault for military action in Vietnam, French high commissioner for Indochina Admiral Georges Thierry d'Argenlieu, then in France, cabled his deputy in Saigon, General Jean-Étienne Valluy, who in turn ordered General Louis Constant Morlière, French commander in the Democratic Republic of Vietnam (DRV, North Vietnam), to employ force. Morlière pointed out that the situation had stabilized and that any imprudent act might lead to general hostilities. Unsatisfied with this reply, Valluy telegraphed directly to Colonel Pierre-Louis Debès, commander of French forces at Haiphong, and ordered him to use force. Debès then issued an ultimatum to the Vietnamese that was couched in terms that they were bound to reject. Following the expiration of the ultimatum, French warships, especially the cruiser *Suffren,* opened fire on the Vietnamese quarter of the port, largely destroying it. Estimates of the number killed vary widely. French admiral Robert Marie Joseph Battet reported that more than 6,000 Vietnamese perished, with total casualties as high as 20,000. However, in 1981 Vu Quoc Uy, then chairman of the Haiphong Municipal Committee, put the figure at 500–1,000 dead. Regardless of the number of casualties, the incident shattered what little confidence remained in Vietnamese-French relations. Within a month the Indochinese War had begun.

Primary Source

By order of the General High Commissioner of the French Republic in IndoChina, I demand:

1. That all Viet Nam military or semi-military forces evacuate:

   a) the Chinese quarter, that is, the quarter bounded on the north by the Rue de la Mission; on the west, by the Song Tam-Bac; on the south, by the Darse Bonnal; on the east, by the Blvd. Admiral Courbet;

   b) the quarters to the northeast of the Avenue de Belgique (including that Avenue);

   c) the villages of Lac-Vien.

2. That all the Vietnamese who were in those quarters and villages, whether or not they have their present domicile there, be disarmed and that no depot of arms or ammunition be set up there.

I demand the pure and simple acceptance of these conditions before November 23, at 9 A.M.; failing which, I reserve for myself the right to take any measure which the situation calls for.

Source: Gareth Porter, ed., *Vietnam: A History in Documents* (New York: New American Library, 1981), 52.

29. Dean Acheson, Acting Secretary of State: Telegram to Division Chief Abbot L. Moffat in Saigon, December 5, 1946

Introduction

Although U.S. acting secretary of state Dean Acheson was concerned about the French government's decision to employ force

in Indochina, he cabled Abbot L. Moffat, chief of the State Department's Division of Southeast Asian Affairs, who was then in Saigon. Acheson asks Moffat, when he visits Hanoi, to convey to Ho Chi Minh, president of the Democratic Republic of Vietnam (DRV, North Vietnam), the U.S. view that Ho will have to give up the provision in the Ho-Sainteny Agreement of the previous March for a plebiscite in southern Vietnam that would allow it to join the North Vietnamese government. Washington took the position that Ho would have to accept some sort of "compromise" on the status of the Republic of Cochin China, which had been recently created by France. The Cold War with the Soviet Union had already begun to intrude on U.S. Indochina policy, as Acheson asks Moffat if there is not some alternative to Ho's government, which Washington sees as too dependent on Moscow.

Primary Source

Assume you will see Ho in Hanoi and offer following summary our present thinking as guide.

Keep in mind Ho's clear record as agent international communism, absence evidence recantation Moscow affiliations, confused political situation France and support Ho receiving French Communist Party. Least desirable eventuality would be establishment Communist-dominated, Moscow-oriented state Indochina in view DEPT, which most interested INFO strength non-communist elements Vietnam. Report fully, repeating or requesting DEPT repeat Paris.

Recent occurrences Tonkin cause deep concern. Consider March 6 accord and modus vivendi as result peaceful negotiation provide basis settlement outstanding questions between France and Vietnam and impose responsibility both sides not prejudice future, particularly forthcoming Fontainebleau Conference, by resort force. Unsettled situation such as pertains certain to offer provocations both sides, but for this reason conciliatory patient attitude especially necessary. Intransigence either side and disposition exploit incidents can only retard economic rehabilitation Indochina and cause indefinite postponement conditions cooperation France and Vietnam which both agree essential.

If Ho takes stand non-implementation promise by French of Cochinchina referendum relieves Vietnam responsibility compliance with agreements, you might if you consider advisable raise question whether he believes referendum after such long disorder could produce worthwhile result and whether he considers compromise on status Cochinchina could possibly be reached through negotiation.

May say American people have welcomed attainments Indochinese in efforts realize praiseworthy aspiration greater autonomy in framework democratic institutions and it would be regrettable should this interest and sympathy be imperilled by any tendency Vietnam administration force issues by intransigence and violence.

May inform Ho Caffery discussing situation French similar frankness. For your INFO, Baudet in DEC 3 conversation stated 1) no question reconquest Indochina as such would be counter French public opinion and probably beyond French military resources, 2) French will continue base policy March 6 accord and modus vivendi and make every effort apply them through negotiation Vietnam, 3) French would resort forceful measures only on restricted scale in case flagrant violation agreements Vietnam, 4) d'Argenlieu's usefulness impaired by outspoken dislike Vietnam officials and replacement perhaps desirable, 5) French Communists embarrassed in pose as guardian French international interests by barrage telegraphic appeals from Vietnam. Caffery will express gratification this statement French policy with observation implementation such policy should go far obviate any danger that 1) Vietnamese irreconcilables and extremists might be in position make capital of situation 2) Vietnamese might be turned irrevocably against West and toward ideologies and affiliations hostile democracies which could result perpetual foment Indochina with consequences all Southeast Asia.

Avoid impression US Govt making formal intervention this juncture. Publicity any kind would be unfortunate.

Paris be guided foregoing.

Source: *United States–Vietnam Relations, 1945–1967,* Book 8 (Washington, DC: U.S. Government Printing Office, 1971), 85–86.

30. Abbott L. Moffat: Telegram from Hanoi to the State Department, December 1946 [Excerpt]

Introduction

In this telegram to the State Department from Hanoi, Abbot L. Moffat, chief of the State Department's Division of Southeast Asian Affairs, reports on his meetings with leaders of the Democratic Republic of Vietnam (DRV, North Vietnam). The situation in North Vietnam was then at a critical point: major fighting had occurred in Haiphong, and there was also bloodshed in Hanoi and other places between French and Vietnamese forces. North Vietnamese president Ho Chi Minh and Deputy Foreign Minister Hoang Minh Giam tried to convince the United States to support North Vietnam. The Vietnamese even went so far as to offer the United States a naval base at Cam Ranh Bay, ironically the site of the large U.S. base during the Vietnam War. But Moffat reports that he informed the North Vietnamese leaders that any diplomatic relationship between the United States and North Vietnam would first have to be cleared with the French.

Primary Source

At 5:00 Giam had an official tea for me at the Presidency. Madame Saincanny was there. Morliere, Lami and a few other French. I met some of the other Vietnamese officials, some business men and doctors and admired some rather lovely lacquer pictures which is a Tonkinese specialty. Giam asked if he could talk with me privately and that he had a present for me from Ho Chih Minh and wanted to ask some questions; so I left at 6:00 and went with Jim to the Consulate where Giam joined us presently. There he presented me with an autographed photograph and a piece of "mountain brocade" inscribed to Ho. (The purpose, of course, to show that the hill people also back Ho. The Tonkinese never live above the 25 meter level, occupy the Delta, but not the mountains). Then he started to explain how Vietnam wanted free ports, and the right to trade freely; to get foreign capital where they would; they wanted American capital, commerce; they hoped an American airline would use Hanoi; an American shipline use Haiphong regularly, etc. In short, he kept reiterating they did not always want to be "compressed" by the French. I interrupted finally to explain that under the March 6 Agreement, their status in many respects is unsettled—"subject to further French-Vietnam negotiations"—such as foreign affairs (for which reason we do not recognize and have relations with the Vietnam Government) and finance, etc. (for which reason, until agreement is reached, we assume in such matters French laws still obtain). He demurred on this last—said the customs question was the cause of the Haiphong incident—and passed on. He then stated Vietnam had no navy and had no intention of being war like, but would be glad to cooperate with the US in developing Cam Ranh Bay as a naval base, that it was a very important location between Singapore and Hong Kong and opposite the PI. I replied I knew nothing of the military plans of my Government, but doubted if we would be interested in such a base (Cam Ranh Bay, as you know, is in South Annam and is presently controlled by the French.) I explained that I was sure that the US would want to have trade and commerce with Vietnam; mentioned the proposed route approved by CAB which included Hanoi; but stated before there could be any direct relations, the Vietnamese and French would have to agree on the respective powers of the two governments. Giam also stated the Vietnam desire for an economic federation of Indochina; a customs union and free trade between the three states; and federal collection of customs so that the revenues could be fairly distributed to the states. But, he stated, the Vietnam was strongly opposed to any political power in the federation. I have perhaps given his remarks more coherence than they had. The impression I received was one of extreme naivety.

Source: Robert M. Blum, *The United States and Vietnam: 1944–1947* (Washington, DC: U.S. Government Printing Office, 1972), 42.

31. Ho Chi Minh: Telegram to French Premier Léon Blum, December 15, 1946

Introduction

In a last effort to prevent full-scale war between France and the Democratic Republic of Vietnam (DRV, North Vietnam), on December 15, 1946, President Ho Chi Minh telegraphed French premier Léon Blum. Ho suggests steps that might be carried out by the Vietnamese and French sides to keep the peace. The French were determined to reassert their control in North Vietnam, however. On December 19 General Louis Constant Morlière, French commander in North Vietnam, demanded the disarmament of the Tu Ve, the Viet Minh militia that had been sniping at French troops in Hanoi. That very night, fear and mistrust—fueled by bloodshed and broken promises—finally bring all-out war.

Primary Source

Blum

Occasion your election Presidency French Government,

To show our confidence in you and in people France,

To show our sincere desire fraternal cooperation with French people,

To prove that our only aspiration is independence and territorial integrity of Viet Nam within French Union,

To prove our ardent desire to settle peacefully serious incidents which at present steep our country in blood,

To prove that we have always been prepared to apply loyally agreements signed by our two Governments,

To dispel atmosphere of hostility, reestablish atmosphere of confidence and friendship, and effectively prepare definitive negotiations,

I have the honor to make to you the following concrete proposals:

a) On the Viet Nam side:
   1) To invite the evacuated Viet Nam population to return to the cities.
   2) To take all necessary measures to assure the return to the cities of the economic life disturbed by the present state of hostility.
   3) To put an end to the measures of self-protection taken by the inhabitants of the cities.
   4) To assure the return to normalcy of the Hanoi-Langson thoroughfare.

b) On the French side:
   1) Return of the French and Viet Nam troops to the positions held before November 20, 1946 at Haiphong and Langson, and withdrawal of the reinforcements recently sent to Tourane, contrary to the agreements.
   2) To cease the so-called mopping-up operations and campaigns of repression in Cochin-China and North Annam.

c) On both sides:
   1) To start working immediately the agencies contemplated for the application of the Modus-Vivendi, a part of the Commission at Hanoi, another at Saigon, as the country resort of DALAT offers us no conveniences for work.
   2) To put an end to all unfriendly propaganda in French and Viet Nam radio-broadcasts and press.

Awaiting the honor of your reply, I beg you to accept the expression of my very high consideration.

Source: Gareth Porter, ed., *Vietnam: A History in Documents* (New York: New American Library, 1981), 57–58.

32. Consul Charles Reed in Saigon: Telegram to Secretary of State James F. Byrnes, December 24, 1946

Introduction

Charles Reed, the U.S. consul in Saigon, reports to Secretary of State James Byrnes that while the French government officially eschews any intention of taking back its former colonies by force, French high commissioner for Indochina Georges Thierry d'Argenlieu has confirmed that the French will no longer treat with President Ho Chi Minh's government in the Democratic Republic of Vietnam (DRV, North Vietnam) and will in fact seek to detach Annam (central Vietnam) from North Vietnam, adding it to Cochin China (southern Vietnam) as "independent" states within the Indochina Federation.

Primary Source

Unprovoked premeditated attack by Vietnam, with atrocities against innocent civilians, at time when French Govt sending representative discuss association accords and plan future French-Vietnam relations, leaves French free hand to deal with situation, especially as Vietnam Govt has fled and effectively no such govt. So said High Commissioner in conversation yesterday prior arrival Moutet. He stated French do not plan exploit situation and there is, first, no intention reconquer FIC and, second, no intention return former colonial system—enough troops will be sent restore order and assure opportunity all persons carry on peaceful pursuits. He admitted many mistakes made in past due those persons reluctant give up prewar life and policy in FIC and said mistakes will be made in future but France holds intention aid honest and meritorious aspirations native peoples (but commented difficult to treat with persons whose aim is destruction as recent events have shown to be aim of Ho and his govt) and France desired chiefly promote their economic interests. French prepared deal with any govt in which can place confidence.

He stressed federation plan is only possible solution, giving peoples of FIC measure of autonomy of which they are now capable, but not excluding possibility of larger independence when peoples are capable thereof. He felt majority natives will welcome removal Ho regime which established and maintained by terroristic methods and in no sense democratic—also felt that with fear reprisals removed, Annam would prefer be state, apart from Tonkin confederation, thus being composed of same five states as formed FIC in past. Expressed satisfaction he now had backing French Govt (with certain notable exceptions) and declared his policy vindicated especially his distrust Ho and his associates but made one remark that indicated he might not be here long. He mentioned return General Leclerc, expected here shortly, but I have reason believe High Commissioner not particularly pleased. Factually, situation in north improving and he hoped all under control within 15 days—expressed grave concern fate of French at Vinh from which no news since French surrendered.

In comment [by me?] French have one more chance impress natives their desire deal fairly with them and to give them advantages both economic and social withheld in past, and if French fail to take advantage this opportunity and institute repressive high handed measures (policy of force) of past no settlement of situation can be expected foreseeable future and period guerilla warfare will follow. [Apparent garble] however presupposes willingness Vietnam act with reasonableness and doubt whether French will treat with Ho in view of "treacherous" attack on civilians as well as military. Perhaps mediation third party only solution.

Please repeat Paris, London.

Source: *Foreign Relations of the United States, 1946,* Vol. 8 (Washington, DC: U.S. Government Printing Office, 1971), 78–79.

33. George C. Marshall, Secretary of State: Telegram to Ambassador Jefferson Caffery, February 3, 1947

Introduction

In this telegram of February 3, 1947, to U.S. ambassador to France Jefferson Caffery, new secretary of state George C. Marshall

discusses the dilemma facing the United States in the Indochina War. The United States needs the support of France, then the only major Western military power in continental Europe, in resisting Soviet expansionism in Europe. At the same time, Marshall expresses fears that the French do not understand that the days of European imperialism are over. Despite his major doubts about French policy in Indochina, Marshall believes that French rule is preferable to that of the Communists under Ho Chi Minh and that there appears to be no alternative to supporting the French policy of force there.

Primary Source

There is reason for increasing concern over situation as it is developing in Indochina and for that reason I feel you might well take early occasion to have frank talk with Ramadier or Bidault or both somewhat along lines conversations you have already had with Blum, but at this time going in fact beyond position you took in those talks. We have only very friendliest feelings toward France and we are anxious in every way we can to support France in her fight to regain her economic, political and military strength and to restore herself as in fact one of major powers of world. In spite any misunderstanding which might have arisen in minds French in regard to our position concerning Indochina they must appreciate that we have fully recognized France's sovereign position in that area and we do not wish to have it appear that we are in any way endeavoring undermine that position, and French should know it is our desire to be helpful and we stand ready assist any appropriate way we can find solution for Indochinese problem. At same time we cannot shut our eyes to fact that there are two sides this problem and that our reports indicate both a lack French understanding of other side (more in Saigon than in Paris) and continued existence dangerously outmoded colonial outlook and methods in area. Furthermore, there is no escape from fact that trend of times is to effect that colonial empires in XIX Century sense are rapidly becoming thing of past. Action Brit felt in India and Burma and Dutch in Indonesia are outstanding examples this trend, and French themselves took cognizance of it both in new Constitution and in their agreements with Vietnam. On other hand we do not lose sight fact that Ho Chi Minh has direct Communist connections and it should be obvious that we are not interested in seeing colonial empire administrations supplanted by philosophy and political organizations emanating from and controlled by Kremlin. Fact does remain, however, that a situation does exist in Indochina which can no longer be considered, if it ever was considered, to be of a local character. If that situation continues deteriorate some country in direct interest is very likely to bring matter before Security Council under Chapter 11 of Charter. We have no intention taking such action ourselves at this time, but French will surely appreciate that we do have a vital interest in political and economic well being this area. If some country should bring matter before Security Council we would find it difficult to oppose an investigation Indochinese problem unless negotiations between parties were going on. It might be added that it would not in our estimation be in France's long-range interest to use her veto position to keep matter from coming before Council. Frankly we have no solution of problem to suggest. It is basically matter for two parties to work out themselves and from your reports and those from Indochina we are led to feel that both parties have endeavored to keep door open to some sort of settlement. We appreciate fact that Vietnam started present fighting in Indochina on December 19 and that this action has made it more difficult for French to adopt a position of generosity and conciliation. Nevertheless we hope that French will find it possible to be more than generous in trying to find a solution.

Source: *Foreign Relations of the United States, 1947,* Vol. 6 (Washington, DC: U.S. Government Printing Office, 1974), 67–68.

34. Democratic Republic of Vietnam: Account of Ho Chi Minh–Paul Mus Meeting, May 12, 1947

Introduction

In order to demonstrate that the leadership of the Democratic Republic of Vietnam (DRV, North Vietnam) sought peace and to appeal to those French leaders who sought the same, North Vietnamese president Ho Chi Minh called for a cease-fire in the fighting. At the same time, Foreign Minister Hoang Minh Giam offered to begin peace talks. In response, in May 1947 French high commissioner for Indochina Émile Bollaert appointed his adviser Paul Mus to travel from Hanoi to meet with Ho in the jungle. Mus, an Asian scholar sympathetic to Vietnamese nationalism, carried a plan drawn up by French military commander in Indochina General Jean-Étienne Valluy and approved by Socialist premier Paul Ramadier that called on the Viet Minh to refrain from hostilities, lay down some arms, permit French troops freedom of movement, and return all prisoners, deserters, and hostages. Ho rejected these terms as tantamount to surrender, and on May 15 Bollaert declared that France would remain in Indochina. This North Vietnamese document is a factual representation of the French terms, although it omits two conditions stated above that were confirmed in Mus's subsequent book *Viet-Nam: Sociologie d'une Guerre,* published in 1952: the return of all prisoners held by the Viet Minh as well as all non-Vietnamese serving in their forces.

Primary Source

President HO and Minister of Foreign Affairs GIAM met with a representative of High Commissioner BOLLAERT in a place not far from Hanoi.

This meeting was most cordial for the representative of the High Commissioner is an old acquaintance of President HO and Minister GIAM.

When the discussion began on the question of the cessation of hostilities, the representative of M. BOLLAERT proposed the following conditions:

1) The Vietnam Government will abstain from all reprisals against pro-French people upon the cessation of hostilities.
2) The Vietnamese troops will surrender all their arms and munitions to France.
3) The French troops have the right to circulate and occupy freely throughout the territory of Vietnam. Vietnamese troops will assemble in spots designated by the French Army.

President HO replied to the first condition: After the last worldwide hostilities, if France took action against Frenchmen who delivered France to Germany, we ought to punish Vietnamese who have decided to deliver our country to a foreign nation. However, we can promise leniency toward these individuals.

To the other conditions, President HO replied:

High Commissioner BOLLAERT is a French democrat and also a patriot. I ask you if High Commissioner BOLLAERT has recognized the act by which the Pétain Government delivered arms and munitions to the German Army, permitted German troops freedom of action in French territory and obliged French troops to assemble in determined positions? Is this an armistice?

At this point in the conversation, the representative of M. BOLLAERT said: In these circumstances, we have nothing more to say to you.

The diplomatic interview thus ended.

President HO then asked the French representative: You certainly know the history of Vietnam

Yes, I have made several studies of it.

In that case, you recall the feats of our ancestors. TRAN HUNG DAO who fought for five years against the Mongol armies and LE LOI who resisted for ten years against the Chinese armies. Well, at the present time, we can resist five years, ten years and more. Our compatriots are firmly decided to unite and to obey the government's orders to resist until independence and unification are obtained.

Source: Gareth Porter, ed., *Vietnam: A History in Documents* (New York: New American Library, 1981), 62.

35. George C. Marshall, Secretary of State: Telegram to Jefferson Caffery in Paris, May 13, 1947

Introduction

In this telegram to U.S. ambassador to France Jefferson Caffery, Secretary of State George C. Marshall expresses concern over the failure of French leaders to carry out meaningful reform in Indochina. Marshall warns that this will only strengthen the hands of the Communists and jeopardize Western interests in the region. He believes that without proper guidance from the West, Vietnam and other states of the region will succumb to Communist or militant nationalist influence. Marshall clearly favors an arrangement in which France will grant independence or autonomy to the states of Indochina while maintaining influence in the region.

Primary Source

We becoming increasingly concerned by slow progress toward settlement Indochina dispute. We fully appreciate French are making effort reach satisfactory settlement and hope visit Commissioner Bollaert to Indochina will produce concrete results. The following considerations, however, are submitted for your use any conversations you may have with French authorities at appropriate time this subject. We recognize it might not be desirable make such approach to newly constituted government in first days its reorganization, but nevertheless feel early appropriate opportunity might be found inform French Gov of our concern in this matter.

Key our position is our awareness that in respect developments affecting position Western democratic powers in southern Asia, we essentially in same boat as French, also as British and Dutch. We cannot conceive setbacks to long-range interests France which would not also be setbacks our own. Conversely we should regard close association France and members French Union as not only to advantage peoples concerned, but indirectly our own.

In our view, southern Asia in critical phase its history with seven new nations in process achieving or struggling independence or autonomy. These nations include quarter inhabitants world and their future course, owing sheer weight populations, resources they command, and strategic location, will be momentous factor world stability. Following relaxation European controls, internal racial, religious, and national differences could plunge new nations into violent discord, or already apparent anti-Western Pan-Asiatic tendencies could become dominant political force, or Communists could capture control. We consider as best safeguard against these eventualities a continued close association between newly-autonomous peoples and powers which have long been responsible their welfare. In particular we recognize Vietnamese will for indefinite period require French material and technical assistance and enlightened political guidance which can be provided only by nation steeped like France in democratic tradition and confirmed in respect human liberties and worth individual.

We are equally convinced, however, such association must be voluntary to be lasting and achieve results, and that protraction present situation Indochina can only destroy basis voluntary cooperation, leave legacy permanent bitterness, and irrevocably alienate Vietnamese from France and those values represented by France and other Western democracies.

While fully appreciating difficulties French position this conflict, we feel there is danger in any arrangement which might provide Vietnamese opportunity compare unfavorably their own position and that of other peoples southern Asia who have made tremendous strides toward autonomy since war.

While we are still ready and willing to do anything we can which might be considered helpful, French will understand we not attempting come forward with any solution our own or intervene in situation. However, they will also understand we inescapably concerned with situation Far East generally, upon which developments Indochina likely have profound effect.

Plain fact is that Western democratic system is on defensive in almost all emergent nations southern Asia and, because identified by peoples these nations with what they have considered former denial their rights, is particularly vulnerable to attacks by demagogic leaders political movements of either ultra-nationalist or Communist nature which promise redress and revenge past so-called wrongs and inequalities. Signs development anti-Western Asiatic consciousness already multiplying, of which Inter-Asian Conf an example. Unanimity support for Vietnamese among other Asiatic countries very striking, even leading to moves Burma, India, and Malaya send volunteer forces their assistance. Vietnam cause proving rallying-cry for all anti-Western forces and playing in hands Communists all areas. We fear continuation conflict may jeopardize position all Western democratic powers in southern Asia and lead to very eventualities of which we most apprehensive.

We confident French fully aware dangers inherent in situation and therefore venture express renewed hope they will be most generous attempt find early solution which, by recognizing legitimate desires Vietnamese, will restore peace and deprive anti-democratic forces of powerful weapon.

For your info, evidence that French Communists are being directed accelerate their agitation French colonies even extent lose much popular support France (Urtel 1719 Apr 25) may be indication Kremlin prepared sacrifice temporary gains with 40 million French to long range colonial strategy with 600 million dependent people, which lends great urgency foregoing views. French position Indochina dispute since Dec 19, which based on Vietnam initiative attack, seems Dept dangerously one-sided in ignoring Debès attack Haiphong Nov 23 and understandable Vietnam contention that stand had be made some point view steady French encroachments after Mar 6 on authority and territory Vietnam (e.g., establishment Cochinchinese Rep, occupation southern Annam and Moi Plateau, and Dalat plan French-dominated Federation to which Vietnam would be subservient). Dept much concerned lest French efforts find "true representatives Vietnam" with whom negotiate result creation impotent puppet Govt along lines Cochinchina regime, or that restoration Baodai may be attempted, implying democracies reduced resort monarchy as weapon against Communism. You may refer these further views if nature your conversations French appears warrant.

Saigon and Hanoi should be guided by this tel in any conversations Bollaert.

Source: *Foreign Relations of the United States, 1947,* Vol. 6 (Washington, DC: U.S. Government Printing Office, 1974), 95–97.

36. Charles S. Reed: Airgram to Dean Acheson, June 14, 1947 [Excerpts]

Introduction

In this communication to Undersecretary of State Dean Acheson, U.S. consul in Saigon Charles Reed stresses that something has to be done to make French leaders aware that most Vietnamese regard the Democratic Republic of Vietnam (DRV, North Vietnam), headed by Ho Chi Minh, as their legitimate government and that any French-installed government will be regarded as a puppet regime. At the same time, however, Reed believes that the Vietnamese are incapable of self-government and will require some degree of Western control. He thus favors a compromise between Vietnamese and French interests in Indochina such as a federated solution with three autonomous states, including North Vietnam, within the French Union.

Primary Source

SIR: I have the honor to summarize and analyze, as of possible interest to the Department, the chronological development of the situation in Indochina from the arrival at Saigon of Mr. Emile Bollaert, High Commissioner of the Republic in Indochina, on April 1, 1947, to his departure for France on June 11. This period of 70 days was a particularly critical one, as Mr. Bollaert had the unenviable task of endeavoring to counteract the effect of errors of omission and commission popularly attributed to the regime of Admiral Thierry d'Argenlieu, former High Commissioner, and of

attempting to find a solution of the complex Indochinese political problem which would be acceptable to both the French and the Annamite peoples. The extent of his success, of course, cannot be measured at this time save in relation to the state of affairs obtaining at the date of his arrival in Indochina, and only time will tell whether or not he has carried back to France a feasible plan for the restoration of peace and security and a workable recommendation for the future status of Annamite Indochina.

This then was Mr. Bollaert's heritage on the French side, a people sharply divided as to the best means of dealing with the situation, as to the concessions to be made, and as to the person or persons whom France should recognize as the representatives of the Annamite peoples; on the Annamite side, a people almost universally distrustful of French intentions, convinced that the French would stop at nothing to deny the fulfilment of native aspirations, and cherishing a hatred and rancor engendered by decades of exploitation by a thoroughly selfish colonial regime. In several respects, however, he was fortunate. The situation could not have been worse—I may say with confidence that the present situation is far worse than when I arrived in February 1946. In his consideration of the thorny problem he could disregard any idea of military reconquest, as France as a whole had neither the will nor the means to embark upon such a vast undertaking, one that would be condemned by the world at large—the French were surely aware that the hard won successes of their military in Tonkin were more apparent than real. And he could count on the Kingdoms of Cambodia and Laos being content to accept French guidance, inspiration and tutelage—the Issarak movements could largely be dismissed as attempts to make dynastic changes rather than revolts against the French position in those countries. Moreover, the High Commissioner had the good fortune to arrive at a time when people were tired of fighting and destruction.

What plan if any the High Commissioner has taken back to France is of course not known. Logically, however, any plan likely to succeed will represent a great concession on the part of France and the unquestionable sacrifice of many of her interests. France has already jettisoned the idea of a Federation of the five entities making up the French Indochina of the past, France may well be prepared to throw overboard the Provisional Government of the Republic of Cochinchina, and France appears to be willing to accept a Vietnam Federation so long as both French and native rights are protected and not to be the spoil of an admittedly totalitarian regime. What security France can exact for such protection in the future is difficult to say. France, if Mr. Bollaert's declaration is to be given credence, will refuse to deal with any one faction. On the other hand Ho Chi Minh has always said he is not fighting the French but only the colonialists, and he has given some indication of willingness to make concessions in his acknowledgement of the right of each of the three Kys to have local autonomy. How far communist-trained Ho Chi Minh is to be trusted is problematic and his concession of local autonomy may be merely a blind. Unfortunately, the majority of natives stoutly maintain that Ho Chi Minh is the man, and the only one, who represents them and they will oppose the putting forward of any other candidate as the creation of but another puppet and the erecting of a smoke screen for France's real intentions. While the natives are tired of fighting and are apprehensive of the destruction and famine that impend for the future there is still a determined nucleus who are prepared to wage a bitter and ruthless warfare if the greater part of their claims is not met. To reconcile these differences will be difficult, but for the future of Indochina, for the stability of Southeast Asia, for the good of the whole Far East, and for the prestige of western democracy, whatever plan is adopted must be put into operation without great loss of time.

From a purely practical point of view too great concessions on the part of France might be very disastrous, if such concessions give the natives virtually a free hand. Many observers doubt whether they are capable of running an independent state and point to the fact that the Philippines after 40 odd years of benevolent tutelage, in which the advantages of education and instruction were available to all, are still not a model of good government. How much less chance would the Annamites have of making a success? The majority of these observers opine that without Occidental check or control the result would be chaos—and in that chaos either the Soviet or the Chinese would find their opportunity. The former would be able to establish their ideology in the very heart of teeming Southeast Asia, with millions of people to indoctrinate and to prepare for the ultimate struggle with the western democracies. The latter would be able to realize their age-old desire to dominate if not to take over this part of the Far East, a desire which is even now manifest. To many observers, the Chinese danger is the greater, even if not imminent because of China's preoccupation with her own political problems. Be that as it may, something must be done to eradicate the distrust and almost contempt of the French for the natives, and to eradicate the distrust and hatred of the natives for the French; something must be done to bring home to the French the fact that times have changed and that the natives have a right to more than a semblance of independence, and to bring home to the natives that the French have a legitimate interest and place in Indochina. Mr. Bollaert must have learned that the above are imperative and that they are the stones in the foundation of peace in Indochina.

The High Commissioner has now gathered the necessary data and it is the task of the French Government to supply and apply the answer. While that Government may continue to procrastinate in the hopes of wearing down the native opposition, I believe that that Government will be led to accept a Federated Republic of Vietnam, in which each of the three Kys will have autonomy, freely associated with the French Union. And Ho Chi Minh, if he is really the nationalist and patriot that he claims to be, must accept that his totalitarian government and Tonkin cannot speak for all Annamites.

Source: *Foreign Relations of the United States, 1947,* Vol. 6 (Washington, DC: U.S. Government Printing Office, 1972), 106–107.

37. George C. Marshall, Secretary of State: Telegram to the Consul General at Saigon (Later Repeated for Paris), July 17, 1947

Introduction

This telegram from Secretary of State George Marshall to U.S. consul Charles Reed in Saigon indicates that the U.S. government understands that France might be forced to accept a unified Vietnam under the rule of the Democratic Republic of Vietnam (DRV, North Vietnam). Marshall seeks to learn the degree of Communist influence within the North Vietnamese coalition government (in fact controlled by the Communists) and whether a united Vietnam under Communist rule will be dominated by Moscow. The telegram reveals that Marshall was considering the possibility that the United States might be able to accept a unified Vietnam under national communism.

Primary Source

Request your and Hanoi's appraisal implications relation US objectives stable Southeast Asia friendly to democratic West in event French should be forced deal present Vietnam Govt and this Govt should eventually emerge as controlling power three Annamese provinces. Refer particularly the following:

1. Whether influence Communists in present coalition Govt and behind-scenes Communists like Dang Xuan Khu and Ha Ba Cang would be sufficient put Vietnam in Soviet camp.

2. Position Ho respect above. Whether your opinion evidence increasing opposition to Ho by militants tends substantiate repeated reports his abandonment Party line and to corroborate reported letter to Chiang Kai Shek in which Ho excused past Communists connections on grounds nowhere else turn, and stated only interest now independence his country. (Impression here Ho publicly attempting walk chalked line between nationalism and Communism effort retain backing both forces.)

3. Whether intellectuals backing Vietnam realize what Communism means as international political force distinct its economic aspects and whether nationalists among them feel they can cope in future with Communist leaders Vietnam.

4. Whether, with removal solidifying effect French pressure, coherent Govt likely be extended over Vietnam representing real

interests Annamese and allowing reasonably free political expression or whether coalition would break in factions which would settle differences by terrorism and armed force, resulting chronic disorders or eventual police state under one-party rule.

5. Sensitivity Vietnamese to US opinion and importance this factor future orientation Vietnam Govt. While French Communists exploit every show of US interest developments Indochina to warn of US intervention, Vietnamese apparently welcome this interest.

6. Effect on Laotians and Cambodians should Soviet-oriented Vietnam emerge Dept fully realizes paucity solid info on which base appraisal.

Source: *Foreign Relations of the United States, 1947,* Vol. 6 (Washington, DC: U.S. Government Printing Office, 1974), 117–118.

38. James L. O'Sullivan, Vice-Consul in Hanoi, and Charles S. Reed in Saigon: Telegrams to George C. Marshall, July 21 and 24, 1947 [Excerpts]

Introduction

Responding to Secretary of State George C. Marshall's telegram of July 17, 1947, consuls James L. Sullivan in Hanoi and Charles Reed in Saigon separately telegraphed the State Department. Each concludes that a unified Vietnam controlled by the Communist-dominated government of the Democratic Republic of Vietnam (DRV, North Vietnam) will not necessarily be controlled by the Soviet Union and that the United States should be able to play some role there. Both diplomats also conclude that the removal of French authority would lead to considerable political infighting among the Vietnamese political parties, unrest, and the imposition of a single-party police state.

Primary Source

Reference Department's telegram 66, July 17. Department's assumptions do not make clear how much French influence it expects would remain event French are forced deal directly with Ho Chi Minh. But assuming French will deal with Ho only in last extremity and their control would tend become negligible thereafter:

1. Influence Communists in present government would not be sufficient to put Viet Nam squarely in Soviet camp although there would be pull in that direction. Agreement with French which would satisfy nationalism of Viet Namese people would probably lead to decrease in under-cover activities of characters such as Ha Ba Cang and Dang Xuan Khu and Tongbo members who would

tend to emerge from shadows. Geographic isolation Indochina from Russia and realization by Ho Chi Minh of United States power based in Philippines would be sufficient to prevent him or any government formed here from entering wholeheartedly Soviet camp.

2. Until further information available, am very skeptical regarding apparent opposition of militants to Ho. However, Ho's very great reluctance to admit that he is Nguyen Ai Quoc or to show any connection whatsoever with Russia is indicative of his realization that he must deal with West. Ho wrote 25 years ago that national revolution must precede Communist revolution in Indochina and it is obvious his first concern is get rid of French here. He is trying to obtain aid wherever he can and will tend be oriented toward source from whence assistance comes.

3. Have impression that intellectuals backing Viet Nam do not realize what is meaning Communism as international force and that they really would not care if it was thoroughly explained to them. They have been driven to Communism by French colonial policy here and they consider that nothing can be any worse. Hate for French blinds them to many things and makes them accept others they do not like. Intellectuals backing Vietnam government hate French so much that any future without French is attractive.

4. Removal French pressure would unquestionably have effect of causing present government in first instance to break into factions which would then for time tend develop into more or less full-blown party movements as those understood in Indochina. There probably then would be demand use armed force to some extent as country has widely distributed arms, has held exactly one general election in last 80 years, has no democratic tradition (outside of villages) which would enable it withstand strain political differences. There unquestionably would be danger police state under one-party rule which danger would have to be combatted by whatever French influence might remain and by United States through propaganda, student exchange, etc.

5. Viet Namese people here still regard United States as promised land and earthly paradise. American flag is still best protection available. Viet Namese are exceeding sensitive to United States opinion and unquestionably would accept United States advice and/or advisers and would be more than willing to have United States intervene if such intervention were directed toward satisfaction their political and economic needs.

6. Should Soviet oriented Viet Nam emerge, Cambodia and Laos would probably be subjected to considerable pressure to overthrow present regimes there. Independent Viet Nam, whether Soviet oriented or not, and absence of protecting power such as France, could be expected to resume encroachment upon Mekong delta which was interrupted by French occupation in 1860. Viet

Namese migration to southern plains has gone on for ten centuries and probably will continue.

Independent Viet Nam, not oriented toward Soviet, would probably leave Laos to its own devices.

In effect, there are dangers in French dealing with Viet Nam Government. There are dangers equally as great in French dealing with series of puppets in continuing effort to establish, despite all statements to contrary, something which strongly resembles status quo of before war.

Problem was and remains primarily nationalist problem in overpopulated area with illiterate populace which has no democratic traditions on national level largely because colonial power gave populace no opportunity express itself politically. With middle-class small, intellectuals who are generally ineffective, and Catholics who are split, best possibility of retaining some stability and preventing development of police state seems to be retention some degree French or international control to act as arbiter between parties.

Communist problem here results from fact French have allowed Communist group to seize and monopolize fight for felt necessity of people and Communist problem will remain without hope solution as long as this necessity is not satisfied elsewhere.

O'Sullivan

Have given considerable thought Deptel 122, July 17, and feel if French compelled treat with present Vietnam Govt their position in French Indo China will be definitely weakened, also if this govt emerges as controlling power in three Kys gradual deterioration of ties with democratic West may be expected. Unquestionably aid from western democracies, especially US, will be welcomed at first but query whether this Govt and in fact any native govt not subject to check or control will not develop a definitely oriental orientation and will not become a prey for non-democratic influences. Such a govt without considerable economic and moral support will not be strong enough to resist the impact of a concerted move by either the Communists or the Chinese for both of whom this part of Asia is indeed a happy hunting ground, fertile field for the inculcation of anti-Western sentiment, and expansion. However, it appears improbable that solution situation can be found without treating with present Vietnam Govt but as noted above and hereafter to treat with that Govt alone is a danger but there is equal danger in treating only with puppets. If French cannot reconcile all political elements or if they try to retain any large degree control, denying independence in regard which both present Vietnam Govt and Nationalist Front elements are united, only solution may be neutral intervention to establish a Vietnam state satisfactory to majority Annamites and to exercise control to see the state is run on democratic and equitable lines. If present Vietnam Govt

is honestly nationalistic, it should welcome such solution but am reasonably sure French, particularly French Communists, will view such suggestion with alarm.

Replying ad seriatim.

1. While tendency is toward Soviet camp as result Communist orientation Vietnam leaders, do not believe Vietnam will come out openly on side of Soviets until ground is prepared; present Soviet policy toward Vietnam appears to be one of remote control rather than open support and such policy will probably be pursued until time is ripe for avowal Soviet affiliation; in meantime Ho is straddling the fence and hopes to win support of west on platform dedicated to fulfillment nationalist aspirations.

2. As I have reported, very possible so-called militant opposition to Ho as being too moderate is only a blind; there is no proof he has renounced his Communist training but it is reasonably certain his indoctrination will be soft pedalled until independence is won and the French are out; a wily opportunist, Ho will take any aid coming his way to gain his ends without disclosing ultimate intentions.

3. Most Annamite intellectuals do not realize what communism means except that it symbolized revolution, nor do they care; as their conflict with French is basically revolutionary, they will accept communism or any other 'is[m]" as a means to the end.

. . . Pure nationalists among these intellectuals want independence and the future can take care of itself; average Annamite not good Communist prospect but strong leaders of aggressive minority can easily bring about evolution Communist state.

4. Removal French pressure and absence Western democracy control will result in chaos as factional fighting with accompanying terrorism will ensue; great bulk of population not prepared for self-government and destinies of country would be in hands of few, those now strongly suspected of Communist leanings; unless active steps were taken, through economic and political pressure, there would be little possibility preventing and combatting resultant police state.

5. American opinion still highly valued by all Annamites, including present Vietnam Government, and American aid is definitely desired to any other; however, if American advice and action run counter to what they think is full sum their desiderata, US might not be so popular; this difference must be noted—present Vietnam Government welcomes American aid in gaining independence, getting rid of French and helping establish national economy but National Front elements in addition to foregoing want American aid to get rid of present Vietnam Government and Communists; if firmly applied, American pressure can be the strongest influence in the country but there can be no temporizing.

6. Strong Vietnam state whether or not Soviet oriented will bring pressure on Laos and Cambodia and definite political and economic encroachments are to be expected; unless full protection given those countries, they would be forced into orbit Buddhist countries to the west and there would follow indefinite period political readjustment and dispute.

While Communist danger exists, it is future one and only when Vietnam Government is firmly established and in position disregard opinion and aid Western democracies will such government align itself with Soviet satellites—events elsewhere may make such alignment only far distant possibility. French overstress this danger. Present dangers are (1) French terms will be such as to prevent any peaceful solution and (2) if Annamites turned loose, only way combatting resultant economic and political chaos will be totalitarian police state, with ruthless suppression opposition. Both alternatives are alarming. Also must not overlook Chinese ambitions in this area which are only inactive because of China's internal situation.

Reed

Source: *Foreign Relations of the United States, 1947,* Vol. 6 (Washington, DC: U.S. Government Printing Office, 1974), 121–126.

39. Department of State Policy Statement on Indochina, September 27, 1948 [Excerpts]

Introduction

This U.S. State Department policy statement of September 1948 rejects both a French military pacification of Indochina and military withdrawal. The State Department concludes that if the French withdraw from Indochina, chaos will inevitably result. Yet because the United States refused to accept either French conquest or withdrawal, this left the United States prey to French policy with little ability to influence the course of events in Indochina.

Primary Source

A. Objectives

The immediate objective of US policy in Indochina is to assist in a solution of the present impasse which will be mutually satisfactory to the French and the Vietnamese peoples, which will result in the termination of the present hostilities, and which will be within the framework of US security.

Our long-term objectives are: (1) to eliminate so far as possible Communist influence in Indochina and to see installed a self-governing nationalist state which will be friendly to the US and which, commensurate with the capacity of the peoples involved, will be patterned upon our conception of a democratic state as opposed to the totalitarian state which would evolve inevitably from Communist domination; (2) to foster the association of the peoples of Indochina with the western powers, particularly with France with whose customs, language and laws they are familiar, to the end that those peoples will prefer freely to cooperate with the western powers culturally, economically and politically; (3) to raise the standard of living so that the peoples of Indochina will be less receptive to totalitarian influences and will have an incentive to work productively and thus contribute to a better balanced world economy; and (4) to prevent undue Chinese penetration and subsequent influence in Indochina so that the peoples of Indochina will not be hampered in their natural developments by the pressure of an alien people and alien interests.

B. Policy Issues

To attain our immediate objective, we should continue to press the French to accommodate the basic aspirations of the Vietnamese: (1) unity of Cochinchina, Annam, and Tonkin, (2) complete internal autonomy, and (3) the right to choose freely regarding participation in the French Union. We have recognized French sovereignty over Indochina but have maintained that such recognition does not imply any commitment on our part to assist France to exert its authority over the Indochinese peoples. Since V-J day, the majority people of the area, the Vietnamese, have stubbornly resisted the reestablishment of French authority, a struggle in which we have tried to maintain insofar as possible a position of non-support of either party.

While the nationalist movement in Vietnam (Cochinchina, Annam, and Tonkin) is strong, and though the great majority of the Vietnamese are not fundamentally Communist, the most active element in the resistance of the local peoples to the French has been a Communist group headed by Ho Chi Minh. This group has successfully extended its influence to include practically all armed forces now fighting the French, thus in effect capturing control of the nationalist movement.

The French on two occasions during 1946 attempted to resolve the problem by negotiation with the government established and dominated by Ho Chi Minh. The general agreements reached were not, however, successfully implemented and widescale fighting subsequently broke out. Since early in 1947, the French have employed about 115,000 troops in Indochina, with little result, since the countryside except in Laos and Cambodia remains under the firm control of the Ho Chi Minh government. A series of French-established puppet governments have tended to enhance the prestige of Ho's government and to call into question, on the part of the Vietnamese, the sincerity of French intentions to accord an independent status to Vietnam.

1. Political

We have regarded these hostilities in a colonial area as detrimental not only to our own long-term interests which require as a minimum a stable Southeast Asia but also detrimental to the interest of France, since the hatred engendered by continuing hostilities may render impossible peaceful collaboration and cooperation of the French and the Vietnamese peoples. This hatred of the Vietnamese people toward the French is keeping alive anti-Western feeling among oriental peoples, to the advantage of the USSR and the detriment of the US.

We have not urged the French to negotiate with Ho Chi Minh, even though he probably is now supported by a considerable majority of the Vietnamese people, because of his record as a Communist and the Communist background of many of the influential figures in and about his government.

Postwar French governments have never understood, or have chosen to underestimate, the strength of the nationalist movement with which they must deal in Indochina. It remains possible that the nationalist movement can be subverted from Communist control but this will require of nationalists at least the same concessions demanded by Ho Chi Minh. The failure of French governments to deal successfully with the Indochinese question has been due, in large measure, to the overwhelming internal issues facing France and the French Union, and to foreign policy considerations in Europe. These factors have combined with the slim parliamentary majorities of postwar governments in France to militate against the bold moves necessary to divert allegiance of the Vietnamese nationalists to non-Communist leadership.

In accord with our policy of regarding with favor the efforts of dependent peoples to attain their legitimate political aspirations, we have been anxious to see the French accord to the Vietnamese the largest possible degree of political and economic independence consistent with legitimate French interests. We have therefore declined to permit the export to the French in Indochina of arms and munitions for the prosecution of the war against the Vietnamese. This policy has been limited in its effect as we have allowed the free export of arms to France, such exports thereby being available for re-shipment to Indochina or for releasing stocks from reserves to be forwarded to Indochina.

[...]

D. Policy Evaluation

The objectives of US policy towards Indochina have not been realized. Three years after the termination of war a friendly ally, France, is fighting a desperate and apparently losing struggle in Indochina. The economic drain of this warfare on French recovery, while difficult to estimate, is unquestionably large. The Communist control in the nationalist movement has been increased during this period. US influence in Indochina and Southeast Asia has suffered as a result.

The objectives of US policy can only be attained by such French action as will satisfy the nationalist aspirations of the peoples of Indochina. We have repeatedly pointed out to the French the desirability of their giving such satisfaction and thus terminating the present open conflict. Our greatest difficulty in talking with the French and in stressing what should and what should not be done has been our inability to suggest any practicable solution of the Indochina problem, as we are all too well aware of the unpleasant fact that Communist Ho Chi Minh is the strongest and perhaps the ablest figure in Indochina and that any suggested solution which excludes him is an expedient of uncertain outcome. We are naturally hesitant to press the French too strongly or to become deeply involved so long as we are not in a position to suggest a solution or until we are prepared to accept the onus of intervention. The above considerations are further complicated by the fact that we have an immediate interest in maintaining in power a friendly French Government, to assist in the furtherance of our aims in Europe. This immediate and vital interest has in consequence taken precedence over active steps looking toward the realization of our objectives in Indochina.

We are prepared, however, to support the French in every way possible in the establishment of a truly nationalist government in Indochina which, by giving satisfaction to the aspirations of the peoples of Indochina, will serve as a rallying point for the nationalists and will weaken the Communist elements. By such support and by active participation in a peaceful and constructive solution in Indochina we stand to regain influence and prestige.

Some solution must be found which will strike a balance between the aspirations of the peoples of Indochina and the interests of the French. Solution by French military reconquest of Indochina is not desirable. Neither would the complete withdrawal of the French from Indochina effect a solution. The first alternative would delay indefinitely the attainment of our objectives, as we would share inevitably in the hatred engendered by an attempted military reconquest and the denial of aspirations for self-government. The second solution would be equally unfortunate as in all likelihood Indochina would then be taken over by the militant Communist group. At best, there might follow a transition period, marked by chaos and terroristic activities, creating a political vacuum into which the Chinese inevitably would be drawn or would push. The absence of stabilization in China will continue to have an important influence upon the objective of a permanent and peaceable solution in Indochina.

We have not been particularly successful in our information and education program in orienting the Vietnamese toward the western democracies and the US. The program has been hampered by the failure of the French to understand that such informational activities as we conduct in Indochina are not inimical to their own long-term interests and by administrative and financial considerations which have prevented the development to the maximum extent of contacts with the Vietnamese. An increased effort should be made to explain democratic institutions, especially American institutions and American policy, to the Indochinese by direct personal contact, by the distribution of information about the US, and the encouraging of educational exchange.

Source: *United States–Vietnam Relations, 1945–1967,* Book 8 (Washington, DC: U.S. Government Printing Office, 1971), 144–149.

40. The United States Praises the Elysée Agreements, 1949

Introduction

U.S. policymakers, who rejected both the restoration of French control by military conquest and a French withdrawal from Indochina that they believed likely to lead to civil war, embraced the so-called Bao Dai experiment. In order to secure additional manpower, gain Vietnamese nationalist support, and quiet critics at home and in the United States, Paris sought the facade of an indigenous Vietnamese regime as a competitor to the Viet Minh. Following several years of negotiations, in March 1949 the French government concluded the Elysée Agreements with former emperor Bao Dai, then living in France. These created the State of Vietnam (SVN), with Bao Dai as its head. Importantly, Paris conceded that Vietnam was indeed one country. With the SVN, Paris sought to cast the war as a conflict between a free Vietnam and the Communists and thus not a colonial war at all. The problem for Vietnamese nationalists, however, was that the SVN never had any power. The French continued to control all of its institutions, and its promised army was late in materializing. There were thus only two choices for Vietnamese: the Viet Minh or the French. In effect the French pushed most nationalists into the Viet Minh camp. The Viet Minh meanwhile wrapped itself in the mantle of nationalism and downplayed communism.

Primary Source

The formation of the new unified state of Vietnam and the recent announcement by Bao Dai that the future constitution will be decided by the Vietnamese people are welcome developments which should serve to hasten the reestablishment of peace in that country and the attainment of Vietnam's rightful place in the family of nations.

The United States Government hopes that the agreements of March 8 between President Auriol and Bao Dai, who is making

sincere efforts to unite all truly nationalist elements within Vietnam, will form the basis for the progressive realization of the legitimate aspirations of the Vietnamese people.

Source: "New Unified State of Vietnam Formed," *Department of State Bulletin* 21(524) (1949): 735–736.

41. Dean Acheson, Secretary of State: Telegram to the Embassy in France, February 25, 1949

Introduction

In this telegram to U.S. ambassador to France Jefferson Caffery, new secretary of state Dean Acheson (he took office in January 1949) reviews the past French record in Indochina and states that the United States cannot support the return of former emperor Bao Dai as head of a new Vietnamese state unless this is accompanied by demonstrated popular support from the Vietnamese people. Acheson points out that even with French arms, without such demonstrated support Bao Dai cannot hope to attract the Vietnamese people away from Ho Chi Minh and the Viet Minh.

Primary Source

Urtel 718, Feb 18. Dept despite reported progress Fr-Bao Dai negots queries whether Fr are really making such concessions as to (1) induce Bao Dai return Indochina (2) give him best opportunity succeed even if he returns there. For months, even though Commie successes China should have induced Fr make outstanding effort, negots have dragged, with Fr unable or unwilling put question status Cochinchina before Fr Assembly. Foregoing connection Dept fully realizes polit difficulties present Fr Govt putting this question before Assembly but Dept equally aware that over past three years Fr have shown no impressively sincere intention or desire make concessions which seem necessary solve Indochina question. Present formula solving status Cochinchina may have virtue but in Dept's thinking it may be but another device to obtain delay and unless proof is adduced to offset record of past three years Dept is now far from inclined give public approval any arrangements with Bao Dai. This disinclination springs from Dept's considered belief it would be unwise give public support to any arrangements for Indochina concluded by Fr unless that arrangement embodies means clearly sufficient insure its success or until it achieves substantial measure of success. Thus even though Bao Dai induced return Indochina Dept views failure Fr Govt take decisive action, at very least re status Cochinchina, as seriously weakening possibility ex-Emperor will obtain support any appreciable portion population. Without such support Bao Dai cannot hope, even though supported by Fr arms as he must necessarily be, wean away militant and organized followers of Ho Chi Minh.

Dept believes therefore, it should not now be committed in any way to approval Fr action vis-à-vis Bao Dai and must reserve aforementioned public expression until Fr have provided Bao Dai with means to succeed and he has demonstrated ability use successfully such means to obtain support appreciable portion Vietnamese population. This connection, Emb may recall doubts expressed in several Fr quarters re Bao Dai's capacities and abilities when negots were first undertaken with him two years ago. Accordingly Emb should make clear to FonOff that for these reasons US not prepared give public indication its approval until, in Dept's opinion, conditions noted above fulfilled.

At same time Emb may state while US remains willing reconsider its ECA Indochinese policy such reconsideration must await developments.

Sent Paris as 598. Rptd Saigon as 15.

Emb should note particularly with respect to first part para 1 that above tel was drafted before receipt embtel 771 Feb. 24, 4 p.m.

Source: *Foreign Relations of the United States, 1949,* Vol. 7, Part 1 (Washington, DC: U.S. Government Printing Office, 1975), 8–9.

42. Dean Acheson, Secretary of State: Telegram to the Consulate General in Saigon, May 10, 1949

Introduction

In this telegram to the U.S. consulate in Saigon, Secretary of State Dean Acheson reacts to the signing of the Elysée Agreements of March 1949 and the return to Vietnam of former emperor Bao Dai as head of the new State of Vietnam (SVN). Acheson expresses caution regarding possible U.S. diplomatic recognition of the SVN and suggests that recognition of the new regime by independent Asian governments would go a long way toward dispelling the notion that this was somehow the result of collusion among the French, British, and U.S. governments.

Primary Source

Assumption urtel 141 Dept desires success Baodai experiment entirely correct. Since appears be no other alternative to estab Commie pattern Vietnam, Dept considers no effort shld be spared by Fr, other Western powers, and non-Commie Asian nations to assure experiment best chance succeeding.

At proper time and under proper circumstances Dept will be prepared do its part by extending recognition Baodai Govt and by exploring possibility of complying with any request by such Govt for US arms and econ assistance. Must be understood however aid program this nature wld require Congressional approval. Since US cld however scarcely afford backing govt which wld have color and be likely suffer fate of puppet regime, it must first be clear Fr will offer all necessary concessions to make Baodai solution attractive to nationalists. This is step of which Fr themselves must see urgent necessity view possibly short time remaining before Commie successes Chi are felt Indochina. Moreover, Baodai Govt must through own efforts demonstrate capacity organize and conduct affairs wisely so as to ensure maximum opportunity obtaining requisite popular support inasmuch as govt created Indochina analogous Kuomintang wld be foredoomed failure.

Assuming essential Fr concessions are forthcoming, best chance success Baodai wld appear lie in persuading Vietnamese nationalists (1) their patriotic aims may be realized promptly through Fr-Baodai agreement (2) Baodai govt will be truly representative even to extent including outstanding non-Commie leaders now supporting Ho and (3) Baodai solution probably only means safeguarding Vietnam from aggressive designs Commie Chi. While attainment these objectives depends initially upon attitude Fr and Baodai circle, Dept believes more will ultimately be required. Best hope might lie in active demonstration of interest in and support of Baodai solution by other non-Commie Asian govts. Appeal such solution to Vietnam nationalists wld presumably be far greater if it appeared sponsored by free Asian nations animated by interest self-determination Asian peoples and their own self-preservation in face immed Commie menace rather than if it had appearance gambit engineered by Fr, US and UK as part strategy of West-East conflict.

Dept giving closest consideration to means whereby US might assist attainment these ends.

From above, you will see Dept thinking closely parallels your own. Dept agrees when time comes Baodai must certainly be fully warned of danger yielding to any temptation include Commies his govt and this connection again believes other Asian govts cld serve most useful purpose since India, Siam, Philippines, and Indonesians (both Repubs and Federalists) are fully alive growing Commie threat Asia.

Re last para urtel 141 "reliability Baodai solution" was error. Deptel 70 shld have read "viability" meaning able live.

While Dept continues believe it wld be premature and unwise for you make special point (such as trip Dalat) see Baodai, there no objection your talking informally with polit personalities close to him with whom you have doubtless already made contact in normal course carrying out your functions. In such talks you might well as suggested urtel 141 take occasion cite examples futility collaboration Commies and grave danger such course.

Source: *Foreign Relations of the United States, 1949,* Vol. 7, Part 1 (Washington, DC: U.S. Government Printing Office, 1975), 23–25.

43. Dean Acheson: Telegram to the Consulate in Hanoi, May 20, 1949

Introduction

In this telegram to the U.S. consulate in Hanoi, Secretary of State Dean Acheson responds to charges by some pro-French Vietnamese that the U.S. government might not oppose Viet Minh participation in a future Vietnamese government. Acheson states that should the anti-Communists not prevail, Vietnam will surely lose its independence to either the Soviet Union or China. He largely dismisses the notion that a Communist Vietnamese state might also be nationalist and operate independently, and he styles Ho an "outright Commie." Acheson believes that the best opportunity to prevent the Communists from taking power is an all-out French effort while its military is still in place.

Primary Source

Reur informative tel 36: In talks Xuan and reps his govt you may take fol line as representing consensus informed Americans:

In light Ho's known background, no other assumption possible but that he outright Commie so long as (1) he fails unequivocally repudiate Moscow connections and Commie doctrine and (2) remains personally singled out for praise by intenatl Commie press and receives its support. Moreover, US not impressed by nationalist character red flag with yellow stars. Question whether Ho as much nationalist as Commie is irrelevant. All Stalinists in colonial areas are nationalists. With achievement natl aims (i.e., independence) their objective necessarily becomes subordination state to Commie purposes and ruthless extermination not only opposition groups but all elements suspected even slightest deviation. On basis examples eastern Eur it must be assumed such wld be goal Ho and men his stamp if included Baodai Govt. To include them in order achieve reconciliation opposing polit elements and "national unity" wld merely postpone settlement issue whether Vietnam to be independent nation or Commie satellite until circumstances probably even less favorable nationalists than now. It must of course be conceded theoretical possibility exists estab National Communist state on pattern Yugoslavia in any area beyond reach Soviet army. However, US attitude cld take acct such possibility only if every other possible avenue closed to

preservation area from Kremlin control. Moreover, while Vietnam out of reach Soviet army it will doubtless be by no means out of reach Chi Commie hatchet men and armed forces.

Fol is for urinfo and such reference as you deem judicious:

Dept naturally considers only Fr can through concessions to nationalist movement lay basis for solution Indochina problem. As suggested Deptel 83 to Saigon, if nationalists find concessions Mar 8 agreements inadequate, much may depend upon willingness Fr put agreements in most favorable possible context by emphasizing expectations rapid evolution Vietnam beyond status envisaged those agreements. Provided Fr display realistic and generous attitude, most important part remainder immed program—viz, winning support nationalists away from Commie leadership—must devolve upon Baodai and Xuan group seconded by other South Asian govts who stand in most immed danger from Commie conquest Indochina and who by full polit and propaganda support Baodai solution might more that anyone else be able to deprive Ho of talking-points in event he continues demand armed resistance Baodai regardless circumstances (which appears certain in light vitriolic tone current Vietminh broadcasts on Baodai which give no recognition any Fr concessions to nationalist demands). Even with conditions for US support Baodai realized, it futile expect US be able assist effectively this initial task beyond stressing requirements situation in talks South Asian govts and providing materials evidencing realities of Communism through USIS for distribution as you and Congen Saigon consider desirable in conjunction with Baodai efforts arouse compatriots to Commie menace. Experience Chi has shown no amt US mil and econ aid can save govt, even if recognized by all other powers and possessed full opportunity achieve natl aims, unless it can rally support people against Commies by affording representation all important natl groups, manifesting devotion to natl as opposed to personal or party interests, and demonstrating real leadership.

Re Viet opinion reported Saigon's 145 that US abandonment Nationalist China presents unfavorable augury for non-Commie regime Vietnam, there no objection emphasizing to persons with this view that Nationalist China came to present pass through deficiency above qualities and lack will to fight, not because US "wrote it off."

Re Xuan query whether US wld propose Vietnam for membership UN shld Fr renege, you shld avoid discussion this matter, at most if pressed state circumstances at moment will of course determine US action. For urinfo only it unlikely US cld even vote for Vietnam membership UN if as it appears now Fr wld remain in control Vietnam fon relations.

Source: *Foreign Relations of the United States, 1949,* Vol. 7, Part 1 (Washington, DC: U.S. Government Printing Office, 1975), 29–30.

44. Memorandum of Conversation among Secretary of State Dean Acheson, French Foreign Minister Robert Schuman, and British Foreign Secretary Ernest Bevin, September 17, 1949 [Excerpt]

Introduction

In the course of a meeting with French foreign minister Robert Schuman and British foreign secretary Ernest Bevin, U.S. secretary of state Dean Acheson retreated from the position taken early in the year that the United States should insist on full independence for Vietnam. Acheson commits the U.S. government to trying to win diplomatic recognition from other Asian nations, especially the Philippines and Thailand (Siam) of the French-backed State of Vietnam (SVN), and holds out hope of additional U.S. aid.

Primary Source

Mr. Schuman then talked about Indochina. He said the Bao Dai government was not quite complete but it was satisfactory. The government was not yet fully established but it would be and it was the only way for a permanent solution. There is no love lost between the Chinese and the Indochinese. The Indochinese are afraid of China. Some of Ho's men, if there was a threat of invasion from China, might go over to Bao Dai. If the Southeast Asian countries recognize the Bao Dai government, its prestige would be increased. Perhaps the United Kingdom and the United States could help the French with Southeast Asia. The agreement with the Bao Dai government would be ratified by the French Parliament soon. Siam perhaps could be encouraged to recognize, by a word from the United States or the United Kingdom, the Bao Dai government. Bevin asked when the French Parliament would ratify the agreement. Schuman replied that Parliament meets on October 18 and should ratify it a few weeks after that—perhaps in November. Bevin remarked that France has to ratify the agreement before anyone else can help.

The Secretary said that if the French ratify the March 8 Agreement and transfer dealings with Bao Dai to the Foreign Office, we could help with the Philippines and Siam. The Southeast Asian countries should take the first steps, otherwise recognition by the United Kingdom and the United States in advance of other countries would make the Bao Dai government look like a Western "front." Congress may take up the question of Point Four Program after the Military Assistance Pact. Perhaps we can arrange technical assistance and Export-Import Bank funds.

Source: *Foreign Relations of the United States, 1949,* Vol. 7, Part 1 (Washington, DC: U.S. Government Printing Office, 1975), 88–89.

45. Raymond B. Fosdick, Consultant to the Secretary of State on Far Eastern Policy: Memorandum for Ambassador-at-Large Philip Jessup, November 4, 1949

Introduction

As the United States moved closer to a full embrace of the new State of Vietnam (SVN) headed by Bao Dai, opinion in the State Department was not unanimous. In this memorandum, Raymond B. Fosdick, a consultant to the State Department on Far Eastern policy, presents a very pessimistic view of the new SVN. Fosdick argues that the Elysée Agreements are nothing more than "semi-colonialism." The Bao Dai regime is "doomed," and nothing can stop the Vietnamese people in their drive for "complete nationalism."

Primary Source

In his memorandum of November 1 on Indochina, Mr. Yost argues that "a further major advance of communism will be considered as, and will in fact be, a defeat for the United States, whether or not we are directly involved." He therefore recommends, among other steps, support of the Bao Dai government (after the March 8 agreements are ratified) economic assistance to Bao Dai, etc.

It seems to me this point of view fails to take into consideration the possible, and I think the probable consequences of such a decision. In grasping one horn of the dilemma, it ignores the other. My belief is that the Bao Dai regime is doomed. The compromises which the French are so reluctantly making cannot possibly save it. The Indochinese are pressing toward complete nationalism and nothing is going to stop them. They see all too clearly that France is offering them a kind of semi-colonialism; and to think that they will be content to settle for less than Indonesia has gained from the Dutch or India from the British is to underestimate the power of the forces that are sweeping Asia today.

What kind of independence is France offering the Indochinese today in the March 8th agreements?

(1) The foreign policy of Indochina is to be under the final control of France.

(2) French military bases are to be established and the Indochinese Army in time of war is to be under French direction.

(3) France is to be in charge of the so-called General Services:

(a) Control of immigration
(b) Communications
(c) Industrial development of Indochina

(4) Customs receipts are to be divided between France and Indochina in accordance with a formula to be agreed upon.

(5) Extraterritorial courts for French citizens are to be continued.

This shabby business is a mockery of all the professions we have made in the Indonesian case. It probably represents an improvement over the brutal colonialism of earlier years, but it is now too late in the history of the world to try to settle for the price of this cheap substitute. For the United States to support France in this attempt will cost us our standing and prestige in all of Southeast Asia. A lot of that prestige went down the drain with Chiang Kaishek; the rest of it will go down with the Bao Dai regime if we support it. Ambassador Stuart calls our relationship to this regime "shameful" and I am inclined to agree with him.

Ev Case argued yesterday that it is too late to do anything else except support Bao Dai. I disagree. It is never too late to change a mistaken policy, particularly when the policy involves the kind of damage that our adherence to the Generalissimo brought us. Why get our fingers burned twice?

Ho Chi Minh as an alternative is decidedly unpleasant, but as was pointed out at our meeting with FE [Far Eastern Bureau] yesterday, there may be unpredictable and unseen factors in this situation which in the end will be more favorable to us than now seems probable. The fundamental antipathy of the Indochinese to China is one of the factors. Faced with a dilemma like this the best possible course is to wait for the breaks. Certainly we should not play our cards in such a way that once again, as in China, we seem to be allied with reaction. Whether the French like it or not, independence is coming to Indochina. Why, therefore, do we tie ourselves to the tail of their battered kite?

Source: Gareth Porter, ed., *Vietnam: A History in Documents* (New York: New American Library, 1981), 83–84.

46. National Security Council Paper No. 64, 1950

Introduction

By the beginning of 1950 the Cold War was in full bloom. In Asia the Communists had taken power in China, and the Truman administration found itself under attack by Republicans for having "lost" China. In these circumstances, as evidenced by National Security Council Paper No. 64, the Truman administration ignored the nationalist aspects of the struggle in Indochina, saw Ho Chi Minh simply as "a communist agent," and styled the fighting as "communist aggression against Indochina" and part of a wider Communist plan to seize all of Southeast Asia. The paper also holds that it is "important to United States security interests" to prevent further Communist inroads in Southeast Asia.

Primary Source

The Position of the United States with Respect to Indochina

The Problem

1. To undertake a determination of all practicable United States measures to protect its security in Indochina and to prevent the expansion of communist aggression in that area.

Analysis

2. It is recognized that the threat of communist aggression against Indochina is only one phase of anticipated communist plans to seize all of Southeast Asia. It is understood that Burma is weak internally and could be invaded without strong opposition or even that the Government of Burma could be subverted. However, Indochina is the area most immediately threatened. It is also the only area adjacent to communist China which contains a large European army, which along with native troops is now in armed conflict with the forces of communist aggression. A decision to contain communist expansion at the border of Indochina must be considered as a part of a wider study to prevent communist aggression into other parts of Southeast Asia.

3. A large segment of the Indochinese nationalist movement was seized in 1945 by Ho Chi Minh, a Vietnamese who under various aliases has served as a communist agent for thirty years. He has attracted noncommunist as well as communist elements to his support. In 1946, he attempted, but failed to secure French agreement to his recognition as the head of a government of Vietnam. Since then he has directed a guerrilla army in raids against French installations and lines of communication. French forces which have been attempting to restore law and order found themselves pitted against a determined adversary who manufactures effective arms locally, who received supplies of arms from outside sources, who maintained no capital or permanent headquarters and who was, and is able, to disrupt and harass almost any area within Vietnam (Tonkin, Annam and Cochinchina) at will.

4. The United States has, since the Japanese surrender, pointed out to the French Government that the legitimate nationalist aspirations of the people of Indochina must be satisfied, and that a return to the prewar colonial rule is not possible. The Department of State has pointed out to the French Government that it was and is necessary to establish and support governments in Indochina

particularly in Vietnam, under leaders who are capable of attracting to their causes the non-communist nationalist followers who had drifted to the Ho Chi Minh communist movement in the absence of any non-communist nationalist movement around which to plan their aspirations.

5. In an effort to establish stability by political means, where military measures had been unsuccessful, i.e., by attracting non-communist nationalists, now followers of Ho Chi Minh, to the support of anti-communist nationalist leaders, the French Government entered into agreements with the governments of the Kingdoms of Laos and Cambodia to elevate their status from protectorates to that of independent states within the French Union. The State of Vietnam was formed, with similar status, out of the former French protectorates of Tonkin, Annam and the former French Colony of Cochinchina. Each state received an increased degree of autonomy and sovereignty. Further steps towards independence were indicated by the French. The agreements were ratified by the French Government on 2 February 1950.

6. The Governments of Vietnam, Laos and Cambodia were officially recognized by the United States and the United Kingdom on February 7, 1950. Other Western powers have, or are committed to do likewise. The United States has consistently brought to the attention of non-communist Asian countries the danger of communist aggression which threatens them if communist expansion in Indochina is unchecked. As this danger becomes more evident it is expected to overcome the reluctance that they have had to recognize and support the three new states. We are therefore continuing to press those countries to recognize the new states. On January 18, 1950, the Chinese Communist Government announced its recognition of the Ho Chi Minh movement as the legal Government of Vietnam, while on January 30, 1950, the Soviet Government, while maintaining diplomatic relations with France, similarly announced its recognition.

7. The newly formed States of Vietnam, Laos and Cambodia do not as yet have sufficient political stability nor military power to prevent the infiltration into their areas of Ho Chi Minh's forces. The French Armed Forces, while apparently effectively utilized at the present time, can do little more than to maintain the status quo. Their strength of some 140,000 does, however, represent an army in being and the only military bulwark in that area against the further expansion of communist aggression from either internal or external forces.

8. The presence of Chinese Communist troops along the border of Indochina makes it possible for arms, material and troops to move freely from Communist China to the northern Tonkin area now controlled by Ho Chi Minh. There is already evidence of movement of arms.

9. In the present state of affairs, it is doubtful that the combined native Indochinese and French troops can successfully contain Ho's forces should they be strengthened by either Chinese Communist troops crossing the border, or Communist-supplied arms and material in quantity from outside Indochina strengthening Ho's forces.

Conclusions

10. It is important to United States security interests that all practicable measures be taken to prevent further communist expansion in Southeast Asia. Indochina is a key area of Southeast Asia and is under immediate threat.

11. The neighboring countries of Thailand and Burma could be expected to fall under Communist domination if Indochina were controlled by a Communist-dominated government. The balance of Southeast Asia would then be in grave hazard.

12. Accordingly, the Departments of State and Defense should prepare as a matter of priority a program of all practicable measures designed to protect United States security interests in Indochina.

> **Source:** *The Pentagon Papers: The Defense Department History of United States Decisionmaking on Vietnam,* Vol. 1. Senator Gravel edition (Boston: Beacon, 1971), 361–362.

47. Dean Acheson, Secretary of State: Telegram to the Embassy in the United Kingdom, January 30, 1950

Introduction

In this telegram to U.S. ambassador to Great Britain Lewis W. Douglas, Secretary of State Dean Acheson explains the U.S. decision to extend full de jure recognition of the Bao Dai State of Vietnam (SVN) and seeks to draw British policy into alignment with that of the United States.

Primary Source

Re Lond's 479, rptd Paris 137, Jan 27. Fol comments on recognition Viet Nam shld be passed to Brit:

As Dept understands it the purpose of according recognition to Bao Dai is to give him stature in the eyes of non-communist nationalists elements in Viet Nam and thus increase his following. This being the case recognition, if accorded by U.K. or ourselves, wld appear most effective if given without any strings attached, i.e.

the defacto step contemplated by Brit as a bargaining point with the Fr in order obtain further concessions. Dept has come to view that the Fr have for the moment gone as far as they can in according independence. This does not mean of course that either we, the Brit or the Fr shld not continue to view the Mar 8 Agreements as an evolutionary step in the independence of Viet Nam.

We are of course aware of fact that the UK does not have unanimous support of the commonwealth re recognition and that no formula re Viet Nam cld be found at Colombo acceptable to all participants. We nevertheless believe that a straightforward recognition without the qualification of defacto, or for that matter de jure, wld best serve our and UK interests and this viewpoint shld be pressed upon the commonwealth govts. In this connection, it shld be borne in mind that simultaneous recognition will have to be accorded to Laos and Cambodia, whose govts fulfill the requirements for the "de jure" status. The Mao Tse Tung govt on the other hand appears indeed to be a "de facto" form of govt altho it was simply "recognized" without qualifications.

Along the lines above Dept is of opinion that merely to give the UK ConGen in Saigon the "courtesy of rank of minister" is a skittish and timorous approach to problem of according diplomatic recognition to Viet Nam which wld tend in large measure to negate the benefits of such recognition. Dept considering making ConGen Saigon a diplomatic agent accredited to all 3 govts with personal rank of minister if this appears indicated.

Source: *Foreign Relations of the United States, 1950,* Vol. 6 (Washington, DC: U.S. Government Printing Office, 1976), 703–704.

48. Paper on Military Aid for Indochina by a Working Group in the Department of State, February 1, 1950 [Excerpts]

Introduction

A working group involving various divisions within the Department of State was formed to discuss the possibility of U.S. military aid to Indochina. Massive amounts of Marshall Plan aid were already freeing up French resources to fight the war in Indochina. Although unwarranted by the facts on the ground, the working group's conclusions reflect U.S. government optimism regarding the possibility of a French military victory in Indochina.

Primary Source

Military Aid for Indochina

I. The Problem

Should the United States provide military aid in Indochina and, if so, how much and in what way.

II. Assumption

A. There will not be an effective split between the USSR and Communist China within the next three years.

B. The USSR will not declare war on any Southeast Asian country within the next three years.

C. Communist China will not declare war on any Southeast Asian country within the next three years.

D. The USSR will endeavor to bring about the fall of Southeast Asian governments which are opposed to Communism by using all devices short of war, making use of Communist China and indigenous communists in this endeavor. . . .

IV. Discussion

8. Ho Chi Minh, a Moscow-trained Communist, controls the Viet Minh movement which is in conflict with the government of Bao Dai for control of Vietnam. Ho actually exercises control of varying degree over more than two-thirds of Vietnam territory and his "government" maintains agents in Thailand, Burma and India. This communist "government" has been recognized by Communist China and the USSR.

9. Most Indochinese, both the supporters of Bao Dai and those of Ho Chi Minh, regard independence from the French as their primary objective. Protection from Chinese Communist imperialism has been considered, up to now, a secondary issue.

10. Unavoidably, the United States is, together with France, committed in Indochina. That is, failure of the French Bao Dai "experiment" would mean the communization of Indochina. It is Bao Dai (or a similar anti-Communist successor) or Ho Chi Minh (or a similar Communist successor); there is no other alternative. The choice confronting the United States is to support the French in Indochina or face the extension of Communism over the remainder of the continental area of Southeast Asia and, possibly, farther westward. We then would be obliged to make staggering investments in those areas and in that part of Southeast Asia remaining outside Communist domination or

withdraw to a much-contracted Pacific line. It would seem a case of "Penny wise, Pound foolish" to deny support to the French in Indochina.

11. The US plans on extending recognition to the newly-created states of Vietnam, Laos and Cambodia, following French legislative action which is expected in early February 1950.

12. Another approach to the problem is to apply the practical test of probability of success. In the present case we know from the complex circumstances involved that the French are going to make literally every possible effort to prevent the victory of Communism in Indochina. Briefly, then, we would be backing a determined protagonist in this venture. Added to this is the fact that French military leaders such as General Cherrière are soberly confident that, in the absence of an invasion in mass from Red China, they (the French) can be successful in their support of the anti-Communist governments in Indochina.

13. Still another approach to the problem is to recall that the United States has undertaken to provide substantial aid to France in Europe. Failure to support French policy in Indochina would have the effect of contributing toward the defeat of our aims in Europe.

V. Conclusions

A. Significant developments have taken place in Indochina since the Mutual Defense Assistance Act of 1949 was drawn up, these changes warranting a reexamination of the question of military aid.

B. The whole of Southeast Asia is in danger of falling under Communist domination.

C. The countries and areas of Southeast Asia are not at present in a position to form a regional organization for self-defense nor are they capable of defending themselves against militarily aggressive Communism, without the aid of the great powers. Despite their lack of military strength, however, there is a will on the part of the legal governments of Indochina toward nationalism and a will to resist whatever aims at destroying that nationalism.

D. The French native and colonial troops presently in Indochina are engaged in military operations aimed at denying the expansion southward of Communism from Red China and of destroying its power in Indochina.

E. In the critical areas of Indochina France needs aid in its support of the legally-constituted anti-Communist states.

VI. Recommendations

1. The United States should furnish military aid in support of the anti-Communist nationalist governments of Indochina, this aid to be tailored to meet deficiencies toward which the United States can make a unique contribution, not including United States troops.

2. This aid should be financed out of funds made available by Section 303 of the Mutual Defense Assistance Act of 1949.

> **Source:** *Foreign Relations of the United States, 1950,* Vol. 6 (Washington, DC: U.S. Government Printing Office, 1976), 711–715.

49. Dean Acheson, Secretary of State: Telegram to U.S. Ambassador to France David Bruce, March 4, 1950

Introduction

Military aid from the People's Republic of China (PRC) to the Viet Minh fighting the French in Indochina was the final straw for Washington, and on February 7, 1950, the United States formally recognized Bao Dai's State of Vietnam (SVN). In May, Washington agreed to provide $20 million to $30 million in direct aid and more the next fiscal year.

Primary Source

In connection with possible military assistance to be given to Indochina Dept is interested in knowing your views on Fr plans regarding the manner and extent of participation by Bao Dai in this aid. Bao Dai's extravagant requests as presented in his memo to Jessup (which we are assuming has not been seen by the Fr) indicate that he may soon raise the question. The granting of arms to Bao Dai raises question about Fr supervision. In order to build up his political position in Vietnam the Dept considers it important that some formula be found to make Bao Dai appear to be the overt recipient of such aid. This may, of course, involve more of a concession than the Fr are prepared to make at this time, but may, from US viewpoint, be necessary. Dept may wish to ask you to discuss with Fr an approach by us to Bao Dai along the fol lines:

1) That his ideas for equipping Vietnamese army, militia, air force and navy, as set forth in his memo to Jessup seem beyond the realm of practical possibility.

2) That for long time to come he will have to look primarily to Fr for supplies of arms, training and military assistance in general.

3) It is up to him as much as it is to Fr to establish a modus vivendi re this question which will enable him to receive from them adequate support to pacify the country without jeopardizing his own position as the chief of an independent Viet Nam.

4) We are considering making a contribution to the joint Fr-Vietnamese war effort in the area. However, in view of urgency of their joint need for assistance it will, for purely practical reasons, be necessary to extend material assistance to them thru the Fr., but preserving Bao Dai as publicized recipient.

5) Since the appearance of it being a joint Franco-Vietnamese operation is of great importance politically we are likewise suggesting to the Fr that they associate him in their request for an arms program for Indochina.

Emb's comments urgently requested. No action should be taken with Fr on above without further instructions.

Rptd Saigon as 122 for info only.

Source: *Foreign Relations of the United States, 1950,* Vol. 6 (Washington, DC: U.S. Government Printing Office, 1976), 748–749.

50. Dean Acheson: Press Release Urging Aid for Indochina, May 22, 1950

Introduction

In this press release, U.S. secretary of state Dean Acheson describes his meeting with French foreign minister Robert Schuman and their exchange of views on Indochina. Glossing over the reality of the situation, which is that the French still retain control, Acheson notes the "independence" of Cambodia, Laos, and Vietnam within the French Union and announces that the United States is providing both economic and military aid to help bring about the "restoration of security" in order to "pursue their peaceful and democratic development." As noted earlier, because the State of Vietnam (SVN) was in fact dominated by France, the Vietnamese had only two choices: join the Communists or support the French. In refusing to grant real independence to Vietnam, France continued to drive Vietnamese nationalists to the Communist side.

Primary Source

The [French] Foreign Minister [Robert Schuman] and I have just had an exchange of views on the situation in Indochina and are in general agreement both as to the urgency of the situation in that area and as to the necessity for remedial action. We have noted the fact that the problem of meeting the threat to the security of Viet Nam, Cambodia, and Laos which now enjoy independence within the French union is primarily the responsibility of France and the Governments and peoples of Indochina. The United States recognizes that the solution of the Indochina problem depends both upon the restoration of security and upon the development of genuine nationalism and that United States assistance can and should contribute to these major objectives.

The United States Government, convinced that neither national independence nor democratic evolution exist[s] in any area dominated by Soviet imperialism, considers the situation to be such as to warrant its according economic aid and military equipment to the associated states of Indochina and to France in order to assist them in restoring stability and permitting these states to pursue their peaceful and democratic development.

Source: "Economic and Military Aid Urged for Indochina," *Department of State Bulletin* 22(568) (1950): 821.

51. President Harry S. Truman: Statement Announcing Direct U.S. Military Aid to Indochina, June 27, 1950

Introduction

The Korean War, which began on June 25, 1950, solidified the position of President Harry S. Truman's administration toward Indochina. Containing the spread of communism now completely subsumed anticolonialism. Washington and Paris saw Korea and Vietnam as mutually dependent theaters in a common Western struggle against the spread of communism. On June 27, 1950, in his statement granting U.S. military assistance to the Republic of Korea (ROK, South Korea), Truman also announced that the United States was changing its policy of providing only indirect aid to the war in Indochina. On June 30 eight C-47 transport aircraft arrived in Saigon with the first direct shipment of U.S. military equipment. U.S. support for the French effort in Indochina grew steadily. With the establishment of the Military Assistance Advisory Group (MAAG), U.S. military aid rose from $100 million in 1950 to $300 million in 1952 and to more than $1 billion in 1954, when the United States was financing some 80 percent of the French effort. Overall U.S. military assistance amounted to nearly $3 billion, or nearly 60 percent of the war's cost.

Primary Source

In Korea the Government forces, which were armed to prevent border raids and to preserve internal security, were attacked by invading forces from North Korea. The Security Council of the United Nations called upon the invading troops to cease hostilities and to withdraw to the 38th parallel. This they have not done, but on the contrary have pressed the attack. The Security Council called upon all members of the United Nations to render every assistance to the United Nations in the execution of this resolution. In these circumstances I have ordered United States air and sea forces to give the Korean Government troops cover and support.

The attack upon Korea makes it plain beyond all doubt that communism has passed beyond the use of subversion to conquer independent nations and will now use armed invasion and war. It has defied the orders of the Security Council of the United Nations issued to preserve international peace and security. In these circumstances the occupation of Formosa by Communist forces would be a direct threat to the security of the Pacific area and to United States forces performing their lawful and necessary functions in that area.

Accordingly I have ordered the 7th Fleet to prevent any attack on Formosa. As a corollary of this action I am calling upon the Chinese Government on Formosa to cease all air and sea operations against the mainland. The 7th Fleet will see that this is done. The determination of the future status of Formosa must await the restoration of security in the Pacific, a peace settlement with Japan, or consideration by the United Nations.

I have also directed that United States Forces in the Philippines be strengthened and that military assistance to the Philippine Government be accelerated.

I have similarly directed acceleration in the furnishing of military assistance to the forces of France and the Associated States in Indochina and the dispatch of a military mission to provide close working relations with those forces.

I know that all members of the United Nations will consider carefully the consequences of this latest aggression in Korea in defiance of the Charter of the United Nations. A return to the rule of force in international affairs would have far-reaching effects. The United States will continue to uphold the rule of law.

I have instructed Ambassador Austin, as the representative of the United States to the Security Council, to report these steps to the Council.

Source: *Public Papers of the Presidents of the United States: Harry S. Truman, 1950* (Washington, DC: U.S. Government Printing Office, 1965), 492.

52. Ho Chi Minh: Answers to Questions Put by the Press Regarding U.S. Intervention in Indochina, July 25, 1950

Introduction

In these remarks, President Ho Chi Minh of the Democratic Republic of Vietnam (DRV, North Vietnam) openly denounces assistance by "U.S. imperialists" to the French in Indochina. Ho expresses his complete confidence in an eventual Viet Minh victory over the "French colonialists and the U.S. interventionists."

Primary Source

Question: What is, Mr. President, the present situation of the U.S. imperialists' interventionist policy in Indochina?

Answer: The U.S. imperialists have of late openly interfered in Indochina's affairs. It is with their money and weapons and their instructions that the French colonialists have been waging war in Viet-Nam, Cambodia, and Laos.

However, the U.S. imperialists are intensifying their plot to discard the French colonialists so as to gain complete control over Indochina. That is why they do their utmost to redouble their direct intervention in every field—military, political, and economic. It is also for this reason that the contradictions between them and the French colonialists become sharper and sharper.

Question: Mr. President, what influence does this intervention exert on the Indochinese people?

Answer: The U.S. imperialists supply their henchmen with armaments to massacre the Indochinese people. They dump their goods in Indochina to prevent the development of local handicrafts. Their pornographic culture contaminates the youth in areas placed under their control. They follow the policy of buying up, deluding, and dividing our people. They drag some bad elements into becoming their tools and use them to invade our country.

Question: What shall we do against them?

Answer: To gain independence, we, the Indochinese people, must defeat the French colonialists, our number-one enemy. At the same time, we will struggle against the U.S. interventionists. The deeper their interference, the more powerful are our solidarity and our struggle. We will expose their maneuvers before all our people, especially those living in areas under their control. We will expose all those who serve as lackeys for the U.S. imperialists to coerce, deceive, and divide our people.

The close solidarity between the peoples of Viet-Nam, Cambodia, and Laos constitutes a force capable of defeating the French colonialists and the U.S. interventionists. The U.S. imperialists failed in China, they will fail in Indochina.

We are still laboring under great difficulties but victory will certainly be ours.

Source: Ho Chi Minh, *Selected Writings: 1920–1969* (Hanoi: Foreign Languages Publishing House, 1977), 94–95.

53. John F. Melby, Chairman of the Joint Survey Mission: Telegram to Dean Rusk, Assistant Secretary of State for Far Eastern Affairs, August 7, 1950 [Excerpt]

Introduction

In this pessimistic report to the Far Eastern Division of the State Department, John F. Melby, who headed a survey team on Indochina, reports that there will be no military solution there. Melby flatly denies that the French have indeed granted independence to the states of the region and notes that nationalism continues to fuel the Viet Minh. He also points out that the complete identification of the United States with France has greatly weakened American influence in the region. The only possible solution is a French pledge to grant genuine independence to the states of Indochina within a specified time period, as with the United States and the Philippines.

Primary Source

In summary then there is good reason to believe that proper application of sufficient military force, plus goading the French into a more offensive spirit, can hold the aid [*sic:* lid?] on the Indochinese kettle for the predictable, if relatively limited, future. It will not however solve the long-range problem. Neither can the French do it on their present promises or without a radical change of heart and approach. If American interests can be served by the short-range approach then the rest need not concern us. This must be determined with relationship to over-all world situation, prospects, and time factors. If however the longer alley is important, then Franco-Vietnamese behavior in that alley, to borrow from the Churchillian analogy of the gorilla in the jungle, is a matter of the gravest concern.

If the latter be the case and the foregoing analysis valid, a satisfactory solution can only be found when the French have been persuaded to sweeter reasonableness and the Vietnamese firmly led by the hand through the growing pains of adolescence. Recent Korean precedent may be suggestive. I could propose

consideration of following: French undertaking for Vietnam independence within specified period of 5, 10, 20, or 30 years with certain special compensations for French such as are found in Philippines-American arrangements.

French would undertake to guarantee inviolability Indochina border. Vietnam national army would be rapidly created to assure responsibility internal situation and as this progressed French forces would withdraw to border areas or where unnecessary depart. Civil administration would increasingly be Vietnam responsibility. All such agreements would have UN public guarantee and such supervision as necessary. Assumably [*sic*] US would as usual pay most of bills. If US can bring its Korean responsibilities within UN framework, there is little solid reason why French cannot do same for Indochina.

Ever recognizing that this form is hardly likely to provoke dancing in the streets of Paris, it may well be that this or something similar is only real prospect for salvaging anything and French must be coerced into realizing it and behaving accordingly. If Vietnam has determined on complete independence as all evidence suggests, it probably cannot get it for a long time in face of French opposition, but it can create the kind of uproar which will constitute a continuing drain on French strength and in end benefit only Communists. Coincidentally, American identification with French in such eventuality will further weaken American influence in Asia. Historically no ruling group has ever remained more or less indefinitely in power in face of active or even passive resistance from the governed, or without ruining itself in the process. There is no convincing evidence Nationalism in Indochina proposes to be an exception.

Source: *Foreign Relations of the United States, 1950,* Vol. 6 (Washington, DC: U.S. Government Printing Office, 1976), 847–848.

54. Dean Acheson, Secretary of State: Telegram to Ambassador to France David Bruce, November 11, 1950

Introduction

After British ambassador to France Sir Oliver Harvey had urged the French government to grant full independence to the states of Indochina, U.S. secretary of state Dean Acheson cabled David Bruce, the ambassador to France. Acheson expresses concern over the impact of such a move on the morale of French troops, making it impossible for them to win the war. Acheson believes that pressure on the French government for such a statement should come only after the military situation is more favorable to the French. (Note: The Paris Conference of 1950 referred to in this cable had brought together representatives of the Indochina states to discuss the possible future framework of institutions there.) As it worked out, France continued to dominate Indochina affairs down to the end of the war.

Primary Source

Dept has followed developments concerning suggestion that UK Amb Paris inform Fr Govt that "they make formal statement of intention release control Indochina without, however, mentioning time limit" with interest (Lond's tel 2234, Oct 18).

We had agreed fully with reasoning behind Harvey's request that he use discretion as to timing approach to Schuman and that it be delayed at least until end Pau Conference. As matter has and will, undoubtedly, continue to be discussed with Fr by Malcolm McDonald Dept now considering suggestion to Brit Govt that their démarche to Fr through McDonald or Harvey be coordinated not joined with similar one on our part. Do not believe joint démarche advisable as traditional Fr suspicion UK FE might lead them resent Brit action. Joining Brit might thus reduce effectiveness our approach.

In forming approach to Fr we do not wish to overlook consideration that morale of troops fighting in Indochina is of prime importance and that, therefore, Fr Govt should not be urged to make any statement concerning further relinquishment Fr controls except under most favorable conditions. Dept would include among factors which might constitute "favorable conditions" (re: Embtel 2436, Nov 3): (1) demonstration renewed Fr mil potential in form absence further deterioration, (2) visible proof of formation National Armies beyond present paper steps which are excellent beginning, (3) further evidence Bao Dai's intention and ability assume active leadership his govt, still waited.

Moreover, Dept agrees that considerations morale troops Indochina and public opinion Fr in face expenditures lives and money will make it necessary that statement be not so extreme as to remove whatever stake for Fr in Indochina is sufficient to assure their continued acceptance of "primary responsibility" to extent of proceeding with present program. Dept eager in this matter, as in others relating to Indochina, to strengthen ties Fr Union and maximize protection Fr economic interests Indochina.

Nevertheless Dept is increasingly of conviction that further evolutionary statement is required to consolidate gains which development National Armies, support Franco-Vietnamese mil potential and enhancement Bao Dai Govt's authority either as result decisions Pau Conference or, possibly, as we hope, through his own revitalization. We are also obviously concerned to see that every means to increase effectiveness of use our own considerable financial and military aid be brought to bear. This would include as a minimum, official declaration by Fr at highest level (Auriol or Schuman) on present and future intentions regarding Indochina,

as they have been stated to us by various high officials including Schuman, Moch and Letourneau, on several recent occasions.

Points outlined in Embtel 2436, Nov 3, Para two, are those which we consider should be included. Without attempting suggest actual form we would view something along lines of Letourneau's statements at Saigon press conference (Saigon 657, Oct 24) and Embassys suggestions in reftel as basic text to build on.

Todays Paris press despatches report McDonald will continue discussions re Indochina with Fr officials during coming week. We would welcome invitation Emb officer participate but as approach shld not be joint realize this might be impossible. Emb shld continue exchange views with McDonald and Fr separately, informing former of our thoughts on concurrent Anglo-U.S. approach to Fr and latter of our agreement with Brit views as expressed to Bruce by McDonald.

London note and, after consultation Paris, inform ForOff our views and general concurrence theirs as expressed McDonald; sound out possibilities similar approach Fr.

Source: *Foreign Relations of the United States, 1950,* Vol. 6 (Washington, DC: U.S. Government Printing Office, 1976), 920–921.

55. John Ohly, Deputy Director of the Mutual Defense Assistance Program: Memorandum to Secretary of State Dean Acheson, November 20, 1950 [Excerpts]

Introduction

With the capture by the Viet Minh of the French Army's key posts along the border with China in late 1949, France had in effect lost the Indochina War. The Chinese set up base camps across the border for the training of Viet Minh troops, and aid could now flow freely into the Democratic Republic of Vietnam (DRV, North Vietnam). As the war deteriorated for the French, pressure grew for Washington to take decisive action as a full partner of the French. Here John Ohly, the deputy director of the Mutual Defense Assistance Program that was supplying aid to the French, points out that many independent observers believe that the French cannot defeat the Viet Minh. Ohly urges a reassessment of U.S. policy in Indochina before greater involvement there.

Primary Source

1. This memorandum is designed to stress the urgent necessity for an immediate, thorough and realistic re-examination of our policy

with respect to Indochina. From the standpoint of the Mutual Defense Assistance Program, such a re-examination is imperative, because the continuance of the present policy of substantial aid may, without achieving its intended purpose, make impossible the fulfillment of mutual defense objectives elsewhere in the world. Such a re-examination may well lead to a reaffirmation of this policy without significant change, but in my opinion, and in the light of the considerations set forth below, it would be the height of folly to pursue such policy further in the absence of a far more searching analysis than has heretofore been made of its possibilities of success and its global consequences. Even if the need for such an approach was not urgent before (and I believe it was), it has certainly been made so by the direct Chinese Communist intervention in Korea which (1) places large additional operating demands upon the limited materiel resources available for both U.S. requirements and all foreign military assistance programs and (2) indicates that the Kremlin may be prepared to accept the risks inherent in the actual commitment of Chinese troops to assist Ho Chi Minh, a step which would, as subsequently indicated, completely transform the character of the military problem in Indochina. . . .

IV. Recommendations

I strongly recommend that before any further substantial commitments of equipment, prestige or forces are made in Indochina, the kind of assessment suggested in the preceding pages be undertaken. I suggest that this be done by a special task force under the auspices of the National Security Council, because it is so urgent that it cannot and should not be pursued through slower channels. We have reached a point where the United States, because of limitations in resources, can no longer simultaneously pursue all of its objectives in all parts of the world and must realistically face the fact that certain objectives, even though they may be extremely valuable and important ones, may have to be abandoned if others of even greater value and importance are to be attained. The situation is not unlike that which faced the United States in the early days of the last war, when a choice had to be made between pursuing the offensive in either the West or the East and not in both places at once.

As an after thought, and by way of additional caveat, I would like to point out that the demands on the U.S. for Indochina are increasing almost daily and that, sometimes imperceptibly, by one step after another, we are gradually increasing our stake in the outcome of the struggle there. We are, moreover, slowly (and not too slowly) getting ourselves into a position where our responsibilities tend to supplant rather than complement those of the French, and where failures are attributed to us as though we were the primary party at fault and in interest. We may be on the road to being a scapegoat, and we are certainly dangerously close to the point of being so deeply committed that we may find ourselves completely committed even to direct intervention. These situations, unfortunately, have a way of snowballing.

Source: *Foreign Relations of the United States, 1950,* Vol. 6 (Washington, DC: U.S. Government Printing Office, 1976), 925–930.

56. Joint Chiefs of Staff: Memorandum to Secretary of Defense George C. Marshall, January 10, 1951

Introduction

Queried by U.S. secretary of defense George C. Marshall regarding the French proposal for tripartite military talks among France, Britain, and the United States on Indochina, the Joint Chiefs of Staff (JCS) takes the position that in view of the present situation in the Far East (i.e., the Korean War), the United States should not itself become directly involved militarily in Indochina, even in the event of a Chinese invasion.

Primary Source

Subject: Proposed Military Talks Regarding Defense of Indochina.

1. This memorandum is in response to your memorandum of 21 December 1950 dealing with the matter of proposed military talks regarding defense of Indochina.

2. In view of the present United States military position in the Far East, the Joint Chiefs of Staff believe the following to be basic:

   a. The United States should not permit its military forces to become engaged in French Indochina at this time, and

   b. In the Event of a communist invasion of Indochina, therefore, the United States should under current circumstances limit its support of the French there to an acceleration and expansion of the present military assistance program, together with taking other appropriate action to deny Indochina to communism, short of the actual employment of military forces.

In light of the above, and in view of the considerations expressed in their memorandum to you of 8 December 1950, the Joint Chiefs of Staff feel, from the strictly military point of view, that no additional military staff talks are desirable at this time.

3. On the other hand, the Joint Chiefs of Staff recognize that the political considerations raised in your memorandum of 21 December 1950 may be regarded as overriding. Under such circumstances, the Joint Chiefs of Staff would not interpose further objection to the holding of additional tripartite military staff talks at this time. Any such talks, however, would be restricted in scope

by the Joint Chiefs of Staff and would not be permitted to deal with matters of strategy affecting United States global policies and plans.

4. In the event of a global war, the major United States measures in support of the French in Indochina would of necessity also be limited to the acceleration and expansion of the present military assistance program as feasible, and, operationally, to matters connected with convoy, routing, and protection of shipping. If the decision is made to hold the proposed additional military talks involving military operational commanders, it would be appropriate, therefore, that the chief United States military representative should be an officer designated by the Commander in Chief, Pacific (CINCPAC), and that he should be assisted by General Brink.

Source: *Foreign Relations of the United States, 1951,* Vol. 6, Part 1 (Washington, DC: U.S. Government Printing Office, 1977), 347–348.

57. Dean Acheson, Secretary of State: Telegram to the Legation in Saigon, January 30, 1951

Introduction

In this telegram of January 30, 1951, to the U.S. legation in Saigon, Secretary of State Dean Acheson sums up talks held during September 29–30 in Washington between U.S. president Harry S. Truman and French premier René Pleven. Acheson reports that Pleven is wary of a request from French high commissioner and military commander in Indochina General Jean de Lattre de Tassigny for additional French troops, especially given French commitments to the defense of Western Europe. Pleven is said to be resisting suggestions that the French government undertake talks with representatives of the Democratic Republic of Vietnam (DRV, North Vietnam) regarding an end to the war and is instead seeking a tripartite coordination of efforts there by France, Great Britain, and the United States. He also wants a commitment from Truman that the United States would provide substantial additional aid to enlarge the armies of the French-supported associated states of Laos, Cambodia, and the State of Vietnam (SVN) fighting the Viet Minh.

Primary Source

The fol is rough summary of Truman-Pleven discussions of yesterday as they pertain to IC:

Pleven presented his position as fols:

1) Events in the Far East make it necessary for the Western Powers to coordinate economically, militarily and politically and procedure for permanent consultation between US, Brit and Fr shld

be established. It might include the establishment of a permanent tripartite body for this purpose.

2) As far as IC is concerned three hypotheses shld be considered:

a. The present situation of fighting an internal rebellion which Fr is and has faced for the last five years. With a reinforced VM Fr can only foresee heavier and heavier losses. The only possible daylight in matter lies in the planned development of Viet natl army. Immed question to be faced is whether Gen de Lattre's demands for reinforcement shld be met or declined in the realization that similar demands may be expected regularly hereafter and cannot be met. The fact that Fr present effort entailed a comparable drain on her contribution to the defense of Western Europe is also pertinent. Amt of US aid to be anticipated is dominant consideration in arriving at decision in matter. Formation of four Vietnamese divisions during 1951 under study. Wld involve a cost of 58 billion francs, 25 billion of which cannot be covered in the contemplated contributions from both Fr and Vietnamese budgets. Particular mention was made of the furnishing of an aircraft carrier. Recommended that this and other technical questions shld be studied by Fr-US mil experts.

b. The second possibility is that which wld be created by an overt Chi Commie attack. Before the Fr can make any decision of action to be taken in this eventuality they must ask for further clarification of the US position vis-à-vis aid in both men and material. Fr Govt wld also appreciate info concerning anticipated US aid in the event of a forced evacuation.

The Fr invite us to consider the effect of the loss of Tonkin or of all IC on the rest of SEA (polit, econ and mil). A study of this matter might be considered by the group suggested in para one.

c. The third possibility is that which wld be created if peace negotiations were undertaken. While Fr observe that it is impossible to calculate if such possibility exists they believe consideration must be given to it "especially in the light of the recent reverses suffered by the VM."

Although detailed minutes are not available fol is a brief summary of our replies to various questions:

Although we are not prepared to consider question of tripartite SEA command as suggested by Fr we are prepared under certain specific and limiting conditions to adhere to our agreement to take part in high level tripartite mil conversations as agreed at the Sep FonMin Conf. We are prepared to appoint man from Admiral Radford's staff to represent us.

We assured Fr that our aid program to IC will be carried out as presently planned, barring unforeseen developments. We are prepared to give the Fr more detailed info on the way our aid program works and specific consideration being given to IC in overall picture. We have told the Fr we are not prepared to commit ground forces but wld, dependent on circumstances applicable at time, supply logistic support in the event of a forced evacuation.

Re the 25 billion franc deficit in sum required for natl armies (Fr state only 33 billion of 58 required can be covered by Fr and Viet budgets combined). The Fr made us a formal request for additional aid of 70 million dollars. We have given them no assurance in that regard and are now engaged in detailed studies at specialists level concerning matter. For your info it is very unlikely that this Govt will engage itself to finance the budgetary deficit of another govt but we hope to devise some other method to assure that necessary funds for the development of the natl armies be forthcoming.

Although we did not accede to the Fr request for another aircraft carrier, Gen Marshall informed Pleven that the present restrictions on the use of the Langley wld be removed, thus apparently making Langley available to Fr for use in Far Eastern waters if they so choose. We assured the Fr that the effect of the loss of Tonkin or of all of IC to rest of SEA is constantly under study by this govt.

We had no comment concerning third hypothesis.

The 58 billion franc figure for the formation of the natl armies is based on armies of 41 battalions. Of this sum it is estimated that the Fr budget cld only make a 15 1/2 billion franc contribution and the Viet one of 17 billion as a maximum (40% of estimated total receipts). The deficit is thus 25 1/2 billion francs or roughly $70 million. Of this sum approximately 2/3 wld be required for payroll and 1/3 for equipment and goods payable in francs and piasters. Eventually natl armies wld consist of four Vietnamese divisions of 34 battalions plus five Cambodian and two Laotian battalions. Fr have stated it will be impossible for them to furnish any equipment for battalions still to be formed and they count on the US for that.

Source: *Foreign Relations of the United States, 1951,* Vol. 6, Part 1 (Washington, DC: U.S. Government Printing Office, 1977), 368–369.

58. Dean Acheson, Secretary of State: Report to the National Security Council on Conversations between President Harry S. Truman and French Premier René Pleven, February 23, 1951 [Excerpt]

Introduction

In this report to the National Security Council (NSC), U.S. secretary of state Dean Acheson sums up the impact on U.S. policy from the meeting concerning Indochina between French premier

René Pleven and U.S. president Harry S. Truman in Washington during January 29–30, 1950. While seeking to provide funds to increase the size of the armies of the associated states of Laos, Cambodia, and the State of Vietnam (SVN) fighting the Viet Minh, the Truman administration remains deeply concerned about direct U.S. military involvement in Indochina. Acheson reports the common sentiment that should the People's Republic of China (PRC) intervene militarily, France will have little choice but to quit Indochina. The United States would provide whatever assistance it can to a French evacuation, but its extent would be determined by the existing situation in the Far East. While the Chinese could overrun all of Southeast Asia and although such an event would threaten "critical security interests" of the United States, it is not now in overall U.S. "security interests" to commit U.S. troops there.

Primary Source

Far East

4a. 'The President and the Prime Minister found themselves in complete agreement as to the necessity of resisting aggression and assisting the free nations of the Far East in their efforts to maintain their security and assure their independence.' The U.S. and France should not over-commit themselves militarily in the Far East and thereby endanger the situation in Europe.

b. 'The President and the Prime Minister agreed that continuous contact should be maintained between the interested nations on these problems.' The Prime Minister's suggestion to create a U.S., U.K., French consultative body to coordinate the three governments' Asiatic policies was not accepted by the President, who preferred to rely on existing mechanisms.

c. 'The situation in Korea was discussed and they concurred that every effort must be exerted to bring about an honorable solution there. Until that end can be accomplished, resistance by United Nations forces to aggression must continue. Both France and the United States will support action directed toward deterring aggression and toward preventing the spread of hostilities beyond Korea.'

d. With regard to Indochina, 'the Prime Minister declared that France was determined to do its utmost to continue' its efforts to resist 'the Communist onslaught in order to maintain the security and independence of the Associated States, Viet Nam, Cambodia, and Laos.'

e. It was desirable to build up the native Indochinese forces as rapidly as possible. We held out no hope for the provision of U.S. budgetary assistance for the National Army in Indochina. We cannot become directly involved in local budgetary deficits of other countries.

f. 'The President informed the Prime Minister that United States aid for the French Union forces and for the National Armies of the Associated States will continue, and that the increased quantities of material to be delivered under the program authorized for the current fiscal year will be expedited.' Additional measures for aid to Indochina included: (1) an indication of our willingness to relax the original restrictions placed on the use by the French of the U.S. aircraft carrier Langley in the Mediterranean in view of our inability to provide another U.S. carrier for service in Indochina; and (2) an agreement to study the possibility of reallocating funds now available in an effort to provide equipment for four Vietnamese divisions.

g. The President said that the United States was agreeable to U.S., U.K., French military consultations on Indochinese matters.

h. In the event of a Chinese Communist attack on Indochina, the U.S. desires to assist in the evacuation of French forces if such action becomes necessary. The extent of the aid would be limited by other demands on our forces, such as Korea, which exist at the time any request for assistance is made.

Source: *Foreign Relations of the United States, 1951,* Vol. 6, Part 1 (Washington, DC: U.S. Government Printing Office, 1977), 367.

59. R. Allen Griffin, Special Far East Representative, Economic Cooperation Administration: Telegram to Richard M. Bissell Jr., Acting Administrator, Economic Cooperation Administration, November 30, 1951

Introduction

Following a visit to Indochina, R. Allen Griffin, formerly the chief of staff of the first U.S. mission to Southeast Asia on economic assistance, provides a pessimistic view of the French-backed government of the State of Vietnam (SVN). Griffin notes that the SVN has no programs to lift the bulk of the Vietnamese population from poverty and calls it "a relic of the past as much as Fr[ench] colonialism." Despite this very negative assessment, Griffin calls for more U.S. involvement to create a representative Vietnamese government.

Primary Source

613. Dept pass ECA. To Bissell from Griffin.

1. US econ aid program Viet basically on right track for US objectives and should be contd as orig conceived. Those objectives remain sound and practical if new govt is to be supported in policies necessary to build loyalty and appreciation among population. However, I believe it is necessary for US clearly to realize the greatest impediment to success of US program and attainment objectives is nature of present Huu Govt, its lack of vitality and public leadership, its lack of enthusiasm for progressive progress that wld improve the gen welfare of peasants.

2. We are dealing with able land owners—mandarin type—functionaire govt. Its weakness is not that it is subordinate in many ways to Fr but that it is in no sense the servant of the people. It has no grass roots. It therefore has no appeal whatsoever to the masses. It evokes no popular support because it has no popular program. It has no popular program because nature of its leaders tends to an attitude that this wld be a "concession." This govt might reluctantly try to mollify public opinion, but it does not consist of men who wld lead public opinion. Therefore though France-Vietnam Armed Forces may cont to win small engagements for ltd objectives, no real progress is being made in winning war, which depends equally on polit solution.

3. It has been perhaps error in judgment in believing essential struggle has been between the constricting polit influence and pressure of Fr—which undoubtedly still exists and patriotic effort of Viets to win increasing degree of independence. Perhaps the essential struggle is one not undertaken—which is to get grass roots ability, conviction and patriotism on behalf of people of Viet into the govt. So-called independence Huu Govt represents means nothing to masses. It simply means a change of functionaires, not a change of social direction, not a drive to advance lot of the people. Revolution will continue and Ho Chi-minh will remain popular hero, so long as "independence" leaders with Fr support are simply native mandarins who are succeeding foreign mandarins. The period of mandarin and functionaire govt in Asia is over. The present type of govt in Viet is a relic of the past as much as Fr colonialism.

4. I believe this predicament is now fully realized by Fr. There is little doubt of fact they know they are fighting war that cannot be won without a polit solution, and the polit solution depends at least as much upon the relationship of Govt of Viet with masses of people of Viet as upon the relationship with Fr on subj of independence. The issue in Viet, in my mind, is more than nationalism and Francophobia. It is old Asian issue that destroyed the Kuomintang in Chi, Communist opportunity to exploit insecurity, and hunger and wretchedness of masses of people to whom their govt has failed to make an effective appeal. The Huu Govt makes no such appeal. Its heart is not in that kind of appeal. If it talked land reform it wld never be believed. It is my opinion that Fr are now fully awake to this predicament. They realize that their interests are not being served by a Viet Govt that not only has no appeal to masses but that has no program and perhaps only

doubtful sympathy for masses. Such condition will not help the Fr to extricate themselves from the milit burden. Nor will it help US to lessen the load of increasing costs the Fr require us to share. It is my opinion that we shld consider this problem jointly with the Fr, to the end that a govt with some grass roots instincts, intentions and social purpose may result.

5. It may be pointed out that US is now engaged in massive milit assistance in Indochina and an econ program of great potential social and polit impact. Fr are insisting on an even greater Amer participation in Fr costs of defending this semi-independent state. US has paid for right to exercise stronger voice in determination of policies. Fr failure to achieve satis polit results out of compliant, obedient landowners nonreform Cabinet may now make possible a practical and farsighted program for improving polit situation, which in itself awaits improvement of social outlook Viet Govt, a condition now obvious to Fr. I believe Fr are ready for that. If we fail to secure their collaboration for setting up a govt fitted for its job by something better than obedience to Fr, then one day we will discover that the Fr in disgust and discouragement will abandon their attempt to defend this flank of sea.

6. I have discussed this outlook with Heath but did not have time to draft cable before leaving Saigon.

Source: *Foreign Relations of the United States, 1951,* Vol. 6 (Washington, DC: U.S. Government Printing Office, 1977), 548–550.

60. National Security Council Staff Study on Objectives, Policies, and Course of Action in Asia (Annex to NSC 48/4), May 17, 1951 [Excerpts]

Introduction

In this National Security Council (NSC) study, the staff outlines the long-range security objectives of the United States. The study concludes that China is the central problem for the United States in Asia. Given its considerable commitments elsewhere, the United States does not have unlimited resources available to meet the Communist threat in Southeast Asia and must constantly evaluate its options. It is not now in the security interests of the United States to commit any of its armed forces in the defense of Southeast Asia, and America cannot guarantee that the region will remain non-Communist.

Primary Source

National Security Council Study on Objectives, Policies, and Courses of Action in Asia (Annex to NSC 48/4) [Extract]

Problem

1. To determine United States national objectives, policies, and courses of action with respect to Asia.

United States Long-Range National Objectives in Asia

2. The long-range national security objectives of the United States with respect to Asia are:

a. Development by the nations and peoples of Asia, through self-help and mutual aid, of stable and self-sustaining non-communist governments, oriented toward the United States, acting in accordance with the purposes and principles of the United Nations Charter, and having the will and ability to maintain internal security and prevent communist aggression.

b. Elimination of the preponderant power and influence of the USSR in Asia or its reduction to such a degree that the Soviet Union will not be capable of threatening from that area the security of the United States or its friends, or the peace, national independence and stability of the Asiatic nations.

c. Development of power relationships in Asia which will make it impossible for any nation or alliance to threaten the security of the United States from that area.

d. In so far as practicable, securing for the United States and the rest of the free world, and denying to the communist world, the availability through mutually advantageous arrangements, of the material resources of the Asian area.

Analysis of the Situation

3. United States objectives, policies, and courses of action in Asia should be designed to contribute toward the global objectives of strengthening the free world vis-a-vis the Soviet orbit, and should be determined with due regard to the relation of United States capabilities and commitments throughout the world. However, in view of the communist resort to armed force in Asia, United States action in that area must be based on the recognition that the most immediate threats to United States security are currently presented in that area.

4. Current Soviet tactics appear to concentrate on bringing the mainland of Eastern Asia and eventually Japan and the other principal off-shore islands in the Western Pacific under Soviet control, primarily through Soviet exploitation of the resources of communist China. The attainment of this objective on the mainland of Eastern Asia would substantially enhance the global position of the USSR at the expense of the United States, by securing the eastern flank of the USSR and permitting the USSR to concentrate its offensive power in other areas, particularly in Europe. Soviet control of the off-shore islands in the Western Pacific, including

Japan, would present an unacceptable threat to the security of the United States.

5. Asia is of strategic importance to the United States.

   a. The strategic significance of Asia arises from its resources, geography, and the political and military force which it could generate. The population of the area is about 1,250,000,000. The demonstrated military capacity of the North Korean and Chinese armies requires a reevaluation of the threat to the free world which the masses of Asia would constitute if they fell under Soviet Communist domination.

   b. The resources of Asia contribute greatly to United States security by helping to meet its need for critical materials and they would be of great assistance in time of war if they remained available. At least until stockpiling levels are met, this phase of the area's importance to the United States will continue. Further, the development of events which might lead to the exhaustion of such stockpiles would magnify the importance of this source of supply. The area produces practically all the world's natural rubber, nearly 5% of the oil, 60% of the tin, the major part of various important tropical products, and strategic materials such as manganese, jute, and atomic materials. Japan's potential in heavy industry is roughly equal to 50% of the Soviet Union's present production. Therefore, it is important to U.S. security interests that U.S. military and economic assistance programs be developed in such a manner as to maximize the availabilities of the material resources of the Asian area to the United States and the free world.

   c. Control by an enemy of the Asiatic mainland would deny to us the use of the most direct sea and air routes between Australia and the Middle East and between the United States and India. Such control would produce disastrous moral and psychological effects in border areas such as the Middle East and a critical effect in Western Europe.

6. The fact of Soviet power and communist aggression in Asia establishes the context within which the policies of the United States must operate.

   a. The problem of China is the central problem which faces the United States in Asia. A solution to this problem, through a change in the regime in control of mainland China, would facilitate the achievement of United States objectives throughout Asia. Therefore, United States policies and courses of action in Asia should be determined in the light of their effect upon the solution of the central problem, that of China.

[…]

Strengthening of Southeast Asia

[…]

41. It is important to the United States that the mainland states of Southeast Asia remain under non-communist control and continue to improve their internal conditions. These states are valuable to the free world because of their strategic position, abundant natural resources, including strategic materials in short supply in the United States, and their large population. Moreover, these states, if adequately developed and organized, could serve to protect and contribute to the economic progress and military defense of the Pacific off-shore islands from Japan to New Zealand. Communist control of both China and Southeast Asia would place Japan in a dangerously vulnerable position and therefore seriously affect the entire security position of the United States in the Pacific. The fall of the mainland states would result in changing the status of the off-shore island chain from supporting bases to front line positions. Further, it would tend to isolate these base areas from each other, requiring a review of our entire strategic deployment of forces. Communist domination of the area would alleviate considerably the food problem of China and make available to the USSR considerable quantities of strategically important materials.

42. In the absence of overt Chinese Communist aggression in Southeast Asia, the general problems facing the United States in this area are: the real threat of Chinese Communist invasion and subversion, the political instability and weak leadership of the non-communist governments, the low standards of living and underdeveloped resources of the peoples of the area, the prevailing prejudice against colonialism and Western "interference" and the insensitivity to the danger of communist imperialism. Further acts of communist aggression in Southeast Asia can be expected to stimulate resistance on the part of countries which have thus far failed to take a positive stand.

43. Therefore, the general objectives of the United States in Southeast Asia are: (1) to contribute to the will and ability of all countries in the region to resist communism from within and without, and (b) to aid in the political, economic and social advancement of the area. For this purpose, the United States has developed support programs to strengthen the governments' administrative and military capabilities, to improve living standards, to encourage pro-Western alignments, and to stave off communist intervention.

44. Chinese Communist conquest of Indochina, Thailand and Burma, by military force and internal subversion, would seriously threaten the critical security interests of the United States. However, in the event of overt Chinese aggression, it is not now in the over-all security interests of the United States to commit any United States armed forces to the defense of the mainland states of Southeast Asia. Therefore, the United States cannot guarantee the

denial of Southeast Asia to communism. The United States should continue its present support programs to strengthen the will and ability to resist the Chinese Communists, to render Communist military operations as costly as possible, and to gain time for the United States and its allies to build up the defenses of the off-shore chain and weaken communist power at its source.

Source: *United States–Vietnam Relations, 1945–1967*, Book 8 (Washington, DC: U.S. Government Printing Office, 1971), 438–443.

61. Minister Donald R. Heath in Saigon: Telegram to Secretary of State Dean Acheson, December 9, 1951 [Excerpt]

Introduction

The French policy of refusing to permit a truly independent Vietnamese government meant that there were only two choices for Vietnamese: to support the Viet Minh or to support the French. For growing numbers of Vietnamese, the choice was the former. In this response to the pessimistic telegram from R. Allen Griffin regarding the government of the State of Vietnam (SVN), U.S. minister in Saigon Donald R. Heath notes that there are no Vietnamese of recognized ability willing to serve in the French-sponsored government.

Primary Source

1156. Re Singapore tels 618 and 621, Nov 30.

1. As Dept aware, I have for some time been concerned re inadequacies Huu Govt and I welcome Griffin corroborations. I am also pleased register my concurrence with his finding that present STEM [Special Technical and Economic Mission] programs fundamentally sound in this trying situation.

2. I am not sure, however, when Griffin speaks of govt with grass roots he means Cabinet nominated by present methods but including agrarian and popular leaders or whether he has in mind govt clothed with some popular mandate based on development forms of popular consultation. As to former, I doubt that much can be done at this time outside possible Catholic participation and acceptance of post by Tri, even this wld be limited advance since Catholics are minority sometimes suspected of too much western orientation and Tri, in entering govt, wld have to swallow disgrace and suppression his Dai Viet backers, who altho in sense "grass roots" have Asiatic fascistic, exotic, secret society aspects.

3. Fact is that no leaders with "grass roots" support presently known who wld join govt constituted on basis existing Franco-Viet

relations and if there were such persons, doubtful if Fr wld accept them or that they wld be proof against Asiatic neutralism or Viet Minh infiltration. Fr know this which accounts for their quandary about replacement for Huu.

Source: *Foreign Relations of the United States, 1951*, Vol. 6 (Washington, DC: U.S. Government Printing Office, 1977), 558.

62. Ambassador David Bruce: Telegram to Secretary of State Dean Acheson, December 26, 1951 [Excerpt]

Introduction

After five years of warfare, growing casualty lists, and no victory in sight, French public opinion turned against the war in Indochina. In this telegram, U.S. ambassador to France David Bruce warns Secretary of State Dean Acheson that the situation is rapidly reaching the point where the French will have to undertake a reexamination of their Indochina policy, from which they would undoubtedly ask for the United States to dramatically increase its economic assistance and make certain military commitments. Without these, Bruce warns, there will be an overwhelming French popular demand to quit Indochina.

Primary Source

14. We may soon be presented with a definite either/or situation: Either we increase our present aid to Indochina to a very considerable extent and make certain definite commitments as to what we will do in the event of a Chi invasion, or the Fr will be compelled to re-examine their entire policy in the area.

15. The issue is not entirely or even primarily whether the Fr will continue their effort at the now existing level. The present level will not be high enough if, even without an actual invasion, the Chi further step up their assistance to the VM. The Fr are becoming increasingly sensitive to the possibility of a sitn in which the Fr govt might be confronted either with the necessity for rapid withdrawal or a military disaster. In the circumstances we must decide whether we wish to go much further than we have heretofore in the direction of a multilateral approach to the problem.

16. If we agree in principle to a multilateral approach, it wld seem that we must immed engage in tripartite conversations, not only at the mil but also at the polit level. Amongst other considerations, we might, for instance, wish to reach a tripartite decision as to the accuracy of present Fr estimates of the mil and polit sitn, and the wisdom of existing plans to deal with them.

17. To conclude, I believe that the snowball has started to form, and public sentiment for withdrawal, in the absence of adoption

of some course of action envisaging either internationalization of Indochina problem or Fr receipt of massive additional aid, will gain steadily and perhaps at accelerated rate. It wld be incorrect to assume that Fr Govt is trying merely to horse trade or bargain with US. It is responding slowly and unwillingly to pressures far stronger than party positions. Consequently, Emb recommends that US re-examine problem in the light of these changing circumstances prior to a final precipitation of these mixed elements in order avoid risk of a sitn threatening the security of all SEA and entailing grave polit and mil repercussions elsewhere.

Source: *Foreign Relations of the United States, 1951,* Vol. 6 (Washington, DC: U.S. Government Printing Office, 1977), 577–578.

63. Ho Chi Minh: Talk to Officers Preparing for the Military Campaign in Northwestern Vietnam, September 9, 1952

Introduction

Thanks in large part to Chinese assistance, by 1952 the Viet Minh had a real army. By the end of that year more than 40,000 People's Army of Vietnam (PAVN, North Vietnamese Army) enlisted men and 10,000 officers had been trained in bases in China. The Chinese had also turned over to the Viet Minh substantial stocks of arms, including artillery supplied earlier by the United States to Guomindang (GMD, Nationalist) China. By mid-1952, the Viet Minh fielded five divisions of well-trained, well-equipped, and highly motivated men. They believed passionately in their cause. In these remarks to military officers, President Ho Chi Minh of the Democratic Republic of Vietnam (DRV, North Vietnam) notes that if the army retains its determination, it will surely defeat the French.

Primary Source

Yesterday it rained heavily and all the streams were flooded. Arriving at a brook with a strong current and seeing a group of compatriots sitting on the other side waiting for the water to subside, I said to myself, "Shouldn't I cross the stream at once so as not to keep you waiting." So a few other comrades and I took off our clothes and, groping our way with sticks, we succeeded in wading across the brook. On seeing my success, the group of compatriots also made up their mind to cross the stream. This is an experience for you, comrades. Whatever we do—big or small—if we are determined we shall be successful and shall imbue other people with the same determination.

Now I speak of the military campaign.

The Party Central Committee and the Party General Committee of the Army have carefully weighed the advantages and difficulties of the coming campaign and are determined that this campaign must be carried out successfully. It is not enough that only the Central Committee has determination. You must weigh and clearly see for yourselves the advantages and difficulties in order to be imbued with this determination. It is not enough that the Central Committee and you are determined, we must act in such a way that this determination permeates every soldier. This determination from the Central Committee must reach the rank and file through you. It must become a monolithic bloc from higher to lower ranks and from lower to higher ranks. To have determination does not mean to speak glibly of it, but to have deep confidence. When meeting with advantages we must be determined to develop them and when encountering difficulties we must be determined to overcome them. Everyone in the army must be deeply imbued with determination.

In this meeting, the Party General Committee of the Army has disseminated in detail the Central Committee's resolutions, and you have debated them. The significance and objectives of the military campaign are: to annihilate the enemy's manpower, to win over the people, and to liberate territory. The main task is to annihilate the enemy's manpower.

You have discussed the advantages and difficulties. When meeting with an advantage, if we are not determined to develop it, it may likely turn into difficulty. When meeting with a difficulty, if we are determined to overcome it, it will become an advantage. In truth, nothing is easy and nothing is difficult. For example, it is easy to break off a branch. But if we are not determined and do it halfheartedly, we may not be able to break it off. It is difficult to carry out the revolution and to wage the Resistance War, but with our determination we will be successful.

Determination does not lie in the meeting place and in words, but in work and deeds. We must have determination to promote a valiant fighting style. We must have determination to oppose all negative, wavering, and selfish acts and false reports.

We must be determined to fight, to endure hardships and difficulties, to overcome them, and be determined to implement the policies of the Central Committee and the Government. In other words, in our behavior, mind, deeds, and fighting, in everything—big or small—we must be determined to win success.

The army is strong when it is well fed. The comrades in the commissariat must have determination to supply the troops with adequate food and weapons.

On their side, the troops must be determined to lightheartedly endure privations, to strive to give a hand to the commissariat if necessary.

Food and weapons are sweat and tears of our compatriots, blood and bones of our troops, so we must value, spare, preserve, and properly use them.

War booty is not a gift from the enemy. It is thanks to the sweat and tears of our compatriots and the blood and bones of our troops that we can capture it. Prior to its capture, it belongs to the enemy, after it, it is ours. Therefore, concerning war booty, we distribute to our compatriots what ought to be distributed, hand over to the Government what should be, and what should be used as reward for the troops must be given in an equitable and rational way. Corruption and waste must be absolutely avoided.

The Government has issued policies concerning the national minorities; you and the troops must implement them correctly. This is a measure to win over the people, frustrating the enemy's scheme of "using Vietnamese to harm Vietnamese." We must so do that each fighter becomes a propagandist. You must behave in such a way that the people welcome you on your arrival and give you willing aid during your stay and miss you on your departure. This would be a great success.

You must be aware that only a small part of enemy troops are Europeans and Africans while the majority are puppet troops. A great number of the latter are press-ganged into the army by the French. If you cleverly carry out the work of agitation among the puppet troops, this would be a way to annihilate enemy manpower.

Our units are helped by civilians moving with them. You must educate and take good care of the volunteer workers, explain our policies to them, and encourage them to work lightheartedly. A close friendship and solidarity must prevail between the troops and the volunteer workers, so that the latter are unwilling to go home, and like to stay on and help the troops. This is one of the factors for victory. If you fail to do so, we shall meet with many difficulties.

It is thanks to good education, correct policies, and strict discipline that the troops are strong. That is why discipline must be strict. There are two points in discipline that call for attention: punishment and reward.

Up to now, punishment and reward have been insufficient, and that is a big mistake. There must be units mentioned in dispatches and awarded with medals. After you have proposed someone for a medal, the proposal has immediately to be made public. The Government, the High Command, and I are ready to reward those who

score achievements. On the other hand, those who have wrongly carried out the orders or made false reports must be punished severely.

The units must emulate with each other and the cadres between themselves to promote the movement for valiant fighting.

We must bear in mind that the revolutionary troops, first of all, the Party members, do not shun difficulties but must overcome them. We must learn the spirit of the Soviet Red Army and of the Chinese Liberation Army: When carrying out some difficult task, the unit which is entrusted with it prides itself on this honor, whereas those which are not appointed feel quite unhappy to find that they have not yet the capacity required.

You can learn from this attitude. I am convinced that thanks to the leadership of the Party and the Government you will be able to take it up.

Divisional commanders down to group leaders must share joy and hardships with the soldiers, take care of, help, and treat each other like blood brothers. This is a tradition of the Soviet Red Army and of the Chinese Liberation Army that our soldiers must learn as well. To succeed in so doing is tantamount to partially triumphing over the enemy before fighting him.

The units must emulate with each other to do as I advise you. Are you determined to emulate with each other?

You are determined, so you must by all means score successes in your fighting. I am waiting for news of victory from you. I promise a reward to the troops in the period from September 2 to December 19. It is a small reward but of great value because I have made it myself. There are other rewards beside this one for the units that are the first to perform feats of arms.

Heroes are not only the troops who exterminate the enemy and perform feats of arms but also the supply men who strive to serve the troops. In each of you exists heroism in the bud, you must develop it.

If you fulfill your task, I shall always be cheerful and in good health.

As is known to some of you, on the setting up of our army, our men were equipped with only a few commodities and the few rifles they got were bought in contraband. We obtained great achievements notwithstanding, and the August Revolution was victorious.

Now that we have numerous troops, good generals, and everyone has determination, we will certainly be successful.

Source: Ho Chi Minh, *On Revolution: Selected Writings, 1920–66*, edited by Bernard B. Fall (New York: Praeger, 1967), 248–252.

64. John Foster Dulles, Secretary of State: Telegram to C. Douglas Dillon, Ambassador to France, March 19, 1953

Introduction

U.S. military aid to the French to fight the war in Indochina increased dramatically. In 1951 military supplies averaged about 6,000 tons a month, but by 1953 military supplies had increased to some 20,000 tons a month. In the spring of 1953, new U.S. secretary of state John Foster Dulles informed ambassador to France C. Douglas Dillon that the Dwight D. Eisenhower administration believed that it was essential that the French develop a plan that would destroy the Viet Minh regular military forces in Indochina within two years. Dulles stresses to Dillon that such a plan is necessary to secure the requisite financial aid from Congress.

Primary Source

Recent Paris working-level discussions added substantially to our factual background on Indochina. Please express to Foreign Minister my appreciation for cooperation all concerned. Also take early opportunity discuss informally on my behalf with Mayer or Bidault forthcoming conversations along following general lines:

QTE Secretary Acheson in December 1952 and I last month have discussed with our French colleagues the Indochina situation. On both occasions we received indications French Government was planning to request US GOVT to increase already considerable share of financial burden of the struggle which it is now bearing. I assume that when Mayer, Bidault and Letourneau come to Washington they will furnish further particulars regarding French Government's plans and resulting requirements. It may be helpful to them in formulating their position to express to them informally some of considerations involved not only in matter of additional aid but also in continuation American assistance at present substantial level. Considerations are:

First, Government and people of US are fully aware of importance to free world of war being waged in Indochina by armies of France and Associated States. They appreciate sacrifices which have been and are being made and degree to which Communist plans have been thwarted by magnificent defense carried out in Indochina against Communist aggression.

Second, we envisage Indochina situation with real sense of urgency. We believe continued military stalemate will produce most undesirable political consequences in Indochina, France and U.S. Therefore, we heartily agree that considerable increased effort having as its aim liquidation principal regular enemy forces within period of, say, twenty-four months is essential. We obviously do not wish share Franco-Vietnamese responsibility for conduct operations. However, if interested Departments this Government are to urge Congress to make necessary appropriations for Indochina for FY 54, those Departments must be convinced that necessarily top secret strategic plans for Indochina are sound and can be and will be aggressively and energetically prosecuted.

Third, I share concern frequently expressed in French circles regarding adequacy of the financial contribution to prosecution of war derived from residents of the Associated States including French businessmen. While I welcome increased Vietnamese Government contribution recently made, I believe there is ground for thoroughgoing re-examination this problem into which balance of payment and rate of exchange considerations enter and which of course is of interest to us in its bearing upon the need for U.S. aid.

Fourth, I look forward to opportunity talking with my French colleagues on question of free world policy in Far East as whole and particularly the policies which we should adopt in order to discourage further Chinese Communist aggression. I hope to reach agreement that speedy defeat of Viet Minh forces in Indochina would deter rather than provoke Chinese Communist aggression in Tonkin since it would be a clear indication of our joint determination to meet force with effective force.

Fifth, I should appreciate receiving any views which my French friends may care to convey regarding relations between the U.S. and the Associated States of Indochina and particularly regarding participation by latter in discussions of military and economic policy and in reception of U.S. aid. END QUOTE

Please handle on strictly oral basis and let me have reaction. The specified points are designed to be exploratory; I would welcome any ideas French may wish to convey on these or other topics prior to our conversations.

Source: *United States–Vietnam Relations, 1945–1967,* Book 9 (Washington, DC: U.S. Government Printing Office, 1971), 15–16.

65. John Foster Dulles, Secretary of State: Telegram to C. Douglas Dillon, Ambassador to France, March 26, 1953 [Excerpt]

Introduction

Here U.S. secretary of state John Foster Dulles shares the results of a March 26, 1953, meeting among President Dwight D. Eisenhower, French premier René Mayer, and Minister of Overseas France Jean Letourneau. In the course of the talks, Eisenhower had expressed American support for the "valiant French struggle" as part of the overall fight against Communist aggression. While he recognized that this was not simply "another colonial war," he emphasized that in order for France to receive increased aid for its effort in Indochina, the American people would have to be convinced that the states of Indochina had indeed been granted full independence and that they were in fact fighting to remain free of Communist control. Eisenhower also urged Mayer to emphasize in his public statements the anti-Communist nature of the struggle, as the American people still thought of the war in terms of anticolonialism. Mayer assured Eisenhower that the French fully expected to be able to reduce the Viet Minh's military forces to a "negligible factor" within two years.

Primary Source

Concerning Indochina President expressed full American sympathy for valiant French struggle as part of over-all fight against Communist aggression.

He recognized this struggle not just another colonial war but advised French to make this very clear as many Americans still under misapprehension. President expressed great American interest in French program leading to solution of Indochina problem making clear that he was not talking in terms of a complete victory. However requests for further American assistance could not be considered without full knowledge of French political and military plans permitting US Government to see why its assistance was required and how it would be used. President expressed great interest in measures being taken by French to obtain greatest possible support by local populations through convincing them they were fighting their own war for their own independence.

Re Indochina Mayer started by referring to NAC Resolution December 1952 re QTE continuing aid UNQTE from NATO Governments. He said French political and military plans would be communicated to us later during the talks. Meanwhile he stressed his full agreement with President that the task was two-fold: militarily, Associated States Armies had to be developed for victory and for internal pacification. Politically it was necessary to develop popular basis for national governments to protect them from eventual take-over by Vietminh forces. While expressing the greatest interest in Gen Clark's report following visit to Indochina Mayer was careful to point out differences between Korea and Indochina.

Le Tourneau said that details of recent Dalat agreements would be given to us later but that in meanwhile he can say that these will permit presentation of a Franco-Vietnamese plan which should lead within two years to reduction of Vietminh to a negligible factor in Indochina if no material increase in Chinese or Soviet aid in meanwhile. Le Tourneau expressed confidence that popular support for local governments was increasing day by day, pointing to success of January elections in Vietnam, to fact that much more officer material is now available for National Armies and that all enlisted men needed under present financial limitations were

available on volunteer basis. Finally he expressed confidence that local populations supported local governments more vigorously now that Vietminh was clearly recognized as the agent not only of Communism but also of traditional Chinese enemy.

Source: *United States–Vietnam Relations, 1945–1967,* Book 9 (Washington, DC: U.S. Government Printing Office, 1971), 17–18.

66. Douglas MacArthur II, Assistant Secretary of State for Congressional Relations: Memorandum, April 27, 1953

Introduction

In the spring of 1953, Viet Minh military commander General Vo Nguyen Giap assembled a powerful force to invade Laos, which had an army of only 10,000 men supported by 3,000 French regulars. Giap employed four divisions totaling 40,000 men, assisted by 4,000 Communist Pathet Lao troops. The French were forced to withdraw and abandon their isolated posts, and the Viet Minh overran most of the northern part of the country. With their own airlift capacity sharply limited, the French government appealed to the United States for Fairchild C-119 Flying Boxcar transport aircraft. The French wanted these to be flown by U.S. military pilots, but the U.S. Joint Chiefs of Staff (JCS) approved only the loan of six transport aircraft to be flown by Civil Air Transport (CAT) civilian personnel. CAT was the airline run by the U.S. Central Intelligence Agency (CIA) and charged with carrying out clandestine air operations in Asia.

Primary Source

At a meeting with the President at the White House this afternoon for the purpose of briefing the President on the recent NATO Paris meeting and bilateral talks with the British and the French, the President asked Secretary Dulles what the French views were on the situation in Laos.

The Secretary replied that the French were very gravely concerned about the situation there. He said that when he had met with Prime Minister René Mayer last evening just prior to departure from Paris, M. Mayer had stated that the French needed more urgently the loan of some C-119 aircraft to help them get tanks and heavy equipment into Laos to assist in its defense. Having such equipment might mean the difference between holding and losing Laos. M. Mayer had envisaged U.S. Air Force personnel operating the aircraft during the period of the loan.

The Secretary said to the President that such a procedure would mean the sending of U.S. personnel on combat missions in

Indochina. This, obviously, was a decision which would have repercussions and would raise many problems. However, there was an alternative, which would be to loan the French the C-119's, which he understood the Department of Defense was willing to do, and have civilian pilots fly them. Following his return to Washington this morning, the Secretary had made inquiry and had ascertained that there were pilots in Formosa who were not members of the U.S. armed forces and who might well be able to carry out these missions. This possibility was being explored on an urgent basis to see whether it would not be possible to have the aircraft loaned and the above-mentioned personnel in Formosa operate them.

Source: *United States–Vietnam Relations, 1945–1967,* Book 9 (Washington, DC: U.S. Government Printing Office, 1971), 38.

67. Lieutenant General John W. O'Daniel: Report to the Joint Chiefs of Staff on the U.S. Joint Military Mission to Indochina, July 14, 1953 [Excerpts]

Introduction

In June 1953 the Joint Chiefs of Staff (JCS) sent Lieutenant General John W. O'Daniel, commander of U.S. forces in the Pacific, to Indochina to assess French requirements for military aid. O'Daniel came back with an optimistic report and support for the so-called Navarre Plan, developed by new French commander in Indochina General Henry Navarre for more aggressive military operations, to include an offensive in Tonkin (northern Vietnam) that would utilize the equivalent of three divisions.

Primary Source

1. The attached Report of the U.S. Joint Military Mission to Indochina is submitted as directed by paragraph 10 of the "Terms of Reference for the Chief of the U.S. Military Mission to Indochina."

2. In summarizing the subject report I wish to emphasize the following:

    a. General Navarre, Commander-in-Chief, French Forces, Far East, submitted to me in writing a new aggressive concept for the conduct of operations in Indochina which, in brief, calls for (a) taking the initiative immediately with local offensives, emphasizing guerrilla warfare, (b) initiating an offensive (utilizing the equivalent of three (3) divisions) in Tonkin by 15 September 1953, (c) recovering a maximum number of units from areas not directly involved in the war, (d) reorganizing battalions into regiments and regiments into divisions, with necessary support units and (e) developing the Armies of the Associated States

and giving them greater leadership responsibility in the conduct of operations.

    b. General Gambiez, Chief of Staff to General Navarre, presented a discussion of operations to take place during the balance of the current rainy season. These operations include four (4) offensive operations outside the Tonkin perimeter aimed at destroying enemy personnel and existent enemy supply dumps, a clearing operation in North Annam, and an offensive operation in South Annam aimed at linking the Phan Thiet beachhead with Plateau forces and thus permanently severing the principal enemy supply line to Cochin China. These operations are to be followed by a large scale offensive in Tonkin on or about 15 September 1953.

    c. General Navarre agreed to establish a French MAAG [Military Assistance Advisory Group] organization to supervise all training of the military forces of the Associated States and to include three (3) U.S. officers. This will provide an excellent opportunity for indirect U.S. participation in the training of indigenous forces and for exercising follow up action on matters already agreed upon with the French and the Associated States.

    d. General Navarre agreed to cooperate wholeheartedly in (1) providing the U.S. with increased intelligence and (2) the stationing of one or two military attaches in Hanoi for this purpose.

    e. General Navarre agreed to keep the Chief, MAAG, Indochina informed of French plans and stated that he will invite MAAG officers to attend all operations.

    f. General Lauzin, Commander-in-Chief, French Air Force, Indochina agreed to (1) the removal of the six (6) C-119's from Indochina, (2) request C-119's in the future on a temporary basis only, (3 or 4 days) to support airborne operations requiring the simultaneous drop of forces in excess of two battalions, (3) step-up pilot and mechanic training and (4) organize a Vietnamese National Air Force.

    g. Admiral Auboyneau agreed to a reorganization of French Naval Forces to include a Joint Amphibious Command for the purpose of (1) attaining increased amphibious effectiveness and (2) delegating increased responsibility to Vietnamese leaders and units.

    h. Once the French became convinced of the soundness of our initial proposals they became increasingly receptive to our subsequent recommendations.

    i. As evidence of French sincerity in carrying out actions designed to improve the status of anti-communist military forces in Indochina, General Navarre and other French officers repeatedly invited me to return in a few months "to witness the progress we will have made."

3. I recommend that the Joint Chiefs of Staff:

    a. Note the contents of the attached report and take appropriate action where required.

b. Propose to the Secretary of Defense that he recommend to the Secretary of State the sending of a small group of qualified experts to Indochina to study the desirability of the U.S. assisting in the development of Associated States small industry capable of producing certain military items or military-support items such as small arms, batteries or recap tires.

c. Approve an increase in artillery units in the force basis for Indochina if MAAG and Department of the Army screening indicates such increase is necessary for a balance of forces in the new divisional organization.

d. Approve my return to Indochina in 3 or 4 months for a follow-up of the mission's activities, and

e. Insure that the Chief, MAAG, Indochina, receives copies of the approved report for his guidance and that he be instructed to take follow-up action where appropriate.

4. I recommend that the Chiefs of the individual Services approve necessary personnel augmentations of the MAAG, Indochina to allow for three (3) U.S. officers (one from each Service) for attachment to the French Training Command, and that the Chief of Staff, U.S. Army assign two (2) additional U.S. Assistant Army Attaches to be used for collecting combat intelligence in conjunction with the French G-2 in the Hanoi area.

Source: *United States–Vietnam Relations, 1945–1967*, Book 9 (Washington, DC: U.S. Government Printing Office, 1971), 69–72.

68. Secretary of State John Foster Dulles: Telegram to C. Douglas Dillon, Ambassador to France, September 9, 1953 [Excerpts]

Introduction

Here U.S. secretary of state John Foster Dulles informs C. Douglas Dillon, ambassador to France, of approval of additional aid for Indochina, contingent on the French furnishing assurances regarding their political and military policies. Dulles calls on Dillon to begin formulating the language that will be required in the response of the French government headed by Premier Joseph Laniel. The response is to include assurance of a continuation of the policy of "perfecting" the independence of the associated states of Indochina.

Primary Source

1. Subject to our receiving necessary assurances from French, NSC today approved additional aid proposed for Indochina based on substance DEPTEL 827, with Presidential approval expected tomorrow. Comments URTELS 939, 940, 941 fully taken into account in presentation to NSC.

2. On most confidential basis you should therefore now informally advise Laniel and Bidault above action and indicate assurances desired are to effect that French Government is determined:

a. put promptly into effect program of action set forth its memorandum Sept 1;

b. carry this program forward vigorously with object of eliminating regular enemy forces in Indochina;

c. continue pursue policy of perfecting independence of Associated States in conformity with July 3 declaration;

d. facilitate exchange information with American military authorities and take into account their views in developing and carrying out French military plans Indochina;

e. assure that no basic or permanent alteration of plans and programs for NATO forces will be made as result of additional effort Indochina;

f. provide appropriate info to US Govt of amount of expenditures for military program set forth in memo of Sept 1.

3. We would expect these assurances be embodied in note which US in reply would acknowledge. US reply would go on to make clear that:

a. appropriately established financial requirements for military program as indicated in Sept 1 memo from French Govt, not rpt not to exceed $385 million or its equivalent in Calendar Year 1954, will be met by US Govt . . . ;

b. amount of $385 million or its equivalent in francs or piasters is deemed to satisfy in full request made by French memo of Sept 1;

c. no further financial assistance may be expected for Calendar Year 1954;

d. US Govt retains right to terminate this additional assistance should for any reason French Govt plan as outlined in memo of Sept 1 prove incapable of execution or should other unforeseen circumstances arise which negate the understandings arrived at between the two govts.

4. You should immediately begin informally to work out language with French covering paragraph 2 above. (We will cable soonest new draft of US reply.) It should be made crystal clear to French that final US Govt agreement will be given only when satisfactory language for exchange notes has been obtained.

[. . .]

Source: *United States–Vietnam Relations, 1945–1967,* Book 9 (Washington, DC: U.S. Government Printing Office, 1971), 150–151.

69. Ho Chi Minh: Replies to a Foreign Correspondent, November 26, 1953

Introduction

In an interview with a correspondent of the Swedish newspaper *Expressen,* President Ho Chi Minh of the Democratic Republic of Vietnam (DRV, North Vietnam) states his readiness to enter into peace talks with France, provided that the French government indicates "sincere respect for the genuine independence of Viet-Nam." Ho also claims that "the U.S. imperialists" are pushing the French "to continue and expand the aggressive war in Viet-Nam."

Primary Source

Question: The debate in the French National Assembly has proved that a great number of French politicians are for a peaceful settlement of the conflicts in Viet-Nam by direct negotiations with the Vietnamese Government. This desire is spreading among the French people. Do your Government and you welcome it?

Answer: The war in Viet-Nam was launched by the French Government. The Vietnamese people are obliged to take up arms and have heroically struggled for nearly eight years against the aggressors, to safeguard our independence and the right to live freely and peacefully. Now, if the French colonialists continue their aggressive war, the Vietnamese people are determined to carry on the patriotic resistance until final victory. However, if the French Government has drawn a lesson from the war they have been waging these last years and want to negotiate an armistice in Viet-Nam and to solve the Viet-Nam problem by peaceful means, the people and Government of the Democratic Republic of Viet-Nam are ready to meet this desire.

Question: Will a cease fire or an armistice be possible?

Answer: A cessation of hostilities is possible, provided that the French Government ends its war of aggression in Viet-Nam. The French Government's sincere respect for the genuine independence of Viet-Nam must be the basis of the armistice.

Question: Would you agree to a neutral country mediating to organize a meeting between you and the representatives of the High Command of the other side? May Sweden be entrusted with this responsibility?

Answer: If there are neutral countries which try to speed up a cessation of hostilities in Viet-Nam by means of negotiations, they

will be welcomed. However, the negotiation for an armistice is mainly the concern of the Government of the Democratic Republic of Viet-Nam and the French Government.

Question: In your opinion, is there any other way to end the hostilities?

Answer: The war in Viet-Nam has brought havoc to the Vietnamese people and at the same time caused countless sufferings to the French people; therefore, the French people are struggling against the war in Viet-Nam.

I have constantly showed my sympathy, affection, and respect for the French people and the French peace fighters. Today not only is the independence of Viet-Nam seriously jeopardized, but the independence of France is also gravely threatened. On the one hand, the U.S. imperialists egg on the French colonialists to continue and expand the aggressive war in Viet-Nam, thus weakening them more and more through fighting, in the hope of replacing France in Indochina; on the other, they oblige France to ratify the European defense treaty that is to revive German militarism.

Therefore, the struggle of the French people to gain independence, democracy, and peace for France and to end the war in Viet-Nam constitutes one of the important factors to settle the Viet-Nam question by peaceful means.

Source: Ho Chi Minh, *On Revolution: Selected Writings, 1920–66,* edited by Bernard B. Fall (New York: Praeger, 1967), 256–257.

70. Ho Chi Minh: Report to the National Assembly, December 1, 1953 [Excerpts]

Introduction

In December 1953, the National Assembly of the Democratic Republic of Vietnam (DRV, North Vietnam) met for the first time since the beginning of the Indochina War. Although the war retained center stage, the primary action before the National Assembly was the passage of land reform legislation. President Ho Chi Minh states here that the goal is nothing less than "to wipe out the feudal system of land ownership, distribute land to the tillers, liberate the productive forces in the countryside, develop production and push forward the war of resistance." Land reform was a particularly difficult issue. That it was undertaken at this time in the middle of war with the French would seem to indicate that Ho sought to enthuse new fervor for the war from the landless peasantry, the bulk of the population. While Ho was undoubtedly correct that the peasants constituted 90 percent of the population in North Vietnam and yet owned only 30 percent of the arable land, redistributing the land proved difficult and ultimately produced wholesale revolt after actions against relatively small landholdings. In November 1956 the army's 325th Division had to be called out to crush rebels in Nghe An Province. In all, some 6,000 farmers were deported or executed.

Primary Source

Our slogan during the war of resistance is "All for the front, all for victory!" The more the war of resistance develops, the more manpower and wealth it requires. Our peasants have contributed the greatest part of this manpower and wealth to the resistance. We must liberate them from the feudal yoke and foster their strength in order fully to mobilize this huge force for the resistance and win victory.

The key victor for the resistance lies in consolidating and enlarging the National United Front, consolidating the worker-peasant alliance and the people's power, strengthening and developing the Army, consolidating the Party and strengthening its leadership in all respects. Only by mobilizing the masses for land reform can we carry out these tasks in favourable conditions.

The enemy actively seeks to use Vietnamese to fight Vietnamese and to feed war with war. They are doing their utmost to deceive, divide and exploit our people. Land reform will exert an influence on our peasant compatriots in the enemy's rear areas and will encourage them to struggle even more vigorously against him in order to liberate themselves, and to give even more enthusiastic support to the democratic Government of the Resistance; at the same time it will have an impact on the puppet armed forces and cause their disintegration because the absolute majority of the puppet soldiers are peasants in enemy-occupied areas.

The overwhelming majority of our people are peasants.

Over these last years, it is thanks to their forces that the war of resistance has been going on successfully. It is also thanks to the peasant forces that it will gain complete victory and our country will be successfully rebuilt.

Our peasants account for almost 90 per cent of the population but they own only 30 per cent of the arable land; they have to work hard all the year round and suffer poverty all their lives.

The feudal landlord class accounts for less than 5 per cent of the population but they and the colonialists occupy about 70 per cent of the arable land and live in clover. This situation is most unjust.

Because of it our country has been invaded and our people are backward and poor. During the years of resistance, the Government has decreed the reduction of land rent, the refunding of excess land rent and the temporary distribution of land belonging to the French and the Vietnamese traitors and that of communal land to the peasants in the free areas. But the key problem remains unsolved: the peasant masses have no land or lack land. This affects the forces of the resistance and the production work of the peasants.

Only by carrying out land reform, giving land to the tillers, liberating the productive forces in the countryside from the yoke of the feudal landlord class can we do away with poverty and backwardness and strongly mobilize the huge forces of the peasants in order to develop production and push the war of resistance forward to complete victory.

The goal set for land reform is to wipe out the feudal system of land ownership, distribute land to the tillers, liberate the productive forces in the countryside, develop production and push forward the war of resistance.

The general line and policy is to rely entirely on the landless and poor peasants, closely unite with the middle peasants, enter into alliance with the rich peasants, wipe out feudal exploitation step by step and with discrimination, develop production, and push forward the war of resistance.

To meet the requirements of the resistance and the National United Front, which consist in satisfying the land demands of the peasants while consolidating and developing the National United Front in the interests of the resistance and production, in the course of land reform we must apply different kinds of treatment to the landlords according to their individual political attitudes. This means that depending on individual cases we shall order confiscation or requisition with or without compensation, but not wholesale confiscation or wholesale requisition without compensation.

The guiding principle for land reform is boldly to mobilize the peasants, rely on the masses, correctly follow the mass line, organize, educate and lead the peasants to struggle according to plan, step by step, with good discipline and under close leadership.

The dispersion of land by landlords after the promulgation of the land rent reduction decree (July 14, 1949) is illegal (except for particular cases mentioned in the circular issued by the Prime Minister's Office on June 1, 1953).

The land confiscated or requisitioned with or without compensation is to be definitively allotted to the peasants who have no or not enough land. These peasants will have the right of ownership over the land thus distributed.

The guiding principle for land distribution is to take the village as unit, to allot land in priority to those who have been tilling it, to take into consideration the area, quality and location of the land, so as to give a fair share to everyone; especial consideration must be given to the peasants who have previously tilled the land to be distributed. As for the diehard elements bent on sabotaging land reform, the traitors, reactionaries, and local despots, those among them who are sentenced to 5 years' imprisonment and more will not receive any land. . . .

In the military field, our peasant compatriots will joint the resistance even more enthusiastically, hence it will be easier to build up the army and recruit voluntary civilian manpower. Our soldiers, with their minds at peace about their families, will fight even more resolutely.

In the political field, political and economic power in the countryside will be in the hands of the peasants, the people's democratic dictatorship will be truly carried into effect, the worker-peasant alliance will be consolidated, the National United Front will include more than 90 per cent of the people in the countryside and will become prodigiously great and strong.

In the economic field, liberated from feudal landlordism, the peasants will enthusiastically carry out production and practise thrift, their purchasing power will increase, industry and commerce will develop and the national economy as a whole will expand.

Thanks to the development of production, the livelihood of the peasants, workers, soldiers and cadres will be improved more rapidly.

In the cultural and social field, the large majority of the people, now having enough food and clothing, will study even harder, in accordance with the saying: "One must have enough to eat before one could practise the good doctrine." Good customs and habits will develop. The experience drawn from localities where mass mobilization has been launched shows that our compatriots are very fond of study and that there are good opportunities for the intellectuals to serve the people.

As said above, land reform is an immense, complex and hard class struggle. It is all the more complex and all the harder because we are conducting a war of resistance. But it is precisely because we want to push the resistance forward to victory that we must be determined to make land reform a success.

Source: Ho Chi Minh, *Selected Writings: 1920–1969* (Hanoi: Foreign Languages Publishing House, 1977), 163–168.

71. Vo Nguyen Giap: Report to Senior Field Commanders on the Dien Bien Phu Campaign, January 14, 1954 [Excerpt]

Introduction

Following successful Viet Minh military operations in northern Laos, in November 1953 French military commander in Indochina General Henri Navarre initiated Operation CASTOR, the creation of a blocking position in far northwestern Vietnam astride the Viet Minh Laos invasion route at the then-obscure village of Dien Bien Phu. President Ho Chi Minh of the Democratic Republic of Vietnam (DRV, North Vietnam) pushed for a major Viet Minh operation against the French there, hoping to influence the course of talks on Asia scheduled for April 1954 in Geneva. Although Viet Minh commander General Vo Nguyen Giap was skeptical, he ultimately committed the bulk of his resources to the effort. As both sides soon realized, the Battle of Dien Bien Phu was the most important military action of the entire Indochina War. Although there was considerable fighting earlier, the siege of the French fortress officially began on March 13, 1954. General Giap here lays out for his senior commanders the goals of the campaign.

Primary Source

Two main objectives:

1. To annihilate an important part of enemy forces.

2. To liberate the whole of the Northwest.

This campaign has a great significance:

a) It will be the greatest positional battle in the annals of our army. Hitherto, we have attacked fortified positions only with forces numbering up to one or two regiments; now we are throwing into action several divisions; we have never before coordinated infantry and artillery action on a large scale; we have succeeded only in capturing positions defended by one or two companies, one battalion at most. This time we shall have to coordinate the action of several branches of the army on a large scale and to annihilate an entrenched camp defended by 13 battalions.

Our victory will mark a big leap forward in the growth of our army, which will have an enormous influence on the future military situation.

b) By annihilating such an important part of enemy forces, by liberating such a wide area, we shall foil the Navarre plan, which is the French and American imperialists' plan for the extension of the war, and shall create conditions for destroying enemy forces on all fronts.

What does this mean, to foil the Navarre plan?

The enemy is seeking to concentrate mobile forces in the delta: we compel him to scatter them in mountain regions where they will be destroyed piecemeal.

He is seeking to increase the size of the puppet army and to bring reinforcements from France: we shall annihilate an important part of his forces to aggravate his manpower crisis beyond retrieve.

He is seeking to pacify the Northern plans and various theatres of operations in the South: our victory at Dien Bien Phu will make it possible for our forces to intensify their action on those various fronts thus creating conditions for the annihilation of important enemy forces and foiling his plans for pacification.

The enemy is seeking to wrest back the initiative; our victory will drive him further to the defensive and will consolidate our offensive situation.

c) From the political point of view, this battle will have a very great influence. On the internal plane, it will consolidate our rear, and ensure the success of the land reform. By winning a victory, the People's Army, which is fighting imperialism by force of arms, will make an effective and glorious complement to the mighty battle being waged in the rear by millions of peasants against feudalism.

This battle is taking place at a time when French imperialism is meeting with numerous difficulties in Vietnam, Laos and Cambodia, when the French people's struggle for an end to the war is increasing and when the struggle of the world's peoples for the defence of peace and an end to the war in Vietnam has reached unequalled designs and will be an important contribution of our army to the defence of world peace.

Source: *Vietnamese Studies: Contribution to the History of Dien Bien Phu,* Vol. 3 (Hanoi: Foreign Languages Publishing House, 1965, 50–52).

72. Joint Chiefs of Staff: Memorandum for Secretary of Defense Charles E. Wilson, March 12, 1954

Introduction

In February 1954 the United States, Britain, and France agreed in the course of their tripartite talks that Indochina would be placed on the agenda at the forthcoming Geneva talks on Asia, scheduled for April. Realizing that the result might well be the creation of a coalition government in Vietnam, the U.S. Joint Chiefs of Staff (JCS) here goes on record as recommending that the United States not agree to any settlement that might impair the "future political and territorial integrity of Indochina." The JCS claimed that if Indochina was "lost to the Communists," the remainder of Southeast Asia "would inevitably follow" (the so-called domino theory). In this memorandum the JCS urges that the French be encouraged not to abandon their "aggressive prosecution of military operations" until a "satisfactory settlement" could be realized. The JCS also for the first time suggests that the United States might have to take up the military struggle there itself without the French.

Primary Source

1. This memorandum is in response to your memorandum dated 5 March 1954, subject as above.

2. In their consideration of this problem, the Joint Chiefs of Staff have reviewed UNITED STATES OBJECTIVES AND COURSES OF ACTION WITH RESPECT TO SOUTHEAST ASIA (NSC 5405), in the light of developments since that policy was approved on 16 January 1954, and they are of the opinion that, from the military point of view, the statement of policy set forth therein remains entirely valid. The Joint Chiefs of Staff reaffirm their views concerning the strategic importance of Indochina to the security interests of the United States and the Free World in general, as reflected in NSC 5405. They are firmly of the belief that the loss of Indochina to the Communists would constitute a political and military setback of the most serious consequences.

3. With respect to the possible course of action enumerated in paragraph 2 of your memorandum, the Joint Chiefs of Staff submit the following views:

   a. Maintenance of the status quo. In the absence of a very substantial improvement in the French Union military situation, which could best be accomplished by the aggressive prosecution of military operations, it is highly improbable that Communist agreement could be obtained to a negotiated settlement which would be consistent with basic United States objectives in Southeast Asia. Therefore, continuation of the fighting with the objective of seeking a military victory appears as the only alternative to acceptance of a compromise settlement based upon one or more of the possible other courses of action upon which the views of the Joint Chiefs of Staff have been specifically requested in your memorandum.

   b. Imposition of a cease-fire. The acceptance of a cease-fire in advance of a satisfactory settlement would, in all probability, lead to a political stalemate attended by a concurrent and irretrievable deterioration of the Franco-Vietnamese military position. (See paragraph 27 of NSC 5405).

c. Establishment of a coalition government. The acceptance of a settlement based upon the establishment of a coalition government in one or more of the Associated States would open the way for the ultimate seizure of control by the Communists under conditions which might preclude timely and effective external assistance in the prevention of such seizure. (See subparagraph 26 b of NSC 5405.)

d. Partition of the country. The acceptance of a partitioning of one or more of the Associated States would represent at least a partial victory for the Viet Minh, and would constitute recognition of a Communist territorial expansion achieved through force of arms. Any partition acceptable to the Communists would in all likelihood include the Tonkin Delta area which is acknowledged to be the keystone of the defense of mainland Southeast Asia, since in friendly hands it cuts off the most favorable routes for any massive southward advance towards central and southern Indochina and Thailand. (See paragraph 4 of NSC 5405.) A partitioning involving Vietnam and Laos in the vicinity of the 16th Parallel, as has been suggested (See State cable from London, No. 3802, dated 4 March 1954), would cede to Communist control approximately half of Indochina, its people and its resources, for exploitation in the interests of further Communist aggression; specifically, it would extend the Communist dominated area to the borders of Thailand, thereby enhancing the opportunities for Communist infiltration and eventual subversion of that country. Any cession of Indochinese territory to the Communists would constitute a retrogressive step in the Containment Policy, and would invite similar Communist tactics against other countries of Southeast Asia.

e. Self-determination through free elections. Such factors as the prevalence of illiteracy, the lack of suitable educational media, and the absence of adequate communications in the outlying areas would render the holding of a truly representative plebiscite of doubtful feasibility. The Communists, by virtue of their superior capability in the field of propaganda, could readily pervert the issue as being a choice between national independence and French Colonial rule. Furthermore, it would be militarily infeasible to prevent widespread intimidation of voters by Communist partisans. While it is obviously impossible to make a dependable forecast as to the outcome of a free election, current intelligence leads the Joint Chiefs of Staff to the belief that a settlement based upon free elections would be attended by almost certain loss of the Associated States to Communist control.

4. The Joint Chiefs of Staff are of the opinion that any negotiated settlement which would involve substantial concessions to the Communists on the part of the Governments of France and the Associated States, such as in c and d above, would be generally regarded by Asian peoples as a Communist victory, and would cast widespread doubt on the ability of anti-Communist forces ultimately to stem the tide of Communist control in the Far East. Any such settlement would, in all probability, lead to the loss of Indochina to the Communists and deal a damaging blow to the national will of other countries of the Far East to oppose Communism.

5. Should Indochina be lost to the Communists, and in the absence of immediate and effective counteraction on the part of the Western Powers which would of necessity be on a much greater scale than that which could be decisive in Indochina, the conquest of the remainder of Southeast Asia would inevitably follow. Thereafter, longer term results involving the gravest threats to fundamental United States security interests in the Far East and even to the stability and security of Europe could be expected to ensue. (See paragraph I of NSC 5405.)

6. Orientation of Japan toward the West is the keystone of United States policy in the Far East. In the judgment of the Joint Chiefs of Staff, the loss of Southeast Asia to Communism would, through economic and political pressures, drive Japan into an accommodation with the Communist Bloc. The communization of Japan would be the probable ultimate result.

7. The rice, tin, rubber, and oil of Southeast Asia and the industrial capacity of Japan are the essential elements which Red China needs to build a monolithic military structure far more formidable than that of Japan prior to World War II. If this complex of military power is permitted to develop to its full potential, it would ultimately control the entire Western and Southwestern Pacific region and would threaten South Asia and the Middle East.

8. Both the United States and France have invested heavily of their resources toward the winning of the struggle in Indochina. Since 1950 the United States has contributed in excess of 1.6 billion dollars in providing logistic support. France is reported to have expended, during the period 1946–1953, the equivalent of some 4.2 billion dollars. This investment, in addition to the heavy casualties sustained by the French and Vietnamese, will have been fruitless for the anti-Communist cause, and indeed may rebound in part to the immediate benefit of the enemy, if control of a portion of Indochina should now be ceded to the Communists. While the additional commitment of resources required to achieve decisive results in Indochina might be considerable, nevertheless this additional effort would be far less than that which would be required to stem the tide of Communist advance once it had gained momentum in its progress into Southeast Asia.

9. If, despite all United States efforts to the contrary, the French Government elects to accept a negotiated settlement which, in the opinion of the United States, would fail to provide reasonably adequate assurance of the future political and territorial integrity of

Indochina, it is considered that the United States should decline to associate itself with such a settlement, thereby preserving freedom of action to pursue directly with the governments of the Associated States and with other allies (notably the United Kingdom) ways and means of continuing the struggle against the Viet Minh in Indochina without participation of the French. The advantages of so doing would, from the military point of view, outweigh the advantage of maintaining political unity of action with the French in regard to Indochina.

10. It is recommended that the foregoing views be conveyed to the Department of State for consideration in connection with the formulation of a United States position on the Indochina problem for the forthcoming Conference and for any conversation with the governments of the United Kingdom, France, and, if deemed advisable, with the governments of the Associated States preliminary to the conference. In this connection, attention is particularly requested to paragraphs 25 and 26 of NSC 5405; it is considered to be of the utmost importance that the French Government be urged not to abandon the aggressive prosecution of military operations until a satisfactory settlement has been achieved.

11. It is further recommended that, in order to be prepared for possible contingencies which might arise incident to the Geneva Conference, the National Security Council considers now the extent to which the United States would be willing to commit its resources in support of the Associated States in the effort to prevent the loss of Indochina to the Communists either:

  a. In concert with the French; or
  b. In the event the French elect to withdraw, in concert with other allies or, if necessary, unilaterally.

12. In order to assure ample opportunity for the Joint Chiefs of Staff to present their views on these matters, it is requested that the Military Services be represented on the Department of Defense working team which, in coordination with the Department of State, will consider all U.S. position papers pertaining to the Geneva discussions on Indochina.

Source: *United States–Vietnam Relations, 1945–1967,* Book 9 (Washington, DC: U.S. Government Printing Office, 1971), 266–270.

73. U.S. Army Position on National Security Council Action No. 1074-A, April 1954

Introduction

With the U.S. military now considering the possibility of active military intervention in Indochina, U.S. Army planners present various options, pointing out that air and naval actions alone could not ensure military victory there.

Primary Source

1. There are important military disadvantages to intervention in Indochina under the assumptions set forth in NSC Action No. 1074-a.

2. A military victory in Indochina cannot be assured by U.S. intervention with air and naval forces alone.

3. The use of atomic weapons in Indochina would not reduce the number of ground forces required to achieve a military victory in Indochina.

4. It is estimated that seven U.S. divisions or their equivalent, with appropriate naval and air support, would be required to win a victory in Indochina if the French withdraw and the Chinese Communists do not intervene. However, U.S. military intervention must take into consideration the capability of the Chinese Communists to intervene.

5. It is estimated that the equivalent of 12 U.S. divisions would be required to win a victory in Indochina if the French withdraw and the Chinese Communists intervene.

6. The equivalent of 7 U.S. divisions would be required to win a victory in Indochina, if the French remain and the Chinese Communists intervene.

7. Requirements for air and naval support for ground force operations are:

  a. Five hundred fighter-bomber sorties per day exclusive of interdiction and counter-air operations.
  b. An airlift capability of a one division drop.
  c. A division amphibious lift.

8. One U.S. airborne regimental combat team can be placed in Indochina in 5 days, one additional division in 24 days, and the remaining divisions in the following 120 days. This could be accomplished partially by reducing U.S. ground strength in the Far East with the remaining units coming from the general reserve in the United States. Consequently, the U.S. ability to meet its NATO commitment would be seriously affected for a considerable period. The time required to place a total of 12 divisions in Indochina would depend upon the industrial and personnel mobilization measures taken by the government.

Source: *United States–Vietnam Relations, 1945–1967,* Book 9 (Washington, DC: U.S. Government Printing Office, 1971), 332.

74. C. Douglas Dillon, Ambassador to France: Telegram to Secretary of State John Foster Dulles, April 4, 1954

Introduction

The situation for the French military at Dien Bien Phu was steadily deteriorating as a result of the Viet Minh being able to place artillery and antiaircraft guns in the hills around the fortress, coupled with inadequate French air support. In these circumstances Admiral Arthur W. Radford, chairman of the U.S. Joint Chiefs of Staff (JCS), lent his support to Operation VULTURE, a plan for U.S. military intervention in the form of air strikes against the Viet Minh positions. Heartened by Radford's support, on April 4, 1954, French premier Joseph Laniel and Foreign Minister Georges Bidault presented to U.S. ambassador C. Douglas Dillon an official request for U.S. carrier aviation intervention. In support of this request they included evidence attesting to the presence of Chinese military personnel in the Democratic Republic of Vietnam (DRV, North Vietnam). In this telegram, Dillon presents the French request to Secretary of States John Foster Dulles.

Primary Source

URGENT. I was called at 11 o'clock Sunday night and asked to come immediately to Matignon where a restricted Cabinet meeting was in progress.

On arrival Bidault received me in Laniel's office and was joined in a few minutes by Laniel. They said that immediate armed intervention of US carrier aircraft at Dien Bien Phu is now necessary to save the situation.

Navarre reports situation there now in state of precarious equilibrium and that both sides are doing best to reinforce—Viet Minh are bringing up last available reinforcements which will way outnumber any reinforcing French can do by parachute drops. Renewal of assault by reinforced Viet Minh probable by middle or end of week. Without help by then fate of Dien Bien Phu will probably be sealed.

Ely brought back report from Washington that Radford gave him his personal (repeat personal) assurance that if situation at Dien Bien Phu required US naval air support he would do his best to obtain such help from US Government. Because of this information from Radford as reported by Ely, French Government now asking for US carrier aircraft support at Dien Bien Phu. Navarre feels that a relatively minor US effort could turn the tide but naturally hopes for as much help as possible.

French report Chinese intervention in Indochina already fully established as follows:

First. Fourteen technical advisors at Giap headquarters plus numerous others at division level. All under command of Chinese Communist General Ly Chen-hou who is stationed at Giap headquarters.

Second. Special telephone lines installed maintained and operated by Chinese personnel.

Third. Forty 37 mm. anti-aircraft guns radar-controlled at Dien Bien Phu. These guns operated by Chinese and evidently are from Korea. These AA guns are now shooting through clouds to bring down French aircraft.

Fourth. One thousand supply trucks of which 500 have arrived since 1 March, all driven by Chinese army personnel.

Fifth. Substantial material help in guns, shells, etc., as is well known.

Bidault said that French Chief of Air Staff wishes US be informed that US air intervention at Dien Bien Phu could lead to Chinese Communist air attack on delta airfields. Nevertheless, government was making request for aid.

Bidault closed by saying that for good or evil the fate of Southeast Asia now rested on Dien Bien Phu. He said that Geneva would be won or lost depending on outcome at Dien Bien Phu. This was reason for French request for this very serious action on our part.

He then emphasized necessity for speed in view of renewed attack which is expected before end of week. He thanked US for prompt action on airlift for French paratroops. He then said that he had received Dulles' proposal for Southeast Asian coalition, and that he would answer as soon as possible later in week as restricted Cabinet session not competent to make this decision.

New Subject. I passed on Norstad's concern that news of airlift (DEPTEL 3470, April 3) might leak as planes assembled, Pleven was called into room. He expressed extreme concern as any leak would lead to earlier Viet Minh attack. He said at all costs operation must be camouflaged as training exercise until troops have arrived. He is preparing them as rapidly as possible and they will be ready to leave in a week. Bidault and Laniel pressed him to hurry up departure date of troops and he said he would do his utmost.

Source: *United States–Vietnam Relations, 1945–1967,* Book 9 (Washington, DC: U.S. Government Printing Office, 1971), 296–297.

75. Draft Report by the President's Special Committee: Southeast Asia, Part II, April 5, 1954 [Excerpt]

Introduction

That the United States was edging toward direct military intervention in Indochina may be seen in the conclusions of this draft report by a presidential special committee formed to discuss the deteriorating French position in Southeast Asia. The report calls for "firm and resolute action" on the part of the United States and concludes that it is "necessary" that Indochina remain in the non-Communist bloc and that the Viet Minh must be defeated in order to halt the spread of communism in Southeast Asia.

Primary Source

IV. Conclusions

A. The Special Committee considers that these factors reinforce the necessity of assuring that Indo-China remain in the non-Communist bloc, and believes that defeat of the Viet Minh in Indo-China is essential if the spread of Communist influence in Southeast Asia is to be halted.

B. Regardless of the outcome of military operations in Indo-China and without compromising in any way the overwhelming strategic importance of the Associated States to the Western position in the area, the U.S. should take all affirmative and practical steps, with or without its European allies, to provide tangible evidence of Western strength and determination to defeat Communism; to demonstrate that ultimate victory will be won by the free world; and to secure the affirmative association of Southeast Asian states with these purposes.

C. That for these purposes the Western position in Indo-China must be maintained and improved by a military victory.

D. That without compromise to C, above, the U.S. should in all prudence reinforce the remainder of Southeast Asia, including the land areas of Malaya, Burma, Thailand, Indonesia, and the Philippines.

V. Recommended Courses of Action

A. The Special Committee wishes to reaffirm the following recommendations which are made in NSC 5405, the Special Committee Report concerning military operations in Indo-China, and the position paper of the Special Committee, concurred in by the Department of Defense, concerning U.S. courses of action and policies with respect to the Geneva Conference:

(1) It be U.S. policy to accept nothing short of a military victory in Indo-China.

(2) It be the U.S. position to obtain French support of this position; and that failing this, the U.S. actively oppose any negotiated settlement in Indo-China at Geneva.

(3) It be the U.S. position in event of failure of (2) above to initiate immediate steps with the governments of the Associated States aimed toward the continuation of the war in Indo-China, to include active U.S. participation and without French support should that be necessary.

(4) Regardless of whether or not the U.S. is successful in obtaining French support for the active U.S. participation called for in (3) above, every effort should be made to undertake this active participation in concert with other interested nations.

B. The Special Committee also considers that all possible political and economic pressure on France must be exerted as the obvious initial course of action to reinforce the French will to continue operations in Indo-China. The Special Committee recognizes that this course of action will jeopardize the existing French Cabinet, may be unpopular among the French public, and may be considered as endangering present U.S. policy with respect to EDC [European Defense Community]. The Committee nevertheless considers that the free world strategic position, not only in Southeast Asia but in Europe and the Middle East as well, is such as to require the most extraordinary efforts to prevent Communist domination of Southeast Asia. The Committee considers that firm and resolute action now in this regard may well be the key to a solution of the entire problem posed by France in the free world community of nations.

Source: *United States–Vietnam Relations, 1945–1967,* Book 9 (Washington, DC: U.S. Government Printing Office, 1971), 348–350.

76. National Security Council Planning Board Report on NSC Action No. 1074-A, April 5, 1954 [Excerpt]

Introduction

With the French position at Dien Bien Phu fast deteriorating, this U.S. National Security Council (NSC) Planning Board report presents the first detailed discussion of possible U.S. military intervention against the Viet Minh in Indochina. The report calls on the U.S. government to exert maximum pressure on the French and the associated states of Indochina to continue to wage war to a successful conclusion. In addition, the report considers possible courses of action, including U.S. cooperation with the French, but notes that French policy in the region—public statements notwithstanding—is regarded as essentially colonialist in character. Should U.S. military intervention occur, this view must be modified.

Primary Source

Problem

1. To analyze the extent to which, and the circumstances and conditions under which, the United States would be willing to commit its resources in support of the effort to prevent the loss of Indochina to the Communists, in concert with the French or in concert with others or, if necessary, unilaterally.

Issues Involved

2. The answer to this problem involves four issues:

   a. Will Indochina be lost to the Communists unless the United States commits combat resources in some form?
   b. What are the risks, requirements and consequences of alternative forms of U.S. military intervention?
   c. Should the United States adopt one of these forms of intervention rather than allow Indochina to be lost to the Communists and if so which alternative should it choose?
   d. When and under what circumstances should this decision be taken and carried into effect?

Prospect of Loss of Indochina

3. The first issue turns on whether the French Union can and will prevent the loss of Indochina and what further actions, if any, the United States can take to bolster or assist the French effort. Some of these questions were covered by the Report of the Special Committee of March 17, 1954. Others are matters of continuous intelligence estimates. At the present time there is clearly a possibility that a trend in the direction of the loss of Indochina to Communist control may become irreversible over the next year in the absence of greater U.S. participation. There is not, however, any certainty that the French have as yet reached the point of being willing to accept a settlement which is unacceptable to U.S. interests or to cease their military efforts. Moreover, regardless of the outcome of the fight at Dienbienphu, there is no indication that a military decision in Indochina is imminent. It is clear that the United States should undertake a maximum diplomatic effort to cause the French and Associated States to continue the fight to a successful conclusion.

Risks, Requirements, and Consequences of U.S. Intervention

4. The attached Annex addresses itself to the second issue: The risks, requirements and consequences of certain alternative forms of U.S. military intervention. In order to permit analysis of military requirements and allied and hostile reactions, this annex assumes that there will be either: (1) a French and Associated States invitation to the United States to participate militarily; or (2) an Associated States invitation to the United States after a French decision to withdraw, and French willingness to cooperate in phasing out French forces as U.S. forces are phased in. If neither of these assumptions proved valid the feasibility of U.S. intervention would be vitiated. If the French, having decided on withdrawal and a negotiated settlement, should oppose U.S. intervention and should carry the Associated States with them in such opposition, U.S. intervention in Indochina would in effect be precluded. If, after a French decision to withdraw, the Associated States should appeal for U.S. military assistance but the French decided not to cooperate in the phasing in of U.S. forces, a successful U.S. intervention would be very difficult.

Desirability and Form of U.S. Intervention

5. The third issue is whether the United States should intervene with combat forces rather than allow Indochina to be lost to the Communists, and which alternative it should select?

   a. U.S. commitment of combat forces would involve strain on the basic western coalition, increased risk of war with China and of general war, high costs in U.S. manpower and money, and possible adverse domestic political repercussions. Moreover, the United States would be undertaking a commitment which it would have to carry through to victory. In whatever form it might intervene, the U.S. would have to take steps at the outset to guard against the risks inherent in intervention. On the other hand, under the principles laid down in NSC 5405, it is essential to U.S. security that Indochina should not fall under Communist control.
   b. Of the alternative courses of action described in the Annex, Course A or B has these advantages over Course C. Neither Course A or B depends on the initial use of U.S. ground forces. For this reason alone, they obviously would be much more acceptable to the American public. For the same reason, they would initially create a less serious drain on existing U.S. military forces. But either Course A or B may turn out to be ineffective without the eventual commitment of U.S. ground forces.
   c. A political obstacle to Course A or Course B lies in the fact that the present French effort is considered by many in Southeast Asia and other parts of the world as essentially colonial or imperialist in character. If the United States joined its combat forces in the Indochina conflict, it would be most important to attempt to counteract or modify the present view of this struggle. This would also be essential in order to mobilize maximum support for the war within Indochina.

d. An advantage of Course B over Course A lies in the association of the Asian States in the enterprise which would help to counteract the tendency to view Indochina as a colonial action. There would be advantages in Course B also in that U.S. opinion would be more favorable if the other free nations and the Asian nations were also taking part and bearing their fair share of the burden.

e. As between UN and regional support it appears that regional grouping would be preferable to UN action, on the ground that UN support would be far more difficult to get and less likely to remain solid until the desired objective was reached.

6. In order to make feasible any regional grouping, it will be essential for the United States to define more clearly its own objectives with respect to any such action. In particular, it would be important to make perfectly clear that this action is not intended as a first step of action to destroy or overthrow Communist China. If the other members of a potential regional grouping thought that we had such a broad objective, they would doubtless be hesitant to join in it. The Western powers would not want to increase the risks of general war which would, in their opinion, flow from any such broad purpose. The Asian countries would be equally reluctant to engage in any such broad activity. Both groups would doubtless want to make very clear that we object essentially to the expansionist tendencies of Communist China and that, if those ceased, we would not go further in attempting to carry on military activities in the Far East. Furthermore, to attract the participation of Asian States in a regional grouping, the United States would undoubtedly have to undertake lasting commitments for their defense.

Timing and Circumstances of Decision to Intervene with U.S. Combat Forces

7. The timing of the disclosure or implementation of any U.S. decision to intervene in Indochina would be of particular importance.

a. In the absence of serious military deterioration in Indochina, it is unlikely that France will agree to the arrangements envisaged in Alternatives A, B, or C in light of the hopes widely held in France and elsewhere that an acceptable settlement can be achieved.

b. On the other hand, inaction until after exhaustive discussions at Geneva, without any indication of U.S. intentions, would tend to increase the chance of the French government and people settling, or accepting the inevitability of settling, on unacceptable terms. Hints of possible U.S. participation would tend to fortify French firmness, but might also tend to induce the Communists to put forward more acceptable terms.

c. On balance, it appears that the United States should now reach a decision whether or not to intervene with combat forces, if that is necessary to save Indochina

from Communist control, and, tentatively, the form and conditions of any such intervention. The timing for communication to the French of such decision, or for its implementation, should be decided in the light of future developments.

8. If the United States should now decide to intervene at some stage, the United States should now take these steps:

a. Obtain Congressional approval of intervention.

b. Initiate planning of the military and mobilization measures to enable intervention.

c. Make publicized U.S. military moves designed to make the necessary U.S. air and naval forces readily available for use on short notice.

d. Make maximum diplomatic efforts to make it clear, as rapidly as possible, that no acceptable settlement can be reached in the absence of far greater Communist concessions than are now envisaged.

e. Explore with major U.S. allies—notably the UK, Australia, and New Zealand, and with as many Asian nations as possible, such as Thailand and the Philippines, and possibly Nationalist China, the Republic of Korea, and Burma—the formation of a regional grouping.

f. Exert maximum diplomatic efforts with France and the Associated States designed to (1) bring about full agreement between them, if possible prior to Geneva, on the future status of the Associated States; (2) prepare them to invite U.S. and if possible group participation in Indochina, if necessary.

Source: *United States–Vietnam Relations, 1945–1967*, Book 9 (Washington, DC: U.S. Government Printing Office, 1971), 298–305.

77. John Foster Dulles, Secretary of State: Telegram to C. Douglas Dillon, Ambassador to France, April 5, 1954

Introduction

At a White House meeting, leaders of Congress informed Secretary of State John Foster Dulles that they could not support U.S. military intervention on the side of the French at Dien Bien Phu unless military intervention was supported by a coalition of nations, the French promised to accelerate real independence for the associated states of Indochina, and the French also promised to continue the war with their ground troops. The next day, President Dwight D. Eisenhower met with Dulles and chairman of the Joint Chiefs of Staff (JCS) Admiral Arthur W. Radford and decided that there would be no U.S. intervention in Indochina unless the three conditions were met.

Primary Source

As I personally explained to Ely in presence of Radford, it is not (rpt not) possible for US to commit belligerent acts in Indochina without full political understanding with France and the other countries. In addition, Congressional action would be required. After conference at highest level, I must confirm this position. US is doing everything possible as indicated my 5175 to prepare public, Congressional and Constitutional basis for united action in Indochina. However, such action is impossible except on coalition basis with active British Commonwealth participation. Meanwhile US prepared, as has been demonstrated, to do everything short of belligerency.

FYI US cannot and will not be put in position of alone salvaging British Commonwealth interests in Malaya, Australia and New Zealand. This matter now under discussion with UK at highest level.

Source: *United States–Vietnam Relations, 1945–1967,* Book 9 (Washington, DC: U.S. Government Printing Office, 1971), 359.

78. President Dwight Eisenhower's News Conference, April 7, 1954

Introduction

President Dwight D. Eisenhower first publicly enunciates the "'falling domino' principle," which became one of the chief justifications for the U.S. involvement in Vietnam. The domino theory held that should Indochina fall to the Communists, the rest of Southeast Asia would inevitably follow.

Primary Source

Q. ROBERT RICHARDS, COPLEY PRESS: Mr. President, would you mind commenting on the strategic importance of Indochina to the free world? I think there has been, across the country, some lack of understanding on just what it means to us.

THE PRESIDENT: You have, of course, both the specific and the general when you talk about such things.

First of all, you have the specific value of a locality in its production of materials that the world needs.

Then you have the possibility that many human beings pass under a dictatorship that is inimical to the free world.

Finally, you have broader considerations that might follow what you would call the "falling domino" principle. You have a row of dominoes set up, you knock over the first one, and what will happen to the last one is the certainty that it will go over very quickly. So you could have a beginning of a disintegration that would have the most profound influences.

Now, with respect to the first one, two of the items from this particular area that the world uses are tin and tungsten. They are very important. There are others, of course, the rubber plantations and so on.

Then with respect to more people passing under this domination, Asia, after all, has already lost some 450 million of its peoples to the Communist dictatorship, and we simply can't afford greater losses.

But when we come to the possible sequence of events, the loss of Indochina, of Burma, of Thailand, of the Peninsula, and Indonesia following, now you begin to talk about areas that not only multiply the disadvantages that you would suffer through loss of materials, sources of materials, but now you are talking really about millions and millions and millions of people.

Finally, the geographical position achieved thereby does many things. It turns the so-called island defensive chain of Japan, Formosa, of the Philippines and to the southward; it moves in to threaten Australia and New Zealand.

It takes away, in its economic aspects, that region that Japan must have as a trading area or Japan, in turn, will have only one place in the world to go—that is, toward the Communist areas in order to live.

So, the possible consequences of the loss are just incalculable to the free world.

Source: *Public Papers of the Presidents of the United States: Dwight D. Eisenhower, 1954* (Washington, DC: U.S. Government Printing Office, 1960), 382–383.

79. Minutes of Meeting among President Dwight Eisenhower, Secretary of State John Foster Dulles, and Special Assistant to the President Robert Cutler, May 7, 1954

Introduction

On May 7, the very day that the last French troops surrendered to the Viet Minh at Dien Bien Phu, U.S. president Dwight D. Eisenhower, Secretary of State John Foster Dulles, and Special Assistant to the President Robert Cutler met to discuss the position of the military members of the National Security Council (NSC) Planning Board that the United States should not support French foreign minister Georges Bidault's proposal for a cease-fire in Indochina but instead should propose to France an internationalization of the war, with the United States becoming a partner with France in the war. Eisenhower stated that he would want as a condition of this the formation of an international coalition and an invitation from the associated states of Indochina for its participation.

Primary Source

At a meeting in the President's office this morning with Dulles, three topics were discussed:

1. Whether the President should approve paragraph 1b of the tentative Record of Action of the 5/6/54 NSC Meeting, which covers the proposed answer to the Eden proposal. The Secretary of State thought the text was correct. Wilson and Radford preferred the draft message to Smith for Eden prepared yesterday by MacArthur and Captain Anderson, and cleared by the JCS, which included in the Five Power Staff Agency Thailand and the Philippines. Radford thinks that the Agency (which has hitherto been not disclosed in SEA) has really completed its military planning; that if it is enlarged by top level personnel, its actions will be necessarily open to the world; that therefore some Southeast Asian countries should be included in it, and he fears Eden's proposal as an intended delaying action.

The President approved the text of paragraph 1b, but suggested that Smith's reply to Eden's proposal should make clear the following:

1. Five Power Staff Agency, alone or with other nations, is not to the United States a satisfactory substitute for a broad political coalition which will include the Southeast Asian countries which are to be defended.
2. Five Power Staff Agency examination is acceptable to see how these nations can give military aid to the Southeast Asian countries in their cooperative defense effort.
3. The United States will not agree to a "white man's party" to determine the problems of the Southeast Asian nations.

I was instructed to advise Wilson and Radford of the above, and have done so.

2. The President went over the draft of the speech which Dulles is going to make tonight, making quite a few suggestions and changes in text. He thought additionally the speech should include some easy to understand slogans, such as "The US will never start a war," "The US will not go to war without Congressional authority," "The US, as always, is trying to organize cooperative efforts to sustain the peace."

3. With reference to the cease-fire proposal transmitted by Bidault to the French Cabinet, I read the following, as views principally of military members of the Planning Board, expressed in their yesterday afternoon meeting:

1. US should not support the Bidault proposal.
2. Reasons for this position:
   a. The mere proposal of the cease-fire at the Geneva Conference would destroy the will to fight of French forces and make fencesitters jump to Vietminh side.
   b. The Communists would evade covertly cease-fire controls.
3. The US should (as a last act to save IndoChina) propose to France that if the following 5 conditions are met, the US will go to Congress for authority to intervene with combat forces:
   a. grant of genuine freedom for Associated States
   b. US take major responsibility for training indigenous forces
   c. US share responsibility for military planning
   d. French forces to stay in the fight and no requirement of replacement by US forces.
   (e. Action under UN auspices?)

This offer to be made known simultaneously to the other members of the proposed regional grouping (UK, Australia, NZ, Thailand, Associated States, Philippines) in order to enlist their participation.

I then summarized possible objections to making the above proposal to the French:

   a. No French Government is now competent to act in a lasting way.
   b. There is no indication France wants to "internationalize" the conflict.
   c. The US proposal would be made without the prior assurance of a regional grouping of SEA States, a precondition of Congress; although this point might be added as another condition to the proposal.
   d. US would be "bailing out colonial France" in the eyes of the world.
   e. US cannot undertake alone to save every situation of trouble.

I concluded that some PB members felt that it had never been made clear to the French that the US was willing to ask for Congressional authority, if certain fundamental preconditions were met; that these matters had only been hinted at, and that the record of history should be clear as to the US position. Dulles was interested to know the President's views, because he is talking with Ambassador Bonnet this afternoon. He indicated that he would mention these matters to Bonnet, perhaps making a more broad hint than heretofore. He would not circulate any formal paper to Bonnet, or to anyone else.

The President referred to the proposition advanced by Governor Stassen at the April 29 Council Meeting as not having been thoroughly thought out. He said that he had been trying to get France to "internationalize" matters for a long time, and they are not willing to do so. If it were thought advisable at this time to point out to the French the essential preconditions to the US asking for Congressional authority to intervene, then it should also be made clear to the French as an additional precondition that the US would never intervene alone, that there must be an invitation by the indigenous people, and that there must be some kind of regional and collective action.

I understand that Dulles will decide the extent to which he cares to follow this line with Ambassador Bonnet. This discussion may afford Dulles guidance in replying to Smith's request about a US alternative to support the Bidault proposal, but there really was no decision as to the US attitude toward the cease-fire proposal itself.

Source: *United States–Vietnam Relations, 1945–1967*, Book 9 (Washington, DC: U.S. Government Printing Office, 1971), 436–438.

80. Treaty of Independence of the State of Vietnam, June 4, 1954

Introduction

On June 4, 1954, France recognized the full sovereignty of Bao Dai's State of Vietnam (SVN), the political entity backed by France and the United States as a rival to Ho Chi Minh's Democratic Republic of Vietnam (DRV, North Vietnam).

Primary Source

Article I:

France recognizes Vietnam as a fully independent and sovereign state and invested of all powers recognized by international law.

Article II:

Vietnam is substituted for France in all laws and obligations resulting from international treaties of conventions contracted by France on behalf of or in the name of the State of Vietnam or all other treaties or conventions concluded by France in the name of French Indochina to the measure in which these acts concerned Vietnam.

Article III:

France pledges to transfer to the Vietnamese government the powers and public services still guaranteed by [France] on Vietnamese territory.

Article IV:

The present treaty, which will enter into force on the date of its signing, abrogates (all) previous acts and provisions contrary to it. The instruments of ratification of the present treaty will be exchanged as of its approval by qualified representatives of France and Vietnam.

Source: Gareth Porter, ed., *Vietnam: A History in Documents* (New York: New American Library, 1981), 151.

81. John Foster Dulles, Secretary of State: Telegram to C. Douglas Dillon, Ambassador to France, June 14, 1954

Introduction

In this telegram to U.S. ambassador to France C. Douglas Dillon, Secretary of State John Foster Dulles discusses the sharp deterioration in the military situation and in French and State of Vietnam (SVN) military morale following the Viet Minh victory at Dien Bien Phu. Dulles blames this situation on French and British indecision (President Dwight Eisenhower having made British participation a condition of U.S. military intervention). While still not completely ruling out U.S. military intervention, Dulles claimed that the French did not really want it as much as they want "a card to play" at the Geneva Conference (May 8–July 21, 1954), which was discussing the future of Indochina.

Primary Source

It is true that there is less disposition now than two months or one month ago to intervene in Indochina militarily. This is the inevitable result of the steady deterioration in Indochina which makes the problem of intervention and pacification more and more difficult. When united defense was first broached, the strength and morale of French and Vietnam forces were such that it seemed that the situation could be held without any great pouring-in of U.S. ground forces. Now all the evidence is that the morale of the Vietnamese Government, armed forces and civilians has deteriorated gravely; the French are forced to contemplate a fallback which would leave virtually the entire Tonkin Delta population in hostile hands and the Saigon area is faced with political disintegration.

What has happened has been what was forecast, as for example by my Embassy Paris 4117 TEDUL 78 of May 17. I there pointed out that probably the French did not really want intervention but wanted to have the possibility as a card to play at Geneva. I pointed out that the Geneva game would doubtless be a long game and that it could not be assumed that at the end the present U.S. position regarding intervention would necessarily exist after the Communists had succeeded in dragging out Geneva by winning military successes in Indochina. This telegram of mine will bear rereading. That point of view has been frequently repeated in subsequent cables.

I deeply regret any sense of bitterness on Bidault's part, but I do not see that he is justified in considering unreasonable the adaptation of U.S. views to events and the consequences of prolonged French and U.K. indecision.

I do not yet wholly exclude possibility U.S. intervention on terms outlined PARIS 402 TEDUL 54. UK it seems is now more disposed to see movement in this direction but apparently the French are less than ever disposed to internationalizing the war.

Source: *United States–Vietnam Relations, 1945–1967*, Book 9 (Washington, DC: U.S. Government Printing Office, 1971), 559–560.

82. Walter Bedell Smith, Head of the U.S. Delegation in Geneva and Undersecretary of State: Telegram to Secretary of State John Foster Dulles, June 17, 1954

Introduction

The U.S. government found itself in an awkward position at the Geneva Conference. The United States wanted the French to continue the war and feared a "sellout" to the Communists. In this telegram to U.S. secretary of state John Foster Dulles, head of the U.S. delegation to the Geneva Conference Walter Bedell Smith passes along a statement from Chinese foreign minister Zhou Enlai (Chou En-lai) that the delegation from the Democratic Republic of Vietnam (DRV, North Vietnam) had agreed to withdraw Viet Minh "volunteers" from both Laos and Cambodia. This became the basis for the independence of both Laos and Cambodia. Resolving the future status of Vietnam would not be as easy. Smith reports that he expressed "contempt" for the proposal by French high commissioner and military commander in Indochina General Paul Ély that France not seek to retain an enclave in the Red River Delta in North Vietnam. Smith regarded this as little more than a "selling-out" with which the United States could not be associated.

Primary Source

Dennis Allen (UK) gave Johnson this morning additional details on conversation with Chou En-lai. Chou stated that in case Cambodia resistance forces were small and all that was necessary was a political settlement by the present royal government with them "which could easily be obtained." In case of Laos, resistance forces were larger, and it would be necessary recognize this fact by formation of regrouping areas along the border with Vietnam and China. The task in both States was twofold: The removal of foreign forces and dealing with the problem of domestic resistance movements. The military staff should get down to this task.

In reply to Eden's query as to whether it would not (repeat not) be difficult obtain Viet Minh admission Viet Minh forces were in Laos and Cambodia, Chou stated it would "not (repeat not) be difficult" to get Viet Minh to agree to withdrawal their forces from these two states in context with withdrawal all foreign forces. Chou made no (repeat no) direct reply to Eden's reference to French-Laotian treaty on French bases in Laos. Eden expressed personal view that Chou wants settlement, but has some doubt with regard to degree of control he exercises over Viet Minh.

In long talk with Bidault this morning Chou substantially repeated what he told Eden yesterday (in conversation with Bidault, Chou referred to Viet Minh forces in Cambodia and Laos as "volunteers"). Bidault had also seen Molotov this morning and reported that both Molotov and Chou are obviously greatly concerned over any break-up Indochina conference in pattern of Korean conference as well as of lowering level conference below level of Foreign Ministers. Bidault said they clearly want to keep the conference going. Bidault and I agree (Eden did not (repeat not) comment) that it was very important we do nothing dispel Chou's worries over US bases in Laos and Cambodia.

I also expressed personal opinion that important Laos and Cambodia move ahead as quickly and as vigorously as possible with appeal to UN. Eden and Bidault agreed, Eden adding that important Vietnam not (repeat not) get mixed up with Laos and Cambodia cases UN.

Chauvel showed me handwritten note from Ely, in his political capacity, urging against attempting hold any enclave in delta and recommending straight partition formula. I could not (repeat not) resist expressing contempt for such an easy "selling-out" of last remaining foothold in north and said we could under no (repeat no) circumstances publicly associate ourselves with such a solution.

Source: *United States–Vietnam Relations, 1945–1967*, Book 9 (Washington, DC: U.S. Government Printing Office, 1971), 574–575.

83. Walter Bedell Smith, Head of the U.S. Delegation in Geneva and Undersecretary of State: Telegram to Secretary of State John Foster Dulles, June 18, 1954

Introduction

In this telegram from Walter Bedell Smith, head of the U.S. delegation to the Geneva Conference, to Secretary of State John Foster Dulles, Smith reports that the U.S. delegation had informed the French that their decision not to retain an enclave in the Red River Delta area of the Democratic Republic of Vietnam (DRV, North Vietnam), which Smith characterized as a "selling-out," had left the U.S. government no choice but to disassociate itself from the Geneva settlement. He had, however, told the French that the United States would continue to support their efforts to secure the best possible settlement. The French government meanwhile claimed that a partition of Vietnam was preferable to a "leopard spot" alternative of enclaves.

Primary Source

Johnson saw Chauvel this morning and discussed with him conference situation in light TEDUL 211. Johnson stated seemed to us that such fundamental questions as composition, voting procedures and authority or international control commission should be dealt with in conference rather than by committee. If conference reached decision on fundamental principles, working out of details could be done by committee of experts of principally interested parties in same pattern as present Franco-Viet Minh military conversations.

Chauvel said this would be agreeable except that question of authority, which he termed "relationship between international commission and joint committees" could be dealt with by technical committee, thus implying France not (repeat not) prepared to maintain principle of subordination joint committees to international commission. As French have already circulated proposal contained SECTO 460 through secretariat, it was agreed we would make suggestion along foregoing lines at today's restricted meeting. Chauvel said they did not (repeat not) yet have any further indication as to what attitude Chinese would take on French proposal entirely clear from conversation with Chauvel that his main interest is in keeping some conference activity of nine going and that if regardless of level representation we prepared continue some conference meetings would probably meet French point of view. Appears French proposal made on assumption that there would be complete recess of conference with departure of Smith and Eden.

Chauvel made reference to his conversation with Smith yesterday (DULTE 193—last paragraph), making inquiry as to exactly what we had in mind. Johnson in reply read to him paragraphs 5, 6 and 7 basic instructions (TOSEC 138) stating that French willingness surrender even minimum enclave in north of Haiphong would so clearly contravene the principles which the US considered essential as to require our public dissociation with such a solution. In reply to Chauvel's questions, Johnson made it clear we were speaking only of public disassociation from such a settlement. The US had in the past and of course would continue working with and supporting France in every possible way and wherever we could. Chauvel indicated full understanding our position. He said they had come to conclusion that what he termed any "leopard spot" solution was entirely impracticable and unenforceable. From standpoint of future it would be much better to retain a reasonably defensible line in Vietnam behind which there would be no (repeat no) enclaves of Viet Minh and do all possible behind that line to build up effective Vietnamese Government and defense. They had no (repeat no) intention of "any immediate surrender of Haiphong" which in any event must remain under their control for a considerable period for purely military reasons to effect evacuation of French Union Forces from the north. However, if, as appeared likely, choice was giving Viet Minh an enclave in south in exchange for French enclave in Haiphong, they thought it preferable to give up Haiphong. He said no (repeat no) French parliament would approve conditions which the US had laid down for its intervention, and French had no (repeat no) choice but made the best deal they could, obtaining as strong position as possible in south. Chauvel understood fully we would probably not (repeat not) be able to publicly associate ourselves with such a solution, but he hoped that when it came time to put it to the Vietnamese the US would consider it possible very discreetly to let the Vietnamese know that we considered it best that could be obtained under the circumstances and our public disassociation would not (repeat not) operate so as to encourage Vietnamese opposition. Johnson replied he did not (repeat not) see how it would be possible for us to do this, and in any event he would of course have to see what the solution was. Chauvel said that such a solution as partition should come as no (repeat no) surprise to the Vietnamese as Buu Loc had sometime ago indicated to Dejean. There had been conversations between Vietnamese and Viet Minh in which Viet Minh had made it clear that only two alternatives were coalition government or partition. Chauvel said Ngo Dinh and Diem are very unrealistic, unreasonable, and would probably prove to be "difficulte".

Chauvel said the line French had in mind had been made available to US defense representatives at some five-power talks, but was vague about time and place. He referred to it as "line of the chalk cliffs", which he said was defensible position running from the sea across Vietnam and Laos to the Mekong. Understand this is a line roughly 19 parallel running from vicinity of Dong Hoi to Thakhek. Replying to query, Chauvel said French Union Forces removed from the north would be deployed along that line.

Chauvel said all indications were Mendès-France would succeed in forming government next day or two and would probably himself assume Foreign Minister post. Said he had been in touch with Mendès-France and had sent emissary to Paris this morning to brief him on situation in Geneva. Chauvel said was anxious to show complete continuity of French effort here in Geneva and hoped there could be another restricted meeting tomorrow. Chauvel said, "Underground military talks" last night had been completely unproductive, Viet Minh obviously taking strong line in view of French Government situation.

Source: *United States–Vietnam Relations, 1945–1967,* Book 9 (Washington, DC: U.S. Government Printing Office, 1971), 578–579.

84. Ho Chi Minh: Report to the Sixth Plenum of the Party Central Committee, July 15, 1954 [Excerpt]

Introduction

Under heavy pressure from the Chinese and the Soviets, the delegation from the Democratic Republic of Vietnam (DRV, North Vietnam) to the Geneva Conference accepted the compromise arrangement of an independent Vietnam temporarily partitioned at the 17th Parallel. The North Vietnamese government would control the north, while the Bao Dai–led State of Vietnam (SVN) would hold power in the south. The French would quit the north, and Viet Minh troops would leave the south. National elections were to take place in 1955. Pham Van Dong, who headed the North Vietnamese delegation to Geneva, was furious at this compromise, for it was less than the Viet Minh had won on the battlefield. Ho Chi Minh and the North Vietnamese leadership accepted the compromise because it kept the United States from intervening militarily. As these remarks make clear, Ho counted on developing differences between France and the United States and on the planned elections, ultimately scheduled for July 1956, to bring about national reunification under control of the Vietnamese Workers' Party (Dang Lao Dong Viet Nam).

Primary Source

2. Home situation

The Vietnamese, Cambodian and Lao peoples are united and their resistance grows ever more vigorous. Our guerilla forces in South, Central and North Viet Nam, not only have stood firm but have grown ever stronger. From the Border Campaign to the Hoa Binh, Tay Bac and other campaigns, our regular forces have recorded repeated successes. These victories plus the major one at Dien Bien Phu have brought about an important change in the situation. The fiasco of the Navarre plan has led to the collapse of the Laniel-Bidault cabinet and the shrinking of French-occupied zones.

We owe our successes to the correct policy of our Party and Government, the heroism of our armed forces and people, and the support of the fraternal countries and the world's people. Our successes also belong to the world movement for peace and democracy.

Besides military successes, initial ones have also been scored on the anti-feudal front. The former have had a good effect on the mobilization of the masses to implement our land policy and the latter, on our struggle against imperialism. Our successes inspire our people and the peoples of the world and reinforce our diplomatic position at Geneva; they have compelled our enemy to enter into talks with us. Compared with what Bollaert put forward in 1947, France's attitude at present has noticeably changed. Thus, since the start of the resistance, our posture has grown stronger and the enemy's weaker. But we should bear in mind that this should be understood in a relative, not absolute, sense. We must guard against subjectiveness and not underrate our enemy. Our successes have awakened the American imperialists. After the Dien Bien Phu campaign, the latter's intentions and plan for intervention have also undergone changes aimed at protracting and internationalizing the Indochina war, sabotaging the Geneva Conference, and ousting the French by every means, in order to occupy Viet Nam, Cambodia and Laos, enslave the peoples of these countries and create further tension in the world.

Therefore, the US imperialists not only are the enemy of the world's people but are becoming the main and direct enemy of the Vietnamese, Cambodian and Lao peoples.

These changes in the world and domestic situation have led to the Geneva Conference. This Conference has further exacerbated the contradictions between the imperialist countries, with France willing to negotiate, Britain wavering, and the United States bent on sabotaging the talks. The Americans have grown ever more isolated.

II. NEW TASKS

The new situation has set new tasks, new guidelines and new tactics. Over nearly nine years of resistance, under the leadership of our Party and Government, our people and army have overcome difficulties, fought heroically, and won glorious victories. Our forces have made headway in all respects. Thanks to the correct policy of our Party and Government, we have recorded good achievements.

At present the situation has changed; so have our tasks and consequently so should our policy and slogans. Up to now we have concentrated our efforts on wiping out the forces of the French imperialist aggressors. But now the French are having talks with us while the American imperialists are becoming our main and direct enemy; so our spearhead must be directed at the latter. Until peace is restored, we shall keep fighting the French; but the brunt of our attack and that of the world's peoples should be focused on the United States. US policy is to expand and internationalize the Indochina war. Ours is to struggle for peace and oppose the US war policy. For some nine years now, our Party has made clear its programme: Complete independence for Viet Nam, Cambodia and Laos, which must be freed from the French yoke; to refuse to recognize the French Union, drive out all French troops from Indochina, destroy the puppet administration and armed forces, confiscate all properties of the imperialists and the traitors, launch a drive for the reduction of land rents and interest rates as a step towards agrarian reform, bring democracy to the whole nation, and carry our war of resistance through to final victory. This programme has won many successes. It is a correct one.

However, in the new situation we cannot maintain the old programme. Our previous motto was "Resistance to the end". At present, we must put forward a new one: "Peace, Unity, Independence, Democracy". We must take firm hold of the banner of peace to oppose the US imperialists' policy of direct interference in, and prolongation and expansion of, the war in Indochina. Our policy must change in consequence: formerly we confiscated the French imperialists' properties; now, as negotiations are going on, we may, in accordance with the principle of equality and mutual benefit, allow French economic and cultural interests to be preserved in Indochina. Negotiations entail reasonable mutual concessions. Formerly we said we would drive out and wipe out all French aggressive forces; now, in the talks held, we have demanded and the French have accepted, that a date be set for the withdrawal of their troops. In the past, our aim was to wipe out the puppet administration and army with a view to national reunification; now we practise a policy of leniency and seek reunification of the country through nationwide elections.

Peace calls for an end to the war; and to end the war one must agree on a cease-fire. A cease-fire requires regrouping zones, that is, enemy troops should be regrouped in a zone with a view to their gradual withdrawal, and ours in another. We must secure a vast area where we would have ample means for building, consolidating and developing our forces so as to exert influence over other regions and thereby advance towards reunification. The setting up of regrouping zones does not mean partition of the country; it is a temporary measure leading to reunification. Owing to the delimitation and exchange of zones, some previously free areas will be temporarily occupied by the enemy; their inhabitants will be dissatisfied; some people might fall prey to discouragement and to enemy deception. We should make it

clear to our compatriots that the trials they are going to endure for the sake of the interests of the whole country, for the sake of our long-range interests, will be a cause for glory and will earn them the gratitude of the whole nation. We should keep everyone free from pessimism and negativism and urge all to continue a vigorous struggle for the complete withdrawal of French forces and for independence.

To set up regrouping zones as a step towards peace, to hold nationwide elections to achieve national reunification, such is our policy. The aims of our war of resistance are independence, unity, democracy and peace. The very restoration of peace is aimed at serving the cause of reunification, independence and democracy. The new situation requires a new policy for securing new successes.

At any juncture, peace or war, we must firmly hold the initiative, show foresight and be in full readiness.

To secure peace is not an easy task: it is a long, hard and complex struggle; with advantageous conditions but also with difficulties. The advantageous conditions: the friendly countries support us, so do the world's people; our people are full of spirit and confidence in our Party and Government, under whose wise leadership they will certainly unite and struggle in peace as in war. The difficulties: the United States is trying its hardest to sabotage the restoration of peace in Indochina, the partisans of peace in France have not completely freed themselves from American influence.

Source: Ho Chi Minh, *Selected Writings: 1920–1969* (Hanoi: Foreign Languages Publishing House, 1977), 174–180.

85. Walter Bedell Smith, Head of the U.S. Delegation in Geneva and Undersecretary of State: Telegram to Secretary of State John Foster Dulles, July 17, 1954

Introduction

Walter Bedell Smith, head of the U.S. delegation in Geneva, here informs Secretary of State John Foster Dulles that French premier Pierre Mendès-France, British foreign secretary Anthony Eden, and Soviet foreign minister Vyacheslav Molotov had failed to reach agreement on either the date for Vietnamese national elections or the location of the temporary partition line. Smith outlines the various proposals. As it worked out, the representatives of the Democratic Republic of Vietnam (DRV, North Vietnam) compromised on the demarcation line in return for what they assumed would be an election date of 1955.

Primary Source

Following account of Mendès-France-Eden-Molotov meeting last night is based on report of this meeting to Foreign Office made available to Johnson by Caccia. This telegram expands upon and supersedes preliminary account transmitted in first three paragraphs SECTO 630 (repeated information Paris 76, Saigon 48).

At Eden's suggestion, French enumerated documents before conference:

(A) Armistice agreements to be signed by local commanders-in-chief. French have prepared drafts for Vietnam and Laos and Cambodians draft for Cambodia. Viet Minh delegation preparing counter draft for Vietnam.

(B) Control arrangements. French have circulated papers for Vietnam, Laos, and Cambodia.

(C) Political arrangements. After having seen military documents, certain delegations might make unilateral statements. For example, Laos and Cambodia are preparing statements on their willingness to limit their armed forces. Conference as whole would then agree upon common statement taking note of military agreements and unilateral declarations. French have circulated draft of such statement. Soviets have prepared counter draft and French second redraft.

French explained that if conference did not (repeat not) have time to agree on all details of armistice, it might approve only parts providing for cessation of hostilities and first stage of regroupment. Remaining aspects of agreements could be covered by statement of general principles for guidance of experts who would work out details after conference had dispersed.

It was agreed that British, French, and Soviet experts would meet July 17 to consider various drafts.

At Eden's suggestion, Mendès-France summarized main outstanding problems as (A) demarcation line for Vietnam; (B) elections, and (C) control arrangements. Concerning demarcation line, he said French had proposed line near 18th parallel whereas Viet Minh proposed 16th parallel. On elections in Vietnam, he said question was whether to fix firm date now (repeat now) (Soviets had proposed June 1955) or whether, as French proposed, to settle now (repeat now) only manner in which date would be set. Elections in Laos and Cambodia already provided for in constitutions for August and September 1955, respectively. On control, he said main questions were: Whether there should

be one commission or three, composition, voting, execution of commissions' recommendations, and freedom of movement for inspection teams.

Molotov added to outstanding issues: (D) time required for regrouping (French have proposed 380 days and Soviets 6 months); and (E) prevention of importation of new arms and military personnel subject to certain exceptions for Laos and Cambodia, prohibition of foreign military bases, and prohibition of military alliances by three states.

Eden added (F) question of regroupment areas for resistance forces in Laos.

Discussion then turned to substantive issues:

(A) Elections in Vietnam. Molotov said conference should fix date for elections. He conceded more flexible formula might be found than firm date of June 1955 previously proposed by Soviets and suggested agreement merely that elections be held during 1955 with precise date to be fixed by Vietnamese and Viet Minh authorities.

Mendès-France argued that it would be prudent to fix date as early as the end of 1955. He suggested two ways of providing necessary flexibility in arrangements: Date for elections might be fixed after completion of regrouping; or exact date might be fixed now (repeat now) and international control commission be given authority to advance date if necessary.

Eden supported Mendès-France on need for flexibility and suggested that two parts of Vietnam fix date after completion of regrouping. Mendès-France agreed to consider this suggestion, but Molotov continued to urge elections during 1955.

(B) Demarcation line. Molotov argued that in moving from 13th to 16th parallel, Viet Minh had made substantial concession which called for proper response from French. Mendès-France disagreed, arguing that Viet Minh would be giving up much less in Annam than they would be getting in Tonkin. He said that Pham Van Dong had admitted that line on 16th parallel would require special arrangements for Tourane, Hue, on route No. 9 leading into Laos. Mendès-France stated that necessity for such special arrangements showed how unnatural demarcation line at 16th parallel would be. He said that there was no (repeat no) chance of persuading French Government to accept line which excluded either Hue or route No. 9. Eden supported Mendès-France.

Molotov suggested that discussion move to question of control arrangements. Mendès-France replied might be better to postpone such discussion. He observed that questions of elections and demarcation line had been discussed together and might be linked in sense that conceivably one party might yield on one question and another party on other.

Source: *United States–Vietnam Relations, 1945–1967,* Book 9 (Washington, DC: U.S. Government Printing Office, 1971), 648–650.

86. Final Declaration of the Geneva Conference on Indochina, July 21, 1954

Introduction

This final agreement of the Geneva Conference (May 8–July 21, 1954) regarding Indochina declared Cambodia, Laos, and Vietnam to be independent states. Cambodia and Laos would hold elections in 1955. Vietnam, while recognized as one state, was temporarily divided at the 17th Parallel, with the Democratic Republic of Vietnam (DRV, North Vietnam) to control north of that line and the State of Vietnam (SVN) south of it. Internationally supervised elections to unite the two were fixed for July 1956. During the 300-day period it would take for all North Vietnamese armed forces to leave southern Vietnam and for all French Union forces to leave North Vietnam, civilians could also move from one zone to the other if they so chose.

Primary Source

1. The Conference takes note of the agreements ending hostilities in Cambodia, Laos, and Vietnam and organizing international control and the supervision of the execution of the provisions of these agreements.

2. The Conference expresses satisfaction at the end of hostilities in Cambodia, Laos, and Vietnam; the Conference expresses its conviction that the execution of the provisions set out in the present declaration and in the agreements of the cessation of hostilities will permit Cambodia, Laos, and Vietnam henceforth to play their part, in full independence and sovereignty, in the peaceful community of nations.

3. The Conference takes note of the declarations made by the Governments of Cambodia and Laos of their intention to adopt measures permitting all citizens to take their place in the national community, in particular by participating in the next general elections, which, in conformity with the constitution of each of these countries, shall take place in the course of the year 1955, by secret ballot and in conditions of respect for fundamental freedoms.

4. The Conference takes note of the clauses in the agreement on the cessation of hostilities in Vietnam prohibiting the introduction into Vietnam of foreign troops and military personnel as well as of all kinds of arms and munitions. The Conference also takes note of the declarations made by the Governments of Cambodia and Laos of their resolution not to request foreign aid, whether in war material, in personnel, or in instructors except for the purpose of the effective defense of their territory and, in the case of Laos, to the extent defined by the agreements of the cessation of hostilities in Laos.

5. The Conference takes note of the clauses in the agreement on the cessation of hostilities in Vietnam to the effect that no military base under the control of a foreign State may be established in the regrouping zones of the two parties, the latter having the obligation to see that the zones allotted to them shall not constitute part of any military alliance and shall not be utilized for the resumption of hostilities or in the service of an aggressive policy. The Conference also takes note of the declarations of the Governments of Cambodia and Laos to the effect that they will not join in any agreement with other States if this agreement includes the obligation to participate in a military alliance not in conformity with the principles of the Charter of the United Nations or, in the case of Laos, with the principles of the agreement on the cessation of hostilities in Laos or, so long as their security is not threatened, the obligation to establish bases on Cambodian or Laotian territory for the military forces of foreign powers.

6. The Conference recognizes that the essential purpose of the agreement relating to Vietnam is to settle military questions with a view to ending hostilities and that the military demarcation line is provisional and should not in any way be interpreted as constituting a political or territorial boundary. The Conference expresses its conviction that the execution of the provisions set out in the present declaration and in the agreement on the cessation of hostilities creates the necessary basis for the achievement in the near future of a political settlement in Vietnam.

7. The Conference declares that, so far as Vietnam is concerned, the settlement of political problems, effected on the basis of respect for the principles of independence, unity, and territorial integrity, shall permit the Vietnamese people to enjoy the fundamental freedoms, guaranteed by democratic institutions established as a result of free general elections by secret ballot. In order to ensure that sufficient progress in the restoration of peace has been made, and that all the necessary conditions obtain for free expression of the national will, general elections shall be held in July 1956 under the supervision of an international commission composed of representatives of the Member States of the International Supervisory Commission, referred to in the agreement on the cessation of hostilities. Consultations will be held on this subject between the competent representative authorities of the two zones from July 20, 1955, onward.

8. The provisions of the agreements on the cessation of hostilities intended to ensure the protection of individuals and of property

must be most strictly applied and must, in particular, allow everyone in Vietnam to decide freely in which zone he wishes to live.

9. The competent representative authorities of the North and South zones of Vietnam, as well as the authorities of Laos and Cambodia, must not permit any individual or collective reprisals against persons who had collaborated in any way with one of the parties during the war, or against members of such persons' families.

10. The Conference takes note of the declaration of the Government of the French Republic to the effect that it is ready to withdraw its troops from the territory of Cambodia, Laos, and Vietnam, at the request of the Governments concerned and within periods which shall be fixed by agreement between the parties except in the cases where, by agreement between the two parties, a certain number of French troops shall remain at specified points and for a specified time.

11. The Conference takes note of the declaration of the French Government to the effect that for the settlement of all the problems connected with the re-establishment and consolidation of peace in Cambodia, Laos, and Vietnam, the French Government will proceed from the principle of respect for the independence and sovereignty, unity and territorial integrity of Cambodia, Laos, and Vietnam.

12. In their relations with Cambodia, Laos, and Vietnam, each member of the Geneva Conference undertakes to respect the sovereignty, the independence, the unity, and the territorial integrity of the above-mentioned States, and to refrain from any interference in their internal affairs.

13. The members of the Conference agree to consult one another on any question which may be referred to them by the International Supervisory Commission, in order to study such measures as may prove necessary to ensure that the agreements on the cessation of hostilities in Cambodia, Laos, and Vietnam are respected.

Source: *The Pentagon Papers: The Defense Department History of United States Decisionmaking on Vietnam,* Vol. 1. Senator Gravel edition (Boston: Beacon, 1971), 571–573.

87. U.S. Government Response to the Geneva Declarations, July 21, 1954

Introduction

In this official response to the agreements reached at the Geneva Conference (May 8–July 21, 1954) regarding Indochina, the Dwight D. Eisenhower administration upheld the principle of self-determination of peoples and declared that it would not use force or the threat of force in an effort to change the agreements but that it would view any new "aggression" that violated the agreements "with grave concern and as seriously threatening international peace and security."

Primary Source

Declaration

The Government of the United States being resolved to devote its efforts to the strengthening of peace in accordance with the principles and purposes of the United Nations takes note of the agreements concluded at Geneva on July 20 and 21, 1954 between (a) the Franco-Laotian Command and the Command of the Peoples Army of Viet-Nam; (b) the Royal Khmer Army Command and the Command of the Peoples Army of Viet-Nam; (c) Franco-Vietnamese Command and the Command of the Peoples Army of Viet-Nam and of paragraphs 1 to 12 inclusive of the declaration presented to the Geneva Conference on July 21, 1954 declares with regard to the aforesaid agreements and paragraphs that (i) it will refrain from the threat or the use of force to disturb them, in accordance with Article 2(4) of the Charter of the United Nations dealing with the obligation of members to refrain in their international relations from the threat or use of force; and (ii) it would view any renewal of the aggression in violation of the aforesaid agreements with grave concern and as seriously threatening international peace and security.

In connection with the statement in the declaration concerning free elections in Viet-Nam my Government wishes to make clear its position which it has expressed in a declaration made in Washington on June 29, 1954, as follows:

In the case of nations now divided against their will, we shall continue to seek to achieve unity through free elections supervised by the United Nations to insure that they are conducted fairly.

With respect to the statement made by the representative of the State of Viet-Nam, the United States reiterates its traditional position that peoples are entitled to determine their own future and that it will not join in an arrangement which would hinder this. Nothing in its declaration just made is intended to or does indicate any departure from this traditional position.

We share the hope that the agreements will permit Cambodia, Laos and Viet-Nam to play their part, in full independence and sovereignty, in the peaceful community of nations, and will enable the peoples of that area to determine their own future.

Source: *The Pentagon Papers: The Defense Department History of United States Decisionmaking on Vietnam,* Vol. 1. Senator Gravel edition (Boston: Beacon, 1971), 570–571.

88. Walter Bedell Smith: Declaration to the Geneva Conference, July 21, 1954

Introduction

The U.S. government was in an awkward place regarding the results of the Geneva Conference, finding itself powerless to prevent a settlement that it did not want. In this statement at the Geneva Conference (May 8–July 21, 1954) regarding the agreements on Indochina, Undersecretary of State Walter Bedell Smith, head of the U.S. delegation, seconds the official announcement that the United States would not seek to undermine the agreements by the use or threat of force but insists that there be United Nations (UN) supervision of the elections scheduled for July 1956 to reunite Vietnam.

Primary Source

The Government of the United States being resolved to devote its efforts to the strengthening of peace in accordance with the principles and purposes of the United Nations.

Takes note of the Agreements concluded at Geneva on July 20 and 21, 1954 between the (a) Franco-Laotian Command and the Command of the People's Army of Viet-Nam; (b) The Royal Khmer Army Command and the Command of the People's Army of Viet-Nam; (c) Franco-Viet-Namese Command and the Command of the People's Army of Viet-Nam, and of paragraphs 1 to 12 inclusive of the Declaration presented to the Geneva Conference on July 21, 1954.

Declares with regard to the aforesaid Agreements and paragraphs (i) it will refrain from the threat or the use of force to disturb them, in accordance with Article 2 (4) of the Charter of the United Nations dealing with the obligation of Members to refrain in their international relations from the threat or use of force; and (ii) it would view any renewal of the aggression in violation of the aforesaid agreements with grave concern and as seriously threatening international peace and security.

In connection with this statement in the Declaration concerning free elections in Viet-Nam, my Government wishes to make clear its position which it has expressed in a Declaration made in Washington June 19, 1954, as follows: "In the case of nations now divided against their will, we shall continue to seek to achieve unity through free elections, supervised by the United Nations to ensure that they are conducted fairly."

With respect to the statement made by the Representative of the State of Viet-Nam, the United States reiterates its traditional position that peoples are entitled to determine their own future and that it will not join in any arrangement which would hinder this.

Nothing in its declaration just made is intended to or does indicate any departure from this traditional position.

We share the hope that the agreement will permit Cambodia, Laos and Viet-Nam to play their part in full independence and sovereignty, in the peaceful community of nations, and will enable the peoples of that area to determine their own future.

Source: "U.S. Declaration on Indochina," *Department of State Bulletin* 31(788) (1954): 162–163.

89. National Intelligence Estimate 63-5-54 on the Post-Geneva Outlook in Indochina, August 3, 1954 [Excerpt]

Introduction

Following the Geneva Conference, the Dwight D. Eisenhower administration found itself opposing the popular will in Vietnam. In this first National Intelligence Estimate (NIE) following Geneva, the intelligence community agrees that Ho Chi Minh's Democratic Republic of Vietnam (DRV, North Vietnam) will undoubtedly increase in popularity among Vietnamese and will "almost certainly" win the elections scheduled for July 1956 to reunite North Vietnam and southern Vietnam. The framers of the NIE believe that the popularity of the State of Vietnam (SVN) in southern Vietnam will be determined entirely by the French and whether they will allow the SVN to be genuinely independent. The NIE concludes that Ngo Dinh Diem, the new premier of the SVN, will have difficulty dealing with the Viet Minh political cadres in southern Vietnam because of provisions in the Geneva Accords that allow them to remain there in order to prepare for the scheduled elections.

Primary Source

23. Outlook in South Vietnam. We believe that the Viet Minh will seek to retain sizeable military and political assets in South Vietnam. Although the agreements provide for the removal to the north of all Viet Minh forces, many of the regular and irregular Viet Minh soldiers now in the south are natives of the area, and large numbers of them will probably cache their arms and remain in South Vietnam. In addition, Viet Minh administrative cadres have been in firm control of several large areas in central and south Vietnam for several years. These cadres will probably remain in place. French and Vietnamese efforts to deal with "stay behind" military and administrative units and personnel will be greatly hampered by armistice provisions guaranteeing the security of pre-armistice dissidents from reprisals.

24. The severe problem of establishing and maintaining security in South Vietnam will probably be increased by certain provisions

of the Geneva agreements which prohibit the import of arms and military equipment, except as replacements, and the introduction of additional foreign military personnel, the establishment of new military bases, and military alliances. These provisions limit the development of a Vietnamese national army to such numbers as may be equipped by stocks evacuated from Tonkin, plus stocks now held in Saigon. However, in the last analysis, Vietnamese security will be determined by the degree of French protection and assistance in the development of a national army, the energy with which the Vietnamese themselves attack the problem, and by the will of the non-Communist powers to provide South Vietnam with effective guarantees.

25. In addition to the activities of stay-behind military and administrative groups, the Viet Minh will make a major effort to discredit any South Vietnam administration, and to exacerbate French-Vietnamese relations, and appeal to the feeling for national unification which will almost certainly continue strong among the South Vietnamese population. The Communist goal will be to cause the collapse of any non-Communist efforts to stabilize the situation in South Vietnam, and thus to leave North Vietnam the only visible foundation on which to re-establish Vietnamese unity. French and anti-Communist Vietnamese efforts to counter the Viet Minh unity appeal and Communist subversive activities will be complicated at the outset by the strong resentment of Vietnamese nationalists over the partitioning of Vietnam and the abandoning of Tonkin to Communist control. It may be difficult to convince many Vietnamese troops, political leaders, and administrative personnel in Tonkin to go south, let alone to assist actively in the development of an effective administration in South Vietnam.

26. Developments in South Vietnam will also depend in large part on French courses of action. Prospects for stability in South Vietnam would be considerably enhanced if the French acted swiftly to insure Vietnam full independence and to encourage strong nationalist leadership. If this were done, anti-French nationalist activity might be lessened. With French military and economic assistance—backed by US aid—the Vietnamese could proceed to develop gradually an effective security force, local government organization, and a long-range program for economic and social reform. Nevertheless, it will be very difficult for the French to furnish the degree of assistance which will be required without at the same time reviving anti-French feeling to the point of endangering the whole effort.

27. On the basis of the evidence we have at this early date, however, we believe that a favorable development of the situation in South Vietnam is unlikely. Unless Mendès-Frances is able to overcome the force of French traditional interests and emotions which have in the past governed the implementation of policy in Indochina, we do not believe there will be the dramatic transformation in

French policy necessary to win the active loyalty and support of the local population for a South Vietnam Government.

At the present time, it appears more likely that the situation will deteriorate in South Vietnam and that the withdrawal from Tonkin will involve recriminations, distrust, and possibly violence. There will be delays in the development of effective administration in the south; the French military will probably be forced to retain a large measure of control for reasons of "security"; and efforts by French colonial interests to develop a puppet Cochin-China state will persist. It is even possible that at some point during the next two years the South Vietnam Government could be taken over by elements that would seek unification with the Viet Minh in the North even at the expense of Communist domination. Even "If the scheduled national elections are held in July 1956, and if the Viet Minh does not prejudice its political prospects, the Viet Minh will almost certainly win."

28. In the interim, Viet Minh propaganda will find ample opportunities to influence Vietnamese attitudes. Within a year, Viet Minh stay-behind units will probably be active politically, and possibly involved in open guerrilla fighting. In these circumstances, the French will probably be able to maintain their "presence" in South Vietnam through mid-1956, but their influence will probably become increasingly restricted to major cities and the perimeters of military installations and bases. The French might be willing to resolve this situation by an arrangement with the Communists which seemed to offer a chance of saving some remnant of the French economic and cultural position in Vietnam. Such an arrangement might include an agreement to hold early elections, even with the virtual certainty of Viet Minh victory. Only if such an arrangement proved impossible, and the situation deteriorated to the point of hopelessness, would the French withdraw completely from the country.

Source: *United States–Vietnam Relations, 1945–1967*, Book 10 (Washington, DC: U.S. Government Printing Office, 1971), 696–697.

90. NSC 5492/2, "Review of U.S. Policy in the Far East", August 20, 1954 [Excerpts]

Introduction

Regarding the recently concluded Geneva Conference as a blow to U.S. prestige and a sellout to the Communists who had provided them an "advance salient" for the future subversion of the non-Communist states of Southeast Asia, the Dwight D. Eisenhower administration sought countermeasures. This National Security Council (NSC) review of U.S. Far Eastern policy calls for the creation of an Asian counterpart to the North Atlantic Treaty Organization (NATO) in Europe that would shore up the non-Communist states of the region and the initiation of "covert operations" to subvert Communist rule in the Democratic Republic of Vietnam (DRV, North Vietnam).

Primary Source

Preface

Consequences of the Geneva Conference

Communist successes in Indochina, culminating in the agreement reached at the Geneva Conference, have produced the following significant consequences which jeopardize the security interests of the U.S. in the Far East and increase Communist strength there:

a. Regardless of the fate of South Vietnam, Laos and Cambodia, the Communists have secured possession of an advance salient in Vietnam from which military and non-military pressures can be mounted against adjacent and more remote non-Communist areas.

b. The loss of prestige in Asia suffered by the U.S. as a backer of the French and the Bao Dai Government will raise further doubts in Asia concerning U.S. leadership and the ability of the U.S. to check the further expansion of Communism in Asia. Furthermore, U.S. prestige will inescapably be associated with subsequent developments in Southeast Asia.

c. By adopting an appearance of moderation at Geneva and taking credit for the cessation of hostilities in Indochina, the Communists will be in a better position to exploit their political strategy of imputing to the United States motives of extremism, belligerency, and opposition to co-existence seeking thereby to alienate the U.S. from its allies. The Communists thus have a basis for sharply accentuating their "peace propaganda" and "peace program" in Asia in an attempt to allay fears of Communist expansionist policy and to establish closer relations with the nations of free Asia.

d. The Communists have increased their military and political prestige in Asia and their capacity for expanding Communist influence by exploiting political and economic weakness and instability in the countries of free Asia without resort to armed attack.

e. The loss of Southeast Asia would imperil retention of Japan as a key element in the off-shore island chain.

Courses of Action

I. Communist China

1. Reduce the power of Communist China in Asia even at the risk of, but without deliberately provoking, war:

a.
  (1) React with force, if necessary and advantageous, to expansion and subversion recognizable as such, supported and supplied by Communist China.
  (2) React with immediate, positive, armed force against any belligerent move by Communist China.

b. Increase efforts to develop the political economic and military strength of non-Communist Asian countries, including the progressive development of the military strength of Japan to the point where she can provide for her own national defense, and, in time, contribute to the collective defense of the Far East.

c. Maintain political and economic pressures against Communist China, including the existing embargo and support for Chinese Nationalist harassing actions.

d. Support the Chinese National Government on Formosa as the Government of China and the representative of China in all UN agencies.

e. Create internal division in the Chinese Communist regime and impair Sino-Soviet relations by all feasible overt and covert means.

[. . .]

IV. Southeast Asia

7. *General.* The U.S. must protect its position and restore its prestige in the Far East by a new initiative in Southeast Asia, where the situation must be stabilized as soon as possible to prevent further losses to Communism through (1) creeping expansion and subversion, or (2) overt aggression.

8. *Security Treaty.* Negotiate a Southeast Asia security treaty with the UK, Australia, New Zealand, France, the Philippines, Thailand and, as appropriate, other free South and Southeast Asian countries willing to participate, which would:

a. Commit each member to treat an armed attack on the agreed area (including Laos, Cambodia and South Vietnam) as dangerous to its own peace, safety and vital interests, and to act promptly to meet the common danger in accordance with its own constitutional processes.

b. Provide so far as possible a legal basis to the President to order attack on Communist China in the event it commits such armed aggression which endangers the peace, safety and vital interests of the United States.

c. Ensure that, in such event, other nations would be obligated in accordance with the treaty to support such U.S. action.

d. Not limit U.S. freedom to use nuclear weapons, or involve a U.S. commitment for local defense or for stationing U.S. forces in Southeast Asia.

The U.S. would continue to provide limited military assistance and training missions, wherever possible, to the states of Southeast Asia in order to bolster their will to fight, to stabilize legal governments, and to assist them in controlling subversion.

9. *Action in the Event of Local Subversion.* If requested by a legitimate local government which requires assistance to defeat local Communist subversion or rebellion not constituting armed attack, the U.S. should view such a situation so gravely that, in addition to giving all possible covert and overt support within Executive Branch authority, the President should at once consider requesting Congressional authority to take appropriate action, which might if necessary and feasible include the use of U.S. military forces either locally or against the external source of such subversion or rebellion (including Communist China if determined to be the source).

10. *Indochina: Political and Covert Action.*

    a. Make every possible effort, not openly inconsistent with the U.S. position as to the armistice agreements, to defeat Communist subversion and influence, to maintain and support friendly non-Communist governments in Cambodia and Laos to maintain a friendly non-Communist South Vietnam, and to prevent a Communist victory through all-Vietnam elections.

    b. Urge that the French promptly recognize and deal with Cambodia, Laos and free Vietnam as independent sovereign nations.

    c. Strengthen U.S. representation and deal directly, wherever advantageous to the U.S., with the governments of Cambodia, Laos, and free Vietnam.

    d. Working through the French only insofar as necessary, assist Cambodia, Laos and free Vietnam to maintain (1) military forces necessary for internal security and (2) economic conditions conducive to the maintenance and strength of non-Communist regimes and comparing favorably with those in adjacent Communist areas.

    e. Aid emigration from North Vietnam and resettlement of peoples unwilling to remain under Communist rule.

    f. Exploit available means to make more difficult the control by the Viet Minh of North Vietnam.

    g. Exploit available means to prevent North Vietnam from becoming permanently incorporated in the Soviet block, using as feasible and desirable consular relations and non-strategic trade.

    h. Conduct covert operations on a large and effective scale in support of the foregoing policies.

Source: *United States–Vietnam Relations, 1945–1967,* Book 10 (Washington, DC: U.S. Government Printing Office, 1971), 731–733, 736–737.

91. Protocol to the SEATO Treaty, September 8, 1954

Introduction

The United States took the lead in the creation of a regional collective security alliance, known as the Southeast Asia Treaty Organization (SEATO). Unlike the North Atlantic Treaty Organization (NATO), SEATO had no standing military force, and there was no specific action required in the event of hostile action. SEATO's members—the United States, France, Britain, New Zealand, Australia, Pakistan, the Philippines, and Thailand—pledged themselves only to "act to meet the common danger" in the event of aggression against any signatory state. A separate protocol extended the treaty's security provisions to Laos, Cambodia, and the "free territory under the jurisdiction of the State of Vietnam."

Primary Source

Designation of States and Territory as to Which Provisions of Article IV and Article III are to be Applicable.

The Parties to the Southeast Asia Collective Defense Treaty unanimously designate for the purposes of Article IV of the Treaty the States of Cambodia and Laos and the free territory under the jurisdiction of the State of Vietnam.

The Parties further agree that the above mentioned states and territory shall be eligible in respect of the economic measures contemplated by Article III.

This Protocol shall enter into force simultaneously with the coming into force of the Treaty.

IN WITNESS WHEREOF, the undersigned Plenipotentiaries have signed this Protocol to the Southeast Asia Collective Defense Treaty.

Done at Manila, this eighth day of September, 1954.

    Source: "Protocol to the Southeast Asia Collective Defense Treaty," *Department of State Bulletin* 31(795) (1954): 395–396.

92. President Dwight Eisenhower: Letter to Ngo Dinh Diem, October 23, 1954

Introduction

Ngo Dinh Diem was premier of the State of Vietnam (SVN). A Catholic in a predominantly Buddhist country, he had powerful support in the United States. Nonetheless, Diem's hold on power appeared tenuous. Opposing him were other political figures as well as the

Binh Xuyen gangsters in Saigon and religious sects that had been armed by the French. Diem also clashed with army chief of staff General Nguyen Van Hinh, who talked openly about a coup. Critical to Diem's survival was U.S. president Dwight D. Eisenhower's decision in October to channel all U.S. aid directly to Diem's government. This greatly upset the French, for it undercut their remaining authority in southern Vietnam. In November, Eisenhower sent former U.S. Army chief of staff General J. Lawton Collins to southern Vietnam as special ambassador with authority over all U.S. government agencies in Vietnam. Collins arrived there in early November and stated that Washington would deal only with Diem. At the end of November, Hinh left Vietnam for exile in France.

Primary Source

Dear Mr. President:

I have been following with great interest the course of developments in Vietnam, particularly since the conclusion of the conference at Geneva. The implications of the agreement concerning Vietnam have caused grave concern regarding the future of the country temporarily divided by an artificial military grouping, weakened by a long and exhausting war, and faced with enemies without and by their subversive collaborators within.

Your recent requests for aid to assist in the formidable project of the movement of several hundred thousand loyal Vietnamese citizens away from areas which are passing under a de facto rule and political ideology which they abhor, are being fulfilled. I am glad that the United States is able to assist in this humanitarian effort.

We have been exploring ways and means to permit our aid to Vietnam to be more effective and to make a greater contribution to the welfare and stability of the Government of Vietnam. I am, accordingly, instructing the American Ambassador to Vietnam [Donald R. Heath] to examine with you in your capacity as Chief of Government, how an intelligent program of American aid given directly to your Government can serve to assist Vietnam in its present hour of trial, provided that your Government is prepared to give assurances as to the standards of performance it would be able to maintain in the event such aid were supplied.

The purpose of this offer is to assist the Government of Vietnam in developing and maintaining a strong, viable state, capable of resisting attempted subversion or aggression through military means. The Government of the United States expects that this aid will be met by performance on the part of the Government of Vietnam in undertaking needed reforms. It hopes that such aid, combined with your own continuing efforts, will contribute effectively toward an independent Vietnam endowed with a strong Government. Such a Government would, I hope, be so responsive to the nationalist aspirations of its people, so enlightened in purpose and effective in performance, that it will be respected at home and abroad and discourage any who might wish to impose a foreign ideology on your free people.

Source: "U.S. Aid to Viet-Nam," *Department of State Bulletin* 31(303) (1954): 735–736.

93. Democratic Republic of Vietnam: Declaration on Normalizing Relations between the Northern and Southern Zones, February 4, 1955

Introduction

With the full support of the U.S. government, Ngo Dinh Diem, premier of the State of Vietnam (SVN), refused to enter into talks called for by the 1954 Geneva Agreements to prepare for the planned July 1956 elections to reunify Vietnam. The government of the Democratic Republic of Vietnam (DRV, North Vietnam) stressed that Vietnam was one nation and that the North Vietnamese government was making every effort to normalize relations between the two Vietnamese states, including entering into agreements with southern Vietnam on a wide range of economic, social, and cultural matters.

Primary Source

Following the appeal made by President Ho-Chi-Minh on New Year's Day, the Council of Ministers of the Democratic Republic of Viet-nam has, in its session early in February 1955, considered the question of restoring normal relations between North and South Viet-nam on either side of the provisional military demarcation line. The Council holds that:

1—Viet-nam is a unified country from the North to the South. The political, economic, cultural, social and sentimental relations and the solidarity of the Vietnamese people are indivisible. During the eight to nine years of the patriotic war, the Vietnamese people from the North to the South have heroically fought to restore peace and struggled together to build up the Fatherland. That is why, after the implementation of the armistice and pending the general elections to bring about the reunification of the country, the reestablishment of normal relations between the Northern and Southern zones fully conforms to the earnest aspiration of the various strata of the population in the two zones and is indispensable for the restoration of a normal and prosperous life of the Vietnamese people throughout the country;

2—The restoration of normal relations between the two zones is in complete conformity with the spirit of the Geneva Armistice Agreement.

The first sentence of the Agreement on the cessation of hostilities in Vietnam stipulates that the demarcation line, on either side of which the forces of the two parties shall be regrouped after their withdrawal, is only provisional.

The Final Declaration of the Geneva Conference clearly mentioned that: "The military demarcation line should not in any way be interpreted as constituting a political or territorial boundary".

The restoration of relations between the two zones does not infringe upon the administrative control of each side. On the contrary, it will provide the authorities of both sides with good opportunity for mutual understanding, thereby creating "the necessary basis for the achievement of a political settlement in Viet-nam," as stipulated in the Final Declaration of the Geneva Conference.

Due to the above-mentioned reasons the Government of the Democratic Republic of Viet-nam declares that:

1—Responding to the earnest desire of the Vietnamese people and in conformity with the spirit of the Geneva Armistice Agreement, the Government of the Democratic Republic of Viet-nam is disposed to grant all facilities to the people in the Northern and Southern zones on either side of the provisional military demarcation line in sending mail, moving, carrying out business or enterprises from one zone to the other, and in exchanging cultural, artistic, scientific, technical, sporting and other activities. The Government of the Democratic Republic of Viet-nam fully encourages and helps the population in the two zones in all economic, cultural and social exchanges advantageous for the restoration of normal life of the people,

2—The Government of the Democratic Republic of Viet-nam hopes that the authorities in South Viet-nam will agree to the restoration of normal relations between the Northern and Southern zones with a view to bringing about solutions favourable for the entire people.

Source: *Documents Related to the Implementation of the Geneva Agreements Concerning Viet-Nam* (Hanoi: Democratic Republic of Vietnam, Ministry of Foreign Affairs, Press and Information Department, 1956), 33–35.

94. John Foster Dulles, Secretary of State: Telegram to the Embassy in Saigon, April 6, 1955 [Excerpt]

Introduction

The U.S. government strongly supported Premier Ngo Dinh Diem of the State of Vietnam (SVN) in his opposition to the free elections, scheduled for July 1956, that were called for by the 1954

Geneva Agreements to reunite the two Vietnamese states. Diem steadfastly refused to enter into the talks that were a necessary prerequisite for the elections. The Dwight D. Eisenhower administration believed that Ho Chi Minh and the Communists would win any free elections. The dilemma for the Eisenhower administration was that while it supported democratic institutions, the Communist regimes had refused to allow free elections once they had come to power. How far the United States was prepared to go on this matter can be seen in this cable from Secretary of State John Foster Dulles to the U.S. embassy in Saigon. Dulles suggests that the U.S. approach to the elections should be that of insisting on "safeguards" and that these should be couched in language that the Communist will have to reject.

Primary Source

FYI. We have been working on problem of elections in Viet-Nam, in great detail over last several weeks. NSC has asked Department submit policy for consideration by mid-April and we sure that elections will be discussed during proposed U.S-French talks Washington April 20. The British have offered give use their views on elections prior these talks.

We feel best solution is for us be in position inform French British our views prior talks and believe it best we can put such forward as support of policy of Free Viet-Nam rather than as unilateral U.S. recommendations.

Our proposal is based on Eden's plan put forward at Berlin-Conference for all German elections and has already been approved by France for use Germany and rejected by the Communists. The basic principle is that Free Viet-Nam will insist to the Viet Minh that unless agreement is first reached by the latter's acceptance of the safeguards spelled out, that no repeat no further discussions are possible regarding the type of elections, the issues to be voted on or any other factors.

After we have Diem's general acceptance we can proceed inform UK and France of this plan which we think only formula which ensures both satisfactory response to Geneva Agreement and at same time plan which is unassailable in intent but probably unacceptable to Communists because of provisions for strict compliance to ensure genuinely free elections. END FYI.

You should speak to Diem privately regarding elections, without showing him formula outlined next telegram. We are not now attempting secure his approval as such to our position but to assure he understands our viewpoint and accepts it to degree we can proceed with French British on broad assumption Free Viet-Nam's position similar our own.

Believe best way accomplish this is to remind him of his and foreign ministers conversations with Secretary on this subject and to continue that in specific cases of elections in Korea and Germany Free World has stood firm on issue of guarantees of genuine free elections, supervised by body having authority guarantee elements free elections PAREN outlined last paragraph following telegram UNPAREN. In each case Communists have refused accept these safeguards which we think basic and fundamental. We believe unless such guarantees previously agreed upon would be dangerous for Free Viet-Nam be drawn into further discussions of other issues of election. Ask Diem if we can assume our thinking is alike on this point.

Since time exceedingly important, hope we can have affirmative answer soonest.

Source: *United States–Vietnam Relations, 1945–1967*, Book 10 (Washington, DC: U.S. Government Printing Office, 1971), 892–893.

95. John Foster Dulles, Secretary of State: Telegram to Special Representative General J. Lawton Collins in Saigon, April 9, 1955

Introduction

Ngo Dinh Diem, premier of the State of Vietnam (SVN), was busy trying to consolidate his power in southern Vietnam. He found himself confronted by a host of opponents, including the Binh Xuyen gangsters who controlled much of the economic life of Saigon, the religious sects that had been armed by the French, and army chief of staff General Nguyen Van Hinh. The Dwight D. Eisenhower administration decided to send former U.S. Army chief of staff General J. Lawton Collins to southern Vietnam as special ambassador. He arrived in November 1954, announced that the United States would support only Diem, and soon arranged for Hinh's departure. Collins then drew up a plan to reform the SVN's army. The issue of army reform touched off a confrontation with the various opposition groups in southern Vietnam that maintained their own military formations. In March and April 1955, fighting erupted between Vietnamese army units loyal to Diem and the Binh Xuyen. Diem adroitly splintered the opposition, and his liberal use of bribes bought off many of those opposed to his rule. By the end of May, government troops had driven the remaining Binh Xuyen from Saigon. Still, Diem's struggle with the religious sects such as the Cao Dai and Hoa Hao led Collins to reconsider his support. Collins believed that Diem lacked the ability to govern and called on the State Department to replace him with a coalition government. In this telegram, Secretary of State John Foster Dulles informs Collins that Washington is inclined to support Diem.

Primary Source

Have this morning discussed situation with highest authority. We are disposed to back whatever your final decision is but before you actually finalize we want to be sure you have weighed all of the factors which concern us here.

We feel that what has happened does not reveal anything new about Diem but rather a basic and dangerous misunderstanding as between France and the U.S.

We have always known the qualities which Diem possesses and those which he lacks. Nevertheless our two countries agreed to support him in default of anyone possessing better qualifications. The only alternatives now suggested are the same persons who were regarded as unacceptable substitutes some months ago.

What has happened is that whereas the United States has been proceeding on the assumption that Diem would be backed as against any who might challenge him assuming that he had the capability, apparently the French have given their support only on the assumption that the Binh Xuyen would also be supported on an autonomous authority and that when they challenged Diem he would not be allowed to use force to assert his authority over it.

We can appreciate the reluctance of the French to see force used but if it cannot be used then what is the point of our supporting at great cost the national army which I thought it had been agreed was primarily to be an army for domestic security rather than an army to fight external aggression.

U.S. recognizes that the Cao Dai and even the Hoa Hao are genuine sects with cultural religious and political roots which cannot be forcibly torn up without grave consequences which should be avoided but we do not believe that any central government can exist as more than a figurehead if it does not have control over the national police and if this control is farmed out to a gang which exploits its privileges to protect vice on a vastly profitable scale and which exists by virtue of the backing of the self-exiled Bao Dai and the French.

We cannot see that replacement of Diem by any persons you mentioned will of itself correct this situation and indeed we have had the impression that Quat was less acceptable to the sects than is Diem.

There are two other factors to be borne in mind.

One is that it is widely known that Diem has so far existed by reason of U.S support despite French reluctance. If, however, when the showdown comes the French view prevails then that will gravely weaken our influence for the future both in Vietnam and elsewhere. Removal of Diem under these circumstances may well be interpreted in Vietnam and Asia as example of U.S. paying lip service to nationalist cause and then forsaking true nationalist leader when QUOTE colonial interests UNQUOTE put enough pressure on us.

The French constantly assert that the U.S. has a primary responsibility in this part of the world but it is difficult to have responsibility without authority. In essence, will not the ouster of Diem on the present conditions mean that from now on we will be merely paying the bill and the French will be calling the tune. Any successor of Diem will clearly know where the real authority lies.

The second factor is that there will be very strong opposition in the Congress to supporting the situation in Indochina generally and Vietnam in particular if Diem is replaced under existing circumstances. We do not say that this opposition may not in the last instance be overcome, particularly if you personally can make a case before the Congressional committees but Mansfield who is looked upon with great respect by his colleagues with reference to this matter, is adamantly opposed to abandonment of Diem under present conditions. I wonder whether there is not some intermediate solution between the present extremes now discussed and that Diem can be allowed to regain his damaged prestige by an assertion of authority over the Binh Xuyen and at the same time other elements be brought into the government under conditions which will assure a real delegation of authority.

I feel that as with most Orientals Diem must be highly suspicious of what is going on about him and that this suspicion exaggerates his natural disposition to be secretive and untrustful. If he ever really felt that the French and ourselves were solidly behind him might he not really broaden his government? We must I think have some sympathy for his predicament as he is constantly called QUOTE the Diem experiment UNQUOTE.

In conclusion I want to reaffirm the very great confidence which we all have in you and in your judgment. You have done and are doing a wonderful job in the face of tremendous difficulties.

Your 4448 has just arrived in Department but is not yet decoded. We will comment on it in subsequent telegram.

Source: *United States–Vietnam Relations, 1945–1967*, Book 10 (Washington, DC: U.S. Government Printing Office, 1971), 907–909.

96. NSC 5519, Draft Statement and National Security Council Staff Study on U.S. Policy on All-Vietnam Elections, May 17, 1955 [Excerpts]

Introduction

The Dwight D. Eisenhower administration opposed the elections called for by the 1954 Geneva Agreements to reunite the two Vietnams. While admitting that Ho Chi Minh and the Communists would have the advantage in the elections, the National Security Council (NSC) staff urges that the United States not be seen as summarily rejecting the elections because of the adverse impact this will have in the Republic of Vietnam (RVN, South Vietnam) and on world opinion.

Primary Source

General Considerations

1. It is U.S. policy to maintain a friendly non-Communist Free Vietnam; to assist Free Vietnam to maintain (a) military forces necessary for internal security, and (b) economic conditions conducive to the maintenance of the strength of the non-Communist regime; and to prevent a Communist victory through all-Vietnam elections.

2. Free Vietnamese strength is essential to any effective approach to the election problem. If Free Vietnam is to cope adequately with national elections it will have to be strong enough to deter or defeat Vietminh insurrections in its territory, to impose and sustain order in its territory, and, to win a free election limited to its own zone and held under its own auspices and control. Otherwise, the Vietminh can take over through internal insurrections or the Government of Free Vietnam will be so weak that it will find it difficult even to give lip service to the idea of national unification through elections, or to insist on adequate conditions for free elections.

3. U.S. policy toward all-Vietnam elections should be predicated on the assumption that there is a possibility of assisting Free Vietnam to achieve the degree of strength described above. If it becomes clear that Free Vietnam cannot achieve such strength, U.S. policy toward Free Vietnam should be reviewed.

4. U.S. Policy must also protect against a Communist take-over of Free Vietnam, even if the Communists were able to win elections under safeguards in North Vietnam. On the other hand, U.S. policy should be prepared to take advantage of the unlikely possibility that North Vietnam might be freed through elections.

Courses of Action

5. Continue to encourage the Government of Free Vietnam to proceed with the consultations about elections called for in July 1955 by the Geneva Agreements.

6. Provide the Government of Free Vietnam with information and advice about Communist positions and tactics with regard to elections elsewhere, e.g., Greece, Germany, Austria and Korea.

7. Assist the Government of Free Vietnam to make it clear that any failure to secure free elections is the fault of the Communists.

8. Encourage the Government of Free Vietnam:

    a. To lay stress on the necessity of compliance with the stipulation of the Geneva Agreements that "all the necessary conditions obtain for free expression of the national will" before all-Vietnam elections can take place. For this purpose the Government of Free Vietnam should insist in the first instance on adequate guarantees of freedom of elections and adequate supervisory powers in a Supervisory Commission.

    b. To adopt positions with respect to the objectives and details of elections which: (1) will avoid terms which would be likely to result in a Communist take-over of Free Vietnam; and (2) to the degree feasible, will maintain a position generally consistent with that adopted by the Free World in other areas such as Korea and Germany.

9. Seek British and French support for the foregoing courses of action.

10. If pursuit of the above policy should result in a renewal of hostilities by the Communists, the U.S., in the light of the general circumstances then prevailing, should be prepared to oppose any Communist attack with U.S. armed forces, if necessary and feasible—consulting the Congress in advance if the emergency permits—preferably in concert with the Manila Pact allies of the U.S., but if necessary alone.

The Problem

Difficulties Involved in Elections

[. . .]

4. The Communists would hold certain advantages in all Vietnam elections, particularly if such elections were not held under conditions of complete freedom and rigorous supervision: (a) Communist popular appeal derived from long identification with the struggle for independence; (b) the greater organizational capacity of the Communists to influence elections through propaganda, control, and coercion; (c) the continuing difficulties of the Free Vietnam Government in consolidating its political control in its own zone and moving ahead with programs of popular appeal.

Problems Involved in Avoiding the Elections

5. Despite these Communist advantages, there are a number of factors which have led the U.S. to encourage Free Vietnam to agree to the preliminary consultations stipulated in the Geneva Agreements in order to determine whether the conditions of free elections and international supervision can be met.

    a. Free Vietnam has already suffered in its contest with the Communists from the fact that the Communists have been able, largely because of the French position in Vietnam, to pre-empt for themselves identification with the slogan of national independence. Actions by Free Vietnam which were clearly directed towards avoiding elections would be seized on by the Communists to demonstrate that Free Vietnam was opposed to unification. To allow the Communists to pose as the sole champions of national unification would greatly increase the problems of Free Vietnam in securing popular support.

    b. The over-all United States position in the world would be harmed by U.S. identification with a policy which appeared to be directed towards avoidance of elections. World public opinion, and for that matter domestic U.S. opinion, would have difficulty in understanding why the U.S. should oppose in Vietnam the democratic procedures which the U.S. has advocated for Korea, Austria and Germany.

    c. It is clear that both the French and the British believe themselves committed as signatories of the Geneva Agreements to a program of encouraging the holding of elections. In addition, the French fear that failure to hold elections would provoke a resumption of hostilities by the Vietminh in which France would be directly and involuntarily involved due to the probable presence of at least large numbers of the French Expeditionary Corps through 1955 and the first half of 1956.

[. . .]

Free Vietnam Position in Election Negotiations

7. It will be advantageous to the U.S. if Free Vietnam, in negotiating on elections with the Communists, adopts a position which: (a) will avoid terms which would be likely to result in a Communist takeover of Free Vietnam; (b) will, to the degree feasible, maintain a position generally consistent with that adopted by the Free World in other areas such as Korea and Germany.

8. In negotiating for conditions of genuine freedom for the holding of elections, Free Vietnam can serve both these objectives by insisting on provisions such as those already supported by the Western Powers at Berlin: Agreement on safeguards to assure conditions of genuine freedom before, after, and during elections; full powers for any Supervisory Commission to act to ensure free elections and to guarantee against prior coercion or subsequent reprisal; adequate guarantees for, among other things, freedom of movement, freedom of presentation of candidates, immunity of candidates, freedom from arbitrary arrest or victimization, freedom of association and political meetings, freedom of expression for all, freedom of press, radio, and free circulation of newspapers,

secrecy of vote, security of polling stations and ballot boxes. The Communists would find it most difficult to accept such conditions or to allow their implementation if accepted. Accordingly, it would be useful for the Free Vietnamese to center their position on securing agreement to conditions for free elections prior to discussion of the forms and objectives of the elections.

9. If the negotiations extend to the subjects of the forms and objectives of elections it will be more difficult for Free Vietnam to adopt positions which clearly protect the interests of Free Vietnam and at the same time are completely consistent with Free World positions on Germany or Korea. Free Vietnam is probably slightly less populous than North Vietnam (although there has been a substantial refugee movement to the South and there are no firm population statistics), so that representation proportionate to population, which we have insisted on in other areas, would be less advantageous in Vietnam than would be equal representation from the two zones. Limitation of the functions of any elected body solely to drafting of a constitution would be clearly desirable in the case of Vietnam, while in other areas we are considering bodies which may have additional functions. It would be advantageous for the Free Vietnam Government to reserve the power to accept or reject any constitution that might be agreed upon in an elected constituent assembly. Such a position is probably not desirable in the other areas. In general, however, it should be possible to devise positions with regard to the details and objectives of elections which would safeguard the non-Communist position of Free Vietnam without violating important principles on which the U.S. is standing elsewhere. Insistence on limiting the powers of any elected body to drafting a constitution, or insisting on a census prior to agreeing to number of representatives, would not, for example, weaken the U.S. position with respect to either German or Korean elections.

Document declassified by the National Security Council, May 11, 1977.

Source: *Foreign Relations of the United States, 1955–1957: Vietnam,* Vol. 1 (Washington, DC: U.S. Government Printing Office, 1985), 411–412.

97. Message from Ho Chi Minh and Foreign Minister Pham Van Dong to the Chief of State of the Republic of Vietnam, July 19, 1955

Introduction

One day before the deadline for the start of talks to discuss the elections to reunite the two Vietnamese states, as specified by the 1954 Geneva Agreements, the leaders of the Democratic Republic of Vietnam (DRV, North Vietnam) sent this message to leaders of the Republic of Vietnam (RVN, South Vietnam) calling on them to name their representatives to the talks. The deadline passed without this occurring.

Primary Source

The holding on schedule of the consultative conference by the competent authorities of the North and the South is of great importance, and has a bearing not only on the prospect of the unity of our country but also on the loyal implementation of the Geneva Agreements, and the consolidation of peace in Indo-China and in the world.

Following the June 6, 1955 declaration by the Government of the Democratic Republic of Viet-nam, Sai-gon Radio on July 16, 1955, made known the "position of the Government of the State of Viet-nam on the problem of general elections for the unification of the national territory". The statement mentioned general elections and reunification but did not touch upon a very important and most realistic issue, that of the meeting of the competent representative authorities of the two zones, of the holding of the consultative conference on the question of general elections and reunification, as provided for by the Geneva Agreements. Moreover there were in the statement things which are untrue and which would not help to create a favourable climate for the convening of the consultative conference.

Our compatriots from the South to the North, irrespective of classes, creeds and political affiliations have deeply at heart the reunification of the country, and are looking forward to the early convening of the consultative conference and to its good outcome. All the countries responsible for the guarantee of the implementation of the Geneva Agreements and in general all the peace-loving countries in the world are anxious to see that the consultative conference will be held and yield good results and that the reunification of our country will be achieved.

The Government of the Democratic Republic of Viet-nam proposes that you appoint your representatives and that they and ours hold the consultative conference from July 20, 1955 onwards, as provided for by the Geneva Agreements, at a place agreeable to both sides, on the Vietnamese territory, in order to discuss the problem of reunification of our country by means of free general elections all over Viet-nam.

Source: *Documents Related to the Implementation of the Geneva Agreements Concerning Viet-nam* (Hanoi: Democratic Republic of Vietnam, Ministry of Foreign Affairs, Press and Information Department, 1956), 41–44.

98. NIE 63-1-55, "Probable Developments in North Vietnam to July 1956", July 19, 1955 [Excerpts]

Introduction

With the issue of the July 1956 elections holding center stage, this U.S. National Intelligence Estimate (NIE) holds that the leadership of the Democratic Republic of Vietnam (DRV, North Vietnam) will be willing to hold "neutral" supervision of the elections but not "complex and elaborate safeguards and guarantees." The NIE does not, however, rule out the possibility of North Vietnam initiating guerrilla activity in the Republic of Vietnam (RVN, South Vietnam) should the elections not occur.

Primary Source

The Problem

To analyze the present strengths and weaknesses of North Vietnam and to estimate probable future developments and trends to July 1956.

Conclusions

1. The immediate concern of the "Democratic Republic of Vietnam" (DRV) is to consolidate its control in the area north of the 17th Parallel and to gain control of South Vietnam. (Para. 14)

2. We believe that the DRV will experience no great difficulty in maintaining effective control of North Vietnam during the period of this estimate and will probably retain a considerable measure of prestige and general acceptance. However, passive resistance and discontent resulting from harsh control measures and poor economic conditions may increase toward the end of the period. If the situation in the South does not deteriorate, the nationalist appeal of Ho Chi Minh and the DRV will probably be reduced throughout Vietnam. (Para. 23)

3. The DRV is confronted by serious economic problems of which the current rice shortage is the most critical. Its present export potential falls far short of providing sufficient funds to pay for necessary imports. However, the Sino-Soviet Bloc will almost certainly provide sufficient economic and technical assistance to meet minimum requirements for stability and control. With such assistance the DRV will probably make gradual progress in gaining control of the economy and in rehabilitating transportation, irrigation, and industrial facilities. (Paras. 24–30)

4. Since the Geneva Conference, the strength of the DRV regular army has been increased substantially by drawing on regional forces to form new units and by the receipt of new and heavier military equipment from Communist China. DRV forces are capable of defeating all military forces, including the French, now located in South Vietnam, Laos, and Cambodia. (Paras. 31–35)

5. The present DRV tactic with respect to South Vietnam is to pose as the champion of Vietnamese independence and unification, and as the defender of the provisions of the Geneva Agreement. The DRV probably still believes that it could emerge from free nationwide elections with control of all Vietnam. It will attempt to appear reasonable in any negotiations concerning procedures for elections. While the Communists almost certainly would not agree to complex and elaborate safeguards and guarantees, they probably would agree to some form of "neutral" (but not UN) supervision. They would probably estimate that such election controls would work to their advantage in the South and, as manipulated, would not adversely affect their position in the North. (Paras. 44–45)

6. In the meantime, the DRV will continue its efforts, through subversion, intimidation, and propaganda, to weaken the Diem government, and to bring to power in the South men prepared to accept a coalition with the DRV. (Para. 46)

7. The Communists in their propaganda have revealed sensitivity to the implication of the Manila Pact which incorporated Vietnam, Cambodia, and Laos in its area of protection. We believe that concern for Western, and particularly US reactions, together with general considerations arising from over-all Bloc policy, will prevent the DRV from openly invading the South during the period of this estimate. Similarly, the resumption of widespread guerrilla activities appears unlikely prior to the election deadline, unless the DRV should come to the conclusion that South Vietnam can be won only by force. Such a conclusion would become more likely should the Diem government persist in refusing to enter the election discussions, should election discussions not proceed favorably for the DRV, or should the Diem government succeed, with US assistance, in consolidating its strength to the point of becoming a nationalist alternative to the Ho regime. Moreover, if during the period of this estimate little progress is made towards relaxing tensions, Peiping and Moscow might permit the DRV greater freedom of action. Should the DRV decide to use force short of open invasion, it would probably attempt to undermine the Saigon government by initiating a campaign of sabotage and terror, seeking to [sic] formation of a new government more amenable to demands for a national coalition. These tactics are likely to include the activation of DRV guerrilla units now in South Vietnam and their reinforcement by the infiltration in small units of regulars from the North. (Para. 47)

[. . .]

Source: *United States–Vietnam Relations, 1945–1967*, Book 10 (Washington, DC: U.S. Government Printing Office, 1971), 994–996.

99. Declaration of the Government of the Republic of Vietnam on Reunification, August 9, 1955

Introduction

His position in the Republic of Vietnam (RVN, South Vietnam) now considerably strengthened, Premier Ngo Dinh Diem in August 1955 summarily rejected the holding of national elections to reunite the two Vietnams as called for by the 1954 Geneva Agreements. With the full support of the U.S. government, Diem declares that while his government supported the principle of national unity, it had not been a party to the Geneva Agreements and thus was not bound by them. He also rejects diplomatic relations with the Democratic Republic of Vietnam (DRV, North Vietnam), where "under the rule of the Vietnamese Communists, the citizens do not enjoy democratic freedoms and fundamental human rights."

Primary Source

Republic of Vietnam Statement on Reunification

In the last July 1955 broadcast, the Vietnamese national Government has made it clear its position towards the problem of territorial unity.

The Government does not consider itself bound in any respect by the Geneva Agreements which it did not sign.

Once more, the Government reasserts that in any circumstance, it places national interests above all, being resolved to achieve at all cost the obvious aim it is pursuing and eventually to achieve national unity, peace and freedom.

The Viet-Minh leaders have had a note dated July 19 transmitted to the Government, in which they asked for the convening of a consultative conference on general elections. This is just a propaganda move aimed at making the people believe that they are the champions of our territorial unity. Everyone still remembers that last year at Geneva, the Vietnamese Communists boisterously advocated the partition of our territory and asked for an economically self-sufficient area whereas the delegation of the State of Viet-nam proposed an armistice without any partition, not even provisional, with a view to safeguarding the sacred rights of the Vietnamese national and territorial unity, national independence and individual freedom. As the Vietnamese delegation states, the Vietnamese Government then stood for the fulfillment of national aspirations by the means which have been given back to Viet-nam by the French solemn recognition of the independence and sovereignty of Viet-nam, as a legal, independent state.

The policy of the Government remains unchanged. Confronted with the partition of the country, which is contrary to the will of the entire people, the Government will see to it that everybody throughout the country may live free from fear, and completely free from all totalitarian oppression. As a champion of justice, of genuine democracy, the Government always holds that the principle of free general election is a peaceful and democratic means only if, first of all, the freedom to live and freedom of vote is sufficiently guaranteed.

In this connection, nothing constructive can be contemplated in the present situation in the North where, under the rule of the Vietnamese Communists, the citizens do not enjoy democratic freedoms and fundamental human rights.

Source: *Documents Related to the Implementation of the Geneva Agreements Concerning Viet-nam* (Hanoi: Democratic Republic of Vietnam, Ministry of Foreign Affairs, Press and Information Department, 1956), 98–99.

100. NIE 63-56, July 17, 1956 [Excerpt]

Introduction

In the Republic of Vietnam (RVN, South Vietnam), Ngo Dinh Diem continued to consolidate his power. Not only was he able to defeat his political rivals, crush the Binh Xuyen gangsters, and neutralize the powerful religious sects, but he also bested Bao Dai. Chief of State Bao Dai, now living in France, named General Nguyen Van Vy, a well-known opponent of Diem, to command the Vietnamese National Army and summoned Diem to France for a meeting. Diem not only refused to go but now called for a referendum in which the people would choose between himself and Bao Dai. Diem would easily have won any honest contest, but he ignored U.S. appeals for such and falsified the results so that the vote was 98 percent in his favor. The announced vote in Saigon was actually a third more than the registered voters in the city. On October 26, 1955, using the results as justification, Diem proclaimed the Republic of Vietnam, with himself as president. In this National Intelligence Estimate (NIE) of the situation in Vietnam, the U.S. intelligence community concludes that the Democratic Republic of Vietnam (DRV, North Vietnam) would refrain from the use of force to achieve reunification, even though the date mandated in the Geneva Agreements for the elections to reunify Vietnam has passed without result. This conclusion was based on the presumed lack of Chinese and Soviet support for such a course because of the failure of the international Communist movement to demand that elections be held. Indeed, the U.S. intelligence community assumed that this implied recognition of Ngo Dinh Diem's Republic of Vietnam as part of the U.S. sphere of influence. (Note: In the document "ICC" refers to the International Control Commission of Canada, India, and Poland, charged by the Geneva Conference with supervising implementation of the 1954 Geneva Agreements, while "GVN" refers to the Government of Vietnam, that is, Diem's Republic of Vietnam.)

Primary Source

IV. The Outlook in Vietnam

Probable Communist Courses of Action Toward South Vietnam

64. The DRV probably estimates that its chances for securing control of South Vietnam by means short of open attack or large-scale guerrilla action supported from the North will gradually diminish with the passage of time. As indicated by Soviet and Chinese Communist performance in the past several months, the DRV probably cannot expect strong support from the Bloc for the "strict implementation" of the Geneva Agreements. The lack of strong Bloc pressure strengthens international acceptance of the status quo in Vietnam and increases confidence in the future in South Vietnam. Although the DRV may still believe that it could obtain control of all Vietnam through ICC supervised nationwide elections, Vietnamese Communist leaders are probably increasingly doubtful on this point because of their own internal difficulties and the growing nationalist stature of Diem. The DRV probably also believes that its covert assets in South Vietnam will gradually decline if the Diem government is permitted to concentrate on internal security and economic problems free of external harassment.

65. Despite the declining prospects for the "peaceful" take-over of South Vietnam, we believe that the USSR and Communist China will almost certainly continue unwilling to support open DRV military action against South Vietnam during the period of this estimate. They are probably unwilling to risk the chance of US or SEATO intervention which would make it difficult to limit the conflict to Vietnam, and probably believe that overt DRV military action would seriously undercut the worldwide effort of the Bloc to win friends and supporters. Although the DRV retains the capability to launch an independent military action against South Vietnam, the chances of such action in the absence of assured Bloc support appear to be extremely small.

66. The only remaining course of action holding out some promise for the early achievement of Communist control in South Vietnam appears to be the development of large scale guerrilla warfare in the south. In recent weeks a number of reports from sources of untested reliability have indicated that the Communists may have started preparations in both South Vietnam and in the north to begin guerrilla action. DRV allegations of Vietnamese violations of the demilitarized zone along the 17th parallel and Communist claims of US-Diem plans to violate the Armistice could be propaganda cover for the initiation of guerrilla action against the south.

67. However, the possible indications of armed action appear inconsistent with the DRV's insistence on the continued functioning of the ICC—which is in a position to make at least limited observations of DRV activities. Moreover, guerrilla action in South Vietnam, if it were to be sustained and not to result simply in the identification and gradual elimination of Communist cadres, would require large scale support from the north. This would involve some risk of detection by the ICC and of intervention by the US and possibly SEATO. It would also tend to prejudice current Communist maneuvers elsewhere in Asia. For these reasons, we believe that the DRV will refrain from instituting large scale guerrilla action within South Vietnam during the period of this estimate. Communist capabilities for guerrilla warfare in South Vietnam will exist for some time, however, and the chances of their being employed would probably increase in the event of any substantial deterioration in the domestic situation in South Vietnam—such as might conceivably occur on the death of Diem. The chances of Communist guerrilla warfare would also be increased by deterioration of the international aspects of the situation, such as a withdrawal of the ICC under circumstances which would permit the Communists to place the blame for this event on the GVN.

Source: *United States–Vietnam Relations, 1945–1967,* Book 10 (Washington, DC: U.S. Government Printing Office, 1971), 1078–1079.

101. Le Duan: "Duong Loi Cach Mang Mien Nam" [The Path of Revolution in the South], 1956

Introduction

Despite the passage of the July 1956 deadline for the elections to reunify Vietnam without them having occurred and with no talks scheduled, the Lao Dong (Workers' Party) in the Democratic Republic of Vietnam (DRV, North Vietnam) continued to hold that reunification could be achieved through the concept of "peaceful political struggle." In truth the North Vietnamese leadership was not displeased at Ngo Dinh Diem's consolidation of power in the Republic of Vietnam (RVN, South Vietnam) in which he had crushed dissident groups. In this November 1956 statement of policy, which was probably approved at the party presidium the next month, the party leader in South Vietnam, Le Duan, notes that the Soviet Union's Communist Party congress of February 1956 had held that revolution could occur peacefully. For the time being, North Vietnam should follow that line both because the sentiment for peace was so strong in South Vietnam and because the Diem regime could easily identify the Viet Minh political cadres who had remained behind there in accordance with the 1954 Geneva Agreements to prepare for the elections. This statement of peaceful revolutionary progress remained official Lao Dong policy for the next three years.

Primary Source

The situation forces bellicose states such as the U.S. and Britain to recognize that if they adventurously start a world war, they themselves will be the first to be destroyed, and thus the movement to demand peace in those imperialist countries is also developing strongly.

Recently, in the U.S Presidential election, the present Republican administration, in order to buy the people's esteem, put forward the slogan "Peace and Prosperity," which showed that even the people of an imperialist warlike country like the U.S. want peace.

The general situation shows us that the forces of peace and democracy in the world have tipped the balance toward the camp of peace and democracy. Therefore we can conclude that the world at present can maintain long-term peace.

On the other hand, however, we can also conclude that as long as the capitalist economy survives, it will always scheme to provoke war, and there will still remain the danger of war.

Based on the above the world situation, the Twentieth Congress of the Communist Party of the Soviet Union produced two important judgments:

1. All conflicts in the world at present can be resolved by means of peaceful negotiations.
2. The revolutionary movement in many countries at present can develop peacefully. Naturally in the countries in which the ruling class has a powerful military-police apparatus and is using fascist policies to repress the movement, the revolutionary parties in those countries must look clearly at their concrete situation to have the appropriate methods of struggle.

Based on the general situation and that judgment, we conclude that, if all conflicts can be resolved by means of peaceful negotiations, peace can be achieved.

Because the interest and aspiration of peaceful reunification of our country are the common interest and aspiration of all the people of the Northern and Southern zones, the people of the two zones did not have any reason to provoke war, nor to prolong the division of the country. On the contrary the people of the two zones are more and more determined to oppose the U.S.-Diem scheme of division and war provocation in order to create favorable conditions for negotiations between the two zones for peaceful unification of the country.

The present situation of division is created solely by the arbitrary U.S.-Diem regime, so the fundamental problem is how to smash the U.S.-Diem scheme of division and war-provocation.

As observed above, if they want to oppose the U.S-Diem regime, there is no other path for the people of the South but the path of revolution. What, then, is the line and struggle method of the revolutionary movement in the South? If the world situation can maintain peace due to a change in the relationship of forces in the world in favor of the camp of peace and democracy, the revolutionary movement can develop following a peaceful line, and the revolutionary movement in the South can also develop following a peaceful line.

First of all, we must determine what it means for a revolutionary movement to struggle according to a peaceful line. A revolutionary movement struggling according to a peaceful line takes the political forces of the people as the base rather than using people's armed forces to struggle with the existing government to achieve their revolutionary objective. A revolutionary movement struggling according to a peaceful line is also different from a reformist movement in that a reformist movement relies fundamentally on the law and constitution to struggle, while a revolutionary movement relies on the revolutionary political forces of the masses as the base. And another difference is that a revolutionary movement struggles for revolutionary objectives, while a reformist movement struggles for reformist goals.

With an imperialist, feudalist, dictatorial, fascist government like the U.S.-Diem, is it possible for a peaceful political struggle line to achieve its objectives?

We must recognize that all accomplishments in every country are due to the people. That is a definite law: it cannot be otherwise. Therefore the line of the revolutionary movement must be in accord with the inclinations and aspirations of the people. Only in that way can a revolutionary movement be mobilized and succeed.

The ardent aspiration of the Southern people is to maintain peace and achieve national unification. We must clearly recognize this longing for peace: the revolutionary movement in the South can mobilize and advance to success on the basis of grasping the flag of peace, in harmony with popular feelings. On the contrary, U.S.-Diem is using fascist violence to provoke war, contrary to the will of the people and therefore must certainly be defeated.

Can the U.S.-Diem regime, by using a clumsy policy of fascist violence, create a strong force to oppose and destroy the revolutionary movement? Definitely not, because the U.S.-Diem regime has no political strength in the country worth mentioning to rely on. On the contrary, nearly all strata of the people oppose them. Therefore the U.S.-Diem government is not a strong government it is only a vile and brutal government. Its vile and brutal character means that it not only has no mass base in the country but is on the way to being isolated internationally. Its cruelty definitely cannot shake the revolutionary movement, and it cannot survive for long.

The proof is that in the past two years, everywhere in the countryside, the sound of the gunfire of U.S.-Diem repression never ceased; not a day went by when they did not kill patriots, but the revolutionary spirit is still firm, and the revolutionary base of the people still has not been shaken.

Once the entire people have become determined to protect the revolution, there is no cruel force that can shake it. But why has the revolutionary movement not yet developed strongly? This is also due to certain objective and subjective factors. Objectively, we see that, after nine years of waging strong armed struggle, the people's movement generally speaking now has a temporarily peaceful character that is a factor in the change of the movement for violent forms of struggle to peaceful forms. It has the correct character of rebuilding to advance later.

With the cruel repression and exploitation of the U.S.-Diem, the people's revolutionary movement definitely will rise up. The people of the South have known the blood and fire of nine years of resistance war, but the cruelty of the U.S.-Diem cannot extinguish the struggle spirit of the people.

On the other hand, subjectively, we must admit that a large number of cadres, those have responsibility for guiding the revolutionary movement, because of the change in the method of struggle and the work situation from public to secret, have not yet firmly grasped the political line of the party, have not yet firmly grasped the method of political struggle, and have not yet followed correctly the mass line, and therefore have greatly reduced the movement's possibilities for development.

At present, therefore, the political struggle movement has not yet developed equally among the people, and a primary reason is that a number of cadres and masses are not yet aware that the strength of political forces of the people can defeat the cruelty, oppression and exploitation of the U.S.-Diem, and therefore they have a halfway attitude and don't believe in the strength of their political forces.

We must admit that any revolutionary movement has times when it falls and times when it rises; any revolutionary movement has times that are favorable for development and times that are unfavorable. The basic thing is that the cadres must see clearly the character of the movement's development to lead the mass struggle to the correct degree, and find a way for the vast determined masses to participate in the movement. If they are determined to struggle from the bottom to the top, no force can resist the determination of the great masses.

In the past two years, the political struggle movement in the countryside and in the cities, either by one form or another, has shown that the masses have much capacity for political struggle with the U.S.-Diem. In those struggles, if we grasp more firmly the struggle line and method, the movement can develop further, to the advantage of the revolution. The cruel policy of U.S.-Diem clearly cannot break the movement, or the people's will to struggle.

There are those who think that the U.S.-Diem's use of violence is now aimed fundamentally at killing the leaders of the revolutionary movement to destroy the Communist Party, and that if the Communist Party is worn away to the point that it doesn't have the capacity to lead the revolution, the political struggle movement of the masses cannot develop.

This judgment is incorrect. Those who lead the revolutionary movement are determined to mingle with the masses, to protect and serve the interest of the masses and to pursue correctly the mass line. Between the masses and communists there is no distinction any more. So how can the U.S.-Diem destroy the leaders of the revolutionary movement, since they cannot destroy the masses? Therefore they cannot annihilate the cadres leading the mass movement.

In fact more than twenty years ago, the French imperialists were determined to destroy the Communists to destroy the revolutionary movement for national liberation, but the movement triumphed. It wasn't the Communist but the French imperialist themselves and their feudal lackeys who were destroyed on our soil.

Now twenty years later, U.S.-Diem are determined to destroy the Communists in the South, but the movement is still firm, and Communists are sill determined to fulfill their duty. And the revolutionary movement will definitely advance and destroy the imperialist, feudalist government. U.S.-Diem will be destroyed, just as the French imperialists and their feudal lackeys were destroyed.

We believe that the peaceful line is appropriate not only to the general situation in the world but also to the situation within the country, both nation-wide and in the South. We believe that the will for peace and the peace forces of the people throughout the country have smashed the U.S.-Diem schemes of war provocation and division.

We believe that the will for peace and Southern people's democratic and peace forces will defeat the cruel, dictatorial and fascist policy of U.S.-Diem and will advance to smash the imperialist, feudalist U.S.-Diem government. Using love and righteousness to triumph over force is a tradition of the Vietnamese nation. The aspiration for peace is an aspiration of the world's people in general and in our own country, including the people of the South, so our struggle line cannot be separated from the peaceful line.

Only the peaceful struggle line can create strong political forces to defeat the scheme of war provocation and the cruel policy of U.S.-Diem. We are determined to carry out our line correctly, and later the development of the situation will permit us to do so. Imperialism and feudalism are on the road to disappearance. The victory belongs to our people's glorious task of unification and independence, to our glorious Communism we must pledge our lives. We shall win.

Source: Le Duan, "Duong Loi Cach Mang Mien Nam" [The Path of Revolution in the South], circa 1956, The Wars for Viet Nam, Vassar College, http://vietnam.vassar.edu/abstracts/index.html.

102. Elbridge Durbrow: Assessment of the Ngo Dinh Diem Regime, January 1, 1957

Introduction

Elbridge Durbrow was U.S. ambassador to the Republic of Vietnam (RVN, South Vietnam) from March 1957 to April 1961. He urged that military aid to South Vietnam be conditioned on Saigon's progress in political and economic reform. At the same time, U.S. Military Assistance and Advisory Group (MAAG) chief Lieutenant General Samuel T. Williams emphasized building the South Vietnamese armed forces. In this document, Durbrow notes South Vietnamese president Ngo Dinh Diem's accomplishments in his first two years in power, including bringing "security and stability," and his pro-West position. At the same time, Durbrow points out Diem's reluctance to bring about genuine economic and social reform that the ambassador believes necessary for long-term stability in favor of placing priority in the military. Certainly Diem was out of touch with the situation in the countryside, and little was done to carry out much-needed land reform, vital in winning the allegiance of the peasants. Until 1960 less than 2 percent of Washington's aid to South Vietnam went for agrarian reform. Corruption was also endemic. While Durbrow minimized the guerrilla threat from the Communists and doubted the need for a 150,000-man army for South Vietnam, the Dwight D. Eisenhower administration's policy of giving priority to the military remained unchanged.

Primary Source

Certain problems now discernible have given us a warning which, if disregarded, might lead to a deteriorating situation in Viet Nam within a few years.

Diem achieved notable successes in the first two years of his regime and remains the only man of stature so far in evidence to guide this country. He has unified free Viet Nam, brought it relative security and stability, and firmly maintains a pro-West, anticommunist position.

In the last year, however, Diem has avoided making decisions required to build the economic and social foundations necessary to secure Viet Nam's future independence and strength. He has made it clear that he would give first priority to the build-up of his armed forces regardless of the country's requirements for economic and social development. Events abroad which increase the danger of communist infiltration and subversion, and which threaten Viet Nam with possible isolation in this area have contributed to his concern and to his determination to strengthen his armed forces.

Certain characteristics of Diem—his suspiciousness and authoritarianism—have also reduced the Government's limited administrative capabilities. He assumes responsibility for the smallest details of Government and grants his Ministers little real authority.

At the same time, discontent is felt in different segments of the population for varied reasons. The base of the regime's popular support remains narrow. The regime might overcome such discontent and finally win over the loyalty of a majority of Vietnamese both in the North and South if it could show its ability to give the country stronger protection and create sound economic and social bases for progress. Progress, which is demanded in Viet Nam as throughout Asia, is perhaps the touchstone of the regime's enduring viability. Yet precisely because Diem is now procrastinating in making decisions affecting fundamental problems of his country's development, the lag between the people's expectations and the Government's ability to show results will grow.

We consider it therefore of importance that we bring strong pressure on the President to reach certain decisions basically in the economic and social fields which have been before him for some months but on which he has not acted. He has resented this and may resent it more, but in ours and his long range interests we must do our utmost to cause him to move forward in these fields.

The purpose of this evaluation of the present situation in Viet Nam is to examine the elements giving rise to some concern regarding certain developments in Viet Nam, to provide the Department [of State] and interested agencies salient background and to set forth conclusions and recommend certain broad courses of action. We feel that a frank discussion of the solution as we see it may be helpful to all concerned.

Source: *Foreign Relations of the United States, 1955–1957: Vietnam,* Vol. 1 (Washington, DC: U.S. Government Printing Office, 1985), 872–873.

103. Conversation between Presidents Ngo Dinh Diem and Dwight Eisenhower Regarding Additional Aid for the Republic of Vietnam, May 9, 1957 [Excerpts]

Introduction

On May 9, 1957, President Ngo Dinh Diem of the Republic of Vietnam (RVN, South Vietnam) visited Washington, D.C., for the first time as head of state and as part of a three-week trip to the United States. The trip had been arranged in part by the Friends of Vietnam, a powerful pro–South Vietnamese lobby that included representatives of both political parties and the Catholic Church. With the Cold War then raging, Diem found himself heralded as the leader of a "free country." In the course of his conversations with U.S. president Dwight D. Eisenhower, Diem urged continuation of U.S. aid at its present level of $250 million a year, $170 million of which went to the military.

Primary Source

After introductory remarks by the President praising President Diem for the excellent achievements he has brought about in the last three years in stabilizing the situation in Viet-Nam, President Eisenhower asked President Diem to outline the principal problems he is facing today.

President Diem replied that his country has gone through a very grave and serious crisis and has been able to hold on despite strong pressures from all sides. The principal problem of establishing internal security and building up their defense posture has been achieved to a considerable extent. The principal reason Viet-Nam has been able to hold out against these pressures has been because of the sympathy and encouragement given by the United States despite the fact that for a time even some people in the United States did not think that the Diem government could maintain itself.

At the present time Viet-Nam is faced with the possibility of a strong Communist offensive from the Vietminh who have 400 thousand men under arms. Fortunately, however, the Vietminh are faced with serious problems such as high taxes needed to maintain this large force and must have other controls which have caused discontent among the population in the North. Diem feels that Red China is faced with the same problems. They are maintaining a large army which requires heavy taxes and controls over the people, which Diem hopes in the long run will force the Chinese Government to demobilize a considerable portion of their forces and treat the people in a more liberal manner. There is, nevertheless, the possibility that the Vietminh with their large army might

try to attack now while they have a superiority in numbers. The Vietminh during the first year after the Geneva Conference did not think it would be necessary to use armed force to take over the South; they thought the government in the South would crumble and they could take over without difficulty. With internal stability in Free Viet-Nam and the build-up of their own armed forces, they have now the possibility of holding out for a few years more during which time Diem reiterated the strain and drain on the economy of the Vietminh may cause them to demobilize some of their forces and adopt a more liberal attitude toward the population. . . .

Diem then reiterated that Viet-Nam has attained stability due primarily to the volume of American aid. He pointed out that the magnitude of American aid permitted the US Government to have a large number of advisers and consultants in Viet-Nam who not only can assist Viet-Nam with its problems but also follow closely developments and the use to which aid is placed. In contrast, the small amounts of aid given to other countries, such as 20/30 million dollars, does not permit the US Government to maintain such close control over developments in other countries as is the case in Viet-Nam. Diem pleaded for the maintenance of the present aid level of 250 million dollars a year of which 170 million dollars is allocated for defense purposes. This aid has permitted Viet-Nam to build up its armed strength and thus play an important role in Southeast Asia. If this aid should be cut both the military and economic progress would have to be reduced. This would cause serious repercussions not only in Viet-Nam but among neighboring countries in Southeast Asia who look on Viet-Nam as an example of the good US aid can bring. Any cut would also bring serious political repercussions in Viet-Nam.

Source: *Foreign Relations of the United States, 1955–1957: Vietnam*, Vol. 1 (Washington, DC: U.S. Government Printing Office, 1985), 794–797.

104. Vo Nguyen Giap: "People's War, People's Army", 1959 [Excerpts]

Introduction

In the late 1950s after the government of the Democratic Republic of Vietnam (DRV, North Vietnam) failed to take action and under increasing pressure from the government of the Republic of Vietnam (RVN, South Vietnam) under President Ngo Dinh Diem, the Viet Minh political cadres who had remained in South Vietnam after 1954 took matters into their own hands and initiated an insurgency against the Diem regime. By late 1958 they had presented the North Vietnamese government with a fait accompli. In response, at the end of the year North Vietnamese president Ho Chi Minh dispatched his trusted lieutenant Le Duan to South Vietnam on a fact-finding mission. A leader there during the Indochina War, Le Duan was then de facto secretary-general of the Lao Dong (Workers' Party) and second in authority only to Ho. Le Duan returned with the recommendation that North Vietnam assume leadership of the insurgency. In January 1959 the Lao Dong Central Committee agreed to support armed insurrection in South Vietnam, although this was to remain secondary to the "political struggle."

Primary Source

On December 22, 1954, the Viet Nam People's Army will celebrate the fifteenth anniversary of its founding. I would like, on this occasion to have a few words with you about the struggle and the building up of the revolutionary armed forces in Viet Nam. At the same time I would like to lay emphasis on the fundamental points which bring out the characteristics of the military policy of the vanguard party of the Vietnamese working class and people—the Indochinese Communist Party—now the Viet Nam Workers' Party.

As Marxism-Leninism teaches us: "The history of all societies up till the present day, has been but the history of class struggle." These struggles can take either the form of political struggle or the form of armed struggle—the armed struggle being only the continuation of the political struggle. In a society which remains divided into classes, we can distinguish two kinds of politics: the politics of the classes and nations of exploiters and oppressors and that of the exploited and oppressed classes and nations. Hence two kinds of wars, of States and armies diametrically opposed to each other, the ones revolutionary, popular and just, and the others counter-revolutionary, anti-popular and unjust.

The Russian October Revolution marked a new era in the history of mankind. A state of a new type appeared, that of proletarian dictatorship, that of the liberated Soviet workers and peasants, toiling people and nationalities. An army of a new type came into being—the Red Army, a genuine people's army placed under the leadership of the Communist Party of the Soviet Union. Born in the October uprising, and steeled and tempered in the combats that followed it, the Red Army was to become, in a short time, the most powerful army in the world, always ready to defend the Soviet Motherland, the first State of workers and peasants.

In Asia, after World War One, the national democratic revolution of the Chinese people made tremendous progress under the good influence of the Russian Revolution. To free themselves, the Chinese people valiantly rose to wage an armed struggle for many decades. It was in this revolutionary war full of heroism and sacrifices that was born and grew up the Chinese Liberation Army, an army equally of a new type, genuinely popular, under the leadership of the Chinese Communist Party.

Only fifteen years of age, the Viet Nam People's Army is a young revolutionary army. It developed in the course of the national liberation war of the Vietnamese people from which it comes, and is now assuming the glorious task of defending the building of socialism in the North while contributing to make it a strong base for the peaceful reunification of the country. It also constitutes an army of a new type, a truly popular army under the leadership of the working class Party of Viet Nam.

In the U.S.S.R. as well as in China and Viet Nam, the revolutionary wars and armies have common fundamental characteristics: their popular and revolutionary nature, and the just cause they serve.

The Vietnamese revolutionary war and army however have their own characteristics. Indeed, from the very start, in the Soviet Union, the revolutionary war evolved within the framework of a socialist revolution. Moreover it proceeded in an independent country possessing a fairly important modern industrial economy, which, under the socialist regime, has not ceased to develop further. As for the revolutionary war in China, it remained for a long period within the framework of a national democratic revolution proceeding in a semi-colonial country, an immensely vast country and with a population of more than 600 million people.

The revolutionary war in Viet Nam, while advancing as in China towards the objectives of a national democratic revolution, differs for the reason that it took place in a colonial country, in a much smaller country than China in both area and population.

Therefore the history of the armed struggle and the building up of the armed forces in Viet Nam is that of a small nation subject to colonial rule and having neither a vast territory nor a large population, which, though lacking a regular army at the beginning had to rise against the aggressive forces of an imperialist power, and triumphed over them in the end, liberating half of the country and enabling it to embark on the socialist path. As for the military policy of the vanguard Party of the Vietnamese working class, it is an application of Marxism-Leninism to the concrete conditions of the war of liberation in a colonial country.

I

Viet Nam is a nation in South-east Asia with a very old history. With its 329,600 square kilometres and 30 million inhabitants and its geographical situation in the Pacific, it has now become one of the outposts of the socialist world.

In the course of its thousands of years of history, many a time, the Vietnamese nation victoriously resisted the invasions of the Chinese feudalists. It can be proud of its traditions of undaunted struggle in safeguarding national independence.

After its invasion of Viet Nam in the second half of the 19th century, French imperialism made it their colony. Since then, the struggle against French colonialism never ceased to extend, uprisings succeeded each other in spite of repression, and daily attracting wider and wider strata belonging to all social classes.

In 1930, the Indochinese Communist Party was founded. Under its firm and clear-sighted leadership, the movement for national liberation of the Vietnamese people made new progress. After ten years of heroic political struggle, at the dawn of World War Two, the Party advocated the preparation for armed struggle, and for that the launching of a guerilla war and the setting up of a free zone. The anti-Japanese movement for national salvation, in its irresistible upsurge, led to the glorious days of the August Revolution of 1945. Taking advantage of the major events in the international situation at the time—the victory of the Soviet Red Army and Allied forces over Japanese fascism—the Vietnamese people rose up as one man in the victorious insurrection and set up the people's power. The Democratic Republic of Viet Nam was born, the first people's democracy in South-east Asia.

The political situation in Viet Nam was then particularly difficult and complicated. Chiang Kai-shek's troops had entered the North, and those of Great Britain the South of the country, to disarm the Japanese who were still in possession of all their armaments in the first days of the capitulation. It was in these conditions that French imperialists, immediately after the founding of the Democratic Republic, unleashed a war of reconquest against Viet Nam hoping to impose their domination on this country.

In response to the appeal of the Party and the Government headed by President Ho Chi Minh, the Vietnamese people rose up as one man for the defence of the Fatherland. A sacred war for national liberation began. All hopes of a peaceful settlement were not lost however. A Preliminary Agreement for the cessation of hostilities was signed in March 1946 between the Government of the Democratic Republic of Viet Nam and that of France. But the French colonialists saw it only as a delaying scheme. Therefore, immediately after the signing of the Agreement, they shamelessly violated it by successively occupying various regions. In December 1946, the war spread to the whole country. It was to rage for nine years, nine years after the end of World War Two. And it ended with the brilliant victory of the Vietnamese people.

Our war of liberation was a people's war, a just war. It was this essential characteristic that was to determine its laws and to decide its final outcome.

At the first gunshots of the imperialist invasion, general Leclerc, the first Commander of the French Expeditionary Corps estimated that the operation for the reoccupation of Viet Nam would be a mere military walk over. When encountering the resistance of the Vietnamese people in the South the French generals considered it as weak and temporary and stuck to their opinion that it would take them ten weeks at the most to occupy and pacify the whole of south

Viet Nam. Why did French colonialists make such an estimation? Because they considered that to meet their aggression, there must be an army. The Vietnamese army had just been created. It was still numerically weak, badly organised, led by inexperienced officers and non-commissioned officers, provided with old and insufficient equipment, a very limited stock of munitions and having neither tanks, airplanes nor artillery. With such an army how could serious resistance be undertaken and the attacks of the powerful and armoured division repelled? All it could do was to use up its stock of munitions before laying down its arms. In fact, the Vietnamese army was then weak in all respects and was destitute of everything. French colonialists were right in this respect. But it was not possible for them to understand a fundamental and decisive fact: this fact was that the Vietnamese army, though very weak materially was a people's army. This fact is that the war in Viet Nam was not only the opposition of two armies. In provoking hostilities, the aggressive colonialists had alienated a whole nation. And, indeed, the whole Vietnamese nation, the entire Vietnamese people rose against them. Unable to grasp this profound truth, the French generals who believed in an easy victory, went instead to certain defeat. They thought they could easily subdue the Vietnamese people, when, in fact, the latter were going to smash them.

Even to this day bourgeois strategists have not yet overcome their surprise at the outcome of the war in Indo-China. How could the Vietnamese nation have defeated an imperialist power such as France which was backed by U.S.? They try to explain this extraordinary fact by the correctness of strategy and tactics, by the forms of combat and the heroism of the Viet Nam People's Army. Of course all these factors contributed to the happy outcome of the resistance. But if the question is put: "Why were the Vietnamese people able to win?" the most precise and most complete answer must be: "The Vietnamese people won because their war of liberation was a people's war."

When the Resistance War spread to the whole country, the Indochinese Communist Party emphasized in its instructions that our Resistance War must be the work of the entire people. Therein lies the key to victory.

Our Resistance War was a people's war, because its political aims were to smash the imperialist yoke to win back national independence, to overthrow the feudal landlord class to bring land to the peasants; in other words, to radically solve the two fundamental contradictions of Vietnamese society—contradiction between the nation and imperialism on the one hand, and contradiction between the people, especially between the peasants and the feudal landlord class on the other—and to pave the socialist path for the Vietnamese revolution.

Holding firmly to the strategy and tactics of the national democratic revolution, the Party pointed out to the people the aims of the struggle: independence and democracy. It was, however, not enough to have objectives entirely in conformity with the fundamental aspirations of the people. It was also necessary to bring everything into play to enlighten the masses of the people, educate and encourage them, organise them in fighting for national salvation. The Party devoted itself entirely to this work, to the regrouping of all the national forces, and to the broadening and strengthening of a national united front, the Viet Minh, and later the Lien Viet which was a magnificent model of the unity of the various strata of the people in the anti-imperialist struggle in a colonial country. In fact, this front united the patriotic forces of all classes and social strata, even progressive landlords; all nationalities in the country—majority as well as minority; patriotic believers of each and every religion. "Unity, the great unity, for victory, the great victory"; this slogan launched by President Ho Chi Minh became a reality, a great reality during the long and hard resistance.

We waged a people's war, and that in the framework of a long since colonised country. Therefore the national factor was of first importance. We had to rally all the forces likely to overthrow the imperialists and their lackeys. On the other hand, this war proceeded in a backward agricultural country where the peasants, making up the great majority of the population, constituted the essential force of the revolution and of the Resistance War. Consequently the relation between the national question and the peasant question had to be clearly defined, with the gradual settlement of the agrarian problem, so as to mobilise the broad peasant masses, one of the essential and decisive factors for victory. Always solicitous about the interests of the peasantry, the Party began by advocating reduction of land rent and interest. Later on, as soon as the stabilisation of the situation allowed it, the Party carried out with great firmness the mobilisation of the masses for land reform in order to bring land to the tillers, thereby to maintain and strengthen the Resistance.

During the years of war, various erroneous tendencies appeared. Either we devoted our attention only to the organisation and growth of the armed forces while neglecting the mobilisation and organisation of large strata of the people, or we mobilised the people for the war without heeding seriously their immediate everyday interests; or we thought of satisfying the immediate interests of the people as a whole, without giving due attention to those of the peasants. The Party resolutely fought all these tendencies. To lead the Resistance to victory, we had to look after the strengthening of the army, while giving thought to mobilising and educating the people, broadening and consolidating the National United Front. We had to mobilise the masses for the Resistance while trying to satisfy their immediate interests to improve their living conditions, essentially those of the peasantry. A very broad national united front was indispensable, on the basis of the worker-peasant alliance and under the leadership of the Party.

The imperatives of the people's war in Viet Nam required the adoption of appropriate strategy and tactics, on the basis of the enemy's characteristics and of our own, of the concrete conditions of the battlefields and balance of forces facing each other. In other words, the strategy and tactics of a people's war, in an economically backward, colonial country.

First of all, this strategy must be the strategy of a long-term war. It does not mean that all revolutionary wars, all people's wars must necessarily be long-term wars. If from the outset, the conditions are favourable to the people and the balance of forces turn in favour of the revolution, the revolutionary war can end victoriously in a short time. But the war of liberation of the Vietnamese people started in quite different conditions: We had to deal with a much stronger enemy. It was patent that this balance of forces took away from us the possibility of giving decisive battles from the opening of the hostilities and of checking the aggression from the first landing operations on our soil. In a word, it was impossible for us to defeat the enemy swiftly.

It was only by a long and hard resistance that we could wear out the enemy forces little by little while strengthening ours, progressively turn the balance of forces in our favour and finally win victory. We did not have any other way.

This strategy and slogan of long term resistance was decided upon by the Indochinese Communist Party from the first days of the war of liberation. It was in this spirit that the Viet Nam People's Army, after fierce street-combats in the big cities, beat strategical retreats to the countryside on its own initiative in order to maintain its bases and preserve its forces.

The long-term revolutionary war must include several different stages: stage of contention, stage of equilibrium and stage of counter-offensive. Practical fighting was, of course, more complicated. There had to be many years of more and more intense and generalised guerilla fighting to realise the equilibrium of forces and develop our war potentiality. When the conjunctures of events at home and abroad allowed it, we went over to counter-offensive first by a series of local operations then by others on a larger scale which were to lead to the decisive victory of Dien Bien Phu.

The application of this strategy of long-term resistance required a whole system of education, a whole ideological struggle among the people and Party members, a gigantic effort of organisation in both military and economic fields, extraordinary sacrifices and heroism from the army as well as from the people, at the front as well as in the rear. Sometimes erroneous tendencies appeared, trying either to by-pass the stages to end the war earlier, or to throw important forces into military adventures. The Party rectified them by a stubborn struggle and persevered in the line it had fixed. In the difficult hours, certain hesitations revealed themselves, the Party faced them with vigour and with determination in the struggle and faith in final victory.

The long-term people's war in Viet Nam also called for appropriate forms of fighting: appropriate to the revolutionary nature of the war as well as to the balance of forces which revealed at that time an overwhelming superiority of the enemy over the still very weak material and technical bases of the People's Army. The adopted form of fighting was guerilla warfare. It can be said that the war of liberation of the Vietnamese people was a long and vast guerilla war proceeding from simple to complex then to mobile war in the last years of the Resistance.

Guerilla war is the war of the broad masses of an economically backward country standing up against a powerfully equipped and well trained army of aggression. Is the enemy strong? One avoids him. Is he weak? One attacks him. To his modern armament one opposes a boundless heroism to vanquish either by harassing or by annihilating the enemy according to circumstances, and by combining military operations with political and economic action; no fixed line of demarcation, the front being wherever the enemy is found.

Concentration of troops to realize an overwhelming superiority over the enemy where he is sufficiently exposed in order to destroy his manpower; initiative, suppleness, rapidity, surprise, suddenness in attack and retreat. As long as the strategic balance of forces remains disadvantageous, resolutely to muster troops to obtain absolute superiority in combat in a given place, and at a given time. To exhaust little by little by small victories the enemy forces and at the same time to maintain and increase ours. In these concrete conditions it proves absolutely necessary not to lose sight of the main objective of the fighting that is the destruction of the enemy manpower. Therefore losses must be avoided even at the cost of losing ground. And that for the purpose of recovering, later on, the occupied territories and completely liberating the country.

In the war of liberation in Viet Nam, guerilla activities spread to all the regions temporarily occupied by the enemy. Each inhabitant was a soldier, each village a fortress, each Party a cell, each village administrative committee a staff.

The people as a whole took part in the armed struggle, fighting according to the principles of guerilla warfare, in small packets, but always in pursuance of the one and same line, and the same instructions, those of the Central Committee of the Party and the Government.

At variance with numerous other countries which waged revolutionary wars, Viet Nam, in the first years of its struggle, did not and could not engage in pitched battles. It had to rest content with guerilla warfare. At the cost of thousands of difficulties and countless sacrifices, this guerilla war developed progressively into a form of mobile war that daily increased in scale. While retaining certain characteristics of guerilla war, it involved regular campaigns with greater attacks on fortified positions. Starting from small operations with the strength of a platoon or a company to annihilate a few men or a group of enemy soldiers, our army went over, later, to more important combats with a battalion or regiment to cut one or several enemy companies to pieces, finally coming to greater campaigns bringing into play many regiments, then many divisions to end at Dien Bien Phu where the French Expeditionary Corps lost 16,000 men of its crack units. It was this process of development that enabled our army to move forward steadily on the road to victory.

People's war, long-term war, guerilla warfare developing step-by-step into mobile warfare, such are the most valuable lessons of the war of liberation in Viet Nam. It was by following that line that the Party led the Resistance to victory. After three thousand days of fighting, difficulties and sacrifices, our people defeated the French imperialists and American interventionists. At present, in the liberated half of our country, sixteen million of our compatriots, by their creative labour, are healing the horrible wounds of war, reconstructing the country and building socialism. In the meantime the struggle is going on to achieve the democratic national revolution throughout the country and to reunify the Fatherland on the basis of independence and democracy.

II

After this account of the main lines of the war of liberation waged by the Vietnamese people against the French and American imperialists, I shall speak of the Viet Nam People's Army.

Being the armed forces of the Vietnamese people, it was born and grew up in the flames of the war of national liberation. Its embryo was the self-defence units created by the Nghe An Soviets which managed to hold power for a few months in the period of revolutionary upsurge in the years 1930–1931. But the creation of revolutionary armed forces was positively considered only at the outset of World War Two when the preparation for an armed insurrection came to the fore of our attention. Our military and paramilitary formations appeared at the Bac Son uprising and in the revolutionary bases in Cao Bang region. Following the setting up of the first platoon of National Salvation, on December 22, 1944, another platoon-strong unit was created: the Progaganda unit of the Viet Nam Liberation Army. Our war bases organised during illegality were at the time limited to a few districts in the provinces of Cao Bang, Bac Can and Lang Son in the jungle of the North. As for the revolutionary armed forces they still consisted of people's units of self-defence and a few groups and platoons completely free from production work. Their number increased quickly and there were already several thousands of guerillas at the beginning of 1945, at the coup de force by the Japanese fascists over the French colonialists. At the time of the setting up of the people's power in the rural regions of six provinces in Viet Bac which were established as a free zone, the existing armed organisations merged to form the Viet Nam Liberation Army.

During the August insurrection, side by side with the people and the self-defence units, the Liberation Army took part in the conquest of power. By incorporating the paramilitary forces regrouped in the course of the glorious days of August, it saw its strength increase rapidly. With a heterogeneous material wrested from the Japanese and their Bao An troops—rifles alone consisted of sixteen different types including old French patterns and even rifles of the czarist forces taken by the Japanese—this young and poorly equipped army soon had to face the aggression of the French Expeditionary Corps which had modern armaments. Such antiquated equipment required from the Vietnamese army and people complete self-sacrifice and superhuman heroism.

Should the enemy attack the regions where our troops were stationed, the latter would give battle. Should he ferret about in the large zones where there were no regular formations, the people would stay his advance with rudimentary weapons: sticks, spears, scimitars, bows, flintlocks. From the first days, there appeared three types of armed forces: paramilitary organisations or guerilla units, regional troops and regular units. These formations were, in the field of organisation, the expression of the general mobilisation of the people in arms. They co-operated closely with one another to annihilate the enemy.

Peasants, workers and intellectuals crowded into the ranks of the armed forces of the Revolution. Leading cadres of the Party and the State apparatus became officers from the first moment. The greatest difficulty to be solved was the equipment problem. Throughout Viet Nam there was no factory manufacturing war materials. Throughout nearly a century, possession and use of arms were strictly forbidden by the colonial administration. Importation was impossible, the neighbouring countries being hostile to the Democratic Republic of Viet Nam. The sole source of supply could only be the battlefront: to take the material from the enemy to turn it against him. While carrying on the aggression against Viet Nam the French Expeditionary Corps fulfilled another task: it became, unwittingly, the supplier of the Viet Nam People's Army with French, even U.S. arms. In spite of their enormous efforts, the arms factories set up later on with makeshift means were far from being able to meet all our needs. A great part of our military materials came from war-booty.

As I have stressed, the Viet Nam People's Army could at first bring into combat only small units such as platoons or companies. The regular forces were, at a given time, compelled to split up into companies operating separately to promote the extension of guerilla activities while mobile battalions were maintained for more important actions. After each victorious combat, the people's armed forces marked a new step forward.

Tempered in combat and stimulated by victories, the guerilla formations created conditions for the growth of the regional troops. And the latter, in their turn, promoted the development of the regular forces. For nine successive years, by following this heroic path bristling with difficulties, our people's army grew up with a determination to win at all costs. It became an army of hundreds of thousands strong, successively amalgamating into regiments and divisions and directing towards a progressive standardisation in organisation and equipment. This force, ever more politically conscious, and better trained militarily, succeeded in fighting and defeating the five hundred thousand men of the French Expeditionary Corps who were equipped and supplied by the United States.

The Vietnamese Army is indeed a national one. In fighting against imperialism and the traitors in its service, it has fought for national independence and the unity of the country. In its ranks are the finest sons of Viet Nam, the most sincere patriots from all revolutionary classes, from all nationalities—majority as well as minority people. It symbolises the irresistible rousing of the national conscience, the union of the entire Vietnamese people in the fight against imperialist aggression to save the country.

Our army is a democratic army, because it fights for the people's democratic interests, and the defence of people's democratic power. Impregnated with the principles of democracy in its internal political life, it submits to a rigorous discipline, but one freely consented to.

Our army is a people's army, because it defends the fundamental interests of the people, in the first place those of the toiling people, workers and peasants. As regards social composition, it comprises a great majority of picked fighters of peasant and worker origin, and intellectuals faithful to the cause of the Revolution.

It is the true army of the people, of toilers, the army of workers and peasants, led by the Party of the working class. Throughout the war of national liberation, its aims of struggle were the very ones followed by the Party and people: independence of the nation, and land to the tillers. Since the return of peace, as a tool of proletarian dictatorship, its mission is to defend the socialist revolution and socialist building in the North, to support the political struggle for the peaceful reunification of the country, and to contribute to the strengthening of peace in Indo-China and South-east Asia.

In the first of the ten points of his Oath of Honour, the fighter of the Viet Nam People's Army swears

"To sacrifice himself unreservedly for the Fatherland, fight for the cause of national independence, democracy and socialism, under the leadership of the Viet Nam Workers' Party and of the Government of the Democratic Republic, to build a peaceful, reunified, independent, democratic and prosperous Viet Nam and contribute to the strengthening of peace in South-east Asia and the world."

This is precisely what makes the Viet Nam People's Army a true child of the people. The people, in return, give it unsparing affection and support. Therein lies the inexhaustible source of its power.

The Viet Nam People's Army has been created by the Party, which ceaselessly trains and educates it. It has always been and will always be under the leadership of the Party which, alone, has made it into a revolutionary army, a true people's army. Since its creation and in the course of its development, this leadership by the Party has been made concrete on the organisational plan. The army has always had its political commissars. In the units, the military and political chiefs assume their responsibilities under the leadership of the Party Committee at the corresponding echelon.

The People's Army is the instrument of the Party and of the revolutionary State for the accomplishment, in armed form, of the tasks of the revolution. Profound awareness of the aims of the Party, boundless loyalty to the cause of the nation and the working class, and a spirit of unreserved sacrifice are fundamental questions for the army, and questions of principle. Therefore, the political work in its ranks is of the first importance. It is the soul of the army. In instilling Marxist-Leninist ideology into the army, it aims at raising the army's political consciousness and ideological level, at strengthening the class position of its cadres and soldiers. During the liberation war, this work imbued the army with the policy of long-drawn-out resistance and the imperative necessity for the people and army to rely on their own strength to overcome difficulties. It instilled into the army the profound significance of mass mobilisation in order to achieve rent reduction and agrarian reform, which had a decisive effect on the morale of the troops. In the new stage entered upon since the restoration of peace, political work centres on the line of socialist revolution in the North and of struggle for the reunification of the country.

But that is not all. Political work still bears upon the correct fulfilment in the army of the programmes of the Party and Government, and the setting up of good relations with the population and between officers and men. It aims at maintaining and strengthening combativeness, uniting true patriotism with proletarian internationalism, developing revolutionary heroism and the great tradition of our army summed up in its slogan: "Resolved to fight, determined to win". Political work is the work of propaganda among and education of the masses; it is, furthermore, the organisational work of the Party in the army. We have always given particular attention to the strengthening of organisations of the Party in the units. From 35 to 40 per cent of officers and armymen have joined it, among the officers, the percentage even exceeds 90 per cent.

The Viet Nam People's Army has always seen to establishing and maintaining good relations with the people. These are based upon the identity of their aims of struggle: in fact, the people and army are together in the fight against the enemy to save the Fatherland, and ensure the full success of the task of liberating the nation and the working class. The people are to the army what water is to fish, as the saying goes. And this saying has a profound significance. Our Army fought on the front; it has also worked to educate the people and helped them to the best of its ability. The Vietnamese fighter has always taken care to observe point 9 of its Oath of Honour:

"In contacts with the people, to follow these three recommendations:

—To respect the people
—To help the people
—To defend the people . . . in order to win their confidence and affection and achieve a perfect understanding between the people and the army."

Our army has always organised days of help for peasants in production work and in the struggle against flood and drought. It has always observed a correct attitude in its relations with the people. It has never done injury to their property, not even a needle or a bit of thread. During the Resistance, especially in the enemy rear, it brought everything into play to defend ordinary people's lives and property; in the newly liberated regions, it strictly carried out the orders of the Party and Government, which enabled it to win the unreserved support of the broadest masses, even in the minority peoples' regions and catholic villages. Since the return of peace, thousands of its officers and men have participated in the great movements for the accomplishment of agrarian reform for agricultural collectivisation and socialist transformation of handicrafts, industry and private trade. It has actively taken part in the economic recovery, and in socialist work days. It has participated in the building of lines of communication, it has built its own barracks and cleared land to found State farms.

The Viet Nam People's Army is always concerned to establish and maintain good relations between officers and men as well as between the officers themselves. Originating from the working strata, officers and men also serve the people's interests and unstintingly devote themselves to the cause of the nation and the working class. Of course every one of them has particular responsibilities which devolve upon him. But relations of comradeship based on political equality and fraternity of class have been established between them. The officer likes his men; he must not only guide them in their work and studies, but take an interest in their life and take into consideration their desires and initiatives. As for the soldier, he must respect his superiors and correctly fulfil all their orders. The officer of the People's Army must set a good example from all points of view: to show himself to be resolute, brave, to ensure discipline and internal democracy, to know how to achieve perfect unity among his men. He must behave like a chief, a leader, vis-à-vis the masses in his unit. The basis of these relations between armymen and officers, like those between officers or between soldiers is solidarity in the fight; and mutual affection of brothers-in-arms, love at the same time pure and sublime, tested and forged in the battle, in the struggle for the defence of the Fatherland and the people.

The Viet Nam People's Army practises a strict discipline, allied to a wide internal democracy. As requires point 2 of its Oath of Honour: "The fighter must rigorously carry out the orders of his superiors and throw himself body and soul into the immediate and strict fulfilment of the tasks entrusted to him". Can we say that guerilla warfare did not require severe discipline? Of course not. It is true that it asked the commander and leader to allow each unit or each region a certain margin of initiative in order to undertake every positive action that it might think opportune. But a centralised leadership and a unified command at a given degree always proved to be necessary. He who speaks of the army, speaks of strict discipline.

Such a discipline is not in contradiction with the internal democracy of our troops. In cells, executive committees of the Party at various levels as well as in plenary meetings of fighting units, the application of principles of democratic centralism is the rule. The facts have proved that the more democracy is respected within the units, the more unity will be strengthened, discipline raised, and orders carried out. The combativeness of the army will thereby be all the greater.

The restoration of peace has created in Viet Nam a new situation. The North is entirely liberated, but the South is still under the yoke of American imperialists and the Ngo Dinh Diem clique, their lackeys. North Viet Nam has entered the stage of socialist revolution while the struggle is going on to free the South from colonial and feudal fetters. To safeguard peace and socialist construction, to help in making the North a strong rampart for the peaceful reunification of the country, the problem of forces of national defence should not be neglected. The People's Army must face the bellicose aims of American imperialists and their lackeys and step by step become a regular and modern army.

First of all, it is important to stress that, in the process of its transformation into a regular and modern army, our army always remains a revolutionary army, a people's army. That is the fundamental characteristic that makes the people's regular and modern army in the North differ radically from Ngo Dinh Diem's army, a regular and modern army too, but anti-revolutionary, anti-popular and in the hands of the people's enemies. The People's Army must necessarily see to the strengthening of the leadership of Party and political work. It must work further to consolidate

the solidarity between officers and men, between the troops and the people, raise the spirit of self-conscious discipline, while maintaining internal democracy. Taking steps to that end, the Party has during the last years, given a prominent place to the activities of its organisations as well as to the political work in the army. Officers, warrant officers and armymen, all of them have followed political courses to improve their understanding of the tasks of socialist revolution and the struggle for national reunification, consolidating their class standpoint and strengthening Marxist-Leninist ideology. This is a particularly important question, more especially as the People's Army has grown up in an agricultural country, and has in its ranks a great majority of toiling peasants and urban petty-bourgeois. Our fighters have gone through a dogged political education and their morale has been forged in the combat. However, the struggle against the influence of bourgeois and petty-bourgeois ideology remains necessary. Thanks to the strengthening of ideological work, the army has become an efficacious instrument in the service of proletarian dictatorship, and has been entirely faithful to the cause of socialist revolution and national reunification. The new advances realised by it in the political plan have found their full expression in the movement "with giant strides, let us overfulfil the norms of the programme," a broad mass movement which is developing among our troops, parallel with the socialist emulation movement among the working people in North Viet Nam.

It is essential actively and firmly to continue, on the basis of a constant strengthening of political army. Thanks to the development realised during the last years of the Resistance War, our army, which was made up of infantry-men only, is now an army composed of different arms. If the problem of improvement of equipments and technique is important, that of cadres and soldiers capable of using them is more important. Our army has always been concerned with the training of officers and warrant officers of worker and peasant origin or revolutionary intellectuals tested under fire. It helps them raise their cultural and technical level to become competent officers and warrant officers of a regular and modern army.

To raise the fighting power of the army, to bring about a strong centralisation of command and a close cooperation between the different arms, it is indispensable to enforce regulations fitted to a regular army. It is not that nothing has been done in this field during the years of the Resistance War; it is a matter of perfecting the existing regulations. The main thing is not to lose sight of the principle that any new regulation must draw its inspiration from the popular character of the army and the absolute necessity of maintaining the leadership of the Party. Along with the general regulations, the statute of officers has been promulgated; a correct system of wages has taken the place of the former regime of allowances in kind; the question of rewards and decorations has been regularised. All these measures have resulted in the strengthening of discipline and solidarity within the army, and of the sense of responsibility among officers and warrant officers as well as among soldiers.

Military training, and political education, are key tasks in the building of the army in peace-time. The question of fighting regulations, and that of tactical concepts and appropriate tactical principles gain a particular importance. The question is to synthesize past experiences, and analyse well the concrete conditions of our army in organization and equipment, consider our economic structure, the terrain of the country—land of forests and jungles, of plains and fields. The question is to assimilate well the modern military science of the armies of the brother countries. Unceasing efforts are indispensable in the training of troops and the development of cadres.

For many years, the Viet Nam People's Army was based on voluntary service: all officers and soldiers voluntarily enlisted for an undetermined period. Its ranks swelled by the affluence of youth always ready to answer the appeal of the Fatherland. Since the return of peace, it has become necessary to replace voluntary service by compulsory military service. This substitution has met with warm response from the population. A great number of volunteers, after demobilisation returned to fields and factories; others are working in units assigned to production work, thus making an active contribution to the building of socialism. Conscription is enforced on the basis of the strengthening and development of the self-defence organisations in the communes, factories and schools. The members of these paramilitary organisations are ready not only to rejoin the permanent army, of which they constitute a particularly important reserve, but also to ensure the security and defence of their localities.

The People's Army was closely linked with the national liberation war, in the fire of which it was born and grew up. At present, its development should neither be disassociated from the building of socialism in the North, nor from the people's struggle for a reunified independent and democratic Viet Nam. Confident of the people's affection and support, in these days of peace as during the war, the People's Army will achieve its tasks: to defend peace and the Fatherland.

III

... As is said above, the history of the national liberation war of the Vietnamese people, that of the Viet Nam People's Army, is the history of the victory of a weak nation, of a colonised people who rose up against the aggressive forces of an imperialist power. This victory is also that of Marxism-Leninism applied to the armed revolutionary struggle in a colonised country, that of the Party of the working class in the leadership of the revolution that it heads, in the democratic national stage as well as in the socialist one.

The vanguard Party of the Vietnamese working people, headed by President Ho Chi Minh, the great leader of the people and the nation, is the organiser and guide that has led the Vietnamese people and their army to victory. In the light of Marxism-Leninism applied to the national democratic revolution in a colonised country, it has made a sound analysis of the contradictions of that society, and stated clearly the fundamental tasks of the revolution. On the question of the national liberation war, it has dialectically analysed the balance of opposing forces and mapped out appropriate strategy and tactics. In the light of Marxism-Leninism, it has created and led a heroic people's army. It has ceaselessly instilled revolutionary spirit and the true patriotism of the proletariat into the people and their army.

The Party has known how to learn from the valuable experiences of the October Revolution which, with the Soviet Red Army, showed the road of liberation not only to the workers of the capitalist countries, but also to colonial people; and those of the Chinese Revolution and Liberation Army which have enriched the theories of the national democratic revolution, of revolutionary war and army in a semi-colonised country. Their wonderful examples have ceaselessly lighted the road of the struggle and successes of the Vietnamese people. In combining the invaluable experiences of the Soviet Union and People's China with its own, our Party has always taken into account the concrete reality of the revolutionary war in Viet Nam, thus is able in its turn to enrich the theories of revolutionary war and army.

At present, on the international plane, the forces of socialist countries, led by the Soviet Union, have become a power previously unknown; the national liberation movement has developed considerably everywhere; the possibilities for achieving lasting peace in the world are greater. However, imperialism is still pursuing its war preparations and seeking to strengthen its military alliance for aggression. While there is a certain relaxation of tension in the international situation, South-east Asia still remains one of the centres of tension in the world. American imperialism is ceaselessly strengthening its military and political hold on the South of our country. It is pursuing the same policy of interference in Laos, aimed at turning it into a colony and military base for a new war of aggression.

Profoundly peace-loving, the Vietnamese people and their army support every effort for disarmament, every effort to relax tension and establish a lasting peace. But they must at the same time heighten their vigilance, strengthen their combativeness, increase their potentiality for defence, and contribute to strengthening the fraternal bonds between the peoples and the revolutionary armed forces of the socialist countries. They are determined to fulfil their sacred duties: to defend the work of socialist revolution and the building of socialism in the North, to pursue the struggle for the peaceful reunification of the Fatherland, to be ready to break every imperialist attempt to provoke a war of aggression, and to contribute to the safeguarding of peace in South-east Asia and throughout the world.

Source: Vo Nguyen Giap, *People's War People's Army,* 2nd ed. (Hanoi: Foreign Languages Publishing House, 1974), 42–74.

105. Republic of Vietnam Law 10/59, May 6, 1959 [Excerpts]

Introduction

For President Ngo Dinh Diem of the Republic of Vietnam (RVN, South Vietnam), reform took a backseat to fighting the Communist insurgency, with the result that the insurgency continued to grow. Diem's response was simply more oppression. In May 1959 the National Assembly passed an internal security measure, known as Law 10/59, that empowered the government to try suspected terrorists by roving tribunals that could impose the death penalty.

Primary Source

Article 1

Sentence of death, and confiscation of the whole or part of his property, . . . will be imposed on whoever commits or attempts to commit one of the following crimes with the aim of sabotage, or upon infringing upon the security of the State, or injuring the lives or property of the people:

1. Deliberate murder, food poisoning, or kidnapping.
2. Destruction, or total or partial damaging, of one of the following categories of objects by means of explosives, fire, or other means:
    (a) Dwelling-houses, whether inhabited or not, churches, pagodas, temples, warehouses, workshops, farms and all outbuildings belonging to private persons;
    (b) Public buildings, residences, offices, workshops, depots, and, in a more general way, all constructions of any kind belonging to the State, and any other property, movable or unmovable, belonging to, or controlled by the State, or which is under the system of concession, or of public management;
    (c) All . . . means of transport, all kinds of vehicles;
    (d) Mines, with machines and equipment;
    (e) Weapons, military material and equipment, posts, buildings, offices, depots, workshops, and constructions of any kind relating to defense or police work;
    (f) crops, draft animals and farm equipment. . . ;
    (g) Installations for telecommunications, postal service, broadcasting, the production and distribution of electricity and water . . . ;

    (h) Dikes, dams, roads, railways, airfields, seaports, bridges, channels, or works relating to them;
    (i) Waterways, large or small, and canals. . . .

Article 3

Whoever belongs to an organization designed to help to prepare or to perpetuate crimes enumerated in Article I . . . , or takes pledges to do so, will be subject to the sentences provided for. . . .

Article 6

Three special military courts are set up and based in Saigon, Ban Me Thuot, and Hue. . . . As the need arises, other special military courts may be set up, by decree. . . .

Article 16

The decisions of the special military court are not subject to appeal. . . .

Article 20

All legal provisions which are contrary to the present law are hereby repealed. . . .

Source: Marvin E. Gettleman, ed., *Vietnam: History, Documents, and Opinions on a Major World Crisis* (Greenwich, CT: Fawcett, 1965), 256–260.

106. Ho Chi Minh: Talk at a Cadres' Meeting Debating the Draft Law on Marriage and Family, October 1959 [Excerpt]

Introduction

Women played an important role in the Communist insurgency within the Republic of Vietnam (RVN, South Vietnam) and occupied key leadership positions. Here President Ho Chi Minh of the Democratic Republic of Vietnam (DRV, North Vietnam) makes a strong case for the proposed North Vietnamese Law on Marriage and Family. He notes that women make up half of the population of Vietnam, and without their emancipation "only half of socialism is built."

Primary Source

There are people who think that as a bachelor I may not have a perfect knowledge of this question. Though I have no family of my own, yet I have a very big family—the working class throughout the world and the Vietnamese people. From that broad family I can judge and imagine the small one.

At present, our entire people want socialist construction. What is to be done to build socialism?

Production must certainly be increased as much as possible. To increase production there must be much labor power, which can be obtained satisfactorily only by emancipating the women's labor power.

Women make up half of society. If they are not liberated, half of society is not freed. If women are not emancipated only half of socialism is built.

It is correct to take a keen interest in the family; many families constitute the society. A good society makes a good family and vice versa. The core of the society is the family. It is precisely to build up socialism that due attention must be paid to this core.

"Living in concord, husband and wife may empty the East Sea," the proverb runs. To enjoy concord in matrimonial life, marriage must be based on genuine love.

The law on marriage to be presented to the National Assembly is a revolution, an integral part of the socialist revolution. Therefore, we should adopt the proletarian stand to understand it. It is not correct if our understanding is based on the feudal, bourgeois, or petitbourgeois stand.

The law on marriage aims at emancipating women, that is, at freeing half of society. The emancipation of the women must be carried out simultaneously with the extirpation of feudal and bourgeois thinking in men. As for themselves, women should not wait until the directives of the Government and the Party free them but they must rely upon themselves and struggle.

The Party must give this law leadership from its preparation to its presentation and execution, because this is a revolution. The leadership by the Party means that all cadres and Party members must apply this law strictly and lead all youth and women's organizations resolutely and correctly put it into effect.

The execution of this law is, on the one hand, favorable, because our people have received the Party education and have made much progress; and on the other, difficult, because of the long-standing and deeply rooted old habits and traditions among the people. That is why everything is not over with the promulgation of this law, but long-term propaganda and education needs to be carried on to obtain good results.

I hope that all of you will do your best, be patient, have a thorough knowledge of this law, and carry it out satisfactorily. In particular, you must be very careful, because this law exerts great influence on the future of the family, the society, and the nation.

Source: Ho Chi Minh, *On Revolution: Selected Writings, 1920–66,* edited by Bernard B. Fall (New York: Praeger, 1967), 336–337.

107. Elbridge Durbrow, U.S. Ambassador in Saigon: Telegram to Secretary of State Christian A. Herter, March 7, 1960

Introduction

By early 1960, security in the Republic of Vietnam (RVN, South Vietnam) had sharply deteriorated. In this cable to Washington, U.S. ambassador Elbridge Durbrow notes the growing dissatisfaction with South Vietnamese president Ngo Dinh Diem. The insurgency in South Vietnam is growing rapidly, fed by government corruption, inattention to the needs of the peasants, and an unwillingness to acknowledge problems. The South Vietnamese leader simply does not understand his culpability. (Note: "GVN" in this document refers to the South Vietnamese government.)

Primary Source

Enclosed is a special report prepared by a Country Team study group on the current internal security situation in Viet-Nam. A summary of this report and an analysis of the main factors in Viet-Nam's current serious internal security problem are given below:

Situation. Internal security, which improved greatly since the nip and tuck period from 1954–56 but which nevertheless has been a steady concern of the GVN over the past few years, has again become its No. 1 problem as a result of intensification of Viet Cong guerrilla and terrorist activities, weaknesses apparent in the GVN security forces and the growth of apathy and considerable dissatisfaction among the rural populace. The situation has grown progressively more disturbing since shortly after the National Assembly elections at the end of August 1959, despite the fact that President DIEM was claiming, up to the end of December, that internal security was continuing to improve. The monthly rate of assassinations rose substantially starting in September, and other signs of increasingly aggressive VC tactics such as ambushes of GVN security forces began to appear about the same time. The full impact of the seriousness of the present situation was brought home by a series of VC incidents in late January and February, particularly an attack on an ARVN regimental post near Tay Ninh, other smaller and less dramatic attacks on security posts elsewhere in the southwest and serious VC depredations in Kien Hoa Province.

President Diem and other GVN officials are now showing a reassuring awareness of the gravity of the situation. They have not permitted themselves to become panic-stricken, and there is no reason to become alarmist if prompt steps are taken to correct the situation.

VC Intentions and Potential. Indications are growing that the VC are mounting a special campaign aimed at undermining the Diem Government. According to CAS [Controlled American Source, for the Central Intelligence Agency] sources, VC armed cadre strength has increased to about 3,000 in the southwest, double the number in September. VC groups now operate in larger strength, and their tactics have changed from attacks on individuals to rather frequent and daring attacks on GVN security forces. A recent CAS report has indicated a VC intention to press general guerrilla warfare in South Viet-Nam in 1960, and indicates the VC are convinced they can mount a coup d'état this year. President Diem also told me in late February about the capture of a VC document indicating their intention to step up aggressive attacks all over the country, including Saigon, beginning in the second quarter.

These signs indicate that aggressively worded statements emanating from the DRV in 1959 may accurately reflect DRV intentions. In May 1959 the central committee of the Lao Dong Party passed a resolution stating that the struggle for reunification of Viet-Nam should be carried out by all "appropriate means". Subsequently in conversations with Western officials, Prime Minister Phan Van DONG made statements to the effect that "We will be in Saigon tomorrow" and "We will drive the Americans into the sea".

It is not completely clear why the DRV has chosen this particular time to mount an intensified guerrilla campaign in South Viet-Nam. Several hypotheses have been put forward. The campaign may be part of general Chicom strategy to increase pressure on non-communist countries all along the southern rim of the Asian communist bloc. Several GVN officials, including President Diem, have said that the present DRV tactics may be related to the forthcoming East-West summit meeting, but they do not seem to be clear as to just what this relationship might be. Diem and others have also expressed the view that the DRV is aiming at disruption of the GVN's economic, social and security programs, many of which have been making steady progress while others, like the agroville program, threaten to weaken the VC position if carried out successfully. The DRV may also have been embittered by its failure to interfere successfully with the GVN National Assembly elections last August and resolved, as a result of this failure, to intensify activities in the South.

GVN Security and Political Weaknesses. At the same time that the DRV guerrilla potential has increased in the South, weaknesses have become more apparent in the GVN security forces. GVN leaders have in recent weeks stressed the need for more anti-guerrilla training of ARVN. The desirability of centralized command in insecure areas and a centralized intelligence service has also become more evident. The need for a capable, well-equipped, well-trained, centrally-controlled Civil Guard is even more keenly felt than previously.

Likewise, at the same time, signs of general apathy and considerable dissatisfaction which the VC can play upon have become more evident among the people in rural areas. Fear among the peasants engendered by sustained VC terrorist activities against which the GVN has not succeeded in protecting them is combined with resentment of the GVN because of the methods which are all too often employed by local officials. Coercion rather than suasion are often used by these officials in carrying out the programs decided upon in Saigon. There is a tendency to disregard the desires and feelings of the peasantry by, for instance, taking them away from their harvests to perform community work. The new agroville program requiring large numbers of "volunteer" laborers has accentuated this trend. Improper actions by local officials such as torture, extortion and corruption, many of which have been reported in the press, have also contributed to peasant dissatisfaction. Favoritism and fear of officials and members of the semi-covert Can Lao Party have likewise contributed to this situation.

Diem cannot be completely absolved of blame for this unsatisfactory situation in the rural areas. Considerable evidence has existed that he has not in the past kept himself properly informed of what is going on. Officials have tended to tell him what he wants to hear, largely because of fear of removal if they indicate that mistakes have been made or reply that projects which he is pushing should not be carried out as rapidly as he desires.

GVN Counteractions. Developments during the last month or so have, however, awakened Diem and other officials to the gravity of the present internal security and political situation. As already indicated, they are now emphasizing the need for increased anti-guerrilla training of the security forces. Diem also has indicated that he is establishing a special commando force with "volunteers" from ARVN, the Civil Guard and reservists who had guerrilla experience during the Indochina war. Diem has also stated that the new commander of the Fifth Military Region (the area of greatest insecurity) has been given full powers over all the security forces in that area, thus recognizing the need for centralized command rather than fragmentation of authority among the province chiefs.

Diem has also indicated that he is replacing local officials who are incompetent or have abused their power. He is placing renewed emphasis with these officials on the necessity of winning the confidence of the people and explaining to them the reasons for the government's programs. He has also indicated that he has ordered a slowdown in the construction of agrovilles, apparently in recognition of the indications that the people were being driven too hard to carry out this new program.

The Embassy's views on these countermeasures of the GVN as well as on certain other actions which should be taken have been expressed in a separate dispatch. As the situation develops, the Embassy expects to make additional recommendations.

Source: *United States–Vietnam Relations, 1945–1967,* Book 10 (Washington, DC: U.S. Government Printing Office, 1971), 1254–1257.

108. Party Central Committee Secret Cable No. 160 to the Cochin China Regional Party Committee, April 28, 1960 [Excerpt]

Introduction

In early 1960 following the adoption of Central Committee Resolution 15 approving the use of "revolutionary violence" in the Republic of Vietnam (RVN, South Vietnam), the Communist leaders in South Vietnam pressed for more aggressive action. However, the Vietnamese Lao Dong (Workers' Party) Politburo in the Democratic Republic of Vietnam (DRV, North Vietnam) was concerned about the possible U.S. military reaction and was caught in the middle of the growing conflict between its two major allies, the Soviet Union and Communist China, neither of which desired a direct military confrontation with the United States in South Vietnam. As a consequence, the Politburo insisted on a slower pace that focused on political "struggle" in South Vietnam and that concealed Communist involvement in the insurrection in South Vietnam behind a supposedly non-Communist front organization that was in the process of being formed. This nascent front organization soon became the National Liberation Front for South Vietnam, usually known as the National Liberation Front (NLF).

Primary Source

The Central Committee has received the Party Committee's February 1960 Resolution reporting on the situation during the last three months of 1959, your 15 March message on the direction of your immediate plans, and the 20 March cable you sent to us. . . . We believe there are a number of fundamental issues that we need to clarify further:

1. *The issue of the assessment of the balance of forces between the enemy and ourselves.*

You comrades have provided a rather meticulous analysis of the balance of forces between the enemy and our side and have provided practical evidence to support your assessment. However, revolutionary leaders in one local area must not rely solely on the direct balance of forces between the two sides in their own local area. They must also view the balance of forces from the global standpoint and from the standpoint of the particular region of the world as well.

The current world situation is basically favorable for the revolution in South Vietnam. That assessment is quite correct. We also must realize, however, that *the struggle between the enemy and ourselves throughout the world is now in a tense, back-and-forth situation. . . . In general, the plans of the imperialists have not fundamentally changed, and in certain limited areas and locations of the world they continue to create tense situations and to incite war.* If we wish to progress toward securing the initiative and driving back the enemy, we need more time. . . . If we want to facilitate the revolution in South Vietnam and to gradually create conditions to allow us to seize the initiative, we need time to let the anti-imperialist movement . . . , and we must work with this movement to weaken and isolate the American imperialists and their allies. . . .

South Vietnam and Laos are currently very "sensitive" locations where the imperialists might directly intervene with their own forces. Our recent experience with the situation in Laos has clearly demonstrated this point. The revolutionary movement in South Vietnam, which is led by our party, is different from the revolutionary movements in Iraq and Cuba. Everyone knows that, even though the role of the Communist parties in both countries was of decisive importance, the revolutions in Cuba and Iraq were led, both in form and in substance, by the capitalist class. That fact made it difficult for the imperialists to intervene directly in those countries, because blatant intervention would isolate them in the eyes of the peoples of the world and even in the eyes of the capitalist classes of the world, the classes that provide the support they need in their effort to oppose the communist movement.

For that reason, *as we lead the effort to advance the cause of the revolutionary movement in South Vietnam, we must weigh the situation very carefully and be very cautious but very determined.* This does not mean that we . . . are afraid to launch an armed struggle in South Vietnam. However, our problem is that we must correctly assess the balance of forces between the enemy and ourselves throughout the world and within the Southeast Asian region in order to take action at the proper moment. . . . The course of the revolution in South Vietnam will certainly require the use of revolutionary violence to oppose the counterrevolutionary violence of the U.S. and Diem. However, the question of the revolution in South Vietnam cannot be separated from the complex, back-and-forth struggle that now exists between the two opposing sides around the world and domestically, within our country. If we push the movement forward without first carefully weighing international and domestic conditions, the movement may encounter difficulties and may even regress. . . .

Another issue that needs attention is that at present in many locations our armed operations usually are conducted *in the name of the Party or under the name of the members of the resistance* [implying the old resistance to the French].... At a time when we must still utilize the Geneva Agreement ..., our armed operations should not be conducted under the name of the Party.... You should use whatever name that ... does not frighten the members of the other classes and strata of the population. For example, ... "teams defending the rights of the people," "democratic organizations," "people's self-defense teams," etc. Once the program of the new Front is announced and Front organizations are formed, the Front will provide a more suitable name to appeal to the masses....

The Central Committee has weighed the opinions expressed above very carefully. The analysis of the situation, the comparison of the balance of forces, and the weighing of timing presented above does not in any way mean that we are pulling back or that we are afraid of U.S. intervention.... On the contrary, it is intended to enable us to resolutely build our forces even stronger and create a powerful and solid posture that will allow us and our movement to advance firmly and secure the conditions needed for certain victory....

Document held in the Archives of the Party Central Committee.

Source: *Van Kien Dang, Toan Tap 21, 1960* [Collected Party Documents, Volume 21, 1960] (Hanoi: Nha Xuat Ban Chinh Tri Quoc Gia, 2002), 288–305. Translated by Merle L. Pribbenow.

109. Resolution of the Vietnamese Workers' Party's Third National Congress of Delegates on the Party's Missions and Policies in This New Era, September 10, 1960 [Excerpt]

Introduction

In January 1959 the Central Committee of the Workers' Party in the Democratic Republic of Vietnam (DRV, North Vietnam) agreed to support armed insurrection in the Republic of Vietnam (RVN, South Vietnam), although the insurrection was to remain secondary to the "political struggle." This position was confirmed by the party leadership at the May Fifteenth Party Plenum. At the Third Party Congress in September 1960, the party went on public record as supporting the establishment of a United Front and approving a program of violent overthrow of the Ngo Dinh Diem government in South Vietnam. There were now two preeminent tasks: carrying out "socialist revolution" in North Vietnam and "liberating the South."

Primary Source

II

After peace was restored and North Vietnam was totally liberated, the Vietnamese revolution shifted into a new era. Under the Party's leadership, North Vietnam is advancing towards socialism in firm, solid steps. It is strengthening its forces in all respects and is becoming the revolutionary bulwark of our entire nation. At the same time, the American imperialists and the Ngo Dinh Diem clique have installed a dictatorial, war-mongering government in South Vietnam and have turned South Vietnam into a new type of colony and an American imperialist military base. Our entire people's goal of unifying the nation is now being blocked and sabotaged.

In this current period, the Vietnamese revolution has two strategic missions:

One, to carry out a socialist revolution in North Vietnam, and

Two, to liberate South Vietnam from the yoke of its American imperialist and lackey rulers, to unify our country, and to bring independence and democracy to our entire country.

These two strategic missions are intimately related to one another, and the two missions stimulate and drive one another forward.

Moving North Vietnam forward into socialism is a necessary mission after our completion of the popular national democratic revolution.

Moving North Vietnam forward into socialism and making North Vietnam increasingly powerful in all respects will benefit the revolution to liberate South Vietnam, will benefit the growth of the revolution throughout our country, and will benefit the maintenance and consolidation of peace in Indochina, Southeast Asia, and throughout the world. For that reason, carrying out a socialist revolution in North Vietnam is the most important duty we have for the development of the entire Vietnamese revolutionary movement and for the cause of unifying our nation. The socialist revolution in North Vietnam is being carried out at a time when South Vietnam is being forced to gather together all nationalist and democratic forces and to expand and strengthen national solidarity in order to isolate the American imperialists and their lackeys and advance our cause of fighting to consolidate peace and unify the Fatherland. For that reason, the formula for carrying out the socialist revolution in North Vietnam is: build up North Vietnam while paying attention to South Vietnam.

As part of our overall goal of completing the popular national democratic revolution throughout our country and unifying our nation, our compatriots in South Vietnam have the direct responsibility for overthrowing their American imperialist and lackey rulers in order to liberate South Vietnam. The revolutionary struggle of our Southern compatriots will also block the U.S.-Diemist scheme of starting up the war again and it will make a positive contribution to the maintenance of peace in Indochina, Southeast Asia, and throughout the world.

Our revolutionary mission in North Vietnam and our revolutionary mission in South Vietnam are two different strategies, each of which is aimed at meeting the specific requirements of each region of the country at a time when our nation is temporarily divided. These two missions are also aimed at resolving the common contradiction of our entire country, which is the contradiction between our people and the American imperialists and their lackeys, and at achieving our common immediate objective, which is the peaceful unification of our Fatherland.

The common missions of the Vietnamese revolution at present are: to strengthen the solidarity of our entire population, to struggle resolutely to maintain peace, and to press forward with the socialist revolution in North Vietnam, while at the same time to advance the popular national democratic revolution in South Vietnam, to unify our country on the basis of independence and democracy, to build Vietnam into a single peaceful, unified, independent, democratic, prosperous, and powerful country, to make a practical contribution to the strengthening of the socialist camp, and to preserve peace in Southeast Asia and throughout the world.

III

1. In South Vietnam, for the past several years the American imperialists and their lackeys, Ngo Dinh Diem and his cohorts, have feverishly implemented a policy of building up their military forces to prepare for war, and they have savagely and barbarically repressed and terrorized the revolutionary movement of the people of South Vietnam. Their goal has been to destroy our nation's independence and unity, to destroy the Geneva Agreement, and to destroy peace in Southeast Asia and the rest of the world. They have exploited, looted, and impoverished all classes of our population. They have driven the South Vietnamese economy into a state of serious collapse, they have disrupted South Vietnam's social order, and they have made the lives of our compatriots in the South incredibly miserable and desperate.

Living in a country that is in flames, our compatriots in South Vietnam have not buckled under to repression, and they have constantly raised high the banner of nationalism, democracy, and solidarity, and in the process have exhibited a heroic enthusiasm for our cause. Throughout the rural countryside and the cities, throughout the lowlands and the mountainous regions, the struggle movement against the U.S. and Diem demanding national independence, freedom, democracy, the improvement of the people's lives, and the peaceful unification of our Fatherland continues to spread ever wider among every class of our population. Ever increasing numbers of South Vietnamese soldiers and government officials have recognized the emptiness and injustice of the U.S. and Diem clique.

The more that the U.S. and the Diem clique increase their acts of repression and terror against the people, the higher will burn the flames of hatred and patriotism in South Vietnam, broadening and tightening the solidarity of our people, making our opponents even more isolated, and making the national democratic movement in South Vietnam grow even stronger.

2. The colonialist and semi-feudalist regime in South Vietnam is an obstacle to peace and to the unification of our nation, and it is the source of all the pain, suffering, and hardship of our compatriots in South Vietnam. The basic mission of the South Vietnamese revolution is: to liberate South Vietnam from the yoke of imperialist and feudalist rule, to achieve national independence and implement land to the tillers, and to contribute to the building of a peaceful, unified, independent, democratic, prosperous, and strong Vietnam.

Currently, the deepest, most profound contradiction in South Vietnam is the contradiction between, on the one side, the South Vietnamese people, consisting of the working class, the peasant class, the petit bourgeois class, the capitalist class, the nationalist capitalist class, and all other patriotic classes and individuals, and on the other side, the American imperialists and their lackeys, who consist of the most reactionary pro-American elements within the landlord and traitorous capitalist classes. The immediate, short-term goals of the South Vietnamese revolution are: to unite the entire population in a resolute struggle against the American imperialist warmongers and aggressors; to overthrow the dictatorial Ngo Dinh Diem clique, the lackeys of the American imperialists; to form a national democratic coalition government in South Vietnam; to implement national independence and the rights to freedom and democracy; to improve the lives of the people; to maintain peace; to unify our nation on the basis of independence and democracy; and to actively contribute to the preservation of peace in Southeast Asia and the rest of the world.

3. The revolutionary struggle in South Vietnam will be a long-term, difficult, arduous, and complicated process that will flexibly combine many different forms of struggle, from low-level struggle to intense struggle, and that will be based on building up, strengthening, and expanding the revolutionary forces of the masses.

During this process special attention must be paid to the work of organizing and educating the people, and first of all the workers, peasants, and intellectuals. We must make maximum use of the patriotic spirit of all classes of our population, we must ceaselessly expose the evil, vicious plans and actions of the American imperialists and their lackeys, and we must divide them and completely isolate them.

In order to ensure that the revolutionary struggle in South Vietnam wins total victory, our compatriots in South Vietnam should strive to build a worker-peasant-soldier alliance and form a broad-based united national front opposed to the U.S. and Diem, a front based on the worker-peasant alliance. This front must unite the different classes, patriotic groups, the majority ethnic group and the minority ethnic groups, patriotic political parties, religions, and everyone who is inclined to oppose the U.S. and Diem. The goals of this front will be peace, national independence, freedom, democracy, improvement of the people's living conditions, and the peaceful unification of the Fatherland. Our front operations must unite all the forces that can possibly be united, win over everyone that we can possibly win over, neutralize those forces that need to be neutralized, and attract the vast majority of the popular masses to join the struggle movement against our common enemy, the U.S. and the Diem clique, in order to liberate South Vietnam and peacefully unify our Fatherland.

4. The revolutionary movement in South Vietnam occupies a very important place in our cause of unifying our nation. In parallel with our effort to build up North Vietnam and advance the North toward socialism, our people also need to strive to preserve and expand the revolutionary forces in South Vietnam in order to create favorable conditions for the peaceful reunification of our nation.

Our people's struggle for the unification of our nation is a just struggle, and we oppose the efforts of the American imperialists and their lackeys to sabotage the Geneva Agreement, which is an international treaty that recognizes the independence, sovereignty, unity, and territorial integrity of our country. Our government and our people are resolved to maintain our policy, which is to peacefully unify our nation and to preserve and respect the Geneva Agreement. We advocate a gradual, step-by-step unification of our country in accordance with the spirit of the Manifesto of Vietnam's Fatherland Front. However, we must always maintain a high state of vigilance and be prepared to deal with any eventuality. If the American imperialists and their lackeys should recklessly start a war with the aim of invading North Vietnam, then the people of our entire nation will resolutely rise up to defeat them and to achieve national independence and the unification of our Fatherland....

Source: *Van Kien Dang, Toan Tap 21, 1960* [Collected Party Documents, Volume 21, 1960] (Hanoi: Nha Xuat Ban Chinh Tri Quoc Gia, 2002), 916–921. Translated by Merle L. Pribbenow.

110. Politburo Cable No. 17-NB Sent to the Cochin China Region Party Committee and the Interzone 5 Region Party Committee, November 11, 1960 [Excerpts]

Introduction

On November 11, 1960, Army of the Republic of Vietnam (ARVN, South Vietnamese Army) paratroopers supported by a number of prominent political figures from the Republic of Vietnam (RVN,

South Vietnam) mounted a coup aimed at overthrowing South Vietnamese president Ngo Dinh Diem. The Communist leadership in Hanoi decided that this coup attempt gave them an excellent opportunity to announce the formation of their long-planned supposedly non-Communist front movement, which was designed to hide the fact that the Communists were in control of the insurgency in South Vietnam. The Politburo also approved and sent to South Vietnam the "Manifesto of the National Liberation Front" (NLF), which the new NLF was to release publicly. These cables provide clear evidence that contrary to the claims made by the government of the Democratic Republic of Vietnam (DRV, North Vietnam) throughout the Vietnam War, the NLF was never a truly independent organization.

Primary Source

1. According to reports we have received from the enemy and through news broadcasts by Saigon, British, American, and French radio stations, a coup began at 3:00 in the morning on 11 November 1960. The coup is being conducted by a number of officers in Diem's army, using airborne units in coordination with police forces and a number of infantry and armored units, all under the command of Colonel Nguyen Chanh Thi and other individuals opposed to Diem.... As of 8:00 tonight, Diem was still dragging his feet, had still not agreed to negotiate, and was moving additional forces from Military Region 5 and elements from Military Regions 1 and 4 up to counter the main coup forces in Saigon. The situation is still unclear. We need to continue to monitor it closely.

No matter what the outcome, this armed clash is beneficial to our side.... Several months ago, based on the situation in South Korea and in Laos, the Politburo sent a directive to you to intensify the political struggle aimed at overthrowing the U.S.-Diem regime. This new situation is very favorable for the implementation of those policies.... The Politburo is providing the following policy guidelines for you to use, based on your assessment of the actual situation down in your area:

Our policy at this time is to exploit the contradictions, disruptions, and confusion in the enemy's ranks to the maximum in order to incite a large mass struggle movement aimed at overthrowing the entire reactionary clique, ... at demanding the formation of a broad-based national democratic coalition government ... and at progressing toward the eventual reunification of the Fatherland. At the same time, we want to use this opportunity to ... form a broad-based united national front.... In order to accomplish these goals, we must publicly issue the program of the National Liberation Front for South Vietnam....

Regarding forms of struggle, we must mobilize large mass forces and coordinate the political struggle with the armed struggle.... In those areas where conditions permit, you might liberate a number of areas or certain towns and cities, but do not publicly use our Party's name and do not display our Party flag or our national flag. Instead, you should use the name of the National

Liberation Front. . . . Depending on the way the situation continues to develop, the Central Committee will send you additional instructions.

Document held in the Archives of the Central Committee.

Source: *Van Kien Dang, Toan Tap 21, 1960* [Collected Party Documents, Volume 21, 1960] (Hanoi: Nha Xuat Ban Chinh Tri Quoc Gia, 2002), 1012–1016. Translated by Merle L. Pribbenow.

111. Manifesto of the National Liberation Front, December 1960

Introduction

On December 20, 1960, Hanoi established the National Front for the Liberation of South Vietnam, usually known as the National Liberation Front (NLF). Designed to replicate the Viet Minh as an umbrella nationalist organization that would appeal to all those disaffected with the regime of President Ngo Dinh Diem in the Republic of Vietnam (RVN, South Vietnam), the manifesto was in fact from the beginning dominated by the Lao Dong (Workers' Party) Central Committee and was North Vietnam's shadow government in South Vietnam.

Primary Source

Compatriots in the country and abroad!

Over the past hundred years the Vietnamese people repeatedly rose up to fight against foreign aggression for the independence and freedom of their fatherland. In 1945, the people throughout the country surged up in an armed uprising, overthrew the Japanese and French domination and seized power. When the French colonialists invaded our country for the second time, our compatriots, determined not to be enslaved again, shed much blood and laid down many lives to defend their national sovereignty and independence. Their solidarity and heroic struggle during nine years led the resistance war to victory. The 1954 Geneva Agreements restored peace in our country and recognized "the sovereignty, independence, unity and territorial integrity of Viet Nam."

Our compatriots in South Viet Nam would have been able to live in peace, to earn their livelihood in security and to build a decent and happy life.

However, the American imperialists, who had in the past helped the French colonialists to massacre our people, have now replaced the French in enslaving the southern part of our country through a disguised colonial regime. They have been using their stooge—the Ngo Dinh Diem administration—in their downright repression and exploitation of our compatriots, in their manoeuvres to permanently divide our country and to turn its southern part into a military base in preparation for war in Southeast Asia.

The aggressors and traitors, working hand in glove with each other, have set up an extremely cruel dictatorial rule. They persecute and massacre democratic and patriotic people, and abolish all human liberties. They ruthlessly exploit the workers, peasants and other labouring people, strangle the local industry and trade, poison the minds of our people with a depraved foreign culture, thus degrading our national culture, traditions and ethics. They feverishly increase their military forces, build military bases, use the army as an instrument for repressing the people and serving the US imperialists' scheme to prepare an aggressive war.

Never, over the past six years, have gun shots massacring our compatriots ceased to resound throughout South Viet Nam. Tens of thousands of patriots here have been murdered and hundreds of thousands thrown into jail. All sections of the people have been living in a stifling atmosphere under the iron heel of the US-Diem clique. Countless families have been torn away and scenes of mourning are seen everywhere as a result of unemployment, poverty, exacting taxes, terror, massacre, drafting of manpower and pressganging, usurpation of land, forcible house removal, and herding of the people into "prosperity zones," "resettlement centres" and other forms of concentration camps.

High anger with the present tyrannical regime is boiling among all strata of the people. Undaunted in the face of barbarous persecution, our compatriots are determined to unite and struggle unflaggingly against the US imperialists' policy of aggression and the dictatorial and nepotic regime of the Ngo Dinh Diem clique. Among workers, peasants and other toiling people, among intellectuals, students and pupils, industrialists and traders, religious sects and national minorities, patriotic activities are gaining in scope and strength, seriously shaking the US-Diem dictatorial regime.

The attempted coup d'etat of November 11, 1960 in Saigon in some respects reflected the seething anger among the people and armymen, and the rottenness and decline of the US-Diem regime. However, there were among the leaders of this coup political speculators who, misusing the patriotism of the armymen, preferred negotiation and compromise rather than to overthrow Ngo Dinh Diem. Like Ngo Dinh Diem, they persisted in following the pro-American and traitorous path, and also used the anticommunist signboard to oppose the people. That is why the coup was not supported by the people and large numbers of armymen and, consequently, ended in failure.

At present, our people are urgently demanding an end to the cruel dictatorial rule; they are demanding independence and democracy, enough food and clothing, and peaceful reunification of the country.

To meet the aspirations of our compatriots, the South Viet Nam National Front for Liberation came into being, pledging itself to shoulder the historic task of liberating our people from the present yoke of slavery.

The South Viet Nam National Front for Liberation undertakes to unite all sections of the people, all social classes, nationalities, political parties, organizations, religious communities and patriotic personalities, without distinction of their political tendencies in order to struggle for the overthrow of the rule of the US imperialists and their stooges—the Ngo Dinh Diem clique—and for the realization of independence, democracy, peace and neutrality pending the peaceful reunification of the fatherland.

The South Viet Nam National Front for Liberation calls on the entire people to unite and heroically rise up as one man to fight along the line of a program of action summarized as follows:

1. To overthrow the disguised colonial regime of the US imperialists and the dictatorial Ngo Dinh Diem administration—lackey of the United States—, and to form a national democratic coalition administration.

2. To bring into being a broad and progressive democracy, promulgate freedom of expression, of the press, of belief, of assembly, of association, of movement and other democratic freedoms. To grant general amnesty to all political detainees, dissolve all concentration camps dubbed "prosperity zones" and "resettlement centres," abolish the fascist 10-59 law and other anti-democratic laws.

3. To abolish the economic monopoly of the United States and its henchmen, to protect home-made products, encourage home industry and trade, expand agriculture and build an independent and sovereign economy. To provide jobs for the unemployed, increase wages for workers, armymen and office employees. To abolish arbitrary fines and apply an equitable and rational tax system. To help those who have gone South to return to their native places if they so desire, and to provide jobs for those among them who want to remain in the South.

4. To carry out land rent reduction, guarantee the peasants' right to till present plots of land, redistribute communal land and advance toward land reform.

5. To do away with enslaving and depraved US-style culture, build a national and progressive culture and education. To wipe out illiteracy, open more schools, carry out reforms in the educational and examination system.

6. To abolish the system of American military advisers, eliminate foreign military bases in Viet Nam and build a national army for the defence of the fatherland and the people.

7. To guarantee equality between men and women and among different nationalities, and the right to autonomy of the national minorities; to protect the legitimate interests of foreign residents in Viet Nam; to protect and take care of the interests of Vietnamese living abroad.

8. To carry out a foreign policy of peace and neutrality, to establish diplomatic relations with all countries which respect the independence and sovereignty of Viet Nam.

9. To re-establish normal relations between the two zones, pending the peaceful reunification of the fatherland.

10. To oppose aggressive war; to actively defend world peace.

Compatriots!

Ours are a heroic people with a tradition of unity and indomitable struggle. We cannot let our country be plunged into darkness and mourning. We are determined to shatter the fetters of slavery, and wrest back independence and freedom.

Let us all rise up and unite!

Let us close our ranks and fight under the banner of the South Viet Nam National Front for Liberation to overthrow the rule of the US imperialists and Ngo Dinh Diem—their henchmen.

Workers, peasants and other toiling people! The oppression and misery which are now heavily weighing on you must be ended. You have the strength of tens of millions of people. Stand up enthusiastically to save your families and our fatherland.

Intellectuals! The dictatorial rulers have stripped us of the most elementary human rights. You are living in humiliation and misery. For our great cause, stand up resolutely!

Industrialists and traders! A country under the sway of foreign sharks cannot have an independent and sovereign economy. You should join in the people's struggle.

Compatriots of all national minorities! Compatriots of all religious communities! Unity is life, disunity is death. Smash all US-Diem schemes of division. Side with the entire people in the struggle for independence, freedom and equality among all nationalities.

Notables! The interests of the nation are above all else. Support actively the struggle for the overthrow of the cruel aggressors and traitors.

Patriotic officers and soldiers! You have arms in your hands. Listen to the sacred call of the fatherland. Be definitely on the side of the people. Your compatriots have faith in your patriotism.

Young men and women! You are the future of the nation. You should devote your youthful ardour to serving the fatherland.

Compatriots living abroad! Turn your thoughts toward the beloved fatherland, contribute actively to the sacred struggle for national liberation.

At present the movement for peace, democracy and national independence is surging up throughout the world. Colonialism is irretrievably disintegrating. The time when the imperialists could plunder and subjugate the people at will is over. This situation is extremely favourable for the struggle to free South Viet Nam from the yoke of the US imperialists and their stooges. Peace-loving and progressive people in the world are supporting us. Justice is on our side, and we have the prodigious strength of the unity of our entire people. We will certainly win! The US imperialist aggressors and the Ngo Dinh Diem traitorous clique will certainly be defeated. The cause of liberation of South Viet Nam will certainly triumph.

Compatriots around the country!

Let us write and march forward confidently and valiantly to score brilliant victories for our people and our fatherland!

"South Vietnam From the N.F.L. to the Provisional Government."

Source: *South Viet Nam National Front for Liberation: Documents* (Saigon: Giai Phong Publishing House, 1968), 11–31.

112. Elbridge Durbrow, U.S. Ambassador in Saigon: Cablegram to Secretary of State Christian A. Herter, December 24, 1960 [Excerpt]

Introduction

Opposition within the Republic of Vietnam (RVN, South Vietnam) to the regime of President Ngo Dinh Diem continued to mount even in the cities, which had been the chief beneficiaries under his regime. In April 1960, 18 prominent South Vietnamese issued a manifesto protesting governmental abuses. They were promptly arrested. In October 1960 with the security situation deteriorating, U.S. ambassador Elbridge Durbrow received approval from Washington to present to Diem a memorandum urging political and administrative reforms. On November 11–12, 1960, American officials were caught by surprise when three battalions of the Army of the Republic of Vietnam (ARVN, South Vietnamese Army) elite paratroop group surrounded the presidential palace in Saigon and demanded reforms, a new government, and more effective prosecution of the war. Diem outmaneuvered them. He agreed to a long list of reforms—including freedom of the press, a coalition government, and new elections—until he could bring loyal army

units to the scene and reverse the situation. Diem refused to see the need for far-reaching political or social reform. Far from pushing him toward reform, the coup attempt merely intensified his distrust of others and caused him to concentrate more authority in his own hands. In this cable to Washington, Durbrow concludes that Diem is convinced that force is the best means of preserving his regime.

Primary Source

On few occasions he let me talk, I urged he adopt reforms soonest since it essential to win further support of the people if Viet Cong menace is to be overcome, but he gave me no indication of reforms he may adopt. Before leaving I again expressed hope that he would accept our suggestion that he announce all liberalizing programs at one time in order to make best impact. Diem replied he would think about this but made no commitment.

Comments. We have heard that Nhu, Thuan and others have been running into resistance when urging Diem to adopt worthwhile reforms. I also received impression he very reluctant to adopt reforms and is still basically thinking in terms of force to save the day, hence his insistence several times that we approve force level increase and his action raising Civil Guard ceiling by 10,000. While I still believe it absolutely essential he adopt more liberal programs, it is not certain from his attitude and remarks that he will take effective action in these matters, although I learned later he has agreed to engage the services of a public relations expert suggested by CAS to make a survey GVN foreign public relations needs.

Source: *United States–Vietnam Relations, 1945–1967,* Book 10 (Washington, DC: U.S. Government Printing Office, 1971), 1350–1351.

113. Gilpatric Task Force Report, April 27, 1961 [Excerpt]

Introduction

New U.S. president John F. Kennedy requested an appraisal of the security situation in the Republic of Vietnam (RVN, South Vietnam). An interagency task force, headed by Undersecretary of Defense Roswell Gilpatric, recommended to Kennedy a modest increase in the number of U.S. military advisers and appropriations sufficient to increase the size of the Army of the Republic of Vietnam (ARVN, South Vietnamese Army) by 200,000 men. Overriding these recommendations, however, was the task force's conclusion that the insurgency in South Vietnam was not so much a response to President Ngo Dinh Diem's repression as it was part of a Communist "master plan" to seize control of all of Southeast Asia.

Primary Source

After meeting in Hanoi on 13 May 1959, the Central Committee of the North Vietnamese Communist Party publicly announced its intention "to smash" the government of President Diem. Following this decision, the Viet Cong have significantly increased their program of infiltration, subversion, sabotage and assassination designed to achieve this end.

At the North Vietnamese Communist Party Congress in September 1960, the earlier declaration of underground war by the Party's Control Committee was reaffirmed. This action by the Party Congress took place only a month after Kong Le's coup in Laos. Scarcely two months later there was a Military uprising in Saigon. The turmoil created throughout the area by this rapid succession of events provides an ideal environment for the Communist "master plan" to take over all of Southeast Asia.

Since that time, the internal security situation in South Vietnam has become critical. What amounts to a state of active guerrilla warfare now exists throughout the country. The number of Viet Cong hard-core Communists has increased from 4400 in early 1960 to an estimated 12,000 today. The number of violent incidents per month now averages 650. Casualties on both sides totaled more than 4500 during the first three months of this year. Fifty-eight percent of the country is under some degree of Communist control, ranging from harassment and night raids to almost complete administrative jurisdiction in the Communist "secure areas."

The Viet Cong over the past two years have succeeded in stepping up the pace and intensity of their attacks to the point where South Vietnam is nearing the decisive phase in its battle for survival. If the situation continues to deteriorate, the Communists will be able to press on to their strategic goal of establishing a rival "National Liberation Front" government in one of these "secure areas" thereby plunging the nation into open civil war. They have publicly announced that they will "take over the country before the end of 1961."

This situation is thus critical, but is not hopeless. The Vietnamese Government, with American aid, has increased its capabilities to fight its attackers, and provides a base upon which the necessary additional effort can be founded to defeat the Communist attack. Should the Communist effort increase, either directly or as a result of a collapse of Laos, additional measures beyond those proposed herein would be necessary.

In short, the situation in South Vietnam has reached the point where, at least for the time being, primary emphasis should be placed on providing a solution to the internal security problem.

The US Objective: To create a viable and increasingly democratic society in South Vietnam and to prevent Communist domination of the country.

Concept of Operations: To initiate on an accelerated basis, a series of mutually supporting actions of a military, political, economic, psychological and covert character designed to achieve this objective. In so doing, it is intended to use, and where appropriate extend, expedite or build upon the existing US and Government of Vietnam (GVN) programs already underway in South Vietnam. There is neither the time available nor any sound justification for "starting from scratch." Rather the need is to focus the US effort in South Vietnam on the immediate internal security problem; to infuse it with a sense of urgency and a dedication to the overall US objective; to achieve, through cooperative interdepartmental support both in the field and in Washington, the operational flexibility needed to apply the available US assets in a manner best calculated to achieve our objective in Vietnam; and, finally, to impress on our friends, the Vietnamese, and on our foes, the Viet Cong, that come what may, the US intends to win this battle.

Source: *United States–Vietnam Relations, 1945–1967,* Book 11 (Washington, DC: U.S. Government Printing Office, 1971), 43–45.

114. Memorandum of Conversation Involving Secretary of State Dean Rusk, Secretary of Defense Robert McNamara, the Joint Chiefs of Staff, and Other Officials, April 29, 1961 [Excerpts]

Introduction

Throughout much of the John F. Kennedy administration, Laos—not Vietnam—was center stage. President Dwight D. Eisenhower had told Kennedy that Laos was the key to Southeast Asia. By the end of 1960, Washington had already provided the Laotian government with $300 million in assistance, of which 85 percent was military. Civil war in Laos now flared anew. A military coup occurred against the rightist government, and both the Democratic Republic of Vietnam (DRV, North Vietnam) and the Soviet Union actively intervened. Key Kennedy administration officials debated an appropriate response. There was general agreement among the conferees that if the United States did not intervene in Laos, the United States would have to fight in Thailand or the Republic of Vietnam (RVN, South Vietnam). Hardliner secretary of state Dean Rusk urged military intervention in Laos, while U.S. Air Force chief of staff General Curtis LeMay called for a preemptive war with China, which he said would have nuclear weapons in a year or two. In the end, Kennedy decided not to send U.S. troops and instead to put his trust in the Geneva Conference on Laos, which opened in July. In this he was to be disappointed.

Primary Source

[...]

The Attorney General asked where would be the best place to stand and fight in Southeast Asia, where to draw the line. Mr. McNamara said he thought we would take a stand in Thailand and South Viet-Nam. The Attorney General asked whether we would save any of Laos, but the major question was whether we would stand up and fight.

Admiral Burke said that we could hold Tourane, and General Le May observed that we could use our air power back as far as necessary, letting the enemy have all of the countryside but that the PL [Pathet Lao] could be stopped by air power.

Mr. McNamara said that we would have to attack the DRV if we gave up Laos.

The Secretary suggested that the part of Laos from the 17th Parallel across to the Mekong might be easier to hold than the entire country.

General Decker thought that there was no good place to fight in Southeast Asia but we must hold as much as we can of Viet-Nam, Cambodia and Laos. At this point the Secretary said we had missed having government troops who were willing to fight.

Mr. Steeves pointed out that we had always argued that we would not give up Laos and that it was on the pleas of our military that we had supported Phoumi; that we had reiterated in the press and to the public what Laos meant to us. If this problem is unsolvable then the problem of Viet-Nam would be unsolvable. If we decided that this was untenable then we were writing the first chapter in the defeat of Southeast Asia. Mr. McNamara said the situation was not as bad five weeks ago as it was now.

Admiral Burke pointed out that each time you give ground it is harder to stand next time. If we give up Laos we would have to put US forces into Viet-Nam and Thailand. We would have to throw enough in to win—perhaps the "works". It would be easier to hold now than later. The thing to do was to land now and hold as much as we can and make clear that we were not going to be pushed out of Southeast Asia. We were fighting for the rest of Asia.

Mr. McNamara wondered whether more Viet Cong would necessarily enter South Vietnam if Laos went down the drain. He mentioned that some 12,000 Viet Cong had entered South Viet-Nam under present conditions and that the Communists held the area south of the 17th Parallel to a depth of twenty-five miles with a supposedly friendly government in South Viet-Nam. (Several of those present questioned the accuracy of the figure of 12,000.)

Turning to the question of the morale of the Southeast Asians, the Secretary recalled that the Thai Foreign Minister had told him during the recent SEATO conference that Thailand was like a "golden bell" which had to be protected from outside. The Secretary said he was not sure the Foreign Minister was wrong. He added that he was less worried about escalation than he was about infectious slackness. He said he would not give a cent for what the Persians would think of us if we did not defend Laos.

General Decker thought that we should have stood last August and wondered what would happen if we got "licked". The Secretary suggested that Thai and US troops might be placed together in Vientiane and, if they could not hold, be removed by helicopter. Even if they were defeated they would be defeated together and this would be better than sitting back and doing nothing. General Decker said we cannot win a conventional war in Southeast Asia; if we go in, we should go in to win, and that means bombing Hanoi, China, and maybe even using nuclear bombs. He pointed out that all the advantage we have in heavy equipment would be lost in the difficult terrain of Laos where we would be at the mercy of the guerrillas. The Secretary pointed out that this fact was also true at the time of the Bangkok Resolution but that we had gone ahead with the resolution anyway and had issued statements indicating that we would back up our words with deeds. Mr. McNamara repeated that the situation is now worse than it was five weeks ago. Mr. Steeves pointed out that the same problems existed in South Viet-Nam, but Admiral Burke thought that South Viet-Nam could be more easily controlled.

General Decker then suggested that troops be moved into Thailand and South Viet-Nam to see whether such action would not produce a cease-fire. Admiral Burke asked what happens if there is still no cease-fire. General Decker said then we would be ready to go ahead.

Mr. Kennedy said we would look sillier than we do now if we got troops in there and then backed down. He reiterated the question whether we are ready to go the distance.

The Secretary said that we would want to get the United Nations "mixed up" in this.

Mr. Behlen [sic: Bohlen] said he saw no need for a fixation on the possibility of a reaction by the Chinese Communists. He said we had no evidence that they want to face the brink of nuclear war. He said that he was more concerned about the objectives we would seek if we took military action.

There followed a discussion about the possibility of restoring the kingdom of Champassak where Boun Oum relinquished the throne and where he is popular. It was thought that Sihanouk would support a partition of Laos. General Decker thought that if a cease-fire could be effected now, it would be possible to secure southern Laos.

General Le May did not believe that it would be possible to get a cease-fire without military action. He admitted that he did not know what US policy is in Laos. He knew what the President had said but he also pointed out that the military had been unable to back up the President's statements. He then enumerated a number of possibilities: 1) do nothing and lose Laos; 2) use B-26's and slow up the enemy; 3) use more sophisticated bombers and stop supplies and then perhaps Phoumi's forces could be brought up to where they could fight; 4) implement Plan 5, backing up troops with air. General Le May did not think the Chinese would escalate but believed on the contrary that a cease-fire would then be brought about. He added that he believed we should go to work on China itself and let Chiang take Hainan Island. He thought Chiang had a good air force. . . .

Mr. Bowles said he thought the main question to be faced was the fact that we were going to have to fight the Chinese anyway in 2, 3, 5 or 10 years and that it was just a question of where, when and how. He thought that a major war would be difficult to avoid. General Le May said that, in that case, we should fight soon since the Chinese would have nuclear weapons within one or two years.

Mr. McNamara said that the situation was worsening by the hour and that if we were going to commit ourselves, then we must do so sooner rather than later.

The Secretary then adjourned the meeting saying he would like to consider the matter further.

> **Source:** *United States–Vietnam Relations, 1945–1967,* Book 11 (Washington, DC: U.S. Government Printing Office, 1971), 63–66.

115. National Security Action Memorandum No. 80, August 29, 1961

Introduction

U.S. president John F. Kennedy was not opposed to a neutralist solution for the Kingdom of Laos, now torn by a three-way struggle involving Communists, neutralists, and rightists. A 14-nation conference convened in Geneva in June 1961, and Kennedy worked to get neutralist prince Souvanna Phouma to agree to his proposals for Laos. As the talks wore on, fighting continued in northeastern Laos between the Communist Pathet Lao, supported by the Democratic Republic of Vietnam (DRV, North Vietnam), and Meo tribesmen, supported by the United States. The North Vietnamese government wanted control of eastern Laos for its Ho Chi Minh Trail infiltration network that funneled men and supplies into the Republic of Vietnam (RVN, South Vietnam), feeding the insurgency there. In this memorandum, President Kennedy approves a modest expansion in military assistance to Laos, including more advisers and the arming of additional Meo.

The failure of the Communists to live up to the subsequent Geneva Agreements concerning neutralization of Laos greatly angered Kennedy and influenced his policies regarding Vietnam.

Primary Source

The President approved the following actions:

1. An intensification of the diplomatic effort to achieve agreement to the Paris proposals on the part of Souvanna, especially by direct conversations between Ambassador Harriman and Souvanna, with an emphasis not only upon the interlocking importance of the Paris proposals, but also upon U.S. support of Souvanna in the event that he accepts the Paris plan.

2. Authorization to undertake conversations with SEATO allies both bilaterally and with the SEATO Council, exploring the possibility of an enlargement of the concept of SEATO Plan 5. It must be understood that this exploration was in the nature of contingency planning and did not represent a flat commitment of the United States to participate in such an enlarged enterprise.

3. An immediate increase in mobile training teams in Laos to include advisers down to the level of the company, to a total U.S. strength in this area of 500, together with an attempt to get Thai agreement to supply an equal amount of Thais for the same purpose.

4. An immediate increase of 2,000 in the number of Meos being supported to bring the total to a level of 11,000.

5. Authorization for photo-reconnaissance by Thai or sanitized aircraft over all of Laos.

It is assumed that these actions will be carried out under the general direction of the Southeast Asia Task Force under the direction of Deputy Under Secretary Johnson.

> **Source:** *United States–Vietnam Relations, 1945–1967,* Book 11 (Washington, DC: U.S. Government Printing Office, 1971), 247–248.

116. General Maxwell Taylor: Cable to President John F. Kennedy Recommending Dispatch of U.S. Forces to South Vietnam, November 1, 1961

Introduction

In October 1961 U.S. president John F. Kennedy's chief military adviser General Maxwell D. Taylor and Special Assistant for National

Security Affairs Walt W. Rostow led a fact-finding trip to the Republic of Vietnam (RVN, South Vietnam). They saw the situation primarily in military terms and recommended a change in the U.S. role from advisory to "limited partnership" with the South Vietnamese government. In this cable, Taylor urges increased U.S. economic aid and military advisory support to include intensive training of local self-defense forces and a significant increase in airplanes, helicopters, and support personnel. Taylor also recommends deployment to South Vietnam of some 8,000 American combat troops to support the Army of the Republic of Vietnam (ARVN, South Vietnamese Army) in military operations. To overcome South Vietnamese president Ngo Dinh Diem's sensitivity regarding foreign troops, these would be called a "flood control team." As it worked out, Diem was opposed to U.S. troops, and Kennedy limited increased U.S. assistance to advisers and air personnel only.

Primary Source

This message is for the purpose of presenting my reasons for recommending the introduction of a U.S. military force into South Vietnam (SVN). I have reached the conclusion that this is an essential action if we are to reverse the present downward trend of events in spite of a full recognition of the following disadvantages:

a. The strategic reserve of U.S. forces is presently so weak that we can ill afford any detachment of forces to a peripheral area of the Communist bloc where they will be pinned down for an uncertain duration.

b. Although U.S. prestige is already engaged in SVN, it will become more so by the sending of troops.

c. If the first contingent is not enough to accomplish the necessary results, it will be difficult to resist the pressure to reinforce. If the ultimate result sought is the closing of the frontiers and the clean-up of the insurgents within SVN, there is no limit to our possible commitment (unless we attack the source in Hanoi).

d. The introduction of U.S. forces may increase tensions and risk escalation into a major war in Asia.

On the other side of the argument, there can be no action so convincing of U.S. seriousness of purpose and hence so reassuring to the people and Government of SVN and to our other friends and allies in SEA as the introduction of U.S. forces into SVN. The views of indigenous and U.S. officials consulted on our trip were unanimous on this point. I have just seen Saigon original 545 to State and suggest that it be read in connection with this message.

The size of the U.S. force introduced need not be great to provide the military presence necessary to produce the desired effect on national morale in SVN and on international opinion. A bare token, however, will not suffice; it must have a significant value.

The kinds of tasks which it might undertake which would have a significant value are suggested in BAGI00005. They are:

(a) Provide a U.S. military presence capable of raising national morale and of showing to Southeast Asia the seriousness of the U.S. intent to resist a Communist take-over.

(b) Conduct logistical operations in support of military and flood relief operations.

(c) Conduct such combat operations as are necessary for self-defense and for the security of the area in which they are stationed.

(d) Provide an emergency reserve to back up the Armed Forces of the GVN [Government of the Republic of Vietnam] in the case of a heightened military crisis.

(e) Act as an advance party of such additional forces as may be introduced if CINCPAC [Commander in Chief, Pacific] or SEATO [Southeast Asia Treaty Organization] contingency plans are invoked.

It is noteworthy that this force is not proposed to clear the jungles and forests of Viet Cong guerrillas. That should be the primary task of the Armed Forces of Vietnam for which they should be specifically organized, trained, and stiffened with ample U.S. advisors down to combat battalion levels. However, the U.S. troops may be called upon to engage in combat to protect themselves, their working parties, and the area in which they live. As a general reserve, they might be thrown into action (with U.S. agreement) against large, formed guerrilla bands which have abandoned the forests for attacks on major targets. But in general, our forces should not engage in small-scale guerrilla operations in the jungle.

As an area for the operations of U.S. troops, SVN is not an excessively difficult or unpleasant place to operate. While the border areas are rugged and heavily forested, the terrain is comparable to parts of Korea where U.S. troops learned to live and work without too much effort. However, these border areas, for reasons stated above, are not the places to engage our forces. In the High Plateau and in the coastal plain where U.S. troops would probably be stationed, these jungle-forest conditions do not exist to any great extent. The most unpleasant feature in the coastal areas would be the heat and, in the Delta, the mud left behind by the flood. The High Plateau offers no particular obstacle to the stationing of U.S. troops.

The extent to which the Task Force would engage in flood relief activities in the Delta will depend upon further study of the problem there. As reported in Saigon 537, I see considerable advantages in playing up this aspect of the Task Force mission. I am presently inclined to favor a dual mission, initially help to the flood area and subsequently use in any other area of SVN where its resources can be used effectively to give tangible support in the struggle against the Viet Cong. However, the possibility of emphasizing the humanitarian mission will wane if we wait long in moving in our forces or in linking our stated purpose with the emergency conditions created by the flood.

The risks of backing into a major Asian war by way of SVN are present but are not impressive. NVN is extremely vulnerable to conventional bombing, a weakness which should be exploited diplomatically in convincing Hanoi to lay off SVN. Both the D.R.V. and the Chicoms [Chinese Communists] would face severe logistical difficulties in trying to maintain strong forces in the field in SEA, difficulties which we share but by no means to the same degree. There is no case for fearing a mass onslaught of Communist manpower into SVN and its neighboring states, particularly if our airpower is allowed a free hand against logistical targets. Finally, the starvation conditions in China should discourage Communist leaders there from being militarily venturesome for some time to come.

By the foregoing line of reasoning, I have reached the conclusion that the introduction of U.S. military Task Force without delay offers definitely more advantage than it creates risks and difficulties. In fact, I do not believe that our program to save SVN will succeed without it. If the concept is approved, the exact size and composition of the force should be determined by Secretary of Defense in consultation with the JCS, the Chief MAAG [Military Assistance Advisory Group] and CINCPAC. My own feeling is that the initial size should not exceed about 8000, of which a preponderant number would be in logistical-type units. After acquiring experience in operating in SVN, this initial force will require reorganization and adjustment to the local scene.

As CINCPAC will point out, any forces committed to SVN will need to be replaced by additional forces to his area from the strategic reserve in the U.S. Also, any troops to SVN are in addition to those which may be required to execute SEATO Plan 5 in Laos. Both facts should be taken into account in current considerations of the FY [fiscal year] 1963 budget which bear upon the permanent increase which should be made in the U.S. military establishment to maintain our strategic position for the long pull.

Source: *United States–Vietnam Relations, 1945–1967,* Book 11 (Washington, DC: U.S. Government Printing Office, 1971), 337–342.

117. Robert McNamara, Defense Secretary: Memorandum to President John F. Kennedy, November 8, 1961

Introduction

In this memorandum, U.S. secretary of defense Robert S. McNamara comments on the recommendations from military adviser General Maxwell D. Taylor following the latter's fact-finding mission to the Republic of Vietnam (RVN, South Vietnam). McNamara warns President John F. Kennedy that the dispatch of ground troops could be the beginning of a long conflict between the United States on one side and the Democratic Republic of Vietnam (DRV, North Vietnam) and the People's Republic of China (PRC) on the other. McNamara, with the support of the Joint Chiefs of Staff (JCS), recommends that the United States not send ground troops unless it "commit[s] itself to the clear objective of preventing the fall of South Vietnam to Communism."

Primary Source

The basic issue framed by the Taylor Report is whether the U.S. shall:

a. Commit itself to the clear objective of preventing the fall of South Vietnam to Communism, and

b. Support this commitment by necessary immediate military actions and preparations for possible later actions.

The Joint Chiefs, Mr. Gilpatric, and I have reached the following conclusions:

1. The fall of South Vietnam to Communism would lead to the fairly rapid extension of Communist control, or complete accommodation to Communism, in the rest of mainland Southeast Asia and in Indonesia. The strategic implications worldwide, particularly in the Orient, would be extremely serious.

2. The chances are against, probably sharply against, preventing that fall by any measures short of the introduction of U.S. forces on a substantial scale. We accept General Taylor's judgment that the various measures proposed by him short of this are useful but will not in themselves do the job of restoring confidence and setting Diem on the way to winning his fight.

3. The introduction of a U.S. force of the magnitude of an initial 8,000 men in a flood relief context will be of great help to Diem. However, it will not convince the other side (whether the shots are called from Moscow, Peiping or Hanoi) that we mean business. Moreover, it probably will not tip the scales decisively. We would be almost certain to get increasingly mired down in an inconclusive struggle.

4. The other side can be convinced we mean business only if we accompany the initial force introduction by a clear commitment to the full objective stated above, accompanied by a warning through some channel to Hanoi that continued support of the Viet Cong will lead to punitive retaliation against North Vietnam.

5. If we act in this way, the ultimate possible extent of our military commitment must be faced. The struggle may be prolonged and Hanoi and Peiping may intervene overtly. In view of the logistic

difficulties faced by the other side, I believe we can assume that the maximum U.S. forces required on the ground in Southeast Asia will not exceed 6 divisions, or about 205,000 men, (CINCPAC Plan 32-59, Phase IV). Our military posture is, or, with the addition of more National Guard or regular Army divisions, can be made, adequate to furnish these forces without serious interference with our present Berlin plans.

6. To accept the stated objective is of course a most serious decision. Military force is not the only element of what must be a most carefully coordinated set of actions. Success will depend on factors many of which are not within our control—notably the conduct of Diem himself and other leaders in the area. Laos will remain a major problem. The domestic political implications of accepting the objective are also grave, although it is our feeling that the country will respond better to a firm initial position than to courses of action that lead us in only gradually, and that in the meantime are sure to involve casualties. The over-all effect on Moscow and Peiping will need careful weighing and may well be mixed; however, permitting South Vietnam to fall can only strengthen and encourage them greatly.

7. In sum:

    a. We do not believe major units of U.S. forces should be introduced in South Vietnam unless we are willing to make an affirmative decision on the issue stated at the start of this memorandum.

    b. We are inclined to recommend that we do commit the U.S. to the clear objective of preventing the fall of South Vietnam to Communism and that we support this commitment by the necessary military actions.

    c. If such a commitment is agreed upon, we support the recommendations of General Taylor as the first steps toward its fulfillment.

Source: *United States–Vietnam Relations, 1945–1967*, Book 11 (Washington, DC: U.S. Government Printing Office, 1971), 343–344.

118. Dean Rusk and Robert S. McNamara: Memorandum to President John F. Kennedy, November 11, 1961 [Excerpts]

Introduction

Unlike President John F. Kennedy, who tended to see the fighting in the Republic of Vietnam (RVN, South Vietnam) more along the lines of a civil war, Secretary of State Dean Rusk was obsessed with the retreat of the Western powers before German dictator Adolf

Hitler's demands at Munich in 1938 and saw the war in terms of "aggression" on the part of the Democratic Republic of Vietnam (DRV, North Vietnam). Secretary of Defense Robert S. McNamara also supported increased U.S. military assistance to South Vietnam. Both men pointed out that a Communist victory in South Vietnam would mean an additional 20 million people living under communism. It would also likely be the end of the Southeast Asia Treaty Organization, would destroy U.S. credibility in the region, and would force the remaining Southeast Asian states to reach accommodation with communism.

Primary Source

1. United States National Interests in South Viet-Nam.

The deteriorating situation in South Viet-Nam requires attention to the nature and scope of United States national interests in that country. The loss of South Viet-Nam to Communism would involve the transfer of a nation of 20 million people from the free world to the Communist bloc. The loss of South Viet-Nam would make pointless any further discussion about the importance of Southeast Asia to the free world; we would have to face the near certainty that the remainder of Southeast Asia and Indonesia would move to a complete accommodation with Communism, if not formal incorporation with the Communist bloc. The United States, as a member of SEATO, has commitments with respect to South Viet-Nam under the Protocol to the SEATO Treaty. Additionally, in a formal statement at the conclusion session of the 1954 Geneva Conference, the United States representative stated that the United States "would view any renewal of the aggression . . . with grave concern as seriously threatening international peace and security."

The loss of South Viet-Nam to Communism would not only destroy SEATO but would undermine the credibility of American commitments elsewhere. Further, loss of South Viet-Nam would stimulate bitter domestic controversies in the United States and would be seized upon by extreme elements to divide the country and harass the Administration. . . .

3. The United States' Objective in South Viet-Nam.

The United States should commit itself to the clear objective of preventing the fall of South Viet-Nam to Communism. The basic means for accomplishing this objective must be to put the Government of South Viet-Nam into a position to win its own war against the Guerillas. We must insist that that Government itself take the measures necessary for that purpose in exchange for large-scale United States assistance in the military, economic and political fields. At the same time we must recognize that it will probably not be possible for the GVN to win this war as long as the flow of men and supplies from North Viet-Nam continues unchecked and the guerillas enjoy a safe sanctuary in neighboring territory.

We should be prepared to introduce United States combat forces if that should become necessary for success. Dependent upon the circumstances, it may also be necessary for United States forces to strike at the source of the aggression in North Viet-Nam.

4. The Use of United States Forces in South Viet-Nam.

The commitment of United States forces to South Viet-Nam involves two different categories: (A) Units of modest size required for the direct support of South Viet-Namese military effort, such as communications, helicopter and other forms of airlift, reconnaissance aircraft, naval patrols, intelligence units, etc., and (B) larger organized units with actual or potential direct military missions. Category (A) should be introduced as speedily as possible. Category (B) units pose a more serious problem in that they are much more significant from the point of view of domestic and international political factors and greatly increase the probabilities of Communist bloc escalation. Further, the employment of United States combat forces (in the absence of Communist bloc escalation) involves a certain dilemma: if there is a strong South Viet-Namese effort, they may not be needed; if there is not such an effort, United States forces could not accomplish their mission in the midst of an apathetic or hostile population. Under present circumstances, therefore, the question of injecting United States and SEATO combat forces should in large part be considered as a contribution to the morale of the South Viet-Namese in their own effort to do the principal job themselves.

5. Probable Extent of the Commitment of United States Forces.

If we commit Category (B) forces to South Viet-Nam, the ultimate possible extent of our military commitment in Southeast Asia must be faced. The struggle may be prolonged, and Hanoi and Peiping may overtly intervene. It is the view of the Secretary of Defense and the Joint Chiefs of Staff that, in the light of the logistic difficulties faced by the other side, we can assume that the maximum United States forces required on the ground in Southeast Asia would not exceed six divisions, or about 205,000 men (CINCPAC Plan 32/59 PHASE IV). This would be in addition to local forces and such SEATO forces as may be engaged. It is also the view of the Secretary of Defense and the Joint Chiefs of Staff that our military posture is, or, with the addition of more National Guard or regular Army divisions, can be made, adequate to furnish these forces and support them in action without serious interference with our present Berlin plans. . . .

Recommendations

In the light of the foregoing, the Secretary of State and the Secretary of Defense recommend that:

1. We now take the decision to commit ourselves to the objective of preventing the fall of South Viet-Nam to Communism and that, in doing so, we recognize that the introduction of United States and other SEATO forces may be necessary to achieve this objective. (However, if it is necessary to commit outside forces to achieve the foregoing objective, our decision to introduce United States forces should not be contingent upon unanimous SEATO agreement thereto.)

2. The Department of Defense be prepared with plans for the use of United States forces in South Viet-Nam under one or more of the following purposes:

   (a) Use of a significant number of United States forces to signify United States determination to defend South Viet-Nam and to boost South Viet-Nam morale.

   (b) Use of substantial United States forces to assist in suppressing Viet Cong insurgency short of engaging in detailed counter-guerrilla operations but including relevant operations in North Viet-Nam.

   (c) Use of United States forces to deal with the situation if there is organized Communist military intervention.

3. We immediately undertake the following actions in support of the GVN: . . .

   (c) Provide the GVN with small craft, including such United States uniformed advisers and operating personnel as may be necessary for quick and effective operations in effecting surveillance and control over coastal waters and inland waterways. . . .

   (e) Provide such personnel and equipment as may be necessary to improve the military-political intelligence system beginning at the provincial level and extending upward through the Government and the armed forces to the Central Intelligence Organization.

   (f) Provide such new terms of reference, reorganization and additional personnel for United States military forces as are required for increased United States participation in the direction and control of GVN military operations and to carry out the other increased responsibilities which accrue to MAAG under these recommendations. . . .

   (i) Provide individual administrators and advisers for insertion into the Governmental machinery of South Viet-Nam in types and numbers to be agreed upon by the two Governments. . . .

5. Very shortly before the arrival in South Viet-Nam of the first increments of United States military personnel and equipment proposed under 3., above, that would exceed the Geneva Accord ceilings, publish the "Jorden report" [by State Department official William J. Jorden and critical of Ngo Dinh Diem] as a United States "white paper," transmitting it as simultaneously as possible to the Governments of all countries with which we have diplomatic relations, including the Communist states.

6. Simultaneous with the publication of the "Jorden report," release an exchange of letters between Diem and the President.

(a) Diem's letter would include: reference to the DRV violations of Geneva Accords as set forth in the October 24 GVN letter to the ICC [International Control Commission] and other documents; pertinent references to GVN statements with respect to its intent to observe the Geneva Accords; reference to its need for flood relief and rehabilitation; reference to previous United States aid and the compliance hitherto by both countries with the Geneva Accords; reference to the USG statement at the time the Geneva Accords were signed; the necessity of now exceeding some provisions of the Accords in view of the DRV violations thereof; the lack of aggressive intent with respect to the DRV; GVN intent to return to strict compliance with the Geneva Accords as soon as the DRV violations ceased; and request for additional United States assistance in framework foregoing policy. The letter should also set forth in appropriate general terms steps Diem has taken and is taking to reform Governmental structure.

(b) The President's reply would be responsive to Diem's request for additional assistance and acknowledge and agree to Diem's statements on the intent promptly to return to strict compliance with the Geneva Accords as soon as DRV violations have ceased. . . .

Source: *United States–Vietnam Relations, 1945–1967,* Book 11 (Washington, DC: U.S. Government Printing Office, 1971), 359–366.

119. McGeorge Bundy, White House Special Assistant for National Security Affairs: National Security Action Memorandum No. 111, November 22, 1961

Introduction

President John F. Kennedy accepted the recommendations from his military adviser General Maxwell D. Taylor and Special Assistant for National Security Affairs Walt W. Rostow with the exception of the introduction of U.S. ground troops, which President Ngo Dinh Diem of the Republic of Vietnam (RVN, South Vietnam) also opposed as a potential Viet Cong (Vietnamese Communist) propaganda bonanza. Kennedy's decision meant that U.S. combat aircraft were soon providing direct combat support to the Army of the Republic of Vietnam troops (ARVN, South Vietnamese Army). From the end of 1961 to the end of 1962, the number of American military personnel in South Vietnam nearly quadrupled to 11,300.

Primary Source

The President has authorized the Secretary of State to instruct our Ambassador to Viet-Nam to inform President Diem as follows:

1. The U.S. Government is prepared to join the Viet-Nam Government in a sharply increased joint effort to avoid a further deterioration in the situation in South Viet-Nam.

2. This joint effort requires undertakings by both Governments as outlined below:

a. On its part the U.S. would immediately undertake the following actions in support of the GVN:

(1) Provide increased air lift to the GVN forces, including helicopters, light aviation, and transport aircraft, manned to the extent necessary by United States uniformed personnel and under United States operational control.

(2) Provide such additional equipment and United States uniformed personnel as may be necessary for air reconnaissance, photography, instruction in and execution of air-ground support techniques, and for special intelligence.

(3) Provide the GVN with small craft, including such United States uniformed advisers and operating personnel as may be necessary for operations in effecting surveillance and control over coastal waters and inland waterways.

(4) Provide expedited training and equipping of the civil guard and the self-defense corps with the objective of relieving the regular Army of static missions and freeing it for mobile offensive operations.

(5) Provide such personnel and equipment as may be necessary to improve the military-political intelligence system beginning at the provincial level and extending upward through the Government and the armed forces to the Central Intelligence Organization.

(6) Provide such new terms of reference, reorganization and additional personnel for United States military forces as are required for increased United States military assistance in the operational collaboration with the GVN and operational direction of U.S. forces and to carry out the other increased responsibilities which accrue to the U.S. military authorities under these recommendations.

(7) Provide such increased economic aid as may be required to permit the GVN to pursue a vigorous flood relief and rehabilitation program, to supply material in support of the security efforts, and to give priority to projects in support of this expanded counter-insurgency program. (This could include

increases in military pay, a full supply of a wide range of materials such as food, medical supplies, transportation equipment, communications equipment, and any other items where material help could assist the GVN in winning the war against the Viet Cong.)

(8) Encourage and support (including financial support) a request by the GVN to the FAO [Food, and Agricultural Organization] or any other appropriate international organization for multilateral assistance in the relief and rehabilitation of the flood area.

(9) Provide individual administrators and advisers for the Governmental machinery of South Viet-Nam in types and numbers to be agreed upon by the two Governments.

(10) Provide personnel for a joint survey with the GVN of conditions in each of the provinces to assess the social, political, intelligence, and military factors bearing on the prosecution of the counter-insurgency program in order to reach a common estimate of these factors and a common determination of how to deal with them.

b. On its part, the GVN would initiate the following actions:

(1) Prompt and appropriate legislative and administrative action to put the nation on a wartime footing to mobilize its entire resources. (This would include a decentralization and broadening of the Government so as to realize the full potential of all non-Communist elements in the country willing to contribute to the common struggle.)

(2) The vitalization of appropriate Governmental wartime agencies with adequate authority to perform their functions effectively.

(3) Overhaul of the military establishment and command structure so as to create an effective military organization for the prosecution of the war and assure a mobile offensive capability for the Army.

Source: *United States–Vietnam Relations, 1945–1967,* Book 11 (Washington, DC: U.S. Government Printing Office, 1971), 419–421.

120. President John F. Kennedy: Letter to President Ngo Dinh Diem, December 14, 1961

Introduction

In this letter to President Ngo Dinh Diem of the Republic of Vietnam (RVN, South Vietnam), U.S. president John F. Kennedy

expresses sympathy for the suffering of the South Vietnamese people caused by "North Vietnam's effort to take over your country" and pledges firm U.S. support for South Vietnamese efforts to maintain its independence.

Primary Source

Dear Mr. President:

I have received your recent letter in which you described so cogently the dangerous conditions caused by North Vietnam's effort to take over your country. The situation in your embattled country is well known to me and to the American people. We have been deeply disturbed by the assault on your country. Our indignation has mounted as the deliberate savagery of the Communist programs of assassination, kidnapping, and wanton violence became clear.

Your letter underlines what our own information has convincingly shown—that the campaign of force and terror now being waged against your people and your Government is supported and directed from outside by the authorities at Hanoi. They have thus violated the provisions of the Geneva Accords designed to ensure peace in Vietnam and to which they bound themselves in 1954.

At that time, the United States, although not a party to the Accords, declared that it "would view any renewal of the aggression in violation of the Agreements with grave concern and as seriously threatening international peace and security." We continue to maintain that view.

In accordance with that declaration, and in response to your request, we are prepared to help the Republic of Vietnam to protect its people and to preserve its independence. We shall promptly increase our assistance to your defense effort as well as help relieve the destruction of the floods which you describe. I have already given the orders to get these programs underway.

The United States, like the Republic of Vietnam, remains devoted to the cause of peace and our primary purpose is to help your people maintain their independence. If the Communist authorities in North Vietnam will stop their campaign to destroy the Republic of Vietnam, the measures we are taking to assist your defense efforts will no longer be necessary. We shall seek to persuade the Communists to give up their attempts to force and subversion. In any case, we are confident that the Vietnamese people will preserve their independence and gain the peace and prosperity for which they have sought so hard and so long.

Source: "President Responds to Request from Viet-Nam for U.S. Aid," *Department of State Bulletin* 46(1175) (1962): 13.

121. Assistant Secretary of State Roger Hilsman: "The Situation and Short-Term Prospects in South Vietnam", December 3, 1962 [Excerpt]

Introduction

Assistant Secretary of State for Far Eastern Affairs Roger Hilsman here posits that a deterioration in the military and security situation in the Republic of Vietnam (RVN, South Vietnam) will greatly enhance the possibility of a coup d'état against South Vietnamese president Ngo Dinh Diem. Hilsman believes that a coup attempt would most likely be non-Communist in nature and would involve elements of the military. In a prescient reading of the situation, Hilsman notes that the United States would likely have advance knowledge of such a coup and that the coup would be accompanied by a worsening of the pacification effort in the countryside.

Primary Source

D. Political Situation

The stability of the government during the next year will continue to depend principally on Diem's handling of the internal security situation. If Diem can demonstrate a continuing improvement in security conditions, he should be able to alleviate concern and boost morale within his bureaucracy and military establishment. However, if the fight against the Viet Cong goes badly, if the Viet Cong launches a series of successful and dramatic military operations, or if South Vietnamese army casualties increase appreciably over a protracted period, the chances of a coup attempt against Diem could increase substantially. Moreover, the possibility of a coup attempt at any time cannot be excluded. Many officials and oppositionists feel that, despite the government's military victories and improved military capabilities and initiative, the GVN is not winning the war principally because of Diem's virtual one-man rule and his failure to follow through with the political and economic measures necessary to gain the support of the peasants.

It is more difficult now than at any time since the crisis in South Vietnam began in late 1959 to estimate reliably the elements that would be most likely to precipitate a coup attempt, the prospects for the success of a coup attempt, or the effects of such an attempt on internal stability and on the counterinsurgency effort itself. During the past year or so, the Viet Cong presumably has improved its ability to initiate a coup and might attempt to do so. However, the Viet Cong probably would not be able to carry out a successful coup, and the odds that it could gain control of a successful coup, although somewhat better than last year, appear to be less than even.

The coup most likely to succeed would be one with non-Communist leadership and support, principally involving South Vietnamese military elements and civilian officials and perhaps some oppositionists outside the government. The abortive coup attempt in November 1960 and the palace bombing in February 1962 have undoubtedly demonstrated to coup plotters the necessity for better preparation and broader participation by the military. Any future non-Communist coup group probably would not be as deficient in this respect and its leaders, unlike the leaders of the 1960 coup attempt, can be expected to be better prepared to execute their plan quickly. Although the possibility of a Kong Letype coup, i.e., a coup led by a junior and relatively unknown officer, cannot be completely discounted, it is more likely that the coup leadership would include some middle and top echelon military officials. While their role is by no means certain, a major polarization of the GVN military leadership into coup and anti-coup groups does not appear likely. Most of them would probably elect to remain uncommitted at the outset of the coup, as they apparently did in November 1960, and would then give their tacit or active support to whatever side appeared to have the best chance of winning. Under these circumstances, a military coup appears to have a better than even chance of succeeding.

Diem's removal—whether by a military coup, assassination, or death from accidental or natural causes—would probably considerably strengthen the power of the military. The odds appear about even between a government led by a military junta or by Vice President Tho, with the army, in the latter case, playing a major if not the predominant role behind the scenes. On the one hand, the military might conclude that a military-led government would be better able to maintain national unity and internal political cohesion and, more importantly, to conduct a determined and effective campaign against the Viet Cong. On the other hand, they might conclude that Tho, who apparently has been on good terms with some of the present top military leaders, would not disagree with their views on the manner of conducting the fight against the Communists and that his constitutional succession would legalize the change in government and possibly avert a serious power struggle. (Although Diem's brothers, Nhu and Can, would probably also be removed by a coup, if Diem left the scene for other reasons his brothers might attempt to retain real political power.) In any event, a government led by the military, by Tho, or by any other civilian approved by the military would probably maintain South Vietnam's pro-US orientation.

If there is a serious disruption of government leadership as a result of a military coup or as a result of Diem's death, any momentum the government's counterinsurgency efforts had achieved would probably be halted and possibly reversed, at least for a time. Moreover, the confusion and suspicion attending the disruption would provide the Viet Cong guerrillas an opportunity to strengthen their position in the countryside and attack some installations in large force, but they would probably fail if they attempted to seize control of the government.

Under most of the foreseeable circumstances involving a coup, the role of the US could be extremely important. Although this is by no means certain, US military and intelligence officials might well have advance notice of an impending coup and might be able to restrain the coup plotters from precipitous action. Even if unable to restrain such action, however, US officials might have greater success in averting widespread fighting and a serious power struggle which would lead to excessive bloodshed and weaken the front against the Viet Cong. The US could also be helpful in achieving agreement among the coup leaders as to who should lead the government in restoring the momentum of the government's counterinsurgency effort.

Source: *United States–Vietnam Relations, 1945–1967,* Book 12 (Washington, DC: U.S. Government Printing Office, 1971), 520–521.

122. Mike Mansfield, Senator: Report to President John F. Kennedy on Southeast Asia and Vietnam, December 18, 1962 [Excerpt]

Introduction

Mike Mansfield (D-Mont.), the majority leader in the U.S. Senate, initially supported the U.S. effort in Vietnam. Following a fact-finding trip to Southeast Asia at the end of 1962, however, Mansfield reports to President John F. Kennedy that the United States is in danger of being drawn into a full-scale war, that it might be seen as playing the role of a "neocolonial" power, and that little thought appears to have been given to the consequences. Mansfield urges Kennedy to undertake a diplomatic effort that will minimize U.S. involvement on the Asian mainland.

Primary Source

Even assuming that aid over a prolonged period would be available, the question still remains as to the capacity of the present Saigon government to carry out the task of social engineering. Ngo Dinh Diem remains a dedicated, sincere, hardworking, incorruptible and patriotic leader. But he is older and the problems which confront him are more complex than those which he faced when he pitted his genuine nationalism against, first, the French and Bao Dai and then against the sects with such effectiveness. The energizing role, which he played in the past appears to be passing to other members of his family, particularly Ngo Dinh Nhu. The latter is a person of great energy and intellect who is fascinated by the operations of political power and has

consummate eagerness and ability in organizing and manipulating it. But it is Ngo Dinh Diem, not Ngo Dinh Nhu, who has such popular mandate to exercise power as there is in South Vietnam. In a situation of this kind there is a great danger of the corruption of unbridled power. This has implications far beyond the persistent reports and rumors of fiscal and similar irregularities which are, in any event, undocumented. More important is its effect on the organization of the machinery for carrying out the new concepts. The difficulties in Vietnam are not likely to be overcome by a handful of paid retainers and sycophants. The success of the new approach in Vietnam presupposes a great contribution of initiative and self-sacrifice from a substantial body of Vietnamese with capacities for leadership at all levels. Whether that contribution can be obtained remains to be seen. For in the last analysis it depends upon a diffusion of political power, essentially in a democratic pattern. The trends in the political life of Vietnam have not been until now in that direction despite lip service to the theory of developing democratic and popular institutions "from the bottom up" through the strategic hamlet program.

To summarize, our policies and activities are designed to meet an existing set of internal problems in south Vietnam. North Vietnam infiltrates some supplies and cadres into the south; together with the Vietnamese we are trying to shut off this flow. The Vietcong has had the offensive in guerrilla warfare in the countryside; we are attempting to aid the Vietnamese military in putting them on the defensive with the hope of eventually reducing them at least to ineffectiveness. Finally, the Vietnamese peasants have sustained the Vietcong guerrillas out of fear, indifference or blandishment and we are helping the Vietnamese in an effort to win the peasants away by offering them the security and other benefits which may be provided in the strategic hamlets.

That, in brief, is the present situation. As noted, there is optimism that success will be achieved quickly. My own view is that the problems can be made to yield to present remedies, provided the problems and their magnitude do not change significantly and provided that the remedies are pursued by both Vietnamese and Americans (and particularly the former) with great vigor and self-dedication.

Certainly, if these remedies do not work, it is difficult to conceive of alternatives, with the possible exception of a truly massive commitment of American military personnel and other resources—in short going to war fully ourselves against the guerrillas—and the establishment of some form of neocolonial rule in south Vietnam. That is an alternative which I most emphatically do not recommend. On the contrary, it seems to me most essential that we make crystal clear to the Vietnamese government and to our own people that while we will go to great lengths to help, the primary responsibility rests with the Vietnamese. Our role is and must remain secondary in present circumstances. It is their country, their future which is most at stake, not ours.

To ignore that reality will not only be immensely costly in terms of American lives and resources but it may also draw us inexorably into some variation of the unenviable position in Vietnam which was formerly occupied by the French. We are not, of course, at that point at this time. But the great increase in American military commitment this year has tended to point us in that general direction and we may well begin to slide rapidly toward it if any of the present remedies begin to falter in practice.

As indicated, our planning appears to be predicated on the assumption that existing internal problems in South Vietnam will remain about the same and can be overcome by greater effort and better techniques. But what if the problems do not remain the same? To all outward appearances, little if any thought has been given in Saigon at least, to the possibilities of a change in the nature of the problems themselves. Nevertheless, they are very real possibilities and the initiative for instituting change rests in enemy hands largely because of the weakness of the Saigon government. The range of possible change includes a step-up in the infiltration of cadres and supplies by land or sea. It includes the use of part or all of the regular armed forces of North Vietnam, reported to be about 300,000 strong, under Vo Nguyen Giap. It includes, in the last analysis, the possibility of a major increase in any of many possible forms of Chinese Communist support for the Vietcong.

None of these possibilities may materialize. It would be folly, however, not to recognize their existence and to have as much clarification in advance of what our response to them will be if they do.

This sort of anticipatory thinking cannot be undertaken with respect to the situation in Vietnam alone. The problem there can be grasped, it seems to me, only as we have clearly in mind our interests with respect to all of Southeast Asia. If it is essential in our own interests to maintain a quasi-permanent position of power on the Asian mainland as against the Chinese then we must be prepared to continue to pay the present cost in Vietnam indefinitely and to meet any escalation on the other side with at least a commensurate escalation of commitment of our own. This can go very far, indeed, in terms of lives and resources. Yet if it is essential to our interests then we would have no choice.

But if on the other hand it is, at best, only desirable rather than essential that a position of power be maintained on the mainland, then other courses are indicated. We would, then, properly view such improvement as may be obtained by the new approach in Vietnam primarily in terms of what it might contribute to strengthening our diplomatic hand in the Southeast Asian region. And we would use that hand as vigorously as possible and in every way possible not to deepen our costly involvement on the Asian mainland but to lighten it.

Source: Mike Mansfield, *Two Reports on Vietnam and Southeast Asia to the President of the U.S.* (Washington, DC: U.S. Government Printing Office, 1973), 139–140.

123. Nguyen Chi Thanh, Lao Dong Political Bureau Member: Article, July 1963 [Excerpt]

Introduction

Here Nguyen Chi Thanh, a member of the powerful Lao Dong (Workers' Party) Political Bureau in the Democratic Republic of Vietnam (DRV, North Vietnam), takes issue with the view of the Soviet Union that armed struggle in the Republic of Vietnam (RVN, South Vietnam) should be avoided because it might lead to world war. Thanh takes the position that the United States should not be feared and that it can be defeated militarily.

Primary Source

Although ultimate conclusions cannot yet be reached insofar as the struggle is still going on in south Viet Nam, we may however put forth the following views:

1. The U.S. imperialists are not invincible. Compared with imperialists of other countries, they are mightier, but compared with the revolutionary forces and the forces of the people of the world, they are not at all strong. If the proletarian revolution and people of the world resolutely struggle against U.S. imperialism, they can surely repel it step by step and narrow down its domain.

We do not have any illusions about the United States. We do not underestimate our opponent—the strong and cunning U.S. imperialism. But we are not afraid of the United States. The strategic concept thoroughly pervades the revolutionary line of south Viet Nam and is the fundamental factor determining the success of the revolution. If, on the contrary, one is afraid of the United States and thinks that to offend it would court failure, and that firm opposition to U.S. imperialism would touch off a nuclear war, then the only course left would be to compromise with and surrender to U.S. imperialism.

2. A powerful north Viet Nam will be a decisive factor in the social development of our entire country. But this does not mean that simply because the north is strong, the revolutionary movement in the south will automatically succeed. The powerful north Viet Nam and the revolutionary movement of the south Vietnamese people are mutually complementary and must be closely coordinated; the

building of the north itself cannot replace the resolution of the inherent social contradictions of south Viet Nam. Adhering to this correct view, we have avoided opportunistic mistakes. If, on the contrary, we had feared the United States and had no faith in the success of our struggles against it, we would have called on the people in south Viet Nam to "wait" and "coexist peacefully" with the U.S.-Diem clique, and committed an irreparable error. We have correctly handled the relations between north and south Viet Nam. This is a Marxist-Leninist strategic concept which is in conformity with the latest experience in the world developments and those in our own country.

Source: Chi Thanh Nguyen, *Who Will Win in South Viet Nam?* (Peking: Foreign Languages Publishing House, 1963).

124. Memorandum for the Record of U.S. State Department Meeting, August 31, 1963

Introduction

Dissatisfaction had steadily grown in the Republic of Vietnam (RVN, South Vietnam), especially among senior commanders of the Army of the Republic of Vietnam (ARVN, South Vietnamese Army), with the leadership of President Ngo Dinh Diem. This was caused by Diem's authoritarian rule, his refusal to listen to the advice of others beyond his own family circle and a few trusted advisers, his appointment of senior officials and army officers on the basis of political loyalty rather than demonstrated ability, his failure to effectively prosecute the war against the Communist insurgents, and rampant corruption. With the U.S. government ambivalent and worried that those planning the coup lacked sufficient strength, the coup planners temporarily suspended their effort, giving pause in Washington and prompting renewed debate among senior U.S. foreign policy officials as to whether the war could indeed be won under Diem's leadership.

Primary Source

1. Secretary Rusk stated that, in his judgment, we were back to where we were about Wednesday of last week, and this causes him to go back to the original problem and ask what in the situation led us to think well of a coup. Ruling out hatred of the Nhus, he said, there would appear to be three things:

   a. The things that the Nhus had done or supported, which tended to upset the GVN internally.
   b. The things that they had done that had an adverse external effect.
   c. The great pressures of U.S. public opinion.

2. Mr. Rusk then asked if we should not pick up Ambassador Lodge's suggestion in his message of today (Saigon 391) and determine what steps are required to re-gird solidarity in South Vietnam—such as improvement in conditions concerning students and Buddhists and the possible departure of Madame Nhu. He said that we should determine what additional measures are needed to improve the international situation—such as problems affecting Cambodia—and to improve the Vietnamese position wherein U.S. public opinion is concerned. He then said that he is reluctant to start off by saying now that Nhu has to go; that it is unrealistic.

3. Mr. McNamara stated that he favored the above proposals of the Secretary of State, with one additional step—that is to establish quickly and firmly our line of communication between Lodge, Harkins and the GVN. He pointed out that at the moment our channels of communication are essentially broken and that they should be reinstituted at all costs.

4. Mr. Rusk added that we must do our best not to permit Diem to decapitate his military command in light of its obviously adverse effect on the prosecution of the war. At this point he asked if anyone present had any doubt in his mind but that the coup was off.

5. Mr. Kattenburg said that he had some remaining doubt; that we have not yet sent the generals a strong enough message; that the VOA statement regarding the withdrawal of aid was most important, but that we repudiated it too soon. He stated further that the group should take note of the fact that General Harkins did not carry out his instructions with respect to communication with the generals. Mr. Rusk interrupted Kattenburg to state that, to the contrary, he believed Harkins' conduct was exactly correct in light of the initial response which he received from General Khiem (they were referring to Harkins' report in MACV 1583).

6. Mr. Hilsman commented that, in his view, the generals are not now going to move unless they are pressed by a revolt from below. In this connect Ambassador Nolting warned that in the uncoordinated Vietnamese structure anything can happen, and that while an organized successful coup is out, there might be small flurries by irresponsible dissidents at any time.

7. Mr. Hilsman undertook to present four basic factors which bear directly on the problem confronting the U.S. now. They are, in his view:

   a. The mood of the people, particularly the middle level officers, noncommissioned officers and middle level bureaucrats, who are most restive. Mr. McNamara interrupted to state that he had seen no evidence of this and General Taylor commented that he had seen none either, but would like to see such evidence as Hilsman could produce. Mr. Kattenburg commented that the middle level officers and bureaucrats are uniformly critical of the government, to which Mr. McNamara commented that if this indeed be the fact we should know about it.

b. The second basic factor, as outlined by Hilsman, was what effect will be felt on our programs elsewhere in Asia if we acquiesce to a strong Nhu-dominated government. In this connection, he reported that there is a Korean study now underway on just how much repression the United States will tolerate before pulling out her aid. Mr. McNamara stated that he had not seen this study and would be anxious to have it.

c. The third basic factor is Mr. Nhu, his personality and his policy. Hilsman recalled that Nhu has once already launched an effort aimed at withdrawal of our province advisors and stated that he is sure he is in conversation with the French. He gave, as supporting evidence, the content of an intercepted message, which Mr. Bundy asked to see. Ambassador Nolting expressed the opinion that Nhu will not make a deal with Ho Chi Minh on Ho's terms.

d. The fourth point is the matter of U.S. and world opinion, Hilsman stated that this problem was moving to a political and diplomatic plane. Part of the problem, he said, is the press, which concludes incorrectly that we have the ability to change the things in Vietnam of which they are critical. To this Mr. Murrow added that this problem of press condemnation is now worldwide.

8. Mr. Kattenburg stated that as recently as last Thursday it was the belief of Ambassador Lodge that, if we undertake to live with this repressive regime, with its bayonets at every street corner and its transparent negotiations with puppet bonzes, we are going to be thrown out of the country in six months. He stated that at this juncture it would be better for us to make the decision to get out honorably. He went on to say that, having been acquainted with Diem for ten years, he was deeply disappointed in him, saying that he will not separate from his brother. It was Kattenburg's view that Diem will get very little support from the military and, as time goes on, he will get less and less support and the country will go steadily down hill.

9. General Taylor asked what Kattenburg meant when he said that we would be forced out of Vietnam within six months. Kattenburg replied that in from six months to a year, as the people see we are losing the war, they will gradually go to the other side and we will be obliged to leave. Ambassador Nolting expressed general disagreement with Mr. Kattenburg. He said that the unfavorable activity which motivated Kattenburg's remarks was confined to the city and, while city support of Diem is doubtless less now, it is not greatly so. He said that it is improper to overlook the fact that we have done a tremendous job toward winning the Vietnam war, working with this same imperfect, annoying government.

10. Mr. Kattenburg added that there is one new factor—the population, which was in high hopes of expelling the Nhus after the VOA announcement regarding cessation of aid; now, under the heel of Nhu's military repression, they would quickly lose heart.

11. Secretary Rusk commented that Kattenburg's recital was largely speculative; that it would be far better for us to start on the firm basis of two things—that we will not pull out of Vietnam until the war is won, and that we will not run a coup; Mr. McNamara expressed agreement with this view.

12. Mr. Rusk then said that we should present questions to Lodge which fall within these parameters. He added that he believes we have good proof that we have been winning the war, particularly the contrast between the first six months of 1962 and the first six months of 1963. He then asked the Vice President if he had any contribution to make.

13. The Vice President stated that he agreed with Secretary Rusk's conclusions completely; that he had great reservations himself with respect to a coup, particularly so because he had never really seen a genuine alternative to Diem. He stated that from both a practical and political viewpoint, it would be a disaster to pull out; that we should stop playing cops and robbers and get back to talking straight to the GVN, and that we should once again go about winning the war. He stated that after our communications with them are genuinely reestablished, it may be necessary for someone to talk rough to them—perhaps General Taylor. He said further that he had been greatly impressed with Ambassador Nolting's views and agreed with Mr. McNamara's conclusions.

14. General Taylor raised the question of whether we should change the disposition of the forces which had been set in motion as a result of the crisis. It was agreed that there should be no change in the existing disposition for the time being.

Source: *The Pentagon Papers: The Defense Department History of United States Decisionmaking on Vietnam,* Vol. 2. Senator Gravel edition (Boston: Beacon, 1971), 741–743.

125. President John F. Kennedy's Remarks on the Situation in Vietnam, September 2, 1963

Introduction

By late 1963, U.S. president John F. Kennedy's position on the war was ambiguous. He told Senate majority leader Mike Mansfield that he was determined to withdraw U.S. forces from Vietnam after the 1964 elections but that any announcement of this before the election would result in a conservative backlash, possibly costing Kennedy the election. On September 2 in the course of an interview with *CBS News* anchorman Walter Cronkite, President Kennedy declares that the government of the Republic of Vietnam (RVN, South Vietnam) is out of touch with the people. He concludes that "In the final analysis, it is their war. They are the ones who have to win it or lose it. . . . But I don't agree with those who say we should withdraw. That would be a great mistake." In a news conference on September 12 he listed three objectives of U.S. policy in Vietnam as: win the war, contain the Communists, and bring Americans home. But on November 12 he listed the objectives as being "to bring Americans home, permit the South Vietnamese to maintain themselves as a free and independent country, and permit democratic forces within the country to operate." There was no mention of winning the war. Kennedy's last statement on Vietnam, made in Fort Worth, Texas, on November 22, reveals the dilemma that he faced: "Without the United States, South Vietnam would collapse overnight." That same day he was killed in Dallas by an assassin. While there is simply no way of knowing what Kennedy would have done about Vietnam had he lived, his statements about withdrawal were made when the United States was seen as having the upper hand.

Primary Source

Mr. Cronkite: Mr. President, the only hot war we've got running at the moment is of course the one in Viet-Nam, and we have our difficulties there, quite obviously.

The President: I don't think that unless a greater effort is made by the Government to win popular support that the war can be won out there. In the final analysis, it is their war. They are the ones who have to win it or lose it. We can help them, we can give them equipment, we can send our men out there as advisers, but they have to win it, the people of Viet-Nam, against the Communists.

We are prepared to continue to assist them, but I don't think that the war can be won unless the people support the effort and, in my opinion, in the last 2 months, the government has gotten out of touch with the people.

The repressions against the Buddhists, we felt, were very unwise. Now all we can do is to make it very clear that we don't think this is the way to win. It is my hope that this will become increasingly obvious to the government, that they will take steps to try to bring back popular support for this very essential struggle.

Mr. Cronkite: Do you think this government still has time to regain the support of the people?

The President: I do. With changes in policy and perhaps with personnel I think it can. If it doesn't make those changes, I would think that the chances of winning it would not be very good.

Mr. Cronkite: Hasn't every indication from Saigon been that President Diem has no intention of changing his pattern?

The President: If he does not change it, of course, that is his decision. He has been there 10 years and, as I say, he has carried this burden when he has been counted out on a number of occasions.

Our best judgment is that he can't be successful on this basis. We hope that he comes to see that, but in the final analysis it is the people and the government itself who have to win or lose this struggle. All we can do is help, and we are making it very clear, but I don't agree with those who say we should withdraw. That would be a great mistake. I know people don't like Americans to be engaged in this kind of an effort. Forty-seven Americans have been killed in combat with the enemy, but this is a very important struggle even though it is far away.

We took all this—made this effort to defend Europe. Now Europe is quite secure. We also have to participate—we may not like it—in the defense of Asia.

Source: *Public Papers of the Presidents of the United States: John F. Kennedy, 1963* (Washington, DC: U.S. Government Printing Office, 1964), 651–652.

126. Report of the McNamara-Taylor Mission to South Vietnam, October 2, 1963 [Excerpt]

Introduction

U.S. secretary of defense Robert S. McNamara and presidential military adviser General Maxwell D. Taylor returned from a fact-finding mission to the Republic of Vietnam (RVN, South Vietnam) with an optimistic view of progress there since the beginning of 1962. At the same time, however, they doubted that South Vietnamese president Ngo Dinh Diem had sufficient support in the cities to enable the government to achieve victory and call for specific actions by the U.S. government to force Diem to institute reforms.

Primary Source

I. Conclusions and Recommendations

A. Conclusions.

1. The military campaign has made great progress and continues to progress.

2. There are serious political tensions in Saigon (and perhaps elsewhere in South Vietnam) where the Diem-Nhu government is becoming increasingly unpopular.

3. There is no solid evidence of the possibility of a successful coup, although assassination of Diem or Nhu is always a possibility.

4. Although some, and perhaps an increasing number, of GVN military officers are becoming hostile to the government, they are more hostile to the Viet Cong than to the government and at least for the near future they will continue to perform their military duties.

5. Further repressive actions by Diem and Nhu could change the present favorable military trends. On the other hand, a return to more moderate methods of control and administration, unlikely though it may be, would substantially mitigate the political crisis.

6. It is not clear that pressures exerted by the U.S. will move Diem and Nhu toward moderation. Indeed, pressures may increase their obduracy. But unless such pressures are exerted, they are almost certain to continue past patterns of behavior.

B. Recommendations.

We recommend that:

1. General Harkins review with Diem the military changes necessary to complete the military campaign in the Northern and Central areas (I, II, and III Corps) by the end of 1954 [1964?], and in the Delta (IV Corps) by the end of 1965. This review would consider the need for such changes as:

   a. A further shift of military emphasis and strength to the Delta (IV Corps).
   b. An increase in the military tempo in all corps areas, so that all combat troops are in the Field an average of 20 days out of 30 and static missions are ended.
   c. Emphasis on "clear and hold operations" instead of terrain sweeps which have little permanent value.
   d. The expansion of personnel in combat units to full authorized strength.
   e. The training and arming of hamlet militia at an accelerated rate, especially in the Delta.
   f. A consolidation of the strategic hamlet program, especially in the Delta, and action to insure that future strategic hamlets are not built until they can be protected, and until civic action programs can be introduced.

2. A program be established to train Vietnamese so that essential functions now performed by U.S. military personnel can be carried out by Vietnamese by the end of 1965. It should be possible to withdraw the bulk of U.S. personnel by that time.

3. In accordance with the program to train progressively Vietnamese to take over military functions, the Defense Department should announce in the very near future presently prepared plans to withdraw 1000 U.S. military personnel by the end of 1963. This action should be explained in low key as an initial step in a long-term program to replace U.S. personnel with trained Vietnamese without impairment of the war effort.

4. The following actions be taken to impress upon Diem our disapproval of his political program.

   a. Continue to withhold commitment of funds in the commodity import program, but avoid a formal announcement. The potential significance of the withholding of commitments for the 1964 military budget should be brought home to the top military officers in working level contacts between USOM and MACV and the Joint General Staff; up to now we have stated $95 million may be used by the Vietnamese as a planning level for the commodity import program for 1964. Henceforth we could make clear that this is uncertain both because of lack of final appropriation action by the Congress and because of executive policy.
   b. Suspend approval of the pending AID [Agency for International Development] loans for the Saigon-Cholon Waterworks and Saigon Electric Power Project. We should state clearly that we are doing so as a matter of policy.
   c. Advise Diem that MAP [Military Assistance Program] and CIA support for designated units, now under Colonel Tung's control (mostly held in or near the Saigon area for political reasons) will be cut off unless these units are promptly assigned to the full authority of the Joint General Staff and transferred to the field.
   d. Maintain the present purely "correct" relations with the top GVN, and specifically between the Ambassador and Diem. Contact between General Harkins and Diem and Defense Secretary Thuan on military matters should not, however, be suspended, as this remains an important channel of advice. USOM and USIA should also seek to maintain contacts where these are needed to push forward programs in support of the effort in the field, while taking care not to cut across the basic picture of U.S. disapproval and uncertainty of U.S. aid intentions. We should work with the Diem government but not support it.

As we pursue these courses of action, the situation must be closely watched to see what steps Diem is taking to reduce repressive practices and to improve the effectiveness of the military effort. We should set no fixed criteria, but recognize that we would have to decide in 2–4 months whether to move to more drastic action or try to carry on with Diem even if he had not taken significant steps.

5. At this time, no initiative should be taken to encourage actively a change in government. Our policy should be to seek urgently to identify and build contacts with an alternative leadership if and when it appears.

6. The following statement be approved as current U.S. policy toward South Vietnam and constitute the substance of the government position to be presented both in Congressional testimony and in public statements.

   a. The security of South Vietnam remains vital to United States security. For this reason, we adhere to the overriding objective of denying this country to Communism and of suppressing the Viet Cong insurgency as promptly as possible. (By suppressing the insurgency we mean reducing it to proportions manageable by the national security forces of the GVN, unassisted by the presence of U.S. military forces.) We believe the U.S. part of the task can be completed by the end of 1965, the terminal date which we are taking as the time objective of our counterinsurgency programs.

   b. The military program in Vietnam has made progress and is sound in principle.

   c. The political situation in Vietnam remains deeply serious. It has not yet significantly affected the military effort, but could do so at some time in the future. If the result is a GVN ineffective in the conduct of the war, the U.S. will review its attitude toward support for the government. Although we are deeply concerned by repressive practices, effective performance in the conduct of the war should be the determining factor in our relations with the GVN.

   d. The U.S. has expressed its disapproval of certain actions of the Diem-Nhu regime and will do so again if required. Our policy is to seek to bring about the abandonment of repression because of its effect on the popular will to resist. Our means consist of expressions of disapproval and the withholding of support from GVN activities that are not clearly contributing to the war effort. We will use these means as required to assure an effective military program.

Source: *United States–Vietnam Relations, 1945–1967*, Book 12 (Washington, DC: U.S. Government Printing Office, 1971), 554–557.

127. John Richardson, CIA Station Chief: Cablegram to CIA Director John McCone, October 5, 1963

Introduction

Here John Richardson, heading the Central Intelligence Agency (CIA) station in Saigon, informs CIA director John A. McCone that he has recommended to U.S. ambassador to the Republic of Vietnam (RVN, South Vietnam) Henry Cabot Lodge that he not "irrevocably" oppose plans by the South Vietnamese generals to assassinate President Ngo Dinh Diem.

Primary Source

1. [Officially deleted.]

2. I have recommended to Ambassador Lodge that:

A. That we proceed with these conversations with Gen. Minh.

B. We do not set ourselves irrevocably against the assassination plot, since the other two alternatives mean either a bloodbath in Saigon or a protracted struggle which could rip the army and the country asunder.

Source: U.S. Congress, Senate, *Select Committee to Study Governmental Activities with Respect to Intelligence, Interim Report: Alleged Assassination Plots Involving Foreign Leaders* (Washington, DC: U.S. Government Printing Office, 1975): 220.

128. White House: Cablegram to U.S. Ambassador to Vietnam Henry Cabot Lodge Jr. on the CIA Channel, October 5, 1963

Introduction

Following government-sponsored attacks by the Republic of Vietnam (RVN, South Vietnam) against Buddhist opposition to the regime, Washington suspended economic subsidies for South Vietnamese commercial imports, froze loans for developmental projects, and cut off financial support of the 2,000-man South Vietnamese Special Forces responsible for the outrages. This action was a clear signal to dissident generals plotting to overthrow South Vietnamese president Ngo Dinh Diem. Fearful of a double-cross, the generals involved refused to reveal the timing of their coup attempt. Nonetheless, General Dong Van Minh had approached a Central Intelligence Agency (CIA) contact in Saigon about a plan to assassinate Diem. Minh requested assurance from the U.S. government that it would not oppose the coup attempt. President John F. Kennedy then cables ambassador to South Vietnam Henry Cabot Lodge and instructs him that while he is not to support a coup attempt, he is to maintain contacts with the dissident generals and monitor the situation closely.

Primary Source

In conjunction with decisions and recommendations in separate EPTEL, President today approved recommendation that no initiative should now be taken to give any active covert encouragement to a coup. There should, however, be urgent covert effort with closest security, under broad guidance of Ambassador to identify and build contacts with possible alternative leadership as and when it appears. Essential that this effort be totally secure and fully deniable and separated entirely from normal political analysis and reporting and other activities of country team. We repeat that this effort is not repeat not to be aimed at active promotion of coup but only at surveillance and readiness. In order to provide plausibility to denial suggest you and no one else in Embassy issue these instructions orally to Acting Station Chief and hold him responsible to you alone for making appropriate contacts and reporting to you alone.

All reports to Washington on this subject should be on this channel.

Source: *The Pentagon Papers: The Defense Department History of United States Decisionmaking on Vietnam,* Vol. 2. Senator Gravel edition (Boston: Beacon, 1971), 766–767.

129. John McCone, CIA Director: Cablegram to Ambassador Henry Cabot Lodge Jr., October 6, 1963

Introduction

Following a conversation with President John F. Kennedy, Central Intelligence Agency (CIA) director John A. McCone cabled U.S. ambassador to the Republic of Vietnam (RVN, South Vietnam) Henry Cabot Lodge to modify instructions of the day before. McCone tells Lodge that while he is not to give the impression that the United States is actively seeking to overthrow Diem, Lodge should make clear to the generals that the United States will not "thwart a change of government." The White House also seeks additional information on the coup planning from General Dong Van Minh in order to gauge the possibility of success.

Primary Source

1. Believe CAP 63560 gives general guidance requested, REFTEL. We have following additional general thoughts which have been discussed with President. While we do not wish to stimulate coup, we also do not wish to leave impression that U.S. would thwart a change of government or deny economic and military assistance to a new regime if it appeared capable of increasing effectiveness of military effort, ensuring popular support to win war and improving working relations with U.S. We would like to be informed on what is being contemplated but we should avoid being drawn into reviewing or advising on operational plans or any other act which might tend to identify U.S. too closely with change in government. We would, however, welcome information which would help us assess character of any alternate leadership.

2. With reference to specific problem of General Minh you should seriously consider having contact take position that in present

state his knowledge he is unable present Minh's case to responsible policy officials with any degree of seriousness. In order to get responsible officials even to consider Minh's problem, contact would have to have detailed information clearly indicating that Minh's plans offer a high prospect of success. At present contact sees no such prospect in the information so far provided.

3. You should also consider with Acting Station Chief whether it would be desirable in order to preserve security and deniability in this as well as similar approaches to others whether appropriate arrangements could be made for follow-up contacts by individuals brought in especially from outside Vietnam. As we indicated in CAP 63560 we are most concerned about security problem and we are confining knowledge these sensitive matters in Washington to extremely limited group, high officials in White House, State, Defense and CIA with whom this message cleared.

Source: *The Pentagon Papers: The Defense Department History of United States Decisionmaking on Vietnam,* Vol. 2. Senator Gravel edition (Boston: Beacon, 1971), 769.

130. Ambassador Henry Cabot Lodge Jr.: Cable to National Security Advisor McGeorge Bundy Discussing Coup Prospects, October 25, 1963

Introduction

In response to the request from the White House of October 6, 1963, U.S. ambassador to the Republic of Vietnam (RVN, South Vietnam) Henry Cabot Lodge cables Washington with details of discussions between U.S. officials and dissident Republic of Vietnam Army (ARVN, South Vietnamese Army) generals planning a coup against President Ngo Dinh Diem. Lodge believes that this is a serious effort.

Primary Source

1. I appreciate the concern expressed by you in ref. a relative to the Gen. Don/Conein relationship, and also the present lack of firm intelligence on the details of the general's plot. I hope that ref. b will assist in clearing up some of the doubts relative to general's plans, and I am hopeful that the detailed plans promised for two days before the coup attempt will clear up any remaining doubts.

2. CAS [Classified American Source, referring to the CIA] has been punctilious in carrying out my instructions. I have personally approved each meeting between Gen. Don and Conein who has carried out my orders in each instance explicitly. While I share your concern about the continued involvement of Conein in this matter, a suitable substitute for Conein as the principal contact is

not presently available. Conein, as you know, is a friend of some eighteen years' standing with Gen. Don, and General Don has expressed extreme reluctance to deal with anyone else. I do not believe the involvement of another American in close contact with the generals would be productive. We are, however, considering the feasibility of a plan for the introduction of an additional officer as a cut-out between Conein and a designee of Gen. Don for communication purposes only. This officer is completely unwitting of any details of past or present coup activities and will remain so.

3. With reference to Gen Harkins' comment to Gen. Don which Don reports to have referred to a presidential directive and the proposal for a meeting with me, this may have served the useful purpose of allaying the General's fears as to our interest. If this were a provocation, the GVN could have assumed and manufactured any variations of the same theme. As a precautionary measure, however, I of course refused to see Gen. Don. As to the lack of information as to General Don's real backing, and the lack of evidence that any real capabilities for action have been developed, ref. b provides only part of the answer. I feel sure that the reluctance of the generals to provide the U.S. with full details of their plans at this time, is a reflection of their own sense of security and a lack of confidence that in the large American community present in Saigon their plans will not be prematurely revealed.

4. The best evidence available to the Embassy, which I grant you is not as complete as we would like it, is that Gen. Don and the other generals involved with him are seriously attempting to effect a change in the government. I do not believe that this is a provocation by Ngo Dinh Nhu, although we shall continue to assess the planning as well as possible. In the event that the coup aborts, or in the event that Nhu has masterminded a provocation, I believe that our involvement to date through Conein is still within the realm of plausible denial. CAS is perfectly prepared to have me disavow Conein at any time it may serve the national interest.

5. I welcome your reaffirming instructions contained in CAS Washington [cable] 74228. It is vital that we neither thwart a coup nor that we are even in a position where we do not know what is going on.

6. We should not thwart a coup for two reasons. First, it seems at least an even bet that the next government would not bungle and stumble as much as the present one has. Secondly, it is extremely unwise in the long range for us to pour cold water on attempts at a coup, particularly when they are just in their beginning stages. We should remember that this is the only way in which the people in Vietnam can possibly get a change of government. Whenever we thwart attempts at a coup, as we have done in the past, we are incurring very long lasting resentments, we are assuming an undue responsibility for keeping the incumbents in office, and in general are setting ourselves in judgment over the affairs of Vietnam. Merely to keep in touch with this situation and a policy merely limited to "not thwarting" are courses both of which entail some risks but these are lesser risks than either thwarting all coups while they are stillborn or our not being informed of what is happening. All the above is totally distinct from not wanting U.S. military advisors to be distracted by matters which are not in their domain, with which I heartily agree. But obviously this does not conflict with a policy of not thwarting. In judging proposed coups, we must consider the effect on the war effort. Certainly a succession of fights for control of the Government of Vietnam would interfere with the war effort. It must also be said that the war effort has been interfered with already by the incompetence of the present government and the uproar which this has caused.

7. Gen. Don's intention to have no religious discrimination in a future government is commendable and I applaud his desire not to be "a vassal" of the U.S. But I do not think his promise of a democratic election is realistic. This country simply is not ready for that procedure. I would add two other requirements. First, that there be no wholesale purges of personnel in the government. Individuals who were particularly reprehensible could be dealt with later by the regular legal process. Then I would be impractical, but I am thinking of a government which might include Tri Quang and which certainly should include men of the stature of Mr. Buu, the labor leader.

8. Copy to Gen. Harkins.

Source: *United States–Vietnam Relations, 1945–1967*, Book 12 (Washington, DC: U.S. Government Printing Office, 1971), 590–591.

131. McGeorge Bundy, National Security Advisor: Cable to Ambassador Henry Cabot Lodge Jr. Expressing Reservations about the Coup, October 30, 1963

Introduction

Washington continued to be of two minds about coup planning by dissident generals to topple President Ngo Dinh Diem of the Republic of Vietnam (RVN, South Vietnam). While U.S. government officials were deeply frustrated with Diem and his policies, there was great concern over the possible consequence of a failed coup as well as what might follow with success. Here National Security Advisor McGeorge Bundy informs U.S. ambassador to South Vietnam Henry Cabot Lodge that President John F. Kennedy seeks assurances that the balance of forces favors the plotters. Without such, Lodge is to discourage the effort.

Primary Source

1. Your [cables] 2023, 2040, 2041 and 2043 examined with care at highest levels here. You should promptly discuss this reply and associated messages with Harkins whose responsibilities toward any coup are very heavy especially after you leave (see para. 7 below). They give much clearer picture group's alleged plans and also indicate chances of action with or without our approval now so significant that we should urgently consider our attitude and contingency plans. We note particularly Don's curiosity your departure and his insistence Conein be available from Wednesday night on, which suggests date might be as early as Thursday.

2. Believe our attitude to coup group can still have decisive effect on its decisions. We believe that what we say to coup group can produce delay of coup and that betrayal of coup plans to Diem is not repeat not our only way of stopping coup. We therefore need urgently your combined assessment with Harkins and CAS (including their separate comments if they desire). We concerned that our line-up of forces in Saigon (being cabled in next message) indicates approximately equal balance of forces, with substantial possibility serious and prolonged fighting or even defeat. Either of these could be serious or even disastrous for U.S. interests, so that we must have assurance balance of forces clearly favorable.

3. With your assessment in hand, we might feel that we should convey message to Don, whether or not he gives 4 or 48 hours notice that would (A) continue explicit hands-off policy, (B) positively encourage coup, or (C) discourage.

4. In any case, believe Conein should find earliest opportunity express to Don that we do not find presently revealed plans give clear prospect of quick results. This conversation should call attention important Saigon units still apparently loyal to Diem and raise serious issue as to what means coup group has to deal with them.

5. From operational standpoint, we also deeply concerned Don only spokesman for group and possibility cannot be discounted he may not be in good faith. We badly need some corroborative evidence whether Minh and others directly and completely involved. In view Don's claim he doesn't handle "military planning" could not Conein tell Don that we need better military picture and that Big Minh could communicate this most naturally and easily to [General Richard] Stilwell [Harkins's chief of staff]? We recognize desirability involving MACV [U.S. Military Assistance Command, Vietnam] to minimum, but believe Stilwell far more desirable this purpose than using Conein both ways.

6. Complexity above actions raises question whether you should adhere to present Thursday schedule. Concur you and other U.S. elements should take no action that could indicate U.S. awareness coup possibility. However, DOD [Department of Defense] is sending berth-equipped military aircraft that will arrive Saigon Thursday and could take you out thereafter as late as Saturday afternoon in time to meet your presently proposed arrival Washington Sunday. You could explain this being done as convenience and that your Washington arrival is same. A further advantage such aircraft is that it would permit your prompt return from any point en route if necessary. To reduce time in transit, you should use this plane, but we recognize delaying your departure may involve greater risk that you personally would appear involved if any action took place. However, advantages your having extra two days in Saigon may outweigh this and we leave timing of flight to your judgment.

7. Whether you leave Thursday or later, believe it essential that prior your departure there be fullest consultation Harkins and CAS and that there be clear arrangements for handling (A) normal activity, (B) continued coup contacts, (C) action in event a coup starts. We assume you will wish Truehart as charge to be head of country team in normal situation, but highest authority desires it clearly understood that after your departure Harkins should participate in supervision of all coup contacts and that in event a coup begins, he become head of country team and direct representative of President, with [William] Truehart [deputy chief of mission] in effect acting as POLAD [political adviser]. On coup contacts we will maintain continuous guidance and will expect equally continuous reporting with prompt account of any important divergences in assessments of Harkins and Smith.

8. If coup should start, question of protecting U.S. nationals at once arises. We can move Marine Battalion into Saigon by air from Okinawa within 24 hours—if available. We are sending instructions to CINCPAC to arrange orderly movement of seaborne Marine Battalion to waters adjacent to South Vietnam in position to close Saigon within approximately 24 hours.

9. We are now examining post-coup contingencies here and request your immediate recommendations on position to be adopted after coup begins, especially with respect to requests for assistance of different sorts from one side or the other also request you forward contingency recommendations for action if coup (A) succeeds, (B) fails, (C) is indecisive.

10. We reiterate burden of proof must be on coup group to show a substantial possibility of quick success; otherwise, we should discourage them from proceeding since a miscalculation could result in jeopardizing U.S. position in Southeast Asia.

Source: *The Pentagon Papers: The Defense Department History of United States Decisionmaking on Vietnam*, Vol. 2. Senator Gravel edition (Boston: Beacon, 1971), 782–783.

132. Phone Conversation between Ngo Dinh Diem and Henry Cabot Lodge Jr., November 1, 1963

Source: *The Pentagon Papers as Published by the New York Times* (New York: Quadrangle, 1971), 238.

Introduction

On November 1, 1963, dissident Army of the Republic of Vietnam (ARVN, South Vietnamese Army) generals launched their coup against President Ngo Dinh Diem. The rebels seized the radio station and police headquarters and besieged the presidential palace. Diem then telephoned U.S. ambassador Henry Cabot Lodge. In the ensuing conversation, Diem informs Lodge of events and inquires about the attitude of the U.S. government. Lodge professes ignorance of what is transpiring and tells Diem that because of the time difference in Washington, it is too early for the U.S. government to take an official position. Lodge professes concern for Diem's safety and tells him that there is a report that the generals have promised him safe passage abroad if he resigns. Early that same evening, Diem and his brother Ngo Dinh Nhu secretly left the presidential palace to seek refuge at St. Francis Xavier Church in Cholon. In an attempt to negotiate with the rebels Diem revealed his hiding place, and he and his brother were arrested there the next day and subsequently executed.

Primary Source

DIEM: Some Units have made a rebellion and I want to know, what is the attitude of the U.S.?

LODGE: I do not feel well enough informed to be able to tell you. I have heard the shootings but with all the facts. Also, it is 4:30 A.M. in Washington and the U.S. Government cannot possibly have a view.

DIEM: But you must have some general ideas. After all, I am Chief of State. I have tried to do my duty. I want to do now what duty and good sense require. I believe in duty above all.

LODGE: You have certainly done your duty. As I told you only this morning, I admire your courage and your great contribution to your country. No one can take away from you the credit for all you have done. Now I am worried about your physical safety. I have a report that those in charge of the current activity offer you and your brother safe conduct out of the country if you resign. Had you heard this?

DIEM: No. [*pause*] You have my phone number.

LODGE: Yes. If I can do anything for your physical safety, please call me.

DIEM: I am trying to re-establish order. [*hangs up*]

133. Joint Chiefs of Staff: Memorandum 46-64, January 22, 1964

Introduction

The assassination of President Ngo Dinh Diem of the Republic of Vietnam (RVN, South Vietnam) did not bring political stability to South Vietnam, for Washington never could find a worthy successor to him. The United States, which could not win the war with Diem, apparently could not win the war without him either. President John F. Kennedy was himself soon assassinated in Dallas, Texas, on November 22, 1963. Vice President Lyndon B. Johnson succeeded him. In early January 1964, ambassador to South Vietnam General Maxwell Taylor (who had succeeded Henry Cabot Lodge the previous July) recommended covert military action against the Democratic Republic of Vietnam (DRV, North Vietnam). In this memorandum to Johnson, the U.S. Joint Chiefs of Staff (JCS) seeks to make the case for additional resources in Vietnam and "bolder actions which may embody greater risk." Among these is pressing the new South Vietnamese leadership to turn over direction of the war to the commander of the Military Assistance Command, Vietnam (MACV), General Paul Harkins, whom they also believe should be given full authority over all U.S. programs in South Vietnam. The JCS also calls for the commitment "as necessary" of U.S. military forces against North Vietnam.

Primary Source

1. National Security Action Memorandum No. 273 makes clear the resolve of the President to ensure victory over the externally directed and supported communist insurgency in South Vietnam. In order to achieve that victory, the Joint Chiefs of Staff are of the opinion that the United States must be prepared to put aside many of the self-imposed restrictions which now limit our efforts, and to undertake bolder actions which may embody greater risks.

2. The Joint Chiefs of Staff are increasingly mindful that our fortunes in South Vietnam are an accurate barometer of our fortunes in all of Southeast Asia. It is our view that if the US program succeeds in South Vietnam it will go far toward stabilizing the total Southeast Asia situation. Conversely, a loss of South Vietnam to the communists will presage an early erosion of the remainder of our position in that subcontinent.

3. Laos, existing on a most fragile foundation now, would not be able to endure the establishment of a communist—or pseudo

neutralist—state on its eastern flank. Thailand less strong today than a month ago by virtue of the loss of Prime Minister Sarit, would probably be unable to withstand the pressures of infiltration from the north should Laos collapse to the communists in its turn. Cambodia apparently has estimated that our prospects in South Vietnam are not promising and, encouraged by the actions of the French, appears already to be seeking an accommodation with the communists. Should we actually suffer defeat in South Vietnam, there is little reason to believe that Cambodia would maintain even a pretense of neutrality.

4. In a broader sense, the failure of our program in South Vietnam would have heavy influence on the judgments of Burma, India, Indonesia, Malaysia, Japan, Taiwan, the Republic of Korea, and the Republic of the Philippines with respect to US durability, resolution, and trustworthiness. Finally, this being the first real test of our determination to defeat the communist wars of national liberation formula, it is not unreasonable to conclude that there would be a corresponding unfavorable effect upon our image in Africa and in Latin America.

5. All of this underscores the pivotal position now occupied in South Vietnam in our world-wide confrontation with the communists and the essentiality that the conflict there be brought to a favorable end as soon as possible. However, it would be unrealistic to believe that a complete suppression of the insurgency can take place in one or even two years. The British effort in Malaya is a recent example of a counterinsurgency effort which required approximately ten years before the bulk of the rural population was brought completely under control of the government, the police were able to maintain order, and the armed forces were able to eliminate the guerrilla strongholds.

6. The Joint Chiefs of Staff are convinced that, in keeping with the guidance in NSAM 273, the United States must make plain to the enemy our determination to see the Vietnam campaign through to a favorable conclusion. To do this, we must prepare for whatever level of activity may be required and, being prepared, must then proceed to take actions as necessary to achieve our purposes surely and promptly.

7. Our considerations, furthermore, cannot be confined entirely to South Vietnam. Our experience in the war thus far leads us to conclude that, in this respect, we are not now giving sufficient attention to the broader area problems of Southeast Asia. The Joint Chiefs of Staff believe that our position in Cambodia, our attitude toward Laos, our action in Thailand, and our great effort in South Vietnam do not comprise a compatible and integrated US policy for Southeast Asia. US objectives in Southeast Asia cannot be achieved by either economic, political, or military measures alone. All three fields must be integrated into a single, broad US program

for Southeast Asia. The measures recommended in this memorandum are a partial contribution to such a program.

8. Currently we and the South Vietnamese are fighting the war on the enemy's terms. He has determined the locale, the timing, and the tactics of the battle while our actions are essentially reactive. One reason for this is the fact that we have obliged ourselves to labor under self-imposed restrictions with respect to impeding external aid to the Viet Cong. These restrictions include keeping the war within the boundaries of South Vietnam, avoiding the direct use of US combat forces, and limiting US direction of the campaign to rendering advice to the Government of Vietnam. These restrictions, while they may make our international position more readily defensible, all tend to make the task in Vietnam more complex, time consuming, and in the end, more costly. In addition to complicating our own problem, these self-imposed restrictions may well now be conveying signals of irresolution to our enemies—encouraging them to higher levels of vigor and greater risks. A reversal of attitude and the adoption of a more aggressive program would enhance greatly our ability to control the degree to which escalation will occur. It appears probable that the economic and agricultural disappointments suffered by Communist China, plus the current rift with the Soviets, could cause the communists to think twice about undertaking a largescale military adventure in Southeast Asia.

9. In adverting to actions outside of South Vietnam, the Joint Chiefs of Staff are aware that the focus of the counterinsurgency battle lies in South Vietnam itself, and that the war must certainly be fought and won primarily in the minds of the Vietnamese people. At the same time, the aid now coming to the Viet Cong from outside the country in men, resources, advice, and direction is sufficiently great in the aggregate to be significant—both as help and as encouragement to the Viet Cong. It is our conviction that if support of the insurgency from outside South Vietnam in terms of operational direction, personnel, and material were stopped completely, the character of the war in South Vietnam would be substantially and favorably altered. Because of this conviction, we are wholly in favor of executing the covert actions against North Vietnam which you have recently proposed to the President. We believe, however, that it would be idle to conclude that these efforts will have a decisive effect on the communist determination to support the insurgency; and it is our view that we must therefore be prepared fully to undertake a much higher level of activity, not only for its beneficial tactical effect, but to make plain our resolution, both to our friends and to our enemies.

10. Accordingly, the Joint Chiefs of Staff consider that the United States must make ready to conduct increasingly bolder actions in Southeast Asia; specifically as to Vietnam to:

a. Assign to the US military commander responsibilities for the total US program in Vietnam.

b. Induce the Government of Vietnam to turn over to the United States military commander, temporarily, the actual tactical direction of the war.

c. Charge the United States military commander with complete responsibility for conduct of the program against North Vietnam.

d. Overfly Laos and Cambodia to whatever extent is necessary for acquisition of operational intelligence.

e. Induce the Government of Vietnam to conduct overt ground operations in Laos of sufficient scope to impede the flow of personnel and material southward.

f. Arm, equip, advise, and support the Government of Vietnam in its conduct of aerial bombing of critical targets in North Vietnam and in mining the sea approaches to that country.

g. Advise and support the Government of Vietnam in its conduct of large-scale commando raids against critical targets in North Vietnam.

h. Conduct aerial bombing of key North Vietnam targets, using US resources under Vietnamese cover, and with the Vietnamese openingly assuming responsibility for the actions.

i. Commit additional US forces, as necessary, in support of the combat action within South Vietnam.

j. Commit US forces as necessary in direct actions against North Vietnam.

11. It is our conviction that any or all of the foregoing actions may be required to enhance our position in Southeast Asia. The past few months have disclosed that considerably higher levels of effort are demanded of us if US objectives are to be attained.

12. The governmental reorganization which followed the coup d'état in Saigon should be completed very soon, giving basis for concluding just how strong the Vietnamese Government is going to be and how much of the load they will be able to bear themselves. Additionally, the five-month dry season, which is just now beginning, will afford the Vietnamese an opportunity to exhibit their ability to reverse the unfavorable situation in the critical Mekong Delta. The Joint Chiefs of Staff will follow these important developments closely and will recommend to you progressively the execution of such of the above actions as are considered militarily required, providing, in each case, their detailed assessment of the risks involved.

13. The Joint Chiefs of Staff consider that the strategic importance of Vietnam and of Southeast Asia warrants preparations for the actions above and recommend that the substance of this memorandum be discussed with the Secretary of State.

Source: *The Pentagon Papers: The Defense Department History of United States Decisionmaking on Vietnam*, Vol. 3. Senator Gravel edition (Boston: Beacon, 1971), 496–499.

134. Robert McNamara, Secretary of Defense: Memorandum for President Lyndon Johnson, March 16, 1964 [Excerpts]

Introduction

On January 30, 1964, another coup occurred in Saigon when General Dong Van Minh was ousted by General Nguyen Thanh. In early March 1964 Secretary of Defense Robert McNamara visited Saigon and there publicly announced U.S. support for General Nguyen Khanh, the new leader of the Republic of Vietnam (RVN, South Vietnam). McNamara also pledged "our complete support.... We'll stay for as long as it takes. We shall provide whatever help is required to win the battle against the Communist insurgents." McNamara returned to Washington with a sobering view of the situation, however. In this report to President Lyndon Johnson, the defense secretary claims that Communist forces now control or have influence over about 40 percent of South Vietnamese territory, that there is widespread indifference among the people as to the outcome of the war, and that another coup is a distinct possibility. McNamara rejects negotiations with the Communists and urges covert military action against the Democratic Republic of Vietnam (DRV, North Vietnam). He also recommends a sharp increase in U.S. military assistance to the South Vietnamese military, which he claims could bring a significant improvement in only six months.

Primary Source

III. The Present Situation in South Vietnam

The key elements in the present situation are as follows:

A. The military tools and concepts of the GVN/US effort are generally sound and adequate. Substantially more can be done in the effective employment of military forces and in the economic and civic action areas. These improvements may require some selective increases in the U.S. presence, but it does not appear likely that major equipment replacement and additions in U.S. personnel are indicated under current policy.

B. The U.S. policy of reducing existing personnel where South Vietnamese are in a position to assume the functions is still sound. Its application will not lead to any major reductions in the near future, but adherence to this policy as such has a sound effect in portraying to the U.S. and the world that we continue to regard the war as a conflict the South Vietnamese must win and take ultimate responsibility for. Substantial reductions in the numbers of U.S. military training personnel should be possible before the end of 1965. However, the U.S. should continue to reiterate that it will provide all the assistance and advice required to do the job regardless of how long it takes.

C. The situation has unquestionably been growing worse, at least since September:

1. In terms of government control of the countryside, about 40% of the territory is under Viet Cong control or predominant influence. In 22 of the 43 provinces, the Viet Cong control 50% or more of the land area, including 80% of Phuoc Tuy; 90% of Binh Duong; 75% of Hau Nghia; 90% of Long An; 90% of Kien Tuong; 90% of Dinh Tuong; 90% of Kien Hoa; and 85% of An Xuyen.

2. Large groups of the population are now showing signs of apathy and indifference, and there are some signs of frustration within the U.S. contingent:
   a. The ARVN and paramilitary desertion rates, and particularly the latter, are high and increasing.
   b. Draft dodging is high while the Viet Cong are recruiting energetically and effectively.
   c. The morale of the hamlet militia and of the Self Defense Corps, on which the security of the hamlets depends, is poor and falling.

3. In the last 90 days the weakening of the government's position has been particularly noticeable. For example:
   a. In Quang Nam province, in the I Corps, the militia in 17 hamlets turned in their weapons.
   b. In Binh Duong province (III Corps) the hamlet militia were disarmed because of suspected disloyalty.
   c. In Binh Dinh province, in the II Corps, 75 hamlets were severely damaged by the Viet Cong (in contrast, during the twelve months ending June 30, 1963, attacks on strategic hamlets were few and none was overrun).
   d. In Quang Ngai province, at the northern edge of the II Corps, there were 413 strategic hamlets under government control a year ago. Of that number, 335 have been damaged to varying degrees or fallen into disrepair, and only 275 remain under government control.
   e. Security throughout the IV Corps has deteriorated badly. The Viet Cong control virtually all facets of peasant life in the southernmost provinces and the government troops there are reduced to defending the administrative centers. Except in An Giang province (dominated by the Hoa Hao religious sect) armed escort is required for almost all movement in both the southern and northern areas of the IV Corps.

4. The political control structure extending from Saigon down into the hamlets disappeared following the November coup. Of the 41 incumbent province chiefs on November 1, 35 have been replaced (nine provinces had three province chiefs in three months; one province had four). Scores of lesser officials were replaced. Almost all major military commands have changed hands twice since the November coup. The faith of the peasants has been shaken by the disruptions in experienced leadership and the loss of physical security. In many areas, power vacuums have developed causing confusion among the people and a rising rate of rural disorders.

5. North Vietnamese support, always significant, has been increasing:
   a. Communications between Hanoi and the Viet Cong (see classified annex).
   b. Since July 1, 1963, the following items of equipment, not previously encountered in South Vietnam, have been captured from the Viet Cong:
      Chicom 75 mm. recoilless rifles.
      Chicom heavy machine guns.
      U.S. .50 caliber heavy machine guns on Chicom mounts.
      In addition, it is clear that the Viet Cong are using Chinese 90 mm rocket launchers and mortars.
   c. The Viet Cong are importing large quantities of munitions and chemicals for the production of explosives: Approximately 50,000 pounds of explosive-producing chemicals destined for the Viet Cong have been intercepted in the 12 months ending March 1964. On December 24, five tons of ammunition, of which one and one-half tons were 75 mm recoilless rifle ammunition, was captured at the Dinh Tuong Viet Cong arsenal. Ninety percent was of Chicom manufacture.
   d. The greatest weakness in the present situation is the uncertain viability of the Khanh government. Khanh himself is a very able man within his experience, but he does not yet have wide political appeal and his control of the Army itself is uncertain (he has the serious problem of the jailed generals). After two coups, as was mentioned above, there has been a sharp drop in morale and organization, and Khanh has not yet been able to build these up satisfactorily. There is a constant threat of assassination or of another coup, which would drop morale and organization nearly to zero. Whether or not French nationals are actively encouraging such a coup, de Gaulle's position and the continuing pessimism and anti-Americanism of the French community in South Vietnam provide constant fuel to neutralist sentiment and the coup possibility. If

a coup is set underway, the odds of our detecting and preventing it in the tactical sense are not high.

e. On the positive side, we have found many reasons for encouragement in the performance of the Khanh government to date. Although its top layer is thin, it is highly responsive to U.S. advice, and with a good grasp of the basic elements of rooting out the Viet Cong. Opposition groups are fragmentary, and Khanh has brought in at least token representation from many key groups hitherto left out. He is keenly aware of the danger of assassination or coup and is taking resourceful steps to minimize these risks. All told, these evidences of energy, comprehension, and decision add up to a sufficiently strong chance of Khanh's really taking hold in the next few months for us to devote all possible energy and resources to his support.

Source: *The Pentagon Papers: The Defense Department History of United States Decisionmaking on Vietnam,* Vol. 3. Senator Gravel edition (Boston: Beacon, 1971), 500–502.

135. President Lyndon Johnson: Telegram to Ambassador Henry Cabot Lodge Jr., March 20, 1964

Introduction

In this telegram of March 20, 1964, U.S. president Lyndon Johnson explains to ambassador to the Republic of Vietnam (RVN, South Vietnam) Henry Cabot Lodge why military operations against the Democratic Republic of Vietnam (DRV, North Vietnam) have been delayed. Johnson tells Lodge that the United States anticipates a "showdown" between the Soviet Union and the People's Republic of China (PRC) that will make it easier for the United States to attack North Vietnam. Johnson agrees with Lodge on the need to bring diplomatic pressure on French president Charles de Gaulle so that he will retract statements calling for the "neutralization" of Vietnam.

Primary Source

1. We have studied your 1776 and I am asking State to have Bill Bundy make sure that you get out latest planning documents on ways of applying pressure and power against the North. I understand that some of this was discussed with you by McNamara mission in Saigon, but as plans are refined it would be helpful to have your detailed comments. As we agreed in our previous messages to each other, judgment is reserved for the present on overt military action in view of the consensus from Saigon conversations of McNamara mission with General Khanh and you on judgment that movement against the North at the present

would be premature. We share General Khanh's judgment that the immediate and essential task is to strengthen the southern base. For this reason our planning for action against the North is on a contingency basis at present, and immediate problem in this area is to develop the strongest possible military and political base for possible later action. There is additional international reason for avoiding immediate overt action in that we expect a showdown between the Chinese and Soviet Communist parties soon and action against the North will be more practicable after than before a showdown. But if at any time you feel that more immediate action is urgent, I count on you to let me know specifically the reasons for such action, together with your recommendations for its size and shape.

2. On dealing with deGaulle, I continue to think it may be valuable for you to go to Paris after Bohlen has made his first try. (State is sending you draft instruction to Bohlen, which I have not yet reviewed, for your comment.) It ought to be possible to explain in Saigon that your mission is precisely for the purpose of knocking down the idea of neutralization wherever it rears its ugly head, and on this point I think that nothing is more important than to stop neutralist talk wherever we can by whatever means we can. I have made this point myself to Mansfield and Lippmann and I expect to use every public opportunity to restate our position firmly. You may want to convey our concern on this point to General Khanh and get his ideas on the best possible joint program to stop such talk in Saigon, in Washington, and in Paris. I imagine that you have kept General Khanh abreast of our efforts in Paris. After we see the results of the Bohlen approach you might wish to sound him out on Paris visit by you.

Source: *The Pentagon Papers: The Defense Department History of United States Decisionmaking on Vietnam,* Vol. 3. Senator Gravel edition (Boston: Beacon, 1971), 511.

136. George W. Ball, Undersecretary of State: Telegram to President Lyndon Johnson and Secretary of State Dean Rusk, June 5, 1964 [Excerpt]

Introduction

U.S. undersecretary of state George W. Ball here reports to President Lyndon Johnson and Secretary of State Dean Rusk regarding a meeting with French president Charles de Gaulle. Ball notes the French president as stating that there can be no military solution for the United States in Vietnam and that the only way to avoid a wider war is through a diplomatic solution in the form of an international peace conference that would include France, the People's Republic of China (PRC), India, Japan, and other nations.

Primary Source

General De Gaulle said he had listened with great attention to what Mr. Ball had said. There was little surprising in it since he had suspected for some time the difficulties of the situation. The US has taken on itself alone the responsibilities which the French had borne in the past.

He said he agreed that South Vietnam was the main problem, with Laos and Cambodia as accessory problems. He referred to our hope that we can bring about a suppression of the insurgency by supplying Vietnam with arms, credits, military advice, etc. I take note, said General De Gaulle, of your hope but I cannot agree with it. I do not believe that you can win in this situation even though you have more aircraft, cannons, and arms of various kinds.

The problem was primarily a political and psychological problem. He was not referring merely to General Khanh but to the people. To them the US was a very big foreign power. "I do not mean that all of the Vietnamese are against you but they regard the US as a foreign power and a very powerful foreign power."

The more the US becomes involved in the actual conduct of military operations the more the Vietnamese will turn against us, as will others, in Southeast Asia.

He said he understood the immense difficulties which the US faced. The US has the possibility and the means of going to war. We could destroy Hanoi, Canton and even Peking. We could link Chiang Kai-shek on the Chinese Mainland and even American troops if we desired. But what would happen when the war began? What would be its consequences? He could not say.

In 1900, at the time of the Boxer Rebellion, it had been very easy. The only problem was that of frightening the Empress. Now continents were involved.

War was, of course, a possibility which the US could envisage. General MacArthur had thought it was a good idea. However, he said, the French would never resume war in Asia. He had told this to President Kennedy. The French consider that Southeast Asia is a "rotten" territory in which to fight. Even if the US were involved France would not get into a war in Asia, as an ally or otherwise.

If the US did not make war we still appeared to think that by reinforcing the existing situation we could strengthen the Vietnamese and win the current struggle. He did not agree with this. The United States might maintain the struggle in this manner for an extended period of time, but we could not bring the affair to an end. Once we realized this, i.e., that we could not put an end to the situation, we might come to the conclusion that we would have to

make peace. This would mean peace with China and others in the area.

He said he noticed that we thought that China was like Russia in 1917—intransigent, warlike, and expansive. He did not know whether this was true or not. Personally he doubted it. He thought it possible that China would see the advantage to itself, at least for a few years, in a passive posture. He did not mean that this would last forever but it might for a few years. China needs rest, it needs help, it needs commerce and technical assistance from other countries. The Russians had been in a different position. Russia had had an intelligentsia, an army, and agriculture. China has none of these things. In any event, the French thought that we should try to see what China was up to. He then asked for Mr. Ball's comments.

Mr. Ball said if we were now to undertake diplomatic efforts with Peking or Hanoi this would threaten the collapse of the existing resistance in South Vietnam. General De Gaulle had said—and he agreed—that the problem was more political and psychological than military. Our task was to help the South Vietnamese create a govt in which the people would have confidence, and to which they would feel allegiance. But if we began, or attempted to begin, negotiations of the type that General De Gaulle was speaking about the result might be a general failure of the will to resist.

Either we must increase the Vietnamese will to resist or we must reduce the subversive efforts of the North. To negotiate before either of these objectives was achieved would destroy the only basis on which we can hope to build in the future. Moreover we said [had?] no reason to believe that an agreement made with the Communists would be carried out. We remembered the agreement of 1962 for the neutralization of Laos, and the attitude of Hanoi and Peking toward it.

De Gaulle said that if a diplomatic operation were undertaken by the US alone, it would, of course, not succeed. What he had in mind was a vast diplomatic operation which would include the participation of France, India, China, Japan, and other countries. This would provide the Vietnamese people—and he was not speaking of General Khanh—with a sense of support and assurance for the future. He doubted that even Ho Chi Minh could continue to kill South Vietnamese while taking part in a conference. World opinion would make it impossible.

He repeated, however, such a diplomatic effort could not be done by the Americans. A large conference had been attempted in 1954 and although the talks had taken a very long time he felt that this in itself was not a bad thing. If a world conference of the type he was thinking of could be put into operation it would change the state of mind of the Vietnamese people and produce a detente. This would render it very difficult for Ho Chi Minh to keep on with his activities. If such a diplomatic operation were undertaken a resulting detente would bring about a new political situation. This, however, was not possible under conditions of civil war.

Mr. Ball said the situation in South Vietnam presented problems of exceptional difficulty. If we were dealing with conventional warfare—with regular armies drawn up in opposing formations—it would be possible to agree to a cease-fire and police it. But in South Vietnam there were scattered groups of guerrillas. Many only came out at night. It would be extremely difficult to police any cease-fire. Moreover, it was not realistic to assume that the insurgents would be willing to lose momentum and thus would be willing to accept a cease-fire. Ho Chi Minh would probably argue with contrived innocence that he had no connection with what was going on in Vietnam. At the same time he would covertly maintain the subversive action. There was enormous danger that a conference would play into the hands of the Communists who would exploit it covertly and dishonestly. Thereafter it might well be impossible to infuse any vitality into a Vietnamese Govt. We would be reluctant to take such a risk.

De Gaulle replied: "All policy involves risks. If it is a policy that does not involve risks there is no choice of policy." He thought a conference of Europeans, Asians and US would produce a very powerful impact on the Vietnamese people and succeed in changing the whole situation, at least for a certain period of time. The present situation, he said, would not result in anything. France has had experience which proved it.

> **Source:** *Foreign Relations of the United States, 1964–1968: Vietnam, 1964,* Vol. 1 (Washington, DC: U.S. Government Printing Office, 1992), 464–470.

137. Blair Seaborn, Canadian International Control Commission Representative: Notes on Meeting with Pham Van Dong, June 18, 1964

Introduction

The International Control Commission (ICC), made up of representatives from Canada, India, and Poland, was the agency charged by the Geneva Conference with supervising implementation of the 1954 Geneva Agreements. Here Canadian ICC representative Blair Seaborn reports on his meeting with Premier Pham Van Dong of the Democratic Republic of Vietnam (DRV, North Vietnam). Seaborn spells out North Vietnam's desire for negotiations to reach a settlement, which must include the participation of the National Front for the Liberation of South Vietnam, usually known as the National Liberation Front (NLF). He reports that Dong has told him that the struggle in the Republic of Vietnam (RVN, South Vietnam) will continue despite increased U.S. aid to the South Vietnamese government. Dong was also emphatic that the NLF would win the war.

Primary Source

President Ho Chi Minh has explained what we mean by a just solution. First it requires an American withdrawal from Indochina. Secondly it means that the affairs of the South must be arranged by the people of the South. It must provide for the participation of the Liberation Front. No other group represents the broad wishes of the people. The programme of the Front is the best one possible. There must be peace and neutrality for South Vietnam, neutrality in the Cambodian manner. Thirdly, a just solution means re-unification of the country. This is a "drame, [as in original document] national, fundamental". But we want peaceful unification, without military pressures. We want negotiation 'round a table. There must be sincere satisfaction with the arrangement for it to be viable. We are in no hurry. We are willing to talk but we shall wait till SVN is ready. We are a divided people, without even personal links across the dividing line.

The United States must show good will, but it is not easy for the USA to do so. Meanwhile the war intensifies. USA aid may increase in all areas, not only for the SVN army but in terms of USA army personnel as well. I suffer to see the war go on, develop, intensify. Yet our people are determined to struggle. It is impossible, quite impossible (excuse me for saying this) for you Westerners to understand the force of the people's will to resist and to continue. The struggle of the people exceeds the imagination. It has astonished us too.

Since the fall of the Ngo brothers, it has been a "cascade". The prospect for the USA and its friends in SVN is "sans issu." Reinforcing the Khanh army doesn't count. The people have had enough. The SVN mercenaries have sacrificed themselves without honour. The Americans are not lovers, for they commit atrocities. How can the people suffer such exactions and terror?

Let me stress, insofar as the internal situation in SVN is concerned, the realistic nature of the Liberation Front's programme. It is impossible to have a representative government which excludes the Front. The idea of a government of national coalition "fait boule de neige" in the South. The Laos pattern of 1962 should serve as a guide for SVN.

To return to Vietnam, it is a question of a "guerre à outrance" which the USA won't win in any event, or neutrality. He had not (as I had suggested) referred to neutrality as a first step only.

Whether SVN would continue neutral would depend upon the people of SVN. He did not prejudge the issue.

Source: *United States–Vietnam Relations, 1945–1967*, VI.C.I (Washington, DC: U.S. Government Printing Office, 1971), 28–29.

138. Maxwell Taylor, Ambassador: Telegram to Secretary of State Dean Rusk, July 25, 1964 [Excerpt]

Introduction

In this cable to U.S. secretary of state Dean Rusk, ambassador to the Republic of Vietnam (RVN, South Vietnam) Maxwell Taylor warns that South Vietnamese premier Nguyen Khanh's public statements about "marching north" could pose major problems for U.S.–South Vietnamese relations. Rusk suggests joint planning talks as the best way for the United States to get control of the situation. The State Department subsequently approved the idea, while it expressed concerns that Khanh might make these talks public for political purposes.

Primary Source

The GVN [Government of Vietnam; South Vietnamese government] public campaign for "Marching North" (reported EMB-TEL 201) may take several courses. In the face of U.S. coolness and absence of evidence of real grassroots support outside certain military quarters, it may die down for a while although it is hardly likely to disappear completely. On the other hand, the proponents of a "Quick Solution" may be able to keep it alive indefinitely as an active issue, in which case it is likely to foment an increasing amount of dissatisfaction with the U.S. (assuming that we continue to give it no support) to the serious detriment of our working relations with the GVN and hence of the ultimate chances of success of the in-country pacification program. In such a case, Vietnamese leaders in and out of government, unable to find a vent to their frustration in "Marching North" may seek other panaceas in various forms of negotiation formulas. General Khanh may find in the situation an excuse or a requirement to resign.

Finally, this "March North" fever can get out of hand in an act of rashness—one maverick pilot taking off for Hanoi with a load of bombs—which could touch off an extension of hostilities at a time and in a form most disadvantageous to U.S. interests.

Faced with these unattractive possibilities, we propose a course of action designed to do several things.

We would try to avoid head-on collision with the GVN which unqualified U.S. opposition to the "March North" campaign would

entail. We could do this by expressing a willingness to engage in joint contingency planning for various forms of extended action against GVN [sic]. Such planning would not only provide an outlet for the martial head of steam now dangerously compressed but would force the generals to look at the hard facts of life which lie behind the neon lights of the "March North" slogans. This planning would also gain time badly needed to stabilize this government and could provide a useful basis for military action if adjudged in our interest at some future time. Finally, it would also afford U.S. an opportunity, for the first time, to have a frank discussion with GVN leaders concerning the political objectives which they would envisage as the purposes inherent in military action against the DRV....

It would be important, however, in initiating such a line of action that we make a clear record that we are not repeat not assuming any commitment to supplement such plans....

Source: *The Pentagon Papers: The Defense Department History of United States Decisionmaking on Vietnam*, Vol. 3. Senator Gravel edition (Boston: Beacon, 1971), 512–513.

139. Admiral Thomas H. Moorer, Commander in Chief, Pacific Fleet: Order to All Subordinate Units, August 2, 1964

Introduction

On August 2, 1964, torpedo boats from the Democratic Republic of Vietnam (DRV, North Vietnam) attacked the U.S. destroyer *Maddox,* which was engaged in an electronic intelligence-collection mission (Operation DE SOTO) in international waters off North Vietnam. There were no casualties. The North Vietnamese reaction was undoubtedly prompted by recent commando raids from the Republic of Vietnam (RVN, South Vietnam) in the vicinity (OPLAN 34A, run out of Saigon). Rather than backing down, the commander of the U.S. Pacific Fleet, Admiral Thomas H. Moorer, ordered the DE SOTO operations to continue but with the addition of a second destroyer. Here Moorer asserts the U.S. intention to force the issue of "freedom of the seas" right up to the international three-mile territorial limit.

Primary Source

1. In view Maddox incident, consider it our best interest that we assert right of freedom of the seas and resume Golf of Tonkin patrol earliest.

2. For COMSEVENTHFLT [Commander, Seventh Fleet] UNODIR [unless otherwise directed] conduct patrol with two destroyers, resuming ASAP [as soon as possible]. When ready, proceed to

Point Charlie arriving first day, thence patrol northward toward Point Delta during daylight hours. Retire to the east during hours of darkness. On second day proceed to Point Delta thence, patrol south toward Point Charlie retiring to night as before. On third day proceed to Point Lima and patrol toward Point Mike, retiring to east at night. On fourth day proceed to Point Mike and patrol toward Point November, retiring night. On fifth day return to [Point] November and retire to south through Points Oscar and Papa and terminate patrol. CPA [closest point of approach] to North Vietnamese coast 8NM [nautical miles]. CPA to North Vietnamese islands 4NM. Above points as specified.

Source: U.S. Congress, *Congressional Record,* 90th Cong., 2nd. sess. (Washington, DC: U.S. Government Printing Office, 1968), 4694.

140. Dean Rusk, Secretary of State: Telegram to Ambassador Maxwell Taylor, August 3, 1964

Introduction

The commander of the now two-destroyer U.S. Navy intelligence-gathering mission (Operation DE SOTO) off the coast of Democratic Republic of Vietnam (DRV, North Vietnam) coast heard reports that intelligence indicated that the North Vietnamese had assumed the *Maddox*—attacked by torpedo boats on August 2, 1964—to be part of the secret OPLAN 34A commando raids by the Republic of Vietnam (RVN, South Vietnam). Here U.S. secretary of state Dean Rusk informs ambassador to South Vietnam Maxwell D. Taylor that the commando raids have "rattled" the North Vietnamese. The telegram also shows that the Lyndon Johnson administration clearly understood, contrary to Defense Secretary Robert McNamara's later testimony before Congress, that the North Vietnamese considered the *Maddox* to be part of the OPLAN 34A operations.

Primary Source

We have been very sensitive here to the considerations you raise reftel. We would hope that part of the problem has been met by President's public statement today, which you have already received. We have asked JCS to insure that you receive copies of the implementing orders to the appropriate commanders through military channels.

Suggestions made in B, C and D reftel are currently being considered in context OPLAN 34A. Significant additions have been made to list of targets for marine operations and these will be transmitted to you shortly.

We believe that present OPLAN 34A activities are beginning to rattle Hanoi, and MADDOX incident is directly related to their

effort to resist these activities. We have no intention yielding to pressure.

In your discretion you may pass these thoughts along to Gen. Khanh. You may also reiterate to him, but only if you believe it appropriate, our concern that actions against the North be limited for the present to the OPLAN 34A type. We do not believe that SVN is yet in a position to mount larger actions so long as the security situation in the near vicinity of Saigon remains precarious. We are impressed with the fact that a battalion-sized attack could have occurred within 4 miles of Saigon without any advance warning.

We would welcome your further comments on Saigon reaction to today's announcement, as well as your continuing assessment of the political temperature there.

Source: *Foreign Relations of the United States, 1964–1968: Vietnam, 1964,* Vol. 1 (Washington, DC: U.S. Government Printing Office, 1992), 603–604.

141. Thomas H. Moorer, Commander in Chief, Pacific Fleet: Message to Captain John Herrick, August 3, 1964 [Excerpts]

Introduction

Believing through radio intercepts that another attack on his two destroyers off the coast of the Democratic Republic of Vietnam (DRV, North Vietnam) was likely, U.S. Navy patrol commander Captain John Herrick requested permission from Pacific Fleet commander Admiral Thomas H. Moorer to terminate his DE SOTO intelligence-gathering mission. In this telegram Moorer refuses Herrick's request, suggesting only that Herrick shift his operational area so that it will not be confused with the OPLAN 34A commando operation being conducted by the Republic of Vietnam (RVN, South Vietnam) but not so far that it would fail to draw North Vietnamese patrol boats away from the South Vietnamese commando operation.

Primary Source

1. Termination of DeSoto patrol after two days of patrol ops [operations] subsequent to Maddox incident does not in my view adequately demonstrate United States resolve to assert our legitimate rights in these international waters.

2. Accordingly, recommend following adjustments in remainder of patrol schedule . . . in order to accommodate COMUSMACV [Commander, United States Military Assistance Command Vietnam] request that patrol ships remain north of LAT [latitude]

19-10 north until [deleted time] to avoid interference with 34-A Ops. 4 August patrol from Point Delta to Charlie remain north of 19-10 North.

The above patrol will (a) clearly demonstrate our determination to continue these operations; (b) possibly draw NVN [North Vietnamese Navy] PGMs [patrol boats] to northward away from area of 34-A Ops; (c) eliminate DeSoto patrol interference with 34-A Ops.

Source: U.S. Congress, *Congressional Record,* 90th Cong., 2nd sess. (Washington, DC: U.S. Government Printing Office, 1968), 4694.

142. President Lyndon Johnson's Message to Congress, August 5, 1964 [Excerpts]

Introduction

On the night of August 4, 1964, U.S. Navy captain John Herrick reported a second patrol boat attack by the Democratic Republic of Vietnam (DRV, North Vietnam) on his two destroyers. He subsequently modified this, saying that he could not be certain that an attack had actually occurred. All evidence suggests that there was no second attack and that the false impression was caused by weather-generated anomalies, seagulls, foam on the crests of waves generated by the destroyers in evasive maneuvers, and other natural disturbances. Leaders of the Lyndon Johnson administration had, however, already decided to use the alleged Gulf of Tonkin Incidents to take direct military action against North Vietnam. In this message to Congress, President Johnson announces retaliatory air strikes against North Vietnam. Known as Operation PIERCE ARROW, these take the form of carrier aviation attacks on North Vietnamese naval vessels at a number of locations along the North Vietnamese coast and a petroleum storage facility at Vinh.

Primary Source

Last night I announced to the American people that the North Vietnamese regime had conducted further deliberate attacks against U.S. naval vessels operating in international waters, and I had therefore directed air action against gunboats and supporting facilities used in these hostile operations. This air action has now been carried out with substantial damage to the boats and facilities. Two U.S. aircraft were lost in the action.

After consultation with the leaders of both parties in the Congress, I further announced a decision to ask the Congress for a resolution expressing the unity and determination of the United States in supporting freedom and in protecting peace in southeast Asia.

These latest actions of the North Vietnamese regime has given a new and grave turn to the already serious situation in southeast Asia. Our commitments in that area are well known to the Congress. They were first made in 1954 by President Eisenhower. They were further defined in the Southeast Asia Collective Defense Treaty approved by the Senate in February 1955.

This treaty with its accompanying protocol obligates the United States and other members to act in accordance with their constitutional processes to meet Communist aggression against any of the parties or protocol states.

Our policy in southeast Asia has been consistent and unchanged since 1954. I summarized it on June 2 in four simple propositions:

1. America keeps her word. Here as elsewhere, we must and shall honor our commitments.
2. The issue is the future of southeast Asia as a whole. A threat to any nation in that region is a threat to all, and a threat to us.
3. Our purpose is peace. We have no military, political, or territorial ambitions in the area.
4. This is not just a jungle war, but a struggle for freedom on every front of human activity. Our military and economic assistance to South Vietnam and Laos in particular has the purpose of helping these countries to repel aggression and strengthen their independence.

The threat to the free nations of southeast Asia has long been clear. The North Vietnamese regime has constantly sought to take over South Vietnam and Laos. This Communist regime has violated the Geneva accords for Vietnam. It has systematically conducted a campaign of subversion, which includes the direction, training, and supply of personnel and arms for the conduct of guerrilla warfare in South Vietnamese territory. In Laos, the North Vietnamese regime has maintained military forces, used Laotian territory for infiltration into South Vietnam, and most recently carried out combat operations—all in direct violation of the Geneva Agreements of 1962.

In recent months, the actions of the North Vietnamese regime have become steadily more threatening. . . .

As President of the United States I have concluded that I should now ask the Congress, on its part, to join in affirming the national determination that all such attacks will be met, and that the United States will continue in its basic policy of assisting the free nations of the area to defend their freedom.

As I have repeatedly made clear, the United States intends no rashness, and seeks no wider war. We must make it clear to all that the United States is united in its determination to bring about the end of Communist subversion and aggression in the area. We seek the full and effective restoration of the international agreements signed in Geneva in 1954, with respect to South Vietnam, and again in Geneva in 1962, with respect to Laos. . . .

Source: *Public Papers of the Presidents of the United States: Lyndon B. Johnson, 1963–64,* Book 2 (Washington, DC: U.S. Government Printing Office, 1965), 930–932.

143. Joint Resolution of Congress H.J. RES 1445: Tonkin Gulf Resolution, August 7, 1964 [Excerpt]

Introduction

Following the alleged second attack on two U.S. Navy destroyers in the Gulf of Tonkin, the Lyndon B. Johnson administration submitted to Congress a resolution that in effect gave it full powers to wage war in Southeast Asia. Contrary to myths surrounding the resolution, its implications were fully discussed in the debate in Congress. The resolution was approved unanimously by the House of Representatives and by a vote of 88 to 2 in the Senate.

Primary Source

Resolved by the Senate and House of Representatives of the United States of America in Congress assembled, That the Congress approves and supports the determination of the President, as Commander in Chief, to take all necessary measures to repel any armed attack against the forces of the United States and to prevent further aggression.

Sec. 2. The United States regards as vital to its national interest and to world peace and security in southeast Asia. Consonant with the Constitution of the United States and the Charter Of the United Nations and in accordance with its obligations under the Southeast Asia Collective Defense Treaty, the United States is, therefore, prepared, as the President determines, to take all necessary steps, including the use of armed force, to assist any member or protocol state of the Southeast Asia Collective Defense Treaty requesting assistance in defense of its freedom.

Sec. 3. This resolution shall expire when the President shall determine that the peace and security of the area is reasonably assured by international conditions created by action of the United Nations or otherwise, except that it may be terminated earlier by concurrent resolution of the Congress.

Source: "Text of Joint Resolution, August 7," *Department of State Bulletin* 51(1313) (1964): 268.

144. Robert S. McNamara Recommends Escalation, July 1, 1965 [Excerpts]

Introduction

Here U.S. secretary of defense Robert S. McNamara spells out the options before the United States in Vietnam: "(1) Cut our losses and withdraw under the best conditions" possible, (2) continue forces at the then existing level and play "for the breaks" with the understanding that conditions would likely worsen, and (3) escalate. Here McNamara makes the case for escalation while estimating its probable consequences.

Primary Source

Introduction

Our objective is to create conditions for a favorable settlement by demonstrating to the VC/DRV that the odds are against their winning. Under present conditions, however, the chances of achieving this objective are small—and the VC are winning now—largely because the ratio of guerrilla to anti-guerrilla forces is unfavorable to the government. With this in mind, we must choose among three courses of action with respect to South Vietnam: (1) Cut our losses and withdraw under the best conditions that can be arranged; (2) continue at about the present level, with US forces limited to, say, 75,000, holding on and playing for the breaks while recognizing that our position will probably grow weaker; or (3) expand substantially the US military pressure against the Viet Cong in the South and the North Vietnamese in the North and at the same time launch a vigorous effort on the political side to get negotiations started. An outline of the third of these approaches follows.

I. Expanded Military Moves

The following military moves should be taken together with the political initiatives in Part II below.

A. *Inside South Vietnam.* Increase US/SVN military strength in SVN enough to prove to the VC that they cannot win and thus to turn the tide of the war. . . .

B. *Against North Vietnam.* While avoiding striking population and industrial targets not closely related to the DRV's supply of war material to the VC, we should announce to Hanoi and carry out actions to destroy such supplies and to interdict their flow into and out of North Vietnam. . . .

II. Expanded Political Moves

Together with the above military moves, we should take the following political initiatives in order (a) to open a dialogue with Hanoi,

Peking, and the VC looking toward a settlement in Vietnam, (b) to keep the Soviet Union from deepening its military involvement and support of North Vietnam until the time when settlement can be achieved, and (c) to cement the support for US policy by the US public, allies and friends, and to keep international opposition at a manageable level. While our approaches may be rebuffed until the tide begins to turn, they nevertheless should be made. . . .

III. Evaluation of the Above Program

A. *Domestic US Reaction.* Even though casualties will increase and the war will continue for some time, the United States public will support this course of action because it is a combined military-political program designed and likely to bring about a favorable solution to the Vietnam problem.

B. *Communist Reaction to the Expanded Programs.*

1. *Soviet.* The Soviets can be expected to continue to contribute materiel and advisors to the North Vietnamese. Increased US bombing of Vietnam, including targets in Hanoi and Haiphong, SAM [surface-to-air missile] sites and airfields, and mining of North Vietnamese harbors, might oblige the Soviet Union to enter the contest more actively with volunteers and aircraft. This might result in minor encounters between US and Soviet personnel.

2. *China.* So long as no US or GVN troops invade North Vietnam and so long as no US or GVN aircraft attack Chinese territory, the Chinese probably will not send regular ground forces or aircraft into the war. However, the possibility of a more active Soviet involvement in North Vietnam might precipitate a Chinese introduction of land forces, probably dubbed volunteers, to preclude the Soviets' taking a pre-eminent position in North Vietnam.

3. *North Vietnam.* North Vietnam will not move towards the negotiating table until the tide begins to turn in the south. When that happens, they may seek to counter it by sending large numbers of men into South Vietnam.

4. *Viet Cong.* The VC, especially if they continue to take high losses, can be expected to depend increasingly upon the PAVN [People's Army of Vietnam, regular forces of North Vietnam] forces as the war moves into a more conventional phase; but they may find ways of continuing almost indefinitely their present intensive military, guerrilla and terror activities, particularly if reinforced with some regular PAVN units. A key question on the military side is whether POL [petroleum-oil-lubricants], ammunition, and cadres can be cut off and if they are cut off whether this really renders the Viet Cong impotent. A key question on the political side is whether any arrangement acceptable to us would be acceptable to the VC.

C. *Estimate of Success*

1. *Militarily.* The success of the above program from a military point of view turns on whether the increased effort stems the tide in the South; that in turn depends on two things—on whether the South Vietnamese hold their own in terms of numbers and fighting spirit, and on whether the US forces can be effective in a quick-reaction reserve role, a role in which they have not been tested. The number of US troops is too small to make a significant difference in the traditional 10–1 government-guerrilla formula, but it is not too small to make a significant difference in the kind of war which seems to be evolving in Vietnam—a "Third Stage" or conventional war in which it is easier to identify, locate and attack the enemy. (South Vietnam has 141 battalions as compared with an estimated equivalent number of VC battalions. The 44 US/3d country battalions mentioned above are the equivalent of 100 South Vietnamese battalions.)

2. *Politically.* It is frequently alleged that such a large expansion of US military personnel, their expanded military role (which would put them in close contact and offer some degree of control over South Vietnamese citizens), and the inevitable expansion of US voice in the operation of the GVN economy and facilities, command and government services will be unpopular; it is said that they could lead to the rejection of the government which supported this American presence, to an irresistible pressure for expulsion of the Americans, and to the greatly increased saleability of Communist propaganda. Whether these allegations are true, we do not know.

    The political initiatives are likely to be successful in the early stages only to demonstrate US good faith; they will pay off toward an actual settlement only after the tide begins to turn (unless we lower our sights substantially). The tide almost certainly cannot begin to turn in less than a few months, and may not for a year or more; the war is one of attrition and will be a long one. Since troops once committed as a practical matter cannot be removed, since US casualties will rise, since we should take call-up actions to support the additional forces in Vietnam, the test of endurance may be as much in the United States as in Vietnam.

3. *Generally (CIA estimate).* Over the longer term we doubt if the Communists are likely to change their basic strategy in Vietnam (i.e., aggressive and steadily mounting insurgency) unless and until two conditions prevail: (1) they are forced to accept a situation in the war in the South which offers them no prospect of an early victory and no grounds for hope that they can simply outlast the US and (2) North Vietnam itself is under continuing and

increasingly damaging punitive attack. So long as the Communists think they scent the possibility of an early victory (which is probably now the case), we believe that they will persevere and accept extremely severe damage to the North. Conversely, if North Vietnam itself is not hurting, Hanoi's doctrinaire leaders will probably be ready to carry on the Southern struggle almost indefinitely. If, however, both of the conditions outlined above should be brought to pass, we believe Hanoi probably would, at least for a period of time, alter its basic strategy and course of action in South Vietnam.

Hanoi might do so in several ways. Going for a conference as a political way of gaining a respite from attack would be one. Alternatively it might reduce the level of insurgent activity in the hopes that this would force the US to stop its punishment of the North but not prevent the US and GVN from remaining subject to wearying harassment in the South. Or, Hanoi might order the VC to suspend operations in the hopes that in a period of temporary tranquillity, domestic and international opinion would force the US to disengage without destroying the VC apparatus or the roots of VC strength. Finally, Hanoi might decide that the US/GVN will to fight could still be broken and the tide of war turned back again in favor of the VC by launching a massive PAVN assault on the South. This is a less likely option in the circumstances we have posited, but still a contingency for which the US must be prepared.

Source: *Foreign Relations of the United States, 1964–1968*, Vol. 3 (Washington, DC: U.S. Government Printing Office, 2001), 97–104.

145. McGeorge Bundy: Memorandum to President Lyndon Johnson, February 7, 1965 [Excerpts]

Introduction

National Security Council adviser McGeorge Bundy was in the Republic of Vietnam (RVN, South Vietnam) on a fact-finding visit and saw for himself the results of a Viet Cong (VC) attack on the U.S. barracks and helicopter base at Pleiku on February 7, 1965. The VC killed 9 Americans, wounded more than 120, and destroyed 16 helicopters, with only minimal casualties for themselves. The Pleiku attack served to confirm Bundy's belief that the U.S. military must launch retaliatory air raids against the Democratic Republic of Vietnam (DRV, North Vietnam). In this memorandum to U.S. president Lyndon Johnson, Bundy urges adoption of a policy of "sustained reprisal."

Primary Source

I. Introductory

We believe that the best available way of increasing our chance of success in Vietnam is the development and execution of a policy of sustained reprisal against North Vietnam a policy in which air and naval action against the North is justified by and related to the whole Viet Cong campaign of violence and terror in the South.

While we believe that the risks of such a policy are acceptable, we emphasize that its costs are real. It implies significant U.S. air losses even if no full air war is joined, and it seems likely that it would eventually require an extensive and costly effort against the whole air defense system of North Vietnam. U.S. casualties would be higher and more visible to American feelings than those sustained in the struggle of South Vietnam. . . . And even if it fails to turn the tide as it may the value of the effort seems to us to exceed its costs. . . .

3. Once a program of reprisals is clearly underway, it should not be necessary to connect each specific act against North Vietnam to a particular outrage in the South. It should be possible, for example, to publish weekly lists of outrages in the South and to have it clearly understood that these outrages are the cause of such action against the North as may be occurring in the current period. Such a more generalized pattern of reprisal would remove much of the difficulty involved in finding precisely matching targets in response to specific atrocities. Even in such a more general pattern, however, it would be important to insure that the general level of reprisal action remained in close correspondence with the level of outrages in the South. We must keep it clear at every stage both to Hanoi and to the world, that our reprisals will be reduced or stopped when outrages in the South are reduced or stopped and that we are not attempting to destroy or conquer North Vietnam.

4. In the early stages of such a course, we should take the appropriate occasion to make clear our firm intent to undertake reprisals on any further acts, major or minor, that appear to us and the GVN as indicating Hanoi's support. We would announce that our two governments have been patient and forebearing in the hope that Hanoi would come to its senses without the necessity of our having to take further action; but the outrages continue and now we must react against those who are responsible; we will not provoke; we will not use our force indiscriminately; but we can no longer sit by in the face of repeated acts of terror and violence for which the DRV is responsible. . . .

9. We are convinced that the political values of reprisal require a continuous operation. Episodic responses geared on a one-for-one basis to "spectacular" outrages would lack the persuasive force of sustained pressure. More important still, they would

leave it open to the Communists to avoid reprisals entirely by giving up only a small element of their own program. The Gulf of Tonkin affair produced a sharp upturn in morale in South Vietnam. When it remained an isolated episode, however, there was a severe relapse. It is the great merit of the proposed scheme that to stop it the Communists would have to stop enough of their activity in the South to permit the probable success of a determined pacification effort. . . .

We emphasize that our primary target in advocating a reprisal policy is the improvement of the situation in South Vietnam. Action against the North is usually urged as a means of affecting the will of Hanoi to direct and support the VC. We consider this an important but longer-range purpose. The immediate and critical targets are in the South in the minds of the South Vietnamese and in the minds of the Viet Cong cadres. . . . The Vietnamese increase in hope could well increase the readiness of Vietnamese factions themselves to join together in forming a more effective government . . .

We think it plausible that effective and sustained reprisals, even in a low key, would have a sustained depressing effect upon the morale of Viet Cong cadres in South Vietnam. This is the strong opinion of CIA Saigon. It is based upon reliable reports of the initial Viet Cong reaction to the Gulf of Tonkin episode, and also upon the solid general assessment that the determination of Hanoi and the apparent timidity of the mighty United States are both major items in Viet Cong confidence. . . .

While emphasizing the importance of reprisals in the South, we do not exclude the impact on Hanoi. We believe, indeed, that it is of great importance that the level of reprisal be adjusted rapidly and visibly to both upward and downward shifts in the level of Viet Cong offenses. We want to keep before Hanoi the carrot of our desisting as well as the stick of continued pressure. We also need to conduct the application of force so that there is always a prospect of worse to come.

We cannot assert that a policy of sustained reprisal will succeed in changing the course of the contest in Vietnam. It may fail, and we cannot estimate the odds of success with any accuracy they may be somewhere between 25% and 75%. What we can say is that even if it fails, the policy will be worth it. At a minimum it will damp down the charge that we did not do all that we could have done, and this charge will be important in many countries, including our own. Beyond that, a reprisal policy to the extent that it demonstrates U.S. willingness to employ this new norm in counterinsurgency will set a higher price for the future upon all adventures of guerrilla warfare, and it should therefore somewhat increase our ability to deter such adventures. We must recognize, however, that that ability will be gravely weakened if there is failure for any reason in Vietnam. . . .

Source: *The Pentagon Papers: The Defense Department History of United States Decisionmaking on Vietnam,* Vol. 3. Senator Gravel edition (Boston: Beacon, 1971), 687–690.

146. Joint Statement of Soviet Premier Aleksai Kosygin and Pham Van Dong in Hanoi, February 10, 1965

Introduction

In November 1964 Soviet premier Aleksei Kosygin sent a message of support to the National Front for the Liberation of South Vietnam (usually known as the National Liberation Front [NLF]), the first by a Soviet leader. In February 1965 Kosygin became the first Soviet premier to visit the Democratic Republic of Vietnam (DRV, North Vietnam). Seeking to restore Soviet influence in Hanoi, he promised North Vietnamese leaders financial aid and signed a defense pact, the beginning of a long military alliance between the two states. This reversed Nikita Khrushchev's policy of disengagement from the war in Vietnam.

Primary Source

The delegation of the Soviet Union emphasized that the Democratic Republic of Vietnam, the outpost of the socialist camp in Southeast Asia, is playing an important role in the struggle against American imperialism and is making its contribution to the defense of peace in Asia and throughout the world.

The governments of the U.S.S.R. and the D.R.V. have examined the situation that has arisen as a result of the increasing provocations and acts of outright aggression by the U.S.A. against the Democratic Republic of Vietnam. Both governments resolutely condemn the aggressive actions of the U.S.A. on Aug. 5, 1964, and especially the barbaric attacks by American aircraft on D.R.V. territory on Feb. 7 and Feb. 8, 1965, in the area of the cities of Donghoi and Vinhlinh as incompatible with both international law and the 1954 Geneva agreements. These highly dangerous actions are at the same time provocations against the whole socialist camp and against all mankind standing for peace, freedom and justice.

The U.S.S.R. government reaffirmed that, adhering to the principles of socialist internationalism, it will not remain indifferent to ensuring the security of a fraternal socialist country and will give the D.R.V. the necessary aid and support. The governments of the two countries reached an understanding on the steps that will be taken to strengthen the defense capacity of the D.R.V. and agreed to hold regular consultations on the above-mentioned questions.

The two sides were unanimous on the fact that for more than ten years now the U.S. government has been breaking the 1954 Geneva agreements on Vietnam, trying to prevent the unification of the country and to turn South Vietnam into a new type of colony and a U.S. military base. It has illegally sent to South Vietnam tens of thousands of its own soldiers and officers and a large quantity of arms and is waging an inhuman and cruel "special war" against the population of South Vietnam. The people of South Vietnam have been forced to wage an armed struggle for their liberation in this highly dangerous situation.

The Soviet Union fully supports the just, heroic struggle by the population of South Vietnam for independence, democracy and neutrality, which they are waging under the leadership of the National Front of Liberations of South Vietnam.

Source: "Joint Statement of Delegations of Union of Soviet Socialist Republics and Democratic Republic of Vietnam," *Current Digest of the Soviet Press* 17(6) (1965): 9–11.

147. Dean Rusk, Secretary of State: Telegram to Ambassador Maxwell Taylor, February 13, 1965 [Excerpt]

Introduction

On February 13, 1965, U.S. president Lyndon Johnson decided to approve the "sustained reprisals" program against the Democratic Republic of Vietnam (DRV, North Vietnam) suggested by National Security Advisor McGeorge Bundy only a few days earlier. The air strikes were at first limited to targets below the 19th Parallel. This operation, known as ROLLING THUNDER, which began on February 24, was to be announced publicly along with the Johnson administration's stated desire for peace talks with the North Vietnamese government to bring its "aggression" against the Republic of Vietnam (RVN, South Vietnam) to an end.

Primary Source

The President today approved the following program for immediate future actions in follow-up decisions he reported to you in Deptel 1653. (The First FLAMING DART reprisal decision.)

1. We will intensify by all available means the program of pacification within SVN.

2. We will execute a program of measured and limited air action jointly with GVN against selected military targets in DRV, remaining south of 19th parallel until further notice.

FYI. Our current expectation is that these attacks might come about once or twice a week and involve two or three targets on each day of operation. END FYI.

3. We will announce this policy of measured action in general terms and at the same time, we will go to UN Security Council to make clear case that aggressor is Hanoi. We will also make it plain that we are ready and eager for 'talks' to bring aggression to an end.

4. We believe that this 3-part program must be concerted with SVN, and we currently expect to announce it by Presidential statement directly after next authorized air action. We believe this action should take place as early as possible next week.

5. You are accordingly instructed to seek immediate GVN agreement on this program. You are authorized to emphasize our conviction that announcement of readiness to talk is stronger diplomatic position than awaiting inevitable summons to Security Council by third parties. We would hope to have appropriate GVN concurrence by Monday (Feb. 14th) if possible here.

In presenting above to GVN, you should draw fully, as you see fit, on following arguments:

a. We are determined to continue with military actions regardless of Security Council deliberations and any 'talks' or negotiations when [words illegible]. [Beginning of sentence illegible] that they cease [words illegible] and also the activity they are directing in the south.

b. We consider the UN Security Council initiative, following another strike, essential if we are to avoid being faced with really damaging initiatives by the USSR or perhaps by such powers as India, France, or even the UN.

c. At an early point in the UN Security Council initiative, we would expect to see calls for the DRV to appear in the UN. If they failed to appear, as in August, this will make doubly clear that it is they who are refusing to desist, and our position in pursuing military actions against the DRV would be strengthened. For some reason we would now hope GVN itself would appear at UN and work closely with U.S.

d. With or without Hanoi, we have every expectation that any 'talks' that may result from our Security Council initiative would in fact go on for many weeks or perhaps months and would above all focus constantly on the cessation of Hanoi's aggression as the precondition to any cessation of military action against the DRV. We further anticipate that any detailed discussions about any possible eventual form of agreement returning to the essentials of the 1954 Accords would be postponed and would be subordinated to the central issue. . . .

Source: *The Pentagon Papers as Published by the New York Times* (New York: Quadrangle, 1971), 438–439.

148. SNIE 10-3/-65: Communist Reactions to Possible U.S. Courses of Action against North Vietnam, February 18, 1965 [Excerpts]

Introduction

In this Special National Intelligence Estimate (SNIE) of February 18, 1965, the U.S. intelligence community held that the likely response by the Democratic Republic of Vietnam (DRV, North Vietnam) to the planned U.S. bombing of North Vietnam would be a reduction in its support for the insurgency in the Republic of Vietnam (RVN, South Vietnam) but that North Vietnam would not abandon the war entirely. There was also the possibility of increased North Vietnamese support for the southern insurgency, but an invasion of South Vietnam by the People's Army of Vietnam (PAVN, North Vietnamese Army) was thought unlikely.

Primary Source

Reactions to a Declared and Sustained US Program of Bombing in the North

[...]

7. Over the past decade the DRV has invested much time, effort, and capital in the development of industry, transportation, and relatively modern military facilities. They will not lightly sacrifice these hard-won gains. Yet a threat by the US to mount sustained attacks on these assets would probably be greeted in Hanoi with mixed feelings of trepidation and skepticism. At the start, the Communists would not be convinced that the US intended really to follow through with this program. They would almost certainly apply a range of pressures in an endeavor to make the US desist. They would maintain strenuous diplomatic and propaganda efforts to organize international influence against the US policy. They would probably threaten dire consequences to US interests in the area. Chinese Communists threats would be more insistent, and Chinese Communist forces would probably be deployed in more threatening postures. Viet Cong attacks would probably continue, though not necessarily at a steady pace.

8. If despite these pressures, the US vigorously continued in its attacks and damaged some important economic or military assets, the DRV leaders would have to reach a decision. They almost certainly believe that, while the US could destroy much in their country by air attacks, these alone would not cause their regime to collapse or prevent them from continuing to support the insurgency in the South. And they may believe that their international political position would improve if they became the object of sustained air attack from the US. Accordingly, they might decide to intensify the struggle, accepting the destructive consequences in the North in the expectation of early victory in the South.

9. It seems to us somewhat more likely however that they would decide to make some effort to secure a respite from US air attack, especially if the US had indicated that such a respite would follow a sharp reduction of Viet Cong activity. We do not know how far they would go in concessions, whether the US would accept what might be offered, or what the international situation might be at such a time. We think it extremely unlikely, however, that Hanoi would concede so far to US demands that it would entail abandoning its support of the insurgency in the South or giving up its intention of unifying Vietnam under Communist control.

10. The Chinese Communists would almost certainly be willing to support the DRV in even the more militant course of action outlined in paragraph 8. We have set forth in SNIE 10-3-65 (paragraphs 16–18, with State Department footnotes of dissent) the use the Chinese would be likely to make of their own forces.

Possible, but Unlikely Reactions

11. Instead of temporarily easing off or intensifying present levels of pressure, the Communist leaders might actually engage in actions which would change the scale and nature of the war. These would be much more dangerous and aggressive courses and, although they seem to us unlikely in the light of logic and prudence, they are possibilities which cannot be ignored:

  a. They might launch a large-scale DRV invasion of South Vietnam and/or Laos. We think it unlikely that they would do this in response to bombings of North Vietnam. They would feel that at best this drastic policy would only accelerate victories in Laos and Vietnam which they are confident they will win before very long through less costly tactics. Such an invasion would virtually require a greater involvement of the Chinese in Vietnam, which is in itself distasteful to the North Vietnamese. The Communists would recognize that to launch such an invasion would be to invite further major destruction upon the DRV and perhaps upon China.

  b. We think it unlikely that the Chinese or DRV would respond to US air raids by air attacks on US aircraft carriers or South Vietnamese airfields. To do so would invite counterattacks on the vulnerable Communist bases and start the escalation of an air war, a form of hostilities most disadvantageous to the North Vietnamese and Chinese. A sneak attack on a carrier by an unidentifiable Chinese submarine is a more difficult possibility to weigh, but we are inclined to think the chance is slim; the risks would be fairly high and Chinese confidence in the ability of their inexperienced submarine force to pull it off is probably low.

c. We also think it unlikely that the Chinese Communists would start another major crisis elsewhere on the periphery of China. Faced with the possibility of a full scale war in Southeast Asia, Peiping would want to have the greatest possible strength focused there. Chinese propaganda has, indeed, said that America's "meager force" in Asia is spread thinly over a "long arc from South Korea to Indochina," and that if the conflict were expanded, the "time, place, and scale of the war would be beyond US control." However, we think this is no more than a general warning of the dangers of expanding the war. Peiping is likely, however, to continue talking of war "over a vast front" and perhaps even to stir up alarms elsewhere to keep US power dispersed and deter the US in Southeast Asia. The Chinese Communists might, for example, increase the apparent military threat in Korea, bombard the offshore islands in order to raise tensions in the Taiwan area, or perhaps make threatening moves on the borders of India.

Source: Central Intelligence Agency, "Communist Reactions to Possible US Actions," Freedom of Information Act Electronic Reading Room, http://www.foia.cia.gov/.

149. "Aggression from the North": State Department White Paper on Vietnam, February 27, 1965 [Excerpts]

Introduction

In February the U.S. State Department released a white paper titled "Aggression from the North: The Record of North Viet-Nam's Campaign to Conquer South Viet-Nam." The position paper holds Hanoi responsible for "aggression" against the Republic of Vietnam (RVN, South Vietnam) and charges that the war is "*not* a spontaneous and local rebellion against the established government." The paper claims that since 1959 Hanoi has sent some 37,100 military personnel south and that three-quarters of 4,400 infiltrators from the Democratic Republic of Vietnam (DRV, North Vietnam) in the first eight months of 1964 have been native northerners, who had been and continue to be the backbone of the entire Viet Cong operation in South Vietnam. The paper also blames Hanoi for arms shipments to South Vietnam, including a trawler sunk in shallow waters off Phu Yen Province on February 16, 1965, that had transported more than 100 tons of arms and ammunition. The paper was clearly designed to justify a U.S. military response.

Primary Source

South Vietnam is fighting for its life against a brutal campaign of terror and armed attack inspired, directed, supplied, and controlled by the Communist regime in Hanoi. This flagrant aggression has been going on for years, but recently the pace has quickened and the threat has now become acute.

The war in Vietnam is a new kind of war, a fact as yet poorly understood in most parts of the world. Much of the confusion that prevails in the thinking of many people, and even governments, stems from this basic misunderstanding. For in Vietnam a totally new brand of aggression has been loosed against an independent people who want to make their way in peace and freedom.

Vietnam is not another Greece, where indigenous guerrilla forces used friendly neighboring territory as a sanctuary.

Vietnam is not another Malaya, where Communist guerrillas were, for the most part, physically distinguishable from the peaceful majority they sought to control.

Vietnam is not another Philippines, where Communist guerrillas were physically separated from the source of their moral and physical support.

Above all, the war in Vietnam is *not* a spontaneous and local rebellion against the established government.

There are elements in the Communist program of conquest directed against South Vietnam common to each of the previous areas of aggression and subversion. But there is one fundamental difference. In Vietnam a Communist government has set out deliberately to conquer a sovereign people in a neighboring state. And to achieve its end, it has used every resource of its own government to carry out its carefully planned program of concealed aggression. North Vietnam's commitment to seize control of the South is no less total than was the commitment of the regime in North Korea in 1950. But knowing the consequences of the latter's undisguised attack, the planners in Hanoi have tried desperately to conceal their hand. They have failed and their aggression is as real as that of an invading army.

This report is a summary of the massive evidence of North Vietnamese aggression obtained by the Government of South Vietnam. This evidence has been jointly analyzed by South Vietnamese and American experts.

The evidence shows that the hard core of the Communist forces attacking South Vietnam were trained in the North and ordered into the South by Hanoi. It shows that the key leadership of the Vietcong (VC), the officers and much of the cadre, many of the technicians, political organizers, and propagandists have come from the North and operate under Hanoi's direction. It shows that the training of essential military personnel and their infiltration into the South is directed by the Military High Command in Hanoi. In recent months new types of weapons have been introduced in the VC army, for which all ammunition must come from outside sources. Communist China and other Communist states have been the prime suppliers of these weapons and ammunition, and they have been channeled primarily through North Vietnam.

The directing force behind the effort to conquer South Vietnam is the Communist Party in the North, the Lao Dong (Workers) Party. As in every Communist state, the party is an integral part of the regime itself. North Vietnamese officials have expressed their firm determination to absorb South Vietnam into the Communist world.

Through its Central Committee, which controls the Government of the North, the Lao Dong Party directs the total political and military effort of the Vietcong. The Military High Command in the North trains the military men and sends them into South Vietnam. The Central Research Agency, North Vietnam's central intelligence organization, directs the elaborate espionage and subversion effort. . . .

Under Hanoi's overall direction the Communists have established an extensive machine for carrying on the war within South Vietnam. The focal point is the Central Office for South Vietnam with its political and military subsections and other specialized agencies. A subordinate part of this Central Office is the liberation Front for South Vietnam. The front was formed at Hanoi's order in 1960. Its principle function is to influence opinion abroad and to create the false impression that the aggression in South Vietnam is an indigenous rebellion against the established Government.

For more than 10 years the people and the Government of South Vietnam, exercising the inherent right of self-defense, have fought back against these efforts to extend Communist power south across the 17th parallel. The United States has responded to the appeals of the Government of the Republic of Vietnam for help in this defense of the freedom and independence of its land and its people.

In 1961 the Department of State issued a report called A Threat to the Peace. It described North Vietnam's program to seize South Vietnam. The evidence in that report had been presented by the Government of the Republic of Vietnam to the International Control Commission (ICC). A special report by the ICC in June 1962 upheld the validity of that evidence. The Commission held that there was "sufficient evidence to show beyond reasonable doubt" that North Vietnam had sent arms and men into South Vietnam to carry out subversion with the aim of overthrowing the legal

Government there. The ICC found the authorities in Hanoi in specific violation of four provisions of the Geneva Accords of 1954.

Since then, new and even more impressive evidence of Hanoi's aggression has accumulated. The Government of the United States believes that evidence should be presented to its own citizens and to the world. It is important for free men to know what has been happening in Vietnam, and how, and why. That is the purpose of this report. . . .

The record is conclusive. It establishes beyond question that North Vietnam is carrying out a carefully conceived plan of aggression against the South. It shows that North Vietnam has intensified its efforts in the years since it was condemned by the International Control Commission. It proves that Hanoi continues to press its systematic program of armed aggression into South Vietnam. This aggression violates the United Nations Charter. It is directly contrary to the Geneva Accords of 1954 and of 1962 to which North Vietnam is a party. It is a fundamental threat to the freedom and security of South Vietnam.

The people of South Vietnam have chosen to resist this threat. At their request, the United States has taken its place beside them in their defensive struggle.

The United States seeks no territory, no military bases, no favored position. But we have learned the meaning of aggression elsewhere in the post-war world, and we have met it.

If peace can be restored in South Vietnam, the United States will be ready at once to reduce its military involvement. But it will not abandon friends who want to remain free. It will do what must be done to help them. The choice now between peace and continued and increasingly destructive conflict is one for the authorities in Hanoi to make.

Source: "Aggression from the North: The Record of North Viet-Nam's Campaign to Conquer South Viet-Nam," *Department of State Bulletin* 52(1343) (1965): 404–426.

150. Le Duan: "Letters to the South", February 1965 [Excerpts]

Introduction

In early 1965 the Viet Cong (VC) were in the middle of a major offensive in the Republic of Vietnam (RVN, South Vietnam) that had inflicted severe losses on forces of the Army of the Republic of Vietnam (ARVN, South Vietnamese Army), particularly during the Battle of Binh Gia southeast of Saigon. The military situation in South Vietnam had become so precarious that the U.S. government was considering sending in U.S. combat troops to prevent the total collapse of South Vietnam. Faced with the possibility of direct U.S. military intervention, the Communist leadership in the Democratic Republic of Vietnam (DRV, North Vietnam) and in South Vietnam debated whether to fall back to a classic protracted-war guerrilla strategy or whether to continue with large-scale military attacks aimed at gaining a quick victory. In February 1965 North Vietnamese Lao Dong (Workers' Party) first secretary Le Duan wrote a letter to the commander of Communist forces in South Vietnam, General Nguyen Chi Thanh, providing his thoughts on this subject. The strategy that Le Duan proposed in this letter, coupling massive military attacks with civilian popular "uprisings," would later evolve into the Communist strategy for the 1968 Tet Offensive. (Note: In this letter, "special war" is the term used by the Communists to describe the counterinsurgency strategy employed by the United States during the early 1960s, while "limited war" referred to a war in which the United States would send American ground combat units into South Vietnam to fight directly against Communist forces, as was the case during the Korean War of 1950–1953.)

Primary Source

My dear Xuan and friends,

The Politburo has met to discuss the situation and missions for 1965. Their resolution will be sent to you separately. Because the resolution may be slow in getting to you, and because there are a number of points that cannot be discussed in a resolution, I am writing this letter to you to give you time to think about them before you discuss the Politburo resolution.

First of all, I would like to inform you that the subject of changing our strategic formula did not even come up during the recent Politburo discussion. All that was discussed was how to apply the agreed-upon formulas in a manner appropriate to the new developments in the situation. Our strategic formulas are still:

—Protracted struggle while striving to create an opportunity to win a decisive victory.
—Conducting parallel military and political struggles leading up to a general offensive and general uprising.

With regards to the first formula, it is our assessment that we have an opportunity at the present time. The primary problem is how to seize the opportunity and not let it escape our grasp. If we want to accomplish this goal, we must fully understand our second formula and make preparations to gradually but continuously build up to the launching of a general offensive while simultaneously making all necessary preparations for launching a general uprising. . . .

Our forces . . . have quickly grown strong. . . . On the enemy side, the primary pillars of support for the enemy cause, the puppet army and the cities, have now undergone a number of important changes. After a series of defeats, the puppet army has begun to

lose faith in American tactics. . . . It is becoming harder and harder for the Americans and their puppets to control the cities. Our revolutionary movement is attracting widespread support among the masses and drawing together a wide group of nationalist, democratic, and peace forces. . . .

The battle of Binh Gia marked a new turning point. . . . Before Binh Gia the Americans . . . still retained some confidence in the mobile units of the puppet regular army. After Binh Gia, however, they recognized clearly that our army was capable of destroying puppet mobile forces. *The U.S. realizes they will lose the "special war" if they do not change their strategy.*

So, has the opportunity to defeat the U.S. in the "special war" arrived? And can we defeat the Americans before they have time to change their strategy? I believe our opportunity has arrived, and I believe it is still possible for us to restrict the enemy sufficiently to defeat them in the "special war." . . . Our problem is to fight in such a way that the Americans and the puppets are defeated while at the same time we . . . virtually eliminate the possibility that the enemy will change his policy and escalate from "special war" to "limited war." . . .

At present, the U.S. relies primarily on the puppet army to carry out the war. They will only accept defeat when that source of support no longer exists. Therefore we must strive to shatter the American source of support. . . . Our goal is to *cause the total disintegration of the puppet army.* That is one point.

A second point: if we cause the total disintegration of the puppet army before the Americans have a chance to react, then their ability to escalate the war into a "limited war" will be reduced to a very low level. Why is that true? Because, first, the U.S. will realize that if they could not win with the puppet army, then if the puppet army no longer exists their chances of being able to defeat us with an American expeditionary army become questionable. . . . The U.S. is very hesitant about becoming bogged down in a particular region for an extended period of time, because that will put the U.S. in a defensive position from a global perspective. Secondly, if they restrict themselves solely to a "special war," if they are forced to end that war the U.S. can withdraw with less loss of face than if they withdraw after becoming bogged down in a "limited war." And if, in addition to defeating the puppet army, we also put the U.S. on the political defensive by overthrowing the puppet government and forming a neutralist government which requests the Americans to withdraw their troops and if we simultaneously further isolate the U.S. internationally, then the possibility that the U.S. will escalate to a "limited war" will be reduced even further.

If we wish to win based on the above requirements, we must cause the complete and utter disintegration of the puppet army before the U.S. has a chance to react, we must put the U.S. on the defensive politically, and at the same time we must come up with a skillful strategy that will allow the U.S. to accept defeat and withdraw without losing face. . . . Can we cause the total disintegration of the puppet army in the near future? I believe this can be accomplished if we closely and skillfully coordinate our military actions with political actions, combining a general offensive with a general uprising. . . .

I shall present below a number of specific issues regarding the military struggle and the political struggle that we need to accomplish and that we are capable of accomplishing in the immediate future.

First of all, I will discuss the military struggle. . . . We need to quickly reinforce our armed forces further to cause a fundamental change in the balance of forces. . . . Our goal is to cause the complete disintegration of the puppet army. The achievement of this goal depends not only on combat operations, but also on the political struggle. In order to allow political factors to have their maximum effect in contributing to the disintegration of the puppet army, however, our military operations must first of all destroy or cause the disintegration of three or four out of the enemy's total of nine regular divisions. . . .

One important battle requirement is to force the enemy to completely exhaust his strategic reserve force in order to drive him into a completely passive and reactive strategic position that leads quickly to disintegration. . . . We must stretch enemy forces thin by launching a truly widespread and powerful guerrilla warfare movement while simultaneously massing *our main forces and preparing sufficient strategic reserve forces to launch a number of offensive campaigns and deal the enemy a number of large annihilation blows on selected battlefields that have been properly prepared.* . . .

One more requirement for our combat operations is to draw the enemy's military forces out of the cities . . . in order to enable our urban movement to grow stronger so we can advance toward general insurrection.

We are capable of achieving the above goals for annihilating enemy forces this year. The battles of Binh Gia and Phu My have demonstrated this fact. . . . In addition to consolidating and expanding our local forces and guerrilla militia throughout the country, we must build three or four powerful main force elements based upon the units we currently possess in key areas while at the same time we rapidly increase our strategic reserve forces. In order to accomplish this quickly, in addition to vigorously recruiting young people into our army, we should mobilize twenty or thirty thousand militia troops and upgrade them into our main force units. Up here in the north we will make even stronger and more urgent efforts to send forces down to you from North Vietnam. . . . The Party Central Committee will mobilize the greatest possible efforts of the entire Party, the entire population, and the entire army to support the front lines.

This is the direction of our military effort. In the following section I will discuss the *direction of our political effort.* . . . The cities will be the focal point for the coming general uprising. . . . Signs of a revolutionary situation have begun to appear in the cities of South Vietnam. However, the revolutionary situation is not yet ripe. If we can render the puppet army . . . ineffective, this will rapidly advance the revolutionary situation until it is ripe. . . .

I will attempt to outline an overall plan for you: As we expand our guerilla warfare operations and shrink the size of those areas occupied by the enemy in the mountain jungles and in the rural lowlands and at the same time raise the struggle movement in the cities to new levels, we can help to "ripen" the situation by attacking and shattering three or four puppet regular divisions in battle. . . . We will then launch a coordinated general uprising with a general military offensive aimed straight at the enemy's heart, his center, to seize control of the government. This will shatter the morale of the puppet army. . . . We will make strong military attacks combined with powerful political and military attacks conducted by the masses to incite military mutinies and create the possibility of causing the collapse of the remaining units of the puppet army. . . . When the situation is ripe, we will launch simultaneous uprisings in Saigon and the other large cities, such as Hue, Danang, My Tho, etc. When we send our soldiers in from the outside to launch powerful attacks aimed at shattering or paralyzing enemy troops stationed in the cities . . . the masses in the cities will rise up in insurrection to seize control of the government. In other words, we will seize the government by coordinating military attacks with popular uprisings. . . .

In order to launch an uprising, our actions must create the greatest possible surprise by first drawing large puppet army units away from the cities through the use of diversionary or deception operations. . . . The primary target for our uprising will be Saigon. We must prevent the enemy from pulling forces back from other locations to relieve Saigon. For this reason, prior to the uprising we will attack and capture the Central Highlands to deny the enemy a place from which he can launch future counterattacks. At the same time we will liberate the remaining rural areas and take control over the entire rural countryside.

In order to attract the middle classes and to create the greatest possible surprise for the Americans, the uprising will be carried out under a different banner: the banner of a *neutralist front.* This neutralist front will have as few external connections with the National Liberation Front as possible. . . . Our troops who attack and occupy the cities will operate under the guise of *neutralist troops.* The Liberation Front will remain on the outside and will announce its support. That will be on the surface, for the eyes of the enemy. With regards to our core mass supporters, however, we will state clearly that the neutral front is something that we advocate and that we support. . . . After the insurrection succeeds, we will form a *neutral government* made up of a wide range of persons who appear to have no connections with us, but naturally we will control the army and the security forces. . . .

The new government will set forward the following demands:

—End the fighting. Establish overt relations with the National Liberation Front for South Vietnam to discuss ending the war.
—Implement a policy of neutrality. Establish relations with France and the United States and raise the issue of requesting the withdrawal of American troops.

—Request that the two joint chairmen of the 1954 Geneva Conference immediately convene a conference to discuss the issue of guaranteeing the neutrality of South Vietnam and a cessation of hostilities.

It may not at first be necessary to raise the issue of establishing relations with North Vietnam.

If we can accomplish the above program, we will have created conditions that will make it easier for the U.S. to agree to withdraw. And if we make full use of our opportunity and rapidly cause the complete disintegration of the puppet army, this will limit to the maximum extent possible the possibility that the U.S. will send in an expeditionary army to conduct a "limited war." . . .

I have presented a number of problems above for you all to consider. As I stated at the beginning, the issue now is to prepare to be able to seize an opportunity to win a decisive victory. Will the opportunity appear soon? We believe it will, if we actively work to create it. . . .

Naturally, what I have presented here deals with only one possibility. . . . How the war situation develops depends in part on the enemy. . . . We also need to make *appropriate preparations to respond to other eventualities* that we have also foreseen.

With wishes for Victory

Ba [alias used by Communist Party first secretary Le Duan]

Source: Le Duan, *Thu Vao Nam* [Letters to the South] (Hanoi: Su That Publishing House, 1986), 70–96. Translated by Merle L. Pribbenow.

151. Maxwell Taylor, Ambassador: Telegram to Secretary of State Dean Rusk, March 18, 1965

Introduction

In early 1965 an immediate concern for the United States was the security of its air bases in Vietnam, and the commander of the Military Assistance Command, Vietnam, General William Westmoreland, sought the support of U.S. ambassador to Vietnam Maxwell Taylor for his recommendation that a battalion of the 9th Marine Expeditionary Brigade be landed to provide this. Westmoreland's request caused General Taylor to visit the wider issue of dispatching U.S. ground forces to the Republic of Vietnam (RVN, South Vietnam), then under active consideration in Washington. Taylor was not necessarily opposed to U.S. ground troops but preferred that they be used as part of an enclave strategy rather than in large-scale combat operations, as Westmoreland wanted. In this telegram to U.S. secretary of state Dean Rusk, Taylor concludes that the presence of U.S. ground troops would likely not

significantly raise the performance level of the Army of the Republic of Vietnam (ARVN, South Vietnamese army) and would be a propaganda bonanza for the Communists in which the United States would be seen as an "alien colonizer and conqueror." Taylor was prescient in his belief that the presence of U.S. ground troops would encourage the ARVN to let the United States fight the war. Taylor departed Vietnam in July 1965.

Primary Source

General Westmoreland has just sought my concurrence in his recommendation for the landing of the Third BLT of the 9th MEB at Phu Bai for the purpose of protecting the 8th RRU and the air strip there. He intends to move helicopters from Da Nang to the strip and thereby reduce field congestion to Da Nang. Because of the military advantages of thus rounding out the MEB, I have no reluctance in agreeing to the merit of his recommendation which, of course, should receive the concurrence of the GVN after that of Washington.

This proposal for introducing the BLT is a reminder of the strong likelihood of additional requests for increases in U.S. ground combat forces in SVN. Such requests may come from the U.S. side, from the GVN side or from both. All of us here are keenly aware of the GVN trained military manpower shortage which will exist throughout 1965 and which probably can be rectified only in part by an accelerated mobilization. We will soon have to decide whether to try to get by with inadequate indigenous forces or to supplement them with Third Country troops, largely if not exclusively U.S. This matter was discussed with General Johnson during his recent visit who no doubt has raised it following his return to Washington. This message examines the pros and cons of such an action—specifically defined as the introduction of a U.S. division (appropriately modified) into SVN.

The purpose of introducing a division would be primarily to relieve the present shortage of ARVN units either by replacing ARVN in the defense of key installations or by engaging in active operations against the VC in conjunction with ARVN. Such a reinforcement would allow a strengthening of military efforts in the I and II Corps areas where the situation is deteriorating and would give a boost to GVN morale, military and civilian. Likewise, it should end any talk of a possible U.S. withdrawal and convince Hanoi of the depth of our resolve to see this thing through to a successful conclusion.

This statement of the purpose of introducing a U.S. division is, in effect, a tabulation of the arguments in favor of so doing. However, there are counter arguments on the other side of the case. The introduction of a U.S. division obviously increases U.S. involvement in the counterinsurgency, exposes greater forces and invites greater losses. It will raise sensitive command questions with our GVN allies and may encourage them to an attitude of "let the United States do it." It will increase our vulnerability to Communist propaganda and Third Country criticism as we appear to assume the old French role of alien colonizer and conqueror. Finally, there is considerable doubt that the number of GVN forces which our action would relieve would have any great significance in reducing the manpower gap.

It is possible to reach a conclusion with regard to the overall merit of this action without first examining in some detail the possible missions which could be assigned a U.S. division. There are two obvious possibilities: the first, the assignment of the division to one or more of the provinces of the high plateau where the climate is good, the terrain relatively open, and the Montagnard population more readily distinguishable from the alien Viet Cong. Here, our forces could utilize their mobility and firepower effectively and make an important contribution in cutting off the growing infiltration into and through this area. For the most part, the Montagnards are friendly to the U.S. and our forces would thus be operating in a relatively friendly environment.

On the other hand, such a mission in the highlands would place our forces in an area with highly exposed lines of communication leading to the coast. Their location in this area would create serious logistic problems because of the difficulty of the movement of land transport through areas infested by the Viet Cong. There would be problems both of reinforcement and of withdrawal because of this precariousness of land communications. Finally, the GVN may question the introduction of sizeable U.S. forces into the Montagnard area where we have often been accused of favoring the Montagnards over the Vietnamese and of encouraging Montagnard separatism.

The other role which has been suggested for U.S. ground forces is the occupation and defense of key enclaves along the coast such as Quang Ngai, Qui Nhon, Tuy Hoa and Nah Trang. Such a disposition would have the advantage of placing our forces in areas of easy access and egress with minimum logistic problems associated with supply and maintenance. The presence of our troops would assure the defense of these important key areas and would relieve some GVN forces for employment elsewhere. The troops would not be called upon to engage in counterinsurgency operation except in their own local defense and hence would be exposed to minimum losses.

On the other hand, they would be engaged in a rather inglorious static defensive mission unappealing to them and unimpressive in the eyes of the Vietnamese. Operating in major population areas would maximize the points of contact with Vietnamese and hence maximize the possible points of friction. The division would be badly fragmented to the extent that its command, control and supervision would be awkward.

The foregoing analysis leads me to the following tentative conclusions. First, it is not desirable to introduce a U.S. division into South Vietnam unless there are clear and tangible advantages outweighing the numerous disadvantages, many of which have been noted above. One must make a definite determination of the numbers and types of GVN forces relieved by the introduction of the U.S. unit and thus the effect of the increased U.S. presence in closing the manpower gap of 1965. Obviously, our division would make some contribution but it remains to be proved that it will be sufficient to reverse the downward trend and give such a lift to the GVN forces that they would perform better by the stimulation of the U.S. presence rather than worse in a mood of relaxation as passing the Viet Cong burden to the U.S.

If the evidence of the probable effectiveness of this U.S. contribution is convincing, then the matter of mission becomes the primary question. The inland mission in the highlands is clearly the more ambitious and, if well done, will make a greater contribution during the present critical period. On the other hand, it is the more exposed and even permits one to entertain the possibility of a kind of Dien Bien Phu if the coastal provinces should collapse and our forces were cut off from the coast except by air.

The coastal enclave mission is safer, simpler but less impressive and less productive than the inland mission. The contrast of the pros and cons of the two suggests the desirability of reexamining the question to see whether the advantages of the inland disposition could not be combined in some way with the retention of a base coastal area, linked with a position inland. In any case, considerable additional study is required before we are prepared to make a recommendation either for the introduction of a division or for the assignment of its mission. In the meantime, we should be giving much thought both in South Vietnam and in Washington as to the right course of action [if] and when this issue becomes pressing—as it shortly will.

Source: *The Pentagon Papers: The Defense Department History of United States Decisionmaking on Vietnam,* Vol. 3. Senator Gravel edition (Boston: Beacon, 1971), 445–447.

152. National Security Action Memorandum No. 328, April 6, 1965

Introduction

In early March 1965, U.S. Army chief of staff General Harold K. Johnson had taken a fact-finding trip to Vietnam, and later that month the Joint Chiefs of Staff (JCS) proposed that U.S. forces in the Republic of Vietnam (RVN, South Vietnam) be permitted to undertake a more active combat role. On April 6 President Lyndon Johnson agreed to the JCS request to deploy substantially greater

U.S. forces to South Vietnam, including two additional marine battalions, and agreed that all marine units in Vietnam could be employed in a "more active role" as advocated by Military Assistance Command, Vietnam (MACV), commander General William Westmoreland. This change was, however, to be presented to the U.S. public as "wholly consistent with existing policy."

Primary Source

On Thursday, April 1, the President made the following decisions with respect to Vietnam:

1. Subject to modifications in the light of experience, and to coordination and direction both in Saigon and in Washington, the President approved the 41-point program of non-military actions submitted by Ambassador Taylor in a memorandum dated March 31, 1965.

2. The President gave general approval to the recommendations submitted by Mr. Rowan in his report dated March 16, with the exception that the President withheld approval of any request for supplemental funds at this time—it is his decision that this program is to be energetically supported by all agencies and departments and by the reprogramming of available funds as necessary within USIA.

3. The President approved the urgent exploration of the 12 suggestions for covert and other actions submitted by the Director of Central Intelligence under date of March 31.

4. The President repeated his earlier approval of the 21-point program of military actions submitted by General Harold K. Johnson under date of March 14 and re-emphasized his desire that aircraft and helicopter reinforcements under this program be accelerated.

5. The President approved an 18–20,000 man increase in U.S. military support forces to fill out existing units and supply needed logistic personnel.

6. The President approved the deployment of two additional Marine Battalions and one Marine Air Squadron and associated headquarters and support elements.

7. The President approved a change of mission for all Marine Battalions deployed to Vietnam to permit their more active use under conditions to be established and approved by the Secretary of Defense in consultation with the Secretary of State.

8. The President approved the urgent exploration, with the Korean, Australian, and New Zealand Governments, of the possibility of rapid deployment of significant combat elements from their armed forces in parallel with the additional Marine deployment approved in paragraph 6.

9. Subject to continuing review, the President approved the following general framework of continuing action against North Vietnam and Laos:

We should continue roughly the present slowly ascending tempo of ROLLING THUNDER operations, being prepared to add strikes in response to a higher rate of VC operations, or conceivably to slow the pace in the unlikely event VC slacked off sharply for what appeared to be more than a temporary operational lull.

The target systems should continue to avoid the effective GCI range of MIGS. We should continue to vary the types of targets, stepping up attacks on lines of communication in the near future, and possibly moving in a few weeks to attacks on the rail lines north and northeast of Hanoi.

Leaflet operations should be expanded to obtain maximum practicable psychological effect on the North Vietnamese population.

Blockade or aerial mining of North Vietnamese ports need further study and should be considered for future operations. It would have major political complications, especially in relation to the Soviets and other third countries, but also offers many advantages.

Air operations in Laos, particularly route blocking operations in the Panhandle area, should be stepped up to the maximum remunerative rate.

10. Ambassador Taylor will promptly seek the reactions of the South Vietnamese Government to appropriate sections of this program and their approval as necessary, and in the event of disapproval or difficulty at that end, these decisions will be appropriately reconsidered. In any event, no action into Vietnam under paragraphs 6 and 7 above should take place without GVN approval or further Presidential authorization.

11. The President desires that with respect to the actions in paragraphs 5 through 7, premature publicity be avoided by all possible precautions. The actions themselves should be taken as rapidly as practicable, but in ways that should minimize any appearance of sudden changes in policy, and official statements on these troop movements will be made only with the direct approval of the Secretary of Defense, in consultation with the Secretary of State. The President's desire is that these movements and changes should be understood as being gradual and wholly consistent with existing policy.

Source: *The Pentagon Papers as Published by the New York Times* (New York: Quadrangle, 1971), 452–453.

153. President Lyndon Johnson, "Peace without Conquest": Address at Johns Hopkins University, April 7, 1965

Introduction

In the course of a major televised address at Johns Hopkins University on April 7, 1965, U.S. president Lyndon Johnson explains his Vietnam policy, including the recent U.S. military escalation there. Johnson offers to participate in discussions to end the war and pledges $1 billion in aid for the development of the Mekong Delta, to include the Democratic Republic of Vietnam (DRV, North Vietnam) and designed to benefit the entire region. As the Johnson administration expected, the North Vietnamese rejected the offer of negotiations without conditions and the economic development program, and this temporarily reduced domestic and foreign criticism of the U.S. military escalation and provided Johnson with broader approval to fight a wider war.

Primary Source

Mr. Garland, Senator Brewster, Senator Tydings, Members of the congressional delegation, members of the faculty of Johns Hopkins, student body, my fellow Americans:

Last week 17 nations sent their views to some two dozen countries having an interest in southeast Asia. We are joining those 17 countries and stating our American policy tonight which we believe will contribute toward peace in this area of the world.

I have come here to review once again with my own people the views of the American Government.

Tonight Americans and Asians are dying for a world where each people may choose its own path to change.

This is the principle for which our ancestors fought in the valleys of Pennsylvania. It is the principle for which our sons fight tonight in the jungles of Viet-Nam.

Viet-Nam is far away from this quiet campus. We have no territory there, nor do we seek any. The war is dirty and brutal and difficult. And some 400 young men, born into an America that is bursting with opportunity and promise, have ended their lives on Viet-Nam's steaming soil.

Why must we take this painful road?

Why must this Nation hazard its ease, and its interest, and its power for the sake of a people so far away?

We fight because we must fight if we are to live in a world where every country can shape its own destiny. And only in such a world will our own freedom be finally secure.

This kind of world will never be built by bombs or bullets. Yet the infirmities of man are such that force must often precede reason, and the waste of war, the works of peace.

We wish that this were not so. But we must deal with the world as it is, if it is ever to be as we wish.

THE NATURE OF THE CONFLICT

The world as it is in Asia is not a serene or peaceful place.

The first reality is that North Viet-Nam has attacked the independent nation of South Viet-Nam. Its object is total conquest.

Of course, some of the people of South Viet-Nam are participating in attack on their own government. But trained men and supplies, orders and arms, flow in a constant stream from north to south.

This support is the heartbeat of the war.

And it is a war of unparalleled brutality. Simple farmers are the targets of assassination and kidnapping. Women and children are strangled in the night because their men are loyal to their government. And helpless villages are ravaged by sneak attacks. Large-scale raids are conducted on towns, and terror strikes in the heart of cities.

The confused nature of this conflict cannot mask the fact that it is the new face of an old enemy.

Over this war—and all Asia—is another reality: the deepening shadow of Communist China. The rulers in Hanoi are urged on by Peking. This is a regime which has destroyed freedom in Tibet, which has attacked India, and has been condemned by the United Nations for aggression in Korea. It is a nation which is helping the forces of violence in almost every continent. The contest in Viet-Nam is part of a wider pattern of aggressive purposes.

WHY ARE WE IN VIET-NAM?

Why are these realities our concern? Why are we in South Viet-Nam?

We are there because we have a promise to keep. Since 1954 every American President has offered support to the people of South Viet-Nam. We have helped to build, and we have helped to defend. Thus, over many years, we have made a national pledge to help South Viet-Nam defend its independence.

And I intend to keep that promise.

To dishonor that pledge, to abandon this small and brave nation to its enemies, and to the terror that must follow, would be an unforgivable wrong.

We are also there to strengthen world order. Around the globe, from Berlin to Thailand, are people whose well-being rests, in part, on the belief that they can count on us if they are attacked. To leave Viet-Nam to its fate would shake the confidence of all these people in the value of an American commitment and in the value of America's word. The result would be increased unrest and instability, and even wider war.

We are also there because there are great stakes in the balance. Let no one think for a moment that retreat from Viet-Nam would bring an end to conflict. The battle would be renewed in one country and then another. The central lesson of our time is that the appetite of aggression is never satisfied. To withdraw from one battlefield means only to prepare for the next. We must say in southeast Asia—as we did in Europe—in the words of the Bible: "Hitherto shalt thou come, but no further."

There are those who say that all our effort there will be futile—that China's power is such that it is bound to dominate all southeast Asia. But there is no end to that argument until all of the nations of Asia are swallowed up.

There are those who wonder why we have a responsibility there. Well, we have it there for the same reason that we have a responsibility for the defense of Europe. World War II was fought in both Europe and Asia, and when it ended we found ourselves with continued responsibility for the defense of freedom.

OUR OBJECTIVE IN VIET-NAM

Our objective is the independence of South Viet-Nam, and its freedom from attack. We want nothing for ourselves—only that the people of South Viet-Nam be allowed to guide their own country in their own way.

We will do everything necessary to reach that objective. And we will do only what is absolutely necessary.

In recent months attacks on South Viet-Nam were stepped up. Thus, it became necessary for us to increase our response and to make attacks by air. This is not a change of purpose. It is a change in what we believe that purpose requires.

We do this in order to slow down aggression.

We do this to increase the confidence of the brave people of South Viet-Nam who have bravely borne this brutal battle for so many years with so many casualties.

And we do this to convince the leaders of North Viet-Nam—and all who seek to share their conquest—of a very simple fact:

We will not be defeated.

We will not grow tired.

We will not withdraw, either openly or under the cloak of a meaningless agreement.

We know that air attacks alone will not accomplish all of these purposes. But it is our best and prayerful judgment that they are a necessary part of the surest road to peace.

We hope that peace will come swiftly. But that is in the hands of others besides ourselves. And we must be prepared for a long continued conflict. It will require patience as well as bravery, the will to endure as well as the will to resist.

I wish it were possible to convince others with words of what we now find it necessary to say with guns and planes: Armed hostility is futile. Our resources are equal to any challenge. Because we fight for values and we fight for principles, rather than territory or colonies, our patience and our determination are unending.

Once this is clear, then it should also be clear that the only path for reasonable men is the path of peaceful settlement.

Such peace demands an independent South Viet-Nam—securely guaranteed and able to shape its own relationships to all others—free from outside interference—tied to no alliance—a military base for no other country.

These are the essentials of any final settlement.

We will never be second in the search for such a peaceful settlement in Viet-Nam.

There may be many ways to this kind of peace: in discussion or negotiation with the governments concerned; in large groups or in small ones; in the reaffirmation of old agreements or their strengthening with new ones.

We have stated this position over and over again, fifty times and more, to friend and foe alike. And we remain ready, with this purpose, for unconditional discussions.

And until that bright and necessary day of peace we will try to keep conflict from spreading. We have no desire to see thousands die in battle—Asians or Americans. We have no desire to devastate that which the people of North Viet-Nam have built with toil and sacrifice. We will use our power with restraint and with all the wisdom that we can command.

But we will use it.

This war, like most wars, is filled with terrible irony. For what do the people of North Viet-Nam want? They want what their neighbors also desire: food for their hunger; health for their bodies; a chance to learn; progress for their country; and an end to the bondage of material misery. And they would find all these things far more readily in peaceful association with others than in the endless course of battle.

A COOPERATIVE EFFORT FOR DEVELOPMENT

These countries of southeast Asia are homes for millions of impoverished people. Each day these people rise at dawn and struggle through until the night to wrestle existence from the soil. They are often wracked by disease, plagued by hunger, and death comes at the early age of 40.

Stability and peace do not come easily in such a land. Neither independence nor human dignity will ever be won, though, by arms alone. It also requires the work of peace. The American people have helped generously in times past in these works. Now there must be a much more massive effort to improve the life of man in that conflict-torn corner of our world.

The first step is for the countries of southeast Asia to associate themselves in a greatly expanded cooperative effort for development. We would hope that North Viet-Nam would take its place in the common effort just as soon as peaceful cooperation is possible.

The United Nations is already actively engaged in development in this area. As far back as 1961 I conferred with our authorities in Viet-Nam in connection with their work there. And I would hope tonight that the Secretary General of the United Nations could use the prestige of his great office, and his deep knowledge of Asia, to initiate, as soon as possible, with the countries of that area, a plan for cooperation in increased development.

For our part I will ask the Congress to join in a billion dollar American investment in this effort as soon as it is underway.

And I would hope that all other industrialized countries, including the Soviet Union, will join in this effort to replace despair with hope, and terror with progress.

The task is nothing less than to enrich the hopes and the existence of more than a hundred million people. And there is much to be done.

The vast Mekong River can provide food and water and power on a scale to dwarf even our own TVA.

The wonders of modern medicine can be spread through villages where thousands die every year from lack of care.

Schools can be established to train people in the skills that are needed to manage the process of development.

And these objectives, and more, are within the reach of a cooperative and determined effort.

I also intend to expand and speed up a program to make available our farm surpluses to assist in feeding and clothing the needy in Asia. We should not allow people to go hungry and wear rags while our own warehouses overflow with an abundance of wheat and corn, rice and cotton.

So I will very shortly name a special team of outstanding, patriotic, distinguished Americans to inaugurate our participation in these programs. This team will be headed by Mr. Eugene Black, the very able former President of the World Bank.

In areas that are still ripped by conflict, of course development will not be easy. Peace will be necessary for final success. But we cannot and must not wait for peace to begin this job.

THE DREAM OF WORLD ORDER

This will be a disorderly planet for a long time. In Asia, as elsewhere, the forces of the modern world are shaking old ways and uprooting ancient civilizations. There will be turbulence and struggle and even violence. Great social change—as we see in our own country now—does not always come without conflict.

We must also expect that nations will on occasion be in dispute with us. It may be because we are rich, or powerful; or because we have made some mistakes; or because they honestly fear our intentions. However, no nation need ever fear that we desire their land, or to impose our will, or to dictate their institutions.

But we will always oppose the effort of one nation to conquer another nation.

We will do this because our own security is at stake.

But there is more to it than that. For our generation has a dream. It is a very old dream. But we have the power and now we have the opportunity to make that dream come true.

For centuries nations have struggled among each other. But we dream of a world where disputes are settled by law and reason. And we will try to make it so.

For most of history men have hated and killed one another in battle. But we dream of an end to war. And we will try to make it so.

For all existence most men have lived in poverty, threatened by hunger. But we dream of a world where all are fed and charged with hope. And we will help to make it so.

The ordinary men and women of North Viet-Nam and South Viet-Nam—of China and India—of Russia and America—are brave people. They are filled with the same proportions of hate and fear, of love and hope. Most of them want the same things for themselves and their families. Most of them do not want their sons to ever die in battle, or to see their homes, or the homes of others, destroyed.

Well, this can be their world yet. Man now has the knowledge—always before denied—to make this planet serve the real needs of the people who live on it.

I know this will not be easy. I know how difficult it is for reason to guide passion, and love to master hate. The complexities of this world do not bow easily to pure and consistent answers.

But the simple truths are there just the same. We must all try to follow them as best we can.

CONCLUSION

We often say how impressive power is. But I do not find it impressive at all. The guns and the bombs, the rockets and the warships, are all symbols of human failure. They are necessary symbols. They protect what we cherish. But they are witness to human folly.

A dam built across a great river is impressive.

In the countryside where I was born, and where I live, I have seen the night illuminated, and the kitchens warmed, and the homes heated, where once the cheerless night and the ceaseless cold held sway. And all this happened because electricity came to our area along the humming wires of the REA. Electrification of the countryside—yes, that, too, is impressive.

A rich harvest in a hungry land is impressive.

The sight of healthy children in a classroom is impressive.

These—not mighty arms—are the achievements which the American Nation believes to be impressive.

And, if we are steadfast, the time may come when all other nations will also find it so.

Every night before I turn out the lights to sleep I ask myself this question: Have I done everything that I can do to unite this country? Have I done everything I can to help unite the world, to try

to bring peace and hope to all the peoples of the world? Have I done enough?

Ask yourselves that question in your homes—and in this hall tonight. Have we, each of us, all done all we could? Have we done enough?

We may well be living in the time foretold many years ago when it was said: "I call heaven and earth to record this day against you, that I have set before you life and death, blessing and cursing: therefore choose life, that both thou and thy seed may live."

This generation of the world must choose: destroy or build, kill or aid, hate or understand.

We can do all these things on a scale never dreamed of before.

Well, we will choose life. In so doing we will prevail over the enemies within man, and over the natural enemies of all mankind.

To Dr. Eisenhower and Mr. Garland, and this great institution, Johns Hopkins, I thank you for this opportunity to convey my thoughts to you and to the American people.

Good night.

Source: *Public Papers of the Presidents of the United States: Lyndon B. Johnson, 1965,* Book 1 (Washington, DC: U.S. Government Printing Office, 1966), 394–399.

154. Pham Van Dong: Report to the Second Session of the Third National Assembly, April 8, 1965 [Excerpts]

Introduction

The leaders of the Democratic Republic of Vietnam (DRV, North Vietnam) had on their part already escalated the war in the Republic of Vietnam (RVN, South Vietnam) with the decision in late 1964 to dispatch native northerners south and to commit regular units of the People's Army of Vietnam (PAVN, North Vietnamese Army) to the fight in South Vietnam. By March 1965, three PAVN regiments were in South Vietnam. In these lengthy remarks to the Third National Assembly of North Vietnam, however, Premier Pham Van Dong condemns U.S. escalation of the war to include the injection of marines from the United States and troops from the Republic of Korea (ROK, South Korea), which he characterizes as part of an effort by Washington to encircle the "socialist countries" with "a network of military bases, and a U.S.-led system of military alliances." He outlines the challenges facing North

Vietnam and pledges that the struggle to reunify Vietnam will continue, even if it takes "20 years or longer."

Primary Source

The U.S. imperialists are intensifying their aggressive war in the southern part of our country. At the same time, they are extending the war to the North with their air force, seriously encroaching on the Democratic Republic of Viet Nam, and directly jeopardizing the peace and security of the peoples of this part of the world.

Allow me, on behalf of the Government of the Democratic Republic of Viet Nam, to present to the National Assembly a report on the new situation brought about by the U.S. aggressors, and on the new tasks to be fulfilled by our people to defeat them.

PART I

NEW SITUATION AND NEW TASKS

The war of aggression waged by the U.S. imperialists on our country is taking very dangerous developments. Therefore, the patriotic struggle of our people has also to take new developments, and to become more determined and vigorous than ever.

In the heat of the present situation, we realize all the more clearly the process of the U.S. imperialists' policy of aggression against our country, and also the growth of our people's patriotic struggle and its prospects of certain victory.

Indictment Against the U.S. Imperialist Aggressors

Today, from the rostrum of the National Assembly the Government of the Democratic Republic of Viet Nam solemnly announces to the entire Vietnamese people and the world peoples the indictment against the aggressive and warlike U.S. imperialists.

After World War II, availing themselves of the collapse of the defeated German, Italian, and Japanese imperialists, and of the serious weakening of the British and French Imperialists in spite of their victory, the U.S. imperialists have been striving to establish world hegemony; they have successively kicked out and replaced the other imperialists to enslave the peoples of Asia, Africa and Latin America, thus playing the role of an international gendarme.

The U.S. imperialists' policy of intervention and aggression in Viet Nam and Indochina is part of their strategy in the Western Pacific area. It is also part of U.S. overall strategy as materialized in the establishment of a network of U.S. military bases, and a U.S.-led system of military alliances aimed at encircling the socialist countries, bringing the national liberation movement under control, preparing for a nuclear war, a world war, and waging limited wars as in Korea formerly and "special war" as in South Viet Nam today.

Immediately after World War II ended with the great victory of the Soviet Army and the world democratic forces, the entire Vietnamese people, under the clearsighted leadership of the Party, stood up, accomplished the August Revolution, founded the Democratic Republic of Viet Nam on September 2, 1945, and established the people's power all over Viet Nam, from North to South. However, only a few months after the proclamation of our independence, the Chiang Kai-shek militarist clique—a tool of the U.S. imperialists—entered North Viet Nam while the British imperialists stepped into South Viet Nam, paving the way for the French colonialists' comeback.

Our resolute and clever struggle in 1946 drove the Chiang Kai-shek militarist clique out of our country, thus avoiding the danger of U.S. imperialist intervention. For their part, the French colonialists gradually encroached on our territory from the South to the North, and finally provoked an outbreak of the war all over our country on December 19, 1946. In recalling our people's heroic resistance war we want to make it clear that the U.S. imperialists began their intervention in our country as early as that time.

In 1949, the great People's Republic of China came into being. One year after, in 1950, the victorious campaign on the Viet Nam-China border broke the imperialists encirclement of the Vietnamese revolution, and connected our country with the mighty socialist camp.

Frightened by the development of our people's resistance war, the U.S. imperialists frenziedly intensified their intervention in Viet Nam, and took a direct part in the aggressive war by sanctioning the French military plans, bearing a great part of the war expenditures, and setting up in Saigon a military mission named M.A.A.G.

While the French were nearing their defeat at Dien Bien Phu, the U.S. imperialists redoubled their efforts to protract and extend the Indochina war. Together with the French advocates of continued war, they mapped out the "Vautour plan" for massive bombing of the northern part of our country in an attempt to save the French from defeat at Dien Bien Phu. However, confronted with the vigorous struggle of our people and army, and the mounting demands of the world's peoples for peace in Indochina, the U.S. imperialists could not carry out their dark schemes. On May 7, 1954, the Dien Bien Phu victory resounded throughout the world. On May 8, 1954, the Geneva Conference on Indochina held its opening session.

It was the Dien Bien Phu victory which, in the main, determined the outcome of the Geneva Conference. In spite of all the sabotage activities of the U.S. imperialists the Conference ended in success. At its closing session, the U.S. Government representative was compelled to pledge respect for the Geneva Agreements on the Indochina countries.

But immediately after the end of the 1954 Geneva Conference, the United States enticed a number of countries to sign the Manila pact and set up S.E.A.T.O., an aggressive military bloc, and disregarding the explicit clauses of the Geneva Agreements, it placed South Viet Nam, Laos and Cambodia in the so-called "protection area" of the bloc.

According to the 1954 Geneva Agreements, Viet Nam was temporarily divided into two zones for the sake of eliminating the state of war, mainly for the French Expeditionary Corps to regroup in South Viet Nam and withdraw thereafter to France. However, the U.S. Imperialists and their flunkeys—the Ngo Dinh Diem clique at that time—blatantly violated a very important provision of the Agreements—the provision on the holding of a nationwide free general election in July 1956 with a view to reunifying Viet Nam.

Here, we clearly see the U.S. imperialists' perfidious design of bringing about a permanent partition of our country, to turn South Viet Nam into a military base and a new-type colony of the United States, and to prepare for a new war of aggression against North Viet Nam and the whole of Southeast Asia.

After the conclusion of the Geneva Agreements, the U.S. imperialists gradually replaced the French colonialists in South Viet Nam, set up the Ngo Dinh Diem puppet administration, wiped out one by one the opposition groupings, and carried out most . . . wicked repressions against the people. They drowned in blood all patriotic forces aspiring to independence, democracy and peace, national identification. They organized camouflaged concentration camps dubbed "prosperity zones", "agricultural settlements", and "strategic hamlets". On the other hand, the U.S.-Diem clique frantically strengthened their military forces: they rigged up a half-a-million–strong mercenary army which a corps of U.S. advisers closely controlled from top to bottom. They build up over a hundred air and naval bases and a whole network of strategic roads. They dream of quickly stabilizing the situation in South Viet Nam, then attacking the North, and carrying out their "March to the North" plan.

But the heroic South Viet Nam people, bringing into play the indomitable tradition of the nation, resolutely stood up against the U.S. imperialists and the puppets. Their patriotic structure surged up all the more impetuously as the enemy resorted to savage terror. The enemy plan for rapid pacification of the South and a march to the North was smashed. In 1960, the South Viet Nam National Front for Liberation came into being, carrying aloft the banner of national salvation and calling on the South Vietnamese people to unite and struggle in accordance with its correct programme. Since then, our Southern compatriots have risen up in actions against the enemy in a still more vigorous drive.

In 1961, the U.S.-Diem clique made a further step in their wicked scheme. It was the May 11, 1961, Johnson–Ngo Dinh Diem joint communiqué which was actually a military pact marking a very serious turning point in U.S. policy of military intervention in South Viet Nam. Immediately after this, the United States set up an operational command in Saigon, brought into South Viet Nam tens of thousands of U.S. servicemen along with a great number of planes, warships, all kinds of modern weapons, napalm bombs and toxic chemicals aimed at increasing the fighting capacities of the South Viet Nam puppet army and stepping up the aggressive war in the South of our country in the form of "special warfare."

The . . . policy of the U.S. aggressors was materialized in the Staley-Taylor plan for "pacification of South Viet Nam within 15 months." This plan aimed at herding the entire South Vietnamese population into "strategic hamlets", isolating and annihilating the patriotic forces, first of all the armed forces, and also preparing conditions for an attack on North Viet Nam after the pacification of South Viet Nam. It has now gone bankrupt. The U.S. imperialists and their agents have suffered heavy losses and landed in a serious military and political crisis.

After being compelled to swap horses in midstream and to remove the Ngo Dinh Diem clique, the U.S. imperialists set forth the Johnson-McNamara plan for the "pacification by priority sectors" in South Viet Nam, that is to say, for the consolidation of a fairly large area surrounding Saigon-Cholon. However, with the ever-stronger struggle of the South Vietnamese people and their successive victories, this plan had to be gradually reduced from 8 provinces to 5, then to 3, and finally to the defence of Saigon-Cholon only. But even in Saigon, the U.S. aggressors and their agents are in a shaky position because of the vigorous growth of the mass struggle.

While intensifying their intervention and aggression in our country, the U.S. imperialists have ceaselessly stepped up their policy of intervention and aggression against the Kingdom of Laos and the Kingdom of Cambodia.

Soon after the 1954 Geneva Conference, the United States brought its military personnel and its satellites' troops into Laos and rekindled the flames of war to annihilate the Lao patriotic forces, and prevent the Kingdom of Laos from going along the path of genuine peace and neutrality. After they failed in this manoeuvre, the U.S. imperialists and their agents were forced to sign in 1962 a new Geneva Agreement recognizing, the neutral status of Laos. But over the past three years, they have frenziedly undermined Lao national concord, sabotaged the tripartite coalition government, torpedoed the policy of peace and neutrality of the Kingdom of Laos, launched repeated military operations to encroach on the area controlled by the Neo Lao Haksat and the genuine neutralist forces, ceaselessly extending the war in Laos and making the situation here more and more strained. The Laotian people and patriotic forces have heroically and persistently struggled against the U.S. imperialist aggressors and their flunkeys to defend the achievements of the revolution and their national rights, and have won glorious victories.

Under the clearsighted leadership of their Head of State, Prince Norodom Sihanouk, the Cambodian Government and people have resolutely steered their country into the path of peace and neutrality. The Government of the Kingdom of Cambodia has rejected the "SEATO protection" and refused to accept U.S. "aid". For the last ten years, the U.S. imperialists and their agents in South Viet Nam, Thailand, and "the Free Khmer", have continuously resorted to perfidious means, from political threat to economic pressure, from attempted assassination and subversion to violation of the Cambodian border and territory. But all these manoeuvres have been defeated by the Cambodian people's struggle. The Kingdom of Cambodia has successfully preserved her independence and neutrality, the anti-U.S. movement there has ceaselessly developed and is now deeper and wider than ever.

The above-mentioned indictment sheds light on the extremely serious crimes committed by the U.S. imperialists in our country:

1. For the last 20 years, the U.S. imperialists have been persistently pursuing their manoeuvres of aggression and enslavement in our country as well as in neighboring Laos and Cambodia. For over four years now they have waged in the southern part of our country the most "dirty" and ruthless war of aggression in the world. Recently, because of their bitter defeats in South Viet Nam, they have brazenly launched air attacks on the Democratic Republic of Viet Nam, an independent and sovereign country and a member of the socialist camp.

2. The U.S. imperialists have heaped up in our country, particularly in the South, the most hideous and unpardonable crimes. Over the past years, they have used most cruel means to raze villages to the ground, and destroy crops and vegetation: they have resorted to napalm bombs, toxic chemicals, and even poison gases to massacre our compatriots with Hitler-like savagery; they have massacred big numbers of innocent people, disembowelled and quartered children, burnt alive old men, raped women; they have endeavoured to propagate depraved ways of life, particularly in towns and cities, and tried by every means to turn our youth into hooligans and poison our people's mind.

3. The U.S. imperialists have systematically and blatantly violated the Geneva Agreements on Viet Nam. All their policies and acts in this area are aimed at doing away with the legal basis and the most important provisions of the said Agreements and denying to the Vietnamese as well as Cambodian and Lao peoples their universally-recognized national rights.

The purpose of this brief indictment is not merely to record the crimes committed by the U.S. aggressors against our people. To condemn the U.S. imperialists is to voice one's will and determination to oppose and defeat them. Like the Vietnamese people, the peoples of Asian, African, Latin American and even European countries can draw similar indictments, denounce similar crimes and by so doing, enhance their will and determination to struggle against them and warlike U.S. Imperialism, the most wicked, aggressive and dangerous enemy of mankind today.

The South Vietnamese People Will Win

The past 20 years or so were years of U.S. imperialist intervention and aggression in our country and also of a persistent and staunch struggle of our people for self-liberation and in defence of their freedom and independence.

In South Viet Nam, the process of development of the U.S. imperialists' policy of intervention and aggression is also a process of development of the people's patriotic struggle. Never before in the history of our nation's struggle against foreign invasion, has there been such a deep and broad mobilization, and this has made it possible to bring into play to a very high extent the strength and intelligence of all social strata from the countryside to the towns, from the coastal areas to the mountainous regions.

In the course of a hard struggle against a modernly-equipped and extremely cruel enemy, in the course of a nationwide, all-out and protracted war waged by the entire people, our South Vietnamese compatriots have created everything, built up a several-million–strong political army with a great variety of effective forms of struggle, built up an ever-stronger armed force, capable of defeating the enemy in ever-bigger battles, and which will deal him crushing blows.

The root cause of the growth of our Southern compatriots and their glorious victories lies in the ardent patriotism, the close unity, and the fighting determination of the entire people. Our army and people's traditional will to fight and to win has been brought into play to a very large extent. Revolution is the work of the masses. Once the masses have risen up, resolved to sacrifice everything and to defeat the enemy with a view to winning back the sacred rights of the country, the right to life and the dignity of human beings, once millions of people are imbued with such determination, they become an invincible force capable of crushing any enemy.

The U.S. aggressors and their agents know very well that to have a "grip" over the people is essential for their "special warfare" in South Viet Nam. That is why all through these long years, they have tried every means—military, political and economic—to mislead and control the people, and thus keep them under their sway. This policy reached its highest peak with the "strategic hamlets" program, the most vicious trick of the U.S. imperialist aggressor and the mad "State policy" of the Ngo Dinh Diem clique who wanted to turn all

South Vietnamese villages and towns into appalling concentration camps and heavily-fortified strongholds. But the people's strength has smashed their schemes. The correct land policy of the South Viet Nam National Front for Liberation, which safeguards the achievements of the revolution and the Resistance war and meets the basic interests of the peasant masses, has powerfully aroused million of South Vietnamese to stand up and destroy the "strategic hamlets". To date, over four-fifths of these hamlets have been completely destroyed, while the rest are in a process of disintegration. A considerable number have been turned into people's fighting villages and strongholds of the patriotic war. The struggle for the destruction of the "strategic hamlets" is an extremely arduous and valiant one. It is a fiercest confrontation between the revolutionary forces of the people and a most ruthless and wicked enemy. The outcome has been victory for the people—the bulk of the "strategic hamlets" system has been razed to the ground, and as a result, the liberated areas have been rapidly expanded, linked together and strengthened in all respects to form a solid base for the liberation struggle. This is shaking to the roots the rule of the U.S. imperialists and their agents.

Parallel to the struggle for the destruction of the "strategic hamlets" and the expansion of the liberated areas is the struggle to counter and foil enemy's mopping-up plans, to wipe out piecemeal its military forces. In the flames of this extremely arduous and glorious fight, the South Viet Nam Liberation Army and other peoples armed forces have rapidly grown up in all fields: in number and quality, in political standard and combat efficiency, in equipment and weapons. This rapid growth has been eloquently demonstrated in all battlefields of South Viet Nam by ever-bigger battles and ever-greater and more significant victories from Nam Bo to the Central Highlands and the plains of South Central Viet Nam: Ap Bac, Bien Hoa, Phel Muong, Cha La, Binh Gia, An Lao, Phu My, Pleiku, Viet An, Phong Phu, etc. In the course of the patriotic war, the South Vietnamese army and people have created from scratch a wonderful force capable of fighting and defeating an enemy several times bigger in number and equipped with all types of planes, naval craft, armoured cars, automatic rifles, artillery, napalm bombs, noxious chemicals, and even toxic gases. The forms of struggle they have used are very original and mark a development of the people's patriotic war to new peaks. At the same time, the mercenary troops are continually weakening, as they realize more and more clearly that they are acting as a vicious tool for the U.S. aggressors to massacre their own compatriots, destroy their homes, and betray their Fatherland. With the fierce patriotic struggle resounding ever more deeply in their hearts and among their ranks, they realize all the more clearly that they are committing crimes. That is why they do not want to fight. In their aggressive war in South Viet Nam, the U.S. imperialists rely mainly on the puppet forces; but it is now obvious that they cannot rely on an army practically demoralized although very well-armed and equipped. This is a victory of tremendous significance for the patriotic war in South Viet Nam.

The struggle for the destruction of the "strategic hamlets" and the ever-greater military victories all over South Viet Nam has had direct, deep and wide repercussions in South Vietnamese towns and cities. Over the recent years, almost all South Vietnamese towns and cities: Saigon, Hue, Da Nang, Ben Tre, My Tho, Nha Trang, Qui Nhon, Quang Tri, etc., have been swept by big mass movements, involving all social strata: workers, pupils, students, intellectuals, Buddhists, etc. These movements powerfully surged up wave after wave in highly vaned forms and with the exalted spirit of people rising up to become masters of their towns, lay bare the traitors and demand a U.S. withdrawal. Once, Saigon students sent an ultimatum to Nguyen Khanh. Saigon workers compelled the elders and the enterprise owners to meet all their claims. On many occasions, the masses managed to secure the control of the streets in Saigon and Hue. In Quy Nhon demonstrating students seized control of the radio broadcasting station. At present, the mass movement is vigorously forging ahead in towns and cities, rallying in its ranks broad social strata, from the labouring masses to public figures, under the slogan of peace and neutrality. In short, the South Vietnamese towns which were bases of the United States and its agents are now becoming the arena of ever more significant struggles of the people.

The "strategic hamlets" network—the backbone of the ruling apparatus of the U.S. Imperialists and their agents—, the mercenary army—the main instrument of the U.S. aggressive war along neo-colonialist pattern—, and the towns—their safest rear area—all these three mainstays are now in a perilous state and a process of disintegration. The ground is crumbling under the U.S. aggressors' feet. In the meantime since the historic Ap Bac battle in spring 1963, the patriotic struggle in South Viet Nam has undergone a wonderfully rapid growth, and the balance of forces between the people and the enemy has changed in favour of the cause of liberation of South Viet Nam. Political and military stages closely combine with each other and impel each other's development; the various regions, the countryside and the towns emulate with one another to score resounding feats of arms, our 14-odd million Southern compatriots are powerfully marching ahead along the path to victory, and no reactionary force whatever can check this advance.

The above situation explains why the U.S. aggressors can not bring up a stable government in Saigon. The successive coups d'état in South Viet Nam are reflections of the strength of the patriotic struggle to defeat the aggressors and the traitors, and also forerunners of their irretrievable collapse. Nowadays, any South Vietnamese hireling administration can be nothing else than a set of puppets in a poor show, and likely to be thrown down at any time. This also shows a basic weakness of the U.S. imperialists and constitutes a heavy defeat of their "special war."

Meanwhile, the South Viet Nam National Front for Liberation, the mobilizer and organizer of the patriotic forces in South Viet Nam, the leader who has taken the people to ever-greater victories, is now controlling 3/4 of the territory and 2/3 of the population of South Viet Nam. It has gained ever-higher international prestige and position, and is being recognized by more and more foreign countries and world opinion as the sole genuine representative of the South Vietnamese people. Its sound programme constitutes the banner of unity and struggle for national salvation which rallies broad social strata in the fight to overthrow the yoke of the U.S. imperialists and their agents with a view to achieving independence, democracy, peace and neutrality—South Viet Nam, and eventual peaceful reunification of the country. The March 22, 1965 Statement of the Front is resounding the world as the strong voice of a people determined to fight and to win, the voice of justice, the voice of the just cause of the Vietnamese people and of the present epoch, the voice filled with national pride and heroism, the voice of a people who are taking the country's destiny into their own hands, the voice of our compatriots of South Viet Nam, the brass citadel of our Fatherland.

The development of the U.S. imperialists' aggressive policy in South Viet Nam as well as the growth of the patriotic war of our Southern compatriots clearly show that the U.S. imperialists' "special warfare" is heading for irretrievable defeat.

The U.S. imperialists have set up a most Machiavellian political and military brain-trust in an attempt to find a way to victory in South Viet Nam; they have used modern weapons, and have brought into this small battlefield 1/4 of their army officers. However, for the U.S aggressors, there is not yet a single ray of light at the end of the tunnel. The situation is such that more and more people in the United States are coming to realize that Washington is being defeated and will be completely defeated in South Viet Nam.

It is very pleasing to note that our Southern compatriots are going on to ever greater victories, as the South Viet Nam National Front for Liberation has worked out a correct and scientific line to meet the U.S. imperialists' counterrevolutionary war of aggression with a patriotic war, a revolutionary war of the people, and gradually and steadily to build its forces and win step by step ever-greater political and military victories. The situation is developing in favour of our Southern compatriots, and no matter what great and frenzied efforts the enemy may make, he cannot possibly reverse the tide to avoid an ignominious defeat.

The Vietnamese People Will Win

Having sustained bitter defeats in South Viet Nam, the U.S. imperialist aggressors, of late, have frenziedly embarked on new and most wicked adventures in an attempt to retrieve their critical position and defeats.

The Government of the Democratic Republic of Viet Nam sternly exposes and denounces to all our compatriots and to the peoples of the world the new and extremely serious war acts of the U.S. imperialists: on the one hand, the later are intensifying the aggressive war in the South, and on the other, they are carrying out air and naval attacks on the North. By engaging in this very dangerous military adventure, they stupidly expect that they can cow our people and also pose a threat to the peace-loving governments and peoples in the world. They hope that our people and the world peoples will flinch out of fear, and thus they will be in a position to shift from a weak to a strong position!

But in face of their new aggressive acts, the Vietnamese people from the South to the North are waging an ever more resolute struggle, and the world peoples are extending us an ever more vigorous support. It is clear that still heavier defeats are in store for the U.S. imperialists.

In an attempt to intensify the aggressive war, the U.S. imperialists have recently brought into South Viet Nam a number of antiaircraft missile units, 3,500 marines, and 2,000 South Korean troops; they are planning to send in more U.S. combat units. U.S.-piloted jet planes are carrying out bombing and strafing raids in increasing numbers in South Viet Nam. More than ever, our 14 million Southern compatriots, responding to the appeal of the South Viet Nam National Front for Liberation, are bringing into play their staunch fighting spirit; the entire people in arms are united and determined to hit vigorously and accurately at the U.S. aggressors and their agents, to liberate South Viet Nam, and achieve national salvation.

Ten years ago, the French Expeditionary Corps in spite of its 200,000 picked troops ended in defeat at Dien Bien Phu. . . . For their part, our Southern compatriots are prepared to "fight with determination, to fight to the end, to fight until not a single U.S. soldier is to be found if they have to struggle for 10 years in our country, even 20 years or longer, however great the difficulties and hardships." [March 22, 1965, Statement of the South Viet Nam National Front for Liberation.]

In intensifying the aggressive war in South Viet Nam, the U.S. imperialists are expanding it to the North with their air force, on the grounds that the Democratic Republic of Viet Nam is at the origin of the patriotic struggle in South Viet Nam! These are obviously impudent acts and perfidious tricks of corsairs.

The Democratic Republic of Viet Nam, a member of the socialist camp, is steadily advancing to socialism; this is the common achievement of the Vietnamese revolution, the fruit of the common endeavour of the people of the whole country. It is a strong base for the patriotic struggle in the South and the peaceful reunification of the country. In laying hands on the North, the U.S. imperialists encroach upon the valuable and sacred achievement of our 30-odd million compatriots and commit an intolerable crime against our Fatherland. By attacking the Democratic Republic of

Viet Nam, they have completely scrapped the Geneva Agreements and grossly violated international law and all human laws. They must pay for their crimes!

In North Viet Nam, since August 5, 1964, the people's armed forces and the population have fought with the greatest heroism, and dealt the U.S. imperialist aggressors ever-stronger blows. The people of the North, closely united, are determined to struggle in a self-sacrificing spirit to defeat all enemy aggressive schemes, to defend the North, and more than ever to stand side by side with our Southern compatriots and wholeheartedly support their liberation struggle till final victory.

Laying hands on the North, the U.S. war-mongers expose themselves not only to well-deserved counter-blows in the North, but also to still more telling blows in the South as was pointed out in the March 22, 1965 Statement of the Liberation Front:

"To defend the beloved North, the army and people of the South have directed the flames of their anger at the U.S. aggressors and their agents. If the U.S. imperialists lay hands on the North of our Fatherland the army and people of the South will deal them much harder blows. In February 1965, while the aggressors and traitors attacked the North, in the South, the Liberation Army launched stormy attacks on important military bases and main forces of the enemy, putting out of action 20,706 enemy troops (including nearly 600 U.S. aggressors killed, wounded or captured), seizing 4,114 guns of various kinds and shooting down, damaging or destroying 111 aircraft of various types."

The U.S. imperialists ceaselessly talk about seeking "a position of strength". Why? Precisely because they are in a weak position. But never will they attain a position Of strength! In the present epoch, in Viet Nam as well as everywhere else in the world, the weakening and defeat of the U.S. imperialists have become a law of nature, an inexorable law governing the present trend of the world, an inexorable law of the development of human society: U.S.-headed imperialism and all other reactionary forces in the world are on the path to defeat and collapse; the more reckless, adventurist, impudent and perfidious they are, the more hatred for them will blaze up everywhere, and the more vigorously the world's peoples will stand up to defeat them! That is a radiant truth of our epoch.

In these circumstances, the more frenzied the U.S. attempts to extend the war to North Viet Nam, the more disastrous will be their defeat! An anti-U.S. wave of indignation is now surging up in the world. The governments and peoples of the socialist countries, newly-independent countries, the international organizations, the peoples the world over, progressive circles and various social strata in the United States are extending an ever more resolute and vigorous support and assistance to our just struggle. Our people, both in the South and in the North, are all the more firmly standing on the frontline of the world people's front against U.S. imperialism, bringing into play their forces to defeat the U.S. imperialists for the sake of their revolutionary cause as well as for peace, national independence, democracy and socialism in the world. That is why the entire Vietnamese people are determined to overcome all difficulties and hardships, to fight to the end in a self-sacrificing spirit and with a rock-like confidence in their certain victory. Even now, our people have already vanquished the U.S. aggressors because theirs is a just cause, and because they have the will and determination and enjoy world-wide sympathy and support. At the start of our national resistance war nearly 20 years ago, our forces were very small, but the entire Vietnamese people were at one in fighting and defeating the aggressors, and the outcome was victory for us. Today, we are much stronger than before, stronger in the North, stronger in the South, and enjoying stronger world support. For their part, the U.S. imperialists are being bogged down in South Viet Nam and encountering great difficulties in various fields and in many places. That is why our people are all the more heightening their will and determination, are animated with even greater enthusiasm and confidence in their just and certainly victorious struggle, and are resolved to devote all their forces to driving the U.S. aggressors out of our country, to defend the North, to liberate the South, eventually to build a peaceful, reunified, independent, democratic and prosperous Viet Nam, and to contribute to the defence of peace in Southeast Asia and the world.

Our people will certainly win, the U.S. imperialist aggressors will surely be defeated. The reasons for our victory can be briefly stated as follows:

1. The Vietnamese people have grasped two points which were tested and proved in the long history of our people's struggle against imperialist aggression, before the August Revolution, and particularly since our resistance war.

   a) To unite the entire people, to wage a resolute and persistent struggle, to be prepared to sacrifice everything for the nation's supreme interests: freedom and happiness of the people, unity and territorial integrity of the Fatherland.

   b) To know how to use a weapon capable of defeating any imperialist aggressors including the U.S. imperialists: the people's revolution war. Our army and people in the South have developed the people's revolutionary war to a high level, in an all-round, uniform and steady manner. This is a valuable contribution to the struggle against U.S. aggression all over the world.

2. The world situation is very favourable to our people:

   a) The socialist camp is becoming ever stronger; all socialist countries are extending wholehearted support and assistance to the Vietnamese people.

b) In the world the newly-independent countries, the international working class, the forces of peace and progress in all countries including the United States, are vigorously supporting us.

3. At the same time the U.S. imperialists and all reactionary forces in the world are suffering defeat after defeat and are in the process of weakening and annihilation.

Over the past few years, the weakening of U.S. imperialists has become still more obvious in economic, political and military fields. The sharpening contradictions between the United States and other imperialist countries and the struggle for democracy, freedom and peace in the United States itself have driven the U.S. imperialists into greater embarrassment and isolation than ever.

In that lies the root cause of the great successive victories of the revolutionary struggle of the world's peoples. In that also lies the root cause of the certain victory of our people.

PART II

THE NORTH CARRIES ON PRODUCTION AND FIGHTING, DEFENDS ITSELF AND SUPPORTS THE SOUTH

Warmly Commending Our People and Army for Their Victories

Since August 5, 1964, and especially since February 7, 1965, the U.S. imperialists have used planes of the U.S. Air Force and Navy and also of the South Vietnamese puppet air force for continual attacks on many places near the Demarcation Line and other areas of the Democratic Republic of Viet Nam. They have put into action hundreds of up-to-date supersonic jets which, starting from their bases in the Pacific (including the Seventh Fleet), in South Viet Nam, in Thailand, and using all kinds of bombs including napalm and phosphorous bombs, have carried out daily raids on populated areas, urban centres, in an attempt to cause losses and cow our people.

A year ago, during the first session of the 3rd National Assembly from this rostrum, we sternly warned the U.S. imperialists: "Beware! Don't play with fire!" Today the fire from the antiaircraft guns of the Democratic Republic of Viet Nam, the flames of hatred of our people, the movement against U.S. aggression throughout the world are dealing telling blows at them.

Vinh Linh, Quang Binh, Ha Tinh, Nghe An, Thanh Hoa, Quang Ninh, Bach Long Vi and other places have been staunchly standing on the frontline of socialist North Viet Nam, repeatedly winning victories over the U.S. aggressors, and setting a brilliant example of both gallantry in fighting and eagerness in production.

The people's armed forces, from anti-aircraft regular units, navy, air force, people's armed security forces to regional troops, militia and self-defence units, have been fighting with admirable gallantry, worthy of the Dien Bien Phu tradition, worthy of heroic South Viet Nam! Our officers have shown high determination and courage, some have refused to leave their fighting positions even after being hit several times by enemy bullets. Political commissar Nguyen Viet Xuan of an anti-aircraft unit had his wounded leg cut off which hindered his movements, ordered other injured fighters to be cared for first, and continued to give effective command to his unit, urging his men to shoot down more U.S. aircraft till he fainted. Navy cadet Tran Gia Tue, amidst the flames calmly, rapidly and accurately aimed at enemy targets; grievously wounded, he continued to fight; after being relieved, he undertook to supply his mates with ammunition instead of leaving the field. Pilot Pham Ngoc Lan cleverly and flexibly reacted to complicated situations, and valiantly dived straight on enemy aircraft to shoot them down, thus achieving together with his mates the first glorious feat of arms of our air force. Security sergeant Nguyen Quoc Co, amidst fierce enemy bombing picked up and threw away a number of steel-pellet bombs about to explode in an air-raid shelter, thus saving the lives of those who were there. These are but a few instances among the many examples of admirable valour in the fight. We warmly hail the splendid feats of the heroic Viet Nam People's Army and other people's armed forces!

The militia, self-defence corps and the people's security played an outstanding part in the fighting. They actively helped in supplying ammunition, extinguishing fires, giving first aid to the wounded, ensuring liaison, capturing prisoners, maintaining security and order, and protecting the people's life and property. Furthermore, using rifles and machine guns, they efficiently coordinated their fire with the air defence forces and navy. A typical example is the shooting down of a U.S. jet with rifle shots by a militia team of Tran Phu Cooperative (Dien Chau district, Nghe An province) comprising four men: Tran Hieu, To Duc Hung, Nguyen Uoc and Pham Nho.

Factory workers and civil servants also valiantly fought to defend their enterprises and offices, and to ensure their normal functioning during enemy attacks.

The recent resounding victories are due to the line of people's war, to the valiant and resolute fighting of our entire people.

They are victories of the unity between the army and people, the army defending the Fatherland and the people, and the latter encouraging, helping the army and participating in the fight together with the army. In all places subjected to enemy attacks the people showed indomitable spirit, calm, and steady morale. Everybody stood firm on his fighting position, enthusiastically took part in the fight against the U.S. aggressors and fulfilled his duties in spite of bombings and strafings. Many old men stood indefatigable in the trenches or by the gun emplacements for many hours at a stretch to lend a hand to the young people fighting U.S. aircraft. Many youths offered their own bodies as mounts for A.A. machine guns and fought with admirable gallantry, others valiantly climbed on elevated and exposed places to be able to shoot more accurately at enemy planes. Many young pioneers moved about under enemy fire to act as liaison agents. Throughout three days' fighting, Mother Suot rowed to and fro across the Nhat Le river 45 times transporting ammunition. Doan, a nurse in the Gianh river area, crawled three kilometres under fire to get medical supplies for the wounded. Even while the fight was raging, the soldiers were fed with hot rice and excellent soup served at their very gun emplacements by local women. The people constantly stood shoulder to shoulder with the troops whom they stimulated, encouraged and efficiently helped. At the same time, all combat duties and preparations: digging of air-raid shelters, evacuation of towns and cities, extinguishing fires and removal of time-bombs after enemy raids, maintenance of security and order, and protection of the people's property, etc., were carried out with a high sense of urgency, great determination and discipline. In these circumstances of hard ordeals, our compatriots showed even greater mutual love and affection, and increased confidence in the Party and Government. They also clearly manifested their ardent patriotism and attachment to socialist construction in the North.

Vinh Linh, Quang Binh, Ha Tinh, Nghe An, Thanh Hoa, Quang Ninh, Bach Long Vi and a number of other places have shown both fierce fighting spirit and ability in production work; there fighting and production are closely linked tasks. The more resounding the victories over the enemy, the greater the people's eagerness in production. Since late 1964, the provinces near the Demarcation Line have gloriously fulfilled three big tasks at one time: shooting down a great number of enemy aircraft, making up for the heavy losses resulting from the recent big floods and typhoons, and ensuring a vigorous development of production in the winter-spring crop. The very provinces which had to fight in the North were those which completed the transplanting of rice-seedlings at an early date. In comparison with the same period last year, they have recorded an increase of nearly 50,000 hectares in acreage and also a marked progress in the application of new farming techniques, especially in irrigation and use of fertilizers. Hundreds of thousands of peasants are daily going to the fields in an exalted spirit, with ploughs in their hands and rifles on their shoulders, fighting the enemy when he comes and resuming production work after he has been driven away. In coastal areas, even on days when U.S. air and naval craft carried out raids, many fishing teams sailed out, and even got greater catches than usual. Whenever a battle is fought in Ho Xa, Dong Hoit, Ha Tinh, Vinh and Thanh Hoa, immediately after the firing ceased, workers of all enterprises and construction yards returned to their work and each time the hours of fierce fighting were followed by even more vigorous emulation drives marked by increased labour productivity.

To engage in fighting and production has become part of the people's daily life. The way of living has been entirely adjusted to the new situation, which means a higher sense of urgency, increased vigour, more practicalness and greater efficiency.

In the face of the ever more impudent and wicked U.S. war acts, every citizen, from old people to little children, have only one wish: to hit at the U.S. aggressors even more vigorously and more accurately, wage a persistent struggle, and be prepared to sacrifice everything to win victory, to carry out production work as vigorously as fighting; to get many aircraft shot down, at the same time to get a good harvest. Only on this condition can we continuously increase our strength and fight persistently until final victory!

We warmly commend the glorious victories recorded by the army and people in Vinh Linh, Quang Binh, Ha Tinh, Nghe An, Thanh Hoa, Quang Ninh, Bach Long Vi and other places. We particularly commend our compatriots who have shown determination and fortitude in face of the enemy, and have done their best to contribute to the fight against the U.S. aggressors, setting a brilliant example and accumulating valuable experience for the entire people.

In the last few months, our army and people in the North have inflicted significant losses on the enemy. However, our greatest victory and the enemy's biggest defeat lie in the fact that he cannot cow our people, indeed he cannot even intimidate our children. Public opinion in the West and in the United States itself has more and more clearly realized that the air attacks on the Democratic Republic of Viet Nam have not brought about any result for the United States except the vigorous counter-blows of our people and the strong condemnation of the world's peoples.

The Whole of North Viet Nam Carries Out Production Work, Fights and Prepares for More Fighting

In the northern part of our country, all regions, branches and social strata are now seething with hatred for the U.S. imperialists, and making every effort to strengthen their fighting capacity, ready to strike at the U.S. aggressors while calmly and unflinchingly boosting production and the building of the material and technical basis of socialism.

The armed forces are strengthening their fighting capacity in all fields. Officers and men are eagerly studying and striving to carry into effect President Ho Chi Minh's teaching: "Be loyal to the Party and the people, fulfil any tasks, overcome any difficulties, defeat any enemies". The entire armed forces are enthusiastically emulating to build the army, to score feats of arms, and to win the honour of keeping President Ho Chi Minh's reward banner bearing the words: "Determined to defeat the U.S. aggressors". Such is the iron will of the armed forces of the North who are the heroic fighters of a heroic people!

Everywhere, our people are doing their best to step up air defence work, develop the militia and self-defence forces, temper themselves physically, undergo military training, carry out marches with full equipment on their backs, prepare their weapons, set up aircraft-hunting teams, first-aid groups, fire brigades, anti-toxic gas groups, patrols. Our entire people are organizing themselves into battle formations!

The leading bodies of the Party and the State, the people's organizations, the economic and cultural branches—industry, agriculture, capital construction, communications and transport, post and broadcasting services, trade, finance, banking, culture, education, public health—are making with a high sense of urgency all necessary preparations to meet the requirements of the new situation and tasks.

Along with the preparations for combat, the emulation movement for the "three high peaks" for the overfulfilment of the State plan is developing more vigorously than ever.

The workers are highlighting the slogans "Let us hold firm both our hammer and our rifle", and "Whenever we lose time once as a result of alerts, we will work twice as hard to make up for the lost time", they are turning their hatred for the U.S. imperialists into a lever for practical actions in production and combat, and striving to make of each enterprise, construction site, State farm, forestry yard, department store, government office a socialist production and fighting unit. Producers are at the same time fighters, and the leaders in production, the commanders in combat.

The peasants are highlighting the slogans "Let us hold firm both our plough and our rifle" and "Let us fight the enemy whenever he comes and resume production after he is put to flight"; they are actively emulating each other to secure a successful winter-spring crop. They have now overfulfilled the State plan in terms of acreage and recorded market progress in the application of new farming techniques. They are determined to develop to the fullest extent the capabilities of the agricultural co-operatives to boost production to an unmatched level, thus enhancing the superiority of the new relations of production. At the same time, all able-bodied peasants are militiamen and members of the self-defence corps, ready to fight the enemy.

Our youth are doing their best to play their role as a shock brigade in production, in fighting as well as in studies and training to defend the Fatherland and to build socialism. So far, more than 1,800,000 youths have volunteered to achieve the "three ready's"—ready to accept any task, ready to fight whenever the enemy comes, and ready to enlist in the army. They are workers, peasants, intellectuals, civil servants, students, pupils, youths from minority nationalities. The ardour and the force of our youth must be closely and vigorously mobilized to further their role on all fronts—the fighting front and the front of economic development and of defence build-up.

Our women are stepping up throughout the North the "three responsibilities" movement as a support for the "three ready's" movement of the youth. Hundreds of thousands of people, from old women to young girls, have volunteered to assume production work in their localities, to look after their families so that their husbands, sons and brothers may confidently enlist in the army, and to serve the front or to participate directly in the fight whenever necessary.

The whole people of the North are warmly responding to the Statement of the South Viet Nam National Front for Liberation and the Statement of the Viet Nam Fatherland Front, they are at the same time carrying out production—fighting and combat preparations, determined to do their best to build and defend the North and to extend wholehearted support to the cause of Liberation of the South. In the present juncture, all social strata, all citizens must work more, with a higher sense of urgency and higher productivity; everybody must, according to his capacity and strength, make the most effective contribution to the common cause of the country.

In response to the appeal of the South Viet Nam National Front for Liberation, the South Viet Nam cadres, army-men and simple citizens regrouped to the North have enthusiastically voiced their readiness to return to their native land to fight with arms in hand or do any work for national salvation. Pending orders to this effect, all of them are striving to boost production and actively work to contribute to the defence and the building of the North. We warmly hail their patriotism and combat-readiness!

New Tasks of Our People and Army in the North

In face of the new and extremely serious juncture due to the U.S. imperialists' aggressive policy in our country, proceeding from the present situation and tasks as expounded in Part I, and on the basis of the experience gained by our people and army in carrying out both production and fighting over the recent period, it is necessary to work out and urgently implement correct and adequate policies and measures so as to strengthen the economic and defence potential of the northern part of our country, thus fully demonstrating our entire people's iron will to increase the strength of the North in all fields, defeat the U.S. imperialists and defend the Fatherland.

Economic Tricks

In the economic field, through the carrying out of the first 5-year plan, the potential of socialist North Viet Nam has been obviously strengthened.

On the basis of the initial achievements in the consolidation of the socialist relations of production, and with the steady growth of the forces of the working class, the cooperative peasantry and the socialist intelligentsia in the political, cultural and technical fields, the economy of the North, organized and managed in a planned way, has gradually become a solid socialist economic system.

On the other hand, the material and technical basis has been further strengthened, production has developed at a fairly quick tempo. The first establishments of heavy industry have already gone into production or are being built; light industry and locally-run industries are much more developed than before. Industry has managed to meet part of its requirements in technical equipment and ensure the supply of raw materials in increasing quantities and that of the major part of consumer goods. With the progress made in water conservancy, intensive cultivation, increased land yield, multiplication of annual crops, reclaiming of waste lands, agriculture is undergoing an all-round development. Food production is in the process of meeting the increasing requirements of the socialist North. In the field of communications, the network of roads has been improved and expanded, the transport capacity on the main lines has been increased. First steps have been made in the way of a sound redistribution of manpower among the various economic branches and between the delta and the highlands.

From a backward and dependent agrarian economy mainly based on small production, we are building an independent and self-supporting economy, and advancing by steady steps to socialism. We are striving to enhance all capabilities of the national economy and at the same time to make the most of the aid from the fraternal countries with a view to meeting the ever greater requirements of economic construction, improvement of the people's livelihood and strengthening of national defence.

We are now in a position to mobilize rapidly and in a planned way much more manpower and material resources than before for the defence of the Fatherland. We must redouble our efforts, endeavour to overcome our weaknesses and shortcomings, strengthen the key branches of the national economy, and adequately consolidate North Viet Nam in order to raise its economic and defence potential.

In the years to come, the economy must be built and developed in line with the new situations. On the one hand, the urgent requirements of the revolutionary tasks must be fully met; we must, at the same time, boost production and stand combat-ready, strengthen our economic potential and defence capabilities, resolutely defend the North and extend all-out support to the revolution for the liberation of the South. On the other, great attention must be paid to securing the advance of the socialist revolution, adequately pursuing the construction of the material and technical basis of socialism, and firmly consolidating the socialist relations of production, in order to strengthen the defence of the North.

The basic contents of this task are:

1. Adequate measures must be taken to strengthen the defence of the people's life and property and of production bases.

2. The reserves of vital materials must be increased, the requirements of economic development and national defence must be met to the highest extent.

3. Strenuous efforts must be made to promote agricultural and industrial production with much attention being paid to locally-run industries, and to develop post and communications in conjunction with the consolidation of the whole rear-area. In this connection, concrete plans must be worked out and efforts made to reach concrete objectives in each stage; marked progress must be recorded after several short stages.

4. While endeavouring to meet the above-mentioned urgent requirements we must adequately pursue the building of the material and technical basis of socialism, strengthen the work of basic survey, geological prospection, scientific research, training of cadres with a view to meeting the new requirements in conjunction with long-term ones.

5. On the basis of boosting production, more resources must be mobilized so as to ensure an adequate supply of manpower and resources for fighting duties and economic development—the requirements of the armed forces are to be satisfied, and the basic needs of the people's livelihood are to be met.

6. Continued efforts must be made to steadily consolidate the socialist relations of production, and to ensure good management of the State-owned enterprises on the basis of the achievements of the "three 'for' and three 'against'" movement; particular attention must be paid to the consolidation of the agricultural cooperatives in the delta and in the highlands, to fishing, and salt-making cooperatives in the costal area, on that basis, to educate, organize and lead the masses in boosting production, fighting, and making combat preparations actively fulfilling all tasks with the determination to win ever-bigger victories.

Strenuous efforts must be made to improve and strengthen the management of our economy . . . , that of production, circulation and distribution, prices and markets. The ranks of cadres and workers must be readjusted actively, rationally, closely and steadily in order to meet the new requirements in the field of production and fighting.

Thrift must be strictly put into practice in production, construction and consumption; corruption, waste and bureaucratism must be fought in all State-run economic branches, government services, agricultural cooperatives, and in the life and activities of everybody.

7. To fulfil the new tasks of the new situation, we must rely mainly on our own resources while doing our best to secure the sympathy and assistance of the world's peoples, first of all, of the fraternal socialist countries.

Defence Tasks

It is necessary to mobilize the whole army and people to urgently strengthen the defence capabilities of our country, resolutely to defeat all acts of sabotage and encroachment on the North, to be prepared to face and smash all the enemy schemes of expanding the war, to maintain security and order, to defend the security of the Fatherland, and defend the socialist construction of our people in the North.

To this end, it is necessary to fulfil the following concrete tasks:

1. To strengthen the armed forces, to promote training and combat readiness, to ensure that our army is ready to fight and to win everywhere and in all circumstances. In order to strengthen the armed forces so as to meet the requirements of the new situation, it is necessary to adequately extend the duration of military service and to carry out partial mobilization.

2. To strengthen particularly the active air defence capacity of the armed forces, along with the strengthening of the civilian air defence with a view to effectively countering enemy raids.

3. To strive to consolidate and develop the regional armed forces: regional troops, guerrillas, militia and self-defence corps, particularly in key areas.

4. To strengthen all rear-area work closely-related to the fighting and combat preparations of the army.

5. To intensify political work in the armed forces, to achieve a vigorous change in thinking, organization and style of work so as to meet the new requirements; to launch in the emulation movement aimed at enhancing its "determination to defeat the U.S. aggressors".

Guiding Principles

In fulfilling the above tasks of economic construction and national defence build-up, it is necessary to grasp the following guiding principles:

1. To work against time, to concentrate our forces so as to meet the most important and urgent requirements of the most essential branches and areas, to combine the immediate tasks of economic construction with those of long-term development, to carry on and promote socialist industrialization in the North.

2. To combine the forces at central and regional levels: at the central level, attention must be paid to the strengthening of forces so as to meet the important requirements which cannot be met at the regional level. The various reasons must rely mainly on their own resources and do their best to bring into play all capabilities with a view to meeting their own requirements.

3. To ensure the centralized leadership and unified management of the central authorities, and on that basis, to increase the power of the various branches and the local authorities in an adequate manner, to enable them to deal in good time with all questions falling within their ability.

4. The leadership should show initiative and diligence and make "timely, practical and effective moves," thus bringing fully into play the role of the leading bodies and officials.

5. To enhance ideological work, to powerfully arouse the revolutionary ardour, combativeness and creative labour of the masses, to mobilize the cadres, labouring people and the whole people of North Viet Nam, to highlight the traditions of heroic struggle and industry, to heighten their sense of response ability and discipline, to step up the emulation movement to redouble efforts, to hold the hammer or the plough in one hand and the rifle in the other, so that all branches, units and individuals may fulfil their tasks.

It should be clearly realized that a good solution of the immediate requirements in the sphere of economy and national defence is basically in keeping with the requirements of economic construction and national defence build-up. We have been endeavouring to develop agriculture, locally-run industries, transport and communications, and to promote economic construction in the mountainous areas. These tasks should now be carried on with stepped-up efforts, with more concentrated forces, and at a quicker tempo. Such efforts are essential and beneficial to the fulfilment of the immediate tasks in the field of production and fighting. At the same time, favourable conditions will thus be brought about to promote socialist construction in the North and to strengthen its economic and defence potential. On the other hand, we must overcome all difficulties to carry on the building of key projects under construction, and start the building of a number of other necessary projects.

We must step up the emulation movement for "three high peaks", strive to raise labour productivity in all branches, to overfulfil the 1965 State Plan and the First Five-Year plan. Particular stress must be laid on the necessity to raise labour productivity in all branches of the national economy. We are facing very heavy tasks in the field of production and fighting, a greatly increased volume of work and rising demands in manpower. More than ever before, urgent steps should be made to readjust and improve organization and guidance in execution, to better technique, rationalize production and popularize the use of improved tools and semimechanized equipment in all branches of production, so that each individual worker may increase productivity twofold, and even three or fourfold.

The new situation and the new tasks require that we determine the direction of economic construction in relatively wide areas with a view to increasing the output of agriculture and locally-run industries, so as to meet on the spot the totality or an important part of the requirements in the field of production and fighting, and the vital needs of the local population. Along with the task of determining and putting into execution the direction of economic construction in each area, care should be taken to ensure the unity and balance of the national economy, to abide by the principle of democratic centralism applied to economic and State management.

Strengthen Ideological and Organizational Work

Ideological work is of decisive importance to the fulfilment of the heavy and urgent tasks mentioned above, and should take pride of place. We must see to it that the entire army and people fully grasp the new situation and the new tasks, and on this basis, raise further their revolutionary ardour, bring into play the nation's tradition of heroism, enhance their sense of responsibility toward the defence and construction of the North, as well as toward the patriotic in the South; we should enhance their fighting will, their determination to defeat the U.S. imperialist aggressors, their readiness to courageously endure hardships and make sacrifices, to overcome all difficulties and to fulfil any task whatever it may be; we should heighten their spirit of self-reliance: every region, every branch, every unit and every individual must rely on their own strength and promote their capabilities to the fullest extent in order to fulfil their production and fighting duties; we should enhance their sense of discipline, their determination to implement with creativeness, diligence and seriousness all initiatives, directives and orders of the competent authorities; we should enhance their revolutionary vigilance, and their sense of strict secrecy; we should overcome pacifism, desire for tranquillity, fear of sacrifice, difficulties and hardships; we should do away with the mentality of relying on outside assistance subjectivism and underestimation of

the enemy, lack of vigilance and combat readiness; we must promote industry, thrift and a simple and healthy life.

Special attention should be given to organizational work in order to fulfil the immediate tasks in production and fighting. We must work out and implement in an active and steady manner the necessary organizational measures desired to strengthen combativeness in all branches and at all levels. Our apparatus should not be cumbersome, it should be light but strong and effective, democratic centralism should be observed, and strict discipline enforced; close coordination of action between the various branches at all levels should be ensured, a diligent and practical style of work should be developed. At the same time, all emulations must be thoroughly observed, especially as regards secrecy.

The slogan of our Northern compatriots is: to carry out production . . . , to defend the North and support the soil. The entire political, economic and cultural life of North Viet Nam should be permeated with this slogan in all its significance and contents.

It must be clearly realized that North Viet Nam is facing a new situation and new tasks in very favourable conditions. We are now given a good opportunity to fulfil, in an exalted spirit of determination to fight and to win, a number of tasks which are bound to confront us in the building of North Viet Nam, namely, boosting agricultural production and locally special run industries, strengthening certain regions of importance, etc. This is also a good opportunity for us to undertake in a more concentrated manner such tasks as basic survey, scientific and technical research, training of cadres, in order to meet the immediate requirements and at the same time prepare for the long-term economic development of North Viet Nam. These tasks in the field of production and fighting provide a strong impetus and inspiration to all branches of the national economy as well as the cultural, educational, public health and art activities. All branches and all levels must step up their activities to a quicker tempo and with a higher spirit in order to score outstanding progress. It is more necessary than ever to maintain security and order so that the most favorable conditions may be ensured for the mobilization of all forces in North Viet Nam for production and fighting. To this end, the responsible State organs must rely on the masses for the successful discharge of their mission.

North Viet Nam is now engaging in a fierce struggle against the U.S. aggressors with the revolutionary optimism of people who have the situation under control, who are firmly taking in hands their own destinies, and are determined to defeat the enemy. The socialist regime in North Viet Nam will grow stronger and more consolidated in the process of production and struggle. The northern part of our country, the Democratic Republic of Viet Nam, will fully play its great role as the base for the liberation of South Viet Nam and the peaceful reunification of the Fatherland.

PART III

OUR PEOPLE'S PATRIOTIC STRUGGLE IS AN INTEGRAL PART OF THE WORLD PEOPLE'S STRUGGLE AGAINST AGGRESSIVE AND WARLIKE U.S. IMPERIALISM

Characteristic Features of the Present-day World

The international situation is developing very favourably for the patriotic struggle of the Vietnamese people. The outstanding features of this situation are: the all-round growth of the forces of socialism, the tempestuous development of the national liberation movement, the new progress of the working class movement in capitalist countries and the growth of the forces of world peace. Meanwhile the imperialists headed by U.S. imperialism, along with all reactionary forces in the world, are facing innumerable difficulties and are declining. Spearheading their struggle at U.S.-headed imperialism, the world's peoples are more and more united in the common struggle for peace, national independence, democracy and socialism.

The mighty socialist camp is developing unceasingly and is becoming a decisive factor in the development of human society. The socialist camp is the bulwark of world revolution and world peace, and a firm support for the national liberation forces. The great and brilliant successes scored by the peoples of the Soviet Union, China and the other socialist countries in the political, economic, cultural, scientific, technological, and national defence fields, constitute important contributions to the consolidation of the socialist camp and the strengthening of the revolutionary and peace forces. China's first successful nuclear and the launching of the Soviet spaceship "Vostok-2" with a stepping into outer space for the first time in history to out scientific observations, are remarkable achievements which bring great enthusiasm to the peoples of the whole world.

In face of the danger of aggression and war created by the U.S. imperialists, the socialist countries will certainly close their ranks and take joint actions, determined together to defeat the common enemy. The peoples of the socialist countries, firmly united under the great banner of Marxism-Leninism, on the basis of the principles of proletarian internationalism, represent an invincible and indestructible force.

During the last twenty years, the national liberation movement, enjoying the encouragement and support of the socialist camp and the international workers' movement, has grown into ever more strongly developed and has revolutionary storms resulting in the collapse of big parts of the colonial system of imperialism. More than fifty colonial and dependent countries have at varying degrees won their political independence. The flames of revolution are burning throughout Asia, Africa and Latin America.

The U.S. imperialists have now to face millions of people who have risen up in arms against them. Like the people of South Viet Nam, the peoples of many countries understand ever more clearly that violence by the masses is the only way to oppose violence by the imperialist aggressors. At present the movement of armed struggle is expanding or has been kindled in many countries: the Congo, Mozambique, Angola, Portuguese, Guinea, South Africa, Venezuela, Colombia, Guatemala, Nicaragua, Panama, Peru, Honduras, Brazil and Argentina. This shows that the struggle against U.S. imperialism is developing into an intense front, with an increasing impetus. Like the Congolese patriots who affirmed their "determination to turn the Congo into a grave for U.S. imperialism", the peoples of many Asian, African and Latin American Countries, victims of U.S. aggression, will turn their homelands into burying grounds for the U.S. brigands, the aggressors and warmongers, in order to reconquer their national independence and freedom in many places.

In the flames of the struggle, the solidarity allying the peoples of Asia, Africa and Latin America is being strengthened. Slogans of support for the Vietnamese, the Cuban and the Congolese peoples, etc., have indeed become slogans of united struggle of the national independence movement and of the world's peoples. The U.S. imperialists in vain endeavoured to divide and sabotage the world people's anti-imperialist front. The 21st Conference of Non-Aligned Countries in Cairo, the Preparatory Meeting for the 2nd Afro-Asian Conference, the Indochinese Peoples' Conference held in Phnom Penh, raised their voices in unison to condemn the U.S. imperialists, express their determination to support the peoples struggling against American aggression, and express their resolute opposition to the imperialists' agents of all kinds, such as the Tshonibe clique.

Due to the U.S. imperialists' frenzied activities, Southeast Asia has become the scene of bitter struggle, a key point of the immense front of the world's peoples against U.S. imperialism. This movement is gaining both in magnitude and strength, and reaching high degrees of development in many countries: Viet Nam, Laos, Cambodia, Indonesia, etc. It is emerging in U.S. satellite countries such as Thailand and the Philippines. The Southeast Asian peoples are doing their utmost to strengthen their solidarity . . . in order to deal ever more decisive blows to the U.S. imperialists . . . ; they are actively contributing to the cause of independence, peace and social progress of the peoples of the world.

As a consequence of the powerful and unrelenting offensive of the national liberation movement in Asian, African and Latin American countries, the rear of imperialism is disintegrating, contradictions within the imperialist camp are deepening, further conditions are created for the development of the worker's movement in capitalist countries. At the same time, this movement constitutes a great support for the building of socialism and communism in the socialist camp, and an important contribution to the preservation of world peace.

In capitalist countries, the struggle against the arms race, for a better life, for democratic rights, is gaining momentum. In the United States itself, jointly with the struggle for their vital interests, the workers and labouring people wage a determined fight to put an end to racial discrimination against the Black people, and to oppose the U.S. policy of armed aggression in Viet Nam. With the participation of millions and millions of people and with an ever stronger impetus, the struggle in capitalist countries for peace and democracy is effective in checking and pushing back the imperialist schemes of aggression and war. This struggle also constitutes a great support for the socialist camp and the national liberation movement in the world.

While the forces of socialism, national liberation, peace and democracy are powerfully and continuously developing, imperialism headed by U.S. imperialism is going deeper into the third stage of the general crisis of capitalism and it is weakening further and further. U.S. imperialism itself encounters more and more difficulties and is becoming more isolated at home and abroad. In the economic field, the United States is facing the prospect of a grave crisis, the number of unemployed (more than five million) remains constant, U.S. economy and finance are so unstable that they are badly shaken by the competition of West European countries in gold and foreign currency. In the political field, at home the Johnson Administration faces mounting protests from the labouring people and a growing struggle of the Black people for political and social rights; abroad, the prestige and influence of the United States are seriously decreasing, as a result of its continuous failures in all parts of the world, especially its bitter failure in the war of aggression in South Viet Nam. The ever-deeper contradictions within the imperialist camp make the United States ever more isolated and embarrassed.

More than ever, U.S. imperialism has laid bare its extremely reactionary and cruel face, exposing itself as the enemy of socialism, national independence and progressive mankind. The more it is cornered, the more frenzied, ferocious and treacherous it becomes. This is its unchanging aggressive, warseeking and reactionary nature. That is why the peoples of the world must further increase their vigilance and resolutely struggle against imperialism, spearheading the fight at U.S. imperialism.

At present, the world situation is rapidly developing in favour of the anti-imperialist struggles. Facts have proved that these struggles have been attacking U.S.-led imperialism, winning successive victories in one area after another, in one field after another. Tempered by struggle, the world's peoples become ever more proficient in the use of every method and form of political, military, economic and cultural struggle against the policy of aggression

and enslavement carried out by imperialism, colonialism and neocolonialism. In this great struggle, the peoples of the world will certainly win complete victory.

The Whole World Support Us

We are standing on the frontline of the world peoples' anti-imperialist struggle. The Viet Nam problem has become a central problem in international political life, a burning issue having a far-reaching impact on the world's peoples.

For more than ten years now, and especially since the U.S. imperialists started brazen acts of war against the Democratic Republic of Viet Nam, the peoples of the fraternal socialist countries, the peoples of the newly-independent countries and peace-loving people throughout the world have constantly been siding with our heroic people in the struggle against aggressive and warlike U.S. imperialism.

The Government of the Soviet Union, the People's Republic of China and the other socialist countries have issued statements severely condemning the U.S. Government for its aggressive war in South Viet Nam, for its brazen air attacks against North Viet Nam, which constitute an aggression against the Democratic Republic of Viet Nam, a member of the socialist camp; they also expressed unreserved support for the just struggle of our entire people, and their determination to do their utmost to help our people (in North and South Viet Nam) in our arduous but certainly victorious struggle. Using varied forms of struggle, such as demonstrations with the participation of millions of people, with a high spirit of struggle, the peoples of the fraternal socialist countries daily express their militant solidarity and their firm determination to support our entire people's just struggle. We are greatly moved and encouraged by this support which makes us believe still more strongly in our final victory.

The governments of many newly-independent countries have raised their voices to demand that the United States stop its aggressive war in South Viet Nam and its acts of war against the Democratic Republic of Viet Nam, and to express deep sympathy and strong support for the just struggle of our people.

Since August 1964, in Cambodia, Laos, Indonesia, Japan, Algeria, Pakistan, Ceylon, Burma, India, Iraq, Guinea, Mali, Ghana, Venezuela, Guatemala . . . millions of people have taken to the streets to demonstrate against U.S. imperialism. They smashed U.S. embassies and U.S. information halls and shouted slogans: "Down with the U.S. imperialists! U.S. imperialists, get out of South Viet Nam!"

In the capitalist countries such as France, Italy, Great Britain, Belgium, Australia, Denmark, Norway, Sweden, Canada, Austria, etc., the movement against the U.S. imperialists' policy of aggression and war in Viet Nam has reached an unprecedented scope and degree, involving millions of people and using varied forms of struggle.

International organizations like the World Peace Council, the World Federation of Trade Unions, the Women's International Democratic Federation, the World Federation of Democratic Youth, the International Association of Democratic Lawyers, the Committee for Solidarity with the People of South Viet Nam, the Afro-Asian Peoples' Solidarity Council, and many others have raised their voices strongly to protest against U.S. aggression in South Viet Nam, and U.S. air attacks against North Viet Nam, to express deep sympathy with our people, and strong support, both moral and material for the patriotic movement in South Viet Nam. The meeting of the International Trade Union Committee for Solidarity with the Workers and People of South Viet Nam and the International Conference for Solidarity with the People of Viet Nam against U.S. Imperialist Aggression and for the Defence of Peace held in Hanoi were warm manifestations of the support extended by the world's peoples to our just struggle.

We are greatly moved and elated by the fact that in recent months, even in the United States, the opposition to the U.S. imperialists' attempt to step up the aggressive war in South Viet Nam and intensify their acts of war against North Viet Nam has been expanding steadily. This movement involves Americans from all walks of life: workers, the youth, women, students, intellectuals clergymen, Congressmen, newsmen.... The forms of struggle are reaching a higher and higher level and becoming more and more varied: statement issued by the American Communist Party to condemn the U.S. aggressive policy in Viet Nam; protest letter sent by 416 American professors and students to U.S. President Johnson; all-night demonstration by 4,200 professors and students; hunger strike by many groups of students and other people; intervention by hundreds of youths to prevent a U.S. ship from carrying troops and weapons to South Viet Nam. We were deeply moved when learning of Mrs. Helga Herz's self immolation by fire to protest against the U.S. policy of war in Viet Nam, thus setting an example of noble sacrifice for peace and friendship between the American and Vietnamese peoples. The American peoples movement of opposition to the "dirty war" in Viet Nam has influenced many U.S. politicians. Never before has the U.S. Government faced such strong opposition by the American people.

The entire Vietnamese people, the National Assembly and the Government of the Democratic Republic of Viet Nam are sincerely grateful to the Governments and peoples of the fraternal socialist countries, to the Governments and peoples of the newly-independent countries, and peace-loving people throughout the world for their sympathy and wholehearted support and assistance. We are resolved to do our utmost to further intensify the patriotic struggle, to uphold our revolutionary cause and at the same time to actively contribute to the cause of peace, national independence, democracy and socialism in the world.

The anti-U.S. struggle of our people has won unprecedented sympathy and support from the world's peoples—the peoples of the fraternal socialist countries and the peoples of the Western countries including the United States. This is a fact of very great international significance. The struggle against U.S. imperialism has become a front comprising the forces of socialism, national liberation, peace and democracy.

In the present epoch, the epoch of transition from capitalism to socialism on a world-wide scale, this then, by its significance, its goal and its achievements, promotes the evolution of world events and influences international life. At the same time, this is a very complex struggle in many forms—military, political, economic and cultural—a struggle which is particularly conspicuous in a number of countries like Viet Nam and Indochina, Berlin, Cuba, the Congo while in other places it is also acute and bitter though less visible.

As they grow weaker and weaker under continual attacks from all sides and are nearing their collapse, the U.S. imperialists are more frantically embarking on the adventurist path of war provocation. That is why the socialist countries and the newly independent countries, the forces of peace and democracy must further unite, and spearhead their struggle at U.S. imperialism to win victories step by step and piece by piece until complete victory.

In this widespread and fierce struggle, the socialist countries extend their full support to the national liberation movement, to the anti-imperialist struggle in all fields—military, political and economic. The socialist countries should also do their utmost to support the newly-independent countries in their struggle against colonialism, old and new, and its camouflaged forms, such as UN intervention.

In their struggle against imperialism, colonialism and neocolonialism, to win and preserve national independence, to build a self-supporting economy, the more the newly-independent countries receive effective support and assistance in all fields from the socialist camp, the greater are their abilities to struggle powerfully and resolutely to the end in order to develop along the non-capitalist path, in conformity with their peoples' aspirations.

Our Foreign Policy

Obviously the peoples of the world are more and more united in their struggle against the aggressive and warlike U.S. imperialists, to defend peace, national independence, democracy and socialism. The Vietnamese people, from North to South, in solidarity with the world's peoples, are determined to struggle against U.S.

imperialism in their own territory and in Asia, Africa and Latin America. That is why in the recent years, the foreign policy of the Democratic Republic of Viet Nam has scored important successes. The whole world is warmly supporting the just and certainly victorious struggle of the Vietnamese people. Doubly significant is the fact that since the U.S. imperialists staged an act of war against the northern part of our country on August 5, 1964, the Republic of Indonesia, the United Arab Republic, Tanzania, . . . and Ghana have established diplomatic relations with the Democratic Republic of Viet Nam. We are happy to see the international status of our country enhanced day by day. These achievements testify to the correctness of our foreign policy. More than ever, we must now spearhead our struggle at the U.S. imperialists, resolutely isolate them and defeat them. We must make great efforts to fan ever stronger and more effective international sympathy and support for our people's patriotic struggle against U.S. aggression.

In response to the warm feelings of the world's peoples, we will contribute all the more actively to the strengthening and expansion of the world peoples' front against the aggressive and war-seeking U.S. imperialists.

We will always struggle together with the peoples of the fraternal socialist countries for the consolidation of the unity of the socialist camp on the basis of Marxism-Leninism and proletarian internationalism, in defence of the socialist camp and world peace, against the manoeuvres of U.S.-led imperialism.

We warmly hail the victory scored by the Chinese people and their Liberation Army in checking the provocative acts of the U.S. imperialists and the Chang Kai-shek reactionary clique. We resolutely support the Chinese people's struggle for the liberation of Taiwan, an integral part of the territory of the People's Republic of China.

We resolutely support the Korean people who are holding firm at the eastern outpost of the socialist camp, and are heroically struggling against the U.S. imperialist aggressors to drive them out of South Korea and peacefully reunify their country.

We resolutely support the German Democratic Republic and the socialist countries members of the Warsaw Treaty in the struggle against the claims of the U.S. imperialists and the West German revanchists for a revision of postwar borders and for the supply of nuclear weapons to West Germany. We resolutely oppose all perfidious plots of the imperialist countries and the West German revanchists, like subversion, peaceful evolution, which create a grave danger for peace and security in Europe and the world.

We resolutely support the heroic Cuban people who are carrying out a staunch struggle against U.S. imperialist aggression and holding aloft the anti-U.S. imperialist banner in the Western Hemisphere. We resolutely support the legitimate 5-point demand put forward by Premier Fidel Castro to ensure the sovereignty, national independence and territorial integrity of the Republic of Cuba.

We resolutely support the peoples of Asia, Africa and Latin America in their struggle for recovering and preserving national independence. We are confident that the holding of the Second Afro-Asian Conference in June 1965 will make an important contribution to the strengthening of Afro-Asian solidarity against imperialism, colonialism and neocolonialism.

We warmly hail the recent victories of the Lao patriotic forces and resolutely support the Lao people in their struggle against U.S. imperialism and its henchmen in order to safeguard the 1962 Geneva Agreement on Laos, the Tripartite National Union Government, and peace and neutrality for Laos. We reaffirm once again our support for the reconvening of the international conference without any preconditions to ensure the implementation of the 1962 Geneva Agreement on Laos.

We resolutely support the just struggle waged by the Cambodian people, under the clearsighted leadership of their Head of State, Prince Norodom Sihanouk, against brazen provocations by the U.S. imperialists and their henchmen, in order to defend the sovereignty, independence, neutrality, and territorial integrity of Cambodia. We fully support the proposal of the Cambodian Royal Government for the holding of an international conference to guarantee the peace, neutrality and territorial integrity of Cambodia.

We warmly welcome and support the resolutions of the Indochinese Peoples' Conference held in Phnom Penh last March. This historic conference opened an era of consolidation of the fraternal solidarity among the peoples of Viet Nam, Cambodia and Laos in their common struggle against the U.S. imperialists, to defend national independence, peace and security in this part of the world. The Democratic Republic of Viet Nam has made and will make every effort to develop good-neighbour relations with the Kingdoms of Cambodia and Laos on the basis of the principles of peaceful co-existence, respect for each other's territorial integrity and sovereignty, nonaggression, non-interference in each other's internal affairs, equality and mutual benefit, and peaceful co-existence.

We resolutely support the Indonesian people who under the clearsighted leadership of President Sukarno, are valiantly struggling to crush Malaysia, an offspring of U.S.-British imperialism. We resolutely support the people of North Kalimantan who are valiantly struggling for freedom and independence. We warmly approve and support the decision taken by the Government of the Republic of Indonesia to withdraw from the UNO and the endeavours made by the Indonesian Government and people in the struggle to defend national independence and to build a self-supporting economy.

We warmly hail the Japanese people who, under the leadership of the Japanese Communist Party, are undauntedly struggling against the U.S. imperialists and the Japanese monopoly capitalists, with a view to building an independent, democratic, peaceful, neutral and prosperous Japan and smashing the U.S. imperialists' scheme in the illegal conclusion of a Japan–South Korea treaty which is aimed at pushing ahead the manoeuvre for the founding of the NEATO aggressive bloc.

We resolutely support the valiant struggle for liberation of the Congolese (Leopoldville) people and other African peoples against the U.S. imperialists and their henchmen, and are confident that this struggle will gain strength and will win glorious victory.

We fully sympathize with and support the valiant struggle of the peoples of the Arab countries against the collusion of U.S. imperialism and West Germany with their Israeli stooges to threaten the national independence and security of these countries.

We resolutely support the ever-widening struggle of the peoples of Venezuela, Colombia, Guatemala and other Latin American countries against U.S. imperialism, to drive the U.S. aggressors out of that part of the Western Hemisphere, their very "backyard", thus making an important contribution to the struggle against U.S. imperialism in the world.

Our Objectives

We often say that the revolutionary cause of the Vietnamese people is closely linked to that of the world's peoples. More than ever this correct view has now been eloquently illustrated by facts. The Vietnamese people are struggling against the U.S. imperialist aggressors, in the interests of their own revolutionary cause, and also of socialism, of the national liberation movement and world peace. On the other hand, the peoples of the socialist countries, newly-independent countries and capitalist countries and peace-loving people the world over are extending us wholehearted support and assistance because victory over the U.S. aggressors in the Viet Nam battlefield not only benefits our people but also peace, national independence, democracy and socialism in the world.

Therefore the great international obligation of our people is, first of all, to fight resolutely to defeat the U.S. imperialist aggressors in our country. At the same time, we should do our best to give more information and better explanation about our struggle to the governments and peoples of other countries and to the international organizations. . . .

The content and aim of this information and explanation work is to tell the truth about the U.S. imperialists' policy of aggression and war and the just struggle of our people, our certain victory and its cause.

This task must be well done, the more so as among the people all over the world who sympathize with and support our cause, many want to know more about our country's situation and our people's struggle. On the other hand, the U.S. imperialists are using every possible means to deceive world opinion, to create misunderstanding and confusion about very simple and clear facts. They are even so perfidious as to mix up wrong and right, calling black white; for instance they say that if they extend the war to the North, this is because the Democratic Republic of Viet Nam has provoked the liberation struggle in the South.

We must in time strongly and sharply expose the U.S. aggressors as a thief saying "Stop thief". We should arouse the world peoples' vigilance to these cunning tricks of the U.S. corsairs. One has to be careful when bandits speak of humanity and justice; they are only trying to enter one's house without having to break the door.

We think that the world's people must be vigilant when President Johnson speaks of coming back to the 1954 Geneva Agreements on Viet Nam! This is really ridiculous! Everybody knows that U.S. imperialism is the enemy of the Geneva Agreements, that the U.S. imperialists and their Saigon lackeys never officially recognized these Agreements, and even refused to officially recognize the International Commission for Supervision and Control of the implementation of the Geneva Agreements. At this very moment, they are more brazenly than ever trampling underfoot the Geneva Agreements on Viet Nam. Nor have they ever observed the 1954 Geneva Agreement on Cambodia and the 1954 and 1962 Geneva Agreements on Laos, and they are now stubbornly opposing the reconvening of a Geneva-type conference on Cambodia and Laos.

The U.S. imperialists are now compelled to speak of the Geneva Agreements on Viet Nam, but they do so only to distort completely the basic principles of the Agreements in an attempt to further their scheme of permanent partition of our country, considering the North and the South as two separate countries. For their part, our Government and people have always been struggling to preserve the Geneva Agreements on Viet Nam as well as those on Cambodia and Laos which we consider as the legal basis of the inalienable and sacred national rights of the three fraternal peoples. President Johnson's speech of April 7, 1965 contains a series of irreconcilable contradictions between the misleading words and the criminal deeds of the U.S. Government in Viet Nam:

1. In his speech, President Johnson talked about peace, about ending the war, and "unconditional discussions". But meanwhile the U.S. Government is intensifying the aggressive war in the South, and extending the war to the North. . . .

2. President Johnson talked a lot about an "Independent" South Viet Nam "free from outside interference, tied to no alliance", "a

military base for no foreign country". But it is the U.S. imperialists who are sticking to South Viet Nam at all costs, bringing in more and more U.S. combat units, and staging attacks on the North precisely in an attempt to cling to the South. It is as clear as daylight that the U.S. Government is the aggressor in South Viet Nam, yet, it has the cheek to slanderously accuse the North of "aggression" in the South!

President Johnson himself stated in his speech: "We will not withdraw either openly or under the cloak of a meaningless agreement!" This impudent assertion exposes the whole of U.S. policy with regard to Viet Nam; this is a challenge to world public opinion.

3. President Johnson also hypocritically talked about economic development, raising the living standards, and about earmarking to this end one million dollars in an attempt to lure the Southeast Asian peoples. But the fact is that the U.S. imperialists are sowing the horrors of war every day in Viet Nam, Laos and other places, committing countless crimes, and even using toxic gases not only in military operations but also to stamp out the struggle of the people in towns and cities.

4. President Johnson threatened to continue using force, determined to fight and to win, they do not fear any but this does not make us flinch. The Vietnamese people are not afraid of difficulty or any enemy. The U.S. imperialists are being defeated, and will certainly suffer complete defeat.

In view of the pressure of public opinion in the United States and the world for the U.S. Government to withdraw its troops from South Viet Nam, and to stop its acts of war against the Democratic Republic of Viet Nam, President Johnson has had to resort to a demagogic language, which is a mere trick, a deceitful manoeuvre aimed at misleading public opinion, and soothing the ever-broader and stronger opposition in the United States and in the world to the aggressive war in Viet Nam.

That is the reason why the Vietnamese people and the world's peoples must heighten their watchfulness in the face of this ignominious trick: to talk about peace and negotiation with a view to intensifying the war, and also to slandering others as bellicose!

It is the unswerving policy of the Government of the Democratic Republic of Viet Nam to strictly respect the 1954 Geneva Agreements on Viet Nam, and to correctly implement their basic provisions as embodied in the following points:

1. Recognition of the basic national rights of the Vietnamese people: peace, independence, sovereignty, unity and territorial integrity. According to the Geneva Agreements, the U.S. Government must withdraw from South Viet Nam all U.S. troops, military personnel and weapons of all kinds, dismantle all U.S. military

bases there, cancel its "military alliance" with South Viet Nam. It must end its policy of intervention and aggression in South Viet Nam. According to the Geneva Agreements, the U.S. Government must stop its acts of war against North Viet Nam, end definitely all encroachments on the territory and sovereignty of the Democratic Republic of Viet Nam.

2. Pending the peaceful reunification of Viet Nam, while Viet Nam is still temporarily divided into two zones, the military provisions of the 1954 Geneva Agreements on Viet Nam must be strictly respected: the two zones must refrain from joining any military alliance with foreign countries; there must be no foreign military bases, troops, and military personnel in their respective territories.

3. The affairs of South Viet Nam must be settled by the South Vietnamese people themselves, in accordance with the proclamations of the South Viet Nam National Front for Liberation, without any foreign interference.

4. The peaceful reunification of Viet Nam is to be settled by the Vietnamese people in both zones, without any foreign interference.

This stand will certainly enjoy the approval and support of all peace- and justice-loving governments and peoples in the world.

The Government of the Democratic Republic of Viet Nam is of the view that the above-explained stand is the basis for the soundest political settlement of the Viet Nam question. If this basis is recognized, favorable conditions will be created for the peaceful settlement of the Viet Nam question and it will be possible to consider the reconvention of an international conference along the pattern of the 1954 Geneva Conference on Viet Nam.

The Government of the Democratic Republic of Viet Nam declares that any approach contrary to the above stand is inappropriate, any approach tending to secure a U.N. intervention in Viet Nam's affairs is also inappropriate because such approaches are basically at variance with the 1954 Geneva Agreements of Viet Nam.

On September 2, 1945, President Ho Chi Minh solemnly proclaimed our country's independence before our people and the peoples of the world. He said, "Viet Nam has the right to enjoy freedom and independence and has actually become a free and independent country. The entire Vietnamese people are determined to devote all their moral and physical strength, their lives and property to the preservation of this freedom and independence."

At present, when the U.S. imperialists are intensifying the aggressive war in the South, brazenly launching air attacks on the North, and violating the territory of the Democratic Republic of Viet

Nam, the Proclamation of Independence and President Ho Chi Minh's Appeal resound all the more deeply in the hearts of our people and stimulate all of us to "devote all our moral and physical strength, our lives and property" to the preservation of freedom and independence in the North, to the recovery of freedom and independence in the South and to eventually achieving peaceful reunification of the country.

The flames of hatred are burning in our hearts! The entire Vietnamese people are determined to fight more vigorously and valiantly than ever for the beloved Fatherland: to defend the Democratic Republic of Viet Nam, homeland of socialism in our country, to liberate the South, to sweep all the invaders out of our territory, so that our land may become again green, our sky again bright and our people from the Red River basin to the Mekong delta may be reunited at an early date "under the same roof." How beautiful and splendid our beloved Fatherland will be then!

U.S. aggressors, beware! During the many thousand years of the history of the Vietnamese nation, each major trial was always followed by a new prodigious growth of our people who defeated the aggressors and consolidated the country. Now more than ever our hearts are filled with national pride, deep attachment to our homeland and affection for our compatriots. Each of us is a staunch fighter, determined to fight to the end in a self-sacrificing spirit, to win a great victory in the patriotic struggle against the U.S. aggressors, to fulfil our internationalist duty toward the peoples of the socialist countries and of the world, and to write down the most glorious pages in the glorious history of the Vietnamese nation!

In these brave hours, we feel all the closer to our Southern brothers. Our Fatherland is very proud of the undaunted South and of its heroic sons and daughters who have been fighting with the utmost gallantry, who are worthy of the title of "Brass Citadel of the Fatherland", and who have recorded resounding feats which give international glory to the Vietnamese people! The people of the North pledge to be worthy of the expectations and confidence of their Southern compatriots, to do their best in production and fighting to develop the economy and strengthen national defence, to defend the North and to extend all-out support to the liberation of the South.

Dear compatriots! Under the glorious banner of the Party and President Ho Chi Minh, let us steadily march forward as the victors, determined to defeat the U.S. imperialist aggressors, build a peaceful, reunified, independent, democratic, prosperous and strong Viet Nam, and contribute to the defence of the socialist camp and of peace in Southeast Asia and the world.

Source: Pham Van Dong, *Selected Writings* (Hanoi: Foreign Languages Publishing House, 1977), 90–158.

155. Robert McNamara, Secretary of Defense: Memorandum for President Lyndon Johnson, April 21, 1965 [Excerpt]

Introduction

U.S. secretary of defense Robert McNamara and other administration officials met in Honolulu on April 20, 1965, to discuss Vietnam policy and assess military requirements with Military Assistance Command, Vietnam (MACV), commander General William Westmoreland; U.S. ambassador to the Republic of Vietnam (RVN, South Vietnam) Maxwell Taylor; and commander in chief, U.S. Pacific Command, Admiral Ulysses Sharp. Here McNamara sums up that meeting for President Lyndon Johnson and details the U.S. forces that should be sent to Vietnam to bolster U.S. marines and troops from the Republic of Korea (ROK, South Korea) already there. McNamara reports that the conferees are in agreement that after a span of as long as a "year or two," the demonstrated military failure of Communist forces in South Vietnam will break their will to continue the struggle and bring about an acceptable political outcome.

Primary Source

Mr. William Bundy, Mr. McNaughton and I met with Ambassador Taylor, General Wheeler, Admiral Sharp and General Westmoreland in Honolulu on Tuesday, April 20. Following is my report of that meeting:

1. None of them expects the DRV/VC to capitulate, or come to a position acceptable to us, in less than six months. This is because they believe that a settlement will come as much or more from VC failure in the South as from DRV pain in the North, and that it will take more than six months, perhaps a year or two, to demonstrate VC failure in the South.

2. With respect to strikes against the North, they all agree that the present tempo is about right, that sufficient increasing pressure is provided by repetition and continuation. All of them envisioned a strike program continuing at least six months, perhaps a year or more, avoiding the Hanoi–Haiphong–Phuc Yen areas during that period. There might be fewer fixed targets, or more restrikes, or more armed reconnaissance missions. Ambassador Taylor stated what appeared to be a shared view, that it is important not to "kill the hostage" by destroying the North Vietnamese assets inside the "Hanoi do-nut." They all believe that the strike program is essential to our campaign—both psychologically and physically—but that it cannot be expected to do the job alone. They all considered it very important that strikes against the North be continued during any talks.

3. None of them sees a dramatic improvement in the South in the immediate future. Their strategy for "victory" over time, is to break the will of the DRV/VC by denying them victory. Ambassador Taylor put it in terms of a demonstration of Communist impotence, which will lead eventually to a political solution. They see slow improvement in the South, but all emphasized the critical importance of holding on and avoiding—for psychological and morale reasons—a spectacular defeat of GVN or US forces. And they all suspect that the recent VC lull is but the quiet before a storm.

4. To bolster the GVN forces while they are building up, they all recommend the following deployments in addition to the 2,000 Koreans and 33,500 US troops already in-country (including the 4 Marine battalions at Danang-Hue):

1 US Army brigade (3 btn) at Bien Hoa/Vung Tau
    4,000 closing 1 May

3 US Marine air sqs + 3 btns at Chu Lai
    6,200 closing 5 May

1 Australian btn at Vun Tau
    1,250 closing 21 May

1 US Army brigade (3 btn) at Qui Nhon/Nha Trang
    4,000 closing 15 Jn.

1 Korean RCT (3 btn) at Quang Ngai
    4,000 closing 15 Jn.

Augmentation of various existing forces
    11,000 already approved

Logistics troops for previously approved force level
    7,000 already approved

Logistics troops for above enclaves and possible 3 divisions
    16,000 not yet approved

TOTAL: US 13 btns 82,000
    ROK & ANZAC 4 btns 7,250

5. Possible later deployments, not recommended now, include a US AirMobile division (9 btns-15,800) to Pleiku/Kontum, and I Corps HQ (1,200) to Nha Trang; and even later, the remainder of the Korean division (6 btns-14,500) to Quang Ngai, and the remainder of the Marine Expeditionary Force (3 btns-24,800) to Danang.

> **Source:** *Foreign Relations of the United States, 1964–1968: Vietnam, January–June 1965*, Vol. 2 (Washington, DC: U.S. Government Printing Office, 1996), 574–575.

156. President Lyndon Johnson: Message to Ambassador Maxwell Taylor, May 10, 1965

Introduction

U.S. president Lyndon Johnson frequently expressed a desire for peace. In early May 1965 he called the first of several halts in the U.S. bombing of the Democratic Republic of Vietnam (DRV, North Vietnam). Here he explains to ambassador to the Republic of Vietnam (RVN, South Vietnam) Maxwell Taylor—himself an advocate of the bombing program—that the planned suspension is designed, should Hanoi reject the demarche, to build support in the United States and abroad for stronger military steps.

Primary Source

I have learned from Bob McNamara that nearly all ROLLING THUNDER operations for this week can be completed by Wednesday noon, Washington time. This fact and the days of Buddha's birthday seem to me to provide an excellent opportunity for a pause in air attacks which might go into next week and which I could use to good effect with world opinion.

My plan is not to announce this brief pause but simply to call it privately to the attention of Moscow and Hanoi as soon as possible and tell them that we shall be watching closely to see whether they respond in any way. My current plan is to report publicly after the pause ends on what we have done.

Could you see Quat [Prime Minister Phan Huy Quat] right away on Tuesday and see if you can persuade him to concur in this plan. I would like to associate him with me in this decision if possible, but I would accept a simple concurrence or even willingness not to oppose my decision. In general, I think it important that he and I should get together in such matters, but I have no desire to embarrass him if it is politically difficult for him to join actively in a pause over Buddha's birthday.

[Words illegible] noted your [words illegible] but do you yet have your appreciation of the political effect in Saigon of acting around Buddha's birthday. From my point of view it is a great advantage to use Buddha's birthday to mask the first days of the pause here, if it is at all possible in political terms for Quat. I assume we could undertake to enlist the Archbishop and the Nuncio in calming the Catholics.

You should understand that my purpose in this plan is to begin to clear a path either toward restoration of peace or toward increased military action, depending upon the reaction of the Communists. We have amply demonstrated our determination and our commitment in the last two months, and I now wish to gain some flexibility.

I know that this is a hard assignment on short notice, but there is no one who can bring it off better.

I have kept this plan in the tightest possible circle here and wish you to inform no one but Alexis Johnson. After I have your report of Quat's reaction, I will make a final decision and it will be communicated promptly to senior officers concerned.

Source: *The Pentagon Papers as Published by the New York Times* (New York: Quadrangle, 1971), 456–457.

157. Message from the U.S. Government to the North Vietnamese Government on the Bombing Pause, May 11, 1965

Introduction

On May 11, 1965, the U.S. government announced a halt in the bombing of the Democratic Republic of Vietnam (DRV, North Vietnam) to take effect at noon Washington time on May 12 and running into the next week, with the stated goal of jump-starting peace negotiations with North Vietnam. After a week of no discernible change, on May 18 the air strikes resumed.

Primary Source

The highest authority in this Government has asked me to inform Hanoi that there will be no air attacks on North Viet-Nam for a period beginning at noon, Washington time, Wednesday, May 12, and running into next week.

In this decision the United States Government has taken account of repeated suggestions from various quarters, including public statements by Hanoi representatives, that there can be no progress toward peace while there are air attacks on North Viet-Nam. The United States Government remains convinced that the underlying cause of trouble in Southeast Asia is armed action against the people and Government of South Vietnam by forces whose actions can be decisively affected from North Vietnam. The United States will be very watchful to see whether in this period of pause there are significant reductions in such armed actions by such forces. (The United States must emphasize that the road toward the end of armed attacks against the people and Government of Vietnam is the only road which will permit the Government of Vietnam (and the Government of the United States) to bring a permanent end to their attacks on North Vietnam.) [Words illegible] be misunderstood as an indication of weakness, and it is therefore necessary for me to point out that if this pause should be misunderstood in this fashion, by any party, it would be necessary to demonstrate

more clearly than ever, after the pause ended, that the United States is determined not to accept aggression without reply in Vietnam. Moreover, the United States must point out that the decision to end air attacks for this limited trial period is one which it must be free to reverse if at any time in the coming days there should be actions by the other side in Vietnam which required immediate reply.

But my Government is very hopeful that there will be no such misunderstanding and that this first pause in the air attacks may meet with a response which will permit further and more extended suspension of this form of military action in the expectation of equally constructive actions by the other side in the future.

Source: *The Pentagon Papers: The Defense Department History of United States Decisionmaking on Vietnam,* Vol. 3. Senator Gravel edition (Boston: Beacon, 1971), 369.

158. George Ball, Undersecretary of State: Memorandum for President Lyndon Johnson, July 1, 1965

Introduction

Undersecretary of State George W. Ball was one of the few dissenting voices in the Lyndon Johnson administration concerning escalation of the war. In this memorandum to Johnson, Ball urges the president to accept a compromise settlement in Vietnam in order to avoid a "long-term catastrophe."

Primary Source

(1) *A Losing War:* The South Vietnamese are losing the war to the Viet Cong. No one can assure you that we can beat the Viet Cong or even force them to the conference table on our terms, no matter how many hundred thousand white, foreign (U.S.) troops we deploy.

No one has demonstrated that a white ground force of whatever size can win a guerrilla war—which is at the same time a civil war between Asians—in jungle terrain in the midst of a population that refuses cooperation to the white forces (and the South Vietnamese) and thus provides a great intelligence advantage to the other side. Three recent incidents vividly illustrate this point: (a) the sneak attack on the Da Nang Air Base which involved penetration of a defense parameter guarded by 9,000 Marines. This raid was possible only because of the cooperation of the local inhabitants; (b) the B-52 raid that failed to hit the Viet Cong who had obviously been tipped off; (c) the search and destroy mission of the 173rd Air Borne Brigade which spent three days looking for the Viet Cong, suffered 23 casualties, and never made contact with the enemy who had obviously gotten advance word of their assignment.

(2) *The Question to Decide:* Should we limit our liabilities in South Vietnam and try to find a way out with minimal long-term costs?

The alternative—no matter what we may wish it to be—is almost certainly a protracted war involving an open-ended commitment of U.S. forces, mounting U.S. casualties, no assurance of a satisfactory solution, and a serious danger of escalation at the end of the road.

(3) *Need for a Decision Now:* So long as our forces are restricted to advising and assisting the South Vietnamese, the struggle will remain a civil war between Asian peoples. Once we deploy substantial numbers of troops in combat it will become a war between the U.S. and a large part of the population of South Vietnam, organized and directed from North Vietnam and backed by the resources of both Moscow and Peiping.

The decision you face now, therefore, is crucial. Once large numbers of U.S. troops are committed to direct combat, they will begin to take heavy casualties in a war they are ill-equipped to fight in a non-cooperative if not downright hostile countryside.

Once we suffer large casualties, we will have started a well-nigh irreversible process. Our involvement will be so great that we cannot—without national humiliation—stop short of achieving our complete objectives. Of the two possibilities I think humiliation would be more likely than the achievement of our objectives—even after we have paid terrible costs.

(4) *Compromise Solution:* Should we commit U.S. manpower and prestige to a terrain so unfavorable as to give a very large advantage to the enemy—or should we seek a compromise settlement which achieves less than our stated objectives and thus cut our losses while we still have the freedom of maneuver to do so.

(5) *Costs of a Compromise Solution:* The answer involves a judgment as to the cost to the U.S. of such a compromise settlement in terms of our relations with the countries in the area of South Vietnam, the credibility of our commitments, and our prestige around the world. In my judgment, if we act before we commit a substantial U.S. truce [*sic*] to combat in South Vietnam we can, by accepting some short-term costs, avoid what may well be a long-term catastrophe. I believe we attended [*sic*] grossly to exaggerate the costs involved in a compromise settlement. An appreciation of probable costs is contained in the attached memorandum.

(6) With these considerations in mind, I strongly urge the following program:

(a) Military Program
   (1) Complete all deployments already announced—15 battalions—but decide not to go beyond a total of 72,000 men represented by this figure.

   (2) Restrict the combat role of the American forces to the June 19 announcement, making it clear to General Westmoreland that this announcement is to be strictly construed.
   (3) Continue bombing in the North but avoid the Hanoi-Haiphong area and any targets nearer to the Chinese border than those already struck.
(b) Political Program
   (1) In any political approaches so far, we have been the prisoners of whatever South Vietnamese government that was momentarily in power. If we are ever to move toward a settlement, it will probably be because the South Vietnamese government pulls the rug out from under us and makes its own deal or because we go forward quietly without advance prearrangement with Saigon.
   (2) So far we have not given the other side a reason to believe there is any flexibility in our negotiating approach. And the other side has been unwilling to accept what in their terms is complete capitulation.
   (3) Now is the time to start some serious diplomatic feelers looking towards a solution based on some application of a self-determination principle.
   (4) I would recommend approaching Hanoi rather than any of the other probable parties, the NLF,—or Peiping. Hanoi is the only one that has given any signs of interest in discussion. Peiping has been rigidly opposed. Moscow has recommended that we negotiate with Hanoi. The NLF has been silent.
   (5) There are several channels to the North Vietnamese, but I think the best one is through their representative in Paris, Mai van Bo. Initial feelers of Bo should be directed toward a discussion both of the four points we have put forward and the four points put forward by Hanoi as a basis for negotiation. We can accept all but one of Hanoi's four points, and hopefully we should be able to agree on some ground rules for serious negotiations—including no preconditions.
   (6) If the initial feelers lead to further secret, exploratory talks, we can inject the concept of self-determination that would permit the Viet Cong some hope of achieving some of their political objectives through local elections or some other device.
   (7) The contact on our side should be handled through a nongovernmental cutout (possibly a reliable newspaper man who can be repudiated).
   (8) If progress can be made at this level a basis can be laid for a multinational conference. At some point, obviously, the government of South Vietnam will have to be brought on board, but I would postpone this step until after a substantial feeling out of Hanoi.

(7) Before moving to any formal conference we should be prepared to agree once the conference is started:

    (a) The U.S. will stand down its bombing of the North

    (b) The South Vietnamese will initiate no offensive operations in the South, and

    (c) The DRV will stop terrorism and other aggressive action against the South.

(8) The negotiations at the conference should aim at incorporating our understanding with Hanoi in the form of a multinational agreement guaranteed by the U.S., the Soviet Union and possibly other parties, and providing for an international mechanism to supervise its execution.

Source: *The Pentagon Papers: The Defense Department History of United States Decisionmaking on Vietnam,* Vol. 4. Senator Gravel edition (Boston: Beacon, 1971), 615–617.

159. Robert McNamara, Secretary of Defense: Memorandum for President Lyndon Johnson, July 20, 1965 [Excerpt]

Introduction

In the spring of 1965, the Lyndon Johnson administration dramatically escalated the Vietnam War with the infusion of significant numbers of U.S. Army ground troops. Here Secretary of Defense Robert S. McNamara points out to President Johnson that a "favorable outcome" in the war is more likely through military force than negotiations. McNamara recommends the dispatch of additional U.S. troops to Vietnam in order to bring U.S. strength there to about 175,000 men, with the deployment of up to another 100,000 early in 1966. Ominously, McNamara states that the deployment of yet additional forces "is possible but will depend on developments." On July 18 President Johnson announced that U.S. troops strength in the Republic of Vietnam (RVN, South Vietnam) would increase from 75,000 to 125,000 men. The Democratic Republic of Vietnam (DRV, North Vietnam) responded by increasing its own troop strength in South Vietnam.

Primary Source

SUBJECT: Recommendations of additional deployments to Vietnam

1. *Introduction.* Our object in Vietnam is to create conditions for a favorable outcome by demonstrating to the VC/DRV that the odds are against their winning. We want to create these conditions, if possible, without causing the war to expand into one with China or the Soviet Union and in a way which preserves support of the

American people and, hopefully, of our allies and friends. The following assessments, made following my trip to Vietnam with Ambassador-designate Lodge and General Wheeler are my own and are addressed to the achievement of that object. My specific recommendations appear in Paragraph 5; they are concurred in by Ambassador Taylor, Ambassador-designate Lodge, Ambassador Johnson, General Wheeler, Admiral Sharp and General Westmoreland. I have neither asked for nor obtained their concurrence in other portions of the paper.

2. *Favorable outcome:* In my view, a "favorable outcome" for purposes of these assessments and recommendations has nine fundamental elements:

    (a) VC stop attacks and drastically reduce incidents of terror and sabotage.

    (b) DRV reduces infiltration to a trickle, with some reasonably reliable method of our obtaining confirmation of this fact.

    (c) US/GVN stop bombing of North Vietnam.

    (d) GVN stays independent (hopefully pro-US, but possibly genuinely neutral).

    (e) GVN exercises governmental functions over substantially all of South Vietnam.

    (f) Communists remain quiescent in Laos and Thailand.

    (g) DRV withdraws PAVN forces and other North Vietnamese infiltrators (not regroupees) from South Vietnam.

    (h) VC/NLF transform from a military to a purely political organization.

    (i) US combat forces (not advisors or AID) withdraw.

[A] favorable outcome could include also arrangements regarding elections, relations between North and South Vietnam, participation in peace-keeping by international forces, membership for North and South Vietnam in the UN, and so on. The nine fundamental elements can evolve with or without an express agreement and, except for what might be negotiated incidental to a cease-fire, are more likely to evolve without an express agreement than with one. We do not need now to address the question whether ultimately we would settle for something less than the nine fundamentals; because deployment of the forces recommended in paragraph 5 is prerequisite to the achievement of any acceptable settlement, and a decision can be made later, when bargaining becomes a reality, whether to compromise in any particular.

3. *Estimate of the situation.* The situation in South Vietnam is worse than a year ago (when it was worse than a year before that). After a few-months of stalemate, the tempo of the war has quickened. A hard VC push is now on to dismember the nation and to maul the army. The VC main and local forces, reinforced by militia and guerrillas, have the initiative and, with large attacks (some in regimental strength), are hurting ARVN forces badly. The main VC efforts have been in southern I Corps, northern and central II Corps and north of Saigon. The central highlands could well be

lost to the National Liberation Front during this monsoon season. Since June 1, the GVN has been forced to abandon six district capitals; only one has been retaken. US combat troop deployments and US/VNAF strikes against the North have put to rest most South Vietnamese fears that the United States will foresake them, and US/VNAF air strikes in-country have probably shaken VC morale somewhat. Yet the government is able to provide security to fewer and fewer people in less and less territory as terrorism increases. Cities and towns are being isolated as fewer and fewer roads and railroads are usable and power and communications lines are cut.

The economy is deteriorating—the war is disrupting rubber production, rice distribution, Dalat vegetable production and the coastal fishing industry, causing the loss of jobs and income, displacement of people and frequent breakdown or suspension of vital means of transportation and communication; foreign exchange earnings have fallen; and severe inflation is threatened.

The odds are less than even that the Ky government will last out the year. Ky is "executive agent" for a directorate of generals. His government is youthful and inexperienced, but dedicated to a "revolutionary" program. His tenure depends upon unity of the armed forces behind him. If the directorate holds together and the downward trend of the war is halted, the religious and regional factions will probably remain quiescent; otherwise there will be political turbulence and possibly uncoordinated efforts to negotiate settlement with the DRV. The Buddhists, Catholics, out-politicians and business community are "wait-and-seeing;" the VC, while unable alone to generate effective unrest in the cities, can "piggyback" on any anti-government demonstration or cause.

Rural reconstruction (pacification) even in the Hop Tac area around Saigon is making little progress. Gains in IV Corps are being held, but in I and II Corps and adjacent III Corps areas it has lost ground fast since the start of the VC monsoon offensive (300,000 people have been lost to the VC, and tens of thousands of refugees have poured out of these areas).

The Government-to-VC ratio over-all is now only a little better than 3-to-1, and in combat battalions little better than 1.5-to-1. Some ARVN units have been mauled; many are understrength and therefore "conservative." Desertions are at a high rate, and the force build-up has slipped badly. The VC, who are undoubtedly suffering badly too (their losses are very high), now control a South Vietnamese manpower pool of 500,000 to 1 million fighting-age men and reportedly are trying to double their combat strength, largely by forced draft (down to 15-year-olds) in the increasing areas they control. They seem to be able more than to replace their losses.

There are no signs that we have throttled the inflow of supplies for the VC or can throttle the flow while their material needs are as low as they are; indeed more and better weapons have been observed in VC hands, and it is probable that there has been further build-up of North Vietnamese regular units in the I and II Corps areas, with at least three full regiments (all of the 325th Division) there. Nor have our air attacks in North Vietnam produced tangible evidence of willingness on the part of Hanoi to come to the conference table in a reasonable mood. The DRV/VC seem to believe that South Vietnam is on the run and near collapse; they show no signs of settling for less than a complete take-over.

4. *Options open to us.* We must choose among three courses of action with respect to Vietnam all of which involve different probabilities, outcomes and costs:

(a) Cut our losses and withdraw under the best conditions that can be arranged—almost certainly conditions humiliating the United States and very damaging to our future effectiveness on the world scene.

(b) Continue at about the present level, with the US forces limited to say 75,000, holding on and playing for the breaks—a course of action which, because our position would grow weaker, almost certainly would confront us later with a choice between withdrawal and an emergency expansion of forces, perhaps too late to do any good.

(c) Expand promptly and substantially the US military pressure against the Viet Cong in the South and maintain the military pressure against the North Vietnamese in the North while launching a vigorous effort on the political side to lay the groundwork for a favorable outcome by clarifying our objectives and establishing channels of communication. This alternative would stave off defeat in the short run and offer a good chance of producing a favorable settlement in the longer run; at the same time it would imply a commitment to see a fighting war clear through at considerable cost in casualties and material and would make any later decision to withdraw even more difficult and even more costly than would be the case today.

My recommendations in paragraph 5 below are based on the choice of the third alternative (Option c) as the course of action involving the best odds of the best outcome with the most acceptable cost to the United States.

5. *Military recommendations.* There are now 15 US (and 1 Australian) combat battalions in Vietnam; they, together with other combat personnel and non-combat personnel, bring the total US personnel in Vietnam to approximately 75,000.

a. I recommend that the deployment of US ground troops in Vietnam be increased by October to 34 maneuver battalions (or, if the Koreans fail to provide the expected 9 battalions promptly, to 43 battalions). The battalions together with increases in helicopter lift, air squadrons, naval units, air defense, combat support and miscellaneous log support and advisory personnel which I also recommend—would bring the total US personnel in Vietnam to approximately 175,000 (200,000 if we must make up for the Korean failure). It should be understood that the deployment of more men (perhaps 100,000) may be necessary in early 1966, and that the deployment of additional forces thereafter is possible but will depend on developments.

b. I recommend that Congress be requested to authorize the call-up of approximately 235,000 men in the Reserve and National Guard. This number—approximately 125,000 Army, 75,000 Marines, 25,000 Air Force and 10,000 Navy—would provide approximately 36 maneuver battalions by the end of this year. The call-up would be for a two-year period; but the intention would be to release them after one year, by which time they could be relieved by regular forces if conditions permitted.

c. I recommend that the regular armed forces be increased by approximately 375,000 men (approximately 250,000 Army, 75,000 Marines, 25,000 Air Force and 25,000 Navy). This would provide approximately 27 additional maneuver battalions by the middle of 1966. The increase would be accomplished by increasing recruitment, increasing the draft and extending tours of duty of men already in the service.

d. I recommend that a supplemental appropriation of approximately $X for FY 1966 be sought from the Congress to cover the first part of the added costs attributable to the build-up in and for the war in Vietnam. A further supplemental appropriation might be required later in the fiscal year.

It should be noted that in mid-1966 the United States would, as a consequence of the above method of handling the build-up, have approximately 600,000 additional men (approximately 63 additional maneuver battalions) as protection against contingencies.

Source: *The Pentagon Papers: The Defense Department History of United States Decisionmaking on Vietnam,* Vol. 4. Senator Gravel edition (Boston: Beacon, 1971), 619–622.

160. Le Duan: Letter to the Central Office for South Vietnam, November 1965

Introduction

Le Duan was the secretary-general of the Democratic Republic of Vietnam (DRV, North Vietnam) Lao Dong (Workers' Party) and later, following the 1969 death of Ho Chi Minh, became the de facto leader of North Vietnam. As direct U.S. involvement in

the war escalated, many in the North Vietnamese leadership grew concerned about the damage that a war against the United States might do to their efforts to develop North Vietnam's economy and "build socialism" in North Vietnam. For the previous six years, North Vietnamese strategy had walked the delicate tightrope of trying to do as much as possible to win the war in the Republic of Vietnam (RVN, South Vietnam) without provoking a direct U.S. military response. Now that this strategy had failed, the leaders debated whether to revert to a low-level protracted guerrilla struggle or to take on the Americans directly in a concerted effort to win a quick victory. In preparation for a Party Central Committee plenum in December 1965, the Politburo approved a compromise resolution stating that while the overall Communist strategy would continue to be one of "protracted war," a major effort should be made to win a "decisive victory" within a "relatively short period of time." In this November 1965 letter, Lao Dong party first secretary Le Duan—clearly an advocate of trying to win a quick victory—writes to the top Communist commanders in South Vietnam to explain how this might be achieved. In joining those who rejected advice from the Chinese to de-escalate, he maintains that only conventional offensive warfare, as had been practiced against the French, could expel the Americans.

Primary Source

Dear friends,

The Politburo has just met to assess the situation and it has issued a new resolution on South Vietnam.

Below I will discuss a number of specific aspects of a number of issues that could not be completely covered in the framework of the Party resolution.

I

1. First of all, I would like to discuss the new characteristics of the war.

We all agreed unanimously that the reason that the U.S. was forced to send tens of thousands of additional troops into South Vietnam was because of the basic failure of their "special war," and that at the same time their attacks against North Vietnam had also failed. The American introduction of additional troops into South Vietnam further demonstrates their defensive, passive political and military posture, not only in South Vietnam and North Vietnam, but also throughout the world.

With the American dispatch of 150,000–200,000 troops, or perhaps even a few more, to South Vietnam, the war in South Vietnam has shifted into a new phase, and there are also new changes in the character of the war.

At the same time, the American action also raises a whole range of new issues for our side.

When I say that the war now has a new character does not mean that the U.S. has changed its entire political and military scheme in South Vietnam or in all of Vietnam. The American war in South

Vietnam is still a neocolonialist war, but one that is now being conducted with new tactics and with the introduction of additional new forces. MacNamara himself stated this in his statement to the U.S. Armed Services Sub-Committee, when he said: "Even though our tactics have changed, our goals remain the same."

However, the American policy of "escalation" in Vietnam still depends on many factors, such as whether or not their goals change, how the balance of forces between the enemy and our side changes, whether the enemy's domestic and international situation is favorable or not, etc.

As for our side, based on the enemy's basic situation and on our own posture and strength, we still affirm that we can restrict the enemy to fighting just in South Vietnam and we are determined to defeat the enemy on that primary battlefield.

For that reason, in the current situation North Vietnam is still a battlefield where the enemy will continue to carry out a war of destruction [bombing campaign]. The enemy may later increase the intensity of his attacks, but no matter how heavy our losses become, North Vietnam will fight resolutely and will defeat the American war of destruction.

In South Vietnam, we need to correctly assess the current massive introduction of massive numbers of expeditionary soldiers. As I stated above, the reason the U.S. was forced to send 150,000–200,000 troops into South Vietnam was because they were being placed increasingly on the defensive and were suffering increasing failures on many fronts.

However, their action also demonstrates that the U.S. is even more determined to hold on to South Vietnam. The U.S. is gradually realizing that their introduction of expeditionary troops into South Vietnam may not, in the short term at least, lead to the outbreak of a major war that would force them to directly confront the large nations of the socialist bloc. The force directly opposing them continues to be the Vietnamese people. The American imperialists have also realized that if they lose in South Vietnam, not only will they lose to the Vietnamese people, they will also suffer a defeat of worldwide proportions. The Vietnam issue has become an issue of international significance. Our people are now confronting the American imperialists, the leading imperialist power and the most brutal enemy of mankind. The battle our people are fighting is taking place in one of the hot-spot areas of the world, it involves many burning contradictions, and it is the focal point of the struggle between two world forces, the forces of the revolution and the forces of the counterrevolution in the world today. For that reason, our people are now carrying out a sacred national duty while at the same time they are performing a noble international mission.

However, we must see that the U.S. is now pouring hundreds of thousands of troops equipped with modern weapons into South Vietnam at a time when our people's revolutionary war is being waged in an extremely powerful way throughout the country, from Quang Tri to Ca Mau, from the mountain jungles and the rural countryside to the cities, and at a time when the puppet army is being dealt crushing blows and the puppet government is increasingly collapsing. That is why the American imperialists' first hope in sending American troops into South Vietnam is to bolster and support the puppet army and puppet government, to prevent them from quickly disintegrating, and to defend a number of key positions as a precaution against major attacks by our forces.

At the same time, with their increased forces, they will gradually, step by step, begin to counterattack in order to regain the initiative and to create a new posture of strength for their side. However, it is clear that the situation will not allow them to achieve that goal.

The fact is that the U.S. is sending in its troops at a time when we have already deployed our forces throughout all South Vietnam, when our three types of troops [main force, local force, guerrilla] have been formed and taken shape, and when the three strategic areas [mountain jungles, rural countryside, the cities] have been built up and consolidated. Our guerrilla militia and province and district local force soldiers have firm footholds in all areas. Our main force units are now being built into powerful "fists," and they have occupied key strategic locations. Throughout the battlefield, guerrilla warfare has been developed to a high level; we have gained the initiative, and we are now attacking the enemy. For that reason, even if the enemy initially strives to mass his forces to mount a counterattack, he will later be forced to disperse his forces to cope with our attacks and will be forced to return to a defensive posture.

2. With respect to forces, previously the American imperialists were forced to rely primarily on the puppet army, but now the puppet army cannot stand against us on its own. Therefore the enemy has been forced to rely on two strategic forces—U.S. troops and puppet troops—to conduct the war.

Although there are not yet as many American troops as there are puppet troops, with their heavy firepower and their tremendous mobility American troops have become the backbone of the enemy's rapid response forces, and they provide the backing that the puppet army needs. American troops have the important political mission of working to prevent the puppet army and puppet government from disintegrating. At the same time, they are also responsible for occupying strategic areas, maintaining the enemy's posture of strength throughout the battlefield, and gradually beginning to mount counterattacks aimed at destroying our key, hard-core forces.

In spite of all this, however, the puppet army is still a large force, and it has a very important political and military mission, which is to provide support and backing for the puppet government at both the national and the local level. The puppet army has been given the missions of attacking and recapturing those areas the enemy has lost, of patching back together the puppet governmental system that has collapsed, of gaining control of the lowlands, of annihilating our guerrilla and local force units, and of cooperating with U.S. troops in launching large military operations to attack our main force troops in order to regain the initiative.

Based on the changes in the balance of forces and on the enemy's new strategic intentions, we conclude that during the current phase, the war in South Vietnam has the characteristics of both a "limited war" as well as a "special war." While we stress the "limited war" nature, which is a new form that is becoming increasingly exhibited in the conduct of the war, we still must correctly assess the level of importance of the remaining "special war" characteristics of the war, because this second aspect is intimately connected to American neocolonialism.

3. Our assessments presented above were made so that we could lay out strategic guidelines and missions designed at defeating the American political objectives and at defeating their military forces.

Working from the above analysis, we have determined that our immediate combat opponent in South Vietnam is no longer primarily the puppet army, but now it is both American troops *and* the puppet army.

We must continue to destroy and cause the disintegration of the puppet army, and we must view that goal as a basic factor that will enable us to bring about the collapse of the puppet government and to crush one of the Americans' most important sources of strength and support. At the same time, however, we must also defeat the American army and shatter this force that provides the backbone of the enemy's war of aggression so that American troops are no longer strong enough to protect the puppet army and puppet government, meaning that they are no longer strong enough to perform their political mission. At the same time, we must make the Americans realize that even if they send in more troops and further reinforce their expeditionary army, they still will not be able to avoid total defeat.

The dialectical relationship in this matter is that we attack U.S. troops in order to create conditions that will enable us to annihilate puppet troops, and, conversely, we annihilate puppet troops in order to create conditions that will enable us to attack and annihilate American troops. And our goal in annihilating both puppet and American troops is to crush the enemy's military forces, to defeat the political goals of his war of aggression, and to defeat the American military strategy. For that reason, we have set forward the overall requirement that we must defeat the enemy in all three of these areas, and only if we are able to defeat the enemy in all three of these areas will we be able to say that we have defeated this war that has both "limited" and "special" characteristics in its current phase. Naturally, when we attack the enemy, we should attack those elements that are weak first and cause them to disintegrate and collapse first. For that reason, in terms of our combat opponents, we must first aim at annihilating puppet soldiers and causing the disintegration of the puppet army while at the same time trying in every way we can to inflict casualties, erode the strength of, and kill large numbers of American troops in order to create conditions that will enable us to destroy puppet forces and cause the disintegration of the puppet army as quickly as possible. Eroding the strength of and killing American soldiers is essential to enable us to retain the initiative on the battlefield, and this task becomes practical and realistic.

At present, it is important to attack both the American army and the puppet army. We are in complete agreement with Brother Nam Cong [alias used by Vo Chi Cong] and the rest of you on this point.

However, I would like to remind you all of one point: When you make your deployments for battle, you must aim first at destroying puppet military forces first, because within the enemy's military forces at present, the puppet army is the weakest element.

When attacking American troops, we must identify their weak points and attack those weak points. We must attack them in situations when they are weak so that we can annihilate them. As for their strengths, or those situations when they are strong, we must avoid them, temporarily at least. However, this instruction is not absolute; it is not cast in stone. In addition to attacking the weaknesses of the Americans, we must also find effective tactics and effective forms of combat that will enable us to defeat their strengths and will prevent them from being their superiority in technology and weaponry.

As for the missions and capabilities of the various battlefields, we must make the following conclusions and assessments very clear:

In the *mountain jungle battlefields* in general, and specifically in the mountain jungles of Region 5, our important and increasingly primary combat opponent is the *American army.* This is because American troops, and also satellite [allied] troops, are increasingly playing the most important role and are being given the mission of directly confronting our troops in this region. At the same time, in this battlefield we must still place emphasis on attacking puppet military forces, because in the mountain jungle areas, the U.S. still uses puppet troops to defend the towns and province capitals, and sometimes the U.S. uses puppet forces in a number of situations for which U.S. troops are not suited or appropriate.

In the *lowland battlefields,* and primarily in the lowlands of Cochin China, our specific and our most important combat opponent is the *puppet army.*

When we go down to lower levels, when we look at smaller-scale battlefields as well as when looking at specific battles, specific attacks, we must take into consideration whether the location has only American troops or whether it has only puppet troops; or, if the specific area has both American troops and puppet troops, we must take into consideration whether there are more American soldiers or more puppet soldiers, and we must also consider when and how each will make their appearance, consider what each force's tactical mission is, etc., in order to determine which type of soldier, American or puppet, should be the specific battlefield target, and then on that basis we should decide on what tactics we will use.

Although we will base our determination of the exact combat opponent, we will engage on each individual battlefield, and in each individual battle on the specific enemy assignment of responsibilities on individual battlefields and on the relationships the various types of enemy troops have with one another, we still must affirm that we fight American troops in order to be able to fight puppet troops and that an individual battlefield fights the Americans so that other battlefields can fight the puppets. On the other hand, we must also affirm that we fight the puppet army precisely in order to fight the Americans, and that an individual battlefield fights the puppets so that another battlefield can kill the Americans.

II

Now I will turn to our strategic guidelines and intentions, the conditions, the capabilities, and the forms of struggle to be used to defeat U.S. and puppet soldiers in order to move forward toward truly gaining mastery of the mountain jungles and the rural countryside, then to surround, split, and isolate the enemy, and eventually to launch a general offensive-general insurrection that gains mastery of the cities and secures decisive victory for our side.

1. Previously, we correctly anticipated that during the course of the battle, as the enemy steadily was defeated and as we won greater and greater victories, the U.S. might send tens of thousands of American combat troops to Vietnam. The Resolution on South Vietnam of the 9th Plenum of the Party Central Committee (Third Congress) stated clearly that the "special war" was the form of warfare best suited to American neocolonialism, but it also said that if they could not win victory in the "special war," under certain conditions the Americans could shift to a "limited war."

Based on that assessment, we made the decision to restrict the enemy to the use of "special war" and to defeat him in the "special war" while at the same time being prepared to deal with the possibility that the enemy might decide to launch a "limited war."

Restricting the enemy to fighting in South Vietnam and defeating the enemy in South Vietnam is the primary issue. It is our largest, main strategic formula. The application of that formula must permeate all of our political, military, and diplomatic activities. Given the current balance of forces in our nation, in Southeast Asia, and in the world, restricting the enemy to South Vietnam and defeating him there is still a realistic and practical possibility. At the same time, we must be prepared and ready to fight the enemy if he should expand the war into North Vietnam using ground forces. At the present time, although there is a possibility that the U.S. might expand the war into North Vietnam using ground forces, that possibility is small. This is because the American imperialists are afraid they would have to contend with the forces of North Vietnam and of the entire socialist bloc while at the same time they would have to deal with a growing and strengthening American people's movement against the war of aggression. The American imperialists are also afraid of becoming more isolated in the face of the increasing powerful movement supporting Vietnam among peaceful, democratic, and national independence forces around the world. In the other imperialist countries, there are some who do not support the U.S. policy, and there are some that support it but do not want to and do not have the ability to join the U.S. in expanding the war.

Both of these groups are looking for opportunities to contest the U.S. for control of areas of influence around the world.

The U.S. war of aggression in South Vietnam could also gradually change into a "limited war" with a number of American ground forces equivalent to the number the U.S. used in the Korean War, but with larger and more powerful air forces. However, no matter how big or how intense the war becomes, South Vietnam's revolutionary forces, with active support and assistance from North Vietnam, still can and must defeat the American imperialists and their lackeys in this "special war." The idea of "special" that I am using here does not have the same meaning that the Americans usually give it. I want to use this word to denote a type of war in which the American imperialists are unable to use all of their strength and in which, in the end, they must accept a certain level of defeat in order to avoid suffering an even larger, more painful defeat and avoid dangerous consequences that they themselves cannot fully predict. In the current international environment, the concrete balance of forces in Vietnam and in Southeast Asia, the strength of the socialist system, of the national democratic movement, and of the peace and democracy movement around the world, and the profound contradictions within the imperialist ranks will not permit the U.S. to unilaterally expand the war to whatever size and scale they may desire.

Currently, the American imperialists have sent more than a hundred thousand troops into South Vietnam. This is a new situation. We must monitor the stages of development of this war in order to have contingency plans ready so that we are certain that we can attain victory in any situation, no matter what happens.

The strategic formula of our revolutionary war in South Vietnam is to fight a protracted struggle, relying primarily on our own strength. This strategic formula is based on the following foundations:

First, initially we must use weakness to fight strength.

Second, the course of the revolution in South Vietnam, from its beginning until it achieves its basic, fundamental goals, will be a long process.

Third, the U.S. is a rich, powerful, and warmongering imperialist nation, and we must anticipate many possible scenarios for the way the situation will develop, especially scenarios in which the war is conducted on many different scales and at many different intensities.

The developments in the war over the past several years and the nature of the war during this current phase have proven that our strategic formula described above was completely correct.

When we saw the grave crisis they faced in their "special war," we decided that, while still operating from the foundation of conducting a protracted struggle, we would seize the opportunity to make an effort to win a decisive victory in a relatively short period of time.

The situation in South Vietnam over the past year and more clearly demonstrates that this strategic guidance stimulated our revolutionary war to gain more and greater victories. We quickly changed the balance of forces in our favor, we exceeded our goals in the destruction of strategic hamlets and in expanding our liberated zones, and we annihilated more than 30 puppet battalions and caused the disintegration of an important portion of the puppet army. In Region 5, we were able to gain the initiative and change the very nature of the battlefield, moving from a defensive posture to a completely offensive posture in which we have the offensive initiative.

We have the ability to defeat the enemy in "special war." That point is now clear, and it is certain.

The above decision must be understood more clearly from another aspect. When we decide to try to score a decisive victory, we are taking as our goal securing a level of fundamental victory in the specific, concrete circumstances of the war as it exists. That is clearly different than securing total victory in any and all circumstances and situations. Using the same definition and meaning of this phrase, we consider the Battle of Dien Bien Phu and the entire 1953–1954 Winter-Spring Campaign to have been a decisive victory, but we do not call it a total victory.

The new problem that presents itself is that now, in the current situation, after the U.S. has sent several scores of thousands of American expeditionary troops into South Vietnam to fight alongside more than half a million puppet troops, do we still have the necessary conditions to win a decisive victory within the next several years? In another scenario, if the war in South Vietnam develops into a large-scale "limited war" with the presence of three hundred thousand, four hundred thousand, or even five hundred thousand American troops, what strategic guidelines should we set and what prospects for victory will we have?

In the first scenario, we have concluded that, on the basis of maintaining a firm grasp on our formula of fighting a protracted struggle, we still have the capability of winning a decisive victory in a relatively short period of time.

In the second scenario, if the U.S. sends in half a million American troops, more or less, and changes the "special war" into a large-scale "limited war" in South Vietnam, with the possibility that the enemy might even send ground forces to invade North Vietnam (even though, in the short-term at least, the prospects for such a move are slight), given the current situation and after assessing both the U.S.'s capabilities and our own capabilities, including all aspects of the situation (political, military, and economic), we are certain that the U.S. cannot fight a protracted war and defeat us, and that in a protracted resistance war, we will certainly be able to win victory in the end.

Under both scenarios, our strategic formula is still correct and we have sufficient conditions to enable us to win victory.

2. On the question of winning a decisive victory within the next several years, I have the following thoughts:

We view the American introduction of several hundred thousand U.S. and satellite [allied] troops into South Vietnam as an important step in the development of the war. During this period, the American imperialists have certain, limited political and military goals, and American troops have their own strengths and weaknesses. The Politburo's resolution mentioned a large number of

issues to deal with this scenario. Here I only want to give you some additional thoughts about fighting American troops and puppet troops and about the political struggle and the possibility of building up to launching a general offensive-general insurrection in this new situation.

In the initial section of this letter, I discussed our new combat opponent and the relationship between fighting American troops and fighting the puppet army. Now I would like to talk more concretely about our goals and our capabilities for fighting the puppet and for fighting the Americans.

When we consider the situation from a military perspective, annihilating [killing] puppet troops is easier than annihilating [killing] American troops. This is because the U.S. troops have little combat experience, so they are subjective [overly optimistic]. They rely on their weapons and, in part at least, on their national pride.

As for the puppet troops, they have suffered defeat on the battlefield, they are now in a state of fear and confusion, and their fighting spirit has suffered. For that reason, we must further emphasize our resolve to annihilate puppet soldiers and to cause the puppet army to disintegrate even more and even faster. In addition, in our propaganda efforts, we must emphasize and stress the slogan, "Seek out the Americans and kill them." On certain battlefields, we must carefully and fully study the most appropriate forms of tactics and fighting methods to annihilate [kill] American troops. With respect to our guerrilla forces that are now surrounding and besieging American bases, we must work to develop in them a courageous fighting spirit. We must give them timely commendations, and we must stimulate their morale so that their resolve to kill large numbers of American troops increases even further.

As for the issue of fighting and defeating the puppet army, the realities of combat over the past several years has clearly shown us the direction to take to attain this goal. Even though today the puppet army still has more than half a million men, and even though it now has American troops to provide it with backup and support, we still assert that we are capable of fundamentally, basically, destroying and disintegrating the puppet army.

In the mountain jungle areas, primarily through the use of our military struggle formula, our main force troops, using relatively powerful "fists," have destroyed and caused the disintegration of many of the puppet army's mobile units. Today, on this battlefield, even though American troops are playing an increasingly important role, we still are capable of annihilating puppet troops in the places where they are based or where they are conducting operations, while at the same time we annihilate American rapid reaction forces.

In the lowland areas, by combining the use of our armed struggle and political struggle formulas, by using our three-pronged attack [military, political, and military proselyting], and in particular with widespread guerrilla warfare and local insurrections in certain locations, our local force troops, guerrilla militia, and revolutionary masses have swept away a rather significant portion of the puppet governmental apparatus at the village and hamlet level, have shattered the enemy's network of strategic hamlets, and have defeated many enemy military sweep operations.

Today, after the arrival of tens of thousands of American expeditionary troops in South Vietnam, the puppet army is able to send additional forces to the lowlands, and he now received a high level of U.S. artillery and air support. Our battles will be fought under even fiercer and more savage conditions, but if we use correct and flexible fighting methods and tactics, we certainly will continue to be able to attack the enemy in the lowlands.

If we want to defeat the puppet army in the lowlands, the most important thing for us is to firmly maintain and expand our mastery and control in the rural countryside. In order to secure and maintain our control in the rural countryside, the first thing we must do is to build and rationally deploy our battlefield armed forces in each district, province, and military region. We must strengthen the forces and improve the fighting skills of our local force troops. We must powerfully and broadly expand our guerrilla network. We must build combat villages and hamlets, and we must equip the guerrillas with additional ordinary weapons (such as punji stakes, mines, rifles, and hand grenades). We must enable the guerrillas to fight the enemy by themselves when enemy troops enter their villages and hamlets, and at the same time enable them to coordinate with our main force and local force troops to annihilate [kill] large numbers of enemy troops.

We must devote attention to consolidating and expanding our mass political army. We must mobilize the various classes of the population to rise up to take control of their villages and hamlets, to maintain and step up production in order to provide for their daily lives while at the same time providing the necessary manpower and resources to kill the enemy and defend their villages and their nation.

We must properly implement our police of greater solidarity to unite the entire population behind us. We must gradually, step by step, provide land to the peasants. We must firmly understand and implement the policies of the Party in the rural countryside and aim the spear-point of our struggle against the American imperialists and against powerful, wicked landlords and enemy lackeys. In addition to stepping up production and combat activities, we must also make sure we properly conduct health, education, cultural, and social activities.

On the rural battlefield, we must set forward missions and goals that are appropriate for each individual area. We must have a plan to tightly coordinate the combat operations of various units and forces and of the different local areas. We must always fully understand and follow our formula of attaining mastery and control to destroy [kill] the enemy and of destroying the enemy in order gain increasingly firm control. This means that we must know how to conduct a solid defense and how to launch powerful attacks, that we must constantly maintain the initiative, that we must protect and expand our forces, that we must use every possible means to mount counterattacks against the enemy to secure and defend each village and hamlet, and that we gradually

expand our area of control and shrink the size of the enemy's area of control. In order to counter the enemy's "pacification" program in the rural countryside and reduce the enemy's advantages and strengths in the lowlands, we must tightly coordinate the three prongs of our attack [military, political, and military proselyting], and we must expand guerrilla warfare to even greater heights. At the same time, we must also step up the political struggle and our military proselyting operations, we must properly consolidate, fortify, and expand our combat villages and hamlets, we must dig underground bunkers to take shelter and hide, and we must build networks of tunnels to use to counter enemy air and artillery strikes and to fight the enemy.

Recently, the enemy massed his forces and conducted extremely intense sweep operations in a number of areas, including the outskirts of Saigon–Cho Lon, Long An, My Tho, Quang Nam, Quang Ngai, Binh Dinh, etc. However, because we had deployed our forces rationally, because we properly coordinated all aspects of our activities, and because we took the initiative in attacking the enemy, we were able to gain and maintain control of these areas and to inflict many casualties on enemy forces.

On the other hand, in a number of other areas in Tri-Thien and western Cochin China [the lower Mekong Delta], because our forces did not carry out the above tasks properly, our defenses were not firm, our attacks were not powerful, and we suffered rather heavy casualties.

To coordinate our attacks against the enemy in the mountain jungles and in the lowlands in the immediate future, we must strive to shatter, disperse, or cause the desertion of around 300,000 to 400,000 puppet army soldiers, and of that total we must destroy at least 70 to 80 enemy battalions. That is one of the requirements for our plan to win a decisive victory.

Attacking puppet troops must go hand in hand with attacking and defeating American troops. The fact that the U.S. is sending several hundred thousand expeditionary troops to fight in South Vietnam means that our people's cause of opposing the Americans to save our nation will be longer, more difficult, and more savage. However, the more American troops that come to Vietnam, the more of them we will be able to kill. If large numbers of American troops are killed, the puppet army will disintegrate even faster, the U.S.'s hope of securing a victory through military means will collapse, and the American people's movement opposed to the U.S.'s dirty war in Vietnam will grow.

In the near future, do we have the capability of annihilating an important portion of the American army? I believe that we have that capability. The victory won by our troops at the recent battle of Van Tuong [the Batangan Peninsula, August 1965] is living proof of that capability. At Van Tuong, the Americans chose the battlefield, they used 9,000 troops, and they massed overwhelming superiority in firepower and military equipment. In spite of this, however, two of our main force battalions dealt them a terrible defeat—our losses were only 1/20th of those suffered by the enemy. If the battle of Ap Bac in early 1963 demonstrated our ability to defeat the American tactics of "helicopter assault" and "armored assault" to support large puppet army forces conducting sweeps in the lowlands, and if the battle of Binh Gia in late 1964 signaled the maturation of our main force troops in their ability to annihilate large enemy regular rapid reaction units, then the battle of Van Tuong has now provided eloquent proof of our ability to defeat American troops even when they have absolute superiority in equipment and firepower.

And after the battle of Van Tuong, in a large number of subsequent battles our soldiers have won glorious victories over American troops.

Currently, we have many possibilities for fighting American troops on mountain jungle and semimountain jungle battlefields and when they are maneuvering out in the field, outside of their defensive fortifications. At the same time, we also have ways of attacking the Americans inside their bases and around their bases. If we want to do this, however, we must clearly recognize the strengths and the weaknesses of American troops.

Fighting on mountain jungle battlefields is something that American troops have been forced into, and something they do with great reluctance, because in that terrain the effectiveness of their superiority in weapons and technology is reduced and their weaknesses are more easily exposed. For us, on the other hand, the mountain jungles are our bases. These are the places where our military units have been built into powerful forces, and these are the battlefields that we know like the back of our hand and where we have a powerful battlefield posture that we can use to destroy both American as well as puppet troops. If we want to defeat the American army in the mountain jungle, the first thing we must do is to gain control of, gain mastery over, the mountain jungles. For a long time we have said that we controlled the mountain jungles, but in fact, there were many vast areas of mountain jungle that the enemy did not completely occupy or where he did not conduct operations, so there were no enemy forces there. As for our side, we too did not have sufficient forces to control these areas. That is the reason that there were instances when the enemy launched attacks into the mountain jungles and struck deep into our base areas, such as in Do Xa in 1963, and in Bien Hoa and Thu Dau Mot in September and October of this year, and yet we failed to annihilate significant numbers of enemy forces and inflicted only light casualties and attrition on the enemy forces.

That demonstrates that in practical terms, we do not yet control the mountain jungle areas. In order to truly control and master the mountain jungles, we must firmly grasp the following points:

First, we must correctly implement the Party's policies toward the ethnic minority peoples living in the mountain areas, and we must build their tribal villages into combat villages.

Second, we must "transplant" people into unpopulated or underpopulated areas and build up local armed forces in order to maintain control throughout all the mountain jungles areas.

Third, we must quickly build up powerful main force units with excellent equipment and a high level of mobility, and we must

ensure that they are properly supplied and that they have good logistics support.

The special characteristics of revolutionary warfare, of national liberation warfare, and of our strategic guidelines in the resistance war against the Americans demand that our armed forces and our political forces must be in control of, must be in control of their own battles. This means that they must have firm footholds, and they must be able to stand their ground firmly on the mountain jungle battlefields as well as in the lowlands in order to fight the enemy. We cannot fight and then run away, abandoning the land and abandoning the people. The mountain jungles have terrain that is favorable to our effort to develop a posture of control and mastery. The more we control the mountain jungles, the better we will be able to gain firm control of other battlefields.

For that reason, we must fully recognize the importance of "transplanting" people in the mountain jungle areas. We must organize powerful guerrilla teams that engage in [agricultural] production in addition to fighting. At the same time, we must also rationally deploy our armed forces in such a way that we gain the initiative, fight off large enemy sweep operations properly, and firmly protect our bases.

In areas where the population is too sparse and where we have no guerrilla militia forces, we must station a small element of our main force troops to help build and develop guerrilla militia forces and local force units. In that way not only will we be able to gain mastery of the mountain jungles; when the enemy does attack, we will be better able to restrict his activities and destroy more of his forces.

In parallel with developing a network of guerrillas and local force units, we must quickly build our main force troops into powerful fists composed of light, tightly organized large units with high fighting spirit, with truly excellent technical and tactical skills, with very heavy firepower (including individual weapons, heavy weapons fire support weapons, antiaircraft guns, and light artillery pieces), with the ability to move rapidly, and with relatively ample food and ammunition reserve stockpiles.

In order to gain the offensive initiative, we usually use such tactics as luring the enemy in to destroy him, as attacking or besieging an outpost in order to lure in and destroy relief forces, as attacking enemy lines of communications and then destroying relief forces sent to reopen them, as attacking puppet army forces as a way to lure American troops out to places where we can kill them, etc. Here, however, I want to discuss the subject of using counterattacks to kill the enemy and to defeat enemy offensive attacks. For a long time we have been unable to accomplish this goal. Almost all of the times when the enemy took the initiative in attacking mountain jungle areas, he encountered only scattered resistance and our armed forces were unable to launch counterattacks against his forces.

We must understand what it means to have the initiative and what it means to be defensive or passive in counterattacks and combating enemy sweep operations. Usually when he drafts an offensive plan and deploys his forces to move into the areas he intends to sweep, the enemy has the initiative, which means he has the initiative in the initial phase.

However, on a battlefield that the enemy has chosen, if we have good control of these areas, if we have deployed our forces in battle positions, and if we take the initiative in combating the enemy sweep, the enemy may gradually lose the initiative he initially enjoyed, and he may gradually be placed more on the defensive and in the passive position of trying to ward off our attacks. In addition, when the enemy has almost finished or has just finished his sweep operation, if we have reserve forces already prepared and if we have a plan ready to mount a determined counterattack, we can drive the enemy totally onto the defensive and inflict heavy losses on his forces, because the enemy troops will be in the process of withdrawing and they will have neither the mental preparations nor the forces available to fend off our attacks.

During the Second World War, Stalin put forward his famous concept about strategic and campaign counteroffensives, and he often talked about the idea of "a counteroffensive of an offensive nature." The battle of Stalingrad was a famous counteroffensive campaign. All of the campaigns fought during 1943, 1944, and early 1945 were part of the Red Army's counteroffensive strategy of fighting on Soviet soil and then attacking across the borders of the Soviet Union all the way to the final fascist lair in Germany.

During our resistance war against the French, we defeated several large French Army offensive operations in the Viet Bac Campaign (1947) and the Hoa Binh Campaign (1952). These were campaigns in which we counterattacked and defeated enemy offensive attacks.

In South Vietnam, there was the battle in which we annihilated a puppet battalion at Phu Tuc (Chau Thanh District, Ben Tre Province, 1964) when the enemy battalion was returning home from a sweep operation. This battle could also be described as a form of counterattack aimed at defeating enemy offensive sweep operations.

During the coming dry season, with additional troops and transportation equipment for mobility, the U.S. is certain to launch many attacks into battlefields in the mountain jungle and semi-mountain jungle areas. The principal forces used on these operations will be American troops, sometimes accompanied by puppet troops and satellite [allied] troops. The American goals in these operations will be to seize the initiative, to score a number of victories to cause political effects favorable to their side, to inflict damage on us and cause us difficulties, and to push us back into a defensive, reactive posture. In order to deal with these new enemy military operations, we must make adequate preparations of all types to counterattack against the enemy. We must view the American dry-season attacks as excellent opportunities that will provide favorable conditions for us to destroy U.S. and puppet military forces, and especially to kill American troops.

Counterattacking against the enemy when he conducts an offensive attack demonstrates that we have a firm understanding of our tactic of fighting the enemy when the enemy is in the field, outside of his fortified defensive positions. If we want to be able to do that, we must obtain a firm understanding of the situation, we must do an excellent job of preparing the battlefield and of preparing our own forces, we must lure the enemy into battle sites that we have prepared beforehand, we must firmly grasp opportunities, and we must take the initiative by attacking the enemy and catching him by surprise. This kind of battle has many advantages over attacking outposts and then destroying enemy relief forces. For that reason, from a tactical standpoint we should not make frontal attacks; instead we can use more flexible fighting methods, such as attacking the enemy's flanks, engaging the enemy in close-quarters battle until he is exhausted, and dividing the enemy force in order to be able to destroy it. The fundamental point is that we must maintain excellent coordination between our three types of troops [main force, local force, guerrillas], we must maintain a firm grasp of the situation on the battlefield, and, most important of all, we must have adequate reserve forces.

In addition to having plans to take the initiative in launching counterattacks, we still must have plans for offensive attacks, the kind that we regularly launched during the recent winter-spring and spring-summer campaigns. However, in these offensive plans we usually use the tactic of attacking a point and then destroying the relief force, and if we do not have a certain amount of reserve forces to commit to the battle at the final moment, after we attack the enemy relief force the enemy can mass his strength to make another counterattack and either put us back on the defensive or force us to withdraw.

That is something that regularly happens in the final phase of our campaigns, such as the Binh Gia and Dong Xoai campaigns, for instance. If at those times we had a reserve force prepared and on hand, ready to use to strike powerful blows during the final phase of the campaign, it is certain that we would have won even greater victories in those battles.

Firmly maintaining an offensive philosophy and initiating attacks in order to defend our positions—those are our strategic and tactical concepts for this revolutionary war. Only if we fully absorb these concepts will we be able to understand the true content of a counterattack, and only then will we be able to recognize possibilities for annihilating U.S. and puppet troops when they are moving in the field, outside of their prepared defensive fortifications, and when they enter our mountain jungle areas. This is the battlefield on which the enemy's superiority in air, artillery, and armor is reduced, and it is the area where our troops can exploit to the maximum our fighting spirit and our superiority in tactics.

In order to further illuminate the way we should conduct counterattacks, I would like to discuss reserve forces and guidelines for employing reserve forces.

Viewing the situation from an overall standpoint, if we want to conduct a protracted war we must build up our forces, from small units all the way up to large forces, in individual areas as well as throughout the battlefield. We must fight at all levels, from scattered guerrilla attacks to large-scale maneuver attacks, we must erode the enemy's strength by inflicting casualties, both in small numbers and in large numbers, and we must build increasingly powerful tactical reserve forces as well as strategic reserve forces.

In any battle or in any campaign, whether we are using large numbers of troops or just small numbers of troops, we must always have a reserve force ready so that we can seize the initiative and ensure victory. This is particularly true when fighting against American troops. We must be able to use reserve forces well in order to deal with sudden, unexpected enemy air attacks or air assault landings by air cavalry units. To be able to resist these strengths of the American army, when we counterattack against the enemy, if we are using a regiment for the counterattack, we must have at least one or two regiments in reserve, and if we are using one battalion for the counterattack, we must have one or two battalions in reserve in order to be ready to engage enemy troops making air assaults. For us, reserve forces do not consist solely of main force troops; they also include guerrilla fighters. Guerrillas are regular combat forces, but they are also a reserve force. When the enemy makes an attack into one of our areas, guerrilla troops cling to the enemy force to fight it. After our main force units make a counterattack, guerrilla teams may be used as a reserve force to continue the pursuit and destruction of the enemy.

Not only do we need to have a military reserve force; we also need to build truly powerful political reserve forces to work with our military forces in striking blows that truly take him by surprise during the conduct of a general offensive–general insurrection. In order to preserve the source of our reserve forces, local Party chapters at all levels must intensify their efforts to incite the masses to struggle against the enemy's plans to draft soldiers into his army.

In the near future, American troops will use the dry season to launch their initial counterattacks in an effort to win a number of military and political victories in order to save the puppet army and puppet government from total collapse. We must coordinate more closely between battlefields and we must take the initiative in launching attacks and counterattacks with the resolute fighting spirit of Van Tuong, Binh Gia, and Ba Gia in order to win clear victory over U.S. troops during the dry season and begin the test of strength between the American imperialists and our own soldiers and civilians in this new phase of the war.

Although there are fewer American troops than there are puppet troops, the Americans had tremendous firepower and they have large bases in our country that are filled with modern military equipment, fuel, and ammunition. For that reason, attacks to inflict damage on American bases, airfields, and large storage facilities and to destroy large puppet and American military units are all of great importance.

As for fighting American forces inside and around their bases in South Vietnam, there are three ways to fight them:

—Make sapper attacks, conducted either independently or in coordination with firepower [shelling] attacks and ground attacks by assault [infantry] forces.
—Shell the Americans from outside their perimeters.
—Fight them in American killing belts using guerrillas and local force units.

Using these three fighting methods, during the recent past our forces have inflicted attrition on and have destroyed a rather large number of American troops and military equipment. These are very creative tactics that exhibit the incredibly courageous spirit and the very high level of technical and tactical skills of our people's armed forces. We must quickly reinforce and strengthen our troops and strongly motivate them to develop the above-mentioned fighting methods so that we can inflict even greater damage on the U.S.'s weapons and military equipment, inflict casualties on his personnel (especially on American pilots and American advisors), cause the Americans further logistical and transportation problems, and force them to use large numbers of their troops to protect their bases.

Sapper tactics are a very unique fighting method that has been developed by our army. We must quickly increase the size of our sapper force and we must organize and train our sappers to turn them into a truly elite branch we can use to attack enemy bases, headquarters, and nerve centers.

We must use specialized sapper teams, powerful explosives, and various specialized types of weapons to attack enemy ammunition stockpiles, fuel dumps, airfields, warships, and locations where large numbers of American officers are concentrated.

Recently the U.S. Military Command in South Vietnam was forced to admit that, given the accuracy displayed during the shelling of Bien Hoa Airbase, the Viet Cong could attack any American base in South Vietnam. That admission shows all the more clearly the need for us to strive to develop and expand the use of this extremely effective fighting method. We must organize and train many units to be able to use mortars, recoilless rifles, mountain howitzers, and other types of long-range weapons skillfully in order to intensify our shelling attacks on U.S. bases. Using the types of weapons we currently have on hand and new weapons that will be soon sent south, we will strike surprise blows that will win great victories and further disrupt and confuse the American efforts to protect their bases in South Vietnam.

Based on the innovations made by our armed forces in Danang and Chu Lai, we need to expand our use of belts of guerrillas and local force troops around U.S. bases. Surrounding, besieging, sniping, and the use of scattered, isolated attacks must become our standard, regular tactics to erode the enemy's manpower strength. The belts must be made very strong; they must be constructed in depth, with many layers, in order to attack and kill enemy troops when they push out from the bases or when they conduct sweep operations. Guerrillas and local force troops must receive careful training, they must be thoroughly familiar with the terrain inside and around the base, they must clearly understand U.S. tactics and the pattern of operations used by U.S. troops, and they must be skilled in the use of many different types of weapons so that they can kill individual enemy soldiers and destroy individual U.S. tanks and small units.

When conditions are favorable, we might also use commando forces to penetrate deep into enemy bases and make powerful attacks against larger enemy units.

In addition to the military struggle, we must devote a great deal of attention to organizing and leading the masses who live in areas around U.S. bases in conducting political struggles and carrying out military proselyting operations directed at American troops with the goal of limiting or restricting enemy sweep operations and bombardments and of protecting the people's lives and property.

During the upcoming spring-summer campaign, we need to strive to kill around 10,000 American soldiers, as was projected, and during the coming few years, we need to kill approximately 40,000–50,000 American soldiers. That is a new goal to help us advance toward scoring a decisive victory in this war.

In addition to killing American and puppet troops, we must inflict heavy losses on the American air forces and at the same time limit the damage caused by air attacks. That is a common mission for both North and South Vietnam, and it is one of the goals we must achieve to win victory.

In North Vietnam, our soldiers and civilians have fought very skillfully and have shot down many U.S. aircraft. In South Vietnam, even though our forces there have only limited air defense forces, our armed forces have found many very effective tactics. They have destroyed rows of enemy aircraft as they sat on their airbases and they have attacked and destroyed enemy bomb storage depots and petroleum storage facilities, thereby restricting enemy air activities. We need to conduct a general review of these activities and quickly disseminate valuable experiences and lessons learned about how to destroy American aircraft and about how to avoid and protect against air attacks.

We must mobilize all our different types of troops [main force, local force, guerrillas] and the different specialty branches and different services of our armed forces to launch an emulation campaign to shoot down or destroy even more enemy aircraft.

Destroying aircraft must go hand in hand with eliminating enemy pilots. According to statements made by U.S. pilots we have captured in North Vietnam and according to other documents and information we have collected, because of our heavy and accurate fire the U.S. is increasingly short of good pilots who are skilled in the use of modern aircraft in all weather and combat conditions. For that reason, we must pay special attention to capturing American pilots when we shoot down their aircraft, and we must make powerful attacks against airfields and against the barracks where American pilots live.

3. On the issue of insurrection [uprisings], the following question has been raised: Now that the U.S. has sent U.S. troops to occupy a number of areas in South Vietnam, is it still possible for us to build up to conducting an insurrection?

In order to reach a clear assessment of this matter, we must first of all understand what an insurrection is and review whether we have had insurrections in South Vietnam during the past few years.

An insurrection is the rising up of the masses in the rural countryside or in the cities and the use of political strength, armed [military] strength, or both political and armed strength to overthrow the enemy's local governments or his national government. Insurrection is also the rising up of large or small units within the enemy's army to stand on the side of the revolution and of the people in opposing the puppet government.

If we agree on this understanding of the term "insurrection," then we can see that over the past several years in South Vietnam the popular masses and a number of puppet military units have conducted insurrections numerous times. Uprisings using primarily political strength, in coordination with the use of mass armed strength, were conducted in a number of mountain jungle areas of Region 5 and the lowlands of Cochin China in later 1959 and early 1960.

These uprisings, which gained control of governmental power at the village and hamlet level, were local insurrections and were our first large high-tide insurrectionary movement. The wave of uprisings conducted in the lowlands of Region 5 for the past year or more are our second large high tide insurrectionary movement. Generally speaking, the movement in which the vast masses of the rural population have risen up to destroy strategic hamlets, to shatter their bonds of repression, and to develop guerrilla warfare to fight the enemy has been a widespread insurrection throughout rural South Vietnam that has lasted for the past several years. The uprisings of the different classes of the urban population in the student movement, the Buddhist movement, and the mass labor movement that led to a change in the puppet government, a change that was not what the U.S. wanted, were actions of a violent nature that can be viewed as practice exercises for an eventual uprising in the cities. The uprisings of a number of small puppet military units in many different provinces to oppose the puppet government and brutal commanders and to support the mass struggle and join the revolution and the National Liberation Front are also a type of small-scale insurrection.

If we understand the term "insurrection" in this manner, then in the near future, after we win greater victories and after both American military forces and the puppet army suffered greater failures, is it not possible that the different classes of the population in areas temporarily under enemy control and puppet soldiers might also rise up in insurrection?

The general insurrection that we put forward as a possibility, a practical guideline to help to win a decisive victory in South Vietnam, certainly must be combined with a general military offensive. In fact, any insurrection that wants to win victory must crush the enemy's military resistance. Conversely, in a revolutionary war, if one wants to completely and totally defeat the enemy, a general military offensive must receive the support and assistance of insurrections of different levels and intensities among the masses and within the enemy army.

During the October Revolution in Russia in 1917, under the leadership of the Bolshevik Party and in the midst of a situation in which the Russian Imperial Army had suffered heavy defeats on the front lines, the workers and an important segment of the Imperial Russian Army in many cities rose up to seize the reins of government. The reasons that our own 1945 August Revolution was able to secure a quick victory was that the French Army and the Japanese Army had both been defeated and because millions of the popular masses, under the leadership of our Party, rose up as one in rebellion to seize control of the government throughout our nation.

In South Vietnam, from late 1959 through early 1960, the reason that the "simultaneous uprisings" of the masses in the rural countryside were able to be successful and that these uprisings have continued to grow and develop right up to the present is that they were closely coordinated with increasingly powerful attacks by military forces conducting a guerrilla war. And the primary reason that the recent waves of violent actions by the masses in Hue, Danang, and Saigon did not develop into insurrections to seize the reins of government was that they lacked any direct coordination with military attacks that would destroy or disperse the puppet army to a major extent, and also that these political struggle lacked close leadership by our Party.

At present, tens of thousands of American troops have been sent into South Vietnam. However, even in those areas where American troops are stationed, there is no reason to believe that the masses cannot rise up in insurrection.

The student uprising in South Korea that overthrew Singman Rhee even though tens of thousands of American troops were stationed in that country is a concrete example of that possibility, is it not?

In addition, as I stated in the analysis I provided above, even the arrival of American troops cannot prevent the disintegration of the puppet army and the puppet government, and the American troops themselves will be annihilated, one piece at a time. In that event, the popular masses in areas behind the enemy's lines and the soldiers in a number of puppet army units could also rise up in revolt. This is a practical, realistic possibility if local Party chapters provide close leadership of the political struggle movement and of military proselyting operations, and if they combine these two attack spearheads with a military struggle to create overwhelming force to defeat our enemies. And the coordination of the waves of military attacks with mass uprisings in the cities and mutinies of a number of puppet army units aimed at overthrowing the puppet government and ending the war is what we call the general offensive-general insurrection.

However, there is one difference from our August Revolution: If the future general military offensive in South Vietnam occurs over a certain period of time and is made up of many attacks and many waves of operations, then the mass insurrection in the cities and the mutinies in a number of units of the puppet army will also take place over a period of time and will consist of many uprisings and many waves of struggle. The practical realities of the progress of the South Vietnamese revolution over the past several years and the historical experience of many insurrections and revolutions in other countries clearly demonstrates the possibility for and the necessity of closely coordinating and combining military attacks with political attacks during the phase when a revolutionary war wins decisive victory.

For that reason, we cannot simply mechanically assert, as a matter of blind faith, that the general insurrection will burst forth simultaneously and proceed as rapidly and as smoothly as did our August Revolution. Instead, we must first derive the fundamental content of the August Revolution, its essence, and then apply it to the new stage of development of the revolution in South Vietnam, the outstanding feature of which is combining military struggle with political struggle.

With this concept in mind, I completely agree with all of you, and also with our comrades in Region 5, that even if the U.S. sends several hundred thousands of expeditionary troops into South Vietnam, we still are capable of progressing to the point of conducting a general offensive-general insurrection.

The decision on how to combine insurrections with military attacks for individual cities and province capitals must be based on the specific situation in each location. For small province capitals where there are large enemy forces, such as the province capitals in the Central Highlands, we might make the military attack our primary effort, and mass uprisings would provide support. In places with large populations but where the number of enemy forces is small, we could conduct insurrection in combination with a limited military attack, but there mass uprisings will play the decisive role. In province capitals with a large civilian population and that also have relatively large numbers of enemy forces, we must closely coordinate military attacks with mass uprisings. In Saigon, Hue, Danang, and other cities with large populations but where enemy forces are both large and powerful, if our revolutionary army lures the enemy out to pre-prepared locations and then launches major attacks, the revolutionary masses can seize the opportunity by relying on their own organized forces, with active assistance provided by people's armed forces operating from springboard positions on the outskirts of the cities and by mutinies inside the puppet army, to rise up to take control of individual parts of the city and to set up a people's government of some appropriate form.

Here I am just illustrating general guidelines, and it is certain that the actual attacks and uprisings will take much more lively, flexible, rich, and varied forms, because in a revolution the creativity of the masses is limitless.

The war in South Vietnam is now developing rapidly. We must constantly keep up with the situation, and especially with changes that are capable of creating turning points in the war. We cannot always correctly anticipate the course of material developments, but we are capable of mastering the situation, because every day we are directing the resistance war on the basis of the laws of revolutionary war that we already understand and based on correct assessments we have made of the enemy's intentions.

III

I am devoting this section to the discussion of a number of issues regarding upcoming operational missions, but before going into these matters, I want to discuss the building of base areas and creation of a battlefield for annihilating the enemy in the mountain jungle region of the provinces of Phuoc Long, Phuoc Thanh, Quang Duc, and Lam Dong. I have frequently told COSVN that the above mountain jungle area occupies a special strategic location for both defensive and offensive operations.

We must work actively to build this area up into a solid base area that can protect COSVN and guarantee that COSVN can continue to guide and direct our operations, and at the same time turn the area into a battlefield in which our large main force units can annihilate large numbers of enemy troops and generate steadily increasing pressure on Saigon.

At present, we have a number of difficulties in this area, such as that it is sparsely populated, it has little food, and communication and transportation routes are poor. However, because of its great strategic location, we can and we must overcome those problems. We must "transplant" into this area additional population taken from the lowlands areas, so that these people can engage in production to support themselves while at the same time we build these people into guerrilla or local force units. We are capable of accomplishing this if we resolutely fight to gain control of the people that the enemy is trying, through his sweep operations, to move into areas he controls. We can propagandize and mobilize them and then select some of them to "transplant" out into the area we control in order to create a rear area that has a civilian population, that has food, that has local armed and paramilitary forces, and that is a source of resources for our resistance war.

In addition to "transplanting" people and stepping up production to attain self-sufficiency, we need to strive to collect more rice from the Cambodia and make better arrangements for transporting this rice to our forces. We will strive to build a number of new routes to increase our transportation of weapons down from North Vietnam in order to overcome our logistics difficulties both in this area and throughout the rest of South Vietnam.

While you prepare to implement the Politburo's resolution, you should pay attention to the following points:

1. During this current phase, it is essential that we gain and firmly maintain the offensive initiative on the battlefield. We must constantly make powerful attacks while at the same time defending ourselves properly. We must constantly expand our mastery and control of the mountain jungles and the rural lowlands, and we must build up to gain control of a number of areas around the cities and inside the cities. If we want to secure and maintain the initiative, we must rationally deploy our armed forces and our mass political forces. We must closely coordinate our operations on the different battlefields, stretch American forces and the puppet army thin, and draw them out in order to attack them. We must surround, cut off, and isolate the enemy in order to destroy him. We must cut the enemy's roads, both major roads and small roads and other lines of communications, for short periods of time and eventually build up to permanently paralyzing his road networks and other lines of communications. At the same time, we must concentrate our military forces and maneuver them to destroy individual large U.S. and puppet army units.

2. In order to ensure close coordination between the different battlefields, we must firmly grasp the special characteristics of the different strategic areas [mountain jungle, rural lowlands, cities], firmly understand our combat opponent, and assign appropriate missions and responsibilities to each individual battlefield. The lowlands battlefield is responsible for inflicting attrition on the enemy, for killing enemy troops, for pinning down enemy troops, and for providing personnel and material resources to our forces. The mountain jungle battlefield is responsible for annihilating enemy troops and pinning down enemy forces, with the primary focus being on U.S. and puppet regular army units. At the same time, it is also responsible for improving and expanding our base areas.

As we get down to smaller, individual battlefields, we must clearly determine which locations and which units are primarily responsible for stretching the enemy thin, pinning him down, and inflicting attrition on his forces, and which locations and which units are responsible for annihilating and destroying enemy troops. For example, in the lowlands, the guerrilla militia, district local force units, and mass political forces will be responsible for pinning down and inflicting attrition on the enemy in a few sectors, so that our provincial local force and regional main force units can attack and annihilate enemy forces in other sectors and areas.

In the mountain jungles we also have the issue of coordinating the missions of inflicting attrition and of annihilating enemy units, and coordinating between primary and secondary battlefields. For instance, the mountain jungle areas of Tri Thien and Region 6 are responsible for stretching enemy forces thin and pinning enemy troops down in order to allow the main force units subordinate to COSVN and to Region 5 to annihilate enemy forces in the mountain jungles of Region 7 and the Central Highlands.

3. Closely coordinate our three types of troops and flexibly employ our different tactical and combat methods. I will not review the ways to coordinate between our different types of troops or review our different tactics and combat methods; instead I just want to emphasize the importance of this subject. The realities of the revolutionary war in South Vietnam clearly show that our people's armed forces can inflict attrition and can kill large numbers of enemy troops, no matter whether they are puppet soldiers, American soldiers, or satellite [allied] soldiers, and no matter what

battlefield they are on or how modern the enemy's equipment is. Even our enemies have had to admit that our army is one of the best armies in the world. This is because, in addition to our absolute political superiority and superiority in morale, our people's armed forces know how to closely coordinate our three types of troops and how to flexibly employ various types of tactics and combat methods suited to the Vietnamese people and the country of Vietnam.

That does not mean that every location, every unit, and every type of soldier always fights well. The truth is that our people's armed forces have not developed uniformly in terms of their quantity or their quality. A number of local areas and a number of units have displayed shortcomings and weaknesses in combat.

We must strive to build different types of troops and different specialty branches that are appropriately organized and equipped, we must strengthen their political and ideological education, and we must increase their military training. In particular, we need to conduct systematic reviews and derive lessons learned in the art of people's war and the art of guerrilla warfare, and especially lessons in fighting methods, so that these lessons can be quickly disseminated in order to improve the combat efficiency of all of our battlefields, all of our units, and all of our different types of troops.

4. We must maintain a firm grasp on our reserve forces and know how to defeat the enemy by taking him by surprise. In Section II, I talked about the issue of reserve forces, so here I would just like to remind you comrades that you must consider this as a principle to follow when you employ your troops throughout your entire battlefield, in individual campaigns, and in individual battles.

Knowing how to defeat the enemy by taking him by surprise does not mean winning by chance or by luck. We must have knowledge and understanding, we must have made prior preparations, we must have plans to overcome all problems and obstacles, and we must have a perfect revolutionary spirit and a very high "determined to fight, determined to win" spirit. If we want to defeat the enemy by taking him by surprise, from the tactical standpoint, we must train our combat units very carefully, and we must take security measures and protect the secrecy of our battle plans. We must quickly discover and identify enemy agents. We must use deception. We must maintain hold onto and correctly employ reserve units. We must know how to pick the right time, the right opportunity, to begin and to end a battle.

If we want to defeat the enemy by taking him by surprise from the strategic standpoint, we must maintain absolute secrecy about our strategic guidelines and intentions. We must build reserve forces among our three types of troops, and, in particular, we must build strategic reserve forces from our main force units. At the same time, we must also build reserve forces in our political army in the large cities. We must also know how to develop and seize opportunities to attack when the enemy is confused, frightened, and disintegrating on the battlefield, or when the U.S. or the puppet government faces a serious political or economic crisis.

5. Study and absorb even more thoroughly our formula of fighting the enemy both militarily and politically. The question of attacking the enemy militarily has been mentioned frequently above, so here I would just like to say a little more about the possibility and the necessity for intensifying the political struggle.

Practical realities have shown that the fact that the U.S. has sent U.S. and satellite troops into South Vietnam has not reduced our people's ability to assemble political forces and conduct political struggles. On the contrary, it has increased our possibilities to do this, and at the same time it has driven the enemy increasingly into a position of political isolation and defeat. The recent reports received from the Region 5 Party Committee have illuminated and proven that assessment.

The reasons for these possibilities are as follows:

—The more American and satellite troops that the U.S. send into South Vietnam, the more military bases they build, the more they expand the areas in which their are based, the more they use modern war-making equipment to conduct brutal destruction, such as using B-52s in carpet-bombing missions and using poisonous chemicals to clear vegetation, etc., the more they intensify the bitter contradictions between our people and the American imperialists, and the more they increase the hatred our compatriots have toward these nation-stealing aggressors.

—Even though the U.S. is intensifying the ferocity of the war with every passing day, it is still pursuing a neocolonialist policy, and it still must use demagoguery to try to win over the people. Because of the rather good and rather profound level of revolutionary awareness that our people have acquired during the course of the struggle, our people can exploit and deepen the enemy's political weaknesses, and they can expose his demagogic schemes in order to intensify the political struggle even further.

—The more expeditionary troops the U.S. sends into South Vietnam, the more internal contradictions are created within the leadership of the puppet army and puppet government and the greater the puppet regime's economic and financial problems will become, and the increasing numbers of American troops will steadily drive up the cost of living becomes for the people residing in the areas the enemy controls. These things will increasingly impel the people to struggle even more vigorously against the enemy.

—The U.S. has sent an expeditionary army into South Vietnam to score victories in order to improve the morale of the puppet army and puppet government. Instead, however, the American troops themselves have been defeated, which has caused the U.S. to begin talking about negotiations. That increases the contradictions between the Americans and the puppets and causes the puppet army to become more frightened and confused, so the puppet army's morale declines even further.

—The more the U.S. leaders intensify the war in South Vietnam and expand the scope of the bombing in North Vietnam, the more the American people and progressive people throughout the world will oppose them.

For these reasons, in the political struggle, and especially in urban operations, we can and we must strive to draw the masses together, draw together every class of the population, and even attract progressives who are part of the puppet army and puppet government to join in one united resistance front to oppose the Americans and save the nation. We must build a truly broad-based national solidarity bloc that aims the sharp spear-point of the struggle straight at the American imperialists and the Vietnamese traitors.

6. Rapidly build up our political forces in the cities and intensify our urban operations. First of all, we must build up hard-core forces made up of grass-roots Party and mass organizations at the local level [wards, subwards] so that we can more easily conceal our forces. We must strive to develop and recruit Party members locally while at the same time we select a number of Party members from the rural countryside to send in to operate inside the cities. We must deploy and assign Party members and loyal, trusted supporters, such as youths, women, and students, to operate in city blocks, in markets, in schools, and in religious organizations, especially Buddhist organizations, in order to propagandize, mobilize, and draw the masses together through appropriate types of organizations.

Relying on our Party members and loyal mass followers, we must aggressively build secret guerrilla units, teams of sappers and commandos, and covert long-term forces that will wait for opportunities to mount military attacks against the enemy.

In order to draw together forces and to intensify the struggle movement in the cities, we should conduct studies to develop a number of appropriate slogans that are capable of sowing division within the enemy's ranks and at the same time of winning over and bringing together large masses of the population. For example, they could be slogans opposing governmental terrorism and forcible military conscription, opposing enemy chemical weapons and B-52 attacks, opposing American interference in Vietnamese affairs, demands for the formation of a broad-based civilian government made up of representatives of all political and religious factions, etc.

7. Further intensify puppet proselyting and enemy proselyting operations. With respect to the puppet army, we must firmly understand our new stratagem, which is to aim the sharp point of our spear directly at the American imperialist aggressors and their traitorous lackeys, to isolate brutal enemy officers and thugs, to neutralize the fence-sitters, and to win over, draw in, and persuade the great masses of enemy troops (including entire military units) who desire peace to either sit still doing nothing or to come over to join us on the side of the revolution. Our goal is to split and divide puppet troops so that, even though the puppet army is large, only a small element of the army will actively and ferociously oppose us.

Then, even though our army is smaller than theirs, we will be able to mass our forces to attack U.S. troops and those puppets who are the most stubborn. Doing this will also enable us to implement our policy of forming a worker-peasant-soldier alliance and to move toward forming a number of neutral army units during localized insurrections and during the general offensive-general insurrection phase in the future.

First of all, we should focus on the general format of appealing to puppet soldiers to return to their homes to make their livings, or when fighting breaks out, appealing to them to run to join the ranks of the liberation army, to turn their guns on the enemy and then bring their weapons with them when they come over to the side of the people. For puppet officers, we need to intensify our secret contact operations and deploy a number of important agents as long-term, stay-behind agents to lie in wait for use when necessary. We must strive to convince a few puppet army battalions and regiments to secede from the enemy's ranks and to either stand on the side of the people or to completely come over to join the liberation army. We will keep such units intact and allow their officers to retain their current ranks. To coordinate with our military and political attacks, we must mobilize all classes of the population to correctly carry out military proselyting operations in order to help stimulate and accelerate the collapse and disintegration of the puppet army.

Currently, a number of localities in South Vietnam are confused and unsure about how to deal with puppet prisoners of war and deserters who are coming over to our side in ever-increasing numbers.

In order to resolve this problem, you should carry out the following three tasks:

a) Properly carry out the work of politically educating these prisoners and deserters.
b) Send most of them to carry out production tasks in your own local liberated areas.
c) Assign a small number whose revolutionary consciences have been awakened to our armed units or to army or headquarters production units. Puppet prisoners of war should no longer be released and allowed to return to enemy-controlled areas, as was done in the past, because we do not want them to be picked up by the enemy again and be sent back as replacements and reinforcements for the puppet army. Naturally, enemy thugs and dangerous elements must be imprisoned for reeducation.

As for American and satellite [allied] troops, the primary thing is to propagandize them so that they understand that America's war is an unjust war of aggression and that the Vietnamese people and the people of their own country are not enemies. We must also spread propaganda among them so that they understand our humane policy of amnesty and forgiveness toward prisoners of war and deserters in order to reduce their arrogance and brutality against the civilian population. Enemy proselyting leaflets and documents should be kept short. We should use excerpts and quotes from the American and foreign press denouncing America's war policy in order to show American soldiers the truth.

In addition, we must try to capture large numbers of American prisoners and to carry out our prisoner of war operations and policies very correctly. Everything, from their detention, administration, and education to how we deal with them on a daily basis, must be conducted strictly in accordance with the policies we have previously promulgated.

We must strengthen our organizations engaged in puppet proselyting and enemy proselyting operations, and we must strengthen the guidance and leadership provided by Party committees at all levels to direct this important work.

8. Build resolve to defeat the American aggressors. We must mobilize the entire Party, the entire population, and the entire army to resolutely overcome all difficulties and hardships and to strive to advance to defeat the war of aggression being conducted by several hundred thousand U.S. troops and half a million puppet troops while at the same time standing ready to fight a protracted war until final victory is secured in the event that the U.S. sends in several hundred thousand more American troops in order to further intensify the war in South Vietnam and if it expands the ground war to include the entire nation [meaning, if the U.S. invades North Vietnam].

Special attention must be devoted to ensuring that we do a good job in our political and ideological operations of educating all classes of the population to profoundly hate the enemy; to ensuring that cadres, Party members, and the broad masses of the population clearly understand the Party's policies and that they fully understand our formula of conducting a protracted war and relying primarily on our own strength; and to ensuring that everyone has firm faith in our final victory, that they do not fear the U.S., and that they have no illusions about the prospects for peace.

9. Mobilize the population to contribute to the resistance war and pay attention to building up the people's strength for a long, protracted battle. In the liberated zones and the areas we partially control, in addition to protecting and ensuring production, we must also increase production. In particular, we must strive to increase our production of rice and food crops by fifty or one hundred percent in order to improve the people's standard of living and to increase our contributions to the resistance war. We must move people who live in the lowlands up into the mountain jungles in order to increase the size of our production forces and to plant large quantities of corn and manioc. At the same time, we must strive to buy food from the lowlands and from outside markets and ship it up to our forces to ensure that our troops have adequate supplies of food.

We must ensure that the level of support [taxes] the people give to the resistance is set at a proper, median level. In Cochin China, I am not sure if the current level of contributions from the people is too high or too low, but in Region 5 the level of support seems to be rather heavy and burdensome.

In this situation, when the enemy is conducting savage military sweeps and bombardments and when he is striving to steal the people's livelihoods and to drain them dry, if we ask the people to contribute too much, I am afraid that the masses will not have sufficient strength to endure a long, protracted struggle. In order to reduce the level of contributions from the people, for the past several years the Central Committee [Hanoi] has tried to meet the financial requirements of the resistance war in South Vietnam. However, our financial capabilities up here [in North Vietnam] are limited. We recommend that you down at the battlefield level make careful calculations in order to limit expenditures and economize.

The issue of providing weapons and ammunition to the battlefields is currently the leading concern of the Party Central Committee and of our military headquarters staff up here [in North Vietnam]. We are making calculations and trying to make use of every possibility, both foreign and domestic, to meet these needs, and at the same time we are trying to overcome all difficulties in order to transport weapons and ammunition from North Vietnam down to you. Within the confines of South Vietnam, however, you all must provide proper guidance and supervision to ensure that all the supplies that we have sent and will send reach their intended destinations.

In addition, we suggest that you pay the utmost attention to economizing on the expenditure of ammunition and that you at the same time place heavy emphasis on capturing enemy weapons and ammunition so that these can be used by our forces.

* * *

The above are a number of ideas I wished to present to you. If there is some issue on which you do not completely agree, please let us know so that we can discuss the matter further.

I wish you all health and victory.

[signed] Ba [alias used by Le Duan]

Source: Le Duan, *Thu Vao Nam* [Letters to the South] (Hanoi: Su That Publishing House, 1986), 119–162. Translated by Merle L. Pribbenow.

161. Robert McNamara, Secretary of Defense: Memorandum to President Lyndon Johnson, November 30, 1965 [Excerpts]

Introduction

Returning to Washington, D.C., after a two-day trip to the Republic of Vietnam (RVN, South Vietnam), U.S. secretary of defense Robert S. McNamara reported to President Lyndon B. Johnson on November 30, 1965. McNamara believes that People's Army of Vietnam (PAVN, North Vietnamese Army) forces in South Vietnam will likely increase by about one-third in the course of a one-year period and that the U.S. troop levels there will thus have to be increased accordingly. He also recommends an escalation of the bombing of the Democratic Republic of Vietnam (DRV, North Vietnam) and suggests the imposition of a bombing halt and an attendant appeal for negotiations to build support for such a step. With both sides fully committed to the war effort, the result was a steady escalation of the war.

Primary Source

The Ky "government of generals" is surviving, but not acquiring wide support or generating actions; pacification is thoroughly stalled, with no guarantee that security anywhere is permanent and no indications that able and willing leadership will emerge in the absence of that permanent security. (Prime Minister Ky estimates that his government controls only 25% of the population today and reports that his pacification chief hopes to increase that to 50% two years from now.)

The dramatic recent changes in the situation are on the military side. They are the increased infiltration from the North and the increased willingness of the Communist forces to stand and fight, even in large-scale engagements. The Ia Drang River Campaign of early November is an example. The Communists appear to have decided to increase their forces in SVN both by heavy recruitment in the South (especially in the Delta) and by infiltration of regular NVN forces from the North. . . . The enemy can be expected to enlarge his present strength of 110 battalion equivalents to more than 150 battalion equivalents by the end of calendar 1966, when hopefully his losses can be made to equal his input.

As for the Communist ability to supply this force, it is estimated that, even taking account of interdiction of routes by air and sea, more than 200 tons of supplies a day can be infiltrated—more than enough, allowing for the extent to which the enemy lives off the land, to support the likely PAVN/VC force at the likely level of operations.

To meet this possible—and in my view likely—Communist buildup, the presently contemplated Phase I forces will not be enough (approx. 220,000 Americans, almost all in place by end of 1965). Bearing in mind the nature of the war, the expected weighted combat force ratio of less than 2-to-1 will not be good enough. Nor will the originally contemplated Phase II addition of 28 more U.S. battalions (112,000 men) be enough; the combat force ratio, even with 32 new SVNese battalions, would still be little better than 2-to-1 at the end of 1966. The initiative which we have held since August would pass to the enemy; we would fall far short of what we expected to achieve in terms of population control and disruption of enemy bases and lines of communications. Indeed, it is estimated that with the contemplated Phase II

addition of 28 U.S. battalions, we would be able only to hold our present geographical positions.

2. We have but two options, it seems to me. One is to go now for a compromise solution (something substantially less than the "favorable outcome" I described in my memo of Nov 3) and hold further deployments to a minimum. The other is to stick with our stated objectives and win the war, and provide what it takes in men and materiel. If it is decided not to move now toward a compromise, I recommend that the US both send a substantial number of additional troops and very gradually intensify the bombing of NVN. Amb. Lodge, Wheeler, Sharp and Westmoreland concur in this prolonged course of action, although Wheeler and Sharp would intensify the bombing of the North more quickly. (recommend up to 74 battalions by end-66: total to approx 400,000 by end-66. And it should be understood that further deployments (perhaps exceeding 200,000) may be needed in 1967.)

3. Bombing of NVN. . . . over a period of the next six months we gradually enlarge the target system in the northeast (Hanoi-Haiphong) quadrant until, at the end of the period, it includes "controlled" reconnaissance of lines of communication throughout the area, bombing of petroleum storage facilities and power plants, and mining of the harbors. (Left unstruck would be population targets, industrial plants, locks and dams).

4. Pause in bombing NVN. It is my belief that there should be a three- or four-week pause in the program of bombing the North before we either greatly increase our troop deployments to VN or intensify our strikes against the North. (My recommendation for a "pause" is not concurred in by Lodge, Wheeler, or Sharp.) The reasons for this belief are, first, that we must lay a foundation in the minds of the American public and in world opinion for such an enlarged phase of the war and, second, we should give NVN a face-saving chance to stop the aggression. I am not seriously concerned about the risk of alienating the SVNese, misleading Hanoi, or being "trapped" in a pause; if we take reasonable precautions, we can avoid these pitfalls. I am seriously concerned about embarking on a markedly higher level of war in VN without having tried, through a pause, to end the war or at least having made it clear to our people that we did our best to end it.

5. Evaluation. We should be aware that deployments of the kind I have recommended will not guarantee success. U.S. killed-in-action can be expected to reach 1000 a month, and the odds are even that we will be faced in early 1967 with a "no-decision" at an even higher level. My overall evaluation, nevertheless, is that the best chance of achieving our stated objectives lies in a pause followed, if it fails, by the deployments mentioned above.

Source: *The Pentagon Papers: The Defense Department History of United States Decisionmaking on Vietnam,* Vol. 4. Senator Gravel edition (Boston: Beacon, 1971), 622–623.

162. Henry Byroade, Ambassador in Rangoon: Aide-Mémoire to North Vietnamese Consul General Vu Huu Binh, December 29, 1965

Introduction

Following the imposition of another bombing halt on December 25, 1965, Washington made increased efforts to open negotiations with the Democratic Republic of Vietnam (DRV, North Vietnam). In this aide-mémoire, U.S. ambassador to Burma (present-day Myanmar) Henry Byroade informs North Vietnamese consul general in Burma Vu Huu Binh that the suspension in bombing can be extended should Hanoi make "a serious contribution toward peace." The halt was extended on the urging of U.S. secretary of defense Robert S. McNamara, but when Hanoi rejected negotiations and following intense lobbying by Admiral Ulysses S. G. Sharp, U.S. Pacific Command commander, the bombing of North Vietnam resumed on January 31, 1966.

Primary Source

1. As you are no doubt aware, there has been no bombing in North Viet-Nam since December 24 although some reconnaissance flights have continued. No decision has been made regarding a resumption of bombings and unless there is a major provocation we would hope that the present stand-down, which is in its fifth day, could extend beyond New Year. If your government will now reciprocate by making a serious contribution toward peace, it would obviously have a favorable effect on the possibility of further extending the suspension.

2. I and other members of my Embassy staff stand available at any time to receive any communication you may wish to address to me or to us.

Source: *Foreign Relations of the United States, 1964–1968: Vietnam, June–December 1965*, Vol. 3 (Washington, DC: U.S. Government Printing Office, 1996), 722.

163. Le Duan, First Secretary: Speech to the 12th Plenum of the Party Central Committee, December 1965 [Excerpts]

Introduction

In December 1965 with almost 200,000 American troops fighting in the Republic of Vietnam (RVN, South Vietnam) and with the U.S. bombing of the Democratic Republic of Vietnam (DRV, North Vietnam) steadily intensifying, the North Vietnamese Lao Dong (Workers' Party) Central Committee met in Hanoi to discuss a resolution that would determine the party's strategy for the conduct of the war against the Americans. There was considerable debate within the party leadership about how the war was going, how the war should be fought, and whether or not North Vietnam should agree to sit down to negotiate with the Americans. Fallout from the growing Sino-Soviet conflict exacerbated this debate, since many party members believed that Vietnam had now aligned itself with China. In a secret speech to the Central Committee during the discussion of the new resolution, First Secretary Le Duan addresses the questions of negotiating with the Americans and of where North Vietnam stands in the Sino-Soviet conflict.

Primary Source

. . . The question of fighting and talking is not an entirely new issue. In our own nation's history, Nguyen Trai implemented the strategy of using weakness to fight strength and of fighting and talking in order to defeat the Ming dynasty's feudal army. Our Chinese comrades decided to fight and talk simultaneously when they were fighting against the American–Chiang Kaishek clique. . . . In military terms, we do not advocate fighting until the enemy is totally destroyed . . . and the American imperialists are compelled to accept unconditional surrender. Instead, we advocate fighting until the puppet army has essentially disintegrated and until we have destroyed an important portion of the American army so that the American imperialist will to commit aggression will have been shattered and they are forced to recognize our conditions! That means the question of fighting and talking . . . involves selecting the correct stratagem, and it is directly linked to our political and military policies. . . .

Currently, the American imperialists are still planning to intensify and expand the war . . . but they also are eager for us to sit down with them at the negotiating table so that they can force us to make concessions. As for our side, we believe we cannot sit down at the table until we have caused the puppet army to disintegrate and until we have crushed the American imperialist will to commit aggression. This is very secret, and we have not yet advised any of the fraternal communist parties of our position on this matter. . . . This issue is very complicated because there are many differing opinions on the question of holding talks. . . . There are the concepts of countries that sincerely support us, but who . . . are worried that in prolonged combat our side's losses and sacrifices will be too great. And there are the concepts of a number of large nations in our camp [the communist bloc] whose strategic missions in the world are different than ours. For that reason everything about their concepts, from the contents of their ideas to the tone of voice in which they couch them, is different than ours. . . .

Maintaining solidarity within our camp and winning the sympathy and assistance of our camp is a strategic problem. The question of fighting and talking, on the other hand, is an issue involving a stratagem. However, the stratagem is very important, because if our stratagem is incorrect we might . . . cause the war to drag on and become protracted, thereby forcing our people to sacrifice more lives and more blood when we might have been able to reduce such losses.

In our situation, we may not have to wait until we have essentially won before we agree to begin talks. At some point in time, under certain specific conditions, we may be able to fight and talk simultaneously in order to restrict our opponent's military actions, to win broader sympathy and support throughout the world, and to conceal our own strategic intentions. The issue right now is when will be the right time to employ this stratagem. That time will come when our forces have won greater and more complete victories on the battlefield, when the enemy's situation has become more desperate and confused, and when the enemy's will to commit aggression has deteriorated further. The timing will also depend on agreement between the fraternal socialist nations and parties about the concept of fighting and talking. . . .

VI—A Number of Thoughts about International Aspects of the Problem of South Vietnam

. . . We are faced with one unfortunate fact: the revolutionary war in the southern half of our country is raging at a time when our camp, and the international communist movement, is not of one accord about the path of the world revolution. At certain times the public disagreements and arguments quieted down for a while, but recently the situation has reemerged and developed so that the tension is now even greater than it was when [Nikita] Khruschev was the leader of the Soviet Union. That is a fact. Previously, before Khruschev was removed from office, the three fraternal communist parties of the Soviet Union, China, and Vietnam, joined by the Lao communist party, sat down together in a meeting to discuss the problem in Laos. Now, however, the prospects for united action by our camp, or for a three-sided or four-sided discussion aimed at joining together to combat the American imperialists on the Vietnam problem, are very dim. Faced with this difficult situation, our Party Central Committee has had to be very cautious. We have had to think carefully and weigh many factors, and we have had to work with all of our might to win the most effective support and assistance from the nations in our camp as well as to try to avoid allowing the worst effects of the disagreement to harm our people's cause of combating the Americans to save the nation.

Our party has always and will always advocate solidarity in the international communist movement and solidarity between the Soviet Union and China, a solidarity based on Marxism-Leninism and on the ideology of the international proletariat. We sincerely believe in such solidarity, because we believe that the Vietnamese revolution in general and the revolution in South Vietnam in particular are integral parts of the world proletarian revolution. . . .

However, from another standpoint, as we work to win support and assistance from parties and nations in our camp and from the international communist movement, we must consider the strategic missions and the political positions of each individual party and country in order to present these parties and countries with logical requests for the correct level of assistance, because we must clearly understand that while the parties and nations that belong to our camp . . . are connected to one another through the spirit of international proletarianism, there are also differences in the concrete relationships between individual nations, differences created by their geographic locations, by their histories, by whether their strategic missions in the world are similar or different, and by regional issues. . . . With respect to the Party Central Committee's domestic and foreign policies, generally speaking all cadre and Party members basically agree with and support these policies. Recently, however, in light of the public arguments within the international communist movement about issues related to the revolutionary situation in our nation of Vietnam, a small number of our Party members have evidenced anxiety and suspicion that, in their eyes at least, it seemed that our Party's international path might have changed. . . . In order to dispel all these suspicions I believe it is necessary to discuss a few vital points. . . .

We must recognize that the strategic policy of our Party differs from the policies of the Soviet Communist Party and of the Chinese Communist Party. Our Party has concluded that the world revolution is now in an offensive position, and our Party advocates an intensification of the revolution's attacks against imperialism . . . so that we can achieve victory for the world proletarian revolution. This revolutionary strategy is fundamentally different than the defensive strategy of détente that is being followed by the Soviet Communist Party. . . .

When we delve more deeply into ideas about current international issues, we can also see many points of difference between the policies of our Party and the policies being followed by the Soviet and Chinese Communist Parties. . . . [However], just because we have differences does not mean that we place the Vietnamese revolutionary movement outside of the world proletarian revolutionary movement or that we place our nation outside of the socialist camp, and it does not mean that we are not determined to maintain solidarity with the Soviet Union and with China. . . . Our Party's policy is to defend the Soviet Union, to defend China, to maintain solidarity with the Soviet Union, and to maintain solidarity with China in order to unite and protect the entire socialist camp and the international communist movement. We are determined never to deviate from that path.

If we want to maintain solidarity with the Soviet Union and with China, then our Party must be independent and self-reliant. . . . We need this spirit of independence and self-reliance, but we must always be very modest. We must always view the Soviet Communist Party and the Chinese Communist Party as our older brothers, as parties with vast experience in revolutionary struggle that we must study and as parties from whom we must learn. . . . However, studying their experiences is one thing, but independence in policy direction is something altogether different. In order to be creative, we must be independent and self-reliant. Mechanical imitation can lead to errors, and sometimes it is even "reactionary," as Comrade Mao Zedong himself has said. . . .

With regard to the problem of South Vietnam, our Party took the initiative in launching a revolution that applied policies, formulas, and methods we had learned through the course of the August [1945] Revolution and during the first resistance war [the war against the French]. When we made the decision to launch the revolution in South Vietnam, Khruschev did not approve, and our Chinese comrades counseled us that we should view this as a long-term effort and that we should hold back to wait for an opportunity. However, we did not do that, and the tremendous victories won by the South Vietnamese revolution over the past several years clearly cannot be separated from our Party's spirit of independence and self-reliance.

In summary, I want to stress that . . . our policies and positions must be independent. . . . The reason I have spoken so much about the spirit of independence and self-reliance is that I believe our party has a serious problem: it lacks independence and self-reliance. Because of this lack of independence and self-reliance, a number of cadres and Party members can be easily swayed and lured off course, especially on international issues, and in that way they begin to suspect the correctness of our Party Central Committee's policies and programs. . . .

I have not talked about these matters in order to make us feel pessimistic and downhearted. . . . Even though there are profound differences of opinion between the two countries, both the Soviet Union and China are continuing to provide us with ample, effective, and ever increasing assistance. We are sincerely thankful for the precious assistance provided to us by the Soviet Union, China, and the other fraternal nations. These are not just polite words spoken from the tips of our tongues, but they come instead from the bottoms of our hearts. . . . Uncle Ho and the Politburo are extremely concerned about solidarity within our camp and within the international communist movement. However, we know that this is a very complex problem that cannot be solved in a short period of time. While our nation is still at war, we need to maintain a truly high degree of agreement and unanimity. The entire Party must unite around the Central Committee. . . . The entire Party must speak and act in strict accordance with the policies and positions of the Central Committee. . . . We must expunge all of the incorrect suspicions I mentioned earlier in order to be able to concentrate our strength and our will on the work of fighting the Americans to save the nation and of defeating the American aggressors. . . .

Source: *Van Kien Dang, Toan Tap 24, 1965* [Collected Party Documents, Volume 24, 1965] (Hanoi: Nha Xuat Ban Chinh Tri Quoc Gia, 2003), 524–621. Translated by Merle L. Pribbenow.

164. William Bundy: Memorandum for Secretary of State Dean Rusk, February 3, 1966 [Excerpt]

Introduction

An advocate of a hard-line approach toward the Democratic Republic of Vietnam (DRV, North Vietnam), William Bundy was assistant secretary of state for East Asian and Pacific affairs and was also a key Vietnam policymaker. Here Bundy writes to Secretary of State Dean Rusk regarding Hanoi's response to the aide-mémoire of December 19, 1965, in which the North Vietnamese leadership denounced U.S. public policy positions; however, the aide-mémoire had been sent only after the bombing pause had ended. Bundy speculates that the reason for the delay was probably the reluctance of the North Vietnamese leadership to open discussions during a pause in the bombing. This would appear to display weakness and indicate that the North Vietnamese government feared the U.S. bombing.

Primary Source

It seems to me that our response to this approach will take careful thought. As a first step, since Byroade's cables are hard to read together, I have done the attached pull-together, which contains the full text of the aide mémoire, and also the points made in the oral conversation. I think this gives us a much better starting point, with numerical headings, for our own reply. (Tab A).

We may know much better, on the basis of Byroade's interim response, whether Hanoi really intended to start a dialogue after the resumption. In the meantime, the present facts appear to indicate that Hanoi may have sent the instructions prior to the resumption, but that it should have been possible to send a last-minute "recall" or "cancel" message if Hanoi had desired. Byroade reports that the DRV interpreter came to him to seek the appointment in the "early afternoon" of January 31, Rangoon time. (Rangoon time is 1½ hours earlier than Saigon time.) This would suggest that the appointment was sought not earlier than 1500 Saigon time, whereas the first bombs had fallen at about 0900 Saigon time. The fact that the aide mémoire was still being typed when Byroade arrived at 1930 Rangoon time would suggest that the instructions must have been freshly received and that there may even have been a preliminary instruction to seek an appointment, followed by the later transmission of the detailed instructions. By 1730 Rangoon time (1900 Saigon time) ten hours had elapsed after the resumption (which we assume was instantaneously reported to Hanoi). We believe that Hanoi's communications to Rangoon may go either by direct commercial cable or by relay through Peiping, using some cryptographic system that is presumably immune to Chicom reading. We are now checking whether NSA [National Security Agency] has any reading on message transmissions of that date, but what stands out is that it would surely have been possible for Hanoi to send a fast commercial cable that need not have said anything more than a short instruction not to carry out prior instructions. In other words, the evidence does add up to a high probability that Hanoi was prepared to go through with the contact notwithstanding the resumption. Indeed, there appears to be a substantial possibility on the timing, that Hanoi even waited till it knew of the resumption before it dispatched the instructions. Paradoxical as it may seem, Hanoi may have been unwilling to open any dialogue during the suspension, lest this appear as a sign of weakness, and fear of our bombing.

Source: *United States–Vietnam Relations, 1945–1967,* VI.C.I (Washington, DC: U.S. Government Printing Office, 1971), 139–140.

165. Aide-Mémoire from the U.S. State Department to the North Vietnamese Government, Delivered to North Vietnamese Consul General Vu Huu Binh in Rangoon, February 16, 1966

Introduction

Responding to the Democratic Republic of Vietnam (DRV, North Vietnam) aide-mémoire of January 31, 1966, denouncing U.S. policy in Vietnam, the U.S. State Department sent an aide-mémoire through its ambassador to Burma (present-day Myanmar), Henry Byroade, to North Vietnamese consul general Vu Huu Binh in Rangoon (present-day Yangon). For the first time, Washington states that it is prepared to withdraw its troops from the Republic of Vietnam (RVN, South Vietnam) as part of a negotiated settlement. The United States defines its Vietnam policy as being in accordance with the military provisions of the 1954 General Accords, while at the same time the United States ignores the political provisions that had identified Vietnam as one state and had called for national elections in 1956. The North Vietnamese leadership subsequently informed Byroade that it was breaking off all diplomatic contact with the U.S. government as long as the bombing continued.

Primary Source

1. The USG [U.S. government] has taken note of the Aide Mémoire delivered to the American Ambassador in Rangoon on January 31, 1966.

2. The USG fully respects the basic rights of the Vietnamese people to peace, independence, sovereignty, unity and territorial integrity, as set forth in the Geneva Accords of 1954. As the USG has repeatedly said, it believes that these Accords, together with the 1962 Accords concerning Laos, are an adequate basis for peace in Southeast Asia or for negotiations looking toward a peaceful settlement.

3. The USG has repeatedly stated and hereby reaffirms that it is prepared to withdraw its forces from South Viet-Nam when peace is restored. The US has never stated that it must be the sole judge of when this condition exists. Plainly, the restoration of peace of the Geneva Accords dealing with the regroupment of opposing forces to their respective areas, and dealing with the obligations that the two zones shall not be utilized for the resumption of hostilities or in the service of an aggressive policy. It is the view of the USG that the DRV in introducing armed forces, military equipment, and political cadres into South Viet-Nam, has breached the provisions of the Accords, and has thus made necessary the actions undertaken by the USG in support of the legitimate right of the Republic of Viet-Nam to self-defense. The withdrawal of US forces would be undertaken in the light of the actions taken by the DRV in this regard, and would necessarily be subject also [to] the existence of adequate measures of verification.

The USG seeks no military bases of any kind in South Viet-Nam and has no desire whatever to retain its forces in South Viet-Nam after peace is secured.

4. With respect to the third of the DRV's four points, the US takes note that Chairman Ho Chi Minh in his letter of January 29 described the program of the NLF as seeking "to achieve independence, democracy, peace and neutrality in South Viet-Nam and to advance toward peaceful reunification." If this is all that is intended when it is stated that the affairs of the South Vietnamese be settled "in accordance with the program of the NLF," the third point would not be an obstacle to negotiations.

However, it appears that in referring to the program of the NLF the DRV may contemplate that the NLF arbitrarily be accorded integral participation in a coalition government or be accepted as the "sole genuine representative of the entire South Vietnamese people" prior to, and without regard to, an election. If this is what is meant by the third point, we would consider it in contradiction of the very objections specified above, and quite without warrant in the Geneva Accords of 1954.

It remains the essence of the USG view that the future political structure in South Viet-Nam should be determined by the South Vietnamese people themselves through truly free elections. The USG is categorically prepared to accept the results of elections held in an atmosphere free from force, intimidation or outside interference.

5. In the light of the foregoing and to make clear our understanding of a possible basis for discussions leading to a peaceful settlement, we submit for consideration of the DRV the following:

Point I—The basic rights of the Vietnamese people to peace, independence, sovereignty, unity and territorial integrity are recognized as set forth in the Geneva Accords of 1954. Obtaining compliance with the essential principles in the Accords is an appropriate subject for immediate, international discussions, or negotiations without preconditions. Such discussions or negotiations should consider, among other things, appropriate means, including agreed stages, for the withdrawal of military and quasi-military personnel and weapons introduced into South Viet-Nam or North Viet-Nam from one area to the other or into either area from any other outside source; the dismantling of any military bases in either areas, and the cancellation of any military alliances, that may contravene the Accords; and the regrouping and redeployment of indigenous forces.

Point II—Strict compliance with the military provisions of the Geneva Accords must be achieved in accordance with schedules and appropriate safeguards to be agreed upon in the said discussions or negotiations.

Point III—The internal affairs of South and North Viet-Nam must be settled respectively by the South and North Vietnamese peoples themselves in conformity with the principles of self-determination. Neither shall interfere in the affairs of the other nor shall there by any interference from any outside source.

Point IV—The issue of reunification of Viet-Nam must be decided peacefully, on the basis of free determination by the people of South and North Viet-Nam without outside interference.

Source: *Foreign Relations of the United States, 1964–1968,* Vol. 4 (Washington, DC: U.S. Government Printing Office, 2002), 228–230.

166. Ho Chi Minh: Replies to an Interview with Japanese NDN TV, April 1966

Introduction

In this interview with the Japanese network NDN TV, Ho Chi Minh, leader of the Democratic Republic of Vietnam (DRV, North Vietnam), comments on the course of the war and diplomatic efforts to end it. He claims that the "U.S. imperialists are waging aggression against Viet-nam" but that the more extensive the U.S. military involvement, the greater will be U.S. defeats. He makes exorbitant claims of U.S. losses in the war and states that the war has made the Vietnamese people more united and determined to push through to victory. He also argues that its policies are increasingly isolating the United States diplomatically.

Primary Source

Question: Mr. President, would you please tell us about the characteristic feature of the war in Viet-Nam in the recent period and its prospects?

Answer: This characteristic feature is: The more the U.S. imperialists bring troops into South Viet-Nam and intensify the air raids against towns and villages of the Democratic Republic of Viet-Nam, the heavier are their defeats.

In South Viet-Nam: During the first two months of 1966 alone, the South Viet-Nam army and people wiped out 32,000 enemy troops (including 16,000 Americans), neatly annihilated seven enemy battalions and thirty enemy companies (including four U.S. battalions), shot down or destroyed over 500 planes, and destroyed about 300 military vehicles.

In North Viet-Nam: The U.S. air attacks have also been defeated. Up to March 8, 1966, the North Viet-Nam army and people have downed over 900 U.S. planes.

On the international front, the U.S. so-called peace offensive has also failed. It has not been able to deceive anybody; instead, it has only increased U.S. isolation.

Now, President Johnson is feverishly preparing to dispatch tens of thousands of additional U.S. troops to South Viet-Nam. The army of aggression from the United States and its satellites is carrying out the savage and criminal "kill all, burn all, destroy all" policy.

But as the enemy grows more ferocious, the Vietnamese people become more closely united and firmly determined to defeat him. In the end, the U.S. imperialists will inevitably be defeated. Although the Vietnamese people's Resistance War against U.S. aggression for national salvation is to be a protracted and arduous one, its victory is left in no doubt.

Question: Mr. President, could we know your views on the recent Honolulu Conference between the U.S. authorities and the South Viet-Nam Administration?

Answer: That conference discussed the question of stepping up real war and sham peace in Viet-Nam. It was a most serious challenge to the Vietnamese people, to the American people, and to peace-loving people in the world. It laid bare the deceitfulness of President Johnson's so-called peace offensive.

The Thieu-Ky puppet clique were summoned to Honolulu to receive directly from their U.S. masters instructions to prepare conditions for an intensification and expansion of the aggressive war in Viet-Nam. This exposed further their nature as traitors to their country and faithful lackeys of the U.S. aggressors, to the peoples of all countries.

Question: How do you assess, Mr. President, the threats uttered by a number of people in the U.S. ruling circles to send U.S. troops for expanding the war in central and southern Laos and the repeated provocations staged by Thailand and South Vietnamese troops against the Kingdom of Cambodia?

Answer: The acts of aggression by the U.S. imperialists and their henchmen against Laos and Cambodia are part of the U.S. scheme to extend the war of aggression to the whole of Indochina.

The United States has been carrying out this scheme step by step: In Laos, it has been savagely intensifying its air attacks on the Liberated Zone. It has been using puppet troops to launch repeated attacks against the Lao people's Liberation Forces. It has been stealthily bringing Thailand troops in increasing numbers into Laos. It is now contemplating to dispatch U.S. troops to central and southern Laos for direct aggression.

With regard to the Kingdom of Cambodia, the U.S. aggressors have not only incited their South Vietnamese and Thailand henchmen to stage repeated provocations on the border, but have also arrogantly stated that U.S. troops may violate the Cambodian territory at any time. These are most brazen encroachments on the independence, sovereignty, and neutrality of the Lao and Khmer peoples, and a serious threat to peace in Indochina and Southeast Asia.

Since the U.S. imperialists want to turn the countries of Indochina into a single battlefield, the Indochinese peoples will unite still more closely and struggle resolutely to defeat them.

Question: Recently, the Japanese Government has engaged in certain activities with a view to carrying out its so-called peace work. What is your opinion on this subject?

Answer: President Johnson's "search for peace" is a hoax. The activities of the Japanese Government to carry out its so-called peace work are aimed at giving publicity to this U.S. swindle. They are also designed to lull into inactivity the Japanese people's resolute struggle against the U.S. war of aggression in Viet-Nam. Another purpose is to cover up the fact that the Japanese Government is helping the U.S. imperialists expand the war in Viet-Nam and allowing them to use Japanese territory as an important base for this war.

Should the Japanese Government really want to contribute to the restoration of peace in Viet-Nam, it would not have colluded with the U.S. aggressors. Unfortunately, it has worked hand in glove with the U.S. imperialists.

Question: As far as we know, your January 24, 1966, letter to the Heads of State of a number of countries has had widespread impact throughout the world. Will you kindly tell us about the significance of that letter?

Answer: The U.S. imperialists are waging aggression against Viet-Nam and jeopardizing ever more seriously the peace and security of the peoples of Indochina and Asia. This is an extremely gross violation of the 1954 Geneva Agreements on Viet-Nam and all norms of international law. Our people have to fight in self-defense, for the independence of their Fatherland, and for world peace.

In the letter I sent to the Heads of State of a number of countries on January 24, 1966, I pointed out these facts and voiced the Vietnamese people's determination to fight against the U.S. imperialist aggressors and fulfill their national and international obligations. Though protracted and arduous, this just struggle of ours is sure to end in victory. I also expounded the fair and reasonable stand of our Government and people regarding a settlement of the Viet-Nam problem.

This stand is a just stand of peace; therefore, it is gaining increasing approval and support from many Heads of State, governments, and the peoples of the world. I take this opportunity to convey our sincere thanks to all our friends throughout the five continents for their valuable support.

Lastly I wish to express our heartfelt thanks to the Japanese people for their warm support of our people's struggle against U.S. aggression, for national salvation.

Source: Ho Chi Minh, *On Revolution: Selected Writings, 1920–66*, edited by Bernard B. Fall (New York: Praeger, 1967), 371–374.

167. Ambassador Henry Cabot Lodge Jr.: Telegram to Secretary of State Dean Rusk, June 29, 1966 [Excerpts]

Introduction

Leaders of the Democratic Republic of Vietnam (DRV, North Vietnam) passed their own peace proposal to the United States through Polish representative to the International Control Commission (ICC) Janusz Lewandowski, then to Italian ambassador to the Republic of Vietnam (RVN, South Vietnam) Giovanni d'Orlandi, and then to U.S. ambassador Henry Cabot Lodge. The North Vietnamese plan called for a "political compromise" rather than focusing on de-escalation. Hanoi sought to explore the U.S. position but by working indirectly through the Soviet government, with the discussions to be kept secret from Beijing. This marked the beginning of Operation MARIGOLD, the abortive diplomatic effort to end the war. Here Ambassador Lodge reports to Washington the essence of the North Vietnamese proposal. Washington remained highly skeptical of the proposal, and in the end nothing came of it.

Primary Source

9. The Pole began by saying that Hanoi has been deeply disappointed by the proposals made by Ronning which, they are sure, had emanated originally from the United States and not from the Canadians. Ronning had proposed that the U.S. stop the bombing if North Viet-Nam stopped the infiltration, and had talked about the exchange of prisoners' parcels and letters. This had bitterly disappointed North Vietnam. The first point, they had said, would be unconditional surrender, and they could not accept it, but they are open to a "political compromise" settling once and for all the entire Viet-Nam question.

10. When D'Orlandi said that he was skeptical, the Pole said that Hanoi was prepared to go "quite a long way." "It is useless for me to add," said the Pole, "that should there not be any kind of a preliminary agreement, Hanoi will deny flatly ever having made any offer." According to the Pole, the North Vietnamese are "tightly controlled" by the Chinese Communists. The preliminary talks, therefore, should be between Moscow and Washington. When and if proposals should emerge which could be considered as a basis for negotiations, Hanoi would at that time and under those circumstances get into it. The Pole said that Hanoi was afraid of the Chinese Communists who have an interest in dragging on the war for many years. D'Orlandi added that the Pole was evidently "proud of himself" for having brought these proposals about.

11. The proposals are as follows:

A. They insist that the so-called National Liberation Front "take part" in the negotiations. The key word is "take part." According to D'Orlandi, there is "no question of their being the representative; they are not to have any monopoly."

B. There must be suspension of the bombing.

12. These are the two proposals.

13. Then there are other points, which D'Orlandi called "negative ones," which are that (a) Hanoi will not ask for immediate reunification, either by elections or otherwise, of North and South Vietnam; (b) They will not ask for establishment of a "socialist" system in South Viet-Nam; (c) They will not ask South Viet-Nam to change the relationships which it has in the field of foreign affairs; and (d) They will not ask for neutralization. (e) Although they will ask for U.S. withdrawal, they are ready to discuss a "reasonable calendar." (f) Although "we would like someone other than Ky"—to quote the words of Hanoi—they do not want to interfere with the South Vietnamese Government.

[. . .]

18. The Pole said that his Government would be willing to arrange for D'Orlandi to meet with appropriate Polish spokesmen anywhere—Hong Kong or Singapore. In response to a question by D'Orlandi as to why they had come to him, the Pole said they wanted "an able debater to put the case to President Johnson, and we feel that the Italian Government has the sympathy of the United States Government." Moreover, the Italians have the same interest we have in agreement between Washington and Moscow, and in shutting out Peking.

19. D'Orlandi's impression is that the Poles are desperately seeking a way out on Moscow's instructions. This, he said, may need further exploration. He had the definite impression that now Hanoi "was amenable to common sense" saying "they do not want anything that would not stop the whole war. They want a political settlement, and are prepared to go a long way."

Source: *Foreign Relations of the United States, 1964–1968,* Vol. 4 (Washington, DC: U.S. Government Printing Office, 2002), 468–470.

168. Ambassador Henry Cabot Lodge Jr.: Telegram to Secretary of State Dean Rusk, November 30, 1966 [Excerpt]

Introduction

Following the U.S. bombing of oil storage areas near Hanoi and Haiphong, Ho Chi Minh, leader of the Democratic Republic of Vietnam (DRV, North Vietnam), declared negotiations with the United States to end the war "out of the question." This U.S. escalation of the ROLLING THUNDER bombing campaign imperiled the indirect talks between North Vietnam and the United States in Operation MARIGOLD now ended. Here U.S. ambassador to the Republic of Vietnam (RVN, South Vietnam) Henry Cabot Lodge reports on the efforts of Polish representative to the International Control Commission (ICC) Janusz Lewandowski to keep the talks alive.

Primary Source

Lewandowski then began his statement. He first thanked me for coming today. He then said: "My trip to Hanoi was very important. You should understand that what has been reached up to now in our conversations in Saigon and in my conversations in Hanoi may be decisive. Both Mr. Rapacki and Mr. Gomulka think so.

D. "I presented to Hanoi my understanding of the U.S. position based on our conversations of November 14 and our previous conversations." He indicated the numbers of the paragraphs as he went along, as follows:

"1. I have insisted that the United States is interested in a peaceful solution through negotiations.

"2. Negotiations should not be interpreted as a way to negotiated surrender by those opposing the United States in Viet-Nam. A political negotiation would be aimed at finding an acceptable solution to all the problems, having in mind that the present status quo in South Viet-Nam must be changed in order to take into account the interests of the parties presently opposing the policy of the United States in South Viet-Nam, and that such a solution may be reached in an honorable and dignified way not detrimental to national pride and prestige.

"3. That the United States are not interested from a point of view of its national interests in having a permanent or long term military presence in South Viet-Nam once a peaceful solution to the conflict has been reached. That is why the offer made in Manila regarding the withdrawal of U.S. troops and the liquidation of American bases should be considered in all seriousness.

"4. The United States would be ready, should other parties show a constructive interest in a negotiated settlement, to work out and to discuss with them proposals of such a settlement covering all important problems involved from a cease-fire to a final solution and withdrawal of U.S. troops.

"5. That the United States, within a general solution, would not oppose the formation of a South Vietnamese Government based on the true will of the Vietnamese people with participation of all through free democratic elections, and that the United States would be prepared to accept the necessary control machinery to secure the democratic and free character of such elections and to respect the results of such elections.

"6. The United States hold the view that unification of Viet-Nam must be decided by the Vietnamese themselves for which the restoration of peace and the formation of proper representative organs of the people in South Viet-Nam is a necessary condition.

"7. The United States are ready to accept and respect a true and complete neutrality of South Viet-Nam.

"8. The United States are prepared to stop the bombing of the territory of North Viet-Nam if this will facilitate such a peaceful solution. In doing so, the United States are ready to avoid any appearance that North Viet-Nam is forced to negotiate by bombings or that North Viet-Nam have negotiated in exchange for cessation of bombing. Stopping of bombings would not involve recognition or confirmation by North Viet-Nam that its armed forces are or were infiltrating into South Viet-Nam.

"9. I have informed the proper governmental sources that at the same time, the United States, while not excluding the unification of Viet-Nam, would not agree to unification under military pressure.

"10. While the United States are seeking a peaceful solution to the conflict, it would be unrealistic to expect that the United States will declare now or in the future its acceptance of North Viet-Nam's four or five points." End of statement.

E. He then stopped and said, "I ask you whether this is a correct statement of the United States point of view."

F. I said that obviously on a matter of such importance, I would have to refer to my government for a definitive reply, but I could say off hand that much of what he cited was in keeping with the spirit of our policy.

G. Personally, I would like to have a closer definition of the language in his paragraph 2 stating that the "present status quo in Viet-Nam must be changed in order to take into account the interested parties opposing the policy of the United States in South Viet-Nam." He said that he would be glad to change the word from "must" to "would." I said that this was obviously something which could be discussed.

H. Another point which I felt might need some clarification would be the first sentence in paragraph 8 which stated: "The United States are prepared to stop the bombing of the territory of North Viet-Nam if this will facilitate a peaceful solution."

I. In general, it was correct to say that we were interested in a peaceful solution, we wished to humiliate nobody, we did not wish anyone to lose pride or prestige, and that our offer at Manila was made in good faith.

J. Lewandowski then said that what he had just read was "very firmly based on conversations with the most respectable government sources in Hanoi" and that it was in addition "vouched for by Mr. Rapacki." He said that he made that statement so as to "avoid any belief on your part that this was not a serious proposition."

K. He added: "I am authorized to say that if the United States are really of the views which I have presented, it would be advisable to confirm them directly by conversation with the North Vietnamese Ambassador in Warsaw."

L. He then repeated once again that "in case of any leak, a denial would be issued." He repeated that "secrecy is of fundamental importance in this case. In fact, it is an essential element of the whole proposition."

M. He then said: "The United States should stop the bombing of North Viet-Nam apart from all other things."

N. He stated: "I was also informed by Hanoi and Warsaw that I should be ready to place myself at your disposal for any comment that you might wish to make."

O. I said that I would be interested in knowing who was the "responsible government source in Hanoi" with whom he spoke. After some hesitation, he said that it was Pham Van Dong, who spoke after "collective debate among all the proper authorities." In other words, this had "the Presidium behind it." He then said:

P. "If you agree that my presentation is in accord with yours and are ready to confirm it with the North Vietnamese Ambassador in Moscow, I would ask for another meeting to clear up things of a practical character." I asked what these were, and he said "the identity of the U.S. representative." He added that both Rapacki and Gomulka attached great importance to his talks with me. "They specifically want to convince you of the importance which should be attached by the United States," he added.

Q. I assured him that we did attach great importance to this. He added that Moscow had been informed.

R. He then said that he hoped we would get at this as "fast as possible." The more delay, the greater the danger. The dangers were two-fold—1) the danger of a leak, and 2) that there would be someone "working against a solution." He felt that we should "keep the present channel" and that we should "not try other channels." To do so would not only create the danger of a leak but also the danger of misinterpretation.

Source: *Foreign Relations of the United States, 1964–1968,* Vol. 4 (Washington, DC: U.S. Government Printing Office, 2002), 890–894.

169. Ambassador Henry Cabot Lodge Jr.: Telegram to Acting Secretary of State Nicholas Katzenbach, December 9, 1966

Introduction

In the first few days of December 1966, at the same time that the U.S. government had informed the leadership of the Democratic Republic of Vietnam (DRV, North Vietnam) of its willingness to enter into direct talks, U.S. fighter-bombers struck oil storage areas in the suburbs of Hanoi and Haiphong. Here U.S. ambassador to the Republic of Vietnam (RVN, South Vietnam) Henry Cabot Lodge reports to Acting Secretary of State Nicholas Katzenbach that Polish representative to the International Control Commission (ICC) Janusz Lewandowski had told Italian ambassador to South Vietnam Giovanni d'Orlandi that it was his belief that Hanoi was not prepared to enter into direct talks with the United States. D'Orlandi, however, informed Lodge that he believed that Lewandowski had in fact persuaded North Vietnamese premier

Pham Van Dong to work to overcome the opposition of the North Vietnamese leadership to such talks.

Primary Source

D'Orlandi asked to see Secretary and Ambassador this evening following dinner party in Secretary's honor. Conversation was as follows:

1. Lewandowski had called urgently on D'Orlandi evening of December 8, on instructions, to express grave concern that U.S. had carried out heavy bombing attacks in Hanoi area on December 2 and December 4, directly following December 1 conversation between Lewandowski and Lodge. Lewandowski conveyed lurid reports from Polish attache Hanoi alleging that December 2 attack had included bombing and machine-gunning within city area and had caused 600 casualties. December 4 attack also described as serious and in Hanoi area. Lewandowski protested to D'Orlandi— urging him to convey message to Lodge and to Secretary if possible—that such attacks could only threaten or destroy possibility of contact in Warsaw. Lewandowski argued that Hanoi could not be expected to enter discussions in face of such escalation. (While whole tenor of message was extremely strong, Lewandowski did not repeat not state that he was actually reporting Hanoi's expressions of view, but rather Warsaw judgment.)

2. D'Orlandi had responded to Lewandowski that no contact had in fact taken place as yet because of apparent refusal of Rapacki to convey firm message, that U.S. had taken forthcoming action in declaring itself ready for discussions and prepared to make contact on December 6, and that it was thus not fair to say possibility of contact destroyed by U.S. action. D'Orlandi went on to say that his hope had been to make contact in any event.

Source: *United States–Vietnam Relations, 1945–1967,* VI.C.4 (Washington, DC: U.S. Government Printing Office, 1971), 77–79.

170. Nguyen Duy Trinh, Foreign Minister: Report to the Party Central Committee on Initiating a New Talk-Fight Strategy, January 23, 1967 [Excerpts]

Introduction

In December 1966 the leadership of the Democratic Republic of Vietnam (DRV, North Vietnam) for the first time permitted an American journalist, Harrison Salisbury of the *New York Times,* to visit North Vietnam. Salisbury's articles about the effects of the U.S. bombing of North Vietnam generated tremendous public attention, especially among those opposed to the war. That same month, however, the secret diplomatic initiative code-named Operation MARIGOLD aimed at initiating direct talks between the United States and North Vietnam collapsed. In January 1967 the North Vietnamese Lao Dong (Workers' Party) Central Committee met to discuss and approve a new stratagem called "Talk-Fight" that was designed to exploit growing opposition to the war in the United States. Here North Vietnamese foreign minister Nguyen Duy Trinh briefs the Central Committee on the outlines of the new stratagem.

Primary Source

I—THE CURRENT SITUATION AND OUR POLICY

1. *The American imperialists are facing increasing defeats and are increasingly confused and on the defensive, both militarily and politically.* . . . *They are facing many internal problems* inside the United States. The desire to bring the war to an end quickly has become relatively widespread because the war of aggression in Vietnam has begun to weigh heavily on the political, the social, and, to some extent, the economic life of the American people. . . . *In the international community, the U.S. is more isolated than ever before.* Even the U.S.'s closest allies do not support the war of aggression in Vietnam. Many neutral countries and many politicians are increasingly critical of the U.S.'s escalation of the bombing of North Vietnam. . . . The U.S. is striving in every way possible to conceal the true "Americanization" of the war. . . . The U.S. has launched a series of "peace campaigns," presenting first 14 points, then seven points, then three points, etc. They have sent representatives to lobby for support from many different nations, and even from U Thant and the Pope. They are also lobbying for the support of a number of socialist Eastern European countries and have sent people to make feelers to us directly. During these "peace offensives," the U.S. has made maximum use of their "bombing" and "cessation of bombing" cards, and their recent attacks against a number of locations in Hanoi were aimed at placing further pressure on us. . . . It is clear that the American imperialists are confused and on the defensive, both militarily and politically.

However, their evil desire to seize and occupy the southern half of our nation has so far remained unchanged. . . . They are now forced to choose between three options:

1/—Expand their limited ground war of aggression into North Vietnam. . . .
2/—Send in additional troops and equipment to fight a protracted war in South Vietnam. . . .
3/—Strive to achieve an important military victory by 1968 and then use their position of strength to achieve a political settlement on terms favorable to them. . . .

The general trend of the American leadership is to try to end the war quickly, before the 1968 elections. . . . [President Lyndon] Johnson himself is following a middle-of-the-road policy (*middle course*) [in English] in order to win the support of both the "hawks" and the "doves," but Johnson usually listens to the "hawks" more than he does to the doves. . . . He wants to choose the third option to seek a way out in order to win the support of the majority and retain the Presidency during the coming elections. . . .

Even though we are facing a few problems in the new stage of our struggle against the Americans to save our nation, *our position is the position of victory,* and the enemy's position is a position of defeat. The enemy's fundamental weak point, his political posture, is increasingly becoming clearer and is causing the enemy to more isolated than ever before.

2. *From the basis of this posture of victory, the situation is becoming increasingly favorable for us to seize the initiative by employing our strategy of fighting while talking, talking while fighting.* . . . We have won increasingly greater and stronger political support and material assistance from the fraternal socialist nations, which has made an important contribution to the intensification of our people's just struggle in both North and South Vietnam. We have also striven to expand and strengthen the united front of the world's population opposed to American imperialist aggression in Vietnam. . . . We have also striven to find ways to create divisions within the ranks of the imperialists, have attracted support from neutralist forces, and have caused our enemy additional difficulties and confusion. . . .

During the recent phase, we have not yet had an opportunity to employ our "fighting while talking, talking while fighting" stratagem because we had only defeated the American imperialist "special war," and the enemy still believed that the massive introduction of American troops into combat operations in South Vietnam could still secure victory. . . . *Now the situation has become favorable for us to seize the initiative by utilizing our stratagem of fighting while talking, talking while fighting.*

It is now favorable because of four factors:

—*First,* . . . The balance of forces is increasingly becoming favorable for our side.
—*Second,* the enemy has clearly recognized that he cannot defeat us, he is undecided and hesitant, and he is tending toward selecting option number three. On our side, . . . we need to make a major effort to concentrate the forces of both North and South Vietnam to create an opportunity to win a decisive victory within a relatively short period of time.
—*Third,* the fraternal socialist nations have clearly recognized our resolve. Even though some of them have some differences with us over strategy or stratagems, they all sympathize with and support us . . . , although their level of support varies. . . .
—*Fourth,* generally speaking, international opinion . . . has strongly supported our four-point program. . . . but they also do not want us to totally reject negotiations while we continue to fight. . . .

During the coming phase, we must, in coordination with the military struggle and the political struggle, further intensify our diplomatic struggle by taking the offensive to attack the enemy politically and employ our stratagem of fighting while talking, talking while fighting. . . . The military struggle will be the directly decisive element. The military struggle must be closely coordinated with the political struggle. . . . The diplomatic struggle must support the military struggle and the political struggle, and success in the military struggle and in the political struggle will create favorable conditions for us to expand the diplomatic struggle.

The mission of the diplomatic struggle is to contribute . . . to the achievement of our current two primary concrete goals:

—Forcing the U.S. to end the bombing of North Vietnam;
—Forcing the U.S. to withdraw its troops from South Vietnam.

. . . On the basis of firmly maintaining our four-point program, we will develop total supremacy on the political front, seize the initiative in attacking the enemy, support the struggle on the battlefield, . . . and create an opportunity to win a decisive victory. We will employ our stratagem of fighting while talking, talking while fighting. This means that, while in South Vietnam we will continue to fight to try to win a decisive victory, there can be talks between the enemy and ourselves in various forms, ranging from individual contacts to a peace conference. Naturally, victory on the battlefield in South Vietnam is the decisive factor. As long as we have not won such a victory, we cannot win victory at the conference table. . . .

On our side . . . we must first of all fight for the demand that the enemy end the bombing of North Vietnam. . . . The enemy knows that if he does not end the bombing there is no possibility of negotiations. After we achieve this first step, we need to continue to struggle to force them to prolong the cessation of the bombing while at the same time we focus on demanding that they withdraw their troops from South Vietnam. . . .

The enemy's position is to stubbornly try to hang on in South Vietnam, and his plan is to link the cessation of the bombing of North Vietnam with a solution to the problem in South Vietnam. The enemy has presented a plan that we must accept or reject *in toto* (a package deal) [in English] to achieve this goal. Meanwhile . . . the most important issue for us is still the liberation of South Vietnam. Our strategy is to demand that they end the bombing unconditionally and not link the end of the bombing with a settlement of the problem in South Vietnam.

The concrete goals of our application of the "fighting while talking, talking while fighting," stratagem are 1) To win additional support from international public opinion. . . . 2) To exacerbate the enemy's domestic problems and his international difficulties. . . . 3) To contribute to the collapse of the puppet army and to . . . strengthen our urban movement in South Vietnam. . . .

Looking at the entire process of our employment of the "fighting while talking, talking while fighting" stratagem, we can visualize three different phases:

—Phase One is the phase in which we force the enemy to end the bombing of North Vietnam without conditions, leading to official and public contacts between North Vietnam and the United States. During this phase, after the U.S. agrees to end the bombing of North Vietnam, North Vietnam and the United States will talk to one another . . . while in South Vietnam, the two sides will continue to fight one another. In reality, we will utilize the forum provided by these talks to denounce the U.S. to the general public.
—Phase Two is the phase when we force the enemy to continue the unconditional cessation of the bombing of North Vietnam, force him to talk to the NLF, and force him to withdraw his troops from South Vietnam. . . . The course of the struggle during this phase will be intimately linked with the military and political struggle on the battlefield in South Vietnam. Only when we secure a decisive victory on the battlefield will we be able to secure success in this phase.
—Phase Three is the phase in which the international community recognizes and confirms the results achieved during Phase Two.

. . . Of the three phases outlined above, Phase Two is the most important phase. It is the decisive phase. However, Phase One is the initial phase and is also of great importance. . . .

The above is our vision of the major features of the process of utilizing our stratagem. . . . The basic situation is advantageous for us, but it will develop in a very complex fashion, because the enemy is very stubborn and devious, because internally there are many differing opinions within the enemy camp, and because the serious disagreement within the socialist camp will also influence, to a certain extent at least, the enemy's attitude. . . . We must be on guard against and overcome misguided assessments and ideas within our own internal ranks. At the same time, we need to develop a plan to persuade both those fraternal socialist nations that may suspect that we are seeking negotiations too soon and may therefore take an attitude that, directly or indirectly, does not agree with us, and those that are so much in favor of negotiations to settle the problem that they pressure us to reach a political settlement too soon, before the situation is ripe. We must be extremely careful to keep our enemy from exploiting disagreements about strategy between us and our fraternal socialist allies. . . .

The goal of the initial phase of the use of our stratagem is to force the enemy to end the bombing of North Vietnam without conditions, and only then will there be talks between North Vietnam and the United States. The two sides will sit down to talk with each other, officially and publicly at the ambassadorial level. The purpose of the talks will not be to resolve the Vietnam problem but to clarify each side's views while the fighting continues in South Vietnam.

This action will be to our advantage both politically and militarily. Even though it will be difficult for the enemy to end the bombing of North Vietnam, the pressure of public opinion demanding that the U.S. end the bombing immediately and unconditionally has turned the bombing of North Vietnam into one of the most prominent issues, and we believe it is possible that at some point the enemy will have to consider taking such an action.

The immediate situation demands that we . . . take the initiative by presenting the issue as follows: If the United States ends the bombing permanently and unconditionally, the Democratic Republic of Vietnam and the United States could hold talks. . . .

Public opinion is now heated and is favorable to our side and not to the enemy. After the recent U.S. bombing of Hanoi, a powerful movement has grown up around the world that is vigorously denouncing the Americans. Taking one more step with respect to the demand that the U.S. end the bombing of North Vietnam, after the U.S. refused U Thant's request and refused to extend the cessation of the bombing through several holidays, international opinion no longer trusts the U.S. and is worried that the U.S. might escalate the bombing further. In this environment, Comrade Pham Van Dong's reception of the American journalist Salisbury and the press conference held by our representative in Paris has caused a great deal of public interest and created a new opportunity to take another step forward in the struggle to demand that the U.S. end the bombing of North Vietnam. . . . The U.S. ruling circles are becoming increasingly divided internally. . . . The Americans clearly see our resolve and have recognized, to some extent, our intentions, so they are afraid that we will step up our supply efforts. They are afraid that if they stop the bombing, they will face both military and political difficulties. They are afraid of a recurrence of the situation of fighting during talks that took place during the Korean War. If they stop the bombing, it will be even harder for them to resume it again. However, they also see that if they do not stop the bombing, it will be difficult to enter into negotiations and that they will become increasingly isolated in the face of public opinion. . . . During his speech to Congress, Johnson clearly portrayed the bleak status of the war of aggression in Vietnam. During the coming days, the debate on the Vietnam issue will become heated.

However, public opinion does not yet clearly realize that we could begin talking to the Americans if they stop the bombing of North Vietnam permanently and unconditionally. For that reason, if we raise this matter publicly, public pressure on the U.S. will increase and the Americans will become even more confused, clumsy, and will be placed on the defensive. It may also deepen internal disagreements, further divide their ranks, and make their stance even shakier.

If we do not take the offensive now, we will be missing an excellent opportunity, because:

—Public opinion is now heated on this subject, and if we do not do something further, it will quiet down. Once that happens, when we raise an issue it will be hard to gain as much attention as we can get at this point in time.

—It is still possible that Johnson will decide to escalate in order to win over the opposing factions. If that happens,

it will be harder for us to employ this stratagem in that situation. Also, if the U.S. sees that we do not take action, they will mount a public offensive and distort and slander our position.

—Our friends may take some misguided action in one direction or another, which would further complicate our effort to utilize this stratagem.

3. How we will publicly present this question to the world: . . .

We will say something like, "recently, the U.S. has suggested that it would like to talk to the Democratic Republic of Vietnam." Finally, we will say,

"After the United States has unconditionally ended the bombing and all other acts of war directed against the Democratic Republic of Vietnam, the Democratic Republic of Vietnam and the United States could talk to one another."

(The above is the general thrust of the content of our statement, which will be given in the form of an answer by our Foreign Minister during a press interview. After it is written out formally as an answer, we will review the wording and tighten it up.)

4. After our statement is made public, there are several possibilities:

—The U.S. will reject it out of hand and will continue to escalate.

—The U.S. will put forward conditions for bargaining purposes. After a period of bargaining, they might:
  + Lie and place the blame on us in order to continue escalating their attacks.
  + Halt the bombing as a practical matter in order to talk to us.
  + Accept our conditions and end the bombing in order to sit down with us for discussions.

At present the first possibility is unlikely because the U.S., like us, wants to win over public opinion. The third possibility is very unlikely. As for the second possibility—that after a period of bargaining they will stop the bombing in practical terms in order to talk to us—there are difficulties here as well. We are not subjective [overoptimistic] about this, but we need to fight hard to push the U.S. into taking this option. Whether we succeed in attaining this option or not, we will still benefit because we will have won over public opinion, which will place pressure on the U.S. and further isolate the Americans. . . . No matter what happens, however, we must fight strongly in the arena of public opinion (while at the same time making even more powerful military and political attacks against them) in order to be able to pressure them into stopping the bombing and sitting down to talk. . . .

We will provide timely notification of our moves to the Soviet Union, China, other fraternal nations, and nations that have good relations with us so that everyone understands what we are doing and supports us. . . . The National Liberation Front will demonstrate its support for the answer given by the Foreign Minister of the Democratic Republic of Vietnam during the interview. At the same time, the Front will emphasize its resolve to hold firm to South Vietnam's demands (the demands that the U.S. immediately and unconditionally end the bombing of North Vietnam, that the U.S. recognize the four point program and the five point proclamation, that it recognize the Front as the only true representative of the people of South Vietnam, and that all U.S. and satellite [allied] military personnel must be withdrawn from South Vietnam)....

Source: *Van Kien Dang, Toan Tap 28, 1967* [Collected Party Documents, Volume 28, 1967] (Hanoi: Nha Xuat Ban Chinh Tri Quoc Gia, 2003), 116–140. Translated by Merle L. Pribbenow.

171. Dean Rusk, Secretary of State: Telegram to Ambassador Henry Cabot Lodge Jr., February 10, 1967 [Excerpt]

Introduction

In early February 1967 Soviet premier Aleksei Kosygin traveled to London for talks with British prime minister Harold Wilson that included the U.S. proposals for peace talks with the Democratic Republic of Vietnam (DRV, North Vietnam). The British then passed along the substance of these discussions with Washington. In the U.S. State Department response, shared by U.S. secretary of state Dean Rusk with ambassador to the Republic of Vietnam (RVN, South Vietnam) Henry Cabot Lodge, the Lyndon Johnson administration reverses the sequence of proposals that had been presented earlier. Now the North Vietnamese government will have to assure the United States that it has halted infiltration into South Vietnam before there can be any halt in the bombing of North Vietnam. The Johnson administration believed that should Hanoi agree to this, the Communist forces in South Vietnam would be significantly weakened.

Primary Source

2. We have provided British with text of proposal. They had already outlined a variation of it orally to Kosygin, who expressed interest today and asked for written text to forward at once to Hanoi. This has been provided and reads as below. You may convey to Ky orally as much of digest of proposal as you deem wise in view of great necessity for secrecy.

QTE A. The United States will order a cessation of bombing of North Vietnam as soon as they are assured that infiltration from North Vietnam to South Vietnam has stopped. This assurance can be communicated in secret if North Vietnam so wishes.

B. Within a few days (with a period to be agreed with the two sides before the bombing stops) the United States will stop further

augmenting their force in South Vietnam. The cessation of bombing of North Vietnam is an action which will be immediately apparent. This requires that the stoppage of infiltration become public very quickly thereafter. If Hanoi is unwilling to announce the stoppage of infiltration, the United States must do so at the time its stops augmentation of US forces. In that case, Hanoi must not deny it.

C. Any assurances from Hanoi can reach the United States direct, or through Soviet channels, or through the Soviet and British Governments. This is for North Vietnam to decide. END QUOTE.

3. In explaining about text, we believe British will have made clear that our stopping "augmenting" would still permit rotation and continued supply. Stoppage of infiltration defined as meaning that men and arms cannot move from DRV into South Vietnam. You should note also that wording of subpara A preclude any sudden last-minute reinforcements after bombing has stopped....

4.... Deprived of additional men and of urgently needed equipment from the North, we believe NVANC forces would be significantly weakened in concrete terms and would probably suffer serious adverse effects on their morale. If infiltration in fact ceases and this word can be picked up by SVN and allied psychological warfare units, we believe there are big chances that Chien Hoi and reconciliation programs would produce substantially larger returns. In short, we think proposal is defensible and forthcoming, if it should ever be surfaced, but at the same time clearly favorable in terms of its effect on the military and morale situation....

Source: U.S. Department of State, Memo, Declassified Top Secret, State 135513, 1967.

172. Ho Chi Minh: Letter to Lyndon Johnson, February 15, 1967

Introduction

On February 15, 1967, in a personal letter to U.S. president Lyndon Johnson, President Ho Chi Minh of the Democratic Republic of Vietnam (DRV, North Vietnam) responds to the U.S. proposal for a bombing halt. In this uncompromising missive, Ho accuses the United States of violating pledges that it had made at the 1954 Geneva Conference, intervening in Vietnamese affairs, and turning the Republic of Vietnam (RVN, South Vietnam) into a U.S. "neocolony and military base." He also accuses the United States of war crimes. The only way to bring about peace is for the United States to cease its "aggression" by immediately halting the bombing of North Vietnam and withdrawing its own and "satellite" troops from South Vietnam, recognizing the National Front for the Liberation of South Vietnam (usually known as the National Liberation Front [NLF]), and permitting the holding of free elections.

Ho does not mention North Vietnam's infiltration of troops into South Vietnam, which the United States had demanded as a precondition to halt the bombing; rather, he says that if the United States is sincere about direct peace talks with the North Vietnamese government, the United States must first halt unconditionally all bombing of North Vietnam.

Primary Source

To His Excellency Mr. Lyndon B. Johnson, President, United States of America

Excellency, on February 10, 1967, I received your message. Here is my response.

Viet-Nam is situated thousands of miles from the United States. The Vietnamese people have never done any harm to the United States. But, contrary to the commitments made by its representative at the Geneva Conference of 1954, the United States Government has constantly intervened in Viet-Nam, it has launched and intensified the war of aggression in South Viet-Nam for the purpose of prolonging the division of Viet-Nam and of transforming South Viet-Nam into an American neo-colony and an American military base. For more than two years now, the American Government, with its military aviation and its navy, has been waging war against the Democratic Republic of Viet-Nam, an independent and sovereign country.

The United States Government has committed war crimes, crimes against peace and against humanity. In South Viet-Nam a half-million American soldiers and soldiers from the satellite countries have resorted to the most inhumane arms and the most barbarous methods of warfare, such as napalm, chemicals, and poison gases in order to massacre our fellow countrymen, destroy the crops, and wipe out the villages. In North Viet-Nam thousands of American planes have rained down hundreds of thousands of tons of bombs, destroying cities, villages, mills, roads, bridges, dikes, dams and even churches, pagodas, hospitals, and schools. In your message you appear to deplore the suffering and the destruction in Viet-Nam. Permit me to ask you: Who perpetrated these monstrous crimes? It was the American soldiers and the soldiers of the satellite countries. The United States Government is entirely responsible for the extremely grave situation in Viet-Nam.

The American war of aggression against the Vietnamese people constitutes a challenge to the countries of the socialist camp, a threat to the peoples' independent movement, and a grave danger to peace in Asia and in the world.

The Vietnamese people deeply love independence, liberty, and peace. But in the face of the American aggression they have risen up as one man, without fearing the sacrifices and the privations. They are determined to continue their resistance until they have won real independence and liberty and true peace. Our just cause enjoys the approval and the powerful support of peoples throughout the world and of large segments of the American people.

The United States Government provoked the war of aggression in Viet-Nam. It must cease that aggression, it is the only road leading to the re-establishment of peace. The United States Government must halt definitively and unconditionally the bombings and all other acts of war against the Democratic Republic of Viet-Nam, withdraw from South Viet-Nam all American troops and all troops from the satellite countries, recognize the National Front of the Liberation of South Viet-Nam, and let the Vietnamese people settle their problems themselves. Such is the basic content of the four-point position of the Government of the Democratic Republic of Viet-Nam, such is the statement of the essential principles and essential arrangements of the Geneva agreements of 1954 on Viet-Nam. It is the basis for a correct political solution of the Vietnamese problem. In your message you suggested direct talks between the Democratic Republic of Viet-Nam and the United States. If the United States Government really wants talks, it must first halt unconditionally the bombings and all other acts of war against the Democratic Republic of Viet-Nam. It is only after the unconditional halting of the American bombings and of all other American acts of war against the Democratic Republic of Viet-Nam that the Democratic Republic of Viet-Nam and the United States could begin talks and discuss questions affecting the two parties.

The Vietnamese people will never give way to force, it will never accept conversation under the clear threat of bombs.

Our cause is absolutely just. It is desirable that the Government of the United States act in conformity to reason.

Sincerely,

Ho Chi Minh

> **Source:** "President Ho Chi Minh's Reply," *Department of State Bulletin* 56(1450) (1967): 596–597.

173. Martin Luther King Jr. Declares His Opposition to the War during a Sermon at New York's Riverside Church, April 4, 1967

Introduction

In a sermon at the Riverside Church in New York City delivered on April 4, 1967, U.S. civil rights leader Dr. Martin Luther King Jr. announces his firm opposition to the Vietnam War. King traces the course of U.S. involvement in Vietnam and points out the enormous financial drain of the war, which is taking funds from the effort to eradicate poverty at home. King sets forth his own five-point peace program: an immediate halt in the U.S. bombing of the Democratic Republic of Vietnam (DRV, North Vietnam), a unilateral cease-fire, an end to the U.S. military buildup in Laos and Thailand, recognition that the National Front for the Liberation of South Vietnam (usually known as the National Liberation Front [NLF]) must play a role in negotiations and a future Vietnamese government, and, in accordance with the 1954 Geneva Agreements, the setting of a date for the withdrawal of all foreign troops from Vietnam.

Primary Source

Mr. Chairman, ladies and gentlemen, I need not pause to say how very delighted I am to be here tonight, and how very delighted I am to see you expressing your concern about the issues that will be discussed tonight by turning out in such large numbers. I also want to say that I consider it a great honor to share this program with Dr. Bennett, Dr. Commager, and Rabbi Heschel, some of the most distinguished leaders and personalities of our nation. And of course it's always good to come back to Riverside Church. Over the last eight years, I have had the privilege of preaching here almost every year in that period, and it's always a rich and rewarding experience to come to this great church and this great pulpit.

I come to this great magnificent house of worship tonight because my conscience leaves me no other choice. I join you in this meeting because I am in deepest agreement with the aims and work of the organization that brought us together, Clergy and Laymen Concerned About Vietnam. The recent statements of your executive committee are the sentiments of my own heart, and I found myself in full accord when I read its opening lines: "A time comes when silence is betrayal." That time has come for us in relation to Vietnam.

The truth of these words is beyond doubt, but the mission to which they call us is a most difficult one. Even when pressed by the demands of inner truth, men do not easily assume the task of opposing their government's policy, especially in time of war. Nor does the human spirit move without great difficulty against all the apathy of conformist thought within one's own bosom and in the surrounding world. Moreover, when the issues at hand seem as perplexing as they often do in the case of this dreadful conflict, we are always on the verge of being mesmerized by uncertainty. But we must move on.

Some of us who have already begun to break the silence of the night have found that the calling to speak is often a vocation of agony, but we must speak. We must speak with all the humility that is appropriate to our limited vision, but we must speak. And we must rejoice as well, for surely this is the first time in our nation's history that a significant number of its religious leaders have chosen to move beyond the prophesying of smooth patriotism to the high grounds of a firm dissent based upon the mandates of conscience and the reading of history. Perhaps a new spirit is rising among us. If it is, let us trace its movement, and pray that our inner being may be sensitive to its guidance. For we are deeply in need of a new way beyond the darkness that seems so close around us.

Over the past two years, as I have moved to break the betrayal of my own silences and to speak from the burnings of my own heart, as I have called for radical departures from the destruction of Vietnam, many persons have questioned me about the wisdom of my path. At the heart of their concerns, this query has often loomed large and loud: "Why are you speaking about the war, Dr. King? Why are you joining the voices of dissent?" "Peace and civil rights don't mix," they say. "Aren't you hurting the cause of your people?" they ask. And when I hear them, though I often understand the source of their concern, I am nevertheless greatly saddened, for such questions mean that the inquirers have not really known me, my commitment, or my calling. Indeed, their questions suggest that they do not know the world in which they live. In the light of such tragic misunderstanding, I deem it of signal importance to state clearly, and I trust concisely, why I believe that the path from Dexter Avenue Baptist Church—the church in Montgomery, Alabama, where I began my pastorate—leads clearly to this sanctuary tonight.

I come to this platform tonight to make a passionate plea to my beloved nation. This speech is not addressed to Hanoi or to the National Liberation Front. It is not addressed to China or to Russia. Nor is it an attempt to overlook the ambiguity of the total situation and the need for a collective solution to the tragedy of Vietnam. Neither is it an attempt to make North Vietnam or the National Liberation Front paragons of virtue, nor to overlook the role they must play in the successful resolution of the problem. While they both may have justifiable reasons to be suspicious of the good faith of the United States, life and history give eloquent testimony to the fact that conflicts are never resolved without trustful give and take on both sides. Tonight, however, I wish not to speak with Hanoi and the National Liberation Front, but rather to my fellow Americans.

Since I am a preacher by calling, I suppose it is not surprising that I have seven major reasons for bringing Vietnam into the field of my moral vision. There is at the outset a very obvious and almost facile connection between the war in Vietnam and the struggle I and others have been waging in America. A few years ago there was a shining moment in that struggle. It seemed as if there was a real promise of hope for the poor, both black and white, through the poverty program. There were experiments, hopes, new beginnings. Then came the buildup in Vietnam, and I watched this program broken and eviscerated as if it were some idle political plaything on a society gone mad on war. And I knew that America would never invest the necessary funds or energies in rehabilitation of its poor so long as adventures like Vietnam continued to draw men and skills and money like some demonic, destructive suction tube. So I was increasingly compelled to see the war as an enemy of the poor and to attack it as such.

Perhaps a more tragic recognition of reality took place when it became clear to me that the war was doing far more than devastating the hopes of the poor at home. It was sending their sons and their brothers and their husbands to fight and to die in extraordinarily high proportions relative to the rest of the population. We were taking the black young men who had been crippled by our society and sending them eight thousand miles away to guarantee liberties in Southeast Asia which they had not found in southwest Georgia and East Harlem. So we have been repeatedly faced with the cruel irony of watching Negro and white boys on TV screens as they kill and die together for a nation that has been unable to seat them together in the same schools. So we watch them in brutal solidarity burning the huts of a poor village, but we realize that they would hardly live on the same block in Chicago. I could not be silent in the face of such cruel manipulation of the poor.

My third reason moves to an even deeper level of awareness, for it grows out of my experience in the ghettos of the North over the last three years, especially the last three summers. As I have walked among the desperate, rejected, and angry young men, I have told them that Molotov cocktails and rifles would not solve their problems. I have tried to offer them my deepest compassion while maintaining my conviction that social change comes most meaningfully through nonviolent action. But they asked, and rightly so, "What about Vietnam?" They asked if our own nation wasn't using massive doses of violence to solve its problems, to bring about the changes it wanted. Their questions hit home, and I knew that I could never again raise my voice against the violence of the oppressed in the ghettos without having first spoken clearly to the greatest purveyor of violence in the world today: my own government. For the sake of those boys, for the sake of this government, for the sake of the hundreds of thousands trembling under our violence, I cannot be silent.

For those who ask the question, "Aren't you a civil rights leader?" and thereby mean to exclude me from the movement for peace, I have this further answer. In 1957, when a group of us formed the Southern Christian Leadership Conference, we chose as our motto: "To save the soul of America." We were convinced that we could not limit our vision to certain rights for black people, but instead affirmed the conviction that America would never be free or saved from itself until the descendants of its slaves were loosed completely from the shackles they still wear. In a way we were agreeing with Langston Hughes, that black bard from Harlem, who had written earlier:

O, yes, I say it plain,
America never was America to me,
And yet I swear this oath—
America will be!

Now it should be incandescently clear that no one who has any concern for the integrity and life of America today can ignore the present war. If America's soul becomes totally poisoned, part of the autopsy must read "Vietnam." It can never be saved so long as it destroys the hopes of men the world over. So it is that those of us who are yet determined that "America will be" are led down the path of protest and dissent, working for the health of our land.

As if the weight of such a commitment to the life and health of America were not enough, another burden of responsibility was placed upon me in 1954 [during the bus boycott in Montgomery, Alabama]. And I cannot forget that the Nobel Peace Prize was also a commission, a commission to work harder than I had ever worked before for the brotherhood of man. This is a calling that takes me beyond national allegiances.

But even if it were not present, I would yet have to live with the meaning of my commitment to the ministry of Jesus Christ. To me, the relationship of this ministry to the making of peace is so obvious that I sometimes marvel at those who ask me why I am speaking against the war. Could it be that they do not know that the Good News was meant for all men—for communist and capitalist, for their children and ours, for black and for white, for revolutionary and conservative? Have they forgotten that my ministry is in obedience to the one who loved his enemies so fully that he died for them? What then can I say to the Vietcong or to Castro or to Mao as a faithful minister of this one? Can I threaten them with death or must I not share with them my life?

Finally, as I try to explain for you and for myself the road that leads from Montgomery to this place, I would have offered all that was most valid if I simply said that I must be true to my conviction that I share with all men the calling to be a son of the living God. Beyond the calling of race or nation or creed is this vocation of sonship and brotherhood. Because I believe that the Father is deeply concerned, especially for His suffering and helpless and outcast children, I come tonight to speak for them. This I believe to be the privilege and the burden of all of us who deem ourselves bound by allegiances and loyalties which are broader and deeper than nationalism and which go beyond our nation's self-defined goals and positions. We are called to speak for the weak, for the voiceless, for the victims of our nation, for those it calls "enemy," for no document from human hands can make these humans any less our brothers.

And as I ponder the madness of Vietnam and search within myself for ways to understand and respond in compassion, my mind goes constantly to the people of that peninsula. I speak now not of the soldiers of each side, not of the ideologies of the Liberation Front, not of the junta in Saigon, but simply of the people who have been living under the curse of war for almost three continuous decades now. I think of them, too, because it is clear to me that there will be no meaningful solution there until some attempt is made to know them and hear their broken cries.

They must see Americans as strange liberators. The Vietnamese people proclaimed their own independence in 1954—in 1945 rather—after a combined French and Japanese occupation and before the communist revolution in China. They were led by Ho Chi Minh. Even though they quoted the American Declaration of Independence in their own document of freedom, we refused to recognize them. Instead, we decided to support France in its reconquest of her former colony. Our government felt then that the Vietnamese people were not ready for independence, and we again fell victim to the deadly Western arrogance that has poisoned the international atmosphere for so long. With that tragic decision we rejected a revolutionary government seeking self-determination and a government that had been established not by China—for whom the Vietnamese have no great love—but by clearly indigenous forces that included some communists. For the peasants this new government meant real land reform, one of the most important needs in their lives.

For nine years following 1945 we denied the people of Vietnam the right of independence. For nine years we vigorously supported the French in their abortive effort to recolonize Vietnam. Before the end of the war we were meeting eighty percent of the French war costs. Even before the French were defeated at Dien Bien Phu, they began to despair of their reckless action, but we did not. We encouraged them with our huge financial and military supplies to continue the war even after they had lost the will. Soon we would be paying almost the full costs of this tragic attempt at recolonization.

After the French were defeated, it looked as if independence and land reform would come again through the Geneva Agreement. But instead there came the United States, determined that Ho should not unify the temporarily divided nation, and the peasants watched again as we supported one of the most vicious modern dictators, our chosen man, Premier Diem. The peasants watched and cringed and Diem ruthlessly rooted out all opposition, supported their extortionist landlords, and refused even to discuss reunification with the North. The peasants watched as all of this was presided over by United States influence and then by increasing numbers of United States troops who came to help quell the insurgency that Diem's methods had aroused. When Diem was overthrown they may have been happy, but the long line of military dictators seemed to offer no real change, especially in terms of their need for land and peace.

The only change came from America as we increased our troop commitments in support of governments which were singularly corrupt, inept, and without popular support. All the while the people read our leaflets and received the regular promises of peace and democracy and land reform. Now they languish under our bombs and consider us, not their fellow Vietnamese, the real enemy. They move sadly and apathetically as we herd them off the land of their fathers into concentration camps where minimal social needs are rarely met. They know they must move on or be destroyed by our bombs.

So they go, primarily women and children and the aged. They watch as we poison their water, as we kill a million acres of their crops. They must weep as the bulldozers roar through their areas preparing to destroy the precious trees. They wander into the hospitals with at least twenty casualties from American firepower for one Vietcong-inflicted injury. So far we may have killed a million of them, mostly children. They wander into the towns and see thousands of the children, homeless, without clothes, running in packs on the streets like animals. They see the children degraded by our soldiers as they beg for food. They see the children selling their sisters to our soldiers, soliciting for their mothers.

What do the peasants think as we ally ourselves with the landlords and as we refuse to put any action into our many words concerning land reform? What do they think as we test out our latest weapons on them, just as the Germans tested out new medicine and new tortures in the concentration camps of Europe? Where are the roots of the independent Vietnam we claim to be building? Is it among these voiceless ones?

We have destroyed their two most cherished institutions: the family and the village. We have destroyed their land and their crops. We have cooperated in the crushing of the nation's only noncommunist revolutionary political force, the unified Buddhist Church. We have supported the enemies of the peasants of Saigon. We have corrupted their women and children and killed their men.

Now there is little left to build on, save bitterness. Soon the only solid physical foundations remaining will be found at our military bases and in the concrete of the concentration camps we call "fortified hamlets." The peasants may well wonder if we plan to build our new Vietnam on such grounds as these. Could we blame them for such thoughts? We must speak for them and raise the questions they cannot raise. These, too, are our brothers.

Perhaps a more difficult but no less necessary task is to speak for those who have been designated as our enemies. What of the National Liberation front, that strangely anonymous group we call "VC" or "communists"? What must they think of the United States of America when they realize that we permitted the repression and cruelty of Diem, which helped to bring them into being as a resistance group in the South? What do they think of our condoning the violence which led to their own taking up of arms? How can they believe in our integrity when now we speak of "aggression from the North" as if there was nothing more essential to the war? How can they trust us when now we charge them with violence after the murderous reign of Diem and charge them with violence while we pour every new weapon of death into their land? Surely we must understand their feelings, even if we do not condone their actions. Surely we must see that the men we supported pressed them to their violence. Surely we must see that our own computerized plans of destruction simply dwarf their greatest acts.

How do they judge us when our officials know that their membership is less than twenty-five percent communist, and yet insist on giving them the blanket name? What must they be thinking when they know that we are aware of their control of major sections of Vietnam, and yet we appear ready to allow national elections in which this highly organized political parallel government will not have a part? They ask how we can speak of free elections when the Saigon press is censored and controlled by the military junta. And they are surely right to wonder what kind of new government we plan to help form without them, the only real party in real touch with the peasants. They question our political goals and they deny the reality of a peace settlement from which they will be excluded. Their questions are frighteningly relevant. Is our nation planning to build on political myth again, and then shore it up upon the power of a new violence?

Here is the true meaning and value of compassion and nonviolence, when it helps us to see the enemy's point of view, to hear his questions, to know his assessment of ourselves. For from his view we may indeed see the basic weaknesses of our own condition, and if we are mature, we may learn and grow and profit from the wisdom of the brothers who are called the opposition.

So, too, with Hanoi. In the North, where our bombs now pummel the land, and our mines endanger the waterways, we are met by a deep but understandable mistrust. To speak for them is to explain this lack of confidence in Western worlds, and especially their distrust of American intentions now. In Hanoi are the men who led this nation to independence against the Japanese and the French, the men who sought membership in the French Commonwealth and were betrayed by the weakness of Paris and the willfulness of the colonial armies. It was they who led a second struggle against French domination at tremendous costs, and then were persuaded to give up the land they controlled between the thirteenth and seventeenth parallel as a temporary measure at Geneva. After 1954 they watched us conspire with Diem to prevent elections which could have surely brought Ho Chi Minh to power over a unified Vietnam, and they realized they had been betrayed again. When we ask why they do not leap to negotiate, these things must be considered.

Also, it must be clear that the leaders of Hanoi considered the presence of American troops in support of the Diem regime to have been the initial military breach of the Geneva Agreement concerning foreign troops. They remind us that they did not begin to send troops in large numbers and even supplies into the South until American forces had moved into the tens of thousands.

Hanoi remembers how our leaders refused to tell us the truth about the earlier North Vietnamese overtures for peace, how the president claimed that none existed when they had clearly been made. Ho Chi Minh has watched as America has spoken of peace and built up its forces, and now he has surely heard the increasing international rumors of American plans for an invasion of the north. He knows the bombing and shelling and mining we are doing are part of traditional pre-invasion strategy. Perhaps only his sense of humor and of irony can save him when he hears the most powerful nation of the world speaking of aggression as it drops thousands of bombs on a poor, weak nation more than eight hundred, or rather, eight thousand miles away from its shores.

At this point I should make it clear that while I have tried to give a voice to the voiceless in Vietnam and to understand the arguments of those who are called "enemy," I am as deeply concerned about our own troops there as anything else. For it occurs to me that what we are submitting them to in Vietnam is not simply the brutalizing process that goes on in any war where armies face each other and seek to destroy. We are adding cynicism to the process of death, for they must know after a short period there that none of the things we claim to be fighting for are really involved. Before long they must know that their government has sent them into a struggle among Vietnamese, and the more sophisticated surely realize that we are on the side of the wealthy, and the secure, while we create a hell for the poor.

Surely this madness must cease. We must stop now. I speak as a child of God and brother to the suffering poor of Vietnam. I speak for those whose land is being laid waste, whose homes are being destroyed, whose culture is being subverted. I speak for the poor in America who are paying the double price of smashed hopes at home, and dealt death and corruption in Vietnam. I speak as a citizen of the world, for the world as it stands aghast at the path we have taken. I speak as one who loves America, to the leaders of our own nation: The great initiative in this war is ours; the initiative to stop it must be ours.

This is the message of the great Buddhist leaders of Vietnam. Recently one of them wrote these words, and I quote:

Each day the war goes on the hatred increased in the hearts of the Vietnamese and in the hearts of those of humanitarian instinct. The Americans are forcing even their friends into becoming their enemies. It is curious that the Americans, who calculate so carefully on the possibilities of military victory, do not realize that in the process they are incurring deep psychological and political defeat. The image of America will never again be the image of revolution, freedom, and democracy, but the image of violence and militarism.

Unquote.

If we continue, there will be no doubt in my mind and in the mind of the world that we have no honorable intentions in Vietnam. If we do not stop our war against the people of Vietnam immediately, the world will be left with no other alternative than to see this as some horrible, clumsy, and deadly game we have decided to play. The world now demands a maturity of America that we may not be able to achieve. It demands that we admit we have been wrong from the beginning of our adventure in Vietnam, that we have been detrimental to the life of the Vietnamese people. The situation is one in which we must be ready to turn sharply from our present ways. In order to atone for our sins and errors in Vietnam, we should take the initiative in bringing a halt to this tragic war.

I would like to suggest five concrete things that our government should do to begin the long and difficult process of extricating ourselves from this nightmarish conflict:

Number one: End all bombing in North and South Vietnam.

Number two: Declare a unilateral cease-fire in the hope that such action will create the atmosphere for negotiation.

Three: Take immediate steps to prevent other battlegrounds in Southeast Asia by curtailing our military buildup in Thailand and our interference in Laos.

Four: Realistically accept the fact that the National Liberation Front has substantial support in South Vietnam and must thereby play a role in any meaningful negotiations and any future Vietnam government.

Five: Set a date that we will remove all foreign troops from Vietnam in accordance with the 1954 Geneva Agreement. [*sustained applause*]

Part of our ongoing [*applause continues*], part of our ongoing commitment might well express itself in an offer to grant asylum to any Vietnamese who fears for his life under a new regime which included the Liberation Front. Then we must make what reparations we can for the damage we have done. We must provide the medical aid that is badly needed, making it available in this country if necessary. Meanwhile [*applause*], meanwhile, we in the churches and synagogues have a continuing task while we urge our government to disengage itself from a disgraceful commitment.

We must continue to raise our voices and our lives if our nation persists in its perverse ways in Vietnam. We must be prepared to match actions with words by seeking out every creative method of protest possible.

As we counsel young men concerning military service, we must clarify for them our nation's role in Vietnam and challenge them with the alternative of conscientious objection. [*sustained applause*] I am pleased to say that this is a path now chosen by more than seventy students at my own alma mater, Morehouse College, and I recommend it to all who find the American course in Vietnam a dishonorable and unjust one. [*applause*] Moreover, I would encourage all ministers of draft age to give up their ministerial exemptions and seek status as conscientious objectors. [*applause*] These are the times for real choices and not false ones. We are at the moment when our lives must be placed on the line if our nation is to survive its own folly. Every man of humane convictions must decide on the protest that best suits his convictions, but we must all protest.

Now there is something seductively tempting about stopping there and sending us all off on what in some circles has become a popular crusade against the war in Vietnam. I say we must enter that struggle, but I wish to go on now to say something even more disturbing.

The war in Vietnam is but a symptom of a far deeper malady within the American spirit, and if we ignore this sobering reality [*applause*], and if we ignore this sobering reality, we will find ourselves organizing "clergy and laymen concerned" committees for the next generation. They will be concerned about Guatemala and Peru. They will be concerned about Thailand and Cambodia. They will be concerned about Mozambique and South Africa. We will be marching for these and a dozen other names and attending rallies without end unless there is a significant and profound change in American life and policy. [*sustained applause*] So such thoughts take us beyond Vietnam, but not beyond our calling as sons of the living God.

In 1957 a sensitive American official overseas said that it seemed to him that our nation was on the wrong side of a world revolution. During the past ten years we have seen emerge a pattern of suppression which has now justified the presence of U.S. military advisors in Venezuela. This need to maintain social stability for our investments accounts for the counterrevolutionary action of American forces in Guatemala. It tells why American helicopters are being used against guerrillas in Cambodia and why American napalm and Green Beret forces have already been active against rebels in Peru.

It is with such activity that the words of the late John F. Kennedy come back to haunt us. Five years ago he said, "Those who make peaceful revolution impossible will make violent revolution inevitable." [*applause*] Increasingly, by choice or by accident, this is the role our nation has taken, the role of those who make peaceful revolution impossible by refusing to give up the privileges and the pleasures that come from the immense profits of overseas investments. I am convinced that if we are to get on to the right side of the world revolution, we as a nation must undergo a radical revolution of values. We must rapidly begin [*applause*], we must rapidly begin the shift from a thing-oriented society to a person-oriented society. When machines and computers, profit motives and property rights, are considered more important than people, the giant triplets of racism, extreme materialism, and militarism are incapable of being conquered.

A true revolution of values will soon cause us to question the fairness and justice of many of our past and present policies. On the one hand we are called to play the Good Samaritan on life's roadside, but that will be only an initial act. One day we must come to see that the whole Jericho Road must be transformed so that men and women will not be constantly beaten and robbed as they make their journey on life's highway. True compassion is more than flinging a coin to a beggar. It comes to see that an edifice which produces beggars needs restructuring. [*applause*]

A true revolution of values will soon look uneasily on the glaring contrast of poverty and wealth. With righteous indignation, it will look across the seas and see individual capitalists of the West investing huge sums of money in Asia, Africa, and South America, only to take the profits out with no concern for the social betterment of the countries, and say, "This is not just." It will look at our alliance with the landed gentry of South America and say, "This is not just." The Western arrogance of feeling that it has everything to teach others and nothing to learn from them is not just.

A true revolution of values will lay hand on the world order and say of war, "This way of settling differences is not just." This business of burning human beings with napalm, of filling our nation's homes with orphans and widows, of injecting poisonous drugs of hate into the veins of peoples normally humane, of sending men home from dark and bloody battlefields physically handicapped and psychologically deranged, cannot be reconciled with wisdom, justice, and love. A nation that continues year after year to spend more money on military defense than on programs of social uplift is approaching spiritual death. [*sustained applause*]

America, the richest and most powerful nation in the world, can well lead the way in this revolution of values. There is nothing except a tragic death wish to prevent us from reordering our priorities so that the pursuit of peace will take precedence over the pursuit of war. There is nothing to keep us from molding a recalcitrant status quo with bruised hands until we have fashioned it into a brotherhood.

This kind of positive revolution of values is our best defense against communism. [*applause*] War is not the answer. Communism will never be defeated by the use of atomic bombs or nuclear weapons. Let us not join those who shout war and, through their misguided passions, urge the United States to relinquish its participation in the United Nations. These are days which demand wise restraint and calm reasonableness. We must not engage in a negative anticommunism, but rather in a positive thrust for democracy [*applause*], realizing that our greatest defense against communism is to take offensive action in behalf of justice. We must with positive action seek to remove those conditions of poverty, insecurity, and injustice, which are the fertile soil in which the seed of communism grows and develops.

These are revolutionary times. All over the globe men are revolting against old systems of exploitation and oppression, and out of the wounds of a frail world, new systems of justice and equality are being born. The shirtless and barefoot people of the land are rising up as never before. The people who sat in darkness have seen a great light. We in the West must support these revolutions.

It is a sad fact that because of comfort, complacency, a morbid fear of communism, and our proneness to adjust to injustice, the Western nations that initiated so much of the revolutionary spirit of the modern world have now become the arch antirevolutionaries. This has driven many to feel that only Marxism has a revolutionary spirit. Therefore, communism is a judgment against our failure to make democracy real and follow through on the revolutions that we initiated. Our only hope today lies in our ability to recapture the revolutionary spirit and go out into a sometimes hostile world declaring eternal hostility to poverty, racism, and militarism. With this powerful commitment we shall boldly challenge the status quo and unjust mores, and thereby speed the day when "every valley shall be exalted, and every mountain and hill shall be made low [audience: Yes]; the crooked shall be made straight, and the rough places plain."

A genuine revolution of values means in the final analysis that our loyalties must become ecumenical rather than sectional. Every nation must now develop an overriding loyalty to mankind as a whole in order to preserve the best in their individual societies.

This call for a worldwide fellowship that lifts neighborly concern beyond one's tribe, race, class, and nation is in reality a call for an all-embracing and unconditional love for all mankind. This oft misunderstood, this oft misinterpreted concept, so readily dismissed by the Nietzsches of the world as a weak and cowardly force, has now become an absolute necessity for the survival of man. When I speak of love I am not speaking of some sentimental and weak response. I'm not speaking of that force which is just emotional bosh. I am speaking of that force which all of the great religions have seen as the supreme unifying principle of life. Love is somehow the key that unlocks the door which leads to ultimate reality. This Hindu-Muslim-Christian-Jewish-Buddhist belief about ultimate reality is beautifully summed up in the first epistle of Saint John: "Let us love one another [audience: Yes], for love is God. [audience: Yes] And every one that loveth is born of God and knoweth God. He that loveth not knoweth not God, for God is love. . . . If we love one another, God dwelleth in us and his love is perfected in us." Let us hope that this spirit will become the order of the day.

We can no longer afford to worship the god of hate or bow before the altar of retaliation. The oceans of history are made turbulent by the ever-rising tides of hate. History is cluttered with the wreckage of nations and individuals that pursued this self-defeating path of hate. As Arnold Toynbee says: "Love is the ultimate force that makes for the saving choice of life and good against the damning choice of death and evil. Therefore the first hope in our inventory must be the hope that love is going to have the last word." Unquote.

We are now faced with the fact, my friends, that tomorrow is today. We are confronted with the fierce urgency of now. In this unfolding conundrum of life and history, there is such a thing as being too late. Procrastination is still the thief of time. Life often leaves us standing bare, naked, and dejected with a lost opportunity. The tide in the affairs of men does not remain at flood—it ebbs. We may cry out desperately for time to pause in her passage, but time is adamant to every plea and rushes on. Over the bleached bones and jumbled residues of numerous civilizations are written the pathetic words, "Too late." There is an invisible book of life that faithfully records our vigilance or our neglect. Omar Khayyam is right: "The moving finger writes, and having writ moves on."

We still have a choice today: nonviolent coexistence or violent coannihilation. We must move past indecision to action. We must find new ways to speak for peace in Vietnam and justice throughout the developing world, a world that borders on our doors. If we do not act, we shall surely be dragged down the long, dark, and shameful corridors of time reserved for those who possess power without compassion, might without morality, and strength without sight.

Now let us begin. Now let us rededicate ourselves to the long and bitter, but beautiful, struggle for a new world. This is the calling of the sons of God, and our brothers wait eagerly for our response. Shall we say the odds are too great? Shall we tell them the struggle is too hard? Will our message be that the forces of American life militate against their arrival as full men, and we send our deepest regrets? Or will there be another message—of longing, of hope, of solidarity with their yearnings, of commitment to their cause, whatever the cost? The choice is ours, and though we might prefer it otherwise, we must choose in this crucial moment of human history.

As that noble bard of yesterday, James Russell Lowell, eloquently stated:

> Once to every man and nation comes a moment to decide,
> In the strife of truth and Falsehood, for the good or evil side;
> Some great cause, God's new Messiah offering each the bloom or blight,
> And the choice goes by forever 'twixt that darkness and that light.
> Though the cause of evil prosper, yet 'tis truth alone is strong
> Though her portions be the scaffold, and upon the throne be wrong
> Yet that scaffold sways the future, and behind the dim unknown
> Standeth God within the shadow, keeping watch above his own.

And if we will only make the right choice, we will be able to transform this pending cosmic elegy into a creative psalm of peace. If we will make the right choice, we will be able to transform the jangling discords of our world into a beautiful symphony of brotherhood. If we will but make the right choice, we will be able to speed up the day, all over America and all over the world, when justice will roll down like waters, and righteousness like a mighty stream. [*sustained applause*]

174. Central Intelligence Agency: Intelligence Memorandum, "Bomb Damage Inflicted on North Vietnam through April 1967", May 12, 1967

Introduction

The U.S. Central Intelligence Agency (CIA) was not optimistic in its assessment of the effects of Operation ROLLING THUNDER, the U.S. bombing of the Democratic Republic of Vietnam (DRV, North Vietnam). In this report of May 1967, the CIA concludes that North Vietnam has been able to offset U.S. efforts to halt the flow of men and supplies into the Republic of Vietnam (RVN, South Vietnam) by increased imports; the dispersion of assets, such as petroleum storage facilities; and the rapid repair of transportation facilities, such as roads and bridges.

Primary Source

Through the end of April 1967 the US air campaign against North Vietnam—Rolling Thunder—had significantly eroded the capacities of North Vietnam's limited industrial and military base. These losses, however, have not meaningfully degraded North Vietnam's material ability to continue the war in South Vietnam.

Total damage through April 1967 was over $233 million, of which 70 percent was accounted for by damage to economic targets. The greatest amount of damage was inflicted on the so-called logistics target system—transport equipment and lines of communication.

By the end of April 1967 the US air campaign had attacked 173 fixed targets, over 70 percent of the targets on the JCS list. This campaign included extensive attacks on almost every major target system in the country. The physical results have varied widely.

All of the 13 targeted petroleum storage facilities have been attacked, with an estimated loss of 85 percent of storage capacity. Attacks on 13 of the 20 targeted electric power facilities have neutralized 70 percent of North Vietnam's power-generating capacity. The major losses in the military establishment include the neutralization of 18 ammunition depots, with a loss capacity of 70 percent. Over three fourths of the 65 JCS-targeted barracks have been attacked, with a loss of about one fourth of national capacity. Attacks on 22 of the 29 targeted supply depots reduced capacity by 17 percent. Through the end of April 1967, five of North Vietnam's airfields had been attacked, with a loss of about 20 percent of national capacity.

North Vietnam's ability to recuperate from the air attacks has been of a high order. The major exception has been the electric power industry. One small plant—Co Dinh—is beyond repair. Most of the other plants would require 3–4 months to be restored to partial operations, although two plants—Haiphong East and Uong Bi—would require one year. For complete restoration, all of the plants would require at least a year. Restoration of these plants would require foreign technical assistance and equipment.

The recuperability problem is not significant for the other target systems. The destroyed petroleum storage system has been replaced by an effective system of dispersed storage and distribution. The damaged military target systems—particularly barracks and storage depots—have simply been abandoned, and supplies and troops dispersed throughout the country. The inventories of transport and military equipment have been replaced by large infusions of military and economic aid from the USSR and Communist China. Damage to bridges and lines of communications is frequently repaired within a matter of days, if not hours, or the effects are countered by an elaborate system of multiple bypasses or pre-positioned spans.

Source: Central Intelligence Agency, "Intelligence Memorandum: Bomb Damage Inflicted on North Vietnam through April 1967," May 12, 1967, Declassified November 17, 1975.

175. President Lyndon Johnson: Address in San Antonio, Texas, September 29, 1967 [Excerpt]

Introduction

In June 1967 two Frenchmen, Dr. Herbert Marcovich and Raymond Aubrac, approached Dr. Henry Kissinger, then a private U.S. citizen and Harvard University professor who was attending a conference in Paris, about establishing contact with the leadership of the Democratic Republic of Vietnam (DRV, North Vietnam) to discuss the possibility of serving as intermediaries between Washington and Hanoi. Aubrac had known Ho since 1946. The Lyndon Johnson administration agreed, and the two Frenchmen traveled to Hanoi in late July to present a new U.S. proposal. The United States would halt the bombing of North Vietnam in return for a pledge from Hanoi to enter into substantive peace talks without Washington insisting on Hanoi's de-escalation of its military effort in the Republic of Vietnam (RVN, South Vietnam). The message did, however, warn against any North Vietnamese effort to "take advantage" of the situation. As it turned out, the North Vietnamese leadership rejected the U.S. offer, which they said still imposed conditions. President Johnson then made the offer public in the course of a speech in San Antonio, Texas, on September 29. The demarche became known as the San Antonio Formula.

Primary Source

Our desire to negotiate peace—through the United Nations or out—has been made very, very clear to Hanoi—directly and many times through third parties.

As we have told Hanoi time and time and time again, the heart of the matter really is this: The United States is willing to stop all aerial and naval bombardment of North Viet-Nam when this will lead promptly to productive discussions. We, of course, assume that while discussions proceed, North Viet-Nam would not take advantage of the bombing cessation or limitation.

But Hanoi has not accepted any of these proposals.

So it is by Hanoi's choice, and not ours and not the rest of the world's, that the war continues.

Why, in the face of military and political progress in the South, and the burden of our bombing in the North, do they insist and persist with the war?

From the many sources the answer is the same. They still hope that the people of the United States will not see this struggle through to the very end. As one Western diplomat reported to me only this week—he had just been in Hanoi—"They believe their staying power is greater than ours and that they can't lose." A visitor from a Communist capital had this to say: "They expect the war to be long, and that the Americans in the end will be defeated by a breakdown in morale, fatigue, and psychological factors." The Premier of North Viet-Nam said as far back as 1962: "Americans do not like long, inconclusive war . . . Thus we are sure to win in the end."

Are the North Vietnamese right about us?

I think not. No. I think they are wrong. I think it is the common failing of totalitarian regimes, that they cannot really understand the nature of our democracy:

—They mistake dissent for disloyalty;
—They mistake restlessness for a rejection of policy;
—They mistake a few committees for a country;
—They misjudge individual speeches for public policy.

They are no better suited to judge the strength and perseverance of America than the Nazi and the Stalinist propagandists were able to judge it. It is a tragedy that they must discover these qualities in the American people, and discover them through a bloody war.

And, soon or late, they will discover them.

In the meantime, it shall be our policy to continue to seek negotiations, confident that reason will some day prevail, that Hanoi will realize that it just can never win, that it will turn away from fighting and start building for its own people.

Source: "Answering Aggression in Viet-Nam," *Department of State Bulletin* 57(1478) (1967): 519–522.

176. General William Westmoreland, Commander of U.S. Forces in Vietnam: National Press Club Address, November 21, 1967 [Excerpts]

Introduction

In mid-November 1967, U.S Military Assistance Command, Vietnam (MACV), commander General William Westmoreland returned to the United States and provided President Lyndon Johnson a decidedly upbeat assessment on the progress of the war. Johnson then asked Westmoreland to make his views public. On November 21 the general appeared before the National Press Club. In his remarks Westmoreland asserts that the United States, the Army of the Republic of Vietnam (ARVN, South Vietnamese Army), and Korean forces are winning the war and that victory is "within our grasp—the enemy's hopes are bankrupt." Westmoreland subsequently told a *Time* interviewer that "I hope they try

something, because we are looking for a fight." That fight occurred in the Communist Tet Offensive of late January 1968.

Primary Source

Improving Vietnamese Effectiveness

With 1968, a new phase is now starting. We have reached an important point when the end begins to come into view. What is this third phase we are about to enter?

In Phase III, in 1968, we intend to do the following:

Help the Vietnamese Armed Forces to continue improving their effectiveness.

Decrease our advisers in training centers and other places where the professional competence of Vietnamese officers makes this possible.

Increase our advisory effort with the younger brothers of the Vietnamese Army: the Regional Forces and Popular Forces.

Use U.S. and free-world forces to destroy North Vietnamese forays while we assist the Vietnamese to reorganize for territorial security.

Provide the new military equipment to revitalize the Vietnamese Army and prepare it to take on an ever-increasing share of the war.

Continue pressure on North to prevent rebuilding and to make infiltration more costly.

Turn a major share of frontline DMZ defense over to the Vietnamese Army.

Increase U.S. support in the rich and populated delta.

Help the Government of Viet-Nam single out and destroy the Communist shadow government.

Continue to isolate the guerrilla from the people.

Help the new Vietnamese government to respond to popular aspirations and to reduce and eliminate corruption.

Help the Vietnamese strengthen their policy forces to enhance law and order.

Open more roads and canals.

Continue to improve the Vietnamese economy and standard of living.

The Final Phase

Now for phase IV—the final phase. That period will see the conclusion of our plan to weaken the enemy and strengthen our friends until we become progressively superfluous. The object will be to show the world that guerrilla warfare and invasion do not pay as a new means of Communist aggression.

I see phase IV happening as follows:

Infiltration will slow.

The Communist infrastructure will be cut up and near collapse.

The Vietnamese Government will prove its stability, and the Vietnamese Army will show that it can handle Viet Cong.

The Regional Forces and Popular Forces will reach a higher level of professional performance.

U.S. units can begin to phase down as the Vietnamese Army is modernized and develops its capacity to the fullest.

The military physical assets, bases and ports, will be progressively turned over to the Vietnamese.

The Vietnamese will take charge of the final mopping up of the Viet Cong (which will probably last several years). The U.S., at the same time, will continue the developmental help envisaged by the President for the community of Southeast Asia.

You may ask how long phase III will take, before we reach the final phase. We have already entered part of phase III. Looking back on phases I and II, we can conclude that we have come a long way.

I see progress as I travel all over Viet-Nam.

I see it in the attitudes of the Vietnamese.

I see it in the open roads and canals.

I see it in the new crops and the new purchasing power of the farmer.

I see it in the increasing willingness of the Vietnamese Army to fight North Vietnamese units and in the victories they are winning.

Parenthetically, I might say that the U.S. press tends to report U.S. actions; so you may not be as aware as I am of the victories won by South Vietnamese forces.

The enemy has many problems:

He is losing control of the scattered population under his influence.

He is losing credibility with the population he still controls.

He is alienating the people by his increased demands and taxes, where he can impose them.

He sees the strength of his forces steadily declining.

He can no longer recruit in the South to any meaningful extent; he must plug the gap with North Vietnamese.

His monsoon offensives have been failures.

He was dealt a mortal blow by the installation of a freely elected representative government.

And he failed in his desperate effort to take the world's headlines from the inauguration by a military victory.

Lastly, the Vietnamese Army is on the road to becoming a competent force. Korean troops in Viet-Nam provide a good example for the Vietnamese. Fifteen years ago the Koreans themselves had problems now ascribed to the Vietnamese. The Koreans surmounted these problems, and so can and will the Vietnamese. . . .

We are making progress. We know you want an honorable and early transition to the fourth and last phase. So do your sons and so do I.

It lies within our grasp—the enemy's hopes are bankrupt. With your support we will give you a success that will impact not only on South Viet-Nam but on every emerging nation in the world.

Source: "Progress Report on the War in Viet-Nam," *Department of State Bulletin* 57(1485) (1967): 785–788.

177. President Lyndon Johnson: News Conference, February 2, 1968 [Excerpts]

Introduction

At the end of January 1968 during the Lunar New Year holiday of Tet, Communist forces launched a massive military offensive all over the Republic of Vietnam (RVN, South Vietnam). Both the timing of the attacks and their intensity caught the United States by surprise. Although Communist forces suffered massive casualties and failed to achieve their goal of triggering a general uprising of the Vietnamese people against the Americans and the South

Vietnamese government, the Tet Offensive stunned the American people, coming as it did on the heels of U.S. commander in Vietnam General William Westmoreland's rosy assessment of two months before. American public opinion now turned decisively against the war. In the course of this news conference on February 2, 1968, U.S. president Lyndon Johnson seeks to place the Communist offensive in proper light and to play up the U.S. and Army of the Republic of Vietnam (ARVN, South Vietnam) success in turning back the North Vietnamese offensive.

Primary Source

Q. Sir, do you see anything in the developments this week in these attacks in Vietnam that causes you to think you need to reevaluate some of the assumptions on which our policies and strategy there has been based? I am thinking in terms of the security ratings, amount of population that is considered under government control? Do you think the basic assumption is still valid?

The President: We do that every week. I see nothing that would indicate that that shouldn't be done. We must, all the time to try to keep up, and to be sure we have not made errors and mistakes. If you are saying, have we felt that what happened could not happen, the answer is no. As a matter of fact, . . . if you have seen any of the intelligence reports, the information has been very clear that two things would happen:

One is that there would be a general uprising, as I stated.

Two, there would be a general invasion and attempt to secure military victory, and that the objective would be to get a military victory and a psychological victory.

That is one of the great problems the President has to deal with. He is sitting there reading these information reports while his own people, a good many of the best intentioned, are supplying him with military strategy, and the two do not fit in.

So you have to be tolerant and understand their best intentions while you are looking at the other fellow's hole card. That is what General Westmoreland has been doing while all of these Monday morning quarterbacks are pointing out to him that this is the way he should move or this is the way you should not move.

This is part of what happens when you look at history. It may be that General Westmoreland makes some serious mistakes or that I make some. We don't know. We are just acting in light of the information we have. We believe we have information about what they are trying to do there. We have taken every precaution we know of. But we don't want to give you assurance that all will be satisfactory. We see nothing that would require any change of great consequence.

We will have to move men from this place to that one. We will have to replace helicopters. Probably we had 100-odd helicopters and planes seriously damaged, and we will have to replace them. Secretary McNamara told me he could have that done very shortly.

We will have to replace the 38 planes lost, but we have approximately 5,900 planes there. We anticipate that we will lose 25 or 30 every month just from normal crashes and so forth. . . .

Now, I am no great strategist and tactician. I know that you are not. But let us assume that the best figures we can have are from our responsible military commanders. They say 10,000 died and we lost 249 and the South Vietnamese lost 500. Now that doesn't look like a Communist victory. I can count. It looks like somebody has paid a very dear price for the temporary encouragement that some of our enemies had.

We have approximately 5,900 planes and have lost 38 completely destroyed. We lost 100-odd that were damaged and have to be repaired. Maybe Secretary McNamara will fly in 150 shortly.

Now, is that a great enemy victory?

In Peking today they say that we are in panic. You have to judge that for yourself. In other Communist capitals today they say that we have definitely exhibited a lack of power and that we do not have any military strength. You will have to judge that for yourself

But General Westmoreland—evaluating this for us and the Joint Chiefs of Staff reviewing it for him tell me—that in their judgment their action has not been a military success.

I am measuring my words. I don't want to overstate the thing. We do not believe that we should help them in making it a psychological success.

Source: *Public Papers of the Presidents of the United States: Lyndon B. Johnson, 1968–69,* Book 1 (Washington, DC: U.S. Government Printing Office, 1970), 159–161.

178. Robert McNamara, Secretary of Defense, and Dean Rusk, Secretary of State: Television Interview, February 4, 1968 [Excerpts]

Introduction

With the Communist Tet Offensive still raging in the Republic of Vietnam (RVN, South Vietnam), U.S. secretary of defense Robert S. McNamara and Secretary of State Dean Rusk defend U.S.

Vietnam policy while answering questions put to them by NBC News State Department correspondent Elie Able.

Primary Source

Able: Secretary McNamara, it is 3 years this week since we started bombing North Viet-Nam. It was also in '65 that we started the big buildup on the ground. What happened this week? How do you relate the ability of the Viet Cong to stage as major an offensive as this one was to the efforts we have been making these past 3 years?

McNamara: Three years ago, or more exactly, 2 1/2 years ago, in July of 1965, President Johnson made the decision—announced to our people the decision to move significant numbers of combat troops into South Viet-Nam. At that time the North Vietnamese and their associates, the Viet Cong, were on the verge of cutting the country in half and of destroying the South Vietnamese Army. We said so at the time, and I think hindsight has proven that a correct appraisal. What has happened since that time, of course, is that they have suffered severe losses, they have failed in their objective to destroy the Government of South Viet-Nam, they have failed in their objective to take control of the country. They have continued to fight.

Just 4 days ago I remember reading in our press that I had presented a gloomy, pessimistic picture of activities in South Viet-Nam. I don't think it was gloomy or pessimistic; it was realistic. It said that while they had suffered severe penalties, they continued to have strength to carry out the attacks which we have seen in the last 2 or 3 days.

Able: Mr. Secretary, are you telling us the fact that the Viet Cong, after all these years, were able to, temporarily at least, grab control of some 20-odd Provincial capitals and the city of Saigon, are you telling us this has no military meaning at all?

McNamara: No; certainly not. I think South Viet-Nam is such a complex situation—one must always look at the pluses and the minuses, and I don't mean to say there haven't been any minuses for the South Vietnamese in the last several days. I think there have been. But there have been many, many pluses. The North Vietnamese and the Viet Cong have not accomplished either one of their major objectives, either to ignite a general uprising or to force a diversion of the troops which the South Vietnamese and the United States have moved into the northern areas of South Viet-Nam, anticipating a major Viet Cong and North Vietnamese offensive in that area. And beyond that, the North Vietnamese and the Viet Cong have suffered very heavy penalties in terms of losses of weapons and losses of men in the past several days. They have, of course, dealt a very heavy blow to many of the cities of South Viet-Nam.

[. . .]

Frankel: Secretary Rusk, the administration has naturally been stressing the things that they think the Viet Cong did not achieve in this week of attacks—didn't cause an uprising, which you say may have been one of their goals, didn't seize cities for any permanent period. But yet we have also been given to understand that the real name of this game out there is "Who can provide safety for whom?" And haven't they in a very serious way humiliated our ability in major cities all up and down this country to provide the South Vietnamese population that is listed as clearly in our control with a degree of assurance and safety that South Vietnamese forces and American forces together could give them?

Rusk: There is almost no way to prevent the other side from making a try. There is a way to prevent them from having a success. I said earlier that I thought there would be a number of South Vietnamese who would take a very grumpy view over the inability of the Government to protect them against some of the things that have happened in the last 3 or 4 days. But the net effect of the transaction is to make it clear that the Viet Cong are not able to come into these Provincial capitals and seize Provincial capitals and hold them; that they are not able to announce the formation of a new committee, or a coalition or a federation, and have it pick up any support in the country. That they are not able to undermine the solidarity of those who are supporting the Government. No; I think there is a psychological factor here that we won't be able to assess until a week or two after the event, and I might say also that we know there is going to be some hard fighting ahead. We are not over this period at all.

As a matter of fact, the major fighting up in the northern part of South Viet-Nam has not yet occurred, so there are some hard battles ahead.

[. . .]

Frankel: Secretary McNamara, let me take advantage of your valedictory mood. Looking back over this long conflict and especially in this rather agonized week in Viet-Nam, if we had to do it all over again, would you make any major changes in our approach?

McNamara: This is not an appropriate time for me to be talking of changes, with hindsight. There is no question but what 5 or 10 or 20 years from now the historians will find actions that might have been done differently. I am sure they will. . . . I am learning more and more about Viet-Nam every day. There is no question I see better today than I did 3 years ago or 5 years ago what might have been done there. On balance, I feel much the way the Asian leaders do. I think the action that this Government has followed, policies it has followed, the objectives it has had in Viet-Nam, are wise. I do not by any means suggest that we have not made mistakes over the many, many years that we have been pursuing those objectives.

Frankel: You seem to suggest that we really didn't—that none of us appreciated what we were really getting into.

McNamara: I don't think any of us predicted 7 years ago or 15 years ago the deployment of 500,000 men to Viet-Nam. I know I didn't.

Source: Peter Braestrup, *Big Story: How the American Press and Television Reported and Interpreted the Crisis of Tet 1968 in Vietnam and Washington,* Vol. 2 (Boulder, CO: Westview, 1977), 95–111.

179. Senator Robert F. Kennedy Calls Vietnam an Unwinnable War, February 8, 1968

Introduction

By February 1968 an overwhelming majority of Americans were opposed to the war or, more accurately, President Lyndon Johnson's handling of it. Already in November 1967, antiwar senator Eugene McCarthy had announced his intention to challenge Johnson in the Democratic Party primaries. Senator Robert F. Kennedy of New York was edging toward the same challenge. On February 8, 1968, Kennedy publicly declares his opposition to the war.

Primary Source

Our enemy, savagely striking at will across all of South Vietnam, has finally shattered the mask of official illusion with which we have concealed our true circumstances, even from ourselves. But a short time ago we were serene in our reports and predictions of progress.

The Vietcong will probably withdraw from the cities, as they were forced to withdraw from the American Embassy. Thousands of them will be dead.

But they will, nevertheless, have demonstrated that no part or person of South Vietnam is secure from their attacks: neither district capitals nor American bases, neither the peasant in his rice paddy nor the commanding general of our own great forces.

No one can predict the exact shape or outcome of the battles now in progress, in Saigon or at Khesanh. Let us pray that we will succeed at the lowest possible cost to our young men.

But whatever their outcome, the events of the last two weeks have taught us something. For the sake of those young Americans who are fighting today, if for no other reason, the time has come to take a new look at the war in Vietnam, not by cursing the past but by using it to illuminate the future.

And the first and necessary step is to face the facts. It is to seek out the austere and painful reality of Vietnam, freed from wishful thinking, false hopes and sentimental dreams. It is to rid ourselves of the "good company," of those illusions which have lured us into the deepening swamp of Vietnam.

We must, first of all, rid ourselves of the illusion that the events of the past two weeks represent some sort of victory. That is not so.

It is said the Vietcong will not be able to hold the cities. This is probably true. But they have demonstrated despite all our reports of progress, of government strength and enemy weakness, that half a million American soldiers with 700,000 Vietnamese allies, with total command of the air, total command of the sea, backed by huge resources and the most modern weapons, are unable to secure even a single city from the attacks of an enemy whose total strength is about 250,000. . . .

For years we have been told that the measure of our success and progress in Vietnam was increasing security and control for the population. Now we have seen that none of the population is secure and no area is under sure control.

Four years ago when we only had about 30,000 troops in Vietnam, the Vietcong were unable to mount the assaults on cities they have now conducted against our enormous forces. At one time a suggestion that we protect enclaves was derided. Now there are no protected enclaves.

This has not happened because our men are not brave or effective, because they are. It is because we have misconceived the nature of the war: It is because we have sought to resolve by military might a conflict whose issue depends upon the will and conviction of the South Vietnamese people. It is like sending a lion to halt an epidemic of jungle rot.

This misconception rests on a second illusion—the illusion that we can win a war which the South Vietnamese cannot win for themselves.

You cannot expect people to risk their lives and endure hardship unless they have a stake in their own society. They must have a clear sense of identification with their own government, a belief they are participating in a cause worth fighting for.

People will not fight to line the pockets of generals or swell the bank accounts of the wealthy. They are far more likely to close their eyes and shut their doors in the face of their government—even as they did last week.

More than any election, more than any proud boast, that single fact reveals the truth. We have an ally in name only. We support a government without supporters. Without the efforts of American arms that government would not last a day.

The third illusion is that the unswerving pursuit of military victory, whatever its cost, is in the interest of either ourselves or the people of Vietnam.

For the people of Vietnam, the last three years have meant little but horror. Their tiny land has been devastated by a weight of bombs and shells greater than Nazi Germany knew in the Second World War.

We have dropped 12 tons of bombs for every square mile in North and South Vietnam. Whole provinces have been substantially destroyed. More than two million South Vietnamese are now homeless refugees.

Imagine the impact in our own country if an equivalent number—over 25 million Americans—were wandering homeless or interned in refugee camps, and millions more refugees were being created as New York and Chicago, Washington and Boston, were being destroyed by a war raging in their streets.

Whatever the outcome of these battles, it is the people we seek to defend who are the greatest losers.

Nor does it serve the interests of America to fight this war as if moral standards could be subordinated to immediate necessities. Last week, a Vietcong suspect was turned over to the chief of the Vietnamese Security Services, who executed him on the spot—a flat violation of the Geneva Convention on the Rules of War.

The photograph of the execution was on front pages all around the world—leading our best and oldest friends to ask, more in sorrow than in anger, what has happened to America?

The fourth illusion is that the American national interest is identical with—or should be subordinated to—the selfish interest of an incompetent military regime.

We are told, of course, that the battle for South Vietnam is in reality a struggle for 250 million Asians—the beginning of a Great Society for all of Asia. But this is pretension.

We can and should offer reasonable assistance to Asia; but we cannot build a Great Society there if we cannot build one in our own country. We cannot speak extravagantly of a struggle for 250 million Asians, when a struggle for 15 million in one Asian country so strains our forces, that another Asian country, a fourth-rate power

which we have already once defeated in battle, dares to seize an American ship and hold and humiliate her crew.

The fifth illusion is that this war can be settled in our own way and in our own time on our own terms. Such a settlement is the privilege of the triumphant: of those who crush their enemies in battle or wear away their will to fight.

We have not done this, nor is there any prospect we will achieve such a victory.

Unable to defeat our enemy or break his will—at least without a huge, long and ever more costly effort—we must actively seek a peaceful settlement. We can no longer harden our terms every time Hanoi indicates it may be prepared to negotiate; and we must be willing to foresee a settlement which will give the Vietcong a chance to participate in the political life of the country.

These are some of the illusions which may be discarded if the events of last week are to prove not simply a tragedy, but a lesson: a lesson which carries with it some basic truths.

First, that a total military victory is not within sight or around the corner; that, in fact, it is probably beyond our grasp; and that the effort to win such a victory will only result in the further slaughter of thousands of innocent and helpless people—a slaughter which will forever rest on our national conscience.

Second, that the pursuit of such a victory is not necessary to our national interest, and is even damaging that interest.

Third, that the progress we have claimed toward increasing our control over the country and the security of the population is largely illusory.

Fourth, that the central battle in this war cannot be measured by body counts or bomb damage, but by the extent to which the people of South Vietnam act on a sense of common purpose and hope with those that govern them.

Fifth, that the current regime in Saigon is unwilling or incapable of being an effective ally in the war against the Communists.

Sixth, that a political compromise is not just the best path to peace, but the only path, and we must show as much willingness to risk some of our prestige for peace as to risk the lives of young men in war.

Seventh, that the escalation policy in Vietnam, far from strengthening and consolidating international resistance to aggression, is injuring our country through the world, reducing the faith of other peoples in our wisdom and purpose and weakening the world's resolve to stand together for freedom and peace.

Eighth, that the best way to save our most precious stake in Vietnam—the lives of our soldiers—is to stop the enlargement of the war, and that the best way to end casualties is to end the war.

Ninth, that our nation must be told the truth about this war, in all its terrible reality, both because it is right—and because only in this way can any Administration rally the public confidence and unity for the shadowed days which lie ahead.

No war has ever demanded more bravery from our people and our Government—not just bravery under fire or the bravery to make sacrifices—but the bravery to discard the comfort of illusion—to do away with false hopes and alluring promises.

Reality is grim and painful. But it is only a remote echo of the anguish toward which a policy founded on illusion is surely taking us.

This is a great nation and a strong people. Any who seek to comfort rather than speak plainly, reassure rather than instruct, promise satisfaction rather than reveal frustration—they deny that greatness and drain that strength. For today as it was in the beginning, it is the truth that makes us free.

Source: U.S. Congress, *Congressional Record,* 90th Cong., 2nd sess., Vol. 119, no. 19 (Washington, DC: U.S. Government Printing Office, 1968).

180. General Earle G. Wheeler, Chairman of the Joint Chiefs of Staff: Report on the Situation in Vietnam, February 27, 1968 [Excerpts]

Introduction

In late February 1968 with the Communist Tet Offensive having been defeated, chairman of the U.S. Joint Chiefs of Staff (JCS) General Earle G. Wheeler traveled to Saigon to confer with Military Assistance Command, Vietnam (MACV), commander General William Westmoreland, who now saw an opportunity to pursue a more aggressive policy. With reinforcements Westmoreland could attack People's Army of Vietnam (PAVN, North Vietnamese Army) base areas and sanctuaries in Laos and Cambodia and even possibly cut the Ho Chi Minh Trail infiltration system fueling the insurgency in the Republic of Vietnam (RVN, South Vietnam). In discussing Vietnam troop requirements, the two generals settled on a figure of 206,756 additional men. Probably by design this represented the total of previous shortfalls in Westmoreland's requests, but such a figure would also force mobilization of the reserve forces. Wheeler wanted to deploy about half this number

to Vietnam by the end of the year and hold the remainder in the United States as a strategic reserve.

Primary Source

1. The Chairman, JCS and party visited SVN on 23, 24 and 25 February. This report summarizes the impressions and facts developed through conversations and briefings at MACV and with senior commanders throughout the country.

2. Summary

—The current situation in Vietnam is still developing and fraught with opportunities as well as dangers.

—There is no question in the mind of MACV that the enemy went all out for a general offensive and general uprising and apparently believed that he would succeed in bringing the war to an early successful conclusion.

—The enemy failed to achieve this initial objectives but is continuing his effort. Although many of his units were badly hurt, the judgment is that he has the will and the capability to continue.

—Enemy losses have been heavy; he has failed to achieve his prime objectives of mass uprisings and capture of a large number of the capital cities and towns. Morale in enemy units which were badly mauled or where the men were oversold the idea of a decisive victory at TET probably has suffered severely. However, with replacements, his indoctrination system would seem capable of maintaining morale at a generally adequate level. His determination appears to be unshaken.

—The enemy is operating with relative freedom in the countryside, probably recruiting heavily and no doubt infiltrating NVA units and personnel. His recovery is likely to be rapid; his supplies are adequate; and he is trying to maintain the momentum of his winter-spring offensive.

—The structure of the GVN held up but its effectiveness has suffered.

—The RVNAF held up against the initial assault with gratifying, and in a way, surprising strength and fortitude. However, ARVN is now in a defensive posture around towns and cities and there is concern about how well they will bear up under sustained pressure.

—The initial attack nearly succeeded in a dozen places, and defeat in those places was only averted by the timely reaction of US forces. In short, it was a very near thing.

—There is no doubt that the RD Program has suffered a severe set back.

—RVNAF was not badly hurt physically—they should recover strength and equipment rather quickly (equipment in 2–3 months—strength in 3–6 months). Their problems are more psychological than physical.

—US forces have lost none of their pre-TET capability.

—MACV has three principal problems. First, logistic support north of Danang is marginal owing to weather, enemy interdiction and harassment and the massive deployment of US forces into the DMZ/Hue area. Opening Route 1 will alleviate this problem but takes a substantial troop commitment. Second, the defensive posture of ARVN is permitting the VC to make rapid inroads in the formerly pacified countryside. ARVN, in its own words, is in a dilemma as it cannot afford another enemy thrust into the cities and towns and yet if it remains in a defensive posture against this contingency, the countryside goes by default. MACV is forced to devote much of its troop strength to this problem. Third, MACV has been forced to deploy 50% of all US maneuver battalions into I Corps, to meet the threat there, while stripping the rest of the country of adequate reserves. If the enemy synchronizes an attack against Khe Sanh/Hue–Quang Tri with an offensive in the Highlands and around Saigon while keeping the pressure on throughout the remainder of the country, MACV will be hard pressed to meet adequately all threats. Under these circumstances, we must be prepared to accept some reverses.

—For these reasons, General Westmoreland has asked for a 3 division–15 tactical fighter squadron force. This force would provide him with a theater reserve and an offensive capability which he does not now have.

3. The situation as it stands today:

a. Enemy capabilities

(1) The enemy has been hurt badly in the populated lowlands, but is practically intact elsewhere. He committed over 67,000 combat maneuver forces plus perhaps 25% or 17,000 more impressed men and boys, for a total of about 84,000. He lost 40,000 killed, at least 3,000 captured, and perhaps 5,000 disabled or died of wounds. He had peaked his force total to about 240,000 just before TET, by hard recruiting, infiltration, civilian impressment, and drawdowns on service and guerrilla personnel. So he has lost about one fifth of his total strength. About two-third of his trained, organized unit strength can continue offensive action. He is probably infiltrating and recruiting heavily in the countryside while allied forces are securing the urban areas. (Discussions of strengths and recruiting are in paragraphs 1, 2 and 3 of Enclosure (1)). The enemy has adequate munitions, stockpiled in-country and available through the DMZ, Laos, and Cambodia, to support major attacks and country-wide pressure; food procurement may be a problem. (Discussion is in paragraph 6 Enclosure (1)). Besides strength losses, the enemy now has morale and training problems which currently limit combat effectiveness of VC guerrilla, main and local forces. (Discussions of forces are in paragraphs 2, 5, Enclosure (1)).

(a) I Corps Tactical Zone: Strong enemy forces in the northern two provinces threaten Quang Tri and Hue cities, and US positions at the DMZ. Two NVA divisions threaten Khe Sanh. Eight enemy battalion equivalents are in the Danang-Hoi An area. Enemy losses in I CTZ have been heavy, with about 13,000 killed; some NVA as well as VC units have been hurt badly. However, NVA replacements in the DMZ area can offset these losses fairly quickly. The enemy has an increased artillery capability at the DMZ, plus some tanks and possibly even a limited air threat in I CTZ.

(b) II Corps Tactical Zone: The 1st NVA Division went virtually unscathed during TET offensive, and represents a strong threat in the western highlands. Seven combat battalion equivalents threaten Dak To. Elsewhere in the highlands, NVA units have been hurt and VC units chopped up badly. On the coast, the 3rd NVA Division had already taken heavy losses just prior to the offensive. The 5th NVA Division, also located on the coast, is not in good shape. Local force strength in coastal II CTZ had dwindled long before the offensive. The enemy's strength in II CTZ is in the highlands where enemy troops are fresh and supply lines short.

(c) III CTZ: Most of the enemy's units were used in the TET effort, and suffered substantial losses. Probably the only major unit to escape heavy losses was the 7th NVA Division. However, present dispositions give the enemy the continuing capability of attacking the Saigon area with 10 to 11 combat effective battalion equivalents. His increased movement southward of supporting arms and infiltration of supplies has further developed his capacity for attacks by fire.

(d) IV Corps Tactical Zone: All enemy forces were committed in IV Corps, but losses per total strength were the lightest in the country. The enemy continues to be capable of investing or attacking cities throughout the area.

(2) New weapons or tactics:

We may see heavier rockets and tube artillery, additional armor, and the use of aircraft, particularly in the I CTZ. The only new tactic in view is infiltration and investment of cities to create chaos, to demoralize the people, to discredit the government, and to tie allied forces to urban security....

4. What does the future hold?

a. Probable enemy strategy. (Reference paragraph 7b, Enclosure (1)). We see the enemy pursuing a reinforced offensive to enlarge his control throughout the country and keep pressures on the government and allies. We expect him to maintain strong threats in the DMZ area, at Khe Sanh, in the highlands, and at Saigon, and to attack in force when conditions seem favorable. He is likely to try to gain control of the country's northern provinces. He will continue efforts to encircle cities and province capitals to isolate and disrupt normal activities, and infiltrate them to create chaos. He will seek maximum attrition of RVNAF elements. Against US forces, he will emphasize attacks by fire on airfields and installations, using assaults and ambushes selectively. His central objective continues to be the destruction of the Government of SVN and its armed forces. As a minimum he hopes to seize sufficient territory and gain control of enough people to support establishment of the groups and committees he proposes for participation in an NLF dominated government.

b. MACV Strategy:

(1) MACV believes that the central thrust of our strategy now must be to defeat the enemy offensive and that if this is done well, the situation overall will be greatly improved over the pre-TET condition.

(2) MACV accepts the fact that its first priority must be the security of Government of Vietnam in Saigon and provincial capitals. MACV describes its objectives as:

—First, to counter the enemy offensive and to destroy or eject the NVA invasion force in the north.

—Second, to restore security in the cities and towns.

—Third, to restore security in the heavily populated areas of the countryside.

—Fourth, to regain the initiative through offensive operations.

c. Tasks:

(1) Security of Cities and Government. MACV recognizes that US forces will be required to reinforce and support RVNAF in the security of cities, towns and government structure. At this time, 10 US battalions are operating in the environs of Saigon. It is clear that this task will absorb a substantial portion of US forces.

(2) Security in the Countryside. To a large extent the VC now control the countryside. Most of the 54 battalions formerly providing security for pacification are now defending district or province towns. MACV estimates that US forces will be required in a number of places to assist and encourage the Vietnamese Army to leave the cities and towns and reenter the country. This is especially true in the Delta.

(3) Defense of the borders, the DMZ and the northern provinces. MACV considers that it must meet the enemy threat in I Corps Tactical Zone and has already deployed there slightly over 50% of all US maneuver battalions. US forces have been thinned out in the highlands, notwithstanding an expected enemy offensive in the early future.

(4) Offensive Operations. Coupling the increased requirement for the cities and subsequent reentry into the rural areas, and the heavy requirement for defense of the I Corps Zone, MACV does not have adequate forces at this time to resume the offensive in the remainder of the country, nor does it have adequate reserves against the contingency of simultaneous large-scale enemy offensive action throughout the country.

5. Force Requirements:

a. Forces currently assigned to MACV, plus the residual Program Five forces yet to be delivered, are inadequate in numbers and balance to carry out the strategy and to accomplish the tasks described above in the proper priority. To contend with, and defeat, the new enemy threat, MACV has stated requirements for forces over the 525,000 ceiling imposed by Program Five. The add-on requested totals 206,756 spaces for a new proposed ceiling of 731,756, with all forces being deployed into country by the end of CY 68. Principal forces included in the add-on are three division equivalents, 15 tactical fighter squadrons and augmentation for current Navy programs. MACV desires that these additional forces be delivered in three packages as follows:

(1) Immediate Increment, Priority One: To be deployed by 1 May 68. Major elements include one brigade of the 5th Mechanized Division with a mix of one infantry, one armored and one mechanized battalion; the Fifth Marine Division (less RLT-26); one armored cavalry regiment; eight tactical fighter squadrons; and a groupment of Navy units to augment on-going programs.

(2) Immediate Increment, Priority Two: To be deployed as soon as possible but prior to 1 Sep. 68. Major elements include the remainder of the 5th Mechanized Division, and four tactical fighter squadrons. It is desirable that the ROK Light Division be deployed within this time frame.

Follow-On Increment: To be deployed by the end of CY 68. Major elements include one infantry division, three tactical fighter squadrons, and units to further augment Navy Programs.

Source: *The Pentagon Papers as Published by the New York Times* (New York: Quadrangle, 1971), 628–634.

181. Walter Cronkite Criticizes U.S. Policy, February 27, 1968 [Excerpts]

Introduction

CBS News television anchorman Walter Cronkite was often held to be "the most trusted man in America." Upon returning from a trip to Vietnam to report on conditions there following the Communist Tet Offensive, Cronkite announces on the evening news that he believes that the United States is not winning the war but is in fact "mired in stalemate" there. President Lyndon B. Johnson reportedly lamented that "If I've lost Cronkite, I've lost America." Although Cronkite was certainly not the only American journalist to take that position, he was the most influential and well-respected reporter to do so.

Primary Source

Walter Cronkite: These ruins are in Saigon, capital and largest city of South Vietnam. They were left here by an act of war, Vietnamese against Vietnamese. Hundreds died here. Here in these ruins can be seen physical evidence of the Vietcong's Tet offensive, but far less tangible is what those ruins mean, and like everything else in this burned and blasted and weary land, they mean success or setback, victory or defeat, depending upon whom you talk to.

President Nguyen Van Thieu: I believe it gives to the VC, it shows first to the VC that the—the Vietnamese people from whom they hoped to have a general uprising, and to welcome the VC in the cities, this is a very bad test for them.

Nguyen Xuan Oanh (critic of government): I think the people have realized now that there [are] no secure areas. Your own home in the heart of the city is not secure. I am stunned myself when I see that the Vietcong can come to your door and open the door and just kill you instantly, without any warning, and without any protection from the government.

Cronkite: There are doubts about the measure of success or setback, but even more, there are doubts about the exact measure of the disaster itself. All that is known with certainty is that on the first two nights of the Tet Lunar New Year, the Vietcong and North Vietnamese Regular Forces, violating the truce agreed on for that holiday, struck across the entire length of South Vietnam, hitting the largest 35 cities, towns, and provincial capitals. How many died and how much damage was done, however, are still but approximations, despite the official figures.

The very preciseness of the figures brings them under suspicion. Anyone who has wandered through these ruins knows that an exact count is impossible. Why, just a short while ago a little old man came and told us that two VC were buried in a hastily dug grave up at the end of the block. Had they been counted? And what about these ruins? Have they gone through all of them for buried civilians and soldiers? And what about those 14 VC we found in the courtyard behind the post office at Hue? Had they been counted and tabulated? They certainly hadn't been buried.

We came to Vietnam to try to determine what all this means to the future of the war here. We talked to officials, top officials, civilian and military, Vietnamese and American. We toured damaged areas like this, and refugee centers. We paid a visit to the Battle at Hue, and to the men manning the northernmost provinces, where the next big communist offensive is expected. All of this is the subject of our report....

We'd like to sum up our findings in Vietnam, an analysis that must be speculative, personal, subjective. Who won and who lost in the great Tet offensive against the cities? I'm not sure. The Vietcong did not win by a knockout, but neither did we. The referees of history may make it a draw. Another stand-off may be coming in the big battles expected south of the Demilitarized Zone. Khe Sanh could well fall, with a terrible loss in American lives, prestige, and morale, and this is a tragedy of our stubbornness there; but the bastion no longer is a key to the rest of the northern regions, and it is doubtful that the American forces can be defeated across the breadth of the DMZ with any substantial loss of ground. Another standoff. On the political front, past performance gives no confidence that the Vietnamese government can cope with its problems, now compounded by the attack on the cities. It may not fall, it may hold on, but it probably won't show the dynamic qualities demanded of this young nation. Another stand-off.

We have been too often disappointed by the optimism of the American leaders, both in Vietnam and Washington, to have faith any longer in the silver linings they find in the darkest clouds. They may be right, that Hanoi's winter-spring offensive has been forced by the communist realization that they could not win the longer war of attrition, and that the communists hope that any success in the offensive will improve their position for eventual negotiations. It would improve their position, and it would also require our realization, that we should have had all along, that any negotiations must be that—negotiations, not the dictation of peace terms. For it seems now more certain than ever that the bloody experience of Vietnam is to end in a stalemate. This summer's almost certain stand-off will either end in real give-and-take negotiations or terrible escalation; and for every means we have to escalate, the enemy can match us, and that applies to invasion of the North, the use of nuclear weapons, or the mere commitment of 100-, or 200-, or 300,000 more American troops to the battle. And with each escalation, the world comes closer to the brink of cosmic disaster.

To say that we are closer to victory today is to believe, in the face of the evidence, the optimists who have been wrong in the past. To suggest we are on the edge of defeat is to yield to unreasonable pessimism. To say that we are mired in stalemate seems the only realistic, yet unsatisfactory, conclusion. On the off chance that military and political analysts are right, in the next few months we must test the enemy's intentions, in case this is indeed his last gasp before negotiations. But it is increasingly clear to this reporter that the only rational way out then will be to negotiate, not as victors, but as an honorable people who lived up to their pledge to defend democracy, and did the best they could.

Source: Peter Braestrup, *Big Story: How the American Press and Television Reported and Interpreted the Crisis of Tet 1968 in Vietnam and Washington*, Vol. 2 (Boulder, CO: Westview, 1977), 180–189.

182. A Communist Party Evaluation of the 1968 Tet Offensive, March 1968

Introduction

In its Resolution No. 6, the Central Office for South Vietnam (COSVN), the organization controlled by the Democratic Republic of Vietnam (DRV, North Vietnam) and running the Communist military effort in the Republic of Vietnam (RVN, South Vietnam), analyzes the recent Communist Tet Offensive. The document trumpets as successes that the Army of the Republic of Vietnam (ARVN, South Vietnamese Army) and U.S. troops have been forced to defend the cities of South Vietnam and that the Communist forces have "liberated" 1.5 million Vietnamese. The report also addresses failures, chief among them being the inability to bring about a general uprising against the South Vietnamese government. COSVN leaders also seek to rally the rank and file for renewed military efforts to bring final victory.

Primary Source

I. Great and unprecedented successes recorded in all fields during the first-month phase of the General Offensive and General Uprising.

Since the beginning of Spring this year, the "Anti-U.S. National Salvation" resistance war of our people in the South has entered a new phase:

In this phase of General Offensive and General Uprising, after a month of continuous offensives and simultaneous uprisings conducted on all battlefields in the South, we have recorded great and unprecedented victories in all fields, inflicting on the enemy heavier losses than those he had suffered in any previous period.

1. We wore down, annihilated and disintegrated almost one-third of the puppet troops' strength, wore down and annihilated about one-fifth of U.S. combat forces, one-third of the total number of aircraft, one-third of the total number of mechanized vehicles, and an important part of U.S. and puppet material installations; destroyed and forced to surrender or withdraw one-third of the enemy military posts, driving the enemy into an unprecedentedly awkward situation: from the position of the aggressor striving to gain the initiative through a two-prong tactic [military action and rural pacification], the enemy has withdrawn into a purely passive and defensive position, with his forces dispersed on all battlefields in the South for the purpose of defending the towns, cities and the main lines of communications. The struggle potential and morale of U.S. and puppet troops have seriously weakened because our army and people have dealt thundering blows at them everywhere, even at their principal lairs, and because they are facing great difficulties in replenishing troops and replacing war facilities destroyed during the past month.

2. We attacked all U.S.-puppet nerve centers, occupied and exerted our control for a definite period and at varying degrees over almost all towns, cities and municipalities in the South, and destroyed and disintegrated an important part of puppet installations at all levels, seriously damaging the puppet administrative machinery.

3. We liberated additional wide areas in the countryside containing a population of 1.5 million inhabitants; consolidated and widened our rear areas, shifted immense resources of manpower and material, which had been previously robbed by the enemy in these areas, to the support of the front-line and of victory; encircled and isolated the enemy, and reduced the enemy's reserves of human and material resources, driving him into a very difficult economic and financial situation.

4. We have quantitatively and qualitatively improved our armed forces and political forces which have become outstandingly mature during the struggle in the past month. Our armed forces have progressed in many aspects, political organizations are being consolidated and have stepped forward, much progress has been realized in leadership activities and methods and we have gained richer experiences.

The above-mentioned great and unprecedented successes in all fields have strongly encouraged and motivated compatriots in towns and cities and areas under temporary enemy control to arise to seize the state power, have created a lively and enthusiastic atmosphere and inspired a strong confidence in final victory among compatriots in both the North and the South. These successes have moreover won the sympathy and support of the socialist countries and the world's progressive people (including the U.S. progressive people) for our people's revolutionary cause, seriously isolated the U.S. imperialists and their lackeys, deepened their internal contradictions and thereby weakened the U.S. will of aggression.

The above-mentioned great successes in all fields have been recorded thanks to the clear-sighted and correct policy, line and strategic determination of the Party, the wise and resolute leadership of the Party Central Committee, the correct implementation of the Party's policy and line by Nam Truong and Party committee echelons, the sacrifice and devotion of all Party cadres and members who have in an exemplary manner carried out the Party's strategic determination, the eagerness for independence and freedom of the people in the South who are ready to shed their blood in exchange for independence and freedom, the absolute loyalty to the Party's and masses' revolution of the People's armed forces who have fought with infinite courage, the great assistance from the northern rear area and brotherly socialist countries, and the sympathy and support from the world people.

We have won great successes but still have many deficiencies and weak points:

1. In the military field—From the beginning, we have not been able to annihilate much of the enemy's live force and much of the reactionary clique. Our armed forces have not fulfilled their role as "lever" and have not created favorable conditions for motivating the masses to arise in towns and cities.

2. In the political field—Organized popular forces were not broad and strong enough. We have not had specific plans for motivating the masses to the extent that they would indulge in violent armed uprisings in coordination with and supporting the military offensives.

3. The puppet troop proselyting failed to create a military revolt movement in which the troops would arise and return to the people's side. The enemy troop proselyting task to be carried out in coordination with the armed struggle and political struggle has not been performed, and inadequate attention had been paid to this in particular.

4. There has not been enough consciousness about specific plans for the widening and development of liberated rural areas and the appropriate mobilization of manpower, material resources and the great capabilities of the masses to support the front line.

5. The building of real strength and particularly the replenishment of troops and development of political forces of the infrastructure has been slow and has not met the requirements of continuous offensives and uprisings of the new phase.

6. In providing leadership and guidance to various echelons, we failed to give them a profound and thorough understanding of the Party's policy, line and strategic determination so that they have a correct and full realization of this phase of General Offensive and General Uprising. The implementation of our policies has not been

sharply and closely conducted. We lacked concreteness, our plans were simple, our coordination poor, control and prodding were absent, reporting and requests for instructions were much delayed.

The above-mentioned deficiencies and weak points have limited our successes and are, at the same time, difficulties which we must resolutely overcome.

II. The present form of the war between the enemy and us and prospects of future developments.

1. Our present "Anti-U.S. National Salvation" resistance war has a very new form and is more favorable to us than ever.

a. We are in a completely active and offensive position; we have brought the war into towns and cities, the enemy's rear areas and important and densely populated areas close to towns and cities; our rear areas have increasingly expanded to form a strong, linked-up position which gradually and tightly encircles the enemy's last strong points. Throughout the three areas, the masses have continuously risen up and strengthened their position of mastery with a higher and higher revolutionary spirit. In towns and cities particularly, in the face of the enemy's recent murderous and savage actions against the people, including puppet troops' and civil servants' dependents, the masses, boiling with anger, have been supporting our troops and awaiting favorable occasions to arise, eradicating wicked [enemy] individuals, sweeping the enemy's state power, and building the people's revolutionary state power. All intermediary classes of people are leaning toward the revolution's side.

b. The enemy is in a passive position, being encircled, divided and dispersed on all battlefields. He is facing difficulties in all aspects such as: a stalemate in strategy; passiveness in tactics; difficulties in replenishing troops and replacing war facilities which had been destroyed; difficulties in the economic field because of the restriction of their reserve of manpower and material resources. Because of their serious isolation in the political field and the state of confusion of the puppet army, the puppet regime is gradually losing authority and running toward total failure.

2. Although the enemy is suffering heavy defeat and is in a passive and confused situation, he still has strength and is very stubborn. In his death throes he will resort to more murderous and savage actions. He will massacre the people, thrust out to break the encirclement and create many new difficulties for us. The struggle between the enemy and us will become fiercer, particularly in areas adjoining the towns and cities. Therefore, we must be extremely vigilant, urgently and actively exploit our past successes, overcome all difficulties and hardships with determination to secure final victory and be ready to fight vigorously should the war be prolonged and widened.

However, it must be clearly realized that this will be but the enemy's convulsions before death, his reaction from a weak, not a strong position. The situation will continue to develop in a way favorable to us and detrimental to the enemy with the possibility of sudden developments which we must be ready to take advantage of in order to secure final victory.

Source: *Viet-Nam Documents and Research Notes, No. 38* (Saigon: U.S. Mission in Viet Nam, July 1968).

183. President Lyndon Johnson: Televised Address, March 31, 1968 [Excerpts]

Introduction

Compounding problems for President Lyndon Johnson, 1968 was an election year. On March 12 in New Hampshire, anti–Vietnam War senator Eugene McCarthy of Minnesota stunned Johnson by winning 42 percent of the vote in that state's Democratic primary (although many of those voting for McCarthy were in fact signaling their displeasure with Johnson for not using greater military force). This prompted antiwar senator Robert Kennedy of New York to join the race. Worried Democratic Party leaders urged the president to do something dramatic to bolster his sagging popularity. On March 31 in a televised address to the nation, Johnson reiterates his Vietnam policies and also announces a halt in the bombing of most of the Democratic Republic of Vietnam (DRV, North Vietnam). Then at the close of his remarks he stuns the nation by announcing that given the nature of the challenges, he cannot in good conscience devote even "an hour" of his time to "personal partisan causes" or to anything other than the "awesome duties" of the presidency and that he will neither seek nor accept another term as president.

Primary Source

Good evening, my fellow Americans. Tonight I want to speak to you of peace in Viet-Nam and Southeast Asia.

No other question so preoccupies our people. No other dream so absorbs the 250 million human beings who live in that part of the world. No other goal motivates American policy in Southeast Asia.

For years, representatives of our Government and others have traveled the world seeking to find a basis for peace talks.

Since last September, they have carried the offer that I made public at San Antonio.

That offer was this: that the United States would stop its bombardment of North Viet-Nam when that would lead promptly to productive discussions—and that we would assume that North Viet-Nam would not take military advantage of our restraint.

Hanoi denounced this offer, both privately and publicly. Even while the search for peace was going on, North Viet-Nam rushed their preparations for a savage assault on the people, the Government, and the allies of South Viet-Nam.

Their attack—during the Tet holidays—failed to achieve its principal objectives.

It did not collapse the elected government of South Viet-Nam or shatter its army, as the Communists had hoped.

It did not produce a "general uprising" among the people of the cities, as they had predicted.

The Communists were unable to maintain control of any of the more than 30 cities that they attacked. And they took very heavy casualties.

But they did compel the South Vietnamese and their allies to move certain forces from the countryside into the cities. They caused widespread disruption and suffering. Their attacks, and the battles that followed, made refugees of half a million human beings.

The Communists may renew their attack any day. They are, it appears, trying to make 1968 the year of decision in South Viet-Nam—the year that brings, if not final victory or defeat, at least a turning point in the struggle.

This much is clear: If they do mount another round of heavy attacks, they will not succeed in destroying the fighting power of South Viet-Nam and its allies.

But tragically, this is also clear: Many men—on both sides of the struggle—will be lost. A nation that has already suffered 20 years of warfare will suffer once again. Armies on both sides will take new casualties. And the war will go on.

There is no need for this to be so.

There is no need to delay the talks that could bring an end to this long and this bloody war.

Tonight I renew the offer I made last August—to stop the bombardment of North Viet-Nam. We ask that talks begin promptly, that they be serious talks on the substance of peace. We assume that during those talks Hanoi will not take advantage of our restraint.

We are prepared to move immediately toward peace through negotiations. So tonight, in the hope that this action will lead to early talks, I am taking the first step to deescalate the conflict. We are reducing—substantially reducing—the present level of hostilities. And we are doing so unilaterally and at once.

Tonight I have ordered our aircraft and our naval vessels to make no attacks on North Viet-Nam, except in the area north of the demilitarized zone where the continuing enemy buildup directly threatens Allied forward positions and where the movements of their troops and supplies are clearly related to that threat.

The area in which we are stopping our attacks includes almost 90 percent of North Viet-Nam's population and most of its territory. Thus there will be no attacks around the principal populated areas or in the food-producing areas of North Viet-Nam.

Even this very limited bombing of the North could come to an early end if our restraint is matched by restraint in Hanoi. But I cannot in good conscience stop all bombing so long as to do so would immediately and directly endanger the lives of our men and our allies. Whether a complete bombing halt becomes possible in the future will be determined by events.

Our purpose in this action is to bring about a reduction in the level of violence that now exists.

It is to save the lives of brave men and to save the lives of innocent women and children. It is to permit the contending forces to move closer to a political settlement.

And tonight I call upon the United Kingdom and I call upon the Soviet Union, as cochairmen of the Geneva conferences and as permanent members of the United Nations Security Council, to do all they can to move from the unilateral act of deescalation that I have just announced toward genuine peace in Southeast Asia.

Now, as in the past, the United States is ready to send its representatives to any forum, at any time, to discuss the means of bringing this ugly war to an end.

I am designating one of our most distinguished Americans, Ambassador Averell Harriman, as my personal representative for such talks. In addition, I have asked Ambassador Llewellyn Thompson, who returned from Moscow for consultation, to be available to join Ambassador Harriman at Geneva or any other suitable place just as soon as Hanoi agrees to a conference.

I call upon President Ho Chi Minh to respond positively and favorably to this new step toward peace.

But if peace does not come now through negotiations, it will come when Hanoi understands that our common resolve is unshakable and our common strength is invincible.

Tonight, we and the other allied nations are contributing 600,000 fighting men to assist 700,000 South Vietnamese troops in defending their little country.

Our presence there has always rested on this basic belief: The main burden of preserving their freedom must be carried out by them—by the South Vietnamese themselves.

We and our allies can only help to provide a shield behind which the people of South Viet-Nam can survive and can grow and develop. On their efforts—on their determinations and resourcefulness—the outcome will ultimately depend. . . .

The actions that we have taken since the beginning of the year to reequip the South Vietnamese forces; to meet our responsibilities in Korea, as well as our responsibilities in Viet-Nam; to meet price increases and the cost of activating and deploying Reserve forces; to replace helicopters and provide the other military supplies we need—all of these actions are going to require additional expenditures.

The tentative estimate of those additional expenditures is $2.5 billion in this fiscal year and $2.6 billion in the next fiscal year.

These projected increases in expenditures for our national security will bring into sharper focus the Nation's need for immediate action, action to protect the prosperity of the American people and to protect the strength and the stability of our American dollar.

On many occasions I have pointed out that without a tax bill or decreased expenditures next year's deficit would again be around $20 billion. I have emphasized the need to set strict priorities in our spending. I have stressed that failure to act—and to act promptly and decisively—would raise very strong doubts throughout the world about America's willingness to keep its financial house in order.

Yet Congress has not acted. And tonight we face the sharpest financial threat in the post-war era—a threat to the dollar's role as the keystone of international trade and finance in the world. . . .

One day, my fellow citizens, there will be peace in Southeast Asia.

It will come because the people of Southeast Asia want it—those whose armies are at war tonight and those who, though threatened, have thus far been spared.

Peace will come because Asians were willing to work for it—and to sacrifice for it—and to die by the thousands for it.

But let it never be forgotten: Peace will come also because America sent her sons to help secure it.

It has not been easy—far from it. During the past 4–1/2 years, it has been my fate and my responsibility to be Commander in Chief. I lived daily and nightly with the cost of this war. I know the pain that it has inflicted. I know perhaps better than anyone the misgivings that it has aroused.

Throughout this entire long period, I have been sustained by a single principle: that what we are doing now in Viet-Nam is vital not only to the security of Southeast Asia, but it is vital to the security of every American.

Surely we have treaties which we must respect. Surely we have commitments that we are going to keep. Resolutions of the Congress testify to the need to resist aggression in the world and in Southeast Asia.

But the heart of our involvement in South Viet-Nam—under three different Presidents, three separate administrations—has always been America's own security.

And the larger purpose of our involvement has always been to help the nations of Southeast Asia become independent and stand alone, self-sustaining as members of a great world community— at peace with themselves and at peace with all others.

With such an Asia, our country—and the world—will be far more secure than it is tonight.

I believe that a peaceful Asia is far nearer to reality because of what America has done in Viet-Nam. I believe that the men who endure the dangers of battle—fighting there for us tonight—are helping the entire world avoid far greater conflicts, far wider wars, far more destruction, than this one.

The peace that will bring them home some day will come. Tonight I have offered the first in what I hope will be a series of mutual moves toward peace.

I pray that it will not be rejected by the leaders of North Viet-Nam. I pray that they will accept it as a means by which the sacrifices of their own people may be ended. And I ask your help and your support, my fellow citizens, for this effort to reach across the battlefield toward an early peace. . . .

Throughout my entire public career I have followed the personal philosophy that I am a free man, an American, a public servant, and a member of my party, in that order always and only.

For 37 years in the service of our nation, first as a Congressman, as a Senator and as Vice President and now as your President, I have put the unity of the people first. I have put it ahead of any divisive partisanship.

And in these times as in times before, it is true that a house divided against itself by the spirit of faction, of party, of region, of religion, of race, is a house that cannot stand.

There is division in the American house now. There is divisiveness among us all tonight. And holding the trust that is mine, as President of all the people, I cannot disregard the peril to the progress of the American people and the hope and the prospect of peace for all peoples.

So I would ask all Americans, whatever their personal interests or concern, to guard against divisiveness and all its ugly consequences.

Fifty-two months and 10 days ago, in a moment of tragedy and trauma, the duties of this Office fell upon me. I asked then for your help and God's, that we might continue America on its course, binding up our wounds, healing our history, moving forward in new unity, to clear the American agenda and to keep the American commitment for all of our people.

United we have kept that commitment. United we have enlarged that commitment.

Through all time to come, I think America will be a stronger nation, a more just society, and a land of greater opportunity and fulfillment because of what we have all done together in these years of unparalleled achievement.

Our reward will come in the life of freedom, peace, and hope that our children will enjoy through ages ahead.

What we won when all of our people united must not now be lost in suspicion, distrust, selfishness, and politics among any of our people.

Believing this as I do, I have concluded that I should not permit the Presidency to become involved in the partisan divisions that are developing in this political year.

With America's sons in the fields far away, with America's future under challenge right here at home, with our hopes and the world's hopes for peace in the balance every day, I do not believe that I should devote an hour or a day of my time to any personal partisan causes or to any duties other than the awesome duties of this Office—the Presidency of your country.

Accordingly, I shall not seek, and I will not accept, the nomination of my party for another term as your President.

But let men everywhere know, however, that a strong, a confident, and a vigilant America stands ready tonight to seek an honorable peace—and stands ready tonight to defend an honored cause—whatever the price, whatever the burden, whatever the sacrifices that duty may require.

Thank you for listening.

Good night and God bless all of you.

Source: *Public Papers of the Presidents of the United States: Lyndon B. Johnson, 1968–69,* Book 1 (Washington, DC: U.S. Government Printing Office, 1970), 469–476.

184. Secret Cable from the North Vietnamese Politburo to COSVN, April 3, 1968 [Excerpts]

Introduction

On April 3, 1968, the Politburo of the Democratic Republic of Vietnam (DRV, North Vietnam) sent a cable to the Central Office for South Vietnam (COSVN), the Communist headquarters in the Republic of Vietnam (RVN, South Vietnam) running the war there, informing the Communist leaders in South Vietnam of its planned response to President Lyndon Johnson's actions in ordering a halt to the bombing of most, but not all, of North Vietnam and calling on the Communist side to enter into peace talks with the United States.

Primary Source

As the result of our massive victories in all areas, military, political, and diplomatic, especially the victories we won in the general offensive and uprisings during the Tet Lunar New Year, the situation on the battlefield in South Vietnam and the situation in the U.S. and throughout the world is developing in directions that are very favorable to us and very unfavorable for the enemy. Because of major political, social, and economic problems, because of the ferocious struggles going on within American leadership circles, especially during the primary elections in the U.S., and because of powerful pressure from U.S. and world public opinion, Johnson has been forced to "restrict the bombing" of North Vietnam. . . .

The Politburo has decided that on the diplomatic front, both North and South Vietnam [North Vietnam and the NLF] must continuously launch sharp and effective attacks against the enemy aimed at supporting our effort to secure even greater military and political victories, at winning even wider sympathy and support from our [the socialist] camp, from the people of the world, and from the American people, and at deepening the contradictions within American political circles, the contradictions between the U.S. and their puppets, the contradictions within the puppet camp,

and the contradictions between the U.S. and the other imperialist countries in order to further isolate the enemy. . . .

To achieve these goals, North Vietnam's government has already issued a public statement that . . . initiates another step in our stratagem by announcing that we have selected a representative who is prepared to meet with an American representative to confirm that the U.S. will unconditionally end the bombing and all other acts of war against the Democratic Republic of Vietnam so that talks may begin. . . .

The Politburo believes that at this time the National Liberation Front must issue a solemn statement presenting its position regarding a political settlement in South Vietnam and announce that it is prepared to enter into talks with the United States based on the Front's position.

The content of the Front's statement will consist of three parts: a) An affirmation of the Front's determination to fight and to win victory, written in strong, resolute language; b) An exposition of the Front's position on a political settlement for South Vietnam . . . ; c) An expression of willingness to talk to the U.S. on the basis of the Front's position.

This statement will be issued approximately one week after the [North Vietnamese] government's statement.

Because this statement must be issued quickly, the Politburo has instructed our staffs up here [in North Vietnam] to draft the statement. The Politburo will review the statement and have it released. We wanted to give COSVN advance notice of what we are doing. . . .

Source: *Van Kien Dang, Toan Tap 29, 1968* [Collected Party Documents, Volume 29, 1968] (Hanoi: Nha Xuat Ban Chinh Tri Quoc Gia, 2004), 203–205. Translated by Merle L. Pribbenow.

185. COSVN Directive, June 10, 1968 [Excerpt]

Introduction

In May 1968 in hopes of strengthening their hand in the Paris Peace Talks, which opened on May 13, the North Vietnamese opened the second phase of their General Offensive, which the Americans dubbed "Mini Tet." The Communist rallying cry was "Blood in May, Peace in June." Although occurring countrywide, these attacks were nowhere near the level of the Tet Offensive and consisted principally of rocket and mortar attacks against cities, towns, and U.S. installations. Widely anticipated by authorities of the United States and the Republic of Vietnam (RVN, South Vietnam), Mini Tet ended in extensive Communist casualties and failure. Nonetheless, the Communist side here claims that they have achieved a significant victory and that they retain the military initiative.

Primary Source

3. Four main weak points stood out in the second phase:

—Militarily, our attacks were concentrated upon main targets, whereas secondary targets were neglected, or were not attacked as vigorously as they should have been.
—The uprising of the people was slow and scattered.
—Troop proselyting was deplorably weak.
—Development of our political armed forces and the strengthening of rear areas was poor.

These four reasons limited our success. . . .

Viewed objectively, our second phase was launched under conditions where the enemy had been warned [officially deleted] and had strengthened his defensive system. We therefore met considerable difficulties created by him. In addition, we did not have enough time for the Party Branches and people to assimilate the resolutions of the Party which caused the forces of the Party, army and people to be less than fully prepared. Subjectively, these weak points and deficiencies originated from our lack of efforts which can be illustrated as follows:

First: We still did not sharply and profoundly assimilate the basic lines of the Party's policy and strategic determination. We did not fully understand the characteristics of the new phase. From the basic assumption that the General Offensive/General Uprising was a "one blow affair" to the realization that it was a phase [of operations], there was a tendency to consider it as a "protracted" struggle and a failure to view it as a phase of continuous offensives and uprising which require a positive urgency in gaining success every hour and every minute. We did not correctly take into consideration the relationship that existed between attacks and uprisings; armed forces and political forces; urban and rural areas; killing the enemy, destroying his key agencies in cities, bases and liberation of the rural areas; attack and building of strength; main points and secondary points; firmness and intrepidity, etc. . . .

Second: In the face of the rigors of war, our ideological indoctrination was not thorough, opportune or persevering, and our soldiers were not taught how to thoroughly rid themselves of their rightist and shirking attitudes.

Among cadre and Party members, including some at leadership levels, inaccurate estimations of the enemy and friendly situations still existed. (They viewed the enemy's forces without considering his serious weaknesses and remarked only on our own difficulties, without realizing the huge potential of our people and the opportunity that was increasingly open for us.) They lacked zeal in attacking the enemy and they were hesitant and sheep-like. They lost their self-confidence, feared to make sacrifices, suffered hardships and had very little sense of responsibility.

Third: The leadership plan at all levels was deficient and the performance of tasks was too simple and lackadaisical. There was no thorough understanding of the Party's policy and strategic determination in general and of the requirements of the second phase in particular. Leadership was not "total, continuous, expedient or daring. . . ." Furthermore, it failed to transform itself into a tool for the people, as it did not realize the potential of the local areas. Leadership at various levels also lacked a sense of urgency and motivation. Close coordination among various levels was poor. The Standing Committee of Nam Truong loosely coordinated with the regions, the regions with the provinces, the provinces with the districts, etc. . . . [sic] A number of Party Committee echelons and cadre did not keep pace with the requirements of the new phase. They were slow, hesitating and reluctant.

Fourth: Two Party branches and popular organizations in the cities and rural areas were as poor in quantity as they were in quality. The Party Committee echelons did not pay enough attention to strengthening leadership and developing the Party's basic structures in accordance with the requirements of the new phase.

These four causes limited our successes, and at the same time, constitute very great obstacles to the future implementation of the strategic determination of the Party. We must do our best to overcome these obstacles with a resolute Revolutionary spirit and a very high sense of responsibility.

Source: Gareth Porter, ed., *Vietnam: A History in Documents* (New York: New American Library, 1981), 151.

186. President Lyndon Johnson: Announcement of U.S. Bombing Halt, October 31, 1968 [Excerpt]

Introduction

During negotiations in Paris, U.S. representative W. Averell Harriman reached an understanding with his counterparts in the Democratic Republic of Vietnam (DRV, North Vietnam). The U.S. would halt the bombing unconditionally, and Hanoi would then cease rocket attacks and shelling cities in the Republic of Vietnam (RVN, South Vietnam) and would respect the demilitarized zone (DMZ). "Meaningful" peace talks would then begin. Although South Vietnamese president Nguyen Van Thieu was strongly opposed, U.S. president Lyndon Johnson on October 31 announced the bombing halt, in effect ending Operation ROLLING THUNDER. The North Vietnamese responded as agreed. The halt in the bombing, long sought by Democratic Party presidential candidate Hubert Humphrey, who had been edging up in the polls, came too late to save his candidacy. Republican Richard Nixon won a narrow election victory a week later.

Primary Source

Good evening my fellow Americans:

I speak to you this evening about very important developments in our search for peace in Vietnam. We have been engaged in discussions with the North Vietnamese in Paris since last May. The discussions began after I announced on the evening of March 31 in a television speech to the nation that the United States—in an effort to get talks started on a settlement of the Vietnam war—had stopped the bombing of North Vietnam in the area where 90 percent of the people live.

When our representatives—Ambassador Harriman and Ambassador Vance—were sent to Paris, they were instructed to insist throughout the discussions that the legitimate elected government of South Vietnam must take its place in any serious negotiations affecting the future of South Vietnam. Therefore, our Ambassadors Harriman and Vance made it abundantly clear to the representatives of North Vietnam in the beginning that—as I had indicated on the evening of March 31—we would stop the bombing of North Vietnamese territory entirely when that would lead to prompt and productive talks, meaning by that talks in which the Government of Vietnam was free to participate. Our Ambassadors also stressed that we could not stop the bombing so long as by doing so we would endanger the lives and the safety of our troops.

For a good many weeks, there was no movement in the talks at all. The talks appeared to really be deadlocked. Then a few weeks ago, they entered a new and a very much more hopeful phase. As we moved ahead, I conducted a series of very intensive discussions with our allies, and with the senior military and diplomatic officers of the U.S. Government, on the prospect for peace. The President also briefed our congressional leaders and all of the presidential candidates.

Last Sunday evening, and throughout Monday, we began to get confirmation of the essential understanding that we had been seeking with the North Vietnamese on the critical issues between us for some time. I spent most of all day Tuesday reviewing every single detail of this matter with our field commander, General Abrams, whom I had ordered home, and who arrived here at the White House at 2:30 in the morning and went into immediate conference with the President and the appropriate members of his Cabinet. We received General Abrams' judgment and we heard his recommendations at some length.

Now, as a result of all of these developments, I have now ordered that all air, naval, and artillery bombardment of North Vietnam cease as of 8 a.m., Washington time, Friday morning. I have reached this decision on the basis of the developments in the Paris talks. And I have reached it in the belief that this action can lead to progress toward a peaceful settlement of the Vietnamese war. I have already informed the three presidential candidates, as well as the congressional leaders of both the Republican and Democratic Parties of the reasons that the Government has made this decision. This decision very closely conforms to the statements that I have made in the past concerning a bombing cessation.

It was on August 19 that the President said:

"This administration does not intend to move further until it has good reasons to believe that the other side intends seriously, seriously, to join us in deescalating the war and moving seriously toward peace."

Then again on September 10, I said:

"The bombing will not stop until we are confident that it will not lead to an increase in American casualties."

The Joint Chiefs of Staff, all military men have assured me—and General Abrams firmly asserted to me on Tuesday in that early, 2:30 a.m. meeting—that in their military judgment this action should be taken now, and this action would not result in any increase in American casualties.

A regular session of the Paris talks will take place on Wednesday, November 6, at which the representatives of the Government of South Vietnam are free to participate. We are informed by the representatives of the Hanoi Government that the representatives of the National Liberation Front will also be present. I emphasize that their attendance in no way involves recognition of the National Liberation Front in any form. Yet, it conforms to the statements that we have made many times over the years that the NLF would have no difficulty making its views known.

What we now expect—what we have a right to expect—are prompt, productive, serious and intensive negotiations in an atmosphere that is conducive to progress. We have reached the stage where productive talks can begin. We have made clear to the other side that such talks cannot continue if they take military advantage of them. We cannot have productive talks in an atmosphere where the cities are being shelled and where the demilitarized zone is being abused.

I think I should caution you, my fellow Americans, that arrangements of this kind are never foolproof. For that matter, even formal treaties are never foolproof, as we have learned from our experience. But in the light of the progress that has been made in recent weeks, and after carefully considering and weighing the unanimous military and diplomatic advice and judgment tendered to the Commander in Chief, I have finally decided to take this step now and to really determine the good faith of those who have assured us that progress will result when bombing ceases and to try to ascertain if an early peace is possible. The overriding consideration that governs us at this hour is the chance and the opportunity that we might have to save human lives, save human lives on both sides of the conflict. Therefore, I have concluded that we should see if they are acting in good faith.

Source: *Public Papers of the Presidents of the United States: Lyndon B. Johnson, 1968–69*, Book 2 (Washington, DC: U.S. Government Printing Office, 1970), 1099–1103.

187. National Security Study Memorandum No. 1, January 21, 1969 [Excerpts]

Introduction

Dr. Henry Kissinger, named by President-elect Richard Nixon as his national security adviser, asked his staff to draw up a list of 28 major questions. These were then submitted to the federal agencies involved in Vietnam policy. The answers ran 548 pages, which are summarized in the document below. Opinions run from relative optimism to relative pessimism, but there is general agreement that the Communist side is negotiating in Paris from strength and that Communist forces in the Republic of Vietnam (RVN, South Vietnam) are fully capable of defeating South Vietnamese armed forces should the United States withdraw.

Primary Source

The responses to the questions posed regarding Vietnam show agreement on some matters as well as very substantial differences of opinion within the U.S. Government on many aspects of the Vietnam situation. While there are some divergencies on the facts, the sharpest differences arise in the interpretation of those facts, the relative weight to be given them, and the implications to be drawn. In addition, there remain certain areas where our information remains inadequate. There is general agreement, assuming we follow our current strategy, on the following—

1. The GVN and allied position in Vietnam has been strengthened recently in many respects.

2. The GVN has improved its political position, but it is not certain that GVN and other non-communist groups will be able to survive a peaceful competition with the NLF for political power in South Vietnam.

3. The RVNAF alone cannot now, or in the foreseeable future, stand up to the current North Vietnamese-Viet Cong forces.

4. The enemy have suffered some reverses but they have not changed their essential objectives and they have sufficient strength to pursue these objectives. We are not attriting his forces faster than he can recruit or infiltrate.

5. The enemy is not in Paris primarily out of weakness. The disagreements within these parameters are reflected in two schools in the government with generally consistent membership. The first school, which we will call Group A, usually includes MACV, CINCPAC, JCS and Embassy Saigon, and takes a hopeful view of current and future prospects in Vietnam within the parameters mentioned. The second school, Group B, usually includes OSD [Office of the Secretary of Defense], CIA and (to a lesser extent) State, and is decidedly more skeptical about the present and pessimistic about the future. There are, of course, disagreements within agencies across the board or on specific issues.

As illustration, these schools line up as follows on some of the broader questions:

In explaining reduced enemy military presence and activities, Group A gives greater relative weight to allied military pressure than does Group B.

The improvements in RVNAF are considered much more significant by Group A than Group B.

Group A underlines advancements in the pacification program, while Group B is skeptical both of the evaluation system used to measure progress and of the solidity of recent advances.

In looking at the political scene, Group A accents recent improvements while Group B highlights remaining obstacles and the relative strength of the NLF.

Group A assigns much greater effectiveness to bombing in Vietnam and Laos than Group B.

Following is a summary of the major conclusions and disagreements about each of six broad areas with regard to Vietnam: the negotiating environment, enemy capabilities, RVNAF capabilities, pacification, South Vietnamese politics, and U.S. military operations. . . .

Negotiating Environment

There is general U.S. government agreement that Hanoi is in Paris for a variety of motives but not primarily out of weakness; that Hanoi is charting a course independent of Moscow, which favors negotiations, and of Peking, which opposes them; and that our knowledge of possible political factions among North Vietnamese leaders is extremely imprecise. There continues wide disagreement about the impact on Southeast Asia of various outcomes in Vietnam.

Various possible North Vietnamese motives for negotiating are discussed, and there is agreement that the DRV is in Paris for mixed reasons. No U.S. agency responding to the questions believes that the primary reason the DRV is in Paris is weakness. All consider it unlikely that Hanoi came to Paris either to accept a face-saving formula for defeat or to give the U.S. a face-saving way to withdraw. There is agreement that Hanoi has been subject to heavy military pressure and that a desire to end the losses and costs of war was an element in Hanoi's decision. The consensus is that Hanoi believes that it can persist long enough to obtain a relatively favorable negotiated compromise. The respondents agree that the DRV is in Paris to negotiate withdrawal of U.S. forces, to undermine GVN and USG [U.S. government] relations and to provide a better chance for FV victory in the South. State believes that increased doubt about winning the war through continued military and international political pressure also played a major role. Hanoi's ultimate goal of a unified Vietnam under its control has not changed.

There continues to be a sharp debate between and within agencies about the effect of the outcome in Vietnam on other nations. The most recent NIE [National Intelligence Estimate] on this subject (NIE 50-58) tended to downgrade the so-called "domino theory." It states that a settlement which would permit the Communists to take control of the Government in South Viet-Nam, not immediately but within a year or two, would be likely to bring Cambodia and Laos into Hanoi's orbit at a fairly early state, but that these developments would not necessarily unhinge the rest of Asia.

The NIE dissenters believe that an unfavorable settlement would stimulate the Communists to become more active elsewhere and that it will be difficult to resist making some accommodation to the pressure than generated. They believe, in contrast to the Estimate, these adjustments would be relatively small and insensitive to subsequent U.S. policy.

Factors entering into the judgments are estimates of (1) Hanoi's and Peking's behavior after the settlement; (2) U.S. posture in the regions; (3) Asian leaders' estimates of future U.S. policy; (4) the reactions of the area's non-Communist leaders to the outcome in Viet-Nam; (5) vulnerabilities of the various governments to insurgency or subversion, and (6) the strengths of opposition groups within each state.

The assessments rest more on judgments and assumptions than on tangible and convincing evidence, and there are major disagreements within the same Department. Within the Defense Department, OSD and DIA [Defense Intelligence Agency] support the conclusions of the NIE, while Army, Navy and Air Force

Intelligence dissent. Within State, the Bureau of Intelligence supports the NIE while the East Asian Bureau dissents.

Both the majority and the dissenters reject the view that an unfavorable settlement in Viet-Nam will inevitably be followed by Communist takeovers outside Indo China.

Indeed, even the dissenters, by phrasing the adverse results in terms such as "pragmatic adjustments" by the Thais and "some means of accommodation" leave it unclear how injurious the adverse effects would be to U.S. security....

The Enemy

Analyses of various enemy tactics and capabilities reveal both significant agreements and sharp controversies within the Government. Among the major points of consensus:

A combination of military pressures and political tacts explains recent enemy withdrawals and lower levels of activity.

Under current rules of engagement, the enemy's manpower pool and infiltration capabilities can outlast allied attrition efforts indefinitely.

The enemy basically controls both side's casualty rates.

The enemy can still launch major offensives, although not at Tet levels, or, probably, with equally dramatic effect.

Major controversies include:

CIA and State assign much higher figures to the VC Order of Battle than MACV, and they include additional categories of VC/NLF organization.

MACV/JCS and Saigon consider Cambodia (and specifically Sihanoukville) an important enemy supply channel while CIA disagrees strongly....

It is generally agreed that the NVN/VC manpower pool is sufficiently large to meet the enemy's replenishment needs over an extended period of time within the framework of current rules of engagement. According to the JCS, "The North Vietnamese and Viet Cong have access to sufficient manpower to meet their replenishment needs—even at the high 1968 loss rate of some 291,000—for at least the next several years.... Present operations are not outrunning the enemy's ability to replenish by recruitment or infiltration."

The South Vietnamese Armed Forces

The emphatic differences between U.S. agencies on the RVNAF outweigh the points of agreement. There is consensus that the

RVNAF is getting larger, better equipped and somewhat more effective. And all agree that it could not now, or in the foreseeable future, handle both the VC and sizable NVA forces without U.S. combat support. On other major points there is vivid controversy. The military community gives much greater weight to RVNAF statistical improvements while OSD and CIA highlight remaining obstacles, with OSD being the most pessimistic. Paradoxically, MACV/CINPAC/JCS see RVNAF as being less capable against the VC alone than does CIA. . . .

Pacification

Two well-defined and divergent views emerged from the agencies on the pacification situation in South Vietnam. One view is held by MACV and Embassy Saigon and endorsed by CINCPAC and JCS. The other view is that of OSD, CIA and State. The two views are profoundly different in terms of factual interpretation and policy implications. Both views agree on the nature of the problem, that is, the obstacles to improvement and complete success. What distinguishes one view from the other is each's assessment of the magnitude of the problem, and the likelihood that obstacles will be overcome.

The first group, consisting of MACV JCS Saigon, maintains that "at the present time, the security situation is better than any time during period in question," i.e., 1961–1968. MACV cites a "dramatic change in the security situation," and finds that the GVN controls three-fourths of the population. JCS suggests that the GVN will control 90% of the population in 1969. The second group, OSD CIA State, on the other hand, is more cautious and pessimistic, their view is not inconsistent with another Tet-offensive-like-shock in the countryside, for example, wiping out the much-touted gains of the 1968 Accelerated Pacification Program, or with more gradual erosion. Representing the latter view, OSD arrives at the following conclusions:

(1) "The portions of the SVN rural population aligned with the VC and aligned with the GVN are apparently the same today as in 1962 [a discouraging year]: 5,000,000 GVN aligned and nearly 3,000,000 VC aligned.

(2) "At the present, it appears that at least 50% of the total rural population is subject to significant VC presence and influence."

CIA agrees, and State (INR) [Bureau of Intelligence and Research] goes even further, saying: "Our best estimate is that the VC have a significant effect on at least two-thirds of the rural population."

The Political Scene

This section on the political situation can be boiled down to three fundamental questions: (1) How strong is the GVN today?

(2) What is being done to strengthen it for the coming political struggle with the NLF? (3) What are the prospects for continued non-Communist government in South Vietnam?

The essence of the replies from U.S. agencies is as follows: (1) Stronger recently than for many years but still very weak in certain areas and among various elites. (2) Some steps are being taken but these are inadequate. (3) Impossible to predict but chancy at best.

Within these broad thrusts of the responses there are decided differences of emphasis among the agencies. Thus MACV/JCS and Saigon, while acknowledging the problems, accent more the increasing stability of the Thieu regime and the overall political system; the significance of the moves being made by the GVN to bolster its strength; and the possibility of continued non-Communist rule in South Vietnam given sufficient U.S. support. CIA and OSD on the other hand, while acknowledging certain progress, are decidedly more skeptical and pessimistic. They note recent political improvements and GVN measures but they tend to deflate their relative impact and highlight the remaining obstacles. State's position, while not so consistent or clear-cut, generally steers closer to the bearishness of OSD and CIA. . . .

U.S. Military Operations

The only major points of agreement with the U.S. Government on these subjects are:

The description of recent U.S. deployment and tactics;

The difficulties of assessing the results of B-52 strikes, but their known effectiveness against known troop concentrations and in close support operations;

The fact that the Soviets and Chinese supply almost all war material to Hanoi and have enabled the North Vietnamese to carry on despite all our operations.

Otherwise there are fundamental disagreements running throughout this section, including the following:

OSD believes, the MACV/JCS deny, that there is a certain amount of "fat" in our current force levels that could be cut back without significant reduction in combat capability.

MACV/JCS and, somewhat more cautiously CIA ascribe much higher casualty estimates to our B-52 strikes.

MACV/JCS assign very much greater effectiveness to our past and current Laos and North Vietnam bombing campaigns than do OSD and CIA.

MACV/JCS believe that a vigorous bombing campaign could choke off enough supplies to Hanoi to make her stop fighting, while OSD and CIA see North Vietnam continuing the struggle even against unlimited bombing.

Source: U.S. Congress, *Congressional Record,* 92nd Cong., 2nd sess. (Washington, DC: U.S. Government Printing Office, 1972), E4977–E4981.

188. Nguyen Van Thieu: Address to the National Assembly, April 7, 1969

Introduction

On April 7, 1969, in a speech to the National Assembly of the Republic of Vietnam (RVN, South Vietnam), President Nguyen Van Thieu presented his own six-point program for peace in South Vietnam and the reunification of the two Vietnamese states.

Primary Source

Today, in this forum, I wish to solemnly confirm once more to the world, to our allies, to our fellow countrymen, and to our enemy that in our constant search for a constructive solution to the conflict, we consider that the following six points constitute a reasonable and solid basis for the restoration of peace in Viet-Nam:

1. Communist aggression should stop.

Communist North Viet-Nam should give up its attempts to conquer the RVN by force. It should stop violating the DMZ and the frontiers of the RVN, and stop its wanton attacks against the innocent population of the RVN.

2. Communist North Vietnamese and auxiliary troops and cadres should be completely withdrawn from the Republic of Viet-Nam.

As the military and subversive forces of Communist North Viet-Nam are withdrawn, infiltration ceases, and the level of violence thus subsides, the RVN will ask its allies to remove their forces, in accordance with the Manila joint-communique of seven nations in October, 1966.

3. The territories of the neighboring countries of the RVN should not be violated and used by Communist North Viet-Nam as bases and staging areas for aggression against the RVN.

Communist North Vietnamese troops and cadres illegally introduced and stationed in Laos and Cambodia should be withdrawn from these countries. Communist North Viet-Nam military installations in these countries should be dismantled.

4. The RVN adopts the policy of National Reconciliation. Those now fighting against us, who renounce violence, respect the laws, and faithfully abide by the democratic processes, will be welcomed as full members of the National Community. As such, they will enjoy full political rights and assume the same obligations as other lawful citizens under the National Constitution.

5. The reunification of the two Viet-Nams is to be decided by the free choice of the entire population of Viet-Nam through democratic processes.

To establish the atmosphere conducive to national reunification, after peace has been reestablished, modalities of economic and cultural exchanges between the two Viet-Nams and other countries of this area, can be actively explored, together with other intermediary measures of peaceful coexistence so that, pending reunification, the two Viet-Nams can participate more fully and more constructively in the various undertakings of the international community.

6. There must be an effective system of international control and reliable international guarantees against the resumption of Communist aggression.

The control mechanisms should be freed from the paralyzing effects of the Veto system. It should have sufficient personnel and adequate means to detect any violation of peace agreement. When violations are committed, and aggression is renewed, there should be prompt and effective response from a reliable system of international guarantees, otherwise any peace agreement will be only a sham device used by the Communists to weaken our system of defense, and not a basis for long lasting peace and stability for this part of the world.

Source: U.S. Congress, Senate, *Background Information Relating to Southeast Asia and Vietnam* (Washington, DC: U.S. Government Printing Office, 1970), 437–438.

189. President Richard Nixon: Televised Address, May 14, 1969 [Excerpt]

Introduction

In the course of a televised address to the American people on May 14, 1969, U.S. president Richard Nixon addressed the matter of negotiations to end the war in Vietnam. The centerpiece was a mutual military withdrawal. In his remarks, Nixon says that he is prepared to withdraw U.S. forces on a specified timetable if the leaders of the Democratic Republic of Vietnam (DRV,

North Vietnam) will do the same—not only from the Republic of Vietnam (RVN, South Vietnam) but also from neighboring Laos and Cambodia—to ensure that these nations would not serve as bases for a renewed war. Internationally supervised elections can then take place. The actual U.S. negotiating position was more demanding, however.

Primary Source

And so this brings us to the matter of negotiations.

We must recognize that peace in Vietnam cannot be achieved overnight. A war that has raged for many years will require detailed negotiations and cannot be settled by a single stroke.

What kind of a settlement will permit the South Vietnamese people to determine freely their own political future? Such a settlement will require the withdrawal of all non–South Vietnamese forces, including our own, from South Vietnam, and procedures for political choice that give each significant group in South Vietnam a real opportunity to participate in the political life of the nation.

To implement these principles, I reaffirm now our willingness to withdraw our forces on a specified timetable. We ask only that North Vietnam withdraw its forces from South Vietnam, Cambodia, and Laos into North Vietnam, also in accordance with a timetable.

We include Cambodia and Laos to ensure that these countries would not be used as bases for a renewed war. Our offer provides for a simultaneous start on withdrawal by both sides, for agreement on a mutually acceptable timetable, and for the withdrawal to be accomplished quickly.

The North Vietnamese delegates have been saying in Paris that political issues should be discussed along with military issues, and that there must be a political settlement in the South. We do not dispute this, but the military withdrawal involves outside forces, and can, therefore, be properly negotiated by North Vietnam and the United States, with the concurrence of its allies.

The political settlement is an internal matter which ought to be decided among the South Vietnamese themselves, and not imposed by outsiders. However, if our presence at these political negotiations would be helpful, and if the South Vietnamese concerned agreed, we would be willing to participate, along with the representatives of Hanoi, if that also were desired.

Recent statements by President Thieu have gone far toward opening the way to a political settlement. He has publicly declared his Government's willingness to discuss a political solution with the National Liberation Front, and has offered free elections. This was a dramatic step forward, a reasonable offer that could lead to a settlement. The South Vietnamese Government has offered to talk without preconditions. I believe the other side should also be willing to talk without preconditions.

The South Vietnamese Government recognizes, as we do, that a settlement must permit all persons and groups that are prepared to renounce the use of force to participate freely in the political life of South Vietnam. To be effective, such a settlement would require two things: first, a process that would allow the South Vietnamese people to express their choice, and, second, a guarantee that this process would be a fair one.

We do not insist on a particular form of guarantee. The important thing is that the guarantees should have the confidence of the South Vietnamese people, and that they should be broad enough and strong enough to protect the interests of all major South Vietnamese groups.

This, then, is the outline of the settlement that we seek to negotiate in Paris. Its basic terms are very simple: mutual withdrawal of non-South Vietnamese forces from South Vietnam and free choice for the people of South Vietnam. I believe that the long-term interests of peace require that we insist on no less, and that the realities of the situation require that we seek no more.

And now, to make very concrete what I have said, I propose the following specific measures which seem to me consistent with the principles of all parties. These proposals are made on the basis of full consultation with President Thieu.

—As soon as agreement can be reached, all non-South Vietnamese forces would begin withdrawals from South Vietnam.

—Over a period of 12 months, by agreed-upon stages, the major portions of all U.S., allied, and other non-South Vietnamese forces would be withdrawn. At the end of this 12-month period, the remaining U.S., allied, and other non-South Vietnamese forces would move into designated base areas and would not engage in combat operations.

—The remaining U.S. and allied forces would complete their withdrawals as the remaining North Vietnamese forces were withdrawn and returned to North Vietnam.

—An international supervisory body, acceptable to both sides, would be created for the purpose of verifying withdrawals, and for any other purposes agreed upon between the two sides.

—This international body would begin operating in accordance with an agreed timetable and would participate in arranging supervised cease-fires in Vietnam.

—As soon as possible after the international body was functioning, elections would be held under agreed procedures and under the supervision of the international body.

—Arrangements would be made for the release of prisoners of war on both sides at the earliest possible time.

—All parties would agree to observe the Geneva Accords of 1954 regarding South Vietnam and Cambodia, and the Laos Accords of 1962.

I believe this proposal for peace is realistic, and takes account of the legitimate interests of all concerned. It is consistent with President Thieu's six points. It can accommodate the various programs put forth by the other side. We and the Government of South Vietnam are prepared to discuss the details with the other side.

Secretary Rogers is now in Saigon and he will be discussing with President Thieu how, together, we may put forward these proposed measures most usefully in Paris. He will, as well, be consulting with our other Asian allies on these measures while on his Asian trip. However, I would stress that these proposals are not offered on a take-it-or-leave-it basis. We are quite willing to consider other approaches consistent with our principles.

We are willing to talk about anybody's program—Hanoi's 4 points, the NLF's [National Liberation Front] 10 points—provided it can be made consistent with the very few basic principles I have set forth here tonight.

Source: *Public Papers of the Presidents of the United States: Richard Nixon, 1969* (Washington, DC: U.S. Government Printing Office, 1971), 372–374.

190. COSVN Resolution No. 9, July 1969 [Excerpts]

Introduction

In the course of its Ninth Conference, the Central Office for South Vietnam (COSVN), the Communist headquarters running the war in the Republic of Vietnam (RVN, South Vietnam), claims that its military effort beginning with the 1968 Tet Offensive has tipped the war in its favor. In this document, COSVN claims that proof of this can be seen in the de-escalation of the U.S. military effort in Vietnam and the negotiations in Paris that include not only representatives of the Democratic Republic of Vietnam (DRV, North Vietnam) but also of the Provisional Revolutionary Government (PRG) in South Vietnam, the rival Communist government for South Vietnam formed in June 1969. While optimistic that Nixon will be forced to seek an early end to the war, COSVN warns that

Nixon could also renew the bombing and expand the war into both Laos and Cambodia.

Primary Source

On our part, the outstanding point is that, on the basis of thoroughly understanding the Central Committee's strategic determination, we have achieved obvious progress since the Spring of 1969 to date in applying the guidelines and methods of struggling and building, both in military and political fields, and making them more fitting to the rules of the General Offensive and Uprising; especially, we have applied and developed the direction and method of fighting with high efficiency which caused very heavy losses to the enemy at very light cost in friendly casualties; we have applied and developed the guidelines and methods for operations in the three areas designed to win and hold control of the weak areas, the areas bordering the cities and parts of the cities and municipalities. This is an improvement in the quality of our Party body's leadership and guidance aimed at securing a more thorough understanding of the Central Committee's lines, policies, and resolutions and fully applying them in a most fitting way to the practical realities of the General Offensive and Uprising in our war theater. This [improvement] has opened up vast possibilities for our army and people to fight strongly and sustainedly, to become stronger as they fight, to win bigger victories as they fight, to launch strong military attacks at the same time as they launch strong political offensives in the cities and countryside, to firmly hold and expand the liberated areas, to widen our mastership, to secure our strategic positions, and to keep up and develop our offensive position and our encirclement of the enemy, especially on the major battlefield under extremely fierce and complicated [fighting] conditions of our war theater. . . .

However, the General Offensive and Uprising is a phase which marks a leap forward of our people's revolutionary warfare; it requires more than ever a strong impulse and improvement in leadership and guidance. Yet the reality of the recent past indicated that the leadership and guidance of our authorities at various echelons did not meet these objective requirements; worse still, in some places and at times, this leadership and guidance evolved too slowly.

a. The key issue which is the origin of all shortcomings and weak points in the leadership and guidance of our authorities at various echelons during the recent period lies in the fact that we did not thoroughly comprehend the basic problems of the General Offensive and Uprising and problems relating to [Party] policies and guidelines; worse still, in some places and at times we made serious mistakes both in ideological concepts, viewpoints, and standpoints, and in the supervision of policy execution. A few of our cadres and Party members, including those at Region and Province Party Committee levels, are usually superficial and narrow-minded in assessing our strength and the enemy's; they only see the manifestations [of things] and fail to see their nature, they overestimate the enemy and underestimate the revolutionary capacities of the masses; therefore, when faced with difficulties, they become skeptical and lack resolution vis-à-vis the Central Committee's strategic determination; and they lose interest in attacking, which is the highest principle of the General Offensive and Uprising. Because they are not firmly anchored in the working class standpoint, they lack absolute determination, and their thinking is subjective and superficial; therefore, they usually have an erroneous conception of the transitional nature of the General Offensive and Uprising, now thinking it is a one-blow affair and consequently lacking vigilance against the enemy plots, now thinking it is a period of protracted struggle and consequently lacking boldness and a sense of urgency; worse still, they become right-leaning and shrink back from action.

Part II. Future Enemy Schemes and Our Immediate Tasks

The Americans' subjective intention is to carry out the precept of deescalating [the war] step by step; to strive to seize the initiative in a passive position; to win a strong position on the battlefield as they de-escalate; to de-escalate in order to "de-Americanize" the war but not to immediately end the war; to reinforce the puppet army as American troops are withdrawn; to have necessary time for having appropriate de-escalation steps; and at every de-escalation step, to strive to launch partial counter-offensives infierce competition with our forces.

b. At present, there is very little possibility that the enemy will carry out a massive troop build-up and expand the limited war to the whole country; however, we still need to keep our alertness. There are two possible developments to the war as follows:

One: In the process of de-escalating the war, the Americans may suffer increasing losses and encounter greater difficulties; therefore they may be forced to seek an early end to the war through a political solution which they cannot refuse. Even in this case, there will be a period of time from the signing of the agreement ending the war until all American troops are withdrawn from South Viet-Nam. During this period of time, our struggle against the enemy will go on with extreme complexity and we will have to be extremely alert.

Two: If our attacks in all aspects are not sufficiently strong and if the Americans are able to temporarily overcome part of their difficulties, they will strive to prolong the war in South Viet-Nam for a certain period of time during which they will try to de-escalate from a strong position of one sort or another, and carry out the de-Americanization in a prolonged war contest before they must admit defeat and accept a political solution.

In both these eventualities, especially in the case of a prolonged de-escalation, the Americans may, in certain circumstances, put pressure on us by threatening to broaden the war through the resumption of bombing in North Viet-Nam within a definite scope and time limit, or the expansion of the war into Laos and Cambodia.

Whether the war will develop according to the first or second eventuality depends principally on the strength of our attacks in the military, political and diplomatic fields, especially our military and political attacks, and on the extent of military, political, economic and financial difficulties which the war causes to the Americans in Viet-Nam, in the U.S.A. itself, and over the world.

Source: U.S. Embassy Vietnam, *COSVN: Resolution No. 9* (Saigon: U.S. Embassy Vietnam, 1969).

191. Final Statement of Ho Chi Minh, September 9, 1969

Introduction

President Ho Chi Minh of the Democratic Republic of Vietnam (DRV, North Vietnam) did not live to see the reunification of Vietnam under Communist rule. He died of a heart attack on September 2, 1969, on the anniversary of his independence speech in 1945. In this statement, released a week after his death, Ho anticipates his own death and calls for the building of a "peaceful unified, independent, democratic and prosperous Vietnam."

Primary Source

Our people's struggle against U.S. aggression, for national salvation, may have to go through even more difficulties and sacrifices, but we are bound to win total victory.

This is a certainty.

I intend, when that comes, to tour both North and South to congratulate our heroic compatriots, cadres and combatants, and visit old people and our beloved youth and children.

Then, on behalf of our people, I will go to the fraternal countries of the socialist camp and friendly countries in the world, and thank them for their wholehearted support and assistance to our people's patriotic struggle against U.S. aggression.

Tu Fu, the well-known Chinese poet of the T'ang period, wrote: "Few have ever reached the age of seventy."

This year, being seventy-nine, I count among those "few"; still, my mind has remained very lucid, though my health has somewhat declined in comparison with previous years. When one is on the wrong side of seventy, health deteriorates with age. This is no wonder.

But who can say how much longer I shall be able to serve the revolution, the Fatherland and the people?

I therefore leave these few lines in anticipation of the day when I shall go and join Karl Marx, V. I. Lenin and other elder revolutionaries; this way, our people throughout the country, our comrades in the Party, and our friends in the world will not be taken by surprise.

First about the Party: Thanks to its close unity and total dedication to the working class, the people and the Fatherland, our Party has been able, since its founding, to unite, organize and lead our people from success to success in a resolute struggle.

Unity is an extremely precious tradition of our Party and people. All comrades, from the Central Committee down to the cell, must preserve the unity and oneness of mind in the Party as the apple of their eye.

Within the Party, to achieve broad democracy and to practice self-criticism and criticism regularly and seriously is the best way to consolidate and further solidarity and unity. Comradely affection should prevail.

Ours is a Party in power. Each Party member, each cadre, must be deeply imbued with revolutionary morality, and show industry, thrift, integrity, uprightness, total dedication to public interests and complete selflessness. Our Party should preserve absolute purity and prove worthy of its role as leader and very loyal servant of the people.

About the working youth and union members and our young people: On the whole they are excellent; they are always ready to come forward, fearless of difficulties and eager for progress. The Party must foster their revolutionary virtues and train them as our successors, both "red" and "expert," in the building of socialism.

Training and educating future revolutionary generations is of great importance and necessity.

About our laboring peoples: In the plains as in the mountain areas, they have for ages endured hardships, feudal and colonial oppression and exploitation; they have moreover experienced many years of war.

Yet, our people have shown great heroism, courage, enthusiasm and industriousness. They have always followed the Party since it came into being, with unqualified loyalty.

The Party must work out a very effective plan for economic and cultural development constantly to raise the living standard of the people.

About the resistance war against U.S. aggression: It may drag on. Our compatriots may have to face new sacrifices in property and life. Whatever may happen, we must keep firm our resolve to fight the U.S. aggressors till total victory.

Our rivers, our mountains, our people will always be.

The American aggressors defeated, we will build a country ten times more beautiful.

Whatever difficulties and hardships may be ahead, our people are sure of total triumph. The U.S. imperialists shall have to quit. Our Fatherland shall be reunified. Our compatriots in the North and in the South shall be reunited under the same roof. We, a small nation, will have earned the unique honor of defeating, through a heroic struggle, two big imperialisms—the French and the American—and making a worthy contribution to the national liberation movement.

About the world communist movement: Having devoted my whole life to the revolution, I am proud of the growth of the international communist and workers' movement as well as grieved at the dissensions now dividing the fraternal parties.

I hope that our Party will do its best to contribute effectively to the restoration of unity among the fraternal parties on the basis of Marxism-Leninism and proletarian internationalism, in a way which conforms to both reason and sentiment.

I am sure that the fraternal parties and countries will have to unite again.

About personal matters: All my life, I have served the Fatherland, the revolution and the people with all my heart and strength. If I should now depart from this world, I would regret nothing, except not being able to serve longer and more.

When I am gone, grand funerals should be avoided so as not to waste the people's time and money.

Finally, to the whole people, the whole Party, the whole army, to my nephews and nieces, the youth and children, I leave my boundless love.

I also convey my cordial greetings of our comrades and friends, to the youth and children of the world.

My ultimate wish is that our whole Party and people, closely joining their efforts, build a peaceful, unified, independent, democratic and prosperous Vietnam, and make a worthy contribution to the world revolution.

Source: *Viet-Nam Documents and Research Notes, No. 68* (Saigon: U.S. Mission in Viet Nam, 1969), 59–61.

192. President Richard Nixon's Speech on Vietnamization, November 3, 1969

Introduction

Although touted as beginning under President Richard Nixon, Vietnamization—the building up of the armed forces of the Republic of Vietnam (RVN, South Vietnam) and turning more of the war over to them—actually began in the last year of the Lyndon Johnson administration. In the course of this televised address to the American people on November 3, 1969, Nixon traces the history of U.S. involvement in Vietnam and his hopes for Vietnamization. Unfortunately, Vietnamization did not work as hoped. Although the South Vietnamese armed forces were larger and better equipped, the same problems remained: too few qualified officers, poor leadership, inability to maintain sophisticated equipment, and rampant corruption. In the course of this speech, Nixon also enunciates what becomes known as the Nixon Doctrine. The United States will honor its current treaty negotiations and provide a nuclear umbrella for its key allies. In the case of aggression, the United States will provide military and economic assistance only.

Primary Source

Good evening, my fellow Americans.

Tonight I want to talk to you on a subject of deep concern to all Americans and to many people in all parts of the world—the war in Vietnam.

I believe that one of the reasons for the deep division about Vietnam is that many Americans have lost confidence in what their Government has told them about our policy. The American people cannot and should not be asked to support a policy which involves the overriding issues of war and peace unless they know the truth about that policy.

Tonight, therefore, I would like to answer some of the questions that I know are on the minds of many of you listening to me.

How and why did America get involved in Vietnam in the first place? How has this administration changed the policy of the previous administration? What has really happened in the negotiations in Paris and on the battlefront in Vietnam? What choices do we have if we are to end the war? What are the prospects for peace? Now, let me begin by describing the situation I found when I was inaugurated on January 20:

* The war had been going on for 4 years. 1,000 Americans had been killed in action.

* The training program for the South Vietnamese was behind schedule.

* 540,000 Americans were in Vietnam with no plans to reduce the number.

* No progress had been made at the negotiations in Paris and the United States had not put forth a comprehensive peace proposal.

* The war was causing deep division at home and criticism from many of our friends as well as our enemies abroad.

In view of these circumstances there were some who urged that I end the war at once by ordering the immediate withdrawal of all American forces.

From a political standpoint this would have been a popular and easy course to follow. After all, we became involved in the war while my predecessor was in office. I could blame the defeat which would be the result of my action on him and come out as the peacemaker. Some put it to me quite bluntly: This was the only way to avoid allowing Johnson's war to become Nixon's war.

But I had a greater obligation than to think only of the years of my administration and of the next election. I had to think of the effect of my decision on the next generation and on the future of peace and freedom in America and in the world.

Let us all understand that the question before us is not whether some Americans are for peace and some Americans are against peace. The question at issue is not whether Johnson's war becomes Nixon's war.

The great question is: How can we win America's peace?

Well, let us turn now to the fundamental issue. Why and how did the United States become involved in Vietnam in the first place? Fifteen years ago North Vietnam, with the logistical support of Communist China and the Soviet Union, launched a campaign to impose a Communist government on South Vietnam by instigating and supporting a revolution.

In response to the request of the Government of South Vietnam, President Eisenhower sent economic aid and military equipment to assist the people of South Vietnam in their efforts to prevent a Communist takeover. Seven years ago, President Kennedy sent 16,000 military personnel to Vietnam as combat advisers. Four years ago, President Johnson sent American combat forces to South Vietnam.

Now, many believe that President Johnson's decision to send American combat forces to South Vietnam was wrong. And many others—I among them—have been strongly critical of the way the war has been conducted.

But the question facing us today is: Now that we are in the war, what is the best way to end it?

In January I could only conclude that the precipitate withdrawal of American forces from Vietnam would be a disaster not only for South Vietnam but for the United States and for the cause of peace.

For the South Vietnamese, our precipitate withdrawal would inevitably allow the Communists to repeat the massacres which followed their takeover in the North 15 years before. They then murdered more than 50,000 people and hundreds of thousands more died in slave labor camps.

We saw a prelude of what would happen in South Vietnam when the Communists entered the city of Hue last year. During their brief rule there, there was a bloody reign of terror in which 3,000 civilians were clubbed, shot to death, and buried in mass graves.

With the sudden collapse of our support, these atrocities of Hue would become the nightmare of the entire nation—and particularly for the million and a half Catholic refugees who fled to South Vietnam when the Communists took over in the North.

For the United States, this first defeat in our Nation's history would result in a collapse of confidence in American leadership, not only in Asia but throughout the world.

Three American Presidents have recognized the great stakes involved in Vietnam and understood what had to be done.

In 1963, President Kennedy, with his characteristic eloquence and clarity, said:

. . . we want to see a stable government there, carrying on a struggle to maintain its national independence. We believe strongly in that. We are not going to withdraw from that effort. In my opinion, for us to withdraw from that effort would mean a collapse not only of South Vietnam, but Southeast Asia. So we are going to stay there.

President Eisenhower and President Johnson expressed the same conclusion during their terms of office.

For the future of peace, precipitate withdrawal would thus be a disaster of immense magnitude.

A nation cannot remain great if it betrays its allies and lets down its friends.

Our defeat and humiliation in South Vietnam without question would promote recklessness in the councils of those great powers who have not yet abandoned their goals of world conquest.

This would spark violence wherever our commitments help maintain the peace—in the Middle East, in Berlin, eventually even in the Western Hemisphere.

Ultimately, this would cost more lives.

It would not bring peace; it would bring more war.

For these reasons, I rejected the recommendation that I should end the war by immediately withdrawing all of our forces. I chose instead to change American policy on both the negotiating front and battlefront. In order to end a war fought on many fronts, I initiated a pursuit for peace on many fronts. In a television speech on May 14, in a speech before the United Nations, and on a number of other occasions I set forth our peace proposals in great detail.

We have offered the complete withdrawal of all outside forces within 1 year.

We have proposed a cease-fire under international supervision.

We have offered free elections under international supervision with the Communists participating in the organization and conduct of the elections as an organized political force. And the Saigon Government has pledged to accept the result of the elections.

We have not put forth our proposals on a take-it-or-leave-it basis. We have indicated that we are willing to discuss the proposals that have been put forth by the other side. We have declared that anything is negotiable except the right of the people of South Vietnam to determine their own future. At the Paris peace conference, Ambassador Lodge has demonstrated our flexibility and good faith in 40 public meetings.

Hanoi has refused even to discuss our proposals. They demand our unconditional acceptance of their terms, which are that we withdraw all American forces immediately and unconditionally and that we overthrow the Government of South Vietnam as we leave.

We have not limited our peace initiatives to public forums and public statements. I recognized, in January, that a long and bitter war like this usually cannot be settled in a public forum. That is why in addition to the public statements and negotiation I have explored every possible private avenue that might lead to a settlement.

Tonight I am taking the unprecedented step of disclosing to you some of our other initiatives for peace—initiatives we undertook privately and secretly because we thought we thereby might open a door which publicly would be closed.

I did not wait for my inauguration to begin my quest for peace.

Soon after my election, through an individual who is directly in contact on a personal basis with the leaders of North Vietnam, I made two private offers for a rapid, comprehensive settlement. Hanoi's replies called in effect for our surrender before negotiations.

Since the Soviet Union furnishes most of the military equipment for North Vietnam, Secretary of State Rogers, my Assistant for National Security Affairs, Dr. Kissinger, Ambassador Lodge, and I, personally, have met on a number of occasions with representatives of the Soviet Government to enlist their assistance in getting meaningful negotiations started. In addition, we have had extended discussions directed toward that same end with representatives of other governments which have diplomatic relations with North Vietnam. None of these initiatives have to date produced results.

In mid-July, I became convinced that it was necessary to make a major move to break the deadlock in the Paris talks. I spoke directly in this office, where I am now sitting, with an individual who had known Ho Chi Minh on a personal basis for 25 years. Through him I sent a letter to Ho Chi Minh. I did this outside of the usual diplomatic channels with the hope that with the necessity of making statements for propaganda removed, there might be constructive progress toward bringing the war to an end. Let me read from that letter to you now:

Dear Mr. President:

I realize that it is difficult to communicate meaningfully across the gulf of four years of war. But precisely because of this gulf, I wanted to take this opportunity to reaffirm in all solemnity my desire to work for a just peace. I deeply believe that the war in Vietnam has gone on too long and delay in bringing it to an end can benefit no one—least of all the people of Vietnam. . . .

The time has come to move forward at the conference table toward an early resolution of this tragic war. You will find us forthcoming and open-minded in a common effort to bring the blessings of peace to the brave people of Vietnam. Let history record that at this critical juncture, both sides turned their face toward peace rather than toward conflict and war.

I received Ho Chi Minh's reply on August 30, 3 days before his death. It simply reiterated the public position North Vietnam had taken at Paris and flatly rejected my initiative.

The full text of both letters is being released to the press.

In addition to the public meetings that I have referred to, Ambassador Lodge has met with Vietnam's chief negotiator in Paris in 11 private sessions.

We have taken other significant initiatives which must remain secret to keep open some channels of communication which may still prove to be productive.

But the effect of all the public, private, and secret negotiations which have been undertaken since the bombing halt a year ago and since this administration came into office on January 20, can be summed up in one sentence: No progress whatever has been made except agreement on the shape of the bargaining table.

Well now, who is at fault?

It has become clear that the obstacle in negotiating an end to the war is not the President of the United States. It is not the South Vietnamese Government.

The obstacle is the other side's absolute refusal to show the least willingness to join us in seeking a just peace. And it will not do so while it is convinced that all it has to do is to wait for our next concession, and our next concession after that one, until it gets everything it wants.

There can now be no longer any question that progress in negotiation depends only on Hanoi's deciding to negotiate, to negotiate seriously.

I realize that this report on our efforts on the diplomatic front is discouraging to the American people, but the American people are entitled to know the truth—the bad news as well as the good news—where the lives of our young men are involved.

Now let me turn, however, to a more encouraging report on another front.

At the time we launched our search for peace I recognized we might not succeed in bringing an end to the war through negotiation. I, therefore, put into effect another plan to bring peace—a plan which will bring the war to an end regardless of what happens on the negotiating front.

It is in line with a major shift in U.S. foreign policy which I described in my press conference at Guam on July 25. Let me briefly explain what has been described as the Nixon Doctrine—a policy which not only will help end the war in Vietnam, but which is an essential element of our program to prevent future Vietnams.

We Americans are a do-it-yourself people. We are an impatient people. Instead of teaching someone else to do a job, we like to do it ourselves. And this trait has been carried over into our foreign policy. In Korea and again in Vietnam, the United States furnished most of the money, most of the arms, and most of the men to help the people of those countries defend their freedom against Communist aggression.

Before any American troops were committed to Vietnam, a leader of another Asian country expressed this opinion to me when I was traveling in Asia as a private citizen. He said: "When you are trying to assist another nation defend its freedom, U.S. policy should be to help them fight the war but not to fight the war for them."

Well, in accordance with this wise counsel, I laid down in Guam three principles as guidelines for future American policy toward Asia:

* First, the United States will keep all of its treaty commitments.

* Second, we shall provide a shield if a nuclear power threatens the freedom of a nation allied with US or of a nation whose survival we consider vital to our security.

* Third, in cases involving other types of aggression, we shall furnish military and economic assistance when requested in accordance with our treaty commitments. But we shall look to the nation directly threatened to assume the primary responsibility of providing the manpower for its defense.

After I announced this policy, I found that the leaders of the Philippines, Thailand, Vietnam, South Korea, and other nations which might be threatened by Communist aggression, welcomed this new direction in American foreign policy.

The defense of freedom is everybody's business—not just America's business. And it is particularly the responsibility of the people whose freedom is threatened. In the previous administration, we Americanized the war in Vietnam. In this administration, we are Vietnamizing the search for peace.

The policy of the previous administration not only resulted in our assuming the primary responsibility for fighting the war, but even more significantly did not adequately stress the goal of strengthening the South Vietnamese so that they could defend themselves when we left.

The Vietnamization plan was launched following Secretary Laird's visit to Vietnam in March. Under the plan, I ordered first a substantial increase in the training and equipment of South Vietnamese forces.

In July, on my visit to Vietnam, I changed General Abrams' orders so that they were consistent with the objectives of our new policies. Under the new orders, the primary mission of our troops is to enable the South Vietnamese forces to assume the full responsibility for the security of South Vietnam.

Our air operations have been reduced by over 20 percent.

And now we have begun to see the results of this long overdue change in American policy in Vietnam.

After 5 years of Americans going into Vietnam, we are finally bringing American men home. By December 15, over 60,000 men will have been withdrawn from South Vietnam, including 20 percent of all of our combat forces.

The South Vietnamese have continued to gain in strength. As a result they have been able to take over combat responsibilities from our American troops.

Two other significant developments have occurred since this administration took office.

* Enemy infiltration, infiltration which is essential if they are to launch a major attack, over the last 3 months is less than 20 percent of what it was over the same period last year.

* Most important—United States casualties have declined during the last 2 months to the lowest point in 3 years.

Let me now turn to our program for the future.

We have adopted a plan which we have worked out in cooperation with the South Vietnamese for the complete withdrawal of all U.S. combat ground forces, and their replacement by South Vietnamese forces on an orderly scheduled timetable. This withdrawal will be made from strength and not from weakness. As South Vietnamese forces become stronger, the rate of American withdrawal can become greater.

I have not and do not intend to announce the timetable for our program. And there are obvious reasons for this decision which I am sure you will understand. As I have indicated on several occasions, the rate of withdrawal will depend on developments on three fronts.

One of these is the progress which can be or might be made in the Paris talks. An announcement of a fixed timetable for our withdrawal would completely remove any incentive for the enemy to negotiate an agreement. They would simply wait until our forces had withdrawn and then move in.

The other two factors on which we will base our withdrawal decisions are the level of enemy activity and the progress of the training programs of the South Vietnamese forces. And I am glad to be able to report tonight progress on both of these fronts has been greater than we anticipated when we started the program in June for withdrawal. As a result, our timetable for withdrawal is more optimistic now than when we made our first estimates in June. Now, this clearly demonstrates why it is not wise to be frozen in on a fixed timetable.

We must retain the flexibility to base each withdrawal decision on the situation as it is at that time rather than on estimates that are no longer valid.

Along with this optimistic estimate, I must—in all candor—leave one note of caution. If the level of enemy activity significantly increases we might have to adjust our timetable accordingly.

However, I want the record to be completely clear on one point.

At the time of the bombing halt just a year ago, there was some confusion as to whether there was an understanding on the part of the enemy that if we stopped the bombing of North Vietnam they would stop the shelling of cities in South Vietnam. I want to be sure that there is no misunderstanding on the part of the enemy with regard to our withdrawal program.

We have noted the reduced level of infiltration, the reduction of our casualties, and are basing our withdrawal decisions partially on those factors. If the level of infiltration or our casualties increase while we are trying to scale down the fighting, it will be the result of a conscious decision by the enemy.

Hanoi could make no greater mistake than to assume that an increase in violence will be to its advantage. If I conclude that increased enemy action jeopardizes our remaining forces in Vietnam, I shall not hesitate to take strong and effective measures to deal with that situation.

This is not a threat. This is a statement of policy, which as Commander in Chief of our Armed Forces, I am making in meeting my responsibility for the protection of American fighting men wherever they may be.

My fellow Americans, I am sure you can recognize from what I have said that we really only have two choices open to us if we want to end this war.

* I can order an immediate, precipitate withdrawal of all Americans from Vietnam without regard to the effects of that action.

* Or we can persist in our search for a just peace through a negotiated settlement if possible, or through continued implementation of our plan for Vietnamization if necessary, a plan in which we will withdraw all of our forces from Vietnam on a schedule in accordance with our program, as the South Vietnamese become strong enough to defend their own freedom.

I have chosen this second course. It is not the easy way. It is the right way.

It is a plan which will end the war and serve the cause of peace—not just in Vietnam but in the Pacific and in the world.

In speaking of the consequences of a precipitate withdrawal, I mentioned that our allies would lose confidence in America.

Far more dangerous, we would lose confidence in ourselves. Oh, the immediate reaction would be a sense of relief that our men were coming home. But as we saw the consequences of what we had done, inevitable remorse and divisive recrimination would scar our spirit as a people.

We have faced other crises in our history and have become stronger by rejecting the easy way out and taking the right way in meeting our challenges. Our greatness as a nation has been our capacity to do what had to be done when we knew our course was right.

I recognize that some of my fellow citizens disagree with the plan for peace I have chosen. Honest and patriotic Americans have reached different conclusions as to how peace should be achieved.

In San Francisco a few weeks ago, I saw demonstrators carrying signs reading: "Lose in Vietnam, bring the boys home."

Well, one of the strengths of our free society is that any American has a right to reach that conclusion and to advocate that point of view. But as President of the United States, I would be untrue to my oath of office if I allowed the policy of this Nation to be dictated by the minority who hold that point of view and who try to impose it on the Nation by mounting demonstrations in the street.

For almost 200 years, the policy of this Nation has been made under our Constitution by those leaders in the Congress and the White House elected by all of the people. If a vocal minority, however fervent its cause, prevails over reason and the will of the majority, this Nation has no future as a free society.

And now I would like to address a word, if I may, to the young people of this Nation who are particularly concerned, and I understand why they are concerned, about this war.

I respect your idealism. I share your concern for peace. I want peace as much as you do. There are powerful personal reasons I want to end this war. This week I will have to sign 83 letters to mothers, fathers, wives, and loved ones of men who have given their lives for America in Vietnam. It is very little satisfaction to me that this is only one-third as many letters as I signed the first week in office. There is nothing I want more than to see the day come when I do not have to write any of those letters.

I want to end the war to save the lives of those brave young men in Vietnam.

But I want to end it in a way which will increase the chance that their younger brothers and their sons will not have to fight in some future Vietnam someplace in the world.

And I want to end the war for another reason. I want to end it so that the energy and dedication of you, our young people, now too often directed into bitter hatred against those responsible for the war, can be turned to the great challenges of peace, a better life for all Americans, a better life for all people on this earth.

I have chosen a plan for peace. I believe it will succeed.

If it does succeed, what the critics say now won't matter. If it does not succeed, anything I say then won't matter.

I know it may not be fashionable to speak of patriotism or national destiny these days. But I feel it is appropriate to do so on this occasion.

Two hundred years ago this Nation was weak and poor. But even then, America was the hope of millions in the world. Today we have become the strongest and richest nation in the world. And the wheel of destiny has turned so that any hope the world has for the survival of peace and freedom will be determined by whether the American people have the moral stamina and the courage to meet the challenge of free world leadership.

Let historians not record that when America was the most powerful nation in the world we passed on the other side of the road and allowed the last hopes for peace and freedom of millions of people to be suffocated by the forces of totalitarianism.

And so tonight—to you, the great silent majority of my fellow Americans—I ask for your support.

I pledged in my campaign for the Presidency to end the war in a way that we could win the peace. I have initiated a plan of action which will enable me to keep that pledge.

The more support I can have from the American people, the sooner that pledge can be redeemed; for the more divided we are at home, the less likely the enemy is to negotiate at Paris.

Let us be united for peace. Let us also be united against defeat. Because let us understand: North Vietnam cannot defeat or humiliate the United States. Only Americans can do that.

Fifty years ago, in this room and at this very desk, President Woodrow Wilson spoke words which caught the imagination of a war-weary world. He said: "This is the war to end war." His dream for peace after World War I was shattered on the hard realities of great power politics and Woodrow Wilson died a broken man.

Tonight I do not tell you that the war in Vietnam is the war to end wars. But I do say this: I have initiated a plan which will end this war in a way that will bring us closer to that great goal to which Woodrow Wilson and every American President in our history has been dedicated—the goal of a just and lasting peace.

As President I hold the responsibility for choosing the best path to that goal and then leading the Nation along it. I pledge to you tonight that I shall meet this responsibility with all of the strength and wisdom I can command in accordance with our hopes, mindful of your concerns, sustained by your prayers.

Thank you and goodnight.

Source: *Public Papers of the Presidents of the United States: Richard Nixon, 1969* (Washington, DC: U.S. Government Printing Office, 1971), 901–909.

193. Vice President Spiro T. Agnew: Criticism of What He Perceives as Biased Television Coverage of the Richard Nixon Administration's Vietnam Policy, November 13, 1969 [Excerpts]

Introduction

Vice President Spiro Agnew was the Richard Nixon administration's point man on Vietnam. Agnew was especially critical of the American news media for what he said was its unfair coverage of Nixon administration Vietnam policy. In these remarks, Agnew accuses the media of bias in reporting and of not reflecting the views of the majority of Americans.

Primary Source

Tonight I want to discuss the importance of the television news medium to the American people. No nation depends more on the intelligent judgment of its citizens. No medium has more profound influence over public opinion. Nowhere in our system are there fewer checks on vast power. So, nowhere should there be more conscientious responsibility exercised than by the news media. The question is, Are we demanding enough of our television news presentations? And are the men of this medium demanding enough of themselves?

Monday night a week ago, President Nixon delivered the most important address of his Administration, one of the most important of our decade.

His subject was Vietnam. His hope was to rally the American people to see the conflict through to a lasting and just peace in the Pacific. For 32 minutes, he reasoned with a nation that has suffered almost a third of a million casualties in the longest war in its history.

When the President completed his address—an address, incidentally, that he spent weeks in the preparation of—his words and policies were subjected to instant analysis and querulous criticism. The audience of 70 million Americans gathered to hear the President of the United States was inherited by a small band of network commentators and self-appointed analysts, the majority of whom expressed in one way or another their hostility to what he had to say.

It was obvious that their minds were made up in advance. . . .

Now every American has a right to disagree with the President of the United States and to express publicly that disagreement. But the President of the United States has a right to communicate directly with the people who elected him, and the people of this country have the right to make up their own minds and form their own opinions about a Presidential address without having a President's words and thoughts characterized through the prejudices of hostile critics before they can even be digested.

When Winston Churchill rallied public opinion to stay the course against Hitler's Germany, he didn't have to contend with a gaggle of commentators raising doubts about whether he was reading public opinion right, or whether Britain had the stamina to see the war through.

When President Kennedy rallied the nation in the Cuban missile crisis, his address to the people was not chewed over by a roundtable of critics who disparaged the course of action he'd asked America to follow.

The purpose of my remarks tonight is to focus your attention on this little group of men who not only enjoy a right of instant rebuttal to every Presidential address, but, more importantly, wield a free hand in selecting, presenting and interpreting the great issues in our nation.

First, let's define that power. At least 40 million Americans every night, it's estimated, watch the network news. Seven million of them view A.B.C., the remainder being divided between N.B.C. and C.B.S.

According to Harris polls and other studies, for millions of Americans the networks are the sole source of national and world news.

In Will Rogers's observation, what you knew was what you read in the newspaper. Today for growing millions of Americans, it's what they see and hear on their television sets.

Now how is this network news determined? A small group of men, numbering perhaps no more than a dozen anchormen, commentators and executive producers, settle upon the 20 minutes or so of film and commentary that's to reach the public. This selection is made from the 90 to 180 minutes that may be available. Their powers of choice are broad.

They decide what 40 to 50 million Americans will learn of the day's events in the nation and in the world.

We cannot measure this power and influence by the traditional democratic standards, for these men can create national issues overnight.

They can make or break by their coverage and commentary a moratorium on the war.

They can elevate men from obscurity to national prominence within a week. They can reward some politicians with national exposure and ignore others. . . .

Nor is their power confined to the substantive. A raised eyebrow, an inflection of the voice, a caustic remark dropped in the middle of a broadcast can raise doubts in a million minds about the veracity of a public official or the wisdom of a Government policy.

One Federal Communications Commissioner considers the powers of the networks equal to that of local, state and Federal Governments all combined. Certainly it represents a concentration of power over American public opinion unknown in history.

Now what do Americans know of the men who wield this power? Of the men who produce and direct the network news the nation knows practically nothing. Of the commentators, most Americans know little other than that they reflect an urbane and assured presence seemingly well-informed on every important matter.

We do know that to a man these commentators and producers live and work in the geographical and intellectual confines of Washington, D.C., or New York City, the latter of which James Reston terms the most unrepresentative community in the entire United States.

Both communities bask in their own provincialism, their own parochialism.

We can deduce that these men read the same newspapers. They draw their political and social views from the same sources. Worse, they talk constantly to one another, thereby providing artificial reinforcement to their shared viewpoints.

Do they allow their biases to influence the selection and presentation of the news? David Brinkley states objectivity is impossible to normal human behavior. Rather, he says, we should strive for fairness.

Another anchorman on a network news show contends, and I quote: "You can't expunge all your private convictions just because you sit in a seat like this and a camera starts to stare at you. I think your program has to reflect what your basic feelings are. I'll plead guilty to that."

Less than a week before the 1968 election, this same commentator charged that President Nixon's campaign commitments were no more durable than campaign balloons. He claimed that, were it not for the fear of hostile reaction, Richard Nixon would be giving into, and I quote him exactly, "his natural instinct to smash the enemy with a club or go after him with a meat axe."

Had this slander been made by one political candidate about another, it would have been dismissed by most commentators as a partisan attack. But this attack emanated from the privileged sanctuary of a network studio and therefore had the apparent dignity of an objective statement.

The American people would rightly not tolerate this concentration of power in Government.

Is it not fair and relevant to question its concentration in the hands of a tiny enclosed fraternity of privileged men elected by no one and enjoying a monopoly sanctioned and licensed by Government?

The views of the majority of this fraternity do not—and I repeat, not—represent the views of America.

That is why such a great gulf existed between how the nation received the President's address and how the networks reviewed it.

Source: Spiro T. Agnew, "Television News Coverage," American Rhetoric, http://www.americanrhetoric.com/speeches/spiroagnewtvnewscoverage.htm.

194. Politburo Resolution No. 194-NQ/TW: Policy toward Captured American Pilots in North Vietnam, November 20, 1969

Introduction

During the summer of 1969 the Richard Nixon administration launched a public campaign on the treatment of American prisoners of war (POWs) in the Democratic Republic of Vietnam (DRV, North Vietnam). The campaign demanded that the North Vietnamese government accept the Geneva Convention provisions regarding the treatment of POWs and allow the International Red Cross to visit the POW camps in North Vietnam. In apparent response to this campaign, in November 1969 the Communist Party Politburo in Hanoi approved this policy resolution regarding the treatment of American POWs.

Primary Source

1. Our humanitarian policy toward American pilots is aimed at further illuminating our just cause in order to win over the American people, support our enemy proselyting operations, and win the sympathy of world opinion for our people's resistance war against the Americans to save the nation.

Even though we do not view American pilots as prisoners of war and we are not bound by the terms of the 1949 Geneva Convention governing the treatment of prisoners of war, we should apply the points of the Geneva Convention that are consistent with our humanitarian policies.

2. For that reason, we must fully implement the following points:

—Provisions for their daily lives (food, clothing, medicine) should be maintained at the current levels.
—Their places of detention must be clean and airy. A program should be implemented to allow them to exercise and work in order to help them maintain their health.
—With regard to political education, we should study appropriate goals and subjects, with the primary focus on making them understand the goals and the justice of our people's cause of resisting the Americans to save the nation, to understand the humanitarian policies of our government, and to cause them to respect the regulations of our prison camps.
—With regard to mail, they should be allowed to send one letter a month, and they should be allowed to receive gifts once every two months. This must be properly organized, implemented, and inspected in order to ensure that the mail is delivered fully and quickly. Inspection of gifts should be focused primarily on preventing the receipt of weapons, explosives, anesthetics, and poisons.
—From now until early 1970, we should gradually allow the American pilots that we are currently detaining in secret to contact their families by sending postcards.
—The personal effects of the pilots must be properly stored and maintained so that they can be returned to them in the future, or, in the event that the prisoner dies, to be returned to their families. Items that have been misplaced should be looked for and recovered so that they can be properly maintained for future return.
—As for the issue of religious services, arrangements should be made for them to attend church services regularly.

We should assign a number of good [reliable] Catholic priests or Protestant pastors (depending on the prisoners' religion) to this task in order to combine holding church services with our efforts to educate them.

—With regards to the graves of those who have died, they need to be concentrated into a number of central location to facilitate administration and so that later we can return the remains to their families.

3. In addition to strengthening the forces assigned to handle the American pilots, we need to ensure that the cadre and enlisted men directly responsible for this task fully understand the political significance of our policy toward the pilots in order to increase their spirit of responsibility, strive to overcome difficulties, and fully implement the policy provisions outlined in this resolution.

4. The Ministry of Foreign Affairs and the General Political Department will study the possibility of allowing the Red Cross Associations of some countries to visit the prisoners.

For the Politburo

[signed] Nguyen Duy Trinh

Source: *Van Kien Dang, Toan Tap 30, 1969* [Collected Party Documents, Volume 30, 1969] (Hanoi: Nha Xuat Ban Chinh Tri Quoc Gia, 2004), 303–305. Translated by Merle L. Pribbenow.

195. President Richard Nixon: Speech on Cambodia, April 30, 1970 [Excerpts]

Introduction

President Richard Nixon sought to demonstrate U.S. resolve and pressure the Democratic Republic of Vietnam (DRV, North Vietnam) in the Paris negotiations by intervening in Cambodia, the border area of which was adjacent to the Republic of Vietnam (RVN, South Vietnam) and honeycombed with People's Army of Vietnam (PAVN, North Vietnamese Army) supply dumps. This step had long been advocated by the U.S. military but had been rejected by President Lyndon Johnson. The secret bombing of the Cambodian border areas by U.S. B-52 bombers—dubbed Operation MENU—began on March 18, 1969, and extended over a span of 14 months. When this action did not have the desired effect, Nixon authorized the use of ground troops. Beginning on April 14, 1970, Army of the Republic of Vietnam (ARVN, South Vietnamese Army) troops entered Cambodia to destroy PAVN border supply caches. Then, despite opposition from Secretary of Defense Melvin Laird and Secretary of State William Rogers, Nixon authorized the use of American ground forces. The resulting Cambodian Incursion involved 50,000 ARVN and 30,000 U.S. troops. On April 30, Nixon informed the American people by television that U.S. troops were invading Cambodia. Nixon says that this is in response to a request from the South Vietnamese government. It is not an invasion but instead is an incursion, an extension of the war "to protect our men who are in Viet-Nam and to guarantee the continued success of our withdrawal and the Vietnamization programs."

Primary Source

Good evening, my fellow Americans.

Ten days ago, in my report to the Nation on Viet-Nam, I announced a decision to withdraw an additional 150,000 Americans from Viet-Nam over the next year. I said then that I was making that decision despite our concern over increased enemy activity in Laos, in Cambodia, and in South Viet-Nam.

At that time, I warned that if I concluded that increased enemy activity in any of these areas endangered the lives of Americans remaining in Viet-Nam, I would not hesitate to take strong and effective measures to deal with that situation.

Despite that warning, North Viet-Nam has increased its military aggression in all these areas, and particularly in Cambodia.

After full consultation with the National Security Council, Ambassador Bunker, General Abrams, and my other advisers, I have concluded that the actions of the enemy in the last 10 days clearly endanger the lives of Americans who are in Viet-Nam now and would constitute an unacceptable risk to those who will be there after withdrawal of another 150,000.

To protect our men who are in Viet-Nam and to guarantee the continued success of our withdrawal and Vietnamization programs, I have concluded that the time has come for action.

Tonight I shall describe the actions of the enemy, the actions I have ordered to deal with that situation, and the reasons for my decision.

Cambodia, a small country of 7 million people, has been a neutral nation since the Geneva agreement of 1954—an agreement, incidentally, which was signed by the Government of North Viet-Nam.

American policy since then has been to scrupulously respect the neutrality of the Cambodian people. We have maintained a skeleton diplomatic mission of fewer than 15 in Cambodia's capital, and that only since last August. For the previous 4 years, from 1965 to 1969, we did not have any diplomatic mission whatever in Cambodia. And for the past 5 years, we have provided no military assistance whatever and no economic assistance to Cambodia.

North Viet-Nam, however, has not respected that neutrality.

For the past 5 years . . . North Viet-Nam has occupied military sanctuaries all along the Cambodian frontier with South Viet-Nam. Some of these extend up to 20 miles into Cambodia. The sanctuaries . . . are on both sides of the border. They are used for hit-and-run attacks on American and South Vietnamese forces in South Viet-Nam.

These Communist-occupied territories contain major base camps, training sites, logistics facilities, weapons and ammunition factories, airstrips, and prisoner of war compounds.

For 5 years neither the United States nor South Viet-Nam has moved against these enemy sanctuaries, because we did not wish to violate the territory of a neutral nation. Even after the Vietnamese Communists began to expand these sanctuaries 4 weeks ago, we counseled patience to our South Vietnamese allies and imposed restraints on our own commanders.

In contrast to our policy, the enemy in the past 2 weeks has stepped up his guerrilla actions, and he is concentrating his main forces in these sanctuaries . . . where they are building up to launch massive attacks on our forces and those of South Viet-Nam.

North Viet-Nam in the last 2 weeks has stripped away all pretense of respecting the sovereignty or the neutrality of Cambodia. Thousands of their soldiers are invading the country from the sanctuaries; they are encircling the Capital of Phnom Penh. Coming from these sanctuaries . . . they have moved into Cambodia and are encircling the Capital.

Cambodia, as a result of this, has sent out a call to the United States, to a number of other nations, for assistance. Because if this enemy effort succeeds, Cambodia would become a vast enemy staging area and a springboard for attacks on South Viet-Nam along 600 miles of frontier, a refuge where enemy troops could return from combat without fear of retaliation.

North Vietnamese men and supplies could then be poured into that country, jeopardizing not only the lives of our own men but the people of South Viet-Nam as well. . . .

In cooperation with the armed forces of South Viet-Nam, attacks are being launched this week to clean out major enemy sanctuaries on the Cambodian-Viet-Nam border.

A major responsibility for the ground operations is being assumed by South Vietnamese forces. For example, the attacks in several areas . . . are exclusively South Vietnamese ground operations under South Vietnamese command, with the United States providing air and logistical support.

There is one area, however . . . where I have concluded that a combined American and South Vietnamese operation is necessary.

Tonight American and South Vietnamese units will attack the headquarters for the entire Communist military operation in South Viet-Nam. This key control center has been occupied by the North Vietnamese and Viet Cong for 5 years in blatant violation of Cambodia's neutrality.

This is not an invasion of Cambodia. The areas in which these attacks will be launched are completely occupied and controlled by North Vietnamese forces. Our purpose is not to occupy the areas. Once enemy forces are driven out of these sanctuaries and once their military supplies are destroyed, we will withdraw.

These actions are in no way directed at the security interests of any nation. Any government that chooses to use these actions as a pretext for harming relations with the United States will be doing so on its own responsibility and on its own initiative, and we will draw the appropriate conclusions.

Now, let me give you the reasons for my decision.

A majority of the American people, a majority of you listening to me, are for the withdrawal of our forces from Viet-Nam. The action I have taken tonight is indispensable for the continuing success of that withdrawal program.

A majority of the American people want to end this war rather than to have it drag on interminably. The action I have taken tonight will serve that purpose.

A majority of the American people want to keep the casualties of our brave men in Viet-Nam at an absolute minimum. The action I take tonight is essential if we are to accomplish that goal.

We take this action not for the purpose of expanding the war into Cambodia, but for the purpose of ending the war in Viet-Nam and winning the just peace we all desire. We have made and we will continue to make every possible effort to end this war through negotiation at the conference table rather than through more fighting on the battlefield. . . .

My fellow Americans, we live in an age of anarchy, both abroad and at home. We see mindless attacks on all the great institutions which have been created by free civilizations in the last 500 years. Even here in the United States, great universities are being systematically destroyed. Small nations all over the world find themselves under attack from within and from without.

If, when the chips are down, the world's most powerful nation, the United States of America, acts like a pitiful, helpless giant, the forces of totalitarianism and anarchy will threaten free nations and free institutions throughout the world.

It is not our power but our will and character that is being tested tonight. The question all Americans must ask and answer tonight is this: Does the richest and strongest nation in the history of the world have the character to meet a direct challenge by a group which rejects every effort to win a just peace, ignores our warning, tramples on solemn agreements, violates the neutrality of an unarmed people, and uses our prisoners as hostages?

If we fail to meet this challenge, all other nations will be on notice that despite its overwhelming power the United States, when a real crisis comes, will be found wanting.

During my campaign for the Presidency, I pledged to bring Americans home from Viet-Nam. They are coming home.

I promised to end this war. I shall keep that promise.

I promised to win a just peace. I shall keep that promise.

We shall avoid a wider war. But we are also determined to put an end to this war. . . .

No one is more aware than I am of the political consequences of the action I have taken. It is tempting to take the easy political path: to blame this war on previous administrations and to bring all of our men home immediately, regardless of the consequences, even though that would mean defeat for the United States; to desert 18 million South Vietnamese people who have put their trust in us and to expose them to the same slaughter and savagery which the leaders of North Viet-Nam inflicted on hundreds of thousands of North Vietnamese who chose freedom when the Communists took over North Viet-Nam in 1954; to get peace at any price now, even though I know that a peace of humiliation for the United States would lead to a bigger war or surrender later.

I have rejected all political considerations in making this decision.

Whether my party gains in November is nothing compared to the lives of 400,000 brave Americans fighting for our country and for the cause of peace and freedom in Viet-Nam. Whether I may be a one-term President is insignificant compared to whether by our failure to act in this crisis the United States proves itself to be unworthy to lead the forces of freedom in this critical period in world history. I would rather be a one-term President and do what I believe is right than to be a two-term President at the cost of seeing America become a second-rate power and to see this nation accept the first defeat in its proud 190-year history.

Source: *Public Papers of the Presidents of the United States: Richard Nixon, 1970* (Washington, DC: U.S. Government Printing Office, 1971), 405–410.

196. Summary of COSVN Directive No. 01/CT71, January–February 1971 [Excerpts]

Introduction

Resolution No. 9 drawn up by the Central Office for South Vietnam (COSVN), the Communist headquarters running the war in the Republic of Vietnam (RVN, South Vietnam), was the guideline for the Communist military effort in South Vietnam until early 1971, when the resolution was apparently superceded by Directive No. 01/CT71. While admitting that U.S. and South Vietnamese pacification efforts have registered some success, the directive points to positive developments for the Communist side such as the expansion of the war to Cambodia, which the directive claims have helped unify the peoples of Indochina; the increased cost of the war to South Vietnam because of Vietnamization; and the growing antiwar movement in the United States.

Primary Source

Following are the characteristics particular to the struggle on the South Viet-Nam battlefield and the general characteristics of the Indochinese theater of operations.

1. Pacification and counterpacification struggles by enemy and friendly forces were and are being conducted under highly violent forms. The enemy has achieved some temporary results, but is steadily failing in implementing his basic schemes. Meanwhile, we have fought courageously and persistently, surmounted all difficulties, and are forging ahead, although some minor difficulties still exist in conducting fierce attacks against the enemy.

During the past two years, the U.S. and puppet focused their efforts on pacifying and encroaching upon rural areas, using the most barbarous schemes. They strengthened puppet forces, consolidated the puppet government, and established an outpost network and espionage and People's Self-Defense Force organizations in many hamlets and villages. They provided more technical equipment for, and increased the mobility of, puppet forces, established blocking lines, and created a new defensive and oppressive system in densely populated rural areas. As a result, they caused many difficulties to and inflicted losses on friendly forces. Generally, however, they were unable to attain their basic objectives. They failed to destroy or wipe out the revolutionary infrastructure or our local and guerrilla forces which continued to remain in their areas of operation. In some areas, we were even able to increase our forces. In spite of his oppressive control, the enemy failed to subdue our people. Along with our cadre and Party members, the people in rural areas continually attacked the enemy and constantly maintained and developed the revolutionary movement. On the other hand, enemy forces and war facilities were increasingly depleted and destroyed. Enemy military forces were thinly dispersed and many of his outposts were encircled or isolated. The noteworthy point is that in implementing his pacification and Vietnamization programs, the enemy was forced to resort to dictatorial and fascist policies which deepened the contradictions between people of various strata, including personnel of the puppet army and administration, and various political factions, on one hand and the U.S.-Thieu-Ky-Khiem clique on the other hand; this situation further aggravated the political, economic and financial crisis of the U.S.-puppets, sapped the internal unity of the puppets and isolated the U.S.-Thieu-Ky-Khiem clique. This created new favorable conditions for popular struggle movements in Saigon and other cities and rural areas.

2. The 18 March 1970 coup d'etat and the subsequent expansion of the war of aggression by the U.S. imperialists to Cambodia, which was intended to support the Vietnamization program in South Viet-Nam, failed to enable them to attain their proposed goals of destroying our agencies, storage facilities, and base areas, destroying and depleting our main forces, halting the revolutionary movement in Cambodia, and saving the Lon Nol clique from a dangerous situation.

On the contrary, this created conditions for the Cambodian revolutionary movement to leap forward and strengthened the unity of the peoples of Laos, Cambodia, and Viet-Nam in their struggles. A unified front was established through which the Indochinese peoples are fighting their common enemy, the U.S. imperialists and their henchmen. A large strategic theater of operations was developed, binding the three countries together, linking the big frontline with the big rear area, and turning Indo-China into a unified battlefield. In this theater, Cambodia is the most vulnerable point of the U.S. and puppets, South Viet-Nam is the main war theater with a decisive bearing on the common victory, and Laos is a significant area of operations.

In 1970, the U.S. imperialists ventured to expand the war in Cambodia, but failed to save themselves from the dangerous situation. On the contrary, they suffered heavier military, political, and diplomatic failures and became further bogged down and strategically deadlocked. The U.S. withdrew its troops while puppet troops had to replace U.S. troops and concurrently play the key role in supporting the puppet Cambodian troops. Since enemy troops were forced to disperse thinly, the enemy experienced increasing difficulties in his pacification and Vietnamization plans and will certainly meet defeat.

3. Because the enemy exerted great efforts to implement the Nixon doctrine in South Viet-Nam and Indo-China, we had to surmount great difficulties and trials in the resistance against the U.S. for national salvation.

The [revolutionary] movement in the rural area was subjected to unprecedented disturbances by barbarous enemy attacks through

his pacification and encroachment programs. However, we were still able to maintain the operational positions of our infrastructure and armed forces.

We managed to maintain and in some areas even expand, our control over villages and hamlets in spite of the presence of enemy outposts. In many areas, we even undermined or reduced the effectiveness of the enemy defensive and oppressive control system.

The [struggle] movement in urban areas against the burden born from the Vietnamization plan developed on a large scale with support from all social classes. They openly demanded U.S. troop withdrawals, an overthrow of the Thieu-Ky-Khiem clique, and the establishment of a Government which would restore peace. The movement was supported by uncommitted factions and many personalities of various [political] parties, including those in the puppet National Assembly and the puppet government. Such a movement has caused continual failures for the U.S.-Thieu-Ky-Khiem clique in its efforts to rally a political force to support its oppression of revolutionary forces and opposition parties.

In this extremely fierce and complicated war, our main force units effectively fulfilled their role by attracting, containing and destroying many enemy mobile forces to successfully support political and armed [struggle] movements in South Viet-Nam and Cambodia. Through their successful maintenance and expansion of our strategic bases and corridors, they have proven to be increasingly significant in the new war position of the Indochinese people.

The great victories achieved on the battlefield by the people of the three Indochinese countries, in conjunction with positive diplomatic activities, won increasingly broad support and cooperation from all democratic and peace-loving people throughout the world and isolated the Nixon clique and its lackey governments. . . .

Noteworthy is the fact that although they would continue to withdraw their troops, they would retain an important element of U.S. and satellite forces to operate with puppet forces which are large in number but low in morale. These troops are reinforced with equipment and given additional training and support from U.S. troops, especially the U.S. Air Force, [and] therefore they have considerable firepower and great mobility. They have a new defensive and oppressive control system designed to safeguard both rural and urban areas [and] therefore they have the hope to maintain and improve their position.

Nevertheless, they also have very fundamental difficulties that cannot be surmounted even with the large military and economic potentials of the ringleader imperialists. They have to deescalate the war, continue to withdraw their troops, and rely on the puppet government and Army which are increasingly demoralized and politically weakened. They have to cope with three Indochinese countries which have power and sound leadership in addition to their tradition of fighting the aggressors. They also have to face the peace movements in the U.S. and throughout the world demanding the end of the war of aggression in Viet-Nam and Indo-China.

The basic enemy weaknesses and our objective advantages are as follows:

The more the U.S. speeds up the Vietnamization program, the more the puppet government is compelled to expedite its dictatorial and fascist policies on conscription, troop upgrading, taxation and inflation, and to send puppet troops to the battlefields to die in the place of U.S. soldiers. By so doing, the puppet government would aggravate the contradictions between itself and the people of various classes, including the uncommitted class and a large number of puppet government personnel. It would make the demands for social welfare, economic improvement, freedom, democracy, culture, the end of war, and restoration of peace become more pressing. It would ripen the political awareness demanding U.S. troop withdrawals and the replacement of the Thieu-Ky-Khiem government by a new one which would restore peace; aggravate the political, economic, and financial crises; and deepen the internal dissensions in the puppet government. These are the objective conditions necessary for us to expand the struggle movement against the Americans for national salvation and rally the new forces including the uncommitted class, puppet soldiers and personnel, and a number of personalities in the puppet government to promote a new movement against the U.S. and the Thieu-Ky-Khiem clique.

Source: *Viet-Nam Documents and Research Notes, No. 99* (Saigon: U.S. Mission in Viet Nam, October 1971).

197. President Richard Nixon: Televised Interview, March 22, 1971 [Excerpt]

Introduction

In this interview with Howard K. Smith broadcast on ABC Television on March 22, 1971, President Richard Nixon attempts to put a positive face on Operation LAM SON 719. Undertaken by the Army of the Republic of Vietnam (ARVN, South Vietnamese Army) supported by U.S. airpower and artillery from within South Vietnam, ARVN forces drove west along Route 9 into southern Laos to Tchepone. The operation was designed to prove that Vietnamization was working, purchase additional time for U.S. troop withdrawals, and weaken Communist forces in South Vietnam by cutting the Ho Chi Minh Trail resupply network. LAM SON 719 lasted from February 8 to March 24, 1971, and ended in an exceedingly costly near rout for ARVN forces.

Primary Source

Mr. Smith: Well, now, sir, they give the impression of retreating from Laos now, and there is still a whole month of dry season before the rains come. If they retreat now, won't the Communists have plenty of time to repair their trails and repair their pipelines before the rains come?

The President: They can never gain back the time, Mr. Smith. Six weeks is a period in which the Communists not only have found, as we pointed out earlier, that the supplies to the South have been drastically cut.

During that 6-week period they have had chewed up great amounts of ammunition, great amounts of materiel that otherwise would have gone south and would have been used, incidentally, against many Americans fighting in South Viet-Nam, and also in that 6-week period the South Vietnamese have developed a considerable capability on their own and considerable confidence on their own. They are better units to handle the situation as we withdraw.

Now, insofar as what they are going to be able to do for the balance of this dry season is concerned, I can only suggest that I cannot predict what will happen today, tomorrow, or the next day. There is going to be some more severe fighting as the South Vietnamese continue to withdraw from Laos. That we expected.

But let me try to put it in perspective. I have noted a considerable amount of discussion on the networks and in the newspapers and so forth, and it is altogether, let me say, understandable and justifiable discussion, as to whether this is a victory or a defeat. And I know that that is a question perhaps that you would raise; certainly, our viewers would raise it.

Let me hit it very directly. This is not the kind of an operation that you can really describe in the traditional terms of victory or defeat, because its purpose was not to conquer territory. Its purpose was not to destroy an army. Its purpose was simply to disrupt supply lines. Its purpose, in other words, was not to conquer or occupy a part of Laos. Its purpose was to defend South Viet-Nam.

Now, let's measure this operation in terms of accomplishing that purpose. For 6 weeks the South Vietnamese have disrupted the enemy's supply lines. For 6 weeks they have tied down some of the enemy's best divisions. For 6 weeks we have seen, too, that the South Vietnamese have been able to handle themselves quite well under very, very difficult circumstances.

Now, what does this mean for the future? Well, I think when we judge whether this operation is going to be labeled a success or a failure, we cannot judge it before it is concluded, and we cannot judge it even after it is concluded. We can only see it in perspective because its goals were long range—long range being, first, to insure the continuation of the American withdrawal; second, to reduce the risk to the remaining Americans as we withdraw; and third, to insure the ability of the South Vietnamese to defend themselves after we have left. Those were the three goals of this operation.

How do we know whether or not those goals will be achieved? Well, I will say this. My interim assessment based on General Abrams' advice and the advice that I get from all people in the field is this: As far as our withdrawal is concerned, it is assured. The next withdrawal announcement will be made in April. It will be at least at the number that I have been withdrawing over the past few months; and second, as far as the danger to the American forces remaining, particularly in the northern part of South Viet-Nam, there are 100,000 there, as you know, that danger has been substantially reduced. That operation has already accomplished that much.

Third, as far as the ARVN [Army of the Republic of Viet-Nam] is concerned—and here I come back to an expert—General Abrams, who tells it like it is and says it like it is, says that some of their units did not do so well but 18 out of 22 battalions conducted themselves with high morale, with great confidence, and they are able to defend themselves man for man against the North Vietnamese.

And so that I would say insofar as achieving our goals of assuring American withdrawal, reducing the threat to the remainder of our forces, and, finally, our goal of seeing to it that the ARVN develops the capability to defend itself, that the operation in Laos at this interim period has made considerable progress in achieving those goals.

Source: *Public Papers of the Presidents of the United States: Richard Nixon, 1971* (Washington, DC: U.S. Government Printing Office, 1972), 451–452.

198. John Kerry: Statement of the Vietnam Veterans Against the War to the Senate Foreign Relations Committee, April 23, 1971 [Excerpts]

Introduction

Founded in April 1967 and dissolved in 1973, the Vietnam Veterans Against the War (VVAW) claimed a membership of several thousand people. The VVAW's stated aim was to lend credence to the antiwar movement by enlisting those who had actually served in Vietnam and had experienced the war firsthand. Here John Kerry, a VVAW member, decorated former U.S. Navy officer, and future U.S. senator and Democratic Party nominee in the 2004 U.S. presidential elections, testifies before the Senate Foreign Relations Committee and details atrocities committed by U.S. troops in what he calls the "civil war" in Vietnam.

Primary Source

I would like to talk on behalf of all those veterans and say that several months ago in Detroit we had an investigation at which over 150 honorably discharged, and many very highly decorated, veterans testified to war crimes committed in Southeast Asia. These were not isolated incidents but crimes committed on a day-to-day basis with the full awareness of officers at all levels of command. It is impossible to describe to you exactly what did happen in Detroit—the emotions in the room and the feelings of the men who were reliving their experiences in Vietnam. They relived the absolute horror of what this country, in a sense, made them do.

They told stories that at times they had personally raped, cut off ears, cut off heads, taped wires from portable telephones to human genitals and turned up the power, cut off limbs, blown up bodies, randomly shot at civilians, razed villages in fashion reminiscent of Ghengis Khan, shot cattle and dogs for fun, poisoned food stocks, and generally ravaged the countryside of South Vietnam in addition to the normal ravage of war and the normal and very particular ravaging which is done by the applied bombing power of this country.

We call this investigation the Winter Soldier Investigation. The term Winter Soldier is a play on words of Thomas Paine's in 1776 when he spoke of the Sunshine Patriots and summertime soldiers who deserted at Valley Forge because the going was rough.

We who have come here to Washington have come here because we feel we have to be winter soldiers now. We could come back to this country, we could be quiet, we could hold our silence, we could not tell what went on in Vietnam, but we feel because of what threatens this country, not the reds, but the crimes which we are committing that threaten it, that we have to speak out. . . .

In our opinion and from our experience, there is nothing in South Vietnam which could happen that realistically threatens the United States of America. And to attempt to justify the loss of one American life in Vietnam, Cambodia or Laos by linking such loss to the preservation of freedom, which those misfits supposedly abuse, is to us the height of criminal hypocrisy, and it is that kind of hypocrisy which we feel has torn this country apart.

We found that not only was it a civil war, an effort by a people who had for years been seeking their liberation from any colonial influence whatsoever, but also we found that the Vietnamese whom we had enthusiastically molded after our own image were hard put to take up the fight against the threat we were supposedly saving them from.

We found most people didn't even know the difference between communism and democracy. They only wanted to work in rice paddies without helicopters strafing them and bombs with napalm burning their villages and tearing their country apart. They wanted everything to do with the war, particularly with this foreign presence of the United States of America, to leave them alone in peace, and they practiced the art of survival by siding with whichever military force was present at a particular time, be it Viet Cong, North Vietnamese or American.

We found also that all too often American men were dying in those rice paddies for want of support from their allies. We saw first hand how monies from American taxes were used for a corrupt dictatorial regime. We saw that many people in this country had a one-sided idea of who was kept free by the flag, and blacks provided the highest percentage of casualties. We saw Vietnam ravaged equally by American bombs and search and destroy missions, as well as by Viet Cong terrorism—and yet we listened while this country tried to blame all of the havoc on the Viet Cong.

We rationalized destroying villages in order to save them. We saw America lose her sense of morality as she accepted very coolly a My Lai and refused to give up the image of American soldiers who hand out chocolate bars and chewing gum.

We learned the meaning of free fire zones, shooting anything that moves, and we watched while America placed a cheapness on the lives of orientals.

We watched the United States falsification of body counts, in fact the glorification of body counts. We listened while month after month we were told the back of the enemy was about to break. We fought using weapons against "oriental human beings." We fought using weapons against those people which I do not believe this country would dream of using were we fighting in the European theater. We watched while men charged up hills because a general said that hill has to be taken, and after losing one platoon or two platoons they marched away to leave the hill for reoccupation by the North Vietnamese. We watched pride allow the most unimportant battles to be blown into extravaganzas, because we couldn't lose, and we couldn't retreat, and because it didn't matter how many American bodies were lost to prove that point, and so there were Hamburger Hills and Khe Sanhs and Hill 81s and Fire Base 6s, and so many others.

Now we are told that the men who fought there must watch quietly while American lives are lost so that we can exercise the incredible arrogance of Vietnamizing the Vietnamese.

Each day to facilitate the process by which the United States washes her hands of Vietnam someone has to give up his life so that the United States doesn't have to admit something that the entire world already knows, so that we can't say that we have made a mistake. Someone has to die so that President Nixon won't be, and these are his words, "the first President to lose a war."

We are asking Americans to think about that because how do you ask a man to be the last man to die in Vietnam? How do you ask a man to be the last man to die for a mistake? . . . . We are here in Washington to say that the problem of this war is not just a question of war and diplomacy. It is part and parcel of everything that we are trying as human beings to communicate to people in this country—the question of racism which is rampant in the military, and so many other questions such as the use of weapons; the hypocrisy in our taking umbrage at the Geneva Conventions and using that as justification for a continuation of this war when we are more guilty than any other body of violations of those Geneva Conventions; in the use of free fire zones, harassment interdiction fire, search and destroy missions, the bombings, the torture of prisoners, all accepted policy by many units in South Vietnam. That is what we are trying to say. It is part and parcel of everything.

An American Indian friend of mine who lives in the Indian Nation of Alcatraz put it to me very succinctly. He told me how as a boy on an Indian reservation he had watched television and he used to cheer the cowboys when they came in and shot the Indians, and then suddenly one day he stopped in Vietnam and he said, "my God, I am doing to these people the very same thing that was done to my people," and he stopped. And that is what we are trying to say, that we think this thing has to end.

We are here to ask, and we are here to ask vehemently, where are the leaders of our country? Where is the leadership? We're here to ask where are McNamara, Rostow, Bundy, Gilpatrick, and so many others? Where are they now that we, the men they sent off to war, have returned? These are the commanders who have deserted their troops. And there is no more serious crime in the laws of war. The Army says they never leave their wounded. The marines say they never even leave their dead. These men have left all the casualties and retreated behind a pious shield of public rectitude. They've left the real stuff of their reputations bleaching behind them in the sun in this country. . . .

We wish that a merciful God could wipe away our own memories of that service as easily as this administration has wiped away their memories of us. But all that they have done and all that they can do by this denial is to make more clear than ever our own determination to undertake one last mission—to search out and destroy the last vestige of this barbaric war, to pacify our own hearts, to conquer the hate and fear that have driven this country these last ten years and more. And more. And so when thirty years from now our brothers go down the street without a leg, without an arm, or a face, and small boys ask why, we will be able to say "Vietnam" and not mean a desert, not a filthy obscene memory, but mean instead where America finally turned and where soldiers like us helped it in the turning.

Source: U.S. Congress, Senate, Committee on Foreign Relations, *Legislative Proposals Relating to the War in Southeast Asia,* 92th Cong., 1st sess. (Washington, DC: U.S. Government Printing Office, April 22, 1971), 180–210.

199. Colonel Robert D. Heinl Jr.: Analysis of the Decline of U.S. Armed Forces, June 7, 1971 [Excerpts]

Introduction

On June 7, 1971, U.S. Marine Corps colonel Robert D. Heinl Jr. published an article titled "The Collapse of the Armed Forces" in the *Armed Forces Journal.* In this scathing critique of the state of the U.S. military, Heinl claims that the military is at its worst level of effectiveness than at any time in the 20th century and possibly in the history of the nation. He asserts that military units in Vietnam are nearly mutinous, drug-ridden, and in a state of near collapse and that elsewhere the situation is almost as serious. It was not easy for critics to dismiss Heinl's views. Heinl was a veteran of 27 years in the U.S. Marine Corps, the distinguished author of five books (including *The Marine Officer's Guide* and *Soldiers of the Sea*), and the former head of the U.S. Marine Corps' military historical program. Although his article was highly controversial and came in for much criticism, much of the criticism was because he had understated the situation in the armed forces.

Primary Source

The morale, discipline and battleworthiness of the U.S. Armed Forces are, with a few salient exceptions, lower and worse than at any time in this century and possibly in the history of the United States.

By every conceivable indicator, our army that now remains in Vietnam is in a state approaching collapse, with individual units avoiding or having refused combat, murdering their officers and noncommissioned officers, drug-ridden, and dispirited where not near-mutinous.

Elsewhere than Vietnam, the situation is nearly as serious.

Intolerably clobbered and buffeted from without and within by social turbulence, pandemic drug addiction, race war, sedition, civilian scapegoatise, draftee recalcitrance and malevolence, barracks theft and common crime, unsupported in their travail by the general government, in Congress as well as the executive branch, distrusted, disliked, and often reviled by the public, the uniformed services today are places of agony for the loyal, silent professionals who doggedly hang on and try to keep the ship afloat.

The responses of the services of these unheard-of conditions, forces and new public attitudes, are confused, resentful, occasionally pollyanna-ish, and in some cases even calculated to worsen the malaise that is wracking them.

While no senior officer (especially one on active duty) can openly voice any such assessment, the foregoing conclusions find virtually unanimous support in numerous non-attributable interviews with responsible senior and midlevel officers, as well as career noncommissioned officers and petty officers in all services.

Historical precedents do exist for some of the services' problems, such as desertion, mutiny, unpopularity, seditious attacks, and racial troubles. Others, such as drugs, pose difficulties that are wholly new. Nowhere, however, in the history of the Armed Forces have comparable past troubles presented themselves in such general magnitude, acuteness, or concentrated focus as today.

By several orders of magnitude, the Army seems to be in worst trouble. But the Navy has serious and unprecedented problems, while the Air Force, on the surface at least still clear of the quicksands in which the Army is sinking, is itself facing disquieting difficulties.

Only the Marines—who have made the news this year by their hard line against indiscipline and general permissiveness—seem, with their expected staunchness and tough tradition, to be weathering the storm.

To understand the military consequences of what is happening to the U.S. Armed Forces, Vietnam is a good place to start. It is in Vietnam that the rearguard of a 500,000-man army, in its day (and in the observation of the writer) the best army the United States ever put into the field, is numbly extricating itself from a nightmare war the Armed Forces feel they had foisted on them by bright civilians who are now back on campus writing books about the folly of it all.

"They have set up separate companies," writes an American soldier from Cu Chi, quoted in the New York Times, "for men who refuse to go out into the field." It is no big thing to refuse to go. If a man is ordered to go to such and such a place he no longer goes through the hassle of refusing; he just packs his shirt and goes to visit some buddies at another base camp. Operations have become incredibly ragtag. Many guys don't even put on their uniforms any more....

"Frag incidents" or just "fragging" is current soldier slang in Vietnam for the murder or attempted murder of strict, unpopular, or just aggressive officers and NCOS. With extreme reluctance (after a young West Pointer from Senator Mike Mansfield's Montana was fragged in his sleep) the Pentagon has now disclosed that fraggings in 1970 (209) have more than doubled those of the previous year (96).

Word of the deaths of officers will bring cheers at troop movies or in bivouacs of certain units.

In one such division—the morale-plagued Americal—fraggings during 1971 have been authoritatively estimated to be running about one a week.

Yet fraggings, though hard to document, form part of the ugly lore of every war. The first such verified incident known to have taken place occurred 190 years ago when Pennsylvania soldiers in the Continental Army killed one of their captains during the night of 1 January 1781.

Bounties, raised by common subscription in amounts running anywhere from $50 to $1,000, have been widely reported put on the heads of leaders whom the privates and Sp4s want to rub out.

Shortly after the costly assault on Hamburger Hill in mid-1969, the GI underground newspaper in Vietnam, "GI Says," publicly offered a $10,000 bounty on LCol Weldon Honeycutt, the officer who ordered (and led) the attack. Despite several attempts, however, Honeycutt managed to live out his tour and return Stateside....

The issue of "combat refusal," an official euphemism for disobedience of orders to fight—the soldier's gravest crime—has only recently been again precipitated on the frontier of Laos by Troop B, 1st Cavalry's mass refusal to recapture their captain's command vehicle containing communication gear, codes and other secret operation orders....

"Search and evade" (meaning tacit avoidance of combat by units in the field) is now virtually a principle of war, vividly expressed by the GI phrase, "CYA (cover your ass) and get home!"

That "search-and-evade" has not gone unnoticed by the enemy is underscored by the Viet Cong delegation's recent statement at the Paris Peace Talks that communist units in Indochina have been ordered not to engage American units which do not molest them. The same statement boasted—not without foundation in fact— that American defectors are in the VC ranks.

Symbolic anti-war fasts (such as the one at Pleiku where an entire medical unit, led by its officers, refused Thanksgiving turkey), peace symbols, "V"-signs not for victory but for peace, booing and cursing of officers and even of hapless entertainers such as Bob Hope, are unhappily commonplace.

As for drugs and race, Vietnam's problems today not only reflect but reinforce those of the Armed Forces as a whole. In April, for example, members of a Congressional investigating subcommittee reported that 10 to 15% of our troops in Vietnam are now using high-grade heroin, and that drug addiction there is "of epidemic proportions."

Only last year an Air Force major and command pilot for Ambassador Bunker was apprehended at Tan Son Nhut air base outside Saigon with $8-million worth of heroin in his aircraft. This major is now in Leavenworth.

Early this year, an Air Force regular colonel was court-martialed and cashiered for leading his squadron in pot parties, while, at Cam Ranh Air Force Base, 43 members of the base security police squadron were recently swept up in dragnet narcotics raids.

All the foregoing facts—and many more dire indicators of the worst kind of military trouble—point to widespread conditions among American forces in Vietnam that have only been exceeded in this century by the French Army's Nivelle mutinies of 1917 and the collapse of the Tsarist armies in 1916 and 1917.

It is a truism that national armies closely reflect societies from which they have been raised. It would be strange indeed if the Armed Forces did not today mirror the agonizing divisions and social traumas of American society, and of course they do.

For this very reason, our Armed Forces outside Vietnam not only reflect these conditions but disclose the depths of their troubles in an awful litany of sedition, disaffection, desertion, race, drugs, breakdowns of authority, abandonment of discipline, and, as a cumulative result, the lowest state of military morale in the history of the country.

Sedition—coupled with disaffection within the ranks, and externally fomented with an audacity and intensity previously inconceivable—infests the Armed Services:

—At best count, there appear to be some 144 underground newspapers published on or aimed at U.S. military bases in this country and overseas. Since 1970 the number of such sheets has increased 40% (up from 103 last fall). These journals are not mere gripe-sheets that poke soldier fun in the "Beetle Bailey" tradition, at the brass and the sergeants. "In Vietnam," writes the Ft Lewis-McChord Free Press, "the Lifers, the Brass, are the true Enemy, not the enemy." Another West Coast sheet advises readers: "Don't desert. Go to Vietnam and kill your commanding officer."

—At least 14 GI dissent organizations (including two made up exclusively of officers) now operate more or less openly. Ancillary to these are at least six antiwar veterans' groups which strive to influence GIs....

Racial conflicts (most but not all sparked by young black enlisted men) are erupting murderously in all services.

At a recent high commanders' conference, General Westmoreland and other senior generals heard the report from Germany that in many units white soldiers are now afraid to enter barracks alone at night for fear of "headhunting" ambushes by blacks.

In the quoted words of one soldier on duty in West Germany, "I'm much more afraid of getting mugged on the post than I am of getting attacked by the Russians."

Other reports tell of jail-delivery attacks on Army stockades and military police to release black prisoners, and of officers being struck in public by black soldiers. Augsburg, Krailsheim, and Hohenfels are said to be rife with racial trouble. Hohenfels was the scene of a racial fragging last year—one of the few so far recorded outside Vietnam.

In Ulm, last fall, a white noncommissioned officer killed a black soldier who was holding a loaded .45 on two unarmed white officers.

Elsewhere, according to Fortune magazine, junior officers are now being attacked at night when inspecting barracks containing numbers of black soldiers.

Kelley Hill, a Ft Benning, Ga., barracks area, has been the scene of repeated nighttime assaults on white soldiers. One such soldier bitterly remarked, "Kelley Hill may belong to the commander in the daytime but it belongs to the blacks after dark."...

The drug problem—like the civilian situation from which it directly derives—is running away with the services. In March, Navy Secretary John H. Chafee, speaking for the two sea services, said bluntly that drug abuse in both Navy and Marines is out of control.

In 1966, the Navy discharged 170 drug offenders. Three years later (1969), 3,800 were discharged. Last year in 1970, the total jumped to over 5,000.

Drug abuse in the Pacific Fleet—with Asia on one side, and kinky California on the other—gives the Navy its worst headaches. To cite one example, a destroyer due to sail from the West Coast last year for the Far East nearly had to postpone deployment when, five days before departure, a ring of some 30 drug users (over 10 percent of the crew) was uncovered.

Only last week, eight midshipmen were dismissed from the Naval Academy following disclosure of an alleged drug ring. While the Navy emphatically denies allegations in a copyrighted article by the Annapolis Capitol that up to 1,000 midshipmen now use marijuana, midshipman sources confirm that pot is anything but unknown at Annapolis.

Yet the Navy is somewhat ahead in the drug game because of the difficulty in concealing addiction at close quarters aboard ship, and because fixes are unobtainable during long deployments at sea.

The Air Force, despite 2,715 drug investigations in 1970, is in even better shape: its rate of 3 cases per thousand airmen is the lowest in the services.

By contrast, the Army had 17,742 drug investigations the same year. According to Col. Thomas B. Hauschild, of the Medical Command of our Army forces in Europe, some 46 percent of the roughly 200,000 soldiers there had used illegal drugs at least once. In one battalion surveyed in West Germany, over 50 percent of the men smoked marijuana regularly (some on duty), while roughly half of those were using hard drugs of some type.

What those statistics say is that the Armed Forces (like their parent society) are in the grip of a drug pandemic—a conclusion underscored by the one fact that, just since 1968, the total number of verified drug addiction cases throughout the Armed Forces has nearly doubled. One other yardstick: according to military medical sources, needle hepatitis now poses as great a problem among young soldiers as VD.

At Ft Bragg, the Army's third largest post, adjacent to Fayetteville, N.C. (a garrison town whose conditions one official likened to New York's "East Village" and San Francisco's "Haight-Ashbury") a recent survey disclosed that 4% (or over 1,400) of the 36,000 soldiers there are hard-drug (mainly heroin and LSD) addicts. In the 82nd Airborne Division, the strategic-reserve unit that boasts its title of "America's Honor Guard," approximately 450 soldier drug abusers were being treated when this reporter visited the post in April. About a hundred were under intensive treatment in special drug wards....

In 1970, the Army had 65,643 deserters, or roughly the equivalent of four infantry divisions. This desertion rate (52.3 soldiers per thousand) is well over twice the peak rate for Korea (22.5 per thousand). It is more than quadruple the 1966 desertion-rate (14.7 per thousand) of the then well-trained, high-spirited professional Army.

If desertions continue to rise (as they are still doing this year), they will attain or surpass the WWII peak of 63 per thousand which, incidentally, occurred in the same year (1945) when more soldiers were actually being discharged from the Army for psychoneurosis than were drafted.

The Air Force—relatively uninvolved in the Vietnam war, all-volunteer, management-oriented rather than disciplinary and hierarchic—enjoys a numerical rate of less than one deserter per thousand men, but even this is double what it was three years ago.

The Marines in 1970 had the highest desertion index in the modern history of the Corps and, for that year at least, slightly higher than the Army's. As the Marines now phase out of Vietnam (and haven't taken a draftee in nearly two years), their desertions are expected to decrease sharply. Meanwhile, grimly remarked one officer, "Let the bastards go. We're all the better without them."

Letting the bastards go is something the Marines can probably afford. "The Marine Corps Isn't Looking for a Lot of Recruits," reads a current recruiting poster, "We just Need a Few Good Men." This is the happy situation of a Corps slimming down to an elite force again composed of true volunteers who want to be professionals.

But letting the bastards go doesn't work at all for the Army and the Navy, who do need a lot of recruits and whose reenlistment problems are dire.

Admiral Elmo R. Zumwalt, Jr, Chief of Naval Operations, minces no words. "We have a personnel crisis," he recently said, "that borders on disaster."

The Navy's crisis, as Zumwalt accurately describes it, is that of a highly technical, material oriented service that finds itself unable to retain the expensively-trained technicians needed to operate warships, which are the largest, most complex items of machinery that man makes and uses. . . .

The trouble of the services—produced by and also in turn producing the dismaying conditions described in this article—is above all a crisis of soul and backbone. It entails—the word is not too strong—something very near a collapse of the command authority and leadership George Washington saw as the soul of military forces. This collapse results, at least in part, from a concurrent collapse of public confidence in the military establishment. . . .

But the fall in public esteem of all three major services—not just the Army—is exceeded by the fall or at least the enfeeblement of the hierarchic and disciplinary system by which they exist and, when ordered to do so, fight and sometimes die. . . .

Source: Col. Robert D. Heinl Jr., "The Collapse of the Armed Forces," *Armed Forces Journal,* June 7, 1971. Reprinted as evidence in *House Committee Hearings on Subversion within the Armed Forces,* Vol. 2 (Washington, DC: U.S. Government Printing Office), 7132–7140.

200. Democratic Republic of Vietnam Peace Proposal, June 26, 1971

Introduction

Beginning in February 1971, Le Duc Tho, representing the Democratic Republic of Vietnam (DRV, North Vietnam), met with U.S. national security adviser Dr. Henry Kissinger in Paris in a series of secret negotiating sessions. On May 31 Kissinger presented a proposal whereby the United States would agree to a timetable for the withdrawal of all of its forces from the Republic of Vietnam (RVN, South Vietnam) in return for the release by North Vietnam of its U.S. prisoners of war (POWs). On June 16 at the next meeting of the two men, Le Duc Tho presented a counterproposal for the a U.S. troop withdrawal and North Vietnamese release of POWs to be accomplished at the same time. The counterproposal also demanded an end to U.S. support for South Vietnamese president Nguyen Van Thieu.

Primary Source

1. The withdrawal of all the forces of the United States and those of the other foreign countries in the U.S. camp for South Vietnam and the other Indochinese countries must be achieved in 1971.

2. The release of all the military men and civilians captured in the war will be carried out at the same time and will be completed at the same moment as the withdrawal of troops mentioned in Point 1.

3. In South Vietnam, the United States ceases supporting Thieu-Ky-Khiem to allow the formation in Saigon of a new administration standing for peace, independence, neutrality, and democracy. The PRGRSV [Provisional Revolutionary Government of the Republic of South Vietnam] will engage in talks with the said administration with a view to settling the internal affairs of South Vietnam and achieving national concord.

4. The U.S. Government must assume the entire responsibility for the damage caused by the United States to the entire Vietnamese people. The DRV Government and the PRGRSV request from the U.S. Government reparations for damage caused by the United States in the two zones of Vietnam.

5. The United States must respect the 1954 Geneva Agreements in Vietnam and Indochina and those of 1962 on Laos. It must cease its aggression against and intervention in the Indochinese countries to let the Indochinese people settle their own affairs.

6. The problems existing between the Indochinese countries will be settled by the Indochinese parties on the basis of mutual respect for independence, sovereignty and territorial integrity, and for

noninterference on internal affairs. For its part, the DRV is prepared to participate in the settlement of these problems.

7. All the parties will observe a cease-fire after the conclusion of agreements of the aforementioned problems.

8. An international supervision will be set-up.

9. An international guarantee will be indispensable for the realization of the basic national rights of the Indochinese people, for the neutrality of South Vietnam, Laos and Cambodia and for the establishment of a lasting peace in this region.

These nine points make up a whole.

> **Source:** "Democratic Republic of Vietnam Peace Proposal, June 26, 1971," The Wars for Viet Nam, Vassar College, http://vietnam.vassar.edu/abstracts/index.html.

201. Peace Proposal of the Provisional Revolutionary Government of South Vietnam, July 1, 1971

Introduction

On July 1, 1971, the Provisional Revolutionary Government of South Vietnam (PRG), the Communist front in the Republic of Vietnam (RVN, South Vietnam) controlled by the Democratic Republic of Vietnam (DRV, North Vietnam), issued a public and more detailed version of the secret North Vietnamese peace proposal presented in Paris the week before.

Primary Source

1—Regarding the deadline for the total withdrawal of U.S. forces.

The U.S. Government must put an end to its war of aggression in Viet Nam, stop its policy of "Vietnamization" of the war, withdraw from South Viet Nam all troops, military personnel, weapons, and war materials of the United States and of the other foreign countries in the U.S. camp, and dismantle all U.S. bases in South Viet Nam, without posing any condition whatsoever.

The U.S. Government must set a terminal date for the withdrawal from South Viet Nam of the totality of U.S. forces and those of the other foreign countries in the U.S. camp.

If the U.S. Government sets a terminal date for the withdrawal from South Viet Nam in 1971 of the totality of U.S. forces and those of the other foreign countries in the U.S. camp, the parties will at the same time agree on the modalities:

A—Of the withdrawal in safety from South Vietnam of the totality of U.S. forces and those of the other foreign countries in the U.S. camp.

B—Of the release of the totality of militarymen of all parties and of the civilians captured in the war (including American pilots captured in North Viet Nam) so that they may all rapidly return to their homes.

These two operations will begin on the same date and will end on the same date.

A cease-fire will be observed between the South Viet Nam People's Liberation Armed Forces and the armed forces of the United States and of the other foreign countries in the U.S. camp as soon as the parties reach agreement on the withdrawal from South Viet Nam of the totality of U.S. forces and those of the other foreign countries in the U.S. camp.

2—Regarding the question of power, in South Viet Nam.

The U.S. Government must really respect the South Viet Nam people's right to self-determination, put an end to its interference in the internal affairs of South Viet Nam, cease backing the bellicose group headed by Nguyen Van Thieu at present in office in Saigon, and stop all maneuvers, including tricks on elections, aimed at maintaining the puppet Nguyen Van Thieu.

The political, social and religious forces in South Viet Nam aspiring to peace and national concord will use various means to form in Saigon a new administration favouring peace, independence, neutrality and democracy. The Provisional Revolutionary Government of the Republic of South Viet Nam will immediately enter into talks with the administration in order to settle the following questions:

A—To form a broad three-segment government of national concord that will assume its functions during the period between the restoration of peace and the holding of general elections and organize general election in South Viet Nam.

A ceasefire will be observed between the South Viet Nam People's Liberation Armed Forces and the armed forces of the Saigon Administration as soon as a government of national concord is formed.

B—To take concrete measures with the required guarantees so as to prohibit all acts of terror, reprisal, and discrimination against persons having collaborated with one or the other party, to ensure every democratic liberty to the South Viet Nam people, to release all persons jailed for political reasons, to dissolve all concentration camps and to liquidate all forms of constraint and coercion so as to permit the people to return to their native places in complete freedom and to freely engage in their occupations.

C—To see that the people's living conditions are stabilized and gradually improve, to create conditions allowing everyone to contribute his talents and efforts to heal the war wounds and rebuild the country.

D—To agree on measures to be taken to ensure the holding of genuinely free, democratic and fair general elections in South Viet Nam.

3—Regarding the question of Vietnamese armed forces in South Viet Nam.

The Vietnamese parties will together settle the question of Vietnamese armed forces in South Viet Nam in a spirit of national concord, equality and mutual respect, without foreign interference, in accordance with the post-war situation and with a view to lightening the people's contribution.

4—Regarding the peaceful reunification of Viet Nam and the relations between the north and south zones.

A—The reunification of Viet Nam will be achieved step by step, by peaceful means, on the basis of discussions and agreements between the two zones, without constraint and annexation from either party, without foreign interference.

Pending the reunification of the country, the north and the south zones will re-establish normal relations, guarantee free movement, free correspondence, free choice of residence and maintain economic and cultural relations on the principle of mutual interests and mutual assistance.

All questions concerning the two zones will be settled by qualified representatives of the Vietnamese people in the two zones on the basis of negotiations, without foreign interference.

B—In keeping with the provisions of the 1954 Geneva agreements on Viet Nam, in the present temporary partition of the country into two zones, the north and the south zones of Viet Nam will refrain from joining any military alliance with foreign countries, from allowing any foreign country to have military bases, troops and military personnel on their soil, and from recognizing the protection of any country, of any military alliance or bloc.

5—Regarding the foreign policy of peace and neutrality of South Viet Nam.

South Viet Nam will pursue a foreign policy of peace and neutrality, establish relations with all countries regardless of their political and social regime, in accordance with the five principles of peaceful coexistence, maintain economic and cultural relations with all countries, accept the cooperation of foreign countries in the exploitation of the resources of South Viet Nam, accept from any country economic and technical aid without any political conditions attached, and participate in regional plans of economic cooperation.

On the basis of these principles, after the end of the war, South Viet Nam and the United States will establish relations in the political, economic and cultural fields.

6—Regarding the damage caused by the United States to the Vietnamese people in the two zones.

The U.S. Government must bear full responsibility for the losses and destruction it has caused to the Vietnamese people in the two zones.

7—Regarding the respect for and international guarantee of the accords that will be concluded.

The parties will find agreement on the forms of respect for and international guarantee of the accords that will be concluded.

Source: U.S. Congress, Senate, *Background Information Relating to Southeast Asia and Vietnam,* 7th rev. ed. (Washington, DC: U.S. Government Printing Office, 1974), 640–641.

202. Le Duc Tho: Cable No. 119, March 27, 1972 [Excerpts]

Introduction

Following the May 1970 Cambodian Incursion by forces of the United States and the Republic of Vietnam (RVN, South Vietnam) that drove Vietnamese Communist forces out of their Cambodian sanctuaries, the bulk of the Democratic Republic of Vietnam (DRV, North Vietnam) main-force units spent the next two years fighting in Cambodia and Laos to rebuild their base areas. As a result, the level of combat activity in South Vietnam dropped precipitously, allowing U.S. and South Vietnamese troops to secure control of almost the entire country. In early 1972 U.S. troop strength in South Vietnam dropped below 100,000 and continued to fall rapidly. With its rear areas and logistics pipelines in Cambodia and Laos now secure, the People's Army of Vietnam (PAVN, North Vietnamese Army) was ready to resume the battle for control of South Vietnam. Anticipating that the upcoming 1972 presidential election campaign in the United States would restrict any response by the Richard Nixon administration and worried that Nixon's new overtures to China and the Soviet Union might affect the level of support that they would receive from their allies in the future, the North Vietnamese prepared to launch an all-out military offensive throughout South Vietnam. On March 27, 1972, four days before this Communist Easter Offensive was scheduled to begin, Politburo member Le Duc Tho, the man in charge of North Vietnam's secret negotiations with the United States, sent a top-secret cable to the Central Office for South Vietnam (COSVN) providing the Politburo's latest assessment of the situation. In it he sets forward the goals of the upcoming offensive and explains the connection between this offensive and North Vietnam's negotiating strategy.

Primary Source

The Central Military Party Committee met recently and sent the resolution it passed to you.... The Politburo agreed with the Central Military Party Committee's assessment of the situation and approved its policy decisions. I am sending you this cable to let you know the Politburo's ideas so you can understand things more clearly. At present the balance of forces between our side and the enemy side is undergoing tremendous changes that are very favorable to our side. As a result of our victories and of the defeats suffered by the Americans and their puppets, the American imperialists and their satellite nations have been forced to withdraw the vast bulk of their troops from the battlefield. They will continue to withdraw additional troops. This is a process that cannot be stopped.... Although the puppet army is now better equipped than it was before, the enemy simply cannot be as strong as he was when there were large numbers of American troops on the battlefield....

Domestically, the U.S. is also facing many insoluble problems. The Vietnam War is still one of the most difficult issues, an issue that has driven the American political and economic situations into a crisis of unprecedented proportions.... The U.S. economic situation continues to deteriorate.... Because of this situation, the vast majority of the American people are very dissatisfied. They want to end the war in order to escape from this morass. Faced with this situation, Nixon wants to use his visits to China and the Soviet Union to break the impasse and deceive the public. However, it will be difficult for him to completely solve ... the problems of Vietnam and Indochina ... because no one else can speak for us in settling the problem. The situation ... is going downhill for the U.S., making the situation in the U.S. even more unsettled in this US Presidential year.

As for our side, in 1971 we won more victories on all three Indochina battlefields than we have won in any years since the Tet Offensive.... Our main force troops have been honed, reinforced, and are better equipped than they were before.... The battlefield situation in the three nations of Indochina is currently developing in our favor. Our Party and our people have high resolve. The peoples of the world continue to strongly support us. China, the Soviet

Union, and the other fraternal socialist nations continue to increase their assistance to us, and up to this point we have encountered no problems as the result of Nixon's recent visit to China.

With the above-described balance of forces, this time we will attack on all battlefields with three strategic punches ... and attack continuously for an extended period of time, so it is certain that the enemy will suffer even greater, more significant defeats.... We have great prospects for winning a great victory in the coming phase. Based on the very favorable situation described above and with a firm understanding of our new opportunities and new capabilities, the Politburo has decided to make a coordinated effort on three fronts (military, political, and diplomatic) to deal a fundamental defeat to the enemy's "Vietnamization" policy by using simultaneous military attacks and popular uprisings to destroy or disperse the bulk of the enemy's forces, to liberate most of the rural countryside, and to intensify the political struggle and uprisings in the cities in order to secure a decisive victory in 1972. The situation is very favorable for our side, but we are not subjective and we do not underestimate our enemy.... We must take precautions against the possibility that the Vietnam problem will not be settled at the conference table ... but we must throw everything we have into this determined effort to secure a decisive victory during 1972, and we have good prospects for being able to achieve that goal.

The time period advantageous for a solution, on the battlefield as well as at the conference table, is after we have achieved success in the spring-summer-fall campaigns and before the U.S. Presidential election is held. That will be the best time for us to secure a decisive victory on all fronts—the military front as well as on the political and diplomatic fronts....

So far during this war ... we have launched only one all-out general offensive and uprising—the 1968 Tet Offensive. This time we will launch another offensive and uprising (at this time we are not officially calling it a general offensive, although in practical terms it is a general offensive and uprising throughout all of South Vietnam). However, the general offensive this time differs from our 1968 general offensive in that its targets, goals, content, and even its scale are all greater than those of the Tet Offensive.... The goals of this offensive are to fundamentally defeat the enemy's "Vietnamization" strategy, to destroy or cause the disintegration of the bulk of the puppet armed forces, to liberate most of the rural countryside, to intensify the political struggle and the mass uprisings in the cities, and, in coordination with the diplomatic struggle, to force the enemy to admit defeat and accept our demands so that we can secure a decisive victory.

The distinctive feature of this offensive is that we will employ the entire strength of our main force army to completely destroy the enemy's elite mobile forces and a number of the enemy's regular divisions.... If a large number of the enemy's regular divisions ... are destroyed, the balance of forces on the battlefield will shift dramatically.... In parallel with our main force attacks, we will also conduct our three-pronged attack [military, political, military proselyting], and that will destroy and shatter the enemy's local level armed forces and forces of oppression. . . . This tide of victory will create favorable conditions for the political struggle movement in the cities to grow strong . . . The destruction of enemy forces, the liberation of the rural countryside, and the uprisings in the cities are intimately and organically linked, and for that reason we must ensure that there is very close coordination between these three strategic blows.

Another special characteristic of this offensive is that we will fight continuously for a long time, through the end of the spring-summer season and into the fall. This is different from our previous offensives, when we stopped to rest and regroup for a time at the end of the spring-summer season before renewing our attacks. . . .

The diplomatic struggle must be closely coordinated with our effort to accomplish our strategic goals on the battlefields, and we must work out carefully coordinated steps to ensure coordination. The battlefield is where victory will be decided. The victories we win on the battlefield will provide the foundation upon which we will reach a successful resolution at the negotiating table. . . .

The goal of the revolution in South Vietnam is to carry out a national, democratic revolution. We may divide the effort to accomplish this into two phases. The first phase began when we launched the resistance war against the Americans and will last until we secure a decisive victory and end the war through a political solution. The second phase will last from the time we secure victory through a political solution until we finally reunite our Fatherland. . . . The level of success achieved in the first phase will determine the conditions required for developments in the second phase. . . .

We will launch continuous attacks throughout the spring, summer, and fall, but these will be divided into two attack waves. The spring-summer attack wave will be the important wave. During this wave our main forces will strike hard blows in parallel with our attacks on the pacification and an intensification of the political struggle and uprisings in the cities throughout the battlefields of all of South Vietnam. If during this phase we win big victories and achieve the goals we set for ourselves by destroying a number of the enemy's elite divisions and liberating the bulk of the rural countryside and a few provincial capitals . . . , the situation will change in a significant manner, and it may progress by leaps and bounds. If that happens . . . the political struggle movement and the mass uprisings in the cities will grow strong and develop rapidly. The enemy's ranks will become more divided and the anti-American, anti-Thieu front will be expanded further. Faced with that situation, the enemy will be forced to replace Thieu, install another enemy lackey in Thieu's place, and open up the government to allow opposition parties and factions to participate so that this government can negotiate with the Provisional Revolutionary Government. . . . That situation will create conditions that will facilitate talks between the Provisional Revolutionary Government and the new government in Saigon to seek a peaceful solution to the Vietnam problem.

Using the victories we win in the spring and summer as our foundation, . . . we will launch the fall offensive wave to deal the enemy a follow-up blow to make his forces disintegrate further and to apply pressure in the diplomatic struggle that will be going on at that time. If we again win a major victory in the fall campaign . . . the U.S. and the new government in Saigon will be forced to accept our demands at the conference table. Our two primary demands will be that the U.S. and its satellite nations must totally withdraw all their troops and that a tripartite coalition government be formed to conduct general elections as demanded in our seven-point program. . . . We will have secured a decisive victory on all three fronts—military, political, and diplomatic.

The above is our projection of the steps we will follow if things progress favorably. However, it is also possible that the level of victory we score in the spring, summer, and fall will not fully meet the goals we set. In that case, it is not certain that the enemy will accept our demands on the negotiating front. Even though, on the military front, the Americans will in the end be forced to withdraw all their troops, on the political front it is not certain that the enemy will agree to replace Thieu immediately. Instead, they may wait until they conclude a treaty with us before they agree to replace him. . . . Based on the actual situation at the time, we will review the pluses and minuses to decide whether to continue to fight or whether to enter into a peace settlement. However, . . . we must resolutely strive to achieve the decisive victory we have projected.

The second phase will last from the time that we secure a political settlement until we complete the national, democratic revolution in Vietnam and move toward the peaceful reunification of our nation. After we secure a political solution, how long it will take us to achieve this goal will depend on the degree of success we achieve on the battle and on the balance of forces between our side and the enemy. . . .

While you make your preparations, it is important for you to remember that the fighting between our side and the enemy in this offensive will be extremely ferocious. We are determined and will throw everything we have into this effort to accomplish our strategic intentions, no matter what it takes. However, the enemy also knows that this offensive will be decisive in determining the outcome of the war on the battlefields of all three nations of Indochina. For that reason, he will take ferocious countermeasures. We need to be on guard against the possibility that the enemy might employ even more powerful and brutal weapons in response to our attacks, because Nixon is a very daring individual who might take that risk, no matter what the consequences. We should not underestimate him. . . .

The Central Committee policies and decisions discussed above should only be disseminated within the COSVN and Region Party Committees. At the provincial level, disseminate these policies gradually, step by step, and only to a certain extent, because they include extremely secret matters and issues that do not need to be discussed right away. After you receive this cable, hold preliminary discussions about it within your current affairs committees and cable us any ideas or thoughts you may have. I may go to Paris around 15 April.

I wish you all good health. Please send my regards to all of our people.

[signed] Le Duc Tho

Source: *Van Kien Dang, Toan Tap 33, 1972* [Collected Party Documents, Volume 33, 1972] (Hanoi: Nha Xuat Ban Chinh Tri Quoc Gia, 2004), 222–223. Translated by Merle L. Pribbenow.

203. President Richard Nixon: Address to the Nation, May 8, 1972 [Excerpts]

Introduction

In response to the massive March 1972 military offensive by the armed forces of the Democratic Republic of Vietnam (DRV, North Vietnam), which included an invasion of the northern provinces of the Republic of Vietnam (RVN, South Vietnam) across the demilitarized zone (DMZ) and was designed to secure more favorable peace terms, U.S. president Richard Nixon ordered a massive bombing of North Vietnam. Dubbed Operation LINEBACKER (and later known as LINEBACKER I), this bombing was much more intense and effective than that of ROLLING THUNDER during the Lyndon Johnson administration. Nixon also ordered the mining of North Vietnam's ports, including Haiphong. In the course of his address to the American people on May 8, 1972, Nixon justifies these actions as necessary to cut off the flow of weapons and military supplies to North Vietnam.

Primary Source

It is plain then that what appears to be a choice among three courses of action for the United States is really no choice at all. The killing in this tragic war must stop. By simply getting out, we would only worsen the bloodshed. By relying solely on negotiations, we would give an intransigent enemy the time he needs to press his aggression on the battlefield.

There is only one way to stop the killing. That is to keep the weapons of war out of the hands of the international outlaws of North Vietnam.

... I therefore concluded that Hanoi must be denied the weapons and supplies it needs to continue the aggression. In full coordination with the Republic of Vietnam, I have ordered the following measures which are being implemented as I am speaking to you.

All entrances to North Vietnamese ports will be mined, to prevent access to these ports and North Vietnamese naval operations from these ports. United States forces have been directed to take appropriate measures within the internal and claimed territorial waters of North Vietnam to interdict the delivery of supplies. Rail and all other communications will be cut off to the maximum extent possible. Air and naval strikes against military targets in North Vietnam will continue.

These actions are not directed against any other nation. Countries with ships presently in North Vietnamese ports have already been notified that their ships will have three daylight periods to leave in safety. After that time, the mines will become active and any ships attempting to leave or enter these ports will do so at their own risk.

These actions I have ordered will cease when the following conditions are met:

First, all American prisoners of war must be returned.

Second, there must be an internationally supervised cease-fire throughout Indochina.

Once prisoners of war are released, once the internationally supervised cease-fire has begun, we will stop all acts of force throughout Indochina, and at that time we will proceed with a complete withdrawal of all American forces from Vietnam within 4 months.

Now these terms are generous terms. They are terms which would not require surrender and humiliation on the part of anybody. They would permit the United States to withdraw with honor. They would end the killing. They would bring our POW'S home. They would allow negotiations on a political settlement between the Vietnamese themselves. They would permit all the nations which have suffered in this long war—Cambodia, Laos, North Vietnam, South Vietnam—to turn at last to the urgent works of healing and of peace. They deserve immediate acceptance by North Vietnam.

Source: *Public Papers of the Presidents of the United States: Richard Nixon, 1972* (Washington, DC: U.S. Government Printing Office, 1974), 584–585.

204. Jane Fonda: Broadcast from Hanoi, August 22, 1972

Introduction

In July 1972 anti–Vietnam War activist and Hollywood movie star Jane Fonda flew to the Democratic Republic of Vietnam (DRV, North Vietnam). During two weeks in North Vietnam, she toured Hanoi and was photographed inspecting bomb damage and seated in a North Vietnamese antiaircraft gun position. Fonda also met with North Vietnamese vice premier Nguyen Duy Trinh and with eight U.S. prisoners of war, and she broadcast statements opposing the war in which she claimed that U.S. air strikes were specifically targeting the North Vietnamese dike system. Fonda was known as "Hanoi Jane" by her detractors and was much reviled by many Americans for this action. In the course of a television interview in 1988, Fonda apologized for her actions and any "hurt" they may have caused.

Primary Source

This is Jane Fonda. During my two week visit in the Democratic Republic of Vietnam, I've had the opportunity to visit a great many places and speak to a large number of people from all walks of life—workers, peasants, students, artists and dancers, historians, journalists, film actresses, soldiers, militia girls, members of the women's union, writers.

I visited the [Dam Xuac] agricultural coop, where the silk worms are also raised and thread is made. I visited a textile factory, a kindergarten in Hanoi. The beautiful Temple of Literature was where I saw traditional dances and heard songs of resistance. I also saw an unforgettable ballet about the guerrillas training bees in the south to attack enemy soldiers. The bees were danced by women, and they did their job well.

In the shadow of the Temple of Literature I saw Vietnamese actors and actresses perform the second act of Arthur Miller's play All My Sons, and this was very moving to me—the fact that artists here are translating and performing American plays while US imperialists are bombing their country.

I cherish the memory of the blushing militia girls on the roof of their factory, encouraging one of their sisters as she sang a song praising the blue sky of Vietnam—these women, who are so gentle and poetic, whose voices are so beautiful, but who, when American planes are bombing their city, become such good fighters.

I cherish the way a farmer evacuated from Hanoi, without hesitation, offered me, an American, their best individual bomb shelter while US bombs fell near by. The daughter and I, in fact, shared the shelter wrapped in each others arms, cheek against cheek. It was on the road back from Nam Dinh, where I had witnessed the systematic destruction of civilian targets—schools, hospitals, pagodas, the factories, houses, and the dike system.

As I left the United States two weeks ago, Nixon was again telling the American people that he was winding down the war, but in the rubble-strewn streets of Nam Dinh, his words echoed with sinister [words indistinct] of a true killer. And like the young Vietnamese woman I held in my arms clinging to me tightly—and I pressed my cheek against hers—I thought, this is a war against Vietnam perhaps, but the tragedy is America's.

One thing that I have learned beyond a shadow of a doubt since I've been in this country is that Nixon will never be able to break the spirit of these people; he'll never be able to turn Vietnam, north and south, into a neo-colony of the United States by bombing, by invading, by attacking in any way. One has only to go into the countryside and listen to the peasants describe the lives they led before the revolution to understand why every bomb that is dropped only strengthens their determination to resist.

I've spoken to many peasants who talked about the days when their parents had to sell themselves to landlords as virtual slaves, when there were very few schools and much illiteracy, inadequate medical care, when they were not masters of their own lives.

But now, despite the bombs, despite the crimes being created—being committed against them by Richard Nixon, these people own their own land, build their own schools—the children learning, literacy—illiteracy is being wiped out, there is no more prostitution as there was during the time when this was a French colony. In other words, the people have taken power into their own hands, and they are controlling their own lives.

And after 4,000 years of struggling against nature and foreign invaders—and the last 25 years, prior to the revolution, of struggling against French colonialism—I don't think that the people of Vietnam are about to compromise in any way, shape or form about the freedom and independence of their country, and I think Richard Nixon would do well to read Vietnamese history, particularly their poetry, and particularly the poetry written by Ho Chi Minh.

> **Source:** U.S. Congress, House, Committee on Internal Security, *Hearings Regarding H.R. 16742: Restraints on Travel to Hostile Areas,* 92th Cong., 2nd sess. (Washington, DC: U.S. Government Printing Office, September 19 and 25, 1972), 7671.

205. Statement of the Provisional Revolutionary Government of South Vietnam, September 11, 1972 [Excerpt]

Introduction

On September 11, 1972, the Provisional Revolutionary Government of South Vietnam (PRG), the Communist alternative or rival to the government of the Republic of Vietnam (RVN, South Vietnam), issued a statement just prior to the next meeting in Paris of the peace negotiators. In a new development, the PRG holds that any solution must recognize the existence in South Vietnam of "two administrations, two armies, and other political forces."

Primary Source

The Provisional Revolutionary Government of the Republic of South Vietnam solemnly declares as follows:

If a correct solution is to be found to the Vietnam problem, and a lasting peace ensured in Vietnam, the U.S. Government must meet the two following requirement:

1—To respect the Vietnamese people's right to true independence and the South Vietnamese people's right to effective self-determination; stop the U.S. war of aggression in Vietnam, the bombing, mining and blockade of the Democratic Republic of Vietnam; completely cease the "Vietnamization" policy; and all U.S. military activities in South Vietnam; rapidly and completely withdraw all U.S. troops, advisors, military personnel, technical personnel, weapons and war materials and those of the other foreign countries in the U.S. camp from South Vietnam; liquidate the U.S. military bases in South Vietnam; end all U.S. military inivolvement in Vietnam; and stop supporting the Nguyen Van Thieu stooge administration.

2—A solution to the internal problem of South Vietnam must proceed from the actual situation that there exist in South Vietnam two administrations, two armies, and other political forces. It is necessary to achieve national concord. The sides in South Vietnam must unite on the basis of equality, mutual respect and mutual nonelimination. Democratic freedoms must be guaranteed to the people. To this end, it is necessary to form in South Vietnam a provisional government of national concord with three equal segments to take charge of the affairs in the period of transition and to organize truly free and democratic general elections.

Source: U.S. Congress, Senate, *Background Information Relating to Southeast Asia and Vietnam,* 7th rev. ed. (Washington, DC: U.S. Government Printing Office, 1974), 648–649.

206. Document by the South Vietnamese Ministry of Foreign Affairs on the Paris Peace Talks, October 24, 1972

Introduction

On October 8, 1972, Le Duc Tho, the representative from the Democratic Republic of Vietnam (DRV, North Vietnam) to the Paris peace talks, agreed for the first time that the government of President Nguyen Van Thieu in the Republic of Vietnam (RVN, South Vietnam) might remain in place and that after a cease-fire the Thieu government would negotiate with the Communist Provisional Revolutionary Government of South Vietnam (PRG), the Communist government in South Vietnam, for a permanent political settlement. U.S. national security adviser Henry Kissinger then flew off to Saigon for talks with Thieu, who strongly objected to the terms of the proposed peace agreement. Chief among them

was that People's Army of Vietnam (PAVN, North Vietnamese Army) units would be allowed to remain in place in South Vietnam after the U.S. military had departed. Thieu characterized the peace agreement as little more than a "decent interval" before South Vietnam would fall to the Communists. This document from the South Vietnamese Foreign Ministry enumerates Thieu's objections.

Primary Source

1. There have been innumerable rumors and speculations with regard to a peaceful solution of the war in Indochina and in Vietnam in particular. The speculations are all the more feverish as the US Presidential elections come closer, and feed on missions carried out by US Presidential adviser Henry Kissinger to Peking, Moscow, Paris and these days to Saigon and Phnom Penh to meet with leaders of friendly and hostile countries.

Meetings in Paris between Dr. Kissinger and Le Duc Tho resulted in agreement on a number of points between the U.S. and North Vietnam, which in turn induced a belief in some quarters of the public opinion that a ceasefire is imminent in Indochina with conditions which are unacceptable to the Republic of Vietnam.

2. The United States has informed the Republic of Vietnam progressively about the evolution of the talks with North Vietnam and the Republic of Vietnam always discussed with the US the course of action to be followed by both parties. Throughout the consultations with the US, the Government of the Republic of Vietnam has observed an absolute discretion so as not to prejudice their outcome, and in order to avoid erroneous speculations about a conflict between the Republic of Vietnam and the US. However, the international press has advanced many stories with regard to those discussions. Those news items, either accurate or misleading, have had an unsettling impact on public opinion in Vietnam.

3. In order to eliminate any doubt, the Republic of Vietnam wishes to affirm that:

Although the Government and people of the Republic of Vietnam fervently wish a return of peace in their land, they cannot accept a peace at all costs, especially a peace that would pave the way to the subjugation of 17 million South Vietnamese people by the Communists. Such a solution would be a betrayal of the many sacrifices consented by combatants of the Republic of Vietnam and the free world who have fought and died for the survival of the Republic of Vietnam.

4. For the aforementioned reasons, and after long and delicate discussion with Dr. Kissinger during the latter's stay in Saigon from October 18th to 23rd, in a frank and cordial atmosphere, President Nguyen Van Thieu had to prepare certain modifications in the cease-fire proposal put forward by North Vietnam. President

Nguyen Van Thieu affirmed the RVN's position after the consultations with the National Security Council.

5. The need for further negotiations is based on the consideration of three essential points of the proposed agreement, as follows:

A. North Vietnam does not explicitly recognize the demilitarized zone at the 17th parallel as established by the 1954 Geneva Agreements. The Geneva Accords recognize that the territory of Vietnam is temporarily separated into two states and as a corollary, that there exists a constitutional and legal government in South Vietnam. It must be clear that North Vietnam cannot assume for itself the right to invade South Vietnam at any moment.

B. The important question of the withdrawal of North Vietnamese forces from South Vietnam is also under negotiation. As a result of infiltrations effected in the past and of the open invasion carried out this year, North Vietnam's army has presently no less than 300,000 troops in South Vietnam, who constitute a mortal threat to the security of the Republic of Vietnam, at present as well as in the future, in case of a cease-fire.

C. Although there has been some change in the proposals previously put forward by the other side, the political arrangements are still under discussion. The Republic of Vietnam is determined to assure arrangements which reflect political realities in South Vietnam and respect basic principles of freedom and democracy as translated in the practice of "one man one vote" in the Republic of Vietnam. Any solution must maintain the constitutional and legal structure adopted by the people of the Republic of Vietnam.

6. There are many other points in the proposed cease-fire agreement which are less important but still require a thorough examination by the Government of the Republic of Vietnam. It is regrettable though that the Government of the Republic of Vietnam had been consulted in a so short period of time that it therefore has not been in a position to examine them in detail.

7. The position of the Government of the Republic of Vietnam is that the Hanoi authorities should hold direct discussions with the Republic of Vietnam to find a solution to the conflict. The Republic of Vietnam has repeatedly proposed bilateral discussions with Hanoi either open or secret, any time anywhere.

8. Problems with regard to the so-called National Liberation Front are a matter of internal affairs of the Republic of Vietnam, and the Government of the Republic of Vietnam has pledged to solve them within the democratic framework and in a spirit of national reconciliation.

Source: Gareth Porter, ed., *Vietnam: A History in Documents* (New York: New American Library, 1981), 410–411.

207. Henry Kissinger, National Security Advisor: News Conference, October 26, 1972 [Excerpt]

Introduction

Returning from Saigon, U.S. national security adviser Henry Kissinger held a nationally televised press conference in which he struck a very positive note about the prospects for peace. In this portion of the transcript, Kissinger glosses over the fundamental objections raised by President Nguyen Van Thieu of the Republic of Vietnam (RVN, South Vietnam), stating only that a half dozen matters needed to be hammered out, including "certain ambiguities," "linguistic problems," and "technical problems." He does not mention that the United States would be presenting substantial demands that will change the character of the document already agreed to and says that it should take no more than one more meeting and "several hours of work" to achieve final agreement.

Primary Source

Now, what is it, then, that prevents the completion of the agreement? Why is it that we have asked for one more meeting with the North Vietnamese to work out a final text? The principal reason is that in a negotiation that was stalemated for five years, and which did not really make a breakthrough until October 8, many of the general principles were clearly understood before the breakthrough, but as one elaborated the text, many of the nuances on which the implementation will ultimately depend became more and more apparent.

It was obvious, it was natural, that when we were talking about the abstract desirability of a cease-fire that neither side was perhaps as precise as it had to become later about the timing and staging of a cease-fire in a country in which there are no clear frontlines. And also the acceptance on our part of the North Vietnamese insistence on an accelerated schedule meant that texts could never be conformed, that English and Vietnamese texts tended to lag behind each other, and that ambiguities in formulation arose that require one more meeting to straighten out.

Let me give you a few examples, and I think you will understand that we are talking here of a different problem than what occupied us in the many sessions I have had with you ladies and gentlemen about the problem of peace in Vietnam, sessions which concerned abstract theories of what approach might succeed.

We are talking here about six or seven very concrete issues that, with anything like the good will that has already been shown, can easily be settled. For example, it has become apparent to us that there will be great temptation for the cease-fire to be paralled by a last effort to seize as much territory as possible and perhaps to extend operations for long enough to establish political control over a given area.

We would like to avoid the dangers of the loss of life, perhaps in some areas even of the massacre that may be inherent in this, and we therefore want to discuss methods by which the international supervisory body can be put in place at the same time that the cease-fire is promulgated.

The Secretary of State has already had preliminary conversations with some of the countries that are being asked to join this body in order to speed up this process.

Secondly, because of the different political circumstances in each of the Indo-Chinese countries, the relationship of military operations there to the end of the war in Viet-Nam, or cease-fires there in relation to the end of the war in Viet-Nam, is somewhat complex; and we would like to discuss more concretely how to compress this time as much as possible.

There were certain ambiguities that were raised by the interview that the North Vietnamese Prime Minister, Pham Van Dong, gave to one of the weekly journals in which he seemed to be, with respect to one or two points, under a misapprehension as to what the agreement contained, and at any rate, we would like to have that clarified.

There are linguistic problems. For example, we call the National Council of Reconciliation an administrative structure in order to make clear that we do not see it as anything comparable to a coalition government. We want to make sure that the Vietnamese text conveys the same meaning.

I must add that the words "administrative structure" were given to us in English by the Vietnamese, so this is not a maneuver on our part.

There are some technical problems as to what clauses of the Geneva accords to refer to in certain sections of the document, and there is a problem which was never settled in which the North Vietnamese, as they have pointed out in their broadcast, have proposed that the agreement be signed by the United States and North Viet-Nam—we on behalf of Saigon, they on behalf of their allies in South Viet-Nam.

We have always held the view that we would leave it up to our allies whether they wanted a two-power document or whether they wanted to sign themselves a document that establishes peace in their country. Now, they prefer to participate in the signing of the peace, and it seems to us not an unreasonable proposal that a country on whose territory a war has been fought and whose population has been uprooted and has suffered so greatly—that

it should have the right to sign its own peace treaty. This, again, strikes us as a not insuperable difficulty, but its acceptance will require the redrafting of certain sections of the document, and that, again, is a job that will require several hours of work.

We have asked the North Vietnamese to meet with us on any date of their choice. We have, as has been reported, restricted our bombing, in effect, to the battle area in order to show our good will and to indicate that we are working within the framework of existing agreements.

We remain convinced that the issues that I have mentioned are soluble in a very brief period of time. We have undertaken, and I repeat it here publicly, to settle them at one more meeting and to remain at that meeting for as long as is necessary to complete the agreement.

Source: U.S. Congress, Senate, *Background Information Relating to Southeast Asia and Vietnam,* 7th rev. ed. (Washington, DC: U.S. Government Printing Office, 1974), 490–491.

208. North Vietnamese Government Statement, October 26, 1972 [Excerpt]

Introduction

Furious that the U.S. government was now demanding changes in the peace treaty that it had already agreed to, the government of the Democratic Republic of Vietnam (DRV, North Vietnam) released its record of the last stages of the Paris negotiations. Washington did not challenge the accuracy of Hanoi's statement.

Primary Source

With a view to making the negotiations progress, at the private meeting on October 8, 1972, the DRV side took a new, extremely important initiative: it put forward a draft "agreement on ending the war and restoring peace in Vietnam," and proposed that the Government of the Democratic Republic of Vietnam, with the concurrence of the Provisional Revolutionary Government of the Republic of South Vietnam, and the Government of the United States of America, with the concurrence of the Government of the Republic of Vietnam, immediately agreed upon and signed [as received] this agreement to rapidly restore peace in Vietnam. In that draft agreement, the DRV side proposed a cessation of the war throughout Vietnam, a cease-fire in South Vietnam, an end to all U.S. military involvement in Vietnam, a total withdrawal from South Vietnam of troops of the United States and those of the foreign countries allied with the United States and with the Republic of Vietnam, and the return of all captured and detained personnel of the parties. From the enforcement of the cease-fire to the installation of the government formed after free and democratic general elections, the two present administrations in South Vietnam will remain in existence with their respective domestic and external functions.

These two administrations shall immediately hold consultations with a view to the exercise of the South Vietnamese people's right to self-determination, achieving national concord, ensuring the democratic liberties of the South Vietnamese people, and forming an administration of national concord which shall have the task of promoting the South Vietnamese parties' implementation of the signed agreements and organizing general elections in South Vietnam. The two South Vietnamese parties shall settle together the internal matters of South Vietnam within three months after the cease-fire comes into effect. Thus the Vietnam problem will be settled in two stages in accordance with the oft-expressed desire of the American side: The first stage will include a cessation of the war in Vietnam, a cease-fire in South Vietnam, a cessation of the U.S. military involvement in South Vietnam and an agreement on the principles for the exercise of the South Vietnamese people's right to self-determination. In the second stage, the two South Vietnamese parties will settle together the internal matters of South Vietnam. The DRV side proposed, that the Democratic Republic of Vietnam and the United States sign this agreement by mid-October 1972.

The above initiative of the Government of the Democratic Republic of Vietnam brought the negotiations on the Vietnam problem, which had dragged on for four years now, onto the path to a settlement. The American side itself admitted that the draft "agreement on ending the war and restoring peace in Vietnam" put forward by the DRV side was indeed an important and very fundamental document which opened up the way to an early settlement.

After several days of negotiations, on October 17, 1972, the Democratic Republic of Vietnam and the United States reached agreement on almost all problems on the basis of the draft agreement of the Democratic Republic of Vietnam, except for only two unagreed issues. With its goodwill, the DRV side did its utmost to remove the last obstacles in accepting the American side's proposals on the two remaining questions in the agreement. In his October 10, 1972 message to the premier of the Democratic Republic of Vietnam, the President of the United States appreciated the goodwill of the Democratic Republic of Vietnam, and confirmed that the formulation of the agreement could be considered complete. But in the same message, he raised a number of complex points. Desirous of rapidly ending the war and restoring peace in Vietnam, the Government of the Democratic Republic of Vietnam clearly explained its views on this subject. In his October 22, 1972 message, the President of the United States expressed satisfaction with the explanations given by the Government of the Democratic Republic of Vietnam. Thus by October 22, 1972, the

formulation of the agreement was complete. The main issues of the agreement which have been agreed upon may be summarized as follows:

(1) The United States respects the independence, sovereignty, unity and territorial integrity of Vietnam as recognized by the 1954 Geneva agreements.

(2) Twenty-four hours after the signing of the agreement, a cease-fire shall be observed throughout South Vietnam. The United States will stop all its military activities, and end the bombing and mining in North Vietnam. Within 60 days, there will be a total withdrawal from South Vietnam of troops and military personnel of the United States and those of the foreign countries allied with the United States and with the Republic of Vietnam. The two South Vietnamese parties shall not accept the introduction of troops, military advisors and military personnel, armaments, munitions, and war material into South Vietnam. The two South Vietnamese parties shall be permitted to make periodical replacements of armaments, munitions, and war material that have been worn out or damaged after the ceasefire, on the basis of piece for piece of similar characteristics and properties. The United States will not continue its military involvement or intervene in the internal affairs of South Vietnam.

(3) The return of all captured personnel of the parties shall be carried out simultaneously with the U.S. troops withdrawal.

(4) The principles for the exercise of the South Vietnamese people's right to self-determination are as follows: The South Vietnamese people shall decide themselves the political future of South Vietnam through genuinely free and democratic general elections under international supervision; the United States is not committed to any political tendency or to any personality in South Vietnam, and it does not seek to impose a pro-American regime in Saigon; national reconciliation and concord will be achieved, the democratic liberties of the people ensured; an administrative structure called the National Council of National Reconciliation and Concord of three equal segments will be set up to promote the implementation of the signed agreements by the Provisional Revolutionary Government of the Republic of South Vietnam and the Government of the Republic of Vietnam and to organize the general elections, the two South Vietnamese parties will consult about the formation of councils at lower levels; the question of Vietnamese armed forces in South Vietnam shall be settled by the South Vietnamese parties in a spirit of national reconciliation and concord, equality and mutual respect, without foreign interference, in accordance with the post-war situation; among the questions to be discussed by the two South Vietnamese parties shall sign an agreement on the internal matters of South Vietnam as soon possible and will do their utmost to accomplish this within three months after the cease-fire comes into effect.

(5) The reunification of Vietnam shall be carried out step by step through peaceful means.

(6) There will be formed a four-party joint military commission, and a joint military commission of the two South Vietnamese parties.

An international commission of control and supervision shall be established.

An international guarantee conference on Vietnam will be convened within 30 days of the signing of this agreement.

(7) The Government of the Democratic Republic of Vietnam, the Provisional Revolutionary Government of the Republic of South Vietnam, the Government of the United States of America, and the Government of the Republic of Vietnam shall strictly respect the Cambodian and Lao peoples' fundamental national rights as recognized by the 1954 Geneva agreements on Indochina and the 1962 Geneva agreements on Laos, i.e., the independence, sovereignty, unity and territorial integrity of these countries. They shall respect the neutrality of Cambodia and Laos. The Government of the Democratic Republic of Vietnam, the Provisional Revolutionary Government of the Republic of South Vietnam, the Government of the United States of America and the Government of the Republic of Vietnam undertake to refrain from using the territory of Cambodia and the territory of Laos to encroach on the sovereignty and security of other countries. Foreign countries shall put an end to all military activities in Laos and Cambodia, totally withdraw from and refrain reintroducing into these two countries troops, military advisers and military personnel, armaments, munitions and war material. The internal affairs of Cambodia and Laos shall be settled by the people of each of these countries without foreign interference.

The problems existing between the three Indochinese countries shall be settled by the Indochinese parties on the basis of respect for each other's independence, sovereignty, and territorial integrity, and non-interference in each other's internal affairs.

(8) The ending of the war, the restoration of peace in Vietnam will create conditions for establishing a new, equal, and mutually beneficial relationship between the Democratic Republic of Vietnam and the United States. The United States will contribute to healing the wounds of war and to post-war reconstruction in the Democratic Republic of Vietnam and throughout Indochina.

(9) This agreement shall come into force as of its signing. It will be strictly implemented by all the parties concerned.

The two parties have also agreed on a schedule for the signing of the agreement. On October 9, 1972, at the proposal of the U.S. side,

it was agreed that on October 18, 1972, the United States would stop the bombing and mining in North Vietnam; on October 19, 1972, the two parties would initial the text of the agreement in Hanoi; on October 26, 1972, the foreign ministers of the two countries would formally sign the agreement in Paris.

On October 11, 1972, the U.S. side proposed the following change to the schedule: On October 21, 1972, the United States would stop the bombing and mining in North Vietnam; on October 22, 1972, the two parties would initial the text of the agreement in Hanoi; on October 30, 1972, the foreign ministers of the two countries would formally sign the agreement in Paris. The Democratic Republic of Vietnam agreed to the new U.S. schedule.

On October 20, 1972, under the pretext that there still remained a number of unagreed points, the U.S. side again put forth another schedule: On October 23, 1972, the United States would stop the bombing and mining in North Vietnam; on October 24, 1972, the two parties would initial the text of the agreement in Hanoi; on October 31, 1972, the foreign ministers of the two countries would formally sign the agreement in Paris. Despite the fact that the U.S. side had changed many times what had been agreed upon, the DRV side with its goodwill again agreed to the U.S. proposal while stressing that the U.S. side should not under any pretext change the agreed schedule.

Thus, by October 22, 1972, the DRV side and the U.S. side had agreed both on the full text of the "agreement on ending the war and restoring peace in Vietnam" and on a schedule to be observed for the formal signing of the agreement on October 31, 1972. Obviously, the two sides had agreed upon an agreement of extremely important significance, which meets the wishes of the peoples in Vietnam, the United States and the world.

But on October 23, 1972, contrary to its pledges, the U.S. side again referred to difficulties in Saigon, demanded that the negotiations be continued for resolving new problems, and did not say anything about the implementation of its commitments under the agreed schedule. This behaviour of the U.S. side has brought about a very serious situation which risks to jeopardize the signing of the "agreement on ending the war and restoring peace in Vietnam."

The so-called difficulties in Saigon represent a mere pretext to delay the implementation of the U.S. commitments, because it is public knowledge that the Saigon administration has been rigged up and fostered by the United States. With a mercenary army equipped and paid by the United States, this administration is a tool for carrying out the "Vietnamization" policy and the neocolonialist policy of the United States in violation of the South Vietnamese people's national rights. It is an instrument for the United States to sabotage all peaceful settlement of the Vietnam problem.

Source: U.S. Congress, Senate, *Background Information Relating to Southeast Asia and Vietnam,* 7th rev. ed. (Washington, DC: U.S. Government Printing Office, 1974), 484–487.

209. President Richard Nixon: Letter to President Nguyen Van Thieu, November 14, 1972

Introduction

President Nguyen Van Thieu of the Republic of Vietnam (RVN, South Vietnam) refused to budge on the peace negotiations. U.S. national security adviser Henry Kissinger urged President Richard Nixon to sign the agreement without him, but the president refused, blaming Hanoi for the impasse. Kissinger has suggested that Nixon rejected implementing the October agreement without Thieu because he would have found it awkward prior to the November 1972 presidential election to risk his support among conservatives who were his political base. In order to regain Thieu's cooperation in the peace negotiations, in November Nixon sent Kissinger's deputy General Alexander Haig to Saigon, and in Operation ENHANCE PLUS the Pentagon turned over massive amounts of military equipment to the South Vietnamese armed forces. In this note to Thieu, Nixon spells out the demands that the United States will make of the negotiators from the Democratic Republic of Vietnam (DRV, North Vietnam) in Paris, including the withdrawal of a number of its troops into North Vietnam, but states that he does not expect all U.S. demands to be met. He also hints at a withdrawal of U.S. assistance if Thieu does not agree to the final text reached.

Primary Source

I was pleased to learn from General Haig that you held useful and constructive discussions with him in Saigon in preparation for Dr. Kissinger's forthcoming meeting with North Vietnam's negotiations in Paris.

After studying your letter of November 11 with great care I have concluded that we have made substantial progress towards reaching a common understanding on many of the important issues before us. You can be sure that we will pursue the proposed changes in the draft agreement that General Haig discussed with you with the utmost firmness and that, as these discussions proceed, we shall keep you fully informed through your Ambassador to the Paris Conference on Vietnam who will be briefed daily by Dr. Kissinger.

I understand from your letter and from General Haig's personal report that your principal remaining concern with respect to the draft agreement is the status of North Vietnamese forces now in South Vietnam. As General Haig explained to you, it is our intention to deal with this problem first by seeking to insert a reference to respect for the demilitarized zone in the proposed agreement and, second, by proposing a clause which provides for the reduction and demobilization of forces on both sides in South Vietnam on a one-to-one basis and to have demobilized personnel return to their homes.

Upon reviewing this proposed language, it is my conviction that such a provision can go a long way towards dealing with your concern with respect to North Vietnamese forces. General Haig tells me, however, that you are also seriously concerned about the timing and verification of such reductions. In light of this, I have asked Dr. Kissinger to convey to you, through Ambassador Bunker, some additional clauses we would propose adding to the agreement dealing with each of these points. In addition, I have asked that Dr. Kissinger send you the other technical and less important substantive changes which General Haig did not have the opportunity to discuss with you because they had not yet been fully developed in Washington. With these proposed modifications, I think you will agree that we have done everything we can to improve the existing draft while remaining within its general framework.

You also raise in your letter the question of participation by other Asian countries in the International Conference. As you know, the presently contemplated composition are the permanent members of the United Nations Security Council, the members of the ICCS, the parties to the Paris Conference on Vietnam and the Secretary General of the United Nations. We seriously considered Cambodian and Laotian participation but decided that these would be unnecessary complications with respect to representation. We do not, however, exclude the possibility of delegations from these countries participating in an observer status at the invitation of the conference. As for Japan, this question was raised earlier in our negotiations with Hanoi and set aside because it inevitably raises the possibility of Indian participation. I have, however, asked that Dr. Kissinger raise this matter again in Paris and he will inform your representative what progress we make on this. What we must recognize as a practical matter is that participation of Japan is very likely to lead to the participation of India. We would appreciate hearing your preference on whether it is better to include both countries or neither of them.

Finally, in respect to the composition of the ICCS, I must say in all candor that I do not share your view that its contemplated membership is unbalanced. I am hopeful that it will prove to be a useful mechanism in detecting and reporting violations of the agreement. In any event, what we both must recognize is that the supervisory mechanism in itself is in no measure as important as our own firm determination to see to it that the agreement works and our vigilance with respect to the prospect of its violation.

I will not repeat here all that I said to you in my letter of November 8, but I do wish to reaffirm its essential content and stress again my determination to work towards an early agreement along the lines of the schedule which General Haig explained to you. I must explain in all frankness that while we will do our very best to secure the changes in the agreement which General Haig discussed with you and those additional ones which Ambassador Bunker will bring you, we cannot expect to secure them all. For example, it is unrealistic to assume that we will be able to secure the absolute assurances which you would hope to have on the troop issue.

But far more important than what we say in the agreement on this issue is what we do in the event the enemy renews its aggression. You have my absolute assurance that if Hanoi fails to abide by the terms of this agreement it is my intention to take swift and severe retaliatory action.

I believe the existing agreement to be an essentially sound one which should become even more so if we succeed in obtaining some of the changes we have discussed. Our best assurance of success is to move into this new situation with confidence and cooperation.

With this attitude and the inherent strength of your government and army on the ground in South Vietnam, I am confident this agreement will be a successful one.

If, on the other hand, we are unable to agree on the course that I have outlined, it is difficult for me to see how we will be able to continue our common effort towards securing a just and honorable peace. As General Haig told you I would with great reluctance be forced to consider other alternatives. For this reason, it is essential that we have your agreement as we proceed into our next meeting with Hanoi's negotiators. And I strongly urge you and your advisors to work promptly with Ambassador Bunker and Our Mission in Saigon on the many practical problems which will face us in implementing the agreement. I cannot overemphasize the urgency of the task at hand nor my unalterable determination to proceed along the course which we have outlined.

Above all we must bear in mind what will really maintain the agreement. It is not any particular clause in the agreement but our joint willingness to maintain its clauses. I repeat my personal assurances to you that the United States will react very strongly and rapidly to any violation of the agreement. But in order to do this effectively it is essential that I have public support and that your Government does not emerge as the obstacle to a peace which [the] American public now universally desires. It is for this reason that I am pressing for the acceptance of an agreement which I am convinced is honorable and fair and which can be made essentially secure by our joint determination.

Mrs. Nixon joins me in extending our warmest personal regards to Madame Thieu and to you. We look forward to seeing you again at our home in California once the just peace we have both fought for so long is finally achieved.

Source: *Foreign Relations of the United States, 1969–1976,* Vol. 9 (Washington, DC: U.S. Government Printing Office, 2010), 395–398.

210. President Richard Nixon: Letter to President Nguyen Van Thieu, January 5, 1973

Introduction

On December 13 with negotiations in Paris, which had resumed in early November, having broken down, U.S. president Richard Nixon chose to blame the government of the Democratic Republic of Vietnam (DRV, North Vietnam) for the impasse rather than blaming President Nguyen Van Thieu of the Republic of Vietnam (RVN, South Vietnam), who had insisted on changes in the document that the United States had already agreed to. Nixon gave Hanoi an ultimatum to return to the conference table within 72 hours "or else." When the North Vietnamese leadership rejected this, on December 18 Nixon launched new air raids against North Vietnam. Dubbed LINEBACKER II and also known as the Christmas Bombings, this 11-day air campaign saw North Vietnam shoot down 15 U.S. B-52 bombers but left the North Vietnamese air defense in a shambles and virtually all military targets destroyed. With the North Vietnamese leaders unwilling to risk attacks on neighborhoods and its vital dike system, they agreed to return to the negotiating table. In this letter to Thieu, Nixon warns the South Vietnamese president that his refusal to agree to the terms hammered out in Paris will jeopardize future U.S. aid, but Nixon also extends a pledge to Thieu—kept secret from the American people—that the United States will response to any North Vietnamese violation of the agreed-upon peace terms with "full force" against North Vietnam.

Primary Source

This will acknowledge your letter of December 20, 1972.

There is nothing substantial that I can add to my many previous messages, including my December 17 letter, which clearly stated my opinions and intentions. With respect to the question of North Vietnamese troops, we will again present your views to the Communists as we have done vigorously at every other opportunity in the negotiations. The result is certain to be once more the rejection of our position. We have explained to you repeatedly why we believe the problem of North Vietnamese troops is manageable under the agreement, and I see no reason to repeat all the arguments.

We will proceed next week in Paris along the lines that General [Alexander] Haig explained to you. Accordingly, if the North Vietnamese meet our concerns on the two outstanding substantive issues in the agreement, concerning the DMZ and the method of signing, and if we can arrange acceptable supervisory machinery, we will proceed to conclude the settlement. The gravest consequences would then ensue if your government chose to reject the agreement and split off from the United States. As I said in my December 17 letter, "I am convinced that your refusal to join us would be an invitation to disaster—to the loss of all that we together have fought for over the past decade. It would be inexcusable above all because we will have lost a just and honorable alternative."

As we enter this new round of talks, I hope that our countries will now show a united front. It is imperative for our common objectives that your government take no further actions that complicate our task and would make more difficult the acceptance of the settlement by all parties. We will keep you informed of the negotiations in Paris through daily briefings of Ambassador Lam.

I can only repeat what I have so often said: The best guarantee for the survival of South Vietnam is the unity of our two countries which would be gravely jeopardized if you persist in your present course. The actions of our Congress since its return have clearly borne out the many warnings we have made.

Should you decide, as I trust you will, to go with us, you have my assurance of continued assistance in the post-settlement period and that we will respond with full force should the settlement be violated by North Vietnam. So once more I conclude with an appeal to you to close ranks with us.

Source: *Foreign Relations of the United States, 1969–1976,* Vol. 9 (Washington, DC: U.S. Government Printing Office, 2010), 906.

211. COSVN Directive 02/73: Policies Related to the Political Settlement and Cease-Fire, January 19, 1973 [Excerpt]

Introduction

Even before a final peace treaty was signed in Paris, the leadership of the Democratic Republic of Vietnam (DRV, North Vietnam) informed the Central Office for South Vietnam (COSVN), the Communist headquarters running the war in the Republic of Vietnam (RVN, South Vietnam), that agreement was near. This COSVN document sets the official Communist position regarding implementation of the peace agreement.

Primary Source

II. Direction of Our Policies in the Event the Agreement Is Signed and the Cease-Fire Goes into Effect

1. In the face of the new situation, in order to ensure the fulfillment of our basic mission which is to achieve the national democratic revolution in the South as a step toward peacefully unifying our country, the direction of our immediate mission when the Agreement is signed is as follows:

"To mobilize the entire Party and people to bring our victory into full play by taking part in the high political movement in the three areas using the slogans calling for 'peace, independence, democracy, rice and clothing for the people, national concord' and demanding the implementation of the Agreement. To disintegrate and seriously collapse the puppet army and Government, take over control of the rural area, seize power at the base level; simultaneously, to build and develop our political and armed forces, build and strengthen the revolutionary administration and liberated area in all aspects, smash all enemy schemes to sabotage the Agreement, prevent large scale conflicts, maintain peace, hold general elections as provided for in the Agreement, bring the South Viet-Nam revolution toward the fulfillment of its basic objectives, at the same time, maintain constant alertness and readiness to deal with the U.S. imperialists' plot to resume hostilities."

In order to fulfill this immediate mission, we must strive to meet the following key requirements:

First, we must reach unity of mind in the entire Party with regard to the victory already gained. We must confidently strive to carry out the Party's immediate political mission at all costs and, at the same time, remain firm in the event the Americans obdurately renege their commitments, sabotage the implementation of the Agreement or even resume hostilities.

Second, we must concentrate efforts to turn the political struggle movement into a high revolutionary movement focussing on the principal slogans mentioned above.

Third, we must strive to severely disintegrate and collapse the puppet army and government, especially at the base level.

Fourth, we must build our forces in every aspect so they become strong, stable and present everywhere, especially in prosperous and populated areas, in the cities, in the religious communities. Development [of our forces] must go hand in hand with consolidation and preservation of forces, cadres and base organizations.

Fifth, we must strengthen our base areas and liberated areas in all aspects, consolidate and expand the revolutionary administration in all areas, and continue to bring the enemy-controlled area and cities to a new step of evolution.

Sixth, we must maintain firmly and improve the development of our armed forces in the new situation, strive to strengthen our three-troop-category forces and make sure that they are ready in any circumstance.

Seventh, we must build up the Party's strength, especially the strength of base-level Party chapters.

2. Strategic principles and struggle guidelines [which] we must fully grasp in the new phase.

a. The following strategic principles must be fully grasped:

One: We must fully grasp the objective of the national democratic revolution and closely combine the national mission with the democratic mission in the new situation.

Therefore, the slogans calling for "peace, independence, democracy, rice and clothing, national concord" are not only principal slogans to be used in the immediate future but also strategic slogans to be used during the whole new phase.

Two: We must fully grasp the offensive strategy of pushing back the enemy step by step and winning victory bit by bit before achieving complete victory. On the basis of persisting in the thought of unceasing and continuous revolution, we must create opportunities and grasp the opportunities in order to accelerate the development of the revolution in the new phase.

Three: We must fully grasp the concept of violence in the context of the new situation, in the political struggle phase. We must absolutely bring into play the masses' political violence, and stand ready to surmount fierceness and bloodshed in the course of promoting the political movement into a high tide. At the same time, we must not neglect military violence. On the contrary, we must stand constantly ready, especially we must unceasingly build up our three-troop–category armed forces as a firm support for our political struggle.

Four: We must closely associate the mission of achieving the national democratic revolution in the South with the mission of protecting and building socialism in the North as a step toward the unification of our country.

Five: We must coordinate the revolutionary movement in South Viet-Nam with the revolutionary movements in Kampuchea and Laos and the Indochinese revolution in general, coordinate the struggle movement for peace, independence, democracy, improvement of living standards with the movement for peace, national liberation and socialism all over the world.

b. We must fully grasp the following guideline and method of operation:

One: We must closely combine political struggle with armed struggle and legalistic struggle, using political struggle as the base, armed struggle as support, while bringing into full play the legalistic effects of the Agreement.

Two: We must closely combine the overt form of organization with the semi-overt and clandestine forms of organization, using the clandestine form as a base.

Three: We must closely coordinate our offensive activities with activities to build our forces in all aspects for the purpose of creating a new position, strength and situation.

Four: We must closely coordinate the masses' struggle in the three strategic areas with the struggle of the overt organizations which are provided for in the Agreement [the Joint Military Commission, the National Council of National Reconciliation and Concord, and the Prisoner Exchange Commission], using the masses' struggle as a base while bringing into full play the struggling effects of the overt organizations.

Source: U.S. Mission in Vietnam, *Viet-Nam and Research Notes, Document 113* (Carlisle Barracks, PA: Library of the U.S. Army Military History Institute, June 1973), 1–8.

212. Paris Peace Agreement, January 27, 1973 [Excerpt]

Introduction

On January 23, 1973, the Democratic Republic of Vietnam (DRV, North Vietnam) and the United States concluded a new peace agreement, which was now imposed on the government of the Republic of Vietnam (RVN, South Vietnam). Four parties signed: the United States, South Vietnam, North Vietnam, and the Provisional Revolutionary Government (PRG), the Communist provisional government in South Vietnam. Despite a few cosmetic changes, the agreement was for all practical purposes identical to that signed the previous October. The agreement acknowledges the "independence, sovereignty, unity and territorial integrity of Viet-Nam as recognized by the 1954 Geneva Agreements on Vietnam." This was what Hanoi had argued for years: that Vietnam was one country and that its effort in South Vietnam was not foreign aggression but rather a legitimate struggle for national independence and unity. The agreement provides for a cease-fire, withdrawal of all U.S. troops and advisers from South Vietnam, release of prisoners, the formation of a Council of National Reconciliation and Concord to resolve disagreements between South

Vietnam and North Vietnam and organize new general elections, new supervisory machinery (the International Commission of Control and Supervision, consisting of representatives of Canada, Hungary, Poland, and Indonesia), and withdrawal of foreign troops from Laos and Cambodia. The agreement also leaves in place in South Vietnam an estimated 150,000 People's Army of Vietnam (PAVN, North Vietnamese Army) troops.

Primary Source

Agreement on Ending the War and Restoring Peace in Vietnam

The Parties participating in the Paris Conference on Viet-Nam,

With a view to ending the war and restoring peace in Viet-Nam on the basis of respect for the Vietnamese people's fundamental national rights and the South Vietnamese people's right to self-determination, and to contributing to the consolidation of peace in Asia and the world.

Have agreed on the following provisions and undertake to respect and to implement them:

Chapter I The Vietnamese People's Fundamental National Rights

Article 1. The United States and all other countries respect the independence, sovereignty, unity, and territorial integrity of Viet-Nam as recognized by the 1954 Geneva Agreements on Viet-Nam.

Chapter II Cessation of Hostilities—Withdrawal of Troops

Article 2. A cease-fire shall be observed throughout South Viet-Nam as of 2400 hours G.M.T., on January 27, 1973.

At the same hour, the United States will stop all its military activities against the territory of the Democratic Republic of Viet-Nam by ground, air and naval forces, wherever they may be based, and end the mining of the territorial waters, ports, harbors, and waterways of the Democratic Republic of Viet-Nam. The United States will remove, permanently deactivate or destroy all the mines in the territorial waters, ports, harbors, and waterways of North Viet-Nam as soon as this Agreement goes into effect.

The complete cessation of hostilities mentioned in this Article shall be durable and without limit of time.

Article 3. The parties undertake to maintain the cease-fire and to ensure a lasting and stable peace.

As soon as the cease-fire goes into effect:

a. The United States forces and those of the other foreign countries allied with the United States and the Republic of Viet-Nam shall remain in-place pending the implementation of the plan of troop withdrawal. The Four-Party Joint Military Commission described in Article 16 [not included here] shall determine the modalities.

b. The armed forces of the two South Vietnamese parties shall remain in-place. The Two-Party Joint Military Commission described in Article 17 [not included here] shall determine the areas controlled by each party and the modalities of stationing.

c. The regular forces of all services and arms and the irregular forces of the parties in South Viet-Nam shall stop all offensive activities against each other and shall strictly abide by the following stipulations:

—All acts of force on the ground, in the air, and on the sea shall be prohibited;
—All hostile acts, terrorism and reprisals by both sides will be banned.

Article 4. The United States will not continue its military involvement or intervene in the internal affairs of South Viet-Nam.

Article 5. Within sixty days of the signing of this Agreement, there will be a total withdrawal from South Viet-Nam of troops, military advisers, and military personnel, including technical military personnel and military personnel associated with the pacification program, armaments, munitions, and war material of the United States and those of the other foreign countries mentioned in Article 3 (a). Advisers from the above-mentioned countries to all paramilitary organizations and the police force will also be withdrawn within the same period of time.

Article 6. The dismantlement of all military bases in South Viet-Nam of the United States and of the other foreign countries mentioned in Article 3 (a) shall be completed within sixty days of the signing of this Agreement.

Article 7. From the enforcement of the cease-fire to the formation of the government provided for in Article 9 (b) and 14 of this Agreement, the two South Vietnamese parties shall not accept the introduction of troops, military advisers, and military personnel including technical military personnel, armaments, munitions, and war material into South Viet-Nam.

The two South Vietnamese parties shall be permitted to make periodic replacement of armaments, munitions and war material which have been destroyed, damaged, worn out or used up after the cease-fire, on the basis of piece-for-piece, of the same characteristics and properties, under the supervision of the Joint Military

Commission of the two South Vietnamese parties and of the International Commission of Control and Supervision.

Chapter III   The Return of Captured Military Personnel and Foreign Civilians, and Captured and Detained Vietnamese Civilian Personnel

Article 8

a. The return of captured military personnel and foreign civilians of the parties shall be carried out simultaneously with and completed not later than the same day as the troop withdrawal mentioned in Article 5. The parties shall exchange complete lists of the above-mentioned captured military personnel and foreign civilians on the day of the signing of this Agreement.

b. The Parties shall help each other to get information about those military personnel and foreign civilians of the parties missing in action, to determine the location and take care of the graves of the dead so as to facilitate the exhumation and repatriation of the remains, and to take any such other measures as may be required to get information about those still considered missing in action.

c. The question of the return of Vietnamese civilian personnel captured and detailed in South Viet-Nam will be resolved by the two South Vietnamese parties on the basis of the principles of Article 21 (b) of the Agreement on the Cessation of Hostilities in Viet-Nam of July 20, 1954. The two South Vietnamese parties will do so in a spirit of national reconciliation and concord, with a view to ending hatred and enmity, in order to ease suffering and to reunite families. The two South Vietnamese parties will do their utmost to resolve this question within ninety days after the cease-fire comes into effect.

Chapter IV   The Exercise of the South Vietnamese People's Right to Self-Determination

Article 9. The Government of the United States of America and the Government of the Democratic Republic of Viet-Nam undertake to respect the following principles for the exercise of the South Vietnamese people's right to self-determination:

a. The South Vietnamese people's right to self-determination is sacred, inalienable, and shall be respected by all countries.

b. The South Vietnamese people shall decide themselves the political future of South Viet-Nam through genuinely free and democratic general elections under international supervision.

c. Foreign countries shall not impose any political tendency or personality on the South Vietnamese people.

Article 10. The two South Vietnamese parties undertake to respect the cease-fire and maintain peace in South Viet-Nam, settle all matters of contention through negotiations, and avoid all armed conflict.

Article 11. Immediately after the cease-fire, the two South Vietnamese parties will:

—achieve national reconciliation and concord, end hatred and enmity, prohibit all acts of reprisal and discrimination against individuals or organizations that have collaborated with one side or the other;

—ensure the democratic liberties of the people: personal freedom, freedom of speech, freedom of the press, freedom of meeting, freedom of organization, freedom of political activities, freedom of belief, freedom of movement, freedom of residence, freedom of work, right to property ownership, and right to free enterprise.

Article 12

a. Immediately after the cease-fire, the two South Vietnamese parties shall hold consultations in a spirit of national reconciliation and concord, mutual respect, and mutual non-elimination to set up a National Council of National Reconciliation and Concord of three equal segments. The Council shall operate on the principle of unanimity. After the National Council of National Reconciliation and Concord has assumed its functions, the two South Vietnamese parties will consult about the formation of councils at lower levels. The two South Vietnamese parties shall sign an agreement on the internal matters of South Viet-Nam as soon as possible and do their utmost to accomplish this within ninety days after the cease-fire comes into effect, in keeping with the South Vietnamese people's aspirations for peace, independence and democracy.

b. The National Council of National Reconciliation and Concord shall have the task of promoting the two South Vietnamese parties' implementation of this Agreement, achievement of national reconciliation and concord and ensurance of democratic liberties. The National Council of National Reconciliation and Concord will organize the free and democratic general elections provided for in Article 9 (b) and decide the procedures and modalities of these general elections. The institutions for which the general elections are to be held will be agreed upon through consultations between the two South Vietnamese parties. The National Council of National Reconciliation and Concord will also decide the procedures and modalities of such local elections as the two South Vietnamese parties agree upon.

Article 13. The question of Vietnamese armed forces in South Viet-Nam shall be settled by the two South Vietnamese parties in a spirit of national reconciliation and concord, equality and mutual respect, without foreign interference, in accordance with the postwar situation. Among the questions to be discussed by the two South Vietnamese parties are steps to reduce their military effectives and to demobilize the troops being reduced. The two South Vietnamese parties will accomplish this as soon as possible.

Article 14. South Viet-Nam will pursue a foreign policy of peace and independence. It will be prepared to establish relations with all countries irrespective of their political and social systems on the basis of mutual respect for independence and sovereignty and accept economic and technical aid from any country with no political conditions attached. The acceptance of military aid by South Viet-Nam in the future shall come under the authority of the government set up after the general elections in South Viet-Nam provided for in Article 9 (b).

Chapter V   The Reunification of Viet-Nam and the Relationship Between North and South Viet-Nam

Article 15. The reunification of Viet-Nam shall be carried out step by step through peaceful means on the basis of discussions and agreements between North and South Viet-Nam, without coercion or annexation by either party, and without foreign interference. The time for reunification will be agreed upon by North and South Viet-Nam.

Pending reunification:

a. The military demarcation line between the two zones at the 17th parallel is only provisional and not a political or territorial boundary, as provided for in paragraph 6 of the Final Declaration of the 1954 Geneva Conference.

b. North and South Viet-Nam shall respect the Demilitarized Zone on either side of the Provisional Military Demarcation Line.

c. North and South Viet-Nam shall promptly start negotiations with a view to reestablishing normal relations in various fields. Among the questions to be negotiated are the modalities of civilian movement across the Provisional Military Demarcation Line.

d. North and South Viet-Nam shall not join any military alliance or military bloc and shall not allow foreign powers to maintain military bases, troops, military advisers, and military personnel on their respective territories, as stipulated in the 1954 Geneva Agreements on Viet-Nam.

[…]

Source: "Agreement on Ending the War and Restoring Peace in Vietnam," *Department of State Bulletin* 68(1755) (1973): 169–172.

213. President Richard Nixon: Letter to Pham Van Dong, February 1, 1973 [Excerpt]

Introduction

During the final phase of the peace negotiations in Paris, U.S. negotiator National Security Advisor Henry Kissinger had promised Le Duc Tho, Kissinger's counterpart from the Democratic Republic of Vietnam (DRV, North Vietnam), that U.S. president Richard Nixon would send a letter to North Vietnamese president Pham Van Dong committing the United States to extend postwar reconstruction aid to North Vietnam. Not released publicly until 1977, this letter pledged the establishment of a join commission to negotiate the aid package, tentatively set at $3.25 billion over a five-year period.

Primary Source

The President wishes to inform the Democratic Republic of Vietnam of the principles which will govern United States participation in the postwar reconstruction of North Vietnam. As indicated in Article 21 of the Agreement on Ending the War and Restoring Peace in Vietnam signed in Paris on Jan. 27, 1973, the United States undertakes this participation in accordance with its traditional policies. These principles are as follows:

1. The Government of the United States of America will contribute to postwar reconstruction in North Vietnam without any political conditions.

2. Preliminary United States studies indicate that the appropriate programs for the United States contribution to postwar reconstruction will fall in the range of $3.25 billion of grant aid over five years. Other forms of aid will be agreed upon between the two parties. This estimate is subject to revision and to detailed discussion between the Government of the United States and the Government of the Democratic Republic [of] Vietnam.

3. The United States will propose to the Democratic Republic of Vietnam the establishment of a United States–North Vietnamese joint Economic Commission within 30 days from the date of this message.

4. The function of the commission will be to develop programs for the United States contribution to reconstruction of North Vietnam. This United States contribution will be based upon such factors as:

(a) the needs of North Vietnam arising from the dislocation of war;

(b) The requirements for postwar reconstruction in the agricultural and industrial sectors of North Vietnam's economy.

5. The Joint Economic Commission will have an equal number of representatives from each side. It will agree upon a mechanism to administer the program which will constitute the United States contribution to the reconstruction of North Vietnam. The commission will attempt to complete this agreement within 60 days after its establishment.

6. The two members of the commission will function on the principle of respect for each other's sovereignty, noninterference in each other's internal affairs, equality and mutual benefit. The offices of the commission will be located at a place to be agreed upon by the United States and the Democratic Republic of Vietnam.

7. The United States considers that the implementation of the foregoing principles will prompt economic, trade and other relations between the United States of America and the Democratic Republic of Vietnam and will contribute to insuring a stable and lasting peace in Indochina. These principles accord with the spirit of Chapter VIII of the Agreement on Ending the War and Restoring Peace in Vietnam which was signed in Paris on Jan. 27, 1973. . . .

Source: "Agreement on Ending the War and Restoring Peace in Vietnam," *Department of State Bulletin* 76(1983) (1977): 674–675.

214. COSVN Directive 03/CT 73, March 1973 [Excerpts]

Introduction

Although the United States was no longer at war, fighting continued in the Republic of Vietnam (RVN, South Vietnam) in what many have called the "Third Vietnam War" of 1973–1975. The Paris accords had not delineated territorial boundaries between the two sides and merely specified a "cease-fire in place." As a result, immediately before the truce took hold, heavy fighting occurred, with both sides endeavoring to seize as much territory as possible. In this document, the leadership of the Central Office for South Vietnam (COSVN), the Communist headquarters controlling the war in South Vietnam, admits that its forces have suffered "a number of losses" and calls for an increase in military forces and predicts final victory.

Primary Source

I. Nature of the Situation, the Form of the Struggle between Us and the Enemy at this Time, the Enemy's Plots, and Facts Concerning the Possibilities for Development of the Situation after 60 Days of Implementation of the Ceasefire Agreement.

1. Message No. 775 of 25 February 1973 made it clear that: The main feature of the situation at this time is that the Agreement to End the War and Restore Peace in Viet-Nam (VN) has been signed, and the U.S. must withdraw all its troops and must cease the bombing and shelling of our people with its fleet. However, the U.S. is, on the other hand, shielding its puppets in their not implementing the Ceasefire order and in violating the Agreement.

The situation in South Viet-Nam (SVN) is not yet stable. The instability and complexity of the situation is seen clearly in the following points: Although there is an Agreement to End the War and Restore Peace in VN, in truth in SVN there are many places where the shooting and bombing and shelling continue, and in some places more than prior to the Agreement.

Armed conflict continues without pause because of the enemy's police operations and aggression and infringement, but the scale and the methods are not what they were when the war was still going on and are concentrated in a limited number of areas. There are no B-52's, artillery, fleet, or, actions by aircraft and infantry of the U.S. and satellites.

The puppets are applying pressure and violating the agreement in this way, but they are still bound by the Paris Agreement. They can postpone and delay the implementation of the Agreement, but they cannot altogether not implement it, as in the cases of the initiation of the FPJMC [Four-Party Joint Military Commission], and the TPJMC [Two-Party Joint Military Commission], the International Commission for Control and Supervision (ICCS), the exchange of POW'S.

The form of the struggle between us and the enemy is: The enemy distorts the Ceasefire Agreement, impedes the implementation of the Agreement, creates suspicion and divisions and hatred among the people, and maintains the tense situation.

We disseminate the Agreement broadly, bring out the significance of the Agreement as a great victory, open up the movement of struggle to demand that the enemy implement the Agreement, and follow the trend in demanding peace and national concord among all classes of people—even within the puppet army and puppet government—and this forms our new struggle position in the new situation.

The enemy launches police operations and oppresses and terrorizes the people, not permitting them freedom of movement in order to make their living. At the same time, he launches military operations with air and artillery support, tries to reoccupy the areas he has lost, does damage to the fields and gardens, gathers the people up, and builds additional outposts.

We are determined to foil enemy oppression and aggression by mobilizing the masses to engage in political, armed and military-proselyting struggle in coordination with legality to defend the lives and property of the people, to defend the liberated areas, to defeat the enemy's plots of obstruction and destruction, and to force the enemy to implement the agreement.

The enemy is delaying, creating problems and even engaging in physical abuse with regard to the initiation of the organizations for the implementation of the Agreement (the ICCS, the JMC's, the negotiations between the two SVN parties). The enemy is fabricating and distorting the provisions of the Cease-fire Agreement and its Protocols. We are determined to struggle to initiate the above-named organizations in order to guarantee the implementation of the Agreement according to the time-schedule and the scope of responsibility set forth in the Agreement and its Protocols. . . .

After 60 days, the situation may change as follows: Firstly, if we evaluate the situation of ourselves and the enemy correctly and in good time, exploit quickly the effects of the Ceasefire Agreement, apply the principles and methods for struggles, prevent the enemy from striking into our territory, bring the political and military-proselyting movements of the masses up to meet requirements, and coordinate the military victories which have forced the enemy to cease his advances and to implement the Cease-fire Agreement—then the situation will develop every day more to our advantage. We will repel the enemy's plot to impede the Ceasefire Agreement and advance our movement another step, continuing to win new victories. As in reality there are two governments, two armies and two areas of control, it is not possible to avoid having scattered, small military engagements, but we must try hard to hold the enemy back and we must know how to defeat the enemy and to force him to implement the Agreement. Secondly, if we make the changes in directions too slowly and are not resolute in attacking the enemy, the enemy will continue to infringe further on us and to create a tense situation to cause us greater difficulties, to limit and paralyze the actions of the TPJMC, and to draw out the talks concerning the establishment of the National Council for National Reconciliation and Concord (NCNRC); the enemy will create a political and military situation to his advantage. Thirdly, it is also possible that, because of his collapse and isolation from which recovery is impossible, the enemy will draw out matters and the current situation will collapse entirely; or, because they hope to achieve victory by arms, we cannot exclude the possibility the enemy may initiate an adventurous civil war. We must be prepared to smother any such action by the enemy and to win a great victory for the nationalist democratic revolution in SVN.

How the situation develops will depend on our subjective efforts, particularly on whether or not we can control our thinking so we can retain the initiative, on whether or not we can change the directions of our policies and methods for struggle to be appropriate, and on whether or not we have the resolve to develop ourselves in every way in order to change the ratio of forces between us and the enemy. . . .

C) We have the Paris Agreement as the new element in the current situation and as the new weapon with which to attack the enemy and to develop our strength. We need to avoid two attitudes:

1. Holding that the Paris Agreement is a complete weapon and can replace the other types of struggle, imagining that with the Agreement we can solve all our problems, not seeing that the ratio of forces is actually the decisive factor. With the Paris Agreement, we have an additional sharp weapon with which to attack the enemy. The agreement creates more advantageous circumstances for us to develop more power and better position and to change the ratio of forces between us and the enemy in our favor.

2. Holding that the enemy has so seriously broken the Agreement that it no longer is valid and has no value, feeling that the current situation is "a return to normal war" as before, or "undeclared war" and, when the U.S. has withdrawn completely they will resume the war immediately. This attitude leads to the idea of going back a step and engaging in armed operations as before; it does not see that the Agreement has been achieved only by the blood of our people in struggle, and the Agreement opens for us a new phase and creates for us a new weapon and new circumstances in our favor for attack upon the enemy. This attitude is the main mistaken attitude at this time. It must be recognized that we have the strength of the masses, the strength of all our armed forces, and now we have the legal sanction to apply to give us the cutting edge of the three strengths in all our struggles, and so we have obtained a new considerable strength for attack upon the enemy. This strength must be shown concretely in the activities of our armed forces and in the three prongs in the villages, in order to develop the new assault posture in the new situation.

D) Because of a lack of deep awareness of the enemy's so very stubborn plots and because of simplistic assessments when the Ceasefire Agreement went into effect, our mental and material preparations to contend steadfastly with the enemy have not been sufficient. In many places the people who have come forth are still confused about the application of the struggle principles and methods in the new situation, while the enemy is infringing on us in many places and is secretly causing us a number of losses and difficulties, but in general the trend of the development of the situation is in our favor. The enemy builds more outposts in many places, but he is drawn-out and has many shortcomings— his soldiers and a large number of the outpost commanders and personnel of the puppet government are now suffering from low morale, are tired and disgusted, and want peace. We must calmly and correctly evaluate the nature of the situation in our own areas, make plans for implementation, and avoid two wrong attitudes:

1. Anxiety and subjectivity in wanting to contend with the enemy's incursions by expanding the scope of military attacks on all the battlefields, as the only way quickly to recover lost territory.

2. Passivity, feeling that even use of the military cannot restore the previous position, and acceptance of Ceasefire Agreement violations just to maintain our position "whereafter we can advance step by step": The essence of this attitude is acceptance of enemy infringements. The above two attitudes: anxiety and subjectivity, and passivity and loss of confidence and struggle orientation, are both in essence rightist; they are wrong evaluations of the situation and represent a failure to recognize strong and weak points and the enemy's new shortcomings, a loss of firm thinking concerning attacks upon the enemy by the right means and in the right form, and a lack of knowledge of the use of the armed forces in conjunction with the political and military-proselyting and of the new weapon, i.e., the Ceasefire Agreement, in each prong of attack as they are joined tightly together.

Source: U.S. Mission in Vietnam, *Viet-Nam and Research Notes, Document 115* (Carlisle Barracks, PA: Library of the U.S. Army Military History Institute, September 1973), 4–10, 11–13.

215. President Richard Nixon: News Conference, March 15, 1973 [Excerpt]

Introduction

In view of the high level of fighting going on in the Republic of Vietnam (RVN, South Vietnam), U.S. president Richard Nixon sought to pressure the government of the Democratic Republic of Vietnam (DRV, North Vietnam) to halt or to at least reduce significantly the resupply of its forces in South Vietnam. In addition to State Department bulletins, Nixon threatens during a news conference on March 15, 1973, to intervene with airpower. Such U.S. military action would have been highly unlikely given the determination of Congress to end U.S. involvement in Indochina and revelations of Nixon's coverup in the Watergate Scandal.

Primary Source

Q. Mr. President, can you say, sir, how concerned you are about the reports of cease-fire violations in Vietnam.

A. Well, I am concerned about the cease-fire violations. As you ladies and gentlemen will recall, I have consistently pointed out in meetings with you, that we would expect violations because of the nature of the war, the guerrilla nature, and that even in Korea, in which we do not have a guerrilla war, we still have violations. They recede each year, but we still have them. Long, 15, 20 years after the war is over.

In the case of these violations, we are concerned about them on two scores. One, because they occur, but two, we are concerned because of another violation that could lead to, we think, rather serious consequences. We do not believe it will. We hope that it will not. And that is the report that you ladies and gentlemen have been receiving from your colleagues in Vietnam with regard to infiltration.

You will note that there have been reports of infiltration by the North Vietnamese into South Vietnam of equipment exceeding the amounts that were agreed upon in the settlement.

Now, some equipment can come in. In other words, replacement equipment, but no new equipment, nothing, which steps up the capacity of the North Vietnamese or the Vietcong to wage war in the South. No new equipment is allowed under the agreement.

Now, as far as that concern is concerned, particularly on the infiltration, that is the more important point, rather than the cease-fire violations which we think, over a period of time, will be reduced—but in terms of the infiltration, I am not going to say publicly what we have said.

I only suggest this: That we have informed the North Vietnamese of our concern about this infiltration and what we believe it to be, a violation of the cease-fire, the cease-fire and the peace agreements. Our concern has also been expressed to other interested parties and I would only suggest that based on my actions over the past four years, that the North Vietnamese should not lightly disregard such expressions of concern, when they are made, with regard to violation. That is all I will say about it.

Q. Mr. President, in connection with this matter, there is a report also that not just equipment, but a new infusion of North Vietnamese combat personnel have been introduced into South Vietnam, which is apart from just equipment. Can you confirm this? Is this partly what you are talking about?

A. Mr. Theis, the reports that we get with regard to infiltration, as you know, are always either too little or too late or too much. And I am not going to confirm that one, except to say that we have noted the report having been made. We, however, are primarily concerned about the equipment, because as far as the personnel are concerned, they could be simply replacement personnel.

Source: *Public Papers of the Presidents of the United States: Richard Nixon, 1973* (Washington, DC: U.S. Government Printing Office, 1975), 205–206.

216. Fulbright-Aiken Amendment: Public Law 93-52, Section 108, July 1, 1973

Introduction

This congressional amendment in effect ties the hands of the Richard Nixon administration regarding Indochina. The amendment specifically prohibits a resumption of bombing or other U.S. combat activity in Indochina.

Primary Source

SEC. 108. Notwithstanding any other provision of law, on or after August 15, 1973, no funds herein or heretofore appropriated may be obligated or expended to finance directly or indirectly combat activities by United States military forces in or over or from off the shores of North Vietnam, South Vietnam, Laos or Cambodia.

Approved July 1, 1973.

> **Source:** U.S. Congress, Senate, *Background Information Relating to Southeast Asia and Vietnam,* 7th rev. ed. (Washington, DC: U.S. Government Printing Office, 1974), 577.

217. War Powers Resolution, November 7, 1973 [Excerpt]

Introduction

First introduced by Senator Jacob K. Javits (R-N.Y.) following the 1970 U.S. invasion of Cambodia, this legislation was related to the American experience in Vietnam and was also the result of an effort by Congress to reassert some of the authority over the military lost to the president from 1941. The law, overwhelmingly passed by Congress on November 7, 1973, limits the war-making powers of the chief executive. The War Powers Resolution of 1973 (Public Law 93-148, 93rd Congress, H.J. Resolution 542, November 7, 1973), simply known as the War Powers Act, requires the president to consult with Congress before military forces are sent into combat abroad or to areas where hostilities are likely and to report in writing within 48 hours after troops are deployed. The president must then terminate the use of military force within 60 to 90 days. The deployment can continue for another 60 days and then for another 30 days beyond that if the president certifies to Congress in writing that the safety of the force so requires. Unless Congress authorizes a continuation through a declaration of war, a concurrent resolution, or other appropriate legislation, the deployment cannot be continued beyond 90 days.

Primary Source

§ 1542. Consultation; initial and regular consultations

The President in every possible instance shall consult with Congress before introducing United States Armed Forces into hostilities or into situations where imminent involvement in hostilities is clearly indicated by the circumstances, and after every such introduction shall consult regularly with the Congress until United States Armed Forces are no longer engaged in hostilities or have been removed from such situations.

§ 1543. Reporting requirement

(a) Written report; time of submission; circumstances necessitating submission; information reported

In the absence of a declaration of war, in any case in which United States Armed Forces are introduced—

(1) into hostilities or into situations where imminent involvement in hostilities is clearly indicated by the circumstances;

(2) into the territory, airspace or waters of a foreign nation, while equipped for combat, except for deployments which relate solely to supply, replacement, repair or training of such forces; or

(3) in numbers which substantially enlarge United States Armed Forces equipped for combat already located in a foreign nation; the President shall submit within 48 hours to the Speaker of the House of Representatives and to the President, pro tempore of the Senate a report, in writing, setting forth—

(A) the circumstances necessitating the introduction of United States Armed Forces;

(B) the constitutional and legislative authority under which such introduction took place; and

(C) the estimated scope and duration of the hostilities or involvement.

(b) Other information reported

The President shall provide such other information as the Congress may request in the fulfillment of its constitutional responsibilities with respect to committing the Nation to war and to the use of United States Armed Forces abroad.

(c) Periodic reports; semiannual requirement

Whenever United States Armed Forces are introduced into hostilities or into any situation described in subsection (a) of this section, the President shall, so long as such armed forces continue to be engaged in such hostilities or situation, report to the Congress periodically on the status of such hostilities or situation as well as on the scope and duration of such hostilities or situation, but in no event shall he report to the Congress less often than once every six months.

§ 1544. Congressional action

(a) Transmittal of report and referral to Congressional Committees; joint request for convening Congress

Each report submitted pursuant to section 1543(a)(1) of this title shall be transmitted to the Speaker of the House of Representatives and to the President pro tempore of the Senate on the same calendar day. Each report so transmitted shall be referred to the Committee on International Relations of the House of Representatives and to the Committee on Foreign Relations of the Senate for appropriate action. If, when the report is transmitted, the Congress has adjourned sine die or has adjourned for any period in excess of three calendar days, the Speaker of the House of Representatives and the President pro tempore of the Senate, if they deem it advisable (or if petitioned by at least 30 percent of the membership of their respective Houses) shall jointly request the President to convene Congress in order that it may consider the report and take appropriate action pursuant to this section.

(b) Termination of use of United States Armed Forces; exceptions; extension period

Within sixty calendar days after a report is submitted or is required to be submitted pursuant to section 1543(a)(1) of this title, whichever is earlier, the President shall terminate any use of United States Armed Forces with respect to which such report was submitted (or required to be submitted), unless the Congress

(1) has declared war or has enacted a specific authorization for such use of United States Armed Forces,
(2) has extended by law such sixty-day period, or
(3) is physically unable to meet as a result of an armed attack upon the United States. Such sixty-day period shall be extended for not more than an additional thirty days if the President determines and certifies to the Congress in writing that unavoidable military necessity respecting the safety of United States Armed Forces requires the continued use of such armed forces in the course of bringing about a prompt removal of such forces.

(c) Concurrent resolution for removal by President of United States Armed Forces

Notwithstanding subsection (b) of this section, at any time that United States Armed Forces are engaged in hostilities outside the territory of the United States, its possessions and territories without a declaration of war or specific statutory authorization, such forces shall be removed by the President if the Congress so directs by concurrent resolution.

> **Source:** The War Powers Resolution, Pub. L. 93-148 [H.J. Res. 542], 87 Stat. 555, 50 U.S.C. §§ 1541–1548, passed over President's veto November 7, 1973, Sec. 2(a).

218. Politburo Resolution No. 236-NQ/TW: Richard Nixon's Resignation of the Presidency of the United States and a Number of Urgent Party Tasks, August 13, 1974 [Excerpts]

Introduction

On August 9, 1974, Richard M. Nixon officially resigned as president of the United States. Four days later the Politburo of the Lao Dong (Workers' Party) in the Democratic Republic of Vietnam (DRV, North Vietnam) approved a resolution providing the party's assessment of the reasons for the resignation, what effect the resignation would have on America's Vietnam policy, and how Communist forces should attempt to exploit the opportunity provided them by Nixon's resignation.

Primary Source

Nixon's resignation as President of the United States is an important political event that signals the weakness and defeat of the American imperialists. . . . We must analyze both the underlying reasons and the direct reasons for Nixon's resignation of the office of President, and from that draw the necessary conclusions. . . .

The state monopoly capitalist clique in the U.S. has been forced to replace America's leader in order to deceive the American people and the people of the world so that the U.S. can, after making some slight adjustments, continue to implement the American world counter-revolutionary strategy that bears the name, the "Nixon Doctrine."

Nixon was not forced to resign from the office of President of the United States solely because of the crimes committed in the Watergate affair. . . . The Watergate affair was just a chance opportunity that set off an explosion of the U.S.'s social contradictions and of the internal contradictions within the American monopoly capitalist class. In fact, the primary cause of these contradictions is the U.S. war of aggression in Vietnam. This war has been so costly, in lives, property, and dollars, that it has caused the American imperialist crises on the economic, political, and military fronts to develop rapidly and to grow more serious with each passing day. . . .

During the final days of the Johnson Administration, the general opinion of the U.S. public was that the U.S. would have to quickly end its war of aggression in Vietnam. Instead, however, under the Nixon Administration the war was prolonged, expanded, and waged even more savagely. The serious crisis of all aspects of American domestic affairs and the weakening position of the United States in the international community were urgent problems that needed to be addressed and solved as far back as the last days of the Johnson Administration. However, throughout his five long years in power, Nixon demonstrated that he was incapable of resolving these problems. After the Paris Agreement on Vietnam was signed, the U.S.'s problems grew even greater.

As a result of this situation, under the Nixon Administration the contradictions between the American people and the American ruling clique grew steadily more serious. . . . In light of the desperate situation facing the United States, for their own interests the American ruling class made Nixon its sacrificial lamb in order to trick the U.S. public and the people of the world. That is the real reason that, in the end, both the Democratic Party and the Republican Party agreed to force Nixon to resign. . . .

Nixon's fall demonstrates the failure of America's world strategy, the crisis and weakness of the American imperialists, and the corruption of the U.S. capitalist regime. . . . It was a powerful political and spiritual blow to the Nguyen Van Thieu puppet government, the lackeys of the Americans, who are now shocked, frightened, and wavering because of Nixon's collapse.

Gerald Ford replaced Nixon as President in the midst of a deep crisis in America, a crisis of unprecedented proportions. First of all, Ford will have to solve that crisis in American society. At the same time, he will also have to deal with a world revolutionary situation that is now growing rapidly because of the U.S.'s weakened position. . . . We have no illusions about the replacement of the U.S. President. This is just a trick by the American monopoly capitalist clique, changing horses in midstream to try to redeem its desperate situation. . . . Ford will continue the Nixon Doctrine without Nixon, he will continue the evil "Vietnamization" policy, and he will continue to sabotage the Paris Agreement on Vietnam. He may use a few more demagogic tricks than Nixon did, but America's basic policies, both domestic and foreign, remain unchanged. For that reason, it is certain that Gerald Ford will not be able to reverse the direction of America's difficult situation, neither domestically nor abroad. By stubbornly following in Nixon's footsteps, Ford will lead the United States down to even greater defeats. . . .

In order to further exacerbate the contradictions, to add to the difficulties of the American imperialists, and to win victory for our people in both North and South Vietnam, we must properly implement the following measures:

In both North and South Vietnam, we must launch a continuous and wide-ranging propaganda campaign aimed at both domestic public opinion and world opinion. . . .

In South Vietnam, we need to exploit Nixon's fall to step up our struggle against the U.S. and the Saigon Government on all fronts—political, military, and diplomatic. We must link the

corruption, the rottenness, the failures, and the stagnation of the Nixon Administration to the corruption, the rottenness, the failures, and the stagnation of the Nguyen Van Thieu Government. We must stress the fact that Nguyen Van Thieu was Nixon's lackey and that only by overthrowing Nguyen Van Thieu will our nation ever be able to enjoy peace and national reconciliation. We need to form a broad-based front against Thieu, a front that demands that Thieu be thrown out, that a government be formed that truly supports the implementation of the Paris Agreement, that this new government implements the exercise of freedom and democracy in the areas controlled by the Saigon government, that it frees political prisoners, and that it implements peace and national reconciliation. . . .

Militarily, we must step up combat operations, shatter the enemy's pacification and land-grabbing military sweep operations, kill enemy troops and erode the enemy's manpower strength, recover those areas that the enemy has seized from us, protect our liberated zones, protect our base areas, and work to implement our policy of mounting a three-pronged attack [military, political, military proselyting] in order to win even greater victories.

In the diplomatic struggle, when the time is right the Provisional Revolutionary Government of South Vietnam may launch a diplomatic offensive to push the Americans and their puppets back up against the wall and to win widespread sympathy and support, both at home and abroad. . . .

In North Vietnam, . . . do everything possible to support and assist South Vietnam to defeat the puppet army, which is controlled and fed by the Americans.

The Party Secretariat and the Central Office for South Vietnam will prepare a plan to disseminate, direct, and push the implementation of this resolution.

[signed] Truong Chinh

Source: *Van Kien Dang, Toan Tap 35, 1974* [Collected Party Documents, Volume 35, 1974] (Hanoi: Nha Xuat Ban Chinh Tri Quoc Gia, 2004), 116–123. Translated by Merle L. Pribbenow.

219. Conclusion of Phase Two of the Politburo Conference of the Lao Dong, January 8, 1975 [Excerpt]

Introduction

In early January 1975 the Politburo of the Lao Dong (Workers' Party) in the Democratic Republic of Vietnam (DRV, North Vietnam) concluded an extended three-week session during which it debated the General Staff's military plan to defeat the forces of the Republic of Vietnam (RVN, South Vietnam) and win the war. A document summarizing the results of the Politburo session laid out the general outlines of the plan and discussed the possibility that the United States might reintervene militarily to try to save South Vietnam from total defeat. (Note: Cochin China is the southern half of South Vietnam, from the southern end of the Central Highlands southward, including Saigon and the Mekong Delta.)

Primary Source

... This final battle is first of all the responsibility of our military and political forces on the battlefields of Cochin China, including the forces of Saigon–Gia Dinh. At the same time, it is also the responsibility of the soldiers and civilians of our entire nation, but the decisive role will be played by COSVN's main force units and by large main force units sent down from other battlefields.

The 1975 operations plan lays out the responsibilities of each individual battlefield and at the same time states that the direction of operations for all battlefields will be aimed at the common goal of moving by the fastest route possible toward fighting the final strategically decisive battle in the enemy's last lair.

The Cochin China [Nam Bo] battlefield has three important missions: to attack the enemy's "pacification" program; to attack puppet main force [regular army] units; and to surround and pressure the cities. To attack "pacification," with the focal point of our attack being the Mekong Delta, we must utilize between 20,000 and 30,000 main force troops from Eastern Cochin China [Dong Nam Bo] to attack down into the delta, in coordination with attacks and uprisings by local armed forces and political forces, and open up a unified, integral liberated zone linking Eastern Cochin China with Regions 8 and 9. At the same time, we must place heavy pressure on My Tho and Saigon, and especially on Saigon, to create conditions that will enable the masses there to rise up. To contribute toward the goal of surrounding and pressuring Saigon, our main force troops must annihilate a significant portion of the puppet's main force [regular] units in Eastern Cochin China.

In the Region 5–Central Highlands area, we will use three main force divisions to attack the Central Highlands to open up a corridor linking the Central Highlands with Eastern Cochin China to create conditions that will enable our main force troops to move rapidly down into Eastern Cochin China to support COSVN's main force units in the attack on Saigon. We will begin the offensive with an opening attack to capture Ban Me Thuot, then strike straight down to Tuy Hoa and Phu Yen, cutting the Region 5 coastal lowlands in two and creating an additional sector through which we can advance rapidly to the south to surround and pressure Saigon.

We will use Military Region 5 forces and the military and political forces of the coastal provinces of Central Vietnam to liberate the area from Binh Dinh northward to put pressure on Da Nang.

In the Tri-Thien Battlefield, we will attack and capture the lowlands and take firm control of the area south of Hue City in order to isolate Hue from Da Nang, to put pressure on both these cities, and to prevent the enemy from regrouping and pulling his forces back to the south. We will incite armed mutinies and secession in Central Vietnam.

When the opportunity arises, we will send three additional divisions down to Eastern Cochin China. We will use two corps to launch lightning attacks to annihilate several of the puppet regular divisions down there and then penetrate straight into Saigon.

We must have plans ready in both South Vietnam and in North Vietnam for how we will respond to possible U.S. resumption of attacks by air and naval forces. The possibility that the U.S. will reintervene in the Vietnam War is low. However, even if that possibility is only five or seven percent, we still must be on guard, because the U.S. is still plotting to maintain its neocolonialist rule. No matter what the U.S. wants to do, it will only be able to take limited action, for example by providing a small amount of additional military and economic aid or, at the very most, by providing air and naval fire support (and only in the event that the puppets are able to resist for a protracted period of time).

These are the primary military attacks in our 1975 strategic plan....

Source: *Dai Thang Mua Xuan, 1975: Van Kien Dang* [Great Spring Victory 1975: Party Documents] (Hanoi: Nha Xuat Ban Chinh Tri Quoc Gia, 2005), 21–31. Translated by Merle L. Pribbenow.

220. Henry Kissinger, Secretary of State: Request for Emergency Aid for the Republic of Vietnam, April 15, 1975

Introduction

In March 1975 three divisions of the People's Army of Vietnam (PAVN, North Vietnamese Army) launched an offensive against forces of the Republic of Vietnam (RVN, South Vietnam) in the Central Highlands of South Vietnam. South Vietnamese president Nguyen Van Thieu then made a fatal decision, ordering the withdrawal of South Vietnamese forces from the region. This soon became a rout. As the South Vietnamese military situation rapidly deteriorated, in early April the Gerald R. Ford administration asked Congress for an emergency appropriation of $800 million to assist South Vietnam. Secretary of State Henry Kissinger appeared before Congress to support the appeal, claiming that the United States had a "moral obligation" to extend the assistance and blaming the military imbalance in South Vietnam on cuts in U.S. aid to the Saigon regime.

Primary Source

The long and agonizing conflict in Indochina has reached a tragic stage. The events of the past month have been discussed at great length before the Congress and require little additional elaboration. In Viet-Nam President Thieu ordered a strategic withdrawal from a number of areas he regarded as militarily untenable.

However, the withdrawal took place in great haste, without adequate advance planning, and with insufficient coordination. It was further complicated by a massive flow of civilian refugees seeking to escape the advancing North Vietnamese Army. Disorganization engendered confusion; fear led to panic. The results, as we all know, were tragic losses—of territory, of population, of material, and of morale.

But to fully understand what has happened, it is necessary to have an appreciation of all that went before. The North Vietnamese offensive, and the South Vietnamese response, did not come about by chance—although chance is always an element in warfare. The origins of these events are complex, and I believe it would be useful to review them briefly.

Since January 1973, Hanoi has violated—continuously, systematically, and energetically—the most fundamental provisions of the Paris agreement. It steadily increased the numbers of its troops in the South. It improved and expanded its logistics system in the South. It increased the armaments and ammunition of its forces in the South. And as you know, it blocked all efforts to account for personnel missing in action. These are facts, and they are indisputable. All of these actions were of course in total violation of the agreement. Parallel to these efforts, Hanoi attempted—with considerable success—to immobilize the various mechanisms established by the agreement to monitor and curtail violations of the cease-fire. Thus, it assiduously prepared the way for further military actions.

South Viet-Nam's record of adherence to the agreement has not been perfect. It is, however, qualitatively and quantitatively far better than Hanoi's. South Viet-Nam did not build up its armed forces. It undertook no major offensive actions—although it traded thrusts and probes with the Communists. It cooperated fully in establishing and supporting the cease-fire control mechanisms provided for in the agreement. And it sought, as did the United States, full implementation of those provisions of the agreement calling for an accounting of soldiers missing in action.

But perhaps more relevant to an understanding of recent events are the following factors.

While North Viet-Nam had available several reserve divisions which it could commit to battle at times and places of its choosing, the South had no strategic reserves. Its forces were stretched thin, defending lines of communication and population centers throughout the country.

While North Viet-Nam, by early this year, had accumulated in South Viet-Nam enough ammunition for two years of intensive combat, South Vietnamese commanders had to ration ammunition as their stocks declined and were not replenished.

While North Viet-Nam had enough fuel in the South to operate its tanks and armored vehicles for at least 18 months, South Viet-Nam faced stringent shortages.

In sum, while Hanoi was strengthening its army in the South, the combat effectiveness of South Viet-Nam's army gradually grew weaker. While Hanoi built up its reserve divisions and accumulated ammunition, fuel, and other military supplies, U.S. aid levels to Viet-Nam were cut—first by half in 1973 and then by another third in 1974. This coincided with a worldwide inflation and a fourfold increase in fuel prices. As a result almost all of our military aid had to be devoted to ammunition and fuel. Very little was available for spare parts, and none for new equipment.

These imbalances became painfully evident when the offensive broke full force, and they contributed to the tragedy which unfolded. Moreover, the steady diminution in the resources available to the Army of South Viet-Nam unquestionably affected the morale of its officers and men. South Vietnamese units in the northern and central provinces knew full well that they faced an enemy superior both in numbers and in firepower. They knew that reinforcements and resupply would not be forthcoming. When the fighting began they also knew, as they had begun to suspect, that the United States would not respond. I would suggest that all of these factors added significantly to the sense of helplessness, despair, and, eventually, panic which we witnessed in late March and early April.

I would add that it is both inaccurate and unfair to hold South Viet-Nam responsible for blocking progress toward a political solution to the conflict. Saigon's proposals in its conversations with PRG [Provisional Revolutionary Government] representatives in Paris were in general constructive and conciliatory. There was no progress toward a compromise political settlement because Hanoi intended that there should not be. Instead, North Viet-Nam's strategy was to lay the groundwork for an eventual military offensive, one which would either bring outright victory or at least allow Hanoi to dictate the terms of a political solution.

Neither the United States nor South Viet-Nam entered into the Paris agreement with the expectation that Hanoi would abide by it in every respect. We did believe, however, that the agreement was sufficiently equitable to both sides that its major provisions could be accepted and acted upon by Hanoi and that the contest could be shifted thereby from a military to a political track. However, our two governments also recognized that, since the agreement manifestly was not self-enforcing, Hanoi's adherence depended heavily on maintaining a military parity in South Viet-Nam. So long as North Viet-Nam confronted a strong South Vietnamese army and so long as the possibility existed of U.S. intervention to offset the strategic advantages of the North, Hanoi could be expected to forgo major military action. Both of those essential conditions were dissipated over the past two years. Hanoi attained a clear military superiority, and it became increasingly convinced that U.S. intervention could be ruled out. It therefore returned to a military course, with the results we have seen.

The present situation in Viet-Nam is ominous. North Viet-Nam's combat forces far outnumber those of the South, and they are better armed. Perhaps more important, they enjoy a psychological momentum which can be as decisive as armaments in battle. South Viet-Nam must reorganize and reequip its forces, and it must restore the morale of its army and its people. These tasks will be difficult, and they can be performed only by the South Vietnamese. However, a successful defense will also require resources— arms, fuel, ammunition, and medical supplies—and these can come only from the United States.

Large quantities of equipment and supplies, totaling perhaps $800 million, were lost in South Viet-Nam's precipitous retreat from the northern and central areas. Much of this should not have been lost, and we regret that it happened. But South Viet-Nam is now faced with a different strategic and tactical situation and different military requirements. Although the amount of military assistance the President has requested is of the same general magnitude as the value of the equipment lost, we are not attempting simply to replace those losses. The President's request, based on [U.S. Army chief of staff] General [Frederick C.] Weyand's assessment, represents our best judgment as to what is needed now, in this new situation, to defend what is left of South Viet-Nam. Weapons, ammunition, and supplies to reequip four divisions, to form a number of ranger groups into divisional units, and to upgrade some territorial forces into infantry regiments will require some $326 million. The balance of our request is for ammunition, fuel, spare parts, and medical supplies to sustain up to 60 days of intensive combat and to pay for the cost of transporting those items. These are minimum requirements, and they are needed urgently.

The human tragedy of Viet-Nam has never been more acute than it now is. Hundreds of thousands of South Vietnamese have sought to flee Communist control and are homeless refugees. They have our compassion, and they must also have our help. Despite commendable efforts by the South Vietnamese Government, the burden of caring for these innocent victims is beyond its capacity. The United States has already done much to assist these people, but many remain without adequate food, shelter, or medical care. The President has asked that additional efforts and additional resources be devoted to this humanitarian effort. I ask that the Congress respond generously and quickly.

The objectives of the United States in this immensely difficult situation remain as they were when the Paris agreement was signed—to end the military conflict and establish conditions which will allow a fair political solution to be achieved. We believe that despite the tragic experience to date, the Paris agreement remains a valid framework within which to proceed toward such a solution. However, today, as in 1973, battlefield conditions will affect political perceptions and the outcome of negotiations. We therefore believe that in order for a political settlement to be reached which preserves any degree of self-determination for the people of South Viet-Nam, the present military situation must be stabilized. It is for these reasons that the President has asked Congress to appropriate urgently additional funds for military assistance for Viet-Nam.

I am acutely aware of the emotions aroused in this country by our long and difficult involvement in Viet-Nam. I understand what the cost has been for this nation and why frustration and anger continue to dominate our national debate. Many will argue that we have done more than enough for the Government and the people of South Viet-Nam. I do not agree with that proposition, however, nor do I believe that to review endlessly the wisdom of our original involvement serves a useful purpose now. For despite the agony of this nation's experience in Indochina and the substantial reappraisal which has taken place concerning our proper role there, few would deny that we are still involved or that what we do—or fail to do—will still weigh heavily in the outcome. We cannot by our actions alone insure the survival of South Viet-Nam. But we can, alone, by our inaction assure its demise.

The United States has no legal obligation to the Government and the people of South Viet-Nam of which the Congress is not aware. But we do have a deep moral obligation—rooted in the history of our involvement and sustained by the continuing efforts of our friends. We cannot easily set it aside. In addition to the obvious consequences for the people of Viet-Nam, our failure to act in accordance with that obligation would inevitably influence other nations' perceptions of our constancy and our determination. American credibility would not collapse, and American honor would not be destroyed. But both would be weakened, to the detriment of this nation and of the peaceful world order we have sought to build.

Source: "Military and Humanitarian Assistance to South Viet-Nam," *Department of State Bulletin* 72(1871) (1975): 583–586.

221. Lao Dong Party Secretariat Directive No. 218-CT/TW: Policy toward Enemy Soldiers Who Are Captured or Surrender in the New Situation, April 18, 1975 [Excerpts]

Introduction

In mid-April 1975 as 15 Communist divisions tightened the noose around Saigon and the imminent collapse of the Republic of Vietnam (RVN, South Vietnam) regime became apparent, the Lao Dong (Workers' Party) in the Democratic Republic of Vietnam (DRV, North Vietnam) issued a directive on the treatment of enemy personnel who were captured or turned themselves in. This document laid the foundation for the establishment of the infamous reeducation camps in which more than 100,000 former South Vietnamese soldiers and civilian officials were imprisoned, many for a decade or more.

Primary Source

In this new situation, currently the number of enemy prisoners of war, of enemy troops who return to our side when their revolutionary consciences are awakened, and of enemy soldiers who mutiny against their superiors is constantly growing, and our liberated zone in South Vietnam is constantly expanding and becoming integrated into one. The Secretariat has decided that these enemy troops will be categorized in the following manner and that our policy for dealing with them will be:

I—Categories

1. Mutineers: Enemy soldiers who carry out actions directed against the enemy and join the revolution. Such actions include uprisings to cause mutinies, serving as our agents inside the enemy's ranks, sabotaging the enemy, or directly or indirectly assisting our side in battle.
2. Soldiers whose revolutionary consciences have been awakened and who return to the revolution (they should not be surrendering soldiers): Enemy soldiers who take the initiative to desert the enemy's ranks in order to join the ranks of the revolution.
3. Prisoners of War: Enemy soldiers that we capture during or after a battle.
4. Soldiers who turn themselves in after fleeing in battle: Enemy soldiers who have been forced to flee and hide after our forces attack and who then turn themselves in to revolutionary governmental authorities.

II—Policies Toward Each Individual Category

1. Mutineers: Politically, they will be considered as revolutionary masses [civilian supporters]. In terms of their lives and rations, they will be treated the same as our own cadre and enlisted soldiers. . . .
2. Soldiers whose revolutionary consciences have been awakened: They will receive the same rights as ordinary citizens and will be dealt with, both in spirit and in material terms, as ordinary citizens.
3. Prisoners of War: They will be dealt with humanely in strict accordance with our policies. In the present situation, they will be handled as follows:
   a) Privates and Non-Commissioned Officers:
      —Those whose families live in liberated zones will have the revolution's policies explained to them and then will be allowed to return home, where local governmental authorities will register, administer, and educate them.
      —Those who come from areas still under enemy control or who are not yet able to return home because they are far from home will be temporarily concentrated together [detained] so that we can administer and educate them and use them to perform work duties. When conditions permit, they will be allowed to return home to their families.
   b) Officers: All officers will be detained for control, education, and labor purposes. Later, depending on the amount of progress made by each, they will be recategorized. Specific detailed policies for handling each category will be set at a later date. Those individuals (including both officers and enlisted men) who have specialized technical skills that we need may be employed in individual tasks for a certain length of time, but we must be vigilant toward them and we must tightly control them. Later, depending on our requirements and on the amount of progress each individual has demonstrated, they may be recruited and employed in various sectors outside the armed forces.
   c) With regards to those who are thugs, intelligence or military security service personnel, psychological warfare officers, pacification or chieu hoi cadre, and leaders of reactionary political parties or party factions within the enemy armed forces, regardless of whether they are privates, noncommissioned officers, or commissioned officers they must be sent to long-term concentrated reeducation. They must be imprisoned separately in secure locations, and they must be tightly controlled and administered.
   d) With regards to those individuals who were formerly soldiers in our army but who deserted to the enemy and joined the puppet army, these individuals are to be dealt with as prisoners of war. Any of them who worked for the enemy as a spy, in psychological warfare operations, in pacification or chieu hoi operations, or who commanded enemy forces in attacks against the revolution will be dealt with as an enemy thug.
4. Soldiers who turn themselves in after fleeing in battle:
   a) Those who turn themselves in and who actively, willingly carry out tasks we entrust to them or who perform services for us by telling us enemy secrets, including the location of enemy supply warehouses, caches, and documents; by informing us of the locations of reactionary leaders who are still hiding from our forces; by helping us to utilize enemy

technical weapons and equipment; by encouraging large numbers of other enemy soldiers to turn themselves in, etc., will be treated as soldiers whose revolutionary consciences have been awakened.

b) As for the rest, in general they will be treated the same as prisoners of war, but attention must be paid to the following issues:

—Privates and noncommissioned officers will be registered, their weapons will be confiscated from them, and our policies will be explained to them. If their homes are in the liberated zone, they will be allowed to return home immediately and responsibility for administering them and educating them will be turned over to the local government. Those who cannot yet return home because their homes are in enemy-controlled areas or because they are too far from home will be concentrated together to be educated and to carry out labor duties.

—Officers must be detained so that they can be reeducated. However, depending on the political situation in individual areas, appropriate measures may be taken so that those who continue to hide out from us will not be too frightened and will be willing to turn themselves in. We may not need to imprison them at first. Based on how the situation develops, we can gradually and systematically concentrate [detain] them later.

—Thugs, spies, and those guilty of numerous crimes must be arrested and detained immediately.

—Those who refuse to turn themselves in within the specified time period must be arrested and detained. Those who hide from us in order to oppose and sabotage us will be punished appropriately according to the existing laws dealing with the crime of sabotage.

5. People's Self-Defense Forces and Popular Forces whose units have disintegrated:

—People's Self-Defense Force units will be disbanded, their weapons and military equipment will be confiscated, and they will be treated as ordinary civilians.

—Popular Forces soldiers will be turned over to local governmental authorities for registration, administration, and education. They will not be concentrated and detained like prisoners of war.

—Regular Army or Regional Forces soldiers who had been detailed to command or to serve as core cadre for Popular Forces or People's Self-Defense Forces units and individuals who are thugs or intelligence agents will be treated the same as those types of individuals in the prisoner of war category (see above).

Enemy enlisted men and officers from all services and all types of units who deserted to return home, who retired from the enemy armed forces, or who were previously discharged from the enemy armed forces will be treated as ordinary civilians. If anyone in this category has committed crimes, the local authorities will deal with them in accordance with our general policy toward criminals.

6. A number of special cases:

—Enemy soldiers detailed to work in governmental or police posts will be dealt with by our security agencies [the Ministry of Public Security].

—If enemy officers who have influence in ethnic minority groups or in one of the religions are needed to win over the civilian masses, an appropriate policy to appeal to them and ease their treatment may be established.

—With respect to officers of the rank of general or colonel, if it is determined that we need to use them for the good of the revolution, a suitable policy for their treatment may be devised. . . .

—Puppet prisoners of war captured in 1972 who are still in detention will be handled like current prisoners of war. Privates and noncommissioned officers who have been successfully reeducated may be allowed to return home to their families.

Note:

1. All military proselyting, military intelligence, and [public] security agents whom we have sent to operate within the enemy's army are considered to be cadre and soldiers in our army. Their cases must be handled carefully and exactly in accordance with our policies, and under no circumstances are they to be mistakenly handled as enemy soldiers.

2. At present, we will not allow prisoners of war or enemy soldiers who have turned themselves in to be used as replacements in our armed forces units.

3. All types of prisoners of war and enemy soldiers who have turned themselves in will be detained in "B" [Code designation for South Vietnam]. They will not be sent to "A" [Code designation for North Vietnam] except in special circumstances in which we need to immediately exploit [interrogate] them in order to support our requirements.

For the Party Secretariat

[signed] To Huu

Source: *Van Kien Dang, Toan Tap 36, 1975* [Collected Party Documents, Volume 36, 1975] (Hanoi: Nha Xuat Ban Chinh Tri Quoc Gia, 2004), 121–125. Translated by Merle L. Pribbenow.

222. Le Duan: Speech at the Meeting Held in Hanoi to Celebrate Victory, May 15, 1975

Introduction

In a speech in Hanoi on May 15, 1975, Le Duan, head of the Lao Dong (Workers' Party) of the Democratic Republic of Vietnam (DRV, North Vietnam), trumpeted the Communist victory in the Ho Chi Minh Campaign in the Republic of Vietnam (RVN, South Vietnam) and the reunification of Vietnam and outlined the reasons behind these successes.

Primary Source

Compatriots and combatants throughout the country,

All Party Comrades,

Comrades and friends,

Today, with boundless joy, throughout the country our 45 million people are jubilantly celebrating the great victory we have won in the general offensive and uprising this Spring of 1975, in completely defeating the war of aggression and the neocolonialist rule of US imperialism, liberating the whole of the southern half of our country so dear to our hearts and gloriously ending the longest, most difficult and greatest patriotic war ever waged in the history of our people's struggle against foreign aggression.

We hail our glorious Fatherland from now on definitively rid of the slavery of foreign domination and the scourge of partition. We hail the beautiful land of Viet Nam from Lang Son to the Cape of Ca Mau, from now on completely independent and free, and independent and free forever.

We hail the new era in our nation's 4,000-year history—an era of brilliant prospects for the development of a peaceful, independent, reunified, democratic, prosperous and strong Viet Nam, an era in which the labouring people have become the complete masters of their destiny and will pool their physical and mental efforts to build a plentiful and happy life for themselves and for thousands of generations to come.

This glory belongs to our great President Ho Chi Minh, the outstanding national hero who brought fame to our land, the first Vietnamese Communist who founded and trained our Party, who steered the ship of the Vietnamese revolution through many a storm to enable it to reach the shore of glory today. In this stirring atmosphere of total victory, our hearts are filled with great emotion at the memory of our beloved Uncle Ho, and we seem to hear again his teaching:

"No matter what difficulties and hardships lie ahead, our people are sure of total victory. The US imperialists will certainly have to quit. Our Fatherland will certainly be reunified. Our fellow countrymen in the South and in the North will certainly be reunited under one roof. We, a small nation, will have earned the signal honour of defeating through heroic struggle, two big imperialisms—the French and the American—and of making a worthy contribution to the world national liberation movement." We are very proud to have thoroughly carried out these recommendations of President Ho Chi Minh in his sacred Testament.

This glory belongs to our heroes, martyrs, compatriots and comrades who have sacrificed their lives for the independence and freedom of the country, for the happiness of the people, for our sacred duty to the nation and our noble internationalist obligation. The Fatherland and the people will forever remember the services of those martyrs, the loyal sons and daughters of the people whose example of courage will shine eternally!

This glory belongs to the heroic people of Viet Nam, in whose veins flows the blood of Trung Sisters, of Lady Trieu, of Ly Thuong Kiet and Tran Hung Dao, of Le Loi, Quang Trung and Phan Dinh Phung, of Hoang Hoa Tham and Truong Cong Dinh and who today under the banner of the Party and of our great President Ho Chi Minh, have upheld their matchless revolutionary heroism and braved untold difficulties and dangers. From the days of blood and fire of the Nghe Tinh Soviets and the Nam Ky Uprising, they marched forward to the glorious victory of the August Revolution. From the resounding victory at Dien Bien Phu, which dealt a mortal blow to old colonialism, they went on to win repeated victories over the successive strategies of neocolonialism, and finally achieved total victory in their marvellous general offensive and uprising in the Spring of 1975.

Today, the day of triumph of the nation, from this historic land of Thang Long, the heart of the country, we send our boundless love and our warmest congratulations to our compatriots and comrades in the South who, battling against waves and wind for 30 years on end, have struggled unflinchingly and indomitably for the great cause under the banner of the National Front for Liberation of South Viet Nam and the Provisional Revolutionary Government of the Republic of South Viet Nam and courageously raised the great storm that has finally swept away the enemy, thus adding still greater renown to the glorious tradition of the "Bronze Citadel" of the Fatherland. We offer our warmest congratulations to our compatriots in the heroic North who over the past decades have been building socialism with industry and thrift, fearing no difficulty and sparing no sacrifice, who have sent tens of thousands of their sons to the frontline to kill the aggressors, and defeated the war of destruction of the US aggressors while firmly defending the North, the powerful base of the revolution in the whole country.

This glory belongs to the heroic Viet Nam people's armed forces, the revolutionary army of the people, completely "loyal to the country and the people and able to fulfil any task, overcome any hardship, and defeat any enemy." Armed at the beginning with mere wooden spears and flintlock, it has grown up at a stupendous speed, like Phu Dong into powerful units which have won all of the hundreds of battles fought across the land of Viet Nam. We send our deepest love and the expression of our boundless pride to all the officers and men of the Viet Nam People's Army. We send our warmest congratulations to the officers and men of all three categories of armed forces and of all arms and services all who, during the 55 recent historic days, fought with peerless valour, great resourcefulness and tremendous power and speed, smashing the enemy and winning resounding victories to give a still brighter hue to their traditional "Determined to Fight and to Win" banner.

This glory belongs to our Party, the experienced and staunch vanguard of the Vietnamese working class, faithful representative of the vital interests and legitimate aspirations of the people and the entire nation of Viet Nam, the leader and organizer of all the victories of the Vietnamese revolution. Our Party has skillfully and successfully combined the revolutionary science of Marxism-Leninism—the culmination of the intelligence of mankind—with the extraordinary revolutionary energy and the inexhaustible creativeness of our people, with the tradition and quintessential qualities of our nation, to work out a correct, creative, independent and sovereign line, mobilize, foster and bring into play all potentials of the country and all forces of the nation, and to combine these with the strength of our times into a tremendous aggregate force, able to defeat all enemies. The Vietnamese communist[s], with their tradition of solidarity and unity, with their iron determination, their courage before all trials, have always marched in the van of the great struggle of the people, and have proved equal to the glorious tasks assigned them by history and the nation.

Our victory is the victory of the unbreakable solidarity of the three Indochinese peoples thoroughly tested in the flames of struggle against the common enemy. In this day of great joy, we hail the great victories of the fraternal peoples of Laos and Cambodia, and express to those companions-in-arms who have been fighting in the same trench as we have our boundless gratitude and our unshakable solidarity.

Our victory is also the victory of the forces of socialism, national independence, democracy and peace throughout the world, who have supported us in the struggle against aggressive US imperialism. On behalf of the Viet Nam Workers' Party and the entire people of Viet Nam, we express our most profound gratitude to the Soviet Union, China and the other fraternal socialist countries, and to all communist and workers' parties, for the very great and precious support and assistance they have given out of their noble internationalist attachment to us. We sincerely thank the working class of all countries in the world, the nationalist countries, the various international democratic organizations, and the whole of progressive mankind for having provided vigorous encouragement and support to our war of resistance for national salvation. To progressive people in the United States who out of their love for peace and justice have given their sympathy and support to our people's just struggle we send our greetings of friendship.

Fellow-countrymen and combatants,

Comrades and friends,

The victory of our war of resistance against the US aggressors and for national salvation is the victory of the banner of national independence, the victory of a patriotism forged by thousands of years of glorious effort to build and defend our nation and now raised to a new height by the Party of the working class. "Nothing is more precious than independence and freedom." This truth has served as the bugle-call urging our people, generation after generation, to rush forward and chase out all invaders and traitors. From it our people have drawn the irresistible strength to break the fetters of old colonialism and, today, the yoke of neocolonialism.

This victory is the victory of socialism, the highest ideal of mankind and the most profound aspiration of the labouring people, which has become a reality over half of our country as well as for one-third of mankind, a system in which the people have become the real masters, free from the exploitation of man by man, a system in which everyone lives in independence and freedom, has enough food and clothing, receives proper education and enjoys a rich and healthy moral life. Such a system is indeed the source of the inexhaustible strength of the People in the North, and a great stimulus to our compatriots in the South.

There can be no genuine independence and freedom for the nation unless the labouring people are freed from oppression and exploitation. Likewise, the labouring people cannot be freed from the yoke of oppression and exploitation so long as national independence and freedom have not been achieved. For the Vietnamese people, the bright road to independence, freedom and socialism was opened up by the triumph of the August Revolution and then by the historic victory of Dien Bien Phu. However, US imperialism, the international gendarme, alarmed by the mounting might of socialism and the national liberation movement throughout the world, ousted the French colonialists and invaded the southern part of our country, turning it into a US neocolony and military base. The scheme of US imperialism was to erase the gains of national independence and socialism of our people and, by so doing, to contain and eventually put down the national liberation movement, contain and push back socialism in this part of the world. As the US aggressors themselves have admitted, Viet Nam became the testing ground for the power and prestige of US imperialism. Viet Nam became the area of the fiercest historic confrontation between the most warlike, the most stubborn aggressive imperialism with the most powerful economic and military potential on one side, and the forces of national independence, democracy and socialism of which the Vietnamese people are the shock force in this region on the other. The victory of Viet Nam, therefore, is not only a victory of national independence and socialism in Viet Nam, but has also a great international significance, and an epoch making character. It has upset the global strategy of US imperialism. It has proved that the three revolutionary torrents of our times are on the offensive, repulsing imperialism step by step and overthrowing it part by part. Today, imperialism, even US imperialism, cannot grab a single square inch of any socialist country; neither can it push back the movement for national independence in the world, nor hinder the advance toward socialism of various countries. In this context, the victory of Viet Nam has opened a new stage of development, extremely favourable, for the world revolutionary movement. Together with the great victories of the fraternal Lao and Cambodian peoples, our victory has made a positive contribution to strengthening the forces of world socialism and created new favourable conditions for the safeguarding of peace and national independence in Indochina and Southeast Asia.

Our victory is the victory of a correct and creative revolutionary line and method, and of the correct and creative line of revolutionary war of our Party. This revolutionary line and method consisted in holding high the two banners of national democratic revolution and socialist revolution, combining the strength of national independence and socialism, mobilizing the strength of our entire people, and combining our nation's might with that of our era, the strength existing in our country with that existing in the world, in order to create a great aggregate strength to fight and defeat US imperialism. The line of our revolutionary war in the stage of our struggle against the US aggressors and for national salvation consisted in constantly applying the strategy of offensive, and also in knowing how to defeat the enemy step by step, forcing him to de-escalate from one rung to another and finally defeating him. It consisted in combining military actions with political struggles, attacks by the armed forces with mass uprisings, seizing control with wiping out the enemy, and wiping out the enemy with seizing control. It consisted in fighting the enemy on three fronts (political struggles, military actions and agitation work among enemy soldiers) and in all three strategic areas, namely the mountain areas, the rural areas, and the urban areas. This line has encouraged and organized millions of people to rush to the front to destroy the enemy and save the country, thus forming an invincible battle-array for the revolutionary war in South Viet Nam exactly as described in the book "Binh Thu Yeu Luoc" [Essentials of Military

Art]: "One man fights a battle, thousands fight a battle, thousands like one man in battle."

This line is the creative application of the revolutionary military science of Marxism-Leninism to the realities of the revolutionary war in our country; it is the result of inheriting and developing the military art of our ancestors, learning from and improving upon the lessons of the August Revolution and the anti-French resistance, and summing up and enhancing the inexhaustible creative experiences of our people. In the light of this line the anti-US struggle for national salvation of the people throughout our country has become the greatest epic of revolutionary war in Viet Nam, radiant with so many glorious and outstanding exploits: the concerted uprisings in 1960 which developed into the revolutionary war to defeat the "special war" strategy; the general offensive and uprising at Tet of the year Mau Than (1968) to defeat the "limited war" strategy; the 1972 strategic offensive in the South and the great triumph over the strategic air blitz in 1972 which forced the US to quit and the general offensive and uprising in Spring 1975 which toppled the puppet regime. Within 55 days and nights of lightning offensives and stormy uprisings we have smashed the one million–odd army of the enemy, giving him no time to organize any significant resistance. This is the highest and most marvelous expression of the all-round revolutionary war strategy in South Viet Nam.

Fellow countrymen and combatants,

Comrades and friends,

With the victory of the anti-US war of resistance for national salvation an extremely brilliant chapter of our country's history has begun.

A new, tremendous and very inspiring task is awaiting our 45 million people. This task is to thoroughly act upon the Testament of our great Uncle Ho: "Our entire Party and people closely joining their efforts will build a peaceful, reunified, independent, democratic, prosperous and strong Viet Nam, and make a worthy contribution to the world revolution." Let us engage in construction and creative labour in order to bring about progress and prosperity to our Viet Nam, happiness and well-being to our people.

Our people have made countless sacrifices and overcome untold hardships and difficulties to recover our country. This country belongs to our people. Let us prove ourselves worthy of our great Fatherland, of our heroic people, of so many martyrs who have laid down their lives, of the great sacrifices of our people. Let us strive to be worthy of Uncle Ho's "boundless love." Let us prove ourselves worthy of being the real masters of the country. Let our compatriots in the North step up socialist construction. Let our compatriots in the South unite and strive to build there a fine national democratic regime, a prosperous national and democratic economy, a progressive and healthy national and democratic culture. In the spirit of national reconciliation and concord, our people have shown leniency to all those who have strayed from the right path and who are now returning to the people, no matter what their past was. Provided they sincerely mend their abilities to the service of the homeland, their place among the people will be guaranteed and all the shame put on them by criminal US imperialist will be washed away.

After so many years of war our people have today fully won the right to build their country in peace, in the South as well as in the North. Let our compatriots in the whole country start a stirring movement of labour. By our creative labour we will rapidly heal the wounds of war, restore and develop the economy, improve our living conditions. By our creative labour we will shake off all vestiges of the parasitic life and the sham prosperity generated in South Viet Nam by our wicked enemy. By our creative labour we will transform the abundant resources of our land into inexhaustible sources of riches for our people, into modern agriculture, modern industry and advanced culture and science. Creative labour will not only embellish our homeland and bring to our people a happy and ever happier life, but will also transform the Vietnamese into new men and women, the masters of nature of society, the masters of their own lives.

As a people who have made tremendous sacrifices to win peace, national independence, democracy and social progress, the Vietnamese people are determined to stand shoulder to shoulder with the other peoples throughout the world to safeguard peace, to struggle tirelessly for national independence, democracy and social progress, and develop friendly relations with all countries on the basis of equality, mutual respect, mutual benefit and peaceful coexistence.

We will do our best to strengthen solidarity and increase mutual support and assistance with the fraternal socialist countries and the international communist and workers' movement in the spirit of proletarian internationalism, in order to win ever more splendid successes for the lofty ideal of Marxism-Leninism.

We pledge to strengthen the unshakable militant friendship between the Vietnamese people and the people in our two fraternal neighbour countries—Laos and Cambodia—on the basis of respect for each other's independence sovereignty and territorial integrity, for the sake of the security growth and prosperity of each people, and for lasting and stable peace in this part of the world.

We will persist in our policy of strengthening solidarity and friendship with our neighbour in Southeast Asia and the countries of the Third World in the struggle to regain and maintain national independence, consolidate sovereignty and oppose all schemes and manoeuvres of imperialism and old and new colonialism.

Fellow countrymen and combatants,

Comrades and friends,

In the four thousand years of our nation's history, the last hundred years were the hardest and fiercest period of struggle against foreign aggression, but they were at the same time the period of our most glorious victories. Our people have overthrown the domination of the Japanese fascists, defeated the old colonialism of France and have now completely defeated the neocolonialism of the United States. By those splendid exploits, our nation has joined the ranks of the vanguard nations of the world and has won the affection and esteem of the whole of progressive mankind. A nation which has recorded such splendid exploits deserves to enjoy peace, freedom and happiness. Such a nation surely has enough determination and energy, strength and talent to overcome all difficulties and reach the great heights of our times, to turn a poor and backward country heavily devastated by war, in which US imperialism has perpetrated so many crimes, into a civilized, prosperous and powerful country, an impregnable bastion of national independence, democracy and socialism in Indochina and Southeast Asia.

With boundless pride, with complete confidence in our success, let our entire Party, our entire people and our entire army march forward! A splendid future is awaiting us!

Long live a peaceful, independent, reunified, democratic, prosperous and strong Viet Nam!

Long live the Viet Nam Workers' Party!

President Ho Chi Minh will live forever in our cause!

Source: Le Duan, *Le Duan: Selected Writings* (Hanoi: Foreign Languages Publishing House, 1977), 516–540.

223. Pham Van Dong: Speech Delivered on National Day, September 2, 1975 [Excerpts]

Introduction

Celebrating the 30th anniversary of Ho Chi Minh's declaration of independence in Hanoi, Premier Pham Van Dong of the Democratic Republic of Vietnam (DRV, North Vietnam) heralds the role of the Lao Dong (Workers' Party) in bringing about the reunification of Vietnam.

Primary Source

Today, the people throughout our country are jubilantly celebrating the 30th anniversary of the victory of the great August Revolution and of the founding of the D.R.V.N. Our joy and enthusiasm are all the greater since we are celebrating these historic events following the glorious victory of Spring 1975 which climaxed in the historic Ho Chi Minh campaign. We have completely defeated the war of aggression of U.S. imperialism, brought to a victorious conclusion the national democratic revolution in the South, firmly defended the cause of socialism in the North, paved the way for our people, now masters of the whole territory of our homeland, to march forward and build a peaceful, unified, independent, democratic and prosperous Viet Nam, a socialist Viet Nam, and now continue to make an active contribution to the revolutionary cause of the peoples of the world.

Today, on the occasion of the great festive day of the nation, on behalf of the Central Committee of the Viet Nam Worker's Party Government of the D.R.V.N., I extend my warmest and most cordial congratulations to our compatriots and combatants throughout the country and to overseas Vietnamese. We convey to the families of fallen heroes and heroines and to all war invalids our most profound sentiments and best Wishes.

Today, on the occasion of the great festive day of our nation, our Party, Government and people warmly greet the Party and Government delegations of the Soviet Union, China and the other fraternal socialist countries, the delegations of Laos and Cambodia, the delegations and representatives of other countries, the delegations of a number of other fraternal Parties, and the delegations of various international democratic organizations.

We express sincere thanks to you, comrades and friends for your kindness in being present here today to join us in celebrating the glorious National Day of our people bringing with you inestimable sympathy and support for our Vietnamese people.

Today, the entire Vietnamese nation is living the most glorious and exciting moments in its history. In this solemn hour, with profound emotion and boundless gratitude, we turn our thoughts to our great President Ho Chi Minh, the founder of our Party and State, the teacher and guide of our people in our persistent revolutionary struggle, who has led us from one victory to another until the complete and glorious victory of today. In this solemn hour, every one of us pledges to do his and her best to continue the great cause of President Ho Chi Minh, carry out in the best possible manner the last recommendations in his Testament, work self-sacrificingly for the victory of the Vietnamese revolution and contribute to the victory of the world revolution.

The greatness of the August Revolution lies in the fact that for the first time in world history, in a colonial and semi-feudal country,

in the favourable conditions created by the brilliant victory of the Soviet Army in World War Two, the Vietnamese people, under the leadership of their Party, staged an armed uprising, overthrew the rule of the French colonialists and the Japanese militarists, won back power for the people and founded the D.R.V.N., the first people's democratic State in Southeast Asia.

The August Revolution opened a new era in the 4,000-year long history of the Vietnamese nation, an era in which the entire country became independent and free and was advancing to socialism. This was also the objective for which our Party had been struggling ever since its foundation fifteen years earlier, an objective which conforms to the deep aspirations of our people and also to the law governing the development of the world.

On September 2, 1945, in the Declaration of Independence, President Ho Chi Minh proclaimed:

"Viet Nam has the right to enjoy freedom and independence, and in fact has become a free and independent country. The entire Vietnamese people are determined to mobilize all their physical and mental strength, to sacrifice their lives and property in order to safeguard their freedom and independence."

However, the imperialist powers headed by U.S. imperialism, the richest and strongest imperialist power at that time, which was nurturing a mad dream of world hegemony, took fright at the success of the Vietnamese revolution and its impact on the world revolution. They gave every possible support and assistance to the French imperialists in launching a war of reconquest in an attempt to reimpose their colonial yoke on Viet Nam. However, the historic Dien Bien Phu victory put a definitive end to the French colonial regime, which had lasted almost a century in our country, and dealt a mortal blow at old-style colonialism on a world scale. Not reconciled to defeat, U.S. imperialism rushed into the South of our country, and waged the longest, most atrocious colonialist war of aggression on the largest scale ever seen in our times. Throughout twenty years of the anti-U.S. war of resistance for national salvation, the Vietnamese people have persevered in an extremely arduous but also extremely glorious struggle and finally won complete victory over the U.S. aggressors, putting a definitive end to U.S. neocolonialism in South Viet Nam, contributing to hastening the bankruptcy of neocolonialism in various forms throughout the world, and upsetting the global strategy of U.S. imperialism. The past thirty years of fighting against imperialist aggression, chiefly U.S. aggression, have demonstrated this eloquent truth of our times: the revolutionary cause of the people—the national democratic revolution and the socialist revolution are closely connected both within a country and on a world scale—is a just and surely victorious cause. It draws its strength from the fact that it is made up of forces deeply rooted in history, and has the capability of surmounting all obstacles standing in its way. U.S. imperialism wanted to use Viet Nam to test its mad design: to check the development of the national democratic revolution as well as the socialist revolution. The Vietnamese people proudly took up this challenge and, as has been rightly pointed out by many persons in the world, Viet Nam became the frontline and our people became the shock army in the fight against U.S. aggression. Thus, the victory of the Vietnamese people is also a very significant victory for the world revolution, for all friends of peace, justice and freedom.

Today, as we review the victories of historic and epochal significance of our Vietnamese people in the past 30 years, we are all the prouder of our Party, the organizer of all victories of our people, and of the correct, clear-sighted, independent, sovereign, intelligent and creative leadership of our Party.

This leadership has been reflected first of all in our Party's revolutionary line, in its political, military and international line.

This line stems from the laws governing the evolution of history in our era, in which Lenin's appeal: "Proletarians and oppressed peoples all over the world, unite!" embodies the revolutionary struggle of the time.

The Party's revolutionary line has brought into play the national tradition of resistance to foreign aggression, achieved the unity of the entire people, mobilized the strength of the armed forces throughout the country, developed the effect of the people's power, of the D.R.V.N., of the P.R.G.R.S.V.N., and carried out a people's war, a revolutionary war, in very diversified forms. This was a sacred war for national salvation carried out under the slogan: "Nothing is more precious than independence and freedom." The more brutal the enemy became and the more crimes they perpetrated, the deeper the hatred of every Vietnamese and the higher their determination to fight, and consequently the revolutionary war of our people became an "immense net covering both sky and earth" from which the enemy found it impossible to escape. This land is our native land, our fatherland. Caught in this encirclement with no escape route, the foreign aggressors and their henchmen were sure to meet with defeat.

The resistance against the French, and especially that against the Americans, were immortal epics of the Vietnamese people and of the combatants of the People's Army in both zones who "are loyal to the country and the people, and will fulfil any task, overcome any difficulty and defeat any enemy." It is the epic of all Vietnamese citizens, men and women, old and young, in all parts of the country, who fought the enemy with legendary courage and intelligence. It can be said that the people, the Vietnamese people, have defeated U.S. technology and defeated blind brute force, because they are men and women armed with lofty ideas and sentiments, and deep confidence in their just and surely victorious fight.

While evoking these exploits of our combatants and people throughout the country in the past two wars of resistance we turn our thoughts, with great emotion and pride to the people and combatants in the South, the "Brass Wall" of the Fatherland. These outstanding sons and daughters of the country, heroes of a heroic nation, have made a worthy contribution to the glorious victory of the nation.

Our Party's revolutionary line has succeeded in enlisting the sympathy, support and assistance of the fraternal socialist countries, the international Communist and workers' movement, the Third World countries and the whole of progressive mankind including progressive people in the United States. The just fight of our people against the criminal war of aggression of U.S. imperialism has had a broad and deep impact on human conscience, giving rise to a world-wide movement of popular support for Vietnam's anti-U.S. resistance. This was one of the largest and most enduring international movements ever seen.

Imbued with the principles of the great doctrine of Marxism-Leninism and noble proletarian internationalism, our Party and our people are deeply conscious that the revolutionary cause of our people is part and parcel of the revolutionary cause of the peoples of the world. We have done our best to win the greatest possible sympathy, support and assistance from our comrades and friends in all continents. Today, we take great pride in having used in the most effective manner the very great and precious support and assistance of the peoples of the other fraternal socialist countries and the world's peoples as a whole. We also take great pride in having contributed a worthy share to the growth of the fraternal socialist countries and the world revolutionary movement.

Today we celebrate with great joy the fraternal friendship and close militant solidarity which have bound our people to the peoples of Laos and Cambodia. This friendship and solidarity has made a very important contribution to the victory of each people. Enhancing this fine tradition, we pledge to do our best to strengthen the fraternal friendship and co-operation among the peoples of our three countries in consolidating our national independence and building our respective countries into prosperous and happy ones.

The Party's leadership has also been reflected in an overall strategy applied in a very flexible and intelligent manner, which caused us to constantly hold the initiative and an offensive posture on all military, political and diplomatic fronts, and constantly drive the enemy into a position of passivity and failure. It was from a position of passivity and failure that the enemy escalated the war and when inevitably they had to de-escalate they found themselves in a still worse position of passivity and failure. That was how we defeated U.S. imperialism step by step: at the end of 1964 we defeated its special war; in the Tet of Mau Than (1968) we defeated its limited war; in 1972 we defeated its "Vietnamization" of the war and with the Paris Agreement, we completely drove more than half a million U.S. aggressor troops from the South of our country. Thus, from the day U.S. imperialism began its war of aggression against our country up to the signing of the Paris Agreement it was a process of fighting to drive the Yankees away. The period that followed was a process of fighting to topple the puppets. In effect, the New Year Message of Uncle Ho was an illustration of a very clever and clearsighted strategy and military art! Our Party's military line and strategy, both in the former anti-French resistance and in the recent anti-U.S. resistance, consisted in waging a protracted war aimed at whittling away and wiping out the enemy forces step by step, while fostering and developing our forces, at the same time creating opportunities to fight and defeat the enemy in battles of a decisive character. This is the dialectics of the strategy of protracted war the anti-French war of resistance began with pointed bamboo sticks, went on to win resounding victories and ended with the famous Dien Bien Phu victory. In the 20-year-long war of resistance against U.S. imperialism, this dialectics led to victories of very important strategic significance, and finally resulted in the victory of Spring 1975. In this battle, within only 55 days, our army, through lightning attacks and with overwhelmingly superior forces, defeated more than one million enemy troops with abundant modern equipment, liberated Saigon and the whole of our beloved South, winning full, total and thorough victory, paving the way for the further development of the great revolutionary cause of our people.

Today, celebrating the 30th anniversary of the D.R.V.N., let us review the exploits in fighting and the achievements in the building of the new system whose superiority has been developed in the flames of war and amidst the innumerable difficulties of national reconstruction following the August Revolution.

The superiority of the new system finds its full expression in the fact that it is the people's democratic regime advancing to socialism without passing through the stage of capitalist development. The invincible strength of the new regime actually lies in the fact that for the first time in our national history, we have a regime of the people, by the people and for the people. It has the capability of mobilizing to the highest level the strength and ardour of the entire nation. Thanks to this, it successfully tided over the worst trials of 1946 and at the end of the same year held high the banner of resistance against the French colonialists in the spirit of a victor.

The nine years of resistance against the French marked an all-sided development of the D.R.V.N. Under the Party's leadership, democratic reforms, especially the land reform, were undertaken, realizing the age-old dream of the peasant masses, bringing about deep changes in the countryside, exerting a positive effect on the whole of the political, economic and social life, and making an important contribution to the war of resistance.

Following the Dien Bien Phu victory and two years after the signing of the 1954 Geneva Agreements on Viet Nam, the whole of Viet Nam should have become a unified country, completely independent and free, and steadily advancing to socialism. But the imperialist powers, headed by U.S. imperialism, blatantly violated the Geneva Agreements, creating conditions for the United States to oust France and intervene in South Viet Nam and launch a new war of aggresion, thus compelling our people to take up arms again to carry out a twenty-year-long war of resistance against the U.S. aggressors.

It was precisely in this glorious fight that the D.R.V.N., the socialist North, has developed to the highest level the superiority and all the capacities of the new system, and proved worthy of being the firm base of the revolution throughout the country: the national-democratic revolution in the South and the socialist revolution in the North.

The Ho Chi Minh Trail along the majestic Truong Son (Long Range) and linking North and South was a marvellous exploit in the history of war, a proud demonstration of the strength of the combative solidarity of our people throughout the country. The harder the enemy tried to block it and destroy it, the more quickly and steadily it developed and grew with the level of the war, and in the Spring of 1975 made an important contribution to our glorious victory in liberating Saigon and completely liberating our beloved South Viet Nam.

In the strategy of U.S. imperialism, to attack North Viet Nam has always been a very important objective. In fact, the United States mobilized major air and naval forces to attack North Viet Nam, destroy economic installations, towns and countryside, destroy the environment in an attempt to "bomb the North back to the Stone Age." However, the strength of our people throughout the country and our extremely effective air defence system caused U.S. imperialism to take heavier and heavier losses as it escalated the air war[;] its losses became so high as to be intolerable and it had to de-escalate after the Nau Than Tet in 1968. However, stubborn by nature, in 1972 and especially in late December of that year, deploying huge air forces including B-52 strategic bombers, the United States launched a frantic air blitz against Hanoi and other cities and towns of North Viet Nam with the intention of nullifying many provisions already agreed upon by the two sides in their negotiations. But this time it incurred a still heavier military and political defeat. World opinion greeted the glorious victory of our people with high elation since it led to the signing of the Paris Agreement on Vietnam.

North Viet Nam has fought and built at the same time, fighting well to defend its building work and building rapidly to increase its combat forces. That is the process of the all-round growth of the D.R.V.N., which is worthy of being the revolutionary base of the entire country and an outpost of socialism in Southeast Asia.

Immediately after the Dien Bien Phu victory, in completely liberated North Viet Nam, in the light of the Party's line on the advance to socialism while bypassing the stage of capitalist development, we moved rapidly to the socialist transformation of agriculture, handicrafts and private capitalist industry and commerce. The land reform and agricultural co-operativization had the effect of boosting agricultural production, doubling rice productivity and output compared with the years before the revolution. At the same time, we stepped up the production of consumer goods, and strove to develop a number of essential branches of heavy industry such as electricity, coal, engineering, metallurgy, chemicals and building materials. We paid particular attention to maintaining and strengthening the communications and transport network with a view to serving the front, the economy and the people's life along with initial steps in the building of the material and technological base of socialism. We attached great importance to the development of science and technology, and exerted great efforts in training a contingent of qualified workers, scientific and technical workers and economic management cadres who are politically staunch and professionally proficient.

We have also done our best to develop socialist culture, education, public health, literature, the arts, physical culture and sports, the protection of mothers and children; we have recorded encouraging achievements, especially in general and higher education.

These profound changes in economic, cultural and social life made North Viet Nam radically different from what it was in the past. The feudal landlord class has been abolished, the bourgeois class has been reformed, the regime of exploitation of man by man has been eliminated and socialist relations of production have been established in two forms: State-run economy and collective economy. The working people, comprising the working class, the peasantry and the socialist intelligentsia have become collective masters of their destiny. Political security and social order have been maintained. North Vietnamese society has become a single united bloc of the working people including people belonging to various nationalities and religions and striving together for national independence and socialism. . . .

At present, under the leadership of the Party and through close co-operation between the Government of the D.R.V.N. and the P.R.G.R.S.V.N., we proceed from the situation and tasks of the revolution in the entire country in the new stage to solve all problems concerning the two zones. In particular, on the economic front, we must strive to give full scope to our new capabilities in order to step up the rehabilitation and development of the national economy—carry out socialist transformation and construction, speed up socialist industrialization and the process of advancing from small to large-scale production, and step by step improve the living standard of our people throughout the country.

In the South we must strive to do away with the long, heavy legacy of dozens of years of aggressive war and U.S. neocolonialism in all spheres—political, economic, cultural, social and ideological. We must rapidly stabilize social order, strengthen political security, set up and consolidate the revolutionary power everywhere. We will also strive, through many effective measures, to care for the life of the working people, and provide jobs for the millions of unemployed left by the old regime and by the war. These tasks benefit from the effective participation of the working people and other patriotic sections of the population. In the economic field, we are encouraging the normal operation of all enterprises and factories of all sizes in order to contribute to economic rehabilitation and development. We call on the working class and other sections of the working people in the towns and countryside to bring into play their role as masters of society under the new regime by working harder than before, working with higher productivity, higher technique and discipline. We also call on the national bourgeoisie, who were formerly held down by foreign competition, to put all their talents and ardour into the service of the great cause of the nation now that the country has become independent and free. Our people in the South are facing difficult and complicated revolutionary tasks which require much courage, intelligence and creativeness. Today we joyfully express to our beloved South Vietnamese compatriots and our confidence and elation at the outstanding achievements they have recorded over the past four months and the prospects of still greater achievements in the days ahead. The South, with its fertile land, is favoured by nature in many other ways. It may carry out large-scale agricultural production in areas with long traditions of rice growing, valuable industrial crops and fruit trees, or stock-breeding and fishing. It is certain that the South of our country will soon become a prosperous centre for agricultural production and fishing to supply the people and provide for exports. In addition, the South has many industrial branches, especially light and food industries which, though mostly of small scale, are capable of producing many items necessary to the people's life and also export items. Communications and transport, and especially the building industry in South Viet Nam, have substantial forces and capabilities that should be utilized in this manner. With the people's support, the new administration will rapidly stabilize the political and economic situation and will normalize the people's life on the basis of a plan for the entire country, the South will make new and very inspiring steps forward. Saigon, Ho Chi Minh city, will have a very important role in many respects and will broaden its foreign relations with countries in Southeast Asia and the rest of the world.

At present, at a time when the entire country has regained independence and freedom and is advancing to socialism, socialist North Viet Nam has all the greater obligation to even fuller play to its achievements and experiences and make the most effective contribution to the rehabilitation and development of the economy in the South. The North must endeavour to develop its co-operativized agriculture, increase the output and productivity of food crops and other plants, develop stock-breeding into a main branch of production, and steadily take agriculture and forestry, from the productive to the processing branches, to large-scale socialist production. The North should attach greater importance to the production of consumer goods, especially those which it has the capacity to produce in great quantities, with high output and low production costs. In particular, North Viet Nam should display courage and intelligence in expanding rapidly the existing heavy industries which are very necessary to itself and to the entire country. Today in North Viet Nam there has taken shape in the most rational [form] a managerial system of the national economy from the centre down to the grassroots, combining management in each branch with management in each locality. The contingent of workers and scientific and technical cadres who have been tempered in fighting and production should make intensive efforts to shoulder the new tasks which are much greater and more complicated than before. Practice has shown that the Party's line on the building of the material and technical basis of socialism is correct and clearsighted. But the organization for the application of this line still falls short of requirements. At present, we are facing very favourable conditions: peace has taken the place of war, our homeland and our cause are now one country and one cause, our position and strength have become many times more powerful in all fields. The new bright situation and new tasks together with the very prospects require that all branches, all levels, all responsible comrades and all the working people make enormous efforts to heighten rapidly their standards and capacities, their organizational and managerial capacities, in order to increase to the highest possible level their effectiveness in the grassroots organizations: factories and cooperatives, which labour to produce material wealth with ever increasing productivity.

In this spirit, we must see to the full achievement of the 1975 State Plan and prepare for the implementation of the 1976 State Plan and the forthcoming five-year plan with still greater progress.

The victory of the revolutionary cause of our people is also a victory of the great doctrine of Marxism-Leninism, the peak of human wisdom, which has lighted our revolutionary path full of glorious victories. Our Party and people plan to study Marxist-Leninist theory and apply it creatively in the new stage of the revolution in order to win still bigger successes for our socialist cause.

Today, celebrating the historic victory of our nation, the Vietnamese people express their sincere and profound gratitude for the sympathy and the great and precious support and assistance extended to us by the peoples of the Soviet Union, China and the other socialist countries, the peoples of our two fraternal neighbours, Laos and Cambodia, the international communist and workers' movement, and the peoples of all other countries in the world including progressive people in the United States. We cordially convey to our comrades and friends in all continents our warmest congratulations.

For us Vietnamese, a glorious page in our history has been turned and a new period has begun: the period of peaceful construction. This new work requires that we strengthen our great friendship and co-operation in all fields with the other socialist countries which are bound to us by the common ideal of building socialism and communism. We will strive to strengthen our great friendship and our relations in all fields with our two fraternal neighbouring countries, relations which have become still closer in the new situation. It is our wish to expand our friendly relations in many respects with other countries in Southeast Asia. Now that peace has been restored, we are provided with favourable conditions to expand our good relations with the bloc of non-aligned countries, the countries of the Third World, for a noble objective—consolidating national independence and building their respective countries into prosperous ones. We are establishing normal relations and expanding economic, cultural, scientific and technical relations with all other countries on the principles of mutual respect for each other's independence and sovereignty, noninterference in each other's internal affairs, equality and mutual benefit. In this spirit, the D.R.V.N. is ready to establish normal relations with the United States on the basis of the Paris Agreement. It is certain that the majority of the American people and many political circles in the United States will support this positive trend.

Our century has witnessed earth-shaking events that have profoundly modified the face of our planet. This revolutionary process is continuing, possibly at a still quicker pace. It will alter the balance of forces in a way more and more favourable for peace, national independence, democracy and socialism, while imperialism and other reactionary forces headed by U.S. imperialism are declining and sustaining more and more defeats caused by mounting difficulties and never-ending crises, and are being continually attacked from all sides. The Vietnamese people are firmly convinced that the revolutionary cause of the peoples in the Arab countries, the peoples in Asia, Africa, Latin America, and other parts of the world will be crowned with glorious victory.

Today, the Vietnamese people as a whole are overwhelmed with joy at the complete and great victories recently won by our nation, victories for peace, independence, democracy and socialism. A new era has opened in our country's history, the era of a regime in which the people are masters of their own destiny and can build with their own hands a happy life, while our Party, as Uncle Ho said, "remains the leader and truly faithful servant of the people."

The entire people of Viet Nam, fired with enthusiasm, are striving to turn their revolutionary heroism in combat into courage in peaceful construction with a view to exploiting the immense riches of the country, mobilizing the very abundant labour forces of the people and step by step building the material and technical basis of socialism, building a modern industry, a modern agriculture, an advanced culture and science, and on this basis, to improve continuously the life of the people. Our people are deeply conscious that to build socialism, it is necessary to have socialist men who love their fatherland, their people, labour and science, who cherish the independence and freedom of their own country and of other countries, who treasure ... their own people and those of the whole of progressive mankind.

Under the banner of the fatherland and socialism, the banner of patriotism combined with proletarian internationalism, let our people steadily march forward to carry out in the best possible way the last behest of our beloved President Ho Chi Minh:

"Let our entire Party and the people, closely joining their efforts, build a peaceful, reunified, independent, democratic and prosperous Vietnam, and make a worthy contribution to the world revolution."

Long live the D.R.V.N.!

Long live a peaceful, reunified, independent, democratic and prosperous Viet Nam!

Long live the Viet Nam Workers' Party, the organizer of all victories of the Vietnamese revolution!

Our great President Ho Chi Minh will live forever in our cause!

Source: Pham Van Dong, *Selected Writings* (Hanoi: Foreign Languages Publishing House, 1977), 375–397.

224. President Bill Clinton Lifts the Trade Embargo on the Socialist Republic of Vietnam, February 3, 1994 [Excerpts]

Introduction

Following the military victory by the Democratic Republic of Vietnam (DRV, North Vietnam) over the forces of the Republic of Vietnam (RVN, South Vietnam) in April 1975, the United States pursued a punitive foreign policy toward the new united Socialist Republic of Vietnam (SRV), established on July 2, 1976. Washington not only refused to normalize relations with the SRV but also actively sought to isolate the SRV politically, economically, and diplomatically. Both sides were intransigent. U.S. leaders were clearly frustrated at the North Vietnamese government's violations of the Paris Peace Accords and the defeat of South Vietnam. On its part, the SRV demanded payment of the $3.3 billion in reconstruction aid pledged by President Richard Nixon. A particularly thorny issue was the fate of some 2,400 Americans missing in action (MIAs) in Southeast Asia. Vietnam's 10-year-long occupation of Cambodia beginning in 1979 further exacerbated the situation. Although efforts had been made under previous administrations, the greatest progress toward normalized U.S.-Vietnamese relations occurred under the Bill Clinton administration, which in February 1994 lifted the American trade embargo on the SRV. That action allowed American trade and investment. The United States also dropped its veto on credits and loans to Vietnam from international lending associations.

Primary Source

From the beginning of my administration, I have said that any decisions about our relationships with Vietnam should be guided by one factor and one factor only: gaining the fullest possible accounting for our prisoners of war and our missing in action. We owe that to all who served in Vietnam and to the families of those whose fate remains unknown.

Today I am lifting the trade embargo against Vietnam because I am absolutely convinced it offers the best way to resolve the fate of those who remain missing and about whom we are not sure. We've worked hard over the last year to achieve progress. On Memorial Day, I pledged to declassify and make available virtually all Government documents related to our POW's and MIA. On Veterans Day, I announced that we had fulfilled that pledge. Last April, and again in July, I sent two Presidential delegations to Vietnam to expand our search for remains and documents. We intensified our diplomatic efforts. We have devoted more resources to this effort than any previous administration. Today, more than 500 dedicated military and civilian personnel are involved in this effort under the leadership of General Shalikashvili, Secretary Aspin, and our Commander in the Pacific, Admiral Larson. Many work daily in the fields, the jungles, the mountains of Vietnam, Cambodia, and Laos, often braving very dangerous conditions, trying to find the truth about those about whom we are not sure.

Last July, I said any improvement in our relations with Vietnam would depend on tangible progress in four specific areas: first, the recovery and return of remains of our POW's and MIA; second, the continued resolution of discrepancy cases, cases in which there is reason to believe individuals could have survived the incident in which they were lost; third, further assistance from Vietnam and Laos on investigations along their common border, an area where many U.S. servicemen were lost and pilots downed; and fourth, accelerated efforts to provide all relevant POW/MIA-related documents.

Today, I can report that significant, tangible progress has been made in all these four areas. Let me describe it. First, on remains: Since the beginning of this administration, we have recovered the remains of 67 American servicemen. In the 7 months since July, we've recovered 39 sets of remains, more than during all of 1992. Second, on the discrepancy cases: Since the beginning of the administration, we've reduced the number of these cases from 135 to 73. Since last July, we've confirmed the deaths of 19 servicemen who were on the list. A special United States team in Vietnam continues to investigate the remaining cases. Third, on cooperation with Laos: As a direct result of the conditions set out in July, the Governments of Vietnam and Laos agreed to work with us to investigate their common border. The first such investigation took place in December and located new remains as well as crash sites that will soon be excavated. Fourth, on the documents: Since July, we have received important wartime documents from Vietnam's military archives that provide leads on unresolved POW/MIA cases.

[. . .]

I have made the judgment that the best way to ensure cooperation from Vietnam and to continue getting the information Americans want on POW's and MIA's is to end the trade embargo. I've also decided to establish a liaison office in Vietnam to provide services for Americans there and help us to pursue a human rights dialog with the Vietnamese Government.

I want to be clear: These actions do not constitute a normalization of our relationships. Before that happens, we must have more progress, more cooperation, and more answers. Toward that end, this spring I will send another high level U.S. delegation to Vietnam to continue the search for remains and for documents.

Earlier today I met with the leaders of our Nation's veterans organizations. I deeply respect their views. Many of the families they represent have endured enormous suffering and uncertainty. And their opinions also deserve special consideration. I talked with them about my decision. I explained the reasons for that decision. Some of them, in all candor, do not agree with the action I am taking today. But I believe we all agree on the ultimate goal: to secure the fullest possible accounting of those who remain missing. And I was pleased that they committed to continue working with us toward that goal.

Whatever the Vietnam war may have done in dividing our country in the past, today our Nation is one in honoring those who served and pressing for answers about all those who did not return. This decision today, I believe, renews that commitment and our constant, constant effort never to forget those until our job is done. Those who have sacrificed deserve a full and final accounting. I am absolutely convinced, as are so many in the Congress who served

there and so many Americans who have studied this issue, that this decision today will help to ensure that fullest possible accounting.

Thank you very much.

Source: *Public Papers of the Presidents of the United States: William J. Clinton, 1994,* Book 1 (Washington, DC: U.S. Government Printing Office, 1995), 178–180.

225. President Bill Clinton: Announcement of Normalization of Diplomatic Relations with Vietnam, July 11, 1995

Introduction

Despite the end of the U.S. trade embargo of the Socialist Republic of Vietnam (SRV), some trade restrictions impeded American companies from taking a greater role in developing the growing SRV economy. U.S. humanitarian aid increased, as did cultural and educational exchanges, and American tourism skyrocketed as veterans and Vietnamese Americans returned to visit friends and relatives. In January 1995 American and Vietnamese officials signed an agreement exchanging liaison offices in their respective capitals. On July 11, 1995, despite some opposition from the lobby for those missing in action (MIA) and from Republican conservatives, President Bill Clinton extended full diplomatic ties to the SRV. The first U.S. envoy to the SRV was Congressman Douglas "Pete" Peterson (D-Fla.), a former Vietnam prisoner of war (POW).

Primary Source

Today I am announcing the normalization of diplomatic relationships with Vietnam.

From the beginning of this administration, any improvement in relationships between America and Vietnam has depended upon making progress on the issue of Americans who were missing in action or held as prisoners of war. Last year, I lifted the trade embargo on Vietnam in response to their cooperation and to enhance our efforts to secure the remains of lost Americans and to determine the fate of those whose remains have not been found.

It has worked. In 17 months, Hanoi has taken important steps to help us resolve many cases. Twenty-nine families have received the remains of their loved ones and at last have been able to give them a proper burial. Hanoi has delivered to us hundreds of pages of documents shedding light on what happened to Americans in Vietnam. And Hanoi has stepped up its cooperation with Laos, where many Americans were lost. We have reduced the number of so-called discrepancy cases, in which we have had reason to believe that Americans were still alive after they were lost, to 55. And we will continue to work to resolve more cases.

Hundreds of dedicated men and women are working on all these cases, often under extreme hardship and real danger in the mountains and jungles of Indochina. On behalf of all Americans, I want to thank them. And I want to pay a special tribute to General John Vessey, who has worked so tirelessly on this issue for Presidents Reagan and Bush and for our administration. He has made a great difference to a great many families. And we as a nation are grateful for his dedication and for his service. Thank you, sir.

I also want to thank the Presidential delegation, led by Deputy Secretary of Veterans Affairs Hershel Gober, Winston Lord, James Wold, who have helped us to make so much progress on this issue. And I am especially grateful to the leaders of the families and the veterans organizations who have worked with the delegation and maintained their extraordinary commitment to finding the answers we seek.

Never before in the history of warfare has such an extensive effort been made to resolve the fate of soldiers who did not return. Let me emphasize, normalization of our relations with Vietnam is not the end of our effort. From the early days of this administration I have said to the families and veterans groups what I say again here: We will keep working until we get all the answers we can. Our strategy is working. Normalization of relations is the next appropriate step. With this new relationship we will be able to make more progress. To that end, I will send another delegation to Vietnam this year. And Vietnam has pledged it will continue to help us find answers. We will hold them to that pledge.

By helping to bring Vietnam into the community of nations, normalization also serves our interest in working for a free and peaceful Vietnam in a stable and peaceful Asia. We will begin to normalize our trade relations with Vietnam, whose economy is now liberalizing and integrating into the economy of the Asia-Pacific region. Our policy will be to implement the appropriate United States Government programs to develop trade with Vietnam consistent with U.S. law.

As you know, many of these programs require certifications regarding human rights and labor rights before they can proceed. We have already begun discussing human rights issues with Vietnam, especially issues regarding religious freedom. Now we can expand and strengthen that dialog. The Secretary of State will go to Vietnam in August where he will discuss all of these issues, beginning with our POW and MIA concerns.

I believe normalization and increased contact between Americans and Vietnamese will advance the cause of freedom in Vietnam, just as it did in Eastern Europe and the former Soviet Union. I strongly believe that engaging the Vietnamese on the broad economic front of economic reform and the broad front of democratic reform will help to honor the sacrifice of those who fought for freedom's sake in Vietnam.

I am proud to be joined in this view by distinguished veterans of the Vietnam war. They served their country bravely. They are of different parties. A generation ago they had different judgments about the war which divided us so deeply. But today they are of a single mind. They agree that the time has come for America to move forward on Vietnam. All Americans should be grateful especially that Senators John McCain, John Kerry, Bob Kerrey, Chuck Robb, and Representative Pete Peterson, along with other Vietnam veterans in the Congress, including Senator Harkin, Congressman Kolbe, and Congressman Gilchrest, who just left, and others who are out here in the audience have kept up their passionate interest in Vietnam but were able to move beyond the haunting and painful past toward finding common ground for the future. Today they and many other veterans support the normalization of relations, giving the opportunity to Vietnam to fully join the community of nations and being true to what they fought for so many years ago.

Whatever we may think about the political decisions of the Vietnam era, the brave Americans who fought and died there had noble motives. They fought for the freedom and the independence of the Vietnamese people. Today the Vietnamese are independent, and we believe this step will help to extend the reach of freedom in Vietnam and, in so doing, to enable these fine veterans of Vietnam to keep working for that freedom.

This step will also help our own country to move forward on an issue that has separated Americans from one another for too long now. Let the future be our destination. We have so much work ahead of us. This moment offers us the opportunity to bind up our own wounds. They have resisted time for too long. We can now move on to common ground. Whatever divided us before let us consign to the past. Let this moment, in the words of the Scripture, be a time to heal and a time to build.

Thank you all, and God bless America.

Source: *Public Papers of the Presidents of the United States: William J. Clinton, 1995,* Book 2 (Washington, DC: U.S. Government Printing Office, 1996), 1073–1074.

Appendices

Appendix A

Unit Designations

The following are some general rules for unit designations, along with the notable exceptions. This is basically the system that is used by the military itself as well as virtually all military historians. Some of this might seem arcane, but knowledgeable readers will spot the deviations right away.

- **Adjectives versus titles**: Words such as "main force," "local force," "VC," "PAVN," "ARVN," and "U.S." are not part of the designations of any units. These are clarifying adjectives. Thus, there are no such units as the 1st U.S. Infantry Division, the 9th VC Division, or the 304th PAVN Infantry Division. They should always be listed as the U.S. 1st Infantry Division, the VC 9th Division, and the PAVN 304th Infantry Division, respectively. Likewise, the words "main force" and "local force" are not part of unit designations. They are allied intelligence classifications. They are not proper nouns and should not be capitalized.
- **Numbering**: With few exceptions, Arabic numerals are used to designate units at every level from squad all the way up to army group.
- **Squads and platoons**: In designating squads and platoons, 2nd Squad or 3rd Platoon, for example, should always be capitalized. These are proper nouns, the official names of units. Those names never change.
- **Companies**: Companies are designated by capital letters (e.g., A Company, C Company, etc.). Sometimes the international phonetic alphabet is used (e.g., Alpha Company, Charlie Company).

  Exception: Company level is one of the places where the People's Army of Vietnam (PAVN, North Vietnamese Army) and the Viet Cong (VC) did it differently. They

kept numerical designations at the company level (e.g., 1st Company, 3rd Company).

  Exception: The New Zealand artillery battery had a unique numerical designation. Following the British practice, its official designation was Number 161 Field Battery, or 161 Field Battery for short.

- **Battalions**: Battalions are designated by Arabic numerals (e.g., 1st Battalion, 3rd Battalion). Most often battalions are part of a larger regiment and are designated as such (e.g., 2nd Battalion, 47th Infantry Regiment).

  Exception: Separate battalions were not elements of larger regiments and had unique numerical designations (e.g., 52nd Aviation Battalion; 95th Military Police Battalion).

- **Regiments**: Regiments are designated by Arabic numerals but are almost always some type of regiment (i.e., of a specific branch), such as the 11th Artillery Regiment, 47th Infantry Regiment. Once the regiment has been introduced, it is acceptable to abbreviate its designation by dropping off the word "Regiment" (e.g., 47th Infantry or even 47th Inf.).

  Exception: All U.S. Marine Corps regiments are designated as Xth Marine Regiment or Xth Marines for short. Even though the 11th Marines is an artillery rather than an infantry regiment, it is still called simply the 11th Marines.

  Important distinction: In the U.S. Army the regiment has not been a tactical command echelon since 1958. In the U.S. Marine Corps it still is. What this means in practice is that all three battalions of a given U.S.

Marine Corps regiment usually operate together under the command of that regiment. In the U.S. Army the 1st, 2nd, and 3rd battalions of a given infantry regiment might not even be in the same division. For example, the 1st and 3rd battalions, 12th Infantry, were assigned to the 4th Infantry Division, while the 2nd Battalion, 12th Infantry, was assigned to the 25th Infantry Division.

Exception: Certain specialized U.S. Army units did operate as separate (nondivisional) regiments. The 11th Armored Cavalry Regiment is the primary example. The Army of the Republic of Vietnam (ARVN, South Vietnamese Army) and the PAVN also had separate regiments.

- **Abbreviating battalions and regiments**: Most army regiments exist in name only, but that name remains an integral part of the battalion designation. Therefore, there is a key distinction in the way that the battalion and regiment designation is abbreviated in the U.S. Army versus the U.S. Marine Corps. This distinction may seem arcane, but it is important.

  U.S. Army: The abbreviation for the 2nd Battalion, 47th Infantry, is 2-47 Infantry. The hyphen (-) indicates that the 2 and the 47 are part of the battalion's full designation and cannot be separated. Only a single echelon of command and control is indicated here.

  U.S. Marine Corps: The abbreviation for the 2nd Battalion, 1st Marines, is 2/1 Marines. The slash (/) indicates two distinct command and control echelons.

  Company designations: One effect of the difference between the U.S. Army and the U.S. Marine Corps is the way the companies are designated. In any given army battalion the companies are designated as A through C, or later A through D when the U.S. Army added a fourth rifle company. Thus, in the 2-47th Infantry. the companies were designated A though D, and in the 3-47th Infantry. they started right back with A through D. In U.S. Marine Corps regiments, all the rifle companies are lettered sequentially throughout the regiment. Hence, the 1/1 Marines has Company A through Company C, the 2/1 Marines has Company D through Company F, and the 3/1 Marines has Company G through Company I.

  General recommendation: I recommend for the most part not even using the word "regiment" when referring to U.S. Army and U.S. Marine Corps divisional units. The name "11th Marines" always stands for 11th Marine Regiment. There is no other way to interpret it. The name "2nd Battalion, 47th Infantry," always stands for 2nd Battalion, 47th Infantry Regiment. There is no other way to interpret

it. Also, it should always be 2nd Battalion, 47th Infantry, and not 2nd Battalion of the 47th Infantry.

- **Brigades**: Brigades are designated by Arabic numerals. Brigades existed in the U.S. Army but not in the U.S. Marine Corps. There were two basic types.

  Divisional brigades: Divisional brigades were the command and control headquarters between the division and the maneuver battalions. These were not standing organizations, as with the U.S. Marine Corps regiments. The maneuver battalions of an army division were attached and detached from the brigades as the operational requirements dictated. Thus, the brigades of a division were numbered as the 1st, 2nd, or 3rd brigades of that division (e.g., 1st Brigade, 9th Infantry Division; 2nd Brigade, 9th Infantry Division; 3rd Brigade, 9th Infantry Division).

  Separate brigades: Nondivisional brigades generally operated directly under the control of a corps-level headquarters. They had unique numbers, and their designations always included the type of unit (e.g., 173rd Airborne Brigade; 196th Light Infantry Brigade; 1st Aviation Brigade; 1st Signal Brigade).

  Non-U.S. brigades: Like the U.S. Marine Corps divisions, the divisions of the Republic of Korea Army (ROKA, South Korean Army), the ARVN, the VC, and the PAVN were organized along regimental lines rather than brigade lines. The sole exceptions to this were the ARVN airborne and marine divisions, both of which were organized into brigades rather than regiments. The ARVN and the PAVN did have nondivisional separate brigades.

- **Groups**: Groups were mostly U.S. Army units that essentially were separate brigades in all but name. They were mostly corps-level assets and were designated by unique Arabic numerals (e.g., 23rd Artillery Group; 11th Aviation Group; 67th Medical Group; 5th Special Forces Group).

- **Divisions**: Divisions are designated by Arabic numerals. Divisions in almost all armies are some specific type of a division that is part of its proper name that must always be included. The 1st Infantry Division, for example, can never be abbreviated as "1st Division." During the Vietnam War the U.S. Army had three different 1st Divisions—the 1st Armored Division, the 1st Infantry Division, and the 1st Cavalry Division—with the latter two being in Vietnam. Nor can the division ever be abbreviated by dropping off the word "division." The name "1st Infantry" always means the 1st Infantry Regiment and not the 1st Infantry Division. The name "1st Cavalry" always means the 1st Cavalry Regiment, not the 1st Cavalry Division. If abbreviations are really necessary, then I recommend using "1st ID" and

"1st CD." Also, there was no such organization as the 1st Air Cavalry Division; it was the 1st Cavalry Division (Airmobile).

- **Corps**: Corps and corps-level organizations are designated by Roman numerals (e.g., XXIV Corps). The general convention is to use XXIV Corps rather than XXIVth Corps. The I Field Force and the II Field Force were corps-level units, as was the III Marine Amphibious Force.

- **Field armies**: Field armies and equivalent U.S. Air Force and U.S. Navy echelons are always designated by spelling out the number (e.g., Seventh Fleet; Seventh Air Force). The U.S. Army equivalent in Vietnam did not have a numerical designation and was called simply the U.S. Army, Vietnam (USARV). The Eighth Army was in Korea at the time.

DAVID T. ZABECKI

Appendix B

Military Ranks

All modern armies have two primary classes of soldiers: officers and enlisted men. This distinction originated in the armies of ancient times. In the medieval period the distinction was between knights and men at arms: nobility and commoners. Up through the beginning of the 20th century the distinction between military officers and enlisted soldiers reflected the social class distinctions of society as a whole. An officer was by definition a gentleman, while a common soldier was not. The breakdown in the old social orders that started during World War I was likewise reflected in the world's armies. By the end of World War II the distinction between officers and enlisted troops in many Western armies had become far more a professional one than a social one. In many East Asian militaries, however, there remained throughout the Vietnam War period a significant class difference between the commissioned and enlisted ranks.

As in the armies of all Communist countries, the officer ranks of the People's Army of Vietnam (PAVN, North Vietnamese Army) and the Viet Cong (VC) were populated by party members whose ideological reliability was beyond question. Unlike Western armies and particularly unlike the Army of the Republic of Vietnam (ARVN, South Vietnamese Army), the vast majority of PAVN and VC officers began their military careers as enlisted men and rose through the ranks, achieving officer rank after their military skills and political loyalty had been tested. PAVN forces in the Democratic Republic of Vietnam (DRV, North Vietnam) did not institute a formal military rank structure until 1958 in North Vietnam, and VC forces in the Republic of Vietnam (RVN, South Vietnam) essentially had no formal rank structure until the end of the war. One's military rank was simply the position that one held (platoon commander, deputy company commander, company commander, battalion commander, etc.) or that one was authorized

to hold; a staff officer, for instance, might hold the rank of company commander (*dai doi truong*) even though he was not actually commanding a company. During the Vietnam War the primary distinction within both the PAVN and the VC was not between "officer" and "enlisted man" but rather between "cadre," which included both officers and noncommissioned officers (NCOs), and privates, who were commonly referred to simply as "fighters" or "warriors" (*chien si*).

Officers comprise 10–15 percent of most modern armies. East Asian militaries with weak NCO corps generally had a much higher percentage of officers, as did all armies that were based on the Soviet model. Officers are further divided into three basic groups. Company-grade officers (lieutenants and captains) are responsible for the leadership of platoons and companies. Field-grade officers (majors and colonels) lead battalions and regiments. General officers command the higher echelons and also coordinate the overall direction of an army and its military activities. It is the generals who answer directly to the political leadership of modern democracies. Navies also recognize three broad groups of officers without necessarily using the army terms. In most militaries, generals and admirals are collectively called flag officers because each one has a personal flag bearing the insignia of his rank.

Although female officers and even flag officers are relatively common in the U.S. military today, this was not the case during most of the Vietnam War era. Many of the female American officers at the time were nurses, doctors, or other medical specialists. The first American female general officer was Brigadier General Anna Mae Hays, who as chief of the Army Nurse Corps was promoted to flag rank on June 11, 1970. Later that same day the chief of the Woman's Army Corps, Colonel Elizabeth P. Hoisington, was also promoted to brigadier general. Neither, however, actually served in Vietnam. Of all the armies that fought in Vietnam, the VC probably had the highest percentage of female officers as well as the highest percentage of female combatants.

Enlisted soldiers, sailors, airmen, and marines are divided into two basic categories: enlisted men and NCOs. The term for NCOs varies from military to military (e.g., petty officer in most navies; *sous officier* in the French Army), but the meaning is universal. In all Western militaries NCOs are the backbone of the organization. They are the ones responsible for training individual soldiers and for training and leading fire teams and squads. They hold key leadership positions in platoons and companies, and at the higher levels they assist staff officers in the planning and execution of operations.

In all armies the larger majority of the enlisted ranks denote the distinctions within the NCO corps. During the 20th century the American and British Commonwealth armies, including Australia and New Zealand, have had the strongest and most professional NCO corps. One of the biggest challenges that faced the American and Australian advisers supporting the ARVN units was the training and development of NCOs.

NCOs include corporals, sergeants, and in some armies warrant officers. It is this category of warrant officer that is most difficult to classify, because the exact status varies from army to army. Many Western armies follow the British Commonwealth model in which warrant officers are the highest category of NCOs. In the American military, on the other hand, warrant officers are a distinct personnel class between officers and enlisted troops. NCOs are considered specialist officers, highly skilled in a certain functional area, and receive pay equivalent to company grade officers but do not have the full range of command authority and responsibilities. The majority of the U.S. Army helicopter pilots who served in Vietnam were warrant officers.

In the American military, warrant officers are much closer to commissioned officers. In the Australian and New Zealand armies, they are clearly the most senior of the NCOs. Contrary to widely held popular belief, the rank of sergeant major, for example, does not exist in military organizations based on the British model. Rather, it is a position title—or an appointment, as the British call it—such as squad leader or company commander. The rank of the NCO holding the sergeant major position is always a warrant officer, but the NCO is always addressed by the position title of sergeant major. The Australians and New Zealanders do not have company first sergeants. The senior NCO in any given company is called the company sergeant major. While the Australian and New Zealand armies each have two grades of warrant officer, the Royal Australian Navy and the Royal Australian Air Force have only one grade of warrant officer.

Thus, there is no real direct comparison between British Commonwealth and American warrant officers, which partially explains the difficulty in correlating exactly the military ranks of the world's armies. The confusion between American and British warrant officers causes problems to this day in many North Atlantic Treaty Organization (NATO) headquarters. During the Vietnam

War period the U.S. Army, the U.S. Navy, and the U.S. Marine Corps all had four grades of warrant officer. The U.S. Air Force also was authorized four grades of warrant officer but stopped making warrant officer appointments in 1959. Many of those who held warrant officer rank at the time later moved into the commissioned grades, but a small handful of U.S. Air Force warrant officers remained on duty up through the late 1970s.

Establishing rank equivalency among armies is an inexact science at best, as the confusion over warrant officers and sergeants major illustrates. Common sense would seem to dictate that two soldiers in different armies with the exact same rank titles would be essentially the same. This, however, is not necessarily always the case.

The problem of rank equivalency is further compounded by the fact that all armies do not have the same number of ranks, especially for enlisted and NCOs. All four of the American military services have nine enlisted grades, but more than one rank can exist within a given pay grade. In the U.S. Army and the U.S. Marine Corps, for example, the second-highest enlisted pay grade, E-8, includes the ranks of master sergeant and first sergeant. Both receive the same pay, but the duties of a first sergeant are more demanding; therefore, first sergeants always take precedence over master sergeants. In the U.S. Air Force, however, the rank of master sergeant is pay grade E-7 and therefore one rank lower than U.S. Army or U.S. Marine Corps master sergeants. U.S. Air Force staff sergeants are also one pay grade lower than those of the U.S. Army and the U.S. Marine Corps.

This misalignment in American rank titles is the result of a major revision in the enlisted rank structure introduced in 1958. All of the services were authorized to increase the number of enlisted pay grades from seven to nine. The U.S. Navy and the U.S. Air Force established two new ranks on the top of their structures, introducing senior chief petty officer and master chief petty officer in the navy and senior master sergeant and chief master sergeant in the air force. The U.S. Army and the U.S. Marine Corps added one rank at the top, establishing the rank of sergeant major (SGM), which since the 1920s had been a position title only but not an actual rank. The army added its second new rank at the bottom, establishing two pay grades of private. The U.S. Marine Corps, however, established its second new rank as lance corporal, placing it above private first class (PFC) and below corporal. Thus, army PFCs to this day hold the pay grade of E-3, while marine PFCs are in pay grade E-2.

Sometimes the number of pay grades and ranks are not even consistent among the military organizations of the same country. The Royal Australian Navy and the Royal Australian Air Force each had six enlisted ranks, while the Australian Army had seven. Soldiers serving in the lowest ranks of the Australian Army had several different titles, depending on their branch. But privates (infantry), troopers (cavalry and armor), gunners (artillery), and sappers (engineers) were all the same rank. Lance corporal is the first rank in the Commonwealth armies that has a rank insignia. A lance corporal wears a single chevron and is an NCO. A U.S. Army soldier who wore a single chevron was only a PFC and not an NCO.

At the start of the Vietnam War, the U.S. Army had specialist ranks in pay grades E-4 through E-9. In theory the specialists were not NCOs, although they received pay at those levels. In practice, however, those holding the rank of specialist 5 though specialist 9 were treated as NCOs, and the distinction quickly blurred between the specialists and the "hard stripe" sergeants. The army eliminated the specialist 8 and specialist 9 ranks in 1965 and the specialist 7 rank in 1978. Today, only the specialist 4 rank remains. Specialist 4 is not an NCO, while corporal, which is also in pay grade E-4, is an NCO.

The U.S. Army made two other important changes to its enlisted rank structure in 1968. Until then, private E-1 and private E-2 had no insignia of rank. Private first class, pay grade E-3, was indicated by the traditional single chevron, popularly called the "mosquito wing." That year, the single chevron became the rank insignia for private E-2, while the insignia for PFC became a single chevron with a "rocker" underneath.

That same year the U.S. Army also introduced a second sergeant major rank. A command sergeant major (CSM) became the senior-ranking NCO at any echelon from battalion through field army. Most of the echelons above battalion also had other sergeants major in key staff positions, but there was only one CSM at each level. Although sergeants major and command sergeants major are both in the same pay grade (E-9), the CSM is the senior in rank. Sergeants major continued to wear their traditional rank insignia of a star between three upper chevrons and three lower rockers. The rank of CSM is indicated by a wreath around the star. Thus, in the 2002 classic Vietnam War movie *We Were Soldiers,* actor Sam Elliot, portraying Sergeant Major Basil Plumley, is seen wearing only the star on his rank insignia, which was correct for the 1964 date of the Battle of the Ia Drang Valley. A sergeant major in the U.S. Marine Corps is the equivalent of a command sergeant major in the U.S. Army. There is only one at any given echelon above company. A marine master gunnery sergeant is the equivalent of an army sergeant major.

There is far more commonality among the officer ranks of the world's armies. Most militaries have three levels each of company grade and field grade officers and four levels of general officers. The initial general officer rank in most armies is brigadier general (one star), although the Commonwealth armies use the rank title of brigadier. In the Royal Australian Navy the first flag officer rank is commodore and the next one up is rear admiral. In the U.S. Navy, however, those ranks are awkwardly designated rear admiral (lower half) and rear admiral (upper half), respectively. Major generals (two stars) typically command divisions. Lieutenant generals (three stars) typically command corps. Generals (four stars) command field armies, theaters, and major commands and serve as national chiefs of staff.

However, the PAVN differed considerably from the standard practice in the rest of the world. Instead of three levels of company- and field-grade officers, the PAVN had four levels of company-grade officers (not counting the sublieutenant rank), four levels of field-grade officers, and four levels of general officers. In the PAVN, battalions were commanded by company-grade officers (usually by captains and senior captains but sometimes by first lieutenants), and regiments and divisions were commanded by field-grade officers (a division commander was usually a lieutenant colonel or colonel and only rarely a senior colonel). Generals never commanded a division; one-star generals (*thieu tuong*) commanded corps, military regions, or even higher-level formations. In terms of his duties and responsibilities, a PAVN senior colonel was probably comparable to a brigadier or major general in most other armies, and a PAVN one-star general was approximately the equivalent of a lieutenant general (three stars). Another complicating factor was linguistic. The Vietnamese word *thieu tuong* was used to refer to a one-star general in the PAVN, but in the ARVN a *thieu tuong* wore two stars and was called a major general; similarly, the PAVN *trung tuong* wore two stars, but in the ARVN a *trung tuong* wore three stars and was called a lieutenant general.

Through the end of World War II many of the world's major armies had a five-star general rank. That rank largely fell into disuse after 1945 but still remained as an official rank and is therefore listed in these tables. American officers holding five-star rank never retire. They draw full active-duty pay for the remainder of their lives, although after a certain point their actual military duties and responsibilities become minimal. During the period of America's involvement in Vietnam there were four American officers still living who held five-star rank, but they held no official positions in the command structure by that point. General of the Army Douglas MacArthur died in 1964, Fleet Admiral Chester Nimitz died in 1966, General of the Army Dwight Eisenhower died in 1969, and General of the Army Omar Bradley died in 1981. (Although Eisenhower had to resign his commission when he became president in 1953, it was reinstated when he left the White House in 1961.) General Jean de Lattre de Tassigny, who commanded French forces in Indochina in 1951, received a posthumous promotion to marshal of France immediately after his death in 1952.

Officer candidates have their own separate rank structures in most armies. But the ranks of cadet, midshipman, aspirant, etc., are essentially temporary training ranks and in most armies do not take part in combat operations until they receive their commissions.

The following table represents an attempt to equate the enlisted and officer ranks of the various militaries of the 1945–1975 wars involving Vietnam. In regard to determining the level at which to place a given rank, the duties and responsibilities of the person holding that rank take precedence over the face value of the rank title or the insignia worn. The tables do not include officer candidates or American-style warrant officers. Warrant officers as NCOs are included. Many armies also have special rank structures and designations for musicians, buglers, and pipers, which likewise are not included in the table.

DAVID T. ZABECKI

Army Ranks

	U.S. Army	French Army	Australian Army	New Zealand Army
Officers	General of the Army	Maréchal de France		
	General	Général d'Armée	General	General
	Lieutenant General	Général de Corps d'Armée	Lieutanant General	Lieutenant General
	Major General	Général de Division	Major General	Major General
	Brigadier General	Géneral de Brigade	Brigadier	Brigadier
	Colonel	Colonel	Colonel	Colonel
	Lieutenant Colonel	Lieutenant Colonel	Lieutenant Colonel	Lieutenant Colonel
	Major	Commandant	Major	Major
	Captain	Capitaine	Captain	Captain
	First Lieutenant	Lieutenant	Lieutenant	Lieutenant
	Second Lieutenant	Sous-Lieutenant	Second Lieutenant	Second Lieutenant
Enlisted	Command Sergeant Major Sergeant Major	Adjutant-Chef	Warrant Officer Class 1	Warrant Officer Class 1
	First Sergeant Master Sergeant	Adjutant	Warrant Officer Class 2	Warrant Officer Class 2
	Platoon Sergeant Sergeant First Class Specialist 7	Sergent-Chef	Staff Sergeant	Staff Sergeant
	Staff Sergeant Specialist 6	Sergent-Comptable	Sergeant	Sergeant
	Sergeant Specialist 5	Sergent	Corporal Bombardier	Corporal Bombardier
	Corporal Specialist 4	Caporal-Chef	Lance Corporal Lance Bombardier	Lance Corporal Lance Bombardier
	Private First Class	Caporal		
	Private (E-2)	Soldat de 1ère Classe		
	Private (E-1)	Soldat de 2ème Classe	Private Trooper Gunner Sapper	Private Trooper Gunner Sapper

		Thailand Army	South Korea Army	Socialist Republic of (North) Vietnam Army	Republic of (South) Vietnam Army
Officers		Chom Pon	Wonsu		Thuong Tuong
		Phon Ek	Taejang	Dai Tuong	Dai Tuong
		Phon Tho	Chungjang	Thuong Tuong	Trung Tuong
		Phon Tri	Sojang	Trung Tuong	Thieu Tuong
		Phan Ek Phiset	Chungjang	Thieu Tuong	Chuan Toung
				Dai Ta	
		Phan Ek	Taeryong	Thuong Ta	Dai Ta
		Phan Tho	Chungryong	Trung Ta	Trung Ta
		Phan Tri	Soryong	Thieu Ta	Thieu Ta
		Roi Ek	Taewi	Dai Uy	Dai Uy
		Roi Tho	Chungwi	Thuong Uy	Trung Uy
				Trung Uy	
		Roi Tri	Sowi	Thieu Uy	Thieu Uy
				Chuan Uy	Chuan Uy
Enlisted		Cha Sip Ek Phiset	Wonsa	Thuong Si	Thoung Si Nhat
		Cha Sip Ek	Sangsa		Thuong Si
		Cha Sip Tho	Chungsa	Trung Si	Trung Si Nhat
		Cha Sip Tri	Hasa		Trung Si
		Sip Ek	Byongjang	Ha Si	Ha Si Nhat
		Sip Tho	Sangbyong		Ha Si
		Sip Tri	Ilbyong	Binh Nhat	Binh Nhat
		Sip Tri Kong Pra	Yibyong		Binh Nhi
		Phon Thahan	Mudungbyong	Binh Nhi	Trung Dinh

Navy Ranks

	United States Navy	Royal Australian Navy	Socialist Republic of (North) Vietnam Navy	Republic of (South) Vietnam Navy
Officers	Fleet Admiral			
	Admiral	Admiral		Dai Tuong
	Vice Admiral	Vice-Admiral	Do Doc	Trung Tuong
	Rear Admiral (Upper Half)	Rear Admiral	Pho Do Doc	Thieu Tuong
	Rear Admiral (Lower Half)	Commodore	Chuan Do Doc	Chuan Toung
			Dai Ta	
	Captain	Captain	Thuong Ta	Dai Ta
	Commander	Commander	Trung Ta	Trung Ta
	Lieutenant Commander	Lieutenant-Commander	Thieu Ta	Thieu Ta
	Lieutanant	Lieutenant	Dai Uy	Dai Uy
	Lieutenant (Junior Grade)	Sub-Lieutenant	Thuong Uy	Trung Uy
			Trung Uy	
	Ensign	Acting Sub-Lieutenant	Thieu Uy	Thieu Uy
			Chuan Uy	Chuan Uy
Enlisted	Master Chief Petty Officer	Warrant Officer	Thuong Si	Thoung Si Nhat
	Senior Chief Petty Officer	Chief Petty Officer		Thuong Si
	Chief Petty Officer		Trung Si	Trung Si Nhat
	Petty Officer First Class	Petty Officer		Trung Si
	Petty Officer Second Class	Leading Seaman	Ha Si	Ha Si Nhat
	Petty Officer Third Class	Able Seaman		Ha Si
	Seaman Airman Fireman		Binh Nhat	Binh Nhat
	Seaman Apprentice Airman Apprentice Fireman Apprentice			Binh Nhi
	Seaman Recruit	Seaman	Binh Nhi	Trung Dinh

Air Force Ranks

	United States Air Force	French Air Force	Royal Australian Air Force	Socialist Republic of (North) Vietnam Air Force	Republic of (South) Vietnam Air Force
Officers	General of the Air Force				
	General	Général d'Armée Aérienne	Air Chief Marshal		Dai Tuong
	Lieutenant General	Général de Corps d'Armée Aérienne	Air Marshal	Thuong Tuong	Trung Tuong
	Major General	Général de Division Aérienne	Air Vice Marshal	Trung Tuong	Thieu Tuong
	Brigadier General	Général de Brigade Aérienne	Air Commodore	Thieu Tuong	Chuan Toung
				Dai Ta	
	Colonel	Colonel	Group Captain	Thuong Ta	Dai Ta
	Lieutenant Colonel	Lieutenant Colonel	Wing Commander	Trung Ta	Trung Ta
	Major	Commandant	Squadron Leader	Thieu Ta	Thieu Ta
	Captain	Capitaine	Flight Lieutenant	Dai Uy	Dai Uy
	First Lieutenant	Lieutenant	Flying Officer	Thuong Uy	Trung Uy
				Trung Uy	
	Second Lieutenant	Sous-Lieutenant	Pilot Officer	Thieu Uy	Thieu Uy
Enlisted	Chief Master Sergeant	Adjutant-Chef	Warrant Officer	Thuong Si	Thoung Si Nhat
	Senior Master Sergeant	Adjutant	Flight Sergeant		Thuong Si
	Master Sergeant	Sergent-Chef		Trung Si	Trung Si Nhat
	Technical Sergeant	Sergent-Comptable	Sergeant		Trung Si
	Staff Sergeant	Sergent	Corporal	Ha Si	Ha Si Nhat
	Sergeant Senior Airman	Caporal-Chef	Leading Aircraftman		Ha Si
	Airman First Class	Caporal		Binh Nhat	Binh Nhat
	Airman	Soldat de 1ère Classe			Binh Nhi
	Airman Basic	Soldat de 2ème Classe	Aircraftman	Binh Nhi	Trung Dinh

Marine Ranks

	United States Marine Corps	South Korea Marines	Republic of (South) Vietnam Marines
Officers			
	General	Taejang	
	Lieutenant General	Chungjang	Trung Tuong
	Major General	Sojang	Thieu Tuong
	Brigadier General	Chungjang	Chuan Toung
	Colonel	Taeryong	Dai Ta
	Lieutenant Colonel	Chungryong	Trung Ta
	Major	Soryong	Thieu Ta
	Captain	Taewi	Dai Uy
	First Lieutenant	Chungwi	Trung Uy
	Second Lieutenant	Sowi	Thieu Uy
Enlisted	Sergeant Major Master Gunnery Sergeant	Wonsa	Thoung Si Nhat
	First Sergeant Master Sergeant	Sangsa	Thuong Si
	Gunnery Sergeant	Chungsa	Trung Si Nhat
	Staff Sergeant	Hasa	Trung Si
	Sergeant	Byongjang	Ha Si Nhat
	Corporal	Sangbyong	Ha Si
	Lance Corporal	Ilbyong	Binh Nhat
	Private First Class	Yibyong	Binh Nhi
	Private	Mudungbyong	Trung Dinh

References

Emerson, William K. *Chevrons: Illustrated History and Catalog of U.S. Army Insignia.* Washington, DC: Smithsonian Institution Press, 1983.

Katcher, Phillip. *Armies of the Vietnam War, 1962–1975.* London: Osprey, 1980.

Larsen, Stanley Robert, and James Lawton Collins Jr. *Allied Participation in Vietnam.* Vietnam Studies Series. Washington, DC: Department of the Army, U.S. Government Printing Office, 1975.

Pike, Douglas. *PAVN: People's Army of Vietnam.* Novato, CA: Presidio, 1986.

Rottman, Gordon L. *Viet Cong Fighter.* Oxford, UK: Osprey, 2007.

Russell, Lee E. *Armies of the Vietnam War (2).* Oxford, UK: Osprey, 1983.

Appendix C

Order of Battle

Order of battle (OB) is the process of determining the identification, disposition, strength, command structure, subordinate units, and equipment of any military force. During military operations, OB is an integral part of the tactical intelligence process, one of the many tools used by military intelligence analysts to determine enemy capabilities and probable courses of action.

All armies go to great lengths to prevent their enemies from obtaining this information. Likewise, all armies engage in deception operations to feed false and misleading information to the opposing forces. For these reasons, OB, like so much else in the realm of military intelligence, is as much an art as a science. Intelligence analysts face the daunting task of building a coherent picture of an enemy from partial, often conflicting, and sometimes false information gathered from a wide variety of sources of varying accuracy and reliability.

The OB picture of an enemy force is never complete and never stable. It is a constantly moving picture that changes shape as units lose or build strength, change location, change commanders, and even exchange subordinate units and elements. The OB picture can be considered true and accurate only after the war is over and perhaps not even then.

The historian uses OB information in much the same manner as the intelligence analyst. Whereas the intelligence analyst is trying to predict the future, the historian is trying to reconstruct the past. Historians use similar research and analytical tools, and they face similar challenges in regard to incomplete, conflicting, and often intentionally misleading information.

Many years after an event, the surviving or available records still might not provide enough information to construct the true picture. The objective of both the intelligence analyst and the military historian is to construct the best picture possible using the best available data.

More than 35 years after the fall of the Republic of Vietnam (RVN, South Vietnam), OB information on the Vietnam War remains incomplete. In the following tables, the information for U.S. military units is virtually complete and accurate. The information for Republic of Vietnam Armed Forces (RVNAF, South Vietnamese Armed Forces) is somewhat less complete. The information for Communist troops—People's Army of Vietnam (PAVN, North Vietnamese Army) and Viet Cong (VC) units—is often incomplete. In many cases, only partial listings of subordinate units are known. In some cases this information is not available at all. In most cases it is possible to reconstruct only partial and spotty listings of commanders.

I. U.S. Order of Battle

A. U.S. Joint Commands

The first U.S. military organization arrived in Vietnam in 1950. The mission of the Military Assistance and Advisory Group, Indochina (MAAG-Indochina), was to provide assistance and advice to the French forces there. In 1955 MAAG-Indochina became MAAG-Vietnam, with a mission of providing joint service support to the South Vietnamese. In 1962 the United States also established the Military Assistance Command, Vietnam (MACV), to coordinate the expanding U.S. military activities in Vietnam.

In 1964 MACV was reorganized and absorbed MAAG-Vietnam, which became the Field Advisory Element, MACV. The Field Advisory Element provided the Army of the Republic of Vietnam (ARVN, South Vietnamese Army) with adviser teams from the corps level down to the regimental level. In essence, the senior

American adviser at any given level functioned as almost a shadow commander. From about mid-1970 the senior U.S. Army officer in each corps tactical zone (CTZ) was considered the senior adviser as well. The one exception was when John Paul Vann became the senior adviser in II CTZ in May 1971. The Field Advisory Element had an assigned strength of 4,741 men in 1964 and reached its peak in 1968 with 9,430 men.

MACV was a subordinate unified command of the U.S. Pacific Command, headquartered in Hawaii. The commander of MACV had control and authority over all U.S. military operations in South Vietnam. This included naval operations in Vietnamese coastal waters and all air missions over South Vietnam. The commander of MACV did not have any control over the air war against the Democratic Republic of Vietnam (DRV, North Vietnam), over the high seas operations of the U.S. Seventh Fleet (including air strikes launched from its carriers), or over any missions carried out by aircraft of the U.S. Air Force's Strategic Air Command (SAC).

In theory the commander of MACV reported to the commander in chief of the Pacific Command (CINCPAC). In practice, however, the commander of MACV often reported directly to the U.S. secretary of defense. In hindsight, it can be seen very clearly that the United States violated the principle of unity of command almost from the start.

Military Assistance Advisory Group, Indochina

Date formed in Vietnam: September 17, 1950
Date reorganized as MAAG-Vietnam: October 31, 1955
Headquarters: Saigon (Cho Lon)

COMMANDING GENERALS

Brigadier General Francis G. Brink	October 1950
Major General Thomas J. H. Trapnell	August 1952
Lieutenant General John W. O'Daniel	April 1954

Military Assistance Advisory Group, Vietnam (MAAG-Vietnam)
Date formed from MAAG-Indochina: November 1, 1955
Date merged with MACV: May 15, 1964
Headquarters: Saigon

COMMANDING GENERALS

Lieutenant General Samuel T. Williams	November 1955
Lieutenant General Lionel C. McGarr	September 1960
Major General Charles J. Timmes	July 1962

Military Assistance Command, Vietnam (MACV)
Date formed in Vietnam: February 8, 1962
Date inactivated in Vietnam: March 29, 1973
Headquarters: Saigon (Tan Son Nhut Air Base)

MAJOR SUBORDINATE COMMANDS
Field Advisory Element, MACV
U.S. Army, Vietnam
I Field Force
II Field Force
XXIV Corps
5th Special Forces Group
III Marine Amphibious Force
Naval Forces, Vietnam
Seventh Air Force

COMMANDING GENERALS

General Paul D. Harkins	February 1962
General William C. Westmoreland	June 1964
General Creighton W. Abrams	July 1968
General Frederick C. Weyand	June 1972

FIELD ADVISORY ELEMENT, MACV
Senior U.S. Army advisers

I CORPS TACTICAL ZONE

Brigadier General A. L. Hamblen Jr.	June 1966
Colonel John J. Beeson III	July 1967
Brigadier General Salve H. Matheson	January 1968
Colonel John J. Beeson III	April 1968
Colonel Ronald H. Renwanz	August 1968
Brigadier General Henry J. Muller Jr.	September 1969
Brigadier General Charles A. Jackson	July 1970
Lieutenant General James W. Sutherland	October 1970
Lieutenant General Welborn G. Dolvin	July 1971
Major General Frederick J. Kroesen	April 1972
Major General Howard H. Cooksey	June 1972

II CORPS TACTICAL ZONE

Brigadier General James S. Timothy	June 1966
Major General Richard M. Lee	August 1966
Colonel Charles A. Cannon	November 1966
Major General John W. Barnes	November 1967
Colonel Robert M. Piper	January 1968
Brigadier General Gordon J. Duquemin	December 1969
Brigadier General Jack MacFarlane	July 1970
Lieutenant General Arthur S. Collins Jr.	October 1970
Major General Charles P. Brown	January 1971
Mr. John Paul Vann	May 1971
Major General Michael D. Healy	June 1972

III CORPS TACTICAL ZONE

Colonel Arndt L. Mueller	June 1966
Colonel Gus S. Peters	November 1967
Brigadier General Donald D. Dunlop	June 1968
Brigadier General Carleton Preer Jr.	May 1969
Brigadier General Dennis P. McAuliffe	January 1970

Lieutenant General Michael S. Davison	October 1970
Major General Jack J. Wagstaff	May 1971
Major General James F. Hollingsworth	January 1972
Major General Marshall B. Garth	September 1972

IV CORPS TACTICAL ZONE

Colonel George A. Barton	June 1964
Colonel Leroy B. Wilson	June 1966
Brigadier General William R. Desorby	August 1966
Major General George S. Eckhardt	January 1967
Major General Roderick Wetheril	June 1969
Major General Hal D. McCown	January 1970
Major General John H. Cushman	May 1971
Brigadier General Frank E. Blazey	February 1972
Major General Thomas M. Tarpley	March 1972

U.S. MILITARY STRENGTH IN VIETNAM

1964	23,310
1965	184,310
1966	385,300
1967	485,600
1968	536,000
1969	484,330
1970	335,790
1971	158,120
1972	24,000

B. U.S. Army Major Commands

U.S. Army, Vietnam (USARV), was established in 1965 to coordinate administrative and logistical support to all U.S. Army units operating in Vietnam. Actual command and control of combat units and operations remained with MACV. On paper, the commander of MACV was also the commander of USARV. In practice, the deputy commander of USARV ran the organization on a day-to-day basis.

In November 1965 the Americans established Field Force, Vietnam, as a corps-level headquarters to control ground combat operations. As the number of U.S. ground combat units grew rapidly, II Field Force, Vietnam, was established in March 1966, with Field Force, Vietnam, redesignated I Field Force, Vietnam. Initially the Americans used the designation "field force" rather than "corps" to avoid confusion with the geographically based corps tactical zones of the ARVN. In February 1968, however, the U.S. Army established its third corps-level headquarters, designating it XXIV Corps. Throughout the war, many U.S. divisions and separate brigades came under the operational control of different field forces/corps at different times.

Most U.S. Army combat forces in Vietnam were organized into divisions. Some units operated as separate brigades. In April 1967 three such separate brigades were organized into a provisional division designated Task Force Oregon. That September, Task Force Oregon was formally organized into the 23rd Infantry Division, re-

taining only one of Task Force Oregon's three brigades and adding two more.

During the war, most U.S. Army units of similar type remained fairly consistent in organization and strength. A typical U.S. division had between 16,570 and 17,730 soldiers. A division's principal combat forces consisted of 10 or 11 maneuver (infantry, armor, or cavalry) battalions and 4 artillery battalions. A typical infantry battalion had 920 officers and soldiers, while a typical artillery battalion had 641 officers and soldiers.

U.S. Army, Vietnam
Date formed in Vietnam: July 20, 1965
Date inactivated in Vietnam: May 15, 1972
Headquarters: Long Binh

MAJOR SUBORDINATE UNITS
1st Logistical Command
1st Aviation Brigade
18th Military Police Brigade
34th General Support Group
525th Military Intelligence Group
U.S. Army Engineer Command (Provisional)

DEPUTY COMMANDING GENERALS, MACV

Major General John Norton	July 1965
Lieutenant General Jean E. Engler	January 1966
Lieutenant General Bruce Palmer Jr.	July 1967
Lieutenant General Frank T. Mildren	June 1968
Lieutenant General William J. McCaffrey	July 1970
Major General Morgan C. Roseborough	September 1972

I Field Force, Vietnam
Date formed in Vietnam: November 15, 1965
Date inactivated in Vietnam: April 30, 1971
Headquarters: Nha Trang

SUBORDINATE COMBAT UNITS
1st Cavalry Division
4th Infantry Division
3rd Brigade, 25th Infantry Division
1st Brigade, 101st Airborne Division
173rd Airborne Brigade
41st Artillery Group
52nd Artillery Group

COMMANDING GENERALS

Lieutenant General Stanley R. Larson	November 1965
Lieutenant General William R. Peers	March 1968
Lieutenant General Charles A. Cocoran	March 1969
Lieutenant General Arthur S. Collins Jr.	March 1970
Major General Charles P. Brown	January 1971

II Field Force, Vietnam
Date formed in Vietnam: March 15, 1966
Date inactivated in Vietnam: May 2, 1971
Headquarters: Long Binh

SUBORDINATE UNITS
1st Cavalry Division
1st Infantry Division
9th Infantry Division
25th Infantry Division
101st Airborne Division
3rd Brigade, 4th Infantry Division
3rd Brigade, 82nd Airborne Division
173rd Airborne Brigade
196th Infantry Brigade
199th Infantry Brigade
11th Armored Cavalry Regiment
23rd Artillery Group
54th Artillery Group

COMMANDING GENERALS

Lieutenant General Jonathan O. Seaman	March 1966
Lieutenant General Bruce Palmer Jr.	March 1967
Major General Frederick C. Weyand	July 1967
Major General Walter T. Kerwin Jr.	August 1968
Lieutenant General Julian J. Ewell	April 1969
Lieutenant General Michael S. Davison	April 1970

XXIV Corps
Date formed in Vietnam: August 15, 1968
Date departed Vietnam: June 20, 1972
Headquarters: Phu Bai, August 1968; Da Nang, March 1970

SUBORDINATE UNITS
III Marine Amphibious Force (after March 1970)
1st Cavalry Division
23rd Infantry Division
101st Airborne Division
1st Brigade, 5th Infantry Division
3rd Brigade, 82nd Airborne Division
196th Infantry Brigade
108th Artillery Group

COMMANDING GENERALS

Lieutenant General William B. Rosson	February 1968
Lieutenant General Richard G. Stilwell	July 1968
Lieutenant General Melvin Zais	June 1969
Lieutenant General James W. Sutherland Jr.	June 1970
Lieutenant General Welborn G. Dolvin	June 1971

1st Cavalry Division (Airmobile) ("The First Team")
Date formed: September 13, 1921

Date arrived in Vietnam: September 11, 1965, from Fort Benning
Date departed Vietnam: April 29, 1971, to Fort Hood
Headquarters: An Khe, September 1965; Bien Hoa, May 1969

SUBORDINATE COMBAT UNITS
1st Battalion, 5th Cavalry
2nd Battalion, 5th Cavalry
1st Battalion, 7th Cavalry
2nd Battalion, 7th Cavalry
5th Battalion, 7th Cavalry
1st Battalion, 8th Cavalry
2nd Battalion, 8th Cavalry
1st Battalion, 12th Cavalry
2nd Battalion, 12th Cavalry
1st Squadron, 9th Cavalry
2nd Battalion, 17th Artillery
2nd Battalion, 19th Artillery
2nd Battalion, 20th Artillery
1st Battalion, 21st Artillery
1st Battalion, 30th Artillery
1st Battalion, 77th Artillery
11th Aviation Group

PRINCIPAL ENGAGEMENTS
Ia Drang Valley
Operation MASHER/WHITE WING
Operation PAUL REVERE II
Operation BYRD
Operation IRVING
Operation PERSHING
Operation BOLLING
Tet Offensive
Khe Sanh
Operation PEGASUS
A Shau Valley
Cambodia, 1970

COMMANDING GENERALS

Major General Harry W. B. Kinnard	July 1965
Major General John Norton	May 1966
Major General John J. Tolson III	April 1967
Major General George I. Forsythe	July 1968
Major General Elvy B. Roberts	May 1969
Major General George W. Casey	May 1970
Brigadier General Jonathan R. Burton	July 1970
Major General George W. Putman Jr.	July 1970

1st Infantry Division ("Big Red One")
Date formed: December 22, 1917
Date arrived in Vietnam: October 2, 1965, from Fort Riley
Date departed Vietnam: April 15, 1970, to Fort Riley

Headquarters: Bien Hoa, October 1965; Di An, February 1966; Lai Khe, October 1967; Di An, November 1969

SUBORDINATE COMBAT UNITS
1st Battalion, 2nd Infantry
2nd Battalion, 2nd Infantry
1st Battalion, 16th Infantry
2nd Battalion, 16th Infantry
1st Battalion, 18th Infantry
2nd Battalion, 18th Infantry
1st Battalion, 26th Infantry
1st Battalion, 28th Infantry
2nd Battalion, 28th Infantry
1st Squadron, 4th Cavalry
1st Battalion, 5th Artillery
8th Battalion, 6th Artillery
1st Battalion, 7th Artillery
6th Battalion, 15th Artillery
2nd Battalion, 33rd Artillery
1st Aviation Battalion

PRINCIPAL ENGAGEMENTS
Operation EL PASO II
Operation ATTLEBORO
Operation CEDAR FALLS
Operation JUNCTION CITY
Tet Offensive
Operation QUYET THANG

COMMANDING GENERALS
Major General Jonathan O. Seaman October 1965
Major General William E. DePuy March 1966
Major General John H. Hay Jr. February 1967
Major General Keith L. Ware March 1968
Major General Orwin C. Talbott September 1968
Major General Albert E. Milloy August 1969
Brigadier General John Q. Herrion March 1970

4th Infantry Division ("Ivy Division")
Date formed: December 1917
Date arrived in Vietnam: September 25, 1966, from Fort Lewis
Date departed Vietnam: December 7, 1970, to Fort Carson
Headquarters: Pleiku, September 1966; Dak To, March 1968; Pleiku, April 1968; An Khe, April 1970

SUBORDINATE COMBAT UNITS
1st Battalion, 8th Infantry
2nd Battalion, 8th Infantry
3rd Battalion, 8th Infantry
1st Battalion, 12th Infantry
2nd Battalion, 12th Infantry
3rd Battalion, 12th Infantry

1st Battalion, 14th Infantry
1st Battalion, 22nd Infantry
2nd Battalion, 22nd Infantry
3rd Battalion, 22nd Infantry
1st Battalion, 35th Infantry
2nd Battalion, 35th Infantry
2nd Battalion, 34th Armor
1st Battalion, 69th Armor
1st Squadron, 10th Cavalry
2nd Battalion, 9th Artillery
5th Battalion, 16th Artillery
6th Battalion, 29th Artillery
4th Battalion, 42nd Artillery
2nd Battalion, 77th Artillery
4th Aviation Battalion

PRINCIPAL ENGAGEMENTS
Operation ATTLEBORO
Operation JUNCTION CITY
Operation FRANCIS MARION
Dak To
Tet Offensive
Cambodia, 1970
Operation WAYNE GREY
Operation PUTNAM TIGER

COMMANDING GENERALS
Brigadier General David O. Byars August 1966
Major General Arthur S. Collins Jr. September 1966
Major General William R. Peers January 1967
Major General Charles P. Stone January 1968
Major General Donn R. Pepke December 1968
Major General Glenn D. Walker November 1969
Major General William A. Burke July 1970
Brigadier General Maurice K. Kendall December 1970

9th Infantry Division ("Old Reliables")
Date formed: August 1, 1940
Date arrived in Vietnam: December 16, 1966, from Fort Riley
Date departed Vietnam: August 27, 1969, to Fort Lewis
Headquarters: Bear Cat, December 1966; Dong Tam, August 1968

SUBORDINATE COMBAT UNITS
6th Battalion, 31st Infantry
2nd Battalion, 39th Infantry
3rd Battalion, 39th Infantry
4th Battalion, 39th Infantry
2nd Battalion, 47th Infantry
3rd Battalion, 47th Infantry
4th Battalion, 47th Infantry
2nd Battalion, 60th Infantry
3rd Battalion, 60th Infantry

5th Battalion, 60th Infantry
3rd Squadron, 5th Cavalry
2nd Battalion, 4th Artillery
1st Battalion, 11th Artillery
3rd Battalion, 34th Artillery
1st Battalion, 84th Artillery
9th Aviation Battalion

PRINCIPAL ENGAGEMENTS
Operation PALM BEACH
Operation ENTERPRISE
Operation JUNCTION CITY II
Tet Offensive
Operation QUYET THANG
Operation DUONG CUA DAN
Operation SPEEDY EXPRESS
Operation RICE FARMER

COMMANDING GENERALS
Major General George C. Eckhart   December 1966
Major General George C. O'Connor   June 1967
Major General Julian J. Ewell   February 1968
Major General Harris W. Hollis   April 1969

Task Force Oregon
Date formed in Vietnam: April 12, 1967
Date converted to 23rd Infantry Division: September 22, 1967
Headquarters: Chu Lai

SUBORDINATE COMBAT UNITS
3rd Brigade, 25th Infantry Division
1st Brigade, 101st Airborne Division
196th Infantry Brigade

COMMANDING GENERALS
Major General William B. Rosson   April 1967
Major General Richard T. Knowles   June 1967

23rd Infantry Division ("Americal Division")
Date formed in Vietnam: September 22, 1967
Date inactivated in Vietnam: November 29, 1971
Headquarters: Chu Lai

SUBORDINATE COMBAT UNITS
11th Infantry Brigade
196th Infantry Brigade
198th Infantry Brigade
2nd Battalion, 1st Infantry
3rd Battalion, 1st Infantry
4th Battalion, 3rd Infantry
1st Battalion, 6th Infantry
1st Battalion, 20th Infantry

3rd Battalion, 21st Infantry
4th Battalion, 21st Infantry
4th Battalion, 31st Infantry
1st Battalion, 46th Infantry
5th Battalion, 46th Infantry
1st Battalion, 52nd Infantry
6th Battalion, 11th Artillery
1st Battalion, 14th Artillery
3rd Battalion, 16th Artillery
3rd Battalion, 18th Artillery
1st Battalion, 82nd Artillery
3rd Battalion, 82nd Artillery
16th Aviation Group

PRINCIPAL ENGAGEMENTS
Operation WHEELER/WALLOWA
Operation MUSCATINE
Tet Offensive
Operation BURLINGTON TRAIL
Operation LAMAR PLAIN

COMMANDING GENERALS
Major General Samuel W. Koster   September 1967
Major General Charles M. Gettys   June 1968
Major General Lloyd B. Ramsey   June 1969
Major General Albert E. Milloy   March 1970
Major General James L. Baldwin   November 1970
Major General Frederick J. Kroesen Jr. July 1971

25th Infantry Division ("Tropic Lightning")
Date formed: October 10, 1941
Date arrived in Vietnam: March 28, 1966, from Schofield
    Barracks
Date departed Vietnam: December 8, 1970, to Schofield Barracks
Headquarters: Cu Chi

SUBORDINATE COMBAT UNITS
1st Battalion, 5th Infantry
4th Battalion, 9th Infantry
2nd Battalion, 12th Infantry
1st Battalion, 14th Infantry
2nd Battalion, 14th Infantry
2nd Battalion, 22nd Infantry
3rd Battalion, 22nd Infantry
4th Battalion, 23rd Infantry
1st Battalion, 27th Infantry
2nd Battalion, 27th Infantry
1st Battalion, 35th Infantry
2nd Battalion, 35th Infantry
2nd Battalion, 34th Armor
1st Battalion, 69th Armor
3rd Squadron, 4th Cavalry

1st Battalion, 8th Artillery
2nd Battalion, 9th Artillery
7th Battalion, 11th Artillery
3rd Battalion, 13th Artillery
2nd Battalion, 77th Artillery
6th Battalion, 77th Artillery
25th Aviation Battalion

PRINCIPAL ENGAGEMENTS
Operation PAUL REVERE
Operation CEDAR FALLS
Operation JUNCTION CITY
Operation YELLOWSTONE
Tet Offensive
Operation QUYET THANG
Operation SARATOGA
Cambodia, 1970

COMMANDING GENERALS

Major General Frederick C. Weyand	January 1966
Major General John C. F. Tillson III	March 1967
Major General Fillmore K. Mearns	August 1967
Major General Ellis W. Williamson	August 1968
Major General Harris W. Hollis	September 1969
Major General Edward Baultz Jr.	April 1970

101st Airborne Division (Airmobile) ("Screaming Eagles")
Date formed: August 15, 1942
Date arrived in Vietnam: November 19, 1967, from Fort Campbell
Date departed Vietnam: March 10, 1972, to Fort Campbell
Headquarters: Bien Hoa, November 1967; Hue, February 1968;
    Bien Hoa, June 1968; Hue/Phu Bai, December 1969

SUBORDINATE COMBAT UNITS
3rd Battalion, 187th Infantry
1st Battalion, 327th Infantry
2nd Battalion, 327th Infantry
1st Battalion, 501st Infantry
2nd Battalion, 501st Infantry
1st Battalion, 502nd Infantry
2nd Battalion, 502nd Infantry
1st Battalion, 506th Infantry
2nd Battalion, 506th Infantry
3rd Battalion, 506th Infantry
2nd Squadron, 17th Cavalry
2nd Battalion, 11th Artillery
1st Battalion, 39th Artillery
4th Battalion, 77th Artillery
2nd Battalion, 319th Artillery
2nd Battalion, 320th Artillery
1st Battalion, 321st Artillery
101st Aviation Group

PRINCIPAL ENGAGEMENTS
Tet Offensive
Operation CARENTAN II
Operation TEXAS STAR
Operation APACHE SNOW
Operation LAMAR PLAIN
Operation RANDOLPH GLEN
Operation JEFFERSON GLENN
Operation LAM SON 719

COMMANDING GENERALS

Major General Olinto M. Barsanti	November 1967
Major General Melvin Zais	July 1968
Major General John M. Wright Jr.	May 1969
Major General John J. Hennessey	May 1970
Major General Thomas M. Tarpley	January 1971

1st Brigade, 5th Infantry Division (Mechanized)
Date arrived in Vietnam: July 25, 1968, from Fort Carson
Date departed Vietnam: August 27, 1971, to Fort Carson
Headquarters: Quang Tri

SUBORDINATE COMBAT UNITS
1st Battalion, 11th Infantry
1st Battalion, 61st Infantry
1st Battalion, 77th Armor
5th Battalion, 4th Artillery

PRINCIPAL ENGAGEMENTS
Operation DEWEY CANYON II

COMMANDING OFFICERS

Colonel Richard J. Glikes	July 1968
Colonel James M. Gibson	October 1968
Colonel John L. Osteen Jr.	June 1969
Brigadier General William A. Burke	April 1970
Brigadier General John G. Hill Jr.	July 1970
Brigadier General Harold H. Dunwoody	May 1971

3rd Brigade, 82nd Airborne Division
Date arrived in Vietnam: February 18, 1968, from Fort Bragg
Date departed Vietnam: December 11, 1969, to Fort Bragg
Headquarters: Hue, February 1968; Saigon, September 1968

SUBORDINATE COMBAT UNITS
1st Battalion, 505th Infantry
2nd Battalion, 505th Infantry
1st Battalion, 508th Infantry
2nd Battalion, 321st Artillery

PRINCIPAL ENGAGEMENTS
Operation CARENTAN II

COMMANDING OFFICERS

Colonel Alex R. Bolling Jr.	February 1968
Brigadier General George W. Dickerson	December 1968

11th Infantry Brigade (Light)
Date arrived in Vietnam: December 19, 1967
Date assigned to 23rd Infantry Division: February 15, 1969
Date departed Vietnam: November 13, 1971
Headquarters: Duc Pho, December 1967; The Loi, July 1971

SUBORDINATE COMBAT UNITS
3rd Battalion, 1st Infantry
4th Battalion, 3rd Infantry
1st Battalion, 20th Infantry
4th Battalion, 21st Infantry
6th Battalion, 11th Artillery

PRINCIPAL ENGAGEMENTS
Operation WHEELER/WALLOWA
Operation MUSCATINE
Tet Offensive
Operation BURLINGTON TRAIL
Operation LAMAR PLAIN

COMMANDING OFFICERS

Brigadier General Andy A. Lipscomb	December 1967
Colonel Oran K. Henderson	March 1968
Colonel John W. Donalson	October 1968
Colonel Jack L. Treadwell	April 1969
Colonel Hugh F. T. Hoffman	September 1969
Colonel Kendrick B. Barlow	March 1970
Colonel John L. Insani	September 1970
Colonel Warner S. Goodwin	March 1971

173rd Airborne Brigade
Date arrived in Vietnam: May 7, 1965, from Okinawa
Date departed Vietnam: August 25, 1971
Headquarters: Bien Hoa, May 1965; An Khe, November 1967;
    Bong Son, May 1969

SUBORDINATE COMBAT UNITS
1st Battalion, 503rd Infantry
2nd Battalion, 503rd Infantry
3rd Battalion, 503rd Infantry
4th Battalion, 503rd Infantry
3rd Battalion, 319th Artillery

PRINCIPAL ENGAGEMENTS
Operation ATTLEBORO
Operation CEDAR FALLS
Operation JUNCTION CITY
Dak To

Tet Offensive
Operation MCLAIN
Operation COCHISE GREEN
Operation WASHINGTON GREEN

COMMANDING OFFICERS

Brigadier General Ellis W. Williamson	May 1965
Brigadier General Paul F. Smith	February 1966
Brigadier General John R. Deane Jr.	December 1966
Brigadier General Leo H. Schweiter	August 1967
Brigadier General Richard J. Allen	April 1968
Brigadier General John W. Barnes	December 1968
Brigadier General Hubert S. Cunningham	August 1969
Brigadier General Elmer R. Ochs	August 1970
Brigadier General Jack MacFarlane	January 1971

196th Infantry Brigade (Light)
Date arrived in Vietnam: August 26, 1966
Date assigned to Task Force Oregon: September 22, 1967
Date relieved from 23rd Infantry Division: November 29, 1971
Date departed Vietnam: June 29, 1972
Headquarters: Tay Ninh, August 1966; Chu Lai, June 1967; Tam
    Ky, November 1967; Phong Dien, April 1968; Hoi An, June
    1968; Chu Lai, July 1968; Da Nang, April 1971

SUBORDINATE COMBAT UNITS
2nd Battalion, 1st Infantry
1st Battalion, 6th Infantry
3rd Battalion, 21st Infantry
4th Battalion, 31st Infantry
1st Battalion, 46th Infantry
3rd Battalion, 82nd Artillery

PRINCIPAL ENGAGEMENTS
Operation ATTLEBORO
Operation JUNCTION CITY
Operation WHEELER/WALLOWA
Operation MUSCATINE
Tet Offensive
Operation BURLINGTON TRAIL
Operation LAMAR PLAIN

COMMANDING OFFICERS

Brigadier General Richard T. Knowles	November 1966
Brigadier General Frank H. Linnell	May 1967
Colonel Louis Gelling	November 1967
Colonel Frederick J. Kroesen Jr.	June 1968
Colonel Thomas H. Tackaberry	May 1969
Colonel James M. Lee	November 1969
Colonel Edwin L. Kennedy	April 1970
Colonel William S. Hathaway	November 1970
Colonel Rutland D. Beard Jr.	June 1971

Brigadier General Joseph P. McDonough   November 1971

198th Infantry Brigade (Light)
Date arrived in Vietnam: October 21, 1967
Date assigned to Task Force Oregon: October 21, 1967
Date departed Vietnam: November 13, 1971
Headquarters: Duc Pho, October 1967; Chu Lai, December 1967

SUBORDINATE COMBAT UNITS
1st Battalion, 6th Infantry
1st Battalion, 46th Infantry
5th Battalion, 46th Infantry
1st Battalion, 52nd Infantry
1st Battalion, 14th Artillery

PRINCIPAL ENGAGEMENTS
Operation WHEELER/WALLOWA
Operation MUSCATINE
Tet Offensive
Operation BURLINGTON TRAIL
Operation LAMAR PLAIN

COMMANDING OFFICERS
Colonel J. R. Waldie   October 1967
Colonel Charles B. Thomas   June 1968
Colonel Robert B. Tully   December 1968
Colonel Jere D. Whittington   May 1969
Colonel Joseph G. Clemons   November 1969
Colonel William R. Richardson   July 1970
Colonel Charles R. Smith   March 1971

199th Infantry Brigade (Light)
Date arrived in Vietnam: December 10, 1966
Date departed Vietnam: October 11, 1970
Headquarters: Song Be, December 1966; Long Binh, March 1967;
    Bien Hoa, April 1967; Long Binh, July 1967; Gao Ho Nai,
    March 1968; Long Binh, July 1968

SUBORDINATE COMBAT UNITS
2nd Battalion, 3rd Infantry
3rd Battalion, 7th Infantry
4th Battalion, 12th Infantry
5th Battalion, 12th Infantry
2nd Battalion, 40th Artillery

PRINCIPAL ENGAGEMENTS
Operation FAIRFAX
Operation UNIONTOWN
Tet Offensive
Phu Tho Racetrack

COMMANDING OFFICERS
Brigadier General Charles W. Ryder Jr.   December 1966
Brigadier General John F. Freund   March 1967
Brigadier General Robert C. Forbes   September 1967
Brigadier General Franklin M. Davis Jr.   May 1968
Colonel Frederic E. Davison   August 1968
Brigadier General Warren K. Bennett   May 1969
Brigadier General William R. Bond   December 1969
Colonel Joseph E. Collins   July 1970
Lieutenant Colonel George E. Williams   September 1970

11th Armored Cavalry Regiment ("Black Horse")
Date arrived in Vietnam: September 8, 1966
Date departed Vietnam: March 5, 1971
Headquarters: Bien Hoa, September 1966; Long Binh, December
    1966; Xuan Loc, March 1967; Lai Khe, February 1969; Long
    Gaio, March 1969; Bien Hoa, October 1969; Di An, July 1970

SUBORDINATE COMBAT UNITS
1st Squadron, 11th Armored Cavalry
2nd Squadron, 11th Armored Cavalry
3rd Squadron, 11th Armored Cavalry

PRINCIPAL ENGAGEMENTS
Operation CEDAR FALLS
Operation JUNCTION CITY
Tet Offensive
Operation TOAN THANG
Cambodia, 1970

COMMANDING OFFICERS
Colonel William W. Cobb   September 1966
Colonel Roy W. Farley   May 1967
Colonel Jack MacFarlane   December 1967
Colonel Charles R. Gorder   March 1968
Colonel Leonard D. Holder   March 1969
Colonel James H. Leach   April 1968
Colonel George S. Patton   July 1969
Colonel Donn A. Starry   December 1969
Colonel John L. Gerrity   June 1970
Colonel Wallace H. Nutting   December 1970

U.S. Army Special Forces, Vietnam (Provisional)
Date formed in Vietnam: September 1962
Date inactivated in Vietnam: September 30, 1964
Headquarters: Nha Trang

SUBORDINATE COMBAT UNITS
C-3 Operational Detachment
B-7 Operational Detachment
B-130 Operational Detachment
B-320 Operational Detachment
B-410 Operational Detachment

COMMANDING OFFICERS

Colonel George C. Morton	September 1962
Colonel Theodore Leonard	November 1963

5th Special Forces Group (Airborne), 1st Special Forces
Date arrived in Vietnam: October 1, 1964, from Fort Bragg
Date departed Vietnam: March 3, 1971, to Fort Bragg
Headquarters: Nha Trang

SUBORDINATE COMBAT UNITS
Joint Combined Coordination Detachment
Operational Detachment B-50 (Project Omega)
Operational Detachment B-51
Operational Detachment B-52 (Project Delta)
Operational Detachment B-53
Operational Detachment B-55 (5th Mobile Strike Force
  Command)
Operational Detachment B-56 (Project Sigma)
Operational Detachment B-57 (Project Gamma)
Company A (C-3 Operational Detachment)
Company B (C-2 Operational Detachment)
Company C (C-1 Operational Detachment)
Company D (C-4 Operational Detachment)
Company E (C-5 Operational Detachment)

COMMANDING OFFICERS

Colonel John H. Spears	August 1964
Colonel William A. McKean	July 1965
Colonel Francis J. Kelly	June 1968
Colonel Jonathan F. Ladd	June 1968
Colonel Harlod R. Aaron	June 1968
Colonel Robert B. Rheault	May 1969
Colonel Alexander Lemberes	July 1969
Colonel Michael D. Healy	August 1969

1st Aviation Brigade
Date formed in Vietnam: May 25, 1966
Date departed Vietnam: March 28, 1973
Headquarters: Tan Son Nhut, May 1966; Long Binh, December
  1967; Tan Son Nhut, December 1972

SUBORDINATE OPERATIONAL AND COMBAT UNITS
11th Aviation Group
12th Aviation Group
16th Aviation Group
17th Aviation Group
160th Aviation Group
164th Aviation Group
165th Aviation Group
10th Aviation Battalion
11th Aviation Battalion
13th Aviation Battalion

14th Aviation Battalion
52nd Aviation Battalion
58th Aviation Battalion
145th Aviation Battalion
210th Aviation Battalion
212th Aviation Battalion
214th Aviation Battalion
222nd Aviation Battalion
223rd Aviation Battalion
268th Aviation Battalion
269th Aviation Battalion
307th Aviation Battalion
308th Aviation Battalion
7th Squadron, 1st Cavalry
1st Squadron, 9th Cavalry
3rd Squadron, 17th Cavalry
7th Squadron, 17th Cavalry

COMMANDING OFFICERS

Brigadier General George P. Seneff	May 1966
Major General Robert R. Williams	November 1967
Brigadier General Allen M. Burdett Jr.	April 1969
Brigadier General George W. Putnam Jr.	January 1970
Colonel Samuel G. Cockerham	August 1970
Brigadier General Jack W. Hemingway	August 1970
Brigadier General Robert N. Mackinnon	September 1971
Brigadier General Jack V. Mackmull	September 1972

C. U.S. Marine Corps Major Commands

The major Marine Corps headquarters in Vietnam was the III Marine Amphibious Force (III MAF), roughly the equivalent of a U.S. Army corps. Initially III MAF reported directly to MACV and was responsible for all U.S. combat operations in the north of the country. The U.S. Army's XXIV Corps was subordinate to III MAF. The U.S. Marine Corps started withdrawing from Vietnam in 1969, and by early 1970 the U.S. Army had the preponderance of U.S. forces in northern South Vietnam. In April 1970 the command relationships reversed, with XXIV Corps now the major subordinate command under MACV and with III MAF subordinates reporting to XXIV Corps.

A U.S. Marine Corps division was roughly the equivalent of a U.S. Army division although slightly smaller and more lightly equipped. Whereas U.S. Army divisions were organized into three or more brigades, U.S. Marine Corps divisions were organized into three or more regiments. The key difference between U.S. Army brigades and U.S. Marine Corps regiments is that the regiments are composed of permanently organic battalions. U.S. Army brigades are purely command and control headquarters, with no permanent battalions. A U.S. Army division's combat battalions can be grouped and regrouped under the various brigade headquarters as the mission dictates.

The 1st Marine Air Wing (1st MAW) reported directly to III MAF and provided air support independent of the Seventh Air Force. At its peak, the 1st MAW had three helicopter groups and three fighter-bomber groups, for a total of approximately 225 rotary and 250 fixed-wing aircraft.

III Marine Amphibious Force
Date formed in Vietnam: May 7, 1967
Date departed Vietnam: April 14, 1971
Headquarters: Da Nang

MAJOR SUBORDINATE COMMANDS
XXIV Corps (until March 1970)
1st Marine Division
3rd Marine Division
1st Marine Air Wing

COMMANDING OFFICERS

Major General William R. Collins	May 1965
Major General Lewis W. Walt	June 1965
Major General Keith B. McCutcheon	February 1966
Lieutenant General Lewis W. Walt	March 1966
Lieutenant General Robert E. Cushman	June 1967
Lieutenant General Herman Nickerson Jr.	March 1969
Lieutenant General Keith B. McCutcheon	March 1970
Lieutenant General Donn J. Robertson	December 1970

1st Marine Division
Date formed: 1942
Date arrived in Vietnam: February 1966
Date departed Vietnam: April 1971
Headquarters: Chu Lai, February 1966; Da Nang, November 1966

SUBORDINATE COMBAT UNITS
1st Marine Regiment
5th Marine Regiment
7th Marine Regiment
11th Marine Regiment (Artillery)
27th Marine Regiment (attached February 1968 from the 5th Marine Division)

PRINCIPAL ENGAGEMENTS
Operation UNION
Operation SWIFT
Hue
Operation HOUSTON
Operation MAMELUKE THRUST
Operation TAYLOR COMMON

COMMANDING GENERALS

Major General Lewis J. Fields	February 1966
Major General Herman Nickerson Jr.	October 1966
Major General Donn J. Robertson	October 1967
Major General Ormond R. Simpson	December 1968
Major General Edwin B. Wheeler	December 1969
Major General Charles F. Widdecke	April 1970

3rd Marine Division
Date formed: 1942
Date arrived in Vietnam: May 6, 1965
Date departed Vietnam: November 30, 1969
Headquarters: Da Nang, May 1965; Hue, October 1966; Quang Tri, March 1968; Dong Ha, June 1968; Da Nang, November 1969

SUBORDINATE COMBAT UNITS
3rd Marine Regiment
4th Marine Regiment
9th Marine Regiment
12th Marine Regiment (Artillery)
26th Marine Regiment (attached April 1967 from the 5th Marine Division)

PRINCIPAL ENGAGEMENTS
Operation STARLITE
Operation HASTINGS
Operation PRAIRIE
Operation PRAIRIE II
Operation BUFFALO
Operation KENTUCKY
Khe Sanh
Operation LANCASTER II
Operation DEWEY CANYON
Operation APACHE SNOW

COMMANDING GENERALS

Major General William R. Collins	March 1965
Major General Lewis W. Walt	June 1965
Major General Wood B. Kyle	March 1966
Major General Bruno A. Hochmuth	March 1967
Major General Rathvon McC. Tompkins	November 1967
Major General Raymond G. Davis	May 1968
Major General William K. Jones	April 1969

1st Marine Air Wing
Date arrived in Vietnam: May 1965
Date departed Vietnam: April 14, 1971
Headquarters: Da Nang

COMMANDING GENERALS

Major General Paul J. Fontana	May 1965
Major General Keith B. McCutcheon	June 1965
Major General Louis B. Robertshaw	May 1966
Major General Norman J. Anderson	June 1967

Major General Charles J. Quilter	June 1968
Major General William G. Thrash	July 1969
Major General Alan J. Armstrong	July 1970

D. U.S. Air Force Major Commands

The 2nd Air Division controlled air operations in South Vietnam from October 1962 until the division was converted to the Seventh Air Force in April 1966. The commander of the Seventh Air Force also served as MACV's deputy commander for air. Not all Seventh Air Force's operations, however, came directly under MACV's control.

When operating against targets in North Vietnam or Laos, the commander of the Seventh Air Force took his orders from the commander of the Pacific Air Force, who reported to the CINCPAC. The Seventh Air Force also did not directly control operations of the 1st MAW. Further muddling the air command and control structure, the U.S. Strategic Air Command, based in Omaha, Nebraska, retained direct control over all B-52 bomber missions flown against Southeast Asian targets.

Another organizational anomaly was the Seventh/Thirteenth Air Force, stationed in Udorn, Thailand. The Seventh/Thirteenth Air Force was an air division–size organization taking orders from two different higher headquarters. In operational matters, the Seventh/Thirteenth Air Force took its orders from the Seventh Air Force; for logistical matters, it took its orders from the Thirteenth Air Force, based in the Philippines.

When the 2nd Air Division was converted to the Seventh Air Force, it had approximately 30,000 personnel and almost 1,000 aircraft. In 1968 the Seventh/Thirteenth Air Force had 35,000 personnel and 600 aircraft.

2nd Air Division
Date formed in Vietnam: October 8, 1962
Date converted to Seventh Air Force: April 1, 1966
Headquarters: Tan Son Nhut Air Base

COMMANDING GENERALS

Brigadier General Rollen H. Anthis	October 1962
Brigadier General Robert R. Rowland	December 1962
Brigadier General Milton B. Adams	December 1963
Lieutenant General Joseph H. Moore	January 1964

Seventh Air Force
Date formed in Vietnam: April 1, 1966
Date departed Vietnam: March 1973
Headquarters: Tan Son Nhut Air Base

SUBORDINATE COMBAT UNITS

834th Air Division
483rd Tactical Airlift Wing
315th Special Operations Wing
Airlift Control Center

3rd Tactical Fighter Wing
12th Tactical Fighter Wing
31st Tactical Fighter Wing
35th Tactical Fighter Wing
366th Tactical Fighter Wing
Air Force Advisory Group

COMMANDING GENERALS

Lieutenant General Joseph H. Moore	April 1966
General William W. Momyer	June 1966
General George S. Brown	August 1968
General Lucius D. Clay Jr.	September 1970
General John D. Lavelle	August 1971
General John W. Vogt Jr.	April 1972

SEVENTH/THIRTEENTH AIR FORCE
Date formed in Thailand: January 6, 1966
Date departed Thailand: April 1973
Headquarters: Udorn, Thailand

SUBORDINATE COMBAT UNITS
8th Tactical Fighter Wing
355th Tactical Fighter Wing
388th Tactical Fighter Wing
432nd Tactical Reconnaissance Wing
553rd Tactical Reconnaissance Wing
56th Special Operations Wing

COMMANDING GENERALS

Major General Charles R. Bond	January 1966
Major General William C. Lindley	June 1967
Major General Louis T. Seith	June 1968
Major General Robert L. Petit	June 1969
Major General James F. Kirkendall	March 1970
Major General Andrew Evans Jr.	October 1970
Major General DeWitt R. Searles	June 1971
Major General James D. Hughes	September 1972

E. U.S. Navy Major Commands

The American naval effort in Vietnam was almost as fragmented as the air effort. U.S. Naval Forces, Vietnam, established in April 1966, reported directly to MACV and controlled operations on inland waterways and coastal operations in the II, III, and IV CTZs. Naval operations in the I CTZ were the responsibility of the III MAF. The U.S. Seventh Fleet, which reported to the commander of the Pacific Fleet and then to the CINCPAC, controlled all naval operations beyond South Vietnamese coastal waters and all operations directly against North Vietnam.

The main striking force of the Seventh Fleet was Task Force 77. Consisting of two to three attack carriers and supporting escorts, Task Force 77 first operated from Dixie Station and then, after mid-1966, from Yankee Station. Task Group 70.8, a cruiser and destroyer force, conducted antishipping and shore gunfire operations against North Vietnam. Task group 70.8's subordinate Task Unit 70.8.9 provided naval gunfire support to MACV's ground forces in South Vietnam. Task Force 73 was the fleet's logistical support element, including the hospital ships *Sanctuary* and *Repose*. Task Force 76 was the fleet's amphibious element and conducted the initial landings in Da Nang in March 1965. In 1969 Task Force 76 conducted Operation BOLD MARINER, the largest amphibious operation of the war.

U.S. Naval Forces, Vietnam, consisted of three main task forces. Task Force 115 was the Coastal Surveillance Force, operating 81 fast patrol boats and 24 Coast Guard cutters. Task Force 116 operated as the River Patrol Force and controlled up to three Sea Air Land (SEAL) platoons at any one time. Task Force 117 was the Riverine Assault Force, the U.S. Navy component of the joint U.S. Army–U.S. Navy Mobile Riverine Force. Naval Forces, Vietnam, also controlled operations of the approximately 50 U.S. Coast Guard vessels that served in Vietnam.

Seventh Fleet
Date began operating in Vietnam waters: 1961
Date ceased major operations in Vietnam waters: mid-1973
Headquarters: Japan

MAJOR SUBORDINATE COMMANDS
Task Force 73
Task Force 76
Task Force 77
Task Group 70.8

COMMANDING OFFICERS
Vice Admiral Roy L. Johnson	June 1964
Vice Admiral Paul P. Blackburn Jr.	March 1965
Rear Admiral Joseph W. Williams	October 1965
Vice Admiral John J. Hyland	December 1965
Vice Admiral William F. Bringle	November 1967
Vice Admiral Maurice F. Weisner	March 1970
Vice Admiral William P. Mack	June 1971
Vice Admiral James L. Holloway III	May 1972

Naval Forces, Vietnam
Date formed in Vietnam: April 1, 1966
Date inactivated in Vietnam: March 29, 1973
Headquarters: Saigon

SUBORDINATE OPERATIONAL UNITS
Task Force 115
Task Force 116
Task Force 117
Naval Advisory Group
3rd Naval Construction Brigade
Military Sea Transportation Service Office, Vietnam

Coast Guard Command, Vietnam
Coast Guard Squadron 1
Coast Guard Squadron 3

COMMANDING OFFICERS
Rear Admiral Norvell G. Ward	April 1966
Rear Admiral Kenneth L. Veth	April 1967
Vice Admiral Elmo R. Zumwalt	September 1968
Vice Admiral Jerome H. King	May 1970
Rear Admiral Robert S. Salzer	April 1971
Rear Admiral Arthur W. Price Jr.	June 1972
Rear Admiral James B. Wilson	August 1972

II. Allied Forces Order of Battle

Seven U.S. allies sent military units and personnel to Vietnam. Both Korea and Thailand provided division-sized units. Australia, New Zealand, and the Philippines sent smaller units. Nationalist China and Spain also sent very small groups of advisers and observers to Vietnam. Between 1964 and 1970, the Republic of China (ROC), also known as Taiwan and Nationalist China, had between 20 and 31 soldiers in Vietnam, and from 1966 to 1970 Spain had between 7 and 13. A very small number of British officers also served in Vietnam while seconded to Australian and New Zealand units.

A. Republic of Korea Forces in Vietnam

Of all America's allies, the Republic of Korea (ROK, South Korea) sent the largest contingent of combat forces to Vietnam. At their peak in 1968, Korean forces were organized into two divisions, a Marine Corps brigade and associated support elements for a total of 22 maneuver battalions. They were grouped under a corps-sized headquarters, established in August 1966. Highly respected militarily by both allies and foes, the bulk of the Korean forces did not start to withdraw from Vietnam until January 1973.

Republic of Korea Forces, Vietnam Field Command
Date arrived in Vietnam: August 1966
Date departed Vietnam: March 17, 1973
Headquarters: Nha Trang

MAJOR SUBORDINATE UNITS
Capital Division
9th Infantry Division
2nd Marine Corps Brigade
100th Logistical Command

Capital Division ("Tigers")
Date arrived in Vietnam: September 29, 1965
Date departed Vietnam: March 10, 1973
Headquarters: Qui Nhon

SUBORDINATE COMBAT UNITS
The Cavalry Regiment
1st Infantry Regiment
26th Infantry Regiment
10th Field Artillery Battalion
60th Field Artillery Battalion
61st Field Artillery Battalion
628th Field Artillery Battalion

9th Infantry Division ("White Horse")
Date arrived in Vietnam: September 27, 1966
Date departed Vietnam: March 16, 1973
Headquarters: Ninh Ho

SUBORDINATE COMBAT UNITS
28th Infantry Regiment
29th Infantry Regiment
30th Infantry Regiment
30th Field Artillery Battalion
51st Field Artillery Battalion
52nd Field Artillery Battalion
966th Field Artillery Battalion

2nd Marine Corps Brigade ("Blue Dragons")
Date arrived in Vietnam: October 19, 1965
Date departed Vietnam: February 1972
Headquarters: Hoi An

SUBORDINATE COMBAT UNITS
1st Marine Battalion
2nd Marine Battalion
3rd Marine Battalion
5th Marine Battalion

B. Thailand Forces in Vietnam

The Royal Thai Army Regiment arrived in Vietnam in September 1967 and operated in conjunction with the U.S. 9th Infantry Division. That regiment rotated back to Thailand in August 1968 and was replaced by the Royal Thai Expeditionary Division. At their peak in 1970, Thai forces fielded six maneuver battalions. They began withdrawing shortly thereafter. By September 1971 only one maneuver brigade and its supporting units remained. That force was redesignated the Royal Thai Army Volunteer Force.

Royal Thai Army Regiment ("Queen's Cobras")
Date arrived in Vietnam: September 19, 1967
Date departed Vietnam: August 15, 1968
Headquarters: Bear Cat

Royal Thai Expeditionary Division ("Black Panthers")
Date arrived in Vietnam: February 25, 1969
Date reorganized to brigade strength: August 31, 1971
Headquarters: Bear Cat

SUBORDINATE COMBAT UNITS
1st Royal Thai Army Brigade
2nd Royal Thai Army Brigade
3rd Royal Thai Army Brigade
1st Artillery Battalion (155-millimeter [mm])
1st Artillery Battalion (105-mm)
2nd Artillery Battalion
3rd Artillery Battalion
1st Armored Cavalry Squadron

Royal Thai Army Volunteer Force
Date formed in Vietnam: September 1, 1971
Date departed Vietnam: March 1972
Headquarters: Saigon

SUBORDINATE COMBAT UNITS
2nd Royal Thai Army Brigade
1st Artillery Battalion (155-mm)
1st Artillery Battalion (105-mm)
2nd Artillery Battalion

C. Australian Forces in Vietnam

The Australians were the first U.S. allies to send military forces to Vietnam. The Australian Army Training Team arrived in July 1962. In 1965 the Australian government decided to commit combat forces to Vietnam, establishing the Australian Army Force, Vietnam. In May 1966 this headquarters was converted to the Australian Forces, Vietnam, a joint headquarters controlling both army and air force units. The 1st Australian Task Force was the principal Australian ground combat headquarters.

The Australians rotated entire battalions in and out of Vietnam. At least 12 different maneuver battalions served in Vietnam at one time or another, with 3 being the maximum number of maneuver battalions in Vietnam at any one time between 1968 and 1970.

Australian Army Training Team, Vietnam
Date arrived in Vietnam: July 31, 1962
Date departed Vietnam: December 18, 1972
Headquarters: Saigon

Australian Army Force, Vietnam
Date arrived in Vietnam: May 25, 1965
Date reorganized as Australian Forces, Vietnam: May 2, 1966
Headquarters: Saigon

Australian Forces, Vietnam
Date organized from Australian Army Force, Vietnam: May 3, 1966
Date departed Vietnam: March 15, 1972
Headquarters: Saigon

SUBORDINATE COMBAT UNITS
1st Australian Task Force

1st Australian Logistic Support Group
Royal Australian Air Force, Vietnam

1st Australian Task Force
Date formed in Vietnam: April 1, 1966
Date departed Vietnam: March 12, 1972
Headquarters: Nui Dat

SUBORDINATE COMBAT UNITS
1st Battalion, Royal Australian Regiment
2nd Battalion, Royal Australian Regiment
3rd Battalion, Royal Australian Regiment
4th Battalion, Royal Australian Regiment
5th Battalion, Royal Australian Regiment
6th Battalion, Royal Australian Regiment
7th Battalion, Royal Australian Regiment
8th Battalion, Royal Australian Regiment
9th Battalion, Royal Australian Regiment
Number 1 Armoured Personnel Carrier Squadron
3rd Cavalry Regiment
1st Armoured Regiment
4th Field Artillery Regiment
12th Field Artillery Regiment
Number 1 Special Air Service Squadron
Number 2 Special Air Service Squadron
Number 3 Special Air Service Squadron

Australian Army Assistance Group, Vietnam
Date formed in Vietnam: March 6, 1972
Date departed Vietnam: January 31, 1973
Headquarters: Saigon

D. New Zealand Forces in Vietnam
Throughout most of the Vietnam War, the New Zealand Battalion of the 28th Commonwealth Brigade was serving in Malaysia. The New Zealanders did, however, send the 161st Field Battery, Royal New Zealand Artillery, to provide fire support for Australian forces. Later New Zealand sent one and then another rifle company.

New Zealand "V" Force
Date arrived in Vietnam: July 21, 1965
Date departed Vietnam: June 1972

SUBORDINATE COMBAT UNITS
"V" Rifle Company, Royal New Zealand Infantry
"W" Rifle Company, Royal New Zealand Infantry
Number 161 Field Battery, Royal New Zealand Artillery
Number 4 Troop, Royal New Zealand Special Air Service

E. Philippine Forces in Vietnam
In 1965 the Philippine Army had approximately 70 soldiers in Vietnam. In September 1966 the 1st Philippine Civic Action Group arrived and concentrated on pacification missions in Tay Ninh Province. Philippine forces reached their peak strength of slightly more than 2,000 in 1966 and 1967. The 1st Philippine Civic Action Group left Vietnam by the end of 1969.

1st Philippine Civic Action Group, Vietnam
Date formed in Vietnam: September 14, 1966
Date departed Vietnam: December 13, 1969
Headquarters: Tay Ninh

SUBORDINATE UNITS
Philippine Security Infantry Battalion
Philippine Field Artillery Battalion
Philippine Construction Engineer Battalion
Philippine Medical and Dental Battalion

III. Republic of Vietnam Armed Forces
Many units of the ARVN traced their origins to French colonial units that fought against the Viet Minh. Most of those units originally were turned over to the State of Vietnam. After the establishment of the Republic of Vietnam on October 26, 1955, all ARVN units went through a confusing series of reorganizations and mergers.

While the vast bulk of ARVN consisted of ground forces, the Republic of Vietnam Navy (VNN, South Vietnamese Navy) and the Republic of Vietnam Air Force (VNAF, South Vietnamese Air Force) played significant roles, and by the early 1970s both had developed into large well-equipped services.

A. Republic of Vietnam Navy
The VNN was formed in 1952. Initially commanded by French officers, the VNN came under Vietnamese command in early 1954. By the early 1970s the VNN had grown from a few small amphibious ships and a few dozen landing craft in 1954 to a force equipped with more than 2,000 warships and smaller naval craft, including former U.S. Navy destroyer escorts and tank landing ships, and organized into an oceangoing fleet, five coastal zones, two river patrol zones, and a SEAL special operations unit.

COMMANDERS

Lieutenant Commander Le Quang My	1955
Lieutenant Commander Tran Van Chon	1957
Lieutenant Commander Ho Tan Quyen	1959
Navy Captain Chung Tan Cang	1963
Commander Tran Van Phan	1965
Navy Captain Tran Van Chon	1966
Commodore Lam Nguon Tanh	1974
Vice Admiral Chung Tan Cang	1975

B. Republic of Vietnam Air Force
Formed as a separate service in 1955, the VNAF began as a small force of a few thousand personnel and was equipped with a few squadrons of small transport aircraft (C-47 and C-45),

light observation aircraft, and F8F "Bearcat" propeller-driven fighter-bombers. By 1972 the VNAF had grown to a force of more than 60,000 men organized into six air divisions and equipped with more than 1,500 aircraft, including supersonic F-5 fighter-bombers; A-37 jet and A-1 propeller-driven attack bombers; AC-47 and AC-119 gunships; C-130, C-123, C-47, and C-7 transports; O-1 observation aircraft; and UH-1 and CH-47 helicopters.

COMMANDERS

Lieutenant Colonel Nguyen Khanh	1955
Major Tran Van Ho	1955
Lieutenant Colonel Nguyen Xuan Vinh	1957
Lieutenant Colonel Huynh Huu Hien	1962
Colonel Do Khac Mai	1963
Colonel (later Major General) Nguyen Cao Ky	1964
Colonel (later Lieutenant General) Tran Van Minh	1967

Republic of Vietnam Air Force Air Divisions (1973)
1st Air Division, based at Da Nang
2nd Air Division, based at Nha Trang
3rd Air Division, based at Bien Hoa
4th Air Division, based at Can Tho
5th Air Division, based at Tan Son Nhut
6th Air Division, based at Pleiku

C. Regional Commands

Between 1957 and 1963 the ARVN established four corps-level commands that divided responsibility for the security of the country into four CTZs. Each of the ARVN's 11 infantry divisions were allocated to a corps. Two elite divisions, the Airborne Division and the Marine Division, constituted the country's strategic reserve and were controlled directly by the Joint General Staff.

Within each of the CTZs, the ARVN designated at least one semiautonomous Special Tactical Zone (STZ) for the purpose of focusing military efforts and resources in critical areas. In addition to the regular forces, the commander of each CTZ also controlled the territorial forces, which consisted of the Civil Guard and the Self-Defense Corps. The latter was later designated the Popular Forces (PF), and the former became the Regional Forces (RF).

I Corps
Date formed: June 1, 1957
Headquarters: Da Nang
Area of responsibility: Quang Tri Province, Thua Thien Province, Quang Nam Province, Quang Tin Province, Quang Ngai Province (after November 1963)

MAJOR SUBORDINATE UNITS
1st Infantry Division
2nd Infantry Division
3rd Infantry Division
1st Ranger Group

1st Armor Brigade
STZ: Quang Da Special Zone

COMMANDING GENERALS

Lieutenant General Thai Quang Hung	November 25, 1956
Lieutenant General Tran Van Don	October 15, 1957
Major General Le Van Nghiem	December 7, 1962
Major General Do Cao Tri	August 21, 1963
Lieutenant General Nguyen Khanh	December 11, 1963
Major General Ton That Xung	January 30, 1964
Lieutenant General Nguyen Chanh Thi	November 14, 1964
Major General Nguyen Van Chuan	March 14, 1966
Lieutenant General Ton That Dinh	April 9, 1966
Major General Huynh Van Cao	May 15, 1966
General Tran Thanh Phong	May 20, 1966
Lieutenant General Hoang Xuan Lam	May 30, 1966
Lieutenant General Ngo Quang Truong	May 3, 1972

II Corps
Date formed: October 1, 1957
Headquarters: Pleiku
Area of responsibility: Kontum Province, Binh Dinh Province, Pleiku Province, Phu Bon Province, Phu Yen Province, Darlac Province, Khanh Hoa Province, Quang Duc Province, Tuyen Duc Province, Ninh Thuan Province, Lam Dong Province, Binh Thuan Province

MAJOR SUBORDINATE UNITS
22nd Infantry Division
23rd Infantry Division
2nd Ranger Group
2nd Armor Brigade
STZ: 24th STZ

COMMANDING GENERALS

Major General Tran Ngoc Tam	October 1, 1957
Major General Ton That Dinh	August 13, 1958
Lieutenant General Nguyen Khanh	December 20, 1962
Lieutenant General Do Cao Tri	December 12, 1963
Major General Nguyen Huu Co	September 15, 1964
Lieutenant General Vinh Loc	June 23, 1965
Lieutenant General Lu Lan	February 28, 1968
Lieutenant General Ngo Dzu	August 28, 1970
Major General Nguyen Van Toan	May 10, 1972
Major General Pham Van Phu	October 30, 1974

III Corps
Date formed: March 1, 1959 (provisional); May 20, 1960 (permanent)
Headquarters: Bien Hoa
Area of responsibility: Phuoc Long Province, Long Khanh Province, Binh Tuy Province, Binh Long Province, Binh

Duong Province, Bien Hoa Province, Phuoc Tuy Province, Tay Ninh Province, Hau Nghia Province, Long An Province

MAJOR SUBORDINATE UNITS

5th Infantry Division
18th Infantry Division
25th Infantry Division
81st Ranger Group
3rd Armor Brigade
STZs: Capital Military District; Rung Sat Special Zone

COMMANDING GENERALS

Lieutenant General Thai Quang Hoang	March 1, 1959
Lieutenant General Nguyen Ngoc Le	October 11, 1959
Major General Le Van Nghiem	May 5, 1960
Major General Ton That Dinh	December 7, 1962
Lieutenant General Tran Thien Khiem	January 5, 1964
Major General Lam Van Phat	February 2, 1964
Lieutenant General Tran Ngoc Tam	April 4, 1964
Major General Cao Van Vien	October 12, 1964
Major General Nguyen Bao Tri	October 11, 1965
Lieutenant General Le Nguyen Khang	June 9, 1966
Lieutenant General Do Cao Tri	August 5, 1968
Lieutenant General Nguyen Van Minh	February 23, 1971
Lieutenant General Pham Quoc Thuan	October 29, 1973
Lieutenant General Du Quoc Dong	October 30, 1974
Lieutenant General Nguyen Van Toan	January 1975

IV Corps

Date formed: January 1, 1963

Headquarters: Can Tho

Area of responsibility: Go Cong Province, Kien Tuong Province, Dinh Tuong Province, Kien Hoa Province, Kien Phong Province, Sa Dec Province, Vinh Long Province, Vinh Binh Province, Chau Doc Province, An Giang Province, Phong Dinh Province, Ba Xuyen Province, Kien Giang Province, Chuong Thien Province, Bac Lieu Province, An Xuyen Province

MAJOR SUBORDINATE UNITS

7th Infantry Division
9th Infantry Division
21st Infantry Division
4th Ranger Group
4th Armor Brigade
STZ: 44th STZ

COMMANDING GENERALS

Major General Huynh Van Cao	January 1, 1963
Major General Nguyen Huu Co	November 4, 1963
Major General Duong Van Duc	March 4, 1964
Major General Nguyen Van Thieu	September 15, 1964
Lieutenant Colonel Dang Van Quang	January 20, 1965

Major General Nguyen Van Manh	November 23, 1966
Lieutenant General Nguyen Duc Thang	February 29, 1968
Lieutenant General Nguyen Viet Thanh	July 1, 1968
Major General Ngo Dzu	May 1, 1970
Lieutenant General Ngo Quang Truong	August 21, 1970
Major General Nguyen Vinh Nghi	May 4, 1972
Major General Nguyen Khoa Nam	October 30, 1974

1st Infantry Division

Date formed: January 1, 1955

Origins and redesignations: 21st Mobile Group (French), September 1, 1953; 21st Infantry Division, January 1, 1955; 21st Field Division, August 1, 1955; 1st Field Division, November 1, 1955; 1st Infantry Division, January 1, 1959

Headquarters: Hue

SUBORDINATE COMBAT UNITS

1st Infantry Regiment
3rd Infantry Regiment
51st Infantry Regiment
54th Infantry Regiment

PRINCIPAL ENGAGEMENTS

Hue Uprising, 1966
Defense of Hue City, Tet Offensive, 1968
Operation LAM SON 719
Easter Offensive, 1972, Hue
Hue, spring of 1975

COMMANDING OFFICERS

Lieutenant Colonel Le Van Nghiem	January 1, 1955
Colonel Nguyen Khanh	1956
Colonel Ton That Dinh	1957
Colonel Nguyen Van Chuan	1958
Colonel Ton That Xung	1959
Colonel Nguyen Duc Thang	1960
Colonel Nguyen Van Thieu	1961
General Do Cao Tri	1962
Colonel Tran Thanh Phong	1963
General Nguyen Chanh Thi	ca. 1964
Major General Nguyen Van Chuan	November 1964
General Phan Xuan Nhuan	March 12, 1966
Lieutenant General Ngo Quang Truong	June 1966
Major General Pham Van Phu	August 21, 1970
Brigadier General Le Van Than	1972
Major General Nguyen Van Diem	October 31, 1974

2nd Infantry Division

Date formed: February 1, 1955

Origins and redesignations: 32nd Mobile Group (French), November 3, 1953; 32nd Infantry Division, February 1, 1955;

32nd Field Division, August 1, 1955; 2nd Field Division, November 1, 1955; 2nd Infantry Division, January 1, 1959

Headquarters: Da Nang, 1955; Quang Ngai, 1965; Chu Lai, 1972; Ham Tan, 1975

SUBORDINATE COMBAT UNITS

4th Infantry Regiment
5th Infantry Regiment
6th Infantry Regiment

PRINCIPAL ENGAGEMENTS

Chu Lai, spring of 1975
Tam Ky, spring of 1975
Phan Rang, spring of 1975

COMMANDING OFFICERS

Colonel Ton That Dinh	January 1, 1955
Lieutenant Colonel Dang Van Son	November 22, 1956
Lieutenant Colonel Le Quang Trong	June 14, 1957
Colonel Duong Ngoc Lam	August 23, 1958
Colonel Lam Van Phat	June 8, 1961
Colonel Truong Van Chuong	June 18, 1963
Brigadier General Ton That Xung	December 6, 1963
Brigadier General Ngo Dzu	January 30, 1964
Colonel Nguyen Thanh Sang	July 29, 1964
Major General Hoang Xuan Lam	October 15, 1964
Major General Nguyen Van Toan	January 10, 1967
Brigadier General Phan Hoa Hiep	January 22, 1972
Brigadier General Tran Van Nhut	August 27, 1972

3rd Infantry Division

Date formed: October 1, 1971
Origins and redesignations: None
Headquarters: Ai Tu, 1971; Da Nang, 1972

SUBORDINATE COMBAT UNITS

2nd Infantry Regiment
56th Infantry Regiment
57th Infantry Regiment

PRINCIPAL ENGAGEMENTS

Easter Offensive, 1972, Quang Tri
Da Nang, spring of 1975

COMMANDING OFFICERS

Brigadier General Vu Van Giai	October 1, 1971
Major General Nguyen Duy Hinh	May 1972

5th Infantry Division

Date formed: February 1, 1955
Origins and redesignations: 6th Infantry Division, February 1, 1955; 6th Field Division, August 1, 1955; 41st Field Division, September 1, 1955; 3rd Field Division, November 1, 1955; 5th Infantry Division, January 1, 1959

Headquarters: Song Mao, 1955; Bien Hoa, 1961; Phu Loi, 1964; Lai Khe, 1970

SUBORDINATE COMBAT UNITS

7th Infantry Regiment
8th Infantry Regiment
9th Infantry Regiment

PRINCIPAL ENGAGEMENTS

Cambodia, 1970
Easter Offensive, 1972, An Loc
Phuoc Long
Ben Cat, spring of 1975

COMMANDING OFFICERS

Colonel Vong A Sang	March 1, 1955
Colonel Pham Van Dong	October 25, 1956
Lieutenant Colonel Nguyen Quang Thong	March 18, 1958
Colonel Ton That Xung	September 16, 1958
Lieutenant Colonel Dang Van Son	November 19, 1958
Colonel Nguyen Van Chuan	August 3, 1959
Brigadier General Tran Ngoc Tam	May 20, 1961
Colonel Nguyen Duc Thang	October 16, 1961
Colonel Nguyen Van Thieu	December 20, 1962
Brigadier General Dang Thanh Liem	February 2, 1964
Brigadier General Cao Hao Hon	June 5, 1964
Brigadier General Tran Thanh Phong	October 21, 1964
Major General Pham Quoc Thuan	July 19, 1965
Major General Nguyen Van Hieu	August 15, 1969
Brigadier General Le Van Hung	June 14, 1971
Brigadier General Tran Quoc Lich	September 4, 1972
Colonel Le Nguyen Vy	November 7, 1973

7th Infantry Division

Date formed: January 1, 1955
Origins and redesignations: 7th Mobile Group (French); 2nd Mobile Group (French); 31st Mobile Group (French), September 1, 1953; 31st Infantry Division, January 1, 1955; 31st Field Division, August 1, 1955; 11th Field Division, August 1955; 4th Field Division, November 1, 1955; 7th Infantry Division, January 1, 1959

Headquarters: Tam Ky, 1955; Bien Hoa, 1955; My Tho, 1961; Dong Tam, 1969

SUBORDINATE COMBAT UNITS

10th Infantry Regiment
11th Infantry Regiment
12th Infantry Regiment

PRINCIPAL ENGAGEMENTS

Operations against Hoa Hao Forces, 1956

Tet Offensive, 1968, My Tho

Cambodia, 1970

Easter Offensive, 1972, Cambodian Border

Tan An, spring of 1975

COMMANDING OFFICERS

Lieutenant Colonel Nguyen Huu Co	January 1, 1955
Colonel Ton That Xung	June 15, 1955
Lieutenant Colonel Ngo Dzu	April 27, 1957
Colonel Tran Thien Khiem	March 17, 1958
Colonel Huynh Van Cao	March 30, 1959
Colonel Bui Dinh Dam	December 22, 1962
Brigadier General Nguyen Huu Co	November 1, 1963
Colonel Pham Van Dong	November 5, 1963
Brigadier General Lam Van Phat	December 2, 1963
Colonel Bui Huu Nhon	February 2, 1964
Colonel Huynh Van Ton	March 7, 1964
Brigadier General Nguyen Bao Tri	September 16, 1964
Brigadier General Nguyen Viet Thanh	October 9, 1965
Brigadier General Nguyen Thanh Hoang	July 3, 1968
Major General Nguyen Khoa Nam	January 16, 1970
General Tran Van Hai	October 30, 1974

9th Infantry Division

Date formed: January 1, 1962

Origins and redesignations: None

Headquarters: Phu Thanh, 1962; Sa Dec, 1963; Vinh Long, 1972

SUBORDINATE COMBAT UNITS

14th Infantry Regiment

15th Infantry Regiment

16th Infantry Regiment

PRINCIPAL ENGAGEMENTS

Cambodia, 1970

Easter Offensive, 1972, An Loc

Mekong Delta, spring of 1975

COMMANDING OFFICERS

Colonel Bui Dzinh	January 1, 1962
Colonel Doan Van Quang	November 7, 1963
Brigadier General Vinh Loc	February 9, 1964
Brigadier General Lam Quang Thi	May 29, 1965
Major General Tran Ba Di	July 3, 1968
Brigadier General Huynh Van Lac	October 26, 1973

18th Infantry Division

Date formed: May 16, 1965 (provisional); August 1, 1965 (permanent)

Origins and redesignations: 10th Infantry Division, May 16, 1965; 18th Infantry Division, January 1, 1967

Headquarters: Xuan Loc

SUBORDINATE COMBAT UNITS

43rd Infantry Regiment

48th Infantry Regiment

52nd Infantry Regiment

PRINCIPAL ENGAGEMENTS

Easter Offensive, 1972, An Loc

Xuan Loc, spring of 1975

COMMANDING OFFICERS

Colonel Nguyen Van Manh	June 5, 1965
Brigadier General Lu Lan	August 20, 1965
Brigadier General Do Ke Giai	September 16, 1966
Major General Lam Quang Tho	August 20, 1969
Brigadier General Le Minh Dao	April 4, 1972

21st Infantry Division

Date formed: June 1, 1959

Origins and redesignations: 1st Light Division, August 1, 1955; 11th Light Division, November 1, 1955; 3rd Light Division, August 1, 1955; 13th Light Division, November 1, 1955; merged as 21st Infantry Division, June 1, 1959

Headquarters: Sa Dec, 1959; Bac Lieu, 1960

SUBORDINATE COMBAT UNITS

31st Infantry Regiment

32nd Infantry Regiment

33rd Infantry Regiment

PRINCIPAL ENGAGEMENTS

Operations against Hoa Hao Forces, 1956

U Minh Forest

Easter Offensive, 1972, An Loc

Mekong Delta, spring of 1975

COMMANDING OFFICERS

Lieutenant Colonel Nguyen Bao Tri	June 1, 1959
Lieutenant Colonel Tran Thanh Chieu	September 8, 1959
Colonel Tran Thien Khiem	February 2, 1960
Colonel Bui Huu Nhon	December 1962
Colonel Cao Hao Hon	November 1963
Brigadier General Dang Van Quang	June 1, 1964
Colonel Nguyen Van Phuoc	January 20, 1965
Brigadier General Nguyen Van Minh	March 21, 1965
Major General Nguyen Vinh Nghi	June 13, 1968
Brigadier General Ho Trung Hau	May 3, 1972
Brigadier General Chuong Dzenh Quay	August 21, 1972
Brigadier General Le Van Hung	June 9, 1973
Brigadier General Mach Van Truong	1974

22nd Infantry Division
Date formed: April 1, 1959
Origins and redesignations: 2nd Light Division, August 1, 1955; 12th Light Division, November 1, 1955 (disbanded March 31, 1959, and troops incorporated into the 22nd Infantry Division); 4th Light Division, August 1, 1955; 14th Light Division, November 1, 1955; 22nd Infantry Division, April 1, 1959
Headquarters: Kontum, 1959; Ba Gi, 1965; Binh Dinh, 1972; Tan An, 1975

SUBORDINATE COMBAT UNITS
40th Infantry Regiment
42nd Infantry Regiment
47th Infantry Regiment

PRINCIPAL ENGAGEMENTS
Operations against Hoa Hao Forces, 1956
Easter Offensive, 1972, Kontum
Binh Dinh, spring of 1975
Tan An, spring of 1975

COMMANDING OFFICERS

Lieutenant Colonel Tran Thanh Chieu	April 1, 1959
Lieutenant Colonel Nguyen Bao Tri	September 8, 1959
Colonel Nguyen Thanh Sang	November 5, 1963
Brigadier General Linh Quang Vien	February 5, 1964
Colonel Nguyen Van Hieu	September 7, 1964
Brigadier General Nguyen Xuan Thinh	October 24, 1964
Brigadier General Nguyen Thanh Sang	March 1, 1965
Brigadier General Nguyen Van Hieu	June 28, 1966
Brigadier General Le Ngoc Trien	August 11, 1969
Colonel Le Duc Dat	March 1, 1972
Brigadier General Phan Dinh Niem	April 28, 1972

23rd Infantry Division
Date formed: April 1, 1959
Origins and redesignations: 5th Light Division, August 1, 1955; 15th Light Division, November 1, 1955; 23rd Infantry Division, April 1, 1959
Headquarters: Nha Trang, 1955; Duc My, 1956; Ban Me Thuot, 1961; Long Hai, 1975

SUBORDINATE COMBAT UNITS
41st Infantry Regiment
44th Infantry Regiment
45th Infantry Regiment
53rd Infantry Regiment

PRINCIPAL ENGAGEMENTS
Operations against Hoa Hao Forces, 1956
Cambodia, 1970

Easter Offensive, 1972, Kontum
Ban Me Thuot, spring of 1975

COMMANDING OFFICERS

Lieutenant Colonel Nguyen The Nhu	1955
Lieutenant Colonel Nguyen Van Vinh	1956
Lieutenant Colonel Bui Dzenh	1958
Lieutenant Colonel Tran Thanh Phong	May 19, 1959
Colonel Le Quang Trong	May 17, 1963
Brigadier General Hoang Xuan Lam	December 14, 1963
Brigadier General Lu Lan	October 14, 1964
Brigadier General Nguyen Van Manh	August 20, 1965
Brigadier General Truong Quang An	November 24, 1966
Brigadier General Vo Van Canh	September 9, 1968
Brigadier General Ly Tong Ba	January 25, 1972
Brigadier General Tran Van Cam	October 20, 1972
Brigadier General Le Trung Tuong	November 24, 1973
Colonel Nguyen Van Duc	mid-March 1975

25th Infantry Division
Date formed: July 1, 1962
Origins and redesignations: None
Headquarters: Thuan Hoa, 1962; Cay Diep, 1964; Cu Chi, 1970

SUBORDINATE COMBAT UNITS
46th Infantry Regiment
49th Infantry Regiment
50th Infantry Regiment

PRINCIPAL ENGAGEMENTS
Cambodia, 1970
Easter Offensive, 1972, An Loc
Tay Ninh, spring of 1975
Cu Chi, spring of 1975

COMMANDING OFFICERS

Colonel Nguyen Van Chuan	July 1962
Colonel Lu Lan	December 28, 1962
Colonel Nguyen Viet Dam	March 19, 1964
Brigadier General Nguyen Thanh Sang	December 1964
Brigadier General Phan Trong Chinh	March 16, 1965
Lieutenant General Nguyen Xuan Thinh	January 10, 1968
Brigadier General Le Van Tu	January 25, 1972
Colonel Nguyen Huu Toan	November 7, 1973
Brigadier General Ly Tong Ba	late 1974

Airborne Division
Date formed: May 1, 1955
Origins and redesignations: 1st Airborne Battalion (French), August 1, 1951; Groupment Aeroporte 3 (French), May 1, 1954; Airborne Group, May 1, 1955; Airborne Brigade, December 1, 1959; Airborne Division, December 1, 1965

Headquarters: Tan Son Nhut, 1955; Quang Tri (Forward
   Headquarters), 1972

SUBORDINATE COMBAT UNITS

1st Airborne Brigade

2nd Airborne Brigade

3rd Airborne Brigade

7th Ranger Group

PRINCIPAL ENGAGEMENTS

Dak To

Tet Offensive

Cambodia, 1970

Operation LAM SON 719

Easter Offensive, 1972, Binh Long

Easter Offensive, 1972, Quang Tri

Nha Trang, spring of 1975

Phan Rang, spring of 1975

Xuan Loc, spring of 1975

COMMANDING OFFICERS

Lieutenant Colonel Do Cao Tri	March 1, 1955
Colonel Nguyen Chanh Thi	September 1, 1956
Colonel Cao Van Vien	November 12, 1960
Lieutenant General Du Quoc Dong	December 19, 1964
Brigadier General Le Quang Luong	November 11, 1972

Marine Division

Date Formed: October 1, 1954

Origins and redesignations: 1st and 2nd Battalions de Marche
   (French); Marine Infantry Battalion, October 1, 1954; Marine
   Infantry Group, April 16, 1956; Marine Brigade, January 1,
   1962; Marine Division, October 1, 1968

Headquarters: Saigon, 1954; Vung Tau, 1975

SUBORDINATE COMBAT UNITS

147th Marine Brigade

258th Marine Brigade

369th Marine Brigade

468th Marine Brigade

PRINCIPAL ENGAGEMENTS

Tet Offensive

Cambodia, 1970

Operation LAM SON 719

Easter Offensive, 1972, Quang Tri

Da Nang, spring of 1975

Vung Tau, spring of 1975

COMMANDING OFFICERS

Lieutenant Colonel Le Quang Trong	October 1, 1954
Major Pham Van Lieu	January 16, 1956

Captain Bui Pho Chi	July 31, 1956
Major Le Nhu Hung	September 30, 1956
Major Le Nguyen Khang	May 7, 1960
Lieutenant Colonel Nguyen Ba Lien	December 16, 1963
Lieutenant General Le Nguyen Khang	February 26, 1964
Brigadier General Bui The Lan	May 5, 1972

IV. People's Army of Vietnam and the National Liberation Front

The PAVN was the lineal successor of the Viet Minh force that defeated the French. All of the Viet Minh divisions that fought in the Red River Delta and at Dien Bien Phu continued with the same designations through 2010.

As with armies of all Communist nations, the PAVN was organized to give the Vietnamese Communist Party (VCP) tremendous influence over its daily operations. At all echelons, political officers had equal authority with commanders but theoretically different responsibilities.

In October 1945 the Viet Minh organized all of Vietnam into 14 military regions. In 1950 the 14 regions were reorganized into 9 military regions, with a special military zone in the Central Highlands, another for Hanoi, and later another for Saigon–Gia Dinh. The PAVN retained this system after the 1954 partition and throughout the Vietnam War. Military Regions V through IX comprised South Vietnam. In 1961 Major General Tran Luong (Tran Nam Trung) established the Central Office for South Vietnam (COSVN), representing the VCP Central Committee to coordinate all military operations in Military Regions VI, VII, VIII, and IX, and the Saigon–Gia Dinh Special Zone. COSVN was primarily located just inside Cambodia, opposite Tay Ninh Province.

The People's Liberation Armed Forces (PLAF) was officially the armed wing of the National Front for the Liberation of South Vietnam (National Liberation Front [NLF]), also known as the Viet Cong (VC). Despite the official fiction that the PAVN and the PLAF were separate and distinct, VC military units actually operated under the direct command of COSVN. As the war progressed, PAVN and VC regiments and battalions often were grouped in the same division. VC units suffered huge losses in the 1968 Tet Offensive, and many were never again battlefield-effective units. After the Tet Offensive, PAVN units increasingly carried the weight of the war. The PAVN officially absorbed the PLAF in June 1976.

The distinction between PAVN units and VC units was one made only by the allied side as part of the effort to denounce North Vietnamese aggression. The Communists made no distinction at all between PAVN and VC units and never referred to a unit as a PAVN or North Vietnamese unit or as a VC unit. As far as they were concerned, all of their units were part of one big army. All units operating in South Vietnam were overtly referred to as part of the PLAF, which was supposedly the military arm of the NLF or, from 1969, of the Provisional Revolutionary Government (PRG) of South Vietnam. From the very beginning, however, the PLAF was considered to be a part of PAVN, and the chain of command for all units, including both those that the allies called the PAVN and those that we called the VC, ran straight back to the PAVN General Staff and the PAVN high command in Hanoi. Indeed, the first commanders of every Communist division formed in South Vietnam, including the VC 5th and 9th divisions, were all natives of North Vietnam. The first commander of the VC 9th Division, for instance, was Hoang Cam, a native of northern Vietnam who had never even set foot in South Vietnam until he arrived there a few months before the 9th Division was formed in September 1965. Indeed, up until his departure from North Vietnam by ship in early 1965, Hoang Cam was the commander of the PAVN 312th Division in North Vietnam. Hoang Cam and the PLAF's deputy political commissar Tran Do, another native of northern Vietnam, sailed from China to Sihanoukville posing as crew members on a Chinese ship and then slipped across the Cambodian border to COSVN headquarters.

The PLAF's first corps-level organization was the 559th Transportation Group. Composed of an infantry division, an engineering division, a transportation division, an antiaircraft division, and three sector divisions, the 559th Transportation Group ran operations along the Ho Chi Minh Trail. The PLAF's first corps of main-force combat units was LXX Corps, established in October 1970.

The 301st Group, established with three main-force divisions in March 1971, was redesignated IV Corps in July 1974. Between October 1973 and March 1975 the PAVN established three other corps, all of which played key command and control roles in the final spring 1975 campaign.

Starting in March 1965, PAVN divisions deploying to South Vietnam started the practice of leaving cadre units, or frame units, in North Vietnam. The frame units raised and trained replacement units and provided the strategic reserve for the defense of North Vietnam. Replacement units received the same numerical designation as the frame unit, followed by a letter designation. Thus, the 325th Infantry Division spawned the 325-B, 325-C, and 325-D Infantry divisions between 1964 and 1966. In 1964 the 325th Infantry Division was redesignated 325-A. The 325-B and 325-C Infantry divisions were eventually devastated by long combat operations in South Vietnam. In 1972 the 325-D Infantry Division was redesignated the 325th Infantry Division. This practice, of course, caused a great deal of confusion among allied OB analysts.

When the Vietnam War ended in 1975, the North Vietnamese had 685,000 regular troops under arms. The ground forces consisted of 24 divisions, 3 training divisions, 15 surface-to-air missile (SAM) regiments, and 40 antiaircraft artillery gun regiments. North Vietnam's navy had 3,000 troops, and its air force had another 12,000 troops. North Vietnam's air force had two MiG-21 interceptor regiments, one MiG-19 interceptor regiment, one MiG-17 fighter-bomber regiment, one air transport regiment (fixed-wing transports and helicopters), and one air training regiment. In addition to the regular forces, the North Vietnamese had some 50,000 troops in the Frontier Force, the Coast Security Force, and the People's Armed Security Force, plus a militia of nearly 1.5 million.

A. PAVN High Command
COMMANDER IN CHIEF AND MINISTER OF NATIONAL DEFENSE

Senior General Vo Nguyen Giap	December 1945–February 1980

CHIEFS OF STAFF

Major General Hoang Van Thai	December 1945–1953
Senior General Van Tien Dung	1953–1980

COMMANDING GENERALS, POLITICAL GENERAL DIRECTORATE

General Nguyen Chi Thanh	June 1950–1961
Lieutenant General Song Hao	1961–ca. December 1975
Sen. General Chu Huy Man	ca. April 1977–ca. October 1984

COMMANDING GENERALS, REAR SERVICES GENERAL DIRECTORATE

Major General Dinh Duc Thien	1965–?
Lieutenant General Bui Phung	1977–1982

First Secretaries, COSVN

MILITARY COMMITTEE/MILITARY AFFAIRS PARTY COMMITTEE

Major General Tran Luong	May 1961–October 1963
Nguyen Van Linh	October 1963–1964
Senior General Nguyen Chi Thanh	1964–June 1967
Pham Hung	June 1967–May 1975

COMMANDING GENERALS, SOUTHERN REGIONAL MILITARY HEADQUARTERS

Colonel General Tran Van Tra	October 1963–January 1967
Lieutenant General Hoang Van Thai	January 1967–1973
Colonel General Tran Van Tra	1973–May 1975

B. Navy Branch
Date formed: May 7, 1955

NAVY UNITS (1973)

171st Patrol Boat Regiment (originally 130th Patrol Boat Group)

172nd Torpedo Boat Regiment (originally 135th Torpedo Boat Group)

125th Maritime Transportation Regiment (originally Maritime Infiltration Group 759)

126th Water Sapper Regiment (originally 8th Water Sapper Group)

128th Fishing Boat Regiment (heavily armed fishing boats responsible for patrol/coastal surveillance duties in addition to fishing)

COMMANDING OFFICERS
Major General Ta Xuan Thu   January 1959
Senior Colonel Nguyen Ba Phat   March 1967
Senior Colonel Doan Ba Khanh   late 1974
Senior Colonel Giap Van Cuong   1980–1990

POLITICAL OFFICERS
Major General Ta Xuan Thu   January 1959
Senior Colonel Doan Phung   March 1967
Hoang Tra   April 1970
Senior Colonel Tran Van Giang   late 1974

C. Air Force Branch
Date formed: March 3, 1955

COMMANDING OFFICERS
Senior Colonel Dang Tinh   September 1955
Colonel Nguyen Van Tien   March 1967
Colonel Dao Dinh Luyen   1969–1986

POLITICAL OFFICERS
Colonel Hoang The Thien   September 1956
Colonel Phan Khac Hy   March 1967
Lieutenant Colonel Do Long   1970s

D. Air Defense–Air Force Service (also known as the Air Defense Command)
Date formed: October 22, 1963

SUBORDINATE UNITS
Air Force Branch
Anti-Aircraft Artillery Branch
Missile Branch
Radar Branch
361st Air Defense Division
363rd Air Defense Division
365th Air Defense Division
367th Air Defense Division
371st Air Force Division (see below)
375th Air Defense Division
377th Antiaircraft Artillery Division

COMMANDING OFFICERS
Senior Colonel Phung The Tai   October 1963
Senior Colonel Le Van Tri   April 1973

POLITICAL OFFICERS
Senior Colonel Dang Tinh   October 1963
Hoang Phuong   1975

371st Air Force Division
Date formed: March 24, 1967

COMMANDING OFFICERS
Colonel Nguyen Van Tien   March 1967
Colonel Dao Dinh Luyen   October 1969

POLITICAL OFFICERS
Colonel Pham Khac Hy   March 1967
Colonel Do Long   1969

Subordinate Units
Note: A fighter regiment normally was equipped with 36 fighter aircraft and had 40–50 pilots. However, this varied greatly during the course of the war, depending on aircraft and pilot availability.

921ST FIGHTER REGIMENT (MIG-17S, 1964–1965; MIG-21S, 1966–1975)
Date formed: May 30, 1963, Mengdu Air Base, China

PRINCIPAL ENGAGEMENTS
Operation ROLLING THUNDER, 1965–1968
Operation BOLO, January 1967
Operation LINEBACKER I, May–October 1972
Operation LINEBACKER II, December 1972

COMMANDING OFFICERS
Dao Dinh Luyen   1963
Tran Manh   1965

POLITICAL OFFICERS
Do Long   1964
Chu Duy Kinh   1967

923RD FIGHTER REGIMENT (MIG-17S)
Date formed: September 7, 1965

PRINCIPAL ENGAGEMENTS
Operation ROLLING THUNDER, 1965–1968
Bombing of U.S. Navy destroyer *Higbee*, April 19, 1972
Operation LINEBACKER I, May 1972
Bombing of Tan Son Nhut Air Base, Saigon, April 28, 1975

COMMANDING OFFICER
Nguyen Phuc Trach   1965

POLITICAL OFFICER
Nguyen Van Tieu   1965

925TH FIGHTER REGIMENT (MIG-19S)
Date formed: 1969

PRINCIPAL ENGAGEMENT
Operation LINEBACKER I, May 1972

COMMANDING OFFICERS
Le Quang Trung	1969
Ho Van Quy	1970

POLITICAL OFFICER
Ho Vinh	1969

927TH FIGHTER REGIMENT (MIG-21S)
Date formed: December 1, 1971

PRINCIPAL ENGAGEMENTS
Operation LINEBACKER I, May–October 1972
Operation LINEBACKER II, December 1972

COMMANDING OFFICER
Nguyen Hong Nhi	1972

POLITICAL OFFICER
Tran Ung	1972

Group Z
Composite regiment equipped with MiG-17s and MiG-21s. Group Z's pilots were North Korean, but the group's ground support personnel and aircraft were Vietnamese.

Date formed: 1967

PRINCIPAL ENGAGEMENT
Operation ROLLING THUNDER, early 1967–1968

919th Air Transport Regiment
An-2, An-24, IL-14, IL-18, and Li-2 fixed-wing transport aircraft and Mi-4 and Mi-6 helicopters.

Date formed: May 1, 1959

PRINCIPAL ENGAGEMENTS
An-2 rocket attacks against South Vietnamese commando boats in the Gulf of Tonkin, 1966
An-2 air attack against covert U.S. Air Force radar site in Laos (Lima Site 85), January 12, 1968 (two aircraft lost)
IL-14 resupply flights and air support flights to Hue and Khe Sanh areas, February 1968 (four aircraft lost)

COMMANDING OFFICER
Nguyen Van Giao	1959

POLITICAL OFFICER
Nguyen Dam	1959

929th Light Bomber Battalion
Twelve IL-28 twin-engine light jet bombers.

Date formed: mid-1965

PRINCIPAL ENGAGEMENT
Two-aircraft bombing attack against Lao government position in Xieng Khoang Province, Laos, October 9, 1972

E. Regional Commands
MILITARY REGION I (FORMERLY VIET BAC MILITARY REGION)
Area of responsibility: Viet Bac, northeastern North Vietnam

COMMANDING OFFICERS
Chu Van Tan	1954
Le Quang Ba	1957
Dam Quang Trung	1961

POLITICAL COMMISSAR
Chu Van Tan	1957–1975

Military Region II (formerly Northwest [Tay Bac] Military Region)
Area of responsibility: Tay Bac, northwestern North Vietnam

COMMANDING OFFICERS
Bang Giang	1957
Lieutenant General Vu Lap	1978

Military Region III (1963–1967, 1976–present)
Area of responsibility: Red River Delta, North Vietnam, formed 1963 by merging the Left Bank and Right Bank Military Regions; disbanded 1967 and reestablished 1976

COMMANDING OFFICERS
Major General Hoang Sam	1963
General Dang Kinh	1976

POLITICAL COMMISSARS
Tran Do	1963
Nguyen Quyet	1976

Left Bank Military Region (1957–1963, 1967–1976)
Area of responsibility: Northern half of Red River Delta, North Vietnam

COMMANDING OFFICERS
Hoang Sam	1957
Nguyen Nhu Thiet	1967

POLITICAL OFFICERS

Nguyen Quyet	1957
Dang Kinh	1967

Right Bank Military Region (1957–1963, 1967–1976)
Area of responsibility: Southern half of Red River Delta, North Vietnam

COMMANDING OFFICERS

Vuong Thua Vu	1957
Hoang Sam	1967

POLITICAL OFFICERS

Tran Do	1957
To Ky	1967

Military Region IV
Area of responsibility: Panhandle, North Vietnam

COMMANDING OFFICERS

General Nguyen Don	1967
Major General Tran Van Quang	1965
Lieutenant General Dam Quang Trung	1967–1975
Lieutenant General Le Quang Hoa	ca. December 1975

Military Region V
Area of responsibility: Quang Tri, Thua Thien, Quang Nam, Quang Tin, Quang Ngai, Binh Dinh, Pleiku, Phu Bon, and Phu Yen provinces, South Vietnam

COMMANDING OFFICERS

Major General Nguyen Don	1957
Lieutenant General Hoang Van Thai	August 1966
Lieutenant General Chu Huy Man	1967
Lieutenant General Doan Khue	ca. 1977

Military Region VI
Area of responsibility: Quang Duc, Tuyen Duc, Ninh Thuan, Binh Thuan, Lam Dong, and Binh Tuy provinces, South Vietnam

COMMANDING OFFICERS

Colonel Yblok Eban	July 1961
Colonel Nguyen Minh Chau	June 1963
Sr. Colonel Nguyen Trong Xuyen	mid-1969

Military Region VII
Area of responsibility: Phuoc Long, Long Khanh, Phuoc Tuy, Binh Long, Binh Duong, Bien Hoa, Tay Ninh, and Hau Nghia provinces, South Vietnam

COMMANDING OFFICERS

Nguyen Binh	December 1945

Huynh Van Nghe	1948
Tran Van Tra	1950
Nguyen Huu Xuyen	1961
Colonel Le Van Ngoc	ca. 1975
Colonel General Tran Van Tra	1976–1978

Military Region VIII
Area of responsibility: Long An, Kien Tuong, Kien Phong, Dinh Tuong, Go Cong, and Kien Hoa provinces, South Vietnam

COMMANDING OFFICERS

Tran Van Tra	August 1946
Le Quoc San	1961
Dong Van Cong	October 1972

Military Region IX
Area of responsibility: Chau Doc, An Giang, Vinh Long, Phong Dinh, Vinh Binh, Ba Xuyen, Kien Giang, Bac Lieu, Chuong Thien, and An Xuyen provinces, South Vietnam

COMMANDING OFFICERS

Vu Duc	November 1945
Huynh Phan No	November 1946
Truong Van Giau	1948
Phan Trong Tue	1949
Nguyen Chanh	1950
Duong Quoc Chinh	1952
Dong Van Cong	1963
Le Duc Anh	1969
Phan Ngoc Hung	November 1973

Saigon–Gia Dinh Special Zone
Merged with Military Region VII in October 1967.

Area of responsibility: Rung Sat Special Zone, Long Tao River, Tan Son Nhut Air Base, Long Binh

F. Main-Force Combat Units
I Military Corps (Quyet Thang Corps)
Date formed: October 24, 1973

SUBORDINATE UNITS
308th Infantry Division
312th Infantry Division
320-B Infantry Division
367th Antiaircraft Artillery Division
45th Artillery Brigade
202nd Tank Brigade
299th Engineer Brigade
140th Signal Regiment

PRINCIPAL ENGAGEMENT
Saigon, spring of 1975

COMMANDING OFFICERS
| Major General Le Trong Tan | October 1973 |
| Major General Nguyen Hoa | mid-1974 |

POLITICAL OFFICERS
| Major General Le Quang Hoa | October 1973 |
| Major General Hoang Minh Thi | mid-1974 |

II Military Corps
Date formed: May 17, 1974

SUBORDINATE UNITS
304th Infantry Division
324th Infantry Division
325th Infantry Division
673rd Antiaircraft Artillery Division
203rd Tank Brigade
164th Artillery Brigade
219th Engineer Brigade
463rd Signal Regiment

PRINCIPAL ENGAGEMENTS
Hue, spring of 1975
Da Nang, spring of 1975
Phan Rang, spring of 1975

COMMANDING OFFICERS
| Lieutenant General Hoang Van Thai | 1974 |
| Major General Nguyen Huu An | 1975 |

POLITICAL OFFICER
| Major General Le Linh | 1974 |

III Military Corps (Tay Nguyen Corps)
Date formed: March 26, 1975

SUBORDINATE UNITS
10th Infantry Division
320th Infantry Division
316th Infantry Division
40th Artillery Regiment
675th Artillery Regiment
234th Antiaircraft Regiment
593rd Antiaircraft Artillery Regiment
273rd Tank Regiment
7th Engineer Regiment
29th Signal Regiment

PRINCIPAL ENGAGEMENT
Saigon, spring of 1975

COMMANDING OFFICERS
| Vu Lang | March 1975 |
| Kim Tuan (Nguyen Cong Tien) | 1977 |

POLITICAL OFFICERS
Dang Vu Hiep	March 1975
Phi Trieu Ham	1977
Pham Sinh	ca. 1978

IV Military Corps (Cuu Long Corps)
Date formed: July 20, 1974

SUBORDINATE UNITS
5th Division (VC)
7th Infantry Division
9th Division (VC)
341st Infantry Division
24th Mobile Artillery Regiment
71st Antiaircraft Artillery Regiment
25th Engineer Regiment
429th Sapper Regiment
69th Signals Regiment

PRINCIPAL ENGAGEMENTS
Route 14, spring of 1975
Saigon, spring of 1975

COMMANDING OFFICER
| Major General Hoang Cam | July 1974 |

POLITICAL OFFICER
| Major General Hoang The Thien | March 1975 |

LXX Military Corps
Date formed: October 1970

SUBORDINATE UNITS
304th Infantry Division
308th Infantry Division
320th Infantry Division

PRINCIPAL ENGAGEMENTS
Route 9
Laos

232nd Group
Date formed: February 1975

SUBORDINATE UNITS
3rd Infantry Division
5th Infantry Division
9th Infantry Division (attached from IV Corps)

PRINCIPAL ENGAGEMENT
Saigon, spring of 1975

COMMANDING OFFICERS
Major General Nguyen Minh Chau   February 1975
General Le Duc Anh   April 1975

POLITICAL OFFICERS
Major General Tran Van Phac   February 1975
General Le Van Tuong   March 1975

301st Group
Date formed: March 18, 1971 (reorganized as IV Corps on July 20, 1974)

SUBORDINATE UNITS
5th Division
7th Division
9th Division
28th Artillery Regiment

PRINCIPAL ENGAGEMENT
Cambodia, 1971

COMMANDING OFFICER
Tram Van Tra   March 1971

POLITICAL OFFICER
Tran Do   March 1971

559th Transportation Group
Date formed: May 19, 1959

SUBORDINATE UNITS
377th Air Defense Division
470th Sector Division
471st Sector Division
472nd Sector Division
473rd Engineering Division
571st Transportation Division
968th Infantry Division

PRINCIPAL ENGAGEMENT
Ho Chi Minh Trail

COMMANDING OFFICERS
Sr. Colonel Vo Bam   May 1959

Major General Phan Trong Tue   1965
Sr. Colonel Dong Sy Nguyen   1967

POLITICAL OFFICERS
Sr. Colonel Dang Tinh   1970–1973 (killed by mine explosion)

Major General Hoang The Thien   1973

1st Infantry Division
Date formed: December 20, 1965

SUBORDINATE UNITS (1967)
24th Infantry Regiment
32nd Infantry Regiment
33rd Infantry Regiment
66th Infantry Regiment
88th Infantry Regiment
95-B Infantry Regiment

SUBORDINATE UNITS (1973)
52nd Infantry Regiment
101-D Infantry Regiment
44th Sapper Regiment
Strength: December 1967, 9,525; December 1972, 3,400

PRINCIPAL ENGAGEMENTS
Central Highlands
Cambodia, 1970–1971
Easter Offensive, 1972

COMMANDING OFFICERS
Colonel Nguyen Huu An   1966
Colonel Tran Van Tran   1968

2nd Infantry Division
Date formed: October 20, 1965

SUBORDINATE UNITS (1967)
1st Infantry Regiment (VC)
31st Infantry Regiment
21st Infantry Regiment

SUBORDINATE UNITS (1973)
1st Infantry Regiment
52nd Infantry Regiment (VC)
141st Infantry Regiment
368th Artillery Regiment
Strength: December 1967, 6,450; December 1972, 4,000

PRINCIPAL ENGAGEMENTS
Operation TEXAS
Tet Offensive

Laos
Easter Offensive, 1972, Kontum
Da Nang, spring of 1975
Cambodia, 1979

COMMANDING OFFICERS

Nguyen Nang	October 1965
Le Huu Tru	ca. July 1967
Giap Van Cuong	December 1967
Hoang Anh Tuan (alias Hoang Xuan Anh)	Early 1968
Le Kich	August 1969
Dao Ngoc Tu	1970
Nguyen Chon	late 1971
Duong Ba Loi	June 1972
Nguyen Viet Son	September 1972
Pham Duu	ca. 1973–1974
Nguyen Chon	1974

POLITICAL OFFICERS

Nguyen Minh Duc	October 1965
Nguyen Ngoc Son	December 1967
Nguyen Huy Chuong	October 1969
Le Dinh Yen	ca. February 1972
Mai Thuan	ca. February 1975

3rd Infantry Division
Date formed: September 2, 1965

SUBORDINATE UNITS (1967)
2nd Regiment (VC)
12th Infantry Regiment (also known as the 18th Infantry Regiment)
22nd Infantry Regiment

SUBORDINATE UNITS (1973)
2nd Infantry Regiment
12th Infantry Regiment
21st Infantry Regiment
Strength: December 1967, 2,870; December 1972, 3,500

PRINCIPAL ENGAGEMENTS
Operation MASHER/WHITE WING
Tet Offensive
Easter Offensive, 1972, Binh Dinh
Route 19, northern Binh Dinh, 1972
Qui Nhon, spring of 1975
Vung Tau, spring of 1975

COMMANDING OFFICERS

Sr. Colonel Giap Van Cuong	September 1965
Lu Giang	ca. April 1968
Huynh Huu Anh	July 1970

Tran Trong Son	ca. May 1974
Do Quang Huong	ca. February 1975
Tran Van Khue	ca. March 1975

POLITICAL OFFICERS

Dang Hoa	September 1965
Nguyen Nam Khanh	ca. April 1968
Mai Tan	June 1971

5th Division (VC)
Date formed: November 23, 1965

SUBORDINATE UNITS (1967)
274th Infantry Regiment (VC)
275th Infantry Regiment (VC)

SUBORDINATE UNITS (1973)
174th Infantry Regiment
205th Infantry Regiment
275th Infantry Regiment (VC)
Strength: December 1967, 3,300; December 1972, 3,900

PRINCIPAL ENGAGEMENTS
Vung Tau
Cambodia, 1971
Easter Offensive, 1972, Loc Ninh
Saigon, spring of 1975

COMMANDING OFFICERS

Nguyen Hoa	November 1965
Nguyen The Truyen	April 1966
Tran Minh Tam	1967
Vo Minh Nhu	1968
Nguyen Huy Bien	1969
Bui Thanh Van	1971

POLITICAL OFFICERS

Le Xuan Luu	November 1965
Nguyen Van Cuc	ca. 1972
Nguyen Xuan Hoa	1974

6th Infantry Division
Date formed: ca. 1972

SUBORDINATE UNITS (1973)
4th Infantry Regiment
33rd Regiment
Strength: December 1972, 2,300

PRINCIPAL ENGAGEMENTS
Xuan Loc, spring of 1975
Bien Hoa, spring of 1975

COMMANDING OFFICER

Dang Ngoc Si   ca. August 1974

7th Infantry Division
Date formed: June 13, 1966

SUBORDINATE UNITS (1967)
141st Infantry Regiment
165th Infantry Regiment
52nd Infantry Regiment

SUBORDINATE UNITS (1973)
141st Infantry Regiment
165th Infantry Regiment
209th Infantry Regiment
Strength: December 1967, 5,250; December 1972, 4,100

PRINCIPAL ENGAGEMENTS
JUNCTION CITY, Tay Ninh
Tet Offensive, Tay Ninh
Cambodia, 1970
Easter Offensive, 1972, Binh Long Province
Phuoc Long
Xuan Loc, spring of 1975
Saigon, spring of 1975
Cambodia, 1979–1983

COMMANDING OFFICERS
Nguyen Hoa   June 1966
Nguyen The Bon   1967
Dam Van Nguy   ca. 1970
Le Nam Phong   September 1973

POLITICAL OFFICERS
Duong Thanh   June 1966
Vuong The Hiep   1967
Le Thanh   ca. 1970
Tu Vinh   July 1974
Phan Liem   March 1975

8th Infantry Division
Date formed: August 1974

SUBORDINATE UNITS
24th Infantry Regiment
88th Infantry Regiment
320th Infantry Regiment (also known as the 32nd Infantry
    Regiment)

PRINCIPAL ENGAGEMENTS
My Tho, spring of 1975
Saigon, spring of 1975

COMMANDING OFFICER

Sr. Colonel Huynh Cong Than   August 1974
    (also known as Huynh Van Nhiem)

9th Division (VC)
Date formed: September 2, 1965

SUBORDINATE UNITS (1967)
16th Infantry Regiment (VC) (also known as the 101st Infantry
    Regiment and the 70th Infantry Regiment)
271st Infantry Regiment (VC)
272nd Infantry Regiment (VC)
273rd Infantry Regiment (VC)

SUBORDINATE UNITS (1973)
3rd Infantry Regiment (also known as the 95-C Infantry
    Regiment)
271st Infantry Regiment (VC)
272nd Infantry Regiment (VC)
Strength: December 1967, 10,260; December 1972, 4,100

PRINCIPAL ENGAGEMENTS
Binh Gia
Bau Bang
Operation ATTLEBORO
Operation CEDAR FALLS
Tet Offensive, Saigon
Cambodia, 1970
Easter Offensive, 1972, Route 13
Phuoc Long, spring of 1975
Saigon, spring of 1975
Cambodia, 1978

COMMANDING OFFICERS
Sr. Colonel Hoang Cam   September 1965
Ta Minh Kham   1967
Le Van Nho   1969
Nguyen Thoi Bung   ca. 1969
Vo Van Dan   ca. 1972

POLITICAL OFFICERS
Sr. Colonel Le Van Tuong   September 1965
Nguyen Van Tong   1967
Nguyen Van Quang   ca 1969
Pham Xuan Tung   ca 1972
Tam Tung   ca. July 1974

10th Infantry Division
Date formed: September 20, 1972

SUBORDINATE UNITS (SEPTEMBER 1972)
28th Infantry Regiment

66th Infantry Regiment
95-B Infantry Regiment
Strength: December 1972, 3,800

SUBORDINATE UNITS (MARCH 1975)
24B Infantry Regiment
28th Infantry Regiment
66th Infantry Regiment

PRINCIPAL ENGAGEMENTS
Ban Me Thuot, spring of 1975
Saigon, spring of 1975
Cambodia, 1978

COMMANDING OFFICERS

Nguyen Manh Quan	September 1972
Do Duc Gia	May 1973
Ho De	mid-1974
Hong Son	April 1975
Sr. Colonel Phung Ba Thuong	September 1976

POLITICAL OFFICERS

Sr. Colonel Dang Vu Hiep	September 1972
La Ngoc Chau	May 1973
Luu Quy Ngu	1975

31st Infantry Division
Date formed (Front 31): March 1973
Date formed as 31st Division: July 11, 1974

SUBORDINATE UNITS
335th Infantry Regiment
866th Infantry Regiment

COMMANDING OFFICERS

Vu Lap (Front 31)	March 1973
Sr. Colonel Nguyen Le Hoan	July 1974

POLITICAL OFFICERS

Le Linh (Front 31)	March 1973
Sr. Colonel Le Nguyen Vu	July 1974

303rd Infantry Division
Date formed: August 19, 1974

SUBORDINATE UNITS
201st Infantry Regiment (VC)
205th Infantry Regiment (VC)
271st Infantry Regiment (VC)
262nd Artillery Regiment

PRINCIPAL ENGAGEMENTS
Phuoc Long, January 1975
Tay Ninh, spring of 1975
Saigon, spring of 1975
Cambodia, 1978
Chinese Border, 1979

COMMANDING OFFICERS

Do Quang Huong	August 1974
Sr. Colonel Tran Hai Phung	1977
Colonel Cao Hoai Sai	September 1977

304th Infantry Division
Date formed: January 4, 1950

SUBORDINATE UNITS (1973)
9th Infantry Regiment
24th Infantry Regiment
66th Infantry Regiment
Strength: December 1972, 5,000

PRINCIPAL ENGAGEMENTS
Day River
Dien Bien Phu
Hoa Binh
The Hill Fights, Khe Sanh, 1967
Khe Sanh, 1968
Operation LAM SON 719
Easter Offensive, 1972, Quang Tri
Da Nang, spring of 1975
Saigon, spring of 1975
Cambodia, 1978

COMMANDING OFFICERS

Hoang Minh Thao	February 1950
Hoang Sam	November 1953
Nam Long	late 1955
Ngo Ngoc Duong	ca. 1960s
Mai Hien	March 1965
Hoang Kien	August 1965
Thai Dung	1967
Hoang Dan	June 1968
Le Cong Phe	ca. 1973
Nguyen An	ca. 1974

POLITICAL OFFICERS

Tran Van Quang	February 1950
Le Chuong	1951
Truong Cong Can	late 1955
Tran Huy	ca. 1960s
Truong Cong Can	August 1965

Tran Nguyen Do	January 1968
Hoang The Thien	June 1968

308th Infantry Division
Date formed: August 1949

SUBORDINATE UNITS (1973)
36th Infantry Regiment
88th Infantry Regiment
102nd Infantry Regiment
268th Artillery Regiment (also known as the 58th Artillery
    Regiment)

PRINCIPAL ENGAGEMENTS
Vinh Yen
Day River
Hoa Binh
Tu Vu
Xom Pheo
Black River
Operation LORRAINE
Laos, 1953
Dien Bien Phu
Khe Sanh
Operation LAM SON 719
Easter Offensive, 1972, Quang Tri

COMMANDING OFFICERS

Vuong Thua Vu	August 1949
Vu Yen	1955
Pham Hong Son	1958
Vu Yen	1959
Nguyen Thai Dung	June 1963
Vu Yen	June 1967
Nguyen Huu An	March 1969
Truong Dinh Mau	July 1971
Dao Dinh Sung	April 15, 1972
Nguyen Huu An	July 17, 1972
Nguyen The Bon	Early 1973
Mac Dinh Vinh	October 1973
Pham Duy Tan	1979

POLITICAL OFFICERS

Song Hao	August 1949
Le Vinh Quoc	1955
Dang Quoc Bao	1958
Le Linh	1959
Nguyen Kien	1963
Hoang Phuong	March 1969
Nguyen Hung Phong	May 1970
Hong Kim	October 1973

312th Infantry Division
Date formed: October 27, 1950

SUBORDINATE UNITS (1973)
141st Infantry Regiment
165th Infantry Regiment
209th Infantry Regiment
Strength: December 1972, 6,000

PRINCIPAL ENGAGEMENTS
Vinh Yen
Hoa Binh
Black River
Laos, 1953
Dien Bien Phu
Tet Offensive
Laos, 1969
Laos, 1971–1972
Easter Offensive, 1972, demilitarized zone (DMZ)
Saigon, spring of 1975

COMMANDING OFFICERS

Le Trong Tan	October 1950
Dam Quang Trung	1954
Sr. Colonel Hoang Cam	1956
Nguyen Nang	mid-1960s
La Thai Hoa	October 1971
Nguyen Chuong	early 1975

POLITICAL OFFICERS

Tran Do	ca. 1953
Le Chieu	mid-1969
Pham Sinh	October 1971
Nguyen Xuyen	early 1975

316th Infantry Division
Date formed: May 1, 1951

SUBORDINATE UNITS (1973)
148th Infantry Regiment
149th Infantry Regiment
174th Infantry Regiment
187th Artillery Regiment

PRINCIPAL ENGAGEMENTS
Mao Khe
Black River
Operation LORRAINE
Laos, 1953
Dien Bien Phu
Laos, 1962
Laos, 1964–1965

Laos, 1967–1973
Ban Me Thuot, spring of 1975
Chinese Border, 1979

COMMANDING OFFICERS

Le Quang Ba	1953
Chu Phuong Doi	1958
Sr. Colonel Le Thuy	1964
Le Hoan	ca. 1969
Sr. Colonel Dam Van Nguy	1973

POLITICAL OFFICERS

Chu Huy Man	May 1951
Le Tu Dong	late 1954
Nguyen Kien	1955
Le Vu	ca. 1969–1970
Colonel Ha Quoc Toan	1973

320th Infantry Division
Date formed: January 16, 1951

SUBORDINATE UNITS (1973)
48th Infantry Regiment
64th Infantry Regiment
Strength: December 1972, 3,000

PRINCIPAL ENGAGEMENTS
Day River
Dong Ha-Cam Lo, DMZ, 1968
Operation LAM SON 719
Easter Offensive, 1972, Kontum
Ban Me Thuot, spring of 1975
Phu Bon, spring of 1975
Saigon, spring of 1975

COMMANDING OFFICERS

Van Tien Dung	January 1951
Sung Lam	ca. 1967
Nguyen Cong Tien (Kim Tuan)	1971
Bui Dinh Hoe	March 1975

POLITICAL OFFICERS

Sr. Colonel Luong Tuan Khang	ca. 1965
Phi Trieu Man	ca. 1971
Colonel Bui Huy Bong	March 1975

320-B Infantry Division
Date formed: September 1965 (redesignated the 390th Infantry
    Division on May 4, 1979)

SUBORDINATE UNITS (1973)
27th Infantry Regiment
48-B Infantry Regiment
64-B Infantry Regiment
Strength: December 1972, 3,500

PRINCIPAL ENGAGEMENTS
Easter Offensive, 1972, DMZ
Chinese Border, 1979

COMMANDING OFFICERS

Pham Than Son	September 1965
Bui Sinh	early 1966
Ha Vi Tung	mid-1969
Sr. Colonel Luu Ba Xao	ca. 1973

POLITICAL OFFICERS

Nguyen Duy Tuong	September 1965
Nguyen Huan	early 1966
Tran Ngoc Kien	mid-1969

324-B Infantry Division
Date formed: ca. 1965

SUBORDINATE UNITS (1967)
803rd Infantry Regiment
812th Infantry Regiment
90th Infantry Regiment

SUBORDINATE UNITS (1973)
29th Infantry Regiment
803rd Infantry Regiment
812th Infantry Regiment
Strength: December 1967, 7,800; December 1972, 5,000

PRINCIPAL ENGAGEMENTS
Con Thien, 1967
Hue, 1968
Hamburger Hill (Operation APACHE SNOW), 1969
Operation LAM SON 719
Easter Offensive, 1972, Hue
Hue, spring of 1975

COMMANDING OFFICER

Duy Son	ca. 1975

POLITICAL OFFICER

Nguyen Trong Dan	ca. 1975

325th Infantry Division
Date formed: March 11, 1951 (redesignated the 325-A Infantry
    Division in late 1964)

SUBORDINATE UNITS (1964)
18th Infantry Regiment
95th Infantry Regiment
101st Infantry Regiment

PRINCIPAL ENGAGEMENT
Laos, 1961

COMMANDING OFFICERS
Tran Quy Hai   ca. 1953
Major General Nguyen Huu An   1964

POLITICAL OFFICERS
Chu Van Bien   ca. 1951
Hoang Van Thai   1955
Quach Si Kha   1961
Nguyen Minh Duc   1964

325-B Infantry Division
Date formed: November 1964

SUBORDINATE UNITS (1965)
18-B Infantry Regiment
95-B Infantry Regiment
101-B Infantry Regiment (also known as the 33rd Infantry
   Regiment)

PRINCIPAL ENGAGEMENT
A Shau Valley

COMMANDING OFFICER
Vuong Tuan Kiet   ca. 1964

POLITICAL OFFICER
Quoc Tuan   ca. 1964

325-C Infantry Division
Date formed: 1965

SUBORDINATE UNITS (1967)
18-C Infantry Regiment
95-C Infantry Regiment
101-D Infantry Regiment
Strength: 1967, 7,790

PRINCIPAL ENGAGEMENTS
Khe Sanh
Hue

COMMANDING OFFICER
Chu Phuong Doi   ca. 1965

POLITICAL OFFICER
Nguyen Cong Trang   ca. 1965

325-D Infantry Division
Date formed: 1966 (redesignated the 325th Infantry Division in
   1972)

SUBORDINATE UNITS (1972)
18-D Infantry Regiment
95-D Infantry Regiment
101-E Infantry Regiment
Strength: December 1972, 5,000

PRINCIPAL ENGAGEMENTS
Easter Offensive, 1972, DMZ
Hue, spring of 1975
Da Nang, spring of 1975
Saigon, spring of 1975
Cambodia, 1978

COMMANDING OFFICERS
Thang Binh   1968
Le Kich   ca. 1971
Colonel Pham Minh Tam   May 1974

POLITICAL OFFICERS
Vu Duc Thai   1968
Sr. Colonel Nguyen Cong Trang   ca. 1971
Colonel Le Van Duong   May 1974

341st Infantry Division
Date formed: February 1962 (disbanded ca. 1963; reconstituted
   March 1965; disbanded late 1966; reconstituted November
   1972)

SUBORDINATE UNITS (1973)
266th Infantry Regiment
270th Infantry Regiment
273rd Infantry Regiment

PRINCIPAL ENGAGEMENTS
Xuan Loc, spring of 1975
Saigon, spring of 1975
Cambodia, 1978

COMMANDING OFFICERS
Bao Cuong   December 1972
Tran Van Tran   November 1973

POLITICAL OFFICER

Tran Nguyen Do   November 1973

351st Heavy Division
Date formed: 1953

SUBORDINATE UNITS (1954)
45th Artillery Regiment (Viet Minh)
675th Artillery Regiment (Viet Minh)
367th Antiaircraft Artillery Regiment (Viet Minh)
237th Heavy Weapons Regiment (Viet Minh)
151st Engineer Regiment (Viet Minh)

PRINCIPAL ENGAGEMENT
Dien Bien Phu

COMMANDING OFFICER

Vu Hien   1953

711th Infantry Division
Date formed: June 1972; disbanded June 1973

SUBORDINATE UNITS (1973)
31st Infantry Regiment
38th Infantry Regiment
Strength: December 1972, 3,500

PRINCIPAL ENGAGEMENT
Easter Offensive, 1972

COMMANDING OFFICER

Nguyen Chon   June 1972

968th Infantry Division
Date formed: July 1970

SUBORDINATE UNITS (JANUARY 1970)
9th Infantry Regiment
19th Infantry Regiment
29th Infantry Regiment

PRINCIPAL ENGAGEMENTS
Operation LAM SON 719, 1971
Central Highlands, spring of 1975

COMMANDING OFFICER
Hoang Bien Son

POLITICAL COMMISSAR
Nguyen Ngoc Son

202nd Tank Brigade (formerly 202nd Tank Regiment)
Date formed (regiment): October 5, 1959
Date formed (brigade): October 25, 1973

SUBORDINATE UNITS (1970)
177th Tank Battalion
195th Tank Battalion
397th Tank Battalion

PRINCIPAL ENGAGEMENTS
Laos, Plain of Jars, 1969–1970
Operation LAM SON 719 (one battalion)
Easter Offensive, 1972, Quang Tri
Saigon, spring of 1975

COMMANDING OFFICERS
Dao Huy Vu   October 1959
Le Xuan Kien   June 1965
Nguyen Van Lang   November 1971
Do Phuong Ngu   1972

POLITICAL OFFICERS
Dang Quang Long   October 1959
Vo Ngoc Hai   June 1965
Hoang Khoai   1972
Le Quang Phuoc   December 1973

G. Vietnamese Advisory Groups/Military Commands in Laos
Military Advisory Group 100
Date formed: August 1954; disbanded January 1958

COMMANDING OFFICER
Chu Huy Man   August 1954

Military Specialist Group 959
Later called Command Headquarters 959, the advisory group supporting the Pathet Lao Headquarters and General Staff.

Date formed: September 1959

COMMANDING OFFICERS
Le Chuong   September 1959
Nguyen Trong Vinh   May 1964
Huynh Dac Huong   mid-1972

Military Specialist Group 463
Later called Command Headquarters 463, the advisory group supporting the Pathet Lao in the Plain of Jars–Xieng Khoang Military Region.

Date formed: April 15, 1963; disbanded June 1973

Commanding Officer
Lt. Colonel Nguyen Binh Son   April 1963

Political Officers
Major Le Van   April 1963
Vu Ngan   1971

Military Specialist Group 565
Later called Command Headquarters 565, the advisory group supporting the Pathet Lao in southern Laos.

Date formed: May 19, 1965; disbanded October 1974

Commanding Officer
Sr. Colonel Dong Sy Nguyen   May 1965
Hoang Tuan Khanh   November 1965

Political Officer
Tran Quyet Thang   1969

V. French Forces in Indochina

The French military returned to Indochina immediately following the end of World War II. By the late 1940s, all French Union forces in Indochina came under the control of the French high commissioner, who exercised command through the military commander in chief. In practice, however, French political and military leaders in Paris intervened in local decisions to the point of almost constant interference. That situation improved only slightly between December 1950 and April 1952 when General Jean de Lattre de Tassigny held both offices. French military headquarters was located in Hanoi.

A post–World War II amendment to France's Budget Law restricted the use of conscripted French nationals to the defense of homeland territory, which included France, Algeria, and French-occupied Germany. Thus, all French regular units sent to Vietnam consisted of volunteers. This of course restricted the size of the ethnic French element of the French Expeditionary Force.

French Foreign Legion units in Vietnam consisted largely, but not exclusively, of non-French Europeans. They were organized and equipped the same as regular French units and had French officers.

The North African colonial units were similarly organized, equipped, and led. Because Algeria was considered part of metropolitan France, the Algerian units were allowed to have Algerian officers. Many of the colonial units in Vietnam recruited locally and included varying proportions of Vietnamese in their ranks. The French also raised colonial units in Vietnam, Cambodia, and Laos.

The French Expeditionary Force was supposedly backed by the French-controlled Vietnamese National Army of 100,000 troops. That force, however, never came close to living up to expectations. In 1947 the French had some 115,000 troops in all of Indochina.

In May 1953 the French Expeditionary Force numbered 189,000 troops.

At any given time, as many as 100,000 troops of the French Expeditionary Force were in static defenses and garrisons. Remaining forces available for offensive operations were often organized into Mobile Groups (*groupes mobiles,* or GM). The GMs were the main French striking units in Indochina. They were ad hoc regimental combat teams, usually consisting of three infantry battalions, an artillery battalion, and armor support. GMs often worked in conjunction with parachute battalions.

Some GMs were fairly stable, tending to have the same battalions from operation to operation. Others swapped out battalions on a frequent basis. Typically, GMs numbered some 6,000 men. Variations on the GM concept included several amphibious groups, at least one airborne group, and armored subgroups that operated in conjunction with the GMs.

Much of the fighting in Tonkin between 1951 and 1953 was carried out by GMs 1 through 4. Although ethnic French units were heavily represented in the GMs, some were made up of colonial or Vietnamese units. GM 1 consisted of crack North African and Senegalese battalions, while most of GM 3's soldiers were tough Muong mountain troops. GM 9 fought at Dien Bien Phu, while GM Nord was part of the Operation CASTOR relief column. GM 100, which was decimated by fighting in southern Vietnam, was formed around the two battalions of the Korea Regiment, French troops who had fought under the United Nations Command (UNC) in Korea.

No comprehensive OB sources exist in English for the French forces in Indochina between 1945 and 1954. The following list was compiled from official French military records. Because the GMs were not regularly constituted units, they do not appear on this list. The one exception to this is GM 1, which also bore the designation Groupe Mobile Nord-Africain. That unit is carried on the French list as a regularly constituted infantry unit between August 25, 1949, and August 11, 1954.

A note of explanation: Units designated *marche,* perhaps best translated as "mobile," in the French Army have no equivalent in the U.S. Army. These units were often assembled for a specific purpose, but as with an American task force, they tended to become permanent. Also, French artillery groups, commanded by a lieutenant colonel and containing three or more separate batteries, were the equivalent of a U.S. artillery battalion.

A. French High Commissioners in Indochina

Admiral Georges d'Argenlieu   August 31, 1945
Émile Bollaert   October 1947
Léon Pignon   October 5, 1948
General Jean de Lattre de Tassigny   December 16, 1950
Maurice Dejean   July 3, 1952
General Paul Ély   June 9, 1954
Ambassador Henri Hoppenot   July 27, 1955

B. French Commanders in Chief in Indochina

General Philippe Leclerc	June 1945
General Jean-Étienne Valluy	October 1, 1946
General Raoul Salan	February 10, 1948
Lieutenant General Roger Blaizot	June 10, 1948
General Marcel Carpentier	April 1, 1949
General Jean de Lattre de Tassigny	December 16, 1950
General Raoul Salan	April 1, 1952
General Henri Navarre	May 29, 1953
General Paul Ély	June 9, 1954
General Pierre Elie Jacquot	June 1, 1955

C. Supreme French Headquarters in Indochina

Headquarters, French Expeditionary Corps, Far East
Date formed in Indochina: September 16, 1945
Date reorganized in Indochina: January 1, 1946

Headquarters, Supreme Command of French Troops, Far East
Date formed in Indochina: January 1, 1946
Date reorganized in Indochina: June 11, 1948

Headquarters, Supreme Command of Ground Forces, Far East
Date formed in Indochina: June 12, 1948
Date reorganized in Indochina: September 9, 1949

Headquarters, Commander in Chief of Military Forces, Far East
Date formed in Indochina: September 10, 1949
Date reorganized in Indochina: December 31, 1950

Headquarters, Joint and Ground Forces, Far East
Date formed in Indochina: January 1, 1951
Date inactivated in Indochina: August 11, 1954

D. Major Subordinate French Headquarters

French Forces of Northern Vietnam, China, and Indochina
Date formed in Indochina: End of 1945
Date reorganized in Indochina: November 1, 1946

French Troops in Indochina, North
Date formed in Indochina: November 2, 1946
Date inactivated in Indochina: August 11, 1954

French Troops in Indochina, South
Date formed in Indochina: September 13, 1946
Date reorganized in Indochina: March 9, 1949

Franco-Vietnamese Forces, South
Date formed in Indochina: March 10, 1949
Date reorganized in Indochina: May 5, 1951

Land Forces, South Vietnam
Date formed in Indochina: May 6, 1951
Date inactivated in Indochina: August 11, 1954

French Troops, Central Annam
Date formed in Indochina: August 1, 1947
Date reorganized in Indochina: October 9, 1949

Land Forces, Central Vietnam
Date formed in Indochina: October 10, 1949
Date inactivated in Indochina: August 11, 1954

Land Forces, Montagnard Plateau
Date formed in Indochina: March 15, 1951
Date reorganized in Indochina: December 31, 1952

Southern Montagnard Plateau
Date formed in Indochina: January 1, 1953
Date inactivated in Indochina: August 11, 1954

French Land Forces in Laos and Laotian Land Forces
Date formed in Indochina: End of 1945
Date inactivated in Indochina: August 11, 1954

Military Command, Cambodia
Date formed in Indochina: January 1, 1946
Date reorganized in Indochina: January 19, 1949

Forces Command, Cambodia
Date formed in Indochina: January 20, 1949
Date reorganized in Indochina: March 31, 1951

Land Forces, Cambodia
Date formed in Indochina: April 1, 1951
Date inactivated in Indochina: October 31, 1953

E. Divisions

2nd Armored Division (Elements)
Date arrived in Vietnam: October 14, 1945
Date departed Vietnam: October 7, 1946

3rd Colonial Infantry Division
Date arrived in Vietnam: October 1945
Date departed Vietnam: September 12, 1946

9th Colonial Infantry Division
Date arrived in Vietnam: end of 1945
Date departed Vietnam: November 1, 1956

1st Tonkin Marche Division
Date formed in Vietnam: start of 1951

Date inactivated in Vietnam: August 11, 1954
Zone of responsibility: Tonkin, West

2nd Tonkin Marche Division
Date formed in Vietnam: start of 1951
Date inactivated in Vietnam: August 11, 1954
Zone of responsibility: Tonkin, North

3rd Tonkin Marche Division
Date formed in Vietnam: November 1, 1951
Date inactivated in Vietnam: August 11, 1954
Zone of responsibility: Tonkin, South

4th Tonkin Marche Division
Date formed in Vietnam: June 1, 1954
Date Inactivated in Vietnam: August 11, 1954
Zone of responsibility: Hai Phong

F. Foreign Legion Units
REGIMENTS
1st Foreign Cavalry Regiment
2nd Foreign Infantry Regiment
3rd Foreign Infantry Regiment
5th Foreign Infantry Regiment
13th Foreign Legion Demi-Brigade

SEPARATE BATTALIONS
1st Foreign Parachute Battalion
2nd Foreign Parachute Battalion
Marche Battalion, 1st Foreign Infantry Regiment
5th Battalion, 4th Foreign Infantry Regiment
3rd Battalion, 6th Foreign Infantry Regiment

G. Airborne Units
There were two Free French Special Air Service (SAS) units organized in World War II, trained and operating under the control
of the British SAS. After the war they kept that designation in the
French Army and went to Indochina.

REGIMENTS
Colonial Parachute Commando Demi-Brigade (SAS).
1st Parachute Demi-Brigade (SAS)
1st Parachute Chasseurs Regiment
2nd Colonial Parachute Commando Demi-Brigade

SEPARATE BATTALIONS
1st Colonial Parachute Battalion
2nd Colonial Parachute Battalion
3rd Colonial Parachute Battalion
4th Colonial Parachute Battalion
5th Colonial Parachute Battalion
6th Colonial Parachute Battalion

7th Colonial Parachute Battalion
8th Colonial Parachute Battalion
9th Colonial Parachute Battalion
10th Dismounted Chasseurs Parachute Battalion
Marche Battalion, 35th Airborne Artillery Regiment

H. Infantry Units
REGIMENTS
Korea Regiment
Mobile Group 1
6th Colonial Infantry Regiment
11th Colonial Infantry Regiment
21st Colonial Infantry Regiment
22nd Colonial Infantry Regiment
23rd Colonial Infantry Regiment
43rd Colonial Infantry Regiment
1st Algerian Rifle Regiment
2nd Algerian Rifle Regiment
3rd Algerian Rifle Regiment
7th Algerian Rifle Regiment
22nd Algerian Rifle Regiment
Moroccan Colonial Infantry Regiment
1st Moroccan Rifle Regiment
2nd Moroccan Rifle Regiment
3rd Moroccan Rifle Regiment
4th Moroccan Rifle Regiment
5th Moroccan Rifle Regiment
6th Moroccan Rifle Regiment
24th Senegalese Rifle Marche Regiment
4th Tunisian Rifle Regiment
1st Tonkin Rifle Regiment
Cambodian Composite Regiment

SEPARATE BATTALIONS
Marche Battalion, 35th Infantry Regiment
Marche Battalion, 43rd Infantry Regiment
1st Marche Battalion, 49th Infantry Regiment
Marche Battalion, 110th Infantry Regiment
Marche Battalion, 151st Infantry Regiment
1st Marche Battalion, 1st Colonial Infantry Regiment
1st Marche Battalion, 2nd Colonial Infantry Regiment
Marche Battalion, 5th Colonial Infantry Regiment
Marche Battalion, 16th Colonial Infantry Regiment
Marche Battalion, 19th Colonial Infantry Regiment
1st African Light Infantry Battalion
1st Marche Battalion, 201st North African Pioneer Infantry
    Regiment
1st Marche Battalion, 6th Algerian Rifle Regiment
21st Algerian Rifle Battalion
22nd Algerian Rifle Battalion
23rd Algerian Rifle Battalion
25th Algerian Rifle Battalion

27th Algerian Rifle Battalion
205th Algerian Rifle Battalion
217th Algerian Rifle Battalion
4th Battalion, Chad Marche Regiment
Marche Battalion, 7th Moroccan Rifle Regiment
1st Marche Battalion, 8th Moroccan Rifle Regiment
1st Moroccan Far East Battalion
2nd Moroccan Far East Battalion
3rd Moroccan Far East Battalion
5th Moroccan Far East Battalion
8th Moroccan Far East Battalion
9th Moroccan Far East Battalion
10th Moroccan Far East Battalion
11th Moroccan Far East Battalion
17th Moroccan Far East Battalion
207th Moroccan Far East Rifle Marche Battalion
214th Moroccan Far East Rifle Battalion
Marche Battalion, 13th Senegalese Rifle Regiment
26th Senegalese Rifle Marche Battalion
27th Senegalese Rifle Marche Battalion
28th Senegalese Rifle Marche Battalion
29th Senegalese Rifle Marche Battalion
30th Senegalese Rifle Marche Battalion
31st Senegalese Rifle Marche Battalion
32nd Senegalese Rifle Marche Battalion
104th Senegalese Battalion
1st French East African Marche Battalion
2nd French East African Marche Battalion
3rd French East African Marche Battalion
Marche Battalion, 4th Tonkin Rifle Regiment
Annam Battalion
Saigon–Cholon Garrison Battalion
1st Far Eastern Marche Battalion
2nd Far Eastern Marche Battalion
3rd Far Eastern Marche Battalion
4th Far Eastern Marche Battalion
5th Far Eastern Marche Battalion
6th Far Eastern Marche Battalion
7th Far Eastern Marche Battalion
1st Indochina Marche Battalion
2nd Indochina Marche Battalion
3rd Indochina Marche Battalion
1st Muong Battalion
2nd Muong Battalion
1st Thai Battalion
2nd Thai Battalion
3rd Thai Battalion
1st Laotian Chasseurs Battalion
2nd Laotian Chasseurs Battalion
3rd Laotian Chasseurs Battalion
4th Laotian Chasseurs Battalion

5th Laotian Chasseurs Battalion
6th Laotian Chasseurs Battalion
7th Laotian Chasseurs Battalion
8th Laotian Chasseurs Battalion
Phnom Penh Garrison Battalion

I. Armor and Cavalry Units
REGIMENTS
1st Armored Cavalry Regiment
4th Dragoon Regiment
5th Armored Cavalry Regiment
9th Dragoon Marche Regiment
8th Algerian Spahis Regiment
2nd Moroccan Spahis Regiment
5th Moroccan Spahis Regiment
6th Moroccan Spahis Regiment
Far East Spahis Marche Regiment
Far East Colonial Armored Regiment

SEPARATE SQUADRONS AND BATTALIONS
4th Dragoon Battalion
7th Squadron, 1st Moroccan Spahis Marche Regiment
1st Far East Independent Reconnaissance Squadron
2nd Far East Independent Reconnaissance Squadron
3rd Far East Independent Reconnaissance Squadron
4th Far East Independent Reconnaissance Squadron
5th Far East Independent Reconnaissance Squadron

J. Artillery Units
REGIMENTS
2nd Artillery Regiment
4th Colonial Artillery Regiment
10th Colonial Artillery Regiment
41st Colonial Artillery Regiment
69th African Artillery Regiment
Moroccan Colonial Artillery Regiment

SEPARATE BATTALIONS
Marche Battalion, 64th Artillery Regiment
Marche Battalion, 66th Artillery Regiment
1st Battalion, Far East Colonial Antiaircraft Regiment
21st Aerial Artillery Observation Battalion
22nd Aerial Artillery Observation Battalion
23rd Aerial Artillery Observation Battalion
24th Aerial Artillery Observation Battalion
261st Antiaircraft Battalion
French East African Colonial Artillery Battalion
Levant Colonial Mountain Artillery Battalion
1st Central Annam Artillery Battalion
2nd Central Annam Artillery Battalion

K. Engineer Units

BATTALIONS

22nd Engineer Battalion

26th Engineer Sanitation Battalion

31st Engineer Marche Battalion

61st Engineer Battalion

62nd Engineer Battalion

71st Engineer Battalion

72nd Engineer Battalion

73rd Engineer Battalion

75th Engineer Battalion

61st Colonial Engineer Battalion

71st Colonial Engineer Battalion

72nd Colonial Engineer Battalion

73rd Colonial Engineer Battalion

DAVID T. ZABECKI AND MERLE L. PRIBBENOW II

References

Berger, Carl, ed. *The United States Air Force in Southeast Asia, 1961–1973: An Illustrated Account.* Washington, DC: Office of Air Force History, 1977.

Collins, James Lawton, Jr. *The Development and Training of the South Vietnamese Army, 1950–1972.* Washington, DC: Department of the Army, 1975.

Davidson, Phillip A. *Vietnam at War: The History, 1946–1975.* Novato, CA: Presidio, 1988.

Fall, Bernard B. *Street without Joy: The French Debacle in Indochina.* Rev. ed. Mechanicsburg, PA: Stackpole Books, 1994.

Lanning, Michael Lee, and Dan Cragg. *Inside the VC and the NVA: The Real Story of Vietnam's Armed Forces.* New York: Fawcett Columbine, 1992.

Larsen, Stanley Robert, and James Lawton Collins Jr. *Allied Participation in Vietnam.* Vietnam Studies Series. Washington, DC: Department of the Army, U.S. Government Printing Office, 1975.

Pike, Douglas. *PAVN: People's Army of Vietnam.* Novato, CA: Presidio, 1986.

Pribbenow, Merle L., and William J. Duiker. *Victory in Vietnam: The Official History of the People's Army of Vietnam.* Lawrence: University Press of Kansas, 2002.

Stanton, Shelby L. *Vietnam Order of Battle.* Mechanicsburg, PA: Stackpole Books, 2003.

Chronology

2879 BCE

Establishment of the Kingdom of Van Lang by Hung Vuong (King Hung) of the Hong Bang dynasty (2879–258 BCE), considered by Vietnamese as the founder of Vietnam.

258 BCE

King Thuc Phan of neighboring Tay Au invades Van Lang and annexes it to his own territory. A new kingdom, Au Lac, is established with himself as ruler.

207 BCE

The Chinese warlord Trieu Da (Chao To), who has broken with the Qin (Ch'in) emperor, defeats King An Duong Vuong and conquers Au Lac. Trieu Da combines it with previously held territory to form the new kingdom of Nam Viet (Nan Yueh), or the "southern country of the Viet," with its capital at Phien Ngung (later Canton; present-day Guangzhou).

111 BCE

A Han expeditionary force conquers Nam Viet and adds it to the Chinese empire. For the next 1,000 years present-day northern Vietnam, except for a few brief but glorious rebellions, is a Chinese province.

39–42 CE

Vietnamese, led by Trung Trac, daughter of the Lac lord of Me-Linh Chan, assisted by her sister Trung Nhi, revolt against the Chinese. The two women are revered in Vietnamese history as the Hai Ba Trung (the Two Trung Ladies, or the Trung Sisters).

42

Battle of Lang Bac. Chinese General Ma Yuan (Ma Vien), commanding an invading army, defeats Trung Trac's forces and reestablishes direct Chinese rule over northern Vietnam.

192

The Indianized Kingdom of Champa is established in the vicinity of the present-day city of Hue.

248

Unsuccessful Vietnamese revolt led by Ba Trieu, Lady Trieu.

542

Revolt by Vietnamese nationalist Ly Bon, defeated in the Battle of Dien-Triet Lake (546).

931

Duong Dinh Nghe, ruler of Ai and Hoan (present-day Ha Trung and Thanh Hoa), drives Chinese forces from Giao Chi and wins recognition from them as military governor there.

938

Ngo Quyen defeats the Chinese in the Battle of the Bach Dang River. After more than 1,000 years of Chinese control, the Vietnamese are again independent. Vietnamese now control all of the territory from the foothills of Yunnan to the 17th Parallel.

939

Ngo Quyen takes the title of king of the now independent Nam Viet.

966

Bo Linh declares himself emperor of northern Vietnam, naming his realm Dai Co Viet.

982

Le Hoan (Le Dai Hanh) defeats a Sung invasion, preserving national independence. He also launches a victorious southern expedition against the Kingdom of Champa.

1069

Ly Thanh Tong seizes the Cham capital of Indrapura and imprisons its king, who wins release by ceding the districts of Dia Ly, Ma Ling, and Bo Chinh. These subsequently become the Vietnamese provinces of Quang Binh and Quang Tri.

April 1288

Second Battle of Bach Dang River. The Vietnamese, led by Tran Hung Dao, defeat invading Monguls.

Early 14th Century

Two more Cham districts, the O and the Ri, are given to Dai Viet in exchange for Vietnamese princess Huyen Tran's hand in marriage. In the 15th century Chams cede all territory north of the present-day province of Quang Nam. These 14th- and 15th-century additions become the future Thua Thien Province, with its imperial capital at Hue.

1407–1427

The Ming dynasty of China briefly reestablishes Chinese control over Vietnam.

1418

Le Loi (Le Thai To), proclaiming himself King Binh Dinh Vuong, begins an insurrection against the occupying Ming, defeating them in 1427. Le Loi establishes the Le dynasty that lasts until 1788, when it is ended by the Tay Son Rebellion.

1471

The Vietnamese take the second Cham capital of Vijaya. This provides a permanent Vietnamese foothold south of Hai Van Pass. In the 17th century the remnants of the old Kingdom of Champa are definitively absorbed.

1481

The Vietnamese government creates the Don Dien agricultural settlements as a means of absorbing lands to the south.

1527

Mac Dang Dung, governor of Thang Long (present-day Ha Noi), overthrows the Le dynasty and by 1527 is king in all but name, prompting the southern feudal lord Nguyen Kim to set up a government-in-exile in Laos to support a Le descendant.

1535

The first lasting contact between Vietnam and Europe, resulting from the arrival of Portuguese explorer and sea captain Antônio da Faria, occurs.

1545

Supporters of Mac Dang Dung murder Nguyen Kim, and Vietnam dissolves into a long civil war that lasts for the next two centuries.

1615

The first permanent Catholic mission is established in Vietnam at Tourane (present-day Da Nang).

1626

French priest Alexandre De Rhodes arrives in Vietnam. He is generally credited with the creation of *quoc ngu*, the written Vietnamese language that uses the Latin alphabet and diacritical marks.

1630s

The Nguyen rulers in southern Vietnam build a wooden wall across a narrow waist of Vietnam at Dong Hoi, ironically not far from the 1954 division of the 17th Parallel. Reportedly the wall is 20 feet high and 6 miles long. For the next 150 years Vietnam is divided along that fortified line. The Trinh lords ruled northern Vietnam and the Nguyen family ruled southern Vietnam. Each family claims to rule in the name of the powerless Le king.

1636

The Dutch establish a trading post at Hanoi.

1658

By this date the Vietnamese have taken all of southern Vietnam north of Saigon (then the fishing village of Prey Kor).

Vietnamese troops invade Cambodia to settle a succession struggle. Two years later Cambodia begins paying regular tribute to Vietnam.

1672

Saigon falls to Vietnamese control.

1680

The French establish their first regular trading post in Vietnam at Pho Hien.

1714–1716

Civil war occurs in Cambodia, and Vietnam intervenes.

1739–1749

War occurs between Cambodia and Vietnam in which Cambodians are defeated and lose to Vietnam additional territory in the Mekong River region.

1755–1760

Vietnamese expansion into Cambodia continues.

1769–1773

War occurs between Vietnam and Siam over Cambodia, with Siam regaining control.

1773

The Tay Son Rebellion begins, named for Nguyen Nhac, Nguyen Lu, and Nguyen Hue, three brothers from the village of Tay Son in present-day Binh Dinh Province.

January 1785

19   Battle of Rach Gam-Xoai Mut, in which Nguyen Hue defeats an invading Siamese army.

January 1789

25–30   Victory of Ngoc Hoi–Dong Da, the greatest military achievement in modern Vietnamese history. In a lightning five-day campaign King Quang Trung (Nguyen Hue) defeats a Chinese expeditionary force commanded by Qin dynasty viceroy Sun Shiyi (Sun Shi-yi), assisted by General Xu Shiheng and supporting Le King Chieu Thong as king of Annam.

1789–1802

Reign of Quang Trung.

1802

Nguyen Anh, heir to the Nguyen warlord family ousted by the Tay Son Rebellion, having captured all three Tay Son capitals with the aid of French missionary Pigneau

de Behaine and French mercenaries, reunites Vietnam from the Linh Giang River to Gia Dinh. That same year Nguyen Anh crowns himself emperor with the name of Gia Long, establishing the Nguyen dynasty. He rules during 1802–1820.

1803

The official name of Vietnam is established when Gia Long envoys travel to Beijing (Peking) to establish diplomatic relations with China.

1820–1841

Reign of Emperor Minh Mang.

1841–1845

Vietnamese-Siamese wars over Cambodia occur and end with joint rule over Cambodia by the two invaders.

1841–1847

Reign of Emperor Thieu Tri.

April 1847

15   At Tourane (Da Nang), French warships sink three Vietnamese ships.

1848–1883

Reign of Emperor Tu Duc.

1856

The French warship *Catinat* shells Tourane (Da Nang).

August 1858

31   Admiral Rigault de Genouilly's squadron of 14 vessels with 3,000 troops arrives at Tourane (Da Nang). The troops, including 300 Filipinos sent by Spain, land the next day, storming Tourane's forts after only perfunctory Vietnamese resistance, taking them and the port, and inaugurating the first phase of the French conquest of Indochina.

February 1859

17   The French shift their operations to the south and on this date take the fishing village of Saigon, selected because of its strategic location, its promise as a deep-water port, and the fact that it could be important in controlling the southern rice trade.

March 1860–January 1861

The siege of Saigon, garrisoned by 1,000 French troops against a force of 12,000 Vietnamese, occurs but is raised by the arrival of a French relief expedition.

1862

Emperor Tu Duc is forced to sign a treaty with France providing for an indemnity of 20 million francs, three treaty ports in Annam and Tonkin, and French possession of the eastern provinces of Cochin China, including Saigon.

1866–1867

French Navy lieutenant François Garnier leads an expedition up the Mekong River. The expedition determines that the river is not navigable past the waterfalls at the Lao-Cambodian border.

1867

French forces have conquered all of Cochin China and also occupied three western provinces of Cambodia.

1870s

The French turn their attention to northern Vietnam, where Emperor Tu Duc's hold is weak.

November 1873

Former French Navy lieutenant François Garnier and a force of some 180 men in three small ships seize the citadel at Hanoi. Garnier is killed the next month while endeavoring to take all of Tonkin, and Paris repudiates his actions. Even so, Emperor Tu Duc suffers an irreparable loss of prestige.

March 1874

Emperor Tu Duc recognizes French control of Cochin China and grants concessions in Hanoi and Haiphong.

1882–1885

The Black Flag Wars, also known as the Tonkin Wars, between France and Vietnam/China occur.

December 1884–March 3, 1885

The Chinese siege of Tuyen Quang occurs but is raised by the French.

1885–1913

Vietnamese nationalists, acting in the name of Emperor Ham Nghi against French rule, stage a brief rebellion. Betrayed to the French, Ham Nghi is captured in 1888 and sent into exile in Algeria. Led by Vietnamese nationalist De Tham, resistance to the French in Tonkin continues.

June 1885

9   Treaty of Tientsin between China and France resulting from French military operations against China. As a

consequence of this treaty, China relinquishes nominal suzerainty over Vietnam.

1887

Paris forms its conquests into French Indochina.

1893

Laos is added to French Indochina. Technically only Cochin China is an outright colony; Annam, Tonkin, Cambodia, and Laos are merely "protectorates." The French leave the emperor as a symbol of Vietnamese unity at Hue, although the French governor-general is in overall control, responsible to the minister of colonies in Paris.

1896

Colonel Joseph Galliéni leads an effort against Vietnamese guerrilla leader De Tham, with only partial success. By 1905 De Tham has expanded his activities and established the Nghia Hung party. During the next eight years his forces inflict serious losses on the French.

1904–1905

Russo-Japanese War. For the first time in modern history, an Asian power defeats a European state. During this war the Russian fleet, after sailing from the Baltic and Black seas around the Horn of Africa and across the Indian Ocean, anchors in Cam Ranh Bay along the Vietnamese coast to take on fuel and provisions on its way to the decisive naval battle against Japan in the Tsushima Strait.

March 1913

Vietnamese nationalist leader De Tham is assassinated by an associate, a Vietnamese working for the French. Although De Tham's followers try to continue the struggle, the nationalist movement soon collapses.

1914–1918

World War I. U.S. president Woodrow Wilson raises Vietnamese nationalist hopes by calling for the self-determination of peoples.

1920

Ho Chi Minh, foremost exponent of modern Vietnamese nationalism and member of the French Socialist Party, votes with the majority at the party conference at Tours to form the French Communist Party, becoming its expert on colonial affairs.

1923

Ho Chi Minh travels to the Soviet Union, where he becomes a member of the Comintern and writes for *Pravda* and other Communist publications.

Late 1924

Ho Chi Minh is sent to Kwangzhou, China, as a member of a Soviet advisory group working with the Chinese government. In China, Ho founds the Vietnamese Revolutionary Youth Association (Thanh Nien Cach Mang Dong Chi Hoi, or Thanh Nien for short), the forerunner of the Vietnamese Communist Party.

December 1927

25   Nguyen Thai Hoc and comrades establish the Viet Nam Quoc Dan Dang (VNQDD, Vietnamese Nationalist Party) as the first well-organized nationalist revolutionary party in Vietnam.

1928

Fleeing China, Ho Chi Minh travels to Thailand, where he spends almost one year building a Communist revolutionary organization among the ethnic Vietnamese community living in northeastern Thailand. This Vietnamese organization in Thailand would provide an important source of financial support, personnel, and weapons to the Vietnamese Communists during the Indochina War (1946–1954).

February 1930

3   In Hong Kong, Ho Chi Minh helps carry out a fusion of three Vietnamese Communist parties into what becomes the Indochinese Communist Party (ICP), by World War II the dominant nationalist force in Indochina.

1930–1931

Vietnamese nationalist uprisings occur, most notably at Yen Bai. Easily crushed by the French, these are led by moderate nationalists who take as their model the Chinese Nationalists. Their organization, the Viet Nam Quoc Dan Dang (VNQDD, Vietnam Nationalist Party), seeks an end to French rule and the establishment of a republican form of government.

April 1930

30   Communist cadres lead hundreds of peasants in protests in many districts of Nghe An Province. Sporadic smaller-scale protests continue to the end of the year. Some 100 peasants are killed, but the events are not widely known and do not have the impact of the Yen Bai revolt.

September 1940

24   Under the threat of force, French governor-general of Indochina Admiral Jean Decoux grants the Japanese government the right to build three airfields and to station 6,000 troops in Tonkin.

November 1940–January 1941

War occurs between France and Thailand, ending in a Japanese-brokered peace treaty whereby France transfers to Thailand three Cambodian and two Laotian provinces on the right bank of the Mekong River, in all some 42,000 square miles of territory. These are regained by France after World War II.

November 1940

The ICP stages a revolt in southern Vietnam that is crushed by the French military.

Late 1940

Ho Chi Minh returns to Vietnam for the first time in more than 20 years and establishes a revolutionary base area at Pac Bo in a remote mountain region along the Chinese border.

May 1941

Ho Chi Minh and his lieutenants form the Viet Nam Doc Lap Dong Minh Hoi (League for Independence of Vietnam), commonly known as the Viet Minh.

July 1941

Japan moves into southern Indochina, placing its long-range bombers within striking distance of Malaya, the Dutch East Indies, and the Philippines. Alarmed by this development and endeavoring to force Japan to withdraw, the United States, Great Britain, and the Netherlands impose an embargo on scrap iron and oil against Japan. As a result of this decision, Tokyo opts for war against the United States.

March 1945

9   The Japanese stage a coup d'état against the French government authorities and military and take power directly in Vietnam.

11   Tokyo grants Vietnam its independence, proclaimed by Bao Dai, who for the previous decade was the French-controlled emperor of Annam and had spent the war years at Hue.

June 1945

Provisional president of the French Republic Charles de Gaulle appoints General Jacques Philippe de Hauteclocque Leclerc to command the French Expeditionary Corps to restore French sovereignty in Indochina.

July 1945

16   The U.S. Office of Strategic Services (OSS) Deer Team, consisting of seven American military intelligence personnel, parachutes into Ho Chi Minh's Pac Bo base

area in northern Vietnam to advise and train Communist military forces led by Ho's military commander, Vo Nguyen Giap.

July–August 1945

The Potsdam Conference in Germany produces an agreement regarding the disarmament of Japanese forces in Indochina. Chinese Guomindang (GMD, Nationalist) forces will take surrender of Japanese troops north of the 16th Parallel, and British troops will do so south of that line.

August 1945

15   Provisional president of the French Republic Charles de Gaulle appoints monk-turned-admiral Georges Thierry d'Argenlieu as high commissioner for Indochina with instructions to restore French sovereignty in Indochina.

16   In Hanoi, veteran Vietnamese Communist leader Ho Chi Minh declares himself president of the provisional government of a "free Vietnam."

19   The Viet Minh seize power in Hanoi.

24   In Saigon, Viet Minh leader Tran Van Giau declares the insurrection under way in southern Vietnam.

25   Emperor Bao Dai abdicates, becoming First Citizen Vinh Thuy.

27   Ho Chi Minh convenes his first cabinet meeting at Hanoi.

September 1945

2   Ho Chi Minh publicly announces the formation of the Provisional Government of the Democratic Republic of Vietnam (DRV, North Vietnam), with its capital at Hanoi.

5   French general Jacques Leclerc arrives in Saigon.

13   In accordance with the Potsdam Agreements, 5,000 troops of the 20th Indian Division, commanded by General Douglas Gracey, arrive in southern Indochina. Gracey, who detests the Viet Minh, subsequently rearms some 1,400 French soldiers imprisoned by the Japanese.

14   Nationalist Chinese troops enter North Vietnam to disarm Japanese troops north of the 16th Parallel.

16–22   The North Vietnamese government organizes Tuan Le Vang (Gold Week), appealing to the people to turn in gold and other valuables so that the government might purchase arms from the Chinese. Much of the money goes to bribe Chinese commander Lu Han to secure his support and end aid to the nationalist parties.

22   French troops return to Vietnam.

26   OSS lieutenant colonel A. Peter Dewey is killed in Saigon by the Viet Minh.

October 1945

25   French general Jacques Leclerc begins the reconquest of Indochina for France, predicting that it will take about a month for "mopping-up operations."

November 1945

11   In a bid to widen his base at home and win Western support abroad, North Vietnamese leader Ho Chi Minh overtly dissolves the ICP.

January 1946

6   Elections occur in North Vietnam. Although the elections were not entirely free, there is no doubt that Ho Chi Minh and his supporters have won. The government is Communist-dominated but includes anti-Communist nationalists because Ho still hopes for recognition and aid from the United States.

February 1946

28   The Franco-Chinese Accords secure Chinese withdrawal from North Vietnam in return for France yielding certain concessions in China. Chinese forces leave North Vietnam the next month.

March 1946

6   North Vietnamese leader Ho Chi Minh signs an agreement with French representative Jean Sainteny to set future relationship between North Vietnam and France. North Vietnam agrees to a French military presence in North Vietnam: 15,000 French and 10,000 Vietnamese troops under unified French command to protect French lives and property, although Paris promises to withdraw 3,000 of them each year. All are to be withdrawn by the end of 1951, with the possible exception of those guarding bases. In return, France recognizes North Vietnam as a "free state with its own government, parliament, army and finances, forming part of the Indochinese Federation of the French Union." In a key provision, France also agrees to a referendum in southern Vietnam to see if it desires to join North Vietnam in a unified state, although no date for the vote is specified. Paris also agrees to train and equip units of the new Vietnamese Army.

27   French commander in Indochina General Jacques Leclerc declares, in a report to Paris kept secret from the French people, that there will be no solution through force in Indochina.

April 1946

3   North Vietnamese representative Vo Nguyen Giap and French general Raoul Salan reach agreement on the stationing of French troops in North Vietnam.

June 1946

1   Shortly after the departure of North Vietnamese leader Ho Chi Minh for France to meet with French government officials, French high commissioner for Indochina Georges Thierry d'Argenlieu torpedoes French diplomat Jean Sainteny's work by proclaiming in Saigon the establishment of the "Republic of Cochin China." This in effect nullifies justification for the planned referendum in South Vietnam to see if its people wish to join North Vietnam.

July 6–September 10, 1946

The Fontainebleau Conference between a North Vietnamese delegation headed by Ho Chi Minh and French government officials fails to resolve the issue of Cochin China. The sum of its work is a draft accord reinforcing France's economic rights in North Vietnam.

August 1946

North Vietnam establishes a representative office in Bangkok, Thailand, the first North Vietnamese diplomatic office abroad. This office becomes important for the purchase of weapons and ammunition to be shipped clandestinely to Vietnam.

November 1946

20   An armed clash occurs between French troops, escorting a commission to Lang Son to investigate French dead at the hands of the Japanese, and Vietnamese forces. The French lose six men, and each side accuses the other of responsibility. This is overshadowed by another more ominous event the same day. The French Navy has virtually blockaded Tonkin's principal port of Haiphong, and a French patrol vessel seizes a Chinese junk attempting to smuggle contraband. Vietnamese soldiers on the shore fire on the French vessel, and shooting also breaks out in the city itself. A subsequent agreement between French and Vietnamese officials brings fighting to an end by the afternoon of November 22, however.

22   French high commissioner to Indochina George Thierry d'Argenlieu, then in Paris, seeks to use the violence in Haiphong to teach the Vietnamese a lesson. Obtaining the approval of French premier Georges Bidault, d'Argenlieu cables General Jean-Étienne Valluy, his deputy in Saigon, who in turn orders General Louis Constant Morlière, commander in North Vietnam, to use force against the Vietnamese. Morlière points out in vain that the situation in Haiphong has stabilized and that any imprudent act might lead to general hostilities.

23   French general Jean-Étienne Valluy in Saigon telegraphs Colonel Pierre-Louis Debès, commander of French troops at Haiphong, ordering him to "give a severe lesson to those who have treacherously attacked you. Use all the means at your disposal to make yourself complete master of Haiphong and so bring the Vietnamese army around to a better understanding of the situation." Debès duly delivers an ultimatum to Vietnamese officials at Haiphong, ordering them to withdraw from the French section of the city, the Chinese quarter, and the port. He gives them only two hours to reply. The French then subject Vietnamese military positions to air, land, and sea bombardment, the bulk of the firepower from the French Navy cruiser *Suffren*. Casualty figures of from 200 to 20,000 are cited. Fighting in the port city continues into November 28.

December 1946

19   French general Louis Constant Morlière demands the disarmament of the Tu Ve, the Viet Minh militia that has been sniping at French troops in Hanoi. That night fear and mistrust, fueled by bloodshed and broken promises, finally erupt into full-scale fighting. The Indochina War has begun.

February 1947

15   After almost two months of fighting, Ho Chi Minh orders those Viet Minh military forces still fighting inside Hanoi to withdraw from the city. Ho moves his government and military headquarters into the mountain jungles of the Viet Bac region, north of Hanoi.

May 1947

11   France proclaims Laos an independent state within the French Union.

12   Paul Mus, personal adviser to French high commissioner Émile Bolleart, meets with North Vietnamese leader Ho Chi Minh to present a plan drawn up by General Jean-Étienne Valluy and approved by Socialist premier Paul Ramadier calling on the Viet Minh to refrain from hostilities, lay down some arms, permit French troops freedom of movement, and return prisoners, deserters, and hostages. Ho rejects this as tantamount to surrender.

October 1947

7   The French begin Operation Léa. Directed by General Raoul Salan, Léa involves some 12,000 men during a three-week period over some 80,000 square miles of nearly impenetrable terrain in the northeast Viet Bac region.

November 1947

20   The French launch Operation CEINTURE (BELT), designed to crush enemy forces in a quadrangle northwest of Hanoi

and capture the North Vietnamese leadership, who escape.

January 1948

15–16   The ICP Central Committee decides to shift the fighting from the defensive to a contention stage.

February 1948

The newly independent nation of Burma (present-day Myanmar) recognizes the North Vietnamese government, which establishes diplomatic office in Rangoon, the Burmese capital. Burma covertly provides 500 weapons and ammunition to Viet Minh forces in Laos, the first foreign military assistance to be received by Ho Chi Minh's Viet Minh forces.

April 1948

The French induce Emperor Bao Dai to return to Vietnam.

June 1948

5   High Commissioner Émile Bollaert and General Nguyen Van Xuan sign the Baie d'Along Agreement, which names Bao Dai chief of state and recognizes the independence of Vietnam within the French Union. Vietnamese from all sides condemn the Bao Dai government as a French puppet.

March 1949

8   Paris concludes the Élysée Agreements with former emperor Bao Dai. These create the State of Vietnam, with Paris conceding that Vietnam is in fact one country.

June–October 1949

The Thap Van Dai Son (Ten Thousand Mountains) Campaign takes place. The Viet Minh army sends four battalions across the Chinese border to help Chinese Communist forces defeat Chinese nationalist forces in Yunan, Kwangsi, and Kwanzhou provinces.

July 1949

1   The State of Vietnam is formally established by Bao Dai decrees.

August 1949

28   The Viet Minh 308th Division, the first division formed by the armed forces of North Vietnam, is created.

October 1949

The Communists defeat the GMD and come to power in China.

November 1949

4   North Vietnamese leader Ho Chi Minh decrees mobilization for all adult males between 16 and 55.

January 1950

14   North Vietnamese leader Ho Chi Minh declares the government of North Vietnam as the only legal government of Vietnam.

18   The Peoples' Republic of China (PRC) formally recognizes the North Vietnamese government and agrees to furnish it with military assistance.

30   The Soviet Union extends formal diplomatic recognition to North Vietnam.

January–February 1950

North Vietnamese chairman Ho Chi Minh visits Beijing and Moscow, where he secures promises of military and economic assistance from China and the Soviet Union.

February 1950

7   Great Britain and the United States extend full diplomatic recognition to the State of Vietnam.

21   North Vietnamese leader Ho Chi Minh declares a general mobilization in North Vietnam.

27   The U.S. National Security Council (NSC) signs NSC-64, a memorandum recommending "that all practicable measures be taken" to block further Communist expansion in Southeast Asia.

March 1950

6   A U.S. mission arrives in Saigon to study economic assistance to the State of Vietnam.

May 1950

8   The United States announces plans to extend economic and military aid to the French in Indochina.

30   A U.S. economic mission is established in Saigon.

June 1950

25   The Korean People's Army (KPA, North Korean Army) attacks south across the 38th Parallel in Korea.

27   U.S. president Harry S. Truman authorizes U.S. air and naval operations against North Korean forces south of the 38th Parallel. He also announces the deployment of the U.S. Seventh Fleet in the Taiwan Strait. That same day, the United Nations (UN) Security Council passes a resolution calling upon members to provide assistance to the Republic of Korea (ROK, South Korea) in resisting aggression. Truman also announces the "acceleration in the furnishing of military assistance to the forces of France and the associated states in Indochina and

dispatch of a military mission to provide close working relations with those forces."

30   Eight C-47 transports arrive in Saigon with the first direct shipment of U.S. military equipment to the French fighting in Indochina.

July 1950

26   U.S. president Harry S. Truman signs legislation providing $15 million in aid to the French war effort in Indochina.

August 1950

3   The U.S. Military Assistance and Advisory Group–Indochina (MAAG-I) is established in Saigon. The mission of the 35-man group is to screen French requests for American military aid, assist in the training of South Vietnamese troops, and advise on strategy.

Summer 1950

The Viet Minh 308th Division and two independent regiments cross the border into China, where they are given additional combat training and issued more modern equipment.

September 1950

16   After the newly trained and reequipped Viet Minh units return from China, accompanied by Chinese military advisers, Viet Minh forces launch the Border Campaign, designed to destroy all French forces stationed along the Sino-Vietnamese border.

October 1950

7   The French garrison evacuating Cao Bang and a relief column from That Khe are destroyed by the Viet Minh in fighting at Dong Khe.

17   The French evacuate Lang Son.

December 1950

General Jean de Lattre de Tassigny, one of France's most famous generals, is appointed commander in Indochina and also named high commissioner, giving him civilian as well as military authority.

December 1950

23   The United States signs a mutual defense assistance agreement with France, Vietnam, Cambodia, and Laos.

January 1951

The Viet Minh carries out Operation TRAN HUNG DAO, also known as the General Counteroffensive, by large conventional units against main French defensive line in the Red River delta. Viet Minh commander General Vo Nguyen Giap's goal is to take the city of Hanoi.

February 1951

11–19   Meeting of the Second National Communist Party Congress, which changes the party's name to the Lao Dong Party (Vietnam Workers' Party).

March 1951

In Operation HOANG HOA THAM, Viet Minh forces again try to secure the Red River Delta and are again defeated.

May–June 1951

In Operation HA NAM NINH, the third Viet Minh offensive to try to secure the Red River Delta, the attacks, centered in the southeastern part of the delta, are again blunted by the French.

September 1951

Nguyen Binh, the commander of all Viet Minh military forces in Cochin China, is killed in northeastern Cambodia by a French Army patrol. French commander in Indochina General Jean de Lattre de Tassigny travels to Washington seeking more aid from the United States.

7   The United States signs an agreement with the State of Vietnam to provide it with economic assistance.

November–February 1952

The "meat-grinder" Battle of Hoa Binh is initiated by General Jean de Lattre de Tassigny. Casualty totals suggest a French victory, but the battle is actually something of a stalemate.

July 1952

U.S. president Harry S. Truman upgrades the American legation in Saigon to embassy status.

October 1952

Over the course of the next several months beginning in October 1952, Viet Minh forces undertake the conquest of Thai Highlands in northwestern Vietnam in what becomes known as the Northwest Campaign.

October–November 1952

In Operation LORRAINE, General Raoul Salan, who assumes command in Indochina on General Jean de Lattre de Tassigny's departure for France, employs 30,000 troops in the largest French military operation of the war. Salan hopes that by striking Viet Minh general Vo Nguyen Giap's base areas, he can force Giap to return divisions to their defense and thereby abandon the effort to conquer the Thai highlands. The operation is largely unsuccessful, however.

April 1953

Viet Minh and Communist Pathet Lao troops seize much of northern Laos.

U.S. vice president Richard Nixon visits Vietnam and tells the French that "It is impossible to lay down arms until victory is won."

May 1953

20   General Henri Navarre assumes command of French Union forces in Vietnam.

July 1953

Operation HIRONDELLE (SWALLOW), a 2,000-man paratroop operation initiated by new French commander in Indochina General Henri Navarre, is intended to destroy supplies at the important Viet Minh base of Lang Son.

27   An armistice is signed in Korea.

September 1953

30   U.S. president Dwight D. Eisenhower approves $385 million in military aid for the French in Indochina.

October 1953

Paris grants full independence to the Kingdom of Laos.

November 1953

20   In Operation CASTOR, 2,200 French paratroopers drop into the valley north and south of the village of Dien Bien Phu in northwestern Tonkin to defeat the Viet Minh garrison there, create a new airhead, and draw Viet Minh forces into pitched battle.

December 1953

The Viet Minh begin a drive that overruns much of southern and central Laos against only light resistance.

25   French Union forces evacuate Thakhek on the Mekong River.

January 1954

Operation ATLANTE, a 15-battalion mainly Vietnamese National Army (VNA) land assault northward from Nha Trang with amphibious landing near Tuy Hoa, occurs. Giap anticipates this and orders his forces not to give battle but merely to harass attacking units. The VNA performs poorly, with whole units deserting. ATLANTE bogs down and simply peters out.

March 1954

In a series of raids, Viet Minh commandos attack French air bases at Gia Lam near Hanoi and Do Son and Cat Bi airfields near Haiphong, destroying 22 aircraft vital to the French effort at Dien Bien Phu.

13   The siege of the French entrenched positions at Dien Bien Phu officially begins with a heavy Viet Minh bombardment.

April 1954

26   An international conference to discuss a range of Asian issues, including Indochina, opens at Geneva.

29   U.S. president Dwight D. Eisenhower announces that the United States will not intervene militarily in Indochina.

May 1954

6   American pilot James B. McGovern Jr. and copilot Wallace Buford are shot down and killed while flying an aerial resupply mission for the beleaguered French garrison at Dien Bien Phu. The pilots were flying a C-119 Flying Boxcar for the Taiwan-based Civil Air Transport, a Central Intelligence Agency (CIA) front airline that was later renamed Air America. Following the death of OSS lieutenant colonel Peter Dewey in Saigon on September 26, 1945, McGovern and Buford are the second and third Americans to die in the Indochina War.

7   The last French troops surrender at Dien Bien Phu, officially ending the battle.

8   The Indochina phase of the Geneva Conference begins.

June 1954

French Groupe Mobile 100 is destroyed by two Viet Minh regiments along Route 19. French control in the Central Highlands is now limited to a small area around Ban Me Thuot and Dalat.

17   Pierre Mendès-France becomes French premier and foreign minister.

18   From his chateau in Cannes, France, Bao Dai selects Ngo Dinh Diem as the new premier of the State of Vietnam.

20   French premier Pierre Mendès-France imposes a 30-day timetable for an Indochina agreement, promising to resign if one is not reached by the end of the deadline.

26   New State of Vietnam premier Ngo Dinh Diem arrives in Saigon.

July 1954

7   State of Vietnam premier Ngo Dinh Diem officially forms his new government, which claims to embrace all of Vietnam.

21   The Geneva Conference issues three cease-fire agreements and one final declaration. Cambodia, Laos, and

Vietnam are all declared independent. Vietnam is temporarily divided into northern and southern zones pending nationwide elections, to be held in 1956.

August 1954

Hundreds of thousands of refugees, mostly Catholic, begin moving from North Vietnam to southern Vietnam under the terms of the Geneva Accords.

September 1954

8   The Southeast Asia Collective Defense Treaty and Protocol is signed in Manila. Southeast Asia Treaty Organization (SEATO) member states—the United States, France, Britain, New Zealand, Australia, Pakistan, the Philippines, and Thailand—pledge themselves only to "act to meet the common danger" in the event of aggression against any signatory state. A separate protocol extends the treaty's security provisions to Laos, Cambodia, and the "free territory under the jurisdiction of the State of Vietnam."

October 1954

9   French forces complete their evacuation of Hanoi.

24   U.S. president Dwight Eisenhower writes to State of Vietnam premier Ngo Dinh Diem and promises direct assistance to his government, now in control of southern Vietnam.

November 1954

8   Former U.S. Army chief of staff General J. Lawton Collins arrives in Saigon. Appointed by President Dwight D. Eisenhower as special ambassador with authority over all U.S. government agencies in Vietnam, Collins assures Diem of American support in his test of wills with army chief of staff General Nguyen Van Hinh, who at the end of the month goes into exile.

January 1955

1   Washington begins channeling its aid directly to the Ngo Dinh Diem government of the State of Vietnam.

February 1955

12   The U.S. Military Assistance and Advisory Group (MAAG) takes over responsibility for training and organization of the State of Vietnam Army from the French.

March–April 1955

Fighting occurs between State of Vietnam Army units loyal to Diem and the gangster organization in Saigon known as the Binh Xuyen.

May 1955

10   State of Vietnam premier Ngo Dinh Diem formally requests U.S. military advisers.

16   The French Army completes its withdrawal from the Haiphong area under the terms of the Geneva Agreement, leaving all of North Vietnam in Communist hands.

July 1955

19   The North Vietnamese government in Hanoi proposes to the State of Vietnam government in Saigon the naming of representatives for the conference to negotiate general elections as called for in 1954 Geneva Agreement.

20   The State of Vietnam rejects the request by the North Vietnamese government for the opening of negotiations regarding the elections to reunify Vietnam. The State of Vietnam claims that it was not a party to the Geneva Agreement and that the elections in North Vietnam would not be free.

August 1955

9   The government of the State of Vietnam declares that it will not enter into negotiations with the North Vietnamese government on elections as long as a Communist government continues in North Vietnam.

31   U.S. secretary of state John Foster Dulles supports the position of the government of the State of Vietnam regarding its refusal to hold national elections to reunify the two Vietnamese states.

October 1955

23   After Emperor Bao Dai, still in France, tries to remove Ngo Dinh Diem as premier, Diem organizes a referendum, held on this date. Carefully managed by Diem, it results in a 98 percent vote in his favor.

26   Using the referendum results as justification, State of Vietnam premier Ngo Dinh Diem proclaims the Republic of Vietnam (RVN, South Vietnam) with himself as president.

January 1956

11   South Vietnamese president Ngo Dinh Diem's government issues Ordinance No. 6, allowing arrest and detention of anyone "considered dangerous to national defense and common security."

March 1956

4   South Vietnamese go to the polls and elect a 123-member national legislative assembly.

April 1956

6   The South Vietnamese government again declares that it is a "non-signatory to the Geneva Agreements" and "continues not to recognize their provisions."

26   France officially abolishes its high command in Indochina.

May 1956

11   The North Vietnamese government again proposes convening the Consultative Conference on elections called for in the 1954 Geneva Agreement.

22   The South Vietnamese government, in a diplomatic note to the British government, again rejects talks on country-wide elections.

July 1956

20   The deadline set by the 1954 Geneva Conference for free elections. The date passes without elections being held. South Vietnamese president Ngo Dinh Diem claims that lack of freedom in North Vietnam makes it impossible to hold elections.

August 1956

Le Duan, leader of the covert Communist forces remaining in South Vietnam, writes the "Tenets of the Revolution of South Vietnam," a call to arms that advocates the use of "revolutionary violence" to "liberate" South Vietnam.

September 1956

14   The last French troops leave Saigon.

October 1956

26   The new South Vietnamese constitution, heavily weighted toward control by the executive, goes into effect. South Vietnam is divided into 41 provinces and then subdivided into districts and villages. These apparent reforms are largely a sham, as South Vietnamese president Ngo Dinh Diem increasingly subjects South Vietnam to authoritarian rule.

November 1956

Land reform in North Vietnam leads to outright revolt. The People's Army of Vietnam (PAVN, North Vietnamese Army) 325th Division is called out to crush rebels in Nghe An Province. In all, some 6,000 farmers are deported or executed.

Early 1957

Le Duan is recalled from South Vietnam to take over leadership of the Lao Dong Party in Hanoi following the removal of party secretary-general Truong Chinh as a result of the failure of North Vietnam's land reform program.

January 1957

3   The International Control Commission (ICC) established under the 1954 Geneva Accords report accuses both North Vietnam and South Vietnam of failing to fulfill obligations under the 1954 Geneva Accords during the period December 1955–August 1956.

February 1957

9   The PAVN requests that the ICC investigate the detention of 1,700 former Viet Minh by South Vietnamese authorities at Hoi An in Quang Nam Province.

May 1957

5–19   South Vietnamese president Ngo Dinh Diem visits the United States and addresses a joint session of Congress. President Dwight D. Eisenhower calls him the "miracle man" of Asia and reaffirms U.S. support for the Diem regime.

August 1958

10   Some 400 raiders attack the large Michelin rubber plantation north of Saigon, easily defeating its security force and making off with more than 100 weapons and 5 million piasters (some $143,000).

December 1958

22   North Vietnamese premier Pham Van Dong writes to South Vietnamese premier Ngo Dinh Diem and repeats proposals for mutual force reductions, economic exchanges, free movement between zones, and an end to hostile propaganda.

January 1959

The Central Committee of the ruling North Vietnamese Lao Dong Party meets to debate Resolution 15, which authorizes the use of armed insurrection in South Vietnam although maintaining that it should remain secondary to the "political struggle." After prolonged discussion, the resolution is finally approved in a second Central Committee session held in May.

February 1959

6   The ICC concludes that South Vietnamese authorities have subjected to reprisal former Viet Minh in Quang Nam Province.

April 1959

4   U.S. president Dwight D. Eisenhower, speaking at Gettysburg College, commits the United States to maintaining South Vietnam as a separate national entity.

30   In Saigon, 18 prominent opposition politicians, calling themselves the Committee for Progress and Liberty, issue an open letter to South Vietnamese president Ngo Dinh Diem protesting governmental abuses. They are promptly arrested.

May 1959

U.S. military advisers are assigned at the regimental level in the Army of the Republic of Vietnam (ARVN, South Vietnamese Army).

North Vietnam establishes the 559th Transportation Group (named for the fifth month of 1959) to move supplies south through eastern Laos, thus beginning the Ho Chi Minh Trail complex.

At the invitation of South Vietnamese president Ngo Dinh Diem. three training teams of 10 men each from 77th Special Forces Group on Okinawa arrive in South Vietnam and set up training schools at Da Nang, Nha Trang, and Song Mao.

6   The South Vietnamese legislature passes National Assembly Law 10/59, an internal security measure that empowers government to try suspected terrorists by roving tribunals that can impose the death penalty.

July 1959

North Vietnamese authorities organize Group 759 to oversee the movement of supplies to Communist insurgents in South Vietnam by sea.

8   Two U.S. servicemen are killed in a Communist attack on Bien Hoa in South Vietnam, the first Americans to die in the Vietnam War.

September 1959

North Vietnam forms Military Specialist Group 959 to support and advise dissident Communist Pathet Lao forces and, later, to command Vietnamese regular army units fighting in Laos.

26   The 2nd Liberation Battalion ambushes two companies of the ARVN 23rd Division, killing 12 men and capturing most of their weapons. This attack leads the South Vietnamese government and U.S. officials to begin referring to the rebels as Viet Cong (VC), a pejorative for "Vietnamese Communist."

December 1959

31   Some 760 U.S. military personnel are in South Vietnam.

January 1960

16   An uprising occurs in South Vietnam in Ben Tre Province, some 100 miles from Saigon in the Mekong Delta, largely in reaction to repression on the part of the government of President Ngo Dinh Diem.

Late January 1960

Communist forces attack a regiment of the ARVN 21st Infantry Division at Trang Sup, Tay Ninh Province, securing several hundred weapons.

February 1960

5   The South Vietnamese government requests that Washington double its MAAG strength from 342 to 685 men.

April 1960

North Vietnam imposes universal military conscription.

May 1960

Thirty instructors from the U.S. Army 7th Special Forces Group deploy to South Vietnam.

August 1960

9   Laotian Army captain Kong Le mounts a neutralist coup that overthrows the right-wing Royal Lao government, sparking all-out civil war in Laos.

September 1960

At the Lao Dong Third Congress, held in Hanoi, the leadership goes on public record as supporting the establishment of a united front and approving a program of the violent overthrow of the government led by President Ngo Dinh Diem in South Vietnam. There were now two preeminent tasks: carrying out a "socialist revolution" in North Vietnam and "liberating the South."

November 1960

The leadership of North Vietnam calls for intensified struggle in South Vietnam and establishment of a "broad national united front."

11–12   In Saigon, three battalions of ARVN paratroopers and marines under command of Colonel Nguyen Van Thai and Lieutenant Colonel Vuong Van Dong surround the presidential palace in an effort to force President Ngo Dinh Diem to institute reforms, a new government, and more effective prosecution of the war. Diem outmaneuvers them by agreeing to a long list of reforms—including freedom of the press, a coalition government, and new elections—until he can bring up loyal units. Most ARVN officers participating in the coup flee to Cambodia, returning only after Diem is overthrown.

December 1960

20   The North Vietnamese government announces the formation of the National Front for the Liberation of South Vietnam (National Liberation Front [NLF]). Designed to replicate the Viet Minh as an umbrella nationalist organization, the NLF reaches out to all those disaffected by the government of President Ngo Dinh Diem in South Vietnam. From the beginning, the NLF is completely dominated by the Lao Dong Party Central Committee and is North Vietnam's shadow government in South Vietnam.

31   Some 900 U.S. military personnel are in South Vietnam.

January 1961

19   Outgoing U.S. president Dwight D. Eisenhower tells incoming president John F. Kennedy that Laos is "the key to the entire area of Southeast Asia" and that the situation there may require U.S. armed intervention.

March 1961

27   A regimental cadre core group of several hundred officers and noncommissioned officers, carrying full equipment and weapons, arrives in War Zone D, northeast of Saigon, after infiltrating down the Ho Chi Minh Trail from North Vietnam. After arrival, the first full VC regiment, the 761st Regiment (also known as the 271st Regiment), is formed around this core group.

April 1961

North Vietnamese troops capture Tchepone on Route 9 in Laos and immediately begin construction work to turn it into a major hub on the Ho Chi Minh Trail network to ship supplies and reinforcements to Communist forces in South Vietnam.

9   Ngo Dinh Diem is reelected president of South Vietnam with a reported 89 percent of the vote.

May 1961

9–15   U.S. vice president Lyndon Johnson visits Saigon. Although later expressing reservations privately about South Vietnamese president Ngo Dinh Diem, Johnson publicly hails him as the "Winston Churchill of Southeast Asia." Less than a week after Johnson's return to Washington, Kennedy agrees to an increase in ARVN strength from 170,000 to 270,000 men.

15   The U.S. State Department informs America's allies that the United States will increase MAAG personnel beyond the limit imposed by the 1954 Geneva Accords, citing as justification North Vietnamese violations of the agreement.

June 1961

A 14-nation conference convenes in Geneva and over the next year works out a tripartite coalition government for Laos.

June–July 1961

A U.S. fact-finding mission under Dr. Eugene Staley takes place in South Vietnam. Staley's findings, reported to President John F. Kennedy in August, stress that South Vietnam needs a self-sustaining economy and that military action alone will not work. Only with substantial social and political reform can favorable results be achieved. Staley's recommendations center on protection of the civilian population. He advocates substantial increases in the size of the ARVN, the Civil Guard, and local militias and seeks improved arms and equipment at the local level. Finally, he calls for construction of a network of strategic hamlets, based on South Vietnamese president Ngo Dinh Diem's earlier Agroville Program.

August 1961

Phuong Dong 1 (Vostok 1), a large infiltration group consisting mostly of senior headquarters staff officers (600 officers and men led by PAVN General Staff deputy chief Tran Van Quang), arrives in War Zone D northwest of Saigon after marching down the Ho Chi Minh Trail from North Vietnam.

September 1961

VC forces carry out a series of attacks in Kontum Province.

18   A VC battalion besieges the provincial capital of Phuoc Vinh, some 36 miles north of Saigon.

October 1961

U.S. president John F. Kennedy's chief military adviser General Maxwell D. Taylor and Special Assistant for National Security Affairs Walt W. Rostow lead a second fact-finding trip to South Vietnam. They see the situation there primarily in military terms and recommend to Kennedy a change in the U.S. role from advisory only to a "limited partnership" with South Vietnam. They urge increased U.S. economic aid and military advisory support, to include intensive training of local self-defense forces and a large increase in airplanes, helicopters, and support personnel. A secret appendix recommends deployment of 8,000 American combat troops that might be used to support the ARVN in military operations.

The Central Office for South Vietnam (COSVN) is formed in War Zone D northeast of Saigon to command the Communist effort in South Vietnam.

18   South Vietnamese president Ngo Dinh Diem declares a state of national emergency because of increased VC activity and the severe floods that have beset South Vietnam.

November 1961

16   U.S. president John F. Kennedy announces his decision to increase South Vietnamese military strength but not commit U.S. combat forces there.

22   U.S. National Security Action Memorandum No. 111 authorizes the commitment to South Vietnam of additional helicopters, transport planes, and warplanes as

well as personnel to carry out training and actual combat missions.

December 1961

6   The U.S. Joint Chiefs of Staff (JCS) authorizes Operation FARM GATE. U.S. personnel and aircraft may undertake combat missions, providing at least one Vietnamese national is carried on board strike aircraft for training purposes.

8   The U.S. State Department issues a White Paper accusing the North Vietnamese government of aggression against South Vietnam and warning of a "clear and present danger" of Communist victory.

11   The U.S. Navy ship *Core* arrives at Saigon with the first U.S. helicopter units and 400 air and ground crewmen.

16   The first U.S. FARM GATE mission is flown in South Vietnam.

31   Some 3,200 U.S. military personnel are in South Vietnam.
      Communist troop strength in South Vietnam stands at 24,500 full-time soldiers and 100,000 local guerrillas. During 1961, 7,664 Communist troops from North Vietnam have infiltrated down the Ho Chi Minh Trail to South Vietnam.

January 1962

12   Operation RANCH HAND, the spraying of defoliant herbicides in South Vietnam, begins.

February 1962

4   The first U.S. helicopter is shot down over South Vietnam while ferrying ARVN troops into battle near the village of Hong My.

6   The U.S. Military Assistance Command, Vietnam (MACV), is established, commanded by General Paul D. Harkins, to direct the U.S. war effort inside South Vietnam.

11   First FARM GATE casualties. Nine U.S. and South Vietnamese crewmen are killed in the crash of a C-47 aircraft near Saigon.

14   U.S. president John F. Kennedy authorizes U.S. military advisers in South Vietnam to return fire if fired upon.

27   South Vietnamese president Ngo Dinh Diem survives another coup attempt when Republic of Vietnam Air Force (VNAF, South Vietnam Air Force) pilots Lieutenants Pham Phu Quoc and Nguyen Van Cu try to kill him and his brother Ngo Dinh Nhu by bombing and strafing the presidential palace. As a result, dozens of Diem political opponents disappear, and thousands more are sent to prison camps. Lieutenant Quoc is arrested after his AD-6 crash-lands in Nha Be, near Saigon. Lieutenant

Cu flees to Cambodia, where he remains until November 1963.

May 1962

      Communist forces gain control of a large area of Laos as several thousand Royal Lao Army troops flee into Thailand.

15   U.S. president John F. Kennedy announces the dispatch of U.S. troops to Thailand (at Thai government request) because of the Communist offensive in Laos and the movement of Communist forces toward the Thai border.

June 1962

2   Canadian and Indian members of the ICC declare the North Vietnamese government guilty of violating the 1954 Geneva Accords in carrying out "hostile activities, including armed attacks," against South Vietnamese armed forces and the South Vietnamese administration. All three members of the ICC (Canada, India, and Poland) find South Vietnam guilty of violating the Geneva Accords by receiving additional military aid and entering into a "factual military alliance" with the United States.

July 1962

23   A declaration and protocol on the neutrality of Laos is signed by the 14-nation conference in Geneva. The tripartite coalition government that it establishes proves short-lived, however.

December 1962

      Communist troop strength in North Vietnam stands at 40,000. During 1962 almost 10,000 North Vietnamese infiltrators make their way down the Ho Chi Minh Trail.

31   Some 11,300 U.S. military personnel are in South Vietnam.

January 1963

2   ARVN forces suffer a major defeat in the Battle of Ap Bac, which occurs some 40 miles southwest of Saigon.

February 1963

26   U.S. helicopter crews escorting ARVN troops are ordered to shoot first in encountering enemy soldiers.

May 1963

8   Buddhist riots in Hue occur protesting the South Vietnamese government ban on flying the multicolored flag of the World Fellowship of Buddhists. South Vietnamese riot police kill eight demonstrators, including some children, leading to widespread Buddhist antigovernment demonstrations throughout South Vietnam.

June 1963

11   The elderly Buddhist monk Thich Quang Duc publicly burns himself to death in protest of South Vietnamese government policies.

July 1963

17   In Saigon, South Vietnamese police break up a Buddhist protest demonstration against alleged religious discrimination.

August 1963

20   South Vietnamese president Ngo Dinh Diem declares martial law.

21   South Vietnamese Special Forces loyal to President Ngo Dinh Diem's brother Ngo Dinh Nhu attack Buddhist pagodas in Saigon, Hue, and other cities. Many of the structures are damaged, and more than 1,400 Buddhists are arrested.

22   Henry Cabot Lodge replaces Frederick Nolting as U.S. ambassador to South Vietnam.

24   A U.S. State Department cable to Ambassador Henry Cabot Lodge in Saigon acknowledges Ngo Dinh Nhu's responsibility for the raids on Buddhist pagodas and says that South Vietnamese generals should be told that Washington is prepared to discontinue economic and military aid to Diem.

September 1963

2   U.S. president John F. Kennedy, in a CBS news interview, says that the war in South Vietnam cannot be won "unless the people support the effort," adding "in my opinion, in the last two months, the Government has gotten out of touch with the people."

October 1963

2   The U.S. government decides to suspend economic subsidies for South Vietnamese commercial imports, to freeze loans for developmental projects, and to cut off financial support of Ngo Dinh Nhu's 2,000-man South Vietnamese Special Forces. This is a clear signal to those planning a coup against South Vietnamese president Ngo Dinh Diem.

3   The first clandestine North Vietnamese infiltration trawler arrives at a covert landing site in the Mekong Delta and unloads more than 20 tons of weapons and ammunition.

November 1963

1   A military coup led by major generals Duong Van Minh, Ton That Dinh, and Tran Van Don overthrows the South Vietnamese government of President Ngo Dinh Diem.

2   Both South Vietnamese president Ngo Dinh Diem and his brother and chief adviser Ngo Dinh Nhu, who U.S. leaders assumed would be given safe passage out of the country, are murdered by the coup leaders, who set up a provisional government, suspend the constitution, and dissolve the National Assembly.

4   Washington recognizes the new South Vietnamese provisional government.

14   In Saigon, U.S. Army major general Charles Timnes announces that 1,000 Americans will be returning home by the end of December.

22   U.S. president John F. Kennedy is assassinated in Dallas, Texas. He is succeeded by Vice President Lyndon Johnson.

23   U.S. president Lyndon Johnson reaffirms Washington's commitment to South Vietnam and to the defeat of the Communist forces there.

December 1963

21   U.S. secretary of defense Robert McNamara reports to President Lyndon B. Johnson that the situation in South Vietnam is "very disturbing" and that "current trends, unless reversed in the next 2–3 months, will lead to neutralization at best or more likely to a Communist-controlled state."

31   Some 16,300 U.S. military personnel are in South Vietnam.

Communist troop strength in South Vietnam stands at 70,000. Between early 1959 and the end of 1963, more than 40,000 Communist troops have infiltrated down the Ho Chi Minh Trail from North Vietnam.

The North Vietnamese leadership decides to send PAVN regular army units to South Vietnam.

In Hanoi, the Lao Dong Party Central Committee's 9th Plenum approves resolution condemning "revisionism." This resolution aligns the party firmly with China in the Sino-Soviet split, causing internal divisions within the party that will fester for several years and ultimately result in the 1967 Anti-Party Affair arrests and purges.

January 1964

16   U.S. president Lyndon Johnson authorizes covert operations against North Vietnam (OPLAN 34A). Such operations, to be conducted by South Vietnamese forces supported by U.S. forces, would gather intelligence and conduct sabotage in order to destabilize the North Vietnamese regime. OPLAN 34A operations begin in February.

27   Two PAVN regiments and Pathet Lao forces launch an offensive in central Laos to clear the corridor along the Laotian–North Vietnamese border for expanded troop infiltration and supply shipments down the Ho Chi Minh Trail.

30   Major General Nguyen Khanh ousts the South Vietnam-
       ese government headed by General Duong Van Minh.
       U.S. officials, caught by surprise, promptly hail Khanh
       as the new savior because he promises to rule with a
       strong hand.

March 1964

U.S. secretary of defense Robert McNamara visits South
Vietnam and vows U.S. support for the Nguyen Khanh
government. McNamara barnstorms the country,
describing Khanh in memorized Vietnamese as the
country's "best possible leader."

April 1964

North Vietnam commences infiltration of regular PAVN
units into South Vietnam.

May 1964

15   South Vietnamese leader General Nguyen Khanh signs a
       decree removing the Ngo Dinh Diem regime restrictions
       against Buddhists in South Vietnam and granting them
       the same rights as those enjoyed by Catholics.

June 1964

9   In response to the Communist Pathet Lao/PAVN spring
       offensive in Laos, the United States begins Operation BAR-
       REL ROLL, a bombing campaign to support Royal Laotian
       Army and CIA-trained Hmong irregular forces led by
       General Vang Pao.

20   General William C. Westmoreland replaces General Paul
       D. Harkins as commander of MACV. Both Westmore-
       land and U.S. ambassador Henry Cabot Lodge favor vig-
       orous action to stiffen South Vietnamese leader General
       Nguyen Khanh's resolve.

July 1964

7   General Maxwell Taylor arrives in South Vietnam as the
       new U.S. ambassador to South Vietnam.

25   The government of the Soviet Union calls for reconven-
       ing the Geneva Conference on Laos.

30–31 South Vietnamese naval forces, using American Swift
       Boats, carry out commando raids on Hon Me and Hon
       Nhieu islands, 7 and 2.5 miles, respectively, off the coast
       of North Vietnam. The North Vietnamese govern-
       ment accuses the United States and South Vietnam of
       an "extremely serious" violation of the 1954 Geneva
       Accords.

August 1964

2   North Vietnamese torpedo boats attack the U.S.
       destroyer *Maddox* on patrol in international waters some
       28 miles from the coast of North Vietnam.

3   North Vietnam endorses the Soviet Union's call for
       reconvening the Geneva Conference "to preserve the
       peace of Indochina and Southeast Asia."

4   Captain John Herrick, the commander of the U.S. Navy
       destroyer *Maddox,* claims that his ship and the accom-
       panying destroyer *C. Turner Joy* are under attack by
       North Vietnamese patrol boats. Although doubts are
       quickly raised by Herrick himself as to whether an attack
       has actually occurred, U.S. president Lyndon Johnson
       orders strikes by carrier aircraft (Operation PIERCE ARROW)
       against "gunboats and certain supporting facilities in
       North Vietnam."

5   During the PIERCE ARROW attacks on North Vietnam, two
       American aircraft are shot down. One pilot is killed, and
       Lieutenant (Junior Grade) Everret Alvarez is captured
       and becomes the first U.S. prisoner of war (POW) in
       North Vietnam.

7   The U.S. Congress passes the Gulf of Tonkin Resolu-
       tion, authorizing "all necessary steps, including the
       use of armed force," in Southeast Asia. Senate passage
       comes with only two dissenting votes; the House vote is
       unanimous.
       South Vietnamese leader Nguyen Khanh declares a "state
       of emergency."

16   General Nguyen Khanh, elected president of South Viet-
       nam by the Military Council, ousts General Duong Van
       Minh as chief of state and installs a new constitution,
       which the U.S. embassy had helped draft.

21–25 In South Vietnam, student demonstrations occur against
       President Nguyen Khanh and the South Vietnamese mili-
       tary government. These then turn into riots.

27   The new constitution of South Vietnam is withdrawn,
       and the ruling Revolutionary Council is dissolved. A tri-
       umvirate of generals Nguyen Khanh, Duong Van Minh,
       and Tran Thien Khiem is created.

29   Nguyen Xuan Oanh, former professor at Trinity
       College in Connecticut, is named acting premier
       of South Vietnam. Oanh says that President
       Nguyen Khanh has suffered a mental and physical
       breakdown.

September 1964

5   The North Vietnamese government renews its appeal to
       the 1954 Geneva Conference cochairmen to reconvene
       the conference.

13   In South Vietnam, a bloodless coup by Brigadier General
       Lam Van Phat is aborted.

26   In South Vietnam, a provisional legislature (the High
       National Council) is inaugurated.

30   At the University of California, Berkeley, the first major
       anti–Vietnam War demonstrations occur in the United
       States.

U.S. presidential adviser William Bundy says that bombing North Vietnam would reduce the threat to South Vietnam within months.

September 1964

MACV commander General William Westmoreland initiates HOP TAC, a pacification operation in six provinces around the city of Saigon.

The North Vietnamese Politburo in Hanoi approves a resolution calling for an urgent effort to win a decisive victory in South Vietnam and for sending large PAVN units south to conduct large-scale attacks to secure such a victory.

October 1964

General Nguyen Chi Thanh is sent down from North Vietnam to take over command of the COSVN and direct the effort to win a decisive Communist victory in South Vietnam.

14　Nikita Khrushchev is deposed as leader of the Soviet Union and replaced by Leonid Brezhnev, opening the way for closer Soviet–North Vietnamese relations and resumption of Soviet military aid to North Vietnam.

31　Tran Van Huong is named premier of South Vietnam.

November 1964

1　Communist forces attack Bien Hoa Air Base in South Vietnam, destroying six B-57 bombers and killing 5 U.S. military personnel.

3　Lyndon Johnson is elected president of the United States in a landslide victory, with 61 percent of the vote.

20　The lead element of the PAVN 325th Division departs North Vietnam to infiltrate south. By the spring of 1965 the entire division and a separate independent PAVN regiment (the newly formed 320th Regiment) have arrived in South Vietnam.

December 1964

Communist forces launch their first multiregimental operation of the war, the Binh Gia Campaign, east of Saigon. The campaign, which lasts into January 1965, inflicts heavy losses on the ARVN and gives rise to serious American concerns about ARVN capabilities.

5　The first Medal of Honor awarded to a U.S. serviceman during the Vietnam War is presented to Captain Roger Donlon for his heroic action during a battle at Nam Dong Special Forces Camp on July 6, 1964.

8–20　Student and Buddhist demonstrations in South Vietnam threaten the military-supported Tran Van Huong government.

14　U.S. aircraft begin bombing the Ho Chi Minh Trail network in Laos.

20　Nguyen Khanh and other generals dissolve the High National Council in the Tran Van Huong government, arrest opponents, and conduct a purge of military leadership, despite the opposition by U.S. ambassador Maxwell Taylor.

24　Two Americans are killed when VC sappers bomb U.S. billets in Saigon.

U.S. ambassador to South Vietnam Maxwell Taylor tells the press that South Vietnamese leader General Nguyen Khanh has outlived his usefulness.

31　Some 23,300 U.S. military personnel are in South Vietnam.

During 1964 more than 17,000 Communist troops from North Vietnam have infiltrated down the Ho Chi Minh Trail into South Vietnam. In more than 80 voyages, North Vietnamese infiltration trawlers have delivered 4,000 tons of weapons and ammunition to Communist forces in South Vietnam.

January 1965

4　In his State of the Union address, President Lyndon Johnson reaffirms the U.S. commitment to South Vietnam.

7　The Armed Forces Council (AFC) and General Nguyen Khanh restore a civilian government in South Vietnam under Tran Van Huong.

19–24　Buddhist demonstrations erupt in South Vietnam in the cities of Saigon and Hue. These include the sacking of the United States Information Service (USIS) building. The demonstrators demand military ouster of the Tran Van Huong government.

27　In South Vietnam, the Armed Forces Council ousts the Tran Van Huong government and reinstalls General Nguyen Khanh in power.

February 1965

7　Communist forces attack U.S. installations at Pleiku in South Vietnam, killing 8 U.S. servicemen, wounding 109, and destroying or damaging 20 aircraft.

In retaliation in FLAMING DART I that same day, 49 A-4 and F-8 aircraft from the carriers *Coral Sea* and *Hancock* strike North Vietnamese training installations at Dong Hoi, some 40 miles north of the demilitarized zone (DMZ). One A-4 is lost in the attack.

8　Twenty-four VNAF propeller-driven A-1 Skyraiders, led in person by Air Marshal Nguyen Cao Ky, hit the Chap Le barracks and communication center at Vinh Linh, 15 miles north of the DMZ. The attackers destroy 47 buildings and damage another 22.

9　A U.S. Marine Corps Hawk air defense missile battalion is deployed to Da Nang in South Vietnam.

10   In South Vietnam, VC operatives smuggle 100 pounds of explosives into the four-story Viet Cuong Hotel, used as a billet for U.S. military personnel in the coastal city of Qui Nhon in Binh Dinh Province. The resulting blast, which kills 23 Americans and wounds another 21, reduces the building to rubble. Two VC are slain at the hotel, and dozens more are killed when South Vietnamese gunboats and U.S. helicopters attack some 50 sampans trying to carry out a raid against Qui Nhon Harbor.

11   In retaliation for the Communist Qui Nhon attack in South Vietnam, the United States launches FLAMING DART II. Ninety-nine sorties are launched from the carriers *Coral Sea, Hancock,* and *Ranger* against the PAVN facilities at Chanh Hoa. At the same time, 28 VNAF A-1 aircraft again strike the Chap Le facility. Three U.S. Navy aircraft are shot down in the attack, and one pilot is taken prisoner.

15   The PRC threatens to enter the Vietnam War if the United States invades North Vietnam.

18   South Vietnamese army and marine units oust General Nguyen Khanh from power in a bloodless coup.

20   In South Vietnam, forces loyal to the Armed Forces Council regain control, but the Armed Forces Council demands General Nguyen Khanh's resignation.

27   The U.S. State Department issues a White Paper detailing North Vietnamese "aggression" against South Vietnam.

28   U.S. and South Vietnamese officials declare that President Lyndon Johnson has decided to begin reprisal attacks against North Vietnam to secure a negotiated settlement.

March 1965

2   Operation ROLLING THUNDER, the sustained U.S. bombing of North Vietnam, begins with first an air mission. One hundred U.S. Air Force and VNAF sorties strike the Xom Bang Ammunition Depot 35 miles north of the DMZ.

8   UN secretary-general U Thant proposes a preliminary conference to discuss Vietnam to include the United States, the Soviet Union, Great Britain, France, China, North Vietnam, and South Vietnam.

      The U.S. 9th Marine Expeditionary Brigade (MEB), deployed from Okinawa, begins arriving at Da Nang in South Vietnam.

9   Washington rejects UN secretary-general U Thant's proposal for a peace conference on Vietnam until North Vietnam ends its aggression in South Vietnam.

April 1965

      The United States begins Operation STEEL TIGER, an air interdiction campaign over the Ho Chi Minh Trail in the northern panhandle of Laos.

      Equipment for the first two SA-2 surface-to-air missile (SAM) regiments along with Soviet advisers/instructors arrive by train in North Vietnam to strengthen North Vietnam's air defenses.

2   The U.S. government announces that it will send several thousand additional troops to South Vietnam.

3–4   The first air battles occur between U.S. aircraft and North Vietnamese MiG fighters over North Vietnam. One U.S. aircraft and three MiGs are destroyed.

7   President Lyndon Johnson, speaking at Johns Hopkins University, announces that the United States is willing to hold "unconditional discussions" with the North Vietnamese government and presents the inducement of a $1 billion economic aid program for Southeast Asia.

8   North Vietnamese premier Pham Van Dong rejects U.S. president Lyndon Johnson's peace proposal and announces North Vietnam's four-point position on peace, including settlement of South Vietnam's internal affairs "in accordance with the program of the National Liberation Front of South Vietnam, without any foreign interference."

May 1965

      The U.S. Navy begins Operation MARKET TIME to interdict Communist surface traffic in South Vietnamese coastal waters.

3   Some 3,500 men of the U.S. Army's 173rd Airborne Brigade, deploying from Okinawa, begin landing in South Vietnam.

13–18   A six-day pause occurs in the U.S. bombing of North Vietnam.

26–30   A Communist regiment in Quang Ngai Province inflicts extremely heavy losses on ARVN forces, elevating U.S. worries about the ARVN's ability to defend South Vietnam without the assistance of U.S. ground forces.

June 1965

8   The U.S. State Department reveals that American troops are authorized to participate in direct combat if so requested by the ARVN.

9   Two Communist regiments attack the Dong Xoai District capital and U.S. Special Forces camp northwest of Saigon, mauling several ARVN battalions.

11   In South Vietnam, a National Directorate comprising 10 military leaders forms a war cabinet headed by Air Marshal Nguyen Cao Ky as premier.

16   U.S. secretary of defense Robert McNamara announces new troop deployments to South Vietnam, bringing U.S. troop strength there to 70,000 men.

18   Arc Light operations begin as B-52 bombers strike Communist targets within South Vietnam.

July 1965

8   Henry Cabot Lodge is reappointed U.S. ambassador to South Vietnam, succeeding Maxwell Taylor.

24   The first use of SAMs against U.S. aircraft over North Vietnam occurs. SAMs fired by Soviet missile crews shoot down one U.S. F-4 aircraft. One U.S. pilot is killed, and another is captured.

August 1965

18–19   Operation STARLITE, the first large ground operation by U.S. ground forces in South Vietnam, takes place in Quang Ngai Province. In the operation, the U.S. 3rd Marine Division mauls a VC regiment.

September 1965

11   The U.S. Army 1st Cavalry Division (Airmobile) begins arriving in South Vietnam.

October 1965

15–16   In the United States, the student-run National Coordinating Committee to End the War in Vietnam sponsors nationwide demonstrations in some 40 cities.

November 1965

14–17   In the Battle of the Ia Drang Valley in the Central Highlands between the U.S. 1st Air Cavalry Division and PAVN forces, heavy losses occur on both sides.

27   A March for Peace in Vietnam draws 15,000 to 35,000 marchers in Washington, D.C.

December 1965

        The U.S. Air Force carries out strikes against targets in the southern panhandle of Laos. Operation TIGER HOUND begins, and the Arc Light campaign by B-52s is extended to Laos.

24   The United States begins a second pause in the bombing of North Vietnam in an effort to get the leaders of the North Vietnamese government to negotiate.

31   Some 184,300 U.S. military personnel are in South Vietnam.
        Communist troop strength in South Vietnam is 170,000 full-time soldiers and 174,000 guerrillas. More than 50,000 North Vietnamese troops have infiltrated into South Vietnam during 1965.

January 1966

31   U.S. air strikes in Operation ROLLING THUNDER resume against North Vietnam.

February 1966

1   The UN Security Council meets to consider a U.S. draft resolution calling for an international conference to bring about peace in South Vietnam and Southeast Asia.

2   The Foreign Ministry of North Vietnam formally rejects UN action regarding Vietnam.

4   The U.S. Senate Foreign Relations Committee opens formal televised hearings on the Vietnam War.

6–9   U.S. president Lyndon Johnson holds talks in Honolulu with South Vietnamese premier Nguyen Cao Ky.

March 1966

12   In South Vietnam, Buddhists and students begin demonstrations in Hue and Da Nang to protest the ouster of ARVN I Corps commander General Nguyen Chanh Thi and to demand elections for a new national assembly.

16–20   Mass Buddhist protests occur in Saigon against the South Vietnamese government.

23   In South Vietnam, general strikes occur in the cities of Da Nang and Hue.

April 1966

1   Communist sappers set off explosives in a Saigon hotel, killing three Americans and four South Vietnamese.

2–5   South Vietnamese premier Nguyen Cao Ky threatens to employ troops to quell the antigovernment rebellion in Da Nang and then orders two Ranger battalions flown there.

11   U.S. Air Force B-52s bomb North Vietnam for the first time.

12–14   The National Directorate of South Vietnam promises elections for a constituent assembly within three to five months. Buddhist demonstrations come to an end.

May 1966

15   South Vietnamese premier Nguyen Cao Ky airlifts 1,000 South Vietnamese marines to the city of Da Nang.

June 1966

1   Students in the city of Hue in South Vietnam burn the U.S. cultural center and consulate.

19   The National Directorate in South Vietnam schedules assembly elections for September.

23   South Vietnamese troops seize the chief Buddhist stronghold in Saigon.

29   U.S. aircraft carry out the first strikes against oil installations in the Hanoi and Haiphong areas of North Vietnam.

July 1966

Following the conclusion of a secret agreement with Cambodian ruler Prince Norodom Sihanouk, a covert Vietnamese Communist logistics support group is formed in Cambodia to ship military equipment unloaded from Communist cargo ships at the Cambodian port of Sihanoukville to base camps along the South Vietnamese–Cambodian border. From 1966 to 1969, more than 21,000 tons of weapons and ammunition are shipped through Sihanoukville to Communist forces in South Vietnam.

8 South Vietnamese chief of state General Nguyen Van Thieu states that the allies should invade North Vietnam if necessary to end the war.

30 U.S. aircraft for the first time intentionally strike targets in the DMZ separating North Vietnam and South Vietnam. These air strikes last until August 5, 1966.

September 1966

11 South Vietnamese go to the polls to elect a 117-member constituent assembly from among officially approved anti-Communist slates. Buddhist leaders denounce the election as fraudulent.

October 1966

The U.S. Navy begins Operation SEA DRAGON, the interdiction of Communist supply vessels in coastal waters off North Vietnam.

25 A meeting occurs in Manila of representatives from the United States and five other nations assisting South Vietnam. They offer to withdraw their troops from South Vietnam six months after Hanoi disengages from the war.

26 President Lyndon Johnson visits U.S. troops in South Vietnam.

November 1966

5 U.S. secretary of defense Robert McNamara announces that the number of U.S. troops in South Vietnam will continue to grow in 1967 but at a lower rate than in 1966.

30 Polish ICC representative Janusz Lewandowski formulates a 10-point peace position on which basis North Vietnam would negotiate seriously with the United States.

December 1966

2 The U.S. State Department decides to contact the North Vietnamese representative in Warsaw regarding secret talks.

2–5 U.S. bombers raid truck depots, rail yards, and fuel dumps in the immediate vicinity of Hanoi in North Vietnam.

9 Polish ICC representative Janusz Lewandowski informs U.S. ambassador to South Vietnam Henry Cabot Lodge that no contact can take place in Warsaw in the face of the U.S. escalation of bombing North Vietnam.

14–15 Additional U.S. air strikes occur very close to the city of Hanoi in North Vietnam.

26 Responding to reports by correspondent Harrison Salisbury of the *New York Times*, U.S. officials admit that

U.S. planes have "accidentally struck civilian areas while attempting to bomb military targets."

31 There are now some 385,300 U.S. military personnel in South Vietnam.
Communist troop strength in South Vietnam is 230,000 full-time soldiers. More than 60,000 North Vietnamese troops have arrived in South Vietnam during 1966.

January 1967

The U.S. Navy establishes the Mekong Delta Mobile Riverine Force in South Vietnam.

8 Operation CEDAR FALLS, involving large numbers of U.S. and ARVN troops, commences. The purpose of the operation is clearing the VC from the Iron Triangle, a 60–square mile area of jungle believed to contain numerous VC base camps and supply dumps.

10 In the course of his State of the Union address, U.S. president Lyndon Johnson calls for a 6 percent surcharge on income taxes to support the war.

27 The Vietnamese Lao Dong Party Central Committee's 13th Plenum secretly approves resolution on implementing a talk-fight strategy to begin negotiations with the United States. The strategy specifies that Communist forces must first win a major victory in South Vietnam to give negotiators leverage in the talks.

February 1967

7 U.S. president Lyndon Johnson sends a proposal to British prime minister Harold Wilson for an "assured stoppage" of the infiltration of South Vietnam by North Vietnam in return for a bombing halt and no further augmentation of U.S. forces in South Vietnam.
The United States begins a six-day pause in Operation ROLLING THUNDER, the bombing of North Vietnam.

10 The U.S. government insists that the formula for talks, presented by British prime minister Harold Wilson to Soviet premier Aleksei Kosygin, requires that North Vietnamese infiltration of South Vietnam stop before the institution of a bombing halt, not afterward as Wilson had suggested orally.

22 Operation JUNCTION CITY, the largest American operation of the Vietnam War, is launched to destroy Communist forces in War Zone C, the key Communist base area northwest of Saigon, where the COSVN is located. The operation lasts until April 15.

March 1967

21 The North Vietnamese government releases the February exchange of notes between U.S. president Lyndon Johnson and North Vietnamese leader Ho Chi Minh in which Ho rejected peace talks unless the United States agrees

to unconditionally halt the bombing and all other acts of war against North Vietnam.

April 1967

15   Massive anti–Vietnam War demonstrations occur in cities across the United States.

20   U.S. aircraft strike a power plant in Hanoi for the first time.

24   U.S. aircraft attack two air bases in North Vietnam for the first time.

May 1967

1   Ellsworth Bunker replaces Henry Cabot Lodge as U.S. ambassador to South Vietnam.

13   South Vietnamese premier Nguyen Cao Ky says that he might react "militarily" if a civilian with whose policies he disagrees is elected president.

14   South Vietnamese chief of state Nguyen Van Thieu says that he believes that 50,000 U.S. or allied troops will be needed in South Vietnam for 10 to 20 years after the end of the war.

June 1967

The PAVN General Staff submits to the party Politburo in Hanoi a plan for a major large-unit offensive in 1968. The Politburo concludes that the plan is inadequate.

30   Following three days of meetings of the ruling Armed Forces Council in South Vietnam, Premier Nguyen Cao Ky withdraws from the presidential race and agrees to be the vice presidential candidate on a ticket headed by the more senior general Nguyen Van Thieu.

July 1967

North Vietnamese security officials carry out the first wave of arrests of individuals implicated in the Anti-Party Affair, also called the Hoang Minh Chinh Affair. This is a supposed dissident plot against the party leadership. By the time the arrests end in early 1968, hundreds of party and government officials, including several current or former Central Committee members and senior military officers who are close associates of General Vo Nguyen Giap, will have been arrested or purged.

6   General Nguyen Chi Thanh, commander of all Communist forces in South Vietnam, dies of a heart attack in Hanoi. He is replaced by Politburo member Pham Hung.

16   The U.S. government admits in a diplomatic note to the Soviet Union that U.S. aircraft may have inadvertently struck the Soviet ship *Mikhail Frunze* in Haiphong Harbor on June 29.

18–19   The South Vietnamese Constituent Assembly approves 11 candidate slates for the upcoming presidential election but rejects peace candidate Au Truong Thanh on a trumped-up charge of links to the Communists and exiled South Vietnamese general Duong Van Minh. In the wake of Nguyen Chi Thanh's death, the North Vietnamese Politburo debates a daring new plan for an all-out Communist offensive and uprisings, a plan that will become the 1968 Tet Offensive.

August 1967

31   The U.S. Senate Preparedness Subcommittee declares that Secretary of Defense Robert McNamara has "shackled" the air war against North Vietnam and calls for the "closure, neutralization, or isolation of Haiphong."

September 1967

PAVN general Vo Nguyen Giap travels to Eastern Europe for "medical treatment." He does not return to North Vietnam until February 1968, after the 1968 Tet Offensive has begun.

3   Generals Nguyen Van Thieu and Nguyen Cao Ky are elected president and vice president, respectively, of South Vietnam. The Thieu-Ky slate secures 35 percent of the vote.

10   The first U.S. air raid on North Vietnamese ports occurs when the port area of Cam Pha, 46 miles northeast of Haiphong, is attacked.

11   Heavy U.S. air strikes occur against the port of Haiphong and its suburbs in an effort to cut it off from Hanoi.

29   U.S. president Lyndon Johnson declares in a speech at San Antonio that the United States will stop the bombing of North Vietnam if this "will lead promptly to productive discussions."

October 1967

12   U.S. secretary of state Dean Rusk declares that the Vietnam War is a test of Asia's ability to withstand the threat of "a billion Chinese . . . armed with nuclear weapons."

12–14   Heavy U.S. Navy air strikes occur against Haiphong shipyards and docks in North Vietnam.

16   The U.S. Congress passes the fiscal year 1967 Department of Defense Appropriations Act (Public Law 89-687). An amendment to the act, introduced by Senator Richard B. Russell (D-Ga.), gives President Lyndon Johnson the authority until June 30, 1968, to order to active duty any unit of the Ready Reserve for a period not to exceed 24 months.

20–24   The Lao Dong Party Politburo in Hanoi meets again to debate the plan for the 1968 Tet Offensive. The Politburo approves only a portion of the plan.

21–23   Some 50,000 Americans rally against the war in Washington, D.C., and march on the Pentagon, which is protected by 10,000 troops.

November 1967

The PAVN mounts the Dak To Campaign in the northern Central Highlands. Both PAVN and U.S. forces suffer heavy casualties. The heaviest fighting is that on Hill 875 during November 18–23.

The Lao Dong Party Politburo in Hanoi finally approves the plan for the January 1968 Tet Offensive.

2   U.S. president Lyndon Johnson convenes a meeting of senior unofficial advisers, known as the so-called Wise Men, who recommend that the administration stay the course in Vietnam and provide more upbeat progress reports.

21   MACV commander General William Westmoreland declares in a speech at the National Press Club in Washington that the war has reached the point when "the end begins to come into view."

29   U.S. president Lyndon Johnson announces that Secretary of Defense Robert McNamara will resign to become president of the World Bank.

December 1967

30   The South Vietnamese government announces a 36-hour truce for the Lunar New Year (Tet) holidays.

31   There are some 485,600 U.S. military personnel in South Vietnam.

Communist full-time troop strength in South Vietnam is 278,000, with another 100,000 part-time guerrillas. More than 80,000 North Vietnamese soldiers have infiltrated into South Vietnam during the year.

Early January 1968

The Lao Dong Party Central Committee holds its 14th Plenum in a secret location outside of Hanoi to formally approve the plan for the 1968 Tet Offensive.

January 1968

1   North Vietnamese foreign minister Nguyen Duy Trinh announces for the first time that North Vietnam "will hold talks with the United States" after it has "unconditionally" halted bombing and "other acts of war" against North Vietnam.

21   Communist forces begin the siege of the U.S. Marine Corps base at Khe Sanh near the DMZ and Laos.

23   North Korean naval forces seize the U.S. Navy electronic intelligence ship *Pueblo* and its crew, diverting U.S. military attention and resources, including several carrier battle groups, toward the Korean Peninsula.

25   Clark Clifford, U.S. president Lyndon Johnson's choice to be the new secretary of defense, tells the Senate Armed Services Committee that the no-advantage clause of the San Antonio speech means that North Vietnam could

continue to transport the "normal" level of goods and men into South Vietnam after a U.S. bombing halt.

U.S. president Lyndon Johnson announces the call-up of 28 units of the Air Force Reserve, Air National Guard, and Naval Reserve, totaling 14,787 reservists. Although the mobilizations are in response to the situation in Korea, some of those called up will later serve in Southeast Asia.

30   First attacks, which are premature, occur in the Communist Tet Offensive at Da Nang, Pleiku, Nha Trang, and nine other cities in central South Vietnam.

31   Major attacks occur in the Communist Tet Offensive. The offensive is widespread throughout South Vietnam, including Saigon and Hue, 5 of 6 autonomous cities, 36 of 44 provincial capitals, and 64 of 245 district capitals. The attacks catch allied forces off guard in both their timing and magnitude. Militarily, the Tet Offensive proves to be a tactical disaster for the Communists. By the end of March 1968 they have not achieved a single one of their objectives, and more than 58,000 VC and PAVN troops have been killed. U.S. forces suffer 3,895 dead, and ARVN losses are 4,954. Non-U.S. allies lose 214 troops. More than 14,300 South Vietnamese civilians also die, and hundreds of thousands are rendered homeless.

February 1968

7–8   PAVN troops overrun the U.S. Army Special Forces camp at Lang Vei, southwest of the U.S. Marine Corps base at Khe Sanh.

20   The U.S. Senate Foreign Relations Committee begins hearings on the 1964 Gulf of Tonkin Incident. Senators William Fulbright and Wayne Morse charge the Defense Department with withholding information on U.S. naval activities in the Gulf of Tonkin that might have provoked North Vietnam.

25   ARVN and U.S. forces recapture the city of Hue after 25 days of occupation by Communist troops.

MACV commander William Westmoreland states that additional U.S. troops "will probably be required" in Vietnam.

26   Allied troops discover the first mass graves in the city of Hue. During February 1–25, the occupying Communist forces massacred as many as 7,000 people identified with South Vietnam. Searchers recover only some 2,800 bodies.

27   CBS news anchorman Walter Cronkite, who has just returned from Saigon and Hue, tells Americans during an evening broadcast that he is certain that "the bloody experience of Vietnam is to end in a stalemate."

March 1968

16   A platoon from Charlie Company, 1st Battalion, 20th Infantry, 11th Infantry Brigade (Light) of the 23rd

(Americal) Division, commanded by Lieutenant William Calley, massacres between 200 and 500 unarmed civilians in My Lai, a cluster of hamlets making up Son My village of the Son Tinh District in the coastal lowlands of Quang Ngai Province in the I Corps Tactical Zone.

22   U.S. president Lyndon Johnson announces that MACV commander General William Westmoreland will be returning to Washington as chief of staff of the U.S. Army and will be replaced as commander of MACV by his deputy, General Creighton Abrams.

31   In the course of a televised address, U.S. president Lyndon Johnson announces a bombing halt over North Vietnam except for "the area north of the Demilitarized Zone." He calls on the North Vietnamese government to agree to peace talks. At the end of his remarks, he announces that he is withdrawing from the presidential race.

April 1968

3   The North Vietnamese government offers to send representatives to meet with U.S. officials "with a view to determining with the American side the unconditional cessation of the U.S. bombing raids and all other acts of war against the Democratic Republic of Vietnam so that talks may start." U.S. president Lyndon Johnson agrees.

11   In response to the Tet Offensive, Secretary of Defense Clark Clifford announces a second round of call-ups, totaling 24,500 reservists and National Guardsmen, including 1,028 U.S. Navy reservists. The reporting date of the second call-up is May 13.

26   Massive anti–Vietnam War demonstrations occur on college campuses across the United States, including some 200,000 protesters in New York City.

May 1968

3   After some haggling over the site, President Lyndon Johnson announces U.S. acceptance of the North Vietnamese government's suggestion that preliminary peace talks be held in Paris.

5–13   In what will turn out to be the second phase of the Tet Offensive, the second large-scale Communist offensive of the year occurs. Although it is smaller than the initial phase of the Tet Offensive, it sees Communist forces strike some 119 allied targets. U.S. and ARVN forces defeat all attacks of this so-called Mini–Tet Offensive.

12   Preliminary talks between the United States and North Vietnam open in Paris.

May 25–June 4, 1968

The third widespread Communist offensive of the year occurs in South Vietnam and is defeated by allied forces.

June 1968

10   General Creighton Abrams formally replaces General William Westmoreland as commander of MACV.

27   U.S. troops withdraw from their base at Khe Sanh after a 77-day siege.

October 1968

31   U.S. president Lyndon Johnson announces the end of ROLLING THUNDER, the complete cessation of "all air, naval, and artillery bombardment of North Vietnam" as of November 1.

November 1968

1   The North Vietnamese delegation at Paris announces that a meeting to include representatives of North Vietnam, South Vietnam, the NLF, and the United States will be held in Paris sometime after November 6.

2   South Vietnamese president Nguyen Van Thieu states that his government will not take part in the Paris peace negotiations.

6   Richard Nixon narrowly defeats Hubert Humphrey in the 1968 U.S. presidential election.

12   U.S. secretary of defense Clark Clifford threatens that the United States might proceed with the Paris negotiations without participation of the South Vietnamese government.

27   The South Vietnamese government announces that it will take part in the Paris peace talks after the U.S. government reiterates its nonrecognition of the NLF as a separate entity.

December 1968

23   NLF representative in Paris Tran Buu Kiem rejects direct negotiations between the NLF and South Vietnam and insists on talks only with the United States.

31   There are some 536,000 U.S. military personnel in South Vietnam.
       More than 140,000 North Vietnamese troops, including replacement troops and new units, have arrived in South Vietnam since January 1, 1968.

January 1969

16   After protracted negotiations, the United States and North Vietnam announce agreement on a roundtable conference format for the Paris peace talks.

20   Richard Nixon takes office as president of the United States.

25   Four-party peace talks begin in Paris.

February 1969

23–24 Communist forces launch mortar and rocket attacks on some 115 targets in South Vietnam, including the cities of Saigon, Da Nang, and Hue and the large U.S. base at Bien Hoa.

March 1969

18   Operation MENU, the secret U.S. air strikes inside Cambodia by B-52 bombers, begins. The operation continues until May 26, 1970.

19   U.S. secretary of defense Melvin Laird proclaims Vietnamization of the war.

26   Women Strike for Peace, the first big anti–Vietnam War rally during the Richard Nixon administration, occurs in Washington, D.C.

27   In Paris U.S. ambassador to the peace negotiations Henry Cabot Lodge and South Vietnamese delegation chief Pham Dang Lam declare that a peace settlement must include the withdrawal of all North Vietnamese "regular and subversive forces" from Laos, Cambodia, and South Vietnam.

April 1969

5–6   A weekend of anti–Vietnam War protests occurs in a number of U.S. cities.

7   South Vietnamese president Nguyen Van Thieu says that he would ask the South Vietnamese allies to remove their military forces from South Vietnam after North Vietnam withdraws its regular troops and "auxiliary troops and cadres."

30   Peak U.S. military strength in South Vietnam occurs, with 543,400 personnel in the country.

May 1969

8   The NLF delegate to the Paris peace talks, Tron Buu Kiem, demands an unconditional U.S. troop withdrawal from South Vietnam and the settlement of remaining military and political issues among the Vietnamese parties to exclude South Vietnamese president Nguyen Van Thieu.

10–20   The Battle of Hamburger Hill (Ap Bia Mountain) near the Laotian border in Thua Thien Province results in heavy U.S. casualties and intense domestic political criticism of U.S. military policies in Vietnam.

12   Communist forces launch their largest number of attacks throughout South Vietnam since the 1968 Tet Offensive, shelling 159 cities, towns, and military bases.

14   In his first major speech on Vietnam, U.S. president Richard Nixon proclaims an eight-point peace proposal that calls for simultaneous withdrawal of U.S. troops and "all non–South Vietnamese forces" from South Vietnam.

June 1969

8   During the course of a meeting with South Vietnamese president Nguyen Van Thieu on Midway Island in the Pacific, President Richard Nixon announces that by August the United States will withdraw 25,000 troops from South Vietnam.

10   The PRG of South Vietnam is formed by the NLF and other pro-NLF anti–South Vietnam organizations and individuals.

July 1969

11   South Vietnamese president Nguyen Van Thieu offers internationally supervised elections and Communist participation in an "electoral commission" but on the provision that the Communists first renounce violence. South Vietnam would oversee the election.

25   On the island of Guam, President Richard Nixon announces the Nixon Doctrine. The United States will have primary responsibility for defense of its allies against nuclear attack, but non-Communist Asian states will bear the brunt of their conventional defense as well as be responsible for their own internal security.

August 1969

4   U.S. national security adviser Henry Kissinger meets secretly in Paris with North Vietnamese representative Xuan Thuy.

September 1969

2   North Vietnamese president Ho Chi Minh dies in Hanoi. North Vietnamese officials announce his death the next day.

16   U.S. president Richard Nixon announces the withdrawal from South Vietnam of an additional 35,000 U.S. troops.

October 1969

15   Anti–Vietnam War demonstrations known as the Moratorium to End the War in Vietnam, involving hundreds of thousands of people, occur across the United States.

16   Secretary of Defense Melvin Laird announces U.S. plans to keep a "residual force" of some 6,000–7,000 troops in South Vietnam after hostilities end there.

25   The PAVN launches Campaign 139, a multidivisional operation in cooperation with Communist Pathet Lao forces to capture the Plain of Jars in central Laos. The offensive continues until April 1970.

November 1969

3   In a major address on the Vietnam War, U.S. president Richard Nixon appeals to the "silent majority" of Americans and argues that "precipitate withdrawal" from South Vietnam would lead to a "disaster of immense magnitude."

15   An anti–Vietnam War demonstration at the Washington Monument in Washington, D.C., the largest

demonstration in that city to date, draws some 250,000 people.

16   The U.S. Army announces an investigation into charges that U.S. forces shot more than 100 Vietnamese civilians in the village of My Lai in March 1968.

24   U.S. Army lieutenant William Calley Jr. is ordered to stand trial for the premeditated murder of 109 Vietnamese civilians at the village of My Lai in March 1968.

December 1969

1   The first U.S. military draft lottery since 1942 is held at Selective Service headquarters.

4   A Louis Harris survey reports that 46 percent of those polled indicate sympathy with the goals of the November Moratorium to End the War in Vietnam demonstrations; 45 percent disagree.

12   The last mobilized Reserve Component unit, Company D, 151st Infantry, Indiana National Guard, returns to the United States from Vietnam.

15   President Richard Nixon announces a third reduction in U.S. troop strength in South Vietnam in which 50,000 men are to leave by April 15, 1970.

31   Some 475,200 U.S. military personnel are in South Vietnam.
      More than 80,000 North Vietnamese troops have infiltrated into South Vietnam since January 1, 1969.

January 1970

28   A Gallup Poll shows that 65 percent of those Americans interviewed approve of President Richard Nixon's handling of the Vietnam War, his highest approval rating to date.

February 1970

21   U.S. national security adviser Henry Kissinger begins secret peace talks in Paris with North Vietnamese representative Le Duc Tho.

March 1970

13   With Prince Norodom Sihanouk abroad, the leaders of Cambodia demand that Vietnamese Communist troops withdraw from the country immediately. Cambodian crowds sack the North Vietnamese embassy in Phnom Penh.

17   Cambodian troops, supported by ARVN artillery, attack Vietnamese Communist sanctuaries along the Cambodian-Vietnamese border.

18   The Cambodian National Assembly deposes Prince Sihanouk, declaring General Lon Nol interim chief of state. South Vietnamese president Nguyen Van Thieu announces his hopes of working with the new Cambodian government to control Communist border activity.

23   In Beijing, Cambodian Prince Norodom Sihanouk announces that he will form both a "national union government" and a "national liberation army." The North Vietnamese government and the Pathet Lao, the Communist organization in Laos, declare their support.

27–28   ARVN forces, supported by U.S. forces, launch their first major attack against Communist base areas in Cambodia.

28   The U.S. government announces that American troops will be permitted, on the judgment of field commanders, to cross into Cambodia in response to Communist threats. Washington insists that this does not mean a widened war.

April 1970

4   The largest rally supporting U.S. involvement in the Vietnam War to date is held in Washington, D.C.
     The Politburo of the Lao Dong Party in Hanoi orders Vietnamese Communist forces to seize control of all Cambodian provinces along the South Vietnamese-Cambodian border.

5   Two ARVN battalions push more than 10 miles into Cambodia, this time without U.S. air support.

8   Vietnamese Communist troops drive back Cambodian government forces in heavy fighting some nine miles from the South Vietnamese border.

11   Cambodian government troops begin the massacre of several thousand Vietnamese civilians living in Southeast Cambodia. Some 40,000 Vietnamese in Phnom Penh are sent to concentration camps.
      A Gallup Poll shows that 48 percent of Americans approve of President Richard Nixon's Vietnam policy, while 41 percent disapprove.

20   President Richard Nixon announces in a televised speech his intention to withdraw 150,000 U.S. troops from Vietnam in the course of the next year.

21   ARVN troops cross the Cambodian border for the third time in a week to attack Communist base areas.

30   In a nationally televised address, President Richard Nixon announces that U.S. troops are attacking Communist sanctuaries in Cambodia. The destruction of base areas is the primary goal, but one objective is to locate and destroy the COSVN headquarters in the Fishhook area some 50 miles northwest of Saigon. In reaction to the Cambodian Incursion, widespread antiwar protests erupt on U.S. college campuses.

May 1970

3   The Pentagon confirms that the United States has conducted heavy bombing of targets in North Vietnam, the first major bombing of North Vietnam since the

November 1968 bombing halt. A Pentagon spokesman calls these "protective reaction" strikes.

4   Ohio National Guardsmen fire on antiwar student demonstrators at Kent State University in Ohio, killing 4 people and wounding 11.

6   Some 200 college campuses across the United States shut down in protest of the Vietnam War and events at Kent State University.

9   Some 75,000–100,000 people gather in Washington, D.C., in a hastily organized protest against the U.S. invasion of Cambodia.

12   South Vietnamese vice president Nguyen Cao Ky reveals that on May 9, South Vietnamese and U.S. Navy warships began a blockade of some 100 miles of Cambodian coastline to prevent Communist resupply there by sea to fuel the Sihanouk Trail logistics network.

20   Some 100,000 people demonstrate in New York City in support of President Richard Nixon's Indochina policies.

21   South Vietnamese vice president Nguyen Cao Ky announces that ARVN troops will remain in Cambodia after U.S. troops withdraw from that country.

26   Operation MENU, the U.S. air strikes against Cambodian sanctuaries by B-52 bombers, ends.

June 1970

3   U.S. president Richard Nixon declares in a televised speech that the U.S. and ARVN invasion of Cambodia is the "most successful operation" of the war, enabling him to resume U.S. troop withdrawals.

7   Secretary of State William Rogers says that no U.S. troops will assist Lon Nol's Cambodian government even if its existence should be threatened by Communist forces.

24   The U.S. Senate repeals the Gulf of Tonkin Resolution in a vote of 81 to 10.

30   U.S. forces end two months of operations inside Cambodia. Some ARVN forces remain in Cambodia.
The U.S. Senate approves the Cooper-Church Amendment in a vote of 53 to 37. The amendment is aimed at limiting future presidential action in Cambodia by prohibiting military personnel in either combat or advisory roles or in direct air support of Cambodian forces. This step, the first limitation ever voted on regarding the powers of a president as commander in chief during a war, nevertheless allows strategic bombing.

September 1970

1   The U.S. Senate rejects by a vote of 55 to 39 the McGovern-Hatfield Amendment that sets a deadline of December 31, 1971, for the complete withdrawal of U.S. forces from South Vietnam.

17   The PRG delegation in Paris proposes an eight-point peace plan, calling for the complete U.S. withdrawal from South Vietnam by June 30, 1971, and a political settlement between the PRG and an interim South Vietnamese government that would exclude President Nguyen Van Thieu, Vice President Nguyen Cao Ky, and Premier Tran Thien Khiem.

26   A Gallup Poll finds that 55 percent of Americans surveyed favor the Senate Hatfield-McGovern Amendment to cut off funds for continued U.S. military activities in Indochina unless there is a declaration of war; 36 percent are opposed.

October 1970

7   U.S. president Richard Nixon announces a five-point proposal to end the war, based on a cease-fire in place in South Vietnam, Laos, and Cambodia. He proposes the eventual withdrawal of all U.S. forces, the unconditional release of POWs, and a political solution reflecting the will of the South Vietnamese people.

8   The Communist delegations in Paris reject U.S. president Richard Nixon's five-point proposal, insisting instead on unconditional withdrawal of U.S. forces from Indochina.

November 1970

5   U.S. officials report the lowest weekly toll of U.S. troops killed in action in five years (since October 25, 1965).

17   The U.S. Army court-martial of Lieutenant William L. Calley, charged with killing civilians at My Lai, begins at Fort Benning, Georgia.

20–21   U.S. forces raid the Son Tay POW compound 25 miles from Hanoi but find no U.S. personnel there.

December 1970

10   U.S. president Richard Nixon warns North Vietnamese leaders that he will resume bombing North Vietnam if fighting in South Vietnam intensifies.

31   There are some 334,600 U.S. military personnel in South Vietnam.

January 1971

1   The U.S. Congress forbids the use of U.S. ground troops in Laos and Cambodia although not the use of airpower there.

February 1971

8   ARVN forces invade southern Laos. Dubbed Operation LAM SON 719, its goal is the disruption of the Communist supply and infiltration network in southern Laos. The operation is supported by U.S. airpower and artillery, but no U.S. advisers are allowed to cross the border.

March 1971

6   A total of 120 U.S. Army helicopters, protected by helicopter gunships and U.S. Air Force fighter-bombers, lift two ARVN battalions into Tchepone, Laos, one of Operation LAM SON 719's key objectives.

24   ARVN Operation LAM SON 719 ends precipitously. The ARVN captures extensive quantities of Communist supplies but sustains heavy casualties, particularly among junior officers. More than 100 U.S. helicopters are also lost.

29   At Fort Benning, Georgia, a U.S. Army court finds Lieutenant William Calley guilty of the premeditated murder of 22 Vietnamese civilians at My Lai 4. He is sentenced to life in prison. His sentence is later reduced to 10 years in prison, and in 1974 he will be paroled.

April 1971

7   U.S. president Richard Nixon, in a televised address, states in reference to Operation LAM SON 719 that "Tonight I can report Vietnamization has succeeded." Nixon announces the withdrawal from South Vietnam of an additional 100,000 U.S. troops.

16   U.S. president Richard Nixon announces that a residual U.S. force will remain in South Vietnam as long as it is needed in order for the South Vietnamese "to develop the capacity for self-defense."

24   More than 200,000 people participate in a rally in Washington, D.C., to protest the Vietnam War.

May 1971

    The Lao Dong Party Politburo in Hanoi decides to launch an all-out offensive in South Vietnam in 1972 to seek a "decisive victory" and force the United States to "negotiate an end to the war from a posture of defeat" before the U.S. presidential election in November 1972.

31   In Paris, the U.S. delegation secretly proposes to the delegation from North Vietnam a deadline for the withdrawal of all American troops in return for the repatriation of all American POWs and a cease-fire.

June 1971

13   The *New York Times* begins publication of the Pentagon Papers, the heretofore secret Pentagon analysis of the three-decades-long U.S. involvement in Indochina.

26   The North Vietnamese government offers to release U.S. POWs at the same time as civilian prisoners and withdrawal of U.S. forces but insists that the United States also abandon its support of South Vietnamese president Nguyen Van Thieu.

30   The U.S. Supreme Court rules that the Pentagon Papers can be published.

July 1971

1   The PRG delegation to the Paris peace talks proposes a plan whereby it would negotiate with a neutral coalition government that excludes South Vietnamese president Nguyen Van Thieu, Vice President Nguyen Cao Ky, and Premier Tran Thien Khiem.

15   U.S. president Richard Nixon announces that he will visit the PRC.

August 1971

20   Retired ARVN general Duong Van Minh, the only opposition candidate in the South Vietnamese presidential election, withdraws from the race, charging that it is rigged in President Nguyen Van Thieu's favor.
Lon Nol's pro-American government in Cambodia launches Operation CHENLA II, a major military operation designed to seize control of the key provinces and road networks north of Phnom Penh. By the time the operation ends in failure in December, Vietnamese and Cambodian Communist forces have inflicted extremely heavy losses on Lon Nol's army.

October 1971

3   South Vietnamese president Nguyen Van Thieu is elected to another four-year term.

11   At the Paris peace talks, the American delegation proposes free elections in South Vietnam to be organized by an independent body representing all political forces in South Vietnam, with South Vietnamese president Nguyen Van Thieu resigning one month before the elections.

November 1971

12   U.S. president Richard Nixon announces the withdrawal from South Vietnam of an additional 45,000 U.S. troops.

December 1971

18   The PAVN launches a massive multidivisional offensive campaign to recapture the Plain of Jars.

26–30   U.S. aircraft resume the bombing of North Vietnam, mounting heavy attacks. Washington characterizes these as "protective reaction" strikes.

31   Some 156,800 U.S. military personnel are in South Vietnam.
During the two-year period from January 1, 1970, to December 31, 1971, 195,000 North Vietnamese troops have been sent down the Ho Chi Minh Trail into South Vietnam.

January 1972

2   President Richard Nixon announces that U.S. forces will continue to withdraw from South Vietnam but that

25,000–35,000 U.S. troops will remain until the release of all U.S. POWs.

13 President Richard Nixon announces that 70,000 U.S. troops will leave South Vietnam over the next three months, reducing U.S. troop strength there by May 1 to only 69,000 men.

25 U.S. president Richard Nixon reveals the details of National Security Advisor Henry Kissinger's secret trips to Paris and the text of the October 11, 1971, U.S. peace proposal.

26 Radio Hanoi announces that the North Vietnamese government has rejected the latest U.S. peace proposal.

February 1972

3 At the Paris peace talks, the PRG delegation presents a revised version of its July 1971 peace proposals, calling for the resignation of South Vietnamese president Nguyen Van Thieu in exchange for the immediate discussion of a political settlement, a specific date for the total U.S. withdrawal from South Vietnam and release of all military and civilian prisoners, and an end to Saigon's "warlike policy."

16 A Gallup Poll finds that 52 percent of those Americans interviewed approve of President Richard Nixon's handling of the war; 39 percent disapprove.

21–16 U.S. president Richard Nixon visits the PRC.

March 1972

23 Washington announces the indefinite suspension of the Paris peace talks until the Communist side agrees to "serious discussions" of predetermined issues.

30 PAVN forces launch their Nguyen Hue Campaign, known to the Americans as the Easter Offensive or the Spring Offensive, the largest Communist military action since 1968 that takes the form of a conventional military invasion of South Vietnam by 14 PAVN divisions and 26 separate regiments, including 120,000 troops and some 1,200 tanks and other armored vehicles. The focus of the offensive will be Quang Tri in northern South Vietnam, Kontum in the Central Highlands, and An Loc in Military Region III, just 65 miles north of Saigon.

April 1972

6 The United States resumes heavy bombing of North Vietnam.

7 The Battle of An Loc (April 7–June 18, 1972) begins in South Vietnam.

8 The Battle for Kontum begins in the Central Highlands.

15 U.S. aircraft resume bombing military targets in the vicinity of Hanoi and Haiphong, the first such strikes in four years.

15–20 Widespread anti–Vietnam War demonstrations occur across the United States.

22 Anti–Vietnam War demonstrators hold marches and rallies throughout the United States to protest the renewed U.S. bombing of North Vietnam.

26 U.S. president Richard Nixon announces the withdrawal of 20,000 U.S. troops from South Vietnam to take place during the next two months, reducing U.S. troop strength in South Vietnam by July 1 to 49,000 men.

27 The Paris peace talks resume.

30 U.S. president Richard Nixon warns that the North Vietnamese are "taking a very great risk if they continue their offensive in the South."

May 1972

1 ARVN forces and their U.S. advisers abandon Quang Tri, the northernmost provincial capital of South Vietnam, following five days of heavy fighting.

4 Citing a "complete lack of progress," the U.S. and South Vietnamese governments announce an indefinite halt to the Paris peace talks.

8 U.S. president Richard Nixon announces the mining of all North Vietnamese ports, the interdiction of rail and other communications, and air strikes against military targets in North Vietnam (Operation LINEBACKER) until the return of U.S. POWs and an internationally supervised cease-fire throughout Indochina.

8–12 A wave of antiwar protests takes place across the United States.

June 1972

U.S. Army general Fred Weyand replaces General Creighton Abrams as commander of MACV, with Abrams returning to Washington as army chief of staff.

28 U.S. president Richard Nixon announces that no more draftees will be sent to South Vietnam unless they volunteer for such duty. Additionally, he announces that another 10,000 troops will be withdrawn from South Vietnam by September 1, leaving a total of 39,000 U.S. military personnel there.

July 1972

13 Formal peace talks resume in Paris.

August 1972

27 In the heaviest bombing in four years, U.S. aircraft flatten North Vietnamese barracks near Hanoi and Haiphong as well as bridges along the railroad line to the border with China.

28 U.S. president Richard Nixon announces an end to the military draft by July 1973.

September 1972

11   At the Paris peace talks, the PRG delegation announces that any settlement in South Vietnam must reflect the "reality" of "two administrations, two armies and other political forces."

15   ARVN forces retake Quang Tri. Following the loss of Quang Tri, the North Vietnamese government decides to take advantage of the U.S. presidential campaign by making political concessions designed to entice President Richard Nixon to accept a negotiated peace agreement with the Communists before the November election in exchange for the total withdrawal of all U.S. forces from South Vietnam.

26–27   U.S. national security adviser Henry Kissinger holds additional secret talks in Paris with North Vietnamese representative Le Duc Tho.

October 1972

8   Le Duc Tho, the North Vietnamese representative to the Paris peace talks, presents a draft peace agreement proposing that two separate administrations remain in South Vietnam and negotiate a formula for general elections.

19–20   U.S. national security adviser Henry Kissinger meets in Saigon with South Vietnamese president Nguyen Van Thieu. Thieu opposes the draft treaty provisions that allow North Vietnamese troops to remain in place in South Vietnam.
U.S. president Richard Nixon announces a halt in the bombing of North Vietnam above the 20th Parallel. He also sends a message to North Vietnamese premier Pham Van Dong confirming that the peace agreement is complete and pledging that it will be signed by the two foreign ministers on October 31, but Nixon seeks clarification on several points.

23   A U.S. message to the North Vietnamese government in Hanoi requests further negotiations, citing difficulties raised by the South Vietnamese government.

26   Radio Hanoi announces that the secret talks in Paris have produced a tentative agreement to end the war.
U.S. national security adviser Henry Kissinger says that "Peace is at hand" and that only one additional meeting is needed to complete the agreement.

November 1972

1   South Vietnamese president Nguyen Van Thieu publicly objects to provisions in the draft peace agreement permitting North Vietnamese troops to remain in South Vietnam and providing for a three-segment "administrative structure" to preside over the political settlement and new elections. He denounces the draft agreement as "surrender of the South Vietnamese people to the Communists."

16   U.S. president Richard Nixon sends a letter to South Vietnamese president Nguyen Van Thieu pledging to press the North Vietnamese government for changes demanded by Thieu.

20–21   U.S. national security adviser Henry Kissinger and North Vietnamese representative to the Paris peace talks Le Duc Tho begin the 21st round of secret negotiations near Paris.

December 1972

13   The Paris peace talks deadlock.

16   U.S. national security adviser Henry Kissinger holds a press conference and publicly blames the North Vietnamese government for the breakdown in peace negotiations.

18–29   The United States renews the bombing of the Hanoi-Haiphong area (Operation LINEBACKER II, also known as the Christmas Bombings), now employing B-52 strategic bombers as well as fighter-bombers.

22   The U.S. government announces that the bombing of North Vietnam will continue until the North Vietnamese government agrees to negotiate "in a spirit of good will and in a constructive attitude."

30   The U.S. government announces that negotiations between National Security Advisor Henry Kissinger and North Vietnamese representative to the Paris peace talks Le Duc Tho will resume on January 2 and that U.S. bombing will cease north of the 20th Parallel of North Vietnam.

31   Approximately 24,000 U.S. military personnel remain in South Vietnam, the lowest total in almost eight years.

January 1973

8–12   U.S. national security adviser Henry Kissinger and North Vietnamese representative to the Paris peace talks Le Duc Tho resume their private negotiations in Paris.

15   Citing "progress" in the Paris peace negotiations, President Richard Nixon announces an end to all U.S. offensive military action against North Vietnam.

17   U.S. president Richard Nixon warns South Vietnamese president Nguyen Van Thieu in a private letter that his refusal to sign the agreement reached at Paris would render it impossible for the United States to continue assistance to South Vietnam.

20   U.S. president Richard Nixon sends an ultimatum to South Vietnamese president Nguyen Van Thieu regarding signing the peace agreement reached in Paris. Nixon demands an answer by January 21.

23   U.S. national security adviser Henry Kissinger and North Vietnamese representative Le Duc Tho initial the peace agreement in Paris. A cease-fire will commence on January 27, and all POWs will be released within 60 days.

27 Foreign ministers of the United States, North Vietnam, South Vietnam, and the PRG formally sign the two-party and four-party versions of the peace agreement.

28 At 8:00 a.m. Saigon time the cease-fire goes into effect, although both sides violate it. South Vietnamese forces continue to take back villages occupied by Communists in the two days before the cease-fire deadline.

30 In Washington, U.S. secretary of defense Melvin Laird announces an end to the military draft.

February 1973

1 In a secret letter to North Vietnamese premier Pham Van Dong, U.S. president Richard Nixon pledges to contribute to "postwar reconstruction in North Vietnam" in the "range of $3.25 billion" over five years.

12 The release of U.S. POWs begins in Hanoi.

16 The Four-Party Joint Military Commission set up by the Paris Peace Accords appeals to both sides in South Vietnam to respect the cease-fire and reaffirms prohibition on air combat missions.

17 The governments of the United States and North Vietnam issue a joint communique following a four-day visit by U.S. national security adviser Henry Kissinger to Hanoi. They announce an agreement to establish a Joint Economic Commission to develop economic relations, particularly the U.S. contribution to "healing the wounds of war" in North Vietnam.

21 A peace agreement is signed in Laos. The United States halts its bombing there.

March 1973

15 U.S. president Richard Nixon threatens to take unilateral action to force North Vietnam to suspend or reduce use of the Ho Chi Minh Trail network to move military equipment into South Vietnam.

28 U.S. president Richard Nixon again warns the leaders of North Vietnam that they "should have no doubt as to the consequences if they fail to comply with the [peace] agreement."

29 The last 67 American POWs held by North Vietnam leave Hanoi.
The last U.S. troops leave South Vietnam, and MACV headquarters is disestablished.

April 1973

3 A Joint communique from U.S. president Richard Nixon and South Vietnamese president Nguyen Van Thieu charges Communist violations of the cease-fire agreement by the infiltration of forces into South Vietnam and warns that continued violations "would call for appropriately vigorous reactions." U.S. secretary of defense Elliot Richardson says that the United States will not renew the bombing unless there is a "flagrant" violation of the agreement, such as a full-scale invasion of South Vietnam.

24 The U.S. and South Vietnamese governments publish texts of the North Vietnamese and U.S. notes accusing each other of violations of the peace agreement.

25 The South Vietnamese and PRG delegations to the talks in Paris offer incompatible proposals for a political settlement.

May 1973

10 The U.S. House of Representatives passes a second supplemental appropriations bill with an amendment deleting authorization for the transfer of $430 million by the Defense Department for the bombing of Cambodia. Another amendment prohibits the use of funds for combat activities in or over Cambodia by U.S. forces.

June 1973

9 Although U.S. national security adviser Henry Kissinger and North Vietnamese representative to the Paris peace talks Le Duc Tho negotiate a new agreement for implementation of the Paris Peace Accords, fighting in South Vietnam reaches its highest level since mid-February.

13 The signatories to the Paris Peace Accords issue a joint communiqué on its implementation that calls for a resumption of processes interrupted in April, including meetings of the U.S.–North Vietnamese Joint Economic Commission. National Security Advisor Henry Kissinger notes a "satisfactory conclusion" on points of concern to the United States.

20 Declassified Defense Department documents show that in seven years of war, 3.2 million tons of bombs have been dropped on South Vietnam, 2.1 million tons of bombs have been dropped on Laos, and 340,000 tons of bombs have been dropped on North Vietnam.

29 The U.S. House of Representatives passes a compromise bill with an August 15 deadline to halt all bombing of Cambodia and adds North Vietnam and South Vietnam to areas included in the ban on combat activities. President Richard Nixon reluctantly signs the bill into law on July 1.

July 1973

26 The U.S. House of Representatives passes the Foreign Assistance Bill after agreeing to an amendment prohibiting the use of authorized funds to aid in the reconstruction of North Vietnam unless specifically authorized by the Congress.

August 1973

14 The U.S. bombing of Cambodia ends, bringing to a halt all U.S. military activity in Indochina.

September 1973

10   The South Vietnamese government protests the construction of air bases in the PRG zone in South Vietnam on the basis that it has control of all air space over South Vietnam.

October 1973

1   South Vietnamese president Nguyen Van Thieu declares that the Communists are planning a spring 1974 "general offensive" and calls for "preemptive attacks" against them.

3–7   VNAF airplanes carry out heavy raids against the PRG zone in Tay Ninh Province, beginning a bombing campaign throughout Military Region III.

13   Following an extended debate that began in July, the 21st Plenum of the Central Committee of the Lao Dong Party in Hanoi approves a resolution stating that "revolutionary violence" is the only path to victory and instructing Communist forces in South Vietnam to conduct offensive operations in spite of the cease-fire agreement. The Central Committee's decision results in the drafting of a plan for another major offensive aimed at calling for the resolution authorizing the drafting of a plan aimed at achieving final victory in 1976.

15   The leaders of Communist forces in South Vietnam issue an order to begin counterattacks of South Vietnamese military bases and other points in retaliation for Saigon's earlier offensive operations.

16   U.S. secretary of state Henry Kissinger and North Vietnamese diplomat Le Duc Tho are awarded the Nobel Prize for Peace. Kissinger accepts, but Tho declines the award until such time as "peace is truly established" in Vietnam.

November 1973

7   The U.S. Congress overrides President Richard Nixon's veto of the War Powers Act limiting the president's power to commit U.S. armed forces abroad without congressional approval.

15   The U.S. Congress passes a Military Procurement Authorization bill that prohibits funds for any U.S. military action in any part of Indochina.

December 1973

31   Approximately 50 U.S. uniformed military personnel remain in South Vietnam.
Communist forces in South Vietnam total 380,000 full-time soldiers and 120,000 part-time guerrillas. More than 100,000 North Vietnamese troops with full equipment have been sent down the Ho Chi Minh Trail to fight in South Vietnam in defiance of the provisions of the January 1973 Paris Peace Accords.

January 1974

4   South Vietnamese president Nguyen Van Thieu announces that "as far as the armed forces are concerned, I can tell you the war has restarted."

20   Naval battle between Republic of Vietnam Navy (VNN, South Vietnam Navy) and Chinese Navy ships in which one large VNN ship is sunk and more than 50 Vietnamese sailors are killed. Following the battle, Chinese forces seize and occupy the Paracel Islands in the South China Sea, claiming them as Chinese territory. The United States takes no action in response to the Chinese attack.

February 1974

South Vietnamese forces launch major offensive operations against PRG-controlled areas in Quang Ngai Province and the Cu Chi–Trang Bang area west of the city of Saigon.

March 1974

The Central Military Committee of the North Vietnamese Lao Dong Party passes a resolution that if the United States and South Vietnam "do not implement the agreement," it must "destroy the enemy and liberate the South." This month sees the heaviest fighting in South Vietnam since the cease-fire.

22   In the last major political initiative by either side in the war, the PRG offers to hold elections within one year of the establishment of a National Council of National Reconciliation and Concord.

April 1974

4   The U.S. House of Representatives rejects the Richard Nixon administration request to increase military aid to South Vietnam.

11   The ARVN evacuates the Ranger base at Tong Le Chan, surrounded by Communist troops since the cease-fire.

12   South Vietnamese representatives withdraw from the Paris talks on political reconciliation with representatives of the PRG.

16   The South Vietnamese government withdraws diplomatic "privileges and immunities" of the PRG delegation to the Joint Military Commission.

May 1974

10   The PRG delegation walks out of the Joint Military Commission, refusing to return until the commission's privileges and immunities are restored.

13   The PRG delegation suspends its participation in the Paris political talks, citing the earlier suspension of the conference by South Vietnam, withdrawal of diplomatic privileges for the PRG delegation in Saigon, and what it styles South Vietnamese "land grabbing" operations.

July–August 1974

Communist forces regain major areas of Quang Nam and Quang Ngai provinces in their first major offensive in the South Vietnamese lowlands.

August 1974

6   In a vote of 233 to 157, the U.S. House of Representatives cuts military aid appropriations for South Vietnam from $1 billion to $700 million.

9   Under threat of impeachment for the Watergate Scandal, Richard Nixon resigns the presidency of the United States. He is succeeded by Vice President Gerald R. Ford.

20   The U.S. Congress agrees on a reduction in aid to South Vietnam from $1 billion to $700 million.

September 1974

28   In the northern provinces of South Vietnam, North Vietnamese troops, after a series of successful pushes in July and August, close to within 15 miles of Hue.

October 1974

The Communist political and military leadership in Vietnam concludes that the United States is unlikely to intervene and could not save the regime of President Nguyen Van Thieu even if it did intervene.

8   The PRG calls on public figures and organizations in South Vietnam to work for the overthrow of the Nguyen Van Thieu government and establishment of a new regime in Saigon.

December 1974

13   PAVN general Tran Van Tra and COSVN head and political commissar for Communist forces in South Vietnam Pham Hung order the 7th Division and the newly formed 3rd Division to attack and seize Phuoc Long Province north of Saigon.

31   Approximately 50 U.S. uniformed military personnel remain in South Vietnam.

January 1975

1   The Khmer Rouge (Red Khmer, Cambodian Communists) begin a final offensive against the besieged Cambodian capital of Phnom Penh.

6   Communist forces take Phuoc Binh, the capital of Phuoc Long Province.

8   Communist forces complete the seizure of Phuoc Long Province. The United States does not intervene with airpower.

February 1975

26   A bipartisan U.S. congressional delegation arrives in Saigon to make a firsthand assessment of the situation.

March 1975

10   Communist forces attack Ban Me Thuot in the Central Highlands, opening their Spring Offensive.

12   Ban Me Thuot falls to Communist forces.
The U.S. Congress turns down President Gerald Ford's request for $300 million in emergency military aid for South Vietnam.

14   South Vietnamese president Nguyen Van Thieu orders the precipitous withdrawal of ARVN forces from the Central Highlands.

15   ARVN forces begin a retreat from Kontum and Pleiku that soon becomes a debacle. Tens of thousands of troops and massive amounts of military equipment and weapons, including hundreds of armored vehicles and artillery pieces, are lost during the retreat to the coast.

19   Communist forces capture Quang Tri City following the withdrawal of the South Vietnamese Marine Division from the province.

21   The PAVN II Corps launches an offensive against Hue City. Following contradictory orders from Saigon about whether or not Hue should be defended, the Army of the Republic of Vietnam's (ARVN, South Vietnamese Army) attempt to withdraw south to Da Nang turns into rout and the ARVN 1st Division disintegrates.

25   The North Vietnamese Politburo revises its timetable for ending the war, deciding that Saigon should be taken before the beginning of the mid-May rainy season. Communist commander of the offensive General Van Tien Dung asks permission to call this the Ho Chi Minh Campaign, in the hope of achieving victory before Ho's May 19 birthday anniversary. The Politburo agrees.

26   The city of Hue falls to Communist troops. Da Nang, flooded with refugees, is already under rocket attack.

30   The city of Da Nang falls to Communist forces. North Vietnamese leaders order the commander of their forces in South Vietnam, General Van Tien Dung, to push toward Saigon in the Ho Chi Minh Campaign.

April 1975

1   Cambodian president Lon Nol abdicates and flees Cambodia.
Nha Trang City, the headquarters of the ARVN II Corps, is evacuated, meaning that the entire northern half of South Vietnam is now in Communist hands.

3–26   Operation BABYLIFT evacuates more than 3,300 Amerasian infants and children from Vietnam.

4   A U.S. Air Force C-5A Galaxy evacuating children under Operation BABYLIFT crashes on takeoff from Tan Son Nhut, killing 153 of 328 on board.

9–22   The Battle for Xuan Loc, capital of Long Khanh Province and strategically important to the defense of Saigon, takes place. The ARVN fights well in the battle, its only major stand of the Communist offensive.

10   U.S. president Gerald Ford requests an additional $722 million in military aid to South Vietnam. Congress refuses.

12   Operation EAGLE PULL, the evacuation of U.S. personnel from Phnom Penh, Cambodia, occurs.

16   U.S. president Gerald Ford orders all "unneeded" Americans to leave South Vietnam. The ARVN Phan Rang Air Base, a brigade of paratroopers, and several infantry regiments are overrun by a North Vietnamese armored column. Two ARVN generals and one U.S. government official are captured following this attack.

17   Khmer Rouge forces take the Cambodian capital of Phnom Penh.

21   South Vietnamese president Nguyen Van Thieu resigns in favor of Vice President Tran Van Huong.

26   The final Communist assault on Saigon begins as 270,000 Communist combat troops organized into five corps advance toward the city from all sides.

28   South Vietnamese president Tran Van Huong resigns in favor of Duong Van Minh, who helped overthrow President Ngo Dinh Diem in 1963. Five captured VNAF jets flown by North Vietnamese pilots bomb Tan Son Nhut Air Base on the outskirts of Saigon.

29   After Saigon's Tan Son Nhut Airfield comes under heavy artillery attack, U.S. ambassador to South Vietnam Graham Martin orders a full U.S. evacuation from Saigon. Fearing its negative impact on morale, he has delayed too long. The operation, known as FREQUENT WIND, takes place in chaotic circumstances as helicopters and U.S. marines evacuate 395 Americans and 4,475 Vietnamese. Only a minority of Vietnamese thought to be at risk are evacuated or manage to escape by other means.

30   Communist forces capture Saigon, for all practical purposes bringing the Vietnam War to a close.

May 1975

Communist Pathet Lao forces seize control of the coalition government of Laos and eliminate the last remaining anti-Communist military forces, completing the Communist takeover of all of Indochina.

1   Communist forces complete the occupation of the Mekong Delta, eliminating the last remaining pockets of resistance of ARVN forces.

12–15   Khmer Rouge naval vessels capture the U.S. merchant ship *Mayaguez* off the Cambodian coast, prompting a U.S. military operation to rescue the ship and its crew. Thirty-eight U.S. servicemen are killed and several U.S. helicopters are shot down by Khmer Rouge forces before the ship and its civilian crew are recovered.

May–June 1975

After Khmer Rouge forces seize Vietnamese territory along the border in the Mekong Delta as well as several offshore islands in the Gulf of Thailand, PAVN ground, naval, and air forces launch attacks to recapture the lost territory. The last offshore island is not retaken until June 14. These battles set the stage for full-scale warfare between Vietnam and Cambodia that breaks out several years later, culminating in the Vietnamese overthrow of the Khmer Rouge regime and the 10-year Vietnamese occupation of Cambodia (1979–1989).

July 1976

2   The reunification of Vietnam is completed with the proclamation of the Socialist Republic of Vietnam (SRV).

SPENCER C. TUCKER AND MERLE L. PRIBBENOW II

Glossary

AA — Antiaircraft artillery (also AAA).

ACAV — Armored Cavalry Assault Vehicle. M113 armored personnel carrier modified with two additional 7.62-millimeter (mm) machine guns and shielding for its main .50-caliber machine gun.

Agent Orange — The most widely used of the several color-coded herbicides employed in the defoliation of Vietnamese forests and jungles.

AK-47 — Russian-designed assault rifle. Automvat Kalashinikov (AK), manufactured throughout the Communist bloc, is considered to be one of the most successful infantry weapons of the twentieth century. The AK-47 was used extensively by Communist forces in the Republic of Vietnam (RVN, South Vietnam) from 1965 on.

AID — *See* **USAID**.

American — U.S. 23rd Infantry Division.

AO — Area of operations. Tactical operations area for a specific combat unit.

AOA — Amphibious objective area.

AOI — Area of interest.

AOR — Area of responsibility.

ap — Vietnamese word for "hamlet."

APC — Armored Personnel Carrier.

APERS — Antipersonnel ammunition. *See* **Beehive ammunition**.

APO — Army Post Office.

ARA — Aerial rocket artillery.

A-rations — Hot food prepared by cooks and served in mess halls or flown out to the troops in the field.

Arc Light — Code name for B-52 bombing program within South Vietnam.

ARG/SLF — Amphibious Ready Group/Special Landing Force.

ARVN — Army of the Republic of Vietnam, the pro-American army of South Vietnam.

ASEAN — The Association of South East Asian Nations, founded in 1967 to oppose the threat of feared Communist expansionism. Members include Brunei, Myanmar (Burma), the Philippines, Indonesia, Laos, Malaysia, Singapore, Thailand, and Vietnam (admitted in July 1995).

attack aircraft — Aircraft employed for the delivery of air-to-ground ordnance.

AWCC — Air Warning Control Center, established to broadcast warnings of artillery fire to friendly aircraft in the vicinity.

AWOL — Absent without leave.

B-40 — People's Army of Vietnam (PAVN, North Vietnamese Army) and Viet Cong (VC) term used to refer to the Soviet-designed RPG-2, a rocket-propelled grenade. *See also* **RPG**.

B-41	PAVN and VC term used to refer to the Soviet-designed RPG-7, a rocket-propelled grenade. *See also* **RPG**.
Ba Muoi Ba	A Vietnamese beer, named for its trademark, the number "33."
base area	Area used for the assembly of troops and logistical support.
battalion	An army and marine corps organizational unit of three or more companies, normally commanded by a lieutenant colonel.
battery	The basic army or marine corps artillery firing unit of approximately 100 soldiers and equipped with two to six guns, commanded by a captain.
BCT	Brigade Combat Team.
BDA	Bomb damage assessment.
beehive ammunition	Antipersonnel ammunition for howitzers and recoilless rifles used by U.S. forces. Beehive ammunition was designed to be used against a massed infantry attack and delivered thousands of small metal arrowlike projectiles (fléchettes) instead of shrapnel that exploded in a 30-degree arc.
berm	Built-up dirt wall used as a defensive barrier against an attack.
Big Red One	U.S. 1st Infantry Division.
bird dog	A very small light single-engine fixed-wing observation aircraft (U.S. Air Force designation, O-1).
Black Horse	U.S. 11th Armored Cavalry Regiment.
BLT	Battalion landing team. Marine amphibious group.
BMEO	Brigade Marine l'Extrême Orient (French Far East Naval Brigade), the first French riverine unit.
boonies	Slang term meaning "the field," "enemy territory," "Indian country," or "Apache country."
brigade	For the U.S. Army in Vietnam, a division was grouped into three brigades, each made up of two to four battalions and commanded by a colonel. The number of soldiers would vary according to the purpose of a particular mission. There were also separate U.S. infantry brigades. In the ARVN, only the Airborne Division and the Marine Division used the brigade system of organization. While People's Army of Vietnam (PAVN, North Vietnamese Army) divisions were always organized into regiments, the PAVN did have a small number of independent brigades.
bug out	Slang term meaning to run from the enemy. The term denotes cowardly action.
CAC	Combined Action Companies. Organized by the U.S. Marine Corps beginning in August 1965, CACs were composed of a Vietnamese Popular Forces company (three platoons) and a U.S. Marine Corps rifle platoon. *See also* **CAP**.
cai tang	Vietnamese practice of reburial. Traditionally and especially before 1954, about three to five years after an individual died and was buried in a temporary grave, the individual's relatives would exhume the remains, remove whatever flesh might still remain, wash the bones with scented alcohol, and rebury the remains in a permanent grave. The remains might also be moved to another grave, at a site selected so as to bring success and luck to the dead person's descendants.
CAP	Combined Action Platoon. Organized in February 1967 by the U.S. Marine Corps to wage the "other war." The CAP combined a U.S. Marine Corps rifle squad of 14 men and 1 U.S. Navy corpsman with 3 10-man Popular Force (PF) militia squads and a 5-man platoon headquarters into a combined platoon of 50 American and Vietnamese soldiers to provide security at the local level and initiate civic action programs as part of the pacification effort. *See also* **CAC**.
CAP	Combined Action Program. U.S. Marine Corps program designed to integrate personnel with local security forces at the hamlet and village levels as part of the counterinsurgency program. *See also* **CAC**.
CAP	Combat Air Patrol of fighter aircraft designed to provide protection against enemy fighters striking one's own attack or bomber aircraft. CAPS were also often flown over U.S. 7th Fleet aircraft carriers when they were operating deep inside the Gulf of Tonkin, off the coast of North Vietnam.
Capital Military District	For the ARVN, the area of Saigon and its immediate environs, including Gia Dinh Province and the Rung Sac Special Zone.
CAR	Combat Action Ribbon (U.S. Navy and U.S. Marine Corps).

CAS	Close air support.
CBU	Cluster Bomb Unit.
CDEC	Combined Document Exploitation Center. Joint U.S.-ARVN unit that specialized in translating, analyzing, and exploiting captured VC and PAVN documents. Located on the outskirts of Saigon.
CG	Commanding general.
Charlie	One of the many names for Communist troops; military phonetic for the letter "c"; also a shortened form of Victor Charlie (Viet Cong).
chicken-plate	Bullet- and fragmentation-resistant breastplate worn by helicopter crews.
CHICOM	Chinese Communist; also Chinese Communist-made weaponry.
Chieu Hoi	Open Arms Program, developed to attract Communist deserters.
CHNAVADVGRP	Chief, Naval Advisory Group Vietnam (U.S. Navy).
chogey	A Korean War slang term transferred to Vietnam and meaning to leave an area (e.g., "cut a chogey").
CIA	U.S. Central Intelligence Agency.
CIB	Combat Infantryman Badge, U.S. Army.
CIDG	Civilian Irregular Defense Group. Originally a CIA project that combined self-defense functions with economic programs to win the support of the civilian population, CIDG units were recruited, paid, and advised by U.S. Army Special Forces personnel working alongside Luc Luong Dac Biet (South Vietnamese Special Forces) officers.
CINCPAC	Commander in chief, Pacific Command. Commander of U.S. forces in the Pacific, including Southeast Asia.
CIO	South Vietnamese Central Intelligence Organization.
civic action	Civil affairs program designed to win the loyalty of civilians as part of general pacification programs.
claymore	An antipersonnel mine that produced a directional fan-shaped pattern of fragments. The American Claymore mine was the M18 antipersonnel mine. Light, easily transported, and highly directional, the Claymore mine sprayed out more than 100 steel balls in a 40-degree arc. The M18 could be hand detonated or emplaced to fire electronically (command detonated). The VC and the PAVN also had their own locally manufactured Claymore mines, which they called DH (*dinh huong,* meaning "directional") mines.
clear and hold	A military strategy used in the pacification program. In the clear phase, friendly troops would surround, capture, and search an area to clear it of Communist forces. When the area was cleared, other troops (usually South Vietnamese forces) would be stationed in the area to defend it while the original troops moved on to clear another area.
CMB	Combat Medical Badge (U.S. Army).
CMIC	Combined Military Interrogation Center. Joint U.S.-ARVN interrogation center specializing in the interrogation of VC and PAVN military personnel, including both prisoners of war and defectors, who were believed to have knowledge of information of significant value. The CMIC was located on the outskirts of Saigon.
CNC	Cuc Nghien Cuu (Research Department). North Vietnam's military intelligence organization.
CNO	Chief of naval operations (U.S.).
CO	Commanding officer.
CO	Conscientious objector.
company	A basic military unit of two or more platoons. In the U.S. armed forces (both the U.S. Army and the U.S. Marine Corps), permanent companies usually had alphabetic names (e.g., Alpha Company, Bravo Company, Charlie Company). Vietnamese companies (including ARVN, VC, and PAVN) normally had numerical designations (e.g., 1st Company, 4th Company, 812th Company, etc.).
COMUSMACV	Commander, U.S. Military Assistance Command, Vietnam.
CONUS	Continental United States.
cordon and search	Operations to surround and then search a specific area.
CORDS	Civilian Operations and Revolutionary Development Support; also Civil Operations and Rural Development Support. CORDS, an organization that directed the work of all U.S. civilian agencies engaged in pacification work in South Vietnam, fell under the military chain of command. CORDS was the

successor to the Office of Civilian Operations (OCO). *Note:* The reason for the two different names for CORDS is that the South Vietnamese government refused to accept the American wish to use the word "revolutionary" in the name of the new pacification program. The South Vietnamese called the program "rural development," while the U.S. Government, for political reasons, insisted on calling it "revolutionary development."

corps A military organization consisting of two or more divisions plus combat support and logistics units. In the ARVN table of organization, but not in the U.S. or PAVN systems, a corps was responsible for a military region.

COSVN Central Office for South Vietnam (Trung Uong Cuc Mien Nam), the highest-level Vietnamese Communist Party (then called the Lao Dong Party, or the Communist Workers' Party) headquarters in South Vietnam. Acting as the direct representative of the Communist Party Central Committee in Hanoi, the COSVN directed all aspects of the war in South Vietnam (military, political, governmental, economic, and social). From 1964 through to the end of the war in 1975, the COSVN was always headed by a member of the Communist Party Politburo (General Nguyen Chi Thanh from 1964 to 1967 and Pham Hung from 1967 to 1975).

CP Command post.

C-rats C-rations.

CSA Chief of staff of the U.S. Army.

CTZ Corps tactical zone, a military region. The ARVN divided Vietnam into four military regions, I to IV.

CUPP U.S. Marine Corps–Regional Forces/Popular Forces Combined Unit Pacification Program.

DEROS Date of estimated return from overseas service, the date eligible to return to the United States.

deuce-and-a-half Slang term for the ubiquitous American 2.5-ton military truck.

DIA Defense Intelligence Agency.

dien cai dau (dinky dau) Vietnamese for "crazy," widely used by GIs and by the Vietnamese to describe Americans in Vietnam.

Dinassauts French integrated tactical units composed of naval and army forces for riverine warfare during the Indochina War.

dink Derogatory slang term used by American GIs to refer to Vietnamese, derived from a Vietnamese term for crazy, *dien cai dau,* which GIs pronounced as "dinky dau".

DIOC District Intelligence Operations Center. A joint South Vietnamese–U.S. organization set up as part of the Phoenix Program that coordinated all intelligence regarding VC activities in a district.

DIVARTY Division artillery.

division An organizational and tactical unit that in the U.S. armed forces consisted of 15,000–20,000 men organized into two to three brigades, used for sustained combat. ARVN divisions were slightly smaller and were made up of three to four infantry regiments. VC/PAVN divisions were considerably smaller (8,000–9,000 in theory but in practice usually around 5,000–6,000 men) and were organized into two to three infantry regiments.

DKB PAVN and VC term used to refer to the Soviet-designed single-tube 122-mm rocket.

DKZ PAVN and VC term for recoilless rifles.

DMZ Demilitarized zone. Established in the 1954 Geneva Accords to provisionally divide North Vietnam and South Vietnam at the 17th Parallel, pending elections that were to have been held in 1956. Demarcation line just below the 17th Parallel following the Ben Hai River.

doc lap Vietnamese term for "independence." The South Vietnamese Presidential Palace, South Vietnam's equivalent to the U.S. White House, was called Dinh Doc Lap, or Independence Palace.

DOD Department of Defense.

donut dollies Nickname for workers in the Supplemental Recreation Activities Overseas (SRAO) program in Vietnam, which provided a variety of recreational activities for American troops. The women were so-named because they often dispensed donuts and coffee to the troops, especially in the field. The women also assisted in hospitals and provided games and conversation in the field.

door gunner	A soldier who fired from the open door of a helicopter, a hazardous position usually filled by volunteers.
dragon ship	AC-47 gunship (also called "Puff the Magic Dragon" and "Spooky").
DRV	Democratic Republic of Vietnam (North Vietnam), established on September 2, 1945.
duster	M-42 tracked vehicle mounted with twin 40-mm antiaircraft guns.
dustoff	Helicopter evacuation of wounded.
DZ	Drop zone for airborne forces.
Eagle Flight	A special U.S. helicopter assault force used to observe Communist positions, react to emergencies, and raid and ambush.
ECM	Electronic countermeasures designed to defeat enemy radar systems.
ELINT	Electronic intelligence. Intelligence derived from the collection and analysis of enemy electronic signals (principally enemy radars).
FAC	Forward air controller. Low-flying spotter planes identified Communist positions and called the FAC, who in turn ordered air strikes against these positions.
FADAC	The U.S. Army's first digital fire direction computer.
FANK	Forces Armées Nationale Khmer (Khmer National Armed Forces), the Cambodian armed forces of the Lon Nol government.
FDC	Fire Direction Center.
FDO	Fire direction officer.
field force	U.S. Corps-sized commands subordinate to MACV.
firebase	A small artillery base, usually temporary, used as a base from which to launch patrols and to support ground operations.
firefight	A brief and violent exchange of small-arms fire between two opposing units rather than combat action between two larger forces during an assault.
First Team	U.S. 1st Cavalry Division (Airmobile). Also referred to as "Aircav," "1st Horse," or "1st Aircav."
FISCOORD	Fire-support coordinator for artillery at the company, battalion, or brigade level. Usually the senior artilleryman present who prepared fire plans and integrated all indirect-fire weapons.

Fishhook	Area of Cambodia jutting into South Vietnam along the northern borders of Tay Ninh and Binh Long Province, northwest of Saigon. Location of numerous Communist headquarters, base camps, and supply caches.
flashback	A strong recurrence of memory, usually a reaction from post-traumatic stress disorder (PTSD).
flight	A basic air force organizational and tactical unit; a group of three to five aircraft used together in a common mission.
FMF	Fleet Marine Force.
FMFPAC	Fleet Marine Force, Pacific Command.
FO	Forward observer. A field artillery lieutenant assigned to an infantry or armor company for the purposes of calling for and adjusting artillery fire on a target.
FOB	Forward operating base.
Force Recon	The U.S. Marine Corps' elite reconnaissance element.
four-deuce	Slang term for the American 4.2-inch heavy mortar.
FPO	Fleet Post Office; U.S. Navy address/zip code.
frag	Hand grenade, fragmentation. Also to kill or attempt to kill one's own officers or noncommissioned officers, usually with a fragmentation grenade.
FRAGO	Fragmentary order, the standard type of order issued to U.S. troops conducting combat operations, called a "fragmentary order" because it was short and did not cover the full range of elements that were prescribed in the U.S. Army Field Manual for military orders.
freedom birds	Nickname given to aircraft that carried U.S. soldiers back home to the United States after their tour of duty in Southeast Asia was over.
free fire zone	An area in which targets could be engaged at any time with any and all available weapons systems.
fresh meat	New replacements or new arrivals in Vietnam.
FSB	Fire-support base.
FUNK	Front Unité Nationale Kampuchea (National United Front of Cambodia). The Khmer Rouge–controlled front organization headed by Cambodia's Prince Sihanouk following the

coup that overthrew Sihanouk's government in March 1970. *See* **Khmer Rouge.**

G-1	The deputy chief of staff for personnel at the divisional, corps, field forces, or Department of the Army levels.
G-2	The deputy chief of staff for intelligence at the divisional, corps, field forces, or Department of the Army levels.
G-3	The deputy chief of staff for operations at the divisional, corps, field forces, or Department of the Army levels.
G-4	The deputy chief of staff for logistics at the divisional, corps, field forces, or Department of the Army levels.
GCMA	Groupement de commandos mixtes aéroportés. French Special Forces that conducted long-range penetration missions and clandestine raids into Viet Minh territory during the Indochina War.
GM	Groupe mobile. French military unit equivalent to a U.S. regimental combat team or a light separate brigade.
going downtown	Flying an air strike mission against the Hanoi area.
GPES	Ground Proximity Extraction System. Used during air resupply to extract loads from transport aircraft, as during the siege of Khe Sanh. A long hook attached to cargo in a C-130 would catch an arrester wire on the runway, pulling the cargo from the plane.
Green Berets	Nickname for U.S. Army Special Forces.
group	A command unit of two or more battalions used for combat service and support and usually commanded by a colonel. Also an artillery unit consisting of three or more battalions commanded by a colonel used for general support within a designated area.
grunt	U.S. nickname for an infantry soldier. Also "Boonie Rat," "11 Bang-Bang," "11 Bush," "Bush Buster."
gunship	An armed helicopter or converted fixed-wing cargo plane with loitering ability to provide aerial support to ground troops.
GVN	Government of Vietnam. U.S. term for the Republic of Vietnam (RVN, South Vietnam).
HA	High-angle fire with an elevation greater than 800 mils (45 degrees). All mortars fired HA only. Field artillery howitzers normally fired

	at HA when necessary to clear an intervening mask or attack a target in defilade.
HE	High-explosive artillery shell or bomb.
Headhunters	Nickname for the 1st Squadron, 9th Cavalry, 1st Cavalry Division (Airmobile), also known as the "Blues." The element of the 1st Cavalry Division designated to perform reconnaissance missions. Their mission was to fix and hold Communist forces until the rest of the division could engage.
hearts and minds	In 1965 President Lyndon B. Johnson said, "So we must be ready to fight in Vietnam, but the ultimate victory will depend on the hearts and minds of the people who actually live out there." The U.S. government tried to win the loyalty and trust of the Vietnamese through various pacification programs that included providing security from VC harassment and civic improvements with the objective of encouraging villagers to fight against the Communists.
HEAT	High explosive, antitank.
H&I	Harassment and interdiction fire. Random rounds fired at suspected or likely enemy locations and routes.
HOB	Height of burst. That height above the ground at which a mortar or artillery round detonated, depending on the setting of the mechanical time fuse or the proximity fuse.
Ho Chi Minh Trail	Network of roads and trails leading from North Vietnam through Laos and Cambodia to South Vietnam.
Hoi Chanh	A Communist defector under the Chieu Hoi Program.
hootch	Slang for a soldier's shelter. Also used to refer to the thatched-roof huts in which Vietnamese rural peasants usually lived.
hop tac	Vietnamese for "cooperation." Operation HOP TAC was the unsuccessful 1964 pacification program concentrated around Saigon.
HQ	Headquarters.
Huey	Slang for the UH-1 series of helicopters.
IADS	Integrated air defense system.
ICC	International Control Commission. Established by the 1954 Geneva Conference to supervise implementation of the Geneva Accords, the ICC consisted of representatives of three countries that were not

participants in the conflict but nonetheless represented different points of view: India (neutralist), Canada (Western), and Poland (Communist).

ICCS International Commission of Control and Supervision. The ICCS was an international military peacekeeping force established by the 1973 Paris Peace Accords to supervise the cease-fire in South Vietnam. The ICCS was originally made up of military personnel from Poland, Hungary, Indonesia, and Canada. Canada withdrew from the ICCS after only a few months and was replaced by Iran.

ICM Improved conventional munitions. Artillery rounds that burst in the air and showered the target area with dozens of bomblets called submunitions. Also known by the slang term "firecracker."

Igloo White Code name for the electronic intelligence collection program that monitored, collated, and analyzed data collected by electronic sensors planted along the Ho Chi Minh Trail in Laos.

ILLUM Illumination rounds fired by either artillery or mortars.

IPSD Infantry Platoon (Scout Dog).

IVS International Voluntary Services. A private nonprofit organization that served as a model for the Peace Corps that first came to South Vietnam in 1957. Funded primarily by USAID, support also came from the South Vietnamese government during the early years. IVS workers were required to study Vietnamese and received instruction in Vietnamese culture. Individuals signed up for a two-year stay in-country, with assignments at the village level ranging from agricultural development to the teaching of English. The IVS saw its function as humanitarian and divorced from USAID political objectives. The South Vietnamese government ceased approving IVS projects in 1971.

J-1 The director of personnel on a joint staff such as MACV, the Pacific Command, or the Department of Defense Joint Staff in Washington.

J-2 The director of intelligence on a joint staff such as MACV, the Pacific Command, or the Department of Defense Joint Staff in Washington.

J-3 The director of operations on a joint staff such as MACV, the Pacific Command, or the Department of Defense Joint Staff in Washington.

J-4 The director of logistics on a joint staff such as MACV, the Pacific Command, or the Department of Defense Joint Staff in Washington.

JCS Joint Chiefs of Staff. Heads of the U.S. military, consisting of the chairman, the U.S. Army chief of staff, the chief of naval operations, the U.S. Air Force chief of staff, and the U.S. Marine Corps commandant (ex officio). The JCS advises the president, the secretary of defense, and the National Security Council on military matters.

JGS Joint General Staff. The national-level headquarters of the Army of the Republic of Vietnam (ARVN, South Vietnamese Army). The Chief of the ARVN JGS was, in theory, the commander of all ARVN forces (including army, navy, air force, and territorial forces), although in practice the South Vietnamese president (especially Ngo Dinh Diem and Nguyen Van Thieu) frequently bypassed the JGS and issued orders directly to subordinate military commanders.

Jolly Green Giant U.S. Air Force HH-3 and HH-53 heavy rescue helicopters.

JUSPAO Joint U.S. Public Affairs Office, created in 1965 to take charge of both relations with the news media and psychological warfare operations.

JUWTF Joint Unconventional Warfare Task Force, composed of unconventional warfare personnel from the U.S. Air Force, the U.S. Army, the U.S. Marine Corps, and the U.S. Navy.

Khmer Krom Cambodian word meaning "lower Khmer" and used to refer to ethnic Cambodian residents of South Vietnam's Mekong Delta.

Khmer Rouge Literally "Red Khmer." The Cambodian Communist organization headed by Pol Pot, Ieng Sary, and Khieu Samphan.

KIA Killed in action.

Killer Junior A close-in artillery technique designed to defend firebases against enemy ground attack using mechanical time-fused projectiles set to burst approximately 30 feet off the ground at ranges of 200 to 1,000 meters. Primarily employed by 155-mm artillery and used by U.S. firebases against ground assaults.

Kit Carson Scouts Former Viet Cong (VC) or People's Army of Vietnam (PAVN, North Vietnamese Army) soldiers who were used as scouts by U.S. units.

KKK Khmer Kampuchea Krom. The KKK was an anti-Communist faction loosely allied with the Khmer Serai and seeking automony for Khmer Krom people living in the Mekong Delta of South Vietnam in return for military services. During the 1960s Khmer Krom soldiers made up the bulk of many territorial force and irregular units of the Army of the Republic of Vietnam (ARVN, South Vietnamese Army).

KPNLF Non-Communist Khmer People's Liberation Front in Cambodia, organized following the Vietnamese invasion of Cambodia in 1979 to oppose the Vietnamese occupation of Cambodia.

laager Slang, also lager. A Boer War term that denotes preparing a defensive position, usually at night. This term was more common in U.S. armored or mechanized infantry units. *See also* **NDP**.

LAW Light antitank weapon (M-72). A LAW was a shoulder-fired U.S.-made 66-mm antitank rocket fired from a collapsible, disposable launch tube.

lima sites Rough primitive airstrips in Laos used by the United States to support covert military operations.

LLDB Luc Luong Dac Biet (LLDB, South Vietnamese Special Forces).

LOC Line of communication.

Local force Viet Cong (VC) territorial forces, organized at the province and district levels.

LOH Light observation helicopter (pronounced *loach*).

LP Listening post. Small outposts, usually consisting of a squad or less, placed outside of a defensive perimeter to provide early warning of approaching enemy forces.

LPLA Lao People's Liberation Army, the military arm of the Communist Pathet Lao.

LZ Landing zone for helicopters.

M-14 A 7.62-mm semiautomatic rifle with wooden stock. The M-14 was the standard U.S. infantry weapon during 1957–1967. *See also* **M-16**.

M-16 A 5.65-mm fully automatic U.S. assault rifle, primary an infantry weapon of the war. The M-16 incurred great controversy, as early models tended to jam in combat. Troops initially preferred the M-14.

M-60 Standard American light machine gun firing the 7.62-mm North Atlantic Treaty Organization (NATO) standard round. The M-60 fired from fixed mounts, tripods, or a bipod attached to the barrel.

M-79 U.S. shoulder-fired 40-mm grenade launcher. Also called the "Thumper" or the "Elephant Gun."

MAAG Military Assistance and Advisory Group.

MAC Military Airlift Command.

MACV Military Assistance Command, Vietnam.

MACV-SOG MACV Studies and Observation Group (unconventional warfare units).

mad minute Used by U.S. forces in an effort to force or "trip" a VC or PAVN ambush or assault. Just prior to daybreak, all forces within a position would open fire into the area surrounding the position, utilizing all weapons.

MAF Marine Amphibious Force.

Main force Viet Cong (VC) and People's Army of Vietnam (PAVN, North Vietnamese Army) regular combat units.

MARKET TIME Codeword for interdiction efforts against North Vietnamese seaborne infiltration.

MATS Military Air Transport Service.

MAW Military Air Wing.

MEB Marine Expeditionary Brigade.

mechanized infantry Combat infantry units trained and equipped to be carried into battle in armored personnel carriers.

MEDCAP Medical Civic Action Program that brought military doctors and medics to rural villages and hamlets.

medevac Acronym combining the words "medical" and "evacuation"; term applied to the movement of casualties from the battlefield to more secure locations for immediate medical attention.

MIA	Missing in action.
Montagnard	French term for indigenous Vietnamese mountain people. Often shortened to "Yard."
MOS	Military Occupational Specialty.
MP	Military Police.
MRF	Mobile Riverine Force.
MSC	Military Sealift Command.
MSS	Military Security Service (South Vietnam), an ARVN intelligence and security agency.
Muscle Shoals	Codeword for electronic sensor operations in the DMZ.
MUST	Medical Unit Self-contained, Transportable.
NAG	Naval Advisory Group. NAG was the U.S. Navy Section in MAAG Vietnam until May 1964. In April 1965 NAG became an operational naval command.
napalm	Incendiary weapon used by both France and the United States in Vietnam. A jellylike substance, napalm adheres to a substance while it burns.
NATO	North Atlantic Treaty Organization.
NDP	Night defensive position.
NLF	National Liberation Front, officially the National Front for the Liberation of South Vietnam, also known as the Viet Cong (VC).
no-fire line	U.S. fire-control measure. The no-fire line was the designated point on a map beyond which no indirect-fire weapons or air assets could be employed without permission from the sector commander.
NSA	National Security Agency, the U.S. agency responsible for the centralized coordination, direction, and performance of American signals intelligence.
nug	Short for "nugget," a new arrival or newly arrived replacement in Vietnam.
Nung	Chinese ethnic group. Nungs often served as mercenaries for the French and later the United States.
NVA	North Vietnamese Army. U.S. designation for the People's Army of Vietnam (PAVN, North Vietnamese Army).
OCO	Office of Civilian Operations. The OCO was the predecessor to the Civilian Operations and Revolutionary Development Support (CORDS). The OCO organized all U.S. civilian agencies in South Vietnam under the jurisdiction of the U.S. embassy.
OP	Observation post. A position used for either reconnaissance or for artillery forward observers to call in fire.
opcon	Operation control. For example, the 196th Light Infantry Brigade, Americal Division, was under the Opcon of the 3rd Marines.
OPLAN	Operations plan.
OPORD	Operations order.
OSS	U.S. Office of Strategic Services, forerunner of the CIA.
P-38	GI slang designation for the C-ration can opener.
PAO	Public Affairs officer.
paramilitary	Militia-type forces that operate separately from regular military formations.
Parrot's Beak	The area of Cambodia jutting deep into South Vietnam west of Saigon on the northern edge of the Mekong Delta and bordering the South Vietnamese provinces of Tay Ninh, Hau Nghia, Long An, and Kien Tuong.
pathfinder	Airborne and airmobile term for specially trained soldiers inserted ahead of the main body of troops to mark a drop zone or a landing zone.
PAVN	People's Army of Vietnam (North Vietnamese Army). NVA was the acronym used by U.S. forces for the PAVN during the war.
PBR	Patrol boat, riverine. A small heavily armed naval vessel used by the U.S. and South Vietnamese navies to patrol the rivers of South Vietnam, especially in the Mekong Delta.
PCF	Patrol craft, fast. A small heavily armed coastal patrol boat used by the U.S. and South Vietnamese navies to patrol South Vietnam's coastal waters. *See also* MARKET TIME.
PCS	Permanent change of station.
PD	Point detonating fuse for artillery and mortar rounds.
phougas	Drums of jellied gasoline placed around a fortification that could be used as a defensive weapon (also called "foo-gas").
PIRAZ	Positive Identification Radar Advisory Zone. PIRAZ ships were U.S. destroyers, frigates, and cruisers operating in the Gulf of Tonkin to provide support for allied war planes.

platoon	The basic infantry unit of 22–40 men (two or more squads) commanded by a lieutenant.
POL	Petroleum, oil, and lubricants.
POW	Prisoner of war.
PRC-25	The standard field radio carried by American radio telephone operators (RTOs).
PRU	Provincial Reconnaissance Unit. PRUs were irregular armed units funded and advised by the CIA and under the direct authority of the province chief. Operating as part of the Phoenix Program, the PRUs were responsible for targeting and capturing or eliminating key members of the Viet Cong infrastructure (VCI).
PSDF	People's Self-Defense Forces. Paramilitary South Vietnamese local militia consisting of part-time soldiers, most of whom were young students, older men, and others who were not of military age or were not qualified for military service. The PSDF was formed after the 1968 Tet Offensive.
PSYOPS	Psychological operations.
PSYWAR	Psychological warfare.
Puff (Puff the Magic Dragon)	Nickname for AC-47 aircraft mounting a bank of 7.62-mm electrically driven Gatling guns.
punji stake	A sharpened bamboo stake covered with feces or poison and placed at the bottom of a pit, under water, or along a trail to be stepped on by troops. The punji stake was an effective physical and psychological weapon.
PX	Post Exchange (U.S. Army). In the U.S. Air Force and the U.S. Navy, it was referred to as the Base Exchange (BX) or the Naval Exchange (NEX), respectively.
PZ	Pickup zone for helicopter landing and extraction of personnel.
rallier	An individual defecting from the other side.
RCT	Regimental Combat Team.
RD	Revolutionary Development; also Rural Development. The term for a South Vietnamese pacification program that was begun under U.S. auspices in the mid-1960s. The RD Training Center at Vung Tau trained RD cadre teams that were sent out to operate in rural villages. The program was directed by South Vietnam's Ministry of Revolutionary Development (called by the South Vietnamese the Ministry of Rural Development) and funded by the Civilian Operations and Revolutionary Development Support (CORDS).
RDF	Radio direction finding. RDF was the use of electronic equipment to pinpoint the location of enemy radio transmitters. RDF provided essential information about the command structure and unit deployment of the opposing side. RDF and associated signals intelligence activities were utilized by all major Indochina antagonists.
recon	Reconnaissance patrol, used to secure information about enemy troop strengths, movements, etc.; also called "recce."
redleg	U.S. slang for artillerymen (from red, the color of the artillery).
regiment	Once a basic organizational unit in the U.S. Army, larger than a battalion, smaller than a brigade; now only used for armored cavalry units. In the U.S. Marine Corps, a regiment is a basic organizational unit of three infantry battalions. The regiment, made up of three battalions plus smaller combat support and logistics units, was also a standard military organizational unit in the Army of the Republic of Vietnam (ARVN, South Vietnamese Army), the Viet Cong (VC), and the People's Army of Vietnam (PAVN, North Vietnamese Army).
REMF	A vulgar slang term used to refer to military personnel assigned to noncombat duties in the rear. "RE" meant "Rear Echelon."
restricted fire line	U.S. fire control measure. The restricted fire line was a designated point on a map beyond which targets could be engaged only with indirect-fire weapons or air assets with permission from tactical headquarters or when direct contact was in progress.
RFs/PFs	South Vietnamese Regional Forces and Popular Forces (also known as "Ruff-Puffs"). RFs/PFs were locally recruited South Vietnamese forces not counted as part of the regular military establishment. The RFs were organized in company and battalion size units, some in battle groups of two or three battalions. RFs were the organic forces of the provinces and were under the command and control of the provincial military headquarters. Armed with light weapons, they were equipped and

trained and held ranks similar to the regular army. The PFs belonged to the villages and operated in separate platoons. They were assigned to defend their villages and prevent infiltration by the Viet Cong (VC).

RIF Reconnaissance-in-force. RIF was a sweep by forces to locate the enemy.

Rome Plow A massive bulldozer used for clearing forest, jungle, and brush. The Rome Plow was manufactured by the Rome (Georgia) Caterpillar Company.

RON Remain overnight.

RPG Rocket-propelled grenade (Soviet-designed antitank grenade launcher). The VC and PAVN were equipped with the RPG-2 (B-40) and the larger and more modern RPG-7 (B-41). *See also* **B-40** and **B-41**.

RR Recoilless rifle.

R&R Rest and recuperation.

RT Reconnaissance team.

RTAFB Royal Thai Air Force Base.

RTO Radio telephone operator.

Ruff-Puffs U.S. term for South Vietnamese Regional Forces and Popular Forces (RFs/PFs).

RVN Republic of Vietnam (South Vietnam).

RVNAF Republic of Vietnam Armed Forces (South Vietnamese Armed Forces).

S-1 The administration and personnel staff officer at the battalion, regimental, group, and brigade levels.

S-2 The intelligence staff officer at the battalion, regimental, group, and brigade levels.

S-3 The operations staff officer at the battalion, regimental, group, and brigade levels.

S-4 The logistics staff officer at the battalion, regimental, group, and brigade levels.

S-5 The civil affairs staff officer at the battalion, regimental, group, and brigade levels.

SAC U.S. Strategic Air Command.

Saigon commando The slang derogatory term given by combat troops to soldiers assigned to rear areas. Often soldiers assigned to these billets wore the popular "boonie hats" and camouflage uniforms denied to frontline forces. *See also* **REMF**.

Saigon tea Nonalcoholic drink (soda, cold tea, or colored scented water) that GIs bought for Vietnamese bar girls at exorbitant prices. The girls made a commission from the bar on each Saigon tea that a GI bought for them.

SAM Surface-to-air missile.

sapper Specially trained assault engineers and demolition experts skilled at penetrating enemy defenses to destroy equipment and fortifications. Sappers, often a part of high-risk missions, were organized and deployed in units ranging from squads up to battalion- or regimental-sized groups. During the Vietnam War the term "sapper" always referred to Communist troops. Today, however, both the U.S. Army and the U.S. Marine Corps use the term for their specially trained assault engineers.

SAR Search and rescue.

SCT Sea Commando Team.

Seabees Naval construction engineers (from CB, for Construction Battalion).

SEAL Sea, air, and land. SEAL is the designation used to refer to elite U.S. Navy commandos.

search and destroy Operations designed to search out enemy units and/or logistical installations and then destroy them, superseded by "clear and hold."

SEPES Service des Etudes Politiques et Sociales (Political and Social Research Agency). The SEPES was the South Vietnamese intelligence, secret police, and covert political propaganda agency under the regime of President Ngo Dien Diem.

SHINING BRASS Code name for U.S.-led ground reconnaissance operations into Laos (October 1965–March 1967).

short rounds Artillery or bombs that fall short, sometimes striking noncombatants or friendly forces.

short-timer A person coming to the end of his assignment in Vietnam.

SKS Soviet-designed semiautomatic rifle. The SKS was standard issue for Viet Cong (VC) and People's Army of Vietnam (PAVN, North Vietnamese Army) infantry forces from 1965 onward. Often called the "CKC" because the Cyrillic letters for "SKS" stamped on the rifle by the Soviet manufacturer looked like the Roman letters "CKC."

SLAM	Search, locate, annihilate, and monitor.
SLF	Special Landing Force. Each 2,000-man SLF was composed of a U.S. Marine Corps Battalion Landing Team (BLT) and a helicopter squadron.
slick	A transport helicopter lacking external guns and rockets, the slick got its name from its slick exterior.
Slope	Derogatory slang term used by American GIs to refer to Vietnamese.
SOD	Special Operations Detachment.
SOG	Studies and Observations Group. Operating out of MACV, this organization carried out clandestine operations, such as Road Watch Teams in Laos, in conjunction with the CIA.
sortie	One mission by one aircraft.
SP	Self-propelled (artillery).
special operations	Military missions requiring specialized or elite units.
Spookie	GI slang term for the AC-47 gunship. *See also* **Puff (Puff the Magic Dragon)**.
squad	A basic fighting unit of 8–10 men commanded by a sergeant and grouped for drill, inspection, and other purposes. A squad is part of a platoon.
squadron	A battalion-sized U.S. Army air or armored cavalry unit commanded by a lieutenant colonel. In the U.S. Navy and the U.S. Air Force, a squadron is two or more flights of aircraft.
SRV	Socialist Republic of Vietnam. Vietnam reunified after 1975 as the SRV.
striker	A Civilian Irregular Defense Group (CIDG) soldier, usually an ethnic Montagnard or Khmer Krom.
TAC	Tactical Air Command.
tacair	Tactical air support.
TAOR	Tactical area of responsibility. TAOR is the area for operations by a specific military unit.
TDY	Temporary duty. TDY is usually a six-months assignment.
Tet	Vietnamese lunar new year.
TFS	Tactical Fighter Squadron.
TFW	Tactical Fighter Wing.
Thunder Road	South Vietnam's heavily fought-over Highway 13.
thunder run	Combat movement of an armored column up or down an enemy-contested road.
toe poppers	Slang term for Communist antipersonnel mines designed to maim (break a foot or blow off toes).
tour of duty	The 365 days that a soldier in the U.S. Army or the 13 months that a soldier in the U.S. Marine Corps spent in Vietnam.
Track	Slang term for an armored vehicle.
Tunnel rat	A U.S. soldier, usually slight in stature, detailed to go into tunnels armed with only a pistol and a flashlight. This was extremely hazardous duty, as the men frequently encountered booby traps, poisonous snakes, and flooded tunnels. Psychological stress was profound.
USAF	United States Air Force.
USAID	United States Agency for International Development, which administered U.S. aid to South Vietnam.
USIA	United States Information Agency, the agency responsible for disseminating information about the United States overseas.
USMC	United States Marine Corps.
USOM	United States Operations Mission. Field agency in South Vietnam that administered the USAID program there.
USN	U.S. Navy.
VC	Viet Cong, derived from Cong San Viet Nam, which means Vietnamese Communist. VC was the term used by the U.S. military to designate Communist forces in South Vietnam (the North Vietnamese military or People's Army of Vietnam [PAVN, North Vietnamese Army] being known as NVA). To Vietnamese, VC were everyone who was in or served the Communist military and public security, wherever and of whatever rank.
VCI	Viet Cong infrastructure, the political cadre of the National Front for the Liberation of South Vietnam (National Liberation Front [NLF]) within the South Vietnamese villages.
Victor Charlie	Phonetic alphabetization for Viet Cong (VC). *See also* **Charlie**.
Viet Minh	Common name for the Viet Nam Doc Lap Dong Minh Hoi, the Communist front

organization founded in 1941 to resist French colonial rule and occupying Japanese forces. The Viet Minh fought the French in the Indochina War.

VNAF Republic of Vietnam Air Force (South Vietnamese Air Force).

VNN Republic of Vietnam Navy (South Vietnamese Navy).

VT Variable time. A proximity fuse for field artillery designed to produce a 65-foot height of burst without having to adjust the height of burst by firing.

VVAW Vietnam Veterans Against the War.

White Mice Derogatory term for the South Vietnamese National Police. The term was derived from the white uniforms that the South Vietnamese police wore.

WIA Wounded in action.

Willy Pete White phosphorus shell round used for screening, signaling, incendiary action, and illumination. Also known as Wilson Pickett (WP).

wing A major organizational U.S. Air Force unit in which aircraft fly in a side-by-side formation. A wing includes one primary mission group plus support.

Wise Men A select group of senior advisers to President Lyndon Johnson.

The World Slang term for the continental United States, also called "land of the big PX."

XO Executive officer.

Yankee Station An operating area off the Vietnamese coast in the South China Sea used by the U.S. Navy's Seventh Fleet Attack Carrier Striking Force (Task Force 77). Air strikes against North Vietnam were launched from Yankee Station, which was also the code name for the Gulf of Tonkin.

Yard U.S. GI slang term for a Montagnard.

ZOA Zone of operation.

David Coffey, Stanley S. McGowen, Julius A. Menzoff, Merle L. Pribbenow II, Harve Saal, Spencer C. Tucker, James H. Willbanks, Sandra Wittman, and David T. Zabecki

Selected Bibliography

Ahern, Thomas L. *Vietnam Declassified: The CIA and Counterinsurgency.* Lexington: University Press of Kentucky, 2009.

Allison, William Thomas. *Military Justice: The Rule of Law in an American War.* Lawrence: University Press of Kansas, 2007.

Alvarez, Everett, Jr., and Anthony S. Pitch. *Chained Eagle.* New York: Dell, 1989.

Anderson, Charles B. *The Grunts.* San Rafael, CA: Presidio, 1976.

Anderson, David L., ed. *The Human Tradition in the Vietnam Era.* Wilmington, DE: Scholarly Resources, 2000.

Anderson, David L., ed. *Shadows on the White House: Presidents and the Vietnam War, 1945–1975.* Lawrence: University of Kansas Press, 1993.

Anderson, David L., and John Ernst, eds. *The War That Never Ends: New Perspectives on the Vietnam War.* Lexington: University Press of Kentucky, 2007.

Anderson, William C. *Bat-21.* Englewood Cliffs, NJ: Prentice Hall, 1980.

Andradé, Dale. *America's Last Vietnam Battle: Halting Hanoi's 1972 Easter Offensive.* Lawrence: University Press of Kansas, 2001.

Andradé, Dale. *Ashes to Ashes: The Phoenix Program and the Vietnam War.* Lanham, MD: Lexington Books, 1990.

Andradé, Dale. *Spies and Commandos: How America Lost the Secret War in North Vietnam.* Lawrence: University Press of Kansas, 2000.

Andradé, Dale. *Trial by Fire: The 1972 Easter Offensive, America's Last Vietnam Battle.* New York: Hippocrene Books, 1995.

Appy, Christian G. *Working Class War: American Combat Soldiers & Vietnam.* Chapel Hill: University of North Carolina Press, 1993.

Arlen, Michael. *Living-Room War.* 1969; reprint, New York: Syracuse University Press, 1997.

Arnett, Peter. *Live from the Battle Field: From Vietnam to Baghdad, 35 Years in the World's War Zones.* New York: Simon and Schuster, 1994.

Balaban, John. *Remembering Heaven's Face: A Moral Witness in Vietnam.* New York: Poseidon, 1991.

Ball, George W. *The Past Has Another Pattern.* New York: Norton, 1982.

Baritz, Loren. *Backfire: A History of How American Culture Led Us into Vietnam and Made Us Fight the Way We Did.* New York: Morrow, 1985.

Barrett, David M. *Uncertain Warriors: Lyndon Johnson and His Vietnam Advisers.* Lawrence: University Press of Kansas, 1993.

Bass, Thomas A. *Vietnamerica: The War Comes Home.* New York: Soho Press, 1996.

Beidler, Philip D. *American Literature and the Experience of Vietnam.* Athens: University of Georgia Press, 1982.

Belknap, Michael R. *The Vietnam War on Trial: The My Lai Massacre and the Court-Martial of Lieutenant Calley.* Lawrence: University Press of Kansas, 2002.

Bergerud, Eric M. *The Dynamics of Defeat. The Vietnam War in Hau Nghia Province.* Boulder, CO: Westview, 1991.

Bergerud, Eric M. *Red Thunder, Tropic Lightning: The World of a Combat Division in Vietnam.* Boulder, CO: Westview, 1993.

Berman, Larry. *Lyndon Johnson's War: The Road to Stalemate in Vietnam.* New York: Norton, 1989.

Berman, Larry. *No Peace, No Honor: Nixon, Kissinger, and Betrayal in Vietnam.* New York: Free Press, 2001.

Berman, Larry. *Perfect Spy: The Incredible Double Life of Pham Xuan An,* Time *Magazine Reporter and Vietnamese Communist Agent.* New York: HarperCollins, 2007.

Berman, Larry. *Planning a Tragedy: The Americanization of the War in Vietnam.* New York: Norton, 1982.

Berman, William C. *William Fulbright and the Vietnam War: The Dissent of a Political Realist.* Kent, OH: Kent State University Press, 1988.

Bey, Douglas. *Wizard 6, a Combat Psychiatrist in Vietnam.* College Station: Texas A&M University Press, 2006.

Bigeard, General Marcel. *Pour une parcelle de gloire.* Paris: Plon, 1976.

Bigler, Philip. *Hostile Fire: The Life and Death of First Lieutenant Sharon Lane.* Arlington, VA: Vandamere, 1996.

Billings-Yun, Melanie. *Decision against War: Eisenhower and Dien Bien Phu, 1954.* New York: Columbia University Press, 1988.

Bilton, Michael, and Kevin Sim. *Four Hours in My Lai.* New York: Penguin, 1992.

Blair, Anne E. *Lodge in Vietnam: A Patriot Abroad.* New Haven, CT: Yale University Press, 1995.

Bodard, Lucien. *The Quicksand War: Prelude to Vietnam.* Boston: Little, Brown, 1967.

Botkin, Richard. *Ride the Thunder: A Vietnam War Story of Honor and Triumph.* Los Angeles: WND Books, 2009.

Bowman, John S, ed. *The World Almanac of the Vietnam War.* New York: Pharos Books, 1985.

Brace, Ernest C. *A Code to Keep: The True Story of America's Longest-Held Civilian Prisoner of War.* New York: St. Martin's, 1988.

Bradley, Mark Philip. *Vietnam At War.* Oxford: Oxford University Press, 2009.

Bradley, Mark Philip, and Marilyn B. Young, eds. *Making Sense of the Vietnam Wars: Local, National and Transnational Perspectives.* New York: Oxford University Press, 2008.

Braestrup, Peter. *Big Story: How the American Press and Television Reported and Interpreted the Crisis of Tet 1968 in Vietnam and Washington.* Novato, CA: Presidio, 1994.

Brigham, Robert K. *ARVN: Life and Death in the South Vietnamese Army.* Lawrence: University Press of Kansas, 2006.

Broughton, Jack. *Going Downtown: The War against Hanoi and Washington.* New York: Pocket Books, 1990.

Browne, Malcolm. *Muddy Boots and Red Socks: A Reporter's Life.* New York: Crown, 1993.

Browne, Malcolm. *The New Face of War.* Indianapolis: Bobbs-Merrill, 1965.

Bryan, C. D. B. *Friendly Fire.* New York: Putnam, 1976.

Bui Diem, with David Chanoff. *In the Jaws of History.* Boston: Houghton, Mifflin, 1987.

Burchett, Wilfred G. *The Furtive War: The United States in Vietnam and Laos.* New York: International Publishers, 1963.

Burkett, B. G., and Glenna Whitley. *Stolen Valor: How the Vietnam Generation Was Robbed of Its Heroes and Its History.* Dallas, TX: Verity, 1998.

Butler, David. *The Fall of Saigon: Scenes from the Sudden End of a Long War.* New York: Simon and Schuster, 1985.

Buttinger, Joseph. *The Smaller Dragon: A Political History of Vietnam.* New York: Praeger, 1958.

Buzzanco, Robert. *Masters of War: Military Dissent and Politics in the Vietnam Era.* New York: Cambridge University Press, 1996.

Cable, Larry E. *Conflict of Myths: The Development of American Counterinsurgency Doctrine and the Vietnam War.* New York: New York University Press, 1988.

Cady, John F. *The Roots of French Imperialism in Eastern Asia.* Ithaca, NY: Cornell University Press, 1954.

Cao Van Vien and Dong Van Khuyen. *Reflections on the Vietnam War.* Indochina Monographs. Washington, DC: U.S. Army Center of Military History, 1980.

Capps, Walter H., ed. *The Vietnam Reader.* New York: Routledge, 1991.

Caputo, Philip. *A Rumor of War.* New York: Holt, Rinehart and Winston, 1977.

Castle, Timothy N. *One Day Too Long: Top Secret Site 85 and the Bombing of North Vietnam.* New York: Columbia University Press, 1999.

Catton, Philip E. *Diem's Final Failure: Prelude to America's War in Vietnam.* Lawrence: University of Kansas Press, 2002.

Chandler, David P. *The Tragedy of Cambodian History: Politics, War, and Revolution since 1945.* New Haven, CT: Yale University Press, 1991.

Chanoff, David, and Doan Van Toai. *Portrait of the Enemy.* New York: Random House, 1986.

Chapuis, Oscar M. *A History of Vietnam: From Hong Bang to Tu Duc.* Westport, CT: Greenwood, 1995.

Chapuis, Oscar M. *The Last Emperors of Vietnam: From Tu Duc to Bao Dai.* Westport, CT: Greenwood, 2000.

Charlton, Michael, and Anthony Moncrieff. *Many Reasons Why: The American Involvement in Vietnam.* New York: Hill and Wang, 1978.

Charton, Pierre. *Indochine 1950: La Tragédie de l'évacuation de Cao Bang.* Paris: Société de production littéraire, 1975.

Chen, King C. *China's War with Vietnam, 1979: Issues, Decisions, and Implications.* Stanford, CA: Hoover Institute Press, 1987.

Chomsky, Noam. *Rethinking Camelot: JFK, the Vietnam War, and U.S. Political Culture.* Boston: South End, 1993.

Clayton, Anthony. *Three Marshals of France: Leadership After Trauma.* London: Brassey's, 1992.

Clifford, Clark, with David Holbrooke. *Counsel to the President: A Memoir.* New York: Random House, 1991.

Clodfelter, Mark. *The Limits of Air Power: The American Bombing of North Vietnam.* New York: Free Press, 1989.

Clodfelter, Mark. *Vietnam in Military Statistics: A History of the Indochina Wars, 1772–1991.* Jefferson, NC: McFarland, 1995.

Coan, James P. *Con Thien: The Hill of Angels.* Tuscaloosa: University of Alabama Press, 2004.

Coedès, Georges. *The Making of South East Asia.* Translated by H. M. Wright. Berkeley: University of California Press, 1966.

Colby, William. *Honorable Men: My Life in the CIA*. New York: Simon and Schuster, 1978.

Colby, William, with James McCargar. *Lost Victory: A Firsthand Account of America's Sixteen-Year Involvement in Vietnam*. Chicago: Contemporary Books, 1989.

Coleman, J. D. *Pleiku: The Dawn of Helicopter Warfare in Vietnam*. New York: St. Martin's, 1988.

Conboy, Kenneth J., and James Morrison. *Shadow War: The CIA's Secret War in Laos*. Boulder, CO: Paladin, 1995.

Corfield, Justin. *The History of Vietnam*. Westport, CT: Greenwood, 2008.

Cosmas, Graham A., Terrance P. Murray, William R. Melton, and Jack Shulimson. *U.S. Marines in Vietnam: Vietnamization and Redeployment, 1970–1971*. Washington, DC: History and Museums Division, Headquarters, U.S. Marine Corps, 1986.

Cummings, Dennis J. *The Men behind the Trident: Seal Team One in Vietnam*. Annapolis, MD: Naval Institute Press, 1997.

Currey, Cecil B. *Edward Lansdale: The Unquiet American*. Boston: Houghton Mifflin, 1988.

Currey, Cecil B. *Victory at Any Cost: The Genius of Viet Nam's General Vo Nguyen Giap*. Washington, DC: Brassey's, 1997.

Cutler, Thomas J. *Brown Water, Black Berets: Coastal and Riverine Warfare in Vietnam*. Annapolis, MD: Naval Institute Press, 1988.

Dalloz, Jacques. *The War in Indo-China, 1945–54*. Savage, MD: Barnes and Noble, 1990.

Dang Van Viet. *Highway 4: The Border Campaign (1947–1950)*. Hanoi: Foreign Languages Publishing House, 1990.

Davidson, Phillip A. *Vietnam at War: The History, 1946–1975*. Novato, CA: Presidio, 1988.

Dawson, Alan. *55 Days: The Fall of South Vietnam*. Englewood Cliffs, NJ: Prentice Hall, 1977.

Deac, Wilfred P. *Road to the Killing Fields: The Cambodian War of 1970–1975*. College Station: Texas A&M University Press, 1997.

DeBenedetti, Charles, with Charles Chatfield. *An American Ordeal: The Antiwar Movement of the Vietnam Era*. Syracuse, NY: Syracuse University Press, 1990.

De Folin, Jacques. *Indochine, 1940–1955: La fin d'un rêve*. Paris: Perrin, 1993.

DeForest, Orrin, and David Chanoff. *Slow Burn: The Rise and Bitter Fall of American Intelligence in Vietnam*. New York: Simon and Schuster, 1990.

De Gaulle, Charles. *The War Memoirs of Charles de Gaulle*, Vol. 3, *Salvation, 1944–1946*. Translated by Richard Howard. New York: Simon and Schuster, 1960.

Denton, Jeremiah A., with Ed Brandt. *When Hell Was in Session*. New York: Reader's Digest, 1976.

Devillers, Philippe. *Histoire du Vietnam de 1940 à 1952*. Paris: Editions de Seuil, 1952.

Dillard, Walter Scott. *Sixty Days to Peace: Implementing the Paris Peace Accords, Vietnam 1973*. Washington, DC: National Defense University, 1982.

Dommen, Arthur J. *Conflict in Laos: The Politics of Neutralization*. Rev. ed. New York: Praeger, 1971.

Dommen, Arthur J. *The Indochinese Experience of the French and Americans: Nationalism and Communism in Cambodia, Laos, and Vietnam*. Bloomington: Indiana University Press, 2001.

Dong Van Khuyen. *The Republic of Vietnam Armed Forces*. Washington, DC: U.S. Army Center of Military History, 1980.

Donovan, David. *Once a Warrior King: Memories of an Officer in Vietnam*. New York: McGraw-Hill, 1985.

Dooley, Thomas A. *Deliver Us from Evil: The Story of Viet Nam's Flight to Freedom*. New York: Farrar, Straus and Cudahy, 1956.

Duiker, William J. *The Communist Road to Power in Vietnam*. 2nd ed. Boulder, CO: Westview, 1996.

Duiker, William J. *Historical Dictionary of Vietnam*. Metuchen, NJ: Scarecrow, 1989.

Duiker, William J. *Ho Chi Minh: A Life*. New York: Hyperion, 2000.

Duiker, William J. *The Rise of Nationalism in Vietnam, 1900–1911*. Ithaca, NY: Cornell University Press, 1976.

Duiker, William J. *Vietnam: Revolution in Transition*. 2nd ed. Boulder, CO: Westview, 1995.

Duncanson, Dennis J. *Government and Revolution in Vietnam*. New York: Oxford University Press, 1968.

Ebert, James R. *A Life in a Year: The American Infantryman in Vietnam, 1965–1972*. Novato, CA: Presidio, 1993.

Edelman, Bernard, ed. *Dear America: Letters Home from Vietnam*. New York: Norton, 1985.

Ellsberg, Daniel. *Papers on the War*. New York: Simon and Schuster, 1972.

Ellsberg, Daniel. *Secrets: A Memoir on Vietnam and the Pentagon Papers*. New York: Viking Penguin, 2002.

Elwood-Akers, Virginia. *Women War Correspondents in the Vietnam War, 1961–1975*. Metuchen, NJ: Scarecrow, 1988.

Emerson, Gloria. *Winners and Losers: Battles, Retreats, Gains, Losses, and Ruins from the Vietnam War*. New York: Random House, 1976.

Engelmann, Larry. *Tears before the Rain: An Oral History of the Fall of South Vietnam*. New York: Oxford University Press, 1990.

Esper, George, and the Associated Press. *The Eyewitness History of the Vietnam War, 1961–1975*. New York: Ballantine Books, 1983.

Fall, Bernard B. *Hell in a Very Small Place: The Siege of Dien Bien Phu*. New York: Lippincott, 1966.

Fall, Bernard B. *Last Reflections on a War*. Garden City, NY: Doubleday, 1967.

Fall, Bernard B. *Street without Joy: The French Debacle in Indochina*. Rev. ed. Mechanicsburg, PA: Stackpole Books, 1994.

Fall, Bernard B. *The Two Viet-Nams: A Political and Military Analysis*. 2nd rev. ed. New York: Praeger, 1967.

Fall, Bernard B. *Viet-Nam Witness, 1953–66*. New York: Praeger, 1966.

Fall, Dorothy. *Bernard Fall: Memories of a Soldier-Scholar*. Washington, DC: Potomac Books, 2006.

FitzGerald, Frances. *Fire in the Lake: The Vietnamese and the Americans in Vietnam.* Boston: Little, Brown, 1972.

Ford, Harold P. *CIA and the Policymakers: Three Episodes, 1962–1968.* Washington, DC: CIA Center for the Study of Intelligence, 1988.

Franklin, H. Bruce. *M.I.A. or Mythmaking in America: How and Why Belief in Live POWs Has Possessed a Nation.* New Brunswick, NJ: Rutgers University Press, 1993.

Frankum, Ronald B., Jr. *Like Rolling Thunder: The Air War in Vietnam, 1964–1975.* New York: Rowman and Littlefield, 2005.

Freeman, James M. *Hearts of Sorrow: Vietnamese-American Lives.* Stanford, CA: Stanford University Press, 1989.

Frier, Gilles. *Les trois guerres d'Indochine.* Lyon: Presses Universitaires de Lyon, 1993.

Fry, Joseph A. *Debating Vietnam: Fulbright, Stennis, and Their Senate Hearings.* New York: Rowman and Littlefield, 2006.

Gabriel, Richard A., and Paul L. Savage. *Crisis in Command: Mismanagement in the Army.* New York: Hill and Wang, 1978.

Gaiduk, Ilya V. *The Soviet Union and the Vietnam War.* Chicago, IL: Ivan R. Dee, 1996.

Gargus, John. *The Son Tay Raid: American POWs in Vietnam Were Not Forgotten.* College Station: Texas A&M University Press, 2007.

Garland, Albert N., ed. *A Distant Challenge: The U.S. Infantryman in Vietnam, 1967–1972.* Nashville: Battery, 1983.

Garnier, Francis. *Voyage d'exploration en Indo-Chine, 1866–88.* Paris: Editions la Découverte, 1985.

Gole, Henry G. *General William E. DePuy: Preparing the Army for Modern War.* Lexington: University Press of Kentucky, 2008.

Glasser, Ronald J. *365 Days.* New York: G. Braziller, 1971.

Glenn, Russell W. *Reading Athena's Dance Card: Men against Fire in Vietnam.* Annapolis, MD: Naval Institute Press, 2000.

Goff, Stanley, and Robert Sanders, with Clark Smith. *Brothers: Black Soldiers in the Nam.* Novato, CA: Presidio, 1982.

Goldman, Peter, and Tony Fuller. *Charlie Company: What Vietnam Did to Us.* New York: Morrow, 1983.

Goldstein, Gordon M. *Lessons in Disaster: McGeorge Bundy and the Path to War in Vietnam.* New York: Times Books, 2008.

Gottlieb, Sherry Gershon. *Hell No, We Won't Go! Resisting the Draft During the Vietnam War.* New York: Viking, 1991.

Gould, Lewis L. *1968: The Election That Changed America.* Chicago: Ivan R. Dee, 1993.

Grant, Zalin. *Survivors.* New York: Norton, 1975.

Gras, Yves. *Histoire de la Guerre d'Indochine.* Paris: Éditions Denoël, 1992.

Greene, Bob. *Homecoming: When the Soldiers Returned from Vietnam.* New York: Putnam, 1989.

Greene, John Robert. *The Presidency of Gerald R. Ford.* Lawrence: University Press of Kansas, 1995.

Groom, Winston, and Duncan Spencer. *Conversations with the Enemy: The Story of Pfc. Robert Garwood.* New York: Putnam, 1983.

Guilmartin, John F. *A Very Short War: The* Mayaguez *and the Battle of Koh Tang.* College Station: Texas A&M University Press, 1995.

Gruner, Elliott. *Prisoners of Culture: Representing the Vietnam POW.* New Brunswick, NJ: Rutgers University Press, 1993.

Gustainis, J. Justin. *American Rhetoric and the Vietnam War.* New York: Praeger, 1993.

Ha Mai Viet. *Steel and Blood: South Vietnamese Armor and the War for Southeast Asia.* Annapolis, MD: Naval Institute Press, 2008.

Hackworth, David H., and Eihys England. *Steel My Soldiers' Hearts.* New York: Touchstone, 2003.

Hackworth, Colonel David H., and Julie Sherman. *About Face: The Odyssey of an American Warrior.* New York: Simon and Schuster, 1989.

Halberstam, David. *The Best and the Brightest.* New York: Random House, 1972.

Halberstam, David. *Ho.* Lanham, MD: Rowman and Littlefield, 2007.

Halberstam, David. *The Making of a Quagmire: America and Vietnam during the Kennedy Era.* Rev. ed. Lanham, MD: Rowman and Littlefield, 2008.

Hamilton-Merritt, Jane. *Tragic Mountains: The Hmong, the Americans, and the Secret Wars for Laos, 1942–1992.* Bloomington: Indiana University Press, 1993.

Hammel, Eric. *Fire in the Streets: The Battle for Hue, Tet, 1968.* Chicago: Contemporary Books, 1991.

Hammel, Eric. *Khe Sanh: Siege in the Clouds; An Oral History.* New York: Crown, 1989.

Hammer, Ellen J. *A Death in November: America in Vietnam, 1963.* New York: Dutton, 1987.

Hammer, Ellen J. *The Struggle for Indochina.* Stanford, CA: Stanford University Press, 1954.

Hammond, William M. *Public Affairs: The Military and the Media, 1962–1968.* Washington, DC: Department of the Army, 1988.

Hammond, William M. *Public Affairs: The Military and the Media, 1968–1973.* Honolulu: University Press of the Pacific, 2002.

Hathorn, Reginald. *Here Are the Tigers: The Secret Air War in Laos.* Mechanicsburg, PA: Stackpole Books, 2008.

Hayslip, Le Ly, and Jay Wurts. *When Heaven and Earth Changed Places: A Vietnamese Woman's Journey from War to Peace.* New York: Doubleday, 1989.

Head, William, and Lawrence E. Grinter, ed. *Looking Back on the Vietnam War: A 1990's Perspective on the Decisions, Combat, and Legacies.* Westport, CT: Greenwood, 1993.

Heineman, Kenneth J. *Campus Wars: The Peace Movement at American State Universities in the Vietnam Era.* New York: New York University Press, 1993.

Hellman, John. *American Myth and the Legacy of Vietnam.* New York: Columbia University Press, 1986.

Hemingway, Albert. *Our War Was Different: Marine Combined Action Platoons in Vietnam.* Annapolis, MD: Naval Institute Press, 1994.

Herr, Michael. *Dispatches*. New York: Knopf, 1977.

Herring, George C. *America's Longest War: The United States and Vietnam, 1950–1975*. 4th ed. New York: McGraw-Hill, 2001.

Herring, George C. *LBJ and Vietnam: A Different Kind of War*. Austin: University of Texas Press, 1994.

Herrington, Stuart A. *Silence Was a Weapon: The Vietnam War in the Villages; A Personal Perspective*. Novato, CA: Presidio, 1982.

Hersh, Seymour M. *Cover-Up: The Army's Secret Investigation of the Massacre at My Lai 4*. New York: Random House, 1972.

Hersh, Seymour M. *My Lai 4: A Report on the Massacre and Its Aftermath*. New York: Random House, 1970.

Hess, Gary. R. *Vietnam: Explaining America's Lost War*. Hoboken, NJ: Wiley-Blackwell, 2008.

Hickey, Gerald Cannon. *Window on a War: An Anthropologist in the Vietnam Conflict*. Lubbock: Texas Tech University Press, 2002.

Higham, Charles. *The Archaeology of Mainland Southeast Asia*. Cambridge: Cambridge University Press, 1989.

Hobson, Chris. *Vietnam Air Losses: United States Air Force, Navy, and Marine Corps Fixed-Wing Aircraft Losses in Southeast Asia, 1961–1973*. Hinckley, UK: Midland Publishing, 2001.

Ho Khang. *The Tet Mau Than 1968 Event in South Vietnam*. Hanoi: Gioi Publishers, 2001.

Ho Mai Viet. *Steel and Blood: South Vietnamese Armor and the War for Southeast Asia*. Annapolis, MD: Naval Institute Press, 2008.

Hoang Hai Van and Tan Tu. *Pham Xuan An: A General of the Secret Service*. Hanoi: Gioi Publishers, 2003.

Hoang Van Thai. *How South Vietnam Was Liberated*. Hanoi: Gioi Publishers, 1996.

Hoffmann, Stanley. *Primacy or World Order: American Foreign Policy since the Cold War*. New York: McGraw-Hill, 1978.

Holm, Tom. *Strong Hearts, Wounded Souls: Native American Veterans of the Vietnam War*. Austin: University of Texas Press, 1996.

Hooper, Edwin B., Dean C. Allard, and Oscar P. Fitzgerald. *The United States Navy and the Vietnam Conflict*, Vol. 1, *The Setting of the Stage to 1959*. Washington, DC: U.S. Navy, Naval History Division, 1976.

Hubbell, John G., Andrew Jones, and Kenneth Y. Tomlinson. *P.O.W.: A Definitive History of the American Prisoner-of-War Experience in Vietnam, 1964–1973*. New York: Reader's Digest, 1976.

Hunt, Richard A. *Pacification: The American Struggle for Vietnam's Hearts and Minds*. Boulder, CO: Westview, 1995.

Huynh, Jade Ngoc Quang. *South Wind Changing*. St. Paul, MN: Graywolf, 1994.

Isaacs, Arnold R. *Without Honor: Defeat in Vietnam and Cambodia*. Baltimore: Johns Hopkins University Press, 1983.

Isaacson, Walter. *Kissinger: A Biography*. New York: Simon and Schuster, 1992.

Jensen-Stevenson, Monika, and William Stevenson. *Kiss the Boys Goodbye: How the United States Betrayed Its Own POWs in Vietnam*. New York: Dutton, 1990.

Johnson, Lyndon B. *The Vantage Point: Perspectives of the Presidency, 1963–1969*. New York: Holt, Rinehart and Winston, 1971.

Jones, Charles. *Boys of '67*. Mechanicsburg, PA: Stackpole, 2006.

Kahin, George McT. *Intervention: How America Became Involved in Vietnam*. New York: Knopf, 1986.

Kane, Rod. *Veteran's Day*. New York: Orion Books, 1989.

Karnow, Stanley. *Vietnam: A History*. 2nd rev. and updated ed. New York: Penguin, 1997.

Katsiaficas, George N., ed. *Vietnam Documents: American and Vietnamese Views of the War*. New York: M. E. Sharpe, 1992.

Kelley, Michael P. *Where We Were in Vietnam: A Comprehensive Guide to the Firebases, Military Installations and Naval Vessels of the Vietnam War, 1945–75*. Central Point, OR: Hellgate, 2002.

Kimball, Jeffrey P., ed. *To Reason Why: The Debate about the Causes of Involvement in the Vietnam War*. Philadelphia: Temple University Press, 1990.

King, Peter, ed. *Australia's Vietnam: Australia in the Second Indochina War*. Boston: Allen and Unwin, 1983.

Kinnard, Douglas. *The War Managers*. Hanover, NH: University Press of New England, 1977.

Kirk, Donald. *Wider War: The Struggle for Cambodia, Thailand, and Laos*. New York: Praeger, 1971.

Kissinger, Henry. *White House Years*. Boston: Little, Brown, 1979.

Kissinger, Henry. *Years of Upheaval*. Boston: Little, Brown, 1982.

Kolko, Gabriel. *Anatomy of a War: Vietnam, the United States, and the Modern Historical Experience*. New York: Pantheon, 1985.

Kovic, Ron. *Born on the Fourth of July*. New York: McGraw-Hill, 1976.

Krall, Yung. *A Thousand Tears Falling: The True Story of a Vietnamese Family Torn Apart by War, Communism, and the CIA*. Atlanta: Longstreet, 1995.

Krepinevich, Andrew F., Jr. *The Army and Vietnam*. Baltimore: Johns Hopkins University Press, 1986.

Krohn, Charles A. *The Lost Battalion of Tet: Breakout of the 2–12 Cavalry at Hue*. Annapolis, MD: Naval Institute Press, 2008.

Kutler, Stanley I., ed. *Encyclopedia of the Vietnam War*. New York: Scribner, 1996.

Lacouture, Jean. *Ho Chi Minh: A Political Biography*. New York: Random House, 1968.

Lam Quang Thi. *The Twenty-Five-Year Century: A South Vietnamese General Remembers the Indochina War to the Fall of Saigon*. Denton: University of North Texas Press, 2001.

Lamb, Christopher Jon. *Belief Systems and Decision Making in the Mayaguez Crisis*. Gainesville: University of Florida Press, 1988.

Lane, Mark. *Conversations with Americans*. New York: Simon and Schuster, 1970.

Lang, Daniel. *Casualties of War.* New York: McGraw-Hill, 1969.

Langguth, A. J. *Our Vietnam: The War, 1954–1975.* New York: Simon and Schuster, 2000.

Lansdale, Edward Geary. *In the Midst of Wars: An American's Mission to Southeast Asia.* New York: Harper and Row, 1972.

Larsen, Stanley Robert, and James Lawton Collins Jr. *Allied Participation in Vietnam.* Vietnam Studies Series. Washington, DC: Department of the Army, U.S. Government Printing Office, 1975.

Larzelere, Alex. *The Coast Guard at War: Vietnam, 1965–1975.* Annapolis, MD: Naval Institute Press, 1997.

Le Gro, William E. *Vietnam from Cease-Fire to Capitulation.* Washington, DC: U.S. Army Center of Military History, 1981.

Le Thanh Khoi. *Histoire du Viet Nam des Origines à 1858.* Paris: Sudestasie, 1981.

Lifton, Robert Jay. *Home from the War: Vietnam Veterans, Neither Victims nor Executioners.* New York: Simon and Schuster, 1973.

Luu Van Loi and Nguyen Anh Vu. *Le Duc Tho–Kissinger Negotiations in Paris.* Hanoi: Gioi Publishers, 1996.

Ly Quy Chung, ed. *Between Two Fires: The Unheard Voices of Vietnam.* New York: Praeger, 1970.

Macdonald, Peter. *Giap: The Victor in Vietnam.* New York: Norton, 1993.

MacGarrigle, George L. *Combat Operations: Taking the Offensive, October 1966 to October 1967.* Washington, DC: Center of Military History, U.S. Army, 1998.

Maclear, Michael. *The Ten Thousand Day War: Vietnam, 1945–1975.* New York: St. Martin's, 1981.

MacPherson, Myra. *Long Time Passing: Vietnam and the Haunted Generation.* New York: Doubleday, 1984.

Maneli, Mieczyslaw. *The War of the Vanquished.* New York: Harper and Row, 1969.

Mangold, Tom, and John Penycate. *The Tunnels of Cu Chi.* New York: Random House, 1985.

Marolda, Edward J. *By Sea, Air, and Land: An Illustrated History of the U.S. Navy and the War in Southeast Asia.* Washington, DC: Naval Historical Center, Department of the Navy, 1994.

Marolda, Edward J., and Oscar P. Fitzgerald. *The United States Navy and the Vietnam Conflict: From Military Assistance to Combat, 1959–1965,* Vol. 2. Washington, DC: Naval Historical Center, 1986.

Marr, David G. *Vietnam 1945: The Quest for Power.* Berkeley: University of California Press, 1995.

Marr, David G. *Vietnamese Tradition on Trial, 1920–1945.* Berkeley: University of California Press, 1981.

Marshall, Kathryn. *In the Combat Zone: An Oral History of American Women in Vietnam, 1966–1975.* Boston: Little, Brown, 1987.

Marshall, S. L. A. *Ambush.* New York: Cowles, 1969.

Marshall, S. L. A. *Battles in the Monsoon: Campaigning in the Central Highlands, South Vietnam, Summer, 1966.* New York: William Morrow, 1967.

Marshall, S. L. A. *Bird: The Christmastide Battle.* New York: Cowles, 1968.

Marshall, S. L. A. *West to Cambodia.* New York: Cowles, 1968.

Marshall, S. L. A., and David Hackworth. *DA Pam 525–2 Vietnam Primer.* Washington, DC: U.S. Government Printing Office, 1967.

Mason, Robert. *Chickenhawk.* New York: Viking, 1983.

Mauer, Harry. *Strange Ground: Americans in Vietnam, 1945–1975, an Oral History.* New York: Henry Holt, 1989.

McCallum, Jack E. *Military Medicine: From Ancient Times to the 21st Century.* Santa Barbara, CA: ABC-CLIO, 2003.

McCarthy, Mary. *The Seventeenth Degree.* New York: Harcourt, Brace, Jovanovich, 1974.

McCloud, Bill. *What Should We Tell Our Children about Vietnam?* Norman: University of Oklahoma Press, 1989.

McConnell, Malcolm. *Inside the Hanoi Secret Archives: Solving the MIA Mystery.* New York: Simon and Schuster, 1995.

McMaster, H. R. *Dereliction of Duty: Lyndon Johnson, Robert McNamara, the Joint Chiefs of Staff, and the Lies That Led to Vietnam.* New York: HarperCollins, 1997.

McNab, Chris, and Andy Weist. *The Illustrated History of the Vietnam War.* San Diego: Thunder Bay, 2000.

McNamara, Robert S., with Brian VanDeMark. *In Retrospect, the Tragedy and Lessons of Vietnam.* New York: Vintage Books, 1995.

McNeill, Ian. *To Long Tan: The Australian Army and the Vietnam War, 1950–1966.* St. Leonards, New South Wales: Allen and Unwin/Australian War Memorial, 1993.

Metzner, Edward P. *More Than a Soldier's War: Pacification in Vietnam.* College Station: Texas A&M University Press, 1995.

Metzner, Edward P., Huynh Van Chinh, Tran Van Phuc, and Le Nguyen Binh. *Reeducation in Postwar Vietnam: Personal Postscripts to Peace.* College Station: Texas A&M University Press, 2001.

Michel, Marshall L., III. *Clashes: Air Combat over North Vietnam, 1965–1972.* Annapolis, MD: Naval Institute Press, 1997.

Michel, Marshall L., III. *The Eleven Days of Christmas: America's Last Vietnam Battle.* San Francisco: Encounter Books, 2002.

Military History Institute of Vietnam. *Victory in Vietnam: The Official History of the People's Army of Vietnam, 1954–1975.* Lawrence: University Press of Kansas, 2002.

Miller, John G. *The Bridge at Dong Ha.* Annapolis, MD: Naval Institute Press, 1996.

Moise, Edwin E. *Tonkin Gulf and the Escalation of the Vietnam War.* Chapel Hill: University of North Carolina Press, 1996.

Moore, Harold G., and Joseph L. Galloway. *We Are Soldiers Still: A Journey Back to the Battlefields of Vietnam.* New York: Harper, 2008.

Moore, Harold G., and Joseph L. Galloway. *We Were Soldiers Once . . . and Young: Ia Drang—The Battle That Changed the War in Vietnam.* New York: Random House, 1992.

Morgan, Joseph G. *The Vietnam Lobby: The American Friends of Vietnam, 1955–1975.* Chapel Hill: University of North Carolina Press, 1997.

Morgan, Ted. *Valley of Death: The Tragedy at Dien Bien Phu That Led America into the Vietnam War.* New York: Random House, 2010.

Morrison, Wilbur H. *The Elephant and the Tiger: The Full Story of the Vietnam War.* New York: Hippocrene Books, 1990.

Moss, George. *Vietnam: An American Ordeal.* 2nd ed. Englewood Cliffs, NJ: Prentice Hall, 1994.

Moyar, Mark. *Phoenix and the Birds of Prey: The CIA's Secret Campaign to Destroy the Viet Cong.* Annapolis, MD: Naval Institute Press, 1997.

Moyar, Mark. *Triumph Forsaken: The Vietnam War, 1954–1965.* New York: Cambridge University Press, 2006.

Murphy, Edward F. *Dak To: The 173rd Airborne Brigade in South Vietnam's Central Highlands, June–November 1967.* Novato, CA: Presidio, 1993.

Murphy, Edward F. *The Hill Fights: The First Battle of Khe Sanh.* New York: Random House, 2003.

Murphy, John. *Harvest of Fear: A History of Australia's Vietnam War.* Boulder, CO: Westview, 1994.

Nalty, Bernard C. *The War against Trucks: Aerial Interdiction in Southern Laos, 1968–1972.* Washington, DC: Air Force History and Museums Program, U.S. Air Force, 2005.

Neilands, J. B., et al. *Harvest of Death: Chemical Warfare in Vietnam and Cambodia.* New York: Free Press, 1972.

Newman, John M. *JFK and Vietnam: Deception, Intrigue, and the Struggle for Power.* New York: Warner Books, 1992.

Newman, John M. *Vietnam War Literature: An Annotated Bibliography of Imaginative Works about Americans Fighting in Vietnam.* 3rd ed. Lanham, NJ: Scarecrow, 1996.

Ngo Quang Truong. *Territorial Forces.* Washington, DC: U.S. Army Center of Military History, 1981.

Nguyen Cao Ky. *Twenty Years and Twenty Days.* New York: Stein and Day, 1976.

Nguyen Khac Vien. *The Long Resistance, 1858–1975.* Hanoi: Foreign Languages Publishing House, 1975.

Nguyen Khac Vien. *Vietnam: A Long History.* Hanoi: Foreign Languages Publishing House, 1987.

Nguyen Tien Hung and Jerrold L. Schechter. *The Palace File.* New York: Harper and Row, 1986.

Nichols, John B., and Barrett Tillman. *On Yankee Station: The Naval Air War over Vietnam.* Annapolis, MD: Naval Institute Press, 1987.

Nixon, Richard M. *No More Vietnams.* New York: Arbor House, 1985.

Nixon, Richard M. *The Real War.* New York: Warner, 1980.

Nixon, Richard M. *RN: The Memoirs of Richard Nixon.* New York: Grosset and Dunlap, 1978.

Nolan, Keith William. *Battle for Hue: Tet, 1968.* Novato, CA: Presidio, 1983.

Nolan, Keith William. *The Battle for Saigon: Tet, 1968.* Novato, CA: Presidio, 1996.

Nolan, Keith William. *House to House: Playing the Enemy's Game in Saigon, May 1968.* St. Paul, MN: Zenith, 2006.

Nolan, Keith William. *Into Laos: The Story of Dewey Canyon II/Lam Son 719, Vietnam 1971.* Novato, CA: Presidio, 1986.

Nolan, Keith William. *Ripcord: Screaming Eagles under Siege, Vietnam 1970.* Novato, CA: Presidio, 2000.

Nolting, Frederick. *From Trust to Tragedy: The Political Memoirs of Frederick Nolting, Kennedy's Ambassador to Diem's Vietnam.* New York: Praeger, 1988.

Novosel, Michael J. *Dustoff: The Memoir of an Army Aviator.* Novato, CA: Presidio, 1999.

O'Ballance, Edgar. *The Wars in Vietnam, 1954–1980.* Rev. ed. New York: Hippocrene Books, 1981.

Oberdorfer, Don. *TET! The Turning Point in the Vietnam War.* Baltimore: Johns Hopkins University Press, 2001.

O'Brien, Tim. *If I Die in a Combat Zone.* New York: Delacorte, 1973.

Olson, James S., ed. *Dictionary of the Vietnam War.* New York: Greenwood, 1988.

Olson, James S., and Randy Roberts. *Where the Domino Fell: America and Vietnam, 1945–1990.* New York: St. Martin's, 1991.

Olson, James S., and Randy Roberts. *The Vietnam War: Handbook of the Literature and Research.* Westport, CT: Greenwood, 1993.

An Outline History of the Vietnam Workers' Party, 1930–1975. Hanoi: Foreign Languages Publishing House, 1978.

Palmer, General Bruce, Jr. *The 25-Year War: America's Military Role in Vietnam.* Lexington: University Press of Kentucky, 1984.

Palmer, Dave R. *Summons of the Trumpet: U.S.-Vietnam in Perspective.* San Rafael, CA: Presidio, 1995.

Palmer, Laura. *Shrapnel in the Heart: Letters and Remembrances from the Vietnam Memorial.* New York: Random House, 1987.

Patti, Archimedes L. A. *Why Viet Nam? Prelude to America's Albatross.* Berkeley: University of California Press, 1980.

Pearson, Willard. *The War in the Northern Provinces, 1966–1968.* Washington, DC: Department of the Army, 1975.

Pedroncini, Guy, and General Philippe Duplay, eds. *Leclerc et l'Indochine.* Paris: Albin Michel, 1992.

Personalities of the South Vietnam Liberation Movement. New York: Commission for Foreign Relations of the South Vietnam National Front for Liberation, 1965.

Peterson, Michael E. *The Combined Action Platoons: The U.S. Marines' Other War in Vietnam.* New York: Praeger, 1989.

Pham Cao Duong. *Lich Su Dan Toc Viet Nam,* Quyen I, *Thoi K Lap Quoc* [History of the Vietnamese People, Vol. I, The Making of the Nation]. Fountain Valley, CA: Truyen Thong Viet, 1987.

Phillips, Rufus. *Why Vietnam Matters: An Eyewitness Account of Lessons Not Learned.* Annapolis, MD: Naval Institute Press, 2008.

Phillips, William R. *Night of the Silver Stars: The Battle of Lang Vei.* Annapolis, MD: Naval Institute Press, 1997.

Philpott, Tom. *Glory Denied: The Saga of Jim Thompson, America's Longest-Held Prisoner of War.* New York: Norton, 2001.

Pike, Douglas. *A History of Vietnamese Communism, 1923–1978.* Stanford, CA: Hoover Institute Press, 1978.

Pike, Douglas. *Viet Cong: The Organization and Techniques of the National Liberation Front of South Vietnam.* Cambridge, MA: MIT Press, 1966.

Pisor, Robert. *The End of the Line: The Siege of Khe Sanh.* New York: Norton, 1982.

Plaster, John. *SOG: The Secret Wars of America's Commandos in Vietnam.* New York: Simon and Schuster, 1997.

Porch, Douglas. *The French Foreign Legion: A Complete History of the Legendary Fighting Force.* New York: HarperCollins, 1991.

Porter, Gareth. *A Peace Denied: The United States, Vietnam, and the Paris Agreement.* Bloomington: Indiana University Press, 1975.

Prados, John. *The Blood Road: The Ho Chi Minh Trail and the Vietnam War.* New York: Wiley, 1999.

Prados, John. *Vietnam: The History of an Unwinnable War, 1945–1975.* Lawrence: University Press of Kansas, 2009.

Prados, John, and Ray W. Stubbe. *Valley of Decision: The Siege of Khe Sanh.* Boston: Houghton Mifflin, 1991.

Pratt, John Clark, ed. *Vietnam Voices: Perspectives on the War Years, 1941–1982.* New York: Viking, 1984.

Pribbenow, Merle L., and William J. Duiker. *Victory in Vietnam: The Official History of the People's Army of Vietnam.* Lawrence: University Press of Kansas, 2002.

Prochnau, William. *Once upon a Distant War: David Halberstam, Neil Sheehan, Peter Arnett—Young War Correspondents and Their Early Vietnam Battles.* New York: Vintage Books, 1995.

Puller, Lewis B., Jr. *Fortunate Son: The Autobiography of Lewis B. Puller, Jr.* New York: Grove Weidenfeld, 1991.

Pyle, Richard, and Horst Faas. *Lost over Laos: A True Story of Tragedy, Mystery, and Friendship.* Cambridge, MA: Da Capo, 2003.

Race, Jeffrey. *War Comes to Long An: Revolutionary Conflict in a Vietnamese Province.* Berkeley: University of California Press, 1972.

Randle, Robert F. *Geneva 1954: The Settlement of the Indochinese War.* Princeton, NJ: Princeton University Press, 1969.

Randolph, Stephen P. *Powerful and Brutal Weapons: Nixon, Kissinger, and the Easter Offensive.* Cambridge: Harvard University Press, 2007.

Reardon, Carol. *Launch the Intruders: A Naval Attack Squadron in the Vietnam War, 1972.* Lawrence: University Press of Kansas, 2005.

Robbins, Christopher. *Air America.* New York: Putnam, 1979.

Rotter, Andrew, ed. *Light at the End of the Tunnel: A Vietnam War Anthology.* New York: St. Martin's, 1991.

Rowe, John Crowe, and Rick Berg, ed. *The Vietnam War and American Culture.* New York: Columbia University Press, 1991.

Roy, Jules. *The Battle of Dienbienphu.* New York: Harper and Row, 1965.

Rusk, Dean. *As I Saw It.* Edited by Daniel S. Papp. New York: Norton, 1990.

Sack, John. *M.* New York: New American Library, 1966.

Safer, Morley. *Flashbacks: On Returning to Vietnam.* New York: Random House, 1990.

Sainteny, Jean. *Histoire d'une Paix Manquée: Indochine, 1945–1947.* Paris: Amiot-Dumont, 1953.

Sainteny, Jean. *Ho Chi Minh and His Vietnam: A Personal Memoir.* Chicago: Cowles, 1972.

Salisbury, Harrison E., ed. *Vietnam Reconsidered: Lessons from a War.* New York: Harper and Row, 1984.

Santoli, Al, ed. *Everything We Had: An Oral History of the Vietnam War by Thirty-Three American Soldiers Who Fought It.* New York: Random House, 1981.

Santoli, Al, ed. *To Bear Any Burden: The Vietnam War and Its Aftermath in the Words of Americans and Southeast Asians.* New York: Dutton, 1985.

Schell, Jonathan. *The Military Half.* New York: Knopf, 1968.

Schell, Jonathan. *The Village of Ben Suc.* New York: Knopf, 1967.

Scholl-Latour, Peter. *Death in the Ricefields: An Eyewitness Account of Vietnam's Three Wars, 1945–1979.* New York: St. Martin's, 1985.

Schreadley, R. L. *From the Rivers to the Sea: The United States Navy in Vietnam.* Annapolis, MD: Naval Institute Press, 1992.

Schwenkel, Christina. *The American War in Contemporary Vietnam: Transnational Remembrance and Representation.* Bloomington: Indiana University Press, 2009.

Shultz, Richard H., Jr. *The Secret War against Hanoi.* New York: HarperCollins, 1999.

Schulzinger, Robert D. *A Time for Peace: The Legacy of the Vietnam War.* New York: Oxford University Press, 2006.

Schulzinger, Robert D. *A Time for War: The United States and Vietnam, 1941–1975.* New York: Oxford University Press, 1997.

Scruggs, Jan C., and Joel L. Swerdlow. *To Heal a Nation: The Vietnam Veterans Memorial.* New York: Harper and Row, 1985.

Sevy, Grace, ed. *The American Experience in Vietnam: A Reader.* Norman: University of Oklahoma Press, 1989.

Shapley, Deborah. *Promise and Power: The Life and Times of Robert McNamara.* Boston: Little, Brown, 1993.

Sharp, Ulysses S. Grant. *Strategy for Defeat: Vietnam in Retrospect.* San Rafael, CA: Presidio, 1978.

Shaw, John M. *The Cambodian Campaign: The 1970 Offensive and America's Vietnam War.* Lawrence: University Press of Kansas, 2005.

Shawcross, William. *Sideshow: Kissinger, Nixon, and the Destruction of Cambodia.* New York: Simon and Schuster, 1979.

Shay, Jonathan. *Achilles in Vietnam: Traumatic Stress and the Undoing of Character.* New York: Atheneum, 1994.

Sheehan, Neil. *A Bright Shining Lie: John Paul Vann and America in Vietnam.* New York: Random House, 1988.

Sheppard, Don. *Riverine: A Brown-Water Sailor in the Delta, 1967.* Novato, CA: Presidio, 1992.

Showalter, Dennis E., and John G. Abert, eds. *An American Dilemma: Vietnam, 1964–1973*. Chicago: Imprint Publications, 1993.

Shulimson, Jack. *U.S. Marines in Vietnam, 1965*. Washington, DC: History and Museums Division, Headquarters, U.S. Marine Corps, 1978.

Shulimson, Jack. *U.S. Marines in Vietnam, 1966: An Expanding War*. Marine Corps Vietnam Series. Washington, DC: History and Museums Division, Marine Corps Historical Center, U.S. Marine Corps Headquarters, 1982.

Shulimson, Jack, Leonard A. Blasiol, Charles R. Smith, and David A. Dawson. *U.S. Marines in Vietnam: The Defining Year, 1968*. Washington, DC: History and Museums Division, Headquarters, U.S. Marine Corps, 1997.

Shulimson, Jack, and Charles M. Johnson. *U.S. Marines in Vietnam: The Landing and the Buildup*. Washington, DC: History and Museums Division, Headquarters, U.S. Marine Corps, 1977.

Sigler, David Burns. *Vietnam Battle Chronology: U.S. Army and Marine Corps Combat Operations, 1965–1973*. Jefferson, NC: McFarland, 1992.

Simpson, Howard R. *Dien Bien Phu: The Epic Battle America Forgot*. Washington, DC: Brassey's, 1994.

Simpson, Howard R. *Tiger in the Barbed Wire: An American in Vietnam, 1952–1991*. Washington, DC: Brassey's, 1992.

Smith, Winnie. *American Daughter Gone To War: On the Front Lines With an Army Nurse in Vietnam*. New York: Morrow, 1992.

Snepp, Frank. *Decent Interval: An Insider's Account of Saigon's Indecent End*. New York: Random House, 1977.

Solis, Gary D. *Son Thang: An American War Crime*. Annapolis, MD: Naval Institute Press, 1997.

Sorley, Lewis. *A Better War: The Unexamined Victories and Final Tragedy of America's Last Years in Vietnam*. New York: Harcourt, Brace, 1999.

Sorley, Lewis. *Thunderbolt: General Creighton Abrams and the Army of His Times*. 2nd ed. Bloomington: Indiana University Press, 2008.

Spector, Ronald H. *Advice and Support: The Early Years, 1941–1960*. United States Army in Vietnam Series. Washington, DC: U.S. Army Center of Military History, 1983.

Spector, Ronald H. *After Tet: The Bloodiest Year in Vietnam*. New York: Free Press, 1993.

Stanton, Shelby L. *Green Berets at War: U.S. Army Special Forces in Southeast Asia, 1956–1975*. Novato, CA: Presidio, 1985.

Stanton, Shelby L. *The Rise and Fall of an American Army: The U.S. Ground Forces in Vietnam, 1965–1975*. Novato, CA: Presidio, 1985.

Stanton, Shelby L. *U.S. Army and Allied Ground Forces in Vietnam Order of Battle*. Washington, DC: U.S. News Books, 1981.

Stevens, Fitzgerald. *The Trail*. New York: Garland, 1993.

Stockdale, James B. *A Vietnam Experience: Ten Years of Reflection*. Stanford, CA: Hoover Institute Press, 1984.

Sullivan, John F. *Of Spies and Lies: A CIA Lie Detector Remembers Vietnam*. Lawrence: University Press of Kansas, 2002.

Summers, Harry G. *Historical Atlas of the Vietnam War*. Boston: Houghton Mifflin, 1995.

Summers, Harry G. *On Strategy: A Critical Analysis of the Vietnam War*. Novato, CA: Presidio Press 1995.

Swift, Earl. *On Strategy*. Novato, CA: Presidio, 1982.

Swift, Earl. *Where They Lay: Searching for America's Lost Soldiers*. New York: Houghton Mifflin, 2003.

Taylor, John M. *General Maxwell Taylor: The Sword and the Pen*. New York: Doubleday, 1989.

Taylor, Keith Weller. *The Birth of Vietnam*. Berkeley: University of California Press, 1983.

Taylor, General Maxwell D. *Swords and Plowshares*. New York: Norton, 1972.

Telfer, Gary L. *U.S. Marines in Vietnam: Fighting the North Vietnamese, 1967*. Washington, DC: History and Museums Division, Headquarters, U.S. Marine Corps, 1984.

Terry, Wallace. *Bloods: An Oral History of the Vietnam War by Black Veterans*. New York: Random House, 1984.

Thompson, Virginia. *French Indo-China*. New York: Octagon Books, 1968.

Timberg, Robert. *The Nightingale's Song*. New York: Touchstone, Simon and Schuster, 1996.

Toczek, David M. *The Battle of Ap Bac, Vietnam: They Did Everything but Learn from It*. Annapolis, MD: Naval Institute Press, 2007.

Todd, Olivier. *Cruel April: The Fall of Saigon*. New York: Norton, 1987.

Tourison, Sedgwick D. *Project Alpha: Washington's Secret Military Operations in North Vietnam*. New York: St. Martin's, 1997.

Tourison, Sedgwick D. *Talking with Victor Charlie: An Interrogator's Story*. New York: Ivy, 1991.

Tran Van Nhut. *An Loc: The Unfinished War*. Lubbock: Texas Tech University Press, 2009.

Trujillo, Charley, ed. *Soldados: Chicanos in Viet Nam*. San Jose, CA: Chusma House, 1990.

Truong Nhu Tang, with David Charnoff and Doan Van Toai. *A Viet Cong Memoir: An Inside Account of the Vietnam War and Its Aftermath*. New York: Harcourt Brace Jovanovich, 1985.

Tuchman, Barbara W. *The March of Folly: From Troy to Vietnam*. New York: Knopf, 1984.

Tucker, Spencer C. *Vietnam*. Lexington: University Press of Kentucky, 1999.

Turley, Gerald H. *The Easter Offensive: The Last American Advisors, Vietnam, 1972*. Novato, CA: Presidio, 1985.

U.S. Department of State. *Aggression from the North: The Record of North Viet-Nam's Campaign to Conquer South Viet-Nam*. Washington, DC: U.S. Government Printing Office, 1965.

Valentine, Douglas. *The Phoenix Program*. New York: Morrow, 1990.

Valette, Jacques. *La Guerre d'Indochine, 1945–1954.* Paris: Armand Colin, 1994.

VanDeMark, Brian. *Into the Quagmire: Lyndon Johnson and the Escalation of the Vietnam War.* New York: Oxford University Press, 1991.

Van Devanter, Lynda. *Home before Morning: The Story of an Army Nurse in Vietnam.* New York: Beaufort Books, 1983.

Vo Nguyen Giap. *"Big Victory, Great Task." North Viet-Nam's Minister of Defense Assesses the Course of the War.* New York: Praeger, 1968.

Vo Nguyen Giap. *Dien Bien Phu.* 5th ed., revised and supplemented. Hanoi: Gioi Publishers, 1994.

Vo Nguyen Giap. *The Military Art of People's War: Selected Writings of Vo Nguyen Giap.* Edited with an introduction by Russell Stetler. New York: Monthly Review Press, 1970.

Vo Nguyen Giap. *People's War People's Army: The Viet Cong Insurrection Manual for Underdeveloped Countries.* New York: Praeger, 1962.

Vo Nguyen Giap. *Unforgettable Months and Years.* Translated by Mai Elliott. Ithaca, NY: Cornell University Press, 1975.

Vo Nguyen Giap. *Viet Nam People's War Has Defeated U.S. War of Destruction.* Hanoi: Foreign Languages Publishing House, 1969.

Vo Nguyen Giap and Huu Mai. *Dien Bien Phu: Rendezvous with History, a Memoir.* Hanoi: Gioi Publishers, 2004.

Vo Nguyen Giap and Huu Mai. *Duong Toi Dien Bien Phu* [The Road to Dien Bien Phu]. Hanoi: People's Army Publishing House, 2001.

Vo Nguyen Giap and Huu Mai. *Fighting under Siege: Reminiscences.* Hanoi: Gioi Publishers, 2004.

Vo Nguyen Giap and Huu Mai. *The General Headquarters in the Spring of Brilliant Victory.* Hanoi: Gioi Publishers, 2002.

Walt, Lewis W. *Strange War, Strange Strategy: A General's Report on Vietnam.* New York: Funk and Wagnalls, 1976.

Warr, Nicholas. *Phase Line Green: The Battle for Hue, 1968.* Annapolis, MD: Naval Institute Press, 1997.

Wells, Tom. *The War Within: America's Battle over Vietnam.* Berkeley: University of California Press, 1994.

Westmoreland, William C. *A Soldier Reports.* New York: Doubleday, 1976.

Wexler, Sanford. *The Vietnam War: An Eyewitness History.* New York: Facts on File, 1992.

Wheeler, John. *Touched with Fire: The Future of the Vietnam Generation.* New York: F. Watts, 1984.

Whitlow, Robert H. *U.S. Marines in Vietnam: The Advisory & Combat Assistance Era, 1954–1964.* Washington, DC: History and Museums Division, Headquarters, U.S. Marine Corps, 1977.

Whitlow, Robert, Jack Shulimson, and Gary L. Telfer. *U.S. Marines in Vietnam: An Anthology and Annotated Bibliography, 1954–1973.* Washington, DC: History and Museums Division, Headquarters, U.S. Marine Corps, 1985.

Wiest, Andrew. *Vietnam's Forgotten Army: Heroism and Betrayal in the ARVN.* New York: New York University Press, 2007.

Wiest, Andrew, ed. *Rolling Thunder in a Gentle Land: The Vietnam War Revisited.* Oxford, UK: Osprey, 2006.

Wilcox, Fred A. *Waiting for an Army to Die: The Tragedy of Agent Orange.* New York: Random House, 1983.

Willbanks, James H. *Abandoning Vietnam: How America Left and South Vietnam Lost Its War.* Lawrence: University Press of Kansas, 2004.

Willbanks, James H. *The Battle of An Loc.* Bloomington: Indiana University Press, 2005.

Willbanks, James H. *The Tet Offensive: A Concise History.* New York: Columbia University Press, 2007.

Willbanks, James H. *Thiet Giap! The Battle of An Loc, April 1972.* Fort Leavenworth, KS: Combat Studies Institute, 1993.

Willenson, Kim. *The Bad War: An Oral History of the Vietnam War.* New York: New American Library, 1987.

Williams, Reese. *Unwinding the Vietnam War: From War into Peace.* Seattle, WA: Real Comet, 1987.

Williams, William Appleman, Thomas McCormick, Lloyd Gardner, and Walter LaFaber, eds. *America in Vietnam: A Documentary History.* New York: Norton, 1989.

Windrow, Martin. *The Last Valley: Dien Bien Phu and the French Defeat in Vietnam.* London: Weidenfeld and Nicolson, 2004.

Winters, Francis X. *The Year of the Hare: America in Vietnam, January 25, 1963–February 15, 1964.* Athens: University of Georgia Press, 1997.

Wirtz, James J. *The Tet Offensive: Intelligence Failure in War.* Ithaca, NY: Cornell University Press, 1991.

Wittman, Sandra M. *Writing about Vietnam: The Literature of the Vietnam Conflict.* Boston: G. K. Hall, 1989.

Wolff, Tobias. *In Pharaoh's Army: Memories of the Lost War.* New York: Knopf, 1994.

Wyatt, Clarence R. *Paper Soldiers: The American Press and the Vietnam War.* 2nd ed. Chicago: University of Chicago Press, 1995.

Young, Marilyn B. *The Vietnam Wars, 1945–1990.* New York: HarperCollins, 1991.

Zabecki, David T. ed. *Vietnam: A Reader.* New York: ibooks, 2002.

Zaffiri, Samuel. *Hamburger Hill: The Brutal Battle for Dong Ap Bia, May 11–20, 1969.* Novato, CA: Presidio, 1988.

Zaffiri, Samuel. *Westmoreland: A Biography of General William C. Westmoreland.* New York: William Morrow, 1994.

Zaroulis, N. C., and Gerald Sullivan. *Who Spoke Up? American Protest against the War in Vietnam, 1963–1975.* Garden City, NY: Doubleday, 1984.

Zhai, Qiang. *China and the Vietnam Wars, 1950–1975.* Chapel Hill: University of North Carolina Press, 2000.

Zumwalt, Elmo, Jr. *On Watch: A Memoir.* New York: Quadrangle/New York Times Books, 1976.

Zumwalt, Elmo, Jr., and Elmo Zumwalt III, with John Pekkanen. *My Father, My Son.* New York: Macmillan, 1986.

Spencer C. Tucker and Sandra M. Wittman

List of Editors and Contributors

Editor
Dr. Spencer C. Tucker
Senior Fellow
Military History, ABC-CLIO, LLC

Associate Editor
Dr. Paul G. Pierpaoli Jr.
Fellow
ABC-CLIO, LLC

Assistant Editors
Merle L. Pribbenow II
Retired Central Intelligence Agency officer
Independent Scholar

Lieutenant Colonel James H. Willbanks,
    PhD, United States Army (Ret.)
Director, Department of Military History
U.S. Army Command and General Staff
    College

Major General David T. Zabecki, PhD,
    Army of the United States (Ret.)
Senior Research Fellow in War Studies, the
    University of Birmingham, England

Contributors
Elizabeth Urban Alexander
Department of History
Texas Christian University

Dr. Donna Alvah
Assistant Professor & Margaret Vilas Chair
    of U.S. History
St. Lawrence University

Kevin Arceneaux
Institution for Social and Policy Studies
Yale University

Dr. Gayle Avant
Baylor University

Lacie A. Ballinger
Department of History
Texas Christian University

Captain Patrick K. Barker
U.S. Air Force Academy

John M. Barcus
Department of History
Louisiana State University

Dr. Mark Barringer
Department of History
Texas Tech University

Dr. Harry Basehart
Department of Political Science
Salisbury State University

Dr. Jeffrey D. Bass
Quinnipiac University

Dr. Randal Scott Beeman
Bakersfield College

Dr. John L. Bell Jr.
Department of History
Western Carolina University

Walter F. Bell
Information Services Librarian
Aurora University

Dr. David M. Berman
School of Education
Department of Curriculum
    and Education
University of Pittsburgh

Andrew J. Birtle
Independent Scholar

Dr. Ernest C. Bolt Jr.
Mitchell-Billikopf Professor of History
University of Richmond

Colonel Walter J. Boyne (Retired)
U.S. Air Force

Dr. Robert K. Brigham
Department of History
Vassar College

George M. Brooke III
Department of History
Virginia Military Institute

Dr. Stefan M. Brooks
Lindsey Wilson College

Robert M. Brown
U.S. Army Command and General Staff
  College

Dean Brumley
Department of History
Texas Christian University

Peter W. Brush
Librarian
Vanderbilt University

Dr. Hum Dac Bui
Independent Scholar

Dr. Robert J. Bunker
CEO, Counter-OPFOR Corporation

Dr. Laura M. Calkins
Texas Tech University

Dr. Paul R. Camacho
Director
William Joiner Center
University of Massachusetts, Boston

J. Nathan Campbell
Department of History
Episcopal School of Dallas

Dr. Ralph G. Carter
Department of Political Science
Texas Christian University

Thomas R. Carver
Independent Scholar

Albert T. Chapman
Government Information & Political Sci-
  ence Librarian
Purdue University

Rajesh H. Chauhan
Independent Scholar

Dr. Edwin Clausen
Arizona International College
University of Arizona

Dr. Francis M. Coan
Tunxis Community College

Dr. David Coffey
Professor and Chair
Department of History and Philosophy
University of Tennessee at Martin

Dr. Jeffery B. Cook
North Greenville University

Justin J. Corfield
Geelong Grammar School
Australia

Kelly E. Crager
Head, Oral History Project
Vietnam Center and Archive
Texas Tech University

Michael H. Creswell
Independent Scholar

Matthew A. Crump
Department of History
Texas Christian University

Dr. Cecil B. Currey
University of South Florida

Dr. Arthur I. Cyr
Clausen Distinguished Professor
Director, Clausen Center
Carthage College

Dr. Paul S. Daum
Department of History
New England College

Christopher R. W. Dietrich
University of Texas at Austin

Scott R. DiMarco
Director of Library and Information
  Resources
Mansfield University of Pennsylvania

Dr. Paul William Doerr
Department of History and Classics
Acadia University

Dr. Arthur J. Dommen
The Indochina Institute
George Mason University

Michael E. Donoghue
Independent Scholar

Dr. Timothy G. Dowling
Department of History
Virginia Military Institute

Benjamin C. Dubberly
Department of History
Texas Tech University

Dr. Joe P. Dunn
Department of History and Politics
Converse College

R. Blake Dunnavent
Department of History
Lubbock Christian College

Dr. Bruce Elleman
History Department
Texas Christian University

Dr. Mark A. Esposito
Department of History
West Virginia University

Colonel Peter Faber
National War College

Dr. Will E. Fahey Jr.
Independent Scholar

Dr. Charles N. Fasanaro
Independent Scholar

Dr. Richard M. Filipink
Department of History
Western Illinois University

Dr. Arthur Thomas Frame
Professor of Strategy and Operational
　Warfare
U.S. Army Command and General Staff
　College

Dr. Ronald B. Frankum Jr.
Department of History
Millersville University

Dr. Christos G. Frentzos
Department of History
Austin Peay State University

James Friguglietti
Department of History
Montana State University, Billings

Dr. Peter K. Frost
Department of History
Williams College

First Lieutenant Noel D. Fulton
Department of History
U.S. Air Force Academy

George J. Gabera
Independent Scholar

Charles J. Gaspar
Department of Humanities and Communi-
　cation Arts
Brenau University

John M. Gates
Department of History
Wooster College

Captain Larry Gatti
Department of History
U.S. Air Force Academy

Laurie Geist
Department of Humanities
Illinois Institute of Technology

Dr. Marc J. Gilbert
Department of History
North Georgia College

Dr. Mark Gilderhus
Department of History
Texas Christian University

Dr. James T. Gillam
Spelman College

Dr. Harold J. Goldberg
Department of History
University of the South

Timothy G. Grammer
Independent Scholar

Benjamin P. Greene
United States Naval Academy

John Robert Greene
Department of History
Cazenovia College

Captain John E. Grenier
Department of History
U.S. Air Force Academy

Dr. Charles J. Gross
Departments of the Army and the Air Force
National Guard Bureau

Brian Gurian
Independent Scholar

Debra Hall
Department of History
Cazenovia College

Dr. Michael R. Hall
Department of History
Armstrong Atlantic State University

Dr. Mitchell K. Hall
Department of History
Central Michigan University

Dr. William P. Head
Historian/Chief, WR-ALC Office of History
U.S. Air Force

Glenn E. Helm
Director
Navy Department Library
Washington Navy Yard

Pia C. Heyn
Independent Scholar

Second Lieutenant Joel E. Higley
Department of History
U.S. Air Force Academy

Second Lieutenant Lincoln Hill
Department of History
U.S. Air Force Academy

Ho Dieu Anh
Independent Scholar

Dr. Charles Francis Howlett
Molloy College

Dr. Richard A. Hunt
Center for Military History

Dr. Arnold R. Isaacs
Independent Scholar

Dr. Eric Jarvis
Department of History
King's College
Canada

Susan G. Kalaf
Independent Scholar

Sean N. Kalic
Department of Military History
U.S. Army Command and General Staff
　College

Dr. Robert B. Kane
Troy University

Rhonda Keen-Payne
School of Nursing
Texas Christian University

David M. Keithly
Independent Scholar

Mary L. Kelley
Department of History
Texas Christian University

Ann L. Kelsey
Independent Scholar

Dr. Gary Kerley
North Hall High School

Dr. Jeff Kinard
Guilford Technical Community College

Lieutenant Colonel Richard L. Kiper
Independent Scholar

Dr. Arne Kislenko
Department of History
Ryerson University
Canada

Srikanth Kondapalli
Associate Professor
Jawaharlal Nehru University
India

Dr. Nicholas A. Krehbiel
Washburn University

Second Lieutenant Brent Langhals
Department of History
U.S. Air Force Academy

Captain Alex R. Larzelere (Retired)
U.S. Coast Guard

Dr. Clayton D. Laurie
Intelligence Historian
Center for the Study of Intelligence
Central Intelligence Agency

Dr. William M. Leary
Department of History
University of Georgia

Mark F. Leep
Independent Scholar

Jonathan H. L'Hommedieu
Department of Contemporary History
University of Turku
Finland

Lorenz M. Lüthi
Independent Scholar

Dr. Robert G. Mangrum
Department of History, Political Science,
    and Geography
Howard Payne University

Dr. Sanders Marble
Office of Medical History
U.S. Army

Steven Fred Marin
Victor Valley College

J. David Markham
President
International Napoleonic Society

Justin Marks
Department of History
Cazenovia College

Dr. Edward J. Marolda
Senior Historian
Naval Historical Center
Department of the Navy
Washington Navy Yard

Dr. Daniel P. Marston
Strategic and Defence Studies Centre
Australian National University

Dr. Joseph P. Martino
Colonel
U.S. Air Force, Retired

Stephen R. Maynard
Independent Scholar

Terry M. Mays
Department of Political Science
The Citadel

Dr. Jack McCallum
Adjunct Professor
Department of History and Geography
Texas Christian University

Dr. Stanley S. McGowen
Department of History
Texas Christian University

Dr. James McNabb
Independent Scholar

Dr. Edward M. McNertney
Department of Economics
Texas Christian University

Dr. Julius A. Menzoff
Savannah State University

Dr. Edwin E. Moise
Department of History
Clemson University

Louise Mongelluzo
Department of History
Cazenovia College

Kirsty Anne Montgomery
Department of History
University of Chicago

Dr. John Morello
Devry University

Dr. Malcolm Muir Jr.
Department of History
Virginia Military Institute

Dr. Caryn E. Neumann
Department of History
Miami University of Ohio

Ngo Ngoc Trung
Institute for East Asian Studies
University of California, Berkeley

Dr. Michael R. Nichols
Department of History
Tarrant County College

Dr. Long Ba Nguyen
Viet Business Publications
Canada

Nguyen Cong Luan
Independent Scholar

Cynthia Northrup
Department of History
University of Texas at Arlington

Dr. Michael G. O'Loughlin
Department of Political Science
Salisbury State University

Dr. Eric W. Osborne
Department of History
Virginia Military Institute

Edward C. Page
Department of History
Texas Christian University

John Gregory Perdue Jr.
Department of History
University of Texas

Delia Pergande
Department of History
University of Kentucky

Dr. Pham Cao Duong
Independent Scholar

Thomas T. Phu
Independent Scholar

Allene S. Phy-Olsen
Languages/Literature Department
Austin Peay State University

Dr. Paul G. Pierpaoli Jr.
Fellow
Military History, ABC-CLIO, Inc.

Dr. Steve Potts
Independent Scholar

Dr. Charlotte A. Power
Department of History
Black River Technical College

Tammy Prater
Independent Scholar

Dr. John Clark Pratt
Department of English
Colorado State University

Merle L. Pribbenow II
Independent Scholar

Jamie Bryan Price
Reference Librarian and Assistant
    Professor
Jefferson College of Health Sciences

Dr. Michael Richards
Department of History
Sweet Briar College

Dr. Priscilla Roberts
Professor of History, School of Humanities
Honorary Director, Centre of American
    Studies
University of Hong Kong

Glenn M. Robins
Independent Scholar

Dr. John D. Root
Lewis Department of Humanities
Armour College
Illinois Institute of Technology

Dr. Rodney J. Ross
Senior Professor of History/Geography
Harrisburg Area Community College

Karl Lee Rubis
Department of History
University of Kansas

Harve Saal
MACV, Studies and Observations Group
MACV-SOG History Project

Dr. David C. Saffell
Department of History and Political Science
Ohio Northern University

Stephen R. Sagarra
Independent Scholar

Dr. Stanley Sandler
JFK Special Warfare School
Fort Bragg

Dr. Claude R. Sasso
William Jewell College

Captain Carl Otis Schuster (Retired)
U.S. Navy
Hawaii Pacific University

Jeff Seiken
Independent Scholar

Dr. Michael Share
Department of History
University of Hong Kong

Tara K. Simpson
Independent Scholar

Dr. Yushau Sodiq
Department of Religion
Texas Christian University

Dr. Lewis Sorley
Independent Scholar

John Southard
Texas Tech University

Dr. James E. Southerland
Brenau University

Dr. Phoebe S. Spinrad
Independent Scholar

Dr. Richard D. Starnes
Department of History
Western Carolina University

Dr. Barry M. Stentiford
Independent Scholar

Dr. Kenneth R. Stevens
Department of History
Texas Christian University

Leslie-Rahye Strickland
Independent Scholar

First Lieutenant Tracy R. Szczepaniak
Department of History
U.S. Air Force Academy

Dr. Brenda J. Taylor
Department of History
Texas Wesleyan University

Lieutenant Colonel John G. Terino Jr.
School of Advanced Air and Space Studies

Christopher C. Thomas
Texas A&M University

Dr. Francis H. Thompson
Department of History
Western Kentucky University

Dr. Earl H. Tilford Jr.
Army War College

Rebecca Tolley-Stokes
University of Maryland, Baltimore County

Dr. Vincent A. Transano
Naval Facilities Engineering Command
Naval Construction Battalion Center

Dr. Stephanie Lynn Trombley
Global Security and Intelligence Studies
Embry-Riddle Aeronautical University

Dr. Spencer C. Tucker
Senior Fellow
Military History, ABC-CLIO, Inc.

Zsolt J. Varga
Department of History
Texas Christian University

Dr. Richard B. Verrone
Texas Tech University

Dr. Thomas D. Veve
Social Sciences Division
Dalton State College

Dr. John F. Votaw
Independent Scholar

Hieu Dinh Vu
Independent Scholar

Dr. Kathleen Warnes
Independent Scholar

Wes Watters
Department of History
Texas Christian University

Dr. Seth Weitz
Indiana University–Northwest

Dr. James Michael Welsh
English Department
Salisbury State University

Mike Werttheimer
Naval Historical Center
Department of the Navy
Washington Navy Yard

Dr. James Edward Westheider
University of Cincinnati–Clermont College

Donald Whaley
Department of History
Salisbury State University

Dr. Wyndham E. Whynot
Department of History and Political Science
Livingstone College

Dr. James H. Willbanks
Director
Department of Military History
U.S. Army Command and General Staff
    College, Fort Leavenworth

Sandra M. Wittman
Library Services
Oakton Community College

Dr. Anna M. Wittmann
Department of English and Film Studies
University of Alberta

Dr. Laura Matysak Wood
Department of Social Sciences
Tarrant County College

Lee Ann Woodall
Department of History
McMurry University

Dr. David T. Zabecki
Major General
Army of the United States, Retired

Admiral Elmo R. Zumwalt Jr.
U.S. Navy, Retired

Categorical Index

Events

Groups and Organizations

Places

Ideas and Movements

Index